THE COMPLETE HANDBOOK FOR THE ENTREPRENEUR

Gary Brenner, M.B.A., J.D.

Joel Ewan, M.B.A.

Henry Custer, Ph.D., C.P.A.

PRENTICE HALL
Englewood Cliffs, New Jersey 07632

Prentice-Hall International (UK) Limited, *London*
Prentice-Hall of Australia Pty. Limited, *Sydney*
Prentice-Hall Canada, Inc., *Toronto*
Prentice-Hall Hispanoamericana, S.A., *Mexico*
Prentice-Hall of India Private Limited, *New Delhi*
Prentice-Hall of Japan, Inc., *Tokyo*
Simon & Schuster Asia Pte. Ltd., *Singapore*
Editora Prentice-Hall do Brasil, Ltda., *Rio de Janeiro*

1990 *by*

PRENTICE-HALL, Inc.
Englewood Cliffs, NJ

10 9 8 7 6 5 4 3 2 1

Library of Congress Cataloging-in-Publication Data

Brenner, Gary.
  Complete handbook for the entrepreneur: your manual for starting and
operating the successful business / by Gary Brenner, Joel Ewan, Henry Custer.

    p. cm.
  Includes bibliographical references.

  1. New business enterprises—United States—Handbooks, manuals, etc. 2.
Success in business—United States—Handbooks, manuals, etc. I.Ewan, Joel. II.
Custer, Henry. III. Title.
HD62.5.B74 1990
658'.041—dc20   89-22858
                                                                        CIP

ISBN 0-13-155995-8

PRENTICE HALL
BUSINESS & PROFESSIONAL DIVISION
A division of Simon & Schuster
Englewood Cliffs, New Jersey 07632

PRINTED IN THE UNITED STATES OF AMERICA

DEDICATION

Many people dream of beginning a business but few have the discipline and the courage. We dedicate this handbook to our clients: ordinary people who are not afraid to ask questions in order to see opportunities where most others only see problems. These individuals recreate the American dream each day. We salute them and hope this handbook will assist them and others like them to become successful.

Gary Brenner
Joel Ewan
Henry Custer

ABOUT THE AUTHORS

GARY BRENNER is a business attorney in private practice in San Diego, California, representing a variety of businesses — from startups to established corporations. He received his MBA from Northwest Louisiana University and his JD from the University of San Diego School of Law. Mr. Brenner is admitted to the bar for the state of California; U.S. District Court, Southern District; U.S. Court of Appeals Ninth Circuit; and U.S. Tax Court. He is a member of the American Bar Association Section of Corporation, Banking and Business Law, and is adjunct professor of business at Chapman College.

JOEL EWAN is vice-president of a commercial bank in San Diego, California. He earned his MBA in finance from New York University. Mr. Ewan spent 11 years as vice president of a multimillion dollar New York garment manufacturing firm, where he gained experience in manufacturing, operations, sales, and corporate finance. Mr. Ewan's experience also includes 5 years in the banking industry as a commercial lending officer and as a member of a corporate banking group. Mr. Ewan is an adjunct professor of business at Chapman College.

HENRY CUSTER earned his Ph.D. from the University of Alabama and his MBA from the University of Denver. Dr. Custer is also a CPA in private practice in San Diego, California, and is licensed to practice public accounting in both California and Nevada. He has taught accounting courses at the university level for over 17 years and has been in private practice for 14 years. Dr. Custer has written and published numerous articles, including some on cash management for the small businessperson, audit procedures and techniques of IRS agents, and human resource accounting.

WHY WE WROTE THIS BOOK

As a business lawyer, I would make a survey of the various business books that were on the market, every few months, so I could recommend one to my clients. Unfortunately, I was unable to find a single book that was both detailed and practical enough to meet the needs of my clients. The books I found were either abstract academic texts that had little day-to-day application (which I knew my clients would never read) or shallow primers consisting of little more than a compilation of references or war stories from business persons who had "made it."

One evening, during a break between classes at the Chapman College Educational Center, I happened to discuss my findings with two of my teaching colleagues: Joel Ewan, who is vice president of a local bank, and Henry Custer, who is a certified public accountant in private practice and holds a Ph.D in Business Administration. They expressed the same observation and dissatisfaction. We then began discussing the type of information and the subjects we would include if we write our own book. Naturally, each of us thought about our clients; we thought about the many questions they have asked us about starting and operating a business, and the many situations they have experienced in their attempt to become successful entrepreneurs.

After several lengthy discussions, we decided that the best approach would be to write a handbook containing an in-depth treatment of the twenty-one subjects most entrepreneurs will need to address at one time or another while starting or operating their businesses. We then made a master outline. The master outline divided the twenty-one subjects into 120 topics. Once the master outline was complete, we assigned different topics to each of us.

Our goal was to meet as a panel each week with our assignments. At the weekly meeting, each of us would show the others what we had written and then ask for a critique on content and format. Some of these critique sessions became quite heated, and there were several rewrites. We met each week for approximately one and one-half years.

We hope that you will find our handbook to be practical, authoritative, and comprehensive and to be the one source you can continually refer to in order to satisfy your information needs. Finally, we wish to thank our clients for providing us with the inspiration to write this handbook.

Gary Brenner
San Diego, California

INTRODUCTION: HOW THIS HANDBOOK CAN HELP YOU

WHAT THIS HANDBOOK CONTAINS

This handbook is designed to be the most comprehensive desk reference you can buy on starting and operating a successful business. Contained in this handbook, you will find the following:

- **Practical Information from Professionals**

  Three professionals: lawyer, banker, and certified public accountant, combine their training and experience to present you with a thorough treatment of 120 topics that most entrepreneurs will need to address at one time or another while starting or operating their business. Topics include: dealing with a banker, protecting yourself from hidden liabilities when buying a business, monitoring your business cash flow, evaluating a franchise, protecting your secrets, anticipating legal and tax requirements when starting from scratch, promoting your product or service, registering your trademark, using trade shows to your advantage, negotiating a lease, pricing your product or service, establishing employee benefit plans, and licensing your product as another avenue of distribution.

- **Examples Used to Illustrate Key Provisions**

  Throughout this handbook, examples are used that show you how a concept is put into practice. For instance, we show you through examples how to prepare a cash flow spread sheet to anticipate your cash needs, how to read and interpret census tract data to market your product or service, how to use the breakeven equation to set the price of your product, how to calculate depreciation of your assets, how to use certain techniques to speed up the collection of your receivables and the effect it will have on your cash flow, how to calculate coinsurance and pro rata provisions in insurance contracts, how to calculate the optimum amount of inventory you should carry and how to use various inventory valuation techniques to adjust your net income, and how to use financial ratio analysis to determine where you stand compared to others in your industry. We also provide you with key legal cases that illustrate how the law works in certain business situations.

- **Business Plan Is Included**

  This handbook not only tells you how to write and present a business plan, it also includes a sample business plan so that you can review the format and content.

- **Numerous Exhibits of Important Forms and Notices**

  Legal and tax requirements demand that you comply with various regulations. To do so, certain forms need to be completed and filed with the appropriate government agencies. We have included tax forms (many of which we have filled in so that you can see how to complete them,

Registration Statement under the Securities Act of 1933, Notice of Sale of Securities under Regulation D, U.S. Small Business Administration Listing of Small Business Investment Companies, Minority Enterprise Small Business Investment Companies, U.S. Small Business Administration Application for a Business Loan, Statement of Personal History and Personal Financial Statement, federally mandated labor notices that must be posted by employers, U.S. Copyright Application, U.S. Patent Application, and U.S. Trademark Application for registration, and excerpts from the U.S. Patent and Trademark Office's Official Gazette.

- **Topics Are Easily Accessible**

  This handbook is separated into the three phases an entrepreneur goes through when beginning a business. Part I is called "Getting Started" and contains those topics you need to think about before you begin your new business. Part II is called "Nuts and Bolts of Running a Business" and contains information, such as financing, marketing, and accounting to help you succeed in your business. Part III is called "Getting the Most from Your Business" and presents techniques and concepts to help you realize the maximum benefits your business will provide.

YOU ARE NOT ALONE

What do the following individuals and their products have in common?

King C. Gillette	Razor blades
Henry Ford	Automobiles
Helena Rubinstein	Cosmetics
Adolph Coors	Beer
Calvin Klein	Jeans
Mary Kay Ash	Cosmetics
Coco Chanel	Perfumes
Charles Pillsbury	Cake mixes
Levi Strauss	Jeans
George Hormel	Food
Max Factor	Cosmetics
William Wrigley	Chewing gum
Rudolph Diesel	Engines
Elizabeth Arden	Cosmetics
Eddie Bauer	Clothing
Carl Jantzen	Swimwear
John Van Heusen	Clothing

First, their last names are recognized as and associated with the products they make. Second, each of these individuals started at the bottom with little capital other than their savings and perhaps a modest bank loan, and through insight, determination, and some luck they all became very successful.

It is well known that Henry Ford started with relatively few assets. The same is true of Adolph Coors. You, too, can be your own boss and be successful despite any setbacks you may start out with. It is not necessary that you were born to the right parents; that you attended the right college; that your spouse is considered socially acceptable by corporate higher-ups; that you lead a lifestyle that matches a predetermined image; that you are like by the right people; or that you attend the right club, church, or synagogue.

Opening your business is an intense experience and will completely absorb you as well as affect the lives of those who are closely related to you. However, it should not be intimidating or overwhelming. Millions of others have gone before you and have been successful. Three traits they all had in common were *caution, planning,* and *discipline.*

This handbook serves as your trainer, to get you ready, and to channel your energies in the right direction. The goal: to help enhance your chances for success.

The authors are often asked about the risk of failure, and their response is something you have probably heard many times: Nothing in life is guaranteed except death and taxes. Like most endeavors, there is a substantial risk of failure. Even some of the largest corporations have faltered. However, the risk can be justified. Although it is well known that the lessons of failure are more difficult to assimilate than the lessons of success, whatever the outcome of your business venture, the experiences you will have encountered and the knowledge you will have gained will enhance you.

This handbook discusses common types of laws and regulations affecting a business. The information, however, should only serve as a general guideline and is not intended to act as a substitute for legal advice. It is strongly recommended that you seek the advice of both an attorney and a certified public accountant before you start your own business. In addition, as you are probably well aware, laws and procedures are constantly changing; therefore, there are no guarantees concerning the timeliness and accuracy of information or forms contained in this handbook.

TABLE OF CONTENTS

Why We Wrote This Book   ix
How This Handbook Can Help You   xi

PART ONE: GETTING STARTED   1

CHAPTER 1   What Are Your Expectations?   3

Are You the Type?   4
Take Stock of Your Personal Skills   4
Estimate Your Financial Investment   4
Establish Objectives and Define the Word "Success"   4

CHAPTER 2   Starting from Scratch   7

Advantages and Disadvantages   7
Legal, Tax, and Accounting Aspects   8
Other Factors to Consider   10

CHAPTER 3   Buying an Existing Business   13

Advantages and Disadvantages   14
Locating Businesses for Sale   14
How to Determine Which Type of Business Is Best for You   15
How to Negotiate the Purchase of a Business   16
How to Determine the Purchase Price   17
Tax Aspects to Consider When Purchasing a Business   21
Protecting Yourself from Hidden Liabilities   23
Using Escrow to Prevent Problems   28
Potential Problems with Transferring the Lease to The New Owner   28

CHAPTER 3   EXHIBITS   30

EXHIBIT 3.1   WORKSHEET: EVALUATING YOUR SKILLS TO RUN A PARTICULAR BUSINESS

EXHIBIT 3.2   WORKSHEET: DETERMINING THE TYPE OF BUSINESS THAT WILL MEET YOUR PERSONAL NEEDS

EXHIBIT 3.3   WORKSHEET: PROFIT AND LOSS 3 YEARS

EXHIBIT 3.4   WORKSHEET: BALANCE SHEET COMPARISON 3 YEARS

EXHIBIT 3.5   UCC FORM 3 REQUEST FOR INFORMATION (STATE OF FLORIDA)

EXHIBIT 3.6   UCC FORM 3 REQUEST FOR INFORMATION (STATE OF WASHINGTON)

EXHIBIT 3.7   UCC FORM 1 FINANCING STATEMENT (STATE OF NEW YORK)

EXHIBIT 3.8   UCC FORM 1 FINANCING STATEMENT (STATE OF ARIZONA)

EXHIBIT 3.9   NOTICE TO CREDITORS OF BULK TRANSFER (STATE OF CALIFORNIA)

EXHIBIT 3.10 CERTIFICATE REQUEST FROM CALIFORNIA SECRETARY OF STATE

CHAPTER 4   EVALUATING FRANCHISE OPPORTUNITIES   47

Advantages & Disadvantages 48
Locating a Franchise 49
Legal Aspects 50
Tax Aspects 56
What to Expect from a Franchisor 58

CHAPTER 4   EXHIBITS   60

EXHIBIT 4.1   FRANCHISE INVESTMENT PROTECTION LAWS REGARDING DISCLOSURE FOR STATE OF
               WASHINGTON

EXHIBIT 4.2   FRANCHISE INVESTMENT PROTECTION LAWS REGARDING DISCLOSURE AND IMPOUND OF
               FRANCHISE FEES FOR STATE OF ILLINOIS

CHAPTER 5   CHOOSING THE LEGAL FORM OF YOUR BUSINESS   83

Types of Businesses 83
Tax Aspects to Consider 90

CHAPTER 5   EXHIBITS   98

EXHIBIT 5.1   CERTIFICATE OF LIMITED PARTNERSHIP FORM LP-1 FOR STATE OF CALIFORNIA

EXHIBIT 5.2   *COMPLETED WITH EXPLANATION*: U.S. INCOME TAX RETURN FOR AN S CORPORATION (IRS
               FORM 1120S)

EXHIBIT 5.3   PASSIVE ACTIVITY LOSS LIMITATIONS (IRS FORM 8582)

CHAPTER 6   GOVERNMENT REQUIREMENTS YOU MUST BE AWARE OF
REGARDLESS OF THE BUSINESS FORM YOU CHOOSE   107

Why You Should Consider a Fictitious Business Name 108
Obtaining Local and State Licenses 109
Obtaining Sales and Use Tax Permits 110
How to Estimate You Self-Employment Tax, and Knowing When to Use Federal Tax Deposit
    Coupons (Form 8109) 110
How to Obtain Social Security Numbers 112
Knowing When to Report Social Security and Income Tax Withholdings from Your Employees
    Wages 112
Understanding Unemployment Taxes: Federal and State 113
Understanding Worker's Compensation Insurance and Why You are Required to Obtain It 114
Recognizing When You May Be Violating Employee Safety and Health Regulations 115

Complying with Federal and State Laws: Wage-Hour, Child Labor, and Discrimination in the
    Workplace 119
Be Careful: All Employers Must Comply with the Immigration Law of 1986 124
Government Notices That Are Required to Be Displayed 125
Factors You Must Consider When You Sell to Consumers on Credit 127

CHAPTER 6 EXHIBITS 129

EXHIBIT 6.1 FICTITIOUS BUSINESS NAME STATEMENT

EXHIBIT 6.2 CITY OF SAN DIEGO DECLARATION OF BUSINESS TAX

EXHIBIT 6.3 COMPUTATION OF SOCIAL SECURITY SELF-EMPLOYMENT TAX (IRS FROM 1040 SCHEDULE SE)

EXHIBIT 6.4 FEDERAL TAX DEPOSIT COUPON (IRS FORM 8109-B)

EXHIBIT 6.5 *COMPLETED WITH EXPLANATION:* EMPLOYER'S QUARTERLY FEDERAL TAX RETURN
    (IRS FORM 941)

EXHIBIT 6.6 EMPLOYER'S ANNUAL TAX RETURN FOR AGRICULTURAL EMPLOYEES (IRS FORM 943)

EXHIBIT 6.7 *COMPLETED WITH EXPLANATION:* APPLICATION FOR EMPLOYER IDENTIFICATION NUMBER
    (IRS FORM SS-4)

EXHIBIT 6.8 APPLICATION FOR A SOCIAL SECURITY NUMBER CARD (IRS FORM SS-5)

EXHIBIT 6.9 EMPLOYER'S QUARTERLY TAX RETURN FOR HOUSEHOLD EMPLOYEES (IRS FORM 942)

EXHIBIT 6.10 *COMPLETED WITH EXPLANATION:* WAGE AND TAX STATEMENT (IRS FORM W-2) AND
    TRANSMITTAL OF INCOME AND TAX STATEMENTS (IRS FORM W-3)

EXHIBIT 6.11 EMPLOYEE WITHHOLDING ALLOWANCE CERTIFICATE (IRS FORM W-4)

EXHIBIT 6.12 *COMPLETED WITH EXPLANATION:* EMPLOYER'S ANNUAL FEDERAL UNEMPLOYMENT (FUTA)
    TAX RETURN (IRS FORM 940)

EXHIBIT 6.13 OSHA NOTICE: JOB SAFETY AND HEALTH PROTECTION

EXHIBIT 6.14 LOG AND SUMMARY OF OCCUPATIONAL INJURIES AND ILLNESSES (CAL/OSHA NO. 200)

EXHIBIT 6.15 SAFETY AND HEALTH PROTECTION ON THE JOB (CAL/OSHA)

EXHIBIT 6.16 INDUSTRIAL WELFARE COMMISSION ORDER 4-80 PROFESSIONAL, TECHNICAL, CLERICAL, AND
    MECHANICAL OCCUPATIONS (STATE OF CALIFORNIA)

EXHIBIT 6.17 EMPLOYMENT ELIGIBILITY VERIFICATION (FORM I-9)

EXHIBIT 6.18 IMMIGRATION AND NATURALIZATION SERVICE "HANDBOOK FOR EMPLOYERS" (EXCERPT
    REGARDING FORM I-9)

EXHIBIT 6.19 EQUAL EMPLOYMENT OPPORTUNITY NOTICE

EXHIBIT 6.20 TRUTH IN LENDING DISCLOSURE FORM FOR A CREDIT SALE

CHAPTER 7 BUSINESS PLAN THE WAY TO SUCCESS 177

Why a Business Plan Is Necessary 177
What the Business Plan Should Include 178
How to Present a Business Plan 180
Use Your Plan to Make a Strategy 181
Sample Business Plan 182

PART TWO: NUTS AND BOLTS OF RUNNING A BUSINESS 203

CHAPTER 8 MARKETING YOUR BUSINESS 205

How to Conduct Market Research 205
How to Segment the Market 208
Understanding Census Tracts 211
Factors to Consider in Choosing Your Target Market 215
How to Promote Your Product or Service 215
Do You Need a Middleman to distribute Your Product? 224
Factors to Consider in Location Your Business 226
How to Price Your Product or Service 229
How to Use Trade Shows to Your Advantage 242

CHAPTER 8 EXHIBITS 246

EXHIBIT 8.1   CENSUS GEOGRAPHIC AREAS: GEOGRAPHIC IDENTIFICATION CODE SCHEME

EXHIBIT 8.2   INDIVIDUAL TRACTS SUPERIMPOSED ON CENSUS TRACT MAP (SAN DIEGO)

EXHIBIT 8.3   CENSUS TRACTS MAP (SAN DIEGO)

EXHIBIT 8.4   CENSUS TRACT 0002 (SAN DIEGO)

EXHIBIT 8.5   CENSUS TRACT 0083.12 (SAN DIEGO)

CHAPTER 9 ACCOUNTING SYSTEMS 257

Understanding Financial Statements 258
Choosing an Accounting System 266
Accounting Services a CPA Can Provide 267
Depreciation 268
Internal Accounting Controls to Prevent Theft 273
Cash Flow Management: How to Construct a Spread Sheet and Why It Is Necessary 276
Cash Flow Management: How to Project You Business Future Cash Flows and How to Maximize
       Cash Flows 281

CHAPTER 9 EXHIBITS 287

EXHIBIT 9.1   GENERAL JOURNAL

EXHIBIT 9.2   GENERAL LEDGER

EXHIBIT 9.3   COMPARISON OF COMPILATION, REVIEW, AND AUDIT ENGAGEMENTS

CHAPTER 10 FEDERAL EXCISE TAXES YOU NEED TO BE AWARE OF 295

Facilities and Service Taxes 296
Manufacturers Taxes 296
Retail and Use Taxes 297
Crude Oil Windfall Profit Tax 297
Other Federal Excise Taxes 297

CHAPTER 10 EXHIBIT 298

EXHIBIT 10.1 QUARTERLY FEDERAL EXCISE TAX RETURN (IRS FORM 720)

CHAPTER 11 BUSINESS INSURANCE 301

How Losses May Occur because of Unanticipated Events 301
Devising and Insurance Plan to Reduce Your Risk 304
Types of Insurance 304

CHAPTER 12 SOURCES OF FUNDS 313

Will You Have Sufficient Capital? 313
Why Financial Institutions Refuse Funding Requests 314
Borrowing Money 316
Selling Securities 327
Small Business Innovation Research Program 342
Factoring Accounts Receivable 344

CHAPTER 12 EXHIBITS 347

EXHIBIT 12.1 U.S. SMALL BUSINESS ADMINISTRATION APPLICATION FOR A LOAN, STATEMENTS REQUIRED
           BY LAWS AND EXECUTIVE ORDERS, SUMMARY OF COLLATERAL, SCHEDULE OF COLLATERAL,
           LENDER'S CHECKLIST FOR SBA APPLICATIONS

EXHIBIT 12.2 STATEMENT OF PERSONAL HISTORY, PERSONAL FINANCIAL STATEMENT

EXHIBIT 12.3 U.S. SMALL BUSINESS ADMINISTRATION LIST OF SBICS

EXHIBIT 12.4 U.S SMALL BUSINESS ADMINISTRATION LIST OF MESBICS

EXHIBIT 12.5 NOTICE OF SALE OF SECURITIES PURSUANT TO REGULATION D, SECTION 4 (6), AND/OR
           UNIFORM LIMITED OFFERING EXEMPTION (FORM D)

EXHIBIT 12.6 REGISTRATION STATEMENT UNDER THE SECURITIES ACT OF 1933 (FORM S-18)

EXHIBIT 12.7 REGISTRATION STATEMENT UNDER THE SECURITIES ACT OF 1933 (FORM S-1)

EXHIBIT 12.8 LETTER FROM VENTURE CAPITALIST WESTAMCO INVESTMENT COMPANY

CHAPTER 13 TAX SAVINGS AND TAX PITFALLS IN YOUR BUSINESS 471

Using a Corporation as a Tax Shelter 471
Sheltering Profits on Export Sales: DISCS and FSCS 473
How to Withdraw Funds from an Incorporated Business 474
Deducting Expenses That Relate to Your Business 476
Choosing the Best Taxable Year for Your Business 478
Selecting a Tax Accounting Method 479
Tax Problems Unique to Corporations 480
How to Plan for Your Estate When Your Business Accounts for a Large Portion of Your Personal
     Worth 482
How to Receive Tax Credits for Hiring Certain Economically Disadvantaged Groups 490
Putting Your Spouse and Children on the Payroll 490
How to Save on Unemployment Taxes 491

CHAPTER 13   EXHIBITS   493

EXHIBIT 13.1 WAS COMPENSATION REASONABLE? *EDWIN'S, INC. V. UNITED STATES*

EXHIBIT 13.2 *COMPLETED WITH EXPLANATION:* PROFIT OR LOSS FROM BUSINESS OR PROFESSION SCHEDULE C (FORM 1040)

EXHIBIT 13.3 *COMPLETED WITH EXPLANATION:* U.S. PARTNERSHIP RETURN OF INCOME (FORM 1065)

EXHIBIT 13.4 *COMPLETED WITH EXPLANATION* U.S. INCOME TAX RETURN FOR S CORPORATION (IRS FORM 1120S)

EXHIBIT 13.5 APPLICATION FOR CHANGE IN ACCOUNTING PERIOD (IRS FORM 1128)

EXHIBIT 13.6 APPLICATION FOR CHANGE IN ACCOUNTING METHOD (IRS FORM 3115)

EXHIBIT 13.7 JOBS CREDIT (IRS FORM 5884)

PART THREE: GETTING THE MOST FROM YOUR BUSINESS   521

CHAPTER 14   OPERATING YOUR BUSINESS   523

How to Forecast Sales 523
How to Forecast Asset Needs 527
Understanding Ratio Analysis and Why It Is Important 531
Should You Sell on Credit? 541
Accounts Receivable: The Lifeblood of the Business 542
Why You Must Closely Monitor Your Inventory 546
How Much Inventory Should Your Business Carry? 548
How to Value Your Inventory 558
How to Estimate Ending Inventory 560
Using Trade Credit to Your Advantage 562
Importance of the Breakeven Point 564
How to Evaluate Your Competition 569
How to Select and Train Personnel 570

CHAPTER 14   EXHIBITS   574

EXHIBIT 14.1 CENSUS TRACTS: SAN DIEGO SMSA (RACE AND SPANISH ORIGIN)

EXHIBIT 14.2 CENSUS TRACTS: SAN DIEGO SMSA (GENERAL CHARACTERISTICS OF SPANISH ORIGIN PERSONS)

EXHIBIT 14.3 CENSUS TRACTS: SAN DIEGO SMSA (GENERAL CHARACTERISTICS OF SPANISH ORIGIN PERSONS)

EXHIBIT 14.4 ROBERT MORRIS ASSOCIATES WHOLESALERS - HARDWARE AND PAINTS

EXHIBIT 14.5 APPLICATION TO USE LIFO INVENTORY METHOD (IRS FORM 970)

CHAPTER 15   WILL YOU NEED A COMPUTER FOR YOUR BUSINESS?   583

How to Assess Your Needs 583
Components of Computer System 585
Ten of the Most Commonly Used Computer Terms 586

**CHAPTER 16   HOW TO SQUEEZE MORE BENEFITS FROM YOUR BUSINESS
FOR YOU AND YOUR EMPLOYEES 589**

Employee Benefit Plans: How They Work 590
Simplified Employee Pension 597
Self Employment Retirement Plans 598
Fringe Benefits 602

CHAPTER 16 EXHIBITS 608

EXHIBIT 16.1   APPLICATION FOR DETERMINATION FOR DEFINED BENEFIT PLAN: FOR PENSION PLANS
OTHER THAN MONEY PURCHASE PLANS (IRS FORM 5300); INSTRUCTIONS FOR IRS FORMS
5300 AND 5301

EXHIBIT 16.2   SUPPLEMENTAL APPLICATION FOR APPROVAL OF EMPLOYEE BENEFIT PLANS UNDER TEFRA
1984, REA, AND TRA 1986 (SCHEDULE T)

EXHIBIT 16.3   APPLICATION FOR DETERMINATION OF DEFINED CONTRIBUTION PLAN: FOR
PROFIT-SHARING, STOCK BONUS AND MONEY PURCHASE PLANS (IRS FORM 5301)

EXHIBIT 16.4   APPLICATION FOR DETERMINATION FOR COLLECTIVELY BARGAINED PLAN UNDER SECTIONS
401 (A) AND 510(A) OF THE INTERNAL REVENUE CODE (FORM IRS 5303)

EXHIBIT 16.5   EMPLOYEE CENSUS (IRS FORM 5302)

EXHIBIT 16.6   FILING REQUIREMENTS FOR EMPLOYEE BENEFIT PLANS (IRS PUBLICATION 1048)

EXHIBIT 16.7   ANNUAL RETURN/REPORT OF EMPLOYEE BENEFIT PLAN (WITH 100 OR MORE PARTICIPANTS)
(IRS FORM 5500)

EXHIBIT 16.8   RETURN/REPORT OF EMPLOYEE BENEFIT PLAN (WITH FEWER THAN 100 PARTICIPANTS) IRS
FOR 5500-C)

EXHIBIT 16.9   REGISTRATION STATEMENT OF EMPLOYEE BENEFIT PLAN (WITH FEWER THAN 100
PARTICIPANTS) (IRS FORM 5500-R)

EXHIBIT 16.10 ANNUAL RETURN OF ONE-PARTICIPANT (OWNERS AND THEIR SPOUSES) PENSION BENEFIT
PLAN (IRS FORM 5500EZ)

EXHIBIT 16.11 INSURANCE INFORMATION SCHEDULE A (IRS FORM 5500)

EXHIBIT 16.12 ANNUAL RETURN OF FIDUCIARY OF EMPLOYEE BENEFIT TRUST SCHEDULE P (IRS FORM
5500)

EXHIBIT 16.13 ANNUAL REGISTRATION STATEMENT IDENTIFYING SEPARATED PARTICIPANTS WITH
DEFERRED VESTED BENEFITS (SCHEDULE SSA)

CHAPTER 17   PROTECTING YOUR IDEAS AND YOUR PRODUCTS 659

Branding: The Way to Increase Sales and Profits 659
Copyrights: They Apply to More Than Only Books and Records 665
Patents: Does Your New Product Violate Someone's Patent? 672
Trade Secrets: An Alternative to Patents 676

CHAPTER 17 EXHIBITS 680

EXHIBIT 17.1 XEROX ADVERTISEMENTS

EXHIBIT 17.2 NOTICE OF TRADEMARK REGISTRATION FROM THE STATE OF CALIFORNIA

EXHIBIT 17.3 PAGE FROM OFFICIAL GAZETTE

EXHIBIT 17.4 TRADEMARK APPLICATION INDIVIDUAL (FORM PTO-1476FB)

EXHIBIT 17.5 TRADEMARK APPLICATION CORPORATION (FORM PTO1478FB)

EXHIBIT 17.6 COPYRIGHT APPLICATION (FORM TX); INSTRUCTIONS FOR COMPLETING APPLICATION
           FORM TX

EXHIBIT 17.7 COPYRIGHT APPLICATION (FORM SE); INSTRUCTIONS FOR COMPLETING APPLICATION
           FORM SE

EXHIBIT 17.8 CIRCULAR R61: COPYRIGHT REGISTRATION FOR COMPUTER PROGRAMS

EXHIBIT 17.9 PATENTS GRANTED (GENERAL AND MECHANICAL, CHEMICAL, ELECTRICAL)

EXHIBIT 17.10 DECLARATION FOR PATENT APPLICATION

EXHIBIT 17.11 VERIFIED STATEMENT CLAIMING SMALL ENTITY STATUS (FORM PTO-FB-A410)

CHAPTER 18   SHOULD YOU HIRE INDEPENDENT CONTRACTORS OR 704 EMPLOYEES?

Significant Legal Distinctions 704
Taxes Are Also a Factor 707
The Independent Contractor and Your Operation 709

CHAPTER 18   EXHIBITS   710

EXHIBIT 18.1 *EXPLANATION:* COMPUTATION OF SOCIAL SECURITY SELF-EMPLOYMENT TAX (SCHEDULE SE
           IRS FORM 1040)

EXHIBIT 18.2 INFORMATION FOR USE IN DETERMINATION WHETHER A WORKER IS AN EMPLOYEE FOR
           FEDERAL EMPLOYMENT TAXES AND INCOME TAX WITHHOLDING (IRS FORM SS-8)

EXHIBIT 18.3 *COMPLETED WITH EXPLANATION:* MISCELLANEOUS INCOME (FORM 1099-MISC); ANNUAL
           SUMMARY AND TRANSMITTAL OF U.S. INFORMATION RETURNS (FORM 1096)

CHAPTER 19   RESEARCH AND DEVELOPMENT PARTNERSHIPS 721

Origin of the R & D Partnership 721
The Most Common Types of R & D Partnerships 722
Advantages and Disadvantages of Using an R & D Partnership 722
Securities Laws and Disclosures 724
Tax Aspects 724

CHAPTER 19   EXHIBITS   727

EXHIBIT 19.1 CREDIT FOR INCREASING RESEARCH ACTIVITIES (IRS FORM 6765)

EXHIBIT 19.2 GENERAL BUSINESS CREDIT (IRS FORM 3800)

CHAPTER 20   LICENSING AGREEMENTS 731

Why Entrepreneurs Use Licenses 731
Types of Licensing Rights 733

Types of Property That Can Be Licensed 733
Checklist to Analyze Prospective Licensees 734
Licensing Agreements: Issues to Consider 735
Original Equipment Manufacturer and Value Added Reseller Arrangements: Another Avenue of
    Distribution 736
Product Licensing Information 737

CHAPTER 21   LEASING VERSUS BUYING EQUIPMENT 739

Advantages and Disadvantages of Leasing Equipment 739
How to Analyze the Cost of the Lease 740
How to Negotiate a Lease 745
Understanding the Terms of a Lease Contract 747

Index 751

PART ONE

GETTING STARTED

Chapter 1

WHAT ARE YOUR EXPECTATIONS?

The purpose of this chapter is to help you articulate and clarify the reasons you have for wanting to start your own business. Unlike the following chapters, which either describe various business tools or reveal inside information, this chapter merely requests that you ask certain fundamental questions about yourself. Yet, this chapter is the most important chapter in the entire handbook. Why? The tools of business can be learned along the way as well as the savvy that results from business experiences, but it is the critical self-examination of who you are and the nature of your expectations that determines whether you will "succeed" or "fail," both as a business person and as an individual.

Expectations—and putting those expectations into effect—distinguish successful entrepreneurs from everyone else. A clear, straightforward philosophy of who you are and why you are starting a business will determine the nature of your plans, provide you with the analytical framework with which to make decisions, and serve as a source of spiritual strength upon which you can draw in those moments of self-doubt. If you attempt to begin a business without having articulated what you expect the business to provide for you, you will not have the necessary references to rely upon to guide your actions, which is essential if you want to succeed.

There is a four-step procedure you can use in determining whether you should start your own business. The analytical process requires you to critically examine your expectations: expectations of yourself and expectations of the benefits you hope your business will bring you.

This chapter explains the four steps you should take before opening your own business.

* Decide if you are the type
* Take stock of your personal skills
* Estimate your financial investment
* Define the word success

ARE YOU THE TYPE?

The first and most important step you must take in order to be successful is to be honest with yourself. Are you really the type of person who should run your own business? Far too often individuals start their own business in an attempt to "find themselves." Ignorance is the quickest road to failure. Know thyself. The list below contains 12 of the most important questions you should ever ask yourself. Mull these questions over, because it is your personality that will establish the foundation for success.

Twelve Questions You Must Ask Yourself:

1. Are you a self starter?
2. Do you like to take charge and see things through?
3. Can you tolerate hard work for long periods of time?
4. Can you make up your mind in a hurry and not regret the decision you have made?
5. Can people trust what you say?
6. Do you have the energy to do most of the things you want to do?
7. Can you look at a problem and see opportunity?
8. Can you maintain organization?
9. Do you have confidence in your ability to solve problems as they arise?
10. Can you explain your ideas to people and have them adopt your point of view?
11. Are you willing to delegate authority as well as responsibility?
12. Can you maintain that positive attitude day in and day out?

TAKE STOCK OF YOUR PERSONAL SKILLS

To choose the best entrepreneurial path, you must determine those areas where there is a need for a service or product. For example, it may be a service that is needed within a particular industry or it could be something that will satisfy consumer demand. Therefore, the second step is to take an inventory of your own skills. The best match is to be in a business that will center around an activity you do best as well as being able to provide a service or product that fills a particular need in the market.

ESTIMATE YOUR FINANCIAL INVESTMENT

The third step is to estimate the investment, in financial terms, that you intend to make:

* Calculate the amount you will have to invest in your business.
* Calculate the typical return on investment in the type of business you intend to start and determine whether or not that rate will be satisfactory.

ESTABLISH OBJECTIVES AND DEFINE THE WORD "SUCCESS"

Step four is to ask yourself the following question: What are my objectives and how will I determine whether or not my venture is a success? The importance of this question is that it allows you to determine whether or not you have made the right decisions.

Intangibles to Consider

You may want to consider factors other than or in addition to compensation. For example:

* Being able to enjoy a certain lifestyle
* Having others depend on you for their sole source of support
* Decision-making power
* Having your name recognized by the public
* Excitement of running your own business
* Having your ideas come to fruition

Sales Volume Required to Support the Return You Expect

The most common measurement of success is to focus exclusively on compensation. With this approach, however, you should think in specifics—that is, how much compensation must you earn before you cross the threshold of success. Will $50 thousand a year be sufficient or must you earn $1 million a year? If this method is going to be your measure of success then you must analyze the volume of sales you will have to generate in order to reach your objective.

The following example illustrates the concept above and also how you should analyze the amount of sales necessary to reach your objective.

Example: Suppose your objective is to earn $25,000 total return on your investment. Suppose also that you are analyzing three different businesses. Each business is in a different industry. The businesses you are thinking about are:

Manufacturing—Machine shop that performs on a job order basis.

Retailing—Dry goods and general merchandise, less than 25 employees, also known as a small department store.

Service—Janitorial service.

From the Robert Morris Associates (RMA) summary of financial information by SIC (Standard Industrial Classification), we can list the following income statement ratios.

	Manufacturing	Retailing	Service
Net sales	100.0%	100.0%	100.0%
Cost of sales	67.0	68.0	—
Gross profit	33.0	32.0	—
Operating expense	26.5	28.5	94.0
Operating profit	6.5	3.5	6.0
Other expense	2.0	.5	2.0
Pre-tax profit	4.5	3.0	4.0

Based on your objective and the relationships cited through RMA, we can determine the amount of sales necessary to earn $25,000 total return on our investment.

	Manufacturing		Retailing		Service	
Net sales	$555,600	100.0%	$833,300	100.0%	$625,000	100.0%
Cost of sales	(372,300)	67.0	(566,600)	68.0	—	—
Gross profit	183,300	33.0	266,700	32.0	—	—
Expenses	(147,200)	26.5	(237,500)	28.5	(587,500)	94.0
Profit	36,100	6.5	29,200	3.5	37,500	6.0
Other expenses	(11,100)	2.0	(4,200)	.5	(12,500)	2.0
Pre-tax profit	$25,000	4.5	$25,000	3.0	$25,000	4.0

Note that return on total investment includes your salary. The amount of salary owners traditionally pay themselves varies in each industry. In most cases, an owner's salary is calculted as a percentage of sales. Using the RMA ratios provided for each of these industries, we can estimate an owner's salary as follows:

Industry	Percentage of Sales[a]			Amount in Dollars		
Manufacturing	3.7	to	9.9%	$20,600	to	$55,000
Retailing	1.6	to	4.9	13,300	to	40,800
Service	3.5	to	8.5	21,900	to	53,100

[a] Source: Compilation of data derived from *Annual Statement Studies* published by Robert Morris Associates, Philadelphia, PA.

This example gives you an idea of the sales volume required to support a specific amount of return and an appropriate salary. There are numerous perquisites that have not been discussed which will affect your business and your ability to reach your objective. The perquisites may include health insurance, life insurance, disability insurance, and expenses, such as automobile, entertainment, travel, postage, and professional journals and seminars.

Furthermore, the financial structure as well as the legal form of your business will determine how much of the pre-tax profit will be available to you. The topic of legal organization will be discussed in Chapter 5.

Chapter 2

STARTING FROM SCRATCH

This chapter will introduce you to a variety of factors you should consider if you are thinking about starting a business from scratch. This chapter explains:

* Advantages and disadvantages of using this approach
* Legal, tax, and accounting aspects
* Issues to consider regarding marketing, suppliers, employees, inventory, location, equipment, and banking services

ADVANTAGES AND DISADVANTAGES

Starting a business from scratch has various advantages, and many entrepreneurs prefer building their businesses from the ground up rather than buying an existing business. The reasons they cite include:

* Greater leeway in deciding where your product or service will be marketed; where your business will be located; and which individuals you will hire.
* Credit connections are new, and a relationship with the lender can be developed from the beginning.
* No preexisting equipment or inventory: you choose only equipment and inventory that are needed according to the particular needs of your business.
* Customer contacts and relationships are new, which permits you to establish your own reputation and a unique image.
* Suppliers are not predetermined, which means they can be evaluated and chosen according to your needs.
* You can create a business that reflects your personality.
* There is no previous ill will to contend with.
* It gives you the opportunity to provide a unique service or product to the market.

7

Just as there are advantages in starting from scratch, there are also certain disadvantages you should be aware of:

* Obtaining credit or investors for your business may be more difficult because the business is not established.
* Starting and organizing your business will take more time and energy than buying an existing business.
* You may have to supplement your income until the business begins to show a profit.
* A customer base that has confidence in your product or service will have to be established, which may take time.
* You may attempt to bring something to the market that is not needed.
* Costs may be difficult to estimate because the business is not established.

LEGAL, TAX, AND ACCOUNTING ASPECTS

Legal and Tax

The single biggest disadvantage of starting from scratch is the element of surprise. There are many rules, regulations, statutes, and taxes that you may not be aware of at the time you open your business.

You will probably first learn of most of these requirements as you encounter them, which can prove to be quite costly. The advantage of buying an on-going business is that while doing the preliminary investigation you should uncover many of the legal, regulatory, and tax requirements that are associated with the business. As a result, when you buy an on-going business you already know and are anticipating the type of legal and tax requirements the current owner must contend with and when those requirements must be satisfied.

The checklist below provides a quick reference to many of the legal and tax requirements that you must anticipate and satisfy when starting a business from scratch.

- Obtain local business license
- Obtain state occupational license
- File and publish fictitious business name statement, if applicable
- Obtain federal license, if applicable to your business activity
- Comply with city, county, state, and federal licensing requirements
- Comply with state and federal job safety requirements
- Obtain weights and measures permit, if applicable
- Notify health department, if applicable
- File an application for federal employer identification number
- File Quarterly Income Tax Withholding and Unemployment Insurance Returns with the state
- File Employer's Quarterly Federal Tax Return
- File Quarterly Sales/Use Tax Return
- File Declaration of Estimated Corporation Tax if you are conducting business as a corporation
- File Personal Income Tax Withholding with the state
- File Personal Property Statement with County Assessor

- File Income Tax Return with the state
- File Federal Income Tax Return
- File Federal Unemployment Tax Return
- Obtain Worker's Compensation Insurance or Certificate of Consent to Self-Insurance
- Register as an employer with your state employment tax agency
- Remit state Personal Income Tax Withholdings and Disability Insurance Contributions
- Remit personal property taxes
- Remit federal income taxes and FICA taxes
- Furnish withholding statements to employees

Accounting

Accounting provides financial information about your business. Not only will you need this information to assist you in making decisions, but outsiders, such as your banker, potential investors, and the government, will want to see this information as well.

Any accounting system, even if you design your own, must include the following functions: (1) a record of financial activity, (2) classification of the data, and (3) a summary of the data so that it can be understood. If your accounting system does not include these functions, your business is not going to operate efficiently and your chances of survival will be slim.

Reasons for an Accounting System

Many entrepreneurs have asked us why it is necessary to have an accounting system. They believe their day-in, day-out involvement clearly shows them whether the business is successful or not. Moreover, maintaining an accounting system is costly and drains resources from the business. In response, there are five good reasons for the necessity of an accounting system:

Reason One: Good records can quickly point out problem areas.

Reason Two: Payroll, income, and expense records are required by state as well as federal governments. Although federal and state governments do not require you to keep your records in any particular way, they will require you to keep records that are permanent, accurate, and complete.

Reason Three: A sound accounting system will permit your business to legally minimize taxes.

Reason Four: An accounting system provides an audit trail, which is essential for checking the accuracy of financial data as well as assisting you in preventing your employees from stealing from your business.

Reason Five: You will make better decisions because you will know how much inventory you have; how much money is owed to you; the amount of your bills and when they are due; how much profit you are making; and how much cash is coming in and going out of your business each month.

When you start from scratch you will have to devise your own accounting system unless a system has been created for your particular business. The advantage of having your own system is that you can design it to reflect your own thinking. Moreover, you are not inheriting someone else's system, which may be either redundant or inaccurate. The drawback to designing your own accounting system is that if you do not know the business very well you may be forced to make numerous revisions, which is costly, time consuming, and potentially demoralizing.

The following list shows of some of the expenditures you need to be aware of and plan for when starting from scratch:

- Your salary
- Salaries of employees
- Rent (include security deposit; also, if you are opening a retail store in a shopping center, the lease will more than likely be triple net so include real property taxes, build-out, fixtures, and decorating)
- Personal property tax
- Sales tax
- Advertising
- Sales promotion
- Supplies (include purchasing checks, paper, pens, stationery, adding machine tape, accounting records)
- Merchandise
- Telephone (include security deposit and installation charges)
- Insurance
- Interest (if you borrow money)
- Maintenance
- Professional fees (legal and accounting)
- Equipment
- Furniture
- Signs
- Shelving
- Cash register
- Computer
- Licenses and permits

In Chapter 9, we explain how to set up a basic accounting system, how to manage your cash flow through the use of a spread sheet, and how to depreciate certain types of assets. We also suggest that if you want more information concerning taxes and your business you should see IRS Publication 583, "Information for Business Taxpayers," and Publication 334, "Tax Guide for Small Businesses." Both of these publications are free and contain very useful information.

OTHER FACTORS TO CONSIDER

There are other factors you should consider and plan for before you begin your business. If you are starting from scratch, you will not have the luxury of adopting a system that is already established and operative.

The following checklist shows factors you should consider to help you plan your future business operation:

Marketing—Who are your customers; can you articulate your customers' needs; how do you know the product or service will satisfy their needs; how will you reach your customers465 with your advertising message; how much money have you budgeted for advertising, sales promotion, and publicity; who will sell your product or service and how will it be done; is your market determined by geography; can you estimate your first year's sales; are your customers price sensitive or service sensitive or prestige sensitive; can you clearly identify your competitors; and how will you distinguish your product, service, or store from your competition?

Inventory—What type of merchandise will you sell; what type of selection will you offer and how will it be determined; will your prices be competitive; will you sell on credit; will you accept credit cards; how many units must you sell before you break even; and have you established an information source to keep you updated on customer trends?

Banking—Have you opened a checking account; will you need a night deposit bag, keys, credit card drafts, endorsement stamps, credit card terminal, debit card terminal, imprinter, summary drafts and deposit slips?

Supplies—Who are your suppliers; what products and services do they offer; how long will it take for delivery; and will they give you credit?

Employees—Will you hire employees; what source will you use; what will be your hiring criteria; will your employees already be trained or experienced; is your way of doing things different from the way of the industry so that you will have to train your employees regardless of their background; who will do the training and how will it be done; and are you prepared to pay for this training?

Location—How important is location to reach customers; will the manner of transportation of your merchandise to customers be important so that you will need to locate near a major traffic artery or near railway line; is the building you propose to use zoned for the activity of your business; can you live with the terms and conditions of the lease; how much can your business expand before it will become necessary to relocate; and will you need to build out or install fixtures and at what cost?

Equipment—What type of equipment and furniture will you need; how will you finance the purchase of equipment and furniture; and will you be able to buy your furniture and equipment second hand?

Miscellaneous—Will you need stationery, business cards, letterhead, envelopes; will you have telephone service and will you advertise in the Yellow Pages; what type of insurance policies will you obtain? Mandatory policies that are dictated by state statute are worker's compensation and automobile insurance. Fire and liability are usually required by the landlord and the provisions mandating such coverages ordinarily are found in the lease. Other types of coverage you should consider are business interruption insurance, crime, group life for you and your employees, group health for you and your employees, disability for you and your employees, key person, and fidelity bond.

Chapter 3

BUYING AN EXISTING BUSINESS

It has often been said that buying an existing business is fraught with more risk than starting from scratch. This chapter will eradicate much of the mystery involved in buying an on-going business by explaining the process. In addition, the issues you should investigate and the factors you should consider if you are thinking about buying an existing business will be explained. This chapter will show you:

* Advantages and disadvantages of using this approach to get into business
* How to determine the best type of business for you
* How to locate a business for sale
* How to negotiate the purchase price
* How to calculate the purchase price
* Tax aspects of buying a business
* Hidden liabilities you should be aware of
* How escrow is used
* Assignment of the lease to the buyer

The purchase of an existing business can be both complex and intimidating. The key to a successful purchase involves planning and investigation. Scrutinize each opportunity you are presented with to ensure it is not an illusion. Sellers have a habit of emphasizing only the positive aspects of their businesses because they do not want to jeopardize the sale. Buyers, on the other hand, have a tendency to become emotionally attached to a certain business because they become convinced by the seller that it represents the opportunity of a lifetime and will become angry if an attorney or certified public accountant begins asking hard questions and discovering negative aspects. If you are thinking about buying a business, we strongly recommend you consult with both an attorney and a certified public accountant before you make your purchase. These professionals are valuable because they provide the objectivity necessary to analyze the advantages and disadvantages of any particular business for sale.

ADVANTAGES AND DISADVANTAGES

There are numerous advantages to buying an existing business. Some of the advantages are listed below.

* Buying an existing business reduces the time and cost associated with establishing a new business; for instance, the business should already have a reputation and supply of customers so you will not have to build sales from scratch.
* The price asked for the business may be a legitimate bargain because the seller is motivated.
* The right amount of inventories and supplies may already be established and are on hand.
* Credit relationships have already been established.
* Existing records of the business are on hand and can be used as a guide in running the business.
* Employees are familiar with the business and can help you manage it.
* The seller may provide you with valuable assistance in running the business, which will help prevent you from committing costly mistakes.
* Your risk of failure is greatly reduced if the business has been in existence for a long period of time.
* The transaction becomes a single purchase issue.
* You eliminate one competitor.

On the flip side, there may be disadvantages to buying a business when compared to starting from scratch. Some negative aspects are the following.

* Bad will may exist because of the way the business has been managed, and you may inherit it.
* The employees who are currently working for the business may be incompetent or may not be able to adapt to your style of management or may resist change.
* You may pay too much for the business because you were impatient and did not accurately appraise the value of the business.
* You may acquire outdated inventory and obsolete equipment.
* The area in which the business is located may be starting to deteriorate.
* The purchase is predicated upon the past, not on the future; therefore, who will know if the business you are buying is about to lose a major customer?
* You may be stuck with an unfavorable lease.
* The inventory, decor, and fixtures will reflect someone else's tastes and may not suit your style.
* The personality of the business is a reflection of the previous owner; as a result, it may take a long time to change the personality of the business, especially if it is bad.

Businesses fail for many reasons. Be careful: You want to buy an opportunity and not a problem.

LOCATING BUSINESSES FOR SALE

Let's assume you have considered the advantages and disadvantages and have found that the positives of buying an existing business outweigh the negatives. You must now locate that existing business. There are numerous ways you can achieve this objective; some are very good and some not so good. The following list of sources ranges from worst to best and is based on the results of much trial and error.

* *Business Brokers and Realtors.* The main drawback with this source is not the usual 10 percent fee, but the fact that there are so many brokers and realtors that the real professionals get "lost." Often the broker knows little or nothing about business in general and is only providing a "rap" sheet for a specific business. Any financial analysis done is strictly from the seller's point of view. The broker is, in most cases, being paid by the seller and therefore attempts to get the highest possible price. While we are extremely critical of this source, it must be noted that there are highly reputable and professional people in this business.

* *Advertising.* Like the real estate market, businesses listed in the classified section of the newspaper are not selling too well. The price may be too high or the business might be too technical or risky. Occasionally, however, a good business sneaks into the classified ads. If you choose this method, you must learn very quickly which ads are "blue sky" and which are for real, in order to you use your time wisely.

* *Local Chambers of Commerce.* Although Chambers of Commerce have no fee incentive, they are still interested in "selling" their area over other areas. Therefore, your best interests may not be their best interests. Chambers of Commerce can be helpful in providing lists of various businesses within their sphere of influence. These lists could be useful in making a decision based on competitive pressure or supplier availability.

* *The Direct Approach.* Often while working in an industry segment, individuals become aware of worthy competitors who might be amenable to selling. Typical situations include:

  —Owner older than 55 and wants to retire
  —Rift in a partnership
  —Marital problems
  —Long-term illness or death
  —Owner has been in the business longer than 10 years and wants a change

* *Trade Publications and Newspapers.* Many owners of businesses for sale use this media because they target a smaller but more interested and knowledgeable audience. This source is an especially good one for someone who has just moved into the area.

* *Trade Suppliers.* These people know who is doing what, when they are doing it, and to whom. By listening to them and probing, they become an excellent source of industry news, including which businesses are for sale or which businesses may soon be for sale. This is a win-win situation for trade suppliers because they are able to help out an old customer and keep a potential account alive.

* *Accountants, Attorneys, and Bankers.* These are without a doubt the best sources. These professionals know long before any of the other sources when a sale is pending. They also have a win-win situation. They have an incentive to assist in the transition so that they can maintain the client relationship.

HOW TO DETERMINE WHICH TYPE OF BUSINESS IS BEST FOR YOU

Patience is the key that you must have in your search for the right business. Too many individuals make a bad choice because they are in a rush to buy a business. Take your time and investigate each opportunity as it comes along. Do not get emotionally involved with any business deal that is offered to you and always be prepared to walk away from a deal if the negative factors outweigh the positive ones. You must maintain your objectivity and use this objectivity when you discuss the pros and cons of buying a particular business with your attorney and certified public accountant. It is not uncommon for an individual to buy a business first and then ask his or her lawyer whether he or she made the right decision. Operating in this way will only increase the risk of failure and ultimately the amount of your legal bills.

Determining which type of business is best for you requires you to analyze each opportunity presented from two distinct perspectives.

> *First:* You should analyze the skills you already have and determine whether they are sufficient to operate the business that you are considering.

> *Second:* You should determine whether the business you are considering will satisfy your personal needs.

Exhibits 3-1 and 3-2 are worksheets to help you determine which type of business is best for you.

HOW TO NEGOTIATE THE PURCHASE OF A BUSINESS

The key to successful negotiations is to understand how the process works. Following is an overview of the typical negotiation for the purchase of a business.

> *Step One:* The business is offered for sale at a given price.

> *Step Two:* Buyer shows interest and seeks financial disclosure. Warning: If the seller refuses to provide financial information in the form of federal tax returns and business records, run—do not walk—away from this deal.

> *Step Three:* Buyer analyzes financial information. Enter 3 years of financial data onto the Balance Sheet and Income Statement sheets that have been provided in Exhibits 3-3 and 3-4.

> * Look at trends in sales, expenses, costs, and profits. Are profits in line with industry averages? Do costs look reasonable?
> * Determine the value of what the seller is taking in perquisites. Will you take the same perks or will they be available to support debt service?
> * Determine depreciation taken. Do not add it back when determining cash flow or net profit because it should be used to replace assets that are deteriorating and as such should be considered a real expense. *Note:* Depreciation should not be taken into account when constructing cash budget. For a more detailed explanation, see Chapter 9.
> * Look for trends in the balance sheet. Is inventory turnover increasing? Is it seasonal or an indication of obsolete inventory? Is accounts receivable turnover increasing? If so, is this due to poor collection efforts or increasing bad debts? For more detailed information, see Chapter 14.

> *Step Four:* Buyer analyzes the nonfinancial aspects.

> * Why is the business for sale? Are the reasons any of the following: death, divorce, health, retirement, loss of market share, obsolete product, or poor quality control?
> * What are the trends that will affect future sales? Is this a growth, stable, or declining market? Is the product subject to obsolescence?
> * Will the business suffer as a result of the seller's departure?

* Will added capital, besides that required in the selling price, be required to run the business? If you were to buy the assets of the business, would there be a need to supply working capital in the form of accounts receivable and operating expenses for the first 3 months, 6 months, 9 months, etc.?
* Will the down payment be sufficient to reduce debt service burden to a manageable level? *Note:* A banker will not provide a loan if the debt service burden remains high. Therefore, even if the seller is willing to finance the deal, you would be well advised to test your arrangement with your banker and see if he or she can match it.
* Are special business licenses required and do they come with the business?
* Is the customer base stable or will it follow the seller?
* Will a "noncompete" arrangement be part of the sale? If not, is the seller going to remain in the area?

Step Five: Buyer will now counteroffer.

Step Six: Seller will accept, reject, or counteroffer.

Step Seven: Buyer accepts or counteroffers.

Step Eight: If the seller accepts, the negotiations end. Buyer and seller settle on price and terms.

HOW TO DETERMINE THE PURCHASE PRICE

Businesses are either publicly traded or privately held. The purchase price of a business that is publicly traded in an active market is relatively easy to calculate. The price is simply the market value of the equity plus the market value of the debt. These businesses, however, represent perhaps less than 1 percent of all businesses. Therefore, this section will show you the methods available to determine the value of a privately held business.

Book Value

The book value is simply the value of the business after all liabilities are subtracted from all assets. This method should be avoided since it is merely a statement of historical costs and as such does not address the efficiency or fair market value of those assets. Further, it can associate an unrealistic value to intangible assets, should any exist on the balance sheet.

Capitalization Approach

This approach is a simplified version of the constant growth stock valuation model:

$$K = \frac{D}{P} + g$$

Where:
  g = growth rate of earnings of the business over a 3-year period
  D = average earnings of the business over the past 3 years

K = capitalization rate or required rate of return for a business of this risk level

P = price of the business today, the unknown

Restating the equation above to solve for the unknown we get the following:

$$P = \frac{D}{K - g}$$

As you can see, this equation reveals that as the term $K - g$ becomes larger, the price we should be willing to pay for a business decreases. That is the higher the risk for a given level of growth, the less we need to invest to yield a given dollar return of D.

Example: A business for sale has the following characteristics:

D = average net earnings, after owner's draw and taxes, equals $30,000

g = growth rate of earnings equals 5%

K = capitalization rate equals 15%

The reasonable price for this business would be:

$$P = \frac{\$30,000}{.15 - .05}$$

Price = $300,000

Note: The growth factor, g, should only be based on the growth which the current business has exhibited, not the growth you expect it to have as a result of your efforts. Do not consider your potential in calculating the growth factor because if potential exists in the business as it stands, it would have been realized. Remember, no one can sell you your own potential.

The major drawback with the capitalization approach is that it is designed for larger profit-maximizing firms where the capitalization rate is determined by the market. It is very difficult to determine K for small firms because the capital structures vary widely and comparisons are hard to find.

Replacement Cost Approach

This method assumes you are indifferent to either buying the assets of the business for sale or replacing them with equivalent new assets. We believe that depreciated assets do not have the same value as new assets. A better method would be to value the assets at their fair secondary market value. Try to use wholesale price rather than retail price. Replacement cost approach ignores the value that is associated with an on-going business. For instance, there are issues concerning the valuation of certain intangibles, such as customer lists, trademarks, and patents.

Use of Multipliers

This method is similar to the capitalization approach. It employs a multiple of sales to determine the price of the business. This method is valuable at providing a quick estimate of the reasonableness of an asking price. It fails, however, to address operational efficiencies of the business and may ignore the fact that a business is losing money. Even if we use a multiple of net earnings, instead of sales, to determine price we still ignore the issue of asset quality. That is, earnings might be inflated because of the seller's failure to reinvest the proper amount into fixed assets.

Compilation Approach

This approach uses the best aspects of all of the prior methods in determining the value of a business. First, we need to define some useful terms, then generate values for those terms, and finally calculate a price. To simplify this calculation, we will assume that the business for sale does not have a goodwill account.

Terms:

Net FMV of Assets—This is the fair market value (FMV) of the assets purchased less the liabilities assumed by you. Note this figure does not include any value for intangible assets.

Required Amount of Return of Net FMV of Assets—This amount is calculated by multiplying the Net FMV of assets by a chosen rate. The rate will fall somewhere between the risk-free rate and the rate required on risky assets such as commodities. This risk can be determined for each industry and is known as the beta factor. Beta factor is often published in trade journals and financial publications.

Intangible Assets Multiple—This multiple is a function of how well established the business is. The factors involved in this determination are:

- Length of time necessary to replicate the current level of earnings.
- Uniqueness of the intangible assets, for example, patents, copyrights, etc. *Note:* Some intangible assets do not appear on the balance sheet, for example, favorable leasehold interest, covenant not to compete, trade secrets, and customer lists, to name a few.

Guidelines as to Values for the Multiple

- Profitable business in operation more than five years: Assign a value of 6 or more.
- Profitable business in operation two to five years: Assign a value of 2 to 5.
- Start-up business: Assign a value of 0 to 1.

Application of This Method

First: Determine the net FMV of assets.

Second: Determine the required amount of return of net FMV of assets.

Third: Estimate the amount of compensation that a manager would earn to run this type of business.

Fourth: Add net earnings before taxes and manager compensation for a period of at least three years and divide by the number of years in the period chosen. The number that results is called *average net earnings*.

Fifth: Determine the value of the intangible assets. This is simply the intangible asset multiple times average net earnings less manager compensation and required amount of return of net FMV of assets.

Example: Take two businesses, A and B, with net FMV of assets of $150,000. The reasonable manager's compensation is $40,000. The firm is profitable and has been in business for four and one-half years and has been assigned an intangible asset multiple of 4. The required amount of return of net FMV of assets is 15 percent. The calculations are as follows:

	Steps	Business A	Business B
A.	Net FMV of assets	$150,000	$150,000
B.	Required amount of return of net FMV of assets (Line A × 15%)	22,500	22,500
C.	Manager's compensation	40,000	40,000
D.	Average net earnings	75,000	60,000
E.	Earnings associated with intangible assets (Line D – Line B – C)	12,500	(2,500)
F.	Value of intangible assets [intangible asset multiple (4) × Line E]	60,000	None
G.	Purchase price (Line A) plus intangible assets (Line F)	$210,000	$150,000 (Maybe less)

Note that Business B is worth no more than the value of its net FMV of assets. If there are intangible assets, they do not help the profitability of the business. In fact, they may be hindering it. In addition, Business B's tangible assets may not be earning all they should.

Warning: Note that none of these methods may be totally accurate. However, use of all or some of these methods will provide you with a guideline in pricing a business. In addition, other factors such as those below could influence how much you are willing to pay.

* Synergy that results from matching your skills or products with those of the on-going business.
* Your status, as you perceive it, associated with the ownership of that particular business.

Also, as stated earlier, you should never pay for your own potential or value added that results from the purchase of the business. The price paid to seller should reflect the business as it has performed and now stands.

TAX ASPECTS TO CONSIDER WHEN PURCHASING A BUSINESS

Allocating Price

Buyer and seller agree as to the allocation of price. When you buy a business, you are really buying all the individual assets of that business. Because of our tax laws, allocation of the purchase price may become an issue. Therefore, it is necessary to classify the assets you have purchased in order to allocate the purchase price to your benefit. The classification scheme for assets follows.

Asset Classifications:
Cash and cash like

* Accounts and notes receivable
* Installment notes and accounts receivable

Tangible Assets

* Merchandise inventories
* Land and leaseholds
* Buildings, machinery, furniture, and fixtures

Intangible Assets

* Patents
* Copyrights
* Agreements not to compete
* Client or customer lists
* Goodwill

Cost Allocation Rules

The 1986 Tax Reform Act (TRA) requires both buyer and seller in certain asset acquisitions to decide the purchase price among the transferred assets using a prescribed formula. The new law's allocation rules apply only to "applicable asset acquisitions" which is defined in Internal Revenue Code section 1060(a) as ". . . any transfer of assets that amounts to a business in which the seller's basis is determined wholly by reference to the consideration paid for the assets." A group of assets is considered a business if their character is such that goodwill can be attached to the assets. Therefore, you will have to apply the special allocation rule to the following situations:

* Sale of a business by an individual or partnership;
* Sale of a partnership interest in which the basis of the purchasing partner's proportionate share of the partnership's assets is adjusted to reflect the purchase price; or
* Purchase price of assets following a stock purchase.

The 1986 Tax Reform Act applies to transactions after May 6, 1986, unless a contract was binding on and before May 6, 1986.

The allocation method used is prescribed in Temporary Regulation Section 1.338(b)-2T and is as follows:

> *First:* Purchase price of the assets acquired is first reduced by cash and cash-like items.
>
> *Second:* The balance is allocated first to tangible assets, and then to intangible assets.
>
> *Third:* The remainder must be allocated to goodwill.

Note: You cannot allocate more than the assets' fair market value. Since there have been no long-term capital gains provisions since January 1, 1987, the seller should be ambivalent toward allocation of sales price among various assets. Remember, goodwill is not amortizable for tax purposes.

Future Requirements

The Internal Revenue Service is currently formulating regulations that may require the seller and buyer to file information returns disclosing amounts allocated to goodwill and to any other categories of assets.

If a buyer and seller deal at arm's length, their agreement will be such that they will allocate the purchase price among all the assets purchased. If the allocation does not represent realistic values or its purpose is tax evasion, then a reallocation will be performed by the Internal Revenue Service. Therefore, we suggest you ask yourself the following questions when deciding how to allocate the purchase price among the assets you are going to purchase:

> * What is the projected business profit or loss?
> * What is the estimated life of each tangible and intangible asset?
> * How is the purchase price to be allocated among the assets?

Again, remember the following:

> • Goodwill is not amortizable for tax purposes.
> • Long-term capital gains no longer receive preferential tax treatment.

Note: Given the current political climate and discussion about the economy, there is a good chance that favorable tax treatment of long-term capital gains will be restored. As a result, the following table explains how buyer and seller would be affected should preferential long-term capital gains treatment be restored.

Item	Buyer	Seller
Inventory	Cost-related asset	Gain is ordinary
Plant and equipment	More depreciable	Less depreciation recapture
Covenant	More amortizable	Less ordinary income
Leasehold	More amortizable	Less ordinary income
Goodwill	Less no benefit	Long term capital gains

For example, assume the purchase price of the business was $120,000.

Asset	Buyer	Seller
Cash	$ 5,000	$ 5,000
Inventory	20,000	20,000
Plant & equipment	70,000	40,000
Covenant	12,000	20,000
Leasehold	12,000	20,000
Goodwill	1,000	15,000
	$120,000	$120,000

PROTECTING YOURSELF FROM HIDDEN LIABILITIES

The sale of a business will take one of two forms: sale of assets or sale of stock.

If a business is a sole proprietorship, the only form the transaction can take is to be a sale of assets. If the business is a corporation, however, the transaction could be a sale of assets or sale of stock. Generally, the sale of a partnership business will be treated in the same manner as the sale of a sole proprietorship although there are a few instances when the transfer of a partnership business is accomplished through a transfer of partnership shares.

Sale of Assets Versus Sale of Stock

Sale of Assets

In the sale of assets, the buyer, as a rule, does not assume the obligations of the business unless he or she specifically agrees to do so. There are certain issues that usually surface whenever assets of a business are sold. These issues are listed below.

* The sale of assets will require individual documents of transfer, such as deeds, assignments, vehicle registrations, and bill of sale for those assets that are being transferred.
* The sale of business tangible personal property may result in a sales tax if the state taxing agency determines that it is not an occasional sale, whereas the sale of corporate stock will not.
* If loans are to be used to purchase the assets of the acquired business, then the lender's consent to the purchase of those assets will usually be required.

Sale of Stock

When a business transfer occurs because the stock of a corporation has been sold, the entire business is transferred, which includes liabilities as well as assets. Thus, in sale of stock, the buyer should be concerned with inheriting both present and potential liabilities of the business.

As a rule, if you are buying a business through the purchase of its stock, you should pay attention to the representations and warranties made by the seller. Because you are buying the liabilities as well as the assets of the business, you will want legally enforceable assurances that the corporation is in the same condition it was represented to you by the seller. If a representation concerning the business was made to you at a time substantially before the close of escrow, then you should insist that the purchase and sale agreement contain covenants and promises to the effect that the representations will remain the same through the closing of escrow.

In addition, you should insist on an indemnification agreement in which there is some type of remedy in the event the representations turn out to be false. If you are especially concerned about this aspect, you should try to get the seller to agree that a reserve will be held in escrow to be made available for any damages that result from a representation that is determined to be untrue.

Regardless of what some people will tell you, the legal procedures in buying an existing business can be quite complex. It is best to seek the assistance of an attorney when negotiating the sale to protect yourself from assuming hidden liabilities.

Following are five basic questions concerning hidden liabilities when purchasing the assets of a business. Each one of these issues are discussed in detail in this section.

1. Has a security interest been filed against the property of the seller's business?
2. Has there been compliance with the Bulk Transfer Act?
3. Have both an employment release and sales and use release been presented?
4. Are there any federal tax liens?
5. Are there any potential product liability claims?

Has a Security Interest Been Filed Against the Property of the Seller's Business?

The concept of the security interest as credit tool is basic to the business world. A *security interest* is an interest in personal property or fixtures that secures payment or performance of an obligation. The property in which the interest is held is called the *collateral*. The party holding the interest is called the *secured party*.

Perfecting the security interest. A creditor has two main concerns if the debtor defaults. First, satisfaction of the debt out of the collateral, and, second, priority over other creditors. For a business person to have a legally enforceable security interest against the collateral, three requirements must be met:

- The agreement, generally, must be in writing;
- The secured party must give value to the debtor; and
- The debtor must have rights in the collateral.

For the business person to have priority over the claims of other creditors such as lenders or suppliers, he or she must perfect security interests. There are three basic methods to perfect a security interest.

First method: Take possession of the collateral.

Second method: Execute a purchase money security interest in the goods.

Third method: File a financing statement.

The third method, filing a financing statement, is the most popular method of perfecting a security interest. There may be, unbeknownst to you, a lien that has been placed against the seller's property. The

Secretary of State's office for the state in which the business is located or operating will provide, for a small fee, a listing of any security interest that has been recorded as a lien against the personal assets of the business you are buying.

To request this information, you will need to use a UCC-3 form. *Note*: Not all UCC-3 forms are identical. Some states share a common format, while others have a format that is substantially different. The states that use the same format are:

Alabama	Massachusetts
Alaska	Mississippi
Arizona	Montana
Colorado	New Hampshire
Connecticut	New Jersey
Delaware	New Mexico
District of Columbia	North Carolina
Hawaii	North Dakota
Idaho	Oklahoma
Indiana	South Carolina
Kansas	Tennessee
Kentucky	Virginia
Maine	West Virginia
Maryland	Wyoming

Exhibit 3-5 shows a UCC-3 form for the state of Florida. Compare this format to Exhibit 3-6, which shows a UCC-3 form for the state of Washington.

The form that is used as a financing statement is the UCC-1 form. Like the UCC-3, the UCC-1 varies from state to state. Exhibit 3-7 gives an example of New York state's form UCC-1 and Exhibit 3-8 shows a UCC-1 form from the state of Arizona.

If you determine that the assets that you are purchasing include land or a building as well as personal assets, then in addition to requesting information from the Secretary of State, you should conduct a title search at the county recorder's office to see if the seller has a good title and if there are any recorded deeds of trust, judicial liens, tax liens, mechanics liens, or mortgages that have been filed against the property.

Has There Been Compliance with the Bulk Transfer Act?

Many types of businesses, especially retail and wholesale, must prepare, prior to their purchase, a "Notice To Creditors of Bulk Transfer." The object of bulk sales statutes, which are found in the Uniform Commercial Code, is to prevent the seller from pocketing the proceeds from the sale and "skipping town" without paying his or her creditors. The notice requirements of the bulk sales statutes vary from restrictive, as in the cases of Florida and Pennsylvania, to liberal, as in the case of California.

Restrictive. The seller provides the buyer with a list, which is sworn to under penalty of perjury, of existing creditors including those creditors whose claim is disputed by the seller. The buyer must give notice of the proposed sale to each creditor of the seller at least ten days before he or she takes possession of the property or pays for it. The notice must specify the following:

* The sale is about to be made;
* The name and address of the buyer and seller;

 * Whether the liabilities of the seller will be paid by the buyer; and
 * The address to which creditors should send their bills.

A second list is then prepared jointly by seller and buyer, which lists the property being transferred. The buyer must then keep in his or her possession, for a term of not less than six months, both this list and the creditor list and must also permit inspection by any creditor of the seller.

Liberal. Notice must be filed in the county in which the business operates with the county recorder's office. In addition, this same notice must be published in the judicial district in which the seller's main office is located and in the judicial district in which the business is located in a newspaper that has been judicially decreed as one of general circulation. Furthermore, a copy of the notice must be sent by certified mail to the tax collector of the county in which the property is located. Exhibit 3-9 gives an example of the form used in the state of California, called the "Notice to Creditors of Bulk Transfer."

Bulk transfer defined. Generally, a bulk transfer or bulk sale is any transfer of a substantial portion of the seller's equipment, materials, supplies, or merchandise. Also included as a rule are restaurants, bakeries, garages, and cleaners. Service businesses or businesses in which the sale of merchandise is only incidental are not subject to the bulk transfer requirements. The entire business does not have to be sold or transferred in order to invoke bulk transfer requirements. For instance, one case, which applied California law, held that the transfer of as little as 5 percent of the inventory of a retail merchant was a bulk transfer.

Failure to comply. If the required notice has not been given, the transfer is deemed "fraudulent and void," and creditors of the seller may disregard the sale of the business and seize the assets that are in the hands of the buyer. In certain instances, creditors may also go beyond the buyer and seize any property the buyer has sold to its customers.

Provision for payment. If the assets being sold amount to less than $1 million, a provision for payment of the seller's creditors is required. The requisite notice must designate someone, usually an escrow agent, to receive the creditors' claims before the date of transfer. Afterwards, the escrow agent is under a duty to pay these claims with whatever cash is due the seller.

Buyer has the burden. It is not the seller's responsibility to notify the creditors. The buyer has this obligation and will be held liable if he or she fails to give proper notice.

Creditors that are protected. All creditors that have claims arising from transactions or events occurring before the bulk transfer are protected. As a result, those individuals whose claims are contingent (such as tort claimants), as well as suppliers that have definite and ascertainable claims, are protected.

Have Both an Employment Release and a Sales and Use Tax Release Been Presented?

The general rule is that in a sale of a business, the buyer is not responsible for the seller's obligations provided the requirements of bulk sale statutes have been satisfied. In most states, there are exceptions to this rule. Two exceptions are tax liabilities, which can be imposed upon the buyer of the business for amounts owed to the state by the seller for sales and use tax, and for unemployment tax and income tax withholdings. Furthermore, if the buyer fails to withhold from the purchase price of the business sufficient amounts to pay the state then the buyer becomes liable for the amounts owed. Often, the liability is a personal liability and not merely a lien on the assets of the business.

You should always ask the seller if he or she has paid all sales and use taxes and employment taxes due the state. If not, you may be held liable to the state for those unpaid taxes. We strongly recommend that as a condition for the purchase of a business, you require the seller to present you with two releases: The first release should come from the state agency that levies and collects sales and use tax. The second release should come from the state agency that levies and collects employment taxes. In California, for example, you would require the seller to present you with a "Certificate of No Tax Due," which is issued by the State Board of Equalization and is a release from sales and use tax claims, and a "Certificate of Release of Buyer," which is issued by the Employment Development Department and is a release from employment tax claims. Exhibit 3-10 is a list of the state agencies that levy and collect sales and use tax.

Indemnity Provision. In addition to requiring certain releases from state tax agencies, we also recommend that you require an indemnity provision in the Purchase and Sale Agreement which states that the seller will pay all amounts that are owed to any state tax agency. Inserting an indemnity provision will enhance the buyer's ability to enforce his or her legal right to reimbursement if he or she is obligated to pay any hidden taxes. The indemnity provision will allow the buyer to offset any payments that he or she makes to the state against installment obligations that he or she may still owe to the seller.

Are There Any Federal Tax Liens?

The federal government allows the Internal Revenue Service, per Internal Revenue Code section 6321, to use tax liens. However, the lien is not valid against the buyer until notice of the lien has been filed with the proper governmental body as designated by state law.

In most states, federal tax liens on personal property must be filed with the Secretary of State's office if the taxpayer is a corporation or partnership. If the taxpayer is an individual, however, the filing takes place in the county in which the individual taxpayer lives. Thus, a UCC-3 request should uncover any federal tax liens that have been filed against the seller if the seller is a corporation or partnership. For example, see Exhibit 3-11, which shows a report from the California Secretary of State. Note the bottom of the exhibit. It states that the filing officer certifies there are no effective financing statements, federal liens, state tax liens, attachment liens, or judgment liens on file against the debtor.

Are There Any Potential Product Liability Claims?

Generally, the purchase of the assets of a business does not subject the buyer to existing liabilities unless:

* The buyer agrees to assume them;
* The transaction amounts to a consolidation or merger of two corporations;
* The purchasing corporation is a mere continuation of the seller; or
* The transfer to the buyer is for the fraudulent purpose of escaping liability for the seller's debt.

In many states, however, the assumption of liabilities by a buyer of business assets may occur when the seller has manufactured and sold defective products. California was one of the first states to promulgate this rule, and many states have adopted the same rule or a similar one. The rule originated from a landmark case, *Ray* v. *Alad*. In the case, the State Supreme Court of California held that when a buyer acquires the principal assets of a manufacturing business, such as inventory, plant and equipment, and trade name, which later dissolves, and then continues the output of its line of products, it will assume strict tort liability for any defect in those products, even though it did not manufacture or sell the product that caused the injury.

The California Supreme Court justified the imposition of strict liability upon the buyer of the business for the following reasons: (1) the virtual destruction of the plaintiff's remedies against the original manufacturer because of the buyer's acquisition of the business; (2) the buyer's inability to assume the original manufacturer's risk; (3) the fairness of requiring the buyer to assume responsibility for defective products because along with the goodwill associated with the original manufacturer must come the burdens that are necessarily attached to it.

As a result of this case and others like it, be aware that when you purchase a manufacturing business you may incur exposure to potential liability claims.

USING ESCROW TO PREVENT PROBLEMS

Although the use of escrow is not required unless real estate is involved, you want to protect yourself by using an escrow to handle the sale of the business. Escrow is simply an account held by an escrow company, escrow department of a financial institution, or an attorney who is a neutral third party.

The job of the escrow holder is to act as an independent party that holds the agreement, escrow instructions, funds, and related documents until all conditions for the sale have been completed. The escrow holder bears a fiduciary relationship to both buyer and seller. The status as a dual agent for both parties continues at all times prior to the performance of the conditions of escrow.

In addition, the escrow holder has a duty to exercise reasonable skill and ordinary diligence in his or her employment, and he is responsible for any loss caused by his or her negligence. Once both buyer and seller have satisfied the escrow instructions, the escrow holder will disburse the funds to the seller and deliver documents of title to the buyer.

Unlike the purchase of real estate, where the purchaser receives title insurance, which guarantees ownership of the property subject only to specific encumbrances agreed to in advance, the purchase of an existing business may contain a number of liens and claims. As a result, the buyer should get an assurance from the escrow holder that the various liens, notices, and tax releases, which were discussed earlier in this chapter, have been obtained. Escrow holders traditionally try to limit their liability in these areas as much as possible. Therefore, be sure to have your attorney review the escrow instructions.

Escrow fees differ among escrow agents. For a business transfer in which the purchase price is approximately $500 thousand the escrow fee will generally fall between $900 and $1,200. Beyond $500 thousand, escrow fees usually range between .1 percent and .3 percent of the purchase price.

POTENTIAL PROBLEMS WITH TRANSFERRING THE LEASE TO THE NEW OWNER

In most business situations, the lease is one of the most important aspects of the purchase because it enables the business to occupy a specific location. Therefore, if there is a favorable lease be sure to determine before the sale that the lease can and will be assigned to you.

In addition, because the lease represents a major expense be sure to carefully examine the new lease to determine whether you will have to pay for common area maintenance, utilities, real property taxes, insurance, and so on. To be safe, you should seek the assistance of an attorney. Many commercial leases are twenty-five to forty-five pages in length and contain numerous clauses which may seem innocuous at the time you sign the lease but later become major sources of conflict.

Examples of provisions you should be aware of include the following.

PROVISION	ISSUES THAT SHOULD BE ADDRESSED
Rent	Is there a reasonable grace period, such as 10 days, before a penalty for late rent?
Rent increases	Does the rent increase periodically by the increased operating expenses under a pro rata formula, by the consumer price index, or by a fixed percentage? Furthermore, is there a maximum cap on the increase?
Service and utilities	Who provides for and pays for such services as heating, ventilating and air conditioning, electric lighting, water, and janitorial? Are these services provided only during normal business hours?
Security deposit	Under what circumstances and when is the security deposit returned?
Casualty	If the premises are damaged by casualty, does the landlord have an obligation to repair and restore the premises as soon as reasonably possible? And does the tenant's rent obligation abate until the damage is repaired?
Alterations	Will the landlord give consent for you to make alterations and additions to the premises as the need arises?
Use	Can you use the premises for any lawful purpose? (A lease that is too restrictive may preclude your business from changing as times change.)
Assignments	Will you be prohibited from assigning or subleasing the premises without the consent of the landlord? What standards has the landlord established that will determine which assignees or subtenants will be acceptable?
Renewals	Will the lease be renewed automatically unless either party gives notice of the termination? Will you have an option to extend the term of the lease on the same terms and conditions as those found in the original lease? How will the rent for the option period be determined?

Chapter 3 Exhibits

Exhibit 3.1   Worksheet: Evaluating Your Skills to Run a
              Particular Business

Exhibit 3.2   Worksheet: Determining the Type of Business
              that Will Meet Your Personal Needs

Exhibit 3.3   Worksheet: Profit and Loss 3 Years

Exhibit 3.4   Worksheet: Balance Sheet Comparison 3 Years

Exhibit 3.5   UCC Form 3 Request for Information (State
              of Florida)

Exhibit 3.6   UCC Form 3 Request for Information (State
              of Washington)

Exhibit 3.7   UCC Form 1 Financing Statement (State of
              New York)

Exhibit 3.8   UCC Form 1 Financing Statement (State of
              Arizona)

Exhibit 3.9   Notice to Creditors of Bulk Transfer (State of
              California)

Exhibit 3.10   Certificate Request from California
              Secretary of State

Exhibit 3.1 Worksheet

EVALUATING YOUR SKILLS TO RUN A PARTICULAR BUSINESS

Name of Business: _____

Type of Business: _____

How Much Skill and Experience Does This Business Require?

Skill	Much Experience	Some Experience	Little Experience	Rate Your Experience
Accounting				
Selling				
Advertising				
Hiring				
Training				
Purchasing				
Motivating				
Production				
Planning				
Computer use				
Administration				
Technical				
Other:				

Do not be dismayed if you are lacking experience in any of these areas. There are various sources of information to help you become knowledgeable before you enter into a business. Some of the sources are this handbook, and other books on the subject, business consultants, small business administration courses, college courses, and adult education courses.

Exhibit 3.2 Worksheet

Determining the Type of Business That Will Meet Your Personal Needs

Name of Business: _____

Type of Business: _____

How Will This Business Satisfy My Needs?

My Needs	Full Satisfaction	Much Satisfaction	Partial Satisfaction	Little Satisfaction
Income				
Status				
Location				
Work hours				
Excitement				
Growth				
Security				
Other:				

Are You Able to Clearly Answer These Two Questions?

Question #1: Why am I going into business for myself?

_____

_____

Question #2: How will this business satisfy my needs?

_____

_____

Exhibit 3.3 Worksheet

PROFIT AND LOSS
3-YEAR WORKSHEET

Item	Year 1	Percentage of Sales	Year 2	Percentage of Sales	Percentage Change	Year 3	Percentage of Sales	Percentage Change	Comments
Gross sales									
Returns and allowances									
Net sales									
Cost of sales									
Gross margin									
Sales General Administrative Expenses									
Owner's draw									
Employee payroll									
Rent									
Commissions									
Utilities Telephone									
Professional (legal and accounting)									
Insurance									
Promotion									
Auto/truck									
Office expenses									
Bad debts									

Exhibit 3.3 (cont'd.)

Other	
Total expenses	
Depreciation	
Interest	
Net before tax	
Tax	
Net income	
Traditional Cash Flow Net income plus depreciation	

Exhibit 3.4 Worksheet

BALANCE SHEET COMPARISON
3-YEAR WORKSHEET

Assets	Year 1	Percentage of Assets	Year 2	Percentage of Assets	Year 3	Percentage of Assets	Comments
Cash							
Accounts receivable							
Inventory							
Net fixed assets							
Other assets							
Intangibles							
Total Assets		100%		100%		100%	

Liabilities and Net Worth	Year 1	Percentage of Assets	Year 2	Percentage of Assets	Year 3	Percentage of Assets	Comments
Accounts payable							
Notes payable							
CPLTD [a]							
Accruals							
Other liabilities							
Long-term debt							
Capital							
Total Liabilities and Net Worth		100%		100%		100%	

Exhibit 3.4 (Cont'd.)

[a] CPLTD stands for current portion of long-term debt.

1. Calculate each asset, liability, and capital entry as a percentage of total assets.
2. Compare each entry's percentage to the previous year, and note trends.
3. Compare each entry's percentage value with the appropriate Robert Morris Associates industry figure and note those items that do not fall within normal parameters.
4. Request information concerning adverse trends or abnormal entry percentage values.

STATE AGENCIES: SALES AND USE TAX

STATE	AGENCY
Alabama	Department of Revenue Sales and Use Taxes Montgomery, Alabama 36130
Alaska	Department of Revenue Pouch S Juneau, Alaska 99801
Arizona	Sales Tax Division Phoenix, Arizona 85007
Arkansas	Sales and Use Tax Division Department of Finance and Administration Little Rock, Arkansas 72201
California	Department of Business Taxes State Board of Equalization P.O. Box 1799 Sacramento, California 95808
Colorado	Department of Revenue State Capitol Annex Denver, Colorado 80203
Connecticut	Sales, Use, and Excise Tax Division Hartford, Connecticut 06115
Delaware	State Division of Revenue Wilmington, Delaware 19801
District of Columbia	Department of Finance and Revenue 300 Indiana Avenue, N.W. Washington, D.C. 20001
Florida	Sales Tax Bureau Department of Revenue Tallahassee, Florida 32304
Georgia	Sales and Use Tax Unit Department of Revenue Atlanta, Georgia 30334
Hawaii	Department of Taxation State Tax Office Building 425 Queen Street Honolulu, Hawaii 96813

Idaho

Sales Tax Division
State Tax Commission
Boise, Idaho 83707

Illinois

Department of Revenue
Springfield, Illinois 62706

Indiana

Sales Tax Division
Department of Revenue
100 N. Senate Avenue
Indianapolis, Indiana 46204

Iowa

Division of Retail Sales and Use Tax
Department of Revenue
Lucas State Office Building
Des Moines, Iowa 50319

Kansas

Sales and Compensating Tax Division
State Revenue Building
Department of Revenue
Topeka, Kansas 66612

Kentucky

Sales Tax Division
Department of Revenue
Frankfort, Kentucky 40601

Louisiana

Collector of Revenue
Baton Rouge, Louisiana 70821

Maine

Sales Tax Division
Bureau of Taxation
Augusta, Maine 04330

Maryland

Retail Sales Tax Division
Treasury Department
301 West Preston St.
Baltimore, Maryland 21201

Massachusetts

Sales and Use Taxes
Department of Corporations
Boston, Massachusetts 02133

Michigan

Sales and Uses Taxes
Department of Treasury
Revenue Division
Treasury Building
Lansing, Michigan 48922

Minnesota	Sales and Use Tax Division Department of Taxation Centennial Office Building St. Paul, Minnesota 55101
Mississippi	Sales and Use Tax Division State Tax Commission Jackson, Mississippi 39205
Missouri	Sale and Use Tax Bureau P.O. Box 840 Jefferson City, Missouri 65102
Nebraska	Sales and Use Tax Unit Department of Revenue Box 4818, State Capitol Lincoln, Nebraska 65809
Nevada	Nevada Tax Commission Carson City, Nevada 89701
New Jersey	Division of Taxation Department of Treasury Trenton, New Jersey 08625
New Mexico	Bureau of Revenue Santa Fe, New Mexico 87501
New York	Sales Tax Bureau Department of Taxation and Finance Tax and Finance Building 9 State Campus Albany, New York 12226
North Carolina	Sales and Use Tax Division Revenue Building - Main Office Raleigh, North Carolina 27611
North Dakota	Sales Tax State Capitol Building Bismarck, North Dakota 58501
Ohio	Sales and Excise Division Department of Taxation 68 East Gay Street Columbus, Ohio 43151
Oklahoma	Sales and Use Taxes Oklahoma Tax Commission 2101 Lincoln Blvd. Oklahoma City, Oklahoma 73105

Pennsylvannia	Bureau of Taxes for Education Department of Revenue Harrisburg, Pennsylvania 17128
Rhode Island	Department of Adminstration 49 Westminister Street Providence, Rhode Island 02903
South Carolina	Sales and Use Tax Division South Carolina Tax Commission Columbia, South Carolina 29201
South Dakota	Sales and Use Tax Division Department of Revenue Pierre, South Dakota 57501
Tennessee	Sales and Use Tax Division Department of Revenue War Memorial Building Nashville, Tennessee 37219
Texas	Comptroller of Public Accounts Austin, Texas 78711
Utah	Sales Tax State Tax Commission 201 State Office Building Salt Lake City, Utah 84114
Vermont	Department of Taxes State of Vermont P.O. Box 547 Montpelier, Vermont 05602
Virginia	Sales and Use Tax Division Department of Taxation P.O. Box 6L Richmond, Virginia 23215
Washington	Department of Revenue Olympia, Washington 98501

Information in items 1 and 2 must agree exactly with the original filing information or as previously amended.

THIS SPACE FOR USE OF FILING OFFICER
Date, Time, Number & Filing Office

ONLY ONE NAME PER BOX

DEBTOR (Last Name First if a Person)
NAME

1A

MAILING ADDRESS

CITY   STATE

MULTIPLE DEBTOR   (IF ANY)   (Last Name First if a Person)
NAME

1B

MAILING ADDRESS

CITY   STATE

MULTIPLE DEBTOR   (IF ANY)   (Last Name First if a Person)
NAME

1C

MAILING ADDRESS

CITY   STATE

SECURED PARTY (Last Name First if a Person)
NAME

2A

MAILING ADDRESS

CITY   STATE

UPDATE

AUDIT

MULTIPLE SECURED PARTY   (IF ANY)   (Last Name First if a Person)
NAME

2B

MAILING ADDRESS

CITY   STATE

VALIDATION INFORMATION

3. This statement refers to original Financing Statement bearing File Number _____ and filed with

The original was filed on _____ 19___

4. ☐ Continuation.   The original financing statement between the foregoing Debtor(s) and Secured Party(ies) bearing file number shown above, is still effective.

5. ☐ Termination.   Secured party no longer claims a security interest under the financing statement bearing file number shown above.

6. ☐ Partial Assignment   Some of Secured party's rights under the Financing Statement have been assigned to the assignee whose name and address are set forth in Item 11. A description of the collateral subject to the assignment is also set forth in Item 11.

7. ☐ Full Assignment   All of Secured Party's rights under the Financing Statement have been assigned to the assignee whose name and address are set forth in Item 11.

8. ☐ Amendment.   Financing Statement bearing file number shown above is amended as set forth in Item 11. Signature of Debtor required at Item 14 unless amendment changes only name or address of either party.

9. ☐ Release.   Secured party releases only the collateral described in Item 11 from the financing statement bearing file number shown above.

10. ☐ Check if true.   All documentary stamp taxes due and payable or to become due and payable pursuant to Chapter 201.22, F.S. have been paid.

11. If more space is required, attach additional sheets 8½ x 11.

12. No. of Additional Sheets presented:

14. SIGNATURE(S) OF DEBTOR(S) Necessary Only For Amendment. See Item 8.

13. Return Copy to:

NAME
ADDRESS

CITY
STATE   ZIP CODE

15. SIGNATURE(S) OF SECURED PARTY(IES) OR ASSIGNEE

STANDARD FORM — FORM UCC-3

Approved by Secretary of State, State of Florida

FILING OFFICER COPY

Exhibit 3-5

PLEASE TYPE FORM
This CHANGE STATEMENT is presented for filing pursuant to the WASHINGTON UNIFORM COMMERCIAL CODE.

☐ LEASE The terms debtor and secured party are to be construed as LESSEE and LESSOR.
☐ CONSIGNMENT - The terms debtor and secured party are to be construed as CONSIGNEE and CONSIGNOR.

1. DEBTOR(S) (or assignor(s)) (last name first, and address(es))	2. FOR OFFICE USE ONLY
TRADE NAME: (if any)	

3. SECURED PARTY(IES) (or assignee(s)) (name and address)	4. ASSIGNEE(S) OF SECURED PARTY(IES) (if applicable) (last name first, and address(es))

5. This statement refers to original FINANCING STATEMENT number _____ Dated _____

7. ☐ CONTINUATION. The original financing statement between the foregoing Debtor(s) and Secured Party(ies), bearing file number shown above is still effective.

☐ FULL ASSIGNMENT. All of the Secured Party's rights under the financing statement bearing file number shown above have been assigned to the Assignee(s) whose NAME(S) AND ADDRESS(ES) APPEAR ABOVE.

☐ PARTIAL ASSIGNMENT. The Secured Party's rights under the financing statement bearing file number shown above to the property DESCRIBED BELOW have been assigned to the Assignee(s) whose NAME(S) AND ADDRESS(ES) APPEAR ABOVE.

☐ AMENDMENT. Financing statement bearing file number shown above is amended AS SET FORTH BELOW.

☐ PARTIAL RELEASE. Secured Party(ies) releases the collateral DESCRIBED BELOW from the financing statement bearing file number shown above.

☐ TERMINATION. Secured Party(ies) no longer claims a security interest under the financing statement bearing file number shown above.

DESCRIPTION:

8. NUMBER OF ADDITIONAL SHEETS ATTACHED:

9.

_____
TYPE NAME(S) OF DEBTOR(S) (or assignor(s))

_____
TYPE NAME(S) OF SECURED PARTY(IES) (or assignee(s))

_____
SIGNATURE(S) OF DEBTOR(S) (or assignor(s))
(Required if amendment)

_____
SIGNATURE(S) OF SECURED PARTY(IES) (or assignee(s))

10. RETURN ACKNOWLEDGMENT COPY TO:

FILE WITH:

UNIFORM COMMERCIAL CODE DIVISION
DEPARTMENT OF LICENSING
P.O. BOX 9660
OLYMPIA, WA 98504
OR
IF FIXTURE FILING:
COUNTY AUDITOR OF COUNTY WHERE
ORIGINAL FILING WAS MADE.

FOR OFFICE USE ONLY: Images To
                              Be Filmed

FORM APPROVED FOR USE IN THE
STATE OF WASHINGTON

WASHINGTON UCC-3

COPY 2—FILING OFFICER—NUMERIC

Exhibit 3-6

This FINANCING STATEMENT is presented to a Filing Officer for filing pursuant to the Uniform Commercial Code.

No. of Additional Sheets Presented:

3. ☐ The Debtor is a transmitting utility.

1. Debtor(s) (Last Name First) and Address(es):	2. Secured Party(ies) Name(s) and Address(es)	4. For Filing Officer: Date, Time, No. Filing Office

5. This Financing Statement covers the following types (or items) of property:

6. Assignee(s) of Secured Party and Address(es)

☐ Products of the Collateral are also covered.

7. ☐ The described crops are growing or to be grown on: *
☐ The described goods are or are to be affixed to: *
☐ The lumber to be cut or minerals or the like (including oil and gas) is on: *
*(Describe Real Estate Below)

8. Describe Real Estate Here: ☐ This statement is to be indexed in the Real Estate Records:

9. Name of a Record Owner

No. & Street	Town or City	County	Section	Block	Lot

10. This statement is filed without the debtor's signature to perfect a security interest in collateral (check appropriate box)
☐ under a security agreement signed by debtor authorizing secured party to file this statement, or
☐ which is proceeds of the original collateral described above in which a security interest was perfected, or
☐ acquired after a change of name, identity or corporate structure of the debtor, or ☐ as to which the filing has lapsed, or already subject to a security interest in another jurisdiction:
☐ when the collateral was brought into the state, or ☐ when the debtor's location was changed to this state.

By _____
Signature(s) of Debtor(s)

By _____
Signature(s) of Secured Party(ies)

(1) Filing Officer Copy - Numerical
(5/82) **STANDARD FORM - FORM UCC-1** — Approved by Secretary of State of New York

Exhibit 3-7

STATE OF ARIZONA, County of_____ ss. on_____, 19_____ at_____o'clock_____M.

I hereby certify that the within instrument was filed (recorded) at the request of_____

Docket_____ Page_____ File number_____. Records of this office.

WITNESS my hand and offical seal the day and year first above written. _____
County Recorder

By _____

Secretary of State

Return copy or recorded original to:

ARIZONA UNIFORM COMMERCIAL CODE
FINANCING STATEMENT — Form UCC-1

This FINANCING STATEMENT is presented for filing (recording) pursuant to the Arizona Uniform Commercial Code.

1. Debtor(s) (last name first and address):	2. Secured Party(ies) and address:

3. Name and Address of Assignee of Secured Party(ies):	4. Proceeds of collateral are also covered.
	☐ If checked, products of collateral are also covered.

5. This Financing Statement covers the following types (or items) of property:

6. If the collateral is crops, the crops are growing or to be grown on the following described real estate:

7. If the collateral is (a) goods which are or are to become fixtures; (b) timber to be cut; or (c) minerals or the like (including oil and gas), or accounts resulting from the sale thereof at the wellhead or minehead to which the security interest attaches upon extraction, the legal description of the real estate concerned is:

And, this Financing Statement is to be recorded in the office where a mortgage on such real estate would be recorded. If the Debtor does not have an interest of record, the name of a record owner is:

8. This Financing Statement is signed by the Secured Party instead of the debtor to perfect or continue perfection of a security interest in:

☐ collateral already subject to a security interest in another jurisdiction when it was brought into this state.

☐ proceeds of collateral because of a change in type or use.

☐ collateral as to which the filing has lapsed or will lapse.

☐ collateral acquired after a change of name, identity, or corporate structure of the Debtor.

TERMINATION STATEMENT — The financing statement described above is terminated.

Dated: _____

_____
Signature(s) of Secured Party(ies) or Assignee of Record

Standard Form UCC-1 Approved By The Secretary Of State Of Arizona Rev. 3/83

ACKNOWLEDGEMENT AND
TERMINATION COPY

See reverse side for instructions

Exhibit 3-8

NOTICE TO CREDITORS OF BULK TRANSFER

(Secs. 6101-6107 U.C.C.)

Notice is hereby given to creditors of the within named transferor(s) that a bulk transfer is about to be made on personal property hereinafter described.

The name(s) and business address of the intended transferor(s) are:

The name(s) and business address of the intended transferee(s) are:

That the property pertinent hereto is described in general as:

and is located at:

The business name used by the said transferor(s) at said location is:

That said bulk transfer is intended to be consummated at the office of:

_____, _____, California_____ _____

on or after _____, 19_____.

This bulk transfer _____ subject to California Uniform Commercial Code Section 6106.
                     is/is not

The name and address of the person with whom claims may be filed is_____

_____,

and the last day for filing claims by any creditor shall be _____,

which is the business day before the consummation date specified above.

So far as is known to said intended Transferee(s) said intended Transferor(s) used the following additional business names and addesses within the three years last past: (If "none" so state.)

Dated _____, 19_____   _____

                                                        _____

                                                        _____

                                                        _____
                                                              Intended Transferee(s)

Exhibit 3-9

STATE OF CALIFORNIA

MARCH FONG EU
SECRETARY OF STATE
SACRAMENTO

CERTIFICATE REQUESTED ON   4 DEC 86

THE UNDERSIGNED FILING OFFICER HEREBY CERTIFIES THAT THERE ARE NO
EFFECTIVE FINANCING STATEMENTS, FEDERAL LIENS, STATE TAX LIENS,
ATTACHMENT LIENS OR JUDGEMENT LIENS ON FILE REFLECTING THE ABOVE DEBTOR
TOGETHER WITH THE ADDRESS AS SHOWN AS OF 20 NOV 1986 AT 1700 HOURS.

MARCH FONG EU
SECRETARY OF STATE

CERTIFICATE 473424-86324

PAGE   1 OF   1

Exhibit 3-10

Chapter 4

EVALUATING FRANCHISE OPPORTUNITIES

Franchising appeals to entrepreneurs for two reasons: First, it is a way to get into a business that may be less risky than if you started from scratch or bought an existing business. In addition, financing is often easier to obtain because the franchisor, in many instances, will assist the prospective franchisee in securing funds to operate the business. Second, franchising is an excellent method to expand a business. It can be used to increase the number of locations. As a rule, this method is less expensive than if you were to open and own each location yourself because you are using someone else's money and labor. Most entrepreneurs make their money from the licensing fees that franchisees pay them. Ramada Inn, Pizza Time Theatre, Jiffy Lube, Putt-Putt Golf, Pier 1 Imports, Jellystone Campgrounds, Hickory Farms, Nursefinders, and Physicians Weight Loss Centers are all examples of franchise arrangements.

Because of the interest expressed to us by entrepreneurs who want to know more about franchising, from both the perspective of buying a franchise as well as expanding a successful business through the use of a franchise arrangement, we have approached the topic of franchising with the knowledge that some of you are interested in becoming franchisees, while others of you are more concerned with starting your own franchise system. The key to the franchising process is the disclosure of sufficient information to the potential investor so that he or she can make an informed decision. As a result, we have explained the federal requirement of disclosure in detail so that you will have an understanding of your rights as a franchisee as well as your responsibilities if you choose to become a franchisor.

This chapter explains:

* Advantages and disadvantages of a franchise arrangement
* How to locate a franchise
* Types of franchises
* Government mandated disclosure of information to prospective franchisees
* Typical issues in a franchise contract

    *   What to expect from a franchisor

ADVANTAGES AND DISADVANTAGES

Some of the advantages of owning a franchise are:

*   The franchisor will provide a "cookbook" method of business decision making from management of personnel to assistance in purchasing.
*   The products and services are market tested, which reduces the risk of failure.
*   The typical franchisor will promote and advertise their products to your advantage.
*   Some franchisors will provide financial aid packages or assistance in seeking financial aid.

A few of the major disadvantages of owning a franchise are:

*   The franchisee loses a large degree of management freedom, which could be a real minus if you have the personality that relishes freedom.
*   In order to ensure quality control, the franchisor will often require the franchisee to purchase products and services from certain vendors, even when better and less expensive sources are available.
*   Purchasing a franchise can be expensive even though much of the risk has been eliminated.
*   It can be difficult to sell or transfer ownership of a franchise for a variety of reasons. A common situation is when the franchisor refuses to approve the prospective purchaser because of questionable credit or no track record.

Franchisor Control

Many franchisors will exercise a wide latitude of control over your business, which may cause considerable friction if you are not prepared. Below is a list of the various methods that franchisors use to control a franchisee's method of operation.

*   Hours of operation
*   Personnel policies
*   Accounting practices
*   Production techniques
*   Site approval
*   Site design and appearance
*   Promotional campaigns requiring franchisee participation
*   Restrictions on the type of customers that may be solicited
*   Requirements for servicing or repairing products
*   Inventory controls
*   Required display of certain goods in a certain manner

Types of Assistance

A franchisor can offer you a variety of procedures that will help ensure success. Some of these are listed below.

- Select site location
- Establish an accounting system
- Assist in locating financing
- Furnish advice on how to handle personnel
- Offer management training classes
- Offer sales training classes
- Show how successful marketing practices are performed
- Provide detailed operating manuals

Ten Questions You Must Ask Every Franchisor

An ounce of prevention is worth a pound of cure. Not only must you ask intelligent questions but you must listen and observe. Below are ten basic questions that quickly address the important issues.

1. What type of financial backing does the franchisor have?
2. Will the franchisor be in competition with you?
3. When will you get to see the franchisor's disclosure statements?
4. How long has the franchisor been in business; how long has it been offering franchises?
5. Has the franchisor or its directors ever filed for bankruptcy?
6. Has the franchisor ever been involved in litigation?
7. What type of marketing plan does the franchisor have?
8. Does the franchisor pay for initial training, and what is included?
9. Why is the product or service marketable in the territory that the franchisor is offering it in?
10. What type of manual will the franchisor provide for the training of staff and the operation of the franchise?

LOCATING A FRANCHISE

There are numerous sources of information for locating franchise opportunities. We can start with those sources mentioned in Chapter 3. These sources, however, are not the only ones. Additional sources are listed below.

* Contact the franchisor directly
* *The Complete Handbook of Franchises*, D. Seltz, Addison-Wesley, 1981.
* *Directory of Franchising Organizations*. Pilot Industries, Inc., 347 Fifth Ave., NY, NY 10016.
* *Franchising*. Small Business Reporter, Bank of America. Volume 9, No.9, 1978. Check with a local branch.

* *Franchise Index/Profile.* Small Business Administration. U.S. Government Printing Office, Washington, D.C. 20402. N45000-00125-3. Try your local SBA office.
* *Franchise Opportunities Handbook.* U.S. Department of Commerce. 1982, US Government Printing Office, Washington, D.C. 20402.
* *Continental Franchise Review.* P.O.Box 6360, Denver, CO 80206. Bi-weekly.
* Trade shows are held regularly around the country to present franchise and distributorship opportunities. One of the larger promoters is The Quality Show Company. Its telephone number is 305-647-8521. This promoter presented approximately twenty-three shows last year.

In general, the government, and specifically the Small Business Administration, is the single best source of information for the location of franchise opportunities. The second best source for reference material is a library. You might try the business school library at a local university or a main public library.

LEGAL ASPECTS

Definition of a Franchise

Franchises are regulated at the federal level, and, in some instances, at the state level. As a consequence, the definition of what constitutes a franchise sometimes differs from state to state. This issue takes on importance because franchisees receive special government protection that is not afforded to businesses that are defined as mere distributors. This protection, however, varies from state to state depending on whether the state has passed legislation protecting franchisees.

If a state has not passed legislation, then federal law will be used to define a franchise. In addition, a particular state may define a franchise in a manner that covers many more business situations than the federal definition. Thus, whether there will be protection at all, and, if so, the type of protection, will depend on whether the business activity falls within the definition of a franchise. The Federal Trade Commission (FTC) has defined a franchise as "an arrangement in which the owner of a trademark, a trade name, or a copyright licenses others, under specified conditions or limitations, to use the trademark, trade name, or copyright in purveying goods and services."

In addition to the federal definition, some states have further defined the term franchise so that it includes additional activities. California, for example, has a more encompassing definition of the word franchise. According to California law, a franchise relationship exists whenever the following occurs:

A contract or agreement is entered into, either expressed or implied, whether oral or written, between two or more persons by which:

1. A franchisee is granted the right to engage in the business of offering, selling, or distributing goods or services under a marketing plan or system prescribed in substantial part by a franchisor;

2. The operation of the franchisee's business pursuant to such plan or system is substantially associated with the franchisor's trademark, service mark, trade name, logotype, advertising, or other commercial symbol designating the franchisor or its affiliate; and

3. The franchisee is required to pay, directly or indirectly, a franchise fee.

Be sure to check your state's definition of a franchise. A franchisor may attempt to classify his or her relationship with investors as a wholesale distributorship when in actuality it is a franchise.

Types of Franchises

There are three types of franchises: distributorships, chainstyle businesses, and manufacturing or processing plants.

A *distributorship* occurs when a manufacturer licenses a dealer to sell its product. Many times a distributorship will be given an exclusive territory. This type of franchising agreement is one of the oldest, and is predominately used in the auto, truck, shoe, paint, and gasoline industries.

A *chainstyle* business operation occurs when a franchise operates under a franchisor's trade name and is identified as a member of a select group of dealers that engages in the franchisor's business. As a rule, the franchisee is required to follow standard operating procedures as established by the franchisor. In certain instances, the franchisee is obligated to deal exclusively with the franchisor to obtain materials and supplies. Examples of this type of arrangement are Maaco, Kentucky Fried Chicken, Avis, Hertz, Howard Johnson's, Holiday Inn, and H&R Block.

A *manufacturing* or *processing* plant arrangement occurs when the franchisor transmits to the franchisee the essential ingredients or formula to make a particular product. The franchisee then either wholesales or retails the product. This type of arrangement is most common in the soft drink industry, for example, Coca-Cola, Pepsi-Cola, and Royal Crown.

Disclosure and Registration: Protection for the Franchisee

State Law

Many states, as well as the federal government, have certain disclosure requirements that must be satisfied by the franchisor. The objective of the disclosure requirements is to protect the prospective franchisee from deception. The disclosure requirements legally compel the franchisor to provide certain information in document form to the prospective franchisee within a specified period of time, usually ten days before the franchise agreement is signed. The document is not given to the federal government.

Some states, however, go a step further and require the franchisor to register its offering, even though it is not necessary to register it with the federal government. Most of the state registration laws require the franchisor to deliver to the state certain information prior to the offer or sale of a franchise. Failure to do so may result in severe criminal and civil penalties.

Many states have different requirements, which have given franchisors headaches at times. For instance, some states, such as New York, California, Washington, and Illinois have impound rules, which means that if a state regulator, after receiving the franchisor's financial statements, concludes that the franchisor is undercapitalized, the regulator will force the franchisor to place the franchise fee into escrow until the franchisor has performed the promises it has made. Other states may not force the franchise fees into an escrow but insist that the franchisor post a bond as a guarantee of performance.

States that require registration are the following:

California	North Dakota
Connecticut	Oregon
Hawaii	Rhode Island
Illinois	South Dakota
Indiana	Texas
Maryland	Virginia
Michigan	Washington
Minnesota	Wisconsin
New York	

The FTC Rule

Disclosure requirements mandated by the FTC became effective on October 21, 1979. The purpose of the requirements was to compel certain disclosures to be made by all franchisors regardless of the state they were operating in.

Essentially, the franchisor must give a copy of the disclosure document to a prospective franchisee at the first personal meeting held to discuss the sale of the franchise, or ten business days prior to the execution by the prospective franchisee of any agreement or payment of any money, whichever occurs first.

There are two formats that may be used to satisfy the federal disclosure requirements: (1) the format set out in the rule itself, which is contained in volume 16 of the *Code of Federal Regulations* section 436.1 (16 CFR section 436.1) or (2) the *Uniform Franchise Offering Circular* (UFOC).

The FTC rule does not preempt state disclosure laws. If a franchisor wants to follow the FTC rule format, it must first investigate the laws of the particular state it intends to do business in. For instance, California rejects the FTC rule format. For those states that do not have disclosure requirements, the FTC rule disclosure format is permissible. The UFOC is an accepted format in all fifty states.

To assist you in better understanding the demands various states place on franchisors to disclose information to prospective franchisees, we have included in this handbook mandatory disclosure requirements promulgated by the state of Illinois and Washington. We believe these two states typify the approach many states have taken to protect investors in the purchase of a franchise. Exhibits 4-1 and 4-2 contain the statutory requirements as to the amount and format of information that must be disclosed to each prospective franchisee. As you will see, these two states require specific information to be presented to each potential investor. The theory underlying the basis for these statutes is that certain information is necessary if a prospective franchisee is to make an informed decision as to whether to invest his or her money in a particular business operation. To ensure the franchisee receives sufficient information in a format that is organized and understandable, the state mandates that franchisors follow a state prescribed method of disclosure.

Exhibit 4-1 shows the franchise investment protection laws for the state of Washington as they apply to disclosure of information to investors. Exhibit 4-2 shows the franchise investment protection laws for the state of Illinois as they apply to disclosure of information and the impound of franchise fees by the director of licensing.

Federal Requirements for Information Disclosure

According to 16 CFR section 436.1 *et seq.*, information must be disclosed in writing to the prospective franchisee concerning the following topics:

Identity of the Franchisor The official name and address and principal place of business of the franchisor, and of the parent firm or holding company of the franchisor, if any; the name under which the franchisor is doing business or intends to do business; and the trademarks, service marks, trade names, commercial symbols, or advertising that identify the goods, commodities, or services to be offered, sold, or distributed by the prospective franchisee.

Business Experience of the Directors and Officers The business experience during the past five years, including information concerning former employers and principal occupations, of each of the franchisor's current directors and executive officers. Executive officers include chief executive, chief operating officer, and financial, franchise marketing, training, and service officers.

Business Experience of the Franchisor The length of time the franchisor has conducted business of the type to be operated by the franchisee; the length of time the franchisor has offered or sold a franchise for such business operating under the trade name and trademark that it claims to be operating under when it approached the prospective franchisee; and the length of time the franchisor has offered for sale or sold franchises in other lines of business, together with a description of such other lines of business.

Litigation History A statement disclosing which of the directors and executive officers have at any time during the previous seven fiscal years been convicted of a felony or pleaded *nolo contendre* to a felony charge if the felony involved fraud, embezzlement, fraudulent conversion, misappropriation of property, or restraint of trade.

A statement disclosing which of the directors or executive officers have at any time during the previous seven fiscal years been held liable in a civil action resulting in a final judgment or has settled out of court any civil actions or is a party to a civil action involving allegations of fraud, embezzlement, fraudulent conversion, misappropriation of property, restraint of trade, or breach of the franchise relationship.

A statement disclosing which directors or executive officers is subject to any currently effective state or federal agency or court injunctive or restrictive order, or is a party to a proceeding currently pending in which the order is sought relating to franchise activities, franchisor-franchisee relationship, fraud, embezzlement, fraudulent conversion, misappropriation of property, or restraint of trade.

Bankruptcy History Which directors or executive officers at any time during the previous seven years has filed for bankruptcy, been adjudged a bankrupt, been reorganized due to insolvency, or been a principal, director, executive officer, or partner of any other business that filed for bankruptcy or was adjudged bankrupt.

Description of the Franchise A complete factual description of the franchise offered to be sold by the franchisor.

Franchise Fees A statement of the total funds that must be paid by the franchisee to the franchisor in order to obtain the franchise operation, such as initial franchise fees, deposits, down payments, prepaid rent, equipment and inventory purchases. If all or part of the fees or deposits are returnable, under certain conditions, the conditions must be set forth. If none of the fees or deposits are returnable then that fact must be disclosed.

Recurring Fees A statement describing any recurring fees required to be paid, in connection with operating the franchise, by the franchisee to the franchisor. Recurring fees include, but are not limited to, royalty, lease, advertising, training, sign rental fees, rental equipment, and inventory purchases.

Required Affiliations A statement setting forth the name of each person the franchisee is directly or indirectly required or advised to do business with by the franchisor, where such persons are affiliated with the franchisor.

Obligations to Purchase A statement describing any real estate, services, supplies, products, inventories, signs, fixtures, or equipment relating to the establishment or the operation of the franchise business that the franchisee is directly or indirectly required by the franchisor to purchase, lease, or rent. In addition, if a purchase, lease, or rental must be made from specific persons, a list of the names and addresses of those persons must be given to the prospective franchisee in a separate document.

Revenues Received by the Franchisor When a franchisee is obligated to buy from suppliers, a description of the basis for calculating any revenue that the franchisor will receive from those suppliers must be delivered to the prospective franchisee.

Financing Arrangements A statement of all the material terms and conditions of any financing arrangement offered directly or indirectly by the franchisor to the prospective franchisee, and a description of the terms by which any payment is to be received by the franchisor from any person offering financing to a prospective franchisee or any person arranging for financing for a prospective franchisee.

Restriction of Sales A statement describing the material facts of whether, by the terms of the franchise agreement, the franchisee is limited in the goods or services that may be offered for sale or limited to certain types of customers that can be sold, or limited to a geographic area in which sales can be conducted. Also, if a franchisor is going to grant territorial protection to a franchisee, a statement describing how this will be accomplished must be given to the prospective franchisee.

Requirement of Personal Participation A statement of the extent to which the franchisor requires the franchisee to participate personally in the direct operation of the franchise.

Termination, Cancellation, and Renewal Information must be disclosed concerning the conditions under which the franchisee may renew or extend; the conditions under which the franchisee may terminate; the obligations of the franchisee after termination of the franchise by the franchisor, and the obligations of the franchisee after termination of the franchise by the franchisee and after expiration of the franchise; the franchisee's interest upon termination of the franchise, or upon refusal to renew or extend the franchise, whether by the franchisor or by the franchisee; the conditions under which the franchisor may repurchase, whether by right or by first refusal or at the option of the franchisor (and if the franchisor has the option to repurchase the franchise, whether there will be an independent appraisal of the franchise, whether the repurchase price will be determined by a predetermined formula and whether there will be a recognition of goodwill or other intangibles associated with the repurchase price to be given to the franchisee).

In addition, information must be disclosed concerning the conditions under which the franchisee may sell or assign all or any interest in the ownership of a franchise or of the assets of the franchise business; the conditions under which the franchisor may sell or assign, in whole or in part, its interests under such agreements; the conditions under which the franchisee may modify; the rights of the franchisee's heirs or personal representative upon the death or incapacity of the franchisee; and the provisions of any covenant not to compete.

Statistical Information The franchisor must disclose the total number of franchises operating at the end of the preceding fiscal year; the name, addresses, and telephone numbers of either (a) 10 franchised outlets nearest the prospective franchisee's intended location or (b) all of the franchisees or (c) all franchisees of the franchisor in the state in which the prospective franchisee lives or where the proposed franchise is to be located, provided there are more than 10 such franchisees; the number of franchises voluntarily terminated or not renewed by franchisees within, or at the conclusion of, the term of the franchise agreement, during the preceding fiscal year; the number of franchises reacquired by the purchase by the franchisor during the term of the franchise agreement, and upon conclusion of the term of the franchise agreement, during the preceding fiscal year; the number of franchises for which the franchisor refused renewal of the franchise agreement or other agreements related to the franchise during the preceding year;

and the number of franchises that were canceled or terminated by the franchisor during the term of the franchise agreement, and upon conclusion of the term of the franchise agreement, during the preceding year.

Moreover, the franchisor must disclose a general categorization of reasons for the reacquisitions, refusals to renew or terminations and the number falling within each such category, including but not limited to, failure to comply with quality control standards, failure to make sufficient sales, and other breaches of contract.

Site Selection If the franchisor selects the site or must give its approval, the franchisor must disclose the range of time that has elapsed between the signing of the franchise agreement and the actual site selection; if the operating franchise outlets are to be provided by the franchisor, a statement disclosing the range of time that has elapsed between the signing of the franchise agreement and the commencement of the franchisee's business.

Training Programs If the franchisor offers an initial training program or informs the prospective franchisee that it intends to provide such person with initial training then the franchisor must disclose the type and nature of such training; the minimum amount, if any, of training that will be provided a franchisee; and the cost, if any, to be borne by the franchisee for the training to be provided or for obtaining such training.

Public Figure Involvement in the Franchise If the name of a public figure is used in connection with a recommendation to purchase a franchise, or as a part of the name of the franchise operation, or if the public figure is stated to be involved with the management of the franchisor, the franchisor must disclose the nature and extent of the public figure's involvement and obligations to the franchisor, including, but not limited to, the promotional assistance the public figure will provide to the franchisor and to the franchisee; the total investment of the public figure in the franchise operation; and the amount of any fee or fees the franchisee will be obligated to pay for such involvement or assistance provided by the public figure.

Financial Information About the Franchisor The franchisor must disclose a balance sheet for the most recent fiscal year, an income statement, and statement of changes of financial position for the most recent three fiscal years. Such statements are required to have been examined in accordance with generally accepted auditing standards by an independent certified or licensed public accountant.

A franchisor may use unaudited financial statements only to the extent that audited financial statements have not been made and provided that such statements are accompanied by a clear and conspicuous disclosure that they are unaudited.

The Franchise Contract

The two most important documents you will analyze are the *franchise offering circular* and the *franchise agreement*. The relationship between franchisor and franchisee is, in theory, an "arm's length" relationship between two parties in which their respective rights are determined by the contract they enter into. Generally, many franchise agreements last only one year. The reason for this short time frame is to make it clear to the franchisee that in order to keep the franchise, the terms of the franchise must be followed.

Franchise contracts usually specify the causes for which the franchisor can terminate the relationship. Common reasons for termination are the following: death of franchisee, bankruptcy, failure to make payments in a timely manner, or failure to meet sales quota.

Most franchise contracts require that notice of termination be given; however, if no time is set then a reasonable time with notice will be implied. Generally, the courts have concluded that a franchisee must be given a reasonable time to wind up the business, for example, complete accounting records, sell off inventory, or return property to the franchisor.

Franchise contracts, by nature, are long and complex, and you will need the assistance of an attorney to help you decipher and understand its numerous provisions. Although there is no such thing as a typical franchise contract, many of these agreements contain standard provisions. Below is a list of individual topics that are commonly found in franchise agreements. You should become aware of these topics because they are normally addressed in an agreement of this type and you will be better prepared for your discussions with the franchisor.

* Term of the franchise
* Site selection
* Franchisor approval of the lease
* Rights granted franchisee
* Exclusive territory
* Training programs
* Trademark or service mark restriction
* Franchisor assistance in opening and operating the franchise
* Advertising by franchisor and franchisee
* Royalty payments
* Recordkeeping and reports
* Assignment and transfer
* Franchisor's right to inspect
* Quality control
* Terminating the agreement
* Enforcement of the agreement
* Right of first refusal by franchisor
* Noncompetition with franchisee
* Franchisor's right to audit franchisee's accounting records
* Title to the operating manual

TAX ASPECTS

In review, a franchise is an agreement that gives the transferee the right to distribute, sell, or provide goods, services, or facilities within a specified area.

Key Issue

The key tax issue is whether the transfer is a sale or exchange rather than a license. If the transfer is a license, then the costs are expensed by the transferee and treated as ordinary income by the transferor. If the transfer is a sale, then the transaction is treated by the transferee as a capitalized expenditure and amortized over the life of the franchise, while the transferor treats the transaction as a sale of a capital asset. A transfer includes the following:

* Granting of a franchise;
* Transfer of a franchise by a grantee to a third party; or

       *   Renewal of a franchise.

Tax Law

A franchise transfer will not receive capital gain or loss treatment if the transferor keeps any significant power, right, or continuing interest in the franchise. The issue of significant power, right, or continuing interest has been litigated on numerous occasions. Below are some of the factors a taxing agency will analyze in determining whether to classify the transaction as a license or a sale.

* Does the franchisor have the a right to disapprove any assignment of the interest, or any part of it?
* Does the franchisor have the right to end the agreement at will?
* Does the franchisor have the right to set standards of quality?
* Does the franchisor have the right to make the recipient sell or advertise only the franchise products or services?
* Does the franchisor have the right to make the recipient buy most supplies and equipment from the franchisor?
* Does the franchisor have the right to receive payments based on the productivity, use, or disposition of the transferred asset, and, if so, are such payments a substantial part of the transfer agreement?
* Does the franchisor have the right to terminate the franchise at will?

Examples.

CASE I

Most modern franchises involve some of these powers, rights, or continuing interests. As a result, contingent payments made by the transferee are deductible as business expenses and treated as ordinary income by the transferor.

CASE II

Franchise payments made that do not depend on productivity, use, or disposition of the transferred asset are treated according to whether the transferor keeps any significant power, right, or continuing interest in the franchise. If not, franchise payments are part of the purchase price of a capital asset.

CASE III

If the transferor keeps any significant power, right, or continuing interest and receives a lump sum payment from the transferee, then the lump-sum payment is amortized over a period of time.

A lump-sum payment made to the transferor is deductible by the transferee in equal amounts over the shorter of ten years or the life of the agreement.

If the transferee makes approximately equal installments to the transferor over the agreement period or a period of more than ten years, then the payments are deductible in the year paid, which is an ordinary expense.

Note: The tax treatment of the franchise payment must be treated in a consistent manner by both the transferor and transferee.

Example: Transferor grants a franchise to transferee to operate a health club. Payments are contingent on the profitability of the franchise. Therefore, payments are ordinary income to transferor and deductible as a business expense to transferee.

WHAT TO EXPECT FROM A FRANCHISOR

If you have decided that owning a franchise is the best method for you to realize your dreams and you are willing to pay a premium to reduce risk, what should you be looking for from your franchisor? The list below is a sampling of the important factors that need to be resolved prior to the purchase.

* How long has the franchisor been in business? Does it have a successful track record? Is the franchisor new and therefore somewhat more speculative?

* Is the franchisor well financed so that it will have staying power? Or has it expanded too fast and is on the verge of bankruptcy?

* Will you be required to attend a training program? Most good franchisors expect the franchisee to attend a 2-6 week training course, often at the franchisee's expense.

* Will the franchisor provide you with assistance during the start-up phase of your business?

* Will the franchisor provide training to your new employees?

* Will the franchisor create a public relations "happening" to help get your new franchise known in the community? This type of assistance is typical of most well-capitalized franchisors.

* Does the franchisor supply credit or capital? What is your investment requirement?

* Can the franchisor be depended on to assist you with merchandising ideas? Although you may originate some of your own ideas and programs, it is always desirable to be presented with market-tested ideas. Your aim is not to reinvent the wheel but to maximize your efforts with those projects that have the greatest return for the least cost. If the franchisor is good, it will have spent the funds necessary to properly implement, test, and analyze its merchandising ideas.

* How successful has the franchisor been at finding good locations? What is its failure rate? How many franchise locations does it intend to put into your area, and are you protected from overexpansion? *Note*: Even the most successful franchisors have failures. Do not become a statistic. You should critically scrutinize the method the franchisor used in determining your location. You should also insist upon inspecting any demographic data the franchisor relies upon to make its determination. Be sure the data used by the franchisor is accurate and recent.

* Does the franchisor sell other competing franchises?

* Has the franchisor met all the legal requirements of the state in which you intend to operate?

* What are the termination clause conditions, such as quality control standards or delinquency of payment of the franchise fee?

* What are the renewal options? Issues to consider would be additional franchise fees or new royalty rates.

* Can your franchise be transferred? Limited transferability will reduce your ability to sell the franchise should you decide it is time to leave the business.

* Does the franchisor have the power to purchase your franchise and under what conditions?

* How are disputes settled? Is arbitration available? What is the governing law, and in which state shall the dispute be heard?

The bottom line is that a franchise relationship is a partnership much in the same way a marriage is. To protect yourself, you must ask the franchisor the questions above as well as others. Admittedly, some of the questions we think are necessary may appear as if we advocate playing hardball; however, you must never forget that the franchisor expects your money and your time. You are the one who is taking the bigger risk. Therefore, you have the right to expect answers to legitimate questions.

If you are dissatisfied with the answers you receive, ask for explanations. You should never feel that the franchisor is doing you a favor. To operate a successful franchise is not a snap; it requires hard work, and you will need all the assistance you can get. Do not purchase a franchise unless you are going to be satisfied with the relationship.

We also suggest that you check out the franchisor very closely before you sign any document or give the franchisor any money. We recommend you check each one of the following sources before you invest:

- The Better Business Bureau
- The local chamber of commerce
- The Federal Trade Commission
- The State Bureau of Consumer Affairs
- The State Attorney General's Office

Chapter 4 Exhibits

Exhibit 4.1   Franchise Investment Protection Laws
Regarding Disclosure for State of Washington

Exhibit 4.2   Franchise Investment Protection Laws
Regarding Disclosure and Impound of Franchise Fees
for State of Illinois

ILLUSTRATION L Requirements for Preparation of a Uniform Franchise Offering Circular

Cover Page: The outside front cover of the offering circular shall contain the following information:

1. The title in boldface type: **FRANCHISE OFFERING CIRCULAR FOR PROSPECTIVE FRANCHISEES REQUIRED BY THE STATE OF (name of state).**

2. The name, type of business organization, principal business address and telephone number of the franchisor.

3. If different that in 2, above, the name, principal business address and telephone number of the subfranchisor or franchise broker offering in this state the herein described franchise.

4. A sample of the primary business trademark, logotype, trade name, or commercial label or symbol used by the franchisor for marketing its products or services and under which the franchisee will conduct its business. (Place in upper left-hand corner of the cover page.)

5. A brief description of the franchise to be offered.

6. A summary of Items 5 and 7 of the offering circular, to wit: Franchisee's Initial Franchise Fee or Other Payment and Franchisee's Initial Investment, respectively.

7. Effective Date: (Leave blank until notified of effectiveness by state regulatory authority.)

8. The following statement in boldface type:

   THIS OFFERING CIRCULAR IS PROVIDED FOR YOUR OWN PROTECTION AND CONTAINS A SUMMARY ONLY OF CERTAIN MATERIAL PROVISIONS OF THE FRANCHISE AGREEMENT. THIS OFFERING CIRCULAR AND ALL CONTRACTS AND AGREEMENTS SHOULD BE READ CAREFULLY IN THEIR ENTIRETY FOR AN UNDERSTANDING OF ALL RIGHTS AND OBLIGATIONS OF BOTH THE FRANCHISOR AND THE FRANCHISEE.

   A FEDERAL TRADE COMMISSION RULE MAKES IT UNLAWFUL TO OFFER OR SELL ANY FRANCHISE WITHOUT FIRST PROVIDING THIS OFFERING CIRCULAR TO THE PROSPECTIVE FRANCHISEE AT THE EARLIER OF (1) THE FIRST PERSONAL MEETING; OR (2) TEN BUSINESS DAYS BEFORE THE SIGNING OF ANY FRANCHISE OR RELATED AGREEMENT; OR (3) TEN BUSINESS DAYS BEFORE ANY PAYMENT. THE PROSPECTIVE FRANCHISEE MUST ALSO RECEIVE A FRANCHISE AGREEMENT CONTAINING ALL MATERIAL TERMS AT LEAST FIVE BUSINESS DAYS PRIOR TO THE SIGNING OF THE FRANCHISE AGREEMENT.

Exhibit 4-1

IF THIS OFFERING CIRCULAR IS NOT DELIVERED ON TIME, OR IF IT CONTAINS A FALSE, INCOMPLETE, INACCURATE OR MISLEADING STATEMENT, A VIOLATION OF FEDERAL AND STATE LAW MAY HAVE OCCURRED AND SHOULD BE REPORTED TO THE FEDERAL TRADE COMMISSION, WASHINGTON, D.C. 20580 <u>AND</u> TO THE ILLINOIS ATTORNEY GENERAL'S OFFICE, 500 SOUTH SECOND STREET, SPRINGFIELD, ILLINOIS 62706, WHICH ADMINISTERS AND ENFORCES THE ILLINOIS FRANCHISE DISCLOSURE ACT.

9. The name and address of the franchisor's registered agent in this state authorized to receive service of process.

10. The name and address of the subfranchisor's or franchise broker's registered agent in this state authorized to receive service of process.

Table of Contents: Include a table of contents based on the requirements of this offering circular.

BODY OF OFFERING CIRCULAR: The offering circular shall contain the following information clearly and concisely stated in narrative form:

1. THE FRANCHISOR AND ANY PREDECESSORS: Set forth in summary form: (The disclosure regarding predecessors need only cover the 15 year period immediately preceding the close of franchisor's most recent fiscal year.)

   A. The name of the franchisor and any predecessors thereto.

   B. The name under which the franchisor is currently doing or intends to do business.

   C. The franchisor's principal business address and the business address or addresses of any predecessors thereto.

   D. The business form of the franchisor whether corporate, partnership, or otherwise.

   E. A description of the franchisor's business and the franchises to be offered in this state.

   F. The prior business experience of the franchisor and any predecessors thereto including:

      (1) The length of time the franchisor has conducted a business of the type to be operated by the franchisee;

      (2) The length of time each predecessor conducted a business of the type to be operated by the franchisee;

(3) The length of time the franchisor has offered franchises for such business;

(4) The length of time the predecessor offered franchises for such business;

(5) Whether the franchisor has offered franchises in other lines of business including:

(a) a description of such other lines of business;

(b) the number of franchises sold in each other line of business;

(c) the length of time the franchisor has offered each such franchise; and

(6) Whether each predecessor offered franchises in other lines of business, including:

(a) a description of such other lines of business;

(b) the number of franchises sold in each other line of business; and

(c) the length of time each predecessor offered each such franchise.

2. IDENTITY AND BUSINESS EXPERIENCE OF PERSONS AFFILIATED WITH THE FRANCHISOR; FRANCHISE BROKERS: List by name and position held the directors, trustees and/or general partners, as the case may be, the principal officers (including the chief executive and chief operating officer, financial, franchise marketing, training and service officers) and other executives or subfranchisors who will have management responsibility in connection with the operation of the franchisor's business relating to the franchises offered by this offering circular and all franchise brokers. With regard to each person listed, state his principal occupation and employers during the past five years.

3. LITIGATION: State whether the franchisor, any person or franchise broker identified in 2.above:

A. Has any administrative, criminal or material civil action (or a significant number of civil actions irrespective of materiality) pending against himalleging a violation of any franchise law, fraud, embezzlement, fraudulent conversion, restraint of trade, unfair or deceptive practices, misappropriation of property or comparable allegations. If so, set forth the name of the person, the court or other forum, nature, and current status of any such pending action. Franchisor may include a summary opinion of counsel as to any such action, but only if a consent to use of such summary opinion is included as part of this offering circular.

B. Has during the 10 year period immediately preceding the date of the offering circular been convicted of a felony or pleaded nolo contendere to a felony charge or been held liable in a civil action by final judgment or been the subject of a material complaint or other legal proceeding if such felony, civil action, complaint or other legal proceeding involved violation of any franchise law, fraud, embezzlement, fraudulent conversion, restraint of trade, unfair or deceptive practices, misappropriation of property or comparable allegations. If so, set forth the name of the person convicted, the court and date of conviction or person against whom judgment was entered, penalty or damages assessed in connection therewith and/or terms of settlement.

C. Is subject to any currently effective injunctive or restrictive order or decree relating to the franchise or under any federal, state or Canadian franchise, securities, antitrust, trade regulation or trade practice law as a result of a concluded or pending action or proceeding brought by a public agency. If so, set forth the name of the person so subject, the public agency and court, a summary of the allegations or facts found by the agency or court and the date, nature, terms and conditions of the order or decree.

4. BANKRUPTCY: State whether the franchisor or any predecessor, officer or general partner of the franchisor has during the 15 year period immediately preceding the date of the offering circular been adjudged bankrupt or reorganized due to insolvency or was a principal officer of any company or a general partner in any partnership that was adjudged bankrupt or reorganized due to insolvency during or within 1 year after the period that such officer or general partner of the franchisor held such position in such company or partnership, or whether any such bankruptcy or reorganization proceeding has been commenced. If so, set forth the name of the person or company adjudged bankrupt or reorganized or named in any such proceeding and the date thereof and any material facts or circumstances.

5. FRANCHISEE'S INITIAL FRANCHISE FEE OR OTHER INITIAL PAYMENT: Describe in detail the following:

A. The initial franchise fee or other initial payment for the franchise, if any, charged upon the signing of the franchise agreement, and whether payable in lump sum or installments. Set forth the manner in which the franchisor will use or apply such franchise fee or initial payment. State whether such fee or payment is refundable, and if so, under what conditions.

B. If an identical initial franchise fee or other initial payment is not charged in connection with each franchise agreement, state the method or formula by which such fee or payment is determined.

6. OTHER FEES: Describe in detail other recurring or isolated fees or payments, including but not limited to royalties, service fees, training fees, lease payments and advertising fees and charges that the franchisee is required to pay the franchisor or persons affiliated with the franchisor or which the franchisor or such affiliated person imposes or collects in whole or in part on behalf of a third party. Include, if applicable, the formula used to compute such other fees and payments. State whether any such fee or payment is refundable, and if so, under what conditions.

7. FRANCHISEE'S INITIAL INVESTMENT: Describe in detail the following expenditures (which may be estimated or described by a low-high range, if not known exactly), stating for each to whom the payments are to be made, when such payments are to be determined, whether any payment is refundable, and if so, under what conditions and, if any part of the franchisee's initial investment in the franchise will or may be financed, an estimate of the loan repayments, including interest:

A. Real property, whether or not financed by contract, installment, purchase or lease. If neither estimable nor describable by a low-high range, describe the variable requirements, such as property, location and building size which make the real properly expenditure neither estimable nor describable by a low-high range.

B. Equipment, fixtures, other fixed assets, construction, remodeling, leasehold improvements and decorating costs, whether or not financed by contract, installment purchases, lease or otherwise.

C. Inventory required to commence operation.

D. Security deposits, other prepared expenses and working capital required to commence operation.

E. Any other payments which the franchisee will be required to make in order to commence operations.

NOTE: The following statement shall be inserted in the offering circular at this point:

THERE ARE NO OTHER DIRECT OR INDIRECT PAYMENTS IN CONJUNCTION WITH THE PURCHASE OF THE FRANCHISE.

8. OBLIGATIONS OF FRANCHISEE TO PURCHASE OR LEASE FROM DESIGNATED SOURCES: State any obligations of the franchisee or subfranchisor, whether arising by terms of the franchise agreement or other device or practice, to purchase or lease

from the franchisor or his designees, goods, services, supplies, fixtures, equipment, inventory or real estate relating to the establishment or operation of the franchise business. Regarding such obligations, state the following:

A. The goods, services, supplies, fixtures, equipment, inventory or real estate required to be purchased or leased from the franchisor or his designees.

B. Whether, and if so, the precise basis by which, the franchisor, its parent or persons affiliated with the franchisor will or may derive income based on or as a result of any such required purchases or leases.

C. To the extent known or estimable by the franchisor, the magnitude of such required purchases and leases in relation to all purchases and leases by the franchisee of goods and services which the franchisee will make or enter into (1) in the establishment and (2) in the operation of the franchise business.

9. OBLIGATIONS OF FRANCHISEE TO PURCHASE OR LEASE IN ACCORDANCE WITH SPECIFICATIONS OR FROM APPROVED SUPPLIERS: State any obligations of the franchisee or subfranchisor, whether arising by terms of the franchise agreement or other device or practice, to purchase or lease in accordance with specifications issued by the franchisor, or from suppliers approved by the franchisor, goods, services, supplies, fixtures, equipment, inventory or real estate relating to the establishment or operation of the franchise business. Regarding such obligations, state the following:

A. The goods, services, supplies, fixtures, equipment, inventory or real estate required to be purchased or leased in accordance with specifications or from suppliers approved by the franchisor.

B. The manner in which the franchisor issues and modifies specifications or grants and revokes approval to suppliers.

C. Whether, and for what categories of goods and services, the franchisor or persons affiliated with the franchisor are approved suppliers or the only approved suppliers.

D. Whether, and if so, the precise basis by which, the franchisor, its parent or persons affiliated with the franchisor may derive income from purchases made from it or from other approved suppliers, if this is the case.

10. FINANCING ARRANGEMENTS: State the terms and conditions of any financing arrangements offered directly or indirectly by the franchisor, its agent or affiliated company, including:

A. A description of any waiver of defenses or similar provisions in any note, contract or other instrument to be executed by the franchisee or subfranchisor.

B. A statement of any past or present practice or of any intent of the franchisor to sell, assign, or discount to a third party, in whole or in part, any note, contract or other instrument executed by the franchisee or subfranchisor.

C. A description of any payments received by the franchisor from any person for the placement of financing with such person.

11. OBLIGATIONS OF THE FRANCHISOR, OTHER SUPERVISION, ASSISTANCE OR SERVICES: Where applicable, describe the following:

A. The obligations to be met by the franchisor prior to the opening of the franchise business, citing by section and page the provisions of the franchise or related agreement requiring performance.

B. Other supervision, assistance or services to be provided by the franchisor prior to the opening of the franchise business although franchisor is not bound by the franchise or any related agreement to provide the same. As part of this disclosure franchisor must disclose that he is not so bound.

C. The obligations to be met by the franchisor during the operation of the franchise business, including, without limitation, the assistance to the franchisee in the operation of his business. Cite by section and page the provisions of the franchise or related agreement requiring performance.

D. Other supervision, assistance or services to be provided by the franchisor during the operation of the franchise business although franchisor is not bound by the franchise or any related agreement to provide the same. As part of this disclosure franchisor must disclose that he is not so bound.

E. The methods used by the franchisor to select the location for the franchisee's business.

F. The typical length of time between the signing of the franchise agreement or the first payment of any consideration for the franchise and the opening of the franchisee's business.

G. The training program of the franchisor, including:

(1) The location, duration and content of the training program;

(2) When the training program is to be conducted;

(3) The experience that the instructors have had with the franchisor;

(4) Any charges to be made to the franchisee and the extent to which the franchisee will be responsible for travel and living expenses of the person(s) who enroll in the training program;

(5) If the training program is not mandatory, the percentage of new franchisees that enrolled in the training program during the 12 months immediately preceding the date of the offering circular; and

(6) Whether any additional training programs and/or refresher courses are available to the franchisee and whether the franchisee will be required to attend the same.

12. EXCLUSIVE AREA OR TERRITORY: Describe any exclusive area or territory granted the franchisee and with respect to such area or territory state whether:

A. The franchisor has established or may establish a company-owned outlet using the franchisor's trade name or trademark.

B. The franchisor has established or may establish a company-owned outlet using the franchisor's trade name or trademark.

C. The franchisor or its parent or affiliate has established or may establish other franchises or company-owned outlets selling or leasing similar products or services under a different trade name or trademark.

D. Continuation of the franchisee's area or territorial exclusivity is dependent upon achievement of a certain sales volume, market penetration or other contingency and under what circumstances the franchisee's area or territory may be altered.

13. TRADEMARKS, SERVICE MARKS, TRADE NAMES, LOGOTYPES, AND COMMERCIAL SYMBOLS: Describe any trademarks, service marks, trade names, logotypes or other commercial symbols to be license to the franchisee including the following:

A. Whether the trademark, service mark, trade name, logotype or other commercial symbol is registered with the United States Patent Office and, if so, for each such registration state the registration date and number and whether or not the registration is on the principal or supplemental register.

B. Whether the trademark, service mark, trade name, logotype and other commercial symbol are registered in this state or the state in which the franchise business is to be located and the dates of such registrations.

C. A description of any presently effective determination of the Patent Office, the trademark administrator of this state or any court, any pending interference, opposition or cancellation proceeding and any pending material litigation involving such trademarks, service marks, trade names, logotypes or other commercial symbols and which is relevant to their use in this state or the state in which the franchise business is to be located.

D. A description of any agreements currently in effect which significantly limit the rights of the franchisor to use or license the use of such trademarks, service marks, trade names, logotypes or other commercial symbols in any manner material to the franchise.

E. Whether the franchisor is obligated by the franchise agreement or otherwise to protect any or all rights which the franchisee has to use such trademarks, service marks, trade names, logotypes or other commercial symbols and to protect the franchisee against claims of infringement or unfair competition with respect to the same.

F. Whether there are any infringing uses actually known to the franchisor which could materially affect the franchisee's use of such trademarks, service marks, trade names, logotypes or other commercial symbols in this state or state in which the franchise business is to be located.

14. PATENTS AND COPYRIGHTS: If the franchisor owns any rights in or to any patents or copyrights which are material to the franchise, describe such patents and copyrights, their relationship to the franchise and the terms and conditions under which the franchisee may use them, including their duration, whether the franchisor can and intends to renew any copyrights, and, to the extent relevant, the information required by Section 13 above with respect to such patents and copyrights.

15. OBLIGATION OF THE FRANCHISEE TO PARTICIPATE IN THE ACTUAL OPERATION FOR THE FRANCHISE BUSINESS: State fully the obligation of the franchisee or subfranchisor, whether arising by terms of the franchise agreement or other device or practice, to participate personally in the direct operation of the franchise business or whether the franchisor recommends participation in the same.

16. RESTRICTIONS ON GOODS AND SERVICES OFFERED BY FRANCHISEE: State any restriction or condition imposed by the franchisor,

whether by terms of the franchise agreement or by other device or practice of the franchisor, whereby the franchisee is restricted as to the goods or services he may offer for sale, or limited in the customers to whom he may sell such goods or services.

17. RENEWAL, TERMINATION, REPURCHASE, MODIFICATION AND ASSIGNMENT OF THE FRANCHISE AGREEMENT AND RELATED INFORMATION: With respect to the franchise and any related agreements state the following:

A. The term and whether such term is affected by any agreement (including leases or subleases) other than the one from which such term arises.

B. The conditions under which the franchisee may renew or extend.

C. The conditions under which the franchisor may refuse to renew or extend.

D. The conditions under which the franchisee may terminate.

E. The conditions under which the franchisor may terminate.

F. The obligations (including lease or sublease obligations) of the franchisee after termination of the franchise by the franchisor and the obligations of the franchisee including lease or sublease obligations) after termination of the franchise by the franchisee or the expiration of the franchise.

G. The franchisee's interest upon termination or refusal to renew or extend the franchise by the franchisor or by the franchisee.

H. The conditions under which the franchisor may repurchase, whether by right of first refusal or at the option of the franchisor. If the franchisor has the option to repurchase the franchise, state whether there will be an independent appraisal of the franchise, whether the repurchase price will be determined by a predetermined formula and whether there will be recognition of goodwill or other intangibles associated therewith in the repurchase price to be given the franchisee.

I. The conditions under which the franchisee or its owners may sell or assign all or an interest in the ownership of the franchise or of the franchisee or in the assets of the franchise business.

J. The conditions under which the franchisor may sell or assign in whole or in part.

K. The conditions under which the franchisee may modify.

L.   The conditions under which the franchisor may modify.

M.   The rights of the franchisee's heirs or personal representative upon the death or incapacity of the franchisee.

N.   The provisions of any covenant not to compete.

18. ARRANGEMENTS WITH PUBLIC FIGURES: State the following:

A.   Any compensation or other benefit given or promised to a public figure arising, in whole or in part, from:

    (1)   the use of the public figure in the name or symbol of the franchise, or

    (2)   the endorsement or recommendation of the franchise by the pubic figure in advertisements.

B.   Any right the franchisee may have to use the name of a public figure in his promotional efforts or advertisingand any charges to be made to the franchisee in connection with such usage.

C.   The extent to which such public figure is involved in the actual management or control of the franchisor.

D.   The total investment of the public figure in the franchise operation.

19. REPRESENTATIONS REGARDING EARNINGS CAPABILITY:

A.   Any earnings claims made in connection with the offer of a franchise must be included in full in the offering circular and must have a reasonable basis at the time it is made. If no earnings claim is made, in accordance with the Guidelines for the Preparation of the Uniform Franchsie Offering Circular (1987, with no later amendments or editions), Item 19 of the offering circular shall contain the following negative disclosure:

The franchisor does not elect to make any representations regarding earnings capability to prospective franchisees.

B.   Any earnings claim shall include a description of its factual basis and the material assumptions underlying its preparation and presentation.

20. INFORMATION REGARDING FRANCHISES OF THE FRANCHISOR: State the following as of the close of the franchisor's most recent fiscal year:

A.   The total number of franchises, exclusive of company owned or operated distribution outlets, of a type

substantially similar to those offered herein and of
that number, the number of such franchises which were
operational as of the date of this offering circular.

B.   The number of franchises in this state, exclusive of
company owned or operated distribution outlets, of a
type substantially similar to those offered herein and
of that number, the number of such franchises which were
operational as of the date of this offering circular.

C.   The total number of franchises substantially similar to
those offered herein for which a business is not yet
operational although a franchise agreement has been
signed.

D.   The number of franchises in this state substantially
similar to those offered herein for which a business is
not yet operational although a franchise agreement has
been signed.

E.   The names, addresses and telephone numbers of all
franchises under franchise agreement with the franchisor
or its subfranchisor which are located in the state
where the proposed franchise is to be located. To the
extent that there are fewer than 10 such franchises
located in said state, the list shall include at least
the 10 such franchises which are most proximate to the
location of the proposed franchise; and if fewer than 10
such franchises exist, the list shall identify all such
franchises and include a statement to that effect.

In lieu of the above disclosure, the franchisor may
attach to the offering circular a list of the names,
address and telephone numbers of all its franchises
under franchise agreements with the franchisor or its
subfranchisors.

F.   An estimate of the total number of franchises to be sold
or granted during the one year period following the date
of the offering circular.

G.   An estimate of the number of franchises to be sold or
granted in this state during the one year period
following the date of the offering circular.

H.   State the number of franchises in each of the following
categories which within the three-year period
immediately preceding the close of franchisor's most
recent fiscal year have:

(1)   been cancelled or terminated by the franchisor for:

(a)   failure to comply with quality control
standards; and

(b)   other reasons;

(2) not been renewed by the franchisor;

(3) been reacquired through purchase by the franchisor;

(4) been otherwise reacquired by the franchisor.

21. FINANCIAL STATEMENTS: Financial statements shall be prepared in accordance with generally accepted accounting principles. Such financial statements shall be audited by an independent certified public accountant or, if permitted by the franchise law of a particular state, an independent public accountant. Unaudited statements may be used for interim periods.

A. The financial statements required to be filed by a franchisor shall include a balance sheet as of the date within 90 days prior to the date of the application and profit and loss statements for each of the three fiscal years preceding the date of the balance sheet and for the period, if any, between the close of the last of such fiscal years and the date of the balance sheet. The balance sheet as of a date within 90 days prior to the date of the application need not be audited. However, if this balance sheet is not audited, there shall be filed in addition an audited balance sheet as of the end of the franchisor's last fiscal year unless such last fiscal year ended within 90 days of the date of the application in which case there shall be filed an audited balance sheet as of the end of the franchisor's next preceding fiscal year. The profit and loss statement shall be audited up to the date of the last audited balance sheet filed, if any.

B. Controlling company statements: Where state law permits, in lieu of the disclosure required by Item 21.A., complete financial statements of a company controlling the franchisor may be filed, but only if the unaudited financial statements of the franchisor are filed and the controlling company absolutely and unconditionally guarantees to assume the duties and obligations of the franchisor under the franchise agreement should the franchisor become unable to perform its duties and obligations.

C. Consolidated and separate statements:

(1) Where a franchisor owns, directly or beneficially, a controlling financial interest in any other corporation, the financial statements required to be filed should normally reflect on a consolidated basis the financial condition of the franchisor and each of its subsidiaries.

(2) A separate financial statement will normally be required for each substantial franchisor or subfranchisor related entity.

(3) A company controlling 80% or more of a franchisor shall normally be required to file its financial statements.

(4) Consolidated and separate financial statements shall be prepared in accordance with generally accepted accounting principles.

22. CONTRACTS: Attach a copy of all franchise and other contracts or agreements proposed for use or in use of this state, including, without limitation, all lease agreements, option agreements, and purchase agreements.

23. ACKNOWLEDGMENT OR RECEIPT BY PROSPECTIVE FRANCHISEE: The last page of each offering circular shall contain a detachable document acknowledging receipt of the offering circular by the prospective franchisee.

WAC 460–80–190 Time of registration effectiveness. A registration statement for the selling of a franchise under RCW 19.100.060 becomes effective if no stop order is in effect and no proceeding pending under RCW 19.100.120 at 3:00 p.m., P.S.T. on the afternoon of the 15th business day after the filing of the registration or the last amendment or at such earlier time as the director determines. [Order 11, § 460–80–190, filed 3/3/72.]

WAC 460–80–195 Approval is not an endorsement. The filing of the application for registration or the effectiveness of the registration does not constitute a finding by the director that any document filed under this act is true, complete and not misleading. Neither any such fact nor the fact that an exemption is available for a transaction means that the director has passed in any way upon the merits or qualification of, or recommended or given approval to any person, franchise or transaction. [Order 11, § 460–80–195, filed 3/3/72.]

WAC 460–80–300 Receipt of offering circular. Each prospective purchaser of a franchise shall sign a receipt in substantially the following form that they have received the offering circular and that they received the same before signing the receipt and completing the sale.

ACKNOWLEDGEMENT OF RECEIPT OF OFFERING
CIRCULAR BY PROSPECTIVE FRANCHISEE FROM
(NAME OF FRANCHISOR)

The undersigned, personally and/or as an officer or partner of the proposed franchisee, does hereby acknowledge receipt of "the franchise offering circular for prospective franchisees required by the state of Washington" including all exhibits attached thereto, to-wit: (List exhibits to be attached, including, but not limited to, financial statements, franchise agreement, lease agreements, etc.) I acknowledge that I received the offering circular at least 48 hours prior to signing this receipt and completing the sale.

Dated: _____

_____
individually and/or as an officer
or partner of _____
a (_____corporation)
(_____partnership)

[Statutory Authority: RCW 19.100.250. 80–04–036 (Order SDO–38–80), § 460–80–300, filed 3/19/80; Order 11, § 460–80–300, filed 3/3/72.]

WAC 460–80–310 Offering circular. The purpose of the offering circular is to inform prospective franchisees and subfranchisors. Accordingly, the information set forth in the circular should be presented in a clear, concise fashion that will be readily understandable.

(a) All information contained in the offering circular shall be set forth under appropriate captions or headings reasonably indicative of the principal subject matter set forth thereunder. Except as to financial statements and other tabular data, information set forth in the offering

circular should be divided into reasonable short paragraphs or sections.

(b) Each offering circular should contain a reasonable detailed table of contents showing the subject matter of the various sections or subdivisions of the offering circular and the page number on which each section or subdivision begins. [Order 11, § 460–80–310, filed 3/3/72.]

WAC 460–80–315 Content and form of offering circular. The information required to be set forth in the offering circular shall be presented in the following sequence:

COVER PAGE. The outside front cover of the offering circular shall contain the following information:

The title in boldface type: FRANCHISE OFFERING CIRCULAR FOR PROSPECTIVE FRANCHISEES REQUIRED BY THE STATE OF WASHINGTON.

The name, type of business organization, principal business address and telephone number of the franchisor.

If different than above, the name, principal business address and telephone number of the subfranchisor or franchise broker offering in this state the herein described franchise.

A sample of the primary business trademark, logotype, trade name or commercial label or symbol used by the franchisor for marketing its products or services and under which the franchisee will conduct its business. (Place in upper left–hand corner of the cover page.)

A brief description of the franchise to be offered.

A summary of items (5) and (7) of the offering circular, to–wit: Franchisee's initial franchise fee or other payment and franchisee's initial investment, respectively.

Effective date: (Leave blank until notified of effectiveness by securities division.)

The following statement in boldface type:
THIS OFFERING CIRCULAR IS PROVIDED FOR YOUR OWN PROTECTION AND CONTAINS A SUMMARY ONLY OF CERTAIN MATERIAL PROVISIONS OF THE FRANCHISE AGREEMENT. THIS OFFERING CIRCULAR AND ALL CONTRACTS AND AGREEMENTS SHOULD BE READ CAREFULLY IN THEIR ENTIRETY FOR AN UNDERSTANDING OF ALL RIGHTS AND OBLIGATIONS OF BOTH THE FRANCHISOR AND THE FRANCHISEE.

A FEDERAL TRADE COMMISSION RULE MAKES IT UNLAWFUL TO OFFER OR SELL ANY FRANCHISE WITHOUT FIRST PROVIDING THIS OFFERING CIRCULAR TO THE PROSPECTIVE FRANCHISEE AT THE EARLIER OF (1) THE FIRST PERSONAL MEETING, OR (2) TEN BUSINESS DAYS BEFORE THE SIGNING OF ANY FRANCHISE OR RELATED AGREEMENT, OR (3) TEN BUSINESS DAYS BEFORE ANY PAYMENT. THE PROSPECTIVE FRANCHISEE MUST ALSO RECEIVE A FRANCHISE AGREEMENT CONTAINING ALL MATERIAL TERMS AT LEAST FIVE BUSINESS DAYS PRIOR TO THE SIGNING OF THE FRANCHISE AGREEMENT.

IF THIS OFFERING CIRCULAR IS NOT DELIVERED ON TIME, OR IF IT CONTAINS A FALSE, INCOMPLETE, INACCURATE OR MISLEADING STATEMENT A VIOLATION OF FEDERAL AND STATE LAW MAY HAVE OCCURRED AND SHOULD BE REPORTED TO THE FEDERAL TRADE COMMISSION, WASHINGTON, D.C. 20580 AND WASHINGTON STATE DEPARTMENT OF LICENSING, SECURITIES DIVISION, P.O. BOX 648, OLYMPIA, WASHINGTON 98504.

The name and address of the franchisor's registered agent in this state authorized to receive service of process.

Exhibit 4-2

The name and address of the subfranchisor's or franchise broker's registered agent in this state authorized to receive service of process.

TABLE OF CONTENTS: Include a table of contents based on the requirements of this offering circular.

BODY OF OFFERING CIRCULAR: The offering circular shall contain the following information clearly and concisely stated in narrative form:

(1) The franchisor and any predecessors: Set forth in summary form: (The disclosure regarding predecessors need only cover the 15 year period immediately preceding the close of franchisor's most recent fiscal year.)

(a) The name of the franchisor and any predecessors thereto.

(b) The name under which the franchisor is currently doing or intends to do business.

(c) The franchisor's principal business address and the business address or addresses of any predecessors thereto.

(d) The business form of the franchisor whether corporate, partnership or otherwise.

(e) A description of the franchisor's business and the franchises to be offered in this state.

(f) The prior business experience of the franchisor and any predecessors thereto including:

(i) The length of time the franchisor has conducted a business of the type to be operated by the franchisee;

(ii) The length of time each predecessor conducted a business of the type to be operated by the franchisee;

(iii) The length of time the franchisor has offered franchises for such business;

(iv) The length of time each predecessor offered franchises for such business;

(v) Whether the franchisor has offered franchises in other lines of business, including:

(A) A description of such other lines of business;

(B) The number of franchises sold in each other line of business;

(C) The length of time the franchisor has offered each such franchise; and

(vi) Whether each predecessor offered franchises in other lines of business, including:

(A) A description of such other lines of business;

(B) The number of franchises sold in each other line of business; and

(C) The length of time each predecessor offered each such franchise.

(2) Identity and business experience of persons affiliated with the franchisor; franchise brokers: List by name and position held the directors, trustees and/or general partners, as the case may be, the principal officers (including the chief executive and chief operating officer, financial, franchise marketing, training and service officers) and other executives or subfranchisors who will have management responsibility in connection with the operation of the franchisor's business relating to the franchises offered by this offering circular and all franchise brokers. With regard to each person listed, state his principal occupations and employers during the past five years.

(3) Litigation: State whether the franchisor, any person or franchise broker identified in (2) above:

(a) Has any administrative, criminal or material civil action (or a significant number of civil actions irrespective of materiality) pending against them alleging a violation of any franchise law, fraud, embezzlement, fraudulent conversion, restraint of trade, unfair or deceptive practices, misappropriation of property or comparable allegations. If so, set forth the name of the person, the court or other forum, nature, and current status of any such pending action. Franchisor may include a summary opinion of counsel as to any such action, but only if a consent to use of such summary opinion is included as part of this offering circular.

(b) Has during the 10 year period immediately preceding the date of the offering circular been convicted of a felony or plead nolo contendere to a felony charge or been held liable in a civil action by final judgment or been the subject of a material complaint or other legal proceeding if such felony, civil action, complaint or other legal proceeding involved violation of any franchise law, fraud, embezzlement, fraudulent conversion, restraint of trade, unfair or deceptive practices, misappropriation of property or comparable allegations. If so, set forth the name of the person convicted, the court and date of conviction or person against whom judgment was entered, penalty or damages assessed in connection therewith and/or terms of settlement.

(c) Is subject to any currently effective injunctive or restrictive order or decree relating to the franchise or under any federal, state or Canadian franchise, securities, antitrust, trade regulation or trade practice law as a result of a concluded or pending action or proceeding brought by a public agency. If so, set forth the name of the person so subject, the public agency and court, a summary of the allegations or facts found by the agency or court and the date, nature, terms and conditions of the order or decree.

(4) Bankruptcy: State whether the franchisor or any predecessor, officer or general partner of the franchisor has during the 15 year period immediately preceding the date of the offering circular been adjudged bankrupt or reorganized due to insolvency or was a principal officer of any company or a general partner in any partnership that was adjudged bankrupt or reorganized due to insolvency during or within one year after the period that such officer or general partner of the franchisor held such position in such company or partnership, or whether any such bankruptcy or reorganization proceeding has been commenced. If so, set forth the name of the person or company adjudged bankrupt or reorganized or named in any such proceeding and the date thereof and any material facts or circumstances.

(5) Franchisee's initial franchise fee or other initial payment: Describe in detail the following:

(a) The initial franchise fee or other initial payment for the franchise, if any, charged upon the signing of the franchise agreement, and whether payable in lump sum or installments. Set forth the manner in which the franchisor will use or apply such franchise fee or initial payment. State whether such fee or payment is refundable, and if so, under what conditions.

(b) If an identical initial franchise fee or other initial payment is not charged in connection with each franchise agreement, state the method or formula by which such fee or payment is determined.

(6) Other fees: Describe in detail other recurring or isolated fees or payments, including but not limited to royalties, service fees, training fees, lease payments and advertising fees and charges that the franchisee is required to pay to the franchisor or persons affiliated with the franchisor or which the franchisor or such affiliated person imposes or collects in whole or in part on behalf of a third party. Include, if applicable, the formula used to compute such other fees and payments. State whether any such fee or payment is refundable, and if so, under what conditions.

(7) Franchisee's initial investment: Describe in detail the following expenditures (which may be estimated or described by a low–high range, if not known exactly), stating for each to whom the payments are to be made, when such payments are to be determined, whether any payment is refundable, and if so, under what conditions and, if any part of the franchisee's initial investment in the franchise will or may be financed, an estimate of the loan repayments, including interest:

(i) Real property, whether or not financed by contract, installment, purchase or lease. If neither estimate nor describable by a low–high range, describe the variable requirements, such as property, location and building size which make the real property expenditure neither estimable nor describable by a low–high range.

(ii) Equipment, fixtures, other fixed assets, construction, remodeling, leasehold improvements and decorating costs, whether or not financed by contract, installment purchases, lease or otherwise.

(iii) Inventory required to commence operations.

(iv) Security deposits, other prepaid expenses and working capital required to commence operation.

(v) Any other payments which the franchisee will be required to make in order to commence operations.

Note: The following statement shall be inserted in the offering circular at this point:
THERE ARE NO OTHER DIRECT OR INDIRECT PAYMENTS IN CONJUNCTION WITH THE PURCHASE OF THE FRANCHISE.

(8) Obligations of franchisee to purchase or lease from designated sources: State any obligations of the franchisee or subfranchisor, whether arising by terms of the franchise agreement or other device or practice, to purchase or lease from the franchisor or his designees, goods, services, supplies, fixtures, equipment, inventory or real estate relating to the establishment or operation of the franchise business. Regarding such obligations, state the following:

(a) The goods, services, supplies, fixtures, equipment, inventory or real estate required to be purchased or leased from the franchisor or its designees.

(b) Whether, and if so, the precise basis by which, the franchisor, its parent or persons affiliated with the franchisor will or may derive income based on or as a result of any such required purchases or leases.

(c) To the extent known or estimable by the franchisor, the magnitude of such required purchases and leases in relation to all purchases and leases by the franchisee of goods and services which the franchisee will make or enter into (1) in the establishment and (2) in the operation of the franchise business.

(9) Obligations of franchisee to purchase or lease in accordance with specifications or from approved suppliers: State any obligations of the franchisee or subfranchisor, whether arising by terms of the franchise agreement or other device or practice, to purchase or lease in accordance with specifications issued by the franchisor, or from suppliers approved by the franchisor, goods, services, supplies, fixtures, equipment, inventory or real estate relating to the establishment or operation of the franchise business. Regarding such obligations, state the following:

(a) The goods, services, supplies, fixtures, equipment, inventory or real estate required to be purchased or leased in accordance with specifications or from suppliers approved by the franchisor.

(b) The manner in which the franchisor issues and modifies specifications or grants and revokes approval to suppliers.

(c) Whether, and for what categories of goods and services, the franchisor or persons affiliated with the franchisor are approved suppliers or the only approved suppliers.

(d) Whether, and if so, the precise basis by which, the franchisor, its parent or persons affiliated with the franchisor may derive income from it or from other approved suppliers, if this is the case.

(10) Financing arrangements: State the terms and conditions of any financing arrangements offered directly or indirectly by the franchisor, its agent or affiliated company, including:

(a) A description of any waiver of defenses or similar provisions in any note, contract or other instrument to be executed by the franchisee or subfranchisor.

(b) A statement of any past or present practice or of any intent of the franchisor to sell, assign, or discount to a third party, in whole or in part, any note, contract or other instrument executed by the franchisee or subfranchisor.

(c) A description of any payments received by the franchisor from any person for the placement of financing with such person.

(11) Obligations of the franchisor; other supervision, assistance or services: Where applicable, describe the following:

(a) The obligations to be met by the franchisor prior to the opening of the franchise business, citing by section and page the provisions of the franchise or related agreement requiring performance.

(b) Other supervision, assistance or services to be provided by the franchisor prior to the opening of the franchise business although franchisor is not bound by the franchise or any related agreement to provide the same. As part of this disclosure franchisor must disclose that he is not so bound.

(c) The obligations to be met by the franchisor during the operation of the franchise business, including, without limitation, the assistance to the franchisee in the operation of his business. Cite by section and page the provisions of the franchise or related agreement requiring performance.

(d) Other supervision, assistance or services to be provided by the franchisor during the operation of the franchise business although franchisor is not bound by the franchise or any related agreement to provide the same. As part of this disclosure franchisor must disclose that it is not so bound.

(e) The methods used by the franchisor to select the location for the franchisee's business.

(f) The typical length of time between the signing of the franchise agreement or the first payment of any consideration for the franchise and the opening of the franchisee's business.

(g) The training program of the franchisor, including:

(i) The location, duration and content of the training program;

(ii) When the training program is to be conducted;

(iii) The experience that the instructors have had with the franchisor;

(iv) Any charges to be made to the franchisee and the extent to which the franchisee will be responsible for travel and living expenses of the person(s) who enroll in the training program;

(v) If the training program is not mandatory, the percentage of new franchisees that enrolled in the training program during the 12 months immediately preceding the date of the offering circular; and

(vi) Whether any additional training programs and/or refresher courses are available to the franchisee and whether the franchisee will be required to attend the same.

(12) Exclusive area or territory: Describe any exclusive area or territory granted the franchisee and with respect to such area or territory state whether:

(a) The franchisor has established or may establish another franchisee who will also be permitted to use the franchisor's trade name or trademark.

(b) The franchisor has established or may establish a company—owned outlet using the franchisor's trade name or trademark.

(c) The franchisor or its parent or affiliate has established or may establish other franchises or company—owned outlets selling or leasing similar products or services under a different trade name or trademark.

(d) Continuation of the franchisee's area or territorial exclusively is dependent upon achievement of a certain sales volume, market penetration or other contingency and under what circumstances the franchisee's area or territory may be altered.

(13) Trademarks, service marks, trade names, logotypes, and commercial symbols: Describe any trademarks, service marks, trade names, logotypes or other commercial symbols to be licensed to the franchisee including the following:

(a) Whether the trademark, service mark, trade name, logotype or other commercial symbol is registered with the United States Patent Office and, if so, for each such registration state the registration date and number and whether or not the registration is on the principal or supplemental register.

(b) Whether the trademark, service mark, trade name, logotype and other commercial symbol are registered in this state or the state in which the franchise business is to be located and the dates of such registrations.

(c) A description of any presently effective determinations of the patent office, the trademark administrator of this state or any court, any pending interference, opposition or cancellation proceeding and any pending material litigation involving such trademarks, service marks, trade names, logotypes or other commercial symbols and which is relevant to their use in this state or the state in which the franchise business is to be located.

(d) A description of any agreements currently in effect which significantly limit the rights of the franchisor to use or license the use of such trademarks, service marks, trade names, logotypes or other commercial symbols in any manner material to the franchise.

(e) Whether the franchisor is obligated by the franchise agreement or otherwise to protect any or all rights which the franchisee has to use such trademarks, service marks, trade names, logotypes or other commercial symbols and to protect the franchisee against claims of infringement or unfair competition with respect to the same.

(f) Whether there are any infringing uses actually known to the franchisor which could materially affect the franchisee's use of such trademarks, service marks, trade names, logotypes or other commercial symbols in this state or state in which the franchise business is to be located.

(14) Patents and copyrights: If the franchisor owns any rights in or to any patents or copyrights which are material to the franchise, describe such patents and copyrights, their relationship to the franchise and the terms and conditions under which the franchisee may use them, including their duration, whether the franchisor can and intends to renew any copyrights, and, to the extent relevant, the information required by Section 15 above with respect to such patents and copyrights.

(15) Obligation of the franchisee to participate in the actual operation of the franchise business: State fully the obligation of the franchisee or the subfranchisor, whether arising by terms of the franchise agreement or other device or practice, to participate personally in the direct operation of the franchise business or whether the franchisor recommends participation in the same.

(16) Restrictions on goods and services offered by franchisee: State any restriction or condition imposed by the franchisor, whether by terms of the franchise agreement or by other device or practice of the franchisor, whereby the franchisee is restricted as to the goods or

services they may offer for sale, or limited in the customers to whom they may sell such goods or services.

(17) Renewal, termination, repurchase, modification and assignment of the franchise agreement and related information: With respect to the franchise and any related agreements state the following:

(a) The term and whether such term is affected by any agreement (including leases or subleases) other than the one from which such term arises.

(b) The conditions under which the franchisee may renew or extend.

(c) The conditions under which the franchisee may refuse to renew or extend.

(d) The conditions under which the franchisee may terminate.

(e) The conditions under which the franchisor may terminate.

(f) The obligations (including lease or sublease obligations) of the franchisee after termination of the franchise by the franchisor and the obligations of the franchisee (including lease or sublease obligations) after termination of the franchise by the franchisee or the expiration of the franchise.

(g) The franchisee's interest upon termination or refusal to renew or extend the franchise by the franchisor or by the franchisee.

(h) The conditions under which the franchisor may repurchase, whether by right of first refusal or at the opinion of the franchisor. If the franchisor has the option to repurchase the franchise, state whether there will be an independent appraisal of the franchise, whether the repurchase price will be determined by a predetermined formula and whether there will be a recognition of goodwill or other intangibles associated therewith in the repurchase price to be given the franchisee.

(i) The conditions under which the franchisee or its owners may sell or assign all or an interest in the ownership of the franchise or of the franchisee or in the assets of the franchise business.

(j) The conditions under which the franchisor may sell or assign in whole or in part.

(k) The conditions under which the franchisee may modify.

(l) The conditions under which the franchisor may modify.

(m) The rights of the franchisee's heirs or personal representative upon the death or incapacity of the franchisee.

(n) The provisions of any covenant not to compete.

(18) Arrangements with public figures: State the following:

(a) Any compensation or other benefit given or promised to a public figure arising, in whole or in part, from:

(i) The use of the public figure in the name or symbol of the franchise, or

(ii) The endorsement or recommendation of the franchise by the public figure in advertisements.

(b) Any right the franchisee may have to use the name of a public figure in his promotional efforts or advertising and any charges to be made to the franchisee in connection with such usage.

(c) The extent to which such public figure is involved in the actual management or control of the franchisor.

(d) The total involvement of the public figure in the franchise operation.

(19)(a) An earnings claim made in connection with an offer of a franchise must be included in full in the offering circular and must have a reasonable basis at the time it is made. If no earnings claim is made, Item 19 of the offering circular shall contain the following negative disclosure:

Franchisor does not furnish or authorize its salespersons to furnish any oral or written information concerning the actual or potential sales, costs, income or profits of (name of franchise). Actual results vary from unit to unit and franchisor cannot estimate the results of any particular franchise.

(b) An earnings claim shall include a description of its factual basis and the material assumptions underlying its preparation and presentation.

Note #1 Definition: "Earnings claim" means information given to a prospective franchisee by, on behalf of or at the direction of the franchisor or its agent, from which a specific level or range of actual or potential sales, costs, income or profit from franchised or nonfranchised units may be easily ascertained.

A chart, table or mathematical calculation presented to demonstrate possible results based upon a combination of variables (such as multiples of price and quantity to reflect gross sales) is an earnings claim subject to this item.

An earnings claim limited solely to the actual operating results of a specific unit being offered for sale need not comply with this item if it is given only to potential purchasers of that unit and is accompanied by the name and last known address of each owner of the unit during the prior three years.

Note #2 Supplemental earnings claim. If a franchisor has made an earnings claim in accordance with this subsection, the franchisor may deliver to a prospective franchisee a supplemental earnings claim directed to a particular location or circumstance, apart from the offering circular. The supplemental earnings claim must be in writing, explain the departure from the earnings claim in the offering circular, be prepared in accordance with this subsection, and be left with the prospective franchisee.

Note #3 Scope of requirement. An earnings claim is not required in connection with the offer of franchises; if made, however, its presentation must conform with this subsection. If an earnings claim is not made, then negative disclosure prescribed by this subsection must be used.

Note #4 Claims regarding future performance. A statement or prediction of future performance that is prepared as a forecast or projection in accordance with the *Statement on Standards for Accountants' Services on Prospective Financial Information* (or its successor) issued by the *American Institute of Certified Public Accountants, Inc.*, is presumed to have a reasonable basis.

Note #5 Burden of proof. The burden is upon the franchisor to show that it had a reasonable basis for its earnings claim.

Note #6 Factual basis: The factual basis of an earnings claim includes significant matters upon which a franchisee's future results are expected to depend, including, for example, economic or market conditions, and which are basic to a franchisee's operation and encompass matters affecting, among other things, franchisee's sales, the cost of goods or services sold and operating expenses.

In the absence of an adequate operating experience of its own, a franchisor may base an earnings claim upon the results of operations of a substantially similar business of a person affiliated with the franchisor, or franchisees of that person; provided that disclosure is made of any material differences in the economic or market conditions known to, or reasonably ascertainable by, the franchisor.

Note #7   Basic disclosures. The earnings claim must state:

(i) Material assumptions, other than matters of common knowledge, underlying the claim;

(ii) A concise summary of the basis for the claim including a statement of whether the claim is based upon actual experience of franchised units and, if so, the percentage of franchised outlets in operation for the period covered by the earnings claim that have actually attained or surpassed the stated results;

(iii) A conspicuous admonition that a new franchisee's individual financial results are likely to differ from the results stated in the earnings claim; and

(iv) A statement that substantiation of the data used in preparing the earnings claim will be made available to the prospective franchisee on reasonable request.

(20) Information regarding franchises of the franchisor: State the following as of the close of franchisor's most recent fiscal year:

(a) The total number of franchises, exclusive of company owned or operated distribution outlets, of a type substantially similar to those offered herein and of that number, the number of such franchises which were operational as of the date of this offering circular.

(b) The number of franchises in this state, exclusive of a company owned or operated distribution outlets, of a type substantially similar to those offered herein and of that number, the number of such franchises which were operational as of the date of this offering circular.

(c) The total number of franchises substantially similar to those offered herein for which a business is not yet operational although a franchise agreement has been signed.

(d) The number of franchises in this state substantially similar to those offered herein for which a business is not yet operational although a franchise agreement has been signed.

(e) The names, addresses and telephone numbers of all franchises under franchise agreements with the franchisor or its subfranchisor which are located in the state where the proposed franchise is to be located. To the extent that there are fewer than 10 such franchises located in said state, the list shall include at least the 10 such franchises which are most proximate to the location of the proposed franchise; and if fewer than 10 such franchises exist, the list shall identify all such franchises and include a statement to that effect.

In lieu of the above disclosure, the franchisor may attach to the offering circular a list of the names, addresses and telephone numbers of all its franchises under franchise agreements with the franchisor or its subfranchisors.

(f) An estimate of the total number of franchises to be sold or granted during the one year period following the date of the offering circular.

(g) An estimate of the number of franchises to be sold or granted in this state during the one year period following the date of the offering circular.

(h) State the number of franchises in each of the following categories which within the three–year period immediately preceding the close of franchisor's most recent fiscal year have:

(i) Been cancelled or terminated by the franchisor for:

(A) Failure to comply with quality control standards; and

(B) Other reasons;

(ii) Not been renewed by the franchisor;

(iii) Been reacquired through purchase by the franchisor; and

(iv) Been otherwise required by the franchisor.

(i) The name and last known address and telephone number of every franchisee in this state under a franchise agreement with the franchisor or its subfranchisor whose franchise has, within the twelve–month period immediately preceding the effective date of this offering circular, been terminated, canceled, not renewed, or who has, during the same time period, otherwise voluntarily or involuntarily ceased to do business pursuant to the franchise agreement.

(21) Financial statements: Financial statements shall be prepared in accordance with generally accepted accounting principles. Such financial statements shall be audited by an independent certified public accountant. Unaudited statements may be used for interim periods.

(a) The financial statements required to be filed by a franchisor shall include a balance sheet as of a date within 90 days prior to the date of the application and profit and loss statements for each of the three fiscal years preceding the date of the balance sheet and for the period, if any, between the close of the last of such fiscal years and the date of the balance sheet. The balance sheet as of a date within 90 days prior to the date of the application need not be audited. However, if this balance sheet is not audited, there shall be filed in addition an audited balance sheet as of the end of the franchisor's last fiscal year unless such last fiscal year ended within 90 days of the date of the application in which case there shall be filed an audited balance sheet as of the end of the franchisor's next preceding fiscal year. The profit and loss statements shall be audited up to the date of the last audited balance sheet filed, if any.

(b) Controlling company statements: In lieu of the disclosure required by item (21)(a), complete financial statements of a company controlling the franchisor may be filed, but only if the unaudited financial statements of the franchisor are filed and the controlling company absolutely and unconditionally guarantees to assume the duties and obligations of the franchisor under the franchise agreement should the franchisor become unable to perform its duties and obligations.

(c) Consolidated and separate statements:

(i) Where a franchisor owns, directly or beneficially, a controlling financial interest in any other corporation, the financial statements required to be filed should normally reflect on a consolidated basis the financial condition of the franchisor and each of its subsidiaries.

(ii) A separate financial statement will normally be required for each substantial franchisor or subfranchisor related entity.

(iii) A company controlling 80% or more of a franchisor shall normally be required to file its financial statements.

(iv) Consolidated and separate financial statements shall be prepared in accordance with generally accepted accounting principles.

(22) Contracts: Attach a copy of all franchise and other contracts or agreements proposed for use in this state, including, without limitation, all lease agreements, option agreements, and purchase agreements.

(23) Acknowledgment of receipt by prospective franchisee: The last page of each offering circular shall contain a detachable document acknowledging receipt of the offering circular by the prospective franchisee. [Statutory Authority: RCW 19.100.250. 88–01–060 (Order SDO 112B–87), § 460–80–315, filed 12/17/87. Statutory Authority: RCW 19.100.040 (4), (7), and (20), and 19.100.250. 80–04–036 (Order SDO–38–80), § 460–80–315, filed 3/19/80.]

WAC 460–80–400 Impounds. The director may, by rule or order, require as a condition to the effectiveness of the registration the impound of franchise fees if he finds that such requirement is appropriate to protect the prospective franchisee. [Order 11, § 460–80–400, filed 3/3/72.]

WAC 460–80–410 Imposition of impound. In a case where the applicant has failed to demonstrate that adequate financial arrangements have been made to fulfill obligations to provide real estate, improvements, equipment, inventory, training or other items included in the offering, the director or administrator may impose as a condition to the registration of a franchise offering an impoundment of the franchise fees and other funds paid by the franchisee or subfranchisor until no later than the time of opening of the franchise business. [Order 11, § 460–80–410, filed 3/3/72.]

WAC 460–80–420 Operation of impound condition. When an impound condition is imposed in connection with the registration of a franchise offering, one hundred percent of franchisee fees and all other funds paid by the franchisees or subfranchisors for any purpose shall within 48 hours of the receipt of such funds, be placed with the depository until the director takes further action pursuant to WAC 460–80–450.

All checks shall be made payable to the depository. [Order 11, § 460–80–420, filed 3/3/72.]

WAC 460–80–430 Purchase receipts. When an impound condition is imposed, the franchisor shall deliver to each franchisee or subfranchisor, a purchase receipt, in a form approved by the director. Such purchase receipts shall be consecutively numbered and prepared in triplicate and the original given to the franchisee or subfranchisor, the first copy to the depository together with the payment received and the second copy to the franchisor. [Order 11, § 460–80–430, filed 3/3/72.]

WAC 460–80–440 Depository. Funds subject to an impound condition shall be placed in a separate trust account with a national bank located in Washington or a Washington bank or trust company. A written consent of the depository to act in such capacity shall be filed with the director. [Order 11, § 460–80–440, filed 3/3/72.]

WAC 460–80–450 Release of impounds. The director will authorize the depository to release to the franchisor such amounts of the impounded funds applicable to a specified franchisee (or subfranchisor) upon a showing that the franchisor has fulfilled its obligations under the franchise agreement, or that for other reasons the impound is no longer required for protection of franchisees.

An application for an order of the director authorizing the release of impounds to the franchisor shall be verified and shall contain the following:

(a) A statement of the franchisor that all required proceeds from the sale of franchises have been placed with the depository in accordance with the terms and conditions of the impound condition.

(b) A statement of the depository signed by an appropriate officer setting forth the aggregate amount of impounds placed with the depository.

(c) The names of each franchisee (or subfranchisor) and the amount held in the impound for the account of each franchisee (or subfranchisor).

(d) A statement by the franchisee that the franchisor has performed his obligations under the franchise contract.

(e) Such other information as the director may require in a particular case. [Order 11, § 460–80–450, filed 3/3/72.]

WAC 460–80–500 Advertising. All advertising to be used to offer a franchise, subject to the registration requirement, for sale must be filed in the office of the director at least 7 days prior to the publication and all advertising shall be subject to the following statement of policy:

(a) An advertisement should not contain any statement or inference that a purchase of a franchise is a safe investment or that failure, loss or default is impossible or unlikely, or that earnings or profits are assured.

(b) An advertisement should not normally contain a projection of future franchisee earnings unless such projection is (i) based on past earnings records of all franchisees operating under conditions, including location, substantially similar to conditions affecting franchises being offered (ii) for a reasonable period only and (iii) is substantiated by data which clearly supports such projections.

(c) An advertisement should normally contain the name and address of the person using the advertisement.

(d) If the advertisement contains any endorsement or recommendation of the franchises by any public figure,

Chapter 5

CHOOSING THE LEGAL FORM OF YOUR BUSINESS

Once you decide to go into business for yourself, regardless of whether you start from scratch, buy an existing business, or purchase a franchise, you will need to decide the legal form in which you will conduct business. This chapter will explain:

*   The different legal forms available
*   Advantages and disadvantages of each legal form
*   Tax aspects you should consider

TYPES OF BUSINESSES

The most common legal forms in which to conduct business are:

*   Sole proprietorship
*   General partnership
*   Limited partnership
*   Corporation

Sole Proprietorship

A sole proprietorship is the simplest form in which to conduct a business. A sole proprietorship is not a legal entity. Instead, the term refers to a person who directly owns the business and is directly responsible for its debts. Hence the owner is the business, so to speak. Listed below are the advantages and disadvantages of a sole proprietorship.

Advantages

* The owner receives all of the profits because she or he is taking all the risks.
* It is often easier and less costly to start a sole proprietorship.
* The owner controls all the decisions, and therefore there are no disagreements.
* The owner receives all of the profits.
* The owner does not pay corporate income taxes; instead, he or she pays only personal income taxes on profits earned by the business.

Disadvantages

* The owner is subjected to unlimited personal liability; thus, as a sole owner, he or she bears the risk of all losses and puts his or her entire personal assets and wealth at risk. Furthermore, if the owner is married, the community property is liable for contract obligations incurred by either spouse during the marriage.
* The owner's ability to raise capital is limited to his or her personal funds or the funds of those who are willing to make loans; this aspect often impedes the growth of the business.
* Because all contracts are made by the owner or in the owner's name by agents of the owner, the authority to enter into contracts terminates upon the death of the owner, and therefore the business will likely dissolve.

Partnership

Partnerships occur when two or more co-owners engage in business for profit. There are two types of partnerships: *general* and *limited*. Each type has its own unique characteristics.

General Partnership

A general partnership is a hybrid of sorts. The law views general partnerships in certain instances as an aggregate of individuals who happen to be in business together, while in other instances defines a partnership as a separate legal entity. For example:

* It can hold and convey legal title to real property in its own name instead of in the name of the partners.
* It can sue and be sued in the partnership name.
* It is a separate entity for bankruptcy purposes so that a partner's bankruptcy does not bankrupt the partnership and vice versa.

However, in most other aspects, the general partnership is simply co-ownership.

The main advantage of a partnership is that it allows individuals to pool their resources and start and operate their business without corporate formalities. Many partnership agreements are informal and unwritten although this is certainly not advised.

There are numerous disadvantages of conducting business in the partnership form. For example:

* Each partner puts his or her entire personal resources at risk for debts and obligations of the partnership business; moreover, each partner is jointly and seperately liable to partnership creditors. This includes liability for wrongdoing by a co-partner committed

in the ordinary course of partnership business as well as liability for debts incurred by co-partners while carrying on partnership business. Furthermore, even though the partners may agree among themselves as to how they will share losses, creditors will not be affected by such agreements. A creditor may collect the full amount of his or her judgment from any one or a combination of the partners.

* Unless otherwise provided by agreement, the duration of the business is uncertain because the partnership is dissolved by the death or bankruptcy of a partner. Furthermore, if one of the partners simply wants out, the partnership is dissolved unless there has been some prior agreement.

* Management and control are shared. Each partner has an equal right to participate in the management and control of the business. Many partnerships dissolve because partners cannot agree among themselves as to how the business should be run.

* Transferability of interest is limited. Unless provided for by an agreement, no one can become a member of the partnership without the consent of all existing partners. There is a small exception which states that a partnership interest may be assigned but the assignee does not have full right of a partner.

Whenever forming a general partnership, you should ensure that you have a well written agreement that spells out the rights and responsibilities of the partners as well as a formula as to how profits and losses will be divided. Often, when a partnership agreement is not in writing, misunderstandings occur and resentment begins to build. When this occurs it is almost a sure precursor to a partnership that will collapse. Tragically, many of the issues that cause a partnership to rupture could easily be avoided if there was a written agreement between the parties beforehand—a constitution to which the partners could resort for guidance in the determination of how the partnership is to function.

The typical partnership agreement usually addresses the following issues:

- Identity of the partners
- Nature and scope of partnership business
- Term of the partnership
- Capital contribution of each partner
- Formula for division of profits and losses
- Responsibilities of each partner
- Restrictions of the authority of each partner to bind the partnership to contracts
- Salaries, if any, paid to the partners
- Withdrawal of a partner

Limited Partnership

A limited partnership is comprised of one or more general partners, who manage the business and are personally liable to the partnership's creditors, and one or more limited partners who contribute capital and share in profits, but who take no part in running the business. Generally, limited partners risk only their capital contribution and no more.

The objective of a limited partnership is to encourage passive investors, individuals who are not active in management and control of the business, to invest in a business that will allow them to take a share of the profits but at the same time not risk their personal assets.

All states require that a limited partnership file with the Secretary of State in the partnership's home state, a certificate which includes the name of the limited partnership, location, general character of its business, identities and address of at least the general partner, and term of the partnership. Some states require that the certificate also disclose the identities and addresses of the limited partners, the contribution of each limited partner, profit share of each limited partner, whether the limited partners have a right to receive property other than cash, whether the partners will have to make additional contributions, membership termination, and distribution of proceeds. For an example of a typical Certificate of Limited Partnership, see Exhibit 5-1.

There are two statutory acts that govern limited partnerships: Uniform Limited Partnership Act of 1916 and the Revised Uniform Limited Partnership Act of 1976 and subsequent amendments of 1985. All states, except for Louisiana, have adopted either the Uniform Limited Partnership Act or the Revised Uniform Limited Partnership Act.

Regardless of which act your state has adopted, a limited partner shall have certain rights in her or his relationship to the partnership. Those rights are:

* The right to inspect and copy any partnership accounting records.
* The right to demand and receive accurate and complete information of all material transactions that affect the partnership and to receive a formal account of partnership affairs whenever circumstances render it just and reasonable.
* The right to have a dissolution and winding-up by decree of court.

An issue you should consider if you form a limited partnership is the potential exposure of the limited partners to liability. The Revised Uniform Limited Partnership Act states in section 303 (Liability to Third Parties) that a limited partner will be held liable for certain obligations of the limited partnership if he or she takes part in the control of the business, and he or she will be held liable for all of the obligations of the limited partnership if he or she engages in substantially the same exercise of powers as the general partner.

Fortunately, the act does provide some guidelines as to what actions will be permitted and will not be construed as constituting participation in the control of the business.

A limited partner does not participate in the control of the business by solely doing one or more of the following:

• being a contractor for or an agent or employee of the limited partnership or of a general partner;
• consulting with and advising a general partner with respect to the business of the limited partnership;
• acting as surety for the limited partnership;
• approving or disapproving an amendment to the partnership agreement; or
• voting on one or more of the following matters: (1) the dissolution and winding-up of the limited partnership, or (2) the sale, exchange, lease, mortgage, pledge, or other transfer of all or substantially all of the assets of the limited partnership other than in the ordinary course of business, or (3) the incurrence of indebtedness by the limited partnership other than in the ordinary course of its business, or (4) a change in the nature of its business or (5) the removal of a general partner.

CORPORATION

Types of Corporations

Domestic versus Foreign. A domestic corporation is formed under the laws of the state in which it is incorporated by filing Articles of Incorporation with the secretary of state. If a corporation is formed in one state and does business in another state, it is a foreign corporation.

Profit versus Nonprofit. Most states do not give a precise definition for either of these two types of corporations. Instead, the state code usually refers to profit corporations as a business corporation. A nonprofit corporation is a special corporation formed by one or more individuals, for the benefit of the public, the mutual benefit of its members, or religious purposes. As a rule, a state will prohibit the distribution of profits to members of nonprofit corporations; however, mutual benefit corporations are exempted. A nonprofit corporation is generally formed for religious, charitable, literary, scientific, or educational purposes.

Professional Corporations. Until recently, the common law did not allow corporations to practice the "learned professions." However, all states and the District of Columbia have now enacted legislation authorizing professionals to incorporate or to form associations having corporate characteristics. The objective of the legislation is to permit individuals practicing in the professions to take advantage of some of the tax benefits available to corporations and their employees.

A typical example of how most states treat professional corporations is the Moscone-Knox Professional Corporation Act of 1968 which allows professionals to incorporate their practices in the state of California. In essence, the act provides that a professional corporation must be organized under the General Corporation Law and must be engaged in rendering professional services, in a single profession, except as otherwise authorized, pursuant to a certificate of registration issued by the government agency regulating the profession. The term *profession* is defined as a type of service that may be provided only pursuant to a license, certification, or registration authorized by the Business and Professions Code or Chiropractic Act.

Below is a list of professions which, if incorporated, would fall under the category of professional corporations.

- Accountant
- Acupuncturist
- Attorney
- Audiologist
- Chiropractor
- Clinical social worker
- Counselor (marriage, family, child)
- Court reporter
- Dentist
- Doctor
- Nurse
- Optometrist
- Osteopath
- Pharmacist
- Physical therapist
- Physician's assistant
- Podiatrist
- Psychologist
- Speech pathologist

Incorporation for a professional does not change any of the rules regarding professional responsibility and does not alter any contract, tort, or other legal relationship between the person receiving professional services and the professional rendering them.

Business Corporation. A business corporation, like the other types of corporations, is a creature of the state. It is a separate legal entity and has its own identity which is separate and apart from the individuals who created it. As a separate legal entity, it has the power to enter into contracts, to own or transfer property, and to sue or be sued.

The creation of a corporation requires the corporate structure to consist of directors, officers, and shareholders. The shareholders, who are the owners of the business, elect a board of directors that is responsible for the management of the business. The directors then hire officers who run the day-to-day operations of the business and are considered agents of the business.

Advantages of the Corporate Form

Risk of loss is limited. Generally, a shareholder's risk of loss is limited to the amount of capital the shareholder invested in the business.

Transferability of interest is easier. Unlike a partnership, the selling or buying of shares does not affect corporate existence. Because of this aspect, the corporate form becomes attractive as capital needs of the business expand.

A corporation can have perpetual existence. Thus, unlike a partnership in which the death of a general partner dissolves the organization, the death of a stockholder has no legal effect on the corporation.

Business owners as well as employees are allowed to participate in pension and profit sharing plans. These plans allow for a corporation to make contributions into specific interest bearing accounts for its employees and the business owner, as well, if the owner is an employee of the corporation. These contributions are tax deductible to the corporation. The employee does not include the contribution into her or his gross income but defers it until a later time. In addition, the interest earned while the contribution sits in the account is not taxed until it is distributed to the employee. As a result, compensation can be increased without the added taxation that usually accompanies it. This feature is especially attractive to highly compensated individuals who are looking for ways to shelter their income. There are specific requirements that must be satisfied, however. For more information see Chapter 16.

Fringe benefits can be bought with pre-tax dollars. When a business is in the corporate form, the business owner may be treated as an employee. As a consequence, certain fringe benefits, such as term life insurance, medical and dental insurance, and disability insurance can be purchased by the corporation for the benefit of the owner and her or his employees. The cost of these benefits is deducted by the corporation as an expense; yet, for tax purposes, it is not included in the gross income of the employees.

Disadvantages of the Corporate Form

Formalities must be followed. This is perhaps the biggest sore spot among business people. Often they cannot understand that certain issues regarding the operation of the business must be addressed and documented. It is a fact of life, and every lawyer will tell you a corporation can be created only by substantial compliance with state law, and once the corporation has been formed, if the shareholders intend to enjoy the protection of the corporate shield, they should ensure that corporate formalities are satisfied. Requirements include filing the articles of incorporation, which contain certain essential provisions, prepayment of certain fees, electing a board of directors, appointing corporate officers, holding annual shareholder meetings and board-of-directors meetings, maintaining separate books and records, and documenting transactions or events that have a significant impact on the corporation. Failure to satisfy these formalities may result in exposing the directors, officers, or shareholders to personal liability for the corporation's debts.

The following checklist gives some of the issues that a corporation should address and document if it expects to be treated as a corporation by the courts and the state.

Choose a corporate name.

Choose an agent for service of process.

Decide on whether or not to become a closely-held corporation.

Determine the purpose of the corporation.

Decide how to capitalize the corporation, which including:

  (a) dividend preferences
  (b) voting rights
  (c) liquidation preferences
  (d) preemptive rights
  (e) redeemable shares
  (f) conversion rights
  (g) valuation of shares when assets other than cash are contributed to the business
  (h) capital call
  (i) assumption of liabilities
  (j) shareholder loans to the corporation

Prepare bylaws, which including:

  (a) location of principal offices
  (b) shareholders' meetings—notice location, proxy rights, quorum
  (c) directors—power, number, election, term of office, vacancies on the board, quorum, action without a meeting, directors' compensation
  (d) officers—appointment, appointment of subordinate officers, removal and resignation, filling of vacancies

Establish inspection rights for shareholders and directors.

Ensure documentation of each shareholders' meeting and board of directors' meeting.

Decide on whether or not there will be qualification of stock under Internal Revenue Code section 1244.

Decide whether or not there will be an election of Subchapter S tax status.

Determining whether or not there will be shareholders' agreement as to the disposition of shares.

Document the following:

  (a) selection of an accounting period
  (b) issuance of shares
  (c) establishment of a principal executive office
  (d) establishment of a bank account
  (e) selection of directors
  (f) appointment of officers
  (g) shareholders' meeting and any resolutions
  (h) directors' meeting and any resolutions
  (i) buy-out agreements
  (j) executive employment agreements
  (k) director and officer indemnification
  (l) voting trust agreement
  (m) loans to the corporation
  (n) profit-sharing plans
  (o) pension plans

       (p)   purchase of major assets
       (q)   mergers
       (r)   dividends
       (s)   stock splits, stock dividends
       (t)   corporate reacquisition of its stock
       (u)   sale of business assets
       (v)   dissolution of the corporation

Double taxation exists. Income generated by the corporation is taxed. In addition, shareholders are also taxed when they receive that income in the form of dividends.

Personal guarantees may be required. Lending institutions as well as landlords frequently require that shareholders give their personal guarantee for debts or long-term obligations contracted by the corporation.

Piercing the corporate veil may be allowed by the courts. A major reason for establishing a corporation is limited liability. However, this protection is not guaranteed. A major risk any corporation faces is that it may be deemed by the courts as the alter ego of the shareholders rather than as a separate entity. When this situation occurs the corporate shield is pierced, and the shareholders are held personally liable for the corporation's debts. The doctrine of alter ego applies to tort claims and tax liabilities as well as contractual obligations. A common trap that judgment creditors often use to snare the personal assets of the corporate shareholders is to show that either corporate formalities were not followed, the corporation was under-capitalized, or the shareholders had the corporation provide services and goods for their own personal benefit.

There are numerous expenses. The corporate form is the most expensive form of doing business. There are costs in starting up a corporation. In addition, there are various annual taxes that must be paid to the government and fees to be paid to a professional to perform certain legally required services. Costs of incorporating include: lawyer's fee, accountant's fee, franchise taxes to the state for the privilege of conducting business as a corporation, fees to the state to issue stock, fees to the state to conduct a name search, fees to the state to file articles of incorporation, cost of stock certificates, and cost of corporate seal.

TAX ASPECTS TO CONSIDER

The 1986 Tax Reform Act and How It Will Affect You

The 1986 Tax Reform Act (TRA) was a landmark piece of tax legislation that had a profound impact on all taxpayers and which will last for many years to come. In addition to affecting individual taxpayers, the TRA affected businesses to a significant extent. Many of the changes that were made to our tax system as result of this act are still being phased in.

Businesses that suffered under the TRA included heavy manufacturing and commercial and multi-family real estate developers. These businesses suffered for the following reasons:

- Repeal of the Investment Tax Credit
- Longer write-off periods for capital equipment
- Curtailment of many of the tax shelters

Businesses that benefited under the TRA included retailers, wholesalers, service firms and consumer-product companies. As a result, do not invest heavily in plant and equipment.

More easily understood provisions of the TRA that affected business include:

* Reduction in top corporate tax rate from 46 percent to 34 percent
* Repeal of Investment Tax Credit
* New depreciation system that creates eight classes of assets which, in effect, extends the lives over which the assets can be depreciated.
* Deductions for business meals and entertainment are limited to 80 percent of their value. In order to be deductible, the meal must satisfy the following requirements:
    (a) The taxpayer or an employee must be present at the meal;
    (b) There must be a definite business purpose for the meal;
    (c) The meal cannot be lavish or extravagant; and
    (d) The taxpayer must expect to obtain some business benefit from the meal.
* Research and development credit has been extended for three years.
* Internal Revenue Code section 179 expensing deduction is increased to $10,000.
* Fringe benefits that discriminate in favor of higher paid employees will be treated as income to the favored employee.
* Deduction that corporations are allowed for dividends they receive from other corporations is reduced to 80 percent.
* Annual limit is placed on net operating losses that can be used to offset taxes when new owners acquire more than 50 percent of a company that is having losses.
* Targeted jobs credit is extended and is lowered to 40 percent of the first $6,000 of wages.
* 25 percent of the cost of health insurance may be deducted directly from gross income for self-employed taxpayers. *Note*: The deduction will not reduce self-employment income when it comes time to figure self-employment tax.
* Businesses with average annual gross receipts under $5 million can use a simplified last-in first-out (LIFO) accounting method that results in a better inventory valuation during inflationary periods.
* Completed-contract method of accounting is curtailed.
* Use of cash basis accounting is cut back.
* Capital gains treatment is repealed (although there is talk of having it restored).
* Use of installment sales method of deferring tax liability is limited.
* Corporations are subject to a new alternative minimum tax:

An exemption of $40,000 is allowed for small business, 20 percent of alternative minimum taxable income (AMTI), AMTI equals taxable income plus preference items.
Preference items include the following:

• deferred income under the completed contract method
• expensing of mining exploration and development costs
• tax exempt interest earned on nongovernment bonds
• excess accelerated depreciation on real and personal property
• deferred installment sale income
• untaxed appreciation of property deducted as a charitable contribution
• one-half the amount a corporation's adjusted net book income is greater than its AMTI

Income Splitting

Income splitting is a device used by higher bracket tax paying parents to reduce overall taxes by shifting income producing assets to lower tax-bracket children. The income received by the children is defined as unearned income.

There are two rules for taxing unearned income received by children.

Rule One—Children under the age of 14 are taxed at the parent's rate, that is, as if the parent had received the income. Wages earned by the child are exempt from the law, even if the child works in a business owned by a parent, and continues to be taxed at the child's rate.

Rule Two—Children over the age of 14 are taxed at the child's rate.

Earned income is taxed at the child's rate. Therefore, taxpayers should employ their children in their business and pay them a reasonable wage. This approach has two advantages:

* The child's earned income is sheltered by the standard deduction, and
* The taxpayer's business receives a deduction for wages paid.

Retirement Plans

The TRA also had an impact on all types of retirement plans. The tax aspect of retirement plans is a complex area, and your tax advisor should be consulted for advice regarding your specific circumstances. We will briefly explain the most popular types of retirement plans, and how the TRA affected each plan. For a detailed description of how these plans work, see Chapter 16.

Individual Retirement Accounts

- Married couples with an adjusted gross income under $40,000 (singles—$25,000) or individuals not covered by a qualified employer pension plan may continue to fund an IRA and deduct contributions as under current law.

- No deduction is allowed for the contribution when a taxpayer's income is over $50,000 (single—$35,000), although the income earned within the IRA is still deferred until withdrawal.

- The allowable deduction is phased out on income levels between $40,000 and $50,000 if either spouse has an employer's plan.

Defined Benefit Plan. Maximum permissible benefit is 100 percent of compensation or $90,000, whichever is less. All employer contributions are still tax deductible. Greater restrictions are placed on maximum benefits paid before Social Security age of retirement. The amount of $90,000 is still allowed at age 65. The $75,000 safe harbor rule at 55 has been discontinued.

Defined Contribution Plan. Employees may continue to contribute up to 25 percent of earned income, not to exceed $30,000 for each eligible participant.

SEP—IRA. Employers with twenty-five or fewer employees may establish a salary reduction SEP. This plan will operate like a 401K, allowing both salary reductions and employer contributions. Maximum contribution for salary reduction portion is $7,000. Employer contributions will remain at 15 percent compensation not to exceed $30,000. This plan enables the small employer to take advantage of a salary reduction plan without the high cost associated with a 401K plan.

401K Plan. Salary reduction limits reduced to $7,000 indexed to inflation. However, matching contributions from employers can make up the difference between $7,000 and the ceiling under the old law. *Note*: Nondiscrimination rules have become more far reaching. For an explanation of nondiscrimination rules, see Chapter 16.

403(b) Plan. There is a $9,500 limit on tax sheltered investments. However, employers can contribute the difference up to an amount that equals 20 percent of the employee's pay. Note that nondiscrimination rules now apply.

Employee Stock Ownership Plans (ESOP). Stock held in these plans must have fair market value determined by an independent outside appraiser. Dividends may be deducted if used to repay ESOP loans. All 1984 Tax Act incentives are retained. These incentives include the following: Tax-deferred sales of stock to ESOP; lenders may exclude 50 percent of interest received on loans to ESOP; and ESOP may assume estate tax liability. Note that one-half of the proceeds of stocks sold by an estate to ESOP are excluded from estate tax.

Fringe Benefits

A fringe benefit is any one of a wide variety of nonmonetary or indirect benefits that an employer may give her or his employee(s) in addition to regular wage or salary compensation. Included are:

* Benefits on which an exact value can be placed; and
* Benefits on which an exact value cannot be placed.

The TRA establishes a comprehensive set of nondiscrimination rules for certain fringe benefit and cafeteria plans. The plans that must not discriminate are:

- Group term life insurance plans
- Accident and health plans
- Group legal services plans
- Educational assistance programs
- Dependent care assistance programs
- Tuition reduction programs
- Cafeteria plans
- Employee discounts
- Employee provided operating facilities
- Welfare benefit plans

Except as provided in IRS regulations, all employees must include in their income an amount equal to their benefit under a statutory fringe benefit plan unless the following requirements are satisfied:

* The fringe benefit plan is in writing;
* Employees' rights under the plan are legally enforceable;
* Employees are given reasonable notice of benefits available;
* The fringe benefit plan is maintained for the exclusive benefit of employees; and

* The fringe benefit plan was established with the intention of being maintained indefinitely.

Even if the requirements listed above are satisfied, the government may still insist upon the inclusion of fringe benefits in the gross income of certain employees if those individuals are highly compensated employees, and the fringe benefit plan is discriminatory in nature. The portion of the fringe benefit that will be included is the discriminatory portion of the coverage provided, or the discriminatory portion of the benefits provided, as long as the benefits are reported on a timely basis. Otherwise, the entire benefit must be included in gross income.

The IRS defines a highly compensated individual as an employee who qualifies as one or more of the following:

* Is a 5 percent owner;
* Earns more than $75,000 in annual compensation;
* Earns more than $50,000 in annual compensation and whose compensation is in the top 20 percent of all the employer's employees; or
* Is an officer and receives more than 150 percent of the dollar limit in annual additions to a deferred contribution plan.

The IRS defines a fringe benefit plan as discriminatory unless it can show the following characteristics:

* At least 50 percent of all eligible employees are not highly compensated.
* At least 90 percent of the nonhighly compensated employees must be eligible and would receive a benefit that is at least 50 percent of the value of the largest benefit available under all such plans to any highly compensated employee.
* The plan cannot contain any provision relating to eligibility that discriminates in favor of highly compensated employees.
* The average employer-provided benefit received over the plan year by nonhighly compensated employees under all plans is at least 75 percent of the average such benefit received by highly compensated employees.

Certain classes of employees may be disregarded in applying nondiscrimination rules under the TRA. See your tax advisor on whether the provisions apply to your situation.

Subchapter S Corporation

For tax purposes, corporations are classified as either a "C" corporation or an "S" corporation (also known as a Subchapter S Corporation). The "C" corporation has certain tax disadvantages, which are listed below.

* Double taxation
* Losses suffered at the corporate level cannot be passed through to the stockholders
* In the case of a new business, where losses in the early years are anticipated, owners are unable to receive the immediate tax advantages of such losses.

To prevent tax considerations from interfering with exercising sound business judgment as to whether a business should be operated in the corporate form, Congress enacted Subchapter S of the Internal Revenue Code. Subchapter S permits certain corporations to avoid the corporate income tax, and enables them to pass through operating losses to their shareholders.

There are two requirements that must be satisfied for a corporation to elect Subchapter S status.

First—A corporation must be a small business corporation to qualify for S corporation status. A small business corporation qualifying for Subchapter S status is defined by the following characteristics.

(a) It must be a domestic corporation.
(b) It must not be a member of an affiliated group.
(c) It must not have more than 35 shareholders.
(d) Its shareholders must be either individuals, estates, and certain trusts.
(e) It must not have a nonresident alien as a shareholder.
(f) It must issue only one class of stock.

Second—Your corporation must make an election. The following requirements must be satisfied if you decide to elect S corporation status.

- Election is made on IRS Form 2553.
- Election must be filed with the Internal Revenue Service anytime during the preceding taxable years, or, before the fifteenth day of the third month of the current year.

Note: You can lose you election as an S corporation if any of the following occurs: (1) The majority of shareholders file a revocation; (2) your corporation ceases to qualify as a small business corporation; or (3) your corporation has certain passive investment income in excess of 25 percent of gross receipts for three consecutive years.

Subchapter S corporations often are preferred by shareholders in closely held corporations because of the favorable tax impact that results. Generally, what makes this tax status so desirable is that certain corporate transactions flow through to the shareholders "as is." The type of transactions that flow through to the shareholders are:

- Intangible drilling costs
- Depletion
- Nonbusiness income or loss
- Qualifying dividends
- Charitable contributions
- Foreign tax credits
- IRC section 1231 gains and losses
- Tax exempt income
- Short-term capital gains and losses
- Basis of new and used Internal Revenue Code section 38 property (to calculate Internal Revenue Code section 179 election)
- Wagering gains and losses

- Soil and water conservation expenditures
- Recoveries of prior taxes, bad debts, and delinquency amounts
- Mining exploration expenditures
- Amortization of reforestation
- Investment interest, expenditures, income and expenses

Taxable income or loss flows through to the shareholders and is reported by the shareholders on IRS Form 1040.

The TRA makes the S election attractive for the following reasons:

* Individual tax rates are lower than corporate rates.
* The corporate alternative minimum tax (AMT) is more potent in C corporations than in S corporations. The new tax law excuses S corporations from the corporate alternative minimum tax.
* S corporations are not required to recognize gain or loss as liquidating sales and distributions.
* S corporations are permitted to use the cash method of accounting.

However, on the negative side:

* S corporations may not have corporate shareholders or subscribers.
* Deductions for retirement and fringe benefits paid to shareholders may be limited.

The tax year of a newly formed S corporation is required to be a calendar year or any other accounting period for which the corporation establishes a business purpose to the satisfaction of the IRS. The return, which is filed on Form 1120S, is due on or before the fifteenth day of the third month following the close of the taxable year. Instructions for IRS Form 1120S may be found in IRS Publication 334.

To assist you in understanding how Form 1120S is filled out, we have provided an example in Exhibit 5-2 by using a hypothetical company called JEE Manufacturing, Inc.

Should you decide that an S corporation suits your needs, there are a few additional factors to consider.

* It is an elective provision.
* Many states do not recognize the S election.
* S corporations are not treated as either partnerships or C corporations for federal tax laws, although they are taxed much like a partnership.
* Both the courts and IRS require strict compliance with Subchapter S provisions of the law.
* The S election is available only to small business corporations.

Passive Activities

A passive activity is any activity involving the conduct of a trade or business in which the taxpayer does not participate materially. Material participation means the taxpayer is involved in the operations of his or her trade or business on a regular, continuous, and substantial basis. IRS Form 8582, "Passive Activity

Loss Limitations," is used to summarize losses and income from passive activities and to compute the amount allowed. See Exhibit 5-3.

Prior to the TRA, taxpayers could reduce income from some other activity with deductions from any activity. As of January 1, 1987, individuals and certain other taxpayers, such as estates, trusts, and personal service corporations, are no longer allowed to reduce income other than passive income, with losses from passive activities. There is also a rule that prevents offsetting passive activity losses against portfolio income of closely held C corporations (other than personal service corporations) which are subject to the at-risk rules. Passive activity losses and credits not allowed in one tax year may be carried forward to the next tax year.

There are special passive activity rules that apply to losses from rental real estate activities. Your accountant should be consulted if you encounter this situation because interests in passive activities acquired before October 23, 1986, are eligible for a gradual phase-in of the passive activity loss and credit limitations. The table below shows the phase-in and the percentages allowed.

Year	Percent Deductible
1987	65
1988	40
1989	20
1990	10
1991	0

In conclusion, space limitations make it impossible to discuss all the changes in the TRA as they impact on your business, whether it is a proprietorship, partnership, or corporation. The material covered in this section is general in nature and is limited to an overview. Many significant changes are not covered. As a result, decisions based on comments contained in this chapter should not be finalized without first consulting your tax advisor and attorney.

Chapter 5 Exhibits

Exhibit 5.1   Certificate of Limited Partnership Form LP-1
              for State of California

Exhibit 5.2   Completed with Explanation: U.S. Income Tax
              Return for an S Corporation (IRS Form 1120S)

Exhibit 5.3   Passive Activity Loss Limitations (IRS Form
              8582)

STATE OF CALIFORNIA
CERTIFICATE OF LIMITED PARTNERSHIP—FORM LP-1
IMPORTANT—Read instructions on back before completing this form

This Certificate is presented for filing pursuant to Chapter 3, Article 2, Section 15621, California Corporations Code.

1. NAME OF LIMITED PARTNERSHIP

2. STREET ADDRESS OF PRINCIPAL EXECUTIVE OFFICE	3. CITY AND STATE	4. ZIP CODE

5. STREET ADDRESS OF CALIFORNIA OFFICE IF EXECUTIVE OFFICE IN ANOTHER STATE	6. CITY	7. ZIP CODE
	CALIF.	

8. COMPLETE IF LIMITED PARTNERSHIP WAS FORMED PRIOR TO JULY 1, 1984 AND IS IN EXISTENCE ON DATE THIS CERTIFICATE IS EXECUTED.

THE ORIGINAL LIMITED PARTNERSHIP CERTIFICATE WAS RECORDED ON _____ 19 _____ WITH THE

RECORDER OF _____ COUNTY. FILE OR RECORDATION NUMBER _____

9. NAMES AND ADDRESSES OF ALL GENERAL PARTNERS: (CONTINUE ON SECOND PAGE, IF NECESSARY)
NAME:
ADDRESS:
CITY: STATE   ZIP CODE

9A.
NAME:
ADDRESS:
CITY: STATE   ZIP CODE

9B.
NAME:
ADDRESS:
CITY: STATE   ZIP CODE

10. NAME AND ADDRESS OF AGENT FOR SERVICE OF PROCESS
NAME:
ADDRESS:
CITY: STATE   ZIP CODE

11. TERM FOR WHICH THIS PARTNERSHIP IS TO EXIST

12. FOR THE PURPOSE OF FILING AMENDMENTS, DISSOLUTION AND CANCELLATION CERTIFICATES PERTAINING TO THIS CERTIFICATE, THE

ACKNOWLEDGMENT OF [   ] GENERAL PARTNERS IS REQUIRED.

13. ANY OTHER MATTERS THE GENERAL PARTNERS DESIRE TO INCLUDE IN THIS CERTIFICATE MAY BE NOTED ON SEPARATE PAGES AND BY

REFERENCE HEREIN IS A PART OF THIS CERTIFICATE. NUMBER OF PAGES ATTACHED [   ]

14. IT IS HEREBY DECLARED THAT I AM (WE ARE) THE PERSON(S) WHO EXECUTED THIS CERTIFICATE OF LIMITED PARTNERSHIP, WHICH EXECUTION IS MY (OUR) ACT AND DEED (SEE INSTRUCTIONS)

15. THIS SPACE FOR FILING OFFICER USE (FILE NUMBER, DATE OF FILING)

SIGNATURE OF GENERAL PARTNER	DATE	SIGNATURE OF GENERAL PARTNER	DATE
SIGNATURE OF GENERAL PARTNER	DATE	SIGNATURE OF GENERAL PARTNER	DATE
SIGNATURE OF OTHER THAN GENERAL PARTNER		TITLE OR DESIGNATION	DATE

16. RETURN ACKNOWLEDGMENT TO:

NAME
ADDRESS
CITY AND
STATE
ZIP CODE

FORM LP-1—FILING FEE $70
Approved by the Secretary of State

Exhibit 5-1

FORM 1120S - S Corporation Form

We will now demonstrate the use of S Corporation Form 1120S with an example of JEE Manufacturing, Inc. This company fabricates various plastic products. It uses the accrual method of accounting and files its returns on the basis of the calendar year end. The company elected S Corporation status on December 31, 1987 and has three stockholders.

During 1988, the company had gross sales of $4,001,532 and returns/allowances of $43,657. For schedule A purposes, the company had a beginning inventory of $506,320 and an ending inventory of $459,622. Purchases during the year were $1,992,406 and labor costs for Schedule A were $810,516. Schedule A depreciation was $175,000. The company revalued its beginning inventory upward $10,015, which is considered Other Income.

In the deduction section, we find the following expenses. Officer compensation totalled $167,000, while salaries/wages totalled $254,163. Repairs to machinery totalled $14,175. Specific accounts charged to bad debts during the year were $29,684. Rent for the year was $75,000 while taxes amounted to $12,000. Interest on company debt was $110,000. Total depreciation for the company was $202,500 with $175,000 taken in Schedule A. The company spent $17,000 for advertising. Other expenses, which include supplies, sales commissions, legal fees, insurance, etc. amounted to $56,530.

The company had other investments valued at cost equal to $100,000. Form these investments, the company earned dividends of $16,000. The company earned $4,000 from its bank account. The company donated $24,000 to the YMCA as a charitable contribution. The company took advantage of federal job programs and earned a Jobs Credit of $6,000.

For Schedule M calculations, Other Additions amount to $20,000 made up of $4,000 of interest and $16,000 of dividend income. The owners received a total of $65,000 of distributions in materials and property (this value is, also, entered on Schedule K). Other reductions amounted to $30,000 made up of $24,000 of charitable contributions and $6,000 of Jobs Credits. The company received $5,000 of tax free income from municipal bonds.

For other examples of the construction of Form 1120S - S Corporation return, refer to the Department of the Treasury, Internal Revenue Service Publication 334 (Rev. Nov. 88). Every line and every box of this form is explained in detail in this publication.

Exhibit 5-2

Form 1120S

U.S. Income Tax Return for an S Corporation

Department of the Treasury
Internal Revenue Service

For the calendar year 1988 or tax year beginning _____, 1988, ending _____, 19___

▶ For Paperwork Reduction Act Notice, see page 1 of the instructions.

OMB No. 1545-0130

1988

A Date of election as an S corporation: 12-31-87

Use IRS label. Otherwise, please print or type.

Name: **JEE MANUFACTURING, INC.**

Number and street (P.O. Box number if mail is not delivered to street address): **123 'A' STREET**

City or town, state, and ZIP code: **ELM CITY CA 95555**

B Business code no. (see Specific Instructions): 3070

C Employer identification number: 95-1234567

D Date incorporated: 3-1-1972

E Total assets (see Specific Instructions): Dollars $270 8505 Cents

F Check applicable boxes: (1) ☐ Initial return (2) ☐ Final return (3) ☐ Change in address (4) ☐ Amended return

G Check this box if this is an S corporation subject to the consolidated audit procedures of sections 6241 through 6245 (see instructions) ▶ ☐

H Enter number of shareholders in the corporation at end of the tax year ▶ 3

Caution: Include **only** trade or business income and expenses on lines 1a through 21. See the instructions for more information.

Income

1a Gross receipts or sales 4001532 **b** Less returns and allowances 43657 **c** Bal ▶	1c	3957875
2 Cost of goods sold and/or operations (Schedule A, line 7)	2	3024620
3 Gross profit (subtract line 2 from line 1c)	3	933255
4 Net gain (or loss) from Form 4797, line 18 (see instructions)	4	-0-
5 Other income (see instructions—attach schedule)	5	10015
6 **Total** income (loss)—Combine lines 3, 4, and 5 and enter here ▶	6	943270

Deductions (See instructions for limitations.)

7 Compensation of officers	7	167000
8a Salaries and wages 254163 **b** Less jobs credit **c** Bal ▶	8c	254163
9 Repairs	9	14175
10 Bad debts (see instructions)	10	29684
11 Rents	11	75000
12 Taxes	12	12000
13 Deductible interest expense not claimed or reported elsewhere on return (see instructions)	13	110000
14a Depreciation from Form 4562 (attach Form 4562) . . . 14a 202500		
b Depreciation reported on Schedule A and elsewhere on return 14b 175000		
c Subtract line 14b from line 14a	14c	27500
15 Depletion (**Do not deduct oil and gas depletion.** See instructions.)	15	-0-
16 Advertising	16	17000
17 Pension, profit-sharing, etc. plans	17	-0-
18 Employee benefit programs	18	-0-
19 Other deductions (attach schedule)	19	56530
20 **Total** deductions—Add lines 7 through 19 and enter here ▶	20	763052
21 Ordinary income (loss) from trade or business activity(ies)—Subtract line 20 from line 6	21	180278

Tax and Payments

22 Tax:		
a Excess net passive income tax (attach schedule) 22a		
b Tax from Schedule D (Form 1120S) 22b		
c Add lines 22a and 22b	22c	-0-
23 Payments:		
a Tax deposited with Form 7004 23a		
b Credit for Federal tax on fuels (attach Form 4136) 23b		
c Add lines 23a and 23b	23c	-0-
24 Tax due (subtract line 23c from line 22c). See instructions for Paying the Tax ▶	24	-0-
25 Overpayment (subtract line 22c from line 23c) ▶	25	-0-

Please Sign Here

Under penalties of perjury, I declare that I have examined this return, including accompanying schedules and statements, and to the best of my knowledge and belief, it is true, correct, and complete. Declaration of preparer (other than taxpayer) is based on all information of which preparer has any knowledge.

Signature of officer: *John Everette Evans* Date: 3-9-89 Title: President

Paid Preparer's Use Only

Preparer's signature ▶	Date	Check if self-employed ▶ ☐	Preparer's social security number
Firm's name (or yours if self-employed) and address ▶		E.I. No. ▶	
		ZIP code ▶	

Form **1120S** (1988)

Schedule A Cost of Goods Sold and/or Operations (See instructions for Schedule A.)

1 Inventory at beginning of year	1	506 320
2 Purchases	2	1992 406
3 Cost of labor	3	810 516
4a Additional section 263A costs (attach schedule) (see instructions)	4a	—0—
b Other costs (attach schedule)	4b	175,000
5 Total—Add lines 1 through 4b	5	3 484 242
6 Inventory at end of year	6	459 622
7 Cost of goods sold and/or operations—Subtract line 6 from line 5. Enter here and on line 2, page 1	7	3 024 620

8a Check all methods used for valuing closing inventory:
- (i) ☒ Cost
- (ii) ☐ Lower of cost or market as described in Regulations section 1.471-4
- (iii) ☐ Writedown of "subnormal" goods as described in Regulations section 1.471-2(c)
- (iv) ☐ Other (Specify method used and attach explanation) ▶ ....

b Check this box if the LIFO inventory method was adopted this tax year for any goods (if checked, attach Form 970) . . . . ☐

c If the LIFO inventory method was used for this tax year, enter percentage (or amounts) of closing inventory computed under LIFO . . . . | 8c |

d Do the rules of section 263A (with respect to property produced or acquired for resale) apply to the corporation? . . . ☐ Yes ☒ No

e Was there any change in determining quantities, cost, or valuations between opening and closing inventory? (If "Yes," attach explanation.) . . . . ☐ Yes ☒ No

Additional Information Required

	Yes	No
I Did you at the end of the tax year own, directly or indirectly, 50% or more of the voting stock of a domestic corporation? (For rules of attribution, see section 267(c).) If "Yes," attach a schedule showing: (1) name, address, and employer identification number; and (2) percentage owned.		X
J Refer to the listing of business activity codes at the end of the Instructions for Form 1120S and state your principal (1) Business activity ▶.................................; (2) Product or service ▶.............................		
K Were you a member of a controlled group subject to the provisions of section 1561?		X
L At any time during the tax year, did you have an interest in or a signature or other authority over a financial account in a foreign country (such as a bank account, securities account, or other financial account)? (See instructions for exceptions and filing requirements for form TD F 90-22.1.)		X
If "Yes," enter the name of the foreign country ▶.................................		
M Were you the grantor of, or transferor to, a foreign trust which existed during the current tax year, whether or not you have any beneficial interest in it? If "Yes," you may have to file Forms 3520, 3520-A, or 926.		X
N During this tax year did you maintain any part of your accounting/tax records on a computerized system?		X
O Check method of accounting: **(1)** ☐ Cash **(2)** ☐ Accrual **(3)** ☐ Other (specify) ▶.............................		
P Check this box if the S corporation has filed or is required to file **Form 8264**, Application for Registration of a Tax Shelter . . . . ▶☐		
Q Check this box if the corporation issued publicly offered debt instruments with original issue discount . . . . . ▶☐		
If so, the corporation may have to file **Form 8281**, Information Return for Publicly Offered Original Issue Discount Instruments.		
R If the corporation: (1) filed its election to be an S corporation after December 31, 1986, (2) was a C corporation prior to making the election, and (3) at the beginning of the tax year has net unrealized built-in gain as defined in section 1374(d)(1), enter the net unrealized built-in gain (see instructions) ▶		

Designation of Tax Matters Person (See instructions.)

The following shareholder is hereby designated as the tax matters person (TMP) for the tax year for which this tax return is filed:

Name of designated TMP ▶ JOHN EVERRETTE EVANS

Identifying number of TMP ▶ 123-45-6789

Address of designated TMP ▶ 4340 HOLMES PARKWAY
ELM CITY CA 95555

Schedule K	Shareholders' Shares of Income, Credits, Deductions, Etc. (See Instructions.)		

	(a) Distributive share items		(b) Total amount

Income (Loss) and Deductions

1	Ordinary income (loss) from trade or business activity(ies) (page 1, line 21)		**1**	180 278
2a	Gross income from rental real estate activity(ies).	**2a**		
b	Minus expenses (attach schedule)	**2b**		
c	Balance: net income (loss) from rental real estate activity(ies).		**2c**	
3a	Gross income from other rental activity(ies)	**3a**		
b	Minus expenses (attach schedule)	**3b**		
c	Balance: net income (loss) from other rental activity(ies)		**3c**	
4	Portfolio income (loss):			
a	Interest income		**4a**	4 000
b	Dividend income		**4b**	16 000
c	Royalty income		**4c**	
d	Net short-term capital gain (loss) (Schedule D (Form 1120S)).		**4d**	
e	Net long-term capital gain (loss) (Schedule D (Form 1120S))		**4e**	
f	Other portfolio income (loss) (attach schedule)		**4f**	
5	Net gain (loss) under section 1231 (other than due to casualty or theft) (see instructions)		**5**	
6	Other income (loss) (attach schedule)		**6**	
7	Charitable contributions (attach list)		**7**	24000
8	Section 179 expense deduction (attach schedule)		**8**	
9	Expenses related to portfolio income (loss) (attach schedule) (see instructions)		**9**	
10	Other deductions (attach schedule)		**10**	,

Credits

11a	Jobs credit		**11a**	6000
b	Low-income housing credit: (1) Partnership to which section 42(j)(5) applies		**11b(1)**	
	(2) Other.		**11b(2)**	
c	Qualified rehabilitation expenditures related to rental real estate activity(ies) (attach schedule)		**11c**	
d	Credits related to rental real estate activity(ies) other than on lines 11b and 11c (attach schedule)		**11d**	
e	Credit(s) related to other rental activity(ies) (see instructions) (attach schedule)		**11e**	
12	Other credits (attach schedule)		**12**	

Investment Interest

13a	Interest expense on investment debts		**13a**	
b	(1) Investment income included on lines 4a through 4f, Schedule K		**13b(1)**	20 000
	(2) Investment expenses included on line 9, Schedule K		**13b(2)**	

Tax Preference and Adjustment Items

14a	Accelerated depreciation of real property placed in service before 1987		**14a**	
b	Accelerated depreciation of leased personal property placed in service before 1987		**14b**	
c	Depreciation adjustment on property placed in service after 1986		**14c**	
d	Depletion (other than oil and gas)		**14d**	
e	(1) Gross income from oil, gas, or geothermal properties		**14e(1)**	
	(2) Gross deductions allocable to oil, gas, or geothermal properties		**14e(2)**	
f	Other items (attach schedule)		**14f**	

Foreign Taxes

15a	Type of income			
b	Name of foreign country or U.S. possession			
c	Total gross income from sources outside the U.S. (attach schedule)		**15c**	
d	Total applicable deductions and losses (attach schedule)		**15d**	
e	Total foreign taxes (check one): ▶ ☐ Paid ☐ Accrued		**15e**	
f	Reduction in taxes available for credit (attach schedule)		**15f**	
g	Other (attach schedule)		**15g**	

Other Items

16	Total property distributions (including cash) other than dividends reported on line 18, Schedule K		**16**	65000
17	Other items and amounts not included in lines 1 through 16, Schedule K, that are required to be reported separately to shareholders (attach schedule).			
18	Total dividend distributions paid from accumulated earnings and profits contained in other retained earnings (line 26 of Schedule L)		**18**	

Form 1120S (1988) Page **4**

Schedule L — Balance Sheets

	Beginning of tax year		End of tax year	
Assets	(a)	(b)	(c)	(d)
1 Cash		354 010		454 343
2 Trade notes and accounts receivable	495 150		503 340	
a Less allowance for bad debts		495 150		503 340
3 Inventories		506 320		459 622
4 Federal and state government obligations				
5 Other current assets (attach schedule)				
6 Loans to shareholders				
7 Mortgage and real estate loans				
8 Other investments (attach schedule)		100 000		100 000
9 Buildings and other depreciable assets	1 525 700		1 725 700	
a Less accumulated depreciation	350 000	1 175 700	552 500	1 173 200
10 Depletable assets				
a Less accumulated depletion				
11 Land (net of any amortization)				
12 Intangible assets (amortizable only)				
a Less accumulated amortization				
13 Other assets (attach schedule)		15 000		18 000
14 Total assets		2 646 180		2 708 505
Liabilities and Shareholders' Equity				
15 Accounts payable		123 788		125 835
16 Mortgages, notes, bonds payable in less than 1 year		150 000		150 000
17 Other current liabilities (attach schedule)		100 000		200 000
18 Loans from shareholders				
19 Mortgages, notes, bonds payable in 1 year or more		900 000		750 000
20 Other liabilities (attach schedule)				
21 Capital stock		500 000		500 000
22 Paid-in or capital surplus				
23 Accumulated adjustments account	-0-		105 278	
24 Other adjustments account			5 000	
25 Shareholders' undistributed taxable income previously taxed				
26 Other retained earnings (see instructions)	872 392		872 392	
Check this box if the corporation has subchapter C earnings and profits at the close of the tax year ▶ ☐ (see instructions)				
27 Total retained earnings per books—Combine amounts on lines 23 through 26, columns (a) and (c) (see instructions)		872 392		982 670
28 Less cost of treasury stock		( )		( )
29 Total liabilities and shareholders' equity		2 646 180		2 708 505

Schedule M — Analysis of Accumulated Adjustments Account, Other Adjustments Account, and Shareholders' Undistributed Taxable Income Previously Taxed (If Schedule L, column (c), amounts for lines 23, 24, or 25 are not the same as corresponding amounts on line 9 of Schedule M, attach a schedule explaining any differences. See instructions.)

	Accumulated adjustments account	Other adjustments account	Shareholders' undistributed taxable income previously taxed
1 Balance at beginning of year	-0-	-0-	
2 Ordinary income from page 1, line 21	180 278		
3 Other additions	20 000	5 000	
4 Total of lines 1, 2, and 3	200 278	5 000	
5 Distributions other than dividend distributions	65 000	-0-	
6 Loss from page 1, line 21	-0-		
7 Other reductions	30 000	-0-	
8 Add lines 5, 6, and 7	95 000	-0-	
9 Balance at end of tax year—Subtract line 8 from line 4	105 278	5 000	

Passive Activity Loss Limitations

▶ See separate instructions.
▶ Attach to Form 1040 or 1041.

OMB No. 1545-1008

1988

Attachment
Sequence No. **88**

Name(s) as shown on return

Social security or employer identification number

Part I — Computation of 1988 Passive Activity Loss

Caution: See the instructions for Worksheet I before completing Part I.

Rental Real Estate Activities With Active Participation (See the definition of active participation under **Rental Activities** in the instructions.)

Activities acquired before 10-23-86 (Pre-enactment):

1a	Activities with net income, Worksheet 1, Part 1, column (a)	1a
1b	Activities with net loss, Worksheet 1, Part 1, column (b)	1b
1c	Combine lines 1a and 1b	1c

Activities acquired after 10-22-86 (Post-enactment):

1d	Activities with net income, Worksheet 1, Part 2, column (a)	1d
1e	Activities with net loss, Worksheet 1, Part 2, column (b)	1e
1f	Combine lines 1d and 1e	1f
1g	Net income or (loss). Combine lines 1c and 1f.	1g
1h	Prior year unallowed losses from 1987, Worksheet 1, Parts 1 and 2, column (c)	1h
1i	Combine lines 1g and 1h	1i

All Other Passive Activities (See the instructions for lines 2a through 2h.)

Activities acquired before 10-23-86 (Pre-enactment):

2a	Activities with net income, Worksheet 2, Part 1, column (a)	2a
2b	Activities with net loss, Worksheet 2, Part 1, column (b)	2b
2c	Combine lines 2a and 2b	2c

Activities acquired after 10-22-86 (Post-enactment):

2d	Activities with net income, Worksheet 2, Part 2, column (a)	2d
2e	Activities with net loss, Worksheet 2, Part 2, column (b)	2e
2f	Combine lines 2d and 2e	2f
2g	Net income or (loss). Combine lines 2c and 2f.	2g
2h	Prior year unallowed losses from 1987, Worksheet 2, Parts 1 and 2, column (c)	2h
2i	Combine lines 2g and 2h	2i
3	Combine lines 1i and 2i. If the result is net income or -0-, see the instructions for line 3. If this line and line 1c or line 1i are losses, go to line 4. Otherwise, enter -0- on lines 8 and 9 and go to line 10	3

Part II — Computation of the Special Allowance for Rental Real Estate With Active Participation

Note: Before completing Parts II and III, see the instructions for how to treat numbers as if they were all positive.

4	Enter the smaller of the loss on line 1i or the loss on line 3. If line 1i is -0- or net income, enter -0- and complete lines 5 through 9	4
5	Enter $150,000. If married filing separately, see instructions.	5
6	Enter modified adjusted gross income, but not less than -0- (see instructions). If line 6 is equal to or greater than line 5, skip line 7, enter -0- on lines 8 and 9, and then go to line 10. Otherwise, go to line 7	6
7	Subtract line 6 from line 5	7
8	Multiply line 7 by 50% (.5). **Do not** enter more than $25,000. If married filing separately, see instructions	8
9	Enter the smaller of line 4 or line 8	9

Part III — Computation of Passive Activity Loss Allowed

10	Combine lines 1c and 2c and enter the result. If the result is -0- or net income, skip to line 16. (See instructions.)	10
11	If line 1c shows income, has no entry, or shows -0-, enter -0- on line 11. Otherwise, enter the smaller of line 1c or line 8	11
12	Subtract line 11 from line 10. If line 11 is equal to or greater than line 10, enter -0-.	12
13	Subtract line 9 from line 3	13
14	Enter the smaller of line 12 or line 13	14
15	Multiply line 14 by 40% (.4) and enter the result	15
16	Enter the amount from line 9	16
17	**Passive Activity Loss Allowed for 1988.** Add lines 15 and 16	17
18	Add the income, if any, on lines 1a, 1d, 2a, and 2d and enter the result	18
19	**Total losses allowed from all passive activities for 1988.** Add lines 17 and 18. See the instructions to see how to report the losses on your tax return	19

For Paperwork Reduction Act Notice, see separate instructions.

Form **8582** (1988)

☆ U. S. GOVERNMENT PRINTING OFFICE: 1988—205-337

Exhibit 5-3

Chapter 6

GOVERNMENT REQUIREMENTS YOU MUST BE AWARE OF REGARDLESS OF THE BUSINESS FORM YOU CHOOSE

As our society becomes more complex, so do the rules that govern us. Government regulation and taxation of our activities, both at the state and federal level, intensify the moment we take the first step to operate our own business, and, as our business activities expand, so do the regulations. You do not want to run afoul of government regulations. The government can penalize you severely for not obeying its regulations. The adage of an ounce of prevention is worth a pound of cure is on target when dealing with the government. We strongly recommend that you use a lawyer and an accountant to help guide you through the government compliance and tax maze. The money you pay out in professional fees will be far less than government imposed fines, penalties, and down time should you choose to ignore the government's mandates. This chapter explains many of the government requirements you must satisfy:

* Use of a fictitious business name
* Obtaining local and state licenses
* Estimating your self-employment tax and federal tax deposit coupons
* Obtaining social security numbers
* Reporting your employees' social security and income tax withholdings
* Unemployment taxes and how they work
* Worker's compensation insurance and why you must obtain it
* Complying with employee safety and health regulations
* Complying with wage-hour laws, child labor laws, and fair employment practices acts
* Displaying necessary government notices in the workplace
* Selling to consumers on credit

WHY YOU SHOULD CONSIDER A FICTITIOUS BUSINESS NAME

Your business name is important because often it can be used to convey an image of who you are and the product or service you offer. When a business goes by a name other than the owner's real name, the business is operating under a fictitious business name, which is also known as or "doing business" as or dba.

Most states require all for-profit businesses operating under a fictitious business name to file a statement with the county clerk. Further, these businesses must publish a fictitious business name statement in a newspaper of general circulation in the county in which the principal place of business is located at intervals of once a week for four successive weeks. In addition, the state will also require an affidavit proving such publication, which must be filed with the county clerk within thirty days after completion of the publication.

The purpose of this state requirement is to inform the public of the name of the owner of the business. This information is necessary for the following reasons: check litigation history or credit rating, or determine the identity of the parties to initiate a lawsuit. Moreover, filing a fictitious business name statement may prevent any other business in the county from using the same business name.

Fictitious Name Defined by Legal Form of Business

Sole proprietorship. A business name is considered fictitious if it does not contain the surname of the owner.

Partnership. A business name is considered fictitious if it does not contain the surname of all the general partners and suggests the existence of additional owners. For example, if a partnership was to operate under the name "Brenner, Ewan, Custer & Associates," it would need to file and publish a fictitious business name statement because it suggests the existence of additional owners.

Corporation. A corporation is not required to file a fictitious business name statement unless it does business under a name that is different from the one that is used in the articles of incorporation.

Exhibit 6-1 shows a typical example of an application for a fictitious business name statement in San Diego County, California.

Reasons for Using a Fictitious Business Name

There are two reasons to consider using a fictitious business name. First, it may allow you to identify your business with the product or service that you are selling, which is an excellent marketing tool. Second, if you use your own name for the business and it becomes successful, you can relax and even take pride in the fact that your name is associated with the business. However, if the business should fail, many individuals throughout the business community will automatically associate your name with the failure; as a result, it may be difficult for you to start another business, especially if you have to rely on credit.

Name Check

Once you have decided on the name of your business, you will need to find out whether there is another business operating under the same name or one that is similar to it. This means that, at the very least, you will have to make an inquiry with the secretary of state and the clerk of the county in which you will be doing business.

OBTAINING LOCAL AND STATE LICENSES

Local License

You will need a local business license to conduct your business regardless of whether it falls into the category of manufacturing, wholesaling, retailing, or providing a service. Local business licenses are issued by the county or city, or both. Failure to obtain a business license will result in a penalty. Also you will be penalized if you apply for a license long after you have been in business or if you are delinquent in your payment. Exhibit 6-2 shows typical example of an application for a business license in San Diego, California.

Not Transferable. If ownership changes hands, the general rule is that the license is not transferable, and a new business license must be obtained. Therefore, if you buy an existing business, it is necessary to check the local rules. More than likely, you will not be able to use the existing license and will have to obtain a new one.

State License

Occupations such as doctors, lawyers, and CPAs have traditionally been licensed. During the past decade, other occupations or businesses have also undergone licensing requirements because of the demand for consumer protection. It is illegal to engage in any occupation or business that is licensed by the state without first complying with the licensing requirements. Therefore, you must determine whether your particular business requires a state license to operate.

Most states publish a handbook that contains detailed information on licensing requirements and fees for different occupations and businesses. Many individuals believe that only professionals, such as doctors and lawyers, must obtain an occupational license from the state before they can do business; however, there is a variety of other types of businesses that require a state issued license to operate. Following is a partial list of the types of businesses requiring a license in most states.

- Alcoholic beverages
- Banks
- Savings and loan association
- Yacht broker
- Geothermal drilling service
- Boxer
- Barber
- Contractor
- Dry cleaning service
- Bedding manufacturer
- Landscape architect
- Escrow agent
- Talent agency
- Clinical laboratory
- Medical device manufacturer
- Nursery and seed service
- All businesses where blasting takes place

- All businesses that use boilers, air tanks, liquid petroleum gas tanks, elevators, amusement rides
- All businesses that engage in excavation, trenching, demolition
- All businesses engaged in buying, receiving on consignment, soliciting for sale commission, or negotiating the sale of farm products from a producer, dealer, broker, or commission merchant for resale

OBTAINING SALES AND USE TAX PERMITS

Almost every business that sells tangible personal property will have to pay sales or use tax and therefore must apply to the state for a seller's permit. Wholesalers as well as retailers are included. There is no fee for the permit but the business may be required to post a bond as security for payment of the tax. If you are not sure whether the sales or use tax applies to your business, request written advice from the state agency that issues sales and use tax permits. In most states, the law provides that the state may relieve the taxpayer of tax, interest, and penalties where the state finds that the failure to make a timely return or payment of sales or use tax was due to reliance on erroneous written advice by the state taxing agency's staff. Refer to Chapter 3 for further discussion of how sales and use taxes affect the purchase of an existing business. Also see Exhibit 3-10 which shows a list of state agencies that collect sales and use tax and issue the permits.

Sales Tax

The sales tax is imposed for the privilege of selling tangible personal property at retail and thus is not really a tax on sales but an excise tax for the privilege of conducting a retail business. The general sales tax, like the general use tax, is governed primarily by sales and use tax law.

Also, the sales tax is imposed on all retailers, and thus is a tax on the seller, not the buyer.

Use Tax

The use tax is an excise tax imposed on the storage, use, or other consumption within the state of tangible personal property. Generally, all tangible personal property not exempted, and not actually covered by the sales tax, is subject to the use tax. The purpose of the use tax is to act as a complement of the sales tax so that all tangible personal property either sold or utilized in the state is taxable.

The use tax applies to tangible personal property wherever it was purchased, as long as it is purchased for use within the state. A use tax may be imposed, for example, on mail order sales to customers within the state or by a foreign corporation doing business within the state. Also, materials purchased outside the state, shipped into the state, and placed in the user's inventory within the state, which will be used in conducting business, are subject to the use tax.

HOW TO ESTIMATE YOUR SELF-EMPLOYMENT TAX (SE TAX), AND KNOWING WHEN TO USE FEDERAL TAX DEPOSIT COUPONS (FORM 8109)

Self-employment tax (SE tax) is a social security tax for self-employed individuals. You will have to pay self-employment tax if net income from self-employment exceeds $400. The following rules concerning self-employment tax will assist you in keeping current with the government.

* The rate is 13.02% for 1989 [(7.51 × 2) - 2.0% credit].

* Maximum earnings subject to SE tax is $48,000 for 1989.
* No SE tax is due if a self-employed individual has W-2 income of $43,800 or self-employment income of less than $400.
* Estimated tax payments must include SE tax. SE tax is determined by the following calculations.

First. Estimate net earnings from self-employment.

Second. Determine amount of earnings subject to SE tax.

Third. Multiply step 2 by 13.02% for 1988 or 13.02% for 1989. See Exhibit 6-3.

* Federal tax deposit coupons (Exhibit 6-4) are used in cases where withheld social security and income taxes are due before the quarterly IRS Form 941 (Exhibit 6-5) and calendar year IRS Form 943 (Exhibit 6-6) are due.
* Tax deposits are computed separately for each return period and each month of a return period is divided into eight deposit periods: 3rd, 7th, 11th, 15th, 19th, 22nd, 25th, and the last day of every month.

Deposit rules:

If your quarterly payroll taxes are less than $500, you may either pay the taxes with Form 941 or deposit them by the return due date.

If quarterly payroll taxes are more than $500 but less than $3,000, they must be deposited by the 15th of the following month. The deposit is made at a federal reserve bank accompanied by a deposit coupon.

If quarterly payroll taxes exceed $3,000, at the end of any of the eight deposit periods during the month, at least 95% of the amount owed must be made within three banking days. The deposit is accompanied by a deposit coupon and made at a federal reserve bank or other authorized financial institution.

Miscellaneous

* Write your federal ID number on your check.
* To avoid problems with lost paperwork, write the period covered by the payment and type of tax you are paying on your check.
* Your coupon books will be mailed to you by the IRS after you have applied for a federal ID number. Do not mail your deposits directly to the IRS.
* Applications for federal ID numbers are made on IRS Form SS-4. See Exhibit 6-7. Check your state agency to determine which form you should use to register as an employer.
* Remember, taxes paid late are subject to penalties and interest.

HOW TO OBTAIN SOCIAL SECURITY NUMBERS

You must file IRS Form SS-5 (Exhibit 6-8) with your local Social Security Administration office. If you are a United States citizen, you will need to do the following:

- Present proof of age
- Present proof of identity
- Present proof of citizenship
- Appear in person if you are over 18 years of age

If you have any questions about necessary documents to substantiate this type of information, contact any Social Security Administration office. You can find the telephone number of the nearest office by checking the federal government listings that appear in the front portion of your local telephone directory.

KNOWING WHEN TO REPORT SOCIAL SECURITY AND INCOME TAX WITHHOLDING FROM YOUR EMPLOYEES' WAGES

Social security and income tax withholdings are reported together on IRS Form 941 (Exhibit 6-5) except in the following cases:

Agricultural workers. (You will need to use IRS Form 943.)

Household employees. (You will need to use IRS Form 942.) See Exhibit 6-9.

Employees not covered by social security tax. (You will need to use IRS Form 941E).

Filing Requirements

IRS Form 943. Filed annually and due one month after the calendar year ends.
IRS Forms 942, 941E, and 941. Filed quarterly and are due one month after the end of each calendar quarter.

Due dates are the same for fiscal year and calendar year employers. If the due date falls on Saturday, Sunday, or a legal holiday, forms are due the next working day.

The following chart will assist you in remembering the due dates.

Form	Date Due
943	January 31
941, 941E, 942	Quarterly
1st Quarter	April 30
2nd Quarter	July 31
3rd Quarter	October 31
4th Quarter	January 31

IRS Form W-2. This form is a combination of federal and state information used by employers to show withheld income tax and social security tax. See Exhibit 6-10 for an example. It is due no later than January 31 or within 30 days of an employee's written request.

IRS Form W-3. This form is a federal transmittal used annually to accompany IRS Form W-2 to the Social Security Administration. It is due by the last day of February following the calendar year for which form W-2 was prepared. (See Exhibit 6-10.)

WARNING: You must not forget that you will also have to reconcile state income tax withheld. For example, in California business owners must file a Form DE-43, which is an annual reconciliation of state personal income tax withheld. You must check with the appropriate state agency to determine how state withholdings will be reconciled and reported.

IRS Form W-4. Each new employee should complete this form on or before his or her first day of work. An example is shown in Exhibit 6-11. The W-4 is effective for the first payment of wages and will last until the employee files a new one. If an employee does not give you a W-4, you are required to withhold taxes as if the employee were single and claiming zero allowances. As the employer, you should keep the form and use it to compute withholding. However, you must send the W-4 to the IRS if:

- Your employee claims more than ten withholding allowances; or
- Your employee claims exemption from withholding and wages are estimated to exceed $200 a week.

Ordinarily, if an employee has filed a W-4 form, the state requirement will be satisfied. However, in some states an employee may want to file a state form equivalent to the W-4 because those states permit employees to claim a different marital status and number of allowances than are claimed for federal withholding purposes. Therefore, we recommend you consult your accountant regarding mandatory state withholdings from your employees' wages.

UNDERSTANDING UNEMPLOYMENT TAXES: FEDERAL AND STATE

Federal and state unemployment tax systems enable workers who have lost their jobs to apply for payments of unemployment compensation. Federal unemployment tax (FUTA) is computed on the first $7,000 in wages paid to each employee. The tax is an employer's tax and is not deducted from the employee's wages. The FUTA rate is .8 percent (.008) for most employers.

FUTA is reported on IRS Form 940 (see Exhibit 6-12) and is due no later than one month after the end of the calendar year. If, at the end of any calendar quarter, you owe more than $100, you must make a deposit using IRS Form 8109, "Federal Tax Deposit Coupon," by the end of the next month. See Exhibit 6-4 for an example of this form. Deposits are made at a federal reserve bank or other authorized financial institution.

Every state also has its own unemployment tax requirement. You will need to determine which form you must file, when it is due, and when you must make your payment. As a rule, the state assigns the rate that is taken on the first $7,000 in wages paid to each employee. Moreover, many states have established a rule for federal income tax purposes that whenever you are required to make a federal payment within three banking days after the end of an eight-month period, you must simultaneously remit withholdings to the state.

At this point, you may have the impression that state requirements can be more complicated than federal requirements. Again, we strongly recommend that you seek assistance from either your state employment tax agency or your accountant.

The following tables summarize the federal requirements.

FEDERAL—Quarterly

FORM	DUE DATE	DESCRIPTION
941	April 30	Withholding, FICA
	July 31	Withholding, FICA
	October 31	Withholding, FICA
	January 31	Withholding, FICA

FEDERAL—Annually

FORM	DUE DATE	DESCRIPTION
W-2	February 28	Wage and tax statement
W-3	February 28	Transmittal of W-2
940	January 31	FUTA

Note: IRS Form W-2 must be distributed to employees by January 31, but submitted to the Social Security Administration by February 28. Deposit requirements, rates, and wage ceilings are subject to change at any time. Similar to the federal government, state requirements often change with little advance warning or publicity. Do not attempt to complete any of the aforementioned forms without first reading IRS Publication Circular E and any state publications offered by your state taxing agency.

UNDERSTANDING WORKER'S COMPENSATION INSURANCE AND WHY YOU ARE REQUIRED TO OBTAIN IT

All states require you to obtain worker's compensation insurance for your employees. As an employer, you are required to secure and maintain worker's compensation insurance, either through a private insurance carrier or through your state compensation insurance fund, at no cost to your employees. In every state, there are numerous insurance companies that offer worker's compensation coverage.

The requirement is governed by the various worker's compensation acts that have been passed by each state. The procedure is substantially similar from state to state. In each state, a commission determines whether an employee who has been injured is entitled to receive compensation. The amount of compensation for each type of injury is established by statute.

The right of the employee to recover under the worker's compensation act does not take into consideration negligence or fault in the traditional sense. Instead, the focus is on whether the individual was an employee and whether the injury or disease arose from within the course of the employee's work. As a result, the objective of worker's compensation is to provide the following:

* Immediate medical benefits
* Prompt wage replacement computed as a percentage of weekly wages
* Death benefit

The advantage in obtaining worker's compensation insurance, other than complying with the law, is that an employee, as a rule, is not permitted to bring a law suit against the employer for injuries suffered because of the negligence of the employer. The employee, however, is not prevented from filing a law suit against a third party who may have caused the employee's injury or at least contributed to it.

Worker's compensation laws do not only mandate that you obtain worker's compensation insurance, but that you also satisfy the following requirements as well:

* Notify new employees, by the end of their first pay period, of their right to worker's compensation in the event they incur a job-related injury.

* Post a notice to employees in a conspicuous place that gives the insurance carrier's name, the date the coverage expires, the phone number of the nearest state labor commissioner's office, and the person or department responsible for claims adjustment.

* Post a notice to employees in a conspicuous place that substantially states the following: Your employer or its insurance carrier may not be liable for the payment of worker's compensation benefits for any injury arising out of an employee's voluntary participation in any off-duty recreational, social, or athletic activity which is not part of the employee's work-related duties.

* Notify all employees of certain rights concerning their medical care. The content of the notice will be generally the following: The employee has the right to request a change of treating physician if the original treating physician is selected by the employer. The employee has the right to be treated by a physician of the employee's own choice 30 days after reporting an injury. The employee has the right to notify and direct the employer, prior to an injury, of the type of medical treatment that he or she desires, except emergency or first aid, by designating a personal treating physician.

RECOGNIZING WHEN YOU MAY BE VIOLATING EMPLOYEE SAFETY AND HEALTH REGULATIONS

Federal

At the federal level, the dominant legislation for employee health and safety protection is the Occupational Safety and Health Act of 1970 (OSHA). The act was passed to ensure safe and healthful working conditions for employees and also to create the Occupational Safety and Health Review Commission and the National Institute for Occupational Safety and Health.

OSHA promulgates and enforces workers' safety and health standards and conducts investigations and inspections as well. In addition, reporting and record-keeping requirements are imposed by OSHA. These requirements are listed below.

Reporting

As an employer, you must post (a) a permanent notice regarding job safety and health and (b) a notice regarding the rights of employees who are penalized for objecting to unsafe working conditions. Exhibit 6-13 shows an example of this type of notice.

Also, you may be required to maintain a log and report certain summary information to the Bureau of Labor Statistics concerning job-related injuries and illnesses. This report is made on Form 200. Finally, if there is an accident that results in the death of one or more employees or the hospitalization of five or more employees, the employer must notify the area director of OSHA within 48 hours.

Record Keeping

Small employers are exempt from record keeping requirements. The law defines a small employer as one with ten or fewer employees during the previous year. For businesses that are not considered small employers, and which operate as a health service facility, repair, amusement or recreation facility, hotel or other lodging place, general merchandise store, or building material and garden supply store, OSHA requires a log to be maintained of industrial injuries and illnesses. At the end of the year, the information in the log must be summarized and posted in a conspicuous place in the workplace from February 1st through March 1st.

Additional record keeping is required if your employees are exposed to toxic substances, asbestos, radiation, or carcinogens.

State Law Requirements

OSHA allows individual states to substitute their own job safety and health program for federal regulations as long as they have been approved by the U.S. Labor Department. Various states have been given final approval by the Labor Department, while other states have been certified but are waiting for final approval.

Regardless of whether your state has its own job safety and health program or relies upon federal regulations, the approach to employee safety is substantially similar. You will need to familiarize yourself with hazard assessment and correction, accident investigation, record keeping, equipment monitoring and maintenance, control of potential hazards, safety rules, emergency procedures, and new employee safety orientation. Moreover, those states that have had their program certified, as a rule, have enacted laws that give employees certain rights to a safe and healthful work environment. Some of these rights are:

* The right to receive training in general safe working practices and specific training with regard to hazards unique to any job assignment.
* The right to refuse to perform work that would violate an occupational and safety standard or order where such violation would pose a real and apparent hazard to the worker's safety or health.
* The right to be given information the employer has regarding safety data and the right to be given training regarding potential health hazards of materials and chemicals that a worker uses or may be exposed to.
* The right to be told by an employer if he or she is being, or has been, exposed to concentrations of harmful substances higher than the exposure limits allowed by OSHA standards.
* The right to see and copy records of exposure to toxic substances and harmful physical agents and medical records maintained by the employer as well as the records of exposure to toxic substances and harmful physical agents of employees with similar past or present jobs or working conditions.
* The right to see any citation the employer receives posted at or near the place where the violation occurred.
* The right to request an inspection of the worksite by making a complaint about unsafe or unhealthful working conditions to OSHA.

To help you better understand how a typical state job safety and health program works, we will briefly explain the program now used in California. California is typical of many states and can be used as a basis for both guidelines and comparisons. California's program has been certified but is waiting for final approval. The Assistant Secretary of Labor for Occupational Safety and Health, however, has allowed California to institute its own program until final approval is given. As a result, the labor department is not requiring adherence to federal standards.

There is an extensive body of law in California concerning employee health and safety on the job, and it is similar in many respects to the federal law. The core of California's program is the safety order and safety and health standards promulgated by the state OSHA board. California law is usually referred to as CAL/OSHA and it too has both reporting and record-keeping requirements.

Record Keeping

CAL/OSHA requires both private employers and state and local government to maintain records. The only exceptions to this rule are "small employers," employers engaged in "low hazard industries," or industries covered under the Federal Mine and Safety Act of 1977.

Small Employer. CAL/OSHA defines a small employer by the number of employees on the payroll. If the number of employees on the payroll for all shifts combined has not risen above ten during any 24-hour period in the previous calendar year then the employer is defined as a small employer. *Note:*—Part-time and full-time employees as well as employees that work outside the state are also included in the count.

Low Hazard. To be classified as low hazard, the organization must conduct the majority of its business in one of the Standard Industrial Classifications (SIC) listed below:

Retail Trade

* Apparel and accessory stores (SIC 56)
* Eating and drinking places (58)
* Miscellaneous retail (59)

Finance, Insurance, and Real Estate

* Banking (SIC 60)
* Credit agencies other than banks (SIC 61)
* Security and commodity brokers and services (SIC 62)
* Insurance (SIC 63)
* Insurance agents, brokers, and services (SIC 64)
* Real estate (SIC 65)
* Combination of real estate insurance, loans, law offices (SIC 66)
* Holding and other investment offices (SIC 67)

Services

* Personal (SIC 72)
* Business (SIC 73)
* Motion pictures, except motion picture production (SIC 78 except 781)
* Legal (SIC 81)
* Educational (SIC 82)
* Social (SIC 83)
* Museums, art galleries, botanical and zoological gardens (SIC 84)
* Membership organizations (SIC 86)
* Private households (SIC 88)
* Miscellaneous (SIC 89)

CAL/OSHA Form 200, "Log Summary of Occupational Injuries and Illnesses," is the basic document used to record work-related employee injuries and illnesses that CAL/OSHA determines as recordable. See Exhibit 6-14 for an example of Form 200. Entries into the log must be made within six working days of discovering when the injury or illness occurred. In addition, CAL/OSHA requires a supplementary record to be kept with the log to provide detailed information about each occupational injury or illness that has been recorded.

Reporting

Each February 1st, employers are required to display an annual summary of occupational injuries and illnesses in a place where notices to employees are customarily posted. The summary should include the following information:

* Totals from Form 200
* Calendar year covered
* Company name
* Establishment name
* Certification signature, title, and date

If employees do not report to a single establishment or to a fixed establishment, a copy of the annual summary must be given or mailed during the month of February to each employee who receives pay during that month.

In addition, every employer must post a CAL/OSHA notice entitled "Safety and health protection on the job" at each place where it conducts business or performs industrial activity. Exhibit 6-15 gives an example of this notice.

Inspection Checklist

We advise you to compile a checklist for self-inspection. The checklist should, at a minimum, include those areas of inspection that are recommended by OSHA. The following checklist contains an excerpt from the "OSHA Handbook for Small Businesses." We suggest you use this list as a reference point and then amend or revise it to meet your particular needs.

Self-Inspection Scope

Processing, Receiving, Shipping, and Storage— equipment, job planning, layout, heights, floor loads, projection of materials, materials-handling and storage methods.

Building and Grounds Condition—floors, walls, ceilings, exits, stairs, walkways, ramps, platforms, driveways, aisles.

Housekeeping Program—waste disposal, tools, objects, materials, leakage and spillage, cleaning methods, schedules, work areas, remote areas, storage areas.

Electricity—equipment, switches, breakers, fuses, switch boxes, junctions, special fixtures, circuits, insulation, extensions, tools, motors, grounding, NEC compliance.

Lighting—type, intensity, controls, conditions, diffusion, location, glare and shadow control.

Heating and Ventilating—type, effectiveness, temperature, humidity, controls, natural and artificial ventilation and exhausting.

Machinery—points of operation, flywheels, gears, shafts, pulleys, key ways, belts, couplings, sprockets, chains, frames, controls, lighting for tools and equipment, brakes, exhausting, feeding, oiling, adjusting, maintenance, lock out, grounding, work space, location, purchasing standards.

Personnel—training, experience, methods of checking machines before use, clothing type, personal protective equipment, use of guards, tool storage, work practices, method of cleaning, oiling, and adjusting machinery.

Hand and Power Tools—purchasing standards, inspection, storage, repair, types, maintenance, grounding, use and handling.

Chemicals—storage, handling, transportation, spills, disposals, amounts used, toxicity or other harmful effects, warning signs, supervision, training, protective clothing and equipment.

Fire Prevention—extinguishers, alarms, sprinklers, smoking rules, exits, assigned personnel, separation of flammable materials and dangerous operations, explosive-proof fixtures in hazardous locations, waste disposal.

Maintenance—regularity, effectiveness, training of personnel, materials and equipment used, records maintained, method of locking out machinery, general methods.

Personal Protective Equipment—type, size, maintenance, repair, storage, assignment of responsibility, purchasing methods, standards observed, training in care and use, rules of use, method of assignment.

COMPLYING WITH FEDERAL AND STATE LAWS: WAGE-HOUR, CHILD LABOR, AND DISCRIMINATION IN THE WORKPLACE

The major sources of legal protection for employees are the following: The Civil Rights Act of 1866; The Civil Rights Act of 1871; The Civil Rights Act of 1964; The Equal Employment Opportunity Act of 1972, which amended the Civil Rights Act of 1964; The Equal Pay Act of 1963; Executive Order 11246 as amended by Executive Order 11375 under federal contracts; The National Labor Relations Act; and state and local fair employment practice laws.

Federal

There are three acts you should pay special attention to because many entrepreneurs unwittingly run afoul of them. They are: Fair Labor Standards Act, Equal Employment Opportunity Act, and Federal Age Discrimination in Employment Act of 1967. Following are brief descriptions of each act and how each impacts upon a business. The descriptions we have provided are intended to serve as an introduction and not as a substitute for the advice of an attorney.

Wage and Hours and Child Labor. As a rule, employers and employees can enter into an employment contract that binds the two of them to certain terms and conditions. One exception is the Fair Labor Standards Act (FLSA), which is also known as the Wage and Hour Act. The act states that subject to certain exceptions, for instance, executive administrators, professionals, and outside salespersons, individuals working in interstate commerce, or in an industry that produces goods for interstate commerce, cannot be paid less than a specified minimum wage and cannot be employed for more than forty hours a week unless they are paid time and half for overtime. The FLSA takes a single work week as its measuring period and does not permit averaging of hours over two or more weeks. *Note*: Many states have limited the work week for children under the age of sixteen during the period when school is in session.

The act also prohibits the employment of children under the age of fourteen years of age but it does permit the employment of children between the ages of fourteen and sixteen in many industries under certain prescribed conditions: Children cannot engage in any work that will cause them to come into contact with either mining, manufacturing, or processing; they cannot work as public messengers or in occupations involving transportation, warehousing and storage, communications or construction; and they cannot operate power machinery or motor vehicles. Moreover, all children under the age of eighteen are excluded from certain occupations that are designated as hazardous by the secretary of labor. *Note*: Many states require persons under the age of eighteen to obtain a work permit.

Discrimination. The Equal Employment Opportunity Act applies to you if, as an employer, you are involved in interstate commerce (which is liberally construed, so consult your lawyer) and you have fifteen or more employees during each work day in each of twenty or more calendar weeks in the current or preceding calendar year. You may not, as an employer, do the following:

* Fail or refuse to hire or to discharge any individual, or otherwise to discriminate against any individual with respect to his or her compensation, terms, conditions, or privileges of employment, because of such individual's race, color, religion, sex, national origin.
* Limit, segregate, or classify your employees or applicants for employment in any way that would deprive or tend to deprive any individual of employment opportunities or otherwise adversely affect an employee's status as an employee, because of such individual's race, color, religion, sex, or national origin.

Another set of acts that affects employer-employee relationships is the Fair Employment Practices Acts. The acts state that, as a rule, employers of fifteen or more persons are forbidden to discriminate as to compensation or other privileges or conditions of employment on the basis of race, religion, color, sex, national origin, or age. In addition, companies entering into contracts with the federal government are usually required to adopt affirmative action programs in the employment of women, minorities, handicapped individuals, and Vietnam veterans.

Under the affirmative action program, employers are required to make a conscientious effort to hire more individuals from each of the categories mentioned above. Furthermore, the employer is charged with upgrading pay and positions of authority of those group s that have historically been subject to patterns of discrimination.

Note: There are three requirements that must be met in order to substantiate an allegation that neutral employment standards have resulted in unlawful discrimination:

* There must be a significantly discriminatory pattern in the way applicants are selected for hire.
* If the requirement above is satisfied then the employer must prove that any given job requirement is related to the job itself.
* If the employer can substantiate the job requirements, then the complaining employee may show that there are other means of selection available for hiring that will not result in a similar discriminatory effect and yet will serve the employer's legitimate interest in efficient and trustworthy workmanship.

Dothard v. *Rawlinson*, 433 U.S. 321 (1977), is an example of the U.S. Supreme Court's view on evidence presented in the lower court to determine whether an unlawful discrimination claim has been sufficiently substantiated. The following excerpt from the opinion written by Justice Stewart stated:

> Appellee Dianne Rawlinson sought employment with the Alabama Board of Corrections as a prison guard, called in Alabama a "correctional counselor." After her application was rejected, she brought this class suit under Title VII of the Civil Rights Act of 1964...alleging that she had been denied employment because of her sex in violation of federal law. A three-judge Federal District Court for the Middle District of Alabama decided in her favor....We noted probable jurisdiction of this appeal from the District Court's judgment....

At the time she applied for a position as correctional counselor trainee, Rawlinson was a 22 year-old college graduate whose major course of study had been correctional psychology. She was refused employment because she failed to meet the minimum 120-pound weight requirement established ....

Like most correctional facilities in the United States, Alabama's prisons are segregated on the basis of sex. Currently the Alabama Board of Corrections operates four major all-male penitentiaries....Their inmate living quarters are for the most part large dormitories, with communal showers and toilets that are open to the dormitories and hallways. The Draper and Fountain penitentiaries carry on extensive farming operations, making necessary a large number of strip searches for contraband when prisoners re-enter the prison buildings.

A correctional counselor's primary duty within these institutions is to maintain security and control of the inmates by continually supervising and observing their activities. To be eligible for consideration as a correctional counselor, an applicant must possess a valid Alabama driver's license, have a high school education or its equivalent, be free from physical defects, be between the ages of 20 1/2 years and 45 years at the time of appointment, and fall between the minimum height and weight requirements of 5 feet 2 inches, and 120 pounds and the maximum of 6 feet 10 inches, and 300 pounds. Appointment is by merit, with a grade assigned each applicant based on experience and education. No written examination is given.

At the time this litigation was in the District Court, the Board of Corrections employed a total of 435 people in various correctional counselor positions, 56 of whom were women. Of those 56 women, 21 were employed at the Julia Tutwiler Prison for Women, 13 were employed in noncontact positions at the four male maximum-security institutions, and the remaining 22 were employed at the other institutions operated by the Alabama Board of Corrections. Because most of Alabama's prisoners are held at the four maximum security male penitentiaries, 336 of the 435 correctional counselor jobs were in those institutions, a majority of them concededly in the "contact" classification. Thus, even though meeting the statutory height and weight requirements, women applicants could under Regulation 204 compete equally with men for only about 25% of the correctional counselor jobs available in the Alabama prison system....

The gist of the claim that the statutory height and weight requirements discriminate against women does not involve an assertion of purposeful discriminatory motive. It is asserted, rather, that these facially neutral qualification standards work in fact disproportionately to exclude women from eligibility for employment by the Alabama Board of Corrections....

In this environment of violence and disorganization, it would be an oversimplification to characterize Regulation 204 as an exercise in "romantic paternalism."...In the usual case, the argument that a particular job is too dangerous for women may appropriately be met by the rejoinder that it is the purpose of Title VII to allow the individual woman to make that choice for herself. More is at stake in this case, however, than an individual woman's decision to weigh and accept the risks of employment in a "contact" position in a maximum-security male prison.

The essence of a correctional counselor's job is to maintain prison security. A woman's relative ability to maintain order in a male, maximum security, unclassified penitentiary of the type Alabama now runs could be directly reduced by her womanhood. There is a basis in fact for expecting that sex offenders who have criminally assaulted women in the past would be moved to do so again if access to women were established within the prison. There would be a real risk that other inmates, deprived of a normal heterosexual environment would assault women guards because they were women. In a prison system where violence is the order of the day, where inmate access to guards is facilitated by dormitory living arrangements, where every institution is understaffed, and where a substantial portion of the inmate population is composed of sex offenders mixed at random with other prisoners, there are few visible deterrents to inmate assaults on women custodians.

Appellee Rawlinson's own expert testified that dormitory housing for aggressive inmates poses a greater security problem than single-cell lockups, and further testified that it would be unwise to use women guards in a prison where even 10% of the inmates had been convicted of sex crimes and were not segregated from the other prisoners. The likelihood that inmates would assault a woman because she was a woman would pose a real threat not only to the victim of the assault but also to the basic control of the penitentiary and protection of its inmates and the other security personnel. The employee's very womanhood would thus directly undermine her capacity to provide the security that is the essence of a correctional counselor's responsibility.

There was substantial testimony from experts on both sides of this litigation that the use of women as guards in "contact" positions under the existing conditions in Alabama maximum-security male penitentiaries would pose a substantial security problem, directly linked to the sex of the prison guard. On the basis of that evidence, we conclude that the District Court was in error in ruling that being male is not a bona fide occupational qualification for the job of correctional counselor in a "contact" position in an Alabama male maximum-security penitentiary.

Employee testing is another area you must pay special attention to because of past abuses to its use. Although employee testing had been used legitimately by many companies to determine the best person for the job, all too often it became a tool used by many businesses to discriminate against individuals because of their race, religion, or sex. The issue of employee testing was finally brought to the Supreme Court in *Griggs* v. *Duke Power Company*, 401 U.S. 424 (1971). This landmark case established the legal standards for employee testing as it relates to employment discrimination.

Basically, the facts of the case involved the following: The Duke Power Company established standards for promotion within the organization. To qualify for many of the promotions, employees had to register satisfactory scores on two tests that were prepared by professionals at test preparation: the Wonderlic Personal Test, which purports to measure general intelligence, and the Bennett Mechanical Comprehension Test. Neither test, however, was directed nor intended to measure the ability to learn to perform a particular job or category of jobs. Instead, it was used to "improve the overall quality of the workforce."

Willie S. Griggs, a black man, and other blacks applied for a promotion but failed to obtain a passing score. They claimed that the requirement to pass the test was a form of prohibited racial discrimination imposed upon them by the employer. Duke Power Company argued there was no showing of racial purpose or invidious intent in the adoption of the two tests and that the standards had been applied fairly to both whites and blacks.

The U.S. Supreme Court ruled that Congress, in passing statutes to prohibit discrimination in the workplace, had as its objective the equality of employment opportunities and the removal of barriers that have operated in the past to favor an identifiable group of white employees over other employees. Therefore, procedures or tests, even though neutral on their face or in their intent, cannot be maintained if they operate to freeze the status quo of prior discriminatory employment practices. The court further stated it acknowledged the use of testing or measuring procedures as useful but they must measure a person's ability for a job, not the person alone.

Remember, the use of occupational qualifications, employee selection methods, and employee testing is not inherently unlawful at the federal level as long as the following requirements are satisfied.

First. An employer employs a person on the basis of religion, sex, or national origin in those certain instances where religion, sex, or national origin is a bona fide occupational qualification reasonably necessary to the normal operation of that particular business or enterprise.

Second. An employer applies different standards of compensation, or different terms, conditions, or privileges of employment pursuant to a bona fide seniority or merit system, or to a system that measures earnings by quantity or quality of production, or to employees who work in different locations, as long as such differences are not the result of an intention to discriminate because of race, religion, sex, or national origin. However, the test must be job related in order not to be unlawfully discriminatory. In addition, the employer may legally differentiate on the basis of sex in determining the amount of wages or compensation if it is authorized by the Federal Labor Standards Act.

Age Discrimination. The Federal Age Discrimination in Employment Act of 1967 was amended in 1978 and in 1986. The purpose of the law is to promote employment of older persons based on their ability rather than their age; to prohibit arbitrary age discrimination in employment; and to help employers and workers find ways of meeting problems arising from the impact of age on employment.

The act applies to every employer that has an effect on interstate commerce and that has twenty or more employees. Basically, an employer is prohibited from doing the following:

* Failing or refusing to hire or discharge any individual or otherwise discriminate against any individual with respect to his or her compensation, terms, conditions, or privileges of employment, because of such individual's age.

* Limiting, segregating, or classifying employees in any way which would deprive or tend to deprive any individual of employment opportunities or otherwise adversely affect an employee's status as an employee, because of such individual's age.

There is one exception to the prohibition against age discrimination: An employee may be terminated on the basis of age before reaching the age of seventy if it can be shown that age is a bona fide occupational qualification reasonably necessary to the normal operations of a particular business.

State

If you intend to conduct business in your state, you should be aware of the large body of laws governing businesses in your state. They include: (a) wages, hours, and working conditions; (b) child labor; and (c) discrimination. Many of these state laws are more stringent than federal law. Approximately forty eight states have statutes and regulations that independently regulate wages, hours, and child labor and prohibit certain types of discrimination.

Perhaps the most troublesome regulations for businesses that are starting up concern wages, hours, and working conditions. These three areas tend to be the most heavily regulated and most vigorously protected. California is typical of those states that have enacted extensive regulations regarding wages, hours, and working conditions. Following is a brief description of California's regulations in these areas. *Note*: Your state will probably have a similar setup; therefore, use our description as a guide when you make inquiries.

The California Industrial Welfare Commission has the duty of regulating wages, hours, and working conditions. These regulations take the form of *orders* and cover various industries and occupations. Below is a list of the fifteen industries and occupations subject to these orders.

Order Number	Industry/Occupation
1-80	Manufacturing
2-80	Personal service
3-80	Canning, freeing, preserving
4-80*	Professional, technical, clerical, mechanical*
5-80	Housekeeping
6-80	Laundry, linen supply, dry cleaning, dyeing
7-80	Mercantile
8-80	Handling products after harvest
9-80	Transportation
10-80	Amusement and recreation
11-80	Broadcasting
12-80	Motion picture
13-80	Preparing agricultural products for market
14-80	Agriculture
15-80	Household

*See Exhibit 6-16 for an example of order number 4-80, which regulates wages, hours, and working conditions in the professional, technical, clerical, and mechanical occupations.

There are a few exceptions, however, to the Industrial Welfare Commission orders. Employees who occupy positions that are primarily executive, administrative, or professional in nature fall outside of the regulations. The orders also do not apply to outside salespersons.

California defines an administrative, executive, or professional employee as an individual who:

* Engages in work that is primarily intellectual, managerial, or creative, and which requires exercise of discretion and independent judgment, and for which the remuneration is not less than $900 per month; or
* Licensed or certified by the state of California to practice one of the nine professions specifically listed in the wage orders: accounting, architecture, dentistry, engineering, law, medicine, pharmacology, optometry, and teaching.

BE CAREFUL: ALL EMPLOYERS MUST COMPLY WITH THE IMMIGRATION LAW OF 1986

In reaction to the large number of undocumented aliens who continually come into the United States seeking employment, Congress passed, and the President signed into law the Immigration Reform and Control Act of 1986, which is the most comprehensive revision of the immigration laws since 1952. In essence, the law says you should hire only American citizens and aliens who are authorized to work in the United States.

As an employer, you will need to verify employment eligibility of anyone hired after November 6, 1986, and complete and retain Form I-9, entitled "Employment Eligibility Verification." Exhibit 6-17 gives an example of this one-page form.

The law requires you, as an employer, to do five things:

1. Have your employees fill out their part of Form I-9 when they start work.
2. Check documents establishing employees' identity and eligibility to work.
3. Properly complete Form I-9.
4. Retain Form I-9 for at least three years (if you employ the person for more than three years, you must retain Form I-9 until one year after the person leaves your employment).
5. Present Form I-9 for inspection to an Immigration and Naturalization Service (INS) agent or Department of Labor (DOL) officer upon request. You will be given at least three days advance notice.

If you employ persons to perform labor or services in return for wages or other pay, you must complete Form I-9 for:

* Persons hired after May 31, 1987.
* Persons hired between November 7, 1986, and May 31, 1987.

There are civil and criminal penalties for violating the immigration laws. The following activities are illegal:

* Hiring or continuing to employ unauthorized employees.
* Failing to comply with record-keeping requirements.
* Requiring indemnification.
* Recruiting unauthorized seasonal agricultural workers outside the United States.
* Engaging in a pattern of knowingly hiring or continuing employing unauthorized employees.
* Engaging in fraud or false statements, or otherwise misusing visas, immigration permits, and identity documents.

The INS has published a booklet entitled *Handbook for Employers*, which contains information on why employers must verify employment eligibility; when the employer must complete Form I-9; the step-by-step process of filling out Form I-9; unlawful discrimination practices; information on prohibited practices and penalties; information for recruiters and referrers for a fee; and documents that can be used to establish employment eligibility.

Exhibit 6-18 contains an excerpt from the booklet, which will help you to better understand your responsibilities as an employer. The excerpt contains excellent information and advice in a question-and-answer format.

GOVERNMENT NOTICES THAT ARE REQUIRED TO BE DISPLAYED

Both the federal government and your state government will require you, as an employer, to post certain notices to inform your employees of their rights. Some notices must always be posted while others are posted only at certain times. In all cases, notices must be displayed in a conspicuous place where notices to employees are customarily posted.

The number and type of notices you will have to post will depend on the state in which your business is located; however, many states require the same type of notices to be posted. For comparison purposes, the notices required by the federal government and the state of California are listed. Your state may have its own notice requirements. Use the list for California as a guide to determine the type of notices that may be required by your state.

Federal Notice: **MINIMUM WAGE NOTICE**

Permanent notice. Required to be displayed if your employees come under the protection of the U.S. Fair Labor Standards Act. Copies may be obtained from the Wage and Hour Division of the U.S. Department of Labor. Federal contractors have to post another notice at the site of the contract. Copies may be obtained from the Employees Standards Administration of the U.S. Department of Labor.

Federal Notice: **EQUAL EMPLOYMENT OPPORTUNITY NOTICE**

Permanent Notice. Required to be displayed if you have fifteen or more employees during twenty weeks of the year. (See Exhibit 6-19.) Copies may be obtained from the Equal Opportunity Commission. Federal contractors must post additional notices: (1) nondiscrimination and affirmative action based on race, color, religion, sex, or national origin; (2) nondiscrimination and affirmative action based on disabled and Vietnam War era veterans under the Vietnam Era Veterans' Readjustment Assistance Act of 1974; (3) nondiscrimination in relation to handicapped workers. In addition, if you employ twenty or more individuals during twenty weeks of the year then you must display a notice prohibiting discrimination based on age even though you may not be a federal contractor.

Federal or California Notice: **ANNUAL SUMMARY OF INJURIES AND ILLNESSES**

Temporary Notice. Required to be displayed by all employers. Post during the entire month of February. Copies may be obtained from the Department of Industrial Relations, Division of Labor Statistics and Research.

California Notice: **INDUSTRIAL WELFARE COMMISSION ORDERS**

Permanent Notice. Required to be displayed by all employers. Copies may be obtained from the Department of Industrial Relations, Division of Labor Standards of Enforcement.

California Notice: **SAFETY AND HEALTH PROTECTION ON THE JOB**

Permanent Notice. Required to be displayed by all employers. Copies may be obtained from the Department of Industrial Relations, Division of Occupational Safety and Health.

California Notice: **PERMIT TO CONDUCT HAZARDOUS BUSINESS**

Permanent Notice. Required to be displayed by all employers. Certain work that is deemed hazardous must have necessary permits on display.

California Notice: **PAYDAYS**

Permanent Notice. Required to be displayed by all employees. Although no particular form is required, California has prepared a small form for employers. Copies may be obtained from the Department of Industrial Relations.

California Notice: **WORKER'S COMPENSATION**

Permanent Notice. Required to be displayed by all employers. Copies may be obtained from your insurance carrier.

California Notice: **DISABILITY INSURANCE**

Permanent Notice. Required to be displayed by all employers. Copies may be obtained from the Franchise Tax Board.

California Notice: **CITATIONS FOR HEALTH AND SAFETY VIOLATIONS**

Temporary Notice. Required to be displayed by all employers. Citations are issued under labor code section 6317 and must be posted at place of violation for three days or until corrected, whichever is longer.

California Notice: **HAZARDOUS CONDITIONS AND EQUIPMENT**

Temporary Notice. Required to be displayed by all employers. Notice must be attached and not removed until dangerous condition is eliminated. No set form is specified, however, you should contact the Department of Industrial Relations, Division of Occupational Safety and Health for instructions.

California Notice: **TIME OFF FOR VOTING**

Temporary Notice. Ten days before every statewide election. Required to be displayed by all employers. There is not a set form.

California Notice: **LABOR DISPUTE**

Temporary Notice. Required to be displayed by all employers. Advertisements or solicitations to hire must contain a notice of labor dispute during strike, lockout, or labor dispute.

FACTORS YOU MUST CONSIDER WHEN YOU SELL TO CONSUMERS ON CREDIT

There are many legal restrictions involved in the sale of goods or services on credit to consumers. The prime sources of information regarding this sensitive area are:

* Federal regulation B of the Equal Credit Opportunity Act
* The Truth In Lending Act, a federal law
* State law

In general, these laws basically provide that grantors of credit:

* May not discriminate based on age, race, marital status, national origin, or public assistance income.
* Must allow women to apply in their birth names, married names, or hyphenated surnames and must not require the applicant's spouse to cosign if the spouse is not an applicant.
* Must disclose a specific reason or reasons why credit was denied.
* Must disclose name or names of credit bureaus providing information that caused a decline of application.
* Must hold all credit applications and evaluation worksheets for fifteen months.
* Must inform applicants and existing customers of their rights and the procedures in the event of a billing error. (For an example, look at the back of any credit card statement.)
* Must notify all applicants of credit decision either orally or in writing within a reasonable time. (Thirty days is recommended.)
* May not close an account on which a customer refused to pay a disputed amount. Customer must dispute within sixty days in writing and must continue to pay undisputed amounts.
* May not inquire into family's plans to propagate. May, however, ask if sources of income will change in the near future.
* Must provide the following information regarding the specific credit transaction:

   First   Annual percentage rate (APR)

   Second   Point at which finance charges begin to accrue

   Third   Size, due date, and number of payments

   Fourth   Description of any prepayment penalties

   Fifth   An accounting of amount financed, prepaid finance charge, and downpayment, if any

   Sixth   Information regarding security interests

   Seventh   Information regarding rights to rescind the deal

Although all these requirements may seem complex, the Federal Reserve Board has simplified things somewhat by publishing a model disclosure statement that provides users with a safe harbor from civil liabilities. See Exhibit 6-20 for an example of this statement.

We strongly recommend that any foray into the area of consumer credit be guided by your attorney. Although fraught with peril if not handled correctly, consumer credit provides you with an excellent marketing tool to increase sales of your merchandise or services.

Note: All credit transactions involving consumers are subject to these laws. However, business-to-business or commercial transactions, in *most* instances, do not require disclosure of the APR.

Chapter 6 Exhibits

Exhibit 6.1   Fictitious Business Name Statement

Exhibit 6.2   City of San Diego Declaration of Business Tax

Exhibit 6.3   Computation of Social Security Self-Employment Tax (IRS Form 1040 Schedule SE)

Exhibit 6.4   Federal Tax Deposit Coupon (IRS Form 8109-B)

Exhibit 6.5   Completed with Explanation: Employer's Quarterly Federal Tax Return (IRS Form 941)

Exhibit 6.6   Employer's Annual Tax Return for Agricultural Employees (IRS Form 943)

Exhibit 6.7   Completed with Explanation: Application for Employer Identification Number (IRS Form SS-4)

Exhibit 6.8   Application for a Social Security Number Card (IRS Form SS-5)

Exhibit 6.9   Employer's Quarterly Tax Return for Household Employees (IRS Form 942)

Exhibit 6.10 Completed with Explanation: Wage and Tax Statement (IRS Form W-2) and Transmittal of Income and Tax Statements (IRS Form W-3)

Exhibit 6.11 Employee Withholding Allowance Certificate (IRS Form W-4)

Exhibit 6.12 Completed with Explanation: Employer's Annual Federal Unemployment (FUTA) Tax Return (IRS Form 940)

Exhibit 6.13 OSHA Notice: Job Safety and Health Protection

Exhibit 6.14 Log and Summary of Occupational Injuries and Illnesses (Cal/OSHA No. 200)

Exhibit 6.15 Safety and Health Protection on the Job (Cal/OSHA)

Exhibit 6.16 Industrial Welfare Commission Order 4-80 Professional, Technical, Clerical, and Mechanical Occupations (State of California)

Exhibit 6.17 Employment Eligibility Verification (Form I-9)

Exhibit 6.18 Immigration and Naturalization Service "Handbook for Employers" (Excerpt Regarding Form I-9)

Exhibit 6.19 Equal Employment Opportunity Notice

Exhibit 6.20 Truth in Lending Disclosure Form for a Credit Sale

**ROBERT D. ZUMWALT,
COUNTY CLERK**
County Courthouse, 220 West Broadway
P. O. Box 128, San Diego, California 92112-4104
(619) 531-3169

This Space For Use of County Clerk

FILING FEE
$10.00 - FOR FIRST BUSINESS NAME ON STATEMENT
$ 2.00 - FOR EACH ADDITIONAL BUSINESS NAME
FILED ON SAME STATEMENT AND DOING
BUSINESS AT THE SAME LOCATION
$ 2.00 - FOR EACH ADDITIONAL OWNER IN EXCESS
OF ONE OWNER

FICTITIOUS BUSINESS NAME STATEMENT

THE NAME[S] OF THE BUSINESS[ES]:

* ....
(Print Fictitious Business Name[s] on Line Above)

** **LOCATED AT:** ....
(Street Address of Business — If No Street Address Assigned — Give Exact Location of Business Plus P.O. Box or Rural Route)

IN: ....
(City and Zip)

IS [ARE] HEREBY REGISTERED BY THE FOLLOWING OWNER[S]:

*** (#1) ....
(Full Name — Type/Print)

(#2) ....
(Full Name — Type/Print)

....
(Residence address if not incorporated)
(State of incorporation if incorporated)

....
Residence address if not incorporated)
(State of incorporation if incorporated)

....
(City and Zip)

....
(City and Zip)

(#3) ....
(Full Name — Type/Print)

(#4) ....
(Full Name — Type/Print)

....
Residence address if not incorporated)
(State of incorporation If incorporated)

....
Residence address if not incorporated)
(State of incorporation if incorporated)

....
(City and Zip)

....
(City and Zip)

**** This business is conducted by: ☐ an Individual ☐ Individuals — Husband and Wife ☐ a General Partnership
☐ a Limited Partnership ☐ a Corporation ☐ a Business Trust ☐ Co-Partners ☐ a Joint Venture
☐ an Unincorporated Association — other than a Partnership ☐ Other (Specify) ....

***** THE REGISTRANT COMMENCED THE TRANSACTION OF BUSINESS ON: ....

SIGNATURE OF REGISTRANT: ....
....
(Print name of person signing and, if a Corporate Officer, also state title)

THIS STATEMENT WAS FILED WITH ROBERT D. ZUMWALT, COUNTY CLERK OF SAN DIEGO COUNTY
ON DATE INDICATED BY FILE STAMP ABOVE

THE FILING OF THIS STATEMENT DOES NOT OF ITSELF AUTHORIZE THE USE IN THE STATE OF A FICTITIOUS BUSINESS NAME IN VIOLATION OF THE RIGHTS OF ANOTHER UNDER FEDERAL, STATE, OR COMMON LAW (see section 14400 et seq., Business and Professions Code). THIS FICTITIOUS BUSINESS STATEMENT NAME EXPIRES FIVE (5) YEARS FROM THE DATE IT WAS FILED IN THE OFFICE OF THE COUNTY CLERK. IF YOU INTEND TO CONTINUE BUSINESS UNDER THIS NAME A NEW FICTITIOUS BUSINESS NAME STATEMENT **MUST BE FILED PRIOR TO:**

....

ASSIGNED FILE NO. ....

Form 231 Co. CLK (REV. 1-89)

COUNTY CLERK

Exhibit 6-1

CITY OF SAN DIEGO DECLARATION OF BUSINESS TAX

Partnership

Certificate Number_____

Invoice Number_____

Come to 1222 First Avenue, San Diego, CA 92101 (619-236-6173) or mail with fee to the City Treasurer, P.O. Box 121536, San Diego, CA 92112-4165.

If you are applying in person, bring both copies — your certificate will be generated by our computer and mailed to you. If you are applying by mail, return the original and keep the duplicate — certificate will be issued within 30 working days.

IMPORTANT NOTICE — READ CAREFULLY BEFORE COMPLETING THIS DECLARATION

Your business tax certificate will be issued under the provisions of Municipal Code Sections 31.0101 and 31.0121. You are cautioned that the certificate does not permit operation of a business within the City of San Diego in violation of any section of the Municipal Code or regulation adopted by the City Council including, but not limited to: Zoning restrictions, land use specifications as defined in planned districts, redevelopment areas, historical districts or revitalization areas, Business Tax regulations, Police Department regulations, and Fire, Health, or Sanitation permits and regulations. If you have any doubt that your business conforms with requirements of the Municipal Code administered by other departments, you are urged to contact those departments for further information **before** filing this declaration for a business tax certificate.

Tax certificate fees are non-refundable unless collected as a result of an error by the City of San Diego.

NOTE: SALES OR USE TAX MAY APPLY TO YOUR BUSINESS ACTIVITIES. YOU MAY SEEK WRITTEN ADVICE REGARDING THE APPLICATION OF TAX TO YOUR PARTICULAR BUSINESS BY WRITING TO THE NEAREST STATE BOARD OF EQUALIZATION OFFICE.

1. BUSINESS NAME								
2. BUSINESS ADDRESS NUMBER	FRACTION	DIR.	STREET NAME			SUITE	CITY	STATE
ZIP				3. BUSINESS TELEPHONE NUMBER				
4. MAILING ADDRESS ATTN:								
NUMBER	FRACTION	DIR.	STREET NAME			SUITE	CITY	STATE
ZIP	COUNTRY			5. MAIL ADDRESS TELEPHONE NUMBER				

6. BUSINESS TYPE (PLEASE CHECK ALL CATEGORIES THAT APPLY TO YOUR BUSINESS.)

RETAIL ____ SERVICE ____ WHSLE ____ CONSTR ____ FINANCIAL ____ TRANSPORT/UTIL ____ MANUF ____ AGRIC ____ MINING ____

7. BUSINESS STARTING DATE MONTH DAY YEAR	8. NUMBER OF EMPLOYEES (Please do not count yourself)	9. NUMBER OF REGULATORY UNITS	10. CHECK IF THIS IS AN OWNERSHIP CHANGE ____
11. FEDERAL EMPLOYER IDENTIFICATION NUMBER (FEIN)		12. STATE BOARD OF EQUALIZATION ACCOUNT NUMBER (SEAN)	

13. PLEASE DESCRIBE THE PRODUCT OR SERVICE WHICH YOUR BUSINESS PROVIDES:	14. PRINCIPAL BUSINESS ACTIVITY CODE Please place here the Principal Business Activity Code number which you will use to report your Federal income tax. We cannot process your declaration without this number.

15. SIGNATURE OF ONE PARTNER	16. DATE OF APPLICATION

FOR OFFICIAL USE ONLY

PED	POLICE		PT	ZONING		Home OCC	C/L		

PERIOD COVERED	_____ to _____		_____ to _____		_____ to _____
BASIC FEE					
EMPLOYEES _____ X $2.00 =					
ASSESSMENT					
PENALTY					
ZONING FEE					
POLICE REGULATORY FEE					
OTHER REGULATORY FEE					
SUBTOTALS					

PMT DATE _____   TOTAL OWED _____

OWNERSHIP INFORMATION

PARTNER 1

17. NAME (LAST)	(FIRST)	(MIDDLE)

18. RESIDENCE ADDRESS NUMBER	FRACTION	DIR.	STREET NAME		SUITE	CITY	STATE
ZIP	COUNTRY			19. RESIDENCE TELEPHONE NUMBER			

20. STATE BLDG. CONTRACTOR NUMBER	21. 2ND STATE BLDG. CONTRACTOR NUMBER	22. SOCIAL SECURITY NUMBER

PARTNER 2

23. NAME (LAST)	(FIRST)	(MIDDLE)

24. RESIDENCE ADDRESS NUMBER	FRACTION	DIR.	STREET NAME		SUITE	CITY	STATE
ZIP	COUNTRY			25. RESIDENCE TELEPHONE NUMBER			

26. STATE BLDG. CONTRACTOR NUMBER	27. 2ND STATE BLDG. CONTRACTOR NUMBER	28. SOCIAL SECURITY NUMBER

PARTNER 3

29. NAME (LAST)	(FIRST)	(MIDDLE)

30. RESIDENCE ADDRESS NUMBER	FRACTION	DIR.	STREET NAME		SUITE	CITY	STATE

Exhibit 6-2

Social Security Self-Employment Tax

▶ See Instructions for Schedule SE (Form 1040).
▶ Attach to Form 1040.

OMB No. 1545-0074

1988

Attachment
Sequence No. 18

Name of person with **self-employment** income (as shown on social security card)	Social security number of person with **self-employment** income ▶
SUE Z. KEW	123 45 6789

Who Must File Schedule SE

You must file Schedule SE if:

● Your net earnings from self-employment were $400 or more (or you had wages of $100 or more from an electing church or church organization); AND

● You did not have wages (subject to social security or railroad retirement tax) of $45,000 or more.

For more information about Schedule SE, see the Instructions.

Note: *Most taxpayers can now use the new short Schedule SE on this page. But, you may have to use the longer Schedule SE that is on the back.*

Who MUST Use the Long Schedule SE (Section B)

You must use Section B if ANY of the following applies:

● You choose the "optional method" to figure your self-employment tax. See Section B, Part II;

● You are a minister, member of a religious order, or Christian Science practitioner and received IRS approval (from **Form 4361**) not to be taxed on your earnings from these sources, but you owe self-employment tax on other earnings;

● You are an employee of a church or church organization that chose by law not to pay employer social security taxes;

● You have tip income that is subject to social security tax, but you did not report those tips to your employer; OR

● You are a government employee with wages subject ONLY to the 1.45% medicare part of the social security tax.

Section A—Short Schedule SE

(Read above to see if you must use the long Schedule SE on the back (Section B).)

1	Net farm profit or (loss) from Schedule F (Form 1040), line 39, and farm partnerships, Schedule K-1 (Form 1065), line 14a	**1**	
2	Net profit or (loss) from Schedule C (Form 1040), line 31, and Schedule K-1 (Form 1065), line 14a (other than farming). See the Instructions for other income to report	**2**	105,426
3	Add lines 1 and 2. Enter the total. If the total is less than $400, **do not** file this schedule	**3**	105,426
4	The largest amount of combined wages and self-employment earnings subject to social security or railroad retirement tax (tier 1) for 1988 is	**4**	$45,000 00
5	Total social security wages and tips from Forms W-2 and railroad retirement compensation (tier 1)	**5**	–0–
6	Subtract line 5 from line 4. Enter the result. (If the result is zero or less, **do not** file this schedule.)	**6**	45,000
7	Enter the **smaller** of line 3 or line 6	**7**	45,000
	If line 7 is $45,000, enter $5,859 on line 8. Otherwise, multiply line 7 by .1302 and enter the result on line 8		×.1302
8	Self-employment tax. Enter this amount on Form 1040, line 48	**8**	5,859

For Paperwork Reduction Act Notice, see Form 1040 Instructions.

Schedule SE (Form 1040) 1988

Exhibit 6-3

Name of person with **self-employment** income (as shown on social security card)	Social security number of person with **self-employment** income ▶	: :

Section B—Long Schedule SE

(Before completing, see if you can use the short Schedule SE on the other side (Section A).)

A   If your only self-employment income was from earnings as a minister, member of a religious order, or Christian Science practitioner, AND you filed **Form 4361,** then DO NOT file Schedule SE. Instead, write "Exempt-Form 4361" on Form 1040, line 48. However, if you filed Form 4361, but have $400 or more of other earnings subject to self-employment tax, continue with Part I and check here.   ▶ ☐

B   If your only earnings subject to self-employment tax are wages from an electing church or church-controlled organization that is exempt from employer social security taxes and you are not a minister or a member of a religious order, skip lines 1–3b. Enter zero on line 3c and go on to line 5a.

Part I   Figure Social Security Self-Employment Tax

1   Net farm profit or (loss) from Schedule F (Form 1040), line 39, and farm partnerships, Schedule K-1 (Form 1065), line 14a **1**

2   Net profit or (loss) from Schedule C (Form 1040), line 31, and Schedule K-1 (Form 1065), line 14a (other than farming). (See Instructions for other income to report.) Employees of an electing church or church-controlled organization **do not** enter your Form W-2 wages on line 2. See the Instructions   . . .   **2**

3a Enter the amount from line 1 (**or,** if you elected the farm optional method, Part II, line 10) **3a**

  b Enter the amount from line 2 (**or,** if you elected the nonfarm optional method, Part II, line 12) **3b**

  c Add lines 3a and 3b. Enter the total. If the total is less than $400, **do not** file this schedule. **(Exception:** *If you are an employee of an electing church or church-controlled organization and the total of lines 3a and 3b is less than $400, enter zero and complete the rest of this schedule.)* **3c**

4   The largest amount of combined wages and self-employment earnings subject to social security or railroad retirement tax (tier 1) for 1988 is **4** $45,000   00

5a Total social security wages and tips from Forms W-2 and railroad retirement compensation (tier 1). **Note:** *Government employees whose wages are subject only to the 1.45% medicare tax and employees of certain church or church-controlled organizations should **not** include those wages on this line. See Instructions* **5a**

  b Unreported tips subject to social security tax from Form 4137, line 9, or to railroad retirement tax (tier 1) **5b**

  c Add lines 5a and 5b. Enter the total **5c**

6a Subtract line 5c from line 4. Enter the result. (If the result is zero or less, enter zero.) **6a**

  b Enter your medicare qualified government wages if you are required to use the worksheet in the Instructions   . . .   **6b**

  c Enter your Form W-2 wages of $100 or more from an electing church or church-controlled organization   . . .   **6c**

  d Add lines 3c and 6c. Enter the total **6d**

7   Enter the **smaller** of line 6a or line 6d **7**

  If line 7 is $45,000, enter $5,859 on line 8. Otherwise, multiply line 7 by .1302 and enter the result on line 8   . . . .   × .1302

8   Self-employment tax. Enter this amount on Form 1040, line 48   . . . .   **8**

Part II   Optional Method To Figure Net Earnings (See "Who Can File Schedule SE" in the Instructions.)

See Instructions for limitations. Generally, you may use this part **only** if:

A   Your **gross** farm income[1] was not more than $2,400; **or**

B   Your **gross** farm income[1] was more than $2,400 and your **net** farm profits[2] were **less** than $1,600; **or**

C   Your **net** nonfarm profits[3] were less than $1,600 and also **less** than two-thirds (²⁄₃) of your **gross** nonfarm income.[4]

Note: *If line 2 above is two-thirds (²⁄₃) or more of your gross nonfarm income[4], or if line 2 is $1,600 or more, you may **not** use the optional method.*

[1]From Schedule F (Form 1040), line 12, and Schedule K-1 (Form 1065), line 14b.   [3]From Schedule C (Form 1040), line 31, and Schedule K-1 (Form 1065), line 14a.
[2]From Schedule F (Form 1040), line 39, and Schedule K-1 (Form 1065), line 14a.   [4]From Schedule C (Form 1040), line 5, and Schedule K-1 (Form 1065), line 14c.

9   Maximum income for optional methods **9** $1,600   00

10   **Farm Optional Method**—If you meet test A or B above, enter the **smaller** of: two-thirds (²⁄₃) of gross farm income from Schedule F (Form 1040), line 12, and farm partnerships, Schedule K-1 (Form 1065), line 14b; **or** $1,600. Also enter this amount on line 3a above **10**

11   Subtract line 10 from line 9. Enter the result **11**

12   **Nonfarm Optional Method**—If you meet test C above, enter the **smallest** of: two-thirds (²⁄₃) of gross nonfarm income from Schedule C (Form 1040), line 5, and Schedule K-1 (Form 1065), line 14c (other than farming); **or** $1,600; **or,** if you elected the farm optional method, the amount on line 11. Also enter this amount on line 3b above **12**

For Paperwork Reduction Act Notice, see Form 1040 Instructions.   Schedule SE (Form 1040) 1988

AMOUNT OF DEPOSIT (Do NOT type; please print.)

DOLLARS   CENTS

TAX YEAR
MONTH ➡

Darken only one TYPE OF TAX		**a n d Darken only one TAX PERIOD**

EMPLOYER IDENTIFICATION NUMBER ➡

TYPE OF TAX		TAX PERIOD
941	Sch. A	1st Quarter
940	1120	2nd Quarter
943	990-T	3rd Quarter
720	990-C	4th Quarter
CT-1	1042	
990-PF		49

BANK NAME/
DATE STAMP

Name _____

Address _____

City _____
State _____ ZIP _____

Telephone number ( )

FOR BANK USE IN MICR ENCODING

Federal Tax Deposit Coupon
Form **8109-B** (Rev. 1-87)

- - - - - - - - ← SEPARATE ALONG THIS LINE AND SUBMIT TO DEPOSITARY WITH PAYMENT → - - - - - - - -

OMB NO. 1545-0257

IMPORTANT

Read instructions carefully before completing Form 8109-B Federal tax deposit coupons.

Note: The entries other than in the name and address section and the telephone number are processed by optical scanning equipment and must be completed by hand in the manner specified. The name and address section and the telephone number may be completed other than by hand. When completing the hand entries, we suggest you use a soft lead pencil (for example, a # 2 pencil) so that the entries can be read more accurately by the optical scanning equipment. Do **NOT** use photocopies of the coupons to make your deposits.

Paperwork Reduction Act Notice.—We ask for this information to carry out the Internal Revenue laws of the United States. We need it to ensure that taxpayers are complying with these laws and to allow us to figure and collect the right amount of tax. You are required to give us this information.

Purpose of Form.—Use Form 8109-B deposit coupons to make tax deposits only in the following two situations:

(1) You have reordered your preprinted deposit coupons **(Form 8109)** but you have not yet received them; or

(2) You are a new entity and have already been assigned an employer identification number (EIN), but have not yet received your initial supply of preprinted deposit coupons (Form 8109).

Note: *You should get your reordered coupons (or your initial supply) within 5-6 weeks of the reorder (or receipt of your EIN). If you do not, please contact your local IRS office.*

If you have applied for an EIN, have not received it, and a deposit must be made, send your payment to your Internal Revenue Service Center. Make your check or money order payable to IRS and show on it your name (as shown on **Form SS-4**, Application for Employer Identification Number), address, kind of tax, period covered, and date you applied for an EIN. Do **NOT** use Form 8109-B in this situation.

Do not use Form 8109-B to deposit delinquent taxes for which you have been assessed by the IRS. Pay those taxes directly to the IRS.

How To Complete Form 8109-B.—Enter your name exactly as shown on your return or other IRS correspondence, address, and employer identification number in the spaces provided. If you are required to file a Form 1120, Form 990-C, Form 990-PF (with net investment income), Form 990-T, or Form 2438, enter the month in which your tax year ends in the "TAX YEAR MONTH" boxes. For example, if your tax year ends in January, enter 01; if it ends in June, enter 06; if it ends in December, enter 12. Please make your entries for employer identification number and tax year month (if applicable) in the manner specified in *Amount of Deposit* below. Darken one box each in the "Type of Tax" and "Tax Period" columns as explained below.

Amount of Deposit.—

Enter the amount of the deposit in the space provided.

Enter amount legibly, forming the characters as shown below:

Handprint money amounts without using dollar signs, commas, a decimal point, or leading zeros. The commas and decimal point are already shown in the entry area.

For example, a deposit of $7,635.22 would be entered like this:

DOLLARS					CENTS
		7	6	3	5	2	2

If the deposit is for whole dollars only, enter "00" in the "CENTS" boxes.

Types of Tax.—

Form 941	—	Withheld Income and Social Security Taxes. (Includes Form 941 series of returns.)
Form 940	—	Federal Unemployment (FUTA) Tax. (Includes Form 940PR.)
Form 943	—	Agricultural Withheld Income and Social Security Taxes. (Includes Form 943PR.)
Form 720	—	Excise Tax.
Form CT-1	—	Railroad Retirement and Railroad Unemployment Repayment Taxes.
Form 990-PF	—	Excise Tax on Private Foundation Net Investment Income.
Schedule A	—	Backup Withholding. (Reported on Forms 941 and 941E.)
Form 1120	—	Corporation Income Tax. (Includes Form 1120 series of returns and Form 2438.)
Form 990-T	—	Exempt Organization Business Income Tax.

Form 990-C — Farmers' Cooperative Association Income Tax.

Form 1042 — Withholding at Source.

How To Determine the Proper Tax Period.—

(a) Payroll Taxes and Withholding:
(Forms 941, Schedule A (Form 941), 940, 943, 1042, and CT-1)

If your liability was incurred during:

- January—March, darken the 1st quarter box
- April—June, darken the 2nd quarter box
- July—September, darken the 3rd quarter box
- October—December, darken the 4th quarter box

Note: *If the liability was incurred during one quarter and deposited in another quarter, darken the box for the quarter in which the tax liability was incurred. For example: If the liability was incurred in March and deposited in April, darken the 1st quarter box.*

(Continued on back of page.)

Department of the Treasury
Internal Revenue Service

Form 8109-B (Rev. 1-87)

Exhibit 6-4

(b) Excise Taxes (Form 720; also, Form 990-PF (with net investment income)):

For Form 720, generally follow the instructions listed in (a) on the front of this form. For exceptions, see the Form 720 instructions. For Form 990-PF, follow the instructions in (c) below, disregarding the *Note*.

(c) Income Taxes (Forms 1120, 990-C, 990-T, and 2438):

Note: *These instructions below only apply to deposits of income taxes. For all other types of tax follow (a) and (b).*

(1) When making a deposit within the tax year for which the deposit is intended, darken the 1st quarter box. Such deposits apply to estimated income tax payments.

Example 1: If your tax year ends on December 31, 1987, and a deposit for 1987 is being made between January 1 and December 31, 1987, darken the 1st quarter box.

Example 2: If your tax year ends on June 30, 1987, and a deposit for that fiscal year is being made between July 1, 1986, and June 30, 1987, darken the 1st quarter box.

(2) When making a deposit after the end of the tax year for which the deposit is intended, darken the 4th quarter box. Such deposits include:

- Deposits of balance due shown on the return. (Forms 1120, 990-C, and 990-T (corporate filers), and for returns for tax years beginning after December 31, 1986, Forms 990-PF and 990-T (trust filers).)

- Deposits of balance due shown on **Form 7004**, Application for Automatic Extension of Time To File Corporation Income Tax Return (be sure to darken the 1120, 990-C, or 990-T box as appropriate).

- Effective for returns for tax years beginning after December 31, 1986, deposits of balance due (from Forms 990-T (trust filers) and 990-PF filers) shown on **Form 2758**, Application for Extension of Time To File U.S. Partnership, Fiduciary, and Certain Exempt Organization Returns (be sure to darken the 990-PF or 990-T box as appropriate).

- Deposits of tax due shown on Form 2438.

Example 1: If your tax year ends on December 31, 1986, and a deposit for 1986 is being made after that date, darken the 4th quarter box.

Example 2: If your tax year ends on June 30, 1986, and a deposit for that fiscal year is being made after that date, darken the 4th quarter box.

How To Ensure Your Deposit Is Credited To The Correct Account.—

(1) Make sure your name and employer identification number are correct;

(2) Prepare only one coupon for each type of tax deposit;

(3) Darken only one box for the type of tax you are depositing; and

(4) Darken only one box for the tax period for which you are making a deposit.

Telephone Number.—A space is provided on the deposit coupon for you to enter your telephone number. Our purpose for requesting it is to allow us to contact you if we have difficulty processing your deposit coupon.

Miscellaneous.—The "IRS USE ONLY" box is used during our processing to ensure proper crediting to your account. Do not darken this box when making a deposit.

How To Make Deposits.—Mail or deliver the completed coupon together with the appropriate payment for the amount of the deposit to a qualified depositary for Federal taxes or to the Federal Reserve Bank (FRB) servicing your geographic area. Make checks or money orders payable to that depositary or FRB. Federal agencies will make deposits at FRBs only. To help ensure proper crediting of your account, include your employer identification number, the type of tax (e.g., Form 940), and the tax period to which the payment applies on your check or money order.

Note: Deposits at depositaries.—Authorized depositaries are required to accept from a taxpayer cash, postal money orders drawn to the order of the depositary, or checks or drafts drawn on and to the order of the depositary. If you want to make a tax deposit with a depositary by a check drawn on another financial institution, you may do so only if the depositary is willing to accept that payment as a deposit of Federal taxes.

Note: Deposits at FRBs.—If you want to make a deposit by check at an FRB, you must make that deposit with the FRB servicing your geographic area using a check or other payment for which immediate credit is given in accordance with the check collection schedule of the receiving FRB. Checks generally considered as immediate credit items at FRBs include, but are not limited to, checks drawn on commercial banks located in the same city as the receiving FRB. Information concerning the FRB servicing your area and checks which are considered by that FRB as immediate credit items can be obtained from FRBs and commercial banks.

Timeliness of Deposits.—The timeliness of deposits will be determined by the date received by an authorized depositary or FRB. However, a deposit received after the due date of the deposit by the authorized depositary or FRB will be considered timely if the taxpayer establishes that it was mailed on or before the second day before the due date.

Note: *Deposits of $20,000 or more that are made by taxpayers required to deposit any taxes more than once a month must be received by the due date of the deposit to be timely; the 2-day mail rule does not apply to these deposits.*

If you hand deliver your deposit to a depositary on the due date, be sure to deliver it before the depositary closes its business day.

For deposits made at an FRB that do not comply with the payment requirements, the date on which the funds are collected determines timeliness of deposit regardless of when mailed.

When To Make Deposits.—Instructions are provided in IRS publications and tax returns. Copies of these documents and other information concerning tax procedures can be obtained from most IRS offices.

Penalties.—You may be charged a penalty for not making deposits when due or in sufficient amounts, unless you have reasonable cause. The penalty is 10% of the underpayment. This penalty may also apply if you mail or deliver Federal tax deposits to IRS offices, rather than to authorized depositaries or FRBs.

If, on your return, you overstate the amount you deposited, you may be charged a penalty of 25% of the overstated amount, unless you have reasonable cause.

★U.S.GPO:1987-0-171-436

IRS FORM 941 - EMPLOYER'S QUARTERLY FEDERAL TAX RETURN

EXAMPLE:

In 1989, Harry paid one employee $600 a week, one employee $500 a week, and one employe $400 a week. The following illustration involves the 4th quarter only. Every quarter Harry is required to file IRS Form 941 on which he reports federal income taxes withheld from employees' wages and both parts of the social security tax; the amount he withholds from employees' wages; and the part he pays as an employer. Because of the amount of tax owed each month in that quarter was enough to trigger a deposit, Harry made 3 monthly deposits, each accompanied by IRS Form 8109, Federal Tax Deposit Coupon.

The amount of federal tax withheld by Harry is determined by each employee's IRS Form W-4. Based on information that is on the W-4, Harry finds the correct amount to withhold in Publication 15, "Circular E, Employer's Tax Guide," which Harry received as a result of filing IRS Form SS-4. Harry also withheld 7.51% of each employee's wages up to $48,000 as social security tax, and he paid a 7.51% share himself for each employee.

For our illustration, assume that Harry paid $1,500 total wages each pay period and total wages paid for the 4th quarter was $19,500. Also assume that total income tax withheld was $2,262 and total social security (FICA) at 15.02% was $2,929.

IRS Form 941 is to due the IRS on the last day of the month following the end of the quarter. So, Harry must file IRS Form 941 by January 31, 1990. He begins filling out IRS Form 941 by using the preaddressed form with his name, address, and employer identification number (EIN).

Line 1a & 1b: Harry does not have to fill in these lines as this is the 4th quarter and lines 1a & 1b apply to the 1st quarter.

Line 2: Harry enters the total wages paid in the 4th quarter, $19,500.

Line 3: Next, Harry enters the total amount of income tax withheld for that quarter, $2,262.

Exhibit 6-5

Line 5: Because Harry does not have to make any adjustments to correct for errors in the withholding he reported for the first 3 quarters of the year, he enters the amount from line 3 on line 5.

Line 6: Since all of Harry's employees earned less than $48,000 yearly limit, all of the $19,500 paid during the quarter is counted as "taxable social security wages." Harry enters 15.02% x $19,500 or $2,928.90 on this line. The amount of $2,929.90 includes both the amount withheld from the employees'' wages and Harry's share.

Lines 8 & 9: Harry enters the amount from line 6 on lines 8 and 10.

Line 14: Harry adds the income tax withheld and the social security tax and enters that amount, $5,190.90 on the line.

Line 16: Since none of Harry's employees received advance payments of the earned income credit (line 15), he enters the amount from line 14 on line 16.

Lines 16 & 17: Because Harry shows that the amount of tax he owed for the quarter and the amount he deposited are the same, he does not have to make a payment with his return (line 18), nor does he receive a refund (line 19).

After reviewing the Form for completeness, Harry is ready to sign, date, and enter his title as "owner."

For additional information on employment taxes, Publication 539, "Employment Taxes," is available from the Internal Revenue Service.

Form 941

(Rev. July 1988)
Department of the Treasury
Internal Revenue Service

4343

Employer's Quarterly Federal Tax Return

▶ For Paperwork Reduction Act Notice, see page 2.

Please type or print.

OMB No. 1545-0029
Expires: 5-31-91

Your name, address, employer identification number, and calendar quarter of return. (If not correct, please change.)

Name (as distinguished from trade name)   Date quarter ended

Trade name, if any   Employer identification number

Address and ZIP code

FoRM wiLL BE ReADDRESSED

T	
FF	
FD	
FP	
I	
T	

1 1 1 1 1 1 1 1 1 1 1 2 3 3 3 3 3 3 4 4 4

IRS Use

5 5 5 . 6 7 8 8 8 8 8 8 9 9 9 10 10 10 10 10 10 10 10 10 10

If address is different from prior return, check here ▶ ☐

If you do not have to file returns in the future, check here . . . ☐   Date final wages paid . . . .

Complete for First Quarter Only			
1a Number of employees (except household) employed in the pay period that includes March 12th	**1a**		
b If you are a subsidiary corporation AND your parent corporation files a consolidated Form 1120, enter parent corporation employer identification number (EIN) . . . **1b**	—		
2 Total wages and tips subject to withholding, plus other compensation	**2**	19,500	00
3 Total income tax withheld from wages, tips, pensions, annuities, sick pay, gambling, etc. . .	**3**	2,202	00
4 Adjustment of withheld income tax for preceding quarters of calendar year (see instructions) .	**4**		
5 Adjusted total of income tax withheld (see instructions)	**5**	2,202	00
6 Taxable social security wages paid . . . . . $ 19,500 00 × 15.02% (.1502) .	**6**	2,928	90
7a Taxable tips reported . . . . $ _____ × 15.02% (.1502)	**7a**		
b Taxable hospital insurance wages paid . . . $ _____ × 2.9% (.029) . .	**7b**		
8 Total social security taxes (add lines 6, 7a, and 7b)	**8**	2,928	90
9 Adjustment of social security taxes (see instructions for required explanation)	**9**		
10 Adjusted total of social security taxes (see instructions)	**10**	2,928	90
11 Backup withholding (see instructions)	**11**		
12 Adjustment of backup withholding tax for preceding quarters of calendar year	**12**		
13 Adjusted total of backup withholding	**13**		
14 Total taxes (add lines 5, 10, and 13)	**14**	5,190	90
15 Advance earned income credit (EIC) payments, if any	**15**		
16 Net taxes (subtract line 15 from line 14). **This must equal line IV below** (plus line IV of Schedule A (Form 941) if you have treated backup withholding as a separate liability).	**16**	5,190	90
17 Total deposits for quarter, including overpayment applied from a prior quarter, from your records .	**17**	5,190	90
18 Balance due (subtract line 17 from line 16). This should be less than $500. Pay to IRS . . .	**18**		

19 If line 17 is more than line 16, enter overpayment here ___ $ _____ and check if to be:
☐ Applied to next return   **OR**   ☐ Refunded

Record of Federal Tax Liability (Complete if line 16 is $500 or more.) See the instructions under rule 4 for details before checking these boxes.
Check only if you made eighth-monthly deposits using the 95% rule ___   Check only if you are a first time 3-banking-day depositor ___

Show tax liability here, **not deposits.** IRS gets deposit data from FTD coupons.

Date wages paid		First month of quarter		Second month of quarter		Third month of quarter
1st through 3rd	A		I		Q	
4th through 7th	B		J		R	
8th through 11th	C		K		S	
12th through 15th	D		L		T	
16th through 19th	E		M		U	
20th through 22nd	F		N		V	
23rd through 25th	G		O		W	
26th through the last	H		P		X	
Total liability for month	**I**	1,496.50	**II**	1,597.20	**III**	1,597.20

Do NOT Show Federal Tax Deposits Here

IV Total for quarter (add lines **I, II,** and **III**). **This must equal line 16 above** 5,190.90

Under penalties of perjury, I declare that I have examined this return, including accompanying schedules and statements, and to the best of my knowledge and belief, it is true, correct, and complete.

Signature *Jerry C Kaykill*   Title OWNER   Date 1-29-90

Form **943**	**Employer's Annual Tax Return for Agricultural Employees**	OMB No. 1545-0035
Department of the Treasury Internal Revenue Service	(For Social Security Taxes and Withheld Income Tax)	19**88**

	T
	FF
	FD
	FP
	I
	T

Your name, address, employer identification number, and calendar year of return. (If not correct, please change.)

▶

Name (as distinguished from trade name)

Calendar year

Trade name, if any

Employer identification number

Address and ZIP code

If address is different from prior return, check here ▶ ☐

If you do not have to file returns in the future, write "FINAL RETURN" here . . . . ▶

1a	Number of agricultural employees employed in the pay period that includes March 12, 1988 . . . ▶	**1a**	
b	If you are a subsidiary corporation AND your parent corporation files a consolidated Form 1120, enter parent corporation's employer identification number (EIN) . . . . ▶	**1b**	
2	Taxable cash wages paid during the year (see instructions on page 4)	**2**	
3	Social security taxes (multiply line 2 by 15.02%)	**3**	
4	Adjustment of social security taxes (attach statement—see instructions on page 4)	**4**	
5	Social security taxes as adjusted	**5**	
6	Federal income tax withheld (see instructions on page 2)	**6**	
7	Total taxes (add lines 5 and 6)	**7**	
8	Advance earned income credit (EIC) payments, if any (see instructions on page 4)	**8**	
9	Net taxes (subtract line 8 from line 7)	**9**	
10	Total amount deposited for 1988, including any overpayment from 1987, as shown in your records . .	**10**	
11	Undeposited taxes due (subtract line 10 from line 9—this should be less than $500). Pay to Internal Revenue Service . . . . ▶	**11**	

12 If line 10 is more than line 9, enter overpayment here ▶ $ _____ and check if to be: ☐ Applied to next return, or ☐ Refunded.

Check if you are a first-time 3-banking-day depositor (see deposit rules on page 4.) . . . . ▶ ☐

Record of Federal Tax Liability
(See deposit rules on page 4.)

If your tax liability for any month in 1988 is $3,000 or more, do not use the schedule below. Instead, attach **Form 943A**, Agricultural Employer's Record of Federal Tax Liability, or a statement showing your tax liability for each eighth-monthly period during which you had a payday. Copies of Form 943A are in the **1988 Circular A**, Agricultural Employer's Tax Guide, and additional copies can be obtained at IRS offices.

Deposit period ending		Tax liability for month		Instructions
A	January 31	**A**		**Instructions**
B	February 29	**B**		If your taxes for the year (line 9) are less than $500, you do not have to complete this record. You may pay the taxes with Form 943 or deposit them by January 31, 1989.
C	March 31	**C**		
D	April 30	**D**		
E	May 31. . . .	**E**		If your taxes for any month are $500 or more but less than $3,000, show your tax liability next to the month. (If your tax liability for any month is $3,000 or more, attach Form 943A or a statement showing your tax liability for each eighth-monthly period during which you had a payday. See rule (4) under "Deposit Rules" on page 4.)
F	June 30	**F**		
G	July 31	**G**		
H	August 31	**H**		
I	September 30	**I**		
J	October 31	**J**		
K	November 30	**K**		**The total tax liability for the year (line M) should equal net taxes (line 9).**
L	December 31. . . .	**L**		
M	Total liability for year (add lines A through L).	**M**		

Under penalties of perjury, I declare that I have examined this return, including accompanying schedules and statements, and to the best of my knowledge and belief, it is true, correct, and complete.

Date ▶ _____ Signature ▶ _____ Title (Owner, etc.) ▶ _____

Please file this form with your Internal Revenue Service Center (see instructions on "Where To File").

For Paperwork Reduction Act Notice, see page 2.

Form **943** (1988)

Exhibit 6-6

General Instructions

Paperwork Reduction Act Notice.—We ask for this information to carry out the Internal Revenue laws of the United States. We need it to ensure that taxpayers are complying with these laws and to allow us to figure and collect the right amount of tax. You are required to give us this information.

The time needed to complete and file this form will vary depending on individual circumstances. The estimated average time is: **Recordkeeping** 8 hrs., 51 mins.; **Learning about the law or the form** 22 mins.; **Preparing the form** 1 hr., 28 mins.; **Copying, assembling, and sending the form to IRS** 16 mins. If you have comments concerning the accuracy of these time estimates or suggestions for making this form more simple, we would be happy to hear from you. You can write to the **Internal Revenue Service**, Washington, DC 20224, Attention: IRS Reports Clearance Officer, TR:FP; or the **Office of Management and Budget,** Paperwork Reduction Project, Washington, DC 20503.

Changes You Should Note.—For 1988, wages subject to social security (FICA) taxes increased to $45,000 of cash wages you paid to each employee , and the tax rate increased to 7.51% for both the employee and employer. The tax rates for 1989 are scheduled to remain at 7.51% each for the employee and the employer. The amount of wages subject to taxes for 1989 is announced by the SSA by October 31, 1988.

Beginning in 1988, there is a new test to determine if your employees are subject to social security taxes. (See *How To Determine...*)

After 1987, social security coverage has been extended to children age 18 or older employed by parents and to one spouse employed by another.

Reconciliation of Form 943 and W-3.— Amounts reported on Form 943 for 1988 must agree with the totals reported on Form W-3, which summarize the Forms W-2 given to employees. The amounts that must agree are: income tax withheld, social security wages, and the advance earned income credit. If the totals do not agree, IRS will require you to explain any differences and correct any errors. You can avoid this by making sure that correct amounts are reported on returns.

New Filing Addresses.—You may have to send your return to a different address than you had to previously. Use the envelope that came with your package or see *Where To File.*

Additional Information.—Circular A, Agricultural Employer's Tax Guide, has information and forms you may need for social security taxes, Federal unemployment (FUTA) tax, and withheld income tax under voluntary agreements. It includes copies of Forms W-2, W-3, 941c, 943A, and 7018-A (an order blank for forms). It also has a table showing the social security tax to withhold from an employee's wages. Circular A is mailed to Form 943 filers each year in October. **Circular E**, Employer's Tax Guide, covers withholding of income tax and other related subjects. You can get these circulars at IRS offices.

Purpose of Form.—Use Form 943 to report employer and employee social security taxes on farmworkers. Also use this form to report taxes on wages of household employees in a private home on a farm operated for profit. They are considered farm employees. Also use Form 943 if you have one or more farmworkers who asked to have income tax withheld from pay for farmwork. If you and the employee agree to this arrangement, you can withhold income tax from an employee's wages. Use this form to report any withheld income tax. If you paid taxable wages to an employee for services other than farmwork, do not include them on Form 943. Instead, use **Form 941**, Employer's Quarterly Federal Tax Return. If you paid wages for domestic services in your private, nonfarm home, use **Form 942**, Employer's Quarterly Tax Return for Household Employees.

Who Must File.—File Form 943 if you paid cash wages to one or more farmworkers to whom social security taxes apply. Cash wages include checks, money orders, etc. For a definition of agricultural workers ("farmworkers"), see Circular A.

How To Determine If Social Security Taxes Are Due. The $150 Test or The New $2,500 Test.— Employer and employee social security taxes are due if:

● You pay an employee cash wages of $150 or more in a calendar year for farmwork; or

● You pay cash wages of $2,500 or more during the year to all of your employees for farmwork.

Social security taxes apply to most payments of sick pay, including payments made by third parties such as insurance companies. For details, see Circular E, and the instructions on **Form W-3**, Transmittal of Income and Tax Statements.

Withholding of Income Tax.—If an employee asks you to withhold income tax and you agree, you must withhold the correct tax from all wages paid to the employee, both cash and noncash. Show total income tax withheld on line 6, page 1.

An employee who wants Federal income tax withheld from wages must give you a completed **Form W-4 ,** Employee's Withholding Allowance Certificate.

See Circular E for Federal income tax withholding tables. You can get Forms W-4, and Circular E at IRS offices.

When To File Form 943.—For 1988, file Form 943 by January 31, 1989. However, if you made deposits on time in full payment of the taxes due for the year, you may file the return by February 10, 1989.

After you file your first return, we will send you a form every year.

If you receive a form for a year in which you are not liable for filing, write NONE on line 9 and send the form back to the Internal Revenue Service. If you stop paying wages during the year, file a final return for 1988. Be sure to fill in the line at the top. If you later become liable for any of the taxes, notify IRS.

Where To File.—

If your legal residence, principal place of business, office, or agency is in ▼	File with the Internal Revenue Service Center at ▼
Florida, Georgia, South Carolina	Atlanta, GA 39901
New Jersey, New York (New York City and counties of Nassau, Rockland, Suffolk, and Westchester)	Holtsville, NY 00501
New York (all other counties), Connecticut, Maine, Massachusetts, New Hampshire, Rhode Island, Vermont	Andover, MA 05501
Illinois, Iowa, Minnesota, Missouri, Wisconsin	Kansas City, MO 64999
Delaware, District of Columbia, Maryland, Pennsylvania, Virginia	Philadelphia, PA 19255
Indiana, Kentucky, Michigan, Ohio, West Virginia	Cincinnati, OH 45999
Kansas, New Mexico, Oklahoma, Texas	Austin, TX 73301
Alaska, Arizona, California (counties of Alpine, Amador, Butte, Calaveras, Colusa, Contra Costa, Del Norte, El Dorado, Glenn, Humboldt, Lake, Lassen, Marin, Mendocino, Modoc, Napa, Nevada, Placer, Plumas, Sacramento, San Joaquin, Shasta, Sierra, Siskiyou, Solano, Sonoma, Sutter, Tehama, Trinity, Yolo, and Yuba), Colorado, Idaho, Montana, Nebraska, Nevada, North Dakota, Oregon, South Dakota, Utah, Washington, Wyoming	Ogden, UT 84201
California (all other counties), Hawaii	Fresno, CA 93888
Alabama, Arkansas, Louisiana, Mississippi, North Carolina, Tennessee	Memphis, TN 37501
If you have no legal residence or principal place of business in any state	Philadelphia, PA 19255

Penalties and Interest.—There are penalties for filing a return late and paying or depositing taxes late, unless there is reasonable cause. If you are late, please attach an explanation to your return. There is a penalty of 25% of the overstatement if, without reasonable cause, you overstate the amount you deposited. There are also penalties for willful failure to : (1) file returns and pay taxes when due, (2) give Form W-2 to employees, (3) keep records, and (4) for filing false returns or submitting bad checks.

Interest is charged on taxes paid late at the rate set by law.

Forms W-2 and W-3.—By January 31, 1989, give Form W-2 to each employee who was working for you at the end of 1988. If an employee stops working for you before the end of the year, give him or her Form W-2 any time after employment ends but no later than January 31 of the following year. However, if the employee asks you for Form W-2, give him or her the completed form within 30 days of the request or the last wage payment, whichever is later.

By February 28, 1989, send Copy A of all Forms W-2 issued for 1988 to the Social Security Administration. Send them with Form W-3 to the SSA Data Operations Center for your state. The SSA addresses are in the instructions for Form W-3.

We sent you a Form W-3 as part of Circular A during the fourth quarter. If you didn't receive it, get Form W-3 from an IRS office.

Filing on Magnetic Media.—You may be required to use magnetic media instead of filing Copy A of Form W-2. You can get the rules for reporting W-2 information on magnetic media from the Social Security Administration, P.O. Box 2317, Baltimore, MD 21203, Attn: Magnetic Media Section.

APPLICATION FOR EMPLOYER IDENTIFICATION NUMBER (IRS FORM SS-4)

EXAMPLE:

On January 1, 1989, Harry Kayhill started a small accounting business which he operates as a sole proprietorship. He anticipates hiring three full time employees on July 1st. Since Kayhill and Co. will pay wages to one or more employees, Harry must apply for an employer identification number (EIN). Application is made on IRS Form SS-4. He must also apply for an EIN if he is required to use it on any return, statement, or other document, even if he is not an employer.

Harry called the IRS, 1-800-424-FORM, to request an IRS Form SS-4 and the instructions. The following exhibits are copies of the SS-4 and instructions which the IRS mailed to Harry.

Harry begins filling out the SS-4 by entering his name and social security number on lines 1 and 2.

Line 3: Since Harry is a calendar year taxpayer, he enters December as the ending month of his accounting year.

Line 4: Harry's trade name is different from his true name. As a result, he enters his trade name, Harry P. Kayhill, CPA on this line.

Next, Harry enters his address on lines 6 and 8. Since Harry's new business is a sole proprietorship, he marks the appropriate boxes on lines 10 and 12.

Line 11: The county of Harry's principal business location, Sacramento, is entered here.

Line 13: Harry enters his business starting date which was January 1, 1989.

Line 14: Harry describes his principal business as accounting and auditing.

Line 15: On this line, he enters the first date wages will be paid, which will be July 7, 1989.

Harry now enters in the appropriate tax on line 16, the peak number of employees expected within the next 12 months. On lines 17 and 18, Harry indicates by making the appropriate boxes that he operates only one place of business and to whom most of his services will be sold. Finally, Harry indicates on line 20 that he has not personally applied for an EIN for his business.

After reviewing the form for completeness, Harry is ready to sign, date, and enter his business telephone number. The form is mailed to the IRS Center in which Harry's business is located, which is Ogden, Utah.

If Harry had needed his EIN more quickly, he could have contacted the IRS at a specified District telephone number. To find out the number for your district, you will need to telephone 1-800-424-1040 for information concerning the EIN telephone number.

Form **SS-4**
(Rev. November 1985)
Department of the Treasury
Internal Revenue Service

Application for Employer Identification Number

(For use by employers and others. Please read
the separate instructions before completing this form.)

For Paperwork Reduction Act Notice, see separate instructions.

OMB No. 1545-0003

Expires 8-31-88

1 Name (True name. See instructions.) HARRY P. KAYHILL	2 Social security no., if sole proprietor 123-45-6789	3 Ending month of accounting year DECEMBER
4 Trade name of business if different from item 1 HARRY P. KAYHILL, CPA	5 General partner's name, if partnership; principal officer's name, if corporation; or grantor's name, if trust	
6 Address of principal place of business (Number and street) 1 KESINGTON RD.	7 Mailing address, if different	
8 City, state, and ZIP code SACRAMENTO, CA 95691	9 City, state, and ZIP code	

10 Type of organization	☒ Individual ☐ Trust ☐ Partnership ☐ Plan administrator ☐ Other (specify) ☐ Governmental ☐ Nonprofit organization ☐ Corporation	11 County of principal business location SACRAMENTO
12 Reason for applying	☒ Started new business ☐ Purchased going business ☐ Other (specify)	13 Acquisition or starting date (Mo., day, year). See instructions. JANUARY 1, 1989
14 Nature of principal activity (See instructions.) ACCOUNTING AND AUDITING		15 First date wages or annuities were paid or will be paid (Mo., day, year). JULY 7, 1989

16 Peak number of employees expected in the next 12 months (If none, enter "0") ▶	Nonagricultural 3	Agricultural	Household	17 Does the applicant operate more than one place of business? ☐ Yes ☒ No
18 Most of the products or services are sold to whom?	☐ Business establishments (wholesale) ☒ General public (retail) ☐ Other (specify) ☐ N/A			19 If nature of business is manufacturing, state principal product and raw material used.

20 Has the applicant ever applied for an identification number for this or any other business? ☐ Yes ☒ No	
If "Yes," enter name and trade name. Also enter approx. date, city, and state where the application was filed and previous number if known. ▶	

Under penalties of perjury, I declare that I have examined this application, and to the best of my knowledge and belief it is true, correct, and complete.

Signature and Title ▶ Harry P. Kayhill	Date ▶ 6-15-89	Telephone number (include area code) 916-123-4567

Please leave blank ▶	Geo.	Ind.	Class	Size	Reas. for appl.	**Part I**

Department of the Treasury
Internal Revenue Service

Instructions for Form SS-4

(Rev. November 1985)

Application for Employer Identification Number

General Instructions

Paperwork Reduction Act Notice.—We ask for this information to carry out the Internal Revenue laws of the United States. We need it to ensure that taxpayers are complying with these laws. You are required to give us this information.

Purpose.—Use this form to apply for an employer identification number (EIN). Return both parts of this form to the Internal Revenue Service. You will receive your EIN in the mail.

Who Must File.—You must file this form if you have not obtained an EIN before and:

(a) You pay wages to one or more employees;

(b) You are required to have an EIN to use on any return, statement, or other document, even if you are not an employer; or

(c) You are required to withhold taxes on income, other than wages, paid to a nonresident alien (individual, corporation, partnership, etc.). If you are applying for an EIN as a withholding agent, on line 12 check "Other" and write in "New Withholding Agent." Also, in the space to the far right of line 20, enter the date you will begin paying income to a nonresident alien.

Individuals who file Schedules C or F (Form 1040) must use EINs if they are required to file excise, employment, or alcohol, tobacco, or firearms returns.

Individuals who file Form 1042 to report income paid (such as alimony) to nonresident aliens must also have EINs and should follow the instructions in (c) above.

The following entities must use EINs even if they do not have any employees:

- Trusts (not IRA trusts)
- Estates
- Corporations
- Partnerships
- Nonprofit organizations (churches, clubs, etc.)
- Plan administrators

New Owner.—If you have become the new owner of an existing business, you cannot use the EIN of the former owner. If you already have an EIN, use that number. If you do not have an EIN, apply for one on this form.

Incorporated.—If you have incorporated a sole proprietorship or formed a partnership, you must get a new EIN for the corporation or partnership.

File Only One SS-4.—File only one Form SS-4, regardless of the number of businesses operated or the number of trade names a business operates under. However, each corporation of an affiliated group must file a separate application.

If you do not have a number by the time a return is due, write "Applied for" and the date you applied in the space shown for the number. If you do not have a number by the time a tax deposit is due, send your payment to the Internal Revenue Service Center where you file your returns. Make it payable to IRS and show on it your name (as shown on Form SS-4), address, kind of tax, period covered, and date you applied for an EIN.

For more information about EINs, see **Publication 583**, Information for Business Taxpayers.

When To File.—File both parts of this form early enough to allow time for us to process Form SS-4 and to send you an EIN before you need the number for a return or deposit. If possible, file 4 weeks before you will need the number. Make sure you sign and date the application.

Where To File.—

If your principal business, office or agency, or legal residence in the case of an individual, is located in:	File with the Internal Revenue Service Center at:
Alabama, Florida, Georgia, Mississippi, South Carolina	Atlanta, GA 31101
New Jersey, New York City and New York counties of Nassau, Rockland, Suffolk, and Westchester	Holtsville, NY 00501
Connecticut, New York (all other counties), Maine, Massachusetts, Minnesota, New Hampshire, Rhode Island, Vermont	Andover, MA 05501
Illinois, Iowa, Missouri, Wisconsin	Kansas City, MO 64999
Delaware, District of Columbia, Maryland, Pennsylvania	Philadelphia, PA 19255
Kentucky, Michigan, Ohio, West Virginia	Cincinnati, OH 45999
Kansas, Louisiana, New Mexico, Oklahoma, Texas	Austin, TX 73301
Alaska, Arizona, California (counties of Alpine, Amador, Butte, Calaveras, Colusa, Contra Costa, Del Norte, El Dorado, Glenn, Humboldt, Lake, Lassen, Marin, Mendocino, Modoc, Napa, Nevada, Placer, Plumas, Sacramento, San Joaquin, Shasta, Sierra, Siskiyou, Solano, Sonoma, Sutter, Tehama, Trinity, Yolo, and Yuba), Colorado, Idaho, Montana, Nebraska, Nevada, North Dakota, Oregon, South Dakota, Utah, Washington, Wyoming	Ogden, UT 84201
California (all other counties), Hawaii	Fresno, CA 93888
Arkansas, Indiana, North Carolina, Tennessee, Virginia	Memphis, TN 37501

If you have no legal residence, principal place of business, or principal office or agency in any Internal Revenue District, file your return with the Internal Revenue Service Center, Philadelphia, PA 19255.

Specific Instructions

The instructions that follow are for those lines that are not self-explanatory for certain entities. Enter N/A for nonapplicable items.

Lines 1, 2, 4, and 5.

Sole proprietors.—On line 1, enter your first name, middle initial, and last name. On line 2, enter your social security number and, if you have a trade name for business purposes, enter it on line 4.

Partnerships.—On line 1, enter the legal name of the partnership as it appears in the partnership agreement. On line 4, enter the trade name, if any, and if different than the legal name. On line 5, enter the first name, middle initial, and last name of a general partner. A general partner should sign this form.

Corporations.—On line 1, enter the corporate name as set forth in the corporation's charter or other legal document creating it. On line 4, enter the trade name, if any, and if different than the legal name. On line 5, enter the first name, middle initial, and last name of a principal officer. A principal officer should sign this form.

Trusts.—On line 1, enter the name of the trust. On line 4, enter the name of the trustee and on line 5, enter the first name, middle initial, and last name of the grantor. The trustee should sign this form.

Estates of a decedent, insolvent, etc.—On line 1, enter the name of the estate. On line 4, enter the first name, middle initial, and last name of the administrator or other fiduciary. The administrator or other fiduciary should sign this form.

Plan administrators.—On line 1, enter the name of the plan administrator. Items 2, 4, and 5 are not applicable. A plan administrator that has already been assigned an EIN for other purposes (such as the filing of income or employment tax returns) should use that same number for plan administration purpose and should not apply for another number.

Line 3.—If you have not yet established an accounting year, write "not established" on line 3 and notify your IRS Service Center when you establish an accounting year. (Be sure to include your employer identification number when you write.)

Line 10.—Note the following before you check one of the boxes:

Governmental.—This box is for an organization that is a state, county, school district, municipality, etc., or one that is related to such entities, such as a county hospital or city library.

Nonprofit organization (other than governmental).—This box is for religious, charitable, scientific, literary, educational, humane, or fraternal, etc., organizations. Generally, a nonprofit organization must apply to IRS for an exemption from Federal income tax. Details on how to apply are in **Publication 557**, Tax-Exempt Status for Your Organization.

Plan administrator.—The term plan administrator means the person or group of persons specified as the administrator by the instrument under which the plan is operated.

Line 13.—For trusts, enter the date the trust was legally created.

For estates, enter the date of death of the decedent whose name appears on line 1.

Line 14.—Describe the principal business engaged in. See the examples that follow.

(a) Governmental.—State the type of governmental organization (whether it is a state, county, school district, municipality, etc.) or its relationship to such entities (for example, a county hospital, city library, etc.).

(b) Nonprofit (other than governmental).— State whether it is organized for religious, charitable, scientific, literary, educational, or humane purposes, and state the principal activity (for example, religious organization—hospital; charitable organization—home for the aged; etc.).

(c) Mining and quarrying.—State the process and the principal product (for example, mining bituminous coal, contract drilling for oil, quarrying dimension stone, etc.).

(d) Contract construction.—State whether it is general contracting or special trade contracting, and show the type of work normally performed (for example, general contractor for residential buildings, electrical subcontractor, etc.).

(e) Trade.—State the type of sale and the principal line of goods sold (for example, wholesale dairy products, manufacturer's representative for mining machinery, retail hardware, etc.).

(f) Manufacturing.—State the type of establishment operated (for example, sawmill, vegetable cannery, etc.). On line 19 state the principal product manufactured and the raw material used.

(g) Other activities.—State the exact type of business operated (for example, advertising agency, farm, labor union, real estate agency, steam laundry, rental of coin-operated vending machines, investment club, etc.).

Line 16.—For classification purposes, employees are divided into three categories:
- Nonagricultural employees
- Agricultural employees
- Household employees.

Enter in the appropriate category the peak number of employees you expect in the next 12 months. If you do not expect to have any, please enter "0" in all three categories.

Line 17.—Check the "yes" box if the business has more than one location.

Line 18.—Please check the N/A (nonapplicable) box if your business activity is not the selling of products or services.

☆ U.S.G.P.O.: 1985 -491-473/20023

FORM SS-5 — APPLICATION FOR A SOCIAL SECURITY NUMBER CARD (Original, Replacement or Correction)

Unless the requested information is provided, we may not be able to issue a Social Security Number (20 CFR 422-103(b))

INSTRUCTIONS TO APPLICANT ▶ Before completing this form, please read the instructions on the opposite page. Type or print, using pen with dark blue or black ink. Do not use pencil. SEE PAGE 1 FOR REQUIRED EVIDENCE.

NAA	NAME TO BE SHOWN ON CARD	First	Middle	Last
NAB **1**	FULL NAME AT BIRTH (IF OTHER THAN ABOVE)	First	Middle	Last
ONA	OTHER NAME(S) USED			

STT **2**	MAILING ADDRESS (Street/Apt. No., P.O. Box, Rural Route No.)

CTY CITY (Do not abbreviate)	**STE** STATE	**ZIP** ZIP CODE

CSP **3** CITIZENSHIP (Check one only)	**SEX** **4** SEX	**ETB** **5** RACE/ETHNIC DESCRIPTION (Check one only) (Voluntary)
☐ a. U.S. citizen	☐ MALE	☐ a. Asian, Asian-American or Pacific Islander (Includes persons of Chinese, Filipino, Japanese, Korean, Samoan, etc., ancestry or descent)
☐ b. Legal alien allowed to work		☐ b. Hispanic (Includes persons of Chicano, Cuban, Mexican or Mexican-American, Puerto Rican, South or Central American, or other Spanish ancestry or descent)
☐ c. Legal alien not allowed to work	☐ FEMALE	☐ c. Negro or Black (not Hispanic)
		☐ d. Northern American Indian or Alaskan Native
☐ d. Other (See instructions on Page 2)		☐ e. White (not Hispanic)

DOB **6** DATE OF BIRTH ▶ MONTH	DAY	YEAR	**AGE** **7** PRESENT AGE	**PLB** **8** PLACE OF BIRTH	CITY (Do not abbreviate) ▶	STATE OR FOREIGN COUNTRY (Do not abbreviate)	**FCI** ☐

MNA **9**	MOTHER'S NAME AT HER BIRTH	First	Middle	Last (Her maiden name)
FNA	FATHER'S NAME	First	Middle	Last

PNO **10**	a. Has a Social Security number card ever been requested for the person listed in item 1? ☐ YES(2) ☐ NO(1) ☐ Don't know(1)	b. Was a card received for the person listed in item 1? ☐ YES(3) ☐ NO(1) ☐ Don't know(1)

▶ IF YOU CHECKED YES TO A OR B, COMPLETE ITEMS C THROUGH E; OTHERWISE GO TO ITEM 11.

SSN	c. Enter the Social Security number assigned to the person listed in item 1	☐☐☐ — ☐☐ — ☐☐☐☐

NLC	d. Enter the name shown on the most recent Social Security card issued for the person listed in item 1.	**PDB**	e. Date of birth correction (See Instruction 10 on page 2) ▶ MONTH	DAY	YEAR

DON **11** TODAY'S DATE ▶ MONTH	DAY	YEAR	**12** Telephone number where we can reach you during the day. Please include the area code. ▶ HOME	OTHER

ASD **WARNING: Deliberately furnishing (or causing to be furnished) false information on this application is a crime punishable by fine or imprisonment, or both.**

IMPORTANT REMINDER: WE CANNOT PROCESS THIS APPLICATION WITHOUT THE REQUIRED EVIDENCE. SEE PAGE 1.

13 YOUR SIGNATURE	**14** YOUR RELATIONSHIP TO PERSON IN ITEM 1 ☐ Self ☐ Other (Specify) _____
WITNESS (Needed only if signed by mark "X")	WITNESS (Needed only if signed by mark "X")

DO NOT WRITE BELOW THIS LINE (FOR SSA USE ONLY)		
DTC (SSA RECEIPT DATE)	NPN	DOC
NTC	CAN	BIC	IDN	ITV ☐ MANDATORY IN PERSON INTERVIEW CONDUCTED
TYPE(S) OF EVIDENCE SUBMITTED	SIGNATURE AND TITLE OF EMPLOYEE(S) REVIEWING EVIDENCE AND/OR CONDUCTING INTERVIEW
	DATE
	DCL	DATE

Exhibit 6-8

THE PRIVACY ACT AND YOUR REQUEST FOR A SOCIAL SECURITY NUMBER CARD

Before we can give you a Social Security number, there is certain information we need from you. The Privacy Act of 1974 and the Paperwork Reduction Act of 1980 require us to give you the following facts when we ask for this information:

- Why the information is needed
- The legal authority for asking for it
- The information you are required to give
- The effects of not providing the information
- How the information will be used and to whom it may be disclosed

Why Information Is Needed

Your Social Security number is needed for us to keep a correct record of your earnings while you are working. It will also be needed if you die, retire or become disabled so that you or your survivors can receive benefits.

The information we request from you is necessary for us to:

- Assign you a Social Security number
- Issue you a replacement card if you lose your card
- Change information on your Social Security record
- Establish and maintain a record of your earnings, and
- Conduct research programs in income distribution and maintenance and health insurance.

Legal Authority to Collect Information

Section 205(c) of the Social Security Act authorizes us to collect the information needed to assign you a Social Security number and issue you a card. Section 702 of the Social Security Act authorizes us to collect the racial ethnic information needed for statistical purposes.

Required Information

We need the following information to assure that the record we establish for you is your unique and individual record. Specifically, we need your:

- Name as you use it now
- Name at birth
- Place of birth
- Citizenship or alien status
- Date of birth
- Sex
- Mother's name at her birth
- Father's name
- Mailing address
- Signature

We also need to know if you have ever had a Social Security number.

Effects of Withholding Information

You have a right to refuse to give most kinds of information, but usually it is to your advantage to give us the information we ask for. Without it, we will be unable to keep an accurate record of your earnings under Social Security. This could possibly cause you to lose benefits in the future. In some cases, we cannot even give you a number without the information. This could mean you would be unable to get a job, since in most cases you need a number to work.

Disclosure of Information

Sometimes we must disclose information from our records without your written consent. This is done, however, only when necessary and when it is authorized by the law or regulations.

If you would like more information about your rights to privacy, ask any Social Security office for a copy of "Collection and Use of Information by the Social Security Administration" (Form SSA-5000).

Information Concerning Collection of Racial/Ethnic Information

The categories for race and ethnic background have been established by the Office of Federal Statistical Policy and Standards to assure uniform reporting to all Federal agencies. The categories are:

Asian or Pacific Islander

Persons having origins (ancestry) in any of the original peoples of the Far East, Southeast Asia, the Indian subcontinent, or the Pacific Islands. This area includes, for example, China, India, Japan, the Philippine Islands, Korea, Samoa, etc.

Hispanic

Persons of Mexican, Puerto Rican, Cuban, Central or South American, or other Spanish culture or origin (ancestry), regardless of race.

Black or Negro (not Hispanic)

Persons having origins (ancestry) in any of the black racial groups of Africa.

American Indian or Alaskan Native

Persons having origins (ancestry) in any of the original peoples of North America and who maintain cultural identification through tribal affiliation or community recognition.

White (not Hispanic)

Persons having origins (ancestry) in any of the original peoples of Europe, North Africa, or the Middle East.

If you are of mixed racial/ethnic background, choose the category with which you most closely identify yourself.

✿U.S. GOVERNMENT PRINTING OFFICE: 1986 491-371/20112

Employer's Quarterly Tax Return
for Household Employees
(For Social Security and Withheld Income Taxes)

OMB No. 1545-0034

Expires 12-31-90

Your name,
address,
employer
identification
number, and
calendar
quarter of
return.
(If not
correct,
please
change.)

Name

Address and ZIP code

Date quarter ended

Employer identification number

___ – ___

Note: Before completing this form,
see *Making Entries on Form 942*
below

If address is
different from
prior return,
check here.

FOR IRS USE ONLY

1 1 1 1 1 1 1 1 1 1   2 2 2 2 2 2 2 2   3 3 3 3 3 3

4 4 4 5 6   7 7 7 7 7 7   8 8 8 9   10 10 10 10 10 10 10 10 10 10 10 10

Social security taxes are due for each household employee to whom you paid cash wages of $50 or more in the calendar quarter
covered by this return. For income tax withholding, see page 2.

		Dollars	Cents
1	Total cash wages subject to social security taxes (see instructions on page 4) **1**		
2	Social security taxes (multiply line 1 by 15.02% (.1502)) **2**		
3	Federal income tax withheld (if requested by your employee) **3**		
4	Total taxes (add lines 2 and 3) **4**		
5	Advance earned income credit (EIC) payments, if any (see **Notes** below) **5**		
6	Total taxes due (subtract line 5 from line 4). Pay to the Internal Revenue Service . . . **6**		

If you will **NOT** need to file Form 942 in the future, check here ☐   If no tax is due, write NONE on line 6.

Important: You **MUST** give a Form W-2 to each employee and file Copy A with the **Social Security Administration**—see page 4.
Send Form 942 and your payment **ONLY** to your **Internal Revenue Service Center** (see *Where To File* on page 2).

Under the penalties of perjury, I declare that I have examined this return, and to the best of my knowledge and belief, it is true, correct, and complete.

Signature
of employer ▶

Date ▶

Paperwork Reduction Act Notice.—We ask for
this information to carry out the Internal Revenue
laws of the United States. We need it to ensure
that taxpayers are complying with these laws and
to allow us to figure and collect the right amount
of tax. You are required to give us this information.

Earned Income Credit Notification.—You have
to notify any employees not having income tax
withheld that they may be eligible for an income
tax refund because of the earned income credit
(EIC). The EIC can be as much as $874 for 1988.
You can notify your employees by giving them
Notice 797 with their Form W-2 (or within one
week before or after giving Form W-2). You can
get Notice 797 (and **Publication 1325,** which
has notification information for employers) from
the IRS.

Making Entries on Form 942.—When making
entries on lines 1 through 6, **print** the amounts
(do not use dollar signs), use a **soft lead pencil**
(for example, a #2 pencil), and keep the
numbers inside the boxes. If you use whole dollar
amounts, enter a "0" in each of the "Cents"
columns of lines 1 through 6.

Please print your numbers like this.

0 1 2 3 4 5 6 7 8 9

Notes:

Under social security, an employee may qualify for
monthly benefits, generally at age 65, for the
employee and eligible dependents, monthly
disability benefits, health insurance benefits at
age 65 or (after a waiting period) when disabled,
and survivor benefits following the employee's
death.

For 1988, the maximum amount of cash wages
subject to social security taxes is $45,000.

The law provides that an employee will be given
a quarter of social security coverage, up to four
quarters, for each $470 of wages paid to the
employee in 1988.

For 1988, social security tax rates have been
increased to 7.51% each for the employer and
the employee. A 7.51% employee social security
tax deduction table for 1988 is on page 4.

Household employers must also file **Form W-2,**
Wage and Tax Statement, and (except those with
only one employee during the year) **Form W-3,**
Transmittal of Income and Tax Statements. **Note:**
*Forms W-2 and Forms W-3 (if any) are to be filed
with the Social Security Administration, not with
the IRS. See page 4.*

For examples and filled-in copies of Forms W-2
and W-3 for household employees, please get
Publication 503, Child and Dependent Care Credit,
and Employment Taxes for Household Employers.
This publication is available from the IRS.

Advance EIC Payments.—Employees who qualify
can choose to receive advance EIC payments with
their wages during the year, rather than waiting to
claim the EIC on their tax returns. Make the
payments from social security taxes and any
withheld income taxes that would otherwise be
paid to IRS. Employees who are eligible can make
this election by giving you annually a completed
Form W-5, Earned Income Credit Advance
Payment Certificate. Employees who work for you
and any other employers should be advised that
employees can have only one certificate in effect
with a current employer at one time. **Circular E,**
Employer's Tax Guide, has tables and instructions
for figuring advance EIC payments. You can get
this circular from the IRS. (Do not continue
advance EIC payments to any employee on wages
of $18,576 or more in 1988.)

Federal Unemployment (FUTA) Tax.— If you
paid cash wages of $1,000 or more for household
work in any calendar quarter in 1987 or 1988, the
employees you have in 1988 are covered under
FUTA and you must file **Form 940,** Employer's
Annual Federal Unemployment (FUTA) Tax
Return. Form 940 is due by January 31 for the
previous calendar year. (For an example and a
filled-in copy of Form 940 for a household
employer, please get Publication 503.)

Form **942** (Rev. 1-88)

Exhibit 6-9

General Instructions

Purpose of Form.—Use this form to report and pay employer and employee social security taxes, and any income tax withheld at the employee's request, on wages paid to household employees.

Who Must File.—File Form 942 if you paid a household employee cash wages of $50 or more in a calendar quarter for household work in or around your private home. Also file Form 942 if you have household employees who asked to have income tax withheld from pay for household work.

Social Security Taxes.—Both the employer and the employee must pay social security taxes on cash wages the employee receives for household work in or around the employer's private home (not including a private home on a farm operated for profit). Generally, it includes services by cooks, waiters, waitresses, butlers, housekeepers, governesses, maids, cleaning people, valets, babysitters, janitors, laundresses, caretakers, handymen, gardeners, and drivers of cars for family use. The combined social security tax rate is 15.02% (7.51% employer tax plus 7.51% employee tax). It applies to the first $45,000 of cash wages paid in 1988.

How To Determine If Social Security Taxes Are Due. The $50 Test.—Social security taxes are due if you pay an employee cash wages of $50 or more in a calendar quarter for household work. The taxes apply to all cash wages paid in the quarter regardless of when earned. The $50 test applies separately to each household employee. You are not required to pay social security taxes on workers who are not your employees, such as carpenters, painters, or plumbers working for you as independent contractors. If you are not sure whether the taxes apply to a worker, you should see Circular E.

Employers with workers on a farm operated for profit should see **Circular A**, Agricultural Employer's Tax Guide, for more information. Other business employers should see Circular E. You can get these free from the IRS.

What Are Wages Subject to Social Security Taxes?—Social security taxes apply only to cash wages paid to household employees who meet the $50 test. Checks, money orders, etc., are the same as cash. The value of food, lodging, clothing, bus tokens, and other noncash items given to household employees are not subject to social security taxes. Cash given in place of these items is considered wages. It does not matter whether payments are based on the hour, day, week, month, or year, or on piecework.

Social security taxes do not apply to wages for work in your home by your spouse, or by your son or daughter under the age of 21.

Also, these taxes do not apply to wages for domestic work in your home by your mother or father unless both of the following apply:

● You have in your home a son or daughter, or stepson or stepdaughter, who is under age 18 or has a physical or mental condition that requires the personal care of an adult for at least 4 continuous weeks in the quarter, and

● You are a widow or widower, or are divorced, or have a spouse in your home who, because of a physical or mental condition, cannot care for your son or daughter, or stepson or stepdaughter, for at least 4 continuous weeks in the quarter.

When you report cash wages on your quarterly return, show the full amount before tax was deducted. If you pay amounts not subject to social security taxes, do not include those amounts on line 1 of Form 942.

Deducting Employee Social Security Tax.— In 1988 deduct 7.51% from each cash wage payment if you expect the employee to meet the $50 test. (See the 7.51% table on page 4.) Payments in 1988 of fourth quarter 1987 wages must be withheld at the 7.51% rate. Even if you are not sure the $50 test will be met when you pay the wages, you may still deduct the tax. Stop deducting the tax when cash wages for 1988 reach $45,000.

If you do not deduct employee social security tax, or if you deduct too little tax, correct the mistake by deducting it from a later payment to the same employee. If you deduct tax when no tax is due, or if you deduct too much, you should repay your employee.

If you would rather pay the employee's share of social security tax without deducting it from his or her wages, you may do so. If you do not deduct the tax, you must still pay it. Any employee social security tax you pay is additional income to the employee. You must include it in box 10 on the employee's Form W-2 (see *Forms W-2 and W-3* on page 4), but do not count it as cash wages for social security purposes, and do not include it in box 13 on the Form W-2.

Income Tax.—An employee who wants you to withhold Federal income tax from wages must give you a completed **Form W-4**, Employee's Withholding Allowance Certificate.

If an employee asks you to withhold income tax and you agree, you must withhold an amount from each payment based on the Form W-4 the employee gives you. Show the total amount on line 3 of Form 942.

Any income tax withholding you pay for an employee without deducting it from the employee's wages is additional income. You must include it in boxes 10 and 13 on the employee's Form W-2.

See Circular E for Federal income tax withholding tables and other information. You can get Form W-4 and Circular E from the IRS.

What Are Wages Subject to Income Tax Withholding?—They consist of everything paid to your employee for work done. The word "wages" covers all pay, including:

● salaries

● vacation allowances

● bonuses

● meals (unless furnished on your premises and for your convenience)

● lodging (unless furnished on your premises, for your convenience, and as a condition of employment)

● clothing

● bus tokens

● other noncash items.

Measure wages you pay in any form other than money by the value of the goods, lodging, meals, or other consideration you give. See Circular E for details.

Employee's Social Security Number.—When you hire a household employee, record the name and social security number exactly as they appear on the employee's social security card.

An employee who does not have a number must apply for one on **Form SS-5**, Application for a Social Security Number Card. Form SS-5 is available from the Social Security Administration and the Internal Revenue Service.

Employer Identification Number.—The employer identification number is a 9-digit number issued by the IRS. Its arrangement is 2 digits, a hyphen, and 7 digits (for example, 00-0000000). Your Form 942 should show the number assigned to you as an employer of household employees. If you do not have a number, write NONE in the space for the number. IRS will then assign you a number and send you a Form 942 each quarter. It is important that you keep a record of your employer identification number.

When To File.—File starting with the first quarter in which you—

● pay wages subject to social security taxes, or

● withhold income tax if requested by your employee.

Due Dates for Returns

Quarter	Ending	Due Date
Jan.-Feb.-Mar.	Mar. 31	Apr. 30
Apr.-May-June	June 30	July 31
July-Aug.-Sept.	Sept. 30	Oct. 31
Oct.-Nov.-Dec.	Dec. 31	Jan. 31

If the due date for filing a return falls on a Saturday, Sunday, or a legal holiday, you may file the return on the first day afterward that is not a Saturday, Sunday, or legal holiday.

If you receive Form 942 for a quarter when you did not pay any taxable wages, write NONE on line 6, and sign and return Form 942 to IRS.

Final Return.—If you do not expect to pay taxable wages in the future, check the box below line 6 on the return. If you start paying taxable wages again, notify IRS.

Paying the Taxes.—Make your check or money order payable to the Internal Revenue Service and write your employer identification number, the period to which the payment applies (for example, "1st quarter 1988"), and "Form 942" on it. You may pay by mail or in person. To avoid loss, do not mail cash.

Where To File.—

If you are in	File with the Internal Revenue Service Center at
Alabama, Florida, Georgia, Mississippi, South Carolina	Atlanta, GA 39901
New Jersey, New York (New York City and counties of Nassau, Rockland, Suffolk, and Westchester)	Holtsville, NY 00501
New York (all other counties), Connecticut, Maine, Massachusetts, Minnesota, New Hampshire, Rhode Island, Vermont	Andover, MA 05501
Illinois, Iowa, Missouri, Wisconsin	Kansas City, MO 64999
Delaware, District of Columbia, Maryland, Pennsylvania	Philadelphia, PA 19255
Kentucky, Michigan, Ohio, West Virginia	Cincinnati, OH 45999
Kansas, Louisiana, New Mexico, Oklahoma, Texas	Austin, TX 73301
Alaska, Arizona, California (counties of Alpine, Amador, Butte, Calaveras, Colusa, Contra Costa, Del Norte, El Dorado, Glenn, Humboldt, Lake, Lassen, Marin, Mendocino, Modoc, Napa, Nevada, Placer, Plumas, Sacramento, San Joaquin, Shasta, Sierra, Siskiyou, Solano, Sonoma, Sutter, Tehama, Trinity, Yolo, and Yuba), Colorado, Idaho, Montana, Nebraska, Nevada, North Dakota, Oregon, South Dakota, Utah, Washington, Wyoming	Ogden, UT 84201
California (all other counties), Hawaii	Fresno, CA 93888
Arkansas, Indiana, North Carolina, Tennessee, Virginia	Memphis, TN 37501
If you have no legal residence in any state	Philadelphia, PA 19255

Keeping Records.—Keep your copies of Forms 942, W-2, and W-3. Also keep a record of each employee's social security number and name, dates and amounts of cash and noncash wage payments, and employee social security tax and income tax (if any) deducted.

Penalties.—Avoid penalties and interest by filing returns on time and paying tax when due. The law provides a penalty for filing a return late or paying tax late unless you show good reason for the delay. If you cannot avoid filing a return late or paying the tax late, attach an explanation to your return. The law also provides a penalty for not giving Forms W-2 to your employees.

(Continued on page 4)

WAGE AND TAX STATEMENT (IRS FORM W-2) AND TRANSMITTAL OF INCOME AND TAX STATEMENTS (IRS FORM W-3)

Harry is required to file IRS Forms W-2 and W-3 transmittals for his 3 employees who began work on July 1, 1989. Wages paid during the employment period are:

Employee	Wages Paid	Income Tax Withheld	FICA Withheld
A. Ronson	$15,600	$2,340	$1,171.56
T. Jackson	13,000	1,950	976.30
P. Frank	10,400	1,560	781.04
	$39,000	$5,850	$2,928.90

State Taxes Withheld	State Disability Insurance
$468	$140.40
390	117.00
312	93.60
$1,170	$351.00

Lines 2,3,4: Harry enters his firm's name and address on line 1 and his EIN and state ID number on lines 2 and 3.

Lines 8 - 22: Apply to the employees. On line 8 is entered the employee's social security number.

Lines 9,10,11: Harry enters the employee's federal income tax withheld on lines 9,10, and 11 respectively. It should be noted that the amount entered on line 11, social security tax withheld, is the employees share only and not Harry's share. The amount Harry enters is $2,928.90.

Line 13: Wages on which social security tax is computed is entered here.

Exhibit 6-10

Lines 17,18, 19: Harry enters state income tax withheld, state wages and name of state. In California, Harry is required to withhold state disability insurance. This amount is entered on line 20 with an explanation entered on line 22.

Copy A of IRS Form W-2 is transmitted to the Social Security Administration with transmittal IRS Form W-3 by February 28th, 1990. Copies 1,B,C and 2 are given to the employees by February 28th. Copy D is kept by Harry.

Copy A of IRS Form W-2 and IRS Form W-3 are returned to the Social Security Administration address for Harry's state which is listed on the bottom of IRS Form W-3. For Harry, the address is Salinas, California. Harry is ready to complete IRS Form W-3. Since Harry is a "941 employee," he marks the appropriate box on line 2.

Line 5: Harry enters the number of completed W-2 forms, which is 3.

Lines 9,10,11: On these lines, Harry enters the totals of federal income tax withheld and wages and social security taxes withheld.

Line 12: Harry enters is state ID number.

Line 13: Harry now enters total wages on which social security taxes are withheld.

Lines 15,17,19: Next Harry enters is EIN and business name and address. After reviewing this form for completeness, Harry is ready to sign, date, and enter his title as "owner."

Additional information on income, excise, and employment taxes for individuals, partnerships, and corporations may be obtained by ordering IRS Publication 334, "Tax Guide for Small Business,"

Form 1

1 Control number	22222	For Paperwork Reduction Act Notice, see back of Copy D. OMB No. 1545-0008	For Official Use Only ▶	

2 Employer's name, address, and ZIP code	3 Employer's identification number 33-0177583	4 Employer's state I.D. number 1234567
HARRY P. KAYHILL, CPA 1 KENSINGTON RD SACRAMENTO, CA 95691	5 Statutory employee ☐ Deceased ☐ Pension plan ☐ Legal rep. ☐	942 emp. ☐ Subtotal ☐ Deferred compensation ☐ Void ☐
	6 Allocated tips	7 Advance EIC payment

8 Employee's social security number 350-92-8741	9 Federal income tax withheld 2,340.00	10 Wages, tips, other compensation 15,600.00	11 Social security tax withheld 1,171.56
12 Employee's name (first, middle, last) ALAN L. RONSON		13 Social security wages 15,600.00	14 Social security tips
258 MT. ALIFAN SACRAMENTO, CA 95691		16 (See Instr. for Forms W-2/W-2P)	16a Fringe benefits incl. in Box 10
		17 State income tax 468.00	18 State wages, tips, etc. 15,600.00	19 Name of state CA
15 Employee's address and ZIP code		20 Local income tax 140.40	21 Local wages, tips, etc.	22 Name of locality SDI

Form **W-2 Wage and Tax Statement** **1988**

Copy A For Social Security Administration   Dept. of the Treasury—IRS

Do NOT Cut or Separate Forms on This Page

Form 2

1 Control number	22222	For Paperwork Reduction Act Notice, see back of Copy D. OMB No. 1545-0008	For Official Use Only ▶	

2 Employer's name, address, and ZIP code	3 Employer's identification number 33-0177583	4 Employer's state I.D. number 1234567
HARRY P. KAYHILL, CPA 1 KENSINGTON RD. SACRAMENTO, CA 95691	5 Statutory employee ☐ Deceased ☐ Pension plan ☐ Legal rep. ☐	942 emp. ☐ Subtotal ☐ Deferred compensation ☐ Void ☐
	6 Allocated tips	7 Advance EIC payment

8 Employee's social security number 090-34-6574	9 Federal income tax withheld 1,950.00	10 Wages, tips, other compensation 13,000.00	11 Social security tax withheld 976.30
12 Employee's name (first, middle, last) JAMES L. JACKSON		13 Social security wages 13,000.00	14 Social security tips
3268 CHATSWORTH DR. SACRAMENTO, CA 95691		16 (See Instr. for Forms W-2/W-2P)	16a Fringe benefits incl. in Box 10
		17 State income tax 390.00	18 State wages, tips, etc. 13,000	19 Name of state CA
15 Employee's address and ZIP code		20 Local income tax 117.00	21 Local wages, tips, etc.	22 Name of locality SDI

Form **W-2 Wage and Tax Statement** **1988**

Copy A For Social Security Administration   Dept. of the Treasury—IRS

Do NOT Cut or Separate Forms on This Page

Form 3

1 Control number	22222	For Paperwork Reduction Act Notice, see back of Copy D. OMB No. 1545-0008	For Official Use Only ▶	

2 Employer's name, address, and ZIP code	3 Employer's identification number 33-0177583	4 Employer's state I.D. number 1234567
HARRY P. KAYHILL, CPA 1 KENSINGTON RD. SACRAMENTO, CA 95691	5 Statutory employee ☐ Deceased ☐ Pension plan ☐ Legal rep. ☐	942 emp. ☐ Subtotal ☐ Deferred compensation ☐ Void ☐
	6 Allocated tips	7 Advance EIC payment

8 Employee's social security number 279-53-3946	9 Federal income tax withheld 1,560.00	10 Wages, tips, other compensation 10,400.00	11 Social security tax withheld 781.04
12 Employee's name (first, middle, last) PAUL S FRANK		13 Social security wages 10,400.00	14 Social security tips
4250 BALBOA AVE. SACRAMENTO, CA 95691		16 (See Instr. for Forms W-2/W-2P)	16a Fringe benefits incl. in Box 10
		17 State income tax 312.00	18 State wages, tips, etc. 10,400.00	19 Name of state CA
15 Employee's address and ZIP code		20 Local income tax 93.60	21 Local wages, tips, etc.	22 Name of locality SDI

Form **W-2 Wage and Tax Statement** **1988**

Copy A For Social Security Administration   Dept. of the Treasury—IRS

DO NOT STAPLE

1 Control number	33333	For Official Use Only ▶ OMB No. 1545-0008			

| ☐ Kind of Payer ▶ | 2 941/941E ☒ Military ☐ 943 ☐
 CT-1 ☐ 942 ☐ Medicare gov't. emp. ☐ | 3 | 4 | 5 Number of statements attached *3* |

6 Allocated tips	7 Advance EIC payments	8

9 Federal income tax withheld *5,850.00*	10 Wages, tips, and other compensation *39,000.00*	11 Social security tax withheld *2,928.90*

12 Employer's state I.D. number *123456*	13 Social security wages *39,000.00*	14 Social security tips

15 Employer's identification number *33 — 0177583*	16 Establishment number

17 Employer's name *HARRY P. KAYHILL, CPA* *1 KENSINGTON RD* *SACRAMENTO, CA 95691*	18 Gross annuity, pension, etc. (Form W-2P) 20 Taxable amount (Form W-2P) 21 Income tax withheld by third-party payer

19 Employer's address and ZIP code (If available, place label over boxes 15, 17, and 19.)

Under penalties of perjury, I declare that I have examined this return and accompanying documents, and to the best of my knowledge and belief they are true, correct, and complete. In the case of documents without recipients' identifying numbers, I have complied with the requirements of the law in attempting to secure such numbers from the recipients.

Signature ▶ *Harry P. Cahill*   Title ▶ *OWNER*   Date ▶ *2-20-90*

Form **W-3** Transmittal of Income and Tax Statements **1988**   Department of the Treasury Internal Revenue Service

---

Please return this entire page with the accompanying Forms W-2 or W-2P to the Social Security Administration address for your state as listed below. Note: Extra postage may be necessary if the report you send contains more than a few pages or if the envelope is larger than letter size.

If your legal residence, principal place of business, office or agency is located in ▼	Use this address ▼
Alaska, Arizona, California, Colorado, Hawaii, Idaho, Iowa, Minnesota, Missouri, Montana, Nebraska, Nevada, North Dakota, Oregon, South Dakota, Utah, Washington, Wisconsin, Wyoming	Social Security Administration Salinas Data Operations Center Salinas, CA 93911
Alabama, Arkansas, Florida, Georgia, Illinois, Kansas, Louisiana, Mississippi, New Mexico, Oklahoma, South Carolina, Tennessee, Texas	Social Security Administration Albuquerque Data Operations Center Albuquerque, NM 87180
Connecticut, Delaware, District of Columbia, Indiana, Kentucky, Maine, Maryland, Massachusetts, Michigan, New Hampshire, New Jersey, New York, North Carolina, Ohio, Pennsylvania, Rhode Island, Vermont, Virginia, West Virginia	Social Security Administration Wilkes-Barre Data Operations Center Wilkes-Barre, PA 18769
If you have no legal residence or principal place of business in any state	Social Security Administration Wilkes-Barre Data Operations Center Wilkes-Barre, PA 18769

Household employers filing Forms W-2 for household employees should send the forms to the Albuquerque Data Operations Center.

Paperwork Reduction Act Notice.—We ask for this information to carry out the Internal Revenue laws of the United States. We need it to ensure that taxpayers are complying with these laws and to allow us to figure and collect the right amount of tax. You are required to give us this information.

1988

Department of the Treasury
Internal Revenue Service

Instructions for Forms W-2 and W-2P

Highlights

If possible, please file Forms W-2 and W-2P either alphabetically by employees' last name or numerically by employees' SSN. This will help the Social Security Administration locate specific forms if there is trouble processing your submission.

General Instructions

(Section references are to the Internal Revenue Code, unless otherwise noted.)

A. Who Must File Forms W-2 and W-2P.—

(1) Form W-2, Wage and Tax Statement.—To be filed by employers. (See **Circular A,** Agricultural Employer's Tax Guide, or **Circular E,** Employer's Tax Guide. Household employers, see Form 942 instructions.)

(2) Form W-2P, Statement for Recipients of Annuities, Pensions, Retired Pay, or IRA Payments.—To be filed by employees' trusts or funds; Federal, state, or local government systems; life insurance companies; and other payers who make such payments.

B. When to File.—File Forms W-2 and W-2P with accompanying **Forms W-3,** Transmittal of Income and Tax Statements, by February 28, 1989.

If you need an extension of time to file Forms W-2, see the Instructions for Form W-3 under "When To File."

C. Where to File.—See Form W-3.

D. Calendar Year Basis.—You must base entries on Forms W-2 and W-2P on a calendar year.

E. Taxpayer Identification Numbers.—We use them to check the payments you report against the amounts shown on the employees' tax returns. Be sure to show the right social security number on the Forms W-2 or W-2P, or on magnetic media.

Persons in a trade or business use an employer identification number (00-0000000). This includes employee trusts, retirement systems, and so forth. Individuals use a social security number (000-00-0000). When you list a number, please separate the nine digits properly to show the kind of number.

Sole proprietors who are payers should show their employer identification number on the statements they prepare. But if you prepare a statement showing payment *to* a sole proprietor, give the proprietor's social security number in Box 8 of Form W-2 or Form W-2P.

Please show the full name, address, and identification number of the payer and the recipient on the form. If you make payments to more than one individual, show on the first line **ONLY** the name of the recipient whose number is on the statement. Show the other names on the second and following lines. If the recipient is **NOT** an individual and the name runs over the first line, you may continue on the second and following lines.

F. Statements to Income Recipients.—You may give statements to income recipients on government-printed official forms or on privately printed substitute forms.

A Revenue Procedure titled "Specifications for Private Printing of Forms W-2, W-2P, and W-3" and reprinted as **Publication 1141,** explains the format that must be used on all substitute paper forms. You can get a copy from any Internal Revenue Service Center or district office.

(1) Form W-2 Recipients.—Generally, give statements to employees by January 31, 1989. If employment ends before December 31, 1988, you may give copies any time after employment ends. If the employee asks for Form W-2, give him or her the completed copies within 30 days of the request or the final wage payment, whichever is later.

(2) Form W-2P Recipients.—Generally, you should give statements to income recipients by January 31, 1989.

G. Corrections.—Use **Form W-2c,** Statement of Corrected Income and Tax Amounts, to correct errors in previously filed Forms W-2 and W-2P. Use **Form W-3c,** Transmittal of Corrected Income and Tax Statements, to transmit the W-2c forms to the Social Security Administration (SSA). Instructions are on the forms. If an employee (or recipient) loses a statement, write "REISSUED STATEMENT" on the new copy, **but do not send Copy A of the reissued statement to SSA.**

H. Sick Pay.—If you had employees who received sick pay in 1988 from an insurance company or other third-party payer, and the third party notified you of the amount of sick pay involved, you must report the following on the employees' W-2s:

(a) in Box 9, the amount (if any) of income tax withheld from the sick pay by the third-party payer;

(b) in Box 10, the amount the employee must include in income;

(c) in Box 11, the employee social security tax withheld by the third-party payer;

(d) in Box 13, the amount of sick pay that is subject to employer social security tax; and

(e) in Box 16, the amount (if any) not includible in income because the employee contributed to the sick pay plan.

You can include these amounts in the Forms W-2 you issue the employees showing wages, or you can give the employees separate W-2s and state that the amounts are for third-party sick pay. In either case, you must show in Box 21 of Form W-3 the total amount of income tax withheld by third-party payers, even though the amounts are includible in Box 9.

I. Penalties.—You may be assessed a $50 per document penalty if you:

● fail to file a timely Form W-2 with SSA or give the employee a copy;

● fail to file on magnetic media, if required; or

● fail to file paper forms with SSA that are machine readable.

If you fail to file a timely Form W-2P, you may be assessed a $25 per day penalty, up to $15,000 ($50 per failure for IRA information reporting).

There is also a penalty if you fail to include correct information on a statement.

How to Complete Form W-2

Copy A of Forms W-2 and W-2P is printed with three forms to an unperforated page. Send the whole page even if one or two of the forms are blank or void. If you are sending 42 or more Forms W-2, please show subtotals on every 42nd form for the preceding 41 forms to permit checking the transmittal totals. Since this form is processed by optical scanning machines, please type the entries, if possible, using black ink. Please do not make any erasures, whiteouts, or strikeovers on Copy A. Make all dollar entries without the dollar sign but with the decimal point (000.00).

The instructions below are for boxes on Form W-2. If an entry does not apply, leave it blank.

Box 1—Control number.—You may use this to identify individual Forms W-2. *You do not have to use this box.*

Box 3—Employer's identification number.—Show the number assigned to you by IRS (00-0000000). Do not use a prior owner's number.

Box 4—Employer's state I.D. number.—You do not have to complete this box, but you may want to if you use copies of this form for your state return. The number is assigned by the individual states.

Box 5.—Check the boxes that apply.

Statutory employee.—Check this box for statutory employees whose earnings are subject to social security tax but **NOT** subject to Federal income tax withholding. (See Circular E for more information on statutory employees.)

Deceased.—Check this box if the employee is now deceased.

Pension plan.—Check this box if the employee was an active participant (for any part of the year) in a retirement plan (including a simplified employee pension (SEP) plan) maintained by you. See IRS Notice 87-16, published in Internal Revenue Bulletin 1987-5, dated February 2, 1987, for definition of an active participant.

Legal representative.—Check this box when the employee's name is the only name shown but is shown as a trust account (e.g., John Doe Trust), or another name is shown in addition to the employee's name and the other person or business is acting on behalf of the employee.

Representatives are identified by words such as "custodian," "parent," or "attorney"; sometimes the employee is identified as a minor, child, etc. Do **NOT** check this box if the address is simply in care of someone other than the employee (John Doe, c/o Jane Smith).

942 employee.—For household employers only. See Form 942 instructions for information on when to check this box.

Subtotal.—If you are submitting **42 or more Forms W-2 or W-2P,** please give subtotal figures for every 41 individual forms. Check the "Subtotal" box on the form that shows the subtotal dollar amounts for the preceding 41 forms. Void statements are counted in order with good statements (*but do not include the money amounts from the void statements in the subtotal figures*). Subtotal statements should always be the last completed form on a page. The subtotal amounts to be shown are:

Form W-2—Boxes 6, 7, 9, 10, 11, 13, and 14
Form W-2P—Boxes 9, 10, and 11

Example: *An employer with Forms W-2 for 86 employees should show a subtotal on the 42nd statement, the 84th statement (showing the subtotal for statements 43 through 83), and the 89th statement (showing the subtotal for statements 85 through 88).*

Deferred compensation.—Check this box if you made contributions on behalf of the employee to a section 401(k), 403(b), 408(k)(6), 457, or 501(c)(18)(D) retirement plan. See also instruction "(d)" under Box 16.

Void.—Put an X in this square when an error has been made. **(Be sure the amounts shown on void forms are NOT included in your subtotals.)**

Box 6—Allocated tips.—If you are a large food or beverage establishment, show the amount of tips allocated to the employee. (See the instructions for **Form 8027,** Employer's Annual Information Return of Tip Income and Allocated Tips.) Do **NOT** include this amount in Box 10 (Wages, tips, other compensation) or Box 14 (Social security tips).

Box 7—Advance EIC payment.—Show the total amount paid to the employee as advance earned income credit payments.

Box 8—Employee's social security number.—Give the number shown on the employee's social security card. If the employee does not have a number, he or she should apply for one at any SSA office.

Box 10—Wages, tips, other compensation.—Show, before any payroll deductions, the total of:

(1) wages paid,

(2) noncash payments (including fringe benefits),

(3) tips reported, and

(4) all other compensation (including certain scholarships and fellowship grants, payments for moving expenses and reimbursements for employee business expenses if the employee does not account to you for those expenses.). Other compensation is what you pay the employee but do not withhold Federal income tax on. If you prefer not to include it in the total, you may show it on a separate Form W-2.

Note: *Payments to statutory employees, that are subject to social security tax but not subject to Federal income tax withholding, must be shown in Box 10 as other compensation. (See Circular E for definition of a statutory employee.)*

Box 11—Employee social security tax withheld.—Show the total employee social security tax (not your share) deducted and withheld or paid by you for the employee. (But if there was an adjustment in 1988 to correct the tax for a prior year, enter the amount withheld in 1988 increased by the adjustment for an overcollection or decreased by the adjustment for an undercollection.)

Example: *Employee A earned $26,000 in 1987. You withheld $1,759 in employee social security taxes. You should have withheld $1,859 ($26,000 x 7.15%). To correct this, you withheld extra tax in 1988 until you made up the $100. At the end of 1988 your books show $2,052.60 withheld ($1,952.60 ($26,000 × 7.51%) plus $100 to make up the 1987 error). To show the correct tax withheld for 1988, subtract the $100 from $2,052.60 and show $1,952.60 in Box 11 of Form W-2. Please note: You must file Form 941c, Statement to Correct Information Previously Reported on the Employer's Federal Tax Return, with your Form 941, Employer's Quarterly Federal Tax Return, in the quarter you find the error and issue the employee a Form W-2c for 1987.*

Box 12—Employee's name.—Enter the name as shown on the employee's social security card. If the name has changed, have the employee get a corrected card from any SSA office. Use the name on the original card until you see the corrected one.

Box 13—Total social security wages.—Show the total wages paid (before payroll deductions) subject to employer social security tax (but **NOT** including allocated tips). Generally, noncash payments are considered wages. Include employer contributions to certain qualified cash or deferred compensation arrangements, even though the contributions are not includible in Box 10 as wages, tips, and other compensation. (See Circular E for more information.) Include any employee social security tax and employee state unemployment compensation tax you paid for your employee rather than deducting it from wages (see Revenue Procedure 81-48, 1981-2 C.B. 623, for details). Do not enter more than $45,000 (the maximum social security wage base for 1988) in Box 13.

Box 14—Social security tips.—Show the amount the employee reported even if you did not have enough employee funds to collect the social security tax for the tips. When tips and wages subject to employee social security taxes amount to $45,000 **do NOT** show any additional tips in this box. But show all tips reported in Box 10 along with wages and other compensation.

Box 15—Employee's address and ZIP code.—This box has been combined with Box 12 (employee's name) on all copies except Copy A to allow employees' copies to be mailed in a window envelope or as a self-mailer.

Box 16—Employer's use.—Complete and label this box if (a), (b), (c), (d), (e), or (f) apply.

(a) You did **not** collect employee social security tax on all the employee's tips. Show the amount of tax that you could not collect because the employee did not have enough funds to deduct it from. Do not include this amount in Box 11.

(b) You provided your employee more than $50,000 of group-term life insurance. Show the cost of coverage over $50,000. Also include it in Box 10 and Box 13.

(c) You are reporting sick pay. Show the amount of any sick pay **NOT** includible in income because the employee contributed to the sick pay plan. Label it as nontaxable. If you issue a separate W-2 for sick pay, use Box 16 to label the W-2 as "Sick pay."

(d) You made contributions to a section 401(k) cash or deferred arrangement, to a section 403(b) salary reduction agreement to purchase an annuity contract, to a section 408(k)(6) salary reduction SEP, to a section 457 deferred compensation plan for state or local government employees, or to a section 501(c)(18)(D) tax-exempt organization plan. Check the "Deferred compensation" checkbox in Box 5, enter the elective deferral in Box 16, and label it "401(k)," "403(b)," etc.

(e) You are a Federal, state, or local agency with employees paying the 1.45% medicare portion of the social security tax. For these employees, write "Medicare qualified government employment" in Box 16, and show the social security wages and 1.45% tax withheld in Boxes 13 and 11, respectively.

(f) You made excess "golden parachute" payments to certain key corporate employees. If the excess payments are considered wages, the 20% excise tax is treated as income tax withholding. Include this tax in Box 9 and identify the amount as "EPP" in Box 16.

If none of the above apply, you may use Box 16 for any information you want to give the employee. Examples are union dues or health insurance premiums deducted, moving expenses paid, or reimbursements for employee business expenses included in Box 10.

Box 16a—Fringe benefits included in Box 10.—Show the total value of the taxable noncash fringe benefits included in Box 10 as other compensation. If you provided a vehicle and included 100 percent of the value in the employee's income, you must separately report this value to the employee in Box 16a or on a separate statement so the employee can compute the value of any business use of the vehicle.

Boxes 17 through 22—State or local income tax information.—You may use these to report state or local income tax information. You do not have to use them. But you may want to show the amounts on Copy A if you use copies of this form for your state or local tax returns or as recipients' statements.

How to Complete Form W-2P

The instructions below are for Form W-2P. If an entry does not apply, leave it blank. Use this form to report retirement payments other than total distributions that close an account. Examples are pensions, retired or retainer pay, annuities under commercial, individually purchased contracts, payments from individual retirement accounts or individual retirement annuities, and loans treated as distributions under section 72(p).

For treatment of repayments by recipients of erroneous pension benefits, see Circular E, Employer's Tax Guide.

Use Form W-2 to report payments from which you withheld social security tax.

Do **NOT** file Form W-2P for the following cases: (a) You paid retirement benefits that are exempt from tax such as Veterans Administration payments; (b) You made payments as a fiduciary, filed Form 1041, and gave each beneficiary a Schedule K-1 (Form 1041); or (c) You made total distributions reported on Form 1099-R.

Box 1—Control number.—You may use this to identify individual Forms W-2P. *You do not have to use this box.*

Box 3—Payer's Federal identification number.—Show the number assigned to you by the IRS (00-0000000).

Box 4—Payer's state I.D. number.—You do not have to complete this box, but you may want to if you use copies of this form for your state return. The number is assigned by the individual states.

Boxes 5 and 6—State income tax withheld and name of state.—You may use these to report state and local tax information if you use copies of this form for your state returns or as recipients' statements.

Box 7.—Check the boxes that apply.

Taxable amount (Tax amt) NOT determined.—Check this box if you are not able to figure the taxable amount of the annuity, pension, retirement pay, or IRA payment to report in Box 10.

Deceased.—Check this box if the recipient is now deceased.

Legal representative.—Check this box when the recipient's name is the only name shown but it is shown as a trust account (e.g., John Doe Trust), or when another name is shown as well as the recipient's name and the other person or business is acting on behalf of the recipient.

Representatives are identified by words such as custodian, parent, or attorney; sometimes the recipient is identified as a minor, child, etc. Do **NOT** check this box if the address is simply in care of someone other than the recipient (such as John Doe c/o Jane Smith).

Subtotal.—If you are submitting **42 or more Forms W-2P**, please give subtotal figures for every 41 individual forms. See the W-2 instructions for Box 5 for details.

Void.—Put an X in this square when an error has been made. Forms W-2P should have no erasures, whiteouts, or strikeovers on Copy A. **(Be sure the amounts shown on void forms are NOT included in your subtotals.)**

Box 8—Recipient's social security number.—Give the number shown on the recipient's social security card. If the person does not have a number, he or she should apply for one at any SSA office.

Box 9—Gross annuity, pension, retired pay, or IRA payment.—Show total amount paid before income tax or other deductions were withheld. Do not include amounts exempt from tax as workmen's compensation under section 104. Include current insurance premiums (including "PS 58" costs) paid by the trustee or custodian, and loans treated as distributions under section 72(p).

Box 10—Taxable amount.—Show the amount the recipient should include in income (including "PS 58" costs). This often is the same as in Box 9. Also, the amount in Box 9 may include taxable earnings on an excess contribution while the excess contribution may be nontaxable. There may be some years in which none of the payments are taxable. You must make every effort to obtain the information necessary to compute the taxable amount. If you do not have the facts you need to figure the taxable amount, you may have to leave this box blank and check "Tax amt not determined" in Box 7.

For new rules on reporting the distribution of excess deferrals, excess contributions, and excess aggregate contributions, see IRS Notice 87-77, published in Internal Revenue Bulletin 1987-51, dated December 21, 1987.

Box 11.—Federal income tax withheld.

Box 12—Recipient's name.—Enter the name as shown on the recipient's social security card. If the name has changed, have the person get a corrected card from any SSA office. Use the name shown on the original card until you see the corrected one.

Box 13.—You may use Box 13 and the space below Boxes 13 and 14 for any other information that you want to give the recipient.

Box 14—Distribution code.—This box is used to identify distributions that may have special tax consequences. Use it to identify any distributions that are not normal retirement distributions. The code is a four-digit number starting with 555. The fourth digit identifies the type of distribution: 1—Premature distribution (other than codes 2, 3, 4, 8, or P); 2—Rollover; 3—Disability; 4—Death; 6—Other; 7—Normal IRA or SEP distribution; 8—Excess contributions/deferrals plus earnings taxable in 1988; "P"—Excess contributions/deferrals refunded in 1988 plus earnings taxable in the prior year (1987); 9—Current insurance premiums including PS 58 costs. (For example, 5553 for disability.) For code "P" distributions, you should advise the payee, at the time of the distribution, that the earnings are taxable in the prior year.

Box 15.—See Box 15, Form W-2 instructions.

1989 Form W-4

Department of the Treasury
Internal Revenue Service

Purpose. Complete Form W-4 so that your employer can withhold the correct amount of Federal income tax from your pay.

Exemption From Withholding. Read line 6 of the certificate below to see if you can claim exempt status. If exempt, only complete the certificate; but do not complete lines 4 and 5. No Federal income tax will be withheld from your pay.

Basic Instructions. Employees who are not exempt should complete the Personal Allowances Worksheet. Additional worksheets are provided on page 2 for employees to adjust their withholding allowances based on itemized deductions, adjustments to income, or two-earner/two-job situations. Complete all worksheets that apply to your situation. The worksheets will help you figure the number of withholding allowances you are

entitled to claim. However, you may claim fewer allowances than this.

Head of Household. Generally, you may claim head of household filing status on your tax return only if you are unmarried and pay more than 50% of the costs of keeping up a home for yourself and your dependent(s) or other qualifying individuals.

Nonwage Income. If you have a large amount of nonwage income, such as interest or dividends, you should consider making estimated tax payments using Form 1040-ES. Otherwise, you may find that you owe additional tax at the end of the year.

Two-Earner/Two-Jobs. If you have a working spouse or more than one job, figure the total number of allowances you are entitled to claim on all jobs using worksheets from only one Form

W-4. This total should be divided among all jobs. Your withholding will usually be most accurate when all allowances are claimed on the W-4 filed for the highest paying job and zero allowances are claimed for the others.

Advance Earned Income Credit. If you are eligible for this credit, you can receive it added to your paycheck throughout the year. For details, obtain Form W-5 from your employer.

Check Your Withholding. After your W-4 takes effect, you can use **Publication 919,** Is My Withholding Correct for 1989?, to see how the dollar amount you are having withheld compares to your estimated total annual tax. Call 1-800-424-3676 (in Hawaii and Alaska, check your local telephone directory) to obtain this publication.

Personal Allowances Worksheet

A Enter "1" for **yourself** if no one else can claim you as a dependent . . . . **A** _____

B Enter "1" if: { **1.** You are single and have only one job; or
2. You are married, have only one job, and your spouse does not work; or
3. Your wages from a second job or your spouse's wages (or the total of both) are $2,500 or less. } . . . . . . **B** _____

C Enter "1" for your **spouse.** But, you may choose to enter "0" if you are married and have either a working spouse or more than one job (this may help you avoid having too little tax withheld) . . . . **C** _____

D Enter number of **dependents** (other than your spouse or yourself) whom you will claim on your tax return . . . . . **D** _____

E Enter "1" if you will file as a **head of household** on your tax return (see conditions under "Head of Household," above) . . **E** _____

F Enter "1" if you have at least $1,500 of **child or dependent care expenses** for which you plan to claim a credit . . . . **F** _____

G Add lines A through F and enter total here . . . . ▶ **G** _____

For accuracy, do all worksheets that apply. {
• If you plan to **itemize or claim adjustments to income** and want to reduce your withholding, turn to the Deductions and Adjustments Worksheet on page 2.
• If you are **single** and have **more than one job** and your combined earnings from all jobs exceed $25,000 OR if you are **married** and have a **working spouse or more than one job,** and the combined earnings from all jobs exceed $40,000, then turn to the Two-Earner/Two-Job Worksheet on page 2 if you want to avoid having too little tax withheld.
• If **neither** of the above situations applies to you, **stop here** and enter the number from line G on line 4 of Form W-4 below. }

- - - - - - - - - - - - - - - - - - - **Cut here and give the certificate to your employer. Keep the top portion for your records.** - - - - - - - - - - - - - - - - - - -

Form **W-4**
Department of the Treasury
Internal Revenue Service

Employee's Withholding Allowance Certificate
▶ **For Privacy Act and Paperwork Reduction Act Notice, see reverse.**

OMB No. 1545-0010

1989

1 Type or print your first name and middle initial	Last name	2 Your social security number

Home address (number and street or rural route)	**3 Marital Status**	☐ Single ☐ Married
City or town, state, and ZIP code		☐ Married, but withhold at higher Single rate.

Note: *If married, but legally separated, or spouse is a nonresident alien, check the Single box.*

4 Total number of allowances you are claiming (from line G above or from the Worksheets on back if they apply) . . . **4** _____

5 Additional amount, if any, you want deducted from each pay . . . . **5** $ _____

6 I claim exemption from withholding and I certify that I meet **ALL** of the following conditions for exemption:
- Last year I had a right to a refund of **ALL** Federal income tax withheld because I had **NO** tax liability; **AND**
- This year I expect a refund of **ALL** Federal income tax withheld because I expect to have **NO** tax liability; **AND**
- This year if my income exceeds $500 and includes nonwage income, another person cannot claim me as a dependent.

If you meet all of the above conditions, enter the year effective and "EXEMPT" here . . . . . . ▶ **6** 19___

7 Are you a full-time student? **(Note:** *Full-time students are not automatically exempt.)* . . . . **7** ☐ Yes ☐ No

Under penalties of perjury, I certify that I am entitled to the number of withholding allowances claimed on this certificate or entitled to claim exempt status

Employee's signature ▶	Date ▶	. 198___
8 Employer's name and address (**Employer:** Complete 8 and 10 **only if sending to IRS**)	9 Office code (optional)	10 Employer identification number

Exhibit 6-11

Deductions and Adjustments Worksheet

Note: *Use this worksheet only if you plan to itemize deductions or claim adjustments to income on your 1989 tax return.*

1   Enter an estimate of your 1989 itemized deductions. These include: qualifying home mortgage interest, 20% of personal interest, charitable contributions, state and local taxes (but not sales taxes), medical expenses in excess of 7.5% of your income, and miscellaneous deductions (most miscellaneous deductions are now deductible only in excess of 2% of your income) . . . . 1 $ _____

2   Enter: $5,200 if married filing jointly or qualifying widow(er)
$4,550 if head of household
$3,100 if single
$2,600 if married filing separately   . . . . 2 $ _____

3   **Subtract** line 2 from line 1. If line 2 is greater than line 1, enter zero . . . . 3 $ _____

4   Enter an estimate of your 1989 adjustments to income. These include alimony paid and deductible IRA contributions . . 4 $ _____

5   **Add** lines 3 and 4 and enter the total . . . . 5 $ _____

6   Enter an estimate of your 1989 nonwage income (such as dividends or interest income) . . . . . 6 $ _____

7   **Subtract** line 6 from line 5. Enter the result, but not less than zero . . . . 7 $ _____

8   **Divide** the amount on line 7 by $2,000 and enter the result here. Drop any fraction 8   _____

9   Enter the number from Personal Allowances Worksheet, line G, on page 1 9   _____

10   **Add** lines 8 and 9 and enter the total here. If you plan to use the Two-Earner/Two-Job Worksheet, also enter the total on line 1, below. Otherwise, **stop here** and enter this total on Form W-4, line 4 on page 1 10   _____

Two-Earner/Two-Job Worksheet

Note: *Use this worksheet only if the instructions at line G on page 1 direct you here.*

1   Enter the number from line G on page 1 (or from line 10 above if you used the Deductions and Adjustments Worksheet) . 1   _____

2   Find the number in **Table 1** below that applies to the **LOWEST** paying job and enter it here 2   _____

3   If line 1 is **GREATER THAN OR EQUAL TO** line 2, subtract line 2 from line 1. Enter the result here (if zero, enter "0") and on Form W-4, line 4, on page 1. **DO NOT** use the rest of this worksheet 3   _____

Note: *If line 1 is **LESS THAN** line 2, enter "0" on Form W-4, line 4, on page 1. Complete lines 4–9 to calculate the additional dollar withholding necessary to avoid a year-end tax bill.*

4   Enter the number from line 2 of this worksheet 4   _____

5   Enter the number from line 1 of this worksheet 5   _____

6   **Subtract** line 5 from line 4 6   _____

7   Find the amount in **Table 2** below that applies to the **HIGHEST** paying job and enter it here . . . . . 7 $ _____

8   **Multiply** line 7 by line 6 and enter the result here. This is the additional annual withholding amount needed   8 $ _____

9   Divide line 8 by the number of pay periods each year. (For example, divide by 26 if you are paid every other week.) Enter the result here and on Form W-4, line 5, page 1. This is the additional amount to be withheld from each paycheck . . . 9 $ _____

Table 1: Two-Earner/Two-Job Worksheet

Married Filing Jointly		All Others	
If wages from **LOWEST** paying job are—	Enter on line 2 above	If wages from **LOWEST** paying job are—	Enter on line 2 above
0 - $4,000	0	0 - $4,000	0
4,001 - 8,000	1	4,001 - 8,000	1
8,001 - 18,000	2	8,001 - 13,000	2
18,001 - 21,000	3	13,001 - 15,000	3
21,001 - 23,000	4	15,001 - 19,000	4
23,001 - 25,000	5	19,001 and over	5
25,001 - 27,000	6		
27,001 - 32,000	7		
32,001 - 38,000	8		
38,001 - 42,000	9		
42,001 and over	10		

Table 2: Two-Earner/Two-Job Worksheet

Married Filing Jointly		All Others	
If wages from **HIGHEST** paying job are—	Enter on line 7 above	If wages from **HIGHEST** paying job are—	Enter on line 7 above
0 - $40,000	$300	0 - $23,000	$300
40,001 - 84,000	560	23,001 - 50,000	560
84,001 and over	660	50,001 and over	660

EMPLOYER'S ANNUAL FEDERAL UNEMPLOYMENT (FUTA) TAX RETURN
(IRS FORM 940)

EXAMPLE:

During the year, Harry made total payments of $39,000 to his employees. Prior to the end of the calendar year, the IRS will mail IRS Form 940 to Harry. This form is filed annually with the IRS and is due by January 31st. Harry begins filling out IRS Form 940 by using the preaddressed form which contains his name, address, and EIN. Next, Harry marks the appropriate boxes on lines A,B, and C and inserts the required information on lines A, B(1) and B(2) .

PART I

Line 1: Harry enters the total amount he has paid his employees during 1988, which $39,000.

Line 2: Since none of the wages paid during 1989 were exempt from federal unemployment tax, Harry enters "none" on this line.

Line 3: Harry enters the amount of wages he paid to each employee that was over the $7,000 limit, or $18,000, [$39,000 - (3 x 7,000)].

Line 4: Harry enters the sum of lines 2 and 3.

Line 5: On this line, Harry enters the amount of his 1988 wage payments that are subject to federal tax, ($39,000 - $18,000 = $21,000).

PART II

Line 1: Harry enters 0.8% x $21,000 or $168.

Line 2: Harry enters his federal unemployment tax deposit for the 4th quarter which was accompanied by IRS Form 8109, "Federal Tax Deposit Coupon." The amount was $104.

Line 3: The balance due represents the difference between his tax liability and his deposit. ($168 - 104 = $64). Harry writes a check for $64 to accompany IRS Form

Exhibit 6-12

940.

Line 4: This line is left blank as Harry did not overpay the
tax.

After reviewing the form for completeness, Harry is ready to
sign, date, and enter his title as "owner."

Additional information on federal unemployment taxes is
available from the IRS by ordering Publication 539, "Employment
Taxes."

Form **940**	**Employer's Annual Federal Unemployment (FUTA) Tax Return**	OMB No. 1545-0028
Department of the Treasury Internal Revenue Service	▶ For Paperwork Reduction Act Notice, see page 2.	19**88**

		T	
		FF	
		FD	
If Incorrect, make any necessary change. ▶	Name (as distinguished from trade name) — Calendar year	FP	
	Trade name, if any	I	
	Address and ZIP code — L _Form will be PREADDRESSED_	T	
	Employer identification number —		

A Did you pay all required contributions to state unemployment funds by the due date of Form 940? (See instructions if none required.) . . . ☒ **Yes** ☐ **No**

If you checked the "Yes" box, enter the amount of contributions paid to state unemployment funds . . . . . . ▶ $ _714_

B Are you required to pay contributions to only one state? . . . . ☒ **Yes** ☐ **No**

If you checked the "Yes" box: (1) Enter the name of the state where you are required to pay contributions . . . . . ▶ _CALIFORNIA_

(2) Enter your state reporting number(s) as shown on state unemployment tax return. ▶ _12-34567_

C If any part of wages taxable for FUTA tax is exempt from state unemployment tax, check the box. (See the Specific Instructions on page 2.). . . . . ☐

Part I Computation of Taxable Wages and Credit Reduction (to be completed by all taxpayers)

1	Total payments (including exempt payments) during the calendar year for services of employees	**1**	39,000	00
2	Exempt payments. (Explain each exemption shown, attaching additional sheets if necessary.) ▶ _____	Amount paid		
		2	_None_	
3	Payments for services of more than $7,000. Enter only the excess over the first $7,000 paid to individual employees not including exempt amounts shown on line 2. Do not use the state wage limitation.	**3**	_18,000_	
4	Total exempt payments (add lines 2 and 3)	**4**	18,000	00
5	**Total taxable wages** (subtract line 4 from line 1). (If any part is exempt from state contributions, see instructions.) ▶	**5**	21,000	00

Part II Tax Due or Refund (Complete if you checked the "Yes" boxes in both questions A and B and did not check the box in C above.)

1	**Total FUTA tax.** Multiply the wages in Part I, line 5, by .008 and enter here	**1**	168	00
2	Minus: Total FUTA tax deposited for the year, including any overpayment applied from a prior year (from your records)	**2**	104	00
3	**Balance due** (subtract line 2 from line 1). This should be $100 or less. Pay to IRS . . . . ▶	**3**	64	00
4	**Overpayment** (subtract line 1 from line 2). Check if it is to be: ☐ Applied to next return, or ☐ Refunded . ▶	**4**		

Part III Tax Due or Refund (Complete if you checked the "No" box in either question A or B or you checked the box in C above. Also complete Part V.)

1	Gross FUTA tax. Multiply the wages in Part I, line 5, by .062	**1**		
2	Maximum credit. Multiply the wages in Part I, line 5, by .054 . .	**2**		
3	**Credit allowable:** Enter the smaller of the amount in Part V, line 11, or Part III, line 2 . .	**3**		
4	**Total FUTA tax** (subtract line 3 from line 1).	**4**		
5	Minus: Total FUTA tax deposited for the year, including any overpayment applied from a prior year (from your records)	**5**		
6	**Balance due** (subtract line 5 from line 4). This should be $100 or less. Pay to IRS . . . . ▶	**6**		
7	**Overpayment** (subtract line 4 from line 5). Check if it is to be: ☐ Applied to next return, or ☐ Refunded . ▶	**7**		

Part IV Record of Quarterly Federal Tax Liability for Unemployment Tax (Do not include state liability.)

Quarter	First	Second	Third	Fourth	Total for Year
Liability for quarter			104.00	64.00	168.00

Part V Computation of Tentative Credit (Complete if you checked the "No" box in either question A or B or you checked the box in C, on page 1—see instructions.)

Name of state	State reporting number(s) as shown on employer's state contribution returns	Taxable payroll (as defined in state act)	State experience rate period		State experience rate	Contributions if rate had been 5.4% (col. 3 x .054)	Contributions payable at experience rate (col. 3 x col. 5)	Additional credit (col. 6 minus col.7) If 0 or less, enter 0.	Contributions actually paid to the state
			From—	To—					
1	**2**	**3**	**4**		**5**	**6**	**7**	**8**	**9**

10 Totals . . . . ▶

11 Total tentative credit (add line 10, columns 8 and 9—see instructions for limitations) . . . . ▶

If you will not have to file returns in the future, write "Final" here (see general instruction "Who Must File") and sign the return. ▶

Under penalties of perjury, I declare that I have examined this return, including accompanying schedules and statements, and to the best of my knowledge and belief, it is true, correct, and complete, and that no part of any payment made to a state unemployment fund claimed as a credit was or is to be deducted from the payments to employees.

Signature ▶ _Harry P. Kayhill_   Title (Owner, etc.) ▶ _OWNER_   Date ▶ _1-27-90_

Form **940** (1988)

Paperwork Reduction Act Notice.—We ask for this information to carry out the Internal Revenue laws of the United States. We need it to ensure that taxpayers are complying with these laws and to allow us to figure and collect the right amount of tax. You are required to give us this information.

The time needed to complete and file this form will vary depending on individual circumstances. The estimated average time is:

Recordkeeping . . . . . 14 hours, 7 minutes

**Learning about the
law or form** . . . . 18 minutes

**Preparing and sending
the form to IRS** . . . . 32 minutes

If you have comments concerning the accuracy of these time estimates or suggestions for making this form more simple, we would be happy to hear from you. You can write to the **Internal Revenue Service,** Washington, DC 20224, Attention: IRS Reports Clearance Officer, TR:FP; or the Office of **Management and Budget,** Paperwork Reduction Project, Washington, DC 20503.

Changes You Should Note

Extension of the Federal Unemployment (FUTA) Tax Rate.—The gross FUTA tax rate will remain at 6.2% through 1990. Since the credit against the FUTA tax for payments to state unemployment funds stays at a maximum of 5.4%, the net FUTA tax rate for 1988 remains at 0.8% (.008). Therefore, you should have used the .008 rate to figure your deposits for 1988.

Credit Reduction States.—For 1988, there are no credit reduction states. The lines relating to credit reduction amounts have been removed from this form.

General Instructions

Purpose of Form.—Use this form for your annual FUTA tax report. **Only the employer pays this tax.**

Who Must File

Household Employers.—You do not have to file this form unless you paid cash wages of $1,000 or more in any calendar quarter in 1987 or 1988 for household work in a private home, local college club, or a local chapter of a college fraternity or sorority.
Note: *See Pub 926, Employment Taxes for Household Employers, for more information.*

In General.—You must file this form if you were other than a household or agricultural employer during 1987 or 1988, and you: (a) paid wages of $1,500 or more in any calendar quarter, or (b) had one or more employees for some part of a day in any 20 different weeks. Count all regular, temporary, and part-time employees. A partnership should not count its partners. If there is a change in ownership or other transfer of business during the year, each employer who meets test (a) or (b) above must file. Neither should report wages paid by the other. Organizations described in section 501(c)(3) of the Internal Revenue Code do not have to file.

Agricultural Employers.—You must file Form 940 if either of the following applies to you:

(1) You paid cash wages of $20,000 or more to farmworkers during any calendar quarter in 1987 or 1988.

(2) You employed 10 or more farmworkers during some part of a day (whether or not at the same time) for at least one day during any 20 different weeks in 1987 or 1988. Count aliens admitted to the United States on a temporary basis to perform farmwork to determine if you meet either of the above tests. However, wages paid to these aliens are not subject to FUTA tax before 1993.

Completing Form 940

Employers Who Are Not Required To Deposit FUTA Tax.—If your total FUTA tax for 1988 is not more than $100, you do not have to deposit the tax. Make your FUTA tax payment when you file Form 940. If you do not have to deposit FUTA tax and you :

(a) made all required payments to state unemployment funds by the due date of Form 940,

(b) are required to make payments to the unemployment fund of only one state, and

(c) paid wages subject to Federal unemployment tax that are also subject to state unemployment tax,

complete Parts I and II. Otherwise, complete Parts I, III, and V.

Employers Who Are Required To Deposit FUTA Tax.—If you meet tests (a), (b), and (c) above, complete Parts I, II, and IV. Otherwise, complete Parts I, III, IV, and V.

If You Are Not Liable for FUTA Tax.—If you receive Form 940 and are not liable for FUTA tax for 1988, write "Not Liable" across the front and return it to IRS. If you will not have to file returns after this, write "Final" on the line above the signature line and sign the return.

Due Date.—Form 940 for 1988 is due by January 31, 1989. However, if you made timely deposits in full payment of the tax due, your due date is February 10, 1989.

Where To File.—

If your principal business, office or agency is located in:	File with the Internal Revenue Service Center at:
Florida, Georgia, South Carolina	Atlanta, GA 39901
New Jersey, New York (New York City and counties of Nassau, Rockland, Suffolk, and Westchester)	Holtsville, NY 00501
New York (all other counties), Connecticut, Maine, Massachusetts, New Hampshire, Rhode Island, Vermont	Andover, MA 05501
Illinois, Iowa, Minnesota, Missouri, Wisconsin	Kansas City, MO 64999
Delaware, District of Columbia, Maryland, Pennsylvania, Puerto Rico, Virginia, Virgin Islands	Philadelphia, PA 19255
Indiana, Kentucky, Michigan, Ohio, West Virginia	Cincinnati, OH 45999
Kansas, New Mexico, Oklahoma, Texas	Austin, TX 73301
Alaska, Arizona, California (counties of Alpine, Amador, Butte, Calaveras, Colusa, Contra Costa, Del Norte, El Dorado, Glenn, Humboldt, Lake, Lassen, Marin, Mendocino, Modoc, Napa, Nevada, Placer, Plumas, Sacramento, San Joaquin, Shasta, Sierra, Siskiyou, Solano, Sonoma, Sutter, Tehama, Trinity, Yolo, and Yuba), Colorado, Idaho, Montana, Nebraska, Nevada, North Dakota, Oregon, South Dakota, Utah, Washington, Wyoming	Ogden, UT 84201
California (all other counties), Hawaii	Fresno, CA 93888
Alabama, Arkansas, Louisiana, Mississippi, North Carolina, Tennessee	Memphis, TN 37501

If you have no legal residence or principal place of business in any IRS district, file with the Internal Revenue Service Center, Philadelphia, PA 19255.

Employer's Name, Address, and Identification Number.—Use the preaddressed Form 940 mailed to you. If you must use a nonpreaddressed form, type or print your name, trade name, address, and employer identification number on it.

See **Publication 583,** Information for Business Taxpayers, for details on how to make tax deposits, file a return, etc., if these are due before you receive your number.

Identifying Your Payments.—On balance due payments made to IRS (Part II, line 3 and Part III, line 6) and Federal tax deposit payments, write your

employer identification number, "Form 940," and the tax period to which the payment applies on your check or money order. This will help ensure proper crediting of your account.

Penalties and Interest.—Avoid penalties and interest by making tax deposits when due, filing a correct return and paying the proper amount of tax when due. The law provides penalties for late deposits and late filing unless you show reasonable cause for the delay. If you file late, attach an explanation to the return. The law also provides a penalty of 25% of the overstatement if, without reasonable cause, you overstate the amount you deposited.

There are also penalties for willful failure to pay tax, keep records, make returns, and for filing false or fraudulent returns.

Credit for Contributions Paid Into State Funds.—You can claim credit for amounts you pay into a certified state (including Puerto Rico and the Virgin Islands) unemployment fund by the due date of Form 940.

Note: *Be sure to enter your state reporting number where required on Form 940. This number is needed for IRS to verify your state contributions.*

"Contributions" are payments that state law requires you to make to an unemployment fund because you are an employer. These payments are "contributions" only to the extent that they are not deducted or deductible from the employees' pay.

Do not take credit for penalties, interest, surcharges, and special taxes which are in addition to the rate assigned by the state. Also do not take credit for voluntary contributions paid to obtain a lower assigned rate.

If you have been assigned an experience rate lower than 5.4% (.054) by a state for the whole or part of the year, you are entitled to an additional credit. This credit is equal to the difference between actual payments and the amount you would have been required to pay at 5.4%.

The total credit allowable may not be more than 5.4% of taxable FUTA wages.

Special Credit for Successor Employers.—If you are claiming special credit as a successor employer, see Code section 3302(e) or Circular E, for the conditions you must meet.

Amended Returns.—If you are amending a previously filed return, complete a new Form 940, using the amounts that should have been used on the original return, and sign the return. Attach a statement explaining why you are filing an amended return. Be sure to use a Form 940 for the year you are amending. Write "AMENDED RETURN" at the top of the form and file it with the Internal Revenue Service Center where you filed the original return.

Specific Instructions

You must answer questions A and B (check the box in C only if it applies), complete Part I, and sign the return.

Note: *If you have been assigned a zero percent experience rate by your state, so that there are no required contributions to the state unemployment fund, check the "Yes" box in question A and write "0% rate" on the dollar amount line.*

Use Part II only if you checked the "Yes" boxes in questions A and B and did not check the box in C. Otherwise, skip Part II and complete Parts III and V.

Complete Part IV if your total tax for the year is more than $100.

Box C.—Check this box **ONLY** if you pay any wages that are taxable for FUTA tax but are exempt from your state's unemployment tax.

(Instructions continued on page 4.)

JOB SAFETY & HEALTH PROTECTION

The Occupational Safety and Health Act of 1970 provides job safety and health protection for workers by promoting safe and healthful working conditions throughout the Nation. Requirements of the Act include the following:

Employers

All employers must furnish to employees employment and a place of employment free from recognized hazards that are causing or are likely to cause death or serious harm to employees. Employers must comply with occupational safety and health standards issued under the Act.

Employees

Employees must comply with all occupational safety and health standards, rules, regulations and orders issued under the Act that apply to their own actions and conduct on the job.

The Occupational Safety and Health Administration (OSHA) of the U.S. Department of Labor has the primary responsibility for administering the Act. OSHA issues occupational safety and health standards, and its Compliance Safety and Health Officers conduct jobsite inspections to help ensure compliance with the Act.

Inspection

The Act requires that a representative of the employer and a representative authorized by the employees be given an opportunity to accompany the OSHA inspector for the purpose of aiding the inspection.

Where there is no authorized employee representative, the OSHA Compliance Officer must consult with a reasonable number of employees concerning safety and health conditions in the workplace.

Complaint

Employees or their representatives have the right to file a complaint with the nearest OSHA office requesting an inspection if they believe unsafe or unhealthful conditions exist in their workplace. OSHA will withhold, on request, names of employees complaining.

The Act provides that employees may not be discharged or discriminated against in any way for filing safety and health complaints or for otherwise exercising their rights under the Act.

Employees who believe they have been discriminated against may file a complaint with their nearest OSHA office within 30 days of the alleged discrimination.

Citation

If upon inspection OSHA believes an employer has violated the Act, a citation alleging such violations will be issued to the employer. Each citation will specify a time period within which the alleged violation must be corrected

The OSHA citation must be prominently displayed at or near the place of alleged violation for three days, or until it is corrected, whichever is later, to warn employees of dangers that may exist there.

Proposed Penalty

The Act provides for mandatory penalties against employers of up to $1,000 for each serious violation and for optional penalties of up to $1,000 for each nonserious violation. Penalties of up to $1,000 per day may be proposed for failure to correct violations within the proposed time period. Also, any employer who willfully or repeatedly violates the Act may be assessed penalties of up to $10,000 for each such violation.

Criminal penalties are also provided for in the Act. Any willful violation resulting in death of an employee, upon conviction, is punishable by a fine of not more than $10,000, or by imprisonment for not more than six months, or by both. Conviction of an employer after a first conviction doubles these maximum penalties.

Voluntary Activity

While providing penalties for violations, the Act also encourages efforts by labor and management, before an OSHA inspection, to reduce workplace hazards voluntarily and to develop and improve safety and health programs in all workplaces and industries. OSHA's Voluntary Protection Programs recognize outstanding efforts of this nature.

Such voluntary action should initially focus on the identification and elimination of hazards that could cause death, injury, or illness to employees and supervisors. There are many public and private organizations that can provide information and assistance in this effort, if requested. Also, your local OSHA office can provide considerable help and advice on solving safety and health problems or can refer you to other sources for help such as training.

Consultation

Free consultative assistance, without citation or penalty, is available to employers, on request, through OSHA supported programs in most State departments of labor or health.

More Information

Additional information and copies of the Act, specific OSHA safety and health standards, and other applicable regulations may be obtained from your employer or from the nearest OSHA Regional Office in the following locations:

Atlanta, Georgia
Boston, Massachusetts
Chicago, Illinois
Dallas, Texas
Denver, Colorado
Kansas City, Missouri
New York, New York
Philadelphia, Pennsylvania
San Francisco, California
Seattle, Washington

Telephone numbers for these offices, and additional area office locations, are listed in the telephone directory under the United States Department of Labor in the United States Government listing.

Washington, D.C.
1985
OSHA 2203

William E. Brock

William E. Brock, Secretary of Labor

U.S. Department of Labor
Occupational Safety and Health Administration

Under provisions of Title 29, Code of Federal Regulations, Part 1903.2(a)(1) employers must post this notice (or a facsimile) in a conspicuous place where notices to employees are customarily posted.

Exhibit 6-13

Log and Summary of Occupational
Injuries and Illnesses

State of California
Department of Industrial Relations
Division of Labor Statistics and Research

For Calendar Year 19 _____   Page ___ of ___

Form Approved
O.M.B. No. 1220-0029

Company Name

Establishment Name

Establishment Address

NOTE: This form is required by Public Law 91-596 and State of California Labor Code, Section 6410 and must be kept in the establishment for 5 years. Failure to maintain and post can result in the issuance of citations and assessment of penalties.
(See posting requirements on the other side of form.)

RECORDABLE CASES: You are required to record information about every occupational death, every nonfatal occupational illness, and those nonfatal occupational injuries which involve one or more of the following: loss of consciousness, restriction of work or motion, transfer to another job, or medical treatment (other than first aid).
(See definitions on the other side of form.)

Case or File Number	Date of Injury or Onset of Illness	Employee's Name	Occupation	Department	Description of Injury or Illness
Enter a nonduplicating number which will facilitate comparisons with supplementary records.	Enter Mo./day.	Enter first name or initial, middle initial, last name.	Enter regular job title, not activity employee was performing when injured or at onset of illness. In the absence of a formal title, enter a brief description of the employee's duties.	Enter department in which the employee is regularly employed or a description of normal workplace to which employee is assigned, even though temporarily working in another department at the time of injury or illness.	Enter a brief description of the injury or illness and indicate the part or parts of body affected. Typical entries for this column might be: Amputation of 1st joint right forefinger, Strain of lower back, Contact dermatitis on both hands, Electrocution—body.
(A)	(B)	(C)	(D)	(E)	(F)

Extent of and Outcome of INJURY

Fatalities	Nonfatal Injuries				
Injury Related	Injuries With Lost Workdays				Injuries Without Lost Workdays
Enter DATE of death. Mo./day/yr.	Enter a CHECK if injury involves days away from work, or days of restricted work activity, or both.	Enter a CHECK if injury involves days away from work.	Enter number of DAYS away from work.	Enter number of DAYS of restricted work activity.	Enter a CHECK if no entry was made in columns 1 or 2 but the injury is recordable as defined above.
(1)	(2)	(3)	(4)	(5)	(6)

Type, Extent, and Outcome of ILLNESS

Type of Illness	Fatalities	Nonfatal Illnesses			
CHECK Only One Column for Each Illness (See other side of form for terminations or permanent transfers.)	Illness Related	Illnesses With Lost Workdays			Illnesses Without Lost Workdays

Type of Illness columns (a–g):
(a) Occupational skin diseases or disorders
(b) Dust diseases of the lungs
(c) Respiratory conditions due to toxic agents
(d) Poisoning (systemic effects of toxic materials)
(e) Disorders due to physical agents
(f) Disorders associated with repeated trauma
(g) All other occupational illnesses

	Enter DATE of death. Mo./day/yr.	Enter a CHECK if illness involves days away from work, or days of restricted work activity, or both.	Enter a CHECK if illness involves days away from work.	Enter number of DAYS away from work.	Enter number of DAYS of restricted work activity.	Enter a CHECK if no entry was made in columns 8 or 9.
(7)	(8)	(9)	(10)	(11)	(12)	(13)

PREVIOUS PAGE TOTALS →

FOLD

Certification of Annual Summary Totals By _____   Title _____   Date _____

POST ONLY THIS PORTION OF THE LAST PAGE NO LATER THAN FEBRUARY 1.

CAL/OSHA No. 200

Exhibit 6-14

SAFETY AND HEALTH PROTECTION ON THE JOB

State of California
Department of Industrial Relations

The California Occupational Safety and Health Act of 1973 provides job safety and health protection for workers. The Department of Industrial Relations has primary responsibility for administering the CAL/OSHA program. Job safety and health standards are promulgated by the Occupational Safety and Health Standards Board. Employers and employees are required to comply with these standards. Enforcement is carried out by the Division of Occupational Safety and Health within the Department of Industrial Relations.

EMPLOYERS AND EMPLOYEES

California law requires every employer to provide employment and a place of employment which are safe and healthful for the employees therein. Employers and employees are required to comply with the occupational safety and health standards contained in Title 8 of the California Administrative Code and all rules, regulations and orders pursuant to Division 5 of the California Labor Code which are applicable to their employment and actions on the job.

COMPLIANCE WITH JOB SAFETY AND HEALTH REQUIREMENTS

To ensure compliance with State job safety and health requirements, the Division of Occupational Safety and Health conducts periodic job site inspections. The inspections are made by trained safety engineers and industrial hygienists.

The law provides that an authorized representative of the employer and a representative of the employees be given an opportunity to accompany the safety engineer/industrial hygienist for the purpose of aiding the inspection. Where there is no authorized employee representative, the safety engineer/industrial hygienist talks with a reasonable number of employees about the safety and health conditions in the workplace.

Every employee has the right to bring unsafe or unhealthful conditions to the attention of the safety engineer/industrial hygienist making the inspection. In addition, any employee who believes unsafe or unhealthful conditions exist at the worksite has the right to notify the Division of Occupational Safety and Health. The Division upon request will withhold the names of employees who submit or make statements during an inspection or investigation.

If the Division of Occupational Safety and Health believes that an employer has violated a safety and health standard or order, it issues a citation to the employer. Each citation specifies a date by which the alleged violation must be corrected. The law provides for mandatory penalties against employers of up to $2,000 for each serious violation and for optional penalties of up to $1,000 for each general violation. Penalties of up to $2,000 per day may be proposed for failure to correct serious violations and up to $1,000 per day may be proposed for failure to correct general violations by the abatement date. Also any employer who willfully or repeatedly violates any occupational safety and health standard or order may be assessed civil penalties of not more than $20,000 for serious violations and $10,000 for general violations.

A willful violation that causes death or permanent impairment of the body of any employee results, upon conviction, in a fine of not more than $10,000 or imprisonment of not more than six months, or both. A second conviction, after a first conviction, doubles these maximum penalties.

While governmental entities may be cited on the same basis as other employers, and abatement dates set, civil penalties will not be assessed.

An employer who receives a citation, Order to Take Special Action or Special Order must post it prominently at or near the place of the violation for three working days, or until the unsafe condition is corrected, whichever is longer, to warn employees of danger that may exist there. Any employee may protest the time allowed for correction of the violation.

COMPLAINTS

Employees or their representatives who believe unsafe or unhealthful conditions exist in their workplace have the right to file a complaint with any office of the Division of Occupational Safety and Health and thereby request an inspection. The Division keeps confidential the names of complainants unless they request otherwise.

An employee may not be fired or punished in any way for filing a complaint about unsafe or unhealthful working conditions or using any other right given to employees by the CAL/OSHA law. An employee of a private employer who believes that he/she has been fired or punished for exercising such rights may file a complaint about this discrimination with the nearest office of the Department of Industrial Relations—Division of Labor Standards Enforcement (State Labor Commissioner) or with the San Francisco office of the U.S. Department of Labor, Occupational Safety and Health Administration. Employees of state or local government agencies may file discrimination complaints only with the State Labor Commissioner. See addresses below.

OTHER EMPLOYEE RIGHTS

Any employee has the right to refuse to perform work which would violate the CAL/OSHA Act or any occupational safety or health standard or order where such violation would create a real and apparent hazard to the employee or other employees.

Employers who use any substance listed as a hazardous substance in Section 339 of Title 8 of the California Administrative Code or subject to the Federal Hazard Communication Standard (29 CFRS 1910.1200) must provide employees with information on the contents of material safety data sheets (MSDS) or equivalent information about the substance which trains employees to use the substance safely.

Employers shall make available on a timely and reasonable basis a material safety data sheet on each hazardous substance in the workplace upon request of an employee collective bargaining representative, or an employee's physician.

Employees have the right to see and copy their medical records and accurate records of employee exposure to potentially toxic materials or harmful physical agents.

Any employee has the right to observe monitoring or measuring of employee exposure to hazards conducted pursuant to CAL/OSHA standards. Employers must tell their employees when they are being, or have been, exposed to concentrations of harmful substances higher than the exposure limits allowed by CAL/OSHA standards, and the corrective action being taken.

For information and assistance, contact the nearest office of the Division of Occupational Safety and Health. See addresses below.

The law requires each employer in California to post this poster conspicuously in each workplace.

CONSULTATION SERVICE

In order to encourage voluntary compliance, CAL/OSHA provides free, upon request, a full range of occupational safety and health consulting services. The CAL/OSHA Consultation Service is separate from CAL/OSHA enforcement activities.

DIVISION OF LABOR STANDARDS ENFORCEMENT

HEADQUARTERS	OFICINA PRINCIPAL		
San Francisco	P.O. Box 603	94101	(415) 557-3827

DISTRICT OFFICES	OFICINAS DISTRITALES		
Bakersfield	5555 California Ave.	93309	(805) 395-2710
El Centro	380 N. Eighth St.	92243	(619) 353-0585
Eureka	619 Second St.	95501	(707) 442-5748
Fresno	666 W. Shaw Ave.	93704	(209) 221-5005
Hollywood	6430 Sunset Blvd.	90028	(213) 736-3161
Inglewood	1 Manchester Blvd.	90301	(213) 412-6380
Long Beach	245 W. Broadway	90802	(213) 590-5044
Los Angeles	107 S. Broadway	90012	(213) 620-5130
Marysville	922 G Street	95901	(916) 741-4061
Napa	3273 Claremont Way	94558	(707) 257-0660
Oakland	1111 Jackson St.	94607	(415) 464-1353
Pomona	300 S. Park Ave.	91766	(714) 622-4236
Redding	2115 Akard Ave.	96001	(916) 225-2654
Sacramento	2422 Arden Way	95825	(916) 920-6116
Salinas	21 W. Laurel Dr.	93906	(408) 443-3040
San Bernardino	303 W. Third St.	92401	(714) 383-4333
San Diego	8765 Aero Dr.	92123	(619) 237-7334
San Francisco	525 Golden Gate Ave.	94102	(415) 557-0860
San Jose	100 Paseo de San Antonio	95113	(408) 277-1265
San Mateo	1900 S. Norfolk St.	94403	(415) 572-9424
Santa Ana	28 Civic Center Plaza	92701	(714) 558-4115
Santa Barbara	411 E. Canon Perdido St.	93101	(805) 963-1438
Santa Rosa	50 D St.	95404	(707) 576-2390
Stockton	31 E. Channel St.	95202	(209) 948-7770
Van Nuys	6150 Van Nuys Blvd.	91401	(818) 901-5312
Ventura	5720 Ralston St.	93003	(805) 654-4538
Whittier	13215 E. Penn St.	90602	(213) 698-2278

OFFICES OF THE DIVISION OF OCCI

OFICINAS DE LA DIVISION DE SEGI

HEADQUARTERS/OFICINA PRINCIPAL

San Francisco	525 Golden Gate Ave.	94102	(415) 557-1946

REGIONAL OFFICES/OFICINAS REGIONALES

Los Angeles	3460 Wilshire Blvd.	90010	(213) 736-3024
Sacramento	2422 Arden Way	95825	(916) 920-6127
San Francisco	455 Golden Gate Ave.	94102	(415) 557-8640
Santa Ana	28 Civic Center Plaza	92701	(714) 558-4476
Van Nuys	6150 Van Nuys Blvd.	91401	(818) 901-5411

DISTRICT OFFICES/OFICINAS DISTRITALES

Bakersfield	4800 Stockdale Hwy.	93309	(805) 395-2718
Berkeley	1625 Shattuck Ave.	94709	(415) 540-3030
Concord	1465 Enea Circle.	94520	(415) 676-5333
Covina	233 N. Second Ave.	91723	(818) 331-4875
Fresno	2550 Mariposa Street	93721	(209) 445-5302
Long Beach	245 W. Broadway	90802	(213) 590-5035
Los Angeles	3460 Wilshire Blvd.	90010	(213) 736-3041
Modesto	1800 Coffee Road	95355	(209) 576-6260
Redding	1421 Court Street	96001	(916) 225-2885
Sacramento	2422 Arden Way	95825	(916) 920-6123

OCCUPATIONAL CANCER CONTROL/C

San Francisco	525 Golden G...

Persons wishing to register a complaint alleging inadequacy in the administration of the California Occupational Safety and Health Plan may do so at the following address: Occupational Safety and Health Administration, U.S. Department of Labor (OSHA), Federal Building, 450 Golden Gate Ave., Box 36017, San Francisco, California 94102. Phone (415) 556-9497. OSHA monitors the operation of State plans to assure that continued approval is merited.

MAY 1986

Exhibit 6-15

ORDER 4-80
Title 8, Calif. Administrative Code 11040

Replacing former Orders 1-76 and MW-78 effective January 1, 1980

INDUSTRIAL WELFARE COMMISSION ORDER NO. 4-80 REGULATING WAGES, HOURS, AND WORKING CONDITIONS IN THE PROFESSIONAL, TECHNICAL, CLERICAL, MECHANICAL AND SIMILAR OCCUPATIONS

ORDER 4-80
PROFESSIONAL, TECHNICAL, CLERICAL, AND MECHANICAL OCCUPATIONS

TO WHOM IT MAY CONCERN:

TAKE NOTICE: That the Industrial Welfare Commission of the State of California has reviewed the order for these occupations, as mandated by Labor Code Section 1173, for the purpose of updating it to the extent found by the Commission to be necessary to provide reasonable wages, hours, and working conditions appropriate for all employees in the modern society; that the Commission called wage boards as required by Labor Code Sections 1178 and 1184 before promulgating and amending each of the previous succeeding orders setting standards for these occupations and, in this review, considered the recommendations of the wage board for the Professional, Technical, Clerical, Mechanical and Similar Occupations, which met on April 11–12, 1979; that the Commission has proceeded in accord with the authority vested in it by Labor Code Sections 1171 through 1204 and Article 14, Section 1 of the Constitution of the State of California; that it has considered all written material and information submitted and has held public hearings and given notice of said hearings as provided by law; that the Commission has, upon its own motion, concluded that its Order No. 4-76, regulating the Professional, Technical, Clerical, Mechanical and Similar Occupations, should be altered and amended to provide for the welfare of employees as specified in Labor Code Section 1182 and has explained such amendments in a statement as to the basis upon which they are predicated.

NOW, THEREFORE, the Industrial Welfare Commission of the State of California does hereby promulgate this Professional, Technical, Clerical, Mechanical and Similar Occupations Order No. 4-80, which alters, amends and supersedes any previous order regulating said occupations, including Order 4-76 and Minimum Wage Order MW-78, and includes in this Order 4-80 the statement as to the basis upon which said order is predicated, in which a majority of the Commission concurred on September 7, 1979. This statement as to the basis of this order includes all of the above and that which is set forth on the reverse side of this order, which is incorporated herein as if fully set forth.

1. APPLICABILITY OF ORDER

This Order shall apply to all persons employed in the professional, technical, clerical, mechanical and similar occupations whether paid on a time, piece rate, commission, or other basis unless such occupation is performed in an industry covered by an industry order of this commission, except that:

(A) Provisions of Sections 3 through 12 shall not apply to persons employed in administrative, executive or professional capacities. No person shall be considered to be employed in an administrative, executive or professional capacity unless one of the following conditions prevails:

(1) The employee is engaged in work which is primarily intellectual, managerial, or creative, and which requires exercise of discretion and independent judgment, and for which the remuneration is not less than $900.00 per month; or

(2) The employee is licensed or certified by the State of California and is engaged in the practice of one of the following recognized professions: law, medicine, dentistry, pharmacy, optometry, architecture, engineering, teaching, or accounting.

(B) The provisions of this Order shall not apply to employees directly employed by the State or any county, incorporated city or town or other municipal corporation, or to outside salespersons.

(C) Provisions of this Order shall not apply to any individual who is the parent, spouse, child, or legally adopted child of the employer.

2. DEFINITIONS

(A) "Commission" means the Industrial Welfare Commission of the State of California.

(B) "Division" means the Division of Labor Standards Enforcement of the State of California.

(C) "Professional, Technical, Clerical, Mechanical and Similar Occupations" includes professional, semiprofessional, managerial, supervisorial, laboratory, research, technical, clerical, office work, and mechanical occupations. Said occupations shall include, but not be limited to, the following: accountants; agents; appraisers; artists; attendants; audio-visual technicians; bookkeepers; bundlers; billposters; canvassers; carriers; cashiers; checkers; clerks; collectors; communications and sound technicians; compilers; copy holders; copy readers; copy writers; computer programmers and operators; demonstrators and display representatives; dispatchers; distributors; doorkeepers; drafters; elevator operators; estimators; editors; graphic arts technicians; guards; guides; hosts; inspectors; installers; instructors; interviewers; investigators; librarians; laboratory workers; machine operators; mechanics; mailers; messengers; medical and dental technicians and technologists; models; nurses; packagers; photographers; porters and cleaners; process servers; printers; proof readers; salespersons and sales agents; secretaries; sign erectors; sign painters; social workers; solicitors; statisticians; stenographers; teachers; telephone, radio-telephone, telegraph and call-out operators; tellers; ticket agents; tracers; typists; vehicle operators; x-ray technicians; their assistants and other related occupations listed as professional, semiprofessional, technical, clerical, mechanical, and kindred occupations.

(D) "Emergency" means an unpredictable or unavoidable occurrence at unscheduled intervals requiring immediate action.

(E) "Employ" means to engage, suffer, or permit to work.

(F) "Employee" means any person employed by an employer.

(G) "Employer" means any person as defined in Section 18 of the Labor Code, who directly or indirectly, or through an agent or any other person, employs or exercises control over the wages, hours, or working conditions of any person.

(H) "Hours worked" means the time during which an employee is subject to the control of an employer, and includes all the time the employee is suffered or permitted to work, whether or not required to do so.

(I) "Minor" means, for the purpose of this Order, any person under the age of eighteen (18) years.

(J) "Outside Salesperson" means any person, 18 years of age or over, who customarily and regularly works more than half the working time away from the employer's place of business selling tangible or intangible items or obtaining orders or contracts for products, services or use of facilities.

(K) "Primarily" as used in Section 1, Applicability, means more than one-half the employee's work time.

(L) "Split shift" means a work schedule which is interrupted by non-paid non-working periods established by the employer, other than bona fide rest or meal periods.

(M) "Teaching" means, for the purpose of Section 1 of this Order, the profession of teaching under a certificate from the Commission for Teacher Preparation and Licensing or teaching in an accredited college or university.

(N) "Wages" means all amounts paid for labor performed by employees of every description, whether the amount is fixed or ascertained by the standard of time, task, piece, commission basis or other method of calculation.

(O) "Workday" means any consecutive 24 hours beginning at the same time each calendar day.

(P) "Workweek" means any seven (7) consecutive days, starting with the same calendar day each week. "Workweek" is a fixed and regularly recurring

State of California
Department of Industrial Relations
DIVISION OF LABOR STANDARDS ENFORCEMENT
Administrative Office:
525 Golden Gate Ave., San Francisco 94102
(P. O. Box 603, San Francisco 94101)

District offices are located in the following cities. Consult the white pages of your local telephone directory under CALIFORNIA, State of, Industrial Relations, Labor Standards Enforcement, for the address and telephone number.

BAKERSFIELD	SALINAS
EL CENTRO	SAN BERNARDINO
EUREKA	SAN DIEGO
FRESNO	SAN FRANCISCO
HOLLYWOOD	SAN JOSE
INGLEWOOD	SAN MATEO
LONG BEACH	SANTA ANA
LOS ANGELES	SANTA BARBARA
MARYSVILLE	SANTA ROSA
NAPA	STOCKTON
OAKLAND	VAN NUYS
POMONA	VENTURA
REDDING	WHITTIER
SACRAMENTO	

Labor Standards Enforcement is one of the eight major programs administered by the State Department of Industrial Relations to protect Californians at work.

(4) After a lapse of twelve (12) months and upon petition of a majority of the affected employees a new vote shall be held and a two-thirds (2/3) vote of the affected employees will be required to reverse the agreement above. If such agreement is revoked the employer shall comply within sixty (60) days. Upon a proper showing by the employer of undue hardship the Division may grant an extension of the time for compliance.

(C) Provisions of subsections (A) and (B) above shall not apply to any employee whose earnings exceed one and one-half (1½) times the minimum wage if more than half (½) of that employee's compensation represents commissions.

(D) No minor shall be employed more than eight (8) hours in any workday or more than six (6) days in any workweek. One and one-half (1½) times the minor's regular rate of pay shall be paid for all work over forty (40) hours in any workweek. No minor shall be employed before 5 o'clock in the morning or after 10 o'clock in the evening, except that during any evening preceding a non-school day a minor may work the hours authorized by this section until 12:30 o'clock in the morning of such non-school day.

(1) Notwithstanding the preceding provisions of this subsection, minors sixteen (16) and seventeen (17) years old who are not required by law to attend school may be employed for the same hours as an adult. Minors so permitted to work shall be subject to subsection (A) or (B) above.

(E) Minors sixteen (16) and seventeen (17) years of age who are enrolled in work experience education programs approved by the State Department of Education or in work experience education programs conducted by private schools may work after 10 p.m. but not later than 12:30 a.m. providing such employment is not detrimental to the health, education or welfare of the minor and the approval of the parent and the work experience coordinator has been obtained. However, any such minor who works any time during the hours from 10 p.m. to 12:30 a.m., shall be paid for work during that time at a rate which is not less than the minimum wage required for adults.

(VIOLATIONS OF CHILD LABOR LAWS are subject to civil penalties of from $100 to $5,000 as well as to criminal penalties provided herein. Refer to California Labor Code Sections 1285 to 1311 and 1390 to 1398 for additional restrictions on the employment of minors.)

(F) An employee may be employed on seven (7) workdays in one workweek with no overtime pay required when the total hours of employment during such workweek do not exceed thirty (30) and the total hours of employment in any one workday thereof do not exceed six (6).

(G) If a meal period occurs on a shift beginning or ending at or between the hours of 10 p.m. and 6 a.m., facilities shall be available for securing hot food or drink or for heating food or drink, and a suitable sheltered place shall be provided in which to consume such food or drink.

(H) Except as provided in subsections (D), (E), (G), and (J), this section shall not apply to any employee covered by a collective bargaining agreement if said agreement provides premium wage rates for overtime work and a cash wage rate for such employee of not less than one dollar ($1.00) per hour more than the minimum wage.

(I) The provisions of this section are not applicable to employees whose hours of service are regulated by (1) the United States Department of Transportation Code of Federal Regulations, Title 49, Sections 395.1 to 395.13, Hours of Service of Drivers, or (2) Title 13 of the California Administrative Code Subchapter 6.5, sec. 1200 and following sections, regulating hours of drivers.

(J) No employee shall be terminated or otherwise disciplined for refusing to work more than 72 hours in any workweek, except in an emergency as defined in Section 2(D).

4. MINIMUM WAGES

(A) Every employer shall pay to each employee wages not less than three dollars and ten cents ($3.10) per hour for all hours worked, effective January 1, 1980, and three dollars and thirty-five cents ($3.35) per hour for all hours worked, effective January 1, 1981, except:

(1) LEARNERS. Employees 18 years of age or over, during their first one hundred and sixty (160) hours of employment in occupations in which they have no previous similar or related experience, may be paid not less than eighty-five percent (85%) of the minimum wage rounded to the nearest nickel.

(2) MINORS may be paid not less than eighty-five percent (85%) of the minimum wage rounded to the nearest nickel provided that the number of minors employed at said lesser rate shall not exceed twenty-five percent (25%) of the persons regularly employed in the establishment. An employer of less than ten (10) persons may employ three (3) minors at said lesser rate. The twenty-five percent (25%) limitation on the employment of minors shall not apply during school vacations.

NOTE: Under certain conditions, the full minimum wage may be required for

less than the minimum wage. Such licenses shall be granted only upon joint application of employer and employee and employee's representative if any.

A special license may be issued to a nonprofit organization such as a sheltered workshop or rehabilitation facility fixing special minimum rates to enable the employment of such persons without requiring individual licenses of such employees.

All such licenses and special licenses shall be renewed on a yearly basis or more frequently at the discretion of the Division.

See California Labor Code, Sections 1191 and 1191.5.

7. RECORDS

(A) Every employer shall keep accurate information with respect to each employee including the following:

(1) Full name, home address, occupation and social security number.

(2) Birthdate, if under 18 years, and designation as a minor.

(3) Time records showing when the employee begins and ends each work period. Meal periods, split shift intervals and total daily hours worked shall also be recorded. Meal periods during which operations cease and authorized rest periods need not be recorded.

(4) Total wages paid each payroll period, including value of board, lodging, or other compensation actually furnished to the employee.

(5) Total hours worked in the payroll period and applicable rates of pay. This information shall be made readily available to the employee upon reasonable request.

(6) When a piece rate or incentive plan is in operation, piece rates or an explanation of the incentive plan formula shall be provided to employees. An accurate production record shall be maintained by the employer.

(B) Every employer shall semimonthly or at the time of each payment of wages furnish each employee either as a detachable part of the check, draft or voucher paying the employee's wages, or separately, an itemized statement in writing showing: (1) all deductions; (2) the inclusive dates of the period for which the employee is paid; (3) the name of the employee or the employee's social security number; and (4) the name of the employer, provided all deductions made on written orders of the employee may be aggregated and shown as one item.

(C) All required records shall be in the English language and in ink or other indelible form, properly dated, showing month, day and year, and shall be kept on file by the employer for at least three years at the place of employment or at a central location within the State of California. An employee's records shall be available for inspection by the employee upon reasonable request.

(D) Clocks shall be provided in all major work areas or within reasonable distance thereto insofar as practicable.

8. CASH SHORTAGE AND BREAKAGE

No employer shall make any deduction from the wage or require any reimbursement from an employee for any cash shortage, breakage or loss of equipment, unless it can be shown that the shortage, breakage or loss is caused by a dishonest or willful act, or by the gross negligence of the employee. Notwithstanding the foregoing provision, where an employee has the exclusive and personal control of cash funds of the employer and is required by the employer to account, under reasonable accounting procedures, for said funds, the employer may upon prior written notice require reimbursement from such employee for cash shortages.

9. UNIFORMS AND EQUIPMENT

(A) When uniforms are required by the employer to be worn by the employee as a condition of employment, such uniforms shall be provided and maintained by the employer. The term "uniform" includes wearing apparel and accessories of distinctive design or color.

NOTE: This section shall not apply to protective apparel regulated by the Occupational Safety and Health Standards Board.

(B) When tools or equipment are required by the employer or are necessary to the performance of a job, such tools and equipment shall be provided and maintained by the employer, except that an employee whose wages are at least two (2) times the minimum wage may be required to provide and maintain hand tools and equipment customarily required by the trade or craft. This subsection (B) shall not apply to apprentices regularly indentured under the State Division of Apprenticeship Standards.

NOTE: This section shall not apply to protective equipment and safety devices on tools regulated by the Occupational Safety and Health Standards Board.

(C) A reasonable deposit may be required as security for the return of the items furnished by the employer under provisions of subsections (A) and (B) of this section upon issuance of a receipt to the employee for such deposit. Such deposits shall be made pursuant to Section 400 and following of the Labor Code or an employer with the prior written authorization of the employee may deduct from the employee's last check the cost of an item furnished pursuant to (A) and (B) above in the event said item is not returned. No deduction shall be made at any time for normal wear and tear. All items furnished by the employer shall be returned by the employee upon completion of the job.

10. MEALS AND LODGING

(A) "Meal" means an adequate, well-balanced serving of a variety of wholesome, nutritious foods.

"Lodging" means living accommodations available to the employee for full-time occupancy which are adequate, decent, and sanitary according to usual and customary standards. Employees shall not be required to share a bed.

(B) Meals or lodging may not be credited against the minimum wage without a voluntary written agreement between the employer and the employee. When credit for meals or lodging is used to meet part of the employer's minimum wage obligation, the amounts so credited may not be more than the following:

	Effective Jan. 1, 1980	*Effective Jan. 1, 1981*
Room occupied alone	$ 15.00 per week	$ 16.00 per week
Room shared	$ 12.00 per week	$ 13.00 per week
Apartment—two-thirds (2/3) of the ordinary rental value, and in no event more than	$175.00 per month	$190.00 per month
Where a couple are both employed by the employer, two-thirds (2/3) of the ordinary rental value, and in no event more than	$260.00 per month	$290.00 per month
Meals:		
Breakfast	$1.10	$1.20
Lunch	$1.55	$1.65
Dinner	$2.05	$2.20

(C) Meals evaluated as part of the minimum wage must be bona fide meals consistent with the employee's work shift. Deductions shall not be made for meals not received nor lodging not used.

(D) If, as a condition of employment, the employee must live at the place of employment or occupy quarters owned or under the control of the employer, then the employer may not charge rent in excess of the values listed herein.

11. MEAL PERIODS

... employ any person for a work period of more than five

authorized rest period time shall be based on the total hours worked daily at the rate of ten (10) minutes net rest time per four (4) hours or major fraction thereof. However, a rest period need not be authorized for employees whose total daily work time is less than three and one-half (3½) hours. Authorized rest period time shall be counted as hours worked for which there shall be no deduction from wages.

13. CHANGE ROOMS AND RESTING FACILITIES

(A) Employers shall provide suitable lockers, closets, or equivalent for the safekeeping of employees' outer clothing during working hours, and when required, for their work clothing during non-working hours. When the occupation requires a change of clothing, change rooms or equivalent space shall be provided in order that employees may change their clothing in reasonable privacy and comfort. These rooms or spaces may be adjacent to but shall be separate from toilet rooms and shall be kept clean.

NOTE: This section shall not apply to change rooms and storage facilities regulated by the Occupational Safety and Health Standards Board.

(B) Suitable resting facilities shall be provided in an area separate from the toilet rooms and shall be available to employees during work hours.

14. SEATS

(A) All working employees shall be provided with suitable seats when the nature of the work reasonably permits the use of seats.

(B) When employees are not engaged in the active duties of their employment and the nature of the work requires standing, an adequate number of suitable seats shall be placed in reasonable proximity to the work area and employees shall be permitted to use such seats when it does not interfere with the performance of their duties.

15. TEMPERATURE

(A) The temperature maintained in each work area shall provide reasonable comfort consistent with industry-wide standards for the nature of the process and the work performed.

(B) If excessive heat or humidity is created by the work process, the employer shall take all feasible means to reduce such excessive heat or humidity to a degree providing reasonable comfort. Where the nature of the employment requires a temperature of less than 60° F., a heated room shall be provided to which employees may retire for warmth, and such room shall be maintained at not less than 68°.

(C) A temperature of not less than 68° shall be maintained in the toilet rooms, resting rooms, and change rooms during hours of use.

(D) Federal and State energy guidelines shall prevail over any conflicting provision of this section.

16. ELEVATORS

Adequate elevator, escalator or similar service consistent with industry-wide standards for the nature of the process and the work performed shall be provided when employees are employed four floors or more above or below ground level.

17. EXEMPTIONS

If, in the opinion of the Division after due investigation, it is found that the enforcement of any provision contained in Section 7, Records; Section 11, Meal Periods; Section 12, Rest Periods; Section 13, Change Rooms and Resting Facilities; Section 14, Seats; Section 15, Temperature; or Section 16, Elevators, would not materially affect the welfare or comfort of employees and would work an undue hardship on the employer, exemption may be made at the discretion of the Division. Such exemptions shall be in writing to be effective and may be revoked after reasonable notice is given in writing. Application for exemption shall be made by the employer or by the employee and/or the employee's representative to the Division in writing. A copy of the application shall be posted at the place of employment at the time the application is filed with the Division.

18. FILING REPORTS

Every employer shall furnish to the Commission and to the Division at all reasonable times any and all reports or information which may be required to carry out the purpose of this Order, such reports and information to be verified if and when so requested.

19. INSPECTION

The Commission and duly authorized representatives of the Division shall be allowed free access to any office or establishment covered by this Order to investigate and gather data regarding wages, hours, working conditions, and employment practices, and shall be permitted to inspect and make excerpts from any and all relevant records and to question all employees for such purposes.

The investigations and data gathering shall be conducted in a reasonable manner calculated to provide the necessary surveillance of employment practices and the enforcement of the Commission's orders.

20. PENALTIES

Failure, refusal, or neglect to comply with any of the provisions of this Order is a violation of the Labor Code of the State of California and is punishable by fine or imprisonment or both.

See Excerpts from Labor Code, Section 1199.

21. SEPARABILITY

If the application of any provision of this Order, or any section, subsection, subdivision, sentence, clause, phrase, word or portion of this Order should be held invalid or unconstitutional or unauthorized or prohibited by statute, the remaining provisions thereof shall not be affected thereby, but shall continue to be given full force and effect as if the part so held invalid or unconstitutional had not been included herein.

22. POSTING OF ORDER

Every employer shall keep a copy of this Order posted in an area frequented by employees where it may be easily read during the work day. Where the location of work or other conditions make this impractical, every employer shall keep a copy of this Order and make it available to every employee upon request.

Order 4-76, enacted July 27, 1976, and Order MW-78, enacted January 19, 1978, and any prior order regulating this industry are hereby rescinded as and of the date upon which this Order becomes effective, January 1, 1980.

Dated at San Francisco, California, the seventh day of September, 1979.

INDUSTRIAL WELFARE COMMISSION STATE OF CALIFORNIA
Mike R. Elorduy, Chairperson
Jackie Walsh
Yvonne Postello
Howard P. Wachman II
John H. Bennett

James L. Quillin, Chief
Division of Labor Standards Enforcement

Excerpts from Labor Code

SECTION 98.6. (a) No person shall discharge or in any manner discriminate against any employee because such employee has filed any bona fide complaint or claim or instituted or caused to be instituted any proceeding under ... jurisdiction of the Labor

Exhibit 6-16

EMPLOYMENT ELIGIBILITY VERIFICATION (Form I-9)

1 **EMPLOYEE INFORMATION AND VERIFICATION:** (To be completed and signed by employee.)

Name: (Print or Type) Last	First	Middle	Birth Name

Address: Street Name and Number	City	State	ZIP Code

Date of Birth (Month/Day/Year)	Social Security Number

I attest, under penalty of perjury, that I am (check a box):

☐ 1. A citizen or national of the United States.

☐ 2. An alien lawfully admitted for permanent residence (Alien Number A _____).

☐ 3. An alien authorized by the Immigration and Naturalization Service to work in the United States (Alien Number A _____ , or Admission Number _____ , expiration of employment authorization, if any _____).

I attest, under penalty of perjury, the documents that I have presented as evidence of identity and employment eligibility are genuine and relate to me. I am aware that federal law provides for imprisonment and/or fine for any false statements or use of false documents in connection with this certificate.

Signature	Date (Month/Day/Year)

PREPARER/TRANSLATOR CERTIFICATION (To be completed if prepared by person other than the employee). I attest, under penalty of perjury, that the above was prepared by me at the request of the named individual and is based on all information of which I have any knowledge.	
Signature	Name (Print or Type)
Address (Street Name and Number)	City — State — Zip Code

2 **EMPLOYER REVIEW AND VERIFICATION:** (To be completed and signed by employer.)

Instructions:

Examine one document from List A and check the appropriate box, **OR** examine one document from List B **and** one from List C and check the appropriate boxes. Provide the **Document Identification Number** and **Expiration Date** for the document checked.

List A Documents that Establish Identity and Employment Eligibility	List B Documents that Establish Identity	**and**	List C Documents that Establish Employment Eligibility
☐ 1. United States Passport	☐ 1. A State-issued driver's license or a State-issued I.D. card with a photograph, or information, including name, sex, date of birth, height, weight, and color of eyes. (Specify State)_____)		☐ 1. Original Social Security Number Card (other than a card stating it is not valid for employment)
☐ 2. Certificate of United States Citizenship			
☐ 3. Certificate of Naturalization	☐ 2. U.S. Military Card		☐ 2. A birth certificate issued by State, county, or municipal authority bearing a seal or other certification
☐ 4. Unexpired foreign passport with attached Employment Authorization	☐ 3. Other (Specify document and issuing authority)		
☐ 5. Alien Registration Card with photograph	_____		☐ 3. Unexpired INS Employment Authorization Specify form # _____
Document Identification # _____	**Document Identification** # _____		**Document Identification** # _____
Expiration Date (if any) _____	**Expiration Date (if any)** _____		**Expiration Date (if any)** _____

CERTIFICATION: I attest, under penalty of perjury, that I have examined the documents presented by the above individual, that they appear to be genuine and to relate to the individual named, and that the individual, to the best of my knowledge, is eligible to work in the United States.

Signature	Name (Print or Type)	Title
Employer Name	Address	Date

Form I-9 (05/07/87)
OMB No. 1115-0136

U.S. Department of Justice
Immigration and Naturalization Service

Exhibit 6-17

Employment Eligibility Verification

> **NOTICE:** Authority for collecting the information on this form is in Title 8, United States Code, Section 1324A, which requires employers to verify employment eligibility of individuals on a form approved by the Attorney General. This form will be used to verify the individual's eligibility for employment in the United States. Failure to present this form for inspection to officers of the Immigration and Naturalization Service or Department of Labor within the time period specified by regulation, or improper completion or retention of this form, may be a violation of the above law and may result in a civil money penalty.

Section 1. Instructions to Employee/Preparer for completing this form

Instructions for the employee.

All employees, upon being hired, must complete Section 1 of this form. Any person hired after November 6, 1986 must complete this form. (For the purpose of completion of this form the term "hired" applies to those employed, recruited or referred for a fee.)

All employees must print or type their complete name, address, date of birth, and Social Security Number. The block which correctly indicates the employee's immigration status must be checked. If the second block is checked, the employee's Alien Registration Number must be provided. If the third block is checked, the employee's Alien Registration Number *or* Admission Number must be provided, as well as the date of expiration of that status, if it expires.

All employees whose present names differ from birth names, because of marriage or other reasons, must print or type their birth names in the appropriate space of Section 1. Also, employees whose names change after employment verification should report these changes to their employer.

All employees must sign and date the form.

Instructions for the preparer of the form, if not the employee.

If a person assists the employee with completing this form, the preparer must certify the form by signing it and printing or typing his or her complete name and address.

Section 2. Instructions to Employer for completing this form

(For the purpose of completion of this form, the term "employer" applies to employers and those who recruit or refer for a fee.)

Employers must complete this section by examining evidence of identity and employment eligibility, and:
- checking the appropriate box in List A *or* boxes in both Lists B and C;
- recording the document identification number and expiration date (if any);
- recording the type of form if not specifically identified in the list;
- signing the certification section.

NOTE: Employers are responsible for reverifying employment eligibility of employees whose employment eligibility documents carry an expiration date.

Copies of documentation presented by an individual for the purpose of establishing identity and employment eligibility may be copied and retained for the purpose of complying with the requirements of this form and no other purpose. Any copies of documentation made for this purpose should be maintained with this form.

Name changes of employees which occur after preparation of this form should be recorded on the form by lining through the old name, printing the new name and the reason (such as marriage), and dating and initialing the changes. Employers should not attempt to delete or erase the old name in any fashion.

RETENTION OF RECORDS.

The completed form must be retained by the employer for:
- three years after the date of hiring; or
- one year after the date the employment is terminated, whichever is later.

> Employers may photocopy or reprint this form as necessary.

U.S. Department of Justice
Immigration and Naturalization Service

OMB #1115-0136
Form I-9 (05/07/87)

Part Seven

Instructions for Recruiters and Referrers for a Fee

The provisions of the new law that apply to employers also apply to those who **recruit** persons and refer them to potential employers in return for a fee and those who **refer** or provide documents or information about persons to employers in return for a fee. The provisions do not apply to persons who recruit for their own company or business. In addition, union hiring halls that refer union members or non-union individuals who pay membership dues are not considered to be recruiters or referrers for a fee.

Recruiters and referrers for a fee are **not** required to verify the status of persons referred between November 6, 1986, and May 31, 1987. **Starting June 1, 1987, they should complete Form I-9 when a person they refer to an employer is hired by that employer.** The Form should be completed within three business days of the hire.

Recruiters and referrers for a fee may also refer individuals covered by the "special rule" and should follow the procedures for completing the Form I-9 on page 4.

Recruiters and referrers may designate agents to complete the verification procedures on their behalf, such as national associations, or employers. If the employer who hires the referred individual is designated as the agent, the employer needs only to provide the recruiter or referrer with a photocopy of the Form I-9. Recruiters or referrers who designate someone to complete the verification procedures on their behalf are still responsible for compliance with the law and may be found liable for violations of the law.

Recruiters and referrers must **retain** the Form I-9 for three years after the date the referred individual was hired by the employer. They must also present Forms for inspection to an INS or DOL officer after three days advance notice.

The penalties described in Part Five apply to recruiting and referring unauthorized employees for a fee which occurs on or after June 1, 1987.

Part Eight

→ Some Questions You May Have About the Form I-9

Q. Do United States citizens need to prove they are eligible to work?

A. Yes. While United States citizens are automatically eligible for employment, they too must provide the required documents and complete the Form I-9.

Q. Do I need to complete an I-9 for everyone who applies for a job with my company?

A. No. You need to complete I-9's only for people you actually hire. For purposes of the new law, a person is "hired" when he or she begins to work for you.

Q. If someone accepts a job with my company but will not start work for a month, can I complete the I-9 when the employee accepts the job?

A. Yes. While the law requires you to complete the I-9 when the person actually begins working, you may complete the Form when he or she accepts the job.

Q. Do I need to fill out an I-9 for independent contractors or their employees?

A. No. For example, if you contract with another company to provide temporary secretarial services, you do not have to complete I-9's for that company's employees. The other company is responsible for completing the I-9's for its own employees. However, you must not knowingly use contract labor to circumvent the law against hiring unauthorized workers.

Q. Do I need to complete an I-9 for people I hired after November 6, 1986, if they left the job before June 1, 1987?

A. No.

Q. Does the new law apply to my current employees if I hired them before it was passed?

A. No. You are not required to verify status or complete I-9's for current employees hired before November 7, 1986. However, if you choose to complete I-9's for these employees, you should do so for all your current employees hired before November 7, 1986.

Exhibit 6-18

Q. What if a current employee was hired before November 7, 1986, but has recently taken an approved leave of absence?

A. You do not need to complete an I-9 for that employee if he or she was temporarily absent from work for approved paid or unpaid leave, strike, or temporary layoff, or was transferred to another location of your business. However, if you rehire an employee who quit or was terminated, you should complete the employment verification process as you would for others hired after November 6, 1986. You must also verify employment eligibility and complete an I-9 if an employee leaves or is removed from the United States because of an order by a judge or INS.

Those conditions also apply to employees hired after November 6, 1986. Once you have completed an I-9 for those employees, you will not need to fill out a new Form if they have a temporary absence for approved leave, strike, layoff, or transfer.

Q. Will I be subject to employer sanctions penalties if a current employee I hired before November 7, 1986, is an illegal alien?

A. No. You will not be subject to employer sanctions penalties for merely retaining in your workforce an illegal alien hired before November 7, 1986. The fact that an illegal alien was on your payroll before November 7, 1986, does *not* give him or her any right to remain in the United States. Unless the alien is legalized or otherwise obtains permission from INS to remain in the United States, he or she is subject to apprehension and removal.

Q. What should I do if illegal alien employees ask me to help them in legalizing their status?

A. You can assist past and present employees who may qualify by providing documentation of employment history. Employment documentation furnished by employers and presented by legalization applicants will be used only to determine the applicant's eligibility for legal status. The government will not use the documents against the employer except in cases of fraud by the employer.

If aliens do not know how to apply for legal status, they may be able to get help from various organizations, such as churches, community groups, or business associations, which have been designated by INS to advise aliens and help them prepare applications.

You can also advise them that the Internal Revenue Service (IRS) may be able to provide them with documentation to verify residence. To obtain this documentation, employees should contact IRS in person or by correspondence to the service center where they filed their tax return(s). A letter to IRS should include name, address of filing, social security number (both spouses' numbers if a joint return was filed), tax year or years required and copies of any correspondence received from IRS relating to the requested years. IRS will then issue them a Form 6166 (Certification of Filing a Tax Return) if the tax information is verifiable.

Q. May I specify which documents I will accept for verification?

A. No. You must accept any document or combination of documents listed on the I-9 or in Part Nine of this Handbook that appear to be genuine.

Q. What should I do if the person I hire is unable to provide the required documents within three days?

A. If an employee is unable to provide the required document or documents within three days he or she must at least produce a receipt showing that he or she has applied for the document. The employee must produce the document itself within 21 days of the hire.

Q. What is my responsibility concerning the authenticity of documents?

A. You should examine the documents and if they appear to be genuine on their face and to relate to the person, you should accept them. If on their face the documents do not appear to be genuine or to relate to the person, you should not accept them. In addition, if the work authorization documents carry restrictions, you should abide by them.

You should also be aware that any social security number starting with a "9" is an invalid number. Employees who are using such numbers should be instructed to get a proper social security number using Form SS-5, available from the Social Security Administration.

Q. What identity documents are acceptable for minors?

A. If the minor does not have any of the identity documents listed in Part Nine, he or she does not have to produce an identity document if a parent or legal guardian completes the appropriate sections of the Form for the minor.

Q. When do I fill out the I-9 if I hire someone for less than three days?

A. You do need to complete an I-9 before the end of the employee's first working day. However, if the person is providing intermittent domestic service in your home, you do not need to complete an I-9.

Q. What if the person I hire after November 6, 1986, is an illegal alien who has applied or intends to apply for legalization?

A. There is a "special rule" for these applicants. Up until September 1, 1987, you should fill out the I-9 as illustrated on page 4.

After September 1, 1987 even these aliens must provide work authorization documents and you should update the I-9 to reflect the authorization.

Q. What if I rehire someone who previously filled out an I-9?

A. You do not need to complete a new I-9 if you rehire the person within three years of the initial hire, and the information on the Form indicates that the person is still authorized to work.

Q. Do I need to complete a new I-9 when one of my employees is promoted within my company or transfers from one of my company's offices to another at a different location?

A. No. You do not not need to complete a new I-9 if the employee is promoted or transferred within your company.

Q. What do I do when an employee's work authorization expires?

A. You will need to update the I-9 if you want to continue employing the person. At that time, the employee must present a document that either shows an extension of employment eligibility or that is a new grant of work authorization. If the employee cannot produce such a document, that person is no longer eligible to work. Continuing to employ that person is a violation of the law, even if the employee was previously authorized to work.

Q. As an employer, do I have to fill out all the I-9's myself?

A. No, you may designate someone to fill out the Form for you such as a personnel officer, foreman, agent, or anyone else acting in your interest. However, you are still responsible for compliance with the new law.

Q. Can I contract with someone to complete I-9's for my business?

A. Yes. You can contract with another person or business to verify employees' work eligibility and complete the I-9's for you. If you do so, of course, you are still responsible for the contractor's actions and could be liable for any violations of the new law.

Q. As an employer, can I negotiate my responsibility to complete the I-9's in a collective bargaining agreement with a union?

A. Yes. However, you are still responsible for compliance with the new law.

Q. When I review the identity and work authorization documents, should I make photocopies of them?

A. The law does not require you to photocopy documents. However, if you wish to make photocopies, you must retain them with the I-9. Photocopies must not be used for any other purpose.

Q. What are the requirements for retaining the I-9?

A. You must retain the Form for at least three years. If you employ the person for more than three years, you must retain the Form for one year after the person leaves your employment.

Q. Will I get any advance notice if an INS or DOL officer wishes to inspect my I-9's?

A. Yes. The officer will give you at least three days advance notice before the inspection. He or she will not need to show you a subpoena or warrant at that time. Failure to provide the I-9's for inspection could result in civil money penalties.

Q. What happens if I do everything the new law requires and INS discovers that one of my employees is not actually authorized to work?

A. Unless the government can show that you had actual knowledge of the illegal status of the employee, you will have an affirmative defense against the imposition of employer sanctions penalties if you have done the following things:

—Had employees fill out their part of the I-9 when they started to work;

—Checked the required documents (they should appear to be genuine and to relate to the individual);

—Properly completed the I-9;

—Retained the Form for the specified time; and

—Presented the Form upon request to an INS or Department of Labor officer. You will receive at least three days advance notice.

Q. How can I avoid discrimination while complying with the new immigration law?

A. Employers can avoid discrimination by applying the verification procedures of the Act to *all* newly hired employees and by hiring without respect to the national origin or citizenship status of those authorized to work in the United States. Seeking identity and employment eligibility documents only from individuals of a particular national origin or from those who appear or sound foreign violates the new immigration law and may also be a violation of Title VII of the Civil Rights Act of 1964. Employers should not discharge present employees, refuse to hire new employees, or otherwise discriminate on the basis of foreign appearance, language, or name. It is also a violation of Title VII to discriminate against employees or applicants for employment on the basis of national origin.

Q. I have heard that state employment agencies can certify that people they refer are eligible to work. Is that true?

A. Yes. State employment agencies may elect to provide individuals they refer to employers with a certification of employment eligibility. If one of these agencies refers potential employees to you and an employee presents you with one of these certifications, you do not have to check documents or complete an I-9 if you hire that person. However, you must retain the certification as you would an I-9 and present it for inspection if requested. Employers who hire people referred by state employment agencies should become familiar with what an authorized state employment agency certification looks like.

Q. Where can I get the Form I-9?

A. There are two copies of the Form I-9 in this Handbook. If you need more, you can photocopy or print the Forms. You may obtain a limited number of copies from INS. Or you may order them in bulk from the Superintendent of Documents at the following address:

Superintendent of Documents
U.S. Government Printing Office
Washington, D.C. 20402
Tel. (202) 783-3238

Q. What if one of my employees tells me that his or her Social Security Number is invalid?

A. You should tell the employee to get a proper Social Security Number by completing a Form SS-5. This Form is available from the Social Security Administration. You do not need to amend your employment tax returns. However, when the employee gives you the new number, you should file Form W-2C with the Social Security Administration for the years in which you reported income and withholding under the incorrect number.

Q. What advice should I give to my employees applying to legalize their status concerning their Federal Tax obligations?

A. You can advise employees that when they apply to INS for permanent resident status, they will be given an IRS publication explaining requirements for filing Form W-4 or W-4A to insure correct withholding of tax on wages, procedures for correcting prior year tax records (if an invalid social security number was used) and other guidelines relating to tax benefits.

Q. What advice should I give to newly-hired employees who ask about their Federal income tax obligations?

A. First, you can tell them it is important to have a valid social security number and to properly complete a W-4 or W-4A so that the employer can withhold the proper amount for income tax. Second, you can encourage employees to apply for social security numbers for their dependent children who will be five years old or older by the end of the year. Beginning in 1987, such numbers are required to be provided for dependents claimed on tax returns.

Part Nine

Acceptable Documents for Verifying Employment Eligibility

The following documents have been designated for determining employment eligibility by the Immigration Reform and Control Act of 1986 and the implementing regulations. As stated in Part Two, the employee will need to provide a document or documents that establish identity and employment eligibility. A complete list of acceptable documents is given on the next page. Samples of many of the acceptable documents appear on the following pages.

Some documents establish **both** identity and employment eligibility. These are listed on the Form I-9 under *List A*, "Documents that Establish Identity and Employment Eligibility."

If a person does not provide a document from *List A* he or she must provide one document that establishes identity **and** one document that establishes employment eligibility.

In order to establish **identity**, the person must provide a state-issued driver's license, a state-issued identification card, or one of the other documents in *List B*.

In order to establish **employment eligibility**, the person must provide a Social Security card, a United States birth certificate, or one of the immigration documents in *List C*.

If an employee is unable to provide the required document or documents within three days, he or she must at least produce (within three days) a receipt showing that he or she has applied for the document. The employee must produce the document itself within 21 days of the hire.

LIST A
Documents That Establish Identity and Employment Eligibility

- United States Passport
- Certificate of United States Citizenship. (INS Form N-560 or N-561)
- Certificate of Naturalization. (INS Form N-550 or N-570)
- Unexpired foreign passport which:
  - —Contains an unexpired stamp which reads "Processed for I-551. Temporary Evidence of Lawful Admission for permanent residence. Valid until _____. Employment authorized;" or
  - —Has attached thereto a Form I-94 bearing the same name as the passport and contains an employment authorization stamp, so long as the period of endorsement has not yet expired and the proposed employment is not in conflict with any restrictions or limitations identified on the Form I-94.
- Alien Registration Receipt Card (INS Form I-151) or Resident Alien Card (INS Form I-551), provided that it contains a photograph of the bearer.
- Temporary Resident Card. (INS Form I-688)
- Employment Authorization Card. (INS Form I-688A)

LIST B
Documents That Establish Identity

For individuals 16 years of age or older:

- State-issued driver's license or state-issued identification card containing a photograph. If the driver's license or identification card does not contain a photograph, identifying information should be included, such as name, date of birth, sex, height, color of eyes, and address.
- School identification card with a photograph
- Voter's registration card
- United States Military card or draft record
- Identification card issued by federal, state or local government agencies
- Military dependent's identification card
- Native American tribal documents
- United States Coast Guard Merchant Mariner Card
- Driver's license issued by a Canadian government authority

For individuals under age 16 who are unable to produce one of the documents listed above:

- School record or report card
- Clinic doctor or hospital record
- Daycare or nursery school record

LIST C
Documents That Establish Employment Eligibility

- Social Security number card, other than one which has printed on its face "not valid for employment purposes."
  - Note: This must be a card issued by the Social Security Administration; a facsimile (such as a metal or plastic reproduction that people can buy) is not acceptable.
- An original or certified copy of a birth certificate issued by a state, county, or municipal authority bearing an official seal
- Unexpired INS employment authorization
- Unexpired re-entry permit. (INS Form I-327)
- Unexpired Refugee Travel Document. (INS Form I-571)
- Certification of Birth issued by the Department of State. (Form FS-545)
- Certification of Birth Abroad issued by the Department of State. (Form DS-1350)
- United States Citizen Identification Card. (INS Form I-197)
- Native American tribal document
- Identification Card for use of Resident Citizen in the United States. (INS Form I-179)

Equal Employment Opportunity is...
THE LAW

Private Employment, State and Local Government, Educational Institutions

Race, Color, Religion, Sex, National Origin

Title VII of the Civil Rights Act of 1964, as amended, prohibits discrimination in hiring, promotion, discharge, pay, fringe benefits, and other aspects of employment, on the basis of race, color, religion, sex or national origin.

Applicants to and employees of most private employers, State and local governments and public or private educational institutions are protected. Employment agencies, labor unions and apprenticeship programs also are covered.

Age

The Age Discrimination in Employment Act of 1967, as amended, prohibits age discrimination and protects applicants and employees aged 40-70 from discrimination in hiring, promotion, discharge, pay, fringe benefits and other aspects of employment. The law covers most private employers, State and local governments, educational institutions, employment agencies and labor organizations.

Sex (wages)

In addition to the sex discrimination prohibited by Title VII of the Civil Rights Act (see above) The Equal Pay Act of 1963, as amended, prohibits sex discrimination in payment of wages to women and men performing substantially equal work in the same establishment. The law covers most private employers, State and local governments and educational institutions. Labor organizations cannot cause employers to violate the law. Many employers not covered by Title VII, because of size, are covered by the Equal Pay Act.

If you believe that you have been discriminated against under any of the above laws, you should immediately contact:

The U.S. Equal Employment Opportunity Commission
2401 E Street, N.W.
Washington, D.C. 20507
or an EEOC field office
by calling toll free
800-USA-EEOC. (For the
hearing impaired, EEOC's TDD number
is 202-634-7057.)

Employers holding Federal contracts or subcontracts

Race, Color, Religion, Sex, National Origin

Executive Order 11246, as amended, prohibits job discrimination on the basis of race, color, religion, sex or national origin, and requires affirmative action to ensure equality of opportunity in all aspects of employment.

Handicap

Section 503 of the Rehabilitation Act of 1973, as amended, prohibits job discrimination because of handicap and requires affirmative action to employ and advance in employment qualified handicapped individuals who, with reasonable accommodation, can perform the functions of a job.

Vietnam Era and Disabled Veterans

Section 402 of the Vietnam Era Veterans Readjustment Assistance Act of 1974 prohibits job discrimination and requires affirmative action to employ and advance in employment qualified Vietnam era veterans and qualified disabled veterans.

Applicants to and employees of companies with a Federal government contract or subcontract are protected under the authorities above. Any person who believes a contractor has violated its nondiscrimination or affirmative action obligations under Executive Order 11246, as amended, Section 503 of the Rehabilitation Act or Section 402 of the Vietnam Era Veterans Readjustment Assistance Act should contact immediately:

The Office of Federal Contract Compliance Programs (OFCCP)
Employment Standards
Administration
U.S. Department of Labor
200 Constitution Avenue, N.W.
Washington, D.C. 20210
or an OFCCP regional or area office, listed in most telephone directories under U.S. Government, Department of Labor.

Programs or activities receiving Federal financial assistance

Handicap

Section 504 of the Rehabilitation Act of 1973, as amended, prohibits employment discrimination on the basis of handicap in any program or activity which receives Federal financial assistance. Discrimination is prohibited in all aspects of employment against handicapped persons who, with reasonable accommodation, can perform the essential functions of a job.

Race, Color, National Origin

In addition to the protection of Title VII of the Civil Rights Act of 1964, Title VI of the Civil Rights Act prohibits discrimination on the basis of race, color or national origin in programs or activities receiving Federal financial assistance. Employment discrimination is covered by Title VI if the primary objective of the financial assistance is provision of employment, or where employment discrimination causes or may cause discrimination in providing services under such programs.

If you believe you have been discriminated against in a program which receives Federal assistance, you should immediately contact the Federal agency providing such assistance.

Don't Forget...
Equal Employment Opportunity is the Law!

GPO : 1986 O - 154-232

Exhibit 6-19

TRUTH IN LENDING DISCLOSURE FORM FOR A CREDIT SALE

ANNUAL PERCENTAGE RATE	**FINANCE CHARGE**	AMOUNT FINANCED	TOTAL OF PAYMENTS	TOTAL SALE PRICE
The cost of your credit as a yearly rate.	The dollar amount the credit will cost you.	The amount of credit provided to you or on your behalf.	The amount you will have paid after you have made all payments as scheduled.	The total cost of your purchase on credit, including your downpayment of $_____
%	$	$	$	$

1. You have the right to receive at this time an itemization of the Amount Financed.

   ☐ I want an itemization

   ☐ I do not want an itemization

2. Your payment schedule will be:

Number of Payments	Amount of Payment	When Payments Are Due

3. **INSURANCE**

   (a) Credit life insurance and credit disability insurance are not required to obtain credit, and will not be provided unless you sign and agree to pay the additional cost.

Type	Premium	Signature
Credit Life		I want credit life insurance _____ Signature
Credit Disability		I want credit disability insurance _____ Signature
Credit Life and Disability		I want credit life and disability insurance _____ Signature

Exhibit 6-20

(b) You may obtain property insurance from anyone you want that is acceptable to seller. If you get the insurance from seller, you will pay $_____ .

4. SECURITY

(a) You are giving a security interest in ☐ the goods being purchased

☐ _____

Brief description of other property

(b) FILING FEES   NON FILING INSURANCE

$_____ $_____

5. LATE CHARGES

If a payment is late you will be charged ☐ $_____ ☐ _____% of the payment

6. PREPAYMENT

(a) If you pay off early you ☐ may ☐ will not have to pay a penalty. If you pay off early you ☐ may ☐ will not be entitled to a refund of part of the finance charge.

(b) See your contract documents for any additional information about non payment, default, any required repayment in full before the scheduled date and prepayment refunds and penalties.

(c) Buyer acknowledges receipt of a copy of this statement.

Date

_____   _____
Seller   Buyer

_____   _____
Signature   Buyer

Chapter 7

BUSINESS PLAN: THE WAY TO SUCCESS

You can enhance your chances for success by taking the time to write a business plan. The process of thinking about your proposed business venture and then articulating it on paper will assist you in thinking through how you are going to accomplish your goal. There are many successful entrepreneurs who will tell you their business plan was instrumental in keeping them focused on their objective. Entrepreneurs are not the only business people who write and use business plans. Many large corporations engage in planning. The anatomy of their plans resembles in many aspects the basic business plan. This chapter will show you:

* Why a business plan is necessary
* What a business plan should include
* How to present your business plan
* How to use your business plan to develop a strategy
* What a sample business plan looks like

WHY A BUSINESS PLAN IS NECESSARY

A business run without a plan is reactive instead of proactive. In today's changing world, a business person must plan in order to suceed. Without a plan, it is difficult to know when money will be required to support sales, when additional employees, materials, or machinery will be required to support growth, and when products or services will be ready for release to the market.

The major reasons for taking the time and effort to put together a thorough business plan are:

1. The process itself will force you to take a critical and unemotional look at what goals you want to accomplish, and when and how you want to accomplish them.

2. Once the business plan is written and reviewed objectively, it will serve as an operating tool to properly manage your business.

3. Perhaps the most important aspect of the business plan is its use as a tool for obtaining financing from a bank or an investor. A well thought out and well written plan is invaluable to those who need to analyze your request.

Often, the question is asked, "If the business plan is so valuable, why don't all entrepreneurs use them?" When we have asked entrepreneurs this question the answers we receive usually fall within three categories:

Category One. Writing a business plan requires lots of hard work and much time. After the plan has been written, additional time is required to track the plan and analyze variances. Most entrepreneurs care about creating sales, not writing plans.

Category Two. For those business ventures that are self-funded, the perceived value is diminished. There are, however, benefits related to the nonfinancial elements of business. We will cover those elements in detail later in this chapter.

Category Three. Entrepreneurs do plan, but keep their plans in their heads. The obvious question then becomes, "What happens to the business if they are hit by a truck or suffer a lapse of memory?" Aside from that aspect, it makes good managerial sense to communicate ideas to others for the express purpose of testing them. None of us, individually, can be sure that we have explored all aspects of a problem or its possible solutions.

Another comment entrepreneurs often make is, "By the time I write down my plan, the economic environment has changed, invalidating my plan." Our response to this comment is the following: The only certainty in planning is the certainty of change. No plan can be 100 percent accurate. However, when planning is performed properly, changes in the market place can be incorporated quickly so as to determine their effect on your business and point to the most profitable solution. We believe that one of the keys to success is the ability of a business to quickly change as its competitive environment changes. A well-thought-out business plan will provide you with the analytical framework to measure the effect of each change and how to go about implementing it.

The time and energy channeled into planning will manifest themselves in aiding you to control expenses and avoid ill-advised ventures. It also provides your employees with a clear, unambiguous statement of what the business is expected to accomplish.

The well-thought-out business plan should show you what goals are, in fact, achievable. It should separate educated estimates from blue sky dreams, and it should give you a sense of perspective.

WHAT THE BUSINESS PLAN SHOULD INCLUDE

The typical business plan is an amalgamation of the interrelated factors that make up a business in general but which refers specifically to your business. If you are going to show your business plan to a lender or investor, then your written presentation should be:

* Brief and to the point
* Typed and neatly packaged
* Factual, avoiding flowery prose

We cannot emphasize enough the importance of your written presentation. An investor or lender will appreciate a succinct approach which by its very nature reflects a professional attitude toward business. In addition, the typical investor does not like to read a business plan the size of a large novel.

A business plan should be formatted to include certain elements. These elements are listed below.

Title Page. This page provides the name, address, and telephone number of the business and the names of the principals.

Introduction. This element can take the form of a cover letter or statement of purpose and includes information or the loan or funding request, the terms and conditions sought, purpose of the funding, and the timing of funds needs. Be sure to discuss how the funds will accomplish your purpose.

Business History. Include salient historical facts that reflect on your request. Discuss legal form of business and incorporation date and location, if applicable. Relate any structural, management, or ownership changes. Also state any present or past successes that will impact on your request.

Product or Service. Provide a description of your product or service and any unique features that will provide you a competitive advantage. Provide sales breakdown by product, region, and industry type. Discuss the product life cycle and seasonality or cyclicality of your product or service. Do you have a patent, copyright, or exclusive agency? If so, discuss the duration and impact on your competitive advantage. Are there any technological trends that will create obsolescence within your product line? Does your product have a limited shelf life? These factors need to be discussed in your plan.

Market Analysis and Strategy. Describe the market, how large, how diverse, and where located. Describe competitors and their pricing policies, promotional strategies, and relative share of market. "We have no competition" is not acceptable unless you can prove a monopoly will be created when you introduce your product or service. Describe the barriers to your market. Discuss whether the market is growing or shrinking. Describe your channel of distribution and whether you will market your product at retail, wholesale, original equipment manufacturer, or consumer-direct. Discuss trade terms for both suppliers and customers. Present statistics on your customer base. Explain why these individuals or organizations will buy from you. Is it your price, performance, personality, or unique characteristics that will cause them to buy from you? Provide information on projected bad debt expense, warranty expense, and reject rates. Describe how you intend to segment the market and which segments you will target. Describe advertising and promotional budgets. Explain the media you intend to use to reach your target markets?

Manufacturing. Give a description of the facility, which should include size, location, type of building, whether it is leased or owned, and capacity constraints. Discuss sources of supply. Explain whether acceptable alternatives exist. Discuss production methods. Discuss whether they are state of the art. Describe whether your competitive advantage is cost, and if so, discuss how you will protect it. Discuss your production methods and whether they are related to job or mass production runs. Describe your materials and whether they are toxic or hazardous. Discuss whether your business will be closely scrutinized by the EPA and OSHA. Explain your quality control procedures. Provide the age and condition of your fixed assets and whether they will need replacements in order to carry out your plan. Project your capital asset requirements for the next five years.

Personnel. Discuss the structure of management including the board of directors, if applicable. Present an organization chart showing position, name of individual, and lines of authority and responsibility. Provide résumés of key personnel. Is the shop union organized? If so, how responsive is the union to management? Describe the local labor pool for the required level of skill you will need. What is the direct labor cost as a percent of sales? Discuss all other fixed and variable costs of production.

Research and Development. Discuss your research efforts to date and those planned as a percentage of sales. Discuss who will control the research efforts and who the key personnel are. Provide résumés. Describe in general terms, projects underway and planned in the near future. Discuss results to date and successes in terms of rate of return on investment. Describe any R & D partnerships your business is involved in, as well as government funding sources, if applicable. Detail duration and amount of these funds.

Financial Data. If the business has been in existence, then provide five years of CPA prepared financial statements including balance sheets, income statements, and sources and uses statements. For information on how to construct these statements, see Chapter 9. Explain the criteria employed in providing all statements including: cash versus accrual method, inventory valuation method, depreciation method, bad debt method, and amortization rate used for intangible assets. Detail the sources of equity and any dividend requirements. Detail the sources of debt and their repayment terms. Regardless of whether your business is a start-up or has been in existence, provide a pro forma balance sheet showing your company's financial condition after funding of the loan. Provide at least three years of revenue and expense projections. Outline projection assumptions such as expected sales increases, cost of goods sold, and expenses (such as sales expense and general and administrative expense). Discuss whether you expect any major capital expenditures during the projection period to support added sales. If so, discuss how your business will fund growth of current assets as sales grow. Calculate your breakeven point both in dollars and units.

As you can see, writing a thorough business plan is not an easy project. It is necessary to ask these questions and seek answers. By articulating your answers in the form of a business plan, you will bring into focus and anticipate events that will occur in the running of your business. Your business plan will prepare you to deal with these events in a proactive manner. The exercise of writing a business plan takes on added meaning if you can appreciate that problems should really be viewed as opportunities.

HOW TO PRESENT A BUSINESS PLAN

Once you have constructed your business plan, you must put it into a presentable form. We all have a tendency to enhance the positives and mitigate the negatives. In the presentation of your plan, you must use the opposite approach. The positives will take care of themselves as long as you do not radically change your modus operandi. In dealing with negatives, you can make or break the deal. Both bankers and investors alike are heartened by the entrepreneur who realizes he or she has problems and recognizes them. They are further encouraged when that same entrepreneur provides a reasonable plan of attack regarding those problems. There are two important factors to remember: First, proposals are a dime a dozen. Second, bankers and investors know that every endeavor has its problems and appreciate help in weighing the risks. Basically, the investment community is looking for a no-nonsense approach to making money.

With this in mind, we recommend that you adopt the following procedures before you put your business plan into print.

Use a neat but not overly ornate package. A frilly package might have the negative connotation of extravagance. Investments should never be extravagant.

Always type your presentation. The most unprofessional approach you can take is to present a handwritten package to a banker or investor. It implies lack of care, and worse, lack of planning. *Note*: Given a choice of a handwritten business plan versus no plan at all, write it out; however, you must understand that you will have a difficult time raising a significant amount of money this way.

Be brief. We estimate that the average plan will get about ten minutes of concentrated reading. You must get your point across in that period of time if you are to get a full reading of you plan. Extra effort should be put forth in the following key areas: industry description, terms of the deal, financial data, and deal uniqueness, if any.

Match your presentation to your audience. Different aspects of deals appeal to different funding sources. You will learn this from experience. Some sources prefer high-risk high-return deals, while others are interested only in seasoned deals.

When making an oral presentation, be brief. Most people communicate better in an active mode rather than a passive one. Plainly put, they talk better than they listen. Give a brief outline and throw the meeting over to the investors or bankers for questions. They will address the areas of interest to them. At that time go into as much detail as they require, no more or no less. Remember these people are professionals and know what level of information they need to make a decision. Your business plan will serve as a hard copy to substantiate your verbal presentation.

Do not get discouraged. At times you will run into bankers or investors who do not have an "appetite" for your industry or type of deal. Let them help direct you to other sources; most of them will prefer to turn you down on a positive note.

USE YOUR PLAN TO MAKE A STRATEGY

The purpose of your business plan is twofold: (1) to raise funds, and (2) to assist you in running your business. By its nature, the preparation of the business plan will direct you to consider all aspects of business in general and your business in specific. This focusing will force you to identify problems and provide solutions. It has often been said that identification of the problem is fifty percent of the solution. It is certain that you will not be able to identify all potential problems but if you are able to identify and solve eighty to ninety percent of them, your time can be spent running the business and not putting out fires.

The process by which the plan is created and updated provides many benefits. They are:

* *The business plan forces you to manage competition.* By identifying competitors and their advantages, it will assist you to think of ways to minimize their impact on your sales. This analysis can lead you to a decision regarding the most efficient methods of product promotion as well as identifying market segments that can be exploited.

* *The plan provides a clearly outlined path to achieving your goals.* Even though the path changes periodically, the players become a part of that change through the updating process.

* *The plan establishes alternatives.* If "A" happens, you already know that you will "B," but if "C" happens, then you will do "D." Since the plan has considered an uncertain situation in advance, it is no longer uncertain. Alternatives have been established and you can avoid the inefficiencies involved in "fire drills."

* *The business plan gives your banker the impression that you know what you are doing.* The plan shows that you are running the business and the business is not propelled strictly by its own inertia. The plan instills confidence, and, as many of us have

learned, lending is, and probably will continue to be, almost to an extreme, based upon confidence.

* ***The business plan acts as a communications tool.*** If formulated properly, all levels of your organization should understand your goals, the method of achieving those goals, and timing of those goals. By passing your business plan around to the members of your organization to read, it will keep them informed and give everyone a sense of purpose. Furthermore, you will probably receive valuable input from others on how things can be done better, faster, and less expensive.

The business plan is the single most important element of your business. We cannot emphasize enough that before you seek financing or even before you decide to pursue a business venture, you should invest the time to think through and write a business plan. Performing this exercise will make it apparent if your idea has a chance for success. Understand, it is significantly cheaper to invest your time to discover a fatal flaw in your idea than it is to jump into a venture and lose your precious funds.

SAMPLE BUSINESS PLAN

To assist you in writing your business plan, we have provided you with an example of a business plan created for a fictitious business, named Events Unlimited.* In presenting this plan, we are interested in providing an example of form not substance. Your plan will require both. Therefore, as you read this presentation, be aware that the facts and figures are false. You will undoubtedly notice that various sections of the sample business plan differ from the sections we recommended earlier in the chapter. This is simply because every business plan serves a different set of needs, has different requirements, and will thus be structured accordingly. For instance, our sample business plan does not include any information concerning Manufacturing or Research and Development. They are not included in our sample because the fictitious business deals with a service and employs available technology.

In the interest of saving space, we have run each of the sections of the business plan one after the other. In a normal presentation, you would use appropriate page separations.

---

*The concept and original draft of Events Unlimited was written by Janice Dehesh, Colleen Lily, and Victoria Ross.

(Cover page)

Business Plan
EVENTS UNLIMITED
Suite 1515
110 West C Street
San Diego, CA 92101
(619) 237-8899
July 5, 19XX

This business plan has been submitted on a confidential basis.
By accepting delivery of this plan, the recipient agrees
to return this copy to the company at the address listed above.

(Page 1)

TABLE OF CONTENTS

I. Summary

II. The Industry, the Company, and the Service

III. The Management Team

IV. Market Research and Analysis

V. Marketing Plan

VI. Financial Data

(Page 2)

I. SUMMARY

Events Unlimited was formed in July of 19XX in San Diego, California by a highly knowledgeable and experienced team of three business women in response to what they believe to be an attractive business opportunity created by the following conditions:

* The need for a facility equipped to cover the requirements of parties or receptions for large groups of people.
* The present competition (hotels and restaurants) cannot accommodate a large scale event without eighteen months lead time.
* Hotels and restaurants require customers to use their catering services, which are substantially more costly.
* Presently there are no companies that offer a party facility as well as consultation services.

Events Unlimited proposes to provide a facility where large corporations, small companies, and individuals could hold events, conventions and seminars. Events Unlimited would coordinate the caterer, florist, entertainment, invitations, and so on for the client at substantial savings in time, effort, and money. All aspects of the event would be subcontracted at various price ranges by Events Unlimited.

Events Unlimited's target market will be the companies and corporations of San Diego along with couples planning to wed. Our marketing plan will include advertisements in local papers and business journals. We will also utilize the radio and direct mail. The size of the market we are targeting is increasing with the rapid growth of San Diego. Potential individual clients will be from the middle and upper classes, which compose a high percentage of the households in our serving area. Because of the complexity and lack of information on industry trends at this time, it is difficult to estimate sales volume. Each function, depending on the size of the party, complexity of special requests, and season of the year will command a price directly related to the elements of the party itself. Because we are unique in our service business, we anticipate the market share to range from 6.0 to 6.5 percent in the San Diego area.

Pricing of our service will be reviewed on an individual party basis. If the particular request appears to be very time consuming or difficult, our fees would be based on an hourly basis plus costs. If the job appears to be relatively routine, a flat fee (which includes the subcontractor's fees) would be charged.

We at Events Unlimited believe we have a competitive advantage in that we are the only company in San Diego to offer both a facility and a full service consultation team. We will offer flexibility in pricing and quality currently not offered by our competition. Our clients will be able to select an event plan that fits into their budget; they can also choose to use only our facility.

Because of the varied types of services offered by our firm, gross margin may fluctuate between 20 and 30 percent depending upon the time involved in providing a particular service. Profits will experience a seasonal cycle. During the busiest periods, summer (weddings) and fall (office parties), profits should range between 5 and 10 percent. In the slower periods, profits should range between 3 and 5 percent. Based on the information we have gathered, we are anticipating attaining the breakeven point within 18 months. We project a positive cash flow within 12 months.

II. THE INDUSTRY, THE COMPANY, AND THE SERVICES

The Industry

The present catering and party consultation firms in the San Diego area do not have a business similar to Events Unlimited. Within San Diego County, there are 210 catering firms and 11 party planning firms. However, these firms are not full service consultation firms with a party facility.

The Company

The opportunity for a new party facility and consultation firm was perceived by a group of three business women in July 19XX. The business women collectively have more than 19 years of experience in finance, marketing and general management. After analysis of conditions in the industry, they are convinced there is a viable growth opportunity for a business of this type.

The customers of a business of this nature will be companies in need of a facility to hold company parties, seminars, and meetings. Another potential customer will be couples intending to be wed and in need of a facility to house their reception.

It will be Events Unlimited's philosophy to offer an attractive facility of adequate size to our clients. We will also provide them with a full service consulting team that will coordinate their needs without taking them away from the daily operation of their own businesses.

The Services

The following list represents the various services Events Unlimited will provide along with a facility capable of holding a maximum of 500 people.

Catering Service —A group of six caterers will be utilized to fill the varying needs of our clients. Each caterer will be in a different price range or specialty of food service. All prices will be contracted for 12 months.

Florists—A group of at least three florists will be contracted to cover clients' needs at the florist's cost plus 15 percent. If the client chooses to contract the florists themselves, they would pay as much as 35 percent over cost.

Invitations—Events Unlimited will act as distributor for the major invitation printers. This will enable us to sell the invitations to our clients at our cost plus 10 percent instead of the usual 25 percent over cost.

Decorations —Utilizing our wholesale license in purchasing decorations and party favors, we can pass on the cost savings to our clients.

Along with these four services, we will negotiate contract pricing with limousine services, photographers, and bakers and pass those savings on to our clients.

Entry and Growth Strategy

In order to gain a foothold in the market place, we need to devote time to research the needs and growth potential of the San Diego market. Our competitive advantage is the full service nature of our firm in the arrangement of a party including the availability of a fully functional facility. The facility will provide us with the lure we require to entice clients to use our services. Our research of hotels, convention halls, and country clubs indicates that these facilities could be employed but that restrictions were often so severe that the planned party would exceed reasonable costs.

Advertising and promotional efforts will be concentrated in those areas that management experience has demonstrated to be the most effective. The use of local magazines and newspapers will tap the market we desire.

As is true of most new businesses, we expect growth during the first year to be slow. However, as more people become aware of our services through word of mouth and advertisement, we expect the sales volume to triple within five years.

III. THE MANAGEMENT TEAM

The following table lists the members of the management team of Events Unlimited and the responsibility of each member as well as employment prior to organization.

Team Members	Experience
V. L. Ross, Operations	Purchasing Supervisor
	M/A COM
J. A. Dehesh, Marketing	Executive Secretary
	M/A COM
C. F. Lily, Finance	Accountant
	Gabele and Oman, CPAs

Qualifications

Victoria L. Ross—Operations
Ms. Ross is currently enrolled at Chapman College in the undergraduate program seeking her degree in business administration. Her experience includes 8 years of increasing responsibilities in purchasing management for a company generating $50 million in orders in the latest fiscal year. During her 8 years at M/A COM, Ms. Ross has coordinated the day-to-day operations of a purchasing staff of 15 persons and currently has a staff of 5 buyers and 2 clerks. Along with her personnel management experience, she has gained experience in large dollar negotiations. Prior to working for M/A COM, Ms. Ross had 2 years experience working for a catering service and 2 years experience with a greeting card company handling orders for invitations and announcements.

Janice A. Dehesh—Marketing
Ms. Dehesh is presently attending Chapman College completing her degree in business administration. She has a vocational degree in sales, marketing, and management. Her experience includes 8 years of management and administrative responsibilities. In 1979 she managed a boutique in which she supervised sales personnel and took care of all marketing and advertising, including newspaper layout, radio jingles, and so on. In recent years, Ms. Dehesh has broadened her experience to include bookkeeping, budget control, payroll, contract negotiations, and customer contact. She has also prepared major presentation materials for potential customers.

Colleen F. Lily—Finance
Ms. Lily is currently enrolled at Chapman College seeking her degree in accounting. Her initial experience was with Professional Copying, Inc. as an accountant and office administrator, where she implemented a new system in their accounting department. She was in charge of the entire financial

operation as well as initiating administrative policies and procedures. In 1980, she joined the accounting firm of Gabele & Oman as an accountant. Her expertise with this firm includes preparation of financial statements and tax returns as well as financial planning for a variety of clientele. While with Gabele & Oman, Ms. Lily has been placed in charge of their information systems department and has supervised the personnel in this department.

IV. MARKET RESEARCH AND ANALYSIS

Customers

Events Unlimited's potential customer base is large and diverse. The following list represents the major groups we are targeting for our marketing plan.

Corporations—San Diego has experienced significant growth in the area of business, especially in the electronics field. The Sorrento Valley and the Golden Triangle areas are predicted to be the next Silicon Valley. Mission Valley continues to attract the professional service industry. The North Park area has several professional and production businesses. Our corporate clients will be our most important clients. Their interest in our services should be picked by the availability of our facility for seminars, meetings, banquets, and parties. They will also appreciate our full range of consultation services. We are equipped to cater to any type of corporate event. It has been related to us that facilities currently equipped to handle the needs of corporate clients are limited. Events must be booked months in advance to accommodate all the special needs of an event. The availability of our facility within the first two years of operation will be very attractive to these clients. Our full service consulting team will be a must for most of our corporate clients. Most companies do not have a person designated for party consultation only and therefore must take employees away from their designated tasks to coordinate their events. We would take care of all aspects of the event and significantly reduce the time requirements of corporate employees. All preliminary footwork would be handled by our staff and would require only final decisions from the corporate liaison.

Future Brides and Grooms—The needs of couples planning to be married vary with their family traditions, ethnic backgrounds, religious beliefs, and most importantly, their budgets. Events Unlimited will help them coordinate all the aspects of their wedding reception. We will present them with a comprehensive plan and price forecast for all the services they will require. They will then be able to select the plan that best serves their needs and budgets. We will also lease the facility to them at a flat rate and allow them to do their own preparation. The number of attractive facilities available for this type of function is limited and therefore difficult to book. Our availability and flexibility in pricing will be extremely attractive to these potential clients. As each couple comes in to book a reception with us, we will give them a presentation of our services and show them how we can save them time and money in coordinating their reception.

Charitable and Political Fund Raisers —There are several political and charitable fundraisers in San Diego each year. A few of these are Las Patronas "Jewel Ball," La Jolla Museum of Contemporary Art "Night in Monte Carlo," and the Combo Gala. The main requirement for events of this type is a well organized staff to attend to all the various aspects of the event. Events Unlimited is a professional and well organized consulting firm that can handle any type of event. We maintain a selection of party themes complete with ideas for decorations, costumes, fireworks, and ice sculptures.

Quinceneras—Because of the large number of Hispanics in the San Diego area, there are hundreds of quinceneras each year. The quinceneras is an elaborate party given to celebrate the fifteenth birthday of a Mexican or Spanish girl. These parties require the same planning as a wedding reception. They are almost always formal. As with our other prospective clients, these parties would require expert coordination of all aspects of the event. We at Events Unlimited are capable of organizing an event of this scope.

Parties in General—Our remaining client base will require various types of parties, such as Bat and Bar Mitzvahs, birthdays, retirement, and over-the-hill, and twenty-fifth and fiftieth wedding anniversaries. We are expertly equipped to handle any theme or setting required for these types of parties. With our expert guidance, our clients' parties will not only be an event, they will be a memorable experience.

Market Size

The market size for the city of San Diego is estimated to be 10,000 parties per year. This figure represents a combination of both consultation engagements and facility rentals. This market is estimated to increase by 10 percent per year. Of this market, one-third is estimated to be party consultation while two-thirds is estimated to be facility rental. Since a consultation is estimated to be 15 hours at $30 per hour, the total consultation market appears to be approximately $1,500,000 per year. The facility market is estimated at the rate of $1,300 per rental or approximately $3,000,000 per year.

The sources of this data were newspapers, caterers, party consultants, and business consultants. The numbers above represent a consensus of all data received.

Competition

Our competition is limited. No one gives the complete service we provide. Hotels, restaurants, and caterers only provide part of the service we offer. We are the only company that will provide every party detail at our location. Following is a list of our competitors.

* Garden Creations of San Diego
* Conventions in San Diego, Inc.
* ESP (Executive Services Provided)
* Exclusive Coordinators of La Jolla, CA
* JRW Executive Service of Poway, CA
* Carole L. Mullen, On-Site coordinator of Solana Beach, CA
* San Diego in Style
* Host San Diego, Inc.
* Professional Meetings Unlimited of La Jolla, CA

This data was compiled from "Catering to You," a guide to entertaining in San Diego.

Compilation of our competitors' strengths is a difficult task since our business does not directly compete with any of these organizations. Party consultants provide the closest comparison to our firm. Their competitive advantage lies in the fact that they are established in San Diego. In the case of hotels and restaurants, we perceive their strength to be their visibility. The weaknesses that are consistent to all of our competitors are their lack of flexibility, their pricing, and failure to provide all the services required to put on a party. Pricing at hotels and restaurants for food, which is generally handled by an outside caterer, is at least $2 a head higher than we would charge. Facilities provided by these sources are limited in their configuration flexibility. We at Events Unlimited will overcome these strengths and take advantage of these weaknesses as follows: We plan to do a widespread advertising campaign including ads in *San Diego* magazine and through the radio media. In the area of flexibility, our primary philosophy is, and will continue to be, that the client's needs are our first priority. Further, our facility will be designed to provide maximum flexibility to conform with client requirements. We at Events Unlimited believe that these strategies will ensure a strong client base in a matter of months.

Estimated Market Share and Sales

Events Unlimited is capable of handling in a professional manner every aspect of any type of social gathering. We have numerous creative ideas that will make our parties an event. M/A-COM Government Systems and Telecommunication Divisions have committed to a 20-plus party contract with Events Unlimited during the first year. This contract was committed based on the excellent performances of past employees, Janice Dehesh and Victoria Ross. In addition to this contract, contracts from General Instrument, Comstream, and Qualcom are out for final signature. These contracts will amount to another 8 parties minimum. See attachments A and B for market data on the consulting and facilities phases of the business.

Ongoing Market Evaluation

To continue the process of on-going evaluation of our target markets, Events Unlimited will mail questionnaires to previous customers asking pertinent questions regarding customer future needs. This questionnaire will serve both as a marketing tool and a quality control tool. In addition, we will send questionnaires and flyers to all corporations in the San Diego area inquiring as to services they might be interested in using. A sample questionnaire follows.

Questionnaire Number 1—The Business Survey

1. How many parties does your company sponsor per year?
2. What services do you require to put on a party?
3. Do you have a company party consultant?
4. If not, who coordinates your parties, meetings, etc.?
5. If you were to engage a professional party consultant, what would your expectations be?
6. Have you engaged a professional party consultant in the past? (If the answer is no, please skip to question 12.)
7. If you answered yes to question 6, was the service helpful?
8. If the service was inadequate, what were the major drawbacks?
9. Was the service charged at an hourly rate or a flat rate?
10. Do you feel the service was priced fairly?
11. Please circle the hourly rate:

    $ 0—20
    21—40
    41—60
    61—80
    81 or higher

12. What service or services would encourage you to engage an event consultant?

Questionnaire Number 2—Client Survey

1. Were you satisfied with services provided by Events Unlimited?

2. If you were satisfied with our service, what were the best features?

3. What services could be improved?

4. If you were dissatisfied with any of our services, what improvements would you make?

5. Was our price reasonable?

6. Please add any additional comments you may have, or features you would like to see added.

V. MARKETING PLAN

Overall Market Strategy

The general marketing philosophy and strategy of Events Unlimited is to create excitingly original and unique events on or off site. Events Unlimited's target market is companies and corporations in San Diego county as well as couples preparing to wed. In the months after we open, we will extend that market to include charitable and political fund raisers, quinceneras, Bar and Bat Mitzvahs, birthdays, retirement, and over-the-hill parties, and anniversary parties.

To reach our potential corporate clients, we will contact and solicit secretaries and human resource personnel who are normally responsible for planning and organizing corporate functions. Future brides will be contacted through newspaper advertisements and through bridal salons. Other potential clientele will be reached through appropriate ethnic and community newspapers. The objective of this advertising would be to make various ethnic groups such as Hispanics and Chinese Americans aware of our expertise in preparing for their special holidays.

Our total service concept will be emphasized in the generation of sales. Our flexible pricing, unique event themes, and captive facility will be extremely attractive to our potential clients. See Attachments 1 and 2, which show estimated total market and estimated market share of Events Unlimited.

Events Unlimited will start as a regional business with our first facility located in the Mission Valley area, which we believe to be centrally located to our market area. Future growth includes sites in the Golden Triangle area and La Jolla.

Pricing

The pricing policy for services provided by Events Unlimited will of necessity be very flexible. We will establish standard rates for each service based on the fees and rates charged by competitors. Our consulting fees will be based on $30 per hour, which is slightly under market for comparable services. Events Unlimited predicts a gross margin of 20 to 30 percent which may fluctuate based on competitive factors. Gross margins on subcontracted caterer services will be closer to 20 percent, while margins on services such as invitations, flowers and decorations will be closer to 30 percent.

We project that our service will be accepted by consumers because we are very price competitive and provide a mix of unique services that no single competitor offers. Our sales ability will allow us to expand the extras we can sell to clients who wish to throw the truly unique party.

Sales Tactics

For the first year, the owners of Events Unlimited will be the sales force. With our knowledge and experience, we are also capable of managing the business aspects of Events Unlimited. After the initial one-year start-up period, we foresee hiring additional staff, which will include sales help, receptionist, and secretary.

Advertising and Promotion

Our advertising cost will be a significant part of our company's expenses and therefore must be monitored carefully. We feel that employment of an advertising agency will lead to the most efficient use of these funds. The agency will be responsible for establishing an advertising program, layout of business cards, brochures, and flyers, and design of the company logo. Its expertise will enable Events Unlimited to present a more professional and original image.

Newspapers will be the main advertising media. The use of community and ethnic newspapers will allow us to target our advertising dollars. We also anticipate the use of direct mailings from appropriate address lists targeting San Diego corporations of appropriate size. Initial phase advertising costs are estimated to be approximately $5,000.

VI. FINANCIAL DATA

Profit and Loss Forecasts (See Attachments 3 and 4.)

Assumptions: Events Unlimited will require a deposit equal to 50 percent of the estimated job at contract signing with the balance due and payable on the day of the event. We do not foresee any bad debt loss since no terms will be extended beyond event date. This will guarantee cash flow for the payment of our vendors within a 10-day period.

Risks and Sensitivity: We have taken into consideration seasonal trends and forecasted accordingly. By promoting unique nonholiday events, we have tried to reduce seasonal loss of revenue and smooth cash flows during nonseasonal periods.

Pro Forma Cash Flow Analysis (See Attachments 5 and 6.)

Assumptions: As discussed previously all events and rental of facilities will be paid in full by the day of the event. Terms of payments to our vendors will be from day of event (caterers) to 30 days (stationers and florists). Wage increases will occur annually at approximately 10 percent per annum on employee's anniversary date.

Rent, insurance, and miscellaneous expense increases have been projected and accounted for in the three years of pro formas. Advertising will increase as a function of sales due to the importance of expanding our customer base.

Because of the expansion of projected sales, three party consultants and one full-time secretary will be hired by the end of the first year. Capital expenditures include a computer and appropriate software to provide bookkeeping capability. In the third year, we have planned a $15,000 enhancement to our facility to keep current clients and lure new clients.

Cash Flow Sensitivity: As projected, after the partners' initial investment for the business start-up, we should not need to borrow. Any other equipment or furniture for events requested or needed will be rented and in turn included in our contract to the client. Any repairs to facilities are included in our lease agreement and annual cost-of-living increases have been included in our pro formas.

Pro Forma Balance Sheets

With the initial capitalization contributed by each partner, Events Unlimited is able to start business without financing from a lending institution. In order to start business, Events Unlimited needs cash for advertising and promotional material, security deposit for rental of facility, and purchase of kitchen equipment and furnishings. Until year 4, when expansion to a larger and more elegant facility is planned, we see no need for applying for a loan. (See Attachment 7.)

Breakeven Chart

Attachment 8 indicates, that based on our consulting service, we will reach breakeven in June of the first year. We forecast that we will reach breakeven for the rental of our facility by April 1988.

If sales projections should fall short during the first nine months, and we do not reach our breakeven point, Events Unlimited will still be in a position to operate several months after this point. It is of the upmost importance that we continue to advertise our service and facility until Events Unlimited becomes well established in the market place.

Cost Control

Events Unlimited will use a peg board system to record cash receipts and disbursements on a daily basis. This information will be compiled at the end of each month for preparation of financial statements. Each month these financial statements will be reviewed and action taken to adjust costs or our budget. If we find that we are continually over budget, the first step will be to reevaluate our markup on contract services and our consulting fees. This will not cause a problem in the marketplace because our fees are somewhat below market at this point.

Since it is imperative that all outside services be charged to a particular contract, an accounts payable journal with ledger card for each contract will be used. Upon receipt of an invoice, quotation, or contract, the appropriate information will be matched with the correct party contract so as to maintain control of specific costs. Because she has twelve years of accounting experience, Colleen Lily will be responsible for controlling the finances of Events Unlimited.

(1/3 MARKET) CONSULTING ONLY

SALES AND MARKET SHARE DATA

		FIRST YEAR				YEAR		
		1Q	2Q	3Q	4Q	2	3	
ESTIMATED TOTAL MARKET	UNITS	3,500	1,000	3,500	2,000	11,000	12,100	
	DOLLARS	1,575,000	450,000	1,575,000	900,000	4,950,000	5,445,000	
ESTIMATED MARKET SHARE %	UNITS	.333%	.67%	.67%	1.16%	1.33%	1.67%	
	DOLLARS	5,245	3,015	10,553	10,440	65,835	90,932	
ESTIMATED SALES	UNITS	12	7	23	23	146	202	
	DOLLARS	5,400	3,150	10,350	10,350	65,700	90,900	

THE FIGURES LISTED ABOVE ARE BASED ON THE CONSULTATION SERVICE OF OUR BUSINESS ONLY. THE ESTIMATED DOLLARS ARE BASED ON AN AVERAGE CONSULTATION CHARGE OF $30 PER HOUR AND 15 HOURS SERVICE.

W6500-137

Attachment 1

(2/3 MARKET) FACILITIES ONLY

SALES AND MARKET SHARE DATA

		FIRST YEAR				YEAR	
		1Q	2Q	3Q	4Q	2	3
ESTIMATED TOTAL MARKET	UNITS	3,500	1,000	3,500	2,000	11,000	12,100
	DOLLARS	4,550,000	1,300,000	4,550,600	2,600,000	14,300,000	15,730,000
ESTIMATED MARKET SHARE %	UNITS	.67%	1.34%	1.34%	2.32%	2.66%	3.32%
	DOLLARS	30,485	17,420	60,970	60,320	380,380	522,236
ESTIMATED SALES	UNITS	23	13	47	46	293	402
	DOLLARS	29,900	16,900	61,100	59,800	380,900	522,600

THE FIGURES LISTED ABOVE ARE BASED ON THE FACILITIES PROVIDED ONLY.
THE ESTIMATED DOLLARS ARE BASED ON AN AVERAGE FACILITY CHARGE OF $1,300 PER EVENT.

W6500-136

Attachment 2

EVENTS UNLIMITED
PRO FORMA MONTHLY INCOME STATEMENT
FOR THE 12 MONTHS ENDED SEPTEMBER 30, 1988

YEAR 1 1988

	OCT.	NOV.	DEC.	JAN.	FEB.	MAR.	APR.	MAY	JUNE	JULY	AUG.	SEPT.	TOTAL
INCOME													
CONSULTING	900	1,800	2,700	2,250	450	450	1,800	3,600	4,950	4,500	3,150	2,700	29,250
CONTRACT SERVICES	4,000	8,000	12,000	10,000	2,000	2,000	8,000	16,000	22,000	20,000	14,000	12,000	130,000
RENTAL OF FACILITIES	6,500	10,400	13,000	10,400	2,600	3,900	15,600	19,500	26,000	26,000	16,900	16,900	167,700
TOTAL INCOME	11,400	20,200	27,700	22,650	5,050	6,350	25,400	39,100	52,950	50,500	34,050	31,600	326,950
EXPENSES													
ADVERTISING	5,100	1,000	1,000	1,000	1,000	1,000	1,000	1,000	1,000	1,000	1,000	1,000	16,100
CONTRACT LABOR	—	—	—	—	—	—	—	700	700	700	700	700	3,500
DEPRECIATION	406	406	406	406	406	406	406	406	406	406	406	406	4,872
INSURANCE	300	300	300	300	300	300	300	300	300	300	300	300	3,600
MISCELLANEOUS	350	350	350	350	350	350	350	450	450	450	450	450	4,700
OUTSIDE SERVICES	3,640	7,280	10,920	9,100	1,820	1,820	7,280	14,560	20,020	18,200	12,740	10,920	118,300
RENT	—	—	—	—	3,833	3,833	3,833	3,833	3,833	3,833	3,833	3,833	30,664
TELEPHONE	275	200	200	200	200	200	200	200	200	200	200	200	2,475
TOTAL EXPENSES	10,071	9,536	13,176	11,356	7,909	7,909	13,369	21,449	26,909	25,089	19,629	17,809	184,211
(AS % OF SALES)	11.65%	52.79%	52.43%	49.86%	<56.61%>	<24.55%>	47.36%	45.14%	49.18%	50.31%	42.35%	43.64%	43.65%
NET PROFIT (LOSS)	1,329	10,664	14,524	11,294	<2,859>	<1,559>	12,031	17,651	26,041	25,411	14,421	13,791	142,739

Attachment 3

W4500-170

EVENTS UNLIMITED
PRO FORMA QUARTERLY INCOME STATEMENT
FOR THE 12 MONTHS ENDED 1989-1990

	YEAR 2 - 1989					YEAR 3 - 1990				
	1Q	2Q	3Q	4Q	TOTAL	1Q	2Q	3Q	4Q	TOTAL
INCOME:										
CONSULTING	15,750	9,900	20,250	19,800	65,700	21,600	13,500	28,350	27,450	90,900
CONTRACT SERVICES	70,000	44,000	90,000	88,000	292,000	96,000	60,000	126,000	122,000	404,000
RENTAL OF FACILITIES	91,000	57,200	118,300	114,400	380,900	124,800	78,000	162,500	157,300	522,600
TOTAL INCOME	176,750	111,100	228,550	222,200	738,600	242,400	151,500	316,850	306,750	1,017,500
EXPENSES										
ADVERTISING	4,500	6,000	7,500	7,500	25,500	10,000	10,000	10,000	10,000	40,000
DEPRECIATION	1,218	1,470	1,470	1,470	5,628	2,718	2,718	2,718	2,718	10,872
INSURANCE	1,000	1,000	1,000	1,000	4,000	2,450	2,450	2,450	2,450	9,800
MISCELLANEOUS	1,650	1,650	1,650	1,650	6,600	2,750	2,750	2,750	2,750	11,000
OUTSIDE SERVICES	63,700	40,040	81,900	80,080	265,720	87,360	54,600	114,660	111,020	367,640
RENT	11,499	12,113	12,420	12,420	48,452	12,420	13,082	13,413	13,413	52,328
TAXES - PAYROLL	360	1,035	1,716	2,397	5,508	1,608	2,621	1,899	1,737	7,865
TELEPHONE	900	900	900	900	3,600	900	900	900	900	3,600
WAGES	3,120	9,120	15,120	21,120	48,480	22,500	23,100	23,700	24,300	93,600
TOTAL EXPENSES	87,947	73,328	123,676	128,537	413,488	142,706	112,221	172,490	169,288	596,705
NET INCOME	88,803	37,772	104,874	93,663	325,112	99,694	39,279	144,360	137,462	420,795
(AS% OF SALES)	50.24%	39.99%	45.89%	42.15%	44.02%	41.13%	25.93%	45.56%	44.81%	41.36%

	1 OCT	2 NOV	3 DEC	4 JAN	5 FEB	6 MARCH	7 APRIL	8 MAY	9 JUNE	10 JULY	11 AUG	12 SEP	TOTAL
ADD: CASH RECEIPTS													
SALES	11,400	20,200	27,700	22,650	5,050	6,350	25,400	39,100	52,950	50,500	34,050	31,600	326,950
TOTAL CASH RECEIPTS													
LESS: DISBURSEMENTS													
EXPENSES	4,565	9,130	12,770	10,950	7,503	7,503	12,963	21,043	26,503	24,683	19,223	17,403	174,239
PARTNER DRAWS		6,000	9,000	9,000	6,000	6,000	6,000	12,000	12,000	18,000	18,000	18,000	120,000
TOTAL DISBURSEMENTS	4,565	15,130	21,770	19,950	13,503	13,503	18,963	33,043	38,503	42,683	37,223	35,403	294,239
NET INCREASE (DECREASE) IN CASH BAL	6,835	5,070	5,930	2,700	<8,453>	<7,153>	6,437	6,057	14,447	817	<3,173>	<3,803>	32,711
OPENING CASH BALANCE	4,634	11,469	16,539	22,469	25,169	16,716	9,563	16,000	22,057	36,504	44,321	41,148	4,634
CLOSING CASH BALANCE	11,469	16,539	22,469	25,169	16,716	9,563	16,000	22,057	36,504	44,321	41,148	37,345	37,345

Attachment 5

W6500-171

EVENTS UNLIMITED
PRO FORMA QUARTERLY CASH FLOWS
FOR THE 12 MONTHS ENDED SEPTEMBER 30

	1989					1990				
	1Q	2Q	3Q	4Q	TOTAL	1Q	2Q	3Q	4Q	TOTAL
ADD: CASH RECEIPTS										
SALES	176,750	111,100	228,550	222,200	738,600	242,400	151,500	316,850	306,750	1,017,500
LESS: DISBURSEMENTS										
EXPENSES	86,729	76,858	122,206	127,067	412,860	154,988	109,503	169,772	166,570	600,833
PARTNER DRAWS	54,000	54,000	81,000	81,000	270,000	82,500	82,500	82,500	82,500	330,000
TOTAL DISBURSEMENTS	149,729	130,858	203,206	208,067	682,860	237,488	192,003	252,272	249,070	930,833
NET INCREASE (DECREASE) IN CASH BAL.	36,021	<19,758>	25,344	14,133	55,740	4,912	40,503	64,578	57,680	86,667
OPENING CASH BALANCE	37,345	73,366	53,608	78,952	37,345	93,085	97,997	57,494	122,072	93,085
CLOSING CASH BALANCE	73,366	53,608	78,952	93,085	93,085	97,997	57,494	122,072	179,752	179,752

W6500-172

Attachment 6

EVENTS UNLIMITED
PRO FORMA QUARTERLY BALANCE SHEET
FOR THE 12 MONTHS ENDED SEPTEMBER 30, 1988

		1ST YEAR - 1988				2ND YEAR - 1989	3RD YEAR - 1990
	START-UP	1Q	2Q	3Q	4Q		
ASSETS							
CASH	4,634	22,469	9,563	36,504	37,345	93,085	179,752
PREPAID EXPENSES	5,100	0	0	0	0		
FURNITURE & EQUIP.	24,400	24,400	24,400	24,400	24,400	29,450	44,400
ACCUM. DEPR.		<1,218>	<2,436>	<3,654>	<4,872>	<10,500>	<21,372>
NET PROPERTY & EQUIP.		23,182	21,964	20,746	19,528	18,900	23,028
SECURITY DEPOSITS	7,866	7,866	7,866	7,866	7,866	7,866	7,866
TOTAL ASSETS	42,000	53,517	39,393	65,116	64,739	119,851	210,646
LIABILITIES & PARTNER'S EQUITY							
PARTNER'S EQUITY							
CAPITAL, BEG.	42,000	42,000	42,000	42,000	42,000	64,739	119,851
PARTNER WITHDRAWALS		<15,000>	<26,000>	<66,000>	<120,000>	<270,000>	<330,000>
NET INCOME		26,517	33,393	89,116	142,739	325,112	420,795
TOTAL LIABILITIES & PARTNER'S EQUITY	42,000	53,517	39,393	65,116	64,739	119,851	210,646

Attachment 7

EVENTS UNLIMITED
BREAK-EVEN CHART FOR CONSULTING

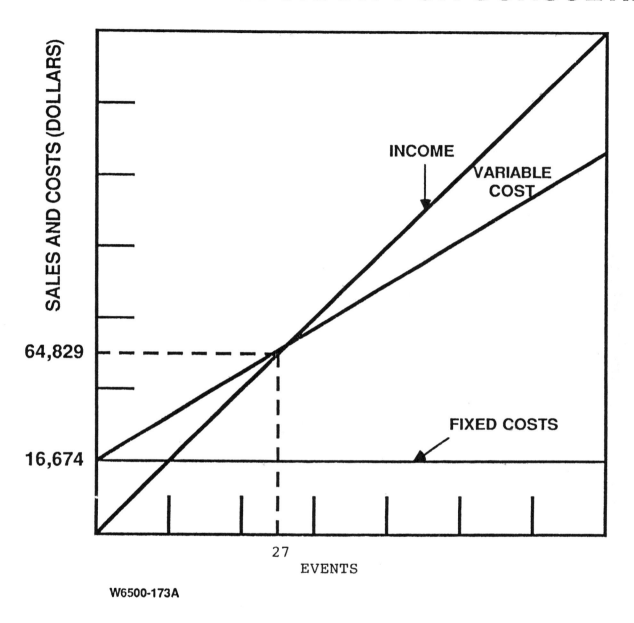

W6500-173A

Attachment 8

PART TWO

NUTS AND BOLTS
OF RUNNING A BUSINESS

Chapter 8

MARKETING YOUR BUSINESS

One of the most critical aspects of running a successful business is to promote and sell your product or service. Similar to other aspects of running a business, this activity can also be mastered once you learn the fundamentals, and consistently apply them. To market your product or service successfully, you must be organized, methodical, and a bit creative. This chapter will show you how to:

* Conduct market research
* Segment the market
* Read and interpret census tracts
* Analyze the various factors in choosing your target market
* Promote your product or service
* Analyze whether you need a "middleman"
* Determine the best location for your business
* Price your product or service
* Use trade shows

HOW TO CONDUCT MARKET RESEARCH

Market research is critical if you expect to launch a successful product or service. As an entrepreneur, your success will be determined by your ability to satisfy customers' perceived needs. The objective of market research is to obtain as much information as possible about the perceived needs of customers so that you can channel your resources into a product or service that will have a high probability of acceptance.

Use Your Library

Your first step in conducting your own market research is to choose an industry that interests you. Therefore, you will need to spend time in the library. There are many industries: publishing, retail, advertising, construction, metallurgy, food service, computers, health care, optics, etc. The Encyclopedia of Associations can be a major source of help. It lists over 20,000 national and international nonprofit, trade, professional, commercial, scientific, engineering, and technical associations. Associations as diverse as the National Bakers Suppliers Association to Metal Fabricating Institute are included in this reference source. Another source is the Encyclopedia of Business Information which contains basic information sources concerning more than 1,100 business related topics. Industries such as metal, agronomy, advertising, biotechnology, computer-aided design, fibers, and photomechanical processes are listed.

Learn the Needs of the Industry You Choose

Once you pick an industry, learn it. Your goal is to seek out those perceived needs within the industry that are not being met. You are looking for a market to serve.

After you have determined which industry or industries you want to channel your energies into, the next step is to ask yourself what the needs of the organizations in this industry are. Almost every industry has a need for a new product or service or needs an existing product or service to be improved. Remember, every problem that confronts an industry, no matter how small, is really an opportunity in disguise.

Shown below are several approaches to take to analyze the needs of an industry.

Approach #1: A Service Needs to Be Improved

REASONS:

* Personality of person or organization providing the service is arrogant or antagonistic.
* Thoroughness of service is poor.
* Quality of service is poor.
* Service is slow.
* Service is overpriced.
* Service is not guaranteed.
* Service is limited.

Approach #2: Product Needs to Be Improved

REASONS:

* Product is overpriced.
* Product is not made to last.
* Product is not guaranteed.
* Product does not fit all sizes or come in all colors.
* Delivery of product is slow.
* Product takes up too much space.
* Product is not stylish.
* There is no service after the sale of product.

Read articles and then ask questions. Do not be afraid to pick up the telephone and call around. Is there really a problem with this type of service? Can it be improved? Would you buy this service from another supplier? How much are you currently paying for this service?

Know Your Market

There are three categories of markets:

* Consumer
* Industrial
* Reseller

A product or service can be aimed at two markets at the same time. For instance, the personal computer satisfies a need at home (consumer market) as well as the office (industrial market). However, the actual promotion for each of these markets is quite different. As a rule, the consumer purchase is based more on impulse whereas the industrial purchase is scrutinized more closely.

Consumer Market. This market is comprised of individuals or households that purchase products or services with the intention of consuming them. Examples of products or services that are supplied to the consumer market are:

Furniture	Recreational equipment
Dental care	Food
Appliances	Television, radio, stereo
Legal services	Housing
Autos, trucks	Computers
Cameras	Stationery
Clothing	Dry cleaning
Pet care	Pet products
Interior decorating	Plumbing
Auto repairs	Jewelry
Art supplies	Therapy
Periodicals	Nursery furniture

As both population and disposable net income continue to increase at a steady rate, the consumer market will expand accordingly and will provide entrepreneurs with new opportunities.

Industrial Market. This market is comprised mostly of organizations that purchase a product or a service to be used in producing another product or for use in daily operations. Examples of products or services that are supplied to the industrial market are:

Food	Fertilizer
Paper bags	Medical equipment
Scanner	Robotics
Floor care products	Industrial security
Ceramics	Material handling
Seed	Office furniture
Forms	Office supplies
Interior design	Insurance

Computer installation	Carpeting
Cleaning materials	Software installation
Fibers	Advertising
Optics	Aerospace

Reseller Market. This market is comprised of wholesalers and retailers who buy finished goods and sell them for a profit. These types of organizations have been traditionally called the "middlemen." There are approximately 418,000 wholesalers and 1,441,700 retailers in the United States. (*Source*: Statistical Abstract of the United States 1985) Resellers usually have three overriding concerns when they choose a supplier: (1) price, (2) quality, and (3) availability.

HOW TO SEGMENT THE MARKET

Once you have decided which industry you are going to enter, the next step is to segment the market.

Rarely is the market a homogeneous block. Instead, it is usually composed of individuals and businesses that have diverse needs. An example is the automobile market. For years, Ford Motor Company made the basic Model T, and, for awhile, led the auto industry in sales. But it was General Motors that realized car buyers wanted cars for different reasons because their perceived needs were different. Some buyers were concerned about economy; other buyers wanted a car to fit their image; while still others bought a car based on comfort and room. General Motors segmented the market by making a car that would precisely fit the needs of each group. Today, General Motors is the single largest domestic producer of cars in the United States.

As the entrepreneur, you have at your disposal four variables to manipulate:

* the product or service itself
* the price of the product or service
* the promotion of the product or service
* the method of distribution of the product or service

Again, using the auto industry as an example, the market can be divided into various groups:

• Individuals who want performance

• Individuals who want luxury

• Individuals who want utility

• Individuals who want status

• Individuals who want economy

• Individuals who want style

A second example is the radio listening market, which is segmented into various groups of listeners. There are groups of individuals who listen to:

• Classical music

• Soft rock

• Hard rock

• Oldies but goodies

• News

- Talk
- Soul
- Sports
- Country and western
- Easy listening
- Jazz
- Top 40

A third example is magazine readership. The market is divided into groups that like to read about:

- Sports
- Current events
- Computers
- Beauty/glamour
- Cooking
- Photography
- Sex
- Body building

- Wealth accumulation
- Art
- Interior decorating
- Housekeeping
- Autos
- Travel
- Self-development
- Fashion

Segmenting the Consumer Market

There are four methods you can choose from to segment the consumer market:

1. Demographic
2. Geographic
3. Psychographic
4. Product-related

Demographic

This is the most popular and easiest method used to segment the market *Demographic* is defined as social statistic. Examples of a demographic would be: age, sex, religion, education, ethnic group, income, race, family size, social class, occupation, and nationality.

As an illustration, consider segmentation by ethnic group. One group that is growing and becoming increasingly important is the U.S. Hispanic market. This group is made up of people of Central and South American heritage as well as people of Mexican, Cuban, and South American ancestry. Recently, demographers have forecasted that by the year 2020, this group, if it continues on its present growth path, will constitute the largest ethnic group in the country. As the table below shows, of the estimated 14,609,000 Hispanics, the largest percentage is concentrated in five states.

State	1980 Population
California	4,544,000
Texas	2,986,000
New York	1,659,000
Florida	858,000
Illinois	636,000

(*Source:* Statistical Abstract of U.S. 1985.)

As the Hispanic population increases, so does its buying power. In 1983 the income of all Hispanic households was $76.5 billion. Hispanic households in the western portion of the United States accounted for $33.9 billion. The mean average salary in 1983 for a Hispanic employed in a managerial or professional specialty was $33,631. (*Source:* Statistical Abstract of U.S. 1985.)

As a result, the Hispanic population has become an important market segment that is attracting increased attention from entrepreneurs.

Geographic

The geographic method includes segmenting the market by population density, region, political subdivisions, climate, or terrain. For example, many companies divide the U.S. market into the following regions: New England, mid-atlantic, south, midwest, southwest, and pacific. Within San Diego county, California, for instance, many companies segment the market into regions: beaches, north county, east county, golden triangle, downtown, southeast San Diego, and south bay.

Psychographic

This method uses psychological and sociological factors to segment the market. Interests that individuals have such as family, home, job, community, fashion, and achievements are used to segment individuals into groups as well as opinions that individuals have of themselves, social issues, their culture and politics. Many companies have segmented individuals into groups based on this method. For example, below is a psychographic profile of the male population, which resulted from a study conducted by a New York newspaper*:

The Traditionalist. This type of male feels secure, has self-esteem, and follows conventional rules. He is proper and respectable and regards himself as altruistic and interested in the welfare of others. As a shopper, he is conservative and likes popular brands and well known manufacturers. This type of male tends to be of low education and low economic status.

The Ethical Highbrow. This type of male is sensitive to people's needs. He is also content with family life, friends, and work; however, he tends to be a puritan. Generally, he is interested in culture, religion, and social reform, and as a consumer, he will buy quality even it means paying a higher price. This type of male tends to be well educated and is in the middle or upper socio-economic class.

The Pleasure-Oriented Male. This type of male oozes with masculinity and rejects those things that appear to be soft or feminine. He views himself as a leader among men. Generally, he is self-centered and dislikes his work or job. He usually seeks immediate gratification for his needs and is an impulsive buyer likely to buy products with a masculine image. This type of male tends to be of low education and in the low socio-economic class.

The Achiever. This type of male is hardworking and dedicated to success and all the trappings that it brings: social prestige, power, and money. He likes diversity, good food, music, and keeps in style. As a consumer, he is status conscious and a discriminating buyer. This type of male tends to be well educated and is in a high socio-economic class.

Source: "Psychographics: A Study of Personality, Lifestyle, and Consumption Patterns." New York: Newspaper Advertising Bureau, 1973.

Product-Related

This method examines the way consumers use a product and the benefits they expect and then groups them accordingly. For instance, why do individuals purchase certain brands of toothpaste? Are their purchase decisions motivated primarily by the toothpaste's ability to: (a) protect against decay, (b) brighten teeth, (c) give fresh breath? What is the primary reason people use under-arm deodorant: (a) to smell good, (b) keep dry, (c) feel secure?

Segmenting the Industrial and Reseller Market

There are at least two methods you can use to segment the industrial and reseller market.

1. Use of Product.

How will your product be used? For example, computers can be used to (a) facilitate business operations, (b) conduct research, or (c) perform engineering calculations. Another example is carpet. It can be used as a floor covering by (a) apartment complexes, (b) retail stores, (c) offices, (d) schools, (e) hospitals, and (f) restaurants.

2. Geographic Location.

Users of your product may tend to congregate around certain regions. Psychologists tend to locate in a larger metropolis; auto makers were traditionally found in and around Detroit; many furniture producers are located in North and South Carolina; a large portion of domestically produced steel is made in Pittsburgh; Silicon Valley is famous for its hi-tech industries, while San Diego's golden triangle and Los Angles' San Fernando Valley are gaining in popularity.

UNDERSTANDING CENSUS TRACTS

The United States Constitution mandates that the federal government conduct a census of the population every ten years. The census has become more probing and sophisticated in its quest for information with each decade. Information such as income, race, sex, type of fuel households use as well as the age of the house, fertility, method of getting to work, years of school completed, marital status, language spoken at home, and the amount of the mortgage on the house is now routinely elicited.

The last census taken was in 1980 and gathered information according to the standard metropolitan statistical areas (SMSA). The concept of the SMSA is as follows: The United States is composed of numerous population nuculei that have adjacent communities with a high degree of social and economic integration within the population center. Most SMSAs have at least one population center, although some may have more. Within the SMSA, there are numerous subdivisions that are called tracts or census tracts. See Exhibit 8-1 as an illustration of how a typical SMSA is subdivided into tracts.

Three important demographics you want to consider whenever you segment the market are income, education, and whether individuals are homeowners or renters.

Income

As income increases, so does buying power. The two most important income figures you need to be aware of are disposable income, which is the amount of money left over after taxes are paid, and discretionary income, which is the amount of money left over after the individual has purchased the basic necessities of life—that is, food, clothing, and shelter. Discretionary income is used to purchase compact disc players, vacations, VCRs, pets, kitchen appliances, furniture, and so on.

Education

Higher education usually means that your customers are likely to be more sophisticated in making their decisions. As a rule, they have been exposed to a broad range of ideas and products; thus, their receptive quotient will tend to be high. If you are offering a product or service that relates to travel, arts, self-improvement, entertainment, gourmet cooking, politics, publishing, high technology, or foreign cultures, this demographic takes on great importance.

At the same time, it should be realized that this type of consumer is likely to be more demanding in the areas of quality, warranty, and knowledge of the product or service.

Homeowners and Renters

Renters generally live in housing units that are smaller in size than those of homeowners. As a result, they are usually interested in products that are efficient and space-saving. Also, there are many products that appeal to the homeowner—for instance, lawn and garden equipment or home improvement equipment—that would not ordinarily appeal to the renter.

Analyzing a Typical Metropolitan Area

To understand how to locate and interpret information from the census tract, we will use San Diego, California as an example. San Diego, like all metropolitan areas, is divided into numerous tracts. An excellent source you can use to locate different tracts throughout a standard metropolitan area is the census tracts map for that area, which is published by the Bureau of the Census. For example, there is a census tracts map for San Diego. We have chosen two tracts to use as an example.

   a. Tract 0002—encompasses a significant portion of Mission Hills

   b. Tract 0083.12—encompasses a significant portion of La Jolla

See Exhibit 8-2 and Exhibit 8-3, which show the individual tracts superimposed on a census tract map. Then look at Exhibit 8-4 and Exhibit 8-5, which show the actual tract information for areas that include a portion of Mission Hills and La Jolla.

From census tracts 0002 (Mission Hills) and 0083.12 (La Jolla), we can surmise the following:

Mission Hills Area

There are 2,989 households in this portion of Mission Hills of which 1,252 are homeowners and 1,737 are renters. The homeowners' median income is $21,182 while the mean income is $27,384. The renters' median income is $11,187 while the mean income is $13,958.

The median monthly rent payment paid is $241.

The median asking price for a housing unit is $125,000 while the median value is $110,600.

Most households (575) fall into the $10,000 to $14,999 category of income; however, there are 683 households that earn $25,000 or more.

Households that have incomes of less than $10,000 spend, on an average, 40 percent of their income on rent; households that have incomes of $10,000 to $19,999 on an average spend 23.7 percent of their income on rent; households that earn more than $20,000 or more spend on an average 14.6 percent of their income on rent.

The total number of individuals who live in this tract is 5,841, of which 2,122 are married, 1,685 are single, and 816 are either separated or divorced. There are 73 widowed males but 471 widowed females.

The percentage of individuals who live alone is 44.9 percent, while occupied housing units that have only two persons living in them amount to 34.3 percent.

Finally, 58.6 percent of the individuals 25 years or older have had at least one year of college.

La Jolla Area

There are 1,534 households in this portion of La Jolla, of which 976 are homeowners and 558 are renters. The homeowners' median income is $41,407 while the mean income is $70,484. The renters' median income is $16,176 while the mean income is $19,932.

The median monthly rent payment is $378.

The median asking price for a house exceeds $200,000 while the median value also exceeds $200,000.

Most households (426) fall into the $500,000 or more category of income. Approximately 53 percent of all households earn $25,000 or more.

Households that have incomes of less than $10,000 spend on an average more than 50 percent of their incomes on rent; households that have incomes of $10,000 to $19,999 on an average spend 35 percent of their income on rent; households that earn over $20,000 spend on an average 17.6 percent of their income on rent.

The total number of individuals who live in the tract is 3,731 of which 1,734 are married, 810 are single, and 352 are either separated or divorced. There are 42 widowed males but 313 widowed females.

The percentage of individuals who live alone is 29.3 percent, while occupied housing units that have only two persons living there amount to 39 percent.

Finally, 78.4 percent of the individuals 25 years or older have at least one year of college.

WARNING NO.1

The government takes the census every ten years. Much can and does occur within a 10-year span, such as inflation, migration, and political events. However, census tracts still provide excellent information but they must be viewed in perspective.

WARNING NO.2

The next census is 1990 and the categorization of data will vary somewhat from the 1980 census. SMSAs will no longer be used. Instead, data will fall into one of three subdivisions:

> CMSA—Consolidated Metropolitan Statistical Areas
> PMSA—Primary Metropolitan Statistical Areas
> MSA—Metropolitan Statistical Areas

1990 Census Will Use TIGER: Topologically Integrated Geographic Encoding and Referencing System

In an effort to improve upon the taking of the census, and in particular maps, address reference files, and geographic reference files, TIGER was developed and will be used for the 1990 census.

TIGER is the Census Bureau's new digital map data base that automates the mapping activities required to support the census. The map data base is computer readable and can be used for automated mapping, geocoding, and geographic information systems.

The TIGER data base includes census statistical area boundaries, such as census tracts and census blocks, political boundaries, address ranges within zip codes, and features, such as roads, rivers, and railroads. The normal geographic coverage for a TIGER/Line file is by county. You can view a prototype of a Tiger/Line file of Boone County, Missouri, by sending either $60 for a single 1.2 megabyte high density flexible diskette or $5 for a paper copy, to:

> Customer Service
> Bureau of the Census
> Washington, D.C. 20233

The files contained on the 1.2 megabyte diskette include:

* Basic data record
* Shape coordinate points
* 1980 census geographic area codes
* Index to alternate feature names
* Feature name list
* Additional address and zip code data

The files contained in the prototype of Boone County representative of the files that will be released for the entire United States.

FACTORS TO CONSIDER IN CHOOSING YOUR TARGET MARKET

After you segment the market and choose your target market, there will be four requirements that you must satisfy to improve your chances of success:

1. When you concentrate on a specific segment of the market you must be able to clearly articulate the needs of that market. For example, individuals who play sports will need appropriate footware. Some individuals run; some play racquetball; while others play a court sport such as tennis or basketball. Each group of individuals has different needs and therefore requires a different type of shoe.

2. Your product must truly satisfy the needs of your target market.

3. If you select only one market segment to serve, it must generate a sufficient return on investment.

4. You must be able to communicate with your target market. The individuals in that market must be able to see or hear your message.

HOW TO PROMOTE YOUR PRODUCT OR SERVICE

The object of promotion is to communicate to your target market that you have the product or service to satisfy its needs. You have at your disposal four tools to use:

> Advertising
> Publicity
> Personal selling
> Sales promotion

Advertising

Advertising can be a very cost-effective way to promote your product or service because it can reach a vast number of people at a low cost per person.

Anyone can develop an "advertising campaign" by following the steps below.

First

Identify and analyze your target market. To be successful, you must be able to clearly articulate the needs of your target market. In addition, you must know the group of individuals your advertising is aimed toward so that you can select the right media.

Second

Define your objective. Do you want to establish a sales goal, say, to increase sales by $150,000? Or do you want to increase brand or product awareness? Many entrepreneurs who introduce a somewhat sophisticated product will place their emphasis on product awareness with the objective of educating potential customers about the features and uses of the product. It is crucial that you carefully establish your objective because it will establish the context within which all of your advertising related decisions will be made.

Third

Create your advertising message. In this step, you will articulate your selling points. These selling points will form the basis of your advertising. One of the best ways to do this is to find out what needs your customers consider the most important. Be sure your advertising addresses and satisfies those needs.

Fourth

Determine which media you will use. You have at your disposal magazines, television, newspapers, radio, trade journals, direct mail, and outdoor displays. You must do your research to determine which media best reaches your target market.

Below is a description of the characteristics of different media and the advantages and disadvantages each one presents.

Newspaper

Types

* City: morning, evening, Sunday, Sunday supplement
* Local: geographic area or subject matter; for example, in San Diego, the *La Jolla Light* caters to only the geographic region of La Jolla, while the San Diego Business Journal caters to persons interested in San Diego's business scene.

Unit of Sale. Column inch: Cost is usually based on depth and width of an ad. The number of lines is the depth and the number of columns is the width. The industry standard is 14 agate lines to the column inch. For example, suppose you want to buy space that is 3 columns wide and 8 inches deep. The space would be 24 column inches (3 x 8) or 336 agate lines (24 x 14). If the newspaper you wanted to advertise in charges $.75 per agate line, the minimum cost of running the ad would be $252.00.

Cost Comparison. The formula that allows you to compare newspaper advertising with other forms of advertising is:

$$\frac{(\text{cost of ad} \times 1{,}000)}{\text{circulation of newspaper}}$$

Example:

$$\frac{(\$252.00 \times 1{,}000)}{10{,}000}$$

The ad costs $25.20 per thousand persons exposed

Advantages. Many people read the newspaper. People can refer back to a specific ad. Advertisements require short lead time; and therefore give you greater flexibility in the event you have to change your message. The selectivity of local newspapers offers you an opportunity to better target your market. Cooperative advertising allowances with manufacturers are common, which in turn will lower your advertising costs.

Disadvantages. The large volume of ads that appear in a newspaper prevents extensive exposure for any one advertisement; thus, unless your ad is truly unique, it may not reach your intended market. Furthermore, much circulation is often wasted.

Magazines and Technical Journals

Types

* Consumer
* Industry

Unit of Sale. Column inches are still used by most magazines/journals as well as measurements of 1/4, 1/2, 3/4 and whole page.

Cost Comparison. The formula for comparing costs is:

$$\frac{\text{cost of ad} \times 1,000}{\text{circulation of magazine}}$$

Advantages. Magazines and journals permit you to effectively reach your target market whether you are using demographics, geographics, psychographics, or product-related variables to segment the market. For example, there are magazines that cater to computer buffs, homeowners, outdoor enthusiasts, gourmets, the showbusiness industry, gardeners, and travelers. In addition, there are numerous magazines and journals written for a particular industry. For example, *Progressive Grocer* targets supermarket personnel, *Rental Owner* targets apartment owners, The *California Therapist* targets marriage and family therapists in California, *Solid Waste* targets the rubbish disposal industry.

Furthermore, there may be a professional or industrial magazine or journal that precisely targets your geographic market. For instance, the *ABA Journal* reaches lawyers throughout the United States; *California Lawyer* is aimed at lawyers who practice in California; and *Dicta* targets lawyers who practice in San Diego County.

A second advantage that magazines and journals offer is that they are normally kept around the house or office for months after they are received. As a result, they are read by many individuals and sometimes reread.

A third advantage is that magazines and journals have the capacity to contain vivid, full color displays and special effects. Magazines and journals, as a rule, have a good reputation for prestige.

Disadvantages. The two biggest disadvantages are the high absolute dollar cost and long lead time. Furthermore, because many journals are monthly or quarterly, the opportunity for rapid follow-up is severely curtailed.

Direct Mail

Types

* Letters
* Brochures
* Newsletters
* Circulars
* Samplers
* Booklets
* Price lists
* Catalogs

Cost Comparison. The costs involved in using mail order include: postage, purchase of mailing list, typesetting, reproduction, labor to stuff the envelopes.

Advantages. There is little wasted circulation. You can be highly selective in choosing your target market. Direct mail is more measurable than newspaper, magazine, or television. You can initiate direct mail at any time without the hurdle of a superimposed lead time. Unlike a magazine or newspaper, there are few distractions and thus your advertising message will stand out.

Disadvantages. Direct mail is expensive. Also, many individuals and companies consider advertising literature to be junk mail and will throw it out before reading it. Mailing lists tend to become outdated quickly because people move and circumstances change. Make sure your mailing list is up to date.

Radio

Types

* AM
* FM

Unit of Sale. Spots: 5, 10, 20, 30, 60 seconds. Programs: sponsor, cosponsor, participative sponsor
Cost Comparison. The formula for comparing costs is:

$$\frac{\text{cost per minute} \times 1,000}{\text{listenership}}$$

Advantages. Using radio is a relatively inexpensive broadcast medium that allows you to change your message quickly. There is a high degree of demographic segmentation as well as geographic selectivity. Buying response is almost immediate, which allows you to measure the success of your ad.

Radio does not have the clutter of advertising messages that are associated with newspapers and magazines. Lead time is usually not more than 3 days.

Disadvantages. Radio provides only an audio message and has a short life. Also, many times listeners' attention is diverted from the radio.

Television

Types

* CATV
* Local
* Network

Unit of Sale. Spots: 5, 10, 15, 30, 60 seconds; programs: sponsor, cosponsor, participative sponsor
Cost Comparison. The formula for cost comparison is:

$$\frac{\text{cost per minute} \times 1,000}{\text{viewership}}$$

Advantages. Television utilizes both sight and sound to get your message across. Television reaches a large audience and the cost-per-exposure is low. Television has some demographic selectivity.

Disadvantages. The absolute dollar cost of television is high. Viewers may leave the room, or engage in conversation during commercial breaks and completely ignore your message. There is tremendous flucuation in audience size, and your rates will vary accordingly. Two well known indexes used to measure audience size are the Nielsen Station Index and the Arbitron Index.

Other Forms

* Inside transit
* Outside transit
* Billboards
* Yellow pages

Legal Aspects to Consider When Advertising

Both the FTC and state enforcement agencies can order you to stop running an advertisement if they consider it to be false or misleading. Furthermore, these agencies may force you to run a retraction stating your prior ad was deceptive . A deceptive ad will severely damage your company's credibility among the users of your company's product or service. In addition to government agencies, you could be sued by the user of the product or service, or even by your competitors. Therefore, there are several do's and don'ts whenever you place an advertisement in any type of medium.

Don't:

* Mislead or deceive: The government does not have to prove the ad actually misled anyone, instead it must merely show that your ad had deceptive qualities.
* Make a false statement: You will be held liable even if you were personally unaware the statement was made.   Your good intentions are irrelevant.
* State that your product or service is free or without charge when there are conditions attached, unless you clearly and conspicuously state the nature of those conditions.
* Claim that your price is a savings unless you previously offered such goods and services at a higher price.
* Offer credit terms unless you generally offer those terms to customers, and, if you advertise specific credit terms be sure to state the down payment, the terms of the repayment, and the annual percentage interest rate.
* Use bait and switch tactics: It is prohibited by both federal law and state law.Telling your customer the item is undesirable or there will be a substantial delay in the delivery of the item is a sufficient indication you never intended to sell the customer the item.

Do:

* Be accurate about your product or service.
* Be truthful about your product or service.
* Be careful about endorsements that may tend to be misleading and also be sure to get permission to use these endorsements.
* Be concise about the words you choose; for example, silverware is not the same as flatware.
* Get releases if your ad features a picture of someone or uses a person's name.
* Have sufficient quantities on hand, and if you don't think you can meet the demand from your ad then state that quantities are limited.

Publicity

Publicity is news. It may be about your product, service, company, or its personnel. Within a large organization, publicity is viewed as part of the public relations function.

Publicity is free. It can be used to shape a total image. If the publicity is sufficiently newsworthy it can be used as a basis for a newspaper or magazine column.

Although publicity is free, the message can be distorted by media personnel because they control content and timing of the communication. Also, your press release may reach a different target market than you intended because control of the message is in the hands of the media.

Types of Publicity

News release. This is the most popular type of publicity and is usually a single page of typewritten copy containing between 50–300 words.

Feature article. This type is usually from 100–300 words and contains an in-depth story about a product or service.

Captioned photograph. This type is a photograph that contains a brief description of the photo's contents. This type of publicity is best whenever you want to show a new or improved product with highly visible features.

Press conference. This type is often used to announce a major news event. The media is invited to the conference and is supplied with written materials.

Publicity Subject Matter

* New product
* New use of product
* Change in credit terms
* Change in guarantee
* Change in distribution policy
* Anniversary of the organization
* Anniversary of the product
* Open house
* Merit awards to employees
* Opening of an exhibition
* Creation of a new service
* Promotion of an employee
* Opening of a new facility
* Visit by a famous person
* Charitable undertaking
* New discovery or production process
* Report on progress of experiment
* Increase in employment
* Opening of new market

Personal Selling

This method involves informing customers about the product's or service's features through personal communication.

The steps involved in personal selling are:

Develop a list of potential customers. Your prospects can come from a variety of sources: tradeshows, newspaper announcements, public records, trade association directories, other customers, telephone directories, etc.

Assess each potential customer's needs. Determine the needs of each prospect and then analyze how your product or service can best satisfy those needs. Your objective is to precisely articulate the characteristics of your customer so that you can use this information in your presentation.

Present your product or service. A successful presentation involves not only talking but listening. You must learn to listen. Make sure to elicit all of your customer's needs. This is your most powerful selling tool. Too many presentations fail because the person making the presentation did not listen when the customer detailed his or her specific needs. A preplanned presentation is important, but you must learn to adjust your presentation quickly. Again, your goal in any presentation is to not only show your product or service but also to communicate to the customer how your product or service will satisfy his or her needs.

Follow-up. Always follow-up after the sale. Check to make sure the order was delivered on time and installed properly. Also check to see whether any problems may have arisen since the installation of the product or use of the service. Also be alert to your customer's future product or service needs.

Promotions

Included in this method are all activities that do not fall within the categories of advertising, publicity, or personal selling. Examples of promotions are:

* coupons - "cents off"
* demonstration of the product or service
* point-of-purchase displays
* free samples
* contests and sweepstakes
* push money offered to wholesalers and retailers
* buying allowance (for example, get one free with a purchase of a dozen)

Never Forget Customer Relations

All the advertising in the world will not help you if you cannot keep your customers satisfied. Customers become dissatisfied usually for one or both of two reasons: (1) your product or service no longer satisfies their needs, or (2) you and your staff are no longer courteous or professional. Usually, it is the second reason that keeps customers away.

Ironically, many business owners and their staff let success go to their heads. They quickly forget that it was customers who made them successful. Doors that were first opened with a touch of anxiety are soon opened with confidence, only to be replaced later with arrogance. This syndrome, which we call "we don't need your business, there are plenty of other customers like you," often exposes itself in those businesses that are successful immediately. Instead of having to struggle to build a large customer base, they open their doors to an immediate success with customers lined up outside the door. Yet, something happens, and almost overnight with the same speed that brought success, the business begins to languish. What was once a booming business is headed toward failure.

We recommend that once you open your doors for business, you perform a self-inspection on a regular basis. Be sure your personnel acts in a professional manner and is courteous. Insist upon all service to be performed in a thorough manner and to be of high quality. Look at your business through the eyes of your customers. Good manners and a courteous demeanor should apply to everyone in your organization.

How to Prepare a Promotion Budget

Promotion costs, such as advertising, personal selling, and sales promotion are controllable, which means you can tailor a program to fit your budget and your marketing needs. We recommend the approach below.

First.

Determine what percentage of your anticipated revenue will be allocated to advertising. Revenue can be estimated. Trade publications and journals will often contain information on how to estimate revenue. In addition, two other methods that can be used to forecast revenue are given in Chapter 14. Percentages can also be obtained from trade journals and publications. Usually the trade association will publish statistics on the percentage of revenue that is spent on marketing efforts.

Second.

Determine the percentage of revenue each month contributes to annual revenue. For example, 15 percent of annual revenue can be attributed to sales in January, and 20 percent of annual revenue can be attributed to sales in February, etc. The total of the percentages must equal 100 percent. Again, if you have a start-up business, we advise you to use trade association figures until you have established your own operating history.

Third.

Establish a budget. It is absolutely imperative that you take the time to make a budget and that you stick to it. It is easy to get sucked into the emotional aspect of your marketing effort and begin spending money without thinking about the negative financial effect it may have on your business. Results from promotion efforts are often difficult to determine; as a consequence, you are never sure whether you are spending enough money for promotional activities and whether the activities are channeled in the right direction. Below is a basic format for a marketing budget, which will assist you in controlling your expenditures. Add to or subtract from the budget as your promotional activities change.

Promotional Activities	Month Actual Budget		Year to Date Actual Budget	
Advertising				
Newspaper				
morning				
evening				
Sunday				
weekly				
shopper				
Magazine				
local				
trade				
Direct Mail				
letters				
brochures				
newsletters				
circulars				
catalogs				
price lists				
Radio				
FM stations				
AM stations				
Television				
local				
CATV				
Publicity				
News release				
Feature article				
Personal Selling				
Indoor				
Outdoor				
Promotion				
Coupons				
Demonstrations				
Free samples				
Displays				

DO YOU NEED A MIDDLEMAN TO DISTRIBUTE YOUR PRODUCT?

As we have seen throughout this handbook, before we can make an educated decision, we must investigate the problem. In this section, we will provide you with a list of various factors and analyses to help you determine whether a middleman is necessary.

Are you a retailer, distributor, or manufacturer? As a retailer, your distribution method is a direct function of your location. If, however, you are a manufacturer or distributor, you will need to consider some method of distribution. The list below contains questions to guide you in considering a method of distribution.

1. Are you able to identify the traditional forms of distribution for your industry?

2. Does your proposed distribution channel compare favorably with the rest of the industry, or is your niche shaped by your unique delivery system?

3. If you compare favorably, is there a more cost effective alternative?

4. Is it less expensive to hire a distribution channel than to recreate it yourself?

If you decide to use an independent distributor, how do you pick the best one? We suggest that your choice be guided by the answers you receive to the following questions:

* What is the distributor's industry reputation?
* Does the distributor service the market you are targeting?
* Does the distributor carry any competing lines or services?
* Are the distributor's goals for market penetration in line with yours?

Remember that any distribution arrangement will become a quasi-partnership and in some cases more than that if you provide territorial exclusivity. Do your homework. Do not accept, at face value, anything middlemen promises you. After all, the goal of all middlemen is to sell you their services—not to relate any negatives about themselves. Check all middlemen out thoroughly.

The bottom line in the decision-making process is: Can your business perform the distribution service better and more cost effectively than the distributor? To answer this question, you will have to make a cost comparison. To assist you in the comparison process, we have provided you with a list of costs you should consider. *Note*: You should perform your cost comparison on the basis of costs as a percentage of your sales.

Cost of Self-Distribution

Outside salespersons—commissions
Inside salespersons—commissions
Sales receptionist salary
Rent, utilities
Investment in fixed assets
Employee benefits
Telephone
Drivers and delivery personnel
Administrative
Invoicing and bookkeeping
Insurance

This list will provide you with an idea of the costs associated with selling and distributing your product. Before comparing costs of self-distribution to a distributor's cost, be sure to compare only those costs that will be eliminated from your operating expenses so that you will be comparing "apples to apples." Should the distributor's costs be lower or the same, choose the distributor since you will now be able to control sales costs directly through performance. If the distributor's cost is higher, you must weigh the intangible cost of breaking into markets that have already been penetrated by the distributor.

Let's assume you have decided a middleman is the best method for your company to distribute its products. What types of middlemen are there? The following list describes various types of middlemen and the services they provide.

Wholesalers. These firms buy in quantity and generally sell to retailers or other wholesalers. They can carry a variety of lines usually dictated by the outlets they service. They can also carry a variety of one item, which they supply to various outlets. They provide value by assuming the duties of assembly and shipping orders, storing merchandise, invoicing, and granting credit to customers. The wholesaler takes title to the goods. By performing these services, the wholesaler reduces the risk associated with credit extension, and provides penetration into outlets that otherwise might be closed.

Rack Jobbers. These firms use retail outlets with rack displays as their selling ground. They replace old and worn merchandise with new, fresh merchandise and charge the retailer for what they supply and credit them for worn or damaged goods. The rack jobber essentially rents space from the retailer. In these arrangements, you must be careful to ensure that sales to the rack jobber are final unless goods are damaged upon receipt by the rack jobbers. Otherwise, you will be assuming the risk the rack jobber is supposed to be taking, which is also incorporated into his or her markup. An example of a rack jobber is the bumper sticker rack. Stickers containing new sayings are rotated into stock and stickers with older sayings are rotated out of stock until they can be brought back at some later time or in some new location.

Manufacturer's Representatives. These individuals carry lines of similar but noncompeting products to service a specific industry, or, a single product to service many industries. This form of distribution can take many forms. Depending on how the product reaches the end user, manufacturer's representatives can sell to wholesalers, to buying offices of major firms, or to companies within some designated territory. The major reason for employing a manufacturer's representative, other than industry tradition, is the ability of that representative to get your product into his or her stable of customers. A good representative will provide you with a selling ground that has already been developed. In this case, the intangible cost of comparison mentioned previously comes into play. The representative does not take title to your goods.

Brokers. These people usually deal in large one-time transactions within a given market. Although the transactions are usually unique in nature, the broker may engage in a number of transactions with the same customer. The major reason why companies deal with brokers is because of their knowledge of the market place, prices within that market, and the buyers in the market. Their value is generally measured in terms of time: They shorten the sales cycle. Brokers do not take title.

Commission Merchants. This type of distributor is also known as a consignment merchant. He or she provides space for a product on the condition that if it is sold, he or she will pay the manufacturer for it. This method has its obvious risks and is usually employed when the manufacturer is new and untried. Because the goods are out of your control and you have not received payment for them, all of the risk has been placed on you. It may be the only way to get started, but avoid this method if at all possible.

Although the list above is not complete, it will give you an idea of what is out there. The ultimate factor in deciding on a distributor is the relative cost of replicating the distributor's service. That service is summarized below:

* Distributors provide expertise.
* Distributors can provide a proven market.
* Distributors can lower your risk.
* Distributors can reduce your out-of-pocket costs.
* Distributors can be more efficient.

Up to this point, we have limited our discussion to distributors that operate outside your business; however, there are numerous other arrangements available to you. Those alternative arrangements involve options closer to your business, and are listed below:

Commission Selling Agents. These independent people work for you on a strict commission basis and are paid as independent contractors. They are supplied a territory and office support but control their own hours. This arrangement works only if the territory has sufficient volume to support them. In many cases, your business will have to give up house accounts in order to develop a territory. The key is to provide a proper incentive that allows the selling agent to earn a spectacular income while you manage to keep your profits high. The two are mutually compatible if done correctly. *Note*: You can never pay a salesperson on straight commission too much.

Salaried Salespeople. These individuals are on your payroll. They are paid a straight salary regardless of what they sell. This method is typical of retail establishments. You may want to provide some goals and commission incentives to get the best out of them.

You. Many of you are reading this handbook because you can sell. It may be that your abilities and connections are the very spark that started this endeavor. If so, you must be prepared to hand over operational control to someone else. We do not discourage this situation; on the contrary, we believe you should leverage your skills with the realization that others will be necessary to run various portions of your business.

As we have seen, there are numerous methods of distributing your product or service. Take the time to find the best one for you and then cultivate it.

FACTORS TO CONSIDER IN LOCATING YOUR BUSINESS

We have a very good friend who is in real estate. When asked what are the three most important factors in determining the value of a piece of property he responded, "Location, location, and location." Little did he know that he was actually talking about the importance of properly placing a business. Factors to consider when locating a business are particularly important because they can be:

* Long-term in nature
* Expensive
* Directly related to the success or failure of your business

We recommend the following method to analyze where you should locate your business.

State

First, you must choose a suitable state in which to operate. It must relate to your position in the channel of distribution. For instance, your business may include manufacturing, wholesaling, or retailing. You may be in the business of providing a service. As you might have suspected, for each category, there is a variety of factors that will affect your decision. The table below represents the major business categories within the channel of distribution.

Position in Distribution Channel	Symbol
Retail	R
Manufacturing	M
Wholesale	W
Service	S

Issues you should consider in the location of your business are listed below.

State

R, S, W—Is the state increasing in population over the national average?

M, R —Is the climate suitable for the business?

R, S—Where are your customers concentrated?

M, R, S—What is labor skill availability? Is labor unionized?

M, W—What are transportation costs and availability?

M—What is the availability of materials and suppliers?

M, R, W—What are construction and land costs?

M, R, W, S—What is your preference?

Metropolitan Area

Once the state has been chosen, you need to further refine your selection to a given metropolitan area within that state. The factors that affect your decision are:

R, S, W—Is the metropolitan area growing?

M—What is the metropolitan area attitude toward your business?

R,S—Where are your customers concentrated?

M, W, R—What is labor skill availability? Is labor unionized?

M, R, S, W—Are police, fire, and utility services adequate?

M, R, S, W—Do tax incentives exist?

M, W—What are transportation costs and availability?

M—What is the availability of materials and supplies?

M, W, R —What is site availability and cost?

M—Are there any environmental issues associated with the community?

As you have probably noticed, similar questions are posed in both the state and metropolitan area selection decision. Once you have selected both state and metropolitan areas, you will need to concentrate on the specific location decision. What are the considerations in choosing a specific location? Each business in the channel of distribution has specific site requirements. To assist you in making the correct decision, you should address the questions below as you analyze each particular site:

Retail

* Is the population in the area sufficient to support your business venture?
* Are you near any competition? For shopping goods, this is essential; for convenience stores, this is the kiss of death.
* What is the traffic density? Can it support your business? Is walk-in traffic important to you?
* Is there public transportation near your site, or is there easy automobile access?
* Is there adequate parking and lighting?
* Do local ordinances allow signage? If so, what type? If not, how much will it cost you to advertise your location?
* Are fire and police protection adequate?
* Will you be near an adequate labor supply?
* Is the markup on your products sufficient to cover your rent expense? Are the terms and conditions of your lease reasonable? *Warning*: Have your lawyer review all commercial leases because they are usually full of traps, such as triple net and percentage rentals. If you know what your costs are before you go into a lease, at least you will be aware of the type of costs and the amount of costs you will incur, and you can make your decision regarding site location accordingly. However, many entrepreneurs attempt to skimp on professional services. In particular, they do not show their lawyer the lease they are about to sign, and only until they are overwhelmed with hidden costs do they seek legal advice, which by then, is usually too late.

Wholesale

* What are the zoning laws in the area?
* What transportation facilities are available and how good is access? Are there sufficient on and off loading facilities? Is rail service available, if needed?
* Is the rent expense reasonable for your activities?
* Where are your customers located? Do you need to be located close by?

Service

* What is your market? Is it upscale? Are appearances important?
* Do you need to be in a high traffic area?
* Is access important?
* Will you need to be near other businesses that supply ancillary services?

Manufacturing

* What is the access to the labor skill level you will require?
* Are transportation services and facilities adequate?
* Are there environmental issues regarding your business?
* Do raw material suppliers need to be close?
* Is the zoning proper for your type of business?
* What is the local political climate like? Will it be hostile to your type of business? Will you receive community support or resistance?

The list of questions above is not comprehensive, but it should get you thinking about the specific location that will best suit your needs. Be prepared, however; few areas will ever be perfect. Specific site location is a series of compromises. You must decide which factors are most important to you and weigh them accordingly. The best advice we can give is to be deliberate in your choice. If you make a decision in haste, you may have a long lease to repent through.

HOW TO PRICE YOUR PRODUCT OR SERVICE

Price is a function of supply and demand. As a general rule, demand for a product normally increases as price decreases and vice versa. If the price of your product or service gets too high, your customers will attempt either to reduce their consumption of your product or service or seek an acceptable substitute. Within this economic framework, there are generally three types of markets you could possibly encounter.

How the Nature of the Market Will Affect Your Pricing Strategy

Your pricing strategy will often depend on the number and types of competitors that you face in the market. Your goal is to seek a market in which you will have some control over the price of your product. There are four types of markets: monopoly oligopoly, monopolistic competition, and competitive. Each market is defined by the competition which operates within that market.

Monopoly Market. This is a market in which one business controls the vast majority of supply. It will have a unique or protected product (for example, a patented invention) or have a temporary edge on the competition due to an existing business structure. In this market, the optimum price you will charge is that amount which will allow marginal revenues to equal marginal costs. *Note*: To charge any higher price or lower price would result in lower profits. However, the monopolist must be wary of causing, through his or her pricing policy, the use of substitutes or conservatism (for example, reduction in the use of oil products due to a quadrupling of prices in the 1970s).

Unless you are very lucky in your patenting process or have a valuable trade secret that cannot be discovered, you probably will not have a perfect monopoly for an extended period of time. Therefore, the approach should be to price your product to cover costs and recover all research and development costs over what you consider to be the monopoly life of your product.

Oligopolistic Market. This market is characterized by few participants with little meaningful product differentiation. In this case, pricing will be a function of competitor pricing such that if you reduce the price of your product your competitors will reduce their price, but if you increase your price your competitor may not. The general model for this type of market is the steel industry, oil industry, or the domestic automobile industry. You may be faced with a smaller oligopolistic market if you operate in a small community, but in most cases you will probably fall into the third type of market.

Competitive Market. Included in this classification is what is known as the monopolistically competitive market. This type of market is characterized by numerous participants with almost no product differentiation and little or no economic bars to market entrance. All the competitors seek to differentiate their product or service through quality, service, or style. In this market, customers, as a whole, determine the price. We will spend our time analyzing pricing and pricing strategies in this market.

In general, as mentioned previously, the price must be high enough to cover costs plus provide a fair return to the owners of the capital as well as be low enough to induce consumers to purchase the product or service. If these two conditions cannot be met, the product or service will become unprofitable and should not be made. There are, however, exceptions to this rule:

* It might be desirable to price one product at or below cost to induce customers to buy other profitable items in the product line. This is known as loss leader pricing.

* It might be desirable to underprice a product to entice a customer to use the product in the hopes that he or she will see its value. This strategy usually results in raising the price at a later date once the customer is "in the fold." *Warning*: You risk customer alienation and some customers will rebel and leave.

* It is sometimes necessary to reduce a price to convert an unwanted item of inventory to cash. This practice is known as the markdown.

These strategies are important; however, if you are to stay in business you must generate a profit. Basically, you must sell, on average, all items on the product list at some average level of profit. Let's take a look at a number of different pricing scenarios to see how you can achieve this end.

Given a highly competitive market where prices are set by competition, one method to create increased profits involves becoming the low-cost producer. This can be accomplished through one or a combination of the following methods:

* Develop a more efficient method of production or product delivery
* Negotiate an advantageous lease
* Purchase labor-saving capital equipment
* Reduce average cost per unit through increased market share
* Improve purchase price through quantity discounts
* Reduce fixed overhead costs

It is obviously easier to list these strategies than to achieve them. However, for competitive markets, there are numerous other influences and strategies for pricing. In a highly competitive environment, you can attempt to differentiate your product or service so that it will command a higher price, or you can target a market segment that is not as price sensitive. Some of the most common methods used to distinguish the product in the mind of the customer are:

* Choose a distinctive and attractive logo
* Choose eye-catching colors
* Advertise your product
* Use personalities to endorse your product
* Obtain good store location
* Enhance quality of your product or service
* Alter the styling of your product

These are just a few of the methods used to differentiate your product from your competition.

Another excellent method to use in determining the price of your product is to analyze the behavior of revenues and costs when your product or service is offered at different prices. This method is based on the concept of breakeven analysis. Breakeven analyis and how to apply it to pricing decisions are discussed below.

Breakeven Analysis

Throughout this chapter, we have stated numerous times that prices must exceed costs or there is no reason to be in business. The use of breakeven analysis will assist you in determining whether or not this relationship exists, and, if so, what quantity–price combination will satisfy your minimum requirement that revenues equal costs.

To accomplish this goal, the various elements of the breakeven equation must be defined.

P = Price

The price at which one unit of a product will be sold. This is generally the unknown; however, it can be established and other variables can be solved for.

Q = Quantity

Amount, in units, that needs to be sold to generate revenues sufficient to cover various costs. This quantity must have the same unit measurement as price. That is, we can deal in gross, each, hundredweights, etc., but the measurement must be used consistently.

F = Fixed Costs

Costs which are present regardless of whether we produce one unit or one thousand units. Note that fixed costs are fixed only to some maximum level of quantity (Q) production. When we exceed that level, we must increase F, fixed costs. For example, if the most widgets we can build in a 10,000 square foot plant is 1,000 widgets, then to produce 1001 widgets we will need to expand our plant. Thus F, fixed costs, will have to increase. Fixed costs will include items such as rent, heat, lights, insurance, administrative salaries, indirect labor expense, and cost of machinery.

V = Variable Costs

Costs associated with each unit of production. These costs are directly associated with the production of each product. Variable costs typically include direct labor expense, raw material expense, and sales commissions.

PF = Profit

The reason we are in business. When we solve for the breakeven level of sales, profit is equal to zero.

Now that all the elements of the breakeven equation have been defined, let's proceed with the equation itself. The basic equation form is:

$$\text{Profit} = (\text{Revenue} - \text{Fixed Costs} - \text{Variable Costs})$$

At this point we need to provide further definitions:

$$* \textbf{Revenue} = (\text{quantity sold}) \times (\text{price per unit})$$

or

$$\textbf{Revenue} = QP$$

$$* \textbf{Variable Costs} = (\text{quantity sold}) \times (\text{variable cost per unit})$$

or

$$\textbf{Variable Costs} = QV$$

We are now ready to state the breakeven equation in its general abbreviated form:

$$\textbf{PF} = (QP - F - QV)$$

You will recall that the objective in breakeven analysis is to determine the level of sales where revenues equal total costs. Note that our general equation has a term for profit. We did this to allow flexibility in determining a level of sales required to provide a desired level of profits (An example follows). At this point, however, let's adjust the general breakeven equation to solve for a breakeven pricing level. Since the breakeven level of sales is the point at which revenues equal total costs, it is also the point at which profit equals zero. Therefore, our general equation now looks like this:

$$0 = PF = QP - F - QV$$

or

$$0 = QP - F - QV$$

Solving the equation for P, we get:

$$P = \frac{F + QV}{Q}$$

Note: We can also solve the equation for Q:

$$Q = \frac{F}{P - V}$$

For those of you who prefer a visual representation, the following graph will present the entire concept of breakeven analysis in a single glance. The three lines are labeled as:

F   =   Fixed cost over the production quantity of interest

TC   =   Total cost to produce Q units of product

R   =   Sales revenue generated by selling Q units of product.

The point labeled B is the breakeven point in terms of sales. Above point B, the firm makes a profit equal to the distance between line R and line TC. Below point B the firm suffers a loss equal to the distance between line TC and line R.

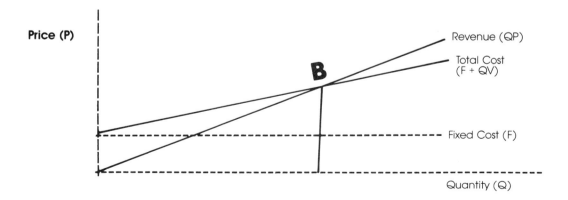

Let's take a look at three examples of the use of breakeven analysis and pricing your product.

Example 1:

Problem: Assume your business will be able to sell everything it can produce and that it produces a maximum of 100,000 units per year. Your fixed costs are $500,000 per year and variable costs are $3.00 per unit. If your business produces and sells at maximum output, what is the breakeven *price*?

Solution: Employ the breakeven equation to solve for price:

$$P = \frac{F + QV}{Q}$$

Where: F = $500,000
        Q = 100,000
        V = $3

Therefore:

$$P = \frac{500,000 + 100,000(3)}{100,000}$$

$$P = \$8.00 \text{ per unit}$$

At $8.00 per unit, your business will just cover fixed and total variable costs.

Example 2:

Problem: Given the same set of circumstances as in the previous example, except that you have set the price at $9.25 per unit, what is the breakeven *quantity* at this price level?

Solution: Employ the second form of the breakeven equation to solve for quantity:

$$Q = \frac{F}{P - V}$$

Where: F = $500,000
        P = $9.25
        V = $3.00

Therefore:

$$Q = \frac{500,000}{9.25 - 3}$$

$$Q = 80,000 \text{ units}$$

At a price of $9.25 per unit, your business can operate below maximum capacity and break even. As a side note, if your business operates at full capacity or 100,000 units and sells all of these units, will it make a profit? Yes, since, by definition, any sales above the breakeven point will cause your business to earn a profit. The amount of the profit is a function of contribution margin. The contribution margin is defined as the difference between the price per unit and its variable cost per unit. In this example, the contribution margin is $6.25 ($9.25 -$3.00). Thus, for every unit above the breakeven point, your business earns $6.25 of profit. This relationship simply relates the fact that all of your fixed overhead will be absorbed at the breakeven point.

Example 3:

Problem: Given the same set of circumstances as in the first example, except now you desire a profit of $100,000 when your business is operating at full capacity, what is the price you must charge?

Solution: This variation assumes that profit is not equal to zero as it was in first and second examples. In fact, profit is targeted at $100,000, and therefore, we must go back to the general formula in order to solve this equation:

$$PF = QP - F - QV$$

Solve the equation for P:

$$P = \frac{PF + F + QV}{Q}$$

Where:

F	=	$500,000
PF	=	$100,000
Q	=	100,000
V	=	$3.00

Therefore:

$$P = \frac{100,000 + 500,000 + 100,000(3)}{100,000}$$

$$P = \$9.00 \text{ per unit}$$

The use of breakeven analysis provides a great deal of latitude in the analysis of our pricing strategy. It allows us to manipulate many variations or combinations of variables to ascertain levels of production/sales, levels of cost, or levels of price necessary to reach a desired profit. It will give us that all important point above which we will create profit and below which we will suffer losses. Knowledge of this point can be extremely important in your pursuit of the market. It will identify products that are profitable to produce and sell versus products that must be dropped.

Note that although we have shown examples of a manufacturing company, the breakeven method will work just as well for wholesalers and retailers. We need only define the appropriate terms of fixed costs, variable costs, selling price or quantity, in order to arrive at the unknown of interest, which could be any of the following:

* The breakeven selling price
* The breakeven quantity
* The price-quantity relationship for a desired amount of profit

The calculation of fixed and variable costs should be a simple task. The key unknown will often be the quantity sold/produced. In the construction of your marketing plan, you will be required to project or forecast the demand for your product or service at various prices. This forecast is important because it will provide you with a quantity that can then be used to test your price and vice versa.

To complete our discussion on pricing, we are now going to introduce you to pricing methods that are used in any general business category.

Commonly Used Pricing Methods

The four general business types are: retail, wholesale, manufacturing, and service. Each business type has its own pricing methods.

Retail

The retailer earns profits by providing site utility—that is, he or she brings a product to the consumer at a time and place of the consumer's choosing. For this service, the retailer is rewarded. Retail pricing strategies can be based on numerous factors such as:

Competition. Perhaps the strongest factor in the pricing equation for a retailer is the issue of competitors' prices. Unless the retailer brings something special, such as time utility (for example, retailer remains open 24 hours a day), he or she cannot charge any more than his or her competitors without losing sales.

Business Conditions. In a robust economy, prices can be maintained and perhaps raised. In a slow economy, it may be necessary to lower prices just to stay in business.

Market Strategy. The retailer should consider the following questions: Does he or she wish to be a low cost, high volume store or vice versa? Will he or she introduce loss leaders to increase volume in more profitable areas? Is his or her target market price sensitive? The answers to these questions will dictate market strategy.

In retailing, there are two basic approaches to pricing: the initial markup method and the market markup method.

Markup Percentage Method

With this method, we want to determine a target profit that is expressed as a percentage of gross sales. To calculate how much we should mark-up our products, the following values must be identified.

* Operating expenses, such as fixed overhead and taxes
* Estimated net sales, which are sales that are not marked down
* Estimated contra-revenues,which consists of discounts to customers, stock shortages, and cost of marked down goods.

For example, if projected net sales are $250,000, operating expenses are $76,660, reductions are $15,000 and the desired profit is $25,000, the initial markup percentage would be determined as follows:

$$\text{Markup \%} = \frac{\text{(operating expenses)} + \text{(contra-revenues)} + \text{(profit)}}{\text{net sales} + \text{contra-revenues}}$$

or

$$\text{Markup \%} = \frac{76,660 + 15,000 + 25,000}{250,000 + 15,000} = 46\%$$

This markup (46%), is to be used to obtain the desired profit. Note that this markup is an average and that some of your products will exceed this markup while others will fall below it.

Market Markup Method

This calculation takes little effort. Simply price your goods similar to those of your competitors. This pricing method is used extensively at grocery stores. In the context of your business, however, you must attempt to somehow differentiate your business from the competition. Areas to concentrate on, which have been proven to be effective include:

* Quality
* Service
* Product performance
* Discounting
* Location
* Hours of operation

Wholesale

In the area of wholesaling, we are faced with a slightly different set of circumstances. Pricing will depend on whether you are distributing unique or nonunique products.

When handling a unique product, the business is generally under some sort of distribution agreement regarding territorial distribution rights. In this case, the manufacturer can determine pricing for the wholesaler or simply provide the wholesaler with goals and allow the wholesaler to price as appropriate to meet those goals and maximize revenues.

When the wholesaler handles nonunique products for which there is much competition, the wholesaler must price his or her product with an eye toward competition. Once again, you should attempt to differentiate your firm. Your economic reward is based on how well you can satisfy your customers' needs through timely deliveries and good service. You should never lose sight that the wholesaler's function is to act as an inventory buffer for his or her customers.

To illustrate pricing methods used by the wholesaler, we will draw information from the Robert Morris Associates (RMA) guide of industry financial data for a wine, liquor, and beer wholesaler, which has a standard classification of SIC 5181. For this type of wholesaler, the gross margin is 24 percent of sales and operating expenses are 22 percent of sales. Note that the lion's share of sales (76 percent) is associated with cost of goods sold. The reason cost of goods sold accounts for such a large portion of sales is that the majority of value for products sold by the wholesaler comes at the manufacturing level. The additional value the wholesaler provides is bringing the product to market and warehousing it until it is needed by the retailer.

Now that we have information concerning the percentage of gross margin, operating expenses, and cost of goods sold, we can examine two approaches that can be used to price your product.

First Approach: We can solve for the breakeven price.

Second Approach: We can calculate a price necessary to charge in order to reach a specific amount of profit.

Let's take a look at how we would handle pricing by using the first approach. As an example, let's use the following set of circumstances:

Fixed costs = $50,000
Quantity = 500,000
Variable cost per unit = $3.00

Solution: From our discussion on breakeven analysis we recall the formula:

$$P = \frac{F + QV}{Q}$$

or

$$P = \frac{50,000 + 500,000(3)}{500,000} = \$3.10$$

Thus, $3.10 is the breakeven price. This is the price you must charge to cover your costs. The example above is typical for wholesalers. They tend to move large quantities of products with relatively low fixed costs. Should you wish to earn a certain amount of profit, say $50,000, simply recalculate the price (P) using the general form of the breakeven formula:

$$P = \frac{PF + F + QV}{Q}$$

or

$$P = \frac{50,000 + 50,000 + 500,000(3)}{500,000} = \$3.20$$

To use, the second approach to calculate a selling price, we need simply to employ the percentage method. Again, let us use the example of the wine, liquor and beer wholesaler. As previously noted, the typical gross margin for this type of wholesaler is 24 percent of sales. If we assume that operating expenses are 22 percent and that we wish to earn a 2 percent pretax profit, we can determine the appropriate price level required by using the following method:

Selling price	100%
Cost of goods	- 76%
Gross profit	24%
Operating expense	- 22%
Pretax profit	2%

As a result, if the cost of the product we sell is $1.00, then the selling price of our product will have to be $1.32, which is calculated by dividing $1.00 by $.76 ($1.00 /.76). The markup on cost is defined as the selling price divided by the cost minus 1, which is 32% [($1.32 / $1.00) -1]. To increase the pretax profit, one of two things can be done:

First: Raise the price for a given level of cost; or

Second: Lower the operating expenses.

For example, using our previous example assume we wish to obtain a pretax profit of 10 percent at the current level of operating expense. Since the operating expense of 22 percent of sales has remained the same, the cost of goods as a percentage of sales will drop to 68 percent [100% - (22% + 10%)]. To determine the selling price, we need simply to divide the cost of our product by the cost of goods sold as a percentage of sales. The result is that the selling price should be $1.47 ($1.00/.68), which is calculated by dividing $1.00 by $.68.

Manufacturing

For manufacturing, as in the other types of businesses, internal cost should not be the only consideration in pricing. Outside influences which may affect prices must be examined in order to determine an appropriate price range. In manufacturing, your price should fall somewhere between the price floor and price ceiling in your industry, assuming there is an established industry for your product. The price floor is defined as the price at which all of your costs are covered, and you earn a desired profit. The price ceiling is the price determined by the general economy, market factors, competition, technological change, and resource availability. If your price floor exceeds your price ceiling you should strongly reconsider your business venture. If the reverse is true, then price will lie somewhere between the price floor and price ceiling.

The first step in determining how to price your product is to establish the price floor. There are several methods by which you can establish the price floor. We will examine three of them: markup on full cost, incremental cost base, and conversion costing.

Markup on Full Cost Method This method is the easiest and the most commonly used. All that is necessary is to add total direct labor cost plus total direct material cost plus total overhead per unit and then multiply this amount by the desired markup percentage. Determining direct material and labor costs is fairly easy and straightforward. The overhead amount, however, is less so. To get the overhead amount, we must calculate total overhead costs per year and divide them by the projected volume of units to be produced during that year. This figure should be reviewed periodically for significant increases or decreases in either volume of units or fixed expenses. An example follows.

Direct labor cost per unit	$10.00
Direct material cost per unit	+ 8.00
Total direct cost	18.00
Overhead cost per unit	+ 4.00
Total cost per unit	22.00
Markup @ 25%	+ 5.50
Selling price per unit	$27.50

Incremental Cost-Base Method. Use this method when overhead costs are considered immaterial to total costs, or overhead costs are assumed to be fully absorbed. An example follows.

Direct labor cost per unit	$10.00
Direct material cost per unit	+ 8.00
Total direct costs	18.00
Markup @ 25%	+ 4 .50
Selling price per unit	$22.50

Note the difference between the incremental method ($22.50) and the full cost method ($27.50). When your entire overhead has been absorbed elsewhere, the incremental price provides a "bare minimum" floor price for your business.

Conversion Costing Method. This method emphasizes value added through labor and overhead and is used where labor or overhead are relatively high compared to material cost. An example follows.

Example:

Direct labor cost per unit	$50.00
Overhead cost per unit	+ 10.00
Total costs	60.00
Mark-up @ 50%	+ 30.00
Cost per unit	90.00

As you can see, the markup in this case will need to be sufficient to cover material costs.

The methods above help us establish a price floor for our product. Now, the next step is to determine a price ceiling. Compared to the price floor the ceiling is far less quantitative in nature. We are faced with two rather nonquantitative methods: market research and trial and error. As a rule, market research is conducted by taking a sampling of your current and potential customers. You can conduct the sampling yourself or have a market research firm do it for you. The cost can range from $1,500 to $25,000 depending on your market, who conducts the research, the depth of information you require, and whether it is primary or secondary research, or both. One of the benefits of market research is that it allows you to determine the price elasticity of your product, which is a formula that allows you to quantify your customers' responses to various prices. For example, if your formula indicates, after calculation, that you have an elasticity coefficient of –2, it means that for every 1 percent change in price, customer demand will change 2 percent in the opposite direction. Thus, using our example, if you increase your price by 1 percent, customer demand will drop by 2 percent, and the pricing decision will follow.

The trial-and-error is usually conducted by simply placing your product on the market at a price above the floor price and seeing what happens. If you are selling all you can produce and then some, perhaps the price is too low. If the item is moving slowly, perhaps the price is too high. Since it is easier to lower prices than to raise them, we recommend that you guess on the high side and lower the price until the item begins to move at a satisfactory rate.

Service

In the service sector, the issue of pricing depends on community standards. When standards are available, a service business will find it difficult to charge more than the going rate unless there is a perceived difference in the reputation of the professionals involved. For instance, Melvin Belli will be able to command a higher rate than our Gary Brenner (at least at this time). Where no community standard is set, the firm can use either (1) the multiplier method or (2) the job method of pricing its services.

Multiplier Method. The multiplier method is based on a target level of sales and profit supported by a target level of direct and indirect costs. For example, if you target direct costs at $100,000; indirect costs at $50,000; and profit at $75,000, you have by default arrived at an annual level of sales of $225,000 ($100,000 + $75,000 + $50,000). Based on total sales of $225,000 and direct costs of $100,000 our multiplier would be:

$$\text{Multiplier} = \text{annual sales} \ / \ \text{direct costs}$$

or

$$\$2.25 = \$225,000 \ / \ \$100,000$$

Since you know the direct labor cost per hour, you simply multiply the multiplier by the direct cost per hour to determine the price you should charge for your service. For example, if direct cost per hour is $10.00, a five-hour job would be billed at:

$$\$2.25 \ \times \ \$10.00 \ \times \ 5 \ = \ \$112.50$$

The Job Method. The job method requires you to add total direct labor used on the job plus total materials used on the job plus allocated overhead to the job as a function of direct labor hours plus the amount of profit required for that job.

Example:

Total direct labor cost	$ 500
Total material cost	125
Total overhead based on direct labor hours @ .75	+ 375
Total cost	1000
Profit margin @ 25%	+ 250
Job price	$1250

As you can see, there are numerous methods, philosophies, and approaches to pricing. Pricing is a personal issue; it is reflective of the image the entrepreneur has of him- or herself. The methods we have shown you will provide you with a starting point from which you can operate. As before, we have surveyed a broad spectrum of methods and leave the choice to you. We believe that experience is the best teacher and when our wallets are affected, we tend to learn very quickly.

HOW TO USE TRADE SHOWS TO YOUR ADVANTAGE

There are approximately 9,000 trade shows each year in North America, according to the Trade Show Bureau. This section will explain the importance of trade shows in terms of marketing your product or service, where to find information regarding trade shows, and how to determine which trade show is right for your business.

Marketing through Trade Show Exhibits

The trade show can be a lucrative marketing tool because the attendees are there for the express purpose of viewing the latest products and services supplied to their industry. The trade show, therefore, brings the market to you and gives you the opportunity to demonstrate your product, contact potential clients, establish leads, and close sales. The atmosphere is similar to that of a department store. With each prospective customer, you will need to quickly ascertain the name of the individual and the individual's firm, or whether the individual is self-employed as well as his or her interest in your product or service, and buying intentions.

If you want a trade show to be a worthwhile investment for your time and money, then you will have to clearly define your marketing objectives. These objectives include the number of leads you wish to develop and the number of sales you wish to close. These objectives must be stressed because far too many individuals view trade shows as a time to have fun or as a get-away from the normal routine of day-to-day activities. Trade shows can be an important marketing tool, and if treated as such can significantly boost your sales.

Many entrepreneurs overlook yet another aspect of the trade show: the importance of the booth design. You will want to create an attractive, uncluttered marketing environment. Your company's name and logo should be prominently and tastefully displayed. You should provide literature but should not hand it out to any and all viewers. Selective give-aways are useful as long as they are used to generate qualified leads.

The presentation of your company at a trade show reflects the personality of your organization. Since you, as an entrepreneur, need to be an expert in many other areas, we suggest that you contact one of the numerous commercial ventures specializing in the presentation of companies at trade shows. These firms can aid in the design, construction, and setup of display booths. They can handle a wide range of services from your printing needs to logo design. Since your budget for marketing is limited, these organizations can help maximize your marketing impact. Before you make your first trade show presentation, we strongly recommend you attend a couple of appropriate trade shows as well as talk to these exhibit specialists.

Where Does the Entrepreneur Find Information Regarding Trade Shows?

Because of the great volume of trade shows presented each year, an industry devoted to providing exposition services has grown and flourished. Numerous associations, such as the Exposition Service Contractors Association of Los Angeles, both create and depend on various sources of information to support their industry, which is the production of trade shows. These professionals look to certain areas for their information; we recommend you do the same. Ten of the most popular sources are listed below.

* U.S. Department of Commerce (DOC)

The DOC is located in Washington, D.C. and provides information on international trade shows through the International Trade Administration (ITA). The ITA publishes periodic lists of overseas shows detailing type, location, and date of exhibition. This information is free.

* Exhibition Validation Council (EVC)

The EVC is part of the Trade Show Bureau. Its purpose is to validate facts related to trade show audiences including type and classification of registrants, job titles, attendance in past years, and geographical origin of attendees. You can contact EVC via the Trade Show Bureau at 49 Locust Avenue, New Canaan, CT 06840.

* Exhibits Schedule

This annual publication is published by *Successful Meeting* magazine and lists trade shows by industry, geographical area, and chronological presentation. It covers both international and domestic shows. New shows are not likely to be found in the magazine because of its infrequent release. The publication does have a semiannual supplement. Information about number of booths, attendance size, frequency of show presentation, and name and address of organizers is available. Exhibit Schedule is located at 633 Third Avenue, New York, NY 10017.

* Trade Association Publications

Trade newspapers, magazines, newsletters, and associations will have the most specific information regarding industry-specific trade shows. In fact, numerous trade associations are responsible for their own trade shows. A simple scan of industry-associated publications will lead you to the proper trade association for your business. *Note:* Your firm could be interested in several different trade associations and trade shows, depending on your market.

* Tradeshow Week

This reference provides a listing of trade shows on a chronological basis. As a weekly publication, this reference provides lists of shows taking place six and twelve months in the future. It distinguishes between domestic and international shows but does not categorize the shows by industry. The publication highlights what it considers to be the top 150 shows each year and provides editorial comments on hundreds of other shows. Tradeshow Week is located at 12233 Olympic Blvd., Los Angeles, CA 90064.

* Trade Show-Related Associations

As mentioned above, associations such as the Exposition Service Contractor Association will be happy to provide industry-specific information. Other associations include the National Association of Exposition Managers, the International Exhibitors Association, and the Exhibit Designers and Producers Association.

* Chambers of Commerce

Local chambers and convention bureaus can provide you with geographical trade show schedules. These local organizations will also be able to provide most of the statistics the sources mentioned above provide.

* Privately Published Lists

These lists are published by various nontrade-related firms such as PennWell Publishing Company. These publications provide the same general listings of trade shows that the sources mentioned above provide.

* Airlines.

Many airlines will provide calendars of trade shows. Some airlines will publish information expressly for certain areas or locales while other airlines publish lists that are international in scope.

* Other Exhibitors.

We have saved perhaps the best source for last. Who better to ask than exhibitors or attendees which trade shows are the best? This word-of-mouth information is probably your best source. Exhibitors, as a rule, are very helpful and will give you their opinion about those shows you should attend.

As you can see, there is no dearth of information regarding trade shows or exhibitions. We suggest you do your research and line up a prospective list of shows.

Because many entrepreneurs' resources are limited, it makes good sense to discuss how to choose the correct trade show or shows in which to invest. Make no mistake; a trade show is an investment from which you should expect a return. Therefore, you need to be selective. Earlier in this chapter, we discussed how you can increase sales by segmenting the market. Market segmentation also applies to trade show selection. As part of your marketing plan, you should determine which segment of the market you will concentrate your promotional efforts on. Once you make your determination, you should then select those trade shows that cater to that particular segment.

In selecting the most appropriate trade show, you should analyze the various types of shows in terms of the shows' exhibitors (sellers) and their attendees (buyers). Trade shows are classified according to the breadth of the market they serve, both in terms of sellers and buyers. The classifications are:

Vertical—This term defines a single market, function, or industry. It is, therefore, very narrow in scope.

Horizontal—This term defines a broad mix of industries or markets.

Because a trade show is made up of both buyers and sellers, we must define various shows in terms of buyer-seller combinations. There are four possible combinations, and therefore, four possible show types. They are:

Vertical Seller	Horizontal Seller
Vertical or Horizontal buyer buyer	Vertical or Horizontal buyer buyer

Below is a brief discussion of each combination:

Vertical Seller—Vertical Buyer. This show is designed for sellers of specific products interested in specific-industry buyers. An example would be the sale of paper mill machinery to paper mills. These shows tend to have relatively low attendance and little interest to fringe buyers.

Vertical Seller—Horizontal Buyer. This type of show provides a narrow range of products to a broad range of industries. An example would be the sale of office automation equipment to businesses. Generally, the audience is diverse and more regional in scope. Attendance is usually relatively high.

Horizontal Seller—Vertical Buyer. Here we have a wide variety of products sold to a specific industry segment. An example would include the sale of various products to the garment industry. Generally, this type of tradeshow has limited attendance. Moreover, there is much competition for the seller because of the wide diversity of products.

Horizontal Seller—Horizontal Buyer. In this show, many products are sold to many markets. This is much akin to swap meets. The drawback is that the diversity of both products and buyers will dilute your importance and the importance of the products you are offering.

Chapter 8 Exhibits

Exhibit 8.1   Census Geographic Areas: Geographic
             Identification Code Scheme

Exhibit 8.2   Individual Tracts Superimposed on Census
             Tract Map (San Diego)

Exhibit 8.3   Census Tracts Map (San Diego)

Exhibit 8.4   Census Tract 0002 (San Diego)

Exhibit 8.5   Census Tract 0083.12 (San Diego)

CENSUS GEOGRAPHIC AREAS

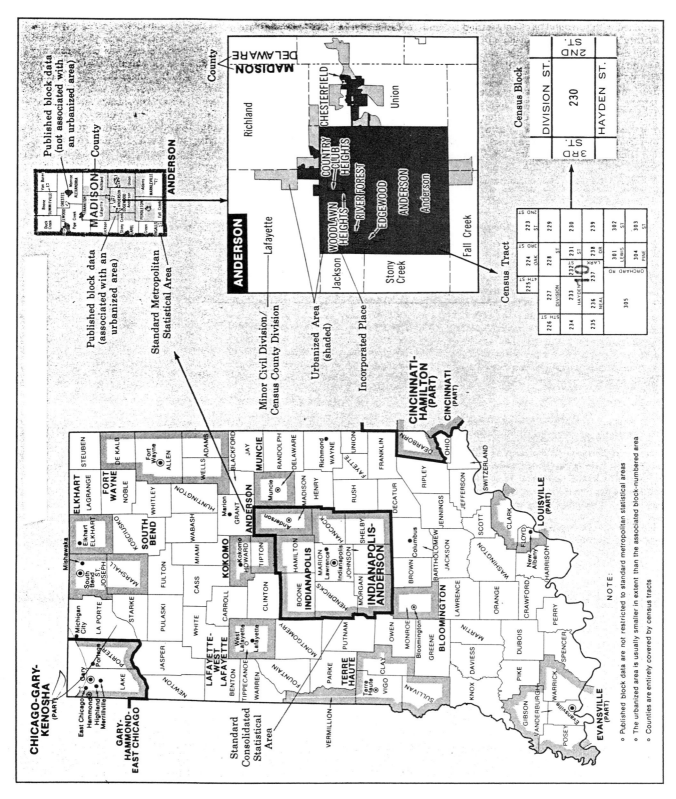

GEOGRAPHIC IDENTIFICATION CODE SCHEME

Exhibit 8-1

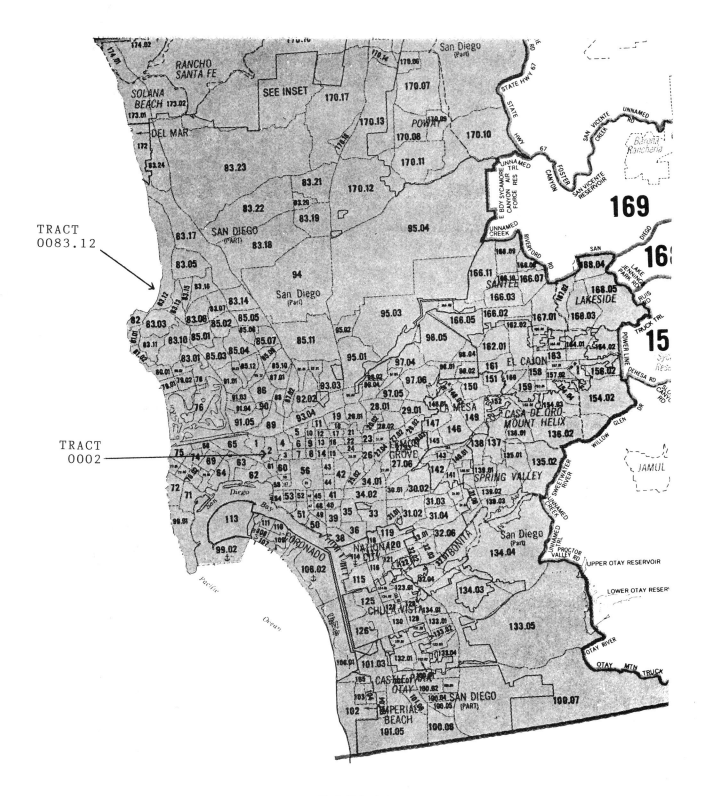

Exhibit 8-2

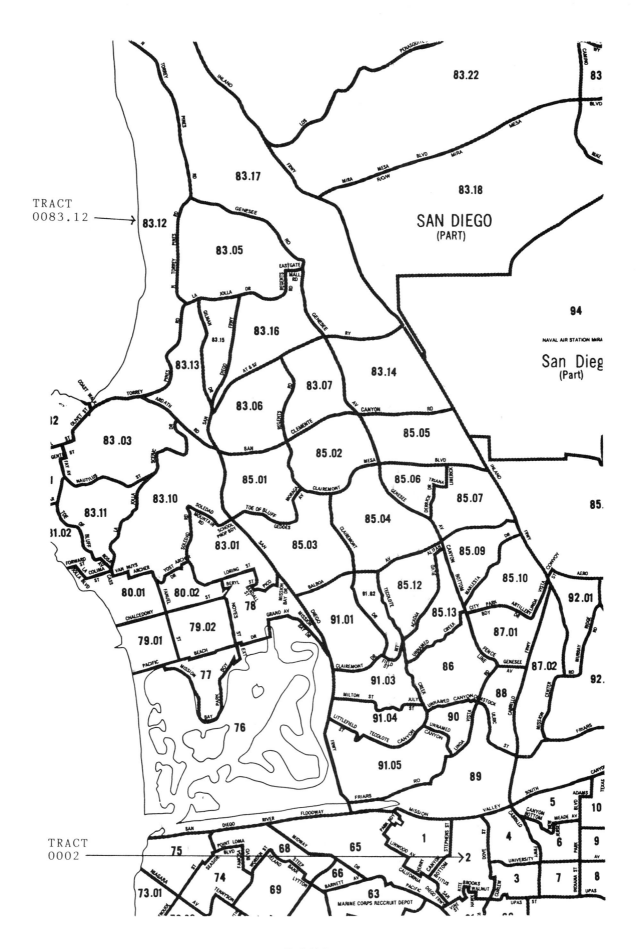

Exhibit 8-3

[Data are estimates based on a sample; see Introduction. For meaning of symbols, see Introduction. For definitions of terms, see appendixes A and B]

Census Tracts	San Diego city, San Diego County												
	Tract 0001	Tract 0002	Tract 0003	Tract 0004	Tract 0005	Tract 0006	Tract 0007	Tract 0008	Tract 0009	Tract 0010	Tract 0011	Tract 0012	Tract 0013
Specified owner-occupied housing units	991	1 058	277	128	416	238	288	359	203	375	253	228	197
MORTGAGE STATUS AND SELECTED MONTHLY OWNER COSTS													
With a mortgage	681	543	130	55	155	83	106	212	101	164	138	80	89
Less than $100	11	–	–	–	–	–	–	–	–	6	8	–	5
$100 to $199	26	27	22	5	6	7	23	27	23	56	29	32	24
$200 to $299	137	137	30	6	36	23	13	45	10	30	21	17	14
$300 to $399	97	98	21	13	20	13	6	39	20	7	39	–	23
$400 to $599	168	92	29	–	20	–	12	77	29	47	8	26	15
$600 or more	242	189	28	31	73	40	52	24	19	18	33	5	8
Median	$488	$452	$381	$619	$563	$389	$542	$391	$394	$242	$329	$224	$305
Not mortgaged	310	515	147	73	261	155	182	147	102	211	115	148	108
Less than $100	105	332	75	41	193	155	134	117	83	170	101	122	92
$100 to $199	184	156	67	24	68	–	39	30	19	41	14	26	16
$200 or more	21	27	5	8	–	–	9	–	–	–	–	–	–
Median	$112	$91	$99	$93	$77	$69	$79	$68	$67	$76	$71	$68	$66
HOUSEHOLD INCOME IN 1979 BY SELECTED MONTHLY OWNER COSTS AS PERCENTAGE OF INCOME													
Less than $10,000	116	226	74	42	97	66	94	81	44	161	105	90	75
Less than 15 percent	22	66	14	17	21	38	30	37	9	68	40	33	8
15 to 24 percent	18	45	12	–	36	14	41	19	29	38	34	15	53
25 to 29 percent	13	9	17	–	20	7	6	8	–	–	8	–	7
30 percent or more	50	99	31	25	20	7	6	17	4	55	8	31	7
Not computed	13	7	–	–	–	–	11	–	2	–	15	11	–
Median	29.4	24.6	28.2	31.4	22.9	13.3	16.6	15.9	22.1	16.6	16.0	17.2	19.9
$10,000 to $19,999	176	256	50	35	108	98	82	105	98	98	73	100	63
Less than 15 percent	67	161	33	10	74	72	54	44	55	50	45	87	50
15 to 24 percent	54	20	8	6	13	12	13	27	13	33	15	13	–
25 to 29 percent	–	16	–	–	15	–	9	8	20	–	5	–	6
30 percent or more	55	59	9	19	6	14	6	26	10	15	8	–	7
Not computed	...	...	...	...	...	...	...	...	...	...	...	...	...
Median	20.8	11.7	7.6	41.7	9.0	10.0	11.7	19.2	12.3	14.7	10.7	8.6	9.3
$20,000 or more	699	576	153	51	211	74	112	173	61	116	75	38	59
Less than 15 percent	449	367	104	29	140	48	60	98	23	82	33	19	43
15 to 24 percent	160	110	22	22	38	10	25	57	9	24	26	7	8
25 to 29 percent	12	31	13	–	11	–	6	6	10	7	–	12	8
30 percent or more	78	68	14	–	22	16	21	12	19	3	16	–	–
Not computed	...	...	...	...	...	...	...	...	...	...	...	...	...
Median	11.5	9.2	11.0	12.1	8.2	7.7	11.7	13.8	24.2	11.3	16.1	17.0	10.8
Specified renter-occupied housing units	164	1 780	1 877	1 541	1 011	1 096	1 647	1 153	2 255	1 731	1 170	2 042	2 237
GROSS RENT													
Less than $80	–	30	13	–	8	14	8	–	100	–	14	7	–
$80 to $99	16	34	26	8	–	46	36	–	51	9	15	14	15
$100 to $149	–	160	120	121	37	87	194	51	271	23	37	69	45
$150 to $199	8	334	347	269	205	203	263	131	239	290	131	206	266
$200 to $249	18	397	417	333	308	320	428	309	618	555	342	692	741
$250 to $299	12	313	385	410	305	178	270	302	608	484	380	688	681
$300 to $349	–	107	228	154	40	125	171	198	254	212	144	235	285
$350 to $399	13	159	90	88	41	38	99	69	47	81	59	66	84
$400 or more	82	226	233	145	59	77	157	86	57	54	48	51	107
No cash rent	15	20	18	13	8	8	21	7	10	23	–	14	13
Median	$420	$241	$251	$253	$242	$231	$239	$261	$238	$248	$255	$251	$253
One-family house, detached or attached	130	556	239	180	399	286	392	356	440	465	267	587	497
Median gross rent	$463	$287	$251	$277	$252	$268	$245	$262	$269	$276	$247	$254	$241
HOUSEHOLD INCOME IN 1979 BY GROSS RENT AS PERCENTAGE OF INCOME													
Less than $10,000	22	795	881	625	424	617	793	534	1 314	769	511	952	1 060
Less than 15 percent	–	–	–	8	–	–	–	–	11	–	8	–	–
15 to 19 percent	–	38	24	16	–	25	20	–	101	–	–	–	–
20 to 24 percent	8	61	26	44	21	41	51	19	125	39	20	26	6
25 to 29 percent	–	101	77	66	38	75	136	65	185	100	43	92	110
30 to 34 percent	–	103	70	84	41	73	97	71	115	67	49	141	74
35 percent or more	7	459	636	400	303	375	474	346	755	511	351	661	841
Not computed	7	33	48	7	21	28	15	33	22	52	40	32	29
Median	24.7	40.0	48.7	42.2	47.0	44.5	41.7	45.6	39.5	46.8	47.4	45.8	49.5
$10,000 to $19,999	59	642	673	566	451	363	536	385	717	691	480	793	867
Less than 15 percent	28	52	69	57	55	20	36	9	44	55	24	50	62
15 to 19 percent	–	147	120	178	81	77	138	68	124	206	100	157	221
20 to 24 percent	–	155	184	123	145	128	150	100	240	175	137	309	274
25 to 29 percent	5	112	148	108	102	86	88	92	160	133	120	168	174
30 to 34 percent	–	77	59	36	48	39	69	60	86	60	57	70	80
35 percent or more	26	87	93	51	12	13	48	56	63	54	42	39	56
Not computed	–	12	–	13	8	–	7	–	–	8	–	–	–
Median	26.5	23.7	24.0	21.7	22.9	23.3	23.0	25.8	24.0	22.3	24.2	23.1	22.7
$20,000 or more	83	343	323	350	136	116	318	234	224	271	179	297	310
Less than 15 percent	8	182	159	176	93	59	186	153	144	173	114	156	193
15 to 19 percent	22	87	64	133	27	43	79	53	66	84	53	119	76
20 to 24 percent	22	55	66	27	8	8	30	19	9	14	12	22	27
25 to 29 percent	14	10	27	14	8	6	–	9	5	–	–	–	7
30 to 34 percent	9	9	–	–	–	–	–	–	–	–	–	–	–
35 percent or more	–	–	–	–	–	–	9	–	–	–	–	–	–
Not computed	8	–	7	–	–	–	14	–	–	–	–	–	7
Median	21.7	14.6	14.9	15.0	13.3	14.9	13.2	13.3	13.5	13.7	13.7	14.6	13.5

Exhibit 8-4

[Data are estimates based on a sample; see Introduction. For meaning of symbols, see Introduction. For definitions of terms, see appendixes A and B]

Census Tracts

San Diego city, San Diego County

	Tract 0001	Tract 0002	Tract 0003	Tract 0004	Tract 0005	Tract 0006	Tract 0007	Tract 0008	Tract 0009	Tract 0010	Tract 0011	Tract 0012	Tract 0013
INCOME IN 1979													
Households	1 265	2 989	2 423	1 770	1 530	1 392	2 065	1 606	2 520	2 187	1 479	2 338	2 518
Less than $5,000	64	473	433	202	248	293	384	211	584	370	258	448	502
$5,000 to $7,499	25	282	366	182	133	199	228	182	430	275	212	228	245
$7,500 to $9,999	60	289	216	266	150	212	287	225	391	286	167	365	413
$10,000 to $14,999	110	575	461	339	370	267	370	297	497	506	342	581	598
$15,000 to $19,999	176	368	328	292	238	215	288	235	321	336	210	350	379
$20,000 to $24,999	85	319	188	185	81	88	185	212	148	236	145	210	192
$25,000 to $34,999	239	290	237	209	171	43	160	150	124	111	100	86	130
$35,000 to $49,999	231	232	100	76	120	59	118	71	17	36	39	53	43
$50,000 or more	275	161	94	19	19	16	45	23	8	31	6	17	16
Median	$30 508	$13 692	$11 833	$13 015	$12 554	$9 906	$11 738	$12 846	$9 073	$11 759	$11 124	$10 938	$10 665
Mean	$39 616	$19 582	$16 426	$15 706	$16 232	$12 438	$15 749	$15 433	$10 969	$13 437	$12 993	$12 407	$12 394
Owner-occupied households	1 090	1 252	549	300	508	269	397	470	204	414	314	252	216
Median income	$32 245	$21 182	$21 224	$17 195	$20 938	$16 250	$17 464	$17 750	$14 306	$13 173	$14 659	$11 524	$12 273
Mean income	$42 425	$27 384	$28 393	$22 066	$25 081	$19 743	$24 179	$19 117	$13 734	$16 336	$16 838	$13 902	$16 115
Renter-occupied households	175	1 737	1 874	1 470	1 022	1 123	1 668	1 136	2 316	1 773	1 165	2 086	2 302
Median income	$18 194	$11 187	$10 504	$12 137	$10 968	$9 081	$10 660	$11 294	$8 796	$11 469	$10 772	$10 858	$10 450
Mean income	$22 119	$13 958	$12 920	$14 408	$11 834	$10 688	$13 742	$13 908	$10 725	$12 761	$11 957	$12 227	$12 045
Families	930	1 279	854	519	644	464	696	758	884	907	609	882	942
Median income	$33 591	$18 681	$19 128	$18 419	$15 980	$13 056	$16 404	$16 552	$11 996	$14 111	$14 114	$12 500	$13 359
Mean income	$45 669	$25 073	$25 108	$20 016	$19 712	$16 157	$22 304	$18 105	$13 431	$16 096	$15 872	$14 372	$14 649
Unrelated individuals 15 years and over	504	2 216	1 953	1 489	1 136	1 179	1 581	1 075	2 068	1 680	1 078	1 778	1 922
Median income	$12 291	$8 927	$7 393	$9 716	$9 208	$7 228	$8 687	$7 629	$6 384	$7 595	$7 707	$7 845	$7 890
Mean income	$15 310	$11 630	$9 571	$11 726	$10 896	$8 336	$10 753	$10 150	$7 681	$8 909	$8 998	$9 086	$9 190
Per capita income	$15 081	$10 018	$9 917	$9 776	$8 770	$7 278	$10 205	$8 157	$6 542	$7 468	$7 515	$7 388	$7 691
INCOME TYPE IN 1979													
Households	1 265	2 989	2 423	1 770	1 530	1 392	2 065	1 606	2 520	2 187	1 479	2 338	2 518
With earnings	1 011	2 280	1 552	1 411	1 203	974	1 246	1 189	1 646	1 713	1 090	1 639	1 439
Mean earnings	$38 703	$20 234	$15 646	$14 969	$15 284	$13 055	$16 999	$15 565	$12 022	$13 729	$13 227	$12 711	$12 815
With Social Security income	356	815	921	390	409	383	803	435	876	528	411	715	1 057
Mean Social Security income	$4 604	$4 112	$4 350	$3 916	$4 207	$4 089	$4 063	$4 093	$3 664	$3 911	$3 572	$3 649	$4 044
With public assistance income	28	196	172	115	157	145	172	123	448	204	132	242	325
Mean public assistance income	$2 283	$2 355	$1 930	$3 145	$2 530	$2 634	$2 516	$3 143	$2 712	$2 425	$2 187	$2 951	$2 180
MEAN FAMILY INCOME IN 1979 BY FAMILY TYPE													
Families	$45 669	$25 073	$25 108	$20 016	$19 712	$16 157	$22 304	$18 105	$13 431	$16 096	$15 872	$14 372	$14 649
With own children under 18 years	$53 172	$25 177	$20 007	$14 327	$17 084	$11 298	$25 604	$16 005	$10 092	$15 240	$14 223	$11 938	$13 703
Without own children under 18 years	$39 804	$25 014	$26 470	$21 459	$21 132	$18 814	$21 221	$19 090	$15 703	$16 665	$16 643	$15 469	$14 948
Married-couple families	$49 527	$26 953	$28 334	$22 453	$22 160	$17 803	$23 539	$19 133	$15 011	$17 322	$16 504	$15 642	$16 609
With own children under 18 years	$60 042	$28 571	$23 701	$17 260	$22 282	$12 585	$31 399	$17 523	$13 157	$19 478	$18 366	$15 157	$21 506
Without own children under 18 years	$42 074	$26 251	$29 268	$23 514	$22 115	$19 980	$21 614	$19 768	$15 757	$16 159	$15 991	$15 807	$15 645
Female householder, no husband present	$20 061	$15 802	$15 222	$13 345	$11 185	$7 269	$16 770	$15 347	$10 129	$12 359	$9 945	$10 724	$7 687
With own children under 18 years	$20 378	$14 493	$12 872	$9 748	$9 916	$7 634	$16 127	$11 628	$7 578	$8 346	$7 380	$6 711	$4 326
Without own children under 18 years	$19 643	$17 593	$16 448	$14 997	$15 822	$6 506	$17 412	$19 995	$15 983	$17 848	$13 985	$14 260	$11 011
ALL INCOME LEVELS IN 1979													
Families	930	1 279	854	519	644	464	696	758	884	907	609	882	942
Householder worked in 1979	744	929	530	340	504	307	452	583	633	644	432	535	457
With related children under 18 years	414	494	191	105	231	164	182	248	363	395	219	274	232
Female householder, no husband present	116	199	178	108	121	71	102	72	280	232	103	190	183
Householder worked in 1979	84	137	87	68	99	35	60	53	195	113	65	108	63
With related children under 18 years	72	132	66	34	95	48	56	40	195	157	77	89	97
With related children under 6 years	12	32	23	10	32	23	15	28	88	86	18	30	81
Householder 65 years and over	228	317	334	157	143	86	214	180	153	219	138	225	372
Unrelated individuals for whom poverty status is determined	504	2 216	1 953	1 489	1 136	1 179	1 581	1 075	2 068	1 680	1 078	1 778	1 922
65 years and over	145	441	511	239	253	242	531	212	703	240	208	382	723
Persons for whom poverty status is determined	3 341	5 709	3 908	2 691	2 876	2 379	3 214	2 992	4 247	4 001	2 571	3 904	4 087
Under 18 years	794	806	225	161	393	314	219	414	512	545	271	368	323
Related children under 18 years	776	799	225	161	388	306	214	411	501	545	271	360	303
Related children 5 to 17 years	594	609	130	100	261	181	124	247	266	320	167	223	159
18 to 59 years	1 773	3 561	2 269	1 883	1 832	1 457	1 810	1 879	2 616	2 701	1 687	2 484	2 106
60 years and over	774	1 342	1 414	647	651	608	1 185	699	1 119	755	613	1 052	1 658
65 years and over	563	993	1 154	505	509	413	972	511	969	575	481	796	1 409
INCOME IN 1979 BELOW POVERTY LEVEL													
Families	16	119	24	16	45	47	22	73	132	70	76	92	119
Percent below poverty level	1.7	9.3	2.8	3.1	7.0	10.1	3.2	9.6	14.9	7.7	12.5	10.4	12.6
Householder worked in 1979	16	63	3	9	28	17	8	49	40	23	33	42	31
With related children under 18 years	6	78	13	9	38	38	15	54	103	61	64	71	80
Female householder, no husband present	6	36	24	5	24	12	7	12	70	46	34	47	70
Householder worked in 1979	6	16	3	5	15	8	–	5	16	9	11	16	13
With related children under 18 years	6	31	13	5	24	12	7	12	70	46	34	44	70
With related children under 6 years	–	14	10	–	24	12	7	5	56	33	–	30	70
Householder 65 years and over	–	29	11	–	–	–	7	–	7	–	14	9	19
Unrelated individuals for whom poverty status is determined	87	363	318	165	137	216	258	127	312	324	170	319	290
Percent below poverty level	17.3	16.4	16.3	11.1	12.1	18.3	16.3	11.8	15.1	19.3	15.8	17.9	15.1
65 years and over	22	40	48	24	59	29	38	31	100	23	45	60	93
Persons for whom poverty status is determined	138	684	377	238	283	405	326	405	679	512	433	544	551
Percent below poverty level	4.1	12.0	9.6	8.8	9.8	17.0	10.1	13.5	16.0	12.8	16.8	13.9	13.5
Under 18 years	35	114	24	40	73	121	33	106	164	94	96	102	108
Related children under 18 years	23	107	24	40	68	113	33	103	153	94	96	94	94
Related children 5 to 17 years	23	66	24	33	18	61	6	50	48	56	63	48	24
18 to 59 years	81	457	244	167	144	233	227	230	396	389	266	333	287
60 years and over	22	113	109	31	66	51	66	69	119	29	71	109	156
65 years and over	22	93	70	24	59	29	52	46	107	23	67	82	129
INCOME IN 1979 BELOW SPECIFIED POVERTY LEVEL													
Percent of persons for whom poverty status is determined:													
Below 75 percent of poverty level	2.9	6.9	6.4	5.4	8.8	11.3	7.9	8.5	10.4	8.8	11.2	8.9	8.7
Below 125 percent of poverty level	5.5	15.9	15.4	13.9	14.6	29.9	15.5	18.7	25.3	19.8	22.7	20.6	18.6
Below 150 percent of poverty level	9.0	22.3	23.2	20.8	21.0	37.0	21.9	24.8	34.3	26.7	30.1	27.2	26.2
Below 200 percent of poverty level	14.8	31.6	35.6	30.7	36.9	47.9	31.0	36.2	52.6	40.6	42.2	41.2	40.9

Table P-1. **General Characteristics of Persons: 1980**—Con.

[For meaning of symbols, see Introduction. For definitions of terms, see appendixes A and B]

San Diego city, San Diego County

Census Tracts	Tract 0001	Tract 0002	Tract 0003	Tract 0004	Tract 0005	Tract 0006	Tract 0007	Tract 0008	Tract 0009	Tract 0010	Tract 0011	Tract 0012	Tract 0013
AGE													
Total persons	3 352	5 841	4 113	2 977	2 816	2 439	3 218	3 008	4 252	4 001	2 583	3 916	4 099
Under 5 years	162	209	67	81	136	104	92	150	237	247	121	188	132
5 to 9 years	193	185	77	62	106	90	50	120	135	137	67	102	76
10 to 14 years	280	280	71	57	96	81	64	101	103	113	53	74	57
15 to 19 years	224	275	89	87	141	95	85	130	226	191	100	159	143
20 to 24 years	172	604	319	365	325	324	242	419	757	689	435	703	516
25 to 34 years	475	1 414	977	866	780	694	724	853	969	1 132	681	898	732
35 to 44 years	493	656	333	285	275	212	286	256	278	322	183	325	252
45 to 54 years	385	486	313	265	202	156	260	183	233	271	197	265	292
55 to 64 years	395	650	533	313	286	236	417	292	349	326	259	404	494
65 to 74 years	353	568	679	315	262	229	512	313	418	320	290	442	669
75 years and over	220	514	655	281	207	218	486	191	547	253	197	356	736
3 and 4 years	72	77	28	22	37	35	24	51	75	72	41	66	40
16 years and over	2 672	5 116	3 883	2 764	2 456	2 151	3 003	2 617	3 762	3 488	2 326	3 534	3 824
18 years and over	2 565	5 020	3 855	2 745	2 421	2 113	2 976	2 583	3 710	3 438	2 297	3 501	3 776
21 years and over	2 458	4 799	3 775	2 639	2 300	2 018	2 899	2 465	3 434	3 214	2 176	3 283	3 612
60 years and over	764	1 390	1 612	731	602	571	1 205	671	1 158	731	619	1 022	1 647
62 years and over	699	1 266	1 517	675	547	534	1 120	597	1 080	667	573	936	1 561
Median	37.4	34.6	49.4	34.4	31.9	31.3	48.1	30.8	30.3	29.3	31.5	32.1	50.7
Female	1 760	3 051	2 279	1 534	1 460	1 307	1 761	1 531	2 377	2 104	1 434	2 135	2 365
Under 5 years	75	104	29	37	67	59	37	80	117	125	65	82	67
5 to 9 years	88	94	34	24	56	42	22	58	69	76	38	51	41
10 to 14 years	140	119	40	32	41	56	36	47	56	61	22	42	29
15 to 19 years	108	130	49	42	73	48	37	69	129	115	66	100	82
20 to 24 years	83	281	144	187	184	172	122	199	365	359	245	358	276
25 to 34 years	256	686	450	375	383	301	340	404	440	504	323	448	321
35 to 44 years	255	313	155	134	108	103	125	105	143	148	81	155	114
45 to 54 years	196	240	165	141	100	78	131	92	123	149	110	136	166
55 to 64 years	216	376	332	186	152	144	237	173	204	205	159	244	298
65 to 74 years	200	328	430	171	159	143	327	181	296	198	188	279	435
75 years and over	143	380	451	205	137	161	347	123	435	164	137	240	536
3 and 4 years	29	38	12	12	16	20	11	26	41	33	24	23	23
16 years and over	1 432	2 715	2 165	1 435	1 287	1 142	1 662	1 335	2 125	1 833	1 301	1 952	2 222
18 years and over	1 382	2 665	2 151	1 425	1 275	1 123	1 651	1 322	2 099	1 805	1 280	1 933	2 196
21 years and over	1 331	2 563	2 113	1 373	1 203	1 075	1 612	1 258	1 949	1 676	1 204	1 799	2 097
60 years and over	449	894	1 065	464	361	380	793	398	848	474	410	650	1 117
62 years and over	414	816	996	426	337	359	747	356	802	430	381	598	1 075
Median	38.4	37.4	57.4	40.4	32.1	33.5	57.0	31.6	35.8	29.9	32.8	34.2	58.1
HOUSEHOLD TYPE AND RELATIONSHIP													
Total persons	3 352	5 841	4 113	2 977	2 816	2 439	3 218	3 008	4 252	4 001	2 583	3 916	4 099
In households	3 352	5 738	3 869	2 690	2 816	2 424	3 218	3 008	4 252	3 999	2 568	3 913	4 066
Householder	1 265	2 991	2 403	1 772	1 525	1 394	2 056	1 575	2 515	2 175	1 478	2 322	2 520
Family householder	927	1 282	792	502	642	465	677	713	860	882	594	869	915
Nonfamily householder	338	1 709	1 611	1 270	883	929	1 379	862	1 655	1 293	884	1 453	1 605
Living alone	261	1 345	1 336	1 062	701	761	1 204	671	1 360	975	737	1 197	1 382
Spouse	790	1 010	624	359	468	333	527	543	591	628	441	621	676
Other relatives	1 120	1 197	440	292	556	450	409	628	740	759	435	633	553
Nonrelatives	177	540	402	267	267	247	226	262	406	437	214	337	317
Inmate of institution	–	103	195	271	–	–	–	–	–	2	–	–	8
Other, in group quarters	–	–	49	16	–	15	–	–	–	–	15	3	25
Persons per household	2.65	1.92	1.61	1.52	1.85	1.74	1.57	1.91	1.69	1.84	1.74	1.69	1.61
Persons per family	3.06	2.72	2.34	2.30	2.60	2.68	2.38	2.64	2.55	2.57	2.47	2.44	2.34
Persons 65 years and over	573	1 082	1 334	596	469	447	998	504	965	573	487	798	1 405
In households	573	991	1 152	493	469	444	998	504	965	572	484	798	1 387
Householder	356	741	850	386	347	352	772	360	806	429	354	620	1 045
Nonfamily householder	143	448	528	266	211	249	546	192	640	256	209	425	708
Living alone	126	430	500	255	202	243	533	182	629	242	204	409	688
Spouse	143	182	235	69	88	72	174	113	112	104	100	139	253
Other relatives	58	52	46	29	27	13	37	26	29	27	22	28	74
Nonrelatives	16	16	21	9	7	7	15	5	18	12	8	11	15
Inmate of institution	–	91	181	97	–	–	–	–	–	1	–	–	–
Other, in group quarters	–	–	1	6	–	3	–	–	–	–	3	–	18
FAMILY TYPE BY PRESENCE OF OWN CHILDREN													
Families	927	1 282	792	502	642	465	677	713	860	882	594	869	915
With own children under 18 years	389	449	147	104	229	161	153	240	315	344	175	254	192
Number of own children under 18 years	744	758	220	139	357	294	217	382	481	509	254	371	279
Married-couple families	790	1 010	624	359	468	333	527	543	591	628	441	621	676
With own children under 18 years	324	319	86	60	129	98	93	156	179	201	100	136	105
Number of own children under 18 years	636	572	134	85	220	206	149	270	286	302	154	203	164
Female householder, no husband present	106	215	135	98	134	96	106	121	206	198	115	194	175
With own children under 18 years	57	114	56	38	90	51	48	64	121	125	62	99	72
Number of own children under 18 years	97	169	80	48	125	73	55	86	176	184	81	142	100
MARITAL STATUS													
Male, 15 years and over	1 260	2 433	1 722	1 336	1 182	1 014	1 346	1 291	1 642	1 662	1 033	1 592	1 606
Single	348	947	731	607	456	436	484	488	702	683	368	593	533
Now married, except separated	811	1 068	665	404	493	354	558	575	626	668	457	659	696
Separated	10	47	50	34	32	40	46	45	77	49	31	53	55
Widowed	33	73	81	56	47	34	66	26	50	36	25	62	82
Divorced	58	298	195	235	154	150	192	157	187	226	152	225	240
Female, 15 years and over	1 457	2 734	2 176	1 441	1 296	1 150	1 666	1 346	2 135	1 842	1 309	1 960	2 228
Single	317	738	550	495	362	334	366	344	564	538	365	559	498
Now married, except separated	814	1 054	663	394	483	355	549	575	620	657	457	661	709
Separated	23	62	64	40	44	42	41	50	74	88	39	68	74
Widowed	184	471	511	251	195	196	417	187	518	250	198	353	616
Divorced	119	409	388	261	212	223	293	190	359	309	250	319	331

Table P-1. **General Characteristics of Persons: 1980**—Con.

[For meaning of symbols, see Introduction. For definitions of terms, see appendixes A and B]

Census Tracts

San Diego city, San Diego County—Con.

AGE	Tract 0082	Tract 0083.01	Tract 0083.03	Tract 0083.05	Tract 0083.06	Tract 0083.07	Tract 0083.10	Tract 0083.11	Tract 0083.12	Tract 0083.13	Tract 0083.14	Tract 0083.15	Tract 0083.16
Total persons	3 185	3 574	3 859	4 752	3 933	4 293	4 567	2 926	3 731	2 478	6 931	3 726	3 366
Under 5 years	38	127	119	155	203	202	146	97	114	86	342	93	133
5 to 9 years	31	181	241	73	301	330	257	119	126	170	473	71	160
10 to 14 years	78	273	310	52	414	449	375	240	240	286	669	90	160
15 to 19 years	73	370	347	2 111	435	478	456	296	282	302	628	182	190
20 to 24 years	164	174	182	1 197	260	291	270	154	275	146	479	636	829
25 to 34 years	414	262	330	634	411	519	389	199	470	223	1 047	1 344	1 043
35 to 44 years	215	487	586	120	694	777	683	399	439	441	1 162	505	378
45 to 54 years	249	579	558	112	625	603	805	477	454	404	771	369	226
55 to 64 years	348	538	521	143	400	417	736	479	578	266	595	316	169
65 to 74 years	572	236	394	82	142	155	339	328	363	109	443	93	63
75 years and over	1 003	347	271	73	48	72	111	138	390	45	322	27	15
3 and 4 years	15	55	62	51	92	83	76	42	50	40	138	37	47
16 years and over	3 026	2 915	3 120	4 467	2 930	3 215	3 720	2 404	3 193	1 862	5 318	3 451	2 886
18 years and over	3 000	2 760	2 951	4 396	2 741	3 008	3 502	2 272	3 071	1 719	5 040	3 399	2 836
21 years and over	2 931	2 574	2 791	1 845	2 509	2 759	3 266	2 134	2 911	1 595	4 710	3 187	2 599
60 years and over	1 753	791	907	228	337	389	749	678	1 019	267	1 028	242	146
62 years and over	1 690	699	807	194	261	314	609	599	907	215	919	188	116
Median	64.4	43.2	41.5	20.0	34.0	33.3	40.4	44.2	43.2	35.7	33.6	30.3	26.5
Female	1 981	1 910	2 034	1 973	1 966	2 140	2 341	1 513	2 027	1 253	3 602	1 866	1 726
Under 5 years	20	64	64	71	95	109	79	36	63	39	166	39	62
5 to 9 years	13	105	108	32	155	153	117	70	61	75	238	38	94
10 to 14 years	40	129	152	28	199	203	204	117	109	158	322	45	90
15 to 19 years	37	173	170	1 017	200	218	217	137	146	133	305	96	112
20 to 24 years	85	76	86	464	107	129	138	75	134	70	182	296	373
25 to 34 years	205	138	192	265	225	277	212	120	221	126	568	670	531
35 to 44 years	106	271	315	47	365	428	377	226	253	247	622	238	200
45 to 54 years	144	303	291	22	323	294	405	244	263	189	392	203	123
55 to 64 years	211	270	265	19	194	199	359	252	312	142	342	183	97
65 to 74 years	373	126	225	4	68	88	168	161	198	47	262	41	34
75 years and over	747	255	166	4	35	42	65	75	267	27	203	17	10
3 and 4 years	10	27	34	23	41	41	40	16	27	16	70	16	20
16 years and over	1 903	1 577	1 680	1 841	1 476	1 628	1 906	1 263	1 764	948	2 812	1 732	1 463
18 years and over	1 891	1 499	1 596	1 798	1 390	1 532	1 798	1 195	1 704	880	2 682	1 705	1 437
21 years and over	1 855	1 416	1 516	630	1 288	1 421	1 684	1 137	1 623	830	2 532	1 602	1 310
60 years and over	1 230	475	519	13	172	210	364	347	618	128	618	128	80
62 years and over	1 190	432	468	11	132	171	296	303	552	107	564	95	66
Median	69.3	45.0	42.1	19.7	35.1	34.5	40.3	44.2	46.3	36.3	35.3	30.3	26.8

HOUSEHOLD TYPE AND RELATIONSHIP

	Tract 0082	Tract 0083.01	Tract 0083.03	Tract 0083.05	Tract 0083.06	Tract 0083.07	Tract 0083.10	Tract 0083.11	Tract 0083.12	Tract 0083.13	Tract 0083.14	Tract 0083.15	Tract 0083.16
Total persons	3 185	3 574	3 859	4 752	3 933	4 293	4 567	2 926	3 731	2 478	6 931	3 726	3 366
In households	2 711	3 255	3 850	1 298	3 931	4 293	4 559	2 926	3 576	2 478	6 931	3 726	3 366
Householder	1 637	1 108	1 477	551	1 193	1 367	1 627	1 058	1 569	805	2 569	2 127	1 648
Family householder	634	962	1 084	355	1 089	1 168	1 355	899	1 007	678	1 840	801	671
Nonfamily householder	1 003	146	393	196	104	199	272	159	562	127	729	1 326	977
Living alone	872	107	315	80	58	135	194	129	460	87	580	966	626
Spouse	500	851	936	278	952	1 028	1 204	802	828	586	1 549	617	441
Other relatives	345	1 204	1 245	299	1 667	1 752	1 562	965	955	990	2 478	498	648
Nonrelatives	229	92	192	170	119	146	166	101	224	97	335	484	629
Inmate of institution	129	319	–	406	–	–	5	–	152	–	–	–	–
Other, in group quarters	345	–	9	3 048	2	–	3	–	3	–	–	–	–
Persons per household	1.66	2.94	2.61	2.36	3.30	3.14	2.80	2.77	2.28	3.08	2.70	1.75	2.04
Persons per family	2.33	3.14	3.01	2.63	3.40	3.38	3.04	2.97	2.77	3.32	3.19	2.39	2.62
Persons 65 years and over	1 575	583	665	155	190	227	450	466	753	154	765	120	78
In households	1 110	268	665	8	190	227	444	466	609	154	765	120	78
Householder	839	147	446	4	91	112	262	289	403	84	498	85	54
Nonfamily householder	539	33	204	1	12	30	65	63	173	9	234	36	23
Living alone	514	27	188	1	11	24	55	58	157	9	229	33	21
Spouse	221	74	176	2	49	62	130	144	158	43	191	22	11
Other relatives	35	45	30	1	49	47	45	27	38	26	66	11	10
Nonrelatives	15	2	13	1	1	6	7	6	10	1	10	2	3
Inmate of institution	129	315	–	147	–	–	5	–	144	–	–	–	–
Other, in group quarters	336	–	–	–	–	–	1	–	–	–	–	–	–

FAMILY TYPE BY PRESENCE OF OWN CHILDREN

	Tract 0082	Tract 0083.01	Tract 0083.03	Tract 0083.05	Tract 0083.06	Tract 0083.07	Tract 0083.10	Tract 0083.11	Tract 0083.12	Tract 0083.13	Tract 0083.14	Tract 0083.15	Tract 0083.16
Families	634	962	1 084	355	1 089	1 168	1 355	899	1 007	678	1 840	801	671
With own children under 18 years	106	422	462	198	626	646	568	342	354	371	981	222	337
Number of own children under 18 years	161	776	872	280	1 148	1 235	1 017	626	631	728	1 828	298	496
Married-couple families	500	851	936	278	952	1 028	1 204	802	828	586	1 549	617	441
With own children under 18 years	57	366	391	127	542	554	495	302	275	319	798	136	174
Number of own children under 18 years	101	685	750	181	1 006	1 070	901	563	508	651	1 488	192	259
Female householder, no husband present	103	88	114	64	111	118	117	78	144	76	232	135	198
With own children under 18 years	42	48	57	62	71	80	58	32	65	47	155	69	147
Number of own children under 18 years	52	80	103	85	122	146	97	52	101	69	296	86	214

MARITAL STATUS

	Tract 0082	Tract 0083.01	Tract 0083.03	Tract 0083.05	Tract 0083.06	Tract 0083.07	Tract 0083.10	Tract 0083.11	Tract 0083.12	Tract 0083.13	Tract 0083.14	Tract 0083.15	Tract 0083.16
Male, 15 years and over	1 130	1 381	1 479	2 630	1 498	1 637	1 848	1 180	1 457	955	2 571	1 728	1 433
Single	310	382	402	1 949	467	494	495	297	444	308	779	781	747
Now married, except separated	604	916	957	501	967	1 046	1 225	817	862	599	1 582	648	468
Separated	31	10	23	32	14	12	19	8	21	8	27	55	39
Widowed	81	29	33	45	13	23	24	23	42	9	51	9	8
Divorced	104	44	64	103	37	62	85	35	88	31	132	235	171
Female, 15 years and over	1 908	1 612	1 710	1 842	1 517	1 675	1 941	1 290	1 794	981	2 876	1 744	1 480
Single	396	337	356	1 437	329	382	410	267	366	229	607	633	611
Now married, except separated	594	925	962	298	977	1 055	1 225	821	872	601	1 590	632	462
Separated	34	21	35	25	23	25	35	24	34	21	51	57	40
Widowed	644	238	226	10	88	92	139	112	313	54	308	93	60
Divorced	240	91	131	72	100	121	132	66	209	76	320	329	307

P—26 SAN DIEGO, CALIF., SMSA

CENSUS TRACTS

Exhibit 8-5

Financial Characteristics of Housing Units: 1980—Con.

[Data are estimates based on a sample; see Introduction. For meaning of symbols, see Introduction. For definitions of terms, see appendixes A and B]

San Diego city, San Diego County—Con.

Census Tracts	Tract 0082	Tract 0083.01	Tract 0083.03	Tract 0083.05	Tract 0083.06	Tract 0083.07	Tract 0083.10	Tract 0083.11	Tract 0083.12	Tract 0083.13	Tract 0083.14	Tract 0083.15	Tract 0083.16
Specified owner-occupied housing units	211	793	996	–	1 033	1 043	1 193	915	688	474	1 331	6	–
MORTGAGE STATUS AND SELECTED MONTHLY OWNER COSTS													
With a mortgage	146	725	731	–	991	1 017	980	744	436	443	1 249	6	–
Less than $100	–	–	–	–	–	9	–	–	–	–	–	–	–
$100 to $199	–	–	–	–	51	50	11	–	6	–	20	–	–
$200 to $299	6	82	44	–	204	170	77	40	29	26	171	–	–
$300 to $399	56	150	32	–	145	218	108	123	37	54	301	–	–
$400 to $599	47	138	141	–	200	231	234	177	88	112	299	6	–
$600 or more	37	355	514	–	391	339	550	404	276	251	458	–	–
Median	$472	$579	$905	–	$510	$461	$669	$637	$718	$691	$480	$425	–
Not mortgaged	65	68	265	–	42	26	213	171	252	31	82	–	–
Less than $100	~	–	–	–	7	7	23	5	11	–	26	–	–
$100 to $199	38	58	127	–	30	19	85	74	124	6	44	–	–
$200 or more	5	10	138	–	5	–	105	92	117	25	12	–	–
Median	$122	$156	$207	–	$133	$121	$194	$207	$193	$263	$114	–	–
HOUSEHOLD INCOME IN 1979 BY SELECTED MONTHLY OWNER COSTS AS PERCENTAGE OF INCOME													
Less than $10,000	18	57	110	–	43	37	81	87	62	18	84	–	–
Less than 15 percent	–	–	–	–	–	–	9	–	–	–	20	–	–
15 to 24 percent	–	–	–	–	–	16	–	18	13	–	–	–	–
25 to 29 percent	–	–	–	–	3	–	–	6	5	–	–	–	–
30 percent or more	11	45	104	–	28	14	38	50	38	18	64	–	–
Not computed	7	12	6	–	12	7	34	13	6	–	–	–	–
Median	50+	50+	50+	–	50+	24.3	50+	50+	50+	50+	50+	–	–
$10,000 to $19,999	40	86	37	–	138	147	122	102	71	24	188	6	–
Less than 15 percent	13	6	15	–	42	18	25	16	40	–	8	–	–
15 to 24 percent	13	13	6	–	30	44	46	49	5	6	37	–	–
25 to 29 percent	–	6	11	–	18	38	11	6	7	6	24	–	–
30 percent or more	14	61	5	–	48	47	40	31	19	12	119	6	–
Not computed	...	...	...	...	...	...	...	...	...	...	...	...	...
Median	17.7	43.7	22.9	–	19.5	26.5	23.1	21.3	14.3	35.0	35.5	37.5	...
$20,000 or more	153	650	849	–	852	859	990	726	555	432	1 059	–	–
Less than 15 percent	87	366	412	–	437	400	468	360	331	211	444	–	–
15 to 24 percent	38	166	198	–	259	289	274	233	160	97	357	–	–
25 to 29 percent	7	42	53	–	64	49	68	31	13	44	97	–	–
30 percent or more	21	72	180	–	92	121	180	102	43	80	161	–	–
Not computed	...	...	...	...	...	...	...	...	...	...	...	...	...
Median	12.2	13.8	15.4	...	14.7	16.0	15.7	15.1	12.1	15.5	16.7	...	...
Specified renter-occupied housing units	1 051	81	270	480	86	265	141	54	569	148	840	1 251	1 053
GROSS RENT													
Less than $80	–	–	–	–	–	–	–	–	–	–	–	–	–
$80 to $99	6	–	–	–	–	–	–	–	–	–	–	–	–
$100 to $149	7	–	–	9	–	–	–	–	27	–	–	–	6
$150 to $199	67	–	13	256	–	4	9	–	96	–	27	–	6
$200 to $249	68	–	13	156	–	11	–	–	23	–	162	4	140
$250 to $299	103	–	19	22	–	–	–	–	14	–	262	192	311
$300 to $349	86	–	50	–	–	6	–	–	73	–	59	213	47
$350 to $399	98	–	20	–	–	22	–	–	72	–	48	198	71
$400 or more	567	74	137	37	80	222	125	54	243	148	263	636	465
No cash rent	49	7	18	–	6	–	7	–	21	–	19	8	13
Median	$424	$500+	$444	$189	$500+	$500+	$500+	$500+	$378	$500+	$274	$406	$361
One-family house, detached or attached	259	81	109	68	86	220	134	54	196	88	342	275	282
Median gross rent	$354	$500+	$500+	$271	$500+	$500+	$500+	$500+	$500+	$500+	$500+	$500+	$463
HOUSEHOLD INCOME IN 1979 BY GROSS RENT AS PERCENTAGE OF INCOME													
Less than $10,000	370	21	100	262	6	28	16	–	196	5	244	421	288
Less than 15 percent	–	–	–	–	–	–	–	–	–	–	–	–	–
15 to 19 percent	–	–	–	–	–	–	–	–	6	–	–	–	–
20 to 24 percent	7	–	–	23	–	–	–	–	12	–	–	–	–
25 to 29 percent	–	–	–	25	–	4	–	–	17	–	4	4	6
30 to 34 percent	11	–	–	48	–	–	–	–	6	–	11	–	33
35 percent or more	311	14	94	148	6	24	–	–	128	–	198	384	244
Not computed	41	7	6	18	–	–	16	–	27	5	31	33	5
Median	50+	50+	50+	41.2	50+	50+	–	–	50+	–	50+	50+	50+
$10,000 to $19,999	282	–	66	163	14	83	49	–	150	36	322	391	444
Less than 15 percent	23	–	–	18	–	7	–	–	11	–	–	–	38
15 to 19 percent	18	–	–	70	–	–	–	–	11	–	41	41	38
20 to 24 percent	56	–	17	36	–	6	–	–	20	–	105	52	71
25 to 29 percent	53	–	5	25	–	6	–	–	31	–	60	49	91
30 to 34 percent	21	–	11	5	–	28	–	–	9	–	63	102	66
35 percent or more	103	–	27	9	14	36	49	–	71	36	53	147	172
Not computed	8	–	–	–	–	–	–	–	–	–	–	–	6
Median	28.8	–	33.6	19.5	45.0	34.0	50+	–	35.0	46.9	26.3	32.6	31.4
$20,000 or more	399	60	104	55	66	154	76	54	223	107	274	439	321
Less than 15 percent	104	8	25	41	6	33	33	24	75	24	97	70	120
15 to 19 percent	96	20	33	–	18	38	28	10	64	–	52	130	89
20 to 24 percent	104	–	5	14	15	61	7	9	51	44	50	101	58
25 to 29 percent	58	8	–	–	14	10	–	11	–	32	31	96	33
30 to 34 percent	18	16	35	–	–	12	8	–	22	7	33	27	14
35 percent or more	–	8	–	–	7	–	–	–	5	–	–	15	–
Not computed	19	–	6	–	6	–	–	–	6	–	11	–	7
Median	19.5	26.3	18.6	12.4	22.0	20.5	15.9	16.5	17.6	23.4	18.3	21.0	17.1

Table H-1. Occupancy, Utilization, and Financial Characteristics of Housing Units: 1980—Con.

[For meaning of symbols, see Introduction. For definitions of terms, see appendixes A and B]

San Diego city, San Diego County—Con.

Census Tracts	Tract 0082	Tract 0083.01	Tract 0083.03	Tract 0083.05	Tract 0083.06	Tract 0083.07	Tract 0083.10	Tract 0083.11	Tract 0083.12	Tract 0083.13	Tract 0083.14	Tract 0083.15	Tract 0083.16
Total housing units	1 956	1 145	1 588	577	1 207	1 402	1 778	1 103	1 829	858	2 731	2 397	1 965
Vacant seasonal and migratory	40	1	3	–	–	–	2	–	22	1	3	5	–
Year-round housing units	1 916	1 144	1 585	577	1 207	1 402	1 776	1 103	1 807	857	2 728	2 392	1 965
YEAR-ROUND HOUSING UNITS													
Tenure by Race and Spanish Origin of Householder													
Owner-occupied housing units	579	1 027	1 207	71	1 100	1 097	1 468	993	997	653	1 631	837	573
Percent of occupied housing units	35.4	92.7	81.7	12.9	92.2	80.2	90.2	93.9	63.5	81.1	63.5	39.4	34.8
White	568	997	1 183	69	1 030	1 042	1 411	973	971	623	1 535	811	534
Black	7	...	...	1	7	7	4	4	2	4	10	5	4
American Indian, Eskimo, and Aleut	...	5	–	...	...	...	...	...	...	...	10	...	–
Asian and Pacific Islander[1]	1	22	10	–	48	41	42	11	13	20	57	15	26
Spanish origin[2]	11	10	32	2	28	24	29	13	15	20	57	33	23
Renter-occupied housing units	1 058	81	270	480	93	270	159	65	572	152	938	1 290	1 075
White	1 023	78	260	348	87	253	147	62	544	140	913	1 184	921
Black	16	...	...	42	1	2	1	1	4	2	2	31	36
American Indian, Eskimo, and Aleut	...	–	–	...	...	...	...	...	...	...	1	...	5
Asian and Pacific Islander[1]	4	1	3	50	3	9	9	1	9	5	18	48	68
Spanish origin[2]	49	4	10	75	4	14	3	2	27	9	23	39	61
Vacancy Status													
Vacant housing units	279	36	108	26	14	35	149	45	238	52	159	265	317
For sale only	22	15	12	2	7	23	92	14	34	10	75	32	8
Vacant less than 6 months	18	13	11	2	4	17	77	10	20	8	74	28	8
Median price asked	200000+	200000+	200000+	–	$156 300	$179 500	200000+	200000+	200000+	200000+	$196 200	$137 500	–
For rent	70	3	13	8	1	9	7	2	59	6	59	137	22
Vacant less than 2 months	41	2	8	8	1	8	3	–	48	6	32	58	18
Median rent asked	$396	500+	$425	$188	$450	$395	500+	500+	500+	500+	$213	$349	$438
Rented or sold, awaiting occupancy	30	7	11	7	1	2	20	12	9	10	7	15	9
Held for occasional use	90	5	33	1	–	1	10	9	85	18	7	37	6
Other vacant	67	6	39	8	5	1	20	8	51	8	11	44	272
Boarded up	8	–	–	–	–	–	–	–	–	–	–	–	–
Lacking Complete Plumbing for Exclusive Use													
Year-round housing units	15	–	2	3	–	–	1	–	6	2	1	1	7
Owner-occupied housing units	4	–	–	–	–	–	–	–	3	1	1	–	1
Renter-occupied housing units	9	–	2	3	–	–	–	–	2	1	–	1	6
Vacant for rent or for sale only	–	–	–	–	–	–	–	–	–	–	–	–	–
Rooms													
Year-round housing units	1 916	1 144	1 585	577	1 207	1 402	1 776	1 103	1 807	857	2 728	2 392	1 965
1 room	125	1	13	–	–	–	1	1	39	2	3	129	21
2 rooms	290	–	38	33	–	6	5	–	90	3	152	275	102
3 rooms	368	3	101	72	8	52	10	3	219	15	418	427	392
4 rooms	556	14	145	341	17	67	61	22	317	47	309	616	490
5 rooms	294	102	187	65	67	131	177	96	294	80	419	411	610
6 rooms	151	358	285	55	352	333	492	316	316	214	556	472	282
7 rooms	69	320	288	10	394	390	446	294	194	190	424	43	56
8 or more rooms	63	346	528	1	369	423	584	371	338	306	447	19	12
Median, year-round housing units	3.8	6.8	6.6	4.0	6.9	6.8	6.8	6.9	5.3	6.9	5.6	4.1	4.5
Median, occupied housing units	3.8	6.8	6.6	4.0	6.9	6.8	6.8	6.9	5.4	6.9	5.6	4.1	4.3
Median, owner-occupied housing units	4.8	6.8	7.0	5.7	6.9	7.0	6.9	6.9	6.3	7.2	6.3	5.0	5.0
Median, renter-occupied housing units	3.2	6.3	3.9	3.9	6.7	5.2	6.3	6.1	3.8	5.3	3.5	3.6	3.9
Persons in Unit													
Occupied housing units	1 637	1 108	1 477	551	1 193	1 367	1 627	1 058	1 569	805	2 569	2 127	1 648
1 person	872	107	315	80	58	135	194	129	460	87	580	966	626
2 persons	590	442	558	280	326	411	672	456	619	268	786	842	542
3 persons	106	203	228	127	274	269	292	178	238	136	436	226	307
4 persons	33	204	213	47	354	336	283	179	143	179	493	70	134
5 persons	21	99	112	13	124	142	133	81	75	91	184	20	35
6 persons	8	39	39	4	42	58	31	22	26	35	63	3	4
7 persons	3	9	9	–	11	9	14	10	6	7	18	–	–
8 or more persons	4	5	3	–	4	7	8	3	2	2	9	–	–
Median, occupied housing units	1.44	2.52	2.26	2.20	3.28	3.01	2.42	2.38	2.02	2.85	2.40	1.62	1.87
Median, owner-occupied housing units	1.69	2.49	2.38	1.52	3.25	3.20	2.41	2.38	2.15	3.03	2.97	1.65	1.81
Median, renter-occupied housing units	1.34	2.97	1.62	2.26	3.59	2.22	2.59	2.34	1.78	2.27	1.79	1.59	1.90
Persons Per Room													
Occupied housing units	1 637	1 108	1 477	551	1 193	1 367	1 627	1 058	1 569	805	2 569	2 127	1 648
1.00 or less	1 601	1 103	1 464	525	1 184	1 360	1 616	1 054	1 554	802	2 549	2 091	1 611
1.01 to 1.50	12	3	8	21	9	7	10	3	7	2	16	11	24
1.51 or more	24	2	5	5	–	–	1	1	8	1	4	25	13
VALUE													
Specified owner-occupied housing units	215	782	1 018	–	1 033	1 043	1 176	915	703	452	1 356	17	1
Less than $10,000	–	–	–	–	–	–	–	–	–	–	–	–	–
$10,000 to $14,999	–	–	–	–	–	–	–	–	–	–	–	–	–
$15,000 to $19,999	–	–	–	–	1	1	–	–	–	–	2	–	–
$20,000 to $24,999	1	–	–	–	1	1	–	–	–	–	1	–	–
$25,000 to $29,999	–	–	2	–	1	1	–	–	1	–	1	–	–
$30,000 to $34,999	–	–	–	–	1	1	–	–	–	–	1	–	–
$35,000 to $39,999	–	1	–	–	1	–	2	–	1	–	2	–	–
$40,000 to $49,999	–	2	–	–	4	3	2	1	–	1	10	–	–
$50,000 to $59,999	6	–	6	–	4	7	3	3	2	1	10	1	–
$60,000 to $79,999	9	11	19	–	18	23	12	10	12	3	41	–	1
$80,000 to $99,999	13	10	16	–	76	72	19	25	17	6	164	3	–
$100,000 to $149,999	47	113	56	–	431	538	92	68	55	22	721	7	–
$150,000 to $199,999	49	240	83	–	369	321	225	111	73	70	312	4	–
$200,000 or more	90	405	836	–	130	75	817	697	543	349	92	2	–
Median	$182 100	200000+	200000+	–	$148 000	$139 000	200000+	200000+	200000+	200000+	$127 500	$139 600	$62 500
CONTRACT RENT													
Specified renter-occupied housing units	1 041	78	266	465	87	266	151	61	564	146	828	1 252	1 053
Median	$394	500+	$442	$190	500+	$454	500+	500+	$373	500+	$253	$382	$300

[1]Excludes "Other Asian and Pacific Islander" groups identified in sample tabulations. [2]Persons of Spanish origin may be of any race.

Chapter 9

ACCOUNTING SYSTEMS

Keeping timely and accurate accounting records of your business activities is fundamental to long-term success. Not only will these records help you to make the right decisions, they will be demanded from third parties, such as a bank or venture capitalist. In addition, accurate accounting records will help keep your taxes to a minimum by providing a firm basis for you to determine your taxable income. Therefore, this chapter explains:

* How to read and understand your balance sheet, income statement, and sources and uses of funds statement
* Basic factors in choosing an accounting system
* Accounting services a CPA can provide
* Depreciation: how it works
* Internal accounting controls
* Cash flow: how to construct a cash flow statement
* Cash flow: how to project your cash needs and maximize your cash flows

In operating a business, the entrepreneur attempts to sell a product or service to the market place at a determined price. The price must be an amount that the customer is willing to pay, yet it must also cover costs; otherwise the entrepreneur is out of business. Generally, before the entrepreneur can sell even one unit of a product or a service, numerous other events must take place: Materials, services, and capital equipment must be purchased by the entrepreneur in order to produce a product or service. Employees, rent, insurance premiums, taxes, utilities, and interest and principal on money borrowed must all be paid in order to finance operations. The entrepreneur may need to arrange for the financing of inventory, accounts receivable, and fixed assets. Therefore, if the entrepreneur expects to remain in business, he or she must ask: "How will I keep track of all of the various cash and noncash transactions affecting my business?" The answer is to set up an accounting system. However, before we explain the various methods available, we will look at the desired end product.

UNDERSTANDING FINANCIAL STATEMENTS

The best and most widely accepted method of presenting the financial data of a business is through the use of three financial statements: the balance sheet, income statement, and statement of sources and uses. Most of your accounting systems will lead to the production of these three statements, which will then be used by you to measure the results of your operations and provide information to interested parties, such as your banker, your board of directors, your investors, and, of course, the government.

Balance Sheet

The balance sheet is a recordation of all assets and liabilities and the net worth or owner's equity. The balance sheet is known as a "snap shot" statement because it literally takes a picture of the business up to the close of business on a certain day. The basic equation is:

$$\text{Assets} = \text{Liabilities} + \text{Net Worth}$$

This equation tells us much. It yields the basic business relationship—that is, how the business has chosen to finance its asset base.

Now let's take a closer look at some basic definitions of assets and liabilities:

Current Assets. These assets are "near" cash—that is, they can be converted to cash within one year. These assets include cash, marketable securities, accounts receivable, inventory, prepaids on which refund is possible, notes receivable within one year, and the cash value of life insurance.

Fixed Assets. These assets generally represent investments that are long-term in nature. As a group, they are not very liquid in nature—that is, it may be difficult to realize cash quickly, if at all. These assets are also generally the subject of depreciation. Fixed assets include machinery and equipment, transportation equipment, furniture and fixtures, leasehold improvements, and plant and land.

Noncurrent Assets. These assets do not fit in either of the two categories mentioned above. This group includes notes receivable due to be collected the following year or beyond, intangible assets, such as goodwill and covenants not to compete, direct investment in subsidiaries or other companies, and purchase options.

Current Liabilities. These are a firm's obligations that are due and payable due within one year. They include trade accounts payable, notes payable, current portion of long-term debt (that is, the amount of long-term liabilities due within one year), income taxes payable, and miscellaneous accruals. Miscellaneous accruals are company payables that are related to the normal operation of the business which have not been paid, but are owed, as the result of a cut-off date for recording the accounting information.

Noncurrent Liabilities. These liabilities are not due within one year. They include long-term debt, that portion of notes payable due to be paid next year or beyond, deferred income taxes (which result from timing differences in the treatment of depreciation for tax and accounting purposes) and deferred revenue (revenue received but not yet earned).

Net Worth or Owner's Equity. This account shows how well a business is doing. It is strictly a measure of the difference between assets and liabilities. Entrepreneurs would like this to be large and positive. This account includes capital contributed to the business, withdrawals by the owner or partners, common and preferred stock issued, capital provided in excess of par value of stock issued, retained earnings from operations and a "contra" account called treasury stock (for stock once issued that has been repurchased by the firm).

A sample balance sheet for "YourCorp" is shown below.

YourCorp
Balance Sheet
December 31, 19XX
(000) Omitted

ASSETS		LIABILITIES & NET WORTH	
Cash	$ 25	Accounts payable	$ 125
Marketable securities	15	Notes payable	100
Accounts receivable	350	Miscellaneous accruals	50
Inventory	200	Current portion of	
Prepaid expense	20	long-term debt	15
Total current assets	610	Total current liabilities	290
Machinery and equipment	$100	Long-term debt	200
Plant and land	300	Deferred taxes	50
Transport equipment	100	Notes payable	100
Leasehold improvement	50	Total noncurrent liabilities	350
Less: accumulated			
depreciation	(150)	Common stock	100
Net fixed assets	400	Capital surplus	50
		less: treasury stock	(10)
Covenant not to compete	50	Retained earnings	330
Goodwill	50	Total net worth	470
Total noncurrent assets	100		
Total assets	$1110	Total liabilities and net worth	$1110
	=====		=====

Note: The YourCorp balance sheet is only an example; it is not meant to express any suggested relationship among assets, liabilities, and net worth. It is a "snap shot" of the business at the close of the business day.

Income Statement

The income statement shows how well a business has done over a period of time. To see how well a business has done, the relationship between revenues and expenses must first be determined. The basic equation for the relationship is:

Revenues greater than Expenses = Profit

Revenues less than Expenses = Loss

We hope that as the result of reading this handbook, you will avoid the second form of the equation. Now let's take a look at some basic definitions.

Revenues. Also known as sales. They are the lifeblood of the business. Sales for the accounting period are accumulated under an account called gross sales. This account is affected by a "contra" account called returns and allowances and/or discounts allowed, which are used to reduce gross sales to arrive at net sales.

Cost of Goods Sold. This account provides us with the direct costs of the product or service we have sold. It can be described by the following equation.

```
      Beginning inventory
      Purchases
+     Freight costs
      Purchase discounts taken
−     Ending inventory

      Cost of goods sold
```

Operating Expenses. These expenses can be broken down into two categories: selling expenses and general and administrative expenses.

Selling Expenses. These expenses are related directly to selling and include commissions, wages of sales personnel, advertising, promotion, entertainment of clients, marketing, and fixed overhead connected with the selling effort.

General and Administrative Expenses. These expenses are not related directly to the cost of the goods produced or the selling of those same goods. These expenses include administrative salaries and wages, utilities, rent, insurance, interest on debts, employee benefits, bad debts, office supplies, and other fixed overhead connected with the administrative effort.

Note : We have not listed depreciation in our discussion. Depreciation should be charged to either selling expenses or general and administrative expenses based on who uses the fixed assets being depreciated. We will address depreciation in more detail later in the chapter.

Income Taxes. Taxes that appear on the income statement can differ substantially from taxes due to governmental entities because of the accounting treatment of certain transactions. For tax accounting purposes, it may be necessary to create an account known as deferred taxes. See your tax advisor concerning this matter.

Net Income. Hopefully the result of your efforts is that you will earn a profit. Profit or net income also results in an increase in the net worth of your business.

A sample income statement for YourCorp is shown below.

YourCorp
Income Statement
for the twelve months ended
December 31, 19XX
(000 Omitted)

Revenue		
Gross sales		$ 3,125
Less returns and allowances		(125)
Net sales		3,000
Cost of goods sold		
Beginning inventory	$ 180	
Plus freight in	20	
Plus purchases	1,500	
Less discounts taken	(40)	
Total goods available	1,660	
Less ending inventory	(200)	
Total cost of goods sold		1,460
Gross profit		1,540
Operating Expenses		
Selling expenses		
Commissions	180	
Advertising	120	
Promotion	100	
Salaries and wages	200	
Depreciation	20	
Overhead expense	80	
Total selling expense	700	
General and administrative expenses		
Salaries and wages	260	
Employee benefits	140	
Insurance	40	
Depreciation	40	
Goodwill/covenant	10	
Overhead expense	150	
Total general and administrative	640	
Total operating expenses		1,340
Total operating income		200
Other revenue and expense		25
Pretax income		225
Tax at 40%		(90)
Net income		$ 135

Again, this is merely an example that illustrates the typical method of presentation of income statements. *Note:* Many accountants use slightly differing formats for the presentation of both the balance sheet and income statement.

Statement of Sources and Uses of Funds (Pre July 1, 1988)

This statement, also known as funds statement, sources and uses and changes in working capital statement, and the statement of changes in financial position, will show you the source of your funds and how they were used. The benefit of this financial statement is that it can be used as a proactive management tool in the financial management of your business. It will point out fund requirements when the business grows or when the business needs to purchase capital equipment or pay dividends. This statement is governed by certain rules, which are presented below.

Sources of Funds	Uses of Funds
Decrease in cash	Increase in cash
Decrease in marketable securities	Increase in marketable securities
Decrease in accounts receivable	Increase in accounts receivable
Decrease in inventory	Increase in inventory
Decrease in prepaids	Increase in prepaids
Decrease in gross fixed assets	Increase in gross fixed assets
Increase in accounts payable	Decrease in accounts payable
Increase in current notes payable	Decrease in current notes payable
Increase in miscellaneous accruals	Decrease in miscellaneous accruals
Increase in long-term debt	Decrease in long-term debt
Increase in deferred taxes	Decrease in deferred taxes
Increase in other notes payable	Decrease in other notes payable
Increase in common stock	Decrease in common stock
Increase in capital surplus	Decrease in capital surplus
Net income	Net loss
Depreciation	

To construct a statement of sources and uses of funds, the balance sheets for two consecutive years should be compared. Any changes that have occurred should be listed in a column called "changes." This column will generate the data needed for the statement of sources and uses of funds. An example is shown below.

YourCorp
Balance Sheet

	December 31, 19XX (000) Omitted	December 31, 19XX Change (000) Omitted		
ASSETS				
Cash	$ 40	$ 25	$ 15	Decrease
Marketable securities	0	15	15	Increase
Accounts receivable	300	350	50	Increase
Inventory	160	200	40	Increase
Prepaid expense	10	20	10	Increase
Total current assets	510	610		
Machinery and equipment	80	100	20	Increase
Plant and land	300	300	0	
Transport equipment	80	100	20	Increase
Leasehold improvements	30	50	20	Increase
Less: accumulated depreciation	(70)	(150)	80	Increase
Net fixed assets	420	400		
Covenant	55	50	5	Decrease
Goodwill	55	50	5	Decrease
Total noncurrent assets	110	100		
Total assets	$ 1040	$ 1110		
LIABILITIES & NET WORTH				
Accounts payable	$ 115	$ 125	10	Increase
Notes payable	140	100	40	Decrease
Miscellaneous accruals	70	50	20	Decrease
Current portion of long-term debt	15	15	0	
Total current liabilities	340	290		
Long-term debt	215	200	15	Decrease
Deferred taxes	45	50	5	Increase
Notes payable	100	100	0	
Total noncurrent liabilities	360	350		
Common stock	100	100	0	
Capital surplus	50	50	0	
Treasury stock	(10)	(10)	0	
Retained earnings	200	330	NA	
Total net worth	340	470		
Total liabilities and net worth	$1040	$1110		

For the purpose of our example, we will assume that YourCorp paid $5,000 in dividends at year end. Given the rules, the appropriate balance sheets, and the income statement, the sources and uses statement will appear as follows:

YourCorp
Statement of Sources and Uses of Funds
For the Twelve Months Ended
December 31, 19XX
(000) Omitted

Sources of Funds	
Decrease in cash	$ 15
Decrease in covenant	5
Decrease in goodwill	5
Increase in accounts payable	10
Increase in deferred taxes	5
Net Income	135
Depreciation	80
Total Sources	$ 255
Uses of Funds	
Increase in marketable securities	$ 15
Increase in accounts receivable	50
Increase in inventory	40
Increase in prepaid expenses	10
Increase in machinery and equipment	20
Increase in transport equipment	20
Increase in leasehold improvements	20
Decrease in notes payable	40
Decrease in miscellaneous accruals	20
Decrease in long-term debt	15
Dividend paid	5
Total uses of funds	$ 255

As expected, the sources of funds equal the uses of funds. This information is useful to managers because it shows precisely where all of the business's profits went. It also illustrates certain principles of business regarding growth and the funding of that growth. *Note:* When you depreciate and amortize assets, it does not create funds, rather it serves as a noncash charge against earnings. We will explain this phenomenon in a later section.

The Statement of Sources and Uses of Funds (Post July 1, 1988)

In November 1987, the Financial Accounting Standards Board (FASB), in Statement No. 95, ruled that a full set of financial statements should only show cash flows for a given period. The reasons for this pronouncement were:

YourCorp
Statement of Cash Flows
For the Year Ended December 31, 199X
Increase (Decrease) in Cash and Cash Equivalents
(000) Omitted

Cash flows from operating activities

Cash received from customers	$13,850	
Cash paid to suppliers and employees	(12,000)	
Dividend received from affiliate	20	
Interest received	55	
Interest paid (net of amount capitalized)	(220)	
Income taxes paid	(325)	
Insurance proceeds received	15	
Cash paid to settle lawsuit for		
trademark infringement	(30)	
Net cash provided by operating activities		$1,365

Cash flows from investing activities

Proceeds from sale of assets	600	
Payment received on note for sale of asset	150	
Capital expenditures	(1,000)	
Payment for purchase of assets		
of another business	(925)	
Net cash used in investing activities		(1,175)

Cash flows from financing activities

Net borrowings under line-of-credit agreement	300	
Principal payments under capital		
lease obligation	(125)	
Proceeds from issuance of long-term debt	400	
Proceeds from issuance of common stock	500	
Dividends paid	(200)	
Net cash provided by financing activities		875

Net increase in cash and cash equivalents[a]		1,065
Cash and cash equivalents at beginning of year		600
Cash and cash equivalents at end of year		$1,665

[a] Cash equivalents are defined as short-term, highly liquid investments.

* Elimination of the ambiguity associated with the word "funds."
* Investors and creditors need a useful statement of cash receipts and cash payments during a period in order to analyze investment and credit risk.
* The statement of cash flows segregates operational, investing (equity), and financing (debt) flows.

FASB 95 has made it much easier for a potential purchaser of a business because it will identify exactly how a business has provided for its cash requirements. Bankers also find FASB 95 to be easier because their entire analysis is designed to distill relevant cash flows.

A typical cash flow statement incorporating almost all of the categories of cash flows follows. You will most likely not encounter all the categories of cash flows we have presented; therefore, simply eliminate the ones that are not applicable. The numbers used in this presentation do not relate in any way to the previous examples.

As we mentioned earlier, this example includes many types of transactions that may not occur in your business. The purpose of the example is to illustrate the usefulness of the cash flow statement to you, the entrepreneur, in highlighting where cash originates. The method we have chosen is the direct method, your accountant may wish to use the indirect method which will allow him or her to arrive at the same result.

CHOOSING AN ACCOUNTING SYSTEM

System Options

Single Entry

A single-entry system is one in which only cash and personal accounts records are maintained. It is not self-balancing, and, therefore, debits do not equal credits. Furthermore, no journal entries are made and as a result, owner's equity on the balance sheet is a "plug" figure. Generally, there is no detailed record of gains or losses. The balance sheet is prepared from whatever data is available. The income statement is prepared from a comparison of beginning and ending balance sheets unless cash transaction totals can provide profit and loss information.

The single-entry system may be adequate where:

• Transactions are infrequent
• Assets and liabilities are few

However, the single-entry system must be carefully maintained.

Double Entry

A double-entry system is universal in its application and is more popular than the single-entry system. It takes its name from the fact that the equality of the accounting equation (assets = liability + owner's equity) is maintained by each entry, which results in recording equal amounts of debits and credits. This system uses journals and ledgers. Transactions are first entered in a journal (see Exhibit 9-1) and then posted to a ledger. A journal is essentially a chronological record containing lists of individual transactions as they occur. A ledger (see Exhibit 9-2) is a loose-leaf book, file, or other record containing all the separate business accounts. Each ledger account contained in the ledger is a means of accumulating all information about changes in a specific asset, liability, or owner's equity.

"Posting" refers to the process of transferring financial information accumulated in chronological order in the general journal to the ledger, where information is accumulated by account.

Each account in the double-entry system has a column on the left side for recording debits and one on the right side for listing credits. It is self-balancing because each transaction is recorded as a debit in one account and a credit in another account. After journal transactions are posted to the ledger, the total debits in the ledger must equal the total credits. If not, an error was made, which must be located and corrected.

At the end of each accounting period, financial statements may be prepared. These statements generally include:

* Income statement
* Balance sheet
* Statement of cash flows

The income statement reflects the results of operations for the period. The balance sheet reflects the financial position of the business on a given date. The statement of cash flows provides relevant information about the cash receipts and cash payments of an enterprise during a period.

In summary, the single-entry system is the simplest to maintain but it has limited application. The double-entry system has a wider variety of application and has built-in checks and balances to help assure accuracy and control. For more information on accounting systems, write to the Superintendent of Documents, Washington, D. C. 20402, and ask for stock number 045-000-00239-9, "Financial Recordkeeping for Small Stores."

Remember, good records are necessary for good management and they will help you:

* Identify source of receipt
* Keep track of deductible expenses
* Compute depreciation allowance
* Keep track of capital gains and losses
* Determine your earnings for self-employment tax purposes
* Support items reported on your tax returns

ACCOUNTING SERVICES A CPA CAN PROVIDE

A CPA can provide you with three types of services: (1) audits, (2) reviews, and (3) compilations. Brief descriptions of each service are given below.

Audits

In business, an audit of financial statements is conducted to determine whether the accounts and statements are kept in conformity with generally accepted accounting principles, and whether they represent a fair statement of the business's condition. If a company goes public, then the SEC requires audited financial statements in compliance with generally accepted accounting principles (GAAP). Also, if a company decides to offer franchises, many state governments, as well as the FTC, will require that audited financial statements be given to the prospective franchisee.

An audit provides a reasonable basis for expressing an opinion regarding the financial statements taken as a whole.

Reviews

A review of financial statements is conducted by performing inquiry and analytical procedures which provide a reasonable basis for expressing limited assurance that there are no material modifications that should be made to the statements in order for them to be in conformity with generally accepted accounting principles.

Compilations

A compilation of financial statements presents, in the form of financial statements, information that is the representation of management (owners) without undertaking to express any assurance on the statements.

A compilation differs from a review in that it is merely a presentation of management's financial information given in the form of financial statements. There is no expression of assurance in a compilation.

In terms of cost, an audit is most expensive and a compilation is least expensive.. The costs relate to how much service is needed. See Exhibit 9-3 for a comparison of audit, review, and compilation engagements.

In summary, the level of service a CPA provides is determined by management's needs. These needs are, in turn, impacted by requirements of third party financial statement users. Because of the varying costs of different levels of service, you should select appropriate levels of service. CPAs can assist in this selection through:

* Evaluating the perceived needs of outside users
* Evaluating the client's system of internal control
* Analyzing prior experience with the client

DEPRECIATION

Depreciation means many things to many people. In common usage, it means an erosion in value. To the business person, depreciation means the provision for "wearing out." To the tax accountant, it means the arbitrary allocation of part of the purchase price of an asset to expenses in a given year. All these definitions have merit. For our discussion, however, we will use the tax accountant's version—that is, we depreciate an asset by assigning to an expense account a certain portion of the asset's original cost according to certain rules. From a philosophical point of view, depreciation can be thought of as a measure of an asset's utility which is consumed over some finite period of time while the asset is used directly or indirectly to produce revenue.

From an everyday perspective, depreciation is a noncash charge to income that reduces income and thus taxes associated with that income. When we say noncash charge, we simply mean that we do not write a check to someone for depreciation. Therefore, from a cash flow point of view, depreciation saves us cash by reducing our tax liability. The more we can employ noncash deductions, the better off our cash flow will be because of tax savings. Recognizing this fact, President Reagan, during the early days of his administration, signed into law a landmark piece of economic legislation, which to this day is still being debated in various circles, entitled the Economic Recovery Act of 1981. Part of that act provided for accelerated depreciation of certain assets and was called the accelerated cost recovery system (ACRS).

ACRS, which is found in Internal Revenue Code section 168, provides a set of depreciation schedules which allow a faster write-off of assets than those already in place for the purpose of stimulating the purchase of capital assets. It was believed that increased activity in the capital asset market would increase activity in the economy in general as well as modernize and increase the productive capacity of the nation. Ultimately, increased productivity would lower unemployment and increase the tax base, which in turn would shrink the deficit.

We have used around the term asset quite a lot, yet we have not looked specifically at a capital or fixed asset. This asset:

* Has a life greater than one year
* Is not bought and sold in the normal course of business
* Is property whose utility diminishes over time
* Is used in the normal course of business to produce income either directly or indirectly
* Must be replaced once it is "used up" if business is to continue at its current level

How is depreciation calculated? There are numerous methods. We will discuss four methods here and compare the results obtained and their effect on taxes.

These four methods will be based on the following example.

Example:

Your company owns a capital asset with the following characteristics:

* It costs $100,000.
* It has an expected useful life of 5 years. (Life expectancy of an asset is the period of time that is commonly determined by the industry in which the asset is employed.)
* It has a salvage value of $6,000.

Straight-line Depreciation

This method simply allocates the cost of the capital asset, less its salvage value equally over the asset's useful life. The general form of this method is:

$$\text{Depreciation Charge} = \frac{(\text{original cost} - \text{salvage value})}{\text{years of useful life}}$$

Note: If salvage value is not in excess of 10 percent of the original cost, it can be ignored. In our example, we will ignore salvage value. Therefore, our calculation will look like:

$$\text{Depreciation charge} = \frac{100,000 - 0}{5}$$

$$\text{Depreciation charge} = \$20,000 \text{ per year}$$

Sum of the Years Digits

The sum of the years digits (SYD) is slightly more complex but allows for acceleration of depreciation in earlier periods. This method compares the number of years left in the asset's life (a declining value in the numerator) to a summation of the digits that make up the asset's life in years (a constant value in the denominator) and calculates the depreciation based on the capital asset's cost minus the asset's salvage value, regardless of what it may be. The general form of this method is:

$$\text{Depreciation charge year } Y = \frac{\text{years remaining}}{\text{summation of } N} \times \text{asset cost}$$

Where:

$$Y = \text{the year of interest}$$

$$\text{Summation of } N = N + N\text{-}1 + N\text{-}2 + \ldots + 1$$

In this example:

$$\text{Summation of } 5 = 5 + 4 + 3 + 2 + 1 = 15$$

Therefore, in our example:

$$\text{Depreciation charge year } 1 = \frac{5}{15} \times 100{,}000$$

$$\text{Depreciation charge year } 1 = \$33{,}333$$

and

$$\text{Depreciation charge year } 2 = \frac{4}{15} \times 100{,}000$$

$$\text{Depreciation charge year } 2 = \$26{,}667$$

Double Declining Balance

The double declining balance (DDB) method is an accelerated method that uses twice the straight-line depreciation factor based on the undepreciated balance. That is, we need to reduce the cost of the asset by the accumulated depreciation times twice the initial straight-line rate. In the case of DDB, we ignore salvage value if it is less than 10 percent of original cost.

In our example, the initial straight-line depreciation factor is 1/5 or 20 percent of the cost of the asset to be written off each year. To get the DDB factor, simply take the straight line rate and multiply it by 2 or 40 percent (2 x 20%).

The general form of DDB is:

$$\text{Depreciation year } Y = (\text{original cost} - \text{accumulated depreciation}) \times \text{DDB}$$

Thus, for Year 1:

$$\text{Depreciation year } 1 = (100{,}000 - 0) \times 40\%$$

$$\text{Depreciation year } 1 = \$40{,}000$$

And for year 2:

$$\text{Depreciation year 2} = (100{,}000 - 40{,}000) \times 40\%$$

$$\text{Depreciation year 2} = \$24{,}000$$

When employing DDB, it will become necessary to switch to straight-line depreciation at some point since we can never fully depreciate the asset by continuing to take 40 percent of some undepreciated balance. In this case, we would switch over in year 4. This may seem strange but it is totally legitimate.

Warning: If the salvage value is greater than 10 percent, we must ensure that net book value (undepreciated balance) does not fall below salvage value. See your tax advisor for clarification.

Accelerated Cost Recovery System (ACRS)

The first three methods discussed are considered accounting methods of depreciation to arrive at a so-called "book" income. The income that is really important to us is taxable income since it is the income on which we will pay taxes in actual cash flow dollars. Accelerated Cost Recovery System (ACRS) is the method used to determine this. ACRS was enacted into federal tax law to allow a tax benefit to businesses that purchase capital goods. As a result, a business using ACRS for tax accounting purposes will pay lower taxes and thereby improve its cash outflows.

To calculate the allowed depreciation the government has set up a depreciation schedule based on the total original cost of the asset ignoring salvage value. For example, under the original ACRS, a five-year asset for book purposes was allowed three-year ACRS treatment using the following schedule:

Year 1	25% of the asset
Year 2	38% of the asset
Year 3	37% of the asset

Therefore, for our example:

$$\text{Depreciation Year 1} = 100{,}000 \times .25$$

$$\text{Depreciation Year 1} = \$25{,}000$$

At this point, you may be wondering about the different methods of depreciation and whether they will create differing taxable incomes for "book" and "tax" statements. Moreover, to complicate the situation, many states, for tax purposes, have not adopted ACRS and mandate accelerated depreciation be calculated according to the SYD or DDB methods. The table below illustrates just how the four methods differ.

Example:

- Property cost is $100,000
- Salvage value is negligible
- Property has an estimated life determined by the trade to be 5 years
- Property qualifies as three-year ACRS property

	Straight-line		Sum of the Years' Digits		Double Declining Balance		ACRS	
Year	Annual Depreciation	Cumulative Depreciation	Annual Depreciation	Cumulative Depreciation	Annual Depreciation	Cumulative Depreciation	Annual Depreciation	Cumulative Depreciation
1	$20,000	$20,000	$33,333	$33,333	$40,000	$40,000	$25,000	25,000
2	20,000	40,000	26,667	60,000	24,000	64,000	38,000	63,000
3	20,000	60,000	20,000	80,000	14,400	78,400	37,000	100,000
4	20,000	80,000	13,333	93,333	10,800	89,200	–0–	100,000
5	20,000	100,000	6,667	100,000	10,800	100,000	–0–	100,000

As you can see, if we use straight-line depreciation for book purposes, ACRS depreciation for federal tax purposes, and double declining balance depreciation for state tax purposes, we will have three different depreciation charges to calculate and apply.

Our reason for showing you these different methods is to point out that it is both legal and desirable to keep three sets of books to conform with accounting principles and to take full advantage of the current tax laws. The following example demonstrates how different depreciation rates will affect your business and create a "deferred tax account."

Example:

- Net profit before taxes and depreciation is $150,000
- Only capital asset is a 5 year $100,000 machine
- Straightline depreciation is employed for "book"
- ACRS depreciation is employed for federal tax purposes
- Double declining balance is employed for state tax purposes
- Asset has negligible salvage value
- Company's federal tax rate is 40%
- Company's state tax rate is 10%

The abbreviated income statements would appear as follows:

YourCorp
December 31, 1989
(000) Omitted

	Book	Federal	Book	State
Net profit before depreciation and tax	$150	$150	$150	$150
depreciation	(20)	(25)	(20)	(40)
Net profit before tax	130	125	130	110
Federal taxes at 40 percent state taxes at 10 percent	(52)	(50)	(13)	(11)
Net profit	$ 78	$ 75	$117	$ 99

As you can see, the difference between book and federal tax net profits is $3,000. Also the actual tax bill is $2,000 less than book calculations would have us believe. In accounting for this difference, we create an account known as "deferred taxes." That is, as the accelerated method of depreciation drops below the amount that would be produced under the book method. Note that these deferred taxes will be repaid at some later period.

For the state tax calculation, we would pay $2,000 less than using the book method. It would also create a deferred tax amount of $18,000. The federal tax deferred would be $3,000.

We hope this discussion has clarified the term depreciation. Its use as an accounting device to record the consumption of capital assets is necessary in the determination of the efficiency of a business. It is also considered to have a positive cash flow to the extent that it is a noncash charge to revenues and as such it can be added back. *Note:* When a business experiences a net loss from operations, depreciation does not supply cash, it simply reduces the arithmetic size of the loss. We have shown how it is legal and necessary to carry different sets of books to account for different methods of depreciation that are available and sometimes mandatory.

Warning: Although this discussion focused on the concept of depreciation, it should be mentioned that ACRS has been changed and that for federal tax purposes, The TRA provides for a modified ACRS method of depreciation. We used ACRS in our example because of its simplicity; you should discuss the MACRS method with your tax accountant. There are also new rules regarding the sale or exchange of depreciated property prior to full depreciation, which should also be discussed with your tax accountant.

INTERNAL ACCOUNTING CONTROLS TO PREVENT THEFT

Internal Crime

The American Institute of Certified Public Accountants Committee on Auditing Procedure defined "internal control" as follows: Internal control comprises the plan of organization and all of the coordinate methods and measures adopted within a business to safeguard its assets, check the accuracy and reliability of its accounting data, promote operational efficiency, and encourage adherence to prescribed managerial policies.

Note that the definition of an internal control system extends beyond those matters directly related to the functions of the accounting and financial departments. That is, it is the means by which you, as the owner, can obtain the information, protection, and control for successful operation of your business enterprise.

Function of Controls

The types of controls adopted by the AICPA are selected by comparing the cost relative to the expected benefits. You, as a business owner, should establish accounting controls to:

* Provide reliable data
* Safeguard your assets and records
* Promote operational efficiency of your business
* Encourage adherence to prescribed policies

An internal control system assists in preventing and detecting embezzlement, fraud, and errors.

Embezzlement involves converting, to a person's own use and benefit, property that has been entrusted to that person's care. Obvious areas of concern are petty cash, cash sales, and inventory.

Fraud involves trickery or deceit and is used by the embezzler to conceal any misappropriation. Fraud is also used to conceal honest errors or to create an appearance of good performance when that is not the case.

Components of Internal Control

In order to fulfill the objectives of internal control, it is necessary for a system to have certain elements: (a) competent, trustworthy personnel with clear lines of authority and responsibility; (b) adequate segregation of duties; (c) proper procedures for authorization; (d) adequate documents and records; (e) proper procedures for record keeping; (f) physical control over assets and records; and (g) independent checks on performance.

Mechanics of Internal Control

The principal way internal control provides protection is by dividing responsibilities for handling various phases of a business transaction. For example, the following responsibilities should be handled by different persons.

* Authorization of the transaction
* Recording of the transaction
* Custody of the assets involved in the transaction

Cross checking results from a segregation of duties and should produce early detection of errors, losses from embezzlement, fraud, carelessness, and as a consequence, discourage improper actions.

Note: Collusion can neutralize a system of internal control. Collusion occurs when two or more dishonest persons work together to overcome internal controls. Bonding employees entrusted with handling the company's assets is a good defense against collusion because bonding is a psychological deterrent. Bonding companies may investigate employees who are to be covered by their insurance and usually insist on prosecuting a dishonest employee who is bonded.

Other Controls

Other controls within an internal control system include:
* Establishing adequate budgets and other reports prepared with sufficient frequency to meet management's needs for control.
* Establishing a chart of accounts.
* Establishing a mandatory vacation policy.
* Establishing a well defined conflict of interest policy, which is strictly adhered to.
* Establishing reasonable record retention policies.
* Performing regular but unannounced comparisons between records establishing accountability for assets and the assets themselves.

External Crime

Every business is subject to crime losses from outsiders because too few business owners understand how losses occur and what can go wrong in their operation. Others are caught up in the day-to-day routine of managing their businesses and cannot find time to implement proper security measures. You must make the time to plan and implement the type of security methods that best fit your particular business. You should think about controlling access to merchandise and other property. This can be achieved through building design, hardware, and labor supervision and accountability.

Any crime prevention program must concentrate on the sources of losses, such as burglary, robbery, shoplifting, passing bad checks, credit card fraud, computer fraud, and internal theft.

An adequate system of internal control and external crime prevention is important for small companies as well as for large ones. Inadequate controls and prevention programs enhance the likelihood of errors in the records and crime losses from outsiders. It is imperative that proper internal controls and crime prevention programs be initiated from the beginning in order for your company's operations not to be permanently damaged.

Steps You Can Take to Prevent Embezzlement

Embezzlement is one of the most emotionally devastating and insidious of property crimes because it is carried out by a person who is in a position of trust. Many a trusted employee, who the owner has relied upon and whose opinion the owner respects, has succumbed to temptation and diverted funds and assets for personal use with no intent of returning them.

Although we recommend you establish controls, we also unequivocally state that no set of controls are foolproof. As you lay awake at night thinking of ways to prevent your employees from stealing from you, we assure you that someone who is working for you, at some time or another, will also be laying awake thinking of ways to rip you off. Controls, however, will keep thefts to a minimum. To assist you in limiting the possibilities of losses through embezzlement, we have provided you with a list of precautions excerpted from the U.S. Small Business Administration Management Aid No. 3.009 "Preventing Embezzlement."

* Check the background of prospective employees. Sometimes you can satisfy yourself by making a few telephone calls or writing a few letters. In other cases, you may want to turn the matter over to a credit bureau or similar agency to run a background check.

* Know your employees to the extent that you may be able to detect signs of financial or other personal problems. Build up a rapport so that they feel free to discuss such things in confidence.

* See that no one is placed on the payroll without authorization from you or a responsible official of the company. If you have a personnel department, require it to approve additions to the payroll, as a double check.

* Have the company mail addressed to a post office box rather than your place of business. In smaller cities, the owner–manager may want to go the post office to collect the mail. In any event, you or your designated key person should personally open the mail and make a record at that time of cash and checks received. Don't delude yourself that checks or money orders payable to your company can't be converted into cash by an enterprising embezzler.

* Either personally prepare the daily cash deposits or compare the deposits made by employees with the record of cash and checks received. Make sure you get a copy of the duplicate deposit slip or other documentation from the bank. Make it a habit to go to the bank and make the daily deposit yourself as often as you can. If you delegate these jobs, make an occasional spot check to see that nothing is amiss.

* Arrange for bank statements and other correspondence from the banks to be sent to the same post office box, and personally reconcile all bank statements with your company's books and records. The owner-manager who has not reconciled the statements for some time may want to get oriented by the firm's outside accountant.

* Personally examine all canceled checks and endorsements to see if there is anything unusual. This also applies to payroll checks.

* Make sure that an employee in a position to mishandle funds is adequately bonded. Let employees know that fidelity coverage is a matter of company policy rather than any feeling of mistrust on your part. If would-be embezzlers know that a bonding company also has an interest in what they do, they may think twice before helping themselves to your funds.

* Spot check your accounting records and assets to satisfy yourself that all is well and that your plan of internal control is being carried out.

* Personally approve unusual discounts and bad-debt write-offs. Approve or spot check credit memos and other documentation for sales returns and allowances.

* Don't delegate the signing of checks and approval of cash disbursements unless absolutely necessary and never approve any payment without sufficient documentation or prior knowledge of the transaction.

* Examine all invoices and supporting data before signing checks. Make sure all merchandise was actually received and the price seems reasonable. In many false purchase schemes, the embezzler neglects to make up receiving forms or other records purporting to show receipt of merchandise.

* Personally cancel all invoices at the time you sign the check to prevent double payment through error or otherwise.

* Don't sign blank checks. Don't leave a supply of signed blank checks when you go on vacation.

* Inspect all prenumbered checkbooks and other prenumbered forms from time to time to ensure that checks or forms from the backs of the books have not been removed and possibly used in a fraudulent scheme.

* Have the preparation of the payroll and the actual paying of employees handled by different persons, especially when cash is involved.

CASH FLOW MANAGEMENT: HOW TO CONSTRUCT A SPREAD SHEET, AND WHY IT IS NECESSARY

Up to this point, we have shown you a number of financial statements and formats and their meaning in the operation of your business. Now we will show you the single most important statement in all of business: the *cash flow statement*. Although balance sheets and income statements are necessary to run the business and report its achievements, the Cash Flow Statement is indispensable in managing your business on a day-to-day basis. The most important aspect of business is cash. Only cash pays the rent, only cash buys supplies, only cash pays your employees, only cash pays the government, and only cash keeps the doors open.

Often, experienced business people have come to us and said, "My accountant told me that my sales are increasing and that I made $15,000 profit this month, yet I am unable to make the next payroll." We found that in each instance these individuals had not run a cash flow projection. Had they done so, they would have observed that an increase in sales converts today's cash into raw materials and labor, and then later into accounts receivable, which will not be collected for a period of at least thirty days. The simple truth is that by creating a cash flow statement, you can identify the effects of taking that next big order. You can see what amount of cash will be necessary to support the current or next level of business activity.

At this point, we will introduce the basic concept of cash flow. The monthly cash flow equation is simply a statement of the following elements:

Beginning cash (cash on hand at beginning of month)

\+ Cash receipts

\- Cash disbursements

= Cash surplus or shortage - Cash paid to bank against line of credit

or

Beginning cash + Cash drawn against bank line of credit

= Cash on hand at end of month

If total cash outflows exceed the total of cash receipts plus beginning cash on hand, we will need to seek additional funds from another source. In the equation, we assumed your business has a bank line of credit, which if you are starting from scratch, is probably tied to the equity in your home. If this is not the case, simply substitute the word "bank" for personal savings or Uncle Harry or whatever your source might be using. On the other hand, if total outflows were less than inflows to such an extent that we did not need all of the cash on hand, we would use the excess funds to pay down the bank line of credit or whatever other source of funds you might have used.

The next step in the process of creating a cash flow statement is to identify the elements that will allow us to construct such a statement. By its very name, the cash flow statement is interested only in those events that have a cash impact on the business. The inflow side of the cash flow equation is concerned with:

* Cash sales
* Collection of accounts receivable
* Refunds of federal or state taxes
* Infusion of capital
* Cash return on investment
* Long-term loans

The other side of the equation is interested in the cash outflows or disbursements required to support our current level of business activity. Those disbursements include, but are not limited to, the following:

* Payroll
* Equipment payments (principal and interest)
* Raw materials and/or other inventory purchases
* Supplies
* Rent
* Utilities
* Selling expenses (such as commissions)
* Long-term loan repayments (principal and interest)
* Transportation costs
* Overhead expenses

     *   Tax installments (federal and state)

Remember, we are only interested in those items that must be paid in cash during a particular month. You will notice we have omitted noncash charges such as depreciation and amortization of goodwill.

Many of you will participate in business ventures in which a majority of your sales will be based on trade credit to your customers. In order to deal with this fact from a cash flow perspective, we present the following rule of thumb: If your terms are net 30 days—that is, payment for your product or service must be paid within 30 days of invoice date, you can expect the following cash collection flow: 60–65 percent of accounts receivable will be collected in the first month after sale (30 days), 20–25 percent of accounts receivable in the second month after sale, about 15–18 percent in the third month after sale, and about 1 percent in the fourth month after sale. For example, we will assume that 1 percent of sales are never collected, which is a fact in business that you must be prepared to accept. Therefore, for those sales on credit, a cash receipts schedule would look something like the following table:

CASH RECEIPTS OF ACCOUNTS RECEIVABLE
(000) omitted

	Month 1	Month 2	Month 3	Month 4	Month 5	Month 6
Sales	100	120	120	130	100	110
Cash receipts						
First month (60%)	0	60	72	72	78	60
Second month (20%)	0	0	20	24	24	26
Third month (18%)	0	0	0	18	22[a]	22[a]
Fourth month (1%)	0	0	0	0	1[a]	1[a]
Total	0	60	92	114	125	109

[a] Rounded

Note that very little cash will flow into the your coffers during the first 90 days. In fact, you will receive only $152,000 during the first 90 days on sales of $340,000. Assuming that you have a net cash margin of 10 percent and that you had to pay cash for all costs of doing business, 90 percent of your sales, or $306,000, will have to be paid out during the first 90 days of operations. Of this amount, you will have only collected $152,000, which leaves a cash deficit of $154,000, which will have to be made up from sources other than the collection of receivables. The smart entrepreneur will be aware of this situation and be prepared for it by calculating his or her cash requirements via the cash flow statement.

Life would indeed be simple if businesses only had to deal with cash inflows; however, the creation of sales involves expenditures. The degree of expenditure is a function of the business type. Some businesses have high fixed costs and low variable costs while others have just the reverse combination. Regardless of the cost structure, each business must make certain cash outlays to support a given level of sales.

Given the following circumstances, we will create a sample cash disbursements schedule. Payroll, as a rule, is a function of sales. In our example, we will use a percentage range that falls within the experience of many businesses, 28 to 30 percent. Insurance will be paid in advance for each six month period of coverage. Commissions are paid at the rate of 6 percent of sales. Supplies are roughly proportional to sales. Inventory is consistently 40 percent of sales and is paid for in the month after purchase. Tax installments are paid quarterly and are based on a 40 percent corporate tax rate (this percentage includes both federal and state income tax). *Note:* In order to arrive at the correct tax figures, you will have to create a proforma income statement that includes noncash deductions, such as amortization and depreciation, and you will have to subtract the amount of principal from the total paydown of any debt paydown of any debt obligation incurred in the purchase of capital equipment. Based on these factors, a cash disbursements schedule might look something like the following:

CASH DISBURSEMENTS
(000 Omitted)

Cash Disbursements	Month 1	Month 2	Month 3	Month 4	Month 5	Month 6
Rent	4	4	4	4	4	4
Payroll	28	36	36	39	28	31
Insurance	6	0	0	0	0	0
Utilities	2	2	2	2	2	2
Commissions (6%)	6	7	7	8	6	7
Equipment payment	7	7	7	7	7	7
Supplies	1	2	2	3	1	2
Inventory	40	48	48	52	40	44
Professionals	1	1	1	1	1	1
Interest at 12%	0	0	0	0	0	0
Tax installments	0	0	14	0	0	193
Total disbursements	96	107	121	116	89	111

Warning: These cash disbursement categories do not necessarily include all cash disbursement items your business may experience. Other disbursements might include advertising, promotion, patent fees, and research and development expenditures. This table includes a typical list, so be sure to include items unique to your business.

Once we have created the table of cash receipts and cash disbursements, all that remains is to construct a cash flow spread sheet. Assuming the beginning balance is $10,000, and you will borrow from an established line of credit at the bank to keep at least $10,000 in the cash account, the cash flow spread sheet will take on the following appearance:

CASH FLOW SPREAD SHEET
(000 omitted)

	Month 1	Month 2	Month 3	Month 4	Month 5	Month 6
Sales	100	120	120	130	100	110
Cash Receipts						
First month (60%)	0	60	72	72	78	60
Second month (20%)	0	0	20	24	24	26
Third month (18%)	0	0	0	18	22 [a]	22 [a]
Fourth month (1%)	0	0	0	0	1 [a]	1 [a]
Total	0	60	92	114	125	109

[a] Rounded

Disbursements	Month 1	Month 2	Month 3	Month 4	Month 5	Month 6
Rent	4	4	4	4	4	4
Payroll	28	36	36	39	28	3
Insurance	6	0	0	0	0	0
Utilities	2	2	2	2	2	2
Commissions (6%)	6	7	7	8	6	7
Equipment payment	7	7	7	7	7	7
Supplies	1	2	2	3	1	2
Inventory	40	48	48	52	40	44
Professionals	1	1	1	1	1	1
Interest at 12%	0	1	1	2	2	1
Tax installments	0	0	14	0	0	13
Total disbursements	96	108	122	118	91	112
Net Cash from Operations	(96)	(48)	(30)	(4)	34	(3)
Beginning cash	10	10	10	10	10	10
Cash on hand or (shortage)	(86)	(38)	(20)	6	44	7
Bank loan required (or paid down)	96	48	30	4	(34)	3
Ending cash	10	10	10	10	10	10
Cumulative bank loan	96	144	174	178	144	147

As you can see, you will need to borrow $178,000 in the first four months. In the fifth month, you will be able to repay $34,000, but you will have to borrow $3,000 in the sixth month in order to finance your sales.

By creating the cash flow spread sheet, you will have a clear, though perhaps discouraging, picture of cash requirements to run a business at this level with these margins. Our feeling is that it is better to know about a problem and deal with it rather than to hope no problem exists. The cash flow spread sheet will clearly inform you of any potential cash flow problems. We cannot urge you strongly enough to prepare cash flow budgets and update them often. In our presentation, we have shown you cash flow spread sheets using six months of data. You should not limit yourself to only six months. We recommend that you construct a cash flow spread sheet for a minimum of twelve months, and that you constantly add a month to this projection as each month elapses.

In the next section, we will show you several ways that you can improve your cash flow to avoid potential cash flow problems.

CASH FLOW MANAGEMENT: HOW TO PROJECT YOUR BUSINESS' FUTURE CASH FLOWS AND HOW TO MAXIMIZE CASH FLOWS

We are often asked by entrepreneurs, "How do I go about constructing a cash flow statement, and where do I get the numbers?" Therefore, we suggest the following approach to estimate cash inflows and outflows.

First:

Estimate sales and be realistic. Meet with your sales and marketing staff (if that's you, put on both hats) and forecast a low, average, and optimistic level of sales and the probability of each level occurring. Chart these sales by product on a month to month basis by month for the next twelve months. Establish a collection rate of accounts receivable based either on experience or industry standards. Again, be realistic.

Second:

Detail all expenses. This step is very important. Bring in everyone who is involved and get their input regarding all possible expenses that will be incurred to meet your sales projections. Include in your considerations any unusual occurrences and their ramifications.

Third:

Quantify all expenses. We recommend being as pessimistic as possible. Remember, you may not achieve your sales projection but odds are that you will make and probably exceed your expense projection. Where possible, establish a percentage relationship of expenses to sales. These expenses are also known as variable expenses, such as inventory, payroll, and commissions. Determine fixed costs, such as rent, insurance, and equipment payments. Remember, your estimates should be high because things rarely go as planned.

Fourth:

Construct a cash flow spread sheet. Determine a level of cash that is necessary to carry on operations on a day-to-day basis. Once receipt and disbursement elements are known, determine the level of outside funds required. Should you not wish to use outside funds then the spread sheet will help you determine the initial capital required. (Refer to Section 9.6 for the mechanics of constructing a cash flow spread sheet.)

Fifth:

Put your plan into action and monitor. A plan is only as good as the tracking, updating, and variance analysis that follows its creation. The follow-up will highlight areas where savings have occurred or where overexpenditure has occurred and management review is required. Furthermore, a continual update is required to account for unexpected sales, expenses, or changes in the timing of expenses or sales already projected. The creation of a cash flow spread sheet lends itself very well to numerous electronic spread sheets available on personal computers.

Often, we are asked by business people whether there are any methods that can be used to improve cash flow. Our answer is yes. There are several steps that can be taken to strengthen cash flow. We will demonstrate how you can improve the cash flow of your business by using the cash flow spread sheet constructed in Section 6 as an example.

CASH FLOW SPREAD SHEET
(000 omitted)

	Month 1	Month 2	Month 3	Month 4	Month 5	Month
Sales	100	120	120	130	100	110
Cash receipts						
First month (60%)	0	60	72	72	78	60
Second month (20%)	0	0	20	24	24	26
Third month (18%)	0	0	0	18	22 [a]	22 [a]
Fourth month (1%)	0	0	0	0	1 [a]	1 [a]
Total	0	60	92	114	125	109

Disbursements	Month 1	Month 2	Month 3	Month 4	Month 5	Month
Rent	4	4	4	4	4	4
Payroll	28	36	36	39	28	31
Insurance	6	0	0	0	0	0
Utilities	2	2	2	2	2	2
Commissions (6%)	6	7	7	8	6	7
Equipment payment	7	7	7	7	7	7
Supplies	1	2	2	3	1	2
Inventory	40	48	48	52	40	44
Professionals	1	1	1	1	1	1
Interest at 12%	0	1	1	2	2	1
Tax installments	0	0	14	0	0	13
Total disbursements	96	108	122	118	91	112
Net cash from operations	(96)	(48)	(30)	(4)	34	(3)
Beginning cash	10	10	10	10	10	10
Cash on hand or (shortage)	(86)	(38)	(20)	6	44	7
Bank loan required (or paid down)	96	48	30	4	(34)	3
Ending cash	10	10	10	10	10	10
Cumulative bank loan	96	144	174	178	144	147

[a] Rounded

There are four areas that affect cash flow, and if approached correctly can significantly enhance your net cash flow. These areas are:

- Collection of accounts receivable
- Payment of accounts payable
- Debt repayment scheduling

• Capitalization

Collection of Accounts Receivable

To construct the cash flow spread sheet in the previous section, we made certain assumptions regarding the terms under which accounts receivable were collected. One assumption is that all payment terms were net 30 days. The collection of receivables was assumed to follow the rule of thumb mentioned earlier. The rule of thumb assumed collection of 60–65 percent of sales in the first month after sales, 18–20 percent in the second month after sales, 18 percent in the third month after sales, and 1 percent in the fourth month after sales. Moreover, 1 percent of sales were assumed to be uncollectible. We ignored the issue of trade discounts in our previous example.

Now is the time to introduce you to the topic of trade discount and its effect on your cash flow. A typical discount used in many industries is 2 percent/10 net 30, which literally means, "pay 98 percent of the invoice amount within 10 days of invoice date or pay 100 percent of the invoice amount within 30 days of the invoice date." If we assume only 10 percent of your customers (which is a conservative figure) takes advantage of your discounted terms, it will radically affect your accounts receivable collections.

Below is a revised schedule of cash receipts in decimal presentation, which is based on the trade discount. Note that by virtue of the discount you will receive 10 percent of your sales in the month of shipment. Note also that you will have to forego 2 percent of the amount otherwise due. The impact of this concept is reflected in the schedule.

CASH RECEIPTS OF ACCOUNTS RECEIVABLE
(000 omitted)

	Month1	Month2	Month3	Month4	Month5	Month6
Sales	$100.0	$120.0	$120.0	$130.0	$100.0	$110.0
Approximate						
Cash receipts						
Month of shipment	$ 9.8	$ 11.8	$ 11.8	$ 12.7	$ 9.8	$ 10.8
First month (60%)	0	54.0	64.8	64.8	70.2	54.0
Second month (20%)	0	0	18.0	21.6	21.6	23.4
Third month (18%)	0	0	0	16.2	19.4	19.4
Fourth month (1%)	0	0	0	0	.9	1.1
Total	$ 9.8	$ 65.8	$ 94.6	$115.3	$121.9	$108.7
Cash receipts						
without discount	$0	$ 60.	$ 92.	$114.	$125.	$109.

As you can see, during the first three months your business collected $170,200 versus $152,000 when no discount was made available. As mentioned previously, we believe that more of your customers will take advantage of the discount and provide you with an even greater cash flow in the earlier periods.

In the area of accounts receivable collection, there are four other tactics that you can use.

1. Establish or tighten credit policy to eliminate slow paying companies. The obvious problem with this tactic is that you may eliminate some very good but slow paying customers. Each industry has its share of large, creditworthy companies that take advantage of small entrepreneurial firms. It seems foolhardy to exclude a company from shipment when sales are profitable and represent a substantial portion of your revenue.

However, this type of customer must not be confused with those customers who are unwilling or unable to pay you and will simply attempt to use your business as an alternative source of financing. Usually they will buy a large quantity of your product and then string out the payments for as long as they can. Although they pay your bill slowly, they will place orders for more products or services from your business, and your dilemma begins. Should you decide not to sell them any more of your product or provide them with any more of your service until they pay their bill, there will be no incentive for them to continue paying you. Therefore, you attempt to negotiate a deal where they are to keep current on all future purchases and make payments to reduce the amount owed on the original purchase. Unfortunately, this situation rarely works out, and the amount owed to you will usually increase. Be prepared to experience strong customer resentment.

2. Establish a collection follow-up system. Companies will first pay those suppliers that pester them on late payments. Never fear that customers will not understand your vigorous collection efforts. They are probably not paying you in order to conserve their own cash and are pestering their customers to pay them.

3. Hold future shipments on customers whose accounts are past due. This may or may not get their attention. If it does not, then the worst you can do is lose the balance of an order and the best you can do is save a larger bad debt.

4. For credit accounts that are slow payers or new accounts, ship on a prepaid or C.O.D. (cash on delivery) basis. Prepayment commonly occurs , especially with new companies. For example, your business, in the beginning, may have to pay cash to receive supplies and materials from suppliers.

There are two additional methods of speeding up the collection of receivables: accounts receivable line of credit and factoring. In the case of an accounts receivable line of credit, a bank will advance some established percentage, generally 60 to 80 percent, against eligible receivables. Eligible receivables are normally defined for this method of financing by the number of days payment is past due and to whom they are shipped. For example, if payment is less than 90 days past due and is not a foreign or government receivable, then it would constitute an eligible receivable.

Factoring is much the same as the accounts receivable line of credit except that the factor will preapprove credit and take over the direct collection of the invoice. In exchange for this privilege, the factor will pay you an amount that represents a discount of the invoice amount. Typical discounts run from 60 to 90 percent—that is, if you present a $100 invoice, the factor would present you with a check for $60 to $90 less any reserve the factor might require against bad invoices.

Accounts receivable line of credit and factoring are presented as alternatives to the methods listed previously. These two methods are explained in greater detail in Chapter 12.

Payment of Accounts Payable

Accounts payable are simply those purchases made by your business and financed through a credit extension from suppliers. Your suppliers will ship on terms established by industry tradition. Terms can vary from very strict, such as C.O.D., to very lenient, such as net 90 days. There is not much you can do as a "small player" in the industry to change these terms. The best the small company can do is keep accounts payable at or near payment terms. That is, pay the payables when they become due. There will be times, however, when a respite in payments is needed to match up your cash inflows with required outflows.

You will find that the trade is very aware of industry and company trends and is generally willing to work with companies who have been good customers and who need help. The use of trade credit to ease company cash flow problems is known as "stretching payables." This is a very popular method of financing company operations since there is generally little or no interest expense associated with extending payments. The drawback to using this method is it may jeopardize your credit rating.

Another area of payables you can manipulate to your advantage is accruals, which are generally defined as internal in nature and include such accounts as wages, commissions, travel and entertainment reimbursement, and payroll taxes. Accruals can be used to a limited extent to finance your operations by establishing policies as to their payment. For instance, in our example, commissions were to be paid in the month of shipment. We could, however, pay them on a 30–day delay basis or even upon collection of the receivable. A similar tactic might be used in the reimbursement of travel and entertainment expenses.

Warning: *Never, never,* delay payment of payroll tax accruals past their due date as a method of funding company operations. The government has a very negative view of this tactic and will go to extremes including shutting down your business and seizing your business and personal assets, in order to get its money.

Debt Repayment

We do not recommend "stretching" debt repayment because banks frown upon erratic repayments. To keep the bank happy, you should be religious in the execution of your repayment schedule. Should you run into trouble, however, be communicative with your banker. Remember, the bank only wants its money back and not the machinery for which it lent you the money. Often, it is possible to negotiate with the bank to ease the upfront payment schedule and delay heavier payments to a time when the business is stronger. Banks have even been know to tier payments to match the seasonal cash flows of certain businesses.

Capital Infusion

Perhaps the best way to avoid a cash flow problem is to provide plenty of capital at the start. Chapter 12 discusses this topic in greater depth; however, we can see that in our previous example an infusion of $200,000 at the outset would have eliminated any cash flow shortage and the need for bank financing.

After you take the following steps, let's take a look at our previous example and see how it relates to capital inusion.

* Infuse the business with beginning capital of $100,000
* Offer 2 percent/10 net 30 terms as a trade discount
* Establish 30-day terms with suppliers
* Pay commissions 30 days after shipment of the product
* Reschedule equipment loan payment to $5000 per month for the first year to increase in subsequent years
* Establish minimum cash on hand at $10,000

Your cash flow spread sheet should look like the one that follows.

CASH FLOW SPREAD SHEET
(000 omitted)

	Month 1	Month 2	Month 3	Month 4	Month 5	Month 6
Sales	$100.0	$120.0	$120.0	$130.0	$100.0	$110.0
Approximate Cash receipts						
Month of shipment	$ 9.8	$ 11.8	$ 11.8	$ 12.7	$ 9.8	$ 10.8
First month (60%)	0	54.0	64.8	64.8	70.2	54.0
Second month (20%)	0	0	18.0	21.6	21.6	23.4
Third month (18%)	0	0	0	16.2	19.4	19.4
Fourth month (1%)	0	0	0	0	.9	1.1
Total	$ 9.8	$ 65.8	$ 94.6	$115.3	$121.9	$108.7
Cash Disbursements						
Rent	$ 4	$ 4	$ 4	$ 4	$ 4	$ 4
Payroll	28	36	36	39	28	31
Insurance	6	0	0	0	0	0
Utilities	2	2	2	2	2	2
Commissions (6%)	0	6	7	7	8	6
Equipment payment	5	5	5	5	5	5
Supplies	1	2	2	3	1	2
Inventory	0	40	48	48	52	40
Professionals	1	1	1	1	1	1
Interest at 12 %	0	0	0	0	0	-0-
Tax installments	0	0	14	0	0	13
Total disbursements	$ 47	$ 96	$119	$109	$101	$104
Net cash from operations	(37.2)	(30.2)	(24.4)	6.3	10.9	4.7
Beginning cash	100	62.8	32.6	10	14.5	25.4
Cash on hand (or shortage)	62.8	32.6	8.2	16.3	25.4	30.1
Bank loan required (or paid down)	0	0	1.8	(1.8)	0	0
Ending cash	62.8	32.6	10	14.5	25.4	30.1
Cumulative bank loan	0	0	1.8	0	0	0
Bank loan required under prior situation	96	144	174	178	144	147

As you can see, the results are dramatic. You went from a situation in which you needed to borrow up to $178,000 during the first six months to borrow up to $178,000 during the first six months to borrowing only $1,800 for the same period. The purpose of this exercise was to illustrate the importance of constructing a cash flow spread sheet and then adjusting it to accomplish your goals. We strongly urge you to make this tool your primary financial planning tool.

Chapter 9 Exhibits

Exhibit 9.1   General Journal

Exhibit 9.2   General Ledger

Exhibit 9.3   Comparison of Compilation, Review, and
Audit Engagements

GENERAL JOURNAL

1987			FOLIO	1	2
MAR	1	Mike Vasily began a yard care			
		business at 3609 Rhodi St, San			
		Diego with the following investment:			
		Cash	1	50000	
		Vehicle	11	400000	
		Equipment	12	90000	
		Note payable	22		250000
		Mike Vasily - Capital	32		290000
		-To record business start up -			
	2	Cash	1	14500	
		Service income	51		14500
		-To record income from service			
	3	Supplies	63	2700	
		Cash	1		2700
		-To record purchase of supplies -			
	3	Cash	1	5000	
		Accounts receivable	5	7000	
		Service income	51		12000
		-To record income from sources -			
	5	Note payable	22	10000	
		Draw	31	4000	
		Vehicle expense	65	1000	
		Cash	1		15000
		-To record cash disbursements -			
	8	Cash	1	19000	
		Accounts Receivable	5	7000	
		Service income	51		26000
		-To record service income and AR collections -			
	15	Cash	1	22500	
		Service income	51		22500
		-To record income from service -			
	15	Equipment	12	25000	
		Vehicle expense	65	5000	
		Cash	1		10000
		Capital	32		20000
		-To record cash disbursements and			
		capital contributions -			

Exhibit 9-1

National® 45-601 Eye-Ease® Made in USA

1987			FOLIO		CASH				FOLIO		
MAR	1		GJ-1		500 00	MAR	3		GJ-1		27 00
	2		GJ-1		145 00		5		GJ-1		150 00
	3		GJ-1		50 00		15		GJ-1		100 00
	8		GJ-1		190 00						
	15		GJ-1		225 00						
					833 00						

Exhibit 9-2

GENERAL LEDGER

GEN SUB	DESCRIPTION	JR REF	BAL FWD	CURR PERIOD	BALANCE
103	CASH ON HAND		500.00		
		2		217.58CR	
		9		217.58	500.00 *
104	CASH IN BANK		2818.95		
		1		25268.53	
		2		18540.74CR	
		9		61.89	
		9		6832.73CR	2775.90 *
121	ACCOUNTS RECEIVABLE-TRADE		1905.08		
		9		1159.52	3064.60 *
130	LESS ALLOW FOR BAD DEBTS		.00	.00	.00 *
153	INVENTORY		27892.00		
		9		12313.19	40205.19 *
211	AUTOMOBILES		8226.57	.00	8226.57 *
212	DEPRECIATION ALLOWANCE		7541.04CR		
		9		685.56CR	8226.60CR*
271	LEASEHOLD IMPROVEMENTS		5069.25	.00	5069.25 *
272	AMORTIZATION ALLOWANCE		5069.25CR	.00	5069.25CR*
277	DO NOT USE		.00	.00	.00 *
278	ACCUMULATED DEPR & AMORT		.00	.00	.00 *
313	ACCOUNTS PAYABLE-TRADE		6274.48CR		
		9		7943.60CR	14218.08CR*
333	PAYROLL TAXES PAYABLE		.00	.00	.00 *
335	FED INCOME TAX WITHHELD		132.00CR		
		2		383.52	
		9		462.00CR	
		9		9.52CR	220.00CR*
337	STATE INCOME TAX WITHHELD		11.20CR		
		2		21.88	
		9		14.70CR	
		9		10.68CR	14.70CR*
341	FED SOC SEC TAX PAYABLE		169.20CR		
		2		479.40	
		9		592.20CR	282.00CR*
342	STATE UNEMPLOYMENT PAY		.00		
		2		257.04	
		9		311.04CR	54.00CR*

GEN SUB	DESCRIPTION	JR REF	BAL FWD	CURR PERIOD	BALANCE
343	STATE DISABILITY PAYABLE		41.68CR		
		2		42.84	
		9		37.80CR	
		9		1.16CR	37.80CR*
344	FED UNEMPLOYMENT PAYABLE		49.73CR		
		2		87.81	
		9		46.08CR	8.00CR*
345	STATE TRAINING FUND		.00	.00	.00 *
350	SALES TAX PAYABLE		1398.99CR		
		1		952.12CR	
		2		1398.99	952.12CR*
385	CONTRACTS PAYABLE		3542.20CR		
		2		462.00	3080.20CR*
397	LESS CURRENT MATURITIES		.00	.00	.00 *
431	DRAWINGS		22494.35		
		9		6630.32	29124.67 *
433	CAPITAL		17802.19CR		
		2		5829.76CR	
		2		3428.28CR	27060.23CR*
497	UNIDENTIFIED ENTRIES		.00	.00	.00 *
502	TAXABLE SALES		67779.78CR		
		1		15868.72CR	
		9		867.06	82781.44CR*
503	LABOR SALES		20324.18CR		
		1		6780.21CR	27104.39CR*
504	WHOLESALE SALES		11600.65CR		
		1		1667.48CR	
		9		2026.58CR	15294.71CR*
517	LESS SALES RETURNS-ALLOW		91.83	.00	91.83 *
651	INVENTORY CHANGE		12396.00CR		
		9		12313.19CR	24709.19CR*
653	PURCHASES		57453.13		
		2		5829.76	
		2		11732.31	
		2		60.00	

GEN SUB	DESCRIPTION	JR REF	BAL FWD	CURR PERIOD	BALANCE
653	PURCHASES		CONTINUED...		
		9		6581.33	81656.53 *)
654	SUPPLIES		179.83		
		2		29.94	209.77 *)
696	LESS PURCHASE DISCOUNTS		.00	.00	.00 *)
801	ADVERTISING		785.46		
		2		311.56	
		9		1362.27	2459.29 *)
803	AMORT LEASEHOLD IMPVT		.00	.00	.00 *)
807	AUTOMOBILE		890.03		
		2		66.93	956.96 *)
809	BAD DEBTS		.00		
		9		61.89	
		9		61.89CR	.00 *)
811	BANK CHARGES		188.39		
		9		40.20	228.59 *)
813	CASH SHORT (OVER)		115.80		
		9		72.06	
		9		149.73CR	38.13 *)
823	DEPRECIATION		2056.66		
		9		685.56	2742.22 *)
825	DUES AND SUBSCRIPTIONS		115.00	.00	115.00 *)
830	FREIGHT OUT		123.27		
		2		136.93	260.20 *)
831	INTEREST		498.96		
		2		166.32	665.28 *)
833	INSURANCE		1320.76		
		2		103.75	1424.51 *)
835	JANITOR		115.00		
		2		30.00	145.00 *)
837	LAUNDRY AND LINEN		57.25		
		2		34.25	91.50 *)

GEN SUB	DESCRIPTION	JR	REF	BAL FWD	CURR PERIOD	BALANCE	
843	MAINTENANCE AND REPAIRS			865.46			
		2			11.97	877.43	*
845	MISCELLANEOUS			.00	.00	.00	*
847	OFFICE EXPENSE			135.00			
		2			600.07		
		2			29.42	764.49	*
853	POSTAGE			6.29			
		2			22.00	28.29	*
855	PROFESSIONAL FEES			1714.39			
		2			329.64	2044.03	*
857	PROMOTION			680.47			
		2			51.86	732.33	*
859	RENT			3000.00			
		2			900.00	3900.00	*
863	SALARIES			10006.60			
		2			3389.40		
		9			810.60	14206.60	*
865	TAXES AND LICENSES			584.23	.00	584.23	*
869	TAXES-PAYROLL			1106.94			
		9			296.10		
		9			378.48	1781.52	*
875	TELEPHONE			3330.11			
		2			1046.77	4376.88	*
877	TRAVEL			.00	.00	.00	*
879	UTILITIES			.00	.00	.00	*
901	INTEREST EARNED			194.49CR			
		9			39.59CR	234.08CR	*
905	MISCELLANEOUS			.00	.00	.00	*
998	UNIDENTIFIED ENTRIES			.00	.00	.00	*
	TOTAL DEBITS			154327.06	84822.94	209346.79	
	TOTAL CREDITS			154327.06CR	84822.94CR	209346.79CR	
	LEDGER TOTALS			.00	.00	.00	

COMPARISON OF COMPILATION, REVIEW, AND AUDIT ENGAGEMENTS

	Compilation Engagement	Review Engagement	Audit Engagement
1. Level of assurance	No assurance as to GAAP	Limited assurance as to GAAP	Statements are fairly presented in accordance with GAAP
2. Entities covered	Nonpublic only	Nonpublic only	Public or nonpublic
3. Knowledge of client's industry	Knowledge of the accounting principles and practices of the industry and general understanding of the client's business	Knowledge same as compilation *plus* an increased understanding of the client's business	Extensive knowledge of the economy, the relevant industry, and the client's business (SAS No. 22)
4. Inquiry procedures required	Inquiries not required unless information supplied by the client is questionable	Inquiry and analytical procedures required *plus* additional procedures if the information appears questionable	Inquiry, analytical procedures (SAS No. 23), and other audit procedures
5. GAAP disclosures omitted	Substantially all disclosures required by GAAP may be omitted, without restriction on use (Exception, See SSARS No. 3)	All disclosures required by GAAP must be included or report must be modified to include the disclosures	Inadequate disclosure requires qualified (except for) or adverse opinion
6. Known departures from GAAP measurement	Disclosure required in modified compilation report (Exception, see SSARS No. 3)	Disclosure required in modified review report	Departure from GAAP requires qualified (except for) or adverse opinion
7. Accountant's independence	Accountant does not have to be independent	Lack of independence precludes issuing review report	Nonpublic company—compilation report (SSARS No. 1) if not independent
			Public company—nonindependence disclaimer (SAS No. 26) if not independent
8. Engagement letter	Recommended	Recommended	Not discussed in SAS
9. Representation letter	No mention	May wish to obtain	Must obtain (SAS No. 19)

Source: Guy, Clay, Meals, "Background Information," Guide to Compilation and Review Engagements, Volume I, sixth edition, November 1984, Fort Worth Texas: Practitioners Publishing Company.

GAAP = Generally Accepted Accounting Principles
SAS = Statements on Auditing Standards
SSARS = Statements on Standards for Accounting and Review Services

Exhibit 9-3

Chapter 10

FEDERAL EXCISE TAXES YOU NEED TO BE AWARE OF

In an age of government deficits, federal excise taxes are often called "hidden" taxes because they are levied and collected by the government even though many individuals are totally unaware of their existence. Excise taxes constitute a significant amount of revenues that are collected by the federal government. As a business person, the federal government expects you to know whether you owe these taxes and, if so, to make prompt payment. This chapter explains the various excise taxes the federal government enacts upon commercial activity. The topics include:

* Facilities and service taxes
* Manufacturers taxes
* Retail and use taxes
* Crude oil windfall profit tax
* Environmental taxes

An *excise* tax is an indirect tax imposed upon manufacturers, wholesalers, and retailers. The federal government imposes excise taxes on various items. It is your responsibility as an entrepreneur to know which taxes should be paid even though many of these taxes are imposed without notification. It is not uncommon for a business to operate for several years and then to suddenly receive notification from the federal government demanding that taxes be paid in addition to interest and penalties.

Since 1982, federal excise taxes have assumed an ever-increasing role in federal revenues. Most federal excise taxes are reported on Form 720, Quarterly Federal Excise Tax Return. (See Exhibit 10-1.) This form is the most frequently used and organizes federal excise taxes into five groups:

* Facilities and service taxes
* Manufacturers taxes
* Retail and use taxes

* Crude oil windfall profit tax
* Environmental taxes

FACILITIES AND SERVICE TAXES

Businesses that transport people or property by air, or provide communication facilities or services usually have to charge an excise tax. Examples of facilities and services that are taxed are:

* Toll telephone service
* Teletypewriter exchange service
* Local telephone service
* Transportation of persons by air
* International air travel facilities

Another type of facility and service tax is imposed on insurance policies issued by foreign insurers or issues of obligations not in registered form.

MANUFACTURERS TAXES

Producers and importers also fall within this category. The tax applies when a business either sells the goods, leases them out, or uses them for its own purpose. The list below shows those items subject to this tax.

• Coal
• Sport fishing equipment
• Firearms
• Shells and cartridges
• Gasoline
• Tires
• Cars that do not meet fuel economy standards*

*This last item is the so-called "gas guzzler" tax on automobiles. According to the Internal Revenue Code Section 4064, the amount of tax for 1986 and later model years is:

Miles Per Gallon	Tax
22.5 or more	$ 0
21.5 - 22.4	500
20.5 - 21.4	650
19.5 - 20.4	850
18.5 - 19.4	1,050
17.5 - 18.4	1,300
16.5 - 17.4	1,500
15.5 - 16.4	1,850
14.5 - 15.4	2,250
13.5 - 14.4	2,700
12.5 - 13.4	3,200
12.4 or less	3,850

RETAIL AND USE TAXES

This excise tax must be charged by the retailer on the sale of heavy trucks, trailers, and tractors (of the kind chiefly used for highway transportation in combination with a trailer or semitrailer). In addition, the owners of the trade or business installing parts or accessories shall be secondarily liable for the retail tax if they install automobile truck chassis, automobile truck bodies, and truck-trailer and semi-trailer chassis or bodies.

Other items that fall within this category are:

- Diesel fuel
- Special motor fuels
- Fuels used on inland waters
- Fuels used in noncommercial aviation

CRUDE OIL WINDFALL PROFIT TAX

This tax is imposed on the "windfall profit of domestically produced crude oil." The tax is paid by producers, which is defined as businesses having an economic interest in underground oil. The process for collecting the tax is complicated and you should seek the advice of your tax advisor.

OTHER FEDERAL EXCISE TAXES

Highway Use. The tax applies to trucks, truck-tractors, and buses on the highway that have a taxable gross vehicle weight of 55,000 pounds or more. As a result, pick-up trucks, panel trucks, and the like are generally not subject to a highway use tax. For more information see Form 2290 and Publication 349, "Federal Highway Use Tax on Heavy Vehicles."

Wagering. This tax applies if you are in the business of accepting bets or running a betting pool or lottery. For more information see Form 730, "Tax on Wagering," and Form 11-C, "Special Tax Return and Application Registry-Wagering."

Alcohol, Tobacco, and Firearms. This excise tax requires you to file Form 11, "Special Tax Return and Application Registry." Form 11 is used to register your place of business and pay an annual tax. The businesses covered by Form 11 are:

Brewers and dealers of liquor, wine, or beer

Distillers, importers, wholesalers, and retailers of distilled spirits

Manufacturers using alcohol to produce nonbeverage products

Manufacturers, importers, and dealers of firearms

Importers and wholesalers of imported perfumes

Most excise taxes can be found in Internal Revenue Code Sections 4041 to 4998. Alcohol and tobacco taxes are in Internal Revenue Code Sections 5001 to 5763.

Chapter 10 Exhibit

Exhibit 10-1 Quarterly Federal Excise Tax Return (IRS
Form 720)

Form **720**

(Rev. January 1988)
Department of the Treasury
Internal Revenue Service

Quarterly Federal Excise Tax Return
Use To Report Excise Taxes for 1988
▶ For Paperwork Reduction Act Notice, see the separate instructions.

OMB No. 1545-0023

Please enter your name, address, employer identification number, and calendar quarter of return if not preprinted. (If not correctly printed, please change.)

If address is different from prior return, check here. ▶ ☐

Quarter ending

Employer identification number

FOR IRS USE ONLY

T	
FF	
FD	
FP	
I	
T	

Note: *Be sure to enter the tax on the correct line to ensure proper credit.* Telephone number (optional) ( )

Part I Computation of Tax Items

			Tax	IRS No.
Crude Oil Windfall Profit Taxes				
Quarterly (production)—Attach Form 6047				50
Quarterly (withholding)—Attach Form 6047				56
Annual return—(See instructions.) (Social security number)				52
Environmental Taxes				
Petroleum (domestic)—Attach Form 6627				53
Petroleum (imported)—Attach Form 6627				16
Chemicals—Attach Form 6627				54

Facilities and Services Taxes	Amount	Rate	Tax	IRS No.
Toll telephone service				
Teletypewriter exchange service		3%		22
Local telephone service				
Transportation of persons by air		8%		26
Transportation of property by air		5%		28

	Number of persons	Rate	Tax	IRS No.
Use of international air travel facilities		$3 per person		27

Fuel Taxes	Number of gallons	Rate	Tax	IRS No.
Alcohol sold as but not used as fuel		$.60/.45		51
Diesel		.15		60
Diesel/alcohol mixture		.09		
Special motor fuels		.09		
Special motor fuels/alcohol mixture		.03		61
Methanol and ethanol		.03		
Produced from natural gas		.045		
Gasoline		.09		62
Gasoline sold for gasohol production		.0333		58
Gasohol		.03		59
Inland waterways fuel use tax		.10		64
Fuel used in noncommercial aviation (other than gasoline)		.14		69
Gasoline used in noncommercial aviation		.029		14
Floor Stocks Taxes (See *Note* on page 2 of instructions about tax rates.)				
Gasoline		.09		65
Gasohol		.03		67
Leaking Underground Storage Tank Taxes				
Diesel		$.001		70
Diesel (railroads)		.001		71
Diesel/alcohol mixture		.001		
Special motor fuels		.001		72
Special motor fuels/alcohol mixture		.001		
Qualified methanol and ethanol		.0005		
Gasoline		.001		73
Gasoline sold for gasohol production		.0011		74
Gasohol		.001		75

Under penalties of perjury, I declare that I have examined this return and accompanying schedules and statements, and, to the best of my knowledge and belief, they are true, correct, and complete.

Signature ▶ _____ **Title (Owner, etc.)** ▶ _____ **Date** ▶ _____
(Please type or print name below signature)

Form **720** (Rev. 1-88)

Exhibit 10-1

Leaking Underground Storage Tank Taxes (continued)	Number of gallons	Rate	Tax	IRS No.
Inland waterways fuel use tax (See *Note* on page 3 of instructions.)		.001		76
Aviation fuel (other than gasoline used in noncommercial aviation)		.001		77
Gasoline used in noncommercial aviation		.001		78

Manufacturers Taxes	Number of tons	Ton price	Rate	Tax	IRS No.
Coal—Underground mined (Enter lower tax) .			$1.10 per ton		36
			4.4% of ton price		37
Coal—Surface mined (Enter lower tax) . . .			$.55 per ton		38
			4.4% of ton price		39

	Total sales	Rate	Tax	IRS No.
Sport fishing equipment		10%		41
Electric outboard motors and sonar devices		3%		42
Bows and arrows		11%		44
Pistols and revolvers		10%		32
Firearms (other than pistols and revolvers)		11%		46
Shells and cartridges		11%		49
Tires (highway type)		(See instructions.)		66
Gas guzzler tax (Attach Form 6197.)		(See instructions.)		40

	Number of doses	Rate	Tax	IRS No.
DPT vaccine		$4.56		81
DT vaccine		.06		82
MMR vaccine		4.44		83
Polio vaccine		.29		84

Retail Taxes	Total sales	Rate	Tax	IRS No.
Truck chassis and bodies				
Trailer and semitrailer chassis and bodies		12% }		33
Tractors				

Other Excise Taxes	Premiums paid	Rate	Tax	IRS No.
Policies issued by foreign insurers				
Casualty insurance and indemnity bonds		(See instructions.) ⎫		
Life insurance, sickness and accident policies, and annuity contracts . . .		(See instructions.) ⎬		30
Reinsurance		(See instructions.) ⎭		

	Amount of obligations	Rate	Tax	IRS No.
Obligations not in registered form		(See instructions.)		31

Part II — Computation of Net Tax Liability

Note: *Do not complete lines 4 through 9 if you are only reporting tax for inland waterways fuel use or sport fishing equipment.*

1 Total tax. Add all amounts from Part I . . . .

2 Adjustments. (See instructions. Attach statement identifying IRS No.) . . . .

3 Tax as adjusted . . . .

4 **(a) Record of Tax Liability**

	Period	Amount of Liability
First Month	1st–15th day	
	16th–last day	
	Total for month	
Second Month	1st–15th day	
	16th–last day	
	Total for month	
Third Month	1st–15th day	
	16th–last day	
	Total for month	

(b) Total liability for quarter . . . .

(c) Total deposits for quarter . . . .

5 Credit for overpaid windfall profit tax (See instructions.) . . . . ▶

6 Overpayment from previous quarter . . . . ▶

7 Total deposits (line 4(c) plus lines 5 and 6) . . . . ▶

8 Undeposited taxes due (line 3 less line 7; this should be $100 or less). Pay to IRS . . . . . . ▶

Note: *If undeposited taxes due at the end of the quarter are more than $100, the entire balance must be deposited.*

If you make semimonthly deposits and claim one of the deposit exceptions explained on page 4 of the instructions, please indicate the exception: 1 ☐ 2 ☐ 3 ☐ 4 ☐

Gasoline refiners or other taxpayers who are eligible for the 14-day depositary due date, please check this box . . . . . . ▶ ☐

9 If line 7 is more than line 3, enter excess here ▶ $ _____ and check if you want it: ☐ applied to your next return, or ☐ refunded to you.

10 If you will not be liable for returns in succeeding quarters, write "FINAL" here ▶ _____ and return this form to your Internal Revenue Service Center.

Chapter 11

BUSINESS INSURANCE

A necessary cost of doing business is the purchase of insurance. Some types of coverage are mandatory while others are optional. This chapter explains:

* Types of unanticipated events
* Key provisions of an insurance policy
* Nature of insurance
* Key terms and definitions of insurance coverage
* How to devise an insurance plan to reduce risk
* Types of insurance

HOW LOSSES MAY OCCUR BECAUSE OF UNANTICIPATED EVENTS

There are a number of unanticipated events that can adversely affect your business. As a result, it is important for you to have an adequate insurance plan to protect your assets. Unnecessarily exposing your business assets to risk not only jeopardizes the future existence of your business but also may expose your personal assets to creditors' claims.

Types of Unanticipated Events

The following list is not all inclusive, but is intended to make you aware of the many types of risks you will encounter when you open your business.

* Damage to business assets because of fire, explosions, and accidents
* Serious bodily injury or death to employees, customers, or delivery personnel, which occur on the premises of your business

* Serious bodily harm or death to individuals who use your product or service
* Accidents your employees are involved in which occur while they are acting within the scope of their employment but away from the premises of your business
* Losses due to criminal activity, such as embezzlement, robbery, theft, forged checks, burglary
* Lawsuits against directors or executive officers by disgruntled shareholders

Key Provisions

Whenever you analyze an insurance package, be alert to its various provisions. Some of these provisions include:

* Scope of loss covered
* Period of time covered
* Property covered
* Individuals covered
* Maximum dollar amount of coverage
* Deductible amount
* Exclusions from coverage

Nature of Insurance

The generally accepted definition of insurance is that it is a contract by which the insurance company promises to pay a sum of money to the beneficiary in the event the insured suffers an injury.

Insurance rests upon the concept of shared risk, which allows the premiums to remain small in comparison to the coverage offered. In theory, only a small percentage of individuals or organizations will make a claim in comparison to the large number who are paying premiums. As long as this ratio remains relatively constant, insurance companies will be able to pay out benefits and make a profit.

Insurance is classified according to the level of risk that is being insured. For example, there is fire insurance, casualty insurance, title insurance, life insurance, product liability insurance, and theft insurance.

Key Terms and Definitions

Policy—the insurance contract itself.
Premium—the amount that is paid to the insurer.
Underwriter—the insurance company.
Parties to an insurance policy—The insurer is the insurance company; the insured is the person or organization covered by the insurance policy's provisions; the agent is an individual who works for the insurance company, and thus the rules of agency law apply, which means that a person who seeks insurance from an agent will usually be protected from the moment the application is received, provided, as a rule, that some premium has been paid, to the time it is either rejected or accepted by the insurance company; the broker, however, is an independent contractor and thus is treated as an agent of the applicant. If the broker does not procure a policy, the individual or business will not be protected.
Key person insurance.—An organization that purchases a life insurance policy for a person who is important to the organization but names itself the beneficiary. Often a partnership will insure the life of

each partner because the death of any partner will legally dissolve the partnership. Also, corporations, as a rule, have an insurable interest in the life expectancy of key executives whose death would cause the corporation financial loss.

Indemnity/Right of Subrogation—Casualty insurance polices usually state that they will pay only for the actual cash value of the loss, which means replacement cost of the property minus depreciation. This is called the *principle of indemnity*. The object is that the insured should not profit from his or her loss even though it was caused by an accident. Once payment is made, these same policies will also state that the insurance company will be entitled to "stand in the shoes of the insured" in pursuing any lawful remedy arising from the incident. This is called the *right of subrogation*.

Coinsurance—This clause is often found in fire insurance contracts. To encourage owners to insure their property as close to full value as possible, many insurance companies will usually insert an 80 percent coinsurance clause, which means that the amount of insurance must be maintained at 80 percent of the property's value. If the amount of insurance at the time of the fire is less than 80 percent, the loss is apportioned between the insurer and the insured in proportion to the amount of the actual insurance versus the insurance required. The formula is given below:

$$\text{Payment} = \frac{(\text{Amount of insurance at the time of the fire}) \times (\text{actual loss})}{80\% \text{ of property's value}}$$

Example:

Suppose the insured has property that is valued at $100,000, under an 80 percent clause the insured agrees to maintain $80,000 of insurance coverage. Suppose, however, there is only $60,000 of coverage at the time a fire erupts, which destroys $40,000 of property. How much would the insured expect to receive from the insurance company?

Solution:

$$\$30,000 = \frac{(\$60,000 \times \$40,000)}{\$80,000}$$

Answer: $30,000

Coinsurance means that the insured coinsures or pays a part of the loss if he does not carry the agreed percentage of insurance.

Pro Rata Clause—This clause is found in many insurance policies and requires that any loss be proportionally shared by all carriers if the property owner is carrying policies from more than one insurance carrier.

Example:

Suppose a business owner has two policies covering inventory. One policy is with Alpha Insurance Co. in the amount of $90,000 and the other is with Beta Insurance Co. in the amount of $30,000. Suppose the business experiences a fire in which $20,000 of inventory is destroyed. If the policies have a pro rata clause, Alpha would pay only $15,000 and Beta would pay $5,000.

Solution:

$$\text{Alpha} = \frac{\$90,000 \times \$20,000}{\$120,000}$$

$$\text{Beta} = \frac{\$30{,}000 \times \$20{,}000}{\$120{,}000}$$

DEVISING AN INSURANCE PLAN TO REDUCE YOUR RISK

Step 1: Look at your business and think about all the ways a loss can occur. Then:

* Prioritize your risks and insure your largest risk factor first
* Make deductibles as high as you can afford; high deductibles will reduce your insurance costs
* Eliminate duplication of insurance coverage; remember, many insurance companies will insist on a pro rata clause
* Buy your insurance in as large a unit as possible; small policies tend to be more expensive for the same coverage; ask your broker or agent about package policies—they may be suitable for your business
* Determine whether your trade association offers an insurance policy; many trade and professional associations offer insurance protection at discount group rates

Step 2: Get professional advice. Be sure you talk to both agents and brokers. To ensure they are credible do not hesitate to ask for their references. Also talk to other business owners. Ask them whether they are satisfied with their insurance coverage.

Step 3: Shop around for your best buy. Prices do vary from company to company. Ideally, you want to select only one agent or broker to handle your business. This fixes responsibility and helps to eliminate the potential for confusion or dishonesty.

Step 4: Always keep accurate records, which includes insurance coverage, premiums, losses, and compensation.

TYPES OF INSURANCE

An insurance checklist is provided below, courtesy of the U.S. Small Business Administration. It was developed by Mark R. Greene, who is a professor at the University of Georgia. The checklist separates insurance coverage into two groups: essential and desirable. Use this checklist to evaluate your insurance needs.

INSURANCE CHECKLIST

	No action needed	Look into this

1. You can add other perils such as windstorm, hail, smoke, explosion, vandalism, and malicious mischief to your basic fire insurance at a relatively small additional cost.

2. If you need comprehensive coverage, your best buy may be one of the all-risk contracts that offer the broadest available protection for the money.

3. The insurance company may indemnify you—that is, compensate you for your losses—in any one of several ways: (1) It may pay actual cash value of the property at the time of loss. (2) It may repair or replace the property with material of similar kind and quality. (3) It may take all the property at the agreed or appraised value and reimburse you for your loss.

4. You can insure property you don't own. You must have an insurable interest—a financial interest—in the property when a loss occurs but not necessarily at the time the insurance contract is made. For instance, a repair shop or drycleaning plant may carry insurance on customers' property in the shop, or a person holding a mortgage on a building may insure the building although he or she doesn't own it.

5. When you sell property, you cannot assign the insurance policy along with the property unless you have permission from the insurance company.

6. Even if you have several policies on your property, you can still collect only the amount of your actual cash loss. All the insurers share the payment proportionately. Suppose, for example, that you are carrying two policies—one for $20,000 and one for $30,000—on a $40,000 building, and fire causes damage to the building amounting to $12,000. The 20,000 policy will pay $4,800—that is, $\frac{\$20,000}{50,000}$ or $\frac{2}{5}$ of $12,000.

The 30,000 policy will pay $7,200; which is $\frac{\$30,000}{\$50,000}$ or $\frac{3}{5}$ of $12,000.

7. Special protection other than the standard fire policy is needed to cover the loss by fire of accounts, bills, currency, deeds, evidences of debt, and money and securities.

8.   If an insured building is vacant or unoccupied for more than 60 consecutive days, coverage is suspended unless you have a special endorsement to your policy canceling this provision.   _____   _____

9.   If, either before or after a loss, you conceal or misrepresent to the insurer any material fact or circumstance concerning your insurance or the interest of the insured, the policy may be voided.   _____   _____

10.   If you increase the hazard of fire, the insurance company may suspend your coverage even for losses not originating from the increased hazard. (An example of such a hazard might be renting part of your building to a drycleaning plant.)   _____   _____

11.   After a loss, you must use all reasonable means to protect the property from further loss or run the risk of having your coverage canceled.   _____   _____

12.   To recover your loss, you must furnish within 60 days (unless an extension is granted by the insurance company) a complete inventory of the damaged, destroyed, and undamaged property showing in detail quantities, costs, actual cash value, and amount of loss claimed.   _____   _____

13.   If you and the insurer disagree on the amount of loss, the question may be resolved through special appraisal procedures provided for in the fire insurance policy.   _____   _____

14.   You may cancel your policy without notice at any time and get part of the premium returned. The insurance company also may cancel at any time with a five-day written notice to you.   _____   _____

15.   By accepting a coinsurance clause in your policy, you get a substantial reduction in premiums. A coinsurance clause states that you must carry insurance equal to 80 or 90 percent of the value of the insured property. If you carry less than this, you cannot collect the full amount of your loss, even if the loss is small. What percent of your loss you can collect will depend on what percent of the full value of the property you have insured it for.   _____   _____

16.   If your loss is caused by someone else's negligence, the insurer has the right to sue this negligent third party for the amount it has paid you under the policy. This is known as the insurer's right of subrogation. However, the insurer will usually waive this right upon request. For example, if you have leased your insured building to someone and have waived your right to recover from the tenant for any insured damages to your property, you should have your agent request the insurer to waive the subrogation clause in the fire policy on your leased building.   _____   _____

17. A building under construction can be insured for fire, lightning, extended coverage, vandalism, and malicious mischief.   _____ _____

Liability Insurance

1. Legal liability limits of $1 million are no longer considered high or unreasonable even for a small business.   _____ _____

2. Most liability policies require you to notify the insurer immediately after an incident on your property that might cause a future claim. This holds true no matter how unimportant the incident may seem at the time it happens.   _____ _____

3. Most liability policies, in addition to bodily injuries, may now cover personal injuries (libel, slander, and so on) if these are specifically insured.   _____ _____

4. Under certain conditions, your business may be subject to damage claims even from trespassers.   _____ _____

5. You may be legally liable for damages even in cases where you used "reasonable care."   _____ _____

6. Even if the suit against you is false or fraudulent, the liability insurer pays court costs, legal fees, and interest on judgments in addition to the liability judgments themselves.   _____ _____

7. You can be liable for the acts of others under contracts you have signed with them. This liability is insurable.   _____ _____

8. In some cases you may be held liable for fire loss to property of others in your care. Yet, this property would normally not be covered by your fire or general liability insurance. This risk can be covered by fire legal liability insurance or through requesting subrogation waivers from insurers of owners of the property.   _____ _____

Automobile Insurance

1. When an employee or subcontractor uses his or her own car on your behalf, you can be legally liable even if you don't own a car or truck yourself.   _____ _____

2. Five or more automobiles or motorcycles under one ownership and operated as a fleet for business purposes can generally be insured under a low-cost fleet policy against both material damage to your vehicle and liability to others for property damage or personal injury.   _____ _____

3. You can often get deductibles of almost any amount, say $250 or $500, and thereby reduce your premiums.

_____ _____

4. Automobile medical payments insurance pays for medical claims, including your own, arising from automobile accidents regardless of the question of negligence.

_____ _____

5. In most states, you must carry liability insurance or be prepared to provide other proof (surety bond) of financial responsibility when you are involved in an accident.

_____ _____

6. You can purchase uninsured motorist protection to cover your own bodily injury claims from someone who has no insurance.

_____ _____

7. Personal property stored in an automobile and not attached to it (for example, merchandise being delivered) is not covered under an automobile policy.

_____ _____

Worker's Compensation

1. Common law requires that an employer (1) provide his or her employees a safe place to work, (2) hire competent fellow employees, (3) provide safe tools, and (4) warn employees of an existing danger.

_____ _____

2. If an employer fails to provide the requirements above, under both common law and worker's compensation laws he or she is liable for damage suits brought by an employee.

_____ _____

3. State law determines the level or type of benefits payable under worker's compensation policies.

_____ _____

4. Not all employees are covered by worker's compensation laws. The exceptions are determined by state law and therefore vary from state to state.

_____ _____

5. In nearly all states, employers are now legally required to cover their employees under worker's compensation.

_____ _____

6. You can save money on worker's compensation insurance by seeing your employees are properly classified.

_____ _____

7. Rates for worker's compensations insurance vary from 0.1 percent of the payroll for "safe" occupations to about 25 percent or more of the payroll for very hazardous occupations.

_____ _____

8. Most employers in most states can reduce their worker's compensation premium cost by reducing their accident rates below the average. They do this by using safety and loss-prevention measures.

_____ _____

DESIRABLE COVERAGES

Some types of insurance coverage, while not absolutely essential, will add greatly to the security of your business. These coverages include business interruption insurance, crime insurance, glass insurance, and rent insurance.

Business Interruption Insurance

1. You can purchase insurance to cover fixed expenses that would continue if a fire shut down your business, for example, salaries to key employees, taxes, interest, depreciation, and utilities as well as the profits you would lose.

2. Under properly written contingent business interruption insurance, you can also collect if fire or other peril closes down the business of a supplier or customer and this interrupts your business.

3. The business interruption policy provides payments for amounts you spend to hasten the reopening of your business after a fire or other insured peril.

4. You can get coverage for the extra expenses you suffer if an insured peril, while not actually closing your business down, seriously disrupts it.

5. When the policy is properly endorsed, you can get business interruption insurance to indemnify you if your operations are suspended because of failure or interruption of the supply of power, light, heat, gas, or water furnished by a public utility company.

Crime Insurance

1. Burglary insurance excludes such property as accounts, fur articles in a showcase window, and manuscripts.

2. Coverage is granted under burglary insurance only if there are visible marks of the burglar's forced entry.

3. Burglary insurance can be written to cover, in addition to money in a safe, inventoried merchandise and damage incurred in the course of a burglary.

4. Robbery insurance protects you from loss of property, money, and securities by force, trickery, or threat of violence on or off your premises.

5.   A comprehensive crime policy written just for small businesses is available. In addition to burglary and robbery, it covers other types of loss by theft, destruction, and disappearance of money and securities. It also covers thefts by your employees.

6.   If you are in a high-risk area and cannot get insurance through normal channels without paying excessive rates, you may be able to get help through the federal crime insurance plan. Your agent or state insurance commissioner can tell you where to get information about these plans.

Glass Insurance

1.   You can purchase a special glass insurance policy that covers all risk to plate-glass windows, glass signs, motion picture screens, glass brick, glass doors, showcases, countertops, and insulated glass panels.

2.   The glass insurance policy covers not only the glass itself, but also its lettering and ornamentation, if these are specifically insured, and the costs of temporary plates or boarding up when necessary.

3.   After the glass has been replaced, full coverage is continued without any additional premium for the period covered.

Rent Insurance

1.   You can buy rent insurance that will pay your rent if the property you lease becomes unusable because of fire or other insured perils and your lease calls for continued payments in such a situation.

2.   If you own property and lease it to others, you can insure against loss if the lease is canceled because of fire and you have to rent the property again at a reduced rental.

Employee Benefit Coverages

Insurance coverages that can be used to provide employee benefits include group life insurance, group health insurance, disability insurance, and retirement income . Key-employee insurance protects the company against financial loss caused by the death of a valuable employee or partner.

Group Life Insurance

1.   If you pay group insurance premiums and cover all employees up to $50,000, the cost to you is deductible for federal income tax purposes, and yet the value of the benefit is not taxable income to your employees.

2.   Most insurers will provide group coverages at low rates even if there are ten or fewer employees in your group.

3. If the employees pay part of the cost of the group insurance, state laws require that 75 percent of them must elect coverage for the plan to qualify as group insurance.

_____ _____

4. Group plans permit an employee leaving the company to convert his or her group insurance coverage to a private plan, at the rate for his or her age, without a medical exam provided this conversion is made within 30 days after termination of employment.

_____ _____

Group Health Insurance

1. Group health insurance costs much less and provides more generous benefits for the worker than individual contracts would.

_____ _____

2. If you pay the entire cost, individual employees cannot be dropped from a group plan unless the entire group policy is cancelled.

_____ _____

3. Generous programs of employee benefits, such as group health insurance, tend to reduce labor turnover.

_____ _____

Disability Insurance

1. Workers' compensation insurance pays an employee only for time lost because of work injuries and work-related sickness—not for time lost because of disabilities incurred off the job. But you can purchase, at a low premium, insurance to replace the lost income of workers who suffer short-term or long-term disability not related to their work.

_____ _____

2. You can get coverage that provides employees with an income for life in case of permanent disability resulting from work-related sickness or accident.

_____ _____

Retirement Income

1. If you are self-employed, you can get an income tax deduction for funds used for retirement for you and your employees through plans of insurance or annuities approved for use under the Employees Retirement Income Security Act of 1974 (ERISA).

_____ _____

2. Annuity contracts may provide for variable payments in the hope of giving the annuitants some protection against the effects of inflation. Whether fixed or variable, an annuity can provide retirement income that is guaranteed for life.

_____ _____

Employee Insurance

1.   One of the most serious setbacks a small company can suffer is the loss of a key employee. However your key employee can be insured with life insurance and disability insurance owned by and payable to your company.

_____   _____

2.   Proceeds of key-employee policy are not subject to income tax, but premiums are not a deductible business expense.

_____   _____

3.   The cash value of key-employee insurance, which accumulates as an asset of the business, can be borrowed against and the interest and dividends are not subject to income tax as long as the policy remains in force.

_____   _____

Chapter 12

SOURCES OF FUNDS

There are numerous sources available to help fund your business venture. Each source has its own advantages and disadvantages, as well as its own set of requirements. This chapter explains:

* The necessity of having sufficient capital
* Reasons financial institutions refuse funding requests
* How to borrow money
* How to sell securities
* Small business innovation research
* How to factor accounts receivable

WILL YOU HAVE SUFFICIENT CAPITAL?

A primary reason small businesses fail is lack of adequate capital. This reason is not meant to frighten you; it is merely a statement of fact which you need to consider. By addressing your business capital needs now, you will avoid a capital shortage in the future.

By financial community standards, capital is defined as the permanent financing of the business through long-term debt and equity, which includes preferred stock, common stock, capital contributions, and retained earnings. Note that this definition excludes short-term debt, trade credit, and accrual accounts. The reason for this exclusion is that these short-term debt accounts should be related directly to current assets which should be liquidated in the short run and therefore are expected to continually turnover and not be part of the permanent financing of the business. In our discussion, however, we will mix short-term and long-term financial requirements as well as include short-term sources of financing as part of the capital base. Take caution, however, that your business should not borrow on a short-term basis to finance long-term assets. For instance, do not borrow funds for one year in order to buy a machine with a useful life of five years. We will discuss the reason for not doing so in more detail in the sections that follow.

The first step to determine how much capital will be sufficienct for your business is address this question: How much cash will I need to run my business? The answer is not as simple as it appears. Many experienced business persons have only a rough "seat of the pants" idea of their cash requirements over the short run. Most of them have no idea of requirements to support their medium and long range plans.

Chapter 9 discussed cash flows and projections of cash needs, and cash requirements in terms of months. In order to address the question above, you will need to look forward at least two years. Within this time frame, you should project (forecast) sales on a conservative basis. Then you must project the expenses necessary to support those sales, including machinery requirements, labor needs, inventory, and accounts receivable, just to mention a few. Once this information is gathered, you must then run a cash budget and determine cash needs. Finally, as cash needs are known, you must determine how they will be met. Will your needs be satisfied as the result of an equity infusion, long-term borrowings, or short-term debt and accruals, or, as more likely, a combination of them all? We recommend you perform a downside picture of cash needs by reducing sales by one- third and increasing expenses by one-fourth. Will your cash flow still satisfy your cash needs? A good rule of thumb in cash flow forecasting is to assume the worst case. Following are a few examples of what can and usually does occur.

* Sales growth will be either much faster or slower than projected. Both cases can be dangerous.
* Accounts receivable will be collected more slowly than expected.
* Suppliers will extend less credit than required.
* Expense budgets are always met and generally exceeded.
* There are only seven days in the week in which to accomplish nine days of work.

WHY FINANCIAL INSTITUTIONS REFUSE FUNDING REQUESTS

The reasons financial institutions refuse funding requests can vary from real concerns regarding the viability of the venture to incompatibility of the loan officer and prospect. The main problems encountered by borrowers in their dealings with financial institutions are addressed in this section. For simplicity, all financial institutions are referred to as banks.

There are as many reasons for refusing loan requests as there are banks. Banks will refuse loan requests when, in their opinion, there is not an excellent chance for repayment of the loan proceeds with interest. Banks view themselves as stewards of the depositors' money and under law have a fiduciary responsibility to depositors. A banker's commodity is money, and once it has left the bank, the banker's control is virtually nonexistent. Banks certainly have methods by which they can legally pursue funds but they are both costly and counterproductive. Therefore, bankers need to feel extremely confident that repayment will occur in a timely manner. The following list explains some of the reasons bankers turn down loan requests.

Lack of Equity. This is probably one of the most important considerations bankers have. Bankers want to see that you have a stake in the deal that is at least as great as the bank's risk. The banker is not your partner and should not be expected to risk as much as you do since the bank will not share in your profits. A banker's goal in making the loan is to recover the bank's principal plus interest.

Lack of Cogent Business Plan. Since repayment of the loan is the banker's primary goal, an ill conceived, "pie-in-the-sky" business plan will hardly instill confidence in the banker.

Lack of Management Experience. Often an entrepreneur will attempt to enter an industry in which he or she has no experience. Bankers realize the world is highly competitive and that experience is essential to survival.

Lack of Financial Information. Bankers like to look at numbers, analyze them, and manipulate them to determine trends. They use these numbers to determine repayment ability. *Note*: The financial information you provide a banker should include projections of how money will be used and how it will be repaid. If the financial statement is poorly done or is nonexistent, there is little chance of obtaining a loan. The one exception is the money-on-money loan or loan against a certificate of deposit.

Industry Type. There will be times when no matter how professional your presentation is or how good your financial statements are, the bank will refuse the loan due to lack of expertise in your industry or bad prior experience in that industry. Try elsewhere.

Type of Loan. As in the case of industry type, some banks will not entertain certain types of loans.

Shoddy Presentation of Request. The world relies on marketing and marketing extensively employs packaging. We write glowing résumés to sell ourselves, and consumer products are attractively bundled for sale. A loan request is no different. A sloppy loan request indicates a lack of care, and if you don't care why should the banker? If you wish your request to be treated seriously then provide a serious presentation. At a minimum, the request should be typed. After all, it is the bank's money you want.

Bank Aggressiveness. At any point in time, banks will either be after business or avoiding it. You will obviously have a better chance with an aggressive bank. Banks react to their own portfolio needs or problems. Research the banks you are interested in before submitting a request.

Failure to Meet One of the Five "Cs" of Credit

Character. This is the probability that an individual or company will honor its obligations in hard times as well as good times. This criteria is very important; failure here is fatal. Banks measure this facet of credit via past performance, credit history, and reputation.

Collateral. This is the collateral that relates directly to the loan. Is the collateral adequate to cover the loan if it needs to be liquidated? Is it controllable?

Capacity. This is the probability that the business can generate cash flows sufficient to service the bank loan and all other debts of the firm. Given the capacity of the business, does it have staying power? How sensitive is the business to changes in the rate of sales?

Capital. This is generally considered to be secondary collateral not directly related to the loan but available to support the loan. It is looked to if the primary collateral is not sufficient.

Conditions. This is the impact economic conditions have on the business which may adversely affect its ability to meet its obligations.

Chemistry. On occasion a borrower will run into a loan officer who is unable to relate to the borrower and his or her needs. This is a fact of life in the business world, move on.

Split Borrowing. This is the practice of borrowing from more than one institution. Banks get very nervous about this prospect because they lose what little control they have if some other bank intends to lend you more money than is believed to be prudent. There are exceptions to this rule. A bank will not be upset if you were to buy a machine that is financed on substantially better terms through the manufacturer unless it puts your financial position in jeopardy.

As you can see, there are quite a few reasons why bankers will not lend you money. In the final analysis, as long as you can convince the banker that you can and will repay his loan, your request will probably be approved.

BORROWING MONEY

Banks

How to Deal with a Banker

To determine how to deal with a banker, you need to know what a bank does. Banks deal in a commodity, and that commodity happens to be money. The bank's source of profit is the lending of money. Thus, for you, the borrower, the first and most important premise in your dealings with a bank is that you represent a potential customer and profit generator. The banker is not doing you a favor by lending you money.

Most people who walk into a bank to borrow money do so with the feeling that they are at a disadvantage. Their approach is timid. The banker commands an aura of fiendish control over their destinies. We recommend that you take the following steps to avoid this perceived disadvantage:

* Present yourself with confidence
* Be forthright
* Be mildly aggressive, if necessary
* Be professional in your presentation
* Dress in neat attire, appearance is important
* Be on time for any appointments
* Provide all the information the banker requests

Deal from a position of strength. By following these steps, any disadvantage, perceived or real, can be eliminated. Until you get into the "big leagues" of borrowing, you will be dealing with bankers who are fairly new at what they do and are just as nervous as you are. Your position should be that there are many banks from which to choose and that the bank you eventually select should be grateful to have your business.

To convince the banker that your venture warrants the loan, you will need to present a number of documents. The personal financial statement is one of these documents.

How to Construct a Personal Financial Statement

The personal financial statement is simply a measure of your personal capital, or, more commonly known as your personal net worth. This statement is the third level of support available to the banker in support of the loan under consideration. The personal financial statement is the basis of the personal guarantee often required of entrepreneurs in single-owner or closely held corporations. Banks will require a personal guarantee as a method of adding a controlling factor in the loan process. The personal guarantee is designed to prevent the owners of a corporation from stripping the corporate assets and then hiding behind the corporate shield. The bank will exercise its rights under the personal guarantee and require payment of monies due.

Physically, the personal financial statement is no more than a balance sheet of personal assets and liabilities. In general, a personal financial statement will also include an income statement and miscellaneous statements regarding personal assets.

Assets

The assets include, in order of liquidity:
Cash in banks. This includes checking and savings accounts.

Certificates of deposit.

Stocks, bonds and other marketable securities. Most banks will provide you with a schedule and ask you to list each instrument, including number of shares held, ownership names, and current market value. Some banks will accept brokerage account statements.

Accounts receivable. This is money due to be received for goods and services that have been provided.

Notes receivable. These obligations are long- term in nature. Again, a schedule will be provided requiring you to list the amounts owed, maturity, payment amount, and frequency.

Cash surrender value of life insurance. This is the cash value of insurance policies and not the face value of the insurance.

Motor vehicles, boats, airplanes, etc. Report the wholesale value. For automobiles, use the *Kelly Blue Book.*

Real estate. Generally this is the largest single asset on the personal financial statement. A schedule of all real estate will be provided which requires you to list ownership names, date of purchase, estimated market value, amount owing, and who holds the mortgage.

Household goods. This is the liquidation value you place on your furnishings.

Other assets. This category of assets includes items such as coin collections, antique automobiles, horses, jewelry, and furs.

Be conservative in your estimations; remember that bankers look at thousands of these personal financial statements each year and can spot over valued assets.

Liabilities

The personal financial statement also includes liability. A list of the liability categories follows.
Accounts payable. These are payables you expect to pay on a monthly basis but that are not necessarily paid off each month. They include charge accounts, doctors bills, and store accounts.

Notes payable. These are generated as a result of secured and unsecured debts. The bank will provide you with a schedule to list each of your notes detailing the term, interest rate, to whom owed, and maturity.

Taxes payable. These are federal, state, or real estate taxes payable.

Real estate loans. These are mortgages secured by the real estate you own. You will need to provide a schedule of these loans including term, interest rate, payment amount, to whom owed, and maturity.

Other liabilities. This section includes court-ordered judgments, settlements of lawsuits, and past due accounts.

Be totally forthright in listing your liabilities. The worst thing a banker can do is discover some impropriety with respect to your liabilities.

Net Worth

The last part of the personal financial statement is the net worth section.The net worth is defined as the difference between assets and liabilities. The net worth is also known as personal capital or wealth. This figure gives the banker a comfort level that, should all else fail, you as the guarantor, shall be able to satisfy the obligations of your business.

The personal financial statement must also include an off balance sheet or contingent liabilities. These are liabilities that are not directly yours but for which you are responsible should another party fail to perform its obligations. Three examples of a contingent liability would be: (1) you were to cosign a loan for someone, such as a friend or relative, (2) you provided your personal guarantee in support of a loan or commercial lease, or (3) you were named as a defendant in a lawsuit.

Banks also want to see the personal equivalent of an income statement. Simply provide all sources of income, including wages, commissions, rents, note collections, stock dividends, bond interest, pension benefits, income from trusts, and so on. On the expense side, banks are interested in real estate payments, income taxes, insurance premiums, alimony, child support, and aggregate payments on installment type accounts. The difference between income and expenses should be positive and represents the cash available to service ordinary living expenses and to place into savings.

Once again, the key issue is to be reasonable in your estimates and to provide sufficient detail and disclose all aspects of your personal finances that will impact upon the banker's decision. *Note*: A strong personal financial statement might swing a moderately weak deal, while a weak personal financial statement may hinder a moderately strong deal.

What Do Bankers Look for?

The first element is the legality of the purpose for which the loan funds are requested. For instance, a bank cannot lend money for the purpose of setting up a lottery. The second element to be satisfied is loan type and borrower's industry. As mentioned previously, many banks are involved in certain industries and loan types in which they consider themselves specialists. The third element is the probability that the loan funds will be repaid. Bankers, therefore, are very interested in existing and projected cash flows. The all important cash flow statement will provide the proof necessary to sell the loan to the bank.

The character of the borrower is another element that is very important to any bank. The bank needs to arrive at a comfort level that the borrower will repay the loan in hard times as well as good times. The next element is the collateral being offered to cover the loan. Is it sufficient? Is it desirable and controllable? If the collateral is undesirable, then will the strength of the cash flow be sufficient to make the amount of exposure to risk acceptable to the bank?

The next element in the review process is that the bank will analyze the secondary collateral or personal capital of the individual entrepreneur or corporation itself. This step provides the banker with an extra level of comfort and therefore is a positive factor in the decision to grant the loan. The last step involves the bank or banker's analysis of the general economic conditions. The bank is concerned with how the economy will impact upon the borrower and the borrower's customers. You can help your case by providing economic summaries and trade projections supporting your position.

These are the major underlying elements upon which banks make their lending decisions. Your presentation of financial information, your business plan, and a face-to- face meeting with the banker are vehicles by which you will sell your request.

Types of Bank Loans

(a) *Unsecured Loans*

An unsecured loan is one in which collateral is neither requested nor given. This type of loan is generally short term in nature—that is, less than one year, and is granted to only the most creditworthy customers. These loans are generally made for a specific purpose such as the purchase of inventory for a specific order. Repayment is generally the conversion of the asset into cash and is made in a lump sum. Interest is collected either monthly or at maturity.

(b) *Secured Loans*

A secured loan is exactly what its name implies. It is secured by some specific piece of collateral or the assets of the company in general. The length of time for payback of this type of loan can be as long as seven to ten years. Typically the collateral for this type of loan is a fixed asset such as machinery. Repayment of the principal is over the term established and comes chiefly from cash flows of the business. Automobiles, trucks, fixtures, and leasehold improvements are examples of secured loan collateral.

(c) *Accounts Receivable Financing*

This type of loan is also known as a secured line of credit. These lines are generally short term in nature and are reviewed each year for renewal. The purpose of this type of loan is to fund investment in accounts receivable. The bank will advance a certain amount based on each acceptable receivable. The amount of the loan usually ranges from 50 to 80 percent of each receivable. Banks define acceptable receivables based on their own preferences. For example, many banks exclude receivables to foreign countries or to related companies. They will also exclude receivables that have not been collected within a reasonable time of shipment, such as 90 days. This type of financing requires significant monitoring by the bank and therefore is relatively costly.

(d) *Inventory Financing*

Similar to accounts receivable financing, inventory financing is a secured line of credit. Advances are made based on a formula established by the bank as to the acceptability and marketability of the inventory being offered. Many banks will not lend on inventory since control is both difficult and expensive and the banks do not want to get involved with liquidation should the need arise. Typical inventory advance rates rarely exceed 50 percent.

(e) *Loans against Real Estate*

These loans are similar in nature to your home mortgage in that they are fully amortized over the loan term. The loan term is often within the 25-year range. The main difference between a residential loan and a commercial real estate loan is the advance rate. For residential loans the advance rate on conventional loans is 80 percent, in commercial real estate, advance rates are rarely over 70 percent. In addition, for a commercial real estate loan, it must be shown that the property can support a multiple of debt service through market value rental analysis. That multiple can range from 1.15 - 1.25 to 1.

We have provided you with a brief overview of the types of loans available to you through the bank. There are situations in which the bank may custom tailor the type of loans we have described to fit its customers' needs. By being aware of the loan types and their uses, you will know what is available and you will be able to relate to the banker on his or her level, thus reducing the advantages bankers are perceived to have.

How To Apply For A Loan Or A Loan Guaranty from Government Agencies

Small Business Administration

One of the objectives of the Small Business Administration (SBA), which is an independent federal agency of the U.S. government, is to help entrepreneurs borrow funds to start up operations. The SBA does not compete with lending institutions but works with them. The SBA may either lend you some or all of the money directly, or much more likely, provide a loan guarantee. There are a number of qualifications you must meet in order to be considered for SBA assistance, however.

First: The SBA must consider you a small business. Size standard eligibility is based on the average number of employees for the preceding twelve months or on sales volume over a three-year period. If you are a manufacturer, the maximum number of employees you are allowed to have could be as low as 500 for certain industries or as high as 1500 for other industries. If you are a wholesaler, the maximum number of employees you are allowed to have may not exceed 500 regardless of the industry. For other types of businesses, the SBA looks at the amount of sales:

Retail—The amount varies depending on the industry. In some industries the maximum amount is $3.5 million. In other industries the maximum amount may be as high as $13.5 million.

Service—The maximum amount varies with each industry. For some industries the ceiling is $3.5 million while for others it may be as high as $14.5 million.

General Construction—Similar to retail and service, the maximum amount varies according to the industry you are in. The limit is $9.5 million for some industries while for others it can be as high as $17 million.

Special Trade Construction—The maximum amount is $7 million regardless of the industry.

Second: Your company must not be dominant in its field.

Third: Your company must comply with all federal employment laws.

Fourth: Your company must pursue traditional lending sources first and then if your company is rejected or unable to get financing at reasonable terms the SBA will accept you.

Fifth: Your business cannot be involved in the creation or distribution of ideas or opinions, which would include newspapers, magazines, and academic schools. Other types of businesses would include those that are engaged in the speculation or investment in rental real estate.

Sixth: You must be able to demonstrate that you have a reasonable investment in your business. Usually 30% to 50% of the total project cost for a new business venture is the rule. The percentage varies according to the degree of risk.

Seventh: You must provide sufficient collateral. The SBA requires that sufficient assets be pledged to adequately secure the loan. This means that liens on personal assets are often required when business assets are considered insufficient to secure the loan. Personal guarantees are also required from all principal owners and from the chief executive officer of the business.

Loan Guaranty. The SBA will evaluate your business proposal. If it accepts it, it will then offer a loan guaranty, which is a guaranty that a lender will be protected from default in the event you can't make your payments. As a rule, the SBA will guarantee up to 90 percent of the principal loan; however, the maximum guaranty percentage of loans exceeding $155,000 is 85 percent. The SBA can guarantee up to $500,000 of a private sector loan. According to the SBA, the average size of a guaranteed business loan is $175,000 and the average maturity is approximately eight years. These loans are usually secured by some type of collateral such as fixed assets, inventory, real property, and so on. In addition, you must put up a sufficient amount of equity. The length of these types of loans ranges from a maximum of seven years for working capital and ten years for fixed assets to twenty-five years for construction projects.

Loan Participation. If you are unable to obtain a loan even with SBA assurances, the SBA may offer to participate with the lending institutions. Generally, a minimum of 25 percent of the principal amount must be funded by the lending institution with the remainder coming from the SBA. The SBA, however, may not lend anymore than $150,000.

Direct Loans. If a loan participation is not possible, the SBA may loan the needed funds directly to you. The principal amount of the loan cannot exceed $150,000. These loans are generally difficult to obtain because funds for this program are usually limited, and , at times, available to only certain types of borrowers such as businesses located in high unemployment areas or owned by handicapped individuals.

Types of Loans. Generally, the SBA provides for two types of loans: working capital and fixed assets. Working capital loans usually mature between five and seven years. However, loans for fixed assets, such as the purchase or renovation of the business premises, have a much longer maturity period. Under the loan guarantee program, interest rates for loans that mature in less than seven years cannot exceed 2 1/4 percent over New York prime. Interest rates for loans that mature after seven years cannot exceed 2 3/4 percent over New York prime.

Loan Paperwork. Many banks participate in an SBA program called the "Certified Lending Program." This program allows banks to handle much of the loan paperwork and review client financial status. As a result, the amount of time it takes to process an SBA loan is reduced greatly. In 1983, the SBA began a pilot program called "Preferred Lenders Program," in which selected banks handle all loan paperwork, loan processing, and also service the loan. Under the preferred lenders program, the percentage of guaranty may be affected; however, the bank is the only institution that has to approve your loan application.

Information Disclosure. The SBA requires you to disclose a variety of information about yourself and your business. The list below describes the kind of information the SBA expects.

Description of Business: Provide a written description of your proposed business or existing business which should include the following information:

* Type of organization
* Date of formation
* Location
* Product or service
* Brief history of business
* Proposed future operation
* Service area
* Competition
* Customers
* Suppliers

Management's Experience: Résumés of each owner and of key management personnel.

Personnel Financial Statements: Financial statements are required of all principal owners and guarantors. A principal owner is defined as having 20 percent or more interest in the business venture. Financial statements should not be older than sixty days. You will also need to attach a copy of last year's federal income tax return.

Money Repayment: You will have to provide a written statement indicating how the loan funds are to be repaid, including repayment sources and time required. The written statement should be supported by cash flow schedules and budgets.

Business Financial Data: If your business is in the proposal stage, you will have to provide a pro forma balance sheet reflecting sources and uses of both equity and borrowed funds. If your business is already in existence, you will have to provide a financial statement for each year for the past three years, which are not older than sixty days and include balance sheets, income statements, and a reconciliation of net worth. Also include a schedule of your accounts receivable and accounts payable.

Projections: You will have to provide a projection of future operations for at least the following year or until a positive cash flow can be shown. The projections should be in income statement format. Be sure to explain all assumptions that you make in your calculations.

Other Items That May Apply:

* Leases or copy of proposal
* Franchise agreement
* Purchase agreement
* Plans, specifications, and cost breakdowns
* Copy of licenses
* Letters of reference
* Letters of intent, contracts, or purchase orders
* Partnership agreement
* Articles of incorporation

See **Exhibit 12-1** for an example of an SBA application for business loan, statements required by laws and executive orders, summary of collateral, schedule of collateral, and lender's checklist for SBA applications.

Also, see **Exhibit 12-2** for an example of a Statement of Personal History and Personal Financial Statement which must be completed along with the application for business loan.

According to the SBA, the top ten lending institutions that have provided long-term credit to small businesses under the SBA loan-guarantee program are shown in the table below.

Lender	Amount in millions	Number of loans granted
The Money Store	$ 143.1	493
Truckee River Bank (California)	69.0	218
Southwestern Commercial Bank (Texas)	52.3	170
ITT Small Business Finance	42.1	168
Gulf American SBLC (Florida)	40.0	134
The Merchants Bank (Vermont)	34.9	198
Independence Mortgage (Texas)	30.5	92
Adobe S&L (California)	30.3	166
Government Funding Calbidco (California)	28.1	128
Banco Popular (Puerto Rico)	24.8	97

The Department of Housing and Urban Development

(HUD) makes Urban Development Action Grants (UDAG) to cities that have economically distressed areas. These grants are used by the cities to make loans to private developers who then leverage these loans by borrowing up to five times the amount from private lenders. The private developers, however, must promise to use the funds for projects that will have a positive economic impact on the distressed areas.

Economic Development Administration

The Economic Development Administration (EDA) is part of the U.S. Department of Commerce and provides loans to those businesses that will benefit certain designated areas determined by the government as needing economic assistance. The objective is to provide jobs to individuals who live in economically distressed areas. As with the SBA, you must be turned down by private lenders before seeking EDA assistance. Unlike the SBA, the EDA does not have a ceiling as to the amount it can lend you. The loan application is more complicated than the SBA's and there are more restrictions.

Farmers Home Administration

The Farmer's Home Administration (FMHA) is operated by the U.S. Department of Agriculture. Its goal is to improve the economic environment of rural life and as such provide supplemental financial support to private lenders to promote business, industrial, and agricultural projects. The FMHA does not compete with private lenders and therefore you must not seek the FMHA as a first resort. As a rule, the FMHA guarantees a loan up to 90 percent. Business and industrial loans are made to large businesses as well as small ones. FMHA wants to promote economic development in rural areas that have a population base of less than 50,000. You must be able to prove to the FMHA that your proposed business will actually create new jobs for the area rather than shift jobs from one area to the next.

Small Business Investment Companies

Small Business Investment Companies (SBICs) were created under the Small Business Investment Act of 1958 and are private profit-making firms. Authentic SBICs are licensed and regulated by the SBA. Usually, an SBIC is started by individuals who have venture capital expertise as well as capital and want to start an investment company. Under federal law, an SBIC can be organized in any state as either a corporation or limited partnership. Most SBICs are owned by small groups of local investors; however, some SBICs are owned by commercial banks, some are subsidiaries of corporations, and some are corporations that have stock that is traded publicly.

SBICs have access to low interest federal funds, which are provided by the SBA. Essentially, SBICs borrow funds from the government to lend out to entrepreneurs. A typical loan is made from five to seven years. SBICs mostly make loans but some will invest in your business by buying stock. Thus, small businesses qualifying for assistance from the SBIC program are able to receive long-term loans and perhaps equity capital as well. According to the *SBIC Digest* for October 1988, the top ten industry groups financed by SBICs during fiscal year 1988 were as follows:

SIC Code*	Description of Industry	Number	Dollar Amount	% of $
15	Building construction	125	$ 50,971,9949	9
48	Communication industry	126	47,286,253	8
67	Holding/other investment office	23	4,423,367	8
73	Business services	195	41,190,623	7
36	Electric equipment (not computer)	175	33,391,068	6
34	abricated metal products	62	31,924,925	5
35	Commercial machinery and computers	118	4,350,986	4
38	Manufacturing of measuring instruments	82	21,622,189	4
27	Printing and publishing	56	1,080,715	
50	Wholesale trade-durable	57	20,744,441	4
	All other industries	1,182	247,452,564	41
	Total	2,201	$584,439,125	100

*SIC stands for Standard Industry Code which is assigned to a business on the basis of its principal product produced or distributed, or on the basis of service rendered. The SIC Code is published by the Office of Management and Budget and appears in the Standard Industrial Classification Manual.

The vast majority of SBIC funding is channeled into businesses that have been in existence less than six years. In fact, 22 percent of the businesses financed by SBICs were start-ups. The following table appeared in the *SBIC Digest* for April 1988 and shows SBIC funding by age of the business.

SBICs
AGE OF SMALL BUSINESS
AT TIME OF SBIC FINANCING

Age of Business	% of Number	% of Dollars
Under 3 years	49.8	57.4
3 to 6 years	22.5	17.1
7 to 10 years	12.7	9.8
Over 10 years	14.9	15.6
Unclassified	0.1	0.1
Total Financing	100.0	100.0

Most of the financing provided by the SBICs are used by small businesses for operating capital. The following table also originated from the *SBIC Digest* for April 1988 and shows the use of financing dollars.

SBICs
USE OF FINANCING DOLLARS
RECEIVED FROM SBICs

Type of Use	% of Number	% of Dollars
Operating capital	66.2	50.3
Acquisition of business	11.5	31.0
Refinance existing debt	10.1	7.8
Research and development	2.3	3.6
Other uses	9.9	7.3
Total Financing	100.0	100.0

Exhibit 12-3 shows the SBA list of all SBICs operating in the United States as of June 1988.

Minority Enterprise Small Business Investment Companies

Americans who are members of minority groups have often found it difficult to raise funds for business purposes. As a result, Section 301(d) of the Small Business Investment Act established the Minority Enterprise Small Business Investment Companies (MESBIC), which is a specialized type of SBIC. A MESBIC's purpose is to provide funds for minority-owned businesses. Like SBICs, they are also regulated and licensed by the SBA and as a result receive funds from the SBA to loan to entrepreneurs. MESBICs also, on occasion, provide equity capital. According to the *SBIC Digest*, for October 1988, the top ten industry groups financed by Section 301(d) SBICs during fiscal year 1988 were:

SIC Code	Description of Industry	Number	Dollar Amount	% of $
41	Local and suburban transit	435	$ 26,684,020	20
58	Eating and drinking places	140	18,070,238	14
54	Food stores	151	11,571,151	9
15	Building construction	41	11,071,799	8
48	Communication	42	7,208,793	5
72	Personal services	70	5,023,636	4
50	Wholesale trade-durable	47	4,826,700	4
80	Health services	71	4,680,703	4
51	Wholesale trade-non-durable	42	4,559,000	3
59	Miscellaneous retail	44	3,615,560	3
	All other industries	384	33,705,726	26
		1,467	$130,963,326	100

Exhibit 12.4 shows the SBA list of all MESBICs or 301(d)s that were operating in the United States as of June 1988.

Local Development Companies

Local Development Comanies (LDCs) are established under SBIC Section 502. LDCs are local companies founded by local residents with the goal of helping local businesses that are in the need of funds. As a rule, LDCs provide only a portion of the costs of a project, usually 10 percent. The rest must come from other sources. The strength of the LDC is that it arranges SBA guaranteed bank loans; as a result, LDCs work closely with the SBA. Generally, in order to be approved for an LDC loan, you must get an approval from three sources: LDC, SBA, and a private lending institution. Expect a lead time of about three to four months. A major restriction in seeking funds from an LDC is that it cannot assist you in seeking funds for working capital, inventory, or freestanding fixtures and equipment.

Certified Development Companies

Certified Development Companies (CDCs) are private nonprofit organizations that arrange low interest loans for small/and medium-sized businesses in order to strengthen the local economy. CDCs receive their charter from the SBA. CDCs can make loans for expansion, remodeling, building acquisition, construction site acquisition, working capital, inventory, debt consolidation, fixtures and equipment, business start-ups, and equipment modernization. In particular, the CDC offers the 504 Loan Program and the 7A Loan Program.

504 Loan Program. Allows the business owner to purchase, construct, or remodel an industrial or commercial building. The loan is a mixture of private capital and federal debenture funds. Eligibility for the 504 program is limited to "for profit" sole proprietorships, partnerships, and corporations which have a minimum business history of one year, a net worth not to exceed $6 million, or a net profit in excess of $2 million after taxes for two consecutive years.

A Loan Program. Loans up to $550,000 can be arranged for small businesses through the SBA to finance critical needs such as start-up costs, equipment purchases, working capital, inventory, and leasehold improvements. Businesses must be classified as "small" according to the SBA definition. One- to six-year loans carry a maximum interest rate of 2 1/4 percent above the prime rate, while loans from seven to twenty-five years carry a maximum interest rate of 2 3/4 percent above the prime rate.

SELLING SECURITIES

Securities are broadly defined by both federal and state laws. A security can be any of the following: stock, bond, membership in an unincorporated association, debenture, beneficial interest in employee benefit plans, investment contract, certificate of interest, or participation in any profit sharing agreement.

If a business is operating in the corporate form, it most likely will issue either stock or bonds.

Difference Between Stocks and Bonds

Stock (also known as equity securities)

Essentially, there are two types of stock: common and preferred. Although both types represent ownership in the firm, each type has different characteristics. As a result, you may decide to issue one type of stock over another because it better suits your particular needs.

Common stock. As a rule, common stockholders have a right to elect the company's directors, who in turn appoint the officers who will manage the business. Both federal and state law dictate how control of the company through stockholder elections will be exercised. Generally, corporations must hold an election of directors at least annually. Often one-third of the directors are elected each year for a three-year term. Each share is given one vote; therefore, an individual who has 5,000 shares would have 5,000 votes. Stockholders can appear in person at the annual meeting and vote in person or they can transfer their right to vote to a second party by means of a document called a *proxy*.

Common stockholders often have a preemptive right to purchase any additional shares sold by the firm. The purchase is on a pro rata basis. In some states, the preemptive right is automatically included in every corporate charter. In other states, the right is not automatic and must be included in the articles of the corporation. You will need to seek the advice of an attorney whenever you issue stock.

Preemptive rights have two purposes: (1) They keep the balance of power that is shared among the stockholders at status quo. For example, if management is under mounting criticism from stockholders it could be tempted to dilute the power that these shareholders possess by issuing additional shares of stock and purchasing these shares itself. By doing so, it could prevent the stockholders from removing it from office and thus effectively securing control of the company. (2) They protect stockholders against dilution of value. As more shares are issued, there is the ever present possibility that the additional shares will be sold at a lower price than the previously issued shares. As a result, the total market value of the company will be less than what it should have been had all the shares sold at the higher price. When this lower value is spread among all the shareholders it dilutes the value of each share and causes the wealth of the company to transfer from previous stockholders to the current ones.

Types of common stock. Most start-up firms will only issue one type of common stock. However, in certain instances, other types of common stock are issued to meet special needs. These different types are designated as class A, class B, class C, etc. For example, some firms offer class A common stock, which the firm defines as paying dividends but has no voting rights for a specified period of time. Class A stock is offered to the general public, and class B common stock, which the firm defines as having voting rights but no right to dividends for a specified period of time or until retained earnings reach a certain level, is issued to the organizers of the corporation. This type of arrangement allows the investing public to receive a share of the profits, yet permits the organizers of the firm to retain absolute control of the company at the early stages of development.

Advantages of Issuing Common Stock
*   The company is not legally obligated to make payments to stockholders so long as the board of directors acts in the best interests of the corporation.
*   It improves the credit rating of the company because the amount of capital in the firm has increased which provides a fixed amount that creditors can look to in the event the business dissolves.
*   Some investors prefer this type of investment because it often provides a better hedge against unanticipated inflation.

Disadvantages of Issuing Common Stock
*   Because this type of stock has voting rights, control may be transferred to the new stockholders.
*   If you are anticipating large profits, the new shareholders will immediately share in the income, while if debt is used, new investors would only receive a fixed return without sharing in the profits.
*   Under current tax law, dividends paid on common stock are not deductible as an expense; interest paid on debt issues may be deducted, however.

Preferred Stock. This stock has certain advantages over common stock, hence the name preferred stock.
*   Preferred stockholders have priority over common stockholders in the distribution of dividends. Dividends must be paid on preferred before they can be paid on the common stock.
*   In the event of dissolution, the claims of preferred stockholders must be satisfied before the common stockholders receive any assets. In addition, most preferred stock certificates have covenant requirements which usually require that a minimum level of retained earnings be maintained before any dividends to common stockholders are distributed.
*   Preferred stock always has either a par value, stated value, or liquidated value. These values are used to establish the amount due to the preferred stockholders in the event of liquidation as well as the amount of dividends each preferred shareholder will receive.
*   Usually preferred stocks provide for cumulative dividends, which means that all past dividends for preferred stock must be paid before any dividends to the common shareholders can be distributed.

The single largest disadvantage to preferred stock is that in most cases it does not have voting rights. Preferred shareholders, as a rule, have no say as to who will be the directors and who will run the company.

Bonds (also known as debt securities)

A bond is a long-term contract in which the issuer, who is the borrower, agrees to make principal and interest payments on specific dates to the holder of the bond. The maturity of bonds ranges from five to thirty years depending on the issuer.

Terms to be aware of:

Mortgage bond—This bond backed by fixed assets. Your company pledges certain assets as security for the bond. If your company defaults then the bond holders can foreclose on those assets to satisfy the bond. Mortgage bonds are given first priority to claims of second mortgage bonds. In the event of liquidation, second mortgage bond holders would have a claim against the specified assets only after the first mortgage bond holders have been paid off in full. Because of the priority that first mortgage bonds have, second mortgages are often called junior mortgages.

Debenture —This is an unsecured bond. A debenture holder is a general creditor. Thus, in the event of liquidation, the debenture holder must wait until the secured creditors' claims are satisfied before receiving a share of the remaining assets. *Subordinated debenture* is a bond that has a claim against the assets of the corporation only after the senior debt has been paid off. Senior debt can be any debt that is listed in the debenture's indenture; for example, promissory notes, bank loans, accounts payable, and so on.

Convertible Bond— This is a security that converts into a share of common stock at the option of the bond holder. The conversion is usually at a fixed price.

Indenture—This is a legal document that specifies the rights of the bond holders and the issuing corporation. The Trust and Indenture Act of 1939 requires that if a debt issue is part of an issue of more than $7.5 million principal amount which is issued publicly, the bond must be issued under an indenture. The indenture itself may range in length from 20 to 200 pages and will include both affirmative and negative covenants. An affirmative covenant requires the corporation to take certain actions, such as maintaining corporate existence, providing periodic financial statements, and maintaining its business and properties in accordance with sound commercial practices. Negative covenants often prohibit the corporation from allowing certain financial ratios to fall below stated levels; for example, assets to debt, debt to equity, revenue to expenses, etc. In addition, negative covenants may prohibit a corporation from making a fundamental change in the nature of its business, replacing individuals holding key management positions, granting certain types of security interests, or incurring capital expenses in excess of a certain amount.

Should You Issue Stocks or Bonds?

A start-up business will usually sell common stock, while an established business that is currently earning a profit will often choose to sell convertible bonds. This approach allows the firm to deduct the interest it pays on the bond, however, there is the ever present option of converting the bond into stock. Thus, in a way, it represents the best of both worlds: it begins as a debt interest and ends as an equity investment. The advantages of using a convertible bond is that (1) it strengthens the capital structure by refunding existing debt, (2) it attracts investors who may not have invested otherwise, and (3) it does not adversely impact, in the beginning, earnings per share while at the same time allows for the retention of control by the current shareholders.

Private Placements

The private offerings of securities, also known as private placements, run the gamut from a direct offering made by a firm to close friends and relatives to an offering conducted by a major investment banking house to institutional investors. Private offerings represent a method to seek funds that many entrepreneurs ignore even though it is an excellent source of capital. Recent reports regarding the dollar volume of private placements in the United States for 1988 place the amount over $60 billion.

There are three major advantages when you seek funds through a private offering:

* A private placement may be exempt from registration with the SEC and state agencies, although notice of the issue will still have to be filed.
* It permits a company to sell stock using a more simplified registration process and fewer disclosure requirements.
* It provides a means of selling stock when the stock market may not be receptive to a public offering.

Although a private placement is simple in concept, federal and state regulations enacted to protect investors make it a complicated procedure that should not be attempted without the advice of professionals such as an attorney, CPA, and a consultant. The discussion following serves as an introduction and is not intended to act as a substitute for a professional's advice and counsel.

Securities and Exchange Commission

You must register your initial offering of security unless it comes within a specific exemption from registration. Traditionally, most start-up companies have relied upon the private offering exemption. Section 4(2) of the Securities Act of 1933 provides an exemption from registration with the SEC for "transactions by an issuer not involving a public offering." This section is usually referred to as the private placement exemption, but the statute does not define what constitutes a private placement.

The ability to rely on Section 4(2) depends heavily on who the potential investors are and the amount of information disclosed to these investors. The courts and the SEC have interpreted the exemption to be available for offerings involving sophisticated offerees and purchasers who have access to the same kind of information that a registered offering would provide and who are able to fend for themselves as knowledgeable investors. A leading case that interprets this exemption is *SEC* v. *Ralston Purina Co.* 346 U.S. 119 (1953). In general, the courts look for the following elements whenever a corporation relies on Section 4(2):

* The transaction is truly a nonpublic offering in which there is not any general advertising or solicitation.
* The offerees and purchasers are limited in number and the purchase is not for resale.
* The offerees and purchasers are either wealthy, institutional investors, have had previous financial or business experience with the issuing corporation, or are in a significant relationship with the issuing corporation, such as director, executive officer, or other policy maker.
* There is substantial disclosure of information made to the offerees and purchasers so that they can evaluate the advantages and disadvantages of the investment.

In order to better understand the requirements necessary to make a private offering, the SEC has issued Release No.33-4552.

Two other exemptions businesses have relied upon are the Intrastate Offering Exemption and Regulation A.

Intrastate Offering Exemption. This exemption, which is found in Section 3(a)(11) of the Securities Act, exempts from registration any security that is part of an issue offered and sold only to residents of a single state or territory, and the issuing business is both a resident of and doing business within that state or territory. This exemption is intended to facilitate the local financing of local business operations. To qualify for the intrastate exemption, the issuing business offering the security must:

* Be incorporated in the state in which it is making its offering;
* Carry out a significant amount of its business in that state; and
* Make offers and sales only to residents of that state.

Note: If any security is offered to or sold to even one out-of-state investor, the exemption may be destroyed.

Regulation A. There is a conditional exemption, which is found in Section 3(b) of the Securities Act, that exempts certain public offerings that do not exceed $1.5 million in any 12-month period. The use of Regulation A as an exemption does not alleviate the issuing corporation from having to supply to potential investors substantially the same type of information and in substantially the same format as would appear in a prospectus. As a result, Regulation A is often referred to as a "short form" of registration.

Regulation D. To coordinate the various limited offering exemptions and to stimulate the existing requirements regarding private offerings, the SEC, in March 1982, adopted under Sections 4(2) and 3(b) of the Securities Act, a set of rules under the heading of Regulation D.

Regulation D is comprised of six rules, 501 through 506, and it establishes three exemptions from the registration requirements of the 1933 act. The SEC's objective in promulgating these rules, according to its Release No.33-6389, was to "simplify existing rules and regulations, to eliminate any unnecessary restrictions that those rules and regulations place on issues, particularly small businesses, and to achieve uniformity between state and federal exemptions in order to facilitate capital formation consistent with the protection of investors." Following is an explanation of these rules:

• Rule 504 — private offering up to $500,000 in a 12-month period
• Rule 505 — private offering up to $5 million in a 12-month period
• Rule 506—- no ceiling on the amount of money that can be raised

Regardless of which rule you choose to issue your securities, it will be necessary to file a notice of sales on SEC Form D with the SEC within fifteen days after the first sale from the offering. Exhibit 12-5 is an example of SEC Form D.

Rule 504. There are no specific disclosure requirements for a private offering for less than $500,000 within a twelve-month period. In addition, there is no limitation on the number of persons purchasing the securities. However, the offering may not be made through any form of general solicitation or general advertising, and the securities that are issued will be "restricted," which means the securities cannot be purchased with the intention of resale, unless the offering is made in a state that provides for the registration of the securities. Although there are no specific requirements for disclosure of information, it must be sufficient for prospective investors to make an informed decision.

Rule 505. This rule permits sales of up to $5 million in any twelve-month period to a theoretically unlimited number of accredited investors plus thirty-five nonaccredited investors. According to Rule 501, an accredited investor is any person who comes within any of the following eight categories or who the issuer reasonably believes comes within one of the categories at the time of the sale of the securities:

* Certain institutional investors: Any small business investment company licensed by the U.S. Small Business Administration; any insurance company as defined by Section 2(13) of the 1933 act; employee benefit plans within the meaning of Title I of ERISA, if the investment decision is made by a plan fiduciary, as defined in Section 3(21) of ERISA, which is either a bank, insurance company, or registered investment advisor, or if the employee benefit plan has total assets in excess of $5,000,000; any investment company registered under the Investment Company Act of 1940, or a business development company as defined in Section 2(a)(48) of that act; and any bank.

* Private business development companies as defined in Section 202(a)(22) of the Investment Advisers Act of 1940.

* Certain tax-exempt organizations.

* Directors, executive officers, and general partners.

* $150,000 investor purchaser as defined as a person, corporation, partnership, or trust that purchases at least $150,000 of securities being offered and the purchaser's total purchase amount does not exceed 20 percent of the purchaser's net worth at the time of the sale.

* Excess of $200,000 of income as defined as any natural person who had an individual income in excess of $200,000 in each of the two most recent years and who reasonably expects an income in excess of $200,00 in the current year.

* Excess of $1 million in net worth as defined as natural persons whose individual or joint net worth at the time of the purchase exceeds $1 million.

* Any corporation in which all of the equity owners are accredited investors.

Substantial disclosure of information is necessary if you use Rule 505 and you issue securities to a non-accredited investor. You must provide the same kind of information as required in Part I of SEC Form S-18 registration statement. See Exhibit 12-6. Although the disclosure requirements of S-18 are not as detailed as Form S-1, which is required in a complete registration, in-depth disclosures about the business and its prospects must be made so that the prospective investor will have full knowledge of the history of the business.

There are two other important restrictions you must not forget: (1) You must take the necessary steps to ensure that investors are not buying your securities with the intention of resale and that they are informed they cannot resell the securities for at least two years after the purchase, and (2) you must not conduct any general advertising or general solicitation to offer or sell your securities.

Rule 506. This rule allows the use of a private placement exemption without regard to dollar amount. In order for the issuer to use Rule 506, certain requirements must be met: (1) The issuer must reasonably believe there are no more than thirty-five nonaccredited purchasers of the securities in the offering; (2) the issuer must reasonably believe that immediately prior to the making of any sale each purchaser, either alone or with his or her purchaser representative, has such knowledge and experience in financial and business matters that he or she is capable of evaluating the merits and risks of the prospective investment. (Rule 501 defines purchaser representative.)

This rule requires the most disclosure of information to potential investors. If any potential investor is offered a securities and is nonaccredited then all investors must receive the same kind of information required on Part I of Form S-1, which is the form used for registration with the SEC for public offerings. Form S-1 requires the following disclosures of information:

* Description of business and properties
* Certain types of financial statements
* Management's discussion and analysis of financial condition and results of operations
* Directors and executive officers
* Executive compensation
* Summary information about the offering
* Risk factors
* Ratio of earnings to fixed charges
* Use of proceeds
* Determination of offering price
* Plan of distribution
* Interests of named experts and counsel
* Description of the securities

See Exhibit 12-7 which is Part I of Form S-1. There are two other restrictions that apply, also. First, the securities that are issued must be restricted. Second, no general solicitation or general advertising is permitted in connection with the offer or sale of the securities.

Underwriters and Investment Bankers. If an entrepreneur is not well known or does not have an established track record, he or she will need to recruit the services of an investment banker for assistance in making a private placement. Until recently, the SEC did not allow sales commissions to be paid for a private placement with the reasoning that small companies would be taken advantage of by investment bankers. Today, however, there are no longer any restrictions. As a result each potential issuer makes the best deal he or she can. Fees to make a private placement differ from banker to banker, but the average is from 8 percent to 12 percent of the offering. If you include legal fees, accounting fees, filing fees, and printing costs, the percentage of the offering that goes to paying the costs of making a private placement may range between 16 percent to 20 percent.

For information concerning matters relating particularly to a small business, you can write:

Office of Small Business Policy
U.S. Securities and Exchange Commission
450 Fifth Street, N.W., Stop 7-10
Washington D.C. 20549
For copies of SEC forms and recently adopted rules, you can write to:

Publication Section
U.S. Securities and Exchange Commission
450 Fifth Street. N.W., Stop 1-2
Washington D.C. 20549

State Law Requirements

The objective of federal securities laws is to ensure that corporations make full disclosures of all necessary facts to prospective purchasers. Each state, however, has its own autonomous securities laws and regulations. Some states have requirements that are much more stringent than the federal government's. They require not only full disclosure of all necessary facts, but also the issuer pass a merit test, unless there is an exemption, and receive a permit to issue securities in that state.

States practicing qualification of securities are known as merit states. Generally, a state official will examine the securities offering to determine whether the offering represents a fair, just, and equitable purchase by the citizens of that state. As a consequence, even if a company complies with registration or filing procedures, the merit state may still refuse to allow that company to offer its securities in that state if it believes the offering does not have sufficient merit.

Venture Capital

What Is Venture Capital?

Venture capital is a source of financing to relatively new businesses. A new business receives cash from the venture capitalist and in turn surrenders either common stock or debt securities that can be readily converted into common stock. Venture capitalists are comprised of private individuals, corporations (many of which are SBICs) and private and publicly-held funds. Venture capitalists provide funding to small businesses with the objective of reaping a lion's share of the new company's profits. Other venture capitalists, however, may look to sharing in the royalties, taking the company public, or selling it to a larger firm. As a rule, venture capitalists attempt to invest in new businesses that have a significant advantage over existing companies. See Exhibit 12-8 for an example of a venture capitalist's investment policy and the type of financing it offers.

Advantages and Disadvantages

Advantages:

* Start-ups are often restricted in their sources of funding; venture capital represents an avenue which would otherwise not be available.

* When an entrepreneur issues common stock, the stock represents equity and thus does not have to be repaid. Nor must interest payments be made. Also, because the issuance of common stock increases the start-up's net worth, the company's credit worthiness is improved. Suppliers and customers may not be as concerned about the start-up's financial strength and whether it will be able to honor its commitments.

* Management assistance becomes available as well as such services as banking and management recruiting.

* The start-up's status within the industry will be enhanced when a professional venture capital firm has decided to invest in the start-up because the start-up's management, product, and chances for success have been determined to be favorable.

* Venture capital is usually less costly in the short run than other sources of funding.

* Venture capitalists, as a rule, do not insist that the owner–manager sign a personal guarantee or execute a security interest in the start-up's assets in exchange for providing capital.

Disadvantages

* Ownership is diluted, which provides the venture capitalist an unlimited benefit from the entrepreneur's hard work and talent.

* In the long run, because a venture capitalist will take a lion's share of the profits, this source of funding can be very costly, usually representing between 25 and 60 percent of the return.
* Absolute control is taken out of the hands of the owner. Thus management decisions are sometimes the result of compromise because of the demands made by venture capitalists.

Venture Capital Industry

The venture capital industry is composed of three types of venture capitalists:

* Independent private venture capital firms
* SBICs licensed by the federal government
* Venture capital subsidiaries of large financial institutions and industrial corporations

Independent private venture capitalists are the most numerous and are usually organized as limited partnerships. The general partnership is comprised collectively of individuals who are responsible for seeking out worthy companies to invest in, and monitoring those companies which have received venture capitalist funds. The general partner usually receives between 1 and 4 percent of the assets of the fund to cover operating expenses, which includes salaries. The limited partners are the true investors. They usually contribute over 95 percent of the capital and receive approximately 80 percent of the profits.

To attract investors, venture capitalists must remain competitive. Two of its main competitors are:

* Riskless investments
* Other venture capitalists

Riskless Investments. To justify its large management fees and its share of the profits, the venture capitalist must pick firms to invest in that will provide a return on investment (ROI), which at least exceeds the return on riskless investments, such as U.S. Treasury bonds, by the amount of the management fees and siphoned profits. For instance, the average length of time a venture capitalist will invest in a company is between four to six years; the average ROI the venture capitalist expects to receive is approximately 30 to 50 percent. This goal is difficult to reach and only a few start-ups will ever reach this percentage. For an example of how difficult this can be see the table below.

<table>
<thead>
<tr><th colspan="2">TEN YEAR INVESTMENT[a]</th></tr>
<tr><th>Number of Times Invested $1 Must Multiply</th><th>Percent Compound ROI</th></tr>
</thead>
<tbody>
<tr><td>6.19</td><td>20</td></tr>
<tr><td>9.13</td><td>25</td></tr>
<tr><td>13.78</td><td>30</td></tr>
<tr><td>20.10</td><td>35</td></tr>
<tr><td>28.92</td><td>40</td></tr>
<tr><td>41.08</td><td>45</td></tr>
<tr><td>57.66</td><td>50</td></tr>
</tbody>
</table>

[a]Formula: $(1+k)^n$

where: k = cost of capital
           n = number of compounding periods

Thus, to achieve a 25 percent compound ROI target, each dollar invested must multiply 9.31 times; for a 50 percent return, the investment dollar must turnover approximately 57 times.

Another way venture capitalists view a prospective investment is to analyze the internal rate of return (IRR) which is the interest rate that causes the net present value of net cash flows to equal zero. To calculate IRR, the venture capitalist will analyze the length of time it will take for him or her to double, triple, or quadruple his or her investment. For an example, see the table below:

INVESTMENT RETURN/INTERNAL RATE OF RETURN[a]

Number of Times Investment Is Returned	Percentage Approximate IRR
2 times the investment in 5 years	15.0
2 times the investment in 10 years	7.0
3 times the investment in 5 years	25.0
3 times the investment in 10 years	11.5
5 times the investment in 5 years	37.0
5 times the investment in 10 years	17.0
10 times the investment in 5 years	58.0
10 times the investment in 10 years	26.0

Formula:
$$PVIF = \frac{cost\ of\ project}{initial\ investment}$$

where:
$$PVIF = \frac{1}{(1+k)^n}$$

(PVIF stands for present value interest factor.)

Thus, a venture capitalist may decide to invest in a start-up if the projected IRR equals or exceeds his or her target. Generally, a venture capitalist will require a start-up to forecast a 50 percent IRR.

Other Venture Capitalists. Venture capitalists compete with each other to find limited partners for funds. As a result, venture capitalists have been forced to segment the market according to investment strategy:

Generalists—does not place an emphasis on either the entrepreneur or the product but places the focus on the company itself.

Specialists—concentrates on specific segments within an industry and often provide expert technical support.

Seed Funds—invest exclusively in start-ups before they are established but require between 60 and 80 percent of the equity.

Business Plan

A well thought out business plan which is well written is absolutely essential if you want to receive venture capital funds. In Chapter 7, we showed you how to write a business plan and gave you an example of what it should look like. The business plan you submit to a venture capitalist is almost identical in format to the type of plan presented in Chapter 7 except you will have to include an "executive summary."

Refer to the discussion on business plans in Chapter 7.

The business plan you submit to a venture capitalist should be organized as follows:

Title Page. Include name, address, and telephone number of the business and the names of the principals.

Executive Summary. This is 1–2 pages and is perhaps the most critical part of your business plan because many venture capitalists will only read this part of your plan. Venture capitalists are presented with perhaps 100 business plans a week and thus there is a tendency not to wade through pages of reports if the essential information is contained in the summary. The objective of the summary is to provide a quick overview of the essential features of your business plan. As a rule, you should write the summary after you have completed your plan. This way you will be able to put everything clearly into perspective. Your executive summary should take the following format:

* Type of business
* Company summary including history
* Product/service
* Potential market and competition
* Management team and its track record
* Amount of funds requested
* Collateral
* Use of funds

Business Description and History. Include legal form of business and any successes business may have had that would impact on your fund request.

Product or Service. Include description of product or service, your market, your industry, your competition, whether you have a patent, and technological trends.

Market Analysis and Strategy. Include information regarding how large your market is, your pricing policies, promotional strategies, relative share of the market, distribution method, and who you think your biggest customers will be.

Manufacturing Plan. Include a description of your production methods, size of plant, materials you will use, type of capital equipment, quality control, and how you will control costs.

Personnel Plan. Include an organizational chart to show how management will be structured, provide résumés of key personnel, and explain whether you think the local labor pool is sufficient for your needs.

Research and Development. Include a description of your company's efforts to date and what you intend to do in the future.

Financial Data. Include financial statements which have been prepared by a CPA and which include a description of the type of depreciation method, inventory valuation method, bad debt method, etc. that your company uses.

Analysis Sheet

Below is a typical analysis sheet used by a venture capitalist to analyze a prospective investment.

ANALYSIS SHEET

Date:
Company:
Product:
Industry:
Name of Entrepreneurs:
Market Potential:
Risks:

PRODUCT
  Description:
  Funding Required to Develop:
  Profit:
  Risks:

MARKETING:
  Target Market:
  Competitors:
  Channels of Distribution:

PERSONNEL:
  President:
  Name:
  College Degree:
  Experience:
  V.P. Marketing:
  Name:
  College Degree:
  Experience:
  V.P. Finance:
  Name:
  College Degree:
  Experience:

FINANCIAL INFORMATION:

                          YEARS
                   1   2   3   4   5

Sales....................
Net Income..........
Assets................
Liabilities............
Net Worth...........

Locating Venture Capitalists

There are two sources available to help you find the right venture capitalist.

Source 1: Firms licensed by the SBA known as (SBICs). The address to obtain a listing of these firms is:

> National Association of Small Business
> Investment Companies (NASBIC)
> 618 Washington Bldg.
> Washington D.C. 20005

Source 2: The firms that fall within this group are not licensed by the government. The address to write for a current list is:

> The National Venture Capital Association
> 1225 19th Street N.W.
> Suite 750
> Washington D.C. 20036

Going Public

Initial Public Offerings (IPOs) can be an excellent source to raise capital. For many entrepreneurs, IPOs represent the ideal way to transform a debt laden operation into one that is equity rich.

How do IPOs work? What is involved? First you must know the difference between closely held and publicly held corporations. A closely held corporation means the company's stock is held by a few individuals who are usually the managers of the firm. A publicly held corporation means that the company's stock is owned by a large number of individuals who usually are not actively involved in its management.

Publicly held stocks are traded in one of two markets: over-the-counter market ("OTC") or organized security exchange.

Stocks traded in the OTC market are called *unlisted* stocks. OTC stock trading takes place through an intricate web of telephone and computer lines that connect dealers and brokers throughout the country. OTC market includes many stocks from small, relatively unknown corporations as well as the issues of large corporations, such as Intel Corp., Apple Computer, Genentech Inc., Adolph Coors, Tandem Computers Inc., and MCI Communications Corp. Generally, there are approximately 30,000 OTC stocks in the United States which are divided into the following categories:

* Approximately 10,000 companies are local companies whose assets and earnings are too small to be of nationwide interest. As a rule, these stocks are listed only with stock brokers in the immediate city, state, or region.
* Approximately 16,000 companies are listed on "pink sheets," which are mailed daily by the National Quotation Bureau to brokers across the country. These stocks represent companies which have substantial amounts of assets and revenues.
* Approximately 3,700 of the most prominent OTC stocks are traded through the National Association of Securities Dealers Automated Quotation System (NASDAQ). Many of the corporations listed on NASDAQ have assets and revenues sufficient to qualify them to be traded on a national exchange but spurn the opportunity because they feel the OTC is more efficient.

Stocks traded on an organized security exchange are called unlisted stocks. There are numerous organized security exchanges, for example Pacific Stock Exchange, which is a regional exchange, and American Stock Exchange and New York Stock Exchange, which are both national exchanges.

Stock market transactions are divided into two markets: secondary and primary. Secondary market is for those stocks that have already been issued and thus are outstanding or used. The corporation whose stock is traded in the secondary market does not receive any additional capital from this type of trading. Primary market is for those newly issued securities that are sold for the first time. When a closely held corporation issues stock to the public at large for the first time, it is called "going public." The process of issuing the stock is called IPO.

<h3 style="text-align:center">Advantages and Disadvantages</h3>

Advantages

* *An offering can provide large sums of cash.* Corporations that are privately held and want to raise cash by selling stock must approach existing owners or shop around for investors. Because of federal and state regulations, the number of investors who can legally purchase stock from this type of corporation is limited. As a result, capital input is limited.

* *Corporate image is enhanced.* In order to be listed on a stock exchange or traded OTC, a corporation must meet certain qualifications. This, in turn, will attract better managers as well as media attention.

Disadvantages

* *Disclosure of sensitive information.* Publicly owned corporations must disclose data concerning their operations to prospective purchasers as well as to the government. Stocks owned by directors, officers, and major shareholders must also be disclosed. Competitors and other groups hostile to the interests of the corporation are permitted to inspect most, if not all, of this information. Those corporations which do not want to submit to intense scrutiny are required to do so anyway or face stiff civil and/or criminal penalties.

* *Disclosure drives up the cost of doing business.* A publicly held corporation must file numerous reports with the SEC. For example, there are quarterly financial reports (Form 10-Q), annual financial reports (Form 10-K), reports about events that have a material impact on the company (Form 8-K). In addition, there are reports that must be sent to the state in which the stock is being offered. There are also proxy statements and annual reports to stockholders. There are considerable costs incurred in the compilation of the required information.

* *The duties owed by the directors and officers to the corporation are magnified.* In a closely held corporation, the owners are usually the managers and the distinction between the two is often blurred. As a result, such dealings as nepotism, high salaries, doing business with the corporation, and fringe benefits which are truly questionable, are overlooked or ignored. For a publicly held corporation, however, these types of transactions must, at the very least, be disclosed to shareholders or else liability attaches. Moreover, government regulatory agencies may conduct a review and inspection which could subject directors and officers to civil and/or criminal penalties.

* *Control will be diluted.* Managers who may have at one time owned the firm often do not own at least 50 percent of the issued stock of a publicly held corporation. As a consequence, they are often pressured to make decisions to appease stockholders but which may not, in their opinion, be in the best interests of the corporation.

* *Going public is an expensive method of raising capital.* Costs are usually higher than other methods of raising funds.

The Investment Banking Process

Investment bankers are used to assist corporations in issuing new securities in the primary market. Some of the topics you need to be aware of when planning an IPO are:

* *Best efforts or underwritten issue.* Best efforts is an underwriting agreement in which brokers use their best efforts to sell the offering as agents of the issuing corporation. In a best efforts issue, the investment banker does not guarantee securities will be sold. In an underwritten agreement, the investment banker gives the issuing corporation a guarantee concerning the sale of the securities. As a consequence, the banker takes a significant risk.
* *Flotation Costs.* Fees to various groups involved in the issuance must be paid by the issuing corporation. These costs normally include the fees of the investment banker, lawyers, accountants, printing, filing fees, public relations, and on-going fees to maintain compliance with various regulations. In addition, there are the following costs to consider:

Costs: Total costs, when legal, accounting, printing, and marketing fees are added in, may consume from 19 to 25 percent of your initial offering. Below is a breakdown of these costs.

Investment Banker—The underwriter's commission usually ranges from 7 to 10 percent of the value of the offering. As a rule, the smaller the offering, the higher the percentage of commission. If the initial public offering is small and the company has no track record, some underwriters will insist on an up-front, nonrefundable deposit which is usually a minimum of 1.5 to 2.5 percent of the value of the offering.

Filing Fees—SEC filing fees cost .02 percent of the maximum aggregate offering price. NASDAQ filing costs are $100 plus .01% of the maximum aggregate offering price, with a $5,100 maximum. There are also state blue-sky fees, registrar, and transfer agent fees.

Public Relations—Information is usually provided to the financial press in order to maintain media attention to the corporation. This is especially critical during the first ninety days after the registration statement has been filed. Thus, public relations firms are sometimes hired to market an institutional image of the corporation.

Registration Statement

Newly issued securities must be registered with the SEC before they are offered publicly. The registration statement provides financial, legal, and other types of information about the company. It is divided into two parts. Part I includes a prospectus, which is a summary of the information contained in the registration and is distributed to underwriters and prospective investors in order to sell the securities. Both registration and prospectus become part of the public record and are analyzed by the SEC to ensure that the information is neither misleading nor inadequate. At a minimum, the prospectus must contain the following:

Cover Page —provides a summary of all key offering facts. A preliminary version of the prospectus distributed to potential buyers of a new security issue prior to approval of the registration statement by the SEC is called a "red herring" prospectus because the cover page is printed in red ink.

Table of Contents

Prospectus Summary—provides an overview of the corporation, describes how the proceeds will be used, and presents certain financial information.

Company Background—provides detailed information about the corporation's primary business.

Risk Factors—analyzes risks involved in the industry as well as the corporation.

Use of Proceeds

Dilution—reports any material dilution of the prospective investors' equity interest. Should there be a material variance between offering price and tangible book value of the share before the offering, it must be reported.

Dividend Policy—discloses whether there are any restrictions placed on dividends.

Capitalization—supplies detailed information regarding the corporation's equity and debt structure prior to and after the offering.

Selected Financial Data—shows financial data of the previous five years and any interim period.

Management Analysis—assesses financial condition and results of operations for the last three years.

Detailed Business Description

Properties of the Business

Legal Proceedings—describes and analyzes litigation that will have a material effect on the corporation.

Management and Security Holder Backgrounds—includes biographical data of the directors along with information such as transactions with promoters or golden parachutes.

Description of the Registered Securities

Underwriting—provides a description of the distribution plan of the securities and principal underwriters in the syndication.

Legal Review—includes the name of the attorneys and a report of their opinions of the validity of the offering.

Financial Statements—includes audited balance sheets, audited income statements, audited statement of changes in financial position, audited statement of stockholders' equity.

SMALL BUSINESS INNOVATION RESEARCH (SBIR) PROGRAM

The Small Business Innovation Research (SBIR) Program came into existence in July 1982 with the enactment of the Small Business Innovation Development Act. In October 1986, the President of the United States signed into legislation a bill that extended the SBIR program through September 1993.

The purpose of SBIR is fourfold: (1) stimulate technological innovation; (2) use small businesses to satisfy federal research and development needs; (3) encourage the participation by disadvantaged and minority persons in technological innovations; and (4) increase private sector commercialization derived from federal research and development.

Under the Small Business Innovation Development Act, each agency with an extramural research and development budget in excess of $100 million must establish an SBIR program. The following agencies are currently participating in the SBIR program:

* Department of Agriculture
* Department of Commerce
* Department of Defense
* Department of Education
* Department of Energy
* Department of Health and Human Services
* Department of Interior
* Department of Transportation
* Environmental Protection Agency
* National Aeronautics and Space Administration
* National Science Foundation
* Nuclear Regulatory Commission

The law requires agencies of the federal government with research and development budgets of more than $20 million to establish small business goals for awarding research and development funding agreements each year. The SBIR program consists of three phases:

Phase I. The purpose is to evaluate the scientific technical merit feasibility of an idea. Awards of up to $50,000 are made within a period of performance usually not to exceed six months.

Phase II. The purpose is to expand on the results of and further pursue the development of Phase I. Awards of $500,000 or less are made, and the period of performance is not to exceed two years.

Phase III. The purpose is for the commercialization of the results of Phase II and requires the use of either private or non-SBIR federal funding. No SBIR funds may be utilized in Phase III.

Any small business with 500 or fewer employees can participate in the SBIR program. There are two restrictions, however: First, the principal investigator for each project must spend more than one half of his or her time employed by the firm at the time of the award and during the conduct of the effort. During Phase I, a minimum of two-thirds of the research and/or analytical effort must be performed by the proposing firm. The remainder of the research and/or analytical effort may be delegated to subcontractors or consultants. During Phase II, at least one-half of the research and/or analytical effort must be performed by the proposing firm.

In an effort to assist small businesses in obtaining these research and development grants, the SBA publishes and distributes, for free, the "Pre-Solicitation Announcement" (PSA). This publication comes out in December, March, June, and September of each year. Every issue of the PSA contains information on the SBIR program along with details on SBIR solicitations that are about to be released. The advantage of obtaining this publication is that it eliminates the need to track the activities of all federal agencies participating in the SBIR program to determine which projects are best for you.

The SBA recommends that to successfully obtain funding, you must select the right project and make the best use of your firm's resources. As a result, there should be an evaluation and comparison procedure to prioritize projects with the greatest chance of success. In selecting projects for SBIR participation, the SBA recommends that you should attempt to maximize the following criteria.

* Your ability to respond to agency needs, problems, or mission area.
* Your ability to conduct the quality technical effort required to make a significant impact.
* Your ability to market and sell a technological innovation resulting from the research and development effort.

It is imperative for you to understand what the federal agencies want. The SBIR solicits proposals to meet agency research and development needs. A proposal should only be submitted if it is in response to a topic presented in an agency SBIR solicitation. Also, all aspects of the proposal must be of high scientific and technical merit. The plausibility of a technical assumption and proposed methodology will be examined in light of current scientific evidence and techniques. According to the SBA's Office of Innovation Research and Technology, the primary reason proposals are rejected is because reviewers disagree with technical claims, dispute the uniqueness of the effort compared to others they are aware of, or downgrade the proposal for leaving out important technical considerations.

If you are interested in obtaining more information on the SBIR program or receiving the PSA, you can write to the SBA at the following address:

> Office of Innovation, Research and Technology
> SBA
> 1441 L Street, N.W.
> Washington, D.C. 20416

FACTORING ACCOUNTS RECEIVABLE

In this chapter numerous financial entities and financial products available for the funding of your business' capital needs have been identified. This section discusses one of the most accessible sources of funds to the new business: factors. The act of factoring is defined as the sale and assignment of the rights to your accounts receivable to a third party in exchange for cash. Of course, you will be charged dearly for this service, as will be explained later.

First, let's look at how a factor works. There are many variations of factoring and some features may be omitted; however, the following example shows a typical factoring plan. The company and the factor enter into an agreement which provides the factor with a blanket security interest in accounts receivable as assigned. The company will normally present a bona fide order to the factor for approval. The factor will perform credit analysis and credit checks on the buyer and will either approve or decline the buyer for factoring. If the credit is denied, the company may either ship the goods for its own account or reject the order. If credit is approved, then the company will normally ship the goods, create an invoice, and present the invoice to the factor for an advance of funds. The factor, in turn, will send the invoice to the buyer with a notification that the invoice has been assigned to the factor and is payable to the factor. This notification sometimes takes the form of a stamped legend directly on the invoice. The buyer then remits payment to the factor and the cycle is complete.

The cost of factoring is high. However, as a practical matter, your business may have no other choice but to factor until sufficient capital can be built up in the business. The cost of factoring will depend on the following elements:

Recourse versus Nonrecourse. Recourse means you will be responsible for paying the factor directly or replacing the uncollectible invoice with one that will be collectible. Nonrecourse is simply the reverse. Due to the risk of nonrecourse factoring, the company will pay a higher rate.

Reserve Accounts. Originally the reserve was established to cover disputes between buyer and seller over damaged or returned goods. Today, factors may require a portion of each account receivable (invoice) to be set aside as "insurance" against non-collection. Reserves can be cash or noncash. The noncash reserve takes the form of a reduction of advance against the invoice. This reserve is paid back when the invoice is collected. If the invoice is never paid, the reserve acts as a loss reduction feature.

Let's see how these features would come into play by looking at two examples of factoring. The first example is an extremely onerous arrangement, while the second example is fairly reasonable.

Example 1:

Assume your company sold a $10,000 product to a buyer of marginal credit quality. The factor has agreed to fund the invoice but only under these conditions:

* 30% collection reserve.
* 10% up-front fee.
* Collection reserve to be returned upon collection.
* Subject to the following fee rebate schedule:

Number of days between assignment & receipt of funds	Fee rebate	Net cost
0 - 30	3.5%	6.5%
31 - 60	2.0	8.0
61 +	-0-	10.0

Under these conditions, the factor would provide cash as follows:

Invoice	$10,000
30% reserve	(3,000)
10% fee	(1,000)
Net cash to company	$ 6,000

If collection occurred within thirty days, total cost to the company would be $650. The reserve and fee rebate would be refunded within seven days of collection of the invoice. What is the borrowing rate your business will have to pay to factor this invoice for thirty days? *Answer:* Your business had use of the $6,000 for thirty days and paid $650 for the privilege. That rate on a simple interest basis is 130% (($650/6000) x 12). Seem high? It is; however, you must consider the risk the factor is taking. Should the invoice be collected at some later date or not at all, the factor's yield will decline significantly.

Example 2:

Your business has an established track record of shipping good saleable merchandise to creditworthy customers. The factor in this case will require no collection reserve, charge an upfront fee of 7 percent regardless of collection receipt, and take the accounts receivable on a nonrecourse basis. Assume your business sells a $10,000 product, net proceeds to your company would be as follows:

Invoice	$10,000
7% fee	700
Net cash to company	$ 9,300

If we assume the invoice is collected in thirty days, the cost to you for the factoring is a simple interest rate of 90.3% [(700/9300) x 12]. *Note*: If the terms of payment were such that the receivable is collected in sixty days, the cost to factor would have been a mere 45.2 percent.

It should be obvious by now that this form of financing is very costly. If it is so costly then why do so many companies use factoring? A few of the reasons provided by the factors are:

* Increased working capital turnover
* Protection and improvement of the company credit rating because timely credit is made to creditors
* The ability to take advantage of trade creditor discounts
* Avoidance of the use of debt since factoring is considered sale of assets
* Increased sales through credit extension approved by factor
* Availability of specialized customer credit qualification assistance.

Although this is one of the most expensive forms of financing, it remains very popular to companies that have not matured to the level necessary to obtain bank financing. The factor provides a valuable service in spreading the company's risks. Factoring has been discussed as a financing alternative; however, it should be used only if other more conventional sources of financing are not available.

Chapter 12 Exhibits

Exhibit 12.1 U.S. Small Business Administration Application for a Loan, Statements Required by Laws and Executive Orders, Summary of Collateral, Schedule of Collateral, Lender's Checklist for SBA Applications

Exhibit 12.2 Statement of Personal History

Exhibit 12.3 U.S. Small Business Administration List of SBICs

Exhibit 12.4 U.S. Small Business Administration List of MESBICs

Exhibit 12.5 Notice of Sale of Securities Pursuant to Regulation D, Section 4(6), and/or Uniform Limited Offering Exemption (Form D)

Exhibit 12.6 Registration Statement Under the Securities Act of 1933 (Form S-18)

Exhibit 12.7 Registration Statement Under the Securities Act of 1933 (Form S-1)

Exhibit 12.8 Letter from Venture Capitalist Westamco Investment Company

U.S. Small Business Administration

Application for Business Loan

Applicant	Full Address

Name of Business	Tax I.D. No.

Full Street Address	Tel. No. (Inc. A/C)

City	County	State	Zip	Number of Employees (Including subsidiaries and affiliates)
Type of Business		Date Business Established		At Time of Application _____
Bank of Business Account and Address				If Loan is Approved _____
				Subsidiaries or Affiliates _____ (Separate from above)

Use of Proceeds: (Enter Gross Dollar Amounts Rounded to Nearest Hundreds)	Loan Requested	SBA USE ONLY
Land Acquisition		
New Construction/ Expansion/Repair		
Acquisition and/or Repair of Machinery and Equipment		
Inventory Purchase		
Working Capital (Including Accounts Payable)		
Acquisition of Existing Business		
Payoff SBA Loan		
Payoff Bank Loan (Non SBA Associated)		
Other Debt Payment (Non SBA Associated)		
All Other		
Total Loan Requested		
Term of Loan		

Collateral

If your collateral consists of (A) Land and Building, (D) Accounts Receivable and/or (E) Inventory, fill in the appropriate blanks. If you are pledging (B) Machinery and Equipment, (C) Furniture and Fixtures, and/or (F) Other, please provide an itemized list (labeled Exhibit A) that contains serial and identification numbers for all articles that had an original value greater than $500. Include a legal description of Real Estate offered as collateral.

	Present Market Value	Present Loan Balance	SBA Use Only Collateral Valuation
A. Land and Building	$	$	$
B. Machinery & Equipment			
C. Furniture & Fixtures			
D. Accounts Receivable			
E. Inventory			
F. Other			
Totals	$	$	$

PREVIOUS SBA OR OTHER GOVERNMENT FINANCING: If you or any principals or affiliates have ever requested Government Financing, complete the following:

Name of Agency	Original Amount of Loan	Date of Request	Approved or Declined	Balance	Current or Past Due
	$			$	
	$			$	

SBA Form 4 (2-85) Previous Editions Obsolete

Exhibit 12-1

INDEBTEDNESS: Furnish the following information on all installment debts, contracts, notes, and mortgages payable. Indicate by an asterisk (*) items to be paid by loan proceeds and reason for paying same (present balance should agree with latest balance sheet submitted).

To Whom Payable	Original Amount	Original Date	Present Balance	Rate of Interest	Maturity Date	Monthly Payment	Security	Current or Past Due
	$		$			$		
	$		$			$		
	$		$			$		
	$		$			$		

MANAGEMENT (Proprietor, partners, officers, directors and all holders of outstanding stock — <u>100% of ownership must be shown</u>). Use separate sheet if necessary.

Name and Social Security Number	Complete Address	% Owned	*Military Service From	To	*Race	*Sex

* This data is collected for statistical purposes only. It has no bearing on the credit decision to approve or decline this application.

ASSISTANCE   List the name(s) and occupation(s) of any who assisted in preparation of this form, other than applicant.

Name and Occupation	Address	Total Fees Paid	Fees Due

Signature of Preparers if Other Than Applicant

THE FOLLOWING EXHIBITS MUST BE COMPLETED WHERE APPLICABLE. ALL QUESTIONS ANSWERED ARE MADE A PART OF THE APPLICATION.

For Guaranty Loans please provide an original and one copy (Photocopy is Acceptable) of the Application Form, and all Exhibits to the participating lender. For Direct Loans submit one original copy of application and Exhibits to SBA.

Submit SBA Form 1261 (Statements Required by Laws and Executive Orders). This form must be signed and dated by each Proprietor, Partner, Principal or Guarantor.

1. Submit SBA Form 912 (Personal History Statement) for each person e.g. owners, partners, officers, directors, major stockholders, etc.; the instructions are on SBA Form 912.

2. Furnish a signed current personal balance sheet (SBA Form 413 may be used for this purpose) for each stockholder (with 20% or greater ownership), partner, officer, and owner. Social Security number should be included on personal financial statement. Label this Exhibit B.

3. Include the statements listed below: 1, 2, 3 for the last three years; also 1, 2, 3, 4 dated within 90 days of filing the application; and statement 5, if applicable. This is Exhibit C (SBA has Management Aids that help in the preparation of financial statements.) All information must be signed and dated.

    1. Balance Sheet   2. Profit and Loss Statement
    3. Reconciliation of Net Worth
    4. Aging of Accounts Receivable and Payable
    5. Earnings projections for at least one year where financial statements for the last three years are unavailable or where requested by District Office.
       (If Profit and Loss Statement is not available, explain why and substitute Federal Income Tax Forms.)

4. Provide a brief history of your company and a paragraph describing the expected benefits it will receive from the loan. Label it Exhibit D.

ALL EXHIBITS MUST BE SIGNED AND DATED BY PERSON SIGNING THIS FORM.

SBA Form 4 (2-85) Previous Editions Obsolete

5. Provide a brief description of the educational, technical and business background for all the people listed under Management. Please mark it Exhibit E.

6. Do you have any co-signers and/or guarantors for this loan? If so, please submit their names, addresses and personal balance sheet(s) as Exhibit F.

7. Are you buying machinery or equipment with your loan money? If so, you must include a list of the equipment and cost as quoted by the seller and his name and address. This is Exhibit G.

8. Have you or any officers of your company ever been involved in bankruptcy or insolvency proceedings? If so, please provide the details as Exhibit H. If none, check here: ☐ Yes ☐ No

9. Are you or your business involved in any pending lawsuits? If yes, provide the details as Exhibit I. If none, check here: ☐ Yes ☐ No

10. Do you or your spouse or any member of your household, or anyone who owns, manages, or directs your business or their spouses or members of their households work for the Small Business Administration, Small Business Advisory Council, SCORE or ACE, any Federal Agency, or the participating lender? If so, please provide the name and address of the person and the office where employed. label this Exhibit J. If none, check here: ☐ Yes ☐ No

11. Does your business, its owners or majority stockholders own or have a controlling interest in other businesses? If yes, please provide their names and the relationship with your company along with a current balance sheet and operating statement for each. This should be Exhibit K.

12. Do you buy from, sell to, or use the services of any concern in which someone in your company has a significant financial interest? If yes, provide details on a separate sheet of paper labeled Exhibit L.

13. If your business is a franchise, include a copy of the franchise agreement and a copy of the FTC disclosure statement supplied to you by the Franchisor. Please include it as Exhibit M.

CONSTRUCTION LOANS ONLY

---

14. Include a separate exhibit (Exhibit N) the estimated cost of the project and a statement of the source of any additional funds.

15. File the necessary compliance document (SBA Form 601).

16. Provide copies of preliminary construction plans and specifications. Include them as Exhibit O. Final plans will be required prior to disbursement.

DIRECT LOANS ONLY

---

17. Include two bank declination letters with your application. These letters should include the name and telephone number of the persons contacted at the banks, the amount and terms of the loan, the reason for decline and whether or not the bank will participate with SBA. In cities with 200,000 people or less, one letter will be sufficient.

EXPORT LOANS

18. Does your business presently engage in Export Trade?
Check here ☐ Yes ☐ No

19. Do you plan to begin exporting as a result of this loan?
Check here ☐ Yes ☐ No

20. Would you like information on Exporting?
Check here ☐ Yes ☐ No

AGREEMENTS AND CERTIFICATIONS

Agreements of Nonemployment of SBA Personnel: I/We agree that if SBA approves this loan application I/We will not, for at least two years, hire as an employee or consultant anyone that was employed by the SBA during the one year period prior to the disbursement of the loan.

Certification: I/We certify: (a) I/We have not paid anyone connected with the Federal Government for help in getting this loan. I/We also agree to report to the SBA office of the Inspector General, 1441 L Street N.W., Washington, D.C. 20416 any Federal Government employee who offers, in return for any type of compensation, to help get this loan approved.

(b) All information in this application and the Exhibits are true and complete to the best of my/our knowledge and are submitted to SBA so SBA can decide whether to grant a loan or participate with a lending institution in a loan to me/us. I/We agree to pay for or reimburse SBA for the cost of any surveys, title or mortgage examinations, appraisals etc., performed by non-SBA personnel provided I/We have given my/our consent.

I/We understand that I/We need not pay anybody to deal with SBA. I/We have read and understand Form 394 which explains SBA policy on representatives and their fees.

If you make a statement that you know to be false or if you over value a security in order to help obtain a loan under the provisions of the Small Business Act, you can be fined up to $5,000 or be put in jail for up to two years, or both.

If Applicant is a proprietor or general partner, sign below:

By: _____
                                                    Date

If Applicant is a Corporation, sign below:

_____
Corporate Name and Seal   Date

_____

By: _____
                    Signature of President

Attested by: _____
                    Signature of Corporate Secretary

ALL EXHIBITS MUST BE SIGNED AND DATED BY PERSON SIGNING THIS FORM.

Federal executive agencies, including the Small Business Administration, are required to withhold or limit financial assistance, to impose special conditions on approved loans, to provide special notices to applicants or borrowers and to require special reports and data from borrowers in order to comply with legislation passed by the Congress and Executive Orders issued by the President and by the provisions of various inter-agency agreements. SBA has issued regulations and procedures that implement these laws and executive orders and they are contained in Parts 112, 113 and 116, Title 13 Code of Federal Regulations Chapter 1, or SOPs.

This form contains a brief summary of the various laws and executive orders that affect SBA's business and disaster loan programs and gives applicants and borrowers the notices required by law or otherwise. The signatures required on the last page provide evidence that SBA has given the necessary notices.

Freedom of Information Act
(5 U.S.C. 552)

This law provides that, with some exceptions, SBA must supply information reflected in agency files and records to a person requesting it. Information about approved loans that will be automatically released includes, among other things, statistics on our loan programs (individual borrowers are not identified in the statistics) and other information such as the names of the borrowers (and their officers, directors, stockholders or partners), the collateral pledged to secure the loan, the amount of the loan, its purpose in general terms and the maturity. Proprietary data on a borrower would not routinely be made available to third parties. All requests under this Act are to be addressed to the nearest SBA office and be identified as a Freedom of Information request.

Privacy Act
(5 U.S.C. 552a)

Disaster home loan files are covered by this legislation because they are normally maintained in the names of individuals. Business loan files are maintained by business name or in the name of individuals in their entrepreneurial capacity. Thus they are not files on individuals and, therefore, are not subject to this Act. Any person can request to see or get copies of any personal information that SBA has in the request's file. Requests for information about another party may be denied unless SBA has the written permission of the individual to release the information to the requester's or unless the information is subject to disclosure under the Freedom of Information Act. (The "Acknowledgement" section of this form contains the written permission of SBA to release information when a disaster victim requests assistance under the family and individual grant program.)

NOTE: Any person concerned with the collection of information, its voluntariness, disclosure or routine use under the Privacy Act or requesting information under the Freedom of Information Act may contact the Director, Freedom of Information/Privacy Acts Division, Small Business Administration, 1441 L Street, N.W., Washington, D.C. 20416, for information about the Agency's procedures on these two subjects.

SBA FORM 1261 (12-86) REF: SOP 50 10 Previous Editions Obsolete

Right to Financial Privacy Act of 1978

(12 U.S.C. 3401)

This is notice to you, as required by the Right to Financial Privacy Act of 1978, of SBA's access rights to financial records held by financial institutions that are or have been doing business with you or your business, including any financial institution participating in a loan or loan guarantee. The law provides that SBA shall have a right of access to your financial records in connection with its consideration or administration of assistance to you in the form of a Government loan or loan guaranty agreement. SBA is required to provide a certificate of its compliance with the Act to a financial institution in connection with its first request for access to your financial records, after which no further certification is required for subsequent accesses. The law also provides that SBA's access rights continue for the term of any approved loan or loan guaranty agreement. No further notice to you of SBA's access rights is required during the term of any such agreement.

The law also authorizes SBA to transfer to another Government authority any financial records included in an application for a loan, or concerning an approved loan or loan guarantee, as necessary to process, service or foreclose a loan or loan guarantee or to collect on a defaulted loan or loan guarantee. No other transfer of your financial records to another Government authority will be permitted by SBA except as required or permitted by law.

Flood Disaster Protection Act

(42 U.S.C. 4011)

Regulations issued by the Federal Insurance Administration (FIA) and by SBA implementing this Act and its amendments. These regulations prohibit SBA from making certain loans in an FIA designated floodplain unless Federal flood insurance is purchased as a condition of the loan. Failure to maintain the required level of flood insurance makes the applicant ineligible for any future financial assistance from SBA under any program, including disaster assistance.

Executive Orders -- Floodplain Management and Wetland Protection

(42 F.R. 26951 and 42 F.R. 2961)

The SBA discourages any settlement in or development of a foodplain or a wetland. This statement is to notify all SBA loan applicants that such actions are hazardous to both life and property and should be avoided. The additional cost of flood preventive construction must be considered in addition to the possible loss of all assets and investments in future floods.

Lead-Based Paint Poisoning Prevention Act

(42 U.S.C. 4821 et seq.)

Borrowers using SBA funds for the construction or rehabilitation of a residential structure are prohibited from using lead-based paint (as defined in SBA regulations) on all interior surfaces, whether accessible or not, and exterior surfaces, such as stairs, decks, porches, railings, windows and doors, which are readily accessible to children under 7 years of age. A "residential structure" is any home, apartment, hotel, motel, orphanage, boarding school, dormitory, day care center, extended care facility, college or other school housing, hospital, group practice or community facility and all other residential or institutional structures where person reside.

Equal Credit Opportunity Act

(15 U.S.C. 1691)

The Federal Equal Credit Opportunity Act prohibits creditors from discriminating against credit applicants on the basis of race, color, religion, national origin, sex, marital status or age (provided that the applicant has the capacity to enter into a binding contract); because all or part of the applicant's income drives from any public assistance program, or because the applicant has in good faith exercised any right under the Consumer Credit Protection Act. The Federal agency that administers compliance with this law concerning this creditor is the Federal Trade Commission, Equal Credit Opportunity, Room 500, 633 Indiana Avenue, N.W., Washington, D.C. 20580.

Civil Rights Legislation

All businesses receiving SBA financial assistance must agree not to discriminate in any business practice, including employment practices and services to the public, on the basis of categories cited in 13 C.F.R., Parts 112 and 113 of SBA Regulations. This includes making their goods and services available to handicapped clients or customers. All business borrowers will be required to display the "Equal Employment Opportunity Poster" prescribed by SBA.

Executive Order 11738 -- Environmental Protection
(38 F.R. 25161)

The Executive Order charges SBA with administering its loan programs in a manner that will result in effective enforcement of the Clean Air Act, the Federal Water Pollution Act and other environmental protection legislation. SBA must, therefore, impose conditions on some loans. By acknowledging receipt of this form and presenting the application, the principals of all small businesses borrowing $100,000 or more in direct funds stipulate to the following:

1.　　That any facility used, or to be used, by the subject firm is not listed on the EPA list of Violating Facilities.

2.　　That subject firm will comply with all the requirements of Section 114 of the Clean Air Act (42 U.S.C. 7414) and Section 308 of the Water Act (33 U.S.C. 1318) relating to inspection, monitoring, entry, reports and information, as well as all other requirements specified in Section 114 and Section 308 of the respective Acts, and all regulations and guidelines issued thereunder.

3.　　That subject firm will notify SBA of the receipt of any communication from the Director of the Environmental Protection Agency indicating that a facility utilized, or to be utilized, by subject firm is under consideration to be listed on EPA List of Violating Facilities.

Occupational Safety and Health Act
(15 U.S.C. 651 et seq.)

This legislation authorizes the Occupational Safety and Health Administration in the Department of Labor to require businesses to modify facilities and procedures to protect employees or pay penalty fees. In some instances the business can be forced to cease operations or be prevented from starting operations in a new facility. Therefore, in some instances SBA may require additional information from an applicant to determine whether the business will be in compliance with OSHA regulations and allowed to operate its facility after the loan is approved and disbursed.

In all instances, signing this form as borrower is a certification that the OSHA requirements that apply to the borrower's business have been determined and the borrower is, to the best of its knowledge, in compliance.

Debt Collection Act of 1982　 Deficit Reduction Act of 1984
(31 U.S.C. 3701 et seq. and other titles)

These laws require SBA to aggressively collect any loan payments which become delinquent. SBA must obtain your taxpayer identification number when you apply for a loan. If you receive a loan, and do not make payments as they come due, SBA may take one or more of the following actions:

- Report the status of your loan(s) to credit bureaus
- Hire a collection agency to collect your loan
- Offset your income tax refund or other amounts due to you from the Federal Government
- Suspend or debar you or your company from doing business with the Federal Government
- Refer your loan to the Department of Justice or other attorneys for litigation
- Foreclose on collateral or take other action permitted in the loan instruments.

Consumer Credit Protection Act

(15 U.S.C. 1601 et seq.)

This legislation gives an applicant who is refused credit because of adverse information about the applicant's credit, reputation, character or mode of living an opportunity to refute or challenge the accuracy of such reports. Therefore, whenever SBA declines a loan in whole or in part because of adverse information in a credit report, the applicant will be given the name and address of the reporting agency so the applicant can seek to have that agency correct its report, if inaccurate. If SBA declines a loan in whole or in part because of adverse information received from a source other than a credit reporting agency, the applicant will be given information about the nature of the adverse information but not the source of the report.

Within 3 days after the consummation of the transaction, any recipient of an SBA loan which is secured in whole or in part by a lien on the recipient's residence or household contents may rescind such a loan in accordance with the "Regulation Z" of the Federal Reserve Board.

Applicant's Acknowledgement

My (our) signature(s) acknowledge(s) receipt of this form, that I (we) have read it and that I (we) have a copy for my (our) files. My (our) signature(s) represents my (our) agreement to comply with the requirements the Small Business Administration makes in connection with the approval of my (our) loan request and to comply, whenever applicable, with the hazard insurance, lead-based paint, civil rights or other limitations contained in this notice.

My (our) signature(s) also represent written permission, as required by the Privacy Act, for the SBA to release any information in my (our) disaster loan application to the Governor of my (our) State or the Governor's designated representative in conjunction with the State's processing of my (our) application for assistance under the Individual and Family Grant Program that is available in certain major disaster areas declared by the President.

Business Name

_____ By _____
Date   Name and Title

Proprietor, Partners, Principals and Guarantors

_____
Date   Signature

_____
Date   Signature

_____
Date   Signature

_____
Date   Signature

SBA Form 1261 (12-86) U.S. Government Printing Office:

OMB Approval No. 3245–0016
Expiration Date 10–31–87

U.S. Small Business Administration
Summary of Collateral
OFFERED BY APPLICANT AS SECURITY FOR LOAN AND SBA APPRAISER'S VALUATION REPORT

	EMPLOYER ID NO.
Name and Address of Applicant: (Include Zip Code) _____	
	SBA LOAN NO.

IMPORTANT INSTRUCTIONS FOR PREPARING THE LISTING OF
COLLATERAL OFFERED AS SECURITY FOR LOAN

Page 1. Summary Of Collateral Offered By Applicant As Security For The Loan: This is a summarization of the detailed listing on SBA Form 4, Schedule A. If collateral is to be acquired, with proceeds of loan describe the collateral in detail *on an attachment* to Schedule A with the notation "To be acquired".

Show exact cost. If assets were acquired from a predecessor company at a price other than cost less depreciation.

The figures to be entered in the net book value column must agree with the figures shown in the balance sheet, on page 2 of the application, except for the assets, if any, not being offered as collateral and non-business assets, if any, which are being offered to secure guarantees.

If a recent appraisal has been made of the collateral offered, it should be submitted with the application.

Any leases on land and buildings must be described, giving date and term of lease, rental, name and address of owner.

Page 2. Real Estate:

Item 1 - Land And Improvements: (a) legal description from deed on the land - location - city where deed is recorded. Book and page numbers of Official Records. Describe the land improvements such as paving, utilities, fence, etc. (b) cost of land when purchased.

Item 2 - Buildings: (a) general description, describe each building or structure on the land. Include size, type of construction, number of stories, date erected, use and condition. (b) amount of taxes and the assessed value from tax bills. (c) total amount of income received by owner from rental of the described property. (d) cost of building when purchased.

INADEQUATE OR POORLY PREPARED LOAN APPLICATION AND LISTING OF COLLATERAL ON PAGE 3 WILL CAUSE DELAY IN THE PROCESSING OF LOAN APPLICATIONS.

Page 3 - It is most **IMPORTANT** that applicants make an **ACTUAL PHYSICAL INVENTORY OF THE EQUIPMENT** being offered as collateral. **DO NOT TAKE FROM BOOK RECORDS.** Actually list each in accordance with the classification, e.g.: 1. Machinery and Equipment; 2. Automotive Equipment; 3. Office furniture and equipment; 4. Other—jigs, dies, fixtures, airplanes, etc.

Page 4 - Is a continuation of Equipment being offered.

Group items in accordance with the above classifications

Show: manufacturer or make, model and serial numbers, size, year, whether purchased new, used, or rebuilt.
BE SURE ITEMS LISTED CAN BE **READILY INSPECTED** BY SBA APPRAISERS.

SUMMARY			
Item	Cost	Net Book Value	Not to be used by applicant
1. Land and land improvements			
2. Buildings			
3. Machinery and Equipment			
4. Automotive Equipment			
5. Office furniture and equipment			
6. Other			
7. Total			
8. Real and chattel mortgages (Not to be paid from SBA loan req.) Attach details	X X X X		
9. Equity	X X X X		
10. To be acquired (Cost)		X X X X	
11. Total			

THE APPRAISER CERTIFIES that he has personally and thoroughly inspected the collateral as listed in this Report. Furthermore, as of _____ the market values shown in the above Summary are fair and reasonable as of that date. Additional comments are attached to this Report.

SBA Appraiser's Signature _____   Date of Report

SBA Form 4 Schedule A (2-85) REF SOP 5010 previous editions are obsolete.

Real Estate

OFFERED BY APPLICANT AS SECURITY FOR LOAN AND SBA APPRAISER'S VALUATION REPORT

Name and Address of Applicant (include Zip Code) _____

Address of Realty Offered _____

Parcel number _____

SBA LOAN No.

Title data: ☐ Title Insurance ☐ Abstract
☐ Other (indicate)

Realty in name of _____

Recorded Book_____ Page_____ County_____

---

1. Land and land improvements (Do not include buildings - see Sec. 2 below)

Cost_____ date acquired_____

Legal description (Attach if too long) *

* If available, attach plat survey.

---

2. Improvements   Cost (If separate from land) $_____

Building description: List each building separately with brief description and dimensions.

Income if Applicable.

Rent $_____ Month ☐ Annually ☐ Lease ☐ _____ Term.

Assessed Value	
Land	_____
Improvements	_____
Taxes	_____

SBA Form 4 Schedule A (2-85) REF SOP 5010 previous editions are obsolete.

Personal Property (Chattels)

OFFERED BY APPLICANT AS SECURITY FOR LOAN AND SBA APPRAISER'S VALUATION REPORT

The following described chattels are located or headquartered at (include Zip Code) ————	EMPLOYER ID NO.
Above location is owned ( ) leased ( )	SBA LOAN NO.

It is most **IMPORTANT** that applicants make an **ACTUAL PHYSICAL INVENTORY OF THE EQUIPMENT** being offered as collateral. **DO NOT TAKE FROM BOOK RECORDS.** Actually list each item in accordance with the classification, e.g.:* 1. Machinery and Equipment 2. Automotive Equipment 3. Office furniture and equipment 4. Other - jigs, dies, fixtures, airplanes, etc.

Show: manufacturer or make, model and serial numbers, size, year, whether purchased new, used or rebuilt.

List chattels at different locations on separate sheets. * Description of _____	Model	Serial Number	New Used Rebuilt	NOT TO BE USED BY APPLICANT	
				Cond.	Market Value
Carry Totals of Each Classification to Page 1 (Summary) Lines 3, 4, 5, and 6.				Total	

INADEQUATE OR POORLY PREPARED LOAN APPLICATION AND LISTING OF COLLATERAL WILL CAUSE DELAY IN THE PROCESSING OF LOAN APPLICATIONS. BE SURE ALL ITEMS CAN BE READILY INSPECTED BY SBA APPRAISER.

I, _____ _____
(Signature of owner, partner, or corporation officer)   (Title)

of the _____
(Name of Firm)

certify that the above machinery and equipment listing represents an *actual physical inventory* taken on (date) _____. Mark items (in column 2) with an asterisk if they are subject to conditional bills of sale or chattel mortgages the balance of which will not be paid off from an SBA loan. Carry total of such balances to line 8, page 1 (Summary).

SBA Form 4 Schedule A (2-85) REF SOP 5010 previous editions are obsolete.

SCHEDULE OF COLLATERAL

Exhibit A

Applicant	
Street Address	
City	State — Zip Code

LIST ALL COLLATERAL TO BE USED AS SECURITY FOR THIS LOAN

Section I—REAL ESTATE

Attach a copy of the deed(s) containing a full legal description of the land and show the location (street address) and city where the deed(s) is recorded. Following the address below, give a brief description of the improvements, such as size, type of construction, use, number of stories, and present condition (use additional sheet if more space is required).

LIST PARCELS OF REAL ESTATE					
Address	Year Acquired	Original Cost	Market Value	Amount of Lien	Name of Lienholder

Description(s):

SECTION II—PERSONAL PROPERTY

All items listed herein must show manufacturer or make, model, year, and serial number. Items with no serial number must be clearly identified (use additional sheet if more space is required).

Description - Show Manufacturer, Model, Serial No.	Year Acquired	Original Cost	Market Value	Current Lien Balance	Name of Lienholder

All information contained herein is TRUE and CORRECT to the best of my knowledge. I understand that FALSE statements may result in forfeiture of benefits and possible fine and prosecution by the U.S. Attorney General (Ref. 18 U.S.C. 100).

_____ Date _____

_____ Date _____

Revised March 18, 1987

LENDER'S CHECKLIST FOR SBA APPLICATIONS

Submission of all applicable items included in this checklist will enable SBA to process your application expeditiously. The application, SBA Forms 4 and 4-I, must be fully completed. We do not start processing a loan request until we are in receipt of all required information. Taking short cuts and not complying with this request may result in your application being returned or withdrawn, and in extensive processing delays.

Be sure that the applicant(s) sign and date all documents, financial statements, and tax returns.

Why risk a two to four week processing delay for the one hour it may take to make a final review of the application package and complete this checklist?

Lenders and packagers ARE TO ASSEMBLE the information in the loan application packages IN THE ORDER PRESENTED IN THIS CHECKLIST. DO NOT USE FANCY BINDERS OR COVERS AS WE MUST REMOVE AND DISCARD THEM.

We are requesting that this completed checklist be submitted with each loan application. This procedure is being implemented in the interest of reducing our processing time and better serving you and your customers.

	YES	NO	N/A

A. APPLICATION AND RELATED ATTACHMENTS:

1. BANK TRANSMITTAL LETTER   ___ ___ ___

2. LENDER'S APPLICATION (FORM 4-I) is fully completed, signed and dated.   ___ ___ ___

   a. Lender has completed the pro-forma Balance Sheet on the reverse of the 4-I.   ___ ___ ___

   b. Lender has completed the Profit & Loss section on the reverse of the 4-I.   ___ ___ ___

   c. Lender has completed pro-forma schedule of Fixed Obligation section.   ___ ___ ___

   d. Lender has provided comments on:

       - Balance Sheet and ratio analysis
       - Repayment ability analysis
       - Management skills analysis
       - Collateral analysis
       - Lender's credit experience with applicant
       - Schedule of insurance requirements
       - Standby Agreements and other requirements

                             ___ ___ ___

3. Lender has submitted a copy of its CREDIT MEMORANDUM.   ___ ___ ___

4. Lender has submitted a copy of its TERM LOAN AGREEMENT.   ___ ___ ___

5. APPLICATION, SBA FORM 4, is completed and signed by applicant
    and preparer/packager. Items 8, 9, and 10 of the form's
    checklist are responded to and appropriate boxes are checked.   ___ ___ ___

6. SBA FORM 912, STATEMENT OF PERSONAL HISTORY, is submitted by
    proprietors, partners, officers, and directors regardless of
    ownership and by shareholders owning 20% or more of the
    stock.   ___ ___ ___

    a. All SBA Forms 912 are signed and dated.   ___ ___ ___

    b. Thorough explanations are provided for each Form 912 where
        questions 6, 7, or 8 are answered yes.   ___ ___ ___

    c. Lender has noted & initialed on the form the date that
        Form 912 was forwarded to SBA's Office of Investigations
        the initials of the sender.   ___ ___ ___

    d. For non-citizens, verification of current alien
        registration status is provided.   ___ ___ ___

NOTE: Applicants who are not U.S. citizens, or who answer yes to questions 6, 7, or 8,
        (although they may be eligible for the loan) cannot be considered under the CLP
        or PLP procedures.

7. Lender has submitted a SCHEDULE DETAILING THE USE OF LOAN
    PROCEEDS. (If not included in its credit memorandum).   ___ ___ ___

8. Applicant has submitted a brief HISTORY OF THE BUSINESS and
    expected loan benefits.   ___ ___ ___

9. Applicant has provided RESUMES FROM THE PRINCIPALS and
    management staff.   ___ ___ ___

10. Lender has submitted CREDIT REPORT AND/OR D&B REPORT on the
    applicant entity and its principals.   ___ ___ ___

B. FINANCIAL INFORMATION:

11. SBA FORM 413, PERSONAL FINANCIAL STATEMENT, is submitted for
    each proprietor, stockholder holding 20% or more of stock,
    each partner, and each officer, for the applicable form of
    entity.   ___ ___ ___

2

a. Form 413 is signed and dated and prepared within 90 days of the application date.   ___ ___ ___

b. All sections of Form 413 are completed in detail.   ___ ___ ___

c. Section 4 of Form 413 is provided for each parcel of real estate owned. (Xerox this section for additional real estate holdings).   ___ ___ ___

d. Form 413 is provided for co-signers and/or guarantors.   ___ ___ ___

e. Personal resources have been used according to the rules of SOP 50 10 paragraph 4(d). Resources available to be used in lieu of the loan are less than $50,000 per family (or 25% of the loan, whichever is greater).   ___ ___ ___

NOTE: ALL FINANCIAL INFORMATION must be prepared in accordance with generally accepted accounting principles. Home-made or in-house prepared financial data that make little or no sense WILL NOT BE ACCEPTED.

AFFILIATES: The same financial information required from the applicant entity will be required from all affiliates.

SBA'S DEFINITION OF AN AFFILIATE is a company that has common ownership, common management, and in some instances, contractual relationship with the applicant company.

12. A one year detailed PROFIT AND LOSS PROJECTION is provided (if repayment is not clearly evident from historical profit results) with a NARRATIVE STATEMENT supporting projected results.   ___ ___ ___

13. Applicant has provided a BALANCE SHEET AND PROFIT & LOSS STATEMENT for the current interim period dated within 90 days of the application.   ___ ___ ___

a. These financial statements are signed and dated by a principal of the company.   ___ ___ ___

14. A SCHEDULE OF ALL BUSINESS TERM DEBT AND/OR LEASES is provided. Term debt totals agree with amounts shown in the current interim period Balance Sheet. (This schedule is signed and dated by the applicant).   ___ ___ ___

NOTE: SBA Form 4 has a debt schedule section; another format may be used, but MUST include the same information on each loan as asked for in the Form 4 schedule.

15. AGING OF ACCOUNTS RECEIVABLE AND ACCOUNTS PAYABLE is provided. Totals agree with amounts shown in the current interim period financial statement.   ___ ___ ___

3

16. A BALANCE SHEET AND PROFIT & LOSS STATEMENT for the last 3 years is provided on the business.   ___ ___ ___

    a. The financial statements are signed and dated by an authorized principal of the company.   ___ ___ ___

17. Copies of the COMPANY'S FEDERAL INCOME TAX RETURNS including all schedules for the last three years are provided. State tax returns are usually duplicative, and should NOT be included.   ___ ___ ___

    a. These tax returns are signed and dated by a principal of the company.   ___ ___ ___

18. A RECONCILIATION OF THE BUSINESS NET WORTH is provided. (A separate schedule if reconciliation is not evident from financial statements).   ___ ___ ___

C. BUSINESS ACQUISITION:

19. COPY OF BUY-SELL AGREEMENT.   ___ ___ ___

20. COPY OF ESCROW INSTRUCTIONS.   ___ ___ ___

21. CURRENT BALANCE SHEET AND PROFIT & LOSS STATEMENT from seller dated within 90 days of the application date. (Signed and dated by the seller).   ___ ___ ___

22. Copies of the company's COMPLETE FEDERAL INCOME TAX RETURNS including all schedules for the past three years from the seller for the business being purchased. (Signed and dated by the seller).   ___ ___ ___

D. MISCELLANEOUS ITEMS:

23. ARTICLES OF INCORPORATION AND BY-LAWS.   ___ ___ ___

24. CERTIFICATE OF CORPORATION IN GOOD STANDING.   ___ ___ ___

25. COMPLETE LIST OF STOCKHOLDERS OR PARTNERS SHOWING PERCENTAGE OF OWNERSHIP OF EACH. (Company's total ownership must be disclosed). For "Alter Ego" loans, copies of stock certificates are also provided for all shares issued and outstanding.   ___ ___ ___

26. PARTNERSHIP AGREEMENTS, if applicable.   ___ ___ ___

27. SCHEDULE OF FIXED ASSETS to be acquired with loan proceeds.   ___ ___ ___

28. Provide REAL ESTATE APPRAISALS for all commercial real estate being acquired with loan proceeds or being used as collateral. Real estate appraisals on residential property to be provided as necessary. ___ ___ ___

29. If applicant is a Franchise, a COPY OF THE FRANCHISE AGREEMENT AND FEDERAL TRADE COMMISSION DISCLOSURE REPORT on the Franchisor should be forwarded to SBA, IN ADVANCE, for legal review. ___ ___ ___

30. COPY OF EXISTING LEASE(S) AND/OR LEASE(S) TO BE ACQUIRED. ___ ___ ___

31. EMPLOYER'S ID NUMBER FROM IRS. ___ ___ ___

32. STANDARD INDUSTRIAL CLASSIFICATION (SIC) CODES. ___ ___ ___

33. IF A NEW BUSINESS, clearly describe the equity capital contribution of the applicant. SBA normally requires a 30% to 50% equity injection for a new business. ___ ___ ___

34. SBA FORM 1261, STATEMENTS REQUIRED BY LAWS AND EXECUTIVE ORDERS. ___ ___ ___

35. SBA FORM 159, COMPENSATION AGREEMENT, is submitted and appropriately signed by packager/representative, applicant, and Bank. ___ ___ ___

    a. A detailed itemization of charges is provided if representatives fee exceeds $300.00. ___ ___ ___

36. Copies of COMPLETE FEDERAL INCOME TAX RETURNS, including all schedules, for the last three years are provided by each principal. ___ ___ ___

    a. PERSONAL TAX RETURNS are signed and dated by the principals. ___ ___ ___

37. SBA FORM 641, REQUEST FOR COUNSELING, is submitted and appropriately signed by applicant. ___ ___ ___

E. CONSTRUCTION, INCLUDING LEASEHOLD IMPROVEMENTS:

38. If loan proceeds are for construction, remodeling, or leasehold improvements, and the cost will exceed $25,000, this office will generally require the following:

    a. Applicant and Contractor must enter into a contract specifying A FIRM FIXED PRICE. ___ ___ ___

b. Contractor must furnish a 100% PERFORMANCE AND PAYMENT BOND. NO EXCEPTIONS without prior SBA approval.   ___ ___ ___

c. FINAL PLANS AND SPEC'S must be submitted to the Lender for final review and approval.   ___ ___ ___

d. Lender to provide for adequate supervision, periodic inspections, and certification of the work to be performed.   ___ ___ ___

e. Lender and applicant TO BE RESPONSIBLE for all cost over-runs resulting from failure to accomplish the above safeguards.   ___ ___ ___

f. Submit SBA FORM 601 AGREEMENT OF COMPLIANCE, for construction projects over $10,000.   ___ ___ ___

g. Where other real estate collateral is inadequate to secure a loan for leasehold improvements, an Assignment of Lease will generally be required.   ___ ___ ___

This checklist completed by:

_____
Lender Representative

_____
Title

_____
Date

United States of America

SMALL BUSINESS ADMINISTRATION

STATEMENT OF PERSONAL HISTORY

Please Read Carefully - Print or Type

Each member of the small business concern requesting assistance or the development company must submit this form in TRIPLICATE for filing with the SBA application. This form must be filled out and submitted by:

1. If a sole proprietorship by the proprietor.
2. If a partnership by each partner.
3. If a corporation or a development company, by each officer, director, and additionally by each holder of 20% or more of the voting stock.
4. Any other person including a hired manager, who has authority to speak for and commit the borrower in the management of the business.

Name and Address of Applicant (Firm Name) (Street, City, State and ZIP Code)	SBA District Office and City
	Amount Applied for:

1. Personal Statement of: (State name in full, if no middle name, state (NMN), or if initial only, indicate initial). List all former names used, and dates each name was used. Use separate sheet if necessary.

First   Middle   Last

2. Date of Birth: (Month, day and year)

3. Place of Birth: (City & State or Foreign Country).

U.S. Citizen? ☐ YES ☐ NO
If no, give alien registration number:
#

4. Give the percentage of ownership or stock owned or to be owned in the small business concern or the Development Company.

Social Security No.

5. Present residence address:

From: To: Address: City   State

Home Telephone No. (Include A/C):   Business Telephone No. (Include A/C):

Immediate past residence address:

From: To: Address:

BE SURE TO ANSWER THE NEXT 3 QUESTIONS CORRECTLY BECAUSE THEY ARE IMPORTANT.

THE FACT THAT YOU HAVE AN ARREST OR CONVICTION RECORD WILL NOT NECESSARILY DISQUALIFY YOU. BUT AN INCORRECT ANSWER WILL PROBABLY CAUSE YOUR APPLICATION TO BE TURNED DOWN.

6. Are you presently under indictment, on parole or probation?

☐ Yes ☐ No   If yes, furnish details in a separate exhibit. List name(s) under which held, if applicable.

7. Have you ever been charged with or arrested for any criminal offense other than a minor motor vehicle violation?

☐ Yes ☐ No   If yes, furnish details in a separate exhibit. List name(s) under which charged, if applicable.

8. Have you ever been convicted of any criminal offense other than a minor motor vehicle violation?

☐ Yes ☐ No   If yes, furnish details in a separate exhibit. List name(s) under which convicted, if applicable.

9. Name and address of participating bank

The information on this form will be used in connection with an investigation of your character. Any information you wish to submit, that you feel will expedite this investigation should be set forth.

Whoever makes any statement knowing it to be false, for the purpose of obtaining for himself or for any applicant, any loan, or loan extension by renewal, deferment or otherwise, or for the purpose of obtaining, or influencing SBA toward, anything of value under the Small Business Act, as amended, shall be punished under Section 16(a) of that Act, by a fine of not more than $5000, or by imprisonment for not more than 2 years, or both.

Signature	Title	Date

It is against SBA's policy to provide assistance to persons not of good character and therefore consideration is given to the qualities and personality traits of a person, favorable and unfavorable, relating thereto, including behavior, integrity, candor and disposition toward criminal actions. It is also against SBA's policy to provide assistance not in the best interests of the United States, for example, if there is reason to believe that the effect of such assistance will be to encourage or support, directly or indirectly, activities inimical to the Security of the United States. Anyone concerned with the collection of this information, as to its voluntariness, disclosure or routine uses may contact the FOIA Office, 1441 "L" Street, N.W., and a copy of §9 "Agency Collection of Information" from SOP 40 04 will be provided.

SBA FORM 912 (5-87) SOP 9020 USE 6-85 EDITION UNTIL EXHAUSTED   **1. SBA FILE COPY**

Exhibit 12-2

OMB Approval No. 3245-0188
Exp. Date: 10-31-89

PERSONAL FINANCIAL STATEMENT
As of _____ 19 _____

Complete this form if 1) a sole proprietorship by the proprietor; 2) a partnership by each partner; 3) a corporation by each officer and each stockholder with 20% or more ownership; 4) any other person or entity providing a guaranty on the loan.

Name	Residence Phone

Residence Address

City, State, & Zip

Business Name of Applicant/Borrower

ASSETS (Omit Cents)	LIABILITIES (Omit Cents)
Cash on hand & in Banks.................$_____	Accounts Payable.......................$_____
Savings Accounts......................... _____	Notes Payable (to Bk & Others
IRA.................................. _____	(Describe in Section 2).................. _____
Accounts & Notes Receivable	Installment Account (Auto)_____
(Describe in Section 6)................ _____	Mo. Payments $_____
Life Insurance—Cash	Installment Account (Other) _____
Surrender Value Only.................. _____	Mo. Payments $ _____
Stocks and Bonds	Loans on Life Insurance.................. _____
(Describe in Section 3)................ _____	Mortgages on Real Estate.................
Real Estate	(Describe in Section 4).................. _____
(Describe in Section 4)................ _____	Unpaid Taxes
Automobile—Present Value............... _____	(Describe in Section 7).................. _____
Other Personal Property..................	Other Liabilities
(Describe in Section 5)................ _____	(Describe in Section 8).................. _____
Other Assets..........................	
(Describe in Section 6)................ _____	Total Liabilities.......................... _____
	Net Worth............................. _____
Total........................$_____	Total..........................$_____

Section 1. Source of Income	Contingent Liabilities
Salary........................ $_____	As Endorser or Co-Maker.........................$_____
Net Investment Income............. _____	Legal Claims & Judgments........................... _____
Real Estate Income............... _____	Provision for Fed Income Tax....................... _____
Other Income (Describe)*.......... _____	Other Special Debt................................ _____

Description of Items Listed in Section I _____

*(Alimony or child support payments need not be disclosed in "Other Income" unless it is desired to have such payments counted toward total income.)

Section 2. Notes Payable to Banks and Others

Name & Address of Noteholder	Original Balance	Current Balance	Payment Amount	Terms (Monthly-etc.)	How Secured or Endorsed—Type of Collateral

SBA Form 413 (10-87)   Use 10-86 edition until exhausted   Refer to SOP 50   10

(Response is required to obtain a benefit)

Licensee	License Number	Private Capital	SBA Leverage	Investment Policy	Owner Code

Alabama

First SBIC of
  Alabama   04/04-0143   2,166,700   6,500,000   Diversified   5
David Delaney, President
16 Midtown Park East
Mobile, AL 36606
(205)476-0700   Date Lic: 07/20/78

Hickory Venture   04/04-0235   8,000,000   0   Diversified   1
  Capital Corporation
J. Thomas Noojin, President
699 Gallatin Street, Suite A-2
Huntsville, AL 35801
(205)539-1931   Date Lic: 03/28/85

Remington Fund,   04/04-0238   3,000,100   0   Diversified   5
  Inc. (The)
Lana Sellers, President
1927 First Avenue North
Birmingham, AL 35202
(205)324-7709   Date Lic: 05/16/86

Alaska

Alaska Business   10/10-0180   2,500,000   0   Diversified   1
  Investment Corp.
James Cloud, Vice President
301 West Northern Lights Blvd.
Mail: P.O. Box 100600; Anchorage 99510
Anchorage, AK 99510
(907)278-2071   Date Lic: 12/10/82

Arizona

Northwest Venture
  Partners
(Main Office: Minneapolis, MN)
88777 E. Via de Ventura
Suite 335
Scottsdale, AZ 85258
(602)483-8940

Norwest Growth Fund,
  Inc.
(Main Office: Minneapolis, MN)
88777 E. Via de Ventura
Suite 335
Scottsdale, AZ 85258
(602)483-8940

3

Exhibit 12-3

Licensee	License Number	Private Capital	SBA Leverage	Investment Policy	Owner Code

Arizona (Cont)

Rocky Mountain Equity   09/09-0289   600,000   500,000   Diversified   5
  Corporation
Anthony J. Nicoli, President
4530 Central Avenue
Phoenix, AZ 85012
(602)274-7534   Date Lic: 09/22/81

Valley National   09/09-0337   15,000,000   0   Diversified   1
  Investors, Inc.
Harley Barnes, President
201 North Central Avenue, Suite 900
Phoenix, AZ 85004
(602)261-1577   Date Lic: 04/04/84

Wilbur Venture   09/09-0372   1,000,000   0   Diversified   5
  Capital Corp.
Jerry F. Wilbur, President
4575 South Palo Verde, Suite 305
Tucson, AZ 85714
(602)747-5999   Date Lic: 05/11/87

Arkansas

Independence Financial 06/06-0257   500,100   0   Diversified   5
  Services, Inc.
Jeffrey Hance, General Manager
Town Plaza Office Park
Mail: P.O. Box 3878
Batesville, AR 72501
(501)793-4533   Date Lic: 10/26/82

Small Business   06/06-0175   1,150,000   3,250,000   Grocery Stores   4
  Inv. Capital, Inc.
Charles E. Toland, President
10003 New Benton Hwy.
Mail: P.O. Box 3627
Little Rock, AR 72203
(501)455-3590   Date Lic: 03/06/75

California

AMF Financial, Inc.   09/09-0302   626,000   0   Diversified   5
William Temple, Vice President
4330 La Jolla Village Drive
Suite 110
San Diego, CA 92122
(619)546-0167   Date Lic: 10/26/82

Licensee	License Number	Private Capital	SBA Leverage	Investment Policy	Owner Code

California (Cont)

Atalanta Investment
  Company, Inc.
(Main Office: New York, NY)
141 El Camino Drive
Beverly Hills, CA 90212
(213)273-1730

BNP Venture Capital Corporation	09/09-0348	1,550,000	0	Diversified	1

Edgerton Scott II, President
3000 Sand Hill Road
Building 1, Suite 125
Menlo Park, CA 94025
(415)854-1084 Date Lic: 10/12/84

Bancorp Venture Capital, Inc.	09/09-0335	2,250,000	2,250,000	Diversified	1

Arthur H. Bernstein, President
11812 San Vicente Boulevard
Los Angeles, CA 90049
(213)820-7222 Date Lic: 05/04/84

BankAmerica Ventures, Inc.	09/12-0007	22,500,000	0	45% Major Groups 26 & 38	1

Patrick Topolski, President
555 California Street
San Francisco, CA 94104
(415)953-3001 Date Lic: 11/12/59

CFB Venture Capital Corporation	09/09-0319	1,000,000	0	Diversified	1

Richard J. Roncaglia, Vice President
530 B. Street, Third Floor
San Diego, CA 92101
(619)230-3304 Date Lic: 08/30/83

CFB Venture Capital
  Corporation
(Main Office: San Diego, CA)
350 California Street, Mezzanine
San Francisco, CA 94104
(415)445-0594

California Capital Investors, Ltd.	09/09-0292	2,525,759	4,000,000	Diversified	5-P

Arthur H. Bernstein, Managing G.P.
11812 San Vincente Blvd.
Los Angeles, CA 90049
(213)820-7222 Date Lic: 09/25/81

Licensee	License Number	Private Capital	SBA Leverage	Investment Policy	Owner Code

Citicorp Venture
   Capital, Ltd.
(Main Office: New York, NY)
2 Embarcadero Place
2200 Geny Road, Suite 203
Palo Alto, CA 94303
(415)424-8000

| City Ventures, Inc. | 09/09-0308 | 2,000,000 | 0 | Diversified | 1 |

Warner Heineman, Vice Chairman
400 N. Roxbury Drive
Beverly Hills, CA 90210
(213)550-5709 Date Lic: 06/04/82

| Crosspoint Investment | 09/09-0245 | 667,500 | 600,000 | Diversified | 3 |

   Corporation
Max Simpson, Pres. & Chief F.O.
1951 Landings Drive
Mountain View, CA 94043
(415)968-0930 Date Lic: 09/26/79

| Developers Equity | 09/14-0079 | 677,000 | 1,010,000 | 100% Real Estate | 5 |

   Capital Corporation
Larry Sade, Chairman of the Board
1880 Century Park East
Suite 311
Los Angeles, CA 90067
(213)277-0330 Date Lic: 06/12/74

| Draper Associates, | 09/09-0242 | 2,015,000 | 4,000,000 | Diversified | 5-P |

   a California LP
Bill Edwards, President
c/o Timothy C. Draper
3000 Sand Hill Road, Bldg. 4, #235
Menlo Park, CA 94025
(415)854-1712 Date Lic: 09/12/79

| First Interstate | 09/09-0224 | 15,000,000 | 0 | Diversified | 1 |

   Capital, Inc.
Ronald J. Hall, Managing Director
5000 Birch Street, Suite 10100
Newport Beach, CA 92660
(714)253-4360 Date Lic: 07/05/78

| First SBIC of | 09/14-0009 | 25,000,000 | 0 | Diversified | 1 |

   California
Tim Hay, President
650 Town Center Drive
Seventeenth Floor
Costa Mesa, CA 92626
(714)556-1964 Date Lic: 01/29/60

Licensee	License Number	Private Capital	SBA Leverage	Investment Policy	Owner Code

California (Cont)

First SBIC of
  California
(Main Office: Costa Mesa, CA)
155 North Lake Avenue, Suite 1010
Pasadena, CA 91109
(818)304-3451

First SBIC of
  California
(Main Office: Costa Mesa, CA)
5 Palo Alto Square, Suite 938
Palo Alto, CA 94306
(415)424-8011

G C & H Partners James C. Gaither, General Partner One Maritime Plaza, 20th Floor San Francisco, CA 94110 (415)981-5252 Date Lic: 04/30/84	09/09-0342	1,287,176	700,000	Diversified	5-P
HMS Capital, Ltd. Michael Hone, President 555 California Street, Room 5070 San Francisco, CA 94109 (415)221-1225 Date Lic: 12/06/83	09/09-0301	1,657,000	0	Diversified	5
Hamco Capital Corp. William R. Hambrecht, President 235 Montgomery Street San Francisco, CA 94104 (415)986-6567 Date Lic: 03/01/82	09/09-0300	3,990,238	11,000,000	Diversified	5
Imperial Ventures, Inc. H. Wayne Snavely, President 9920 South Lacienega Blvd. Mail: P.O. Box 92991; L.A. 90009 Inglewood, CA 90301 (213)417-5888 Date Lic: 08/31/78	09/09-0203	3,001,781	0	Diversified	1
Ivanhoe Venture Capital, Ltd. Alan Toffler, General Partner 737 Pearl Street, Suite 201 LaJolla, CA 92037 (619)454-8882 Date Lic: 12/29/82	09/09-0314	629,061	1,100,000	Diversified	5

Licensee	License Number	Private Capital	SBA Leverage	Investment Policy	Owner Code

California (Cont)

Jupiter Partners
09/12-0079 3,253,720 4,500,000 50% Major Group 36 5-P
John M. Bryan, President
600 Montgomery Street
35th Floor
San Francisco, CA 94111
(415)421-9990 Date Lic: 10/26/62

Latigo Capital
Partners, II
09/09-0357 1,015,000 1,000,000 Diversified 5
Robert A. Peterson, General Partner
1015 Gayley Avenue, Suite 202
Los Angeles, CA 90024
(218)208-3892 Date Lic: 09/20/85

Marwit Capital Corp.
09/02-0175 1,031,178 2,000,000 Diversified 5
Martin W. Witte, President
180 Newport Center Drive
Suite 200
Newport Beach, CA 92660
(714)640-6234 Date Lic: 05/03/62

Merrill Pickard
Anderson & Eyre I
09/09-0271 28,083,735 0 Diversified 1-P
Steven L. Merrill, President
Two Palo Alto Square, Suite 425
Palo Alto, CA 94306
(415)856-8880 Date Lic: 11/26/80

Metropolitan Venture
Company, Inc.
09/09-0293 1,000,000 1,000,000 Diversified 5
Rudolph J. Lowy, Chairman of the Board
5757 Wilshire Blvd.
Suite 670
Los Angeles, CA 90036
(213)938-3488 Date Lic: 09/30/81

Nelson Capital Corp.
(Main Office: Garden City, NY)
10000 Santa Monica Blvd., Suite 300
Los Angeles, CA 90067
(213)556-1944

New West Partners II
09/09-0373 1,003,123 1,000,000 Diversified 5
Timothy P. Haidinger, Manager
4350 Executive Drive, Suite 206
San Diego, CA 92121
(619)457-0723 Date Lic: 02/17/87

8

Licensee	License Number	Private Capital	SBA Leverage	Investment Policy	Owner Code

New West Partners II
(Main Office: San Diego, CA)
4600 Campus Drive, Suite 103
Newport Beach, CA 92660
(714)756-8940

PBC Venture Capital Inc. Henry L. Wheeler, Manager 1408 - 18th Street Mail: P.O. Box 6008; Bakersfield 93386 Bakersfield, CA 93301 (805)395-3555 Date Lic: 09/28/80	09/09-0266	550,000	0	Diversified	1
Peerless Capital Company, Inc. Robert W. Lautz, Jr., President 675 South Arroyo Parkway Suite 320 Pasadena, CA 91105 (818)577-9199 Date Lic: 07/11/86	09/09-0368	1,000,000	0	Diversified	5
Ritter Partners William C. Edwards, President 150 Isabella Avenue Atherton, CA 94025 (415)854-1555 Date Lic: 10/18/62	09/12-0075	3,228,802	4,500,000	50% Major Group 36	5-P
Round Table Capital Corporation Richard Dumke, President 655 Montgomery Street, Suite 700 San Francisco, CA 94111 (415)392-7500 Date Lic: 04/28/80	09/09-0262	900,000	2,700,000	Diversified	5
San Joaquin Capital Corporation Chester Troudy, President 1415 18th Street, Suite 306 Mail: P.O. Box 2538 Bakersfield, CA 93301 (805)323-7581 Date Lic: 05/11/62	09/14-0037	1,086,971	3,235,000	Diversified	5
Seaport Ventures, Inc. Michael Stopler, President 525 B Street, Suite 630 San Diego, CA 92101 (619)232-4069 Date Lic: 11/22/82	09/09-0311	1,355,452	2,000,000	Diversified	5

Licensee	License Number	Private Capital	SBA Leverage	Investment Policy	Owner Code

California (Cont)

Union Venture Corp.   09/12-0145 23,550,000   0   Diversified   1
Jeffrey Watts, President
445 South Figueroa Street
Los Angeles, CA 90071
(213)236-4092 Date Lic: 09/30/67

VK Capital Company   09/09-0365 1,050,505   500,000   Diversified   5-P
Franklin Van Kasper, General Partner
50 California Street, Suite 2350
San Francisco, CA 94111
(415)391-5600 Date Lic: 02/07/86

Vista Capital Corp.   09/09-0310   568,501   0   Diversified   5
Frederick J. Howden, Jr., Chairman
5080 Shoreham Place, Suite 202
San Diego, CA 92122
(619)453-0780 Date Lic: 02/02/83

Walden Capital   09/09-0175 1,294,227 3,350,000   Diversified   2-P
  Partners
Arthur S. Berliner, President
750 Battery Street, Seventh Floor
San Francisco, CA 94111
(415)391-7225 Date Lic: 12/17/74

Westamco Investment   09/14-0024   800,000   0   66-2/3% Real   4
  Company   Estate
Leonard G. Muskin, President
8929 Wilshire Blvd., Suite 400
Beverly Hills, CA 90211
(213)652-8288 Date Lic: 07/24/61

Colorado

Associated Capital   08/08-0039 2,125,000 2,250,000   Grocery Stores   4
  Corporation
Rodney J. Love, President
4891 Independence Street, Suite 201
Wheat Ridge, CO 80033
(303)420-8155 Date Lic: 11/16/76

UBD Capital, Inc.   08/08-0146 2,000,000   0   Diversified   1
Allan R. Haworth, President
1700 Broadway
Denver, CO 80274
(303)863-6329 Date Lic: 10/23/85

Licensee	License Number	Private Capital	SBA Leverage	Investment Policy	Owner Code
Connecticut					
AB SBIC, Inc. Adam J. Bozzuto, President 275 School House Road Cheshire, CT 06410 (203)272-0203 Date Lic: 11/17/76	01/01-0280	500,000	1,000,000	Grocery Stores	4
All State Venture Capital Corporation Ceasar N. Anquillare, President The Bishop House 32 Elm Street, P.O. Box 1629 New Haven, CT 06506 (203)787-5029 Date Lic: 11/02/62	01/02-0215	1,000,000	0	Diversified	6
Capital Impact Corp. William D. Starbuck, President 961 Main Street Bridgeport, CT 06601 (203)384-5670 Date Lic: 03/01/85	01/01-0335	7,216,171	9,000,000	Diversified	1
Capital Resource Co. of Connecticut I. Martin Fierberg, Managing Partner 699 Bloomfield Avenue Bloomfield, CT 06002 (203)243-1114 Date Lic: 03/23/77	01/01-0285	976,365	2,845,000	Diversified	5-P
Dewey Investment Corp. George E. Mrosek, President 101 Middle Turnpike West Manchester, CT 06040 (203)649-0654 Date Lic: 04/09/62	01/02-0145	510,650	910,000	Diversified	5
First Connecticut SBIC David Engelson, President 177 State Street Bridgeport, CT 06604 (203)366-4726 Date Lic: 05/06/60	01/02-0013	9,402,322	25,850,000	50% Real Estate	6
First New England Capital, LP Richard C. Klaffky, President 255 Main Street Hartford, CT 06106 (203)249-4321 Date Lic: 03/25/88	01/01-0344	5,000,000	0	Diversified	2-P

Licensee	License Number	Private Capital	SBA Leverage	Investment Policy	Owner Code
Connecticut (Cont)					
Marcon Capital Corp. Martin A. Cohen, President 49 Riverside Avenue Westport, CT 06880 (203)226-6893 Date Lic: 10/23/75	01/01-0277	776,550	2,250,000	Diversified	4
Northeastern Capital Corporation Joseph V. Ciaburri, Chairman and CEO 209 Church Street New Haven, CT 06510 (203)865-4500 Date Lic: 03/08/61	01/02-0062	588,951	700,000	Diversified	6
Regional Financial Enterprises, L.P. Robert M. Williams, Managing Partner 36 Grove Street New Canaan, CT 06840 (203)966-2800 Date Lic: 07/01/80	01/01-0307	10,107,679	13,000,000	Diversified	1-P
SBIC of Connecticut Inc. (The) Kenneth F. Zarrilli, President 1115 Main Street Bridgeport, CT 06603 (203)367-3282 Date Lic: 01/31/61	01/02-0052	617,160	1,250,000	Diversified	6
Delaware					
Morgan Investment Corporation William E. Pike, Chairman 902 Market Street Wilmington, DE 19801 (302)651-2500 Date Lic: 12/10/87	03/03-0185	30,000,000	0	Diversified	2
D.C.					
Allied Investment Corporation David J. Gladstone, President 1666 K Street, N.W., Suite 901 Washington, DC 20006 (202)331-1112 Date Lic: 12/23/59	03/04-0003	4,784,708	10,700,000	Diversified	6

Licensee	License Number	Private Capital	SBA Leverage	Investment Policy	Owner Code

D.C. (Cont)

American Security 03/03-0174 2,500,000 0 Diversified 1
Capital Corp., Inc.
William G. Tull, President
730 Fifteenth Street, N.W.
Washington, DC 20013
(202)624-4843 Date Lic: 08/13/84

DC Bancorp Venture 03/03-0178 1,500,000 0 Diversified 2
Capital Company
Allan A. Weissburg, President
1801 K Street, N.W.
Washington, DC 20006
(202)955-6970 Date Lic: 07/18/85

Washington Ventures, 03/03-0180 2,000,000 2,000,000 Diversified 1
Inc.
Kenneth A. Swain, President
1320 18th Street, N.W.
Suite 300
Washington, DC 20036
(202)895-2560 Date Lic: 12/03/86

Florida

Allied Investment
Corporation
(Main Office: Washington, DC)
Executive Office Center, Suite 305
2770 N. Indian River Blvd.
Vero Beach, FL 32960
(407)778-5556

Caribank Capital Corp 04/04-0213 1,500,000 4,000,000 Diversified 1
Michael E. Chaney, President
2400 East Commercial Boulevard
Suite 814
Fort Lauderdale, FL 33308
(305)776-1133 Date Lic: 07/07/82

First North Florida 04/05-0022 1,500,108 2,500,000 Grocery Stores 5
SBIC
J.B. Higdon, President
1400 Gadsden Street
P.O. Box 1021
Quincy, FL 32351
(904)875-2600 Date Lic: 12/17/60

13

Licensee	License Number	Private Capital	SBA Leverage	Investment Policy	Owner Code

Florida (Cont)

Gold Coast Capital Corporation
William I. Gold, President
3550 Biscayne Blvd., Room 601
Miami, FL 33137
(305)576-2012 Date Lic: 12/22/59

	04/05-0010	680,000	1,930,092	Diversified	5

J & D Capital Corp.
Jack Carmel, President
12747 Biscayne Blvd.
North Miami, FL 33181
(305)893-0303 Date Lic: 07/09/80

	04/04-0188	694,106	2,050,000	Diversified	5

Market Capital Corp.
E. E. Eads, President
1102 North 28th Street
P.O. Box 22667
Tampa, FL 33630
(813)247-1357 Date Lic: 03/24/64

	04/05-0086	786,000	1,800,000	Grocery Stores	4

Southeast Venture Capital Limited I
James R. Fitzsimons, Jr, President
3250 Miami Center
100 Chopin Plaza
Miami, FL 33131
(305)379-2005 Date Lic: 01/08/68

	04/05-0095	5,970,420	6,500,000	Diversified	1-P

Western Financial Capital Corporation
Dr. F. M. Rosemore, President
1380 N.E. Miami Gardens Drive
Suite 225
N. Miami Beach, FL 33179
(305)949-5900 Date Lic: 02/22/80

	04/04-0183	4,046,744	9,140,000	Medical	6

Georgia

Investor's Equity, Inc.
I. Walter Fisher, President
2629 First National Bank Tower
Atlanta, GA 30383
(404)523-3999 Date Lic: 08/10/61

	04/05-0018	3,083,000	0	Diversified	5

14

Licensee	License Number	Private Capital	SBA Leverage	Investment Policy	Owner Code

Georgia (Cont)

North Riverside 04/04-0230   3,010,500   8,400,000   Diversified   5
  Capital Corporation
Tom Barry, President
50 Technology Park/Atlanta
Norcross, GA 30092
(404)446-5556   Date Lic: 08/24/84

Hawaii

Bancorp Hawaii SBIC   09/09-0340   2,000,000   500,000   Diversified   1
James D. Evans, Jr., President
111 South King Street
Suite 1060
Honolulu, HI 96813
(808)521-6411   Date Lic: 02/17/84

Illinois

ANB Venture   05/05-0207   10,000,000   0   Diversified   1
  Corporation
Kurt L. Liljedahl, Exec. Vice-President
33 North LaSalle Street
Chicago, IL 60690
(312)855-1554   Date Lic: 09/11/87

Alpha Capital Venture   05/05-0191   4,867,307   0   Diversified   2-P
  Partners, L.P.
Andrew H. Kalnow, General Partner
Three First National Plaza, 14th Floor
Chicago, IL 60602
(312)372-1556   Date Lic: 04/23/84

Business Ventures,   05/05-0172   564,750   600,000   Diversified   5
  Incorporated
Milton Lefton, President
20 North Wacker Drive, Suite 550
Chicago, IL 60606
(312)346-1580   Date Lic: 10/31/83

Continental Illinois   05/07-0078   25,200,450   0   Diversified   1
  Venture Corp.
John L. Hines, President
209 South LaSalle Street
Mail: 231 South LaSalle Street
Chicago, IL 60693
(312)828-8023   Date Lic: 04/02/70

15

Licensee	License Number	Private Capital	SBA Leverage	Investment Policy	Owner Code
Illinois (Cont)					
First Capital Corp. of Chicago John A. Canning, Jr., President Three First National Plaza Suite 1330 Chicago, IL 60670 (312)732-5400 Date Lic: 06/08/61	05/07-0042	91,771,742	3,600,000	Diversified	1
Frontenac Capital Corporation David A. R. Dullum, President 208 South LaSalle Street, Room 1900 Chicago, IL 60604 (312)368-0047 Date Lic: 12/29/76	05/05-0114	6,245,622	3,600,000	Diversified	2
La Salle Street Capital Corporation Robert E. Koe, President 200 North La Salle Street 10th Floor Chicago, IL 60601 (312)621-7057 Date Lic: 09/19/80	05/02-0401	2,015,000	0	Diversified	5
Mesirow Capital Partners SBIC, Ltd. Lester A. Morris, General Partner 350 North Clark Street 3rd Floor Chicago, IL 60610 (312)670-6098 Date Lic: 07/07/82	05/05-0168	1,250,000	5,000,000	Diversified	5-P
Walnut Capital Corp. Burton W. Kanter, Chairman of the Board 208 South LaSalle Street Chicago, IL 60604 (312)346-2033 Date Lic: 11/07/83	05/02-0430	5,123,800	10,000,000	Diversified	5
Indiana					
1st Source Capital Corporation Eugene L. Cavanaugh, Jr., Vice President 100 North Michgan Street Mail: P.O: Box 1602; South Bend 46634 South Bend, IN 46601 (219)236-2180 Date Lic: 12/23/83	05/05-0194	1,800,000	0	Diversified	1

Licensee	License Number	Private Capital	SBA Leverage	Investment Policy	Owner Code
Indiana (Cont)					
Circle Ventures, Inc. Robert Salyers, President 2502 Roosevelt Avenue Indianapolis, IN 46218 (317)636-7242 Date Lic: 08/19/83	05/05-0171	1,000,000	0	Diversified	5
Equity Resource Company, Inc. Michael J. Hammes, Vice President One Plaza Place 202 South Michigan Street South Bend, IN 46601 (219)237-5255 Date Lic: 12/27/83	05/05-0193	2,000,000	0	Diversified	1
Raffensperger Hughes Venture Corp. Samuel B. Sutphin, President 20 North Meridian Street Indianapolis, IN 46204 (317)635-4551 Date Lic: 05/05/88	05/05-0209	1,050,000	0	Diversified	5
White River Capital Corporation Thomas D. Washburn, President 500 Washington Street Mail: P.O. Box 929 Columbus, IN 47201 (812)372-0111 Date Lic: 03/31/82	05/05-0165	1,048,000	0	Diversified	1
Iowa					
MorAmerica Capital Corporation Donald E. Flynn, President Suite 200, American Building Cedar Rapids, IA 52401 (319)363-8247 Date Lic: 09/30/59	07/07-0006	5,000,000	10,650,440	Diversified	3
Kansas					
Kansas Venture Capital, Inc. Larry J. High, President 1030 First National Bank Tower One Townsite Plaza Topeka, KS 66603 (913)235-3437 Date Lic: 06/17/77	07/07-0077	3,740,690	0	Diversified	3

Licensee	License Number	Private Capital	SBA Leverage	Investment Policy	Owner Code

Kentucky

Financial   04/04-0113   900,000   3,600,000   Diversified   4
  Opportunities, Inc.
Gary Duerr, Manager
6060 Dutchman's Lane
Mail: PO Box 35710; Louisville, KY 40232
Louisville, KY 40205
(502)451-3800   Date Lic: 10/17/74

Mountain Ventures,   04/04-0145   1,640,000   0   Diversified   5
  Inc.
Roger E. Whitehouse, President
911 North Main Street
Mail: P.O. Box 628
London, KY 40741
(606)864-5175   Date Lic: 12/19/78

Wilbur Venture
  Capital Corp.
(Main Office: Tucson, AZ)
400 Fincastle Building
3rd & Broadway
Louisville, KY 40202
(502)585-1214

Louisiana

Capital Equity Corp.   06/06-0263   1,164,974   0   Diversified   1
Arthur J. Mitchell, General Manager
1885 Wooddale Blvd., Suite 210
Baton Rouge, LA 70806
(504)924-9209   Date Lic: 03/11/83

Capital for   06/06-0195   750,000   480,000   Diversified   5
  Terrebonne, Inc.
Hartwell A. Lewis, President
27 Austin Drive
Houma, LA 70360
(504)868-3930   Date Lic: 01/24/78

Dixie Business   06/06-0173   501,118   1,500,000   Diversified   2
  Investment Company
George Lensing, Chairman
401-1/2 Lake Street
P.O. Box 588
Lake Providence, LA 71254
(318)559-1558   Date Lic: 08/21/74

Licensee	License Number	Private Capital	SBA Leverage	Investment Policy	Owner Code

Louisiana (Cont)

Louisiana Equity 06/06-0169 4,260,639 0 Diversified 1
Capital Corporation
G. Lee Griffin, President
451 Florida Street
Baton Rouge, LA 70821
(504)389-4421 Date Lic: 02/21/74

Maine

Maine Capital Corp. 01/01-0306 1,000,000 1,000,000 Diversified 1
David M. Coit, President
Seventy Center Street
Portland, ME 04101
(207)772-1001 Date Lic: 08/07/80

Maryland

First Maryland 03/03-0169 616,600 0 Diversified 5
Capital, Inc.
Joseph A. Kenary, President
107 West Jefferson Street
Rockville, MD 20850
(301)251-6630 Date Lic: 07/12/84

Greater Washington 03/04-0011 8,485,655 2,513,720 Diversified 6
Investments, Inc.
Don A. Christensen, President
5454 Wisconsin Avenue
Chevy Chase, MD 20815
(301)656-0626 Date Lic: 02/09/60

Jiffy Lube Capital 03/03-0182 2,000,000 1,200,000 Diversified 5
Corporation
Eleanor C. Harding, President
6000 Metro Drive
Mail: PO Box 17223; Baltimore 21203-7223
Baltimore, MD 21215
(301)764-3234 Date Lic: 12/09/87

Massachusetts

Advent Atlantic 01/01-0327 4,956,680 6,000,000 Diversified 5-P
Capital Company, LP
David D. Croll, Managing Partner
45 Milk Street
Boston, MA 02109
(617)338-0800 Date Lic: 11/28/83

Licensee	License Number	Private Capital	SBA Leverage	Investment Policy	Owner Code

Massachusetts (Cont)

Advent IV Capital   01/01-0316 12,050,000   6,000,000 Diversified   5-P
  Company
David D. Croll, Managing Partner
45 Milk Street
Boston, MA 02109
(617)338-0800 Date Lic: 07/27/82

Advent Industrial   01/01-0332   3,326,400   7,000,000 Diversified   3-P
  Capital Company, LP
David D. Croll, Managing Partner
45 Milk Street
Boston, MA 02109
(617)338-0800 Date Lic: 11/09/84

Advent V Capital   01/01-0331 29,075,000 35,000,000 Diversified   5-P
  Company LP
David D. Croll, Managing Partner
45 Milk Street
Boston, MA 02109
(617)338-0800 Date Lic: 09/05/84

Atlas II Capital   01/01-0319   1,000,000   500,000 Diversified   5
  Corporation
Joost E. Tjaden, President
260 Franklin Street, Suite 1501
Boston, MA 02109
(617)439-6160 Date Lic: 07/27/82

BancBoston Ventures,   01/01-0001 25,000,000   0 Diversified   1
  Incorporated
Paul F. Hogan, President
100 Federal Street
Mail: P.O. Box 2016 Stop 01-31-08
Boston, MA 02106
(617)434-2441 Date Lic: 05/08/59

Bever Capital Corp.   01/01-0325   1,000,000   1,500,000 Diversified   5
Joost E. Tjaden, President
260 Franklin Street, 15th Floor
Boston, MA 02109
(617)439-6160 Date Lic: 10/31/83

Boston Hambro Capital   01/01-0299   5,942,914   2,000,000 Diversified   5-P
  Company
Edwin Goodman, President of Corp. G.P.
160 State Street, 9th Floor
Boston, MA 02109
(617)523-7767 Date Lic: 01/04/80

Licensee	License Number	Private Capital	SBA Leverage	Investment Policy	Owner Code

Massachusetts (Cont)

Licensee	License Number	Private Capital	SBA Leverage	Investment Policy	Owner Code
Business Achievement Corporation Michael L. Katzeff, President 1172 Beacon Street, Sutie 202 Newton, MA 02161 (617)965-0550 Date Lic: 08/08/63	01/01-0055	550,000	1,570,000	Diversified	5
Chestnut Capital International II LP David D. Croll, Managing Partner 45 Milk Street Boston, MA 02109 (617)338-0800 Date Lic: 07/10/85	01/01-0336	6,729,124	12,500,000	Diversified	5-P
Chestnut Street Partners, Inc. David D. Croll, President 45 Milk Street Boston, MA 02109 (617)574-6763 Date Lic: 12/03/86	01/01-0339	3,000,000	5,000,000	Diversified	5
First Capital Corp. of Chicago (Main Office: Chicago, IL) 133 Federal Street, 6th Floor Boston, MA 02110 (617)542-9185					
First United SBIC, Inc. Alfred W. Ferrara, Vice President 135 Will Drive Canton, MA 02021 (617)828-6150 Date Lic: 10/29/76	01/01-0284	300,000	0	Diversified	4
Fleet Venture Resources, Inc. (Main Office: Providence, RI) Carlton V. Klein, Vice-President 60 State Street Boston, MA 02109 (617)367-6700					
Mezzanine Capital Corporation David D. Croll, President 45 Milk Street Boston, MA 02109 (617)574-6752 Date Lic: 05/28/87	01/01-0341	30,000,000	25,000,000	Diversified	4

Licensee	License Number	Private Capital	SBA Leverage	Investment Policy	Owner Code

Licensee	License Number	Private Capital	SBA Leverage	Investment Policy	Owner Code
Milk Street Partners, Inc.	01/01-0342	1,000,000	0	Diversified	5

Richard H. Churchill, Jr., President
45 Milk Street
Boston, MA 02109
(617)574-6723 Date Lic: 09/17/87

Monarch-Narragansett Ventures, Inc.	01/01-0340	10,000,000	23,970,000	Diversified	3

George W. Siguler, President
One Financial Plaza
Springfield, MA 01102
(413)781-3000 Date Lic: 12/08/86

New England Capital Corporation	01/01-0023	10,000,000	0	Diversified	1

Z. David Patterson, Vice President
One Washington Mall, 7th Floor
Boston, MA 02108
(617)722-6400 Date Lic: 08/21/61

Northeast SBI Corp.	01/01-0275	378,802	1,130,000	Diversified	5

Joseph Mindick, Treasurer
16 Cumberland Street
Boston, MA 02115
(617)267-3983 Date Lic: 05/07/74

Orange Nassau Capital Corporation	01/01-0313	2,000,000	1,000,000	Diversified	5

Joost E. Tjaden, President
260 Franklin Street, 15th Floor
Boston, MA 02109
(617)439-6160 Date Lic: 07/08/81

Pioneer Ventures Limited Partnership	01/01-0337	3,157,122	0	Diversified	3-P

Christopher W. Lynch, Managing Partner
60 State Street
Boston, MA 02109
(617)742-7825 Date Lic: 11/20/86

Shawmut National Capital Corporation	01/01-0068	1,000,000	0	Diversified	1

William L.G. Lester, President
c/o Shawmut Bank, N.A.
One Federal Street
Boston, MA 02210
(617)292-4128 Date Lic: 12/27/67

Licensee	License Number	Private Capital	SBA Leverage	Investment Policy	Owner Code
Massachusetts (Cont)					
Stevens Capital Corporation Edward Capuano, President 168 Stevens Street Fall River, MA 02721 (617)679-0044 Date Lic: 06/21/84	01/01-0323	506,000	0	Diversified	5
UST Capital Corp. Walter Dick, President 40 Court Street Boston, MA 02108 (617)726-7137 Date Lic: 10/06/61	01/01-0027	1,752,800	2,000,000	Diversified	1
Vadus Capital Corp. Joost E. Tjaden, President 260 Franklin Street, 15th Floor Boston, MA 02109 (617)439-6160 Date Lic: 11/03/81	01/01-0314	2,000,000	1,000,000	Diversified	5
Michigan					
Doan Resources Limited Partnership Herbert D. Doan, Partner 4251 Plymouth Road P.O. Box 986 Ann Arbor, MI 48106 (313)747-9401 Date Lic: 02/25/74	05/05-0098	2,850,000	0	Diversified	3-P
Michigan Tech Capital Corporation Clark L. Pellegrini, President Technology Park 601 West Sharon Avenue; P.O. Box 364 Houghton, MI 49931 (906)487-2970 Date Lic: 08/20/82	05/05-0169	642,500	0	Diversified	5
Minnesota					
FBS SBIC, Limited Partnership Dennis E. Evans, President 1100 First Bank Place East Minneapolis, MN 55480 (612)370-4764 Date Lic: 09/27/84	09/09-0345	11,183,320	0	Diversified	1-P

Licensee	License Number	Private Capital	SBA Leverage	Investment Policy	Owner Code

Hidden Oaks Financial   05/05-0208   1,050,000   0   Grocery Stores   5
  Services, Inc.
C. Patrick Schulke, President
4620 West 77th Street, Suite 155
Edina, MN 55435
(612)897-3902   Date Lic: 05/11/88

Itasca Growth Fund,   05/05-0200   1,056,000   0   Diversified   4
  Inc.
Carroll Bergerson, General Manager
One N.W. Third Street
Grand Rapids, MN 55744
(218)327-6200   Date Lic: 05/06/85

North Star   05/05-0190   6,663,585   13,020,000   Diversified   5
  Ventures II, Inc.
Terrence W. Glarner, President
100 South Fifth Street
Suite 2200
Minneapolis, MN 55402
(612)333-1133   Date Lic: 05/17/84

Northland Capital   05/08-0018   773,822   700,000   Diversified   5-P
  Venture Partnership
George G. Barnum, Jr., President
613 Missabe Building
Duluth, MN 55802
(218)722-0545   Date Lic: 06/30/67

Northwest Venture   05/05-0182   50,446,962   0   Diversified   2-P
  Partners
Robert F. Zicarelli, Managing G.P.
2800 Piper Jaffray Tower
222 South Ninth Street
Minneapolis, MN 55402
(612)372-8770   Date Lic: 10/13/83

Norwest Growth Fund,   05/08-0006   16,350,000   18,504,000   Diversified   1
  Inc.
Daniel J. Haggerty, President
2800 Piper Jaffray Tower
222 South Ninth Street
Minneapolis, MN 55402
(612)372-8770   Date Lic: 02/25/60

Licensee	License Number	Private Capital	SBA Leverage	Investment Policy	Owner Code

Minnesota (Cont)

Shared Ventures, Inc. 05/05-0157   752,000   1,200,000   Diversified   5
Howard W. Weiner, President
6550 York Avenue, South
Suite 419
Edina, MN 55435
(612)925-3411   Date Lic: 09/18/81

Mississippi

Vicksburg SBIC   04/05-0011   950,000   509,000   Diversified   5
David L. May, President
302 First National Bank Building
Vicksburg, MS 39180
(601)636-4762   Date Lic: 06/09/60

Missouri

Bankers Capital Corp. 07/07-0075   632,000   1,010,000   Diversified   5
Raymond E. Glasnapp, President
3100 Gillham Road
Kansas City, MO 64109
(816)531-1600   Date Lic: 02/12/76

Capital for   07/09-0002   6,000,000   0   Diversified   1
   Business, Inc.
James B. Hebenstreit, President
1000 Walnut, 18th Floor
Kansas City, MO 64106
(816)234-2357   Date Lic: 10/15/59

Capital for
   Business, Inc.
(Main Office: Kansas City, MO)
11 South Meramec, Suite 804
St. Louis, MO 63105
(314)854-7427

MBI Venture Capital   07/07-0092   5,500,000   0   Diversified   1
   Investors, Inc.
Anthony Sommers, President
850 Main Street
Kansas City, MO 64105
(816)471-1700   Date Lic: 12/11/84

MorAmerica Capital
   Corporation
(Main Office: Cedar Rapids, IA)
911 Main Street, Suite 2724A
Commerce Tower Building
Kansas City, MO 64105
(816)842-0114

Licensee	License Number	Private Capital	SBA Leverage	Investment Policy	Owner Code

Missouri (Cont)

United Missouri   07/07-0091   2,500,000   0   Diversified   1
   Capital Corporation
Joe Kessinger, Manager
1010 Grand Avenue
Mail: P.O. Box 419226; K.C., MO 64141
Kansas City, MO 64106
(816)556-7333   Date Lic: 09/21/84

Nebraska

United Financial   07/07-0087   500,000   500,000   Grocery Stores   5
   Resources Corp.
Dennis L. Schulte, Manager
6211 L Street
Mail: P.O. Box 1131
Omaha, NE 68101
(402)734-1250   Date Lic: 07/07/83

Nevada

Enterprise Finance Cap   08/08-0059   1,000,000   800,000   Diversified   5
   Development Corp.
Robert N. Hampton, President
First Interstate Bank of Nevada Bldg.
One East First Street, Suite 1100
Reno, NV 89501
(702)329-7797   Date Lic: 12/29/83

New Hampshire

VenCap, Inc.   01/01-0330   1,403,911   1,200,000   Diversified   5
Richard J. Ash, President
1155 Elm Street
Manchester, NH 03101
(603)644-6100   Date Lic: 01/10/85

New Jersey

Bishop Capital, L.P.   02/02-0503   3,000,000   1,000,000   Diversified   2-P
Charles J. Irish
58 Park Place
Newark, NJ 07102
(201)623-0171   Date Lic: 08/27/87

ESLO Capital Corp.   01/01-0300   639,323   1,500,000   Diversified   5
Leo Katz, President
212 Wright Street
Newark, NJ 07114
(201)242-4488   Date Lic: 05/31/79

Licensee	License Number	Private Capital	SBA Leverage	Investment Policy	Owner Code

New Jersey (Cont)

First Princeton Capital Corporation
02/02-0449 — 1,300,897 — 500,000 — Diversified — 5
Michael D. Feinstein, President
Five Garret Mountain Plaza
West Paterson, NJ 07424
(201)278-8111   Date Lic: 03/08/83

Monmouth Capital Corp.
02/02-0088 — 2,453,931 — 6,072,000 — Diversified — 6
Eugene W. Landy, President
125 Wycoff Road
Midland National Bank Bldg.-P.O. Box 335
Eatontown, NJ 07724
(201)542-4927   Date Lic: 05/28/61

Tappan Zee Capital Corporation
02/02-0209 — 750,000 — 2,250,000 — 66% Real Estate — 5
Karl Kirschner, President
201 Lower Notch Road
Little Falls, NJ 07424
(201)256-8280   Date Lic: 11/16/63

Unicorn Ventures II, L.P.
02/02-0477 — 4,553,000 — 2,500,000 — Diversified — 5-P
Frank P. Diassi, General Partner
6 Commerce Drive
Cranford, NJ 07016
(201)276-7880   Date Lic: 10/09/84

Unicorn Ventures, Ltd.
02/02-0405 — 2,508,513 — 6,000,000 — Diversified — 5-P
Frank P. Diassi, President
6 Commerce Drive
Cranford, NJ 07016
(201)276-7880   Date Lic: 11/10/81

United Jersey Venture Capital, Inc.
02/02-0489 — 1,000,000 — 0 — Diversified — 1
Stephen H. Paneyko, President
301 Carnegie Center
P.O. Box 2066
Princeton, NJ 08540
(609)987-3490   Date Lic: 01/20/87

New Mexico

Albuquerque SBIC
06/06-0191 — 502,000 — 1,500,000 — Diversified — 5
Albert T. Ussery, President
501 Tijeras Avenue, N.W.
P.O. Box 487
Albuquerque, NM 87103
(505)247-0145   Date Lic: 11/16/77

Licensee	License Number	Private Capital	SBA Leverage	Investment Policy	Owner Code

New Mexico (Cont)

Equity Capital Corp.   06/06-0274   962,720   1,250,000   Diversified   5
Jerry A. Henson, President
119 East Marcy Street, Suite 101
Santa Fe, NM 87501
(505)988-4273 Date Lic: 01/24/84

Southwest Capital   06/06-0229   830,552   2,180,000   Diversified   3
  Investments, Inc.
Martin J. Roe, President
The Southwest Building
3500-E Comanche Road, N.E.
Albuquerque, NM 87107
(505)884-7161 Date Lic: 04/30/76

United Mercantile   06/06-0184   629,888   1,200,000   Diversified   5
  Capital Corp.
Joe Justice, General Manager
2400 Louisiana Blvd., Bldg 4, Suite 101
Mail: P.O. Box 37487 Albuquerque 87176
Albuquerque, NM 87110
(505)883-8201 Date Lic: 11/16/76

New York

767 Limited   02/02-0464   1,515,152   1,500,000   Diversified   5-P
  Partnership
H. Wertheim and H. Mallement, G.P.
767 Third Avenue
New York, NY 10017
(212)838-7776 Date Lic: 06/18/84

ASEA-Harvest   02/02-0478   1,016,559   1,000,000   Diversified   5-P
  Partners II
Harvey Wertheim, General Partner
767 Third Avenue
New York, NY 10017
(212)838-7776 Date Lic: 10/09/84

American Commercial   02/02-0443   1,000,000   3,000,000   Diversified   5
  Capital Corporation
Gerald J. Grossman, President
310 Madison Avenue, Suite 1304
New York, NY 10017
(212)986-3305 Date Lic: 12/30/82

Licensee	License Number	Private Capital	SBA Leverage	Investment Policy	Owner Code
New York (Cont)					
American Energy Investment Corp. John J. Hoey, Chairman of the Board 645 Fifth Avenue, Suite 1900 New York, NY 10022 (212)688-7307 Date Lic: 02/20/81	02/06-0236	2,500,000	0	Energy Industries	5
Amev Capital Corp. Martin Orland, President One World Trade Center 50th Floor New York, NY 10048 (212)775-9100 Date Lic: 08/14/79	02/02-0370	5,500,000	5,000,000	Diversified	5
Atalanta Investment Company, Inc. L. Mark Newman, Chairman of the Board 450 Park Avenue New York, NY 10022 (212)832-1104 Date Lic: 06/22/79	02/02-0357	6,572,196	11,800,000	Diversified	4
BT Capital Corp. James G. Hellmuth, President 280 Park Avenue - 10 West New York, NY 10017 (212)850-1916 Date Lic: 11/10/72	02/02-0295	78,310,944	25,500,000	Diversified	1
Boston Hambro Capital Company (Main Office: Boston, MA) 17 East 71st Street New York, NY 10021 (212)288-9106					
Bridger Capital Corp. Seymour L. Wane, President 645 Madison Avenue, Suite 810 New York, NY 10022 (212)888-4004 Date Lic: 04/05/88	02/02-0511	2,000,000	2,000,000	Diversified	5
CMNY Capital L.P. Robert Davidoff, General Partner 77 Water Street New York, NY 10005 (212)437-7078 Date Lic: 03/14/62	02/02-0180	2,400,000	7,100,000	Diversified	3-P

Licensee	License Number	Private Capital	SBA Leverage	Investment Policy	Owner Code

Central New York SBIC 02/02-0044 150,000 0 Vending Machine 4
(The)
Robert E. Romig, President
351 South Warren Street
Syracuse, NY 13202
(315)478-5026 Date Lic: 04/28/61

Chase Manhattan 02/02-0228 24,785,000 0 Diversified 1
Capital Corporation
Gustav H. Koven, President
1 Chase Manhattan Plaza - 23rd Floor
New York, NY 10081
(212)552-6275 Date Lic: 08/02/62

Chemical Venture 02/02-0479 69,384,413 0 Diversified 1-P
Capital Associates
Steven J. Gilbert, President
277 Park Avenue, 10th Floor
New York, NY 10172
(212)310-7578 Date Lic: 10/22/84

Citicorp Venture 02/02-0266 127,197,602 10,000,000 Diversified 1
Capital, Ltd.
William Comfort, Chairman of the Board
153 East 53rd Street, 28th Floor
New York, NY 10043
(212)559-1127 Date Lic: 12/18/67

Clinton Capital Corp. 02/02-0410 12,000,000 35,000,000 Diversified 5
Mark Scharfman, President
79 Madison Avenue, Suite 800
New York, NY 10016
(212)696-4334 Date Lic: 10/22/80

Croyden Capital Corp. 02/02-0472 1,457,963 1,500,000 Diversified 5
Lawrence D. Garfinkle, President
45 Rockefeller Plaza, Suite 2165
New York, NY 10111
(212)974-0184 Date Lic: 05/23/84

Diamond Capital Corp. 02/02-0510 2,000,000 0 Diversified 5
Steven B. Kraiety, President
805 Third Avenue, Suite 1100
New York, NY 10017
(212)838-1255 Date Lic: 01/21/88

Licensee	License Number	Private Capital	SBA Leverage	Investment Policy	Owner Code

Licensee	License Number	Private Capital	SBA Leverage	Investment Policy	Owner Code
EAB Venture Corp. Mark R. Littell, President EAB Plaza Uniondale, NY 11555 (516)296-5784 Date Lic: 08/18/80	02/02-0403	5,000,000	9,000,000	Diversified	1
Edwards Capital Company Edward H. Teitlebaum, President 215 Lexington Avenue, Suite 805 New York, NY 10016 (212)686-2568 Date Lic: 06/22/79	02/02-0366	7,200,000	18,450,000	Transportation	5-P
Fairfield Equity Corp. Matthew A. Berdon, President 200 East 42nd Street New York, NY 10017 (212)867-0150 Date Lic: 11/16/61	02/02-0151	997,109	2,400,000	Diversified	5
Ferranti High Technology, Inc. Sandford R. Simon, President & Director 515 Madison Avenue New York, NY 10022 (212)688-9828 Date Lic: 05/31/83	02/02-0457	3,000,000	1,000,000	Diversified	5
Fifty-Third Street Ventures, L.P. Patricia Cloherty & Dan Tessler, G.P. 155 Main Street Cold Spring, NY 10516 (914)265-5167 Date Lic: 07/29/76	02/02-0315	5,790,251	7,960,000	Diversified	5-P
First New York SBIC Israel Mindick, General Partner 20 Squadron Blvd., Suite 480 New City, NY 10956 (914)638-1550 Date Lic: 12/30/85	02/02-0486	1,000,000	0	Diversified	5-P
Franklin Corp. (The) Norman S. Strobel, President 767 Fifth Avenue G.M. Building, 23rd Floor New York, NY 10153 (212)486-2323 Date Lic: 09/17/59	02/02-0005	10,003,114	8,640,000	Diversified	6

Licensee	License Number	Private Capital	SBA Leverage	Investment Policy	Owner Code

Fundex Capital Corp. 02/02-0340 1,551,000 3,900,000 Diversified 5
Howard Sommer, President
525 Northern Blvd.
Great Neck, NY 11021
(516)466-8551 Date Lic: 05/18/78

GHW Capital Corp. 02/02-0491 1,000,000 0 Diversified 1
Nesta Stephens, V.P. & Administrator
489 Fifth Avenue
New York, NY 10017
(212)687-1708 Date Lic: 11/13/85

Genesee Funding, Inc. 02/02-0499 1,000,000 0 Diversified 5
A. Keene Bolton, President, CEO
100 Corporate Woods
Rochester, NY 14623
(716)272-2332 Date Lic: 11/26/86

Hanover Capital Corp. 02/02-0102 1,000,001 1,875,000 Diversified 5
  (The)
Geoffrey T. Selzer, President
150 East 58th Street, Suite 2710
New York, NY 10155
(212)980-9670 Date Lic: 06/22/61

Intergroup Venture 02/02-0345 502,500 0 Diversified 5
  Capital Corp.
Ben Hauben, President
230 Park Avenue
New York, NY 10017
(212)661-5428 Date Lic: 08/07/78

Interstate Capital 02/02-0408 1,250,000 3,500,000 Diversified 5
  Company, Inc.
David Scharf, President
380 Lexington Avenue
New York, NY 10017
(212)986-7333 Date Lic: 10/22/80

Irving Capital Corp. 02/02-0321 10,000,000 0 Diversified 1
Andrew McWethy, President
1290 Avenue of the Americas
New York, NY 10104
(212)408-4800 Date Lic: 12/06/76

Licensee	License Number	Private Capital	SBA Leverage	Investment Policy	Owner Code

Kwiat Capital Corp.   02/02-0416   510,000   500,000   Diversified   5
Sheldon F. Kwiat, President
576 Fifth Avenue
New York, NY 10036
(212)391-2461   Date Lic: 09/25/81

M & T Capital Corp.   02/02-0268   5,007,486   0   Diversified   1
William Randon, President
One M & T Plaza
Buffalo, NY 14240
(716)842-5881   Date Lic: 12/29/67

MH Capital   02/02-0501   20,000,000   0   Diversified   1
   Investors, Inc.
Edward L. Kock III, President
270 Park Avenue
New York, NY 10017
(212)286-3222   Date Lic: 11/06/86

Multi-Purpose Capital   02/02-0232   210,300   165,000   Diversified   5
   Corporation
Eli B. Fine, President
31 South Broadway
Yonkers, NY 10701
(914)963-2733   Date Lic: 03/18/63

NYBDC Capital Corp.   02/02-0303   500,000   770,000   Diversified   4
Robert W. Lazar, President
41 State Street
Albany, NY 12207
(518)463-2268   Date Lic: 11/02/73

NYSTRS/NV Capital,   02/02-0493   5,793,400   0   Diversified   2-P
   Limited Partnership
Raymond A. Lancaster, President
One Norstar Plaza
Albany, NY 12207
(518)447-4050   Date Lic: 02/07/86

NatWest USA Capital   02/02-0492   20,000,000   0   Diversified   1
   Corporation
Orville G. Aarons, General Manager
175 Water Street
New York, NY 10038
(212)602-1200   Date Lic: 02/06/86

Licensee	License Number	Private Capital	SBA Leverage	Investment Policy	Owner Code

Nelson Capital Corp. 02/02-0297 500,000 1,500,000 Diversified 5
Irwin Nelson, President
585 Stewart Avenue, Suite 416
Garden City L.I., NY 11530
(516)222-2555 Date Lic: 06/12/73

Norstar Capital Inc. 02/02-0482 5,396,925 0 Diversified 1
Raymond A. Lancaster, President
One Norstar Plaza
Albany, NY 12207
(518)447-4043 Date Lic: 04/12/85

Onondaga Venture 02/02-0498 2,502,500 0 Diversified 5
   Capital Fund, Inc.
Irving W. Schwartz, Exec. V.P.
327 State Tower Building
Syracuse, NY 13202
(315)478-0157 Date Lic: 09/30/87

Preferential Capital 02/02-0372 509,380 0 Diversified 5
   Corporation
Bruce Bayroff, Secretary-Treasurer
16 Court Street
Brooklyn, NY 11241
(718)855-2728 Date Lic: 09/14/79

Pyramid Ventures, Inc. 02/02-0507 16,002,501 0 Diversified 1
John Popovitch, Treasurer
280 Park Avenue
New York, NY 10015
(212)850-1934 Date Lic: 06/26/87

Questech Capital Corp. 02/02-0415 5,000,000 12,000,000 Diversified 5
John E. Koonce, President
320 Park Avenue, 3rd Floor
New York, NY 10022
(212)891-7500 Date Lic: 06/26/81

R & R Financial Corp. 02/02-0135 505,000 300,000 Diversified 3
Imre Rosenthal, President
1451 Broadway
New York, NY 10036
(212)790-1441 Date Lic: 04/27/62

Rand SBIC, Inc. 02/02-0311 1,605,000 1,800,000 Diversified 6
Donald Ross, President
1300 Rand Building
Buffalo, NY 14203
(716)853-0802 Date Lic: 05/05/76

Licensee	License Number	Private Capital	SBA Leverage	Investment Policy	Owner Code

Realty Growth Capital 02/02-0097 500,000 1,080,000 100% Real Estate Specialist 5
   Corporation
Lawrence Beneson, President
331 Madison Avenue
Fourth Floor East
New York, NY 10017
(212)661-8380 Date Lic: 03/29/63

Republic SBI 02/02-0506 2,000,000 0 Diversified 1
   Corporation
Robert V. Treanor, Senior V.P.
452 Fifth Avenue
New York, NY 10018
(212)930-8639 Date Lic: 04/04/88

SLK Capital Corp. 02/02-0509 1,000,000 0 Diversified 5
Edward A. Kerbs, President
115 Broadway, 20th Floor
New York, NY 10006
(212)587-8800 Date Lic: 01/27/88

Small Bus. Electronics 02/02-0026 600,000 0 Diversified 5
   Investment Corp.
Stanley Meisels, President
1220 Peninsula Blvd.
Hewlett, NY 11557
(516)374-0743 Date Lic: 09/01/60

Southern Tier Capital 02/02-0095 350,111 800,000 Major Group 70 5
   Corporation   (Hotels and
Harold Gold, Secretary-Treasurer   Rooming Houses)
55 South Main Street
Liberty, NY 12754
(914)292-3030 Date Lic: 06/28/61

TLC Funding Corp. 02/02-0380 1,250,000 2,940,000 Diversified 5
Philip G. Kass, President
141 South Central Avenue
Hartsdale, NY 10530
(914)683-1144 Date Lic: 02/29/80

Tappan Zee Capital
   Corporation
(Main Office: Little Falls, NJ)
120 North Main Street
New City, NY 10956
(914)634-8890

Licensee	License Number	Private Capital	SBA Leverage	Investment Policy	Owner Code

Telesciences Capital   02/02-0341   1,250,000   0   Diversified   4
   Corporation
Mike A. Petrozzo, Contact
26 Broadway, Suite 841
New York, NY 10004
(212)425-0320   Date Lic: 09/14/78

Vega Capital Corp.   02/02-0270   2,402,861   6,950,000   Diversified   6
Victor Harz, President
720 White Plains Road
Scarsdale, NY 10583
(914)472-8550   Date Lic: 08/05/68

Venture SBIC, Inc.   02/02-0334   612,000   1,800,000   Diversified   5
Arnold Feldman, President
249-12 Jericho Turnpike
Floral Park, NY 11001
(516)352-0068   Date Lic: 11/23/77

WFG-Harvest Partners,   02/02-0490   3,026,412   0   Diversified   1-P
   Ltd.
Harvey J. Wertheim, General Partner
767 Third Avenue
New York, NY 10017
(212)838-7776   Date Lic: 09/30/85

Winfield Capital Corp. 02/02-0292   1,100,000   3,300,000   Diversified   5
Stanley M. Pechman, President
237 Mamaroneck Avenue
White Plains, NY 10605
(914)949-2600   Date Lic: 04/19/72

Wood River Capital   02/02-0361   15,512,000   31,000,000   Diversified   5
   Corporation
Elizabeth W. Smith, President
645 Madison Avenue
New York, NY 10022
(212)750-9420   Date Lic: 05/09/79

North Carolina

Delta Capital, Inc.   04/10-0086   1,250,000   5,000,000   50% Real Estate   3
Alex B. Wilkins, Jr., President
227 North Tryon Street, Suite 201
Charlotte, NC 28202
(704)372-1410   Date Lic: 11/29/61

Licensee	License Number	Private Capital	SBA Leverage	Investment Policy	Owner Code
North Carolina (Cont)					
Falcon Capital Corp. P.S. Prasad, President 400 West Fifth Street Greenville, NC 27834 (919)752-5918 Date Lic: 04/14/64	04/04-0091	504,237	500,000	Diversified	5
Heritage Capital Corp. William R. Starnes, President 2095 Two First Union Plaza Charlotte, NC 28282 (704)334-2867 Date Lic: 10/21/61	04/04-0047	2,050,265	2,500,114	50% Real Estate	3
Kitty Hawk Capital, Limited Partnership Walter H. Wilkinson, President Independence Center, Suite 1640 Charlotte, NC 28246 (704)333-3777 Date Lic: 07/23/80	04/04-0189	1,905,000	3,000,000	Diversified	5-P
NCNB SBIC Corporation Troy S. McCrory, Jr., President One NCNB Plaza - T05 - 2 Charlotte, NC 28255 (704)374-5583 Date Lic: 07/19/84	04/04-0232	2,500,000	0	Diversified	1
NCNB Venture Company, L.P. S. Epes Robinson, General Partner One NCNB Plaza, T-39 Charlotte, NC 28255 (704)374-5723 Date Lic: 07/19/84	04/04-0231	20,176,039	0	Diversified	1-P
Ohio					
A.T. Capital Corp. Robert C. Salipante, President 900 Euclid Avenue, T-18 Mail: P.O. Box 5937 Cleveland, OH 44101 (216)687-4970 Date Lic: 06/04/84	05/05-0197	1,010,000	0	Diversified	1
Banc One Capital Corporation James E. Kolls, Vice President 100 East Broad Street Columbus, OH 43215 (614)248-5932 Date Lic: 01/17/62	05/06-0020	440,000	0	Diversified	1

Licensee	License Number	Private Capital	SBA Leverage	Investment Policy	Owner Code

Licensee	License Number	Private Capital	SBA Leverage	Investment Policy	Owner Code
Capital Funds Corp.	05/06-0011	5,700,000	0	Communications	1

Capital Funds Corp. 05/06-0011 5,700,000 0 Communications 1
Carl G. Nelson, Chief Inv. Officer
800 Superior Avenue
Cleveland, OH 44114
(216)344-5774 Date Lic: 12/09/60

Clarion Capital Corp. 05/07-0023 8,891,858 10,040,000 Diversified 6
Morton A. Cohen, President
35555 Curtis Blvd.
Eastlake, OH 44094
(216)953-0555 Date Lic: 09/25/68

First Ohio Capital 05/05-0163 2,450,000 1,300,000 Diversified 1
  Corporation
David J. McMacken, General Manager
606 Madison Avenue
Mail: P.O. Box 2061; Toledo, OH 43603
Toledo, OH 43604
(419)259-7146 Date Lic: 04/14/82

Gries Investment 05/06-0031 682,961 1,432,400 Diversified 5
  Company
Robert D. Gries, President
1500 Statler Office Tower
Cleveland, OH 44115
(216)861-1146 Date Lic: 03/24/64

JRM Capital Corp. 05/05-0105 550,000 310,000 Grocery Stores 4
H.F. Meyer, President
110 West Streetsboro Street
Hudson, OH 44236
(216)656-4010 Date Lic: 09/18/75

National City Capital 05/05-0137 2,501,791 4,530,000 Diversified 1
  Corporation
Michael Sherwin, President
629 Euclid Avenue
Cleveland, OH 44114
(216)575-2491 Date Lic: 02/08/79

River Capital
  Corporation
(Main Office: Alexandria, VA)
796 Huntington Building
Cleveland, OH 44114
(216)781-3655

Licensee	License Number	Private Capital	SBA Leverage	Investment Policy	Owner Code
Ohio (Cont)					
SeaGate Venture Management, Inc. Charles A. Brown, Vice-President 245 Summit Street, Suite 1403 Toledo, OH 43603 (419)259-8605 Date Lic: 07/19/85	05/05-0203	1,010,000	1,000,000	Diversified	1
Tamco Investors (SBIC) Incorporated Nathan H. Monus, President 375 Victoria Road Youngstown, OH 44515 (216)792-3811 Date Lic: 06/21/77	05/05-0116	350,000	1,050,000	Grocery Stores	4
Oklahoma					
Alliance Business Investment Company Barry Davis, President 17 East Second Street One Williams Center, Suite 2000 Tulsa, OK 74172 (918)584-3581 Date Lic: 08/12/59	06/10-0012	3,469,367	2,660,000	Diversified	5
Western Venture Capital Corporation William B Baker, Chief Operating Officer 4880 South Lewis Tulsa, OK 74105 (918)749-7981 Date Lic: 08/03/81	06/06-0248	2,007,500	4,000,000	Diversified	2
Oregon					
First Interstate Capital, Inc. (Main Office: Newport Beach, CA) 227 S.W. Pine Street, Suite 200 Portland, OR 97204 (503)223-4334					
Northern Pacific Capital Corporation John J. Tennant, Jr., President 1201 S.W. 12th Avenue, Suite 608 Mail: P.O. Box 1658; Portland, OR 97207 Portland, OR 97205 (503)241-1255 Date Lic: 01/18/62	10/13-0014	911,464	500,000	Diversified	5

Licensee	License Number	Private Capital	SBA Leverage	Investment Policy	Owner Code

Oregon (Cont)

Norwest Growth Fund,
  Inc.
(Main Office: Minneapolis, MN)
1300 S.W. 5th Street, Suite 3108
Portland, OR 97201
(503)223-6622

Pennsylvania

Capital Corporation   03/03-0040   1,302,135   1,315,000   Diversified   6
  of America
Martin M. Newman, President
225 South 15th Street, Suite 920
Philadelphia, PA 19102
(215)732-1666   Date Lic: 08/09/84

Enterprise Venture Cap 03/03-0179   1,147,649   0   Diversified   1
  Corp of Pennsylvania
Don Cowie, C.E.O.
227 Franklin Street, Suite 215
Johnstown, PA 15901
(814)535-7597   Date Lic: 09/11/85

Erie SBIC   03/03-0177   1,080,000   1,000,000   Diversified   5
George R. Heaton, President
32 West 8th Street, Suite 615
Erie, PA 16501
(814)453-7964   Date Lic: 07/19/85

Fidelcor Capital   03/03-0184   5,100,000   0   Diversified   1
  Corporation
Bruce H. Luehrs, President
123 S. Broad Street
Philadelphia, PA 19109
(215)985-7287   Date Lic: 01/14/88

First SBIC of
  California
(Main Office: Costa Mesa, CA)
Daniel A. Dye, Contact
P.O. Box 512
Washington, PA 15301
(412)223-0707

First Valley Capital   03/03-0160   510,000   0   Diversified   1
  Corporation
Matthew W. Thomas, President
640 Hamilton Mall, 8th Floor
Allentown, PA 18101
(215)776-6760   Date Lic: 08/19/83

Licensee	License Number	Private Capital	SBA Leverage	Investment Policy	Owner Code

Pennsylvania (Cont)

Franklin Corp. (The)
(Main Office: New York, NY)
Plymouth Meeting Executive Congress
Suite 461-610 W. germantown Pike
Plymouth Meeting, PA 19462

Licensee	License Number	Private Capital	SBA Leverage	Investment Policy	Owner Code
Meridian Capital Corp.	03/03-0127	1,820,000	0	Diversified	1

Joseph E. Laky, President
Suite 222, Blue Bell West
650 Skippack Pike
Blue Bell, PA 19422
(215)278-8907   Date Lic: 07/22/77

Meridian Venture Partners	03/03-0181	5,000,000	0	Diversified	5-P

Raymond R. Rafferty, General Partner
The Fidelity Court Building
259 Radnor-Chester Road
Radnor, PA 19087
(215)293-0210   Date Lic: 02/24/87

PNC Capital Corp.	03/03-0152	5,044,971	0	Diversified	1

Gary J. Zentner, President
Pittsburgh National Building
Fifth Avenue and Wood Street
Pittsburgh, PA 15222
(412)355-2245   Date Lic: 08/12/82

Rhode Island

Domestic Capital Corp.	01/01-0333	500,000	1,000,000	Diversified	1

Nathaniel B. Baker, President
815 Reservoir Avenue
Cranston, RI 02910
(401)946-3310   Date Lic: 12/11/84

Fleet Venture Resources, Inc.	01/01-0067	10,207,604	1,500,000	Diversified	1

Robert M. Van Degna, President
111 Westminster Street
Providence, RI 02903
(401)278-677Q   Date Lic: 12/18/67

Moneta Capital Corp.	01/01-0322	1,002,500	1,500,000	Diversified	5

Arnold Kilberg, President
285 Governor Street
Providence, RI 02906
(401)861-4600   Date Lic: 05/04/84

Licensee	License Number	Private Capital	SBA Leverage	Investment Policy	Owner Code

Rhode Island (Cont)

Old Stone Capital Corporation Arthur C. Barton, President One Old Stone Square, 11th Floor Providence, RI 02903 (401)278-2559 Date Lic: 07/20/61	01/13-0008	6,991,500	7,270,000	Diversified	3
River Capital Corporation (Main Office: Alexandria, VA) 555 South Main Street Providence, RI 02903 (401)861-7470					
Wallace Capital Corporation Lloyd W. Granoff, President 170 Westminister Street Suite 300 Providence, RI 02903 (401)273-9191 Date Lic: 12/22/86	01/01-0338	1,015,000	0	Diversified	4

South Carolina

Carolina Venture Cap. Corporation Thomas H. Harvey III, President 14 Archer Road Hilton Head Isl., SC 29928 (803)842-3101 Date Lic: 01/19/81	04/04-0201	792,100	700,000	Diversified	5
Charleston Capital Corporation Henry Yaschik, President 111 Church Street P.O. Box 328 Charleston, SC 29402 (803)723-6464 Date Lic: 06/21/61	04/04-0042	1,012,409	500,000	Diversified	5
Floco Investment Company, Inc. (The) William H. Johnson, Sr., President Highway 52 North Mail: P.O. Box 919; Lake City, SC 29560 Scranton, SC 29561 (803)389-2731 Date Lic: 07/05/61	04/04-0032	491,900	0	Food Retailers	5

Licensee	License Number	Private Capital	SBA Leverage	Investment Policy	Owner Code
South Carolina (Cont)					
Lowcountry Investment Corporation Joseph T. Newton, Jr., President 4444 Daley Street P.O. Box 10447 Charleston, SC 29411 (803)554-9880 Date Lic: 07/28/60	04/04-0021	1,908,950	3,000,000	Grocery Stores	4
Reedy River Ventures John M. Sterling, President 400 Haywood Road Mail: P.O. Box 17526 Greenville, SC 29606 (803)297-9198 Date Lic: 07/16/81	04/04-0198	2,607,300	3,200,000	Diversified	5-P
Tennessee					
Financial Resources, Incorporated Milton Picard, Chairman of the Board 2800 Sterick Building Memphis, TN 38103 (901)527-9411 Date Lic: 03/21/62	04/05-0064	1,000,320	0	Diversified	5
Leader Capital Corp. James E. Pruitt Jr., President 158 Madison Avenue P.O. Box 708; Memphis, TN 38101-0708 Memphis, TN 38101 (901)578-2405 Date Lic: 06/23/86	04/04-0237	1,485,000	0	Diversified	3
Texas					
Alliance Business Investment Company (Main Office: Tulsa, OK) 911 Louisiana One Shell Plaza, Suite 3990 Houston, TX 77002 (713)224-8224					
Americap Corporation James L. Hurn, President 7575 San Felipe Houston, TX 77063 (713)780-8084 Date Lic: 03/01/83	06/06-0265	1,045,000	3,600,000	Diversified	1

Licensee	License Number	Private Capital	SBA Leverage	Investment Policy	Owner Code

Texas (Cont)

Ameriway Venture 06/06-0290 1,055,000 1,000,000 Diversified 1-P
  Partners I
James L. Hurn, General Partner
7575 San Felipe
Houston, TX 77063
(713)780-8084 Date Lic: 11/19/85

Brittany Capital 06/10-0152 1,000,000 2,425,000 Diversified 5-P
  Company
Steve Peden, Partner
1525 Elm Street
2424 LTV Tower
Dallas, TX 75201
(214)954-1515 Date Lic: 08/04/69

Business Capital Corp. 06/06-0253 510,000 800,000 Diversified 5
James E. Sowell, Chairman of the Board
4809 Cole Avenue, Suite 250
Dallas, TX 75205
(214)522-3739 Date Lic: 09/30/82

Capital Marketing 06/10-0150 11,082,311 32,390,000 Grocery Stores 4
  Corporation
Ray Ballard, Manager
100 Nat Gibbs Drive
P.O. Box 1000
Keller, TX 76248
(817)656-7309 Date Lic: 06/24/68

Capital Southwest 06/10-0065 5,690,585 16,000,000 Diversified 6
  Venture Corp.
William R. Thomas, President
12900 Preston Road, Suite 700
Dallas, TX 75230
(214)233-8242 Date Lic: 07/13/61

Central Texas SBI 06/10-0076 600,000 0 Diversified 1
  Corporation
David G. Horner, President
P.O. Box 2600
Waco, TX 76702
(817)753-6461 Date Lic: 03/29/62

Charter Venture Group, 06/06-0237 1,000,000 1,000,000 Diversified 1
  Incorporated
Winston C. Davis, President
2600 Citadel Plaza Drive, Suite 600
Houston, TX 77008
(713)863-0704 Date Lic: 10/10/80

Licensee	License Number	Private Capital	SBA Leverage	Investment Policy	Owner Code

Citicorp Venture
  Capital, Ltd.
(Main Office: New York, NY)
717 North Harwood Street
Dallas, TX 75201
(214)880-9670

Energy Assets, Inc.	06/06-0211	1,108,109	500,000	Various Firms In Energy Ind.	4

Laurence E. Simmons, Exec. V.P.
4900 Republic Bank Center
700 Louisiana
Houston, TX 77002
(713)236-9999 Date Lic: 04/12/79

Enterprise Capital Corporation	06/10-0154	5,000,000	8,000,000	Diversified	3

Fred Zeidman, President
4543 Post Oak Place, #130
Houston, TX 77027
(713)621-9444 Date Lic: 05/08/70

FCA Investment Company	06/06-0289	1,017,000	240,000	Diversified	5

Robert S. Baker, Chairman
3000 Post Oak, Suite 1790
Houston, TX 77056
(713)965-0061 Date Lic: 08/19/85

First Interstate Cap. Corp. of Texas	06/06-0219	19,057,008	19,000,000	Diversified	1

Richard S. Smith, President
1000 Louisiana, 7th Floor
Mail: P.O. Box 3326; Houston, TX 77253
Houston, TX 77002
(713)224-6611 Date Lic: 11/01/79

Ford Capital, Ltd.	06/06-0292	8,045,500	0	Diversified	1-P

C. Jeff Pan, President
1525 Elm Street
Mail: P.O. Box 2140; Dallas, TX 75221
Dallas, TX 75201
(214)954-0688 Date Lic: 10/06/86

MCap Corp	06/06-0295	3,500,000	0	Diversified	1

J. Wayne Gaylord, Manager
1717 Main Street, 6th Floor
Momentum Place
Dallas, TX 75201
(214)939-3131 Date Lic: 03/31/88

Licensee	License Number	Private Capital	SBA Leverage	Investment Policy	Owner Code
Texas (Cont)					
MVenture Corp Wayne Gaylord, Sr., Vice President 1717 Main Street, 6th Fl-Momentum Place Mail: P.O. Box 662090; Dallas, TX 75266 Dallas, TX 75201 (214)939-3131 Date Lic: 12/08/76	06/06-0188	16,250,000	35,000,000	Diversified	1
Mapleleaf Capital Ltd. Edward Fink, President 55 Waugh, Suite 710 Houston, TX 77007 (713)880-4494 Date Lic: 10/06/80	06/06-0239	3,000,002	2,000,000	Diversified	2-P
Mid-State Capital Corporation Smith E. Thomasson, President 510 North Valley Mills Drive Waco, TX 76710 (817)772-9220 Date Lic: 03/04/85	06/06-0287	1,400,000	0	Diversified	2
Neptune Capital Corporation Richard C. Strauss, President 5956 Sherry Lane, Suite 800 Dallas, TX 75225 (214)739-1414 Date Lic: 12/23/86	06/06-0293	1,062,707	0	Diversified	5
North Riverside Capital Corporation (Main Office: Atlanta, GA) 400 North St. Paul, Suite 1265 Dallas, TX 75201 (214)220-2717					
Omega Capital Corporation Theodric E. Moor, Jr., President 755 South 11th Street, Suite 250 Mail: P.O. Box 2173 Beaumont, TX 77704 (409)832-0221 Date Lic: 08/12/82	06/06-0260	530,000	500,000	Diversified	5
Republic Venture Group, Incorporated Robert H. Wellborn, Pres. & General Mgr. 325 N. St Paul 2829 Tower II Mail: P.O. Box 655961; Dallas, TX 75265 Dallas, TX 75201 (214)922-3500 Date Lic: 06/26/61	06/10-0059	36,000,044	9,000,000	Diversified	1

Licensee	License Number	Private Capital	SBA Leverage	Investment Policy	Owner Code

Revelation Resources, 06/06-0294 1,123,605 0 Diversified 5-P
  Ltd.
Mr. Chris J. Mathews, Manager
2929 Allen Parkway, Suite 1705
Houston, TX 77019
(713)526-5623 Date Lic: 01/12/88

Rust Capital Limited 06/06-0209 7,000,000 12,000,000 Diversified 3-P
Jeffrey Garvey, Partner
114 West 7th Street, Suite 500
Austin, TX 78701
(512)482-0806 Date Lic: 05/04/79

SBI Capital Corp. 06/06-0244 2,250,000 2,700,000 Diversified 5
William E. Wright, President
6305 Beverly Hill Lane
Mail: P.O. Box 570368; Houston, TX 77257
Houston, TX 77057
(713)975-1188 Date Lic: 10/22/81

San Antonio Venture 06/06-0190 1,051,000 0 Diversified 4
  Group, Inc.
Domingo Bueno, President
2300 West Commerce Street
San Antonio, TX 78207
(512)223-3633 Date Lic: 03/23/78

South Texas SBIC 06/10-0019 1,500,000 1,000,000 Diversified 1
Kenneth L. Vickers, President
120 South Main Street
P.O. Box 1698
Victoria, TX 77902
(512)573-5151 Date Lic: 05/08/61

Southwestern Venture 06/06-0234 1,326,000 1,000,000 Diversified 2
  Cap. of Texas, Inc.
James A. Bettersworth, President
1336 East Court Street
P.O. Box 1719
Seguin, TX 78155
(512)379-0380 Date Lic: 11/24/80

Southwestern Venture
  Cap. of Texas, Inc.
(Main Office: Seguin, TX)
1250 N.E. Loop 410, Suite 300
San Antonio, TX 78209
(512)822-9949

Licensee	License Number	Private Capital	SBA Leverage	Investment Policy	Owner Code
Texas (Cont)					
Sunwestern Capital Corporation Thomas W. Wright, President 3 Forest Plaza 12221 Merit Drive, Suite 1300 Dallas, TX 75251 (214)239-5650 Date Lic: 03/07/83	06/06-0266	2,324,372	5,500,000	Diversified	5
Sunwestern Ventures Company Thomas W. Wright, President 3 Forest Plaza 12221 Merit Drive, Suite 1300 Dallas, TX 75251 (214)239-5650 Date Lic: 10/22/84	06/06-0286	10,076,928	11,500,000	Diversified	5
Texas Commerce Investment Company Fred Lummis, Vice President Texas Commerce Bank Bldg., 30th Floor 712 Main Street Houston, TX 77002 (713)236-4719 Date Lic: 06/09/82	06/06-0258	8,700,000	0	Diversified	1
Wesbanc Ventures, Ltd. Stuart Schube, General Partner 2401 Fountainview, Suite 950 Houston, TX 77057 (713)977-7421 Date Lic: 05/28/85	06/06-0288	2,530,000	1,500,000	Diversified	1-P
Vermont					
Queneska Capital Corporation Albert W. Coffrin, III, President 123 Church Street Burlington, VT 05401 (802)865-1806 Date Lic: 04/25/88	01/01-0345	1,500,000	0	Diversified	1
Virginia					
Crestar Capital A. Hugh Ewing, III, Managing G.P. 9 South 12th Street - Third Floor Richmond, VA 23219 (804)643-7358 Date Lic: 10/29/84	03/03-0175	9,100,000	5,000,000	Diversified	1

Licensee	License Number	Private Capital	SBA Leverage	Investment Policy	Owner Code

Virginia (Cont)

James River Capital   03/03-0146   1,144,875   2,500,000   Diversified   5-P
  Associates
A. Hugh Ewing, Managing Partner
9 South 12th Street
Mail: P.O. Box 1776; Richmond, VA 23219
Richmond, VA 23214
(804)643-7323   Date Lic: 05/15/81

Metropolitan Capital   03/04-0107   2,238,418   3,090,000   Diversified   4
  Corporation
John B. Toomey, President
2550 Huntington Avenue
Alexandria, VA 22303
(703)960-4698   Date Lic: 12/02/70

River Capital   03/01-0320   7,125,000   28,500,000   Diversified   5
  Corporation
Peter Van Oosterhout, President
1033 N. Fairfax Street
Alexandria, VA 22314
(703)739-2100   Date Lic: 06/29/82

Sovran Funding Corp.   03/03-0176   10,000,000   3,000,000   Diversified   1
David A. King, Jr., President
Sovran Center, 6th Floor
One Commercial Plaza; Mail: P.O. Box 600
Norfolk, VA 23510
(804)441-4041   Date Lic: 02/11/85

Tidewater Industrial   03/04-0065   758,200   760,000   Diversified   4
  Capital Corporation
Armand Caplan, President
Suite 1424
United Virginia Bank Building
Norfolk, VA 23510
(804)622-1501   Date Lic: 02/13/62

Tidewater SBI Corp.   03/04-0100   1,000,000   500,000   Diversified   4
Gregory H. Wingfield, President
1214 First Virginia Bank Tower
101 St. Paul's Blvd.
Norfolk, VA 23510
(804)627-2315   Date Lic: 02/05/65

Washington

Capital Resource   10/10-0171   1,087,373   1,000,000   Diversified   5
  Corporation
T. Evans Wyckoff, President
1001 Logan Building
Seattle, WA 98101
(206)623-6550   Date Lic: 05/19/80

Licensee	License Number	Private Capital	SBA Leverage	Investment Policy	Owner Code
Washington (Cont)					
Northwest Business Investment Corp. C. Paul Sandifur, President 929 West Sprague Avenue Spokane, WA 99204 (509)838-3111 Date Lic: 03/16/61	10/13-0005	238,680	0	Diversified	5
Peoples Capital Corporation Robert E. Karns, President 1415 Fifth Avenue Seattle, WA 98171 (206)344-5463 Date Lic: 03/05/81	10/10-0174	1,730,000	0	Diversified	1
Seafirst Capital Corporation R. Bruce Harrod, President Columbia Seafirst Center 701 Fifth Avenue, P.O. Box 34103 Seattle, WA 98124 (206)358-7441 Date Lic: 06/18/80	10/10-0166	3,000,000	5,500,000	Diversified	1
Washington Trust Equity Corp. John M. Snead, President Washington Trust Financial Center P.O. Box 2127 Spokane, WA 99210 (509)455-4106 Date Lic: 02/21/80	10/10-0170	705,000	0	Diversified	1
Wisconsin					
Bando-McGlocklin Capital Corporation George Schonath, Investment Advisor 13555 Bishops Court, Suite 225 Brookfield, WI 53005 (414)784-9010 Date Lic: 09/02/80	05/05-0147	7,175,113	21,520,000	Diversified	5
Capital Investments, Inc. Robert L. Banner, Vice President Commerce Building, Suite 400 744 North Fourth Street Milwaukee, WI 53203 (414)273-6560 Date Lic: 05/25/59	05/07-0003	4,806,833	7,580,000	Diversified	6

Licensee	License Number	Private Capital	SBA Leverage	Investment Policy	Owner Code

Wisconsin (Cont)

M & I Ventures Corp.   05/05-0202   5,448,370   0   Diversified   1
John T. Byrnes, President
770 North Water Street
Milwaukee, WI 53202
(414)765-7910 Date Lic: 08/19/85

Marine Venture   05/05-0195   6,000,000   0   Diversified   1
  Capital, Inc.
H. Wayne Foreman, President
111 East Wisconsin Avenue
Milwaukee, WI 53202
(414)765-2274 Date Lic: 05/02/84

MorAmerica Capital
  Corporation
(Main Office: Cedar Rapids, Iowa)
600 East Mason Street
Milwaukee, WI 53202
(414)276-3839

Super Market   05/05-0136   500,000   750,000   Grocery Stores   4
  Investors, Inc.
David H. Maass, President
23000 Roundy Drive
Mail: P.O. Box 473; Milwaukee 53202
Pewaukee, WI 53072
(414)547-7999 Date Lic: 01/25/79

Wisconsin Community   05/05-0204   1,005,000   0   Diversified   5
  Capital, Inc.
Francis J. David, General Manager
14 West Mifflin Street
Suite 314
Madison, WI 53703
(608)256-3441 Date Lic: 12/17/85

Wyoming

Capital Corporation of 08/08-0048   1,000,000   1,500,000   Diversified   3
  Wyoming, Inc.
Scott Weaver, Manager
P.O. Box 3599
145 South Durbin Street
Casper, WY 82602
(307)234-5351 Date Lic: 09/27/79

State	Size 1	Size 2	Size 3	Size 4	Total	Total Private Cap	Total Obligations to SBA
Alabama	0	1	2	0	3	13,166,800	6,500,000
Alaska	0	1	0	0	1	2,500,000	0
Arizona	2	0	0	1	3	16,600,000	500,000
Arkansas	1	1	0	0	2	1,650,100	3,250,000
California	15	9	4	6	34	157,147,729	50,445,000
Colorado	1	1	0	0	2	4,125,000	2,250,000
Connecticut	5	3	0	3	11	36,695,848	56,805,000
Delaware	0	0	0	1	1	30,000,000	0
Dist. of Col.	1	2	0	1	4	10,784,708	12,700,000
Florida	0	4	1	2	7	15,177,378	27,920,092
Georgia	0	1	0	1	2	6,093,500	8,400,000
Hawaii	0	1	0	0	1	2,000,000	500,000
Idaho	0	0	0	0	0	0	0
Illinois	1	2	3	3	9	147,038,671	22,800,000
Indiana	5	0	0	0	5	6,898,000	0
Iowa	0	0	0	1	1	5,000,000	10,650,440
Kansas	0	1	0	0	1	3,740,690	0
Kentucky	1	1	0	0	2	2,540,000	3,600,000
Louisiana	2	2	0	0	4	6,676,731	1,980,000
Maine	1	0	0	0	1	1,000,000	1,000,000
Maryland	1	1	0	1	3	11,102,255	3,713,720
Massachusetts	6	6	3	8	23	154,724,842	131,170,000
Michigan	1	1	0	0	2	3,492,500	0
Minnesota	4	0	0	4	8	88,275,689	33,424,000
Mississippi	1	0	0	0	1	950,000	509,000
Missouri	1	1	2	0	4	14,632,000	1,010,000
Montana	0	0	0	0	0	0	0
Nebraska	1	0	0	0	1	500,000	500,000
Nevada	1	0	0	0	1	1,000,000	800,000
New Hampshire	0	1	0	0	1	1,403,911	1,200,000
New Jersey	2	3	3	0	8	16,205,664	19,822,000
New Mexico	1	3	0	0	4	2,925,160	6,130,000
New York	18	16	7	16	57	500,729,680	225,030,000
North Carolina	1	3	1	1	6	28,385,541	11,000,114
North Dakota	0	0	0	0	0	0	0
Ohio	4	3	2	1	10	23,586,610	19,662,400
Oklahoma	0	0	2	0	2	5,476,867	6,660,000
Oregon	1	0	0	0	1	911,464	500,000
Pennsylvania	3	3	2	0	8	21,004,755	2,315,000
Puerto Rico	0	0	0	0	0	0	0
Rhode Island	2	1	0	2	5	19,716,604	11,270,000
South Carolina	3	1	1	0	5	6,812,659	7,400,000
South Dakota	0	0	0	0	0	0	0
Tennessee	2	0	0	0	2	2,485,320	0
Texas	10	8	4	8	30	155,835,171	166,655,000
Utah	0	0	0	0	0	0	0
Vermont	1	0	0	0	1	1,500,000	0
Virginia	2	1	1	3	7	31,366,493	43,350,000
Washington	3	1	1	0	5	6,761,053	6,500,000
West Virginia	0	0	0	0	0	0	0
Wisconsin	2	0	2	2	6	24,935,316	29,850,000
Wyoming	0	1	0	0	1	1,000,000	1,500,000
TOTAL	106	84	41	65	296	1,594,554,709	939,271,766

Licensee	License Number	Private Capital	SBA Leverage	Investment Policy	Owner Code
Alabama					
Alabama Capital Corporation David C. Delaney, President 16 Midtown Park East Mobile, AL 36606 (205)476-0700 Date Lic: 07/28/81	04/04-5203	1,550,000	4,650,000	Diversified	5
Alabama Small Business Investment Company Harold Gilchrist, Manager 206 North 24th Street Birmingham, AL 35203 (205)324-5234 Date Lic: 04/05/88	04/04-5243	1,005,000	0	Diversified	1
Tuskegee Capital Corporation A. G. Bartholomew, President 4453 Richardson Road Hampton Hall Building Montgomery, AL 36108 (205)281-8059 Date Lic: 02/09/83	04/04-5215	850,000	0	Diversified	5
Alaska					
Calista Business Investment Corp. Alex Raider, President 503 East Sixth Avenue Anchorage, AK 99501 (907)277-0425 Date Lic: 03/31/83	10/10-5181	750,000	750,000	Diversified	5
Arkansas					
Capital Management Services, Inc. David L. Hale, President 1910 North Grant Street Suite 200 Little Rock, AR 72207 (501)664-8613 Date Lic: 03/14/79	06/06-5207	1,006,310	2,500,000	Diversified	5
Kar-Mal Venture Capital, Inc. Amelia Karam, President 2821 Kavanaugh Blvd. Little Rock, AR 72205 (501)661-0010 Date Lic: 11/23/77	06/06-5185	500,000	1,000,000	Diversified	4

Exhibit 12-4

Licensee	License Number	Private Capital	SBA Leverage	Investment Policy	Owner Code

Arkansas (Cont)

Power Ventures, Inc.   06/06-5235   500,000   1,000,000   Diversified   5
Dorsey D. Glover, President
829 Highway 270 North
Malvern, AR 72104
(501)332-3695 Date Lic: 02/26/81

California

ABC Capital Corp.   09/09-5352   1,000,000   3,000,000   Diversified   5
Anne B. Cheng, President
610 East Live Oak Avenue
Arcadia, CA 91006
(818)570-0653 Date Lic: 01/09/85

Allied Business   09/09-5309   600,000   1,200,000   Diversified   5
  Investors, Inc.
Jack Hong, President
428 South Atlantic Blvd., Suite 201
Monterey Park, CA 91754
(818)289-0186 Date Lic: 12/29/82

Ally Finance Corp.   09/09-5299   600,000   950,000   Diversified   5
Percy P. Lin, President
9100 Wilshire Blvd., Suite 408
Beverly Hills, CA 90212
(213)550-8100 Date Lic: 06/04/82

Asian American Capital 09/09-5279   638,200   1,000,000   Diversified   5
  Corporation
David Der, President
1251 West Tennyson Road
Suite #4
Hayward, CA 94544
(415)887-6888 Date Lic: 02/23/81

Astar Capital Corp.   09/09-5370   1,020,000   2,040,000   Diversified   5
George Hsu, President
7282 Orangethorpe Ave., Suite 8
Buena Park, CA 90621
(714)739-2218 Date Lic: 11/06/86

Bentley Capital   09/09-5375   1,500,000   0   Diversified   5
John Hung, President
592 Vallejo Street, Suite #2
San Francisco, CA 94133
(415)362-2868 Date Lic: 08/27/87

Licensee	License Number	Private Capital	SBA Leverage	Investment Policy	Owner Code
California (Cont)					
Best Finance Corporation Vincent Lee, General Manager 1814 W. Washington Blvd. Los Angeles, CA 90007 (213)731-2268 Date Lic: 06/24/87	09/09-5369	1,001,200	1,000,000	Diversified	5
Business Equity and Development Corp. Leon M.N. Garcia, President/CEO 767 North Hill Street, Suite 401 Los Angeles, CA 90012 (213)613-0351 Date Lic: 03/19/70	09/12-5151	1,877,532	1,000,000	Diversified	5
Charterway Investment Corporation Harold H. M. Chuang, President 222 South Hill Street, Suite 800 Los Angeles, CA 90012 (213)687-8539 Date Lic: 04/04/84	09/09-5338	1,597,336	3,000,000	Diversified	5
Continental Investors, Inc. Lac Thantrong, President 8781 Seaspray Drive Huntington Beach, CA 92646 (714)964-5207 Date Lic: 06/18/80	09/09-5144	2,000,000	5,000,000	Diversified	5
Equitable Capital Corporation John C. Lee, President 855 Sansome Street San Francisco, CA 94111 (415)434-4114 Date Lic: 03/08/79	09/09-5231	642,995	1,505,000	Diversified	5
First American Capital Funding, Inc. Luu TranKiem, Chairman 38 Corporate Park, Suite B Irvine, CA 92714 (714)660-9288 Date Lic: 05/02/84	09/09-5332	734,000	2,202,000	Diversified	5
Helio Capital, Inc. Chester Koo, President 5900 South Eastern Avenue Suite 136 Commerce, CA 90040 (213)721-8053 Date Lic: 09/20/85	09/09-5361	1,000,000	2,000,000	Diversified	5

Licensee	License Number	Private Capital	SBA Leverage	Investment Policy	Owner Code

California (Cont)

LaiLai Capital Corp.   09/09-5285   1,000,000   2,000,000   Diversified   5
Hsing-Jong Duan, Pres. & General Manager
1545 Wilshire Blvd., Suite 510
Los Angeles, CA 90017
(213)484-5085   Date Lic: 11/24/82

Magna Pacific   09/09-5362   1,000,000   1,080,000   Diversified   5
   Investments
David Wong, President
977 North Broadway, Suite 301
Los Angeles, CA 90012
(213)680-2505   Date Lic: 12/03/85

Myriad Capital, Inc.   09/09-5272   1,334,530   5,338,120   Diversified   5
Chuang-I Lin, President
328 South Atlantic Boulevard
Suite 200
Monterey Park, CA 91754
(818)570-4548   Date Lic: 09/16/80

New Kukje Investment   09/09-5343   1,020,000   1,000,000   Diversified   5
   Company
George Su Chey, President
958 South Vermont Avenue
Suite C
Los Angeles, CA 90006
(213)389-8679   Date Lic: 01/10/85

Opportunity Capital   09/12-5155   2,526,043   2,180,500   Diversified   2
   Corporation
J. Peter Thompson, President
One Fremont Place
39650 Liberty Street, Suite 425
Fremont, CA 94538
(415)651-4412   Date Lic: 09/23/71

Positive Enterprises,   09/09-5256   505,000   505,000   Diversified   5
   Inc.
Kwok Szeto, President
399 Arguello Street
San Francisco, CA 94118
(415)386-6606   Date Lic: 06/06/80

RSC Financial Corp.   09/09-5161   526,508   1,900,000   Diversified   3
Frederick K. Bae, President
323 E. Matilija Road, #208
Ojai, CA 93023
(805)646-2925   Date Lic: 09/28/72

Licensee	License Number	Private Capital	SBA Leverage	Investment Policy	Owner Code

California (Cont)

San Joaquin Business 09/09-5376 1,000,000 0 Diversified 5
  Investment Group Inc
Joe Williams, President
2310 Tulare Street, Suite 140
Fresno, CA 93721
(209)233-3580 Date Lic: 04/23/88

Colorado

Colorado Invesco, Inc. 08/08-5058 1,020,600 0 Diversified 5
Samuel E. Matthews, President
1999 Broadway, Suite 2100
Denver, CO 80202
(303)293-2431 Date Lic: 06/18/84

D.C.

Allied Financial 03/03-5163 4,000,000 8,000,000 Diversified 6
  Corporation
David J. Gladstone, President
1666 K Street, N.W., Suite 901
Washington, DC 20006
(202)331-1112 Date Lic: 08/09/83

Broadcast Capital, 03/03-5147 3,050,000 5,000,000 Communications 5
  Inc.   Media
John E. Oxendine, President
1771 N Street, N.W., Suite 421
Washington, DC 20036
(202)429-5393 Date Lic: 11/26/80

Consumers United 03/03-5171 1,008,000 0 Diversified 4
  Capital Corporation
Ester M. Carr-Davis, President
2100 M Street, N.W.
Washington, DC 20037
(202)872-5274 Date Lic: 04/22/85

Fulcrum Venture 03/03-5135 2,000,000 2,000,000 Diversified 3
  Capital Corporation
C. Robert Kemp, Chairman
1030 15th Street, N.W., Suite 203
Washington, DC 20005
(202)785-4253 Date Lic: 07/05/78

Licensee	License Number	Private Capital	SBA Leverage	Investment Policy	Owner Code
D.C. (Cont)					
Minority Broadcast Investment Corp. Walter L. Threadgill, President 450 M Street, S.W. Washington, DC 20024 (202)479-0878 Date Lic: 08/07/79	03/03-5142	1,000,100	1,500,100	Communications	5
Syncom Capital Corp. Herbert P. Wilkins, President 1030 - 15th Street, N.W., Suite 203 Washington, DC 20005 (202)293-9428 Date Lic: 07/10/78	03/03-5137	2,250,000	5,125,000	Communications Media	4
Florida					
Allied Financial Corporation (Main Office: Washington, D.C.) Executive Office Center, Suite 305 2770 N. Indian River Blvd. Vero Beach, FL 32960 (407)778-5556					
First American Lending Corporation (The) Roy W. Talmo, Chairman 1926 10th Avenue North Mail: P.O. Box 24660; W Palm Beach 33416 Lake Worth, FL 33461 (305)533-1511 Date Lic: 09/27/79	04/04-5162	500,000	1,000,000	Diversified	1
Ideal Financial Corporation Ectore T. Reynaldo, General Manager 780 N.W. 42nd Avenue, Suite 303 Miami, FL 33126 (305)442-4665 Date Lic: 03/07/83	04/04-5190	500,000	1,000,000	Diversified	5
Pro-Med Investment Corporation Mrs. Marion Rosemore, President 1380 N.E. Miami Gardens Drive Suite 225 N. Miami Beach, FL 33179 (305)949-5915 Date Lic: 11/28/86	04/04-5240	2,000,000	1,000,000	Diversified	6

Licensee	License Number	Private Capital	SBA Leverage	Investment Policy	Owner Code

Florida (Cont)

Venture Group, Inc.   04/04-5219   500,000   500,000   Diversified   5
Ellis W. Hitzing, President
5433 Buffalo Avenue
Jacksonville, FL 32208
(904)353-7313   Date Lic: 04/25/83

Georgia

Renaissance Capital   04/04-5236   1,000,000   0   Diversified   5
    Corporation
Samuel B. Florence, President
161 Spring Street, NW
Suite 610
Atlanta, GA 30303
(404)658-9061   Date Lic: 12/05/86

Hawaii

Pacific Venture   09/09-5182   1,000,000   700,000   Diversified   4
    Capital, Ltd.
Dexter J. Taniguchi, President
222 South Vineyard Street
PH.1
Honolulu, HI 96813
(808)521-6502   Date Lic: 06/25/80

Illinois

Amoco Venture Capital   05/07-5083   2,976,750   6,603,000   Diversified   4
    Company
Gordon E. Stone, President
200 E. Randolph Drive
Chicago, IL 60601
(312)856-6523   Date Lic: 12/22/70

Chicago Community   05/05-5089   1,005,000   2,005,000   Diversified   4
    Ventures, Inc.
Phyllis George, President
104 South Michigan Avenue
Suite 215-218
Chicago, IL 60603
(312)726-6084   Date Lic: 06/14/72

Combined Fund,   05/07-5080   1,100,250   1,629,000   Diversified   1
    Inc. (The)
E. Patric Jones, President
1525 East 53rd Street
Chicago, IL 60615
(312)753-9650   Date Lic: 05/04/71

Licensee	License Number	Private Capital	SBA Leverage	Investment Policy	Owner Code

Illinois (Cont)

Neighborhood Fund, Inc. (The)
James Fletcher, President
1950 East 71st Street
Chicago, IL 60649
(312)684-8074 Date Lic: 04/03/78

| | 05/05-5124 | 730,000 | 950,000 | Diversified | 1 |

Peterson Finance and Investment Company
James S. Rhee, President
3300 West Peterson Avenue, Suite A
Chicago, IL 60659
(312)583-6300 Date Lic: 02/07/84

| | 05/05-5176 | 1,035,000 | 1,520,000 | Diversified | 2 |

Tower Ventures, Inc.
Robert T. Smith, President
Sears Tower, BSC 43-50
Chicago, IL 60684
(312)875-0571 Date Lic: 06/30/75

| | 05/05-5104 | 2,000,000 | 3,000,000 | Diversified | 4 |

Kentucky

Equal Opportunity Finance, Inc.
Franklin Justice, Jr., V.P. & Manager
420 Hurstbourne Lane, Suite 201
Louisville, KY 40222
(502)423-1943 Date Lic: 09/24/70

| | 04/05-5096 | 1,456,591 | 1,600,000 | Diversified | 4 |

Louisiana

SCDF Investment Corp.
Martial Mirabeau, Manager
1006 Surrey Street
P.O. Box 3885
Lafayette, LA 70502
(318)232-3769 Date Lic: 04/26/73

| | 06/10-5157 | 2,700,010 | 3,119,549 | Diversified | 4 |

Maryland

Albright Venture Capital, Inc.
William A. Albright, President
1355 Piccard Drive, Suite 380
Rockville, MD 20850
(301)921-9090 Date Lic: 08/10/79

| | 03/03-5141 | 505,000 | 750,000 | Diversified | 5 |

Licensee	License Number	Private Capital	SBA Leverage	Investment Policy	Owner Code
Maryland (Cont)					
Security Financial and Investment Corp. Han Y. Cho, President 7720 Wisconsin Avenue, Suite 207 Bethesda, MD 20814 (301)951-4288 Date Lic: 12/29/83	03/03-5158	510,000	500,000	Diversified	5
Massachusetts					
New England MESBIC, Inc. Etang Chen, President 530 Turnpike Street North Andover, MA 01845 (617)688-4326 Date Lic: 10/26/82	01/01-5318	500,000	1,500,000	Diversified	5
Transportation Capital Corp. (Main Office: New York, NY) 230 Newbury Street, Suite 21 Boston, MA 02116 (617)536-0344					
Michigan					
Dearborn Capital Corp. Michael LaManes, President P.O. Box 1729 Dearborn, MI 48121 (313)337-8577 Date Lic: 12/14/78	05/05-5135	2,064,349	1,000,000	Diversified	4
Metro-Detroit Investment Company William J. Fowler, President 30777 Northwestern Highway Suite 300 Farmington Hill, MI 48018 (313)851-6300 Date Lic: 06/01/78	05/05-5126	2,000,000	6,000,000	Grocery Stores	4
Motor Enterprises, Inc. James Kobus, Manager 3044 West Grand Blvd. Detroit, MI 48202 (313)556-4273 Date Lic: 04/13/70	05/15-5024	1,500,000	2,000,000	Diversified	4

Licensee	License Number	Private Capital	SBA Leverage	Investment Policy	Owner Code

Michigan (Cont)

Mutual Investment   05/05-5144   1,964,094   5,808,000   Diversified   5
   Company, Inc.
Jack Najor, President
21415 Civic Center Drive
Mark Plaza Building, Suite 217
Southfield, MI 48076
(313)557-2020   Date Lic: 04/21/80

Minnesota

Capital Dimensions   05/05-5134   7,342,662   10,000,000   Diversified   4
   Ventures Fund, Inc.
Dean R. Pickerell, President
Two Appletree Square, Suite 244
Minneapolis, MN 55425
(612)854-3007   Date Lic: 01/29/79

Mississippi

Sun-Delta Capital   04/04-5175   1,258,100   0   Diversified   5
   Access Center, Inc.
Howard Boutte, Jr., Vice President
819 Main Street
Greenville, MS 38701
(601)335-5291   Date Lic: 09/25/79

New Jersey

Capital Circulation   02/02-5484   1,000,000   200,000   Diversified   5
   Corporation
Judy Kao, Manager
208 Main Street
Fort Lee, NJ 07024
(201)947-8637   Date Lic: 03/28/85

Formosa Captal Corp.   02/02-5485   1,000,000   1,000,000   Diversified   5
Philp Chen, President
605 King George Post Road
Fords, NJ 08863
(201)738-4710   Date Lic: 08/22/85

Rutgers Minority   02/02-5283   1,499,000   905,000   Diversified   4
   Investment Company
Oscar Figueroa, President
92 New Street
Newark, NJ 07102
(201)648-5287   Date Lic: 07/28/70

Licensee	License Number	Private Capital	SBA Leverage	Investment Policy	Owner Code
New Jersey (Cont)					
Transpac Capital Corporation Tsuey Tang Wang, President 1037 Route 46 East Clifton, NJ 07013 (201)470-0706 Date Lic: 05/28/87	02/02-5502	1,000,000	0	Diversified	5
Zaitech Capital Corporation Mr. Fu-Tong Hsu, President 2083 Center Avenue Fort Lee, NJ 07024 (201)944-3018 Date Lic: 06/05/86	02/02-5494	1,000,000	1,000,000	Diversified	5
New Mexico					
Associated Southwest Investors, Inc. John R. Rice, General Manager 2400 Louisiana N.E. Bldg. #4, Suite 225 Albuquerque, NM 87110 (505)881-0066 Date Lic: 12/09/71	09/14-5086	707,000	1,700,000	Diversified	4
New York					
American Asian Capital Corporation Howard H. Lin, President 130 Water Street, Suite 6-L New York, NY 10005 (212)422-6880 Date Lic: 11/12/76	02/02-5316	503,000	500,000	Diversified	5
Avdon Capital Corp. A. M. Donner, President 805 Avenue L Brooklyn, NY 11230 (718)692-0950 Date Lic: 04/21/83	02/02-5456	1,000,000	2,500,000	Diversified	5
CVC Capital Corp. Jeorg G. Klebe, President 131 East 62th Street New York, NY 10021 (212)319-7210 Date Lic: 03/22/78	02/02-5338	3,255,000	6,000,000	Communications, Real Estate, Export Finance	5

Licensee	License Number	Private Capital	SBA Leverage	Investment Policy	Owner Code
New York (Cont)					
Capital Investors & Management Corp. Rose Chao, Manager 210 Canal Street, Suite 607 New York, NY 10013 (212)964-2480 Date Lic: 02/06/80	02/02-5363	900,000	1,500,000	Diversified	5
Cohen Capital Corp. Edward H. Cohen, President 8 Freer Street, Suite 185 Lynbrook, NY 11563 (516)887-3434 Date Lic: 03/01/78	02/02-5335	710,000	1,300,000	Diversified	5
Columbia Capital Corporation Mark Scharfman, President 79 Madison Avenue, Suite 800 New York, NY 10016 (212)696-4334 Date Lic: 09/09/83	02/02-5462	3,831,343	3,660,000	Diversified	5
East Coast Venture Capital, Inc. Zindel Zelmanovitch, President 313 West 53rd Street, Third Floor New York, NY 10019 (212)245-6460 Date Lic: 07/14/86	02/02-5470	1,000,000	2,000,000	Diversified	5
Elk Associates Funding Corporation Gary C. Granoff, President 600 Third Avenue, 38th Floor New York, NY 10016 (212)972-8550 Date Lic: 07/24/80	02/02-5377	5,487,808	8,785,000	Transportation	5
Equico Capital Corp. Duane Hill, President 1290 Avenue of the Americas Suite 3400 New York, NY 10019 (212)397-8660 Date Lic: 05/07/71	02/02-5286	10,550,000	10,295,000	Diversified	4
Everlast Capital Corporation Frank J. Segreto, Gen. Mgr. & V.P. 350 Fifth Avenue, Suite 2805 New York, NY 10118 (212)695-3910 Date Lic: 07/30/84	02/02-5468	2,840,000	5,400,000	Diversified	5

Licensee	License Number	Private Capital	SBA Leverage	Investment Policy	Owner Code

Exim Capital Corp.　02/02-5351　660,000　1,500,000　Diversified　5
Victor K. Chun, President
290 Madison Avenue
New York, NY 10017
(212)683-3375　Date Lic:　01/05/79

Fair Capital Corp.　02/02-5437　508,000　500,000　Diversified　5
Robert Yet Sen Chen, President
c/o Summit Associates
3 Pell Street, 2nd Floor
New York, NY 10013
(201)608-5866　Date Lic:　09/27/82

Freshstart Venture　02/02-5447　708,525　2,310,000　Diversified　5
　Capital Corporation
Zindel Zelmanovich, President
313 West 53rd Street, 3rd Floor
New York, NY 10019
(212)265-2249　Date Lic:　02/24/83

Hanam Capital Corp.　02/02-5497　1,021,000　0　Diversified　5
Dr. Yul Chang, President
One Penn Plaza, Suite 3330
New York, NY 10119
(212)714-9830　Date Lic:　05/06/87

Hop Chung Capital　02/02-5368　510,000　1,000,000　Diversified　5
　Investors, Inc.
Yon Hon Lee, President
185 Canal Street, Room 303
New York, NY 10013
(212)219-1777　Date Lic:　07/18/80

Horn & Hardart Capital 04/04-5228　1,000,000　0　Diversified　5
　Corporation
Morton Farber, Manager
730 Fifth Avenue
New York, NY 10019
(212)484-9600　Date Lic:　09/11/85

Ibero American　02/02-5369　1,246,471　1,897,000　Diversified　5
　Investors Corp.
Emilio Serrano, President
38 Scio Street
Rochester, NY 14604
(716)262-3440　Date Lic:　09/28/79

Licensee	License Number	Private Capital	SBA Leverage	Investment Policy	Owner Code
New York (Cont)					
Intercontinental Capital Funding Corp James S. Yu, President 60 East 42nd Street, Suite 740 New York, NY 10165 (212)286-9642 Date Lic: 09/30/81	02/02-5421	500,000	1,750,000	Diversified	5
International Paper Cap. Formation, Inc. (Main Office: Memphis, TN) Frank Polney, Manager Two Manhattanville Road Purchase, NY 10577 (914)397-1578					
Japanese American Capital Corporation Stephen C. Huang, President 19 Rector Street New York, NY 10006 (212)964-4077 Date Lic: 08/07/79	02/02-5367	525,000	1,490,000	Diversified	5
Jardine Capital Corp. Evelyn Sy Dy, President 8 Chatham Square, Suite 708 New York, NY 10038 (212)406-1799 Date Lic: 12/22/86	02/02-5495	1,000,000	1,000,000	Diversified	5
Manhattan Central Capital Corp. David Choi, President 1255 Broadway, Room 405 New York, NY 10001 (212)684-6411 Date Lic: 06/11/87	02/02-5500	1,000,000	1,000,000	Diversified	5
Medallion Funding Corporation Alvin Murstein, President 205 E. 42nd Street, Suite 2020 New York, NY 10017 (212)682-3300 Date Lic: 06/23/80	02/02-5393	9,234,000	19,734,000	Transportation	5
Minority Equity Cap. Company, Inc. Donald F. Greene, President 275 Madison Avenue New York, NY 10016 (212)686-9710 Date Lic: 05/17/71	02/02-5288	2,615,747	3,104,046	Diversified	4

Licensee	License Number	Private Capital	SBA Leverage	Investment Policy	Owner Code

New York (Cont)

Monsey Capital Corp.   02/02-5474   1,257,040   3,000,000   Diversified   5
Shamuel Myski, President
125 Route 59
Monsey, NY 10952
(914)425-2229 Date Lic: 01/17/85

New Oasis Capital   02/02-5379   500,000   1,500,000   Diversified   5
   Corporation
James Huang, President
114 Liberty Street, Suite 404
New York, NY 10006
(212)349-2804 Date Lic: 02/06/80

North American Funding 02/02-5418   500,000   1,500,000   Diversified   5
   Corporation
Franklin F. Y. Wong, V.P. & Gen. Mgr.
177 Canal Street
New York, NY 10013
(212)226-0080 Date Lic: 03/05/81

North Street Capital   02/02-5285   2,200,000   1,500,000   Diversified   4
   Corporation
Ralph McNeal, President
250 North Street, RA-65
White Plains, NY 10625
(914)335-6306 Date Lic: 10/16/70

Pan Pac Capital Corp. 02/02-5386   503,000   1,505,000   Diversified   5
Dr. In Ping Jack Lee, President
121 East Industry Court
Deer Park, NY 11729
(516)586-7653 Date Lic: 06/11/80

Pierre Funding Corp.   02/02-5396   2,762,074   7,111,800   Transportation   5
Elias Debbas, President
131 South Central Avenue
Hartsdale, NY 10530
(914)683-1144 Date Lic: 01/22/81

Pierre Funding Corp.
(Main Office: Hartsdale, NY)
270 Madison Avenue
New York, NY 10016
(212)689-9361

Licensee	License Number	Private Capital	SBA Leverage	Investment Policy	Owner Code

Licensee	License Number	Private Capital	SBA Leverage	Investment Policy	Owner Code
Pioneer Capital Corp. James G. Niven, President 113 East 55th Street New York, NY 10022 (212)980-9090 Date Lic: 09/02/69	02/02-5274	701,261	700,000	Diversified	5
Situation Venture Corporation Sam Hollander, President 502 Flushing Avenue Brooklyn, NY 11205 (718)855-1835 Date Lic: 02/16/77	02/02-5323	1,000,200	3,000,000	Diversified	5
Square Deal Venture Capital Corp. Mordechai Z. Feldman, President 805 Avenue L Brooklyn, NY 11230 (718)692-2924 Date Lic: 09/28/79	02/02-5374	546,000	1,200,000	Diversified	5
Taroco Capital Corp. David R. C. Chang, President 19 Rector Street, 35th Floor New York, NY 10006 (212)344-6690 Date Lic: 09/10/76	02/02-5318	1,010,000	3,030,000	Chinese Americans	5
Transportation Capital Corp. Melvin L. Hirsch, President 60 East 42nd Street, Suite 3126 New York, NY 10165 (212)697-4885 Date Lic: 06/23/80	02/02-5388	6,561,380	10,148,333	Diversified	5
Triad Capital Corp. of New York Lorenzo J. Barrera, President 960 Southern Blvd. Bronx, NY 10459 (212)589-6541 Date Lic: 11/25/83	02/02-5455	545,253	500,000	Diversified	2
Trico Venture, Inc. Avruhum Donner, President 805 Avenue L Brooklyn, NY 11230 (718)692-0950 Date Lic: 06/27/86	02/02-5496	1,000,000	1,700,000	Diversified	5

Licensee	License Number	Private Capital	SBA Leverage	Investment Policy	Owner Code

New York (Cont)

United Capital
  Investment Corp. 02/02-5480 1,030,000 3,000,000 Diversified 5
Paul Lee, President
60 East 42nd Street, Suite 1515
New York, NY 10165
(212)682-7210 Date Lic: 02/05/85

Venture Opportunities 02/04-5151 875,000 2,300,000 Diversified 5
  Corporation
A. Fred March, President
110 East 59th Street, 29th Floor
New York, NY 10022
(212)832-3737 Date Lic: 12/01/78

Watchung Capital Corp. 02/02-5371 500,000 1,000,000 Diversified 5
S. T. Jeng, President
431 Fifth Avenue, Fifth Floor
New York, NY 10016
(212)889-3466 Date Lic: 02/19/80

Yang Capital Corp. 02/02-5429 500,000 1,500,000 Diversified 5
Maysing Yang, President
41-40 Kissena Blvd.
Flushing, NY 11355
(516)482-1578 Date Lic: 04/12/83

Yusa Capital Corp. 02/02-5467 1,035,000 2,000,000 Diversified 5
Christopher Yeung, Chairman of the Board
622 Broadway
New York, NY 10012
(212)420-1350 Date Lic: 07/31/84

Ohio

Center City MESBIC, 05/05-5153 500,000 500,000 Diversified 5
  Inc.
Michael A. Robinson, President
Centre City Office Building, Suite 762
40 South Main Street
Dayton, OH 45402
(513)461-6164 Date Lic: 07/29/81

Rubber City Capital 05/05-5201 1,000,000 0 Diversified 5
  Corporation
Jesse T. Williams, President
1144 East Market Street
Akron, OH 44316
(216)796-9167 Date Lic: 08/14/85

71

Licensee	License Number	Private Capital	SBA Leverage	Investment Policy	Owner Code
Pennsylvania					
Alliance Enterprise Corporation W. B. Priestley, President 1801 Market Street, 3rd Floor Philadelphia, PA 19103 (215)977-3925 Date Lic: 10/20/71	03/03-5066	3,030,200	2,700,000	Diversified	4
Greater Phila. Venture Capital Corp., Inc. Martin Newman, Manager 920 Lewis Tower Bldg. 225 South Fifteenth Street Philadelphia, PA 19102 (215)732-3415 Date Lic: 03/31/72	03/03-5112	756,583	1,505,000	Diversified	2
Salween Financial Services, Inc. Dr. Ramarao Naidu, President 228 North Pottstown Pike Exton, PA 19341 (215)524-1880 Date Lic: 07/01/83	03/03-5157	800,000	725,000	Diversified	5
Puerto Rico					
North America Inv. Corporation Santigo Ruz Betacourt, President Banco CTR #1710, M Rivera Av Stop 34 Mail: PO BX 1831 Hato Rey Sta., PR 00919 Hato Rey, PR 00936 (809)751-6178 Date Lic: 11/07/74	02/02-5308	750,000	2,250,000	Diversified	5
Tennessee					
Chickasaw Capital Corporation Tom Moore, President 67 Madison Avenue Memphis, TN 38147 (901)523-6404 Date Lic: 08/30/77	04/04-5128	500,000	500,000	Diversified	1
International Paper Cap. Formation, Inc. John G. Herman, V.P. and Controller International Place I 6400 Poplar Avenue, 10-74 Memphis, TN 38197 (901)763-6282 Date Lic: 11/05/81	04/02-5432	1,000,000	1,000,000	Diversified	5

Licensee	License Number	Private Capital	SBA Leverage	Investment Policy	Owner Code
Tennessee (Cont)					
Tennessee Equity Capital Corporation Walter S. Cohen, President 1102 Stonewall Jackson Court Nashville, TN 37220 (615)373-4502 Date Lic: 01/19/79	04/04-5157	837,000	750,000	Diversified	5
Tennessee Venture Capital Corporation Wendell P. Knox, President 162 Fourth Avenue North, Suite 125 Mail: P.O. Box 2567 Nashville, TN 37219 (615)244-6935 Date Lic: 09/28/79	04/04-5176	500,000	500,000	Diversified	5
Valley Capital Corp. Lamar J. Partridge, President 8th Floor Krystal Building 100 W. Martin Luther King Blvd. Chattanooga, TN 37402 (615)265-1557 Date Lic: 10/08/82	04/04-5216	1,145,000	0	Diversified	5
West Tennessee Venture Capital Corporation Robert Fenner, Manager 152 Beale Street, Suite 401 Mail: P.O. Box 300; Memphis, TN 38101 Memphis, TN 38101 (901)527-6091 Date Lic: 12/16/82	04/04-5218	1,250,000	0	Diversified	5
Texas					
Chen's Financial Group, Inc. Samuel S. C. Chen, President 1616 West Loop South, Suite 200 Houston, TX 77027 (713)850-0879 Date Lic: 03/05/84	06/06-5281	1,000,000	2,000,000	Diversified	5
Evergreen Capital Company, Inc. Shen-Lim Lin, Chairman & President 8502 Tybor Drive, Suite 201 Houston, TX 77074 (713)778-9770 Date Lic: 07/07/83	06/06-5264	1,001,000	2,000,000	Diversified	5

Licensee	License Number	Private Capital	SBA Leverage	Investment Policy	Owner Code

Texas (Cont)

MESBIC Financial Corp. of Dallas Donald R. Lawhorne, President 12655 N. Central Expressway Suite 814 Dallas, TX 75243 (214)991-1597 Date Lic: 02/26/70	06/10-5153	4,050,000	3,050,000	Diversified	2
MESBIC Financial Corp. of Houston Lynn H. Miller, President 811 Rusk, Suite 201 Houston, TX 77002 (713)228-8321 Date Lic: 11/12/76	06/06-5180	854,900	854,000	Diversified	2
Minority Enterprise Funding, Inc. Frederick C. Chang, President 17300 El Camino Real, Suite 107-B Houston, TX 77058 (713)488-4919 Date Lic: 03/09/79	06/09-5230	1,000,000	2,650,000	Diversified	5
Southern Orient Capital Corporation Min H. Liang, President 2419 Fannin, Suite 200 Houston, TX 77002 (713)225-3369 Date Lic: 12/29/80	06/06-5240	550,000	1,650,000	Diversified	5
United Oriental Capital Corporation Don J. Wang, President 908 Town & Country Blvd. Suite 310 Houston, TX 77024 (713)461-3909 Date Lic: 07/07/82	06/06-5254	1,000,000	1,500,000	Diversified	5

Virginia

Basic Investment Corp. Frank F. Luwis, President 6723 Whittier Avenue McLean, VA 22101 (703)356-4300 Date Lic: 07/29/83	03/03-5156	500,000	0	Diversified	5

Licensee	License Number	Private Capital	SBA Leverage	Investment Policy	Owner Code
Virginia (Cont)					
East West United Investment Company Bui Dung, President 815 West Broad Street Falls Church, VA 22046 (703)237-7200 Date Lic: 01/22/76	03/03-5125	500,000	1,500,000	Diversified	5
Washington Finance and Investment Corp. Chang H. Lie, President 100 E. Broad Street Falls Church, VA 22046 (703)534-7200 Date Lic: 06/03/82	03/03-5150	1,005,000	2,000,000	Diversified	5
Wisconsin					
Future Value Ventures, Incorporated William P. Beckett, President 622 North Water Street, Suite 500 Milwaukee, WI 53202 (414)278-0377 Date Lic: 11/09/84	05/05-5198	1,020,000	1,000,000	Diversified	5

State	Number of SBICs					Total Private Cap	Total Obligations to SBA
	Size 1	Size 2	Size 3	Size 4	Total		
Alabama	2	0	1	0	3	3,405,000	4,650,000
Alaska	1	0	0	0	1	750,000	750,000
Arizona	0	0	0	0	0	0	0
Arkansas	2	1	0	0	3	2,006,310	4,500,000
California	6	13	2	0	21	23,123,344	37,900,620
Colorado	1	0	0	0	1	1,020,600	0
Connecticut	0	0	0	0	0	0	0
Delaware	0	0	0	0	0	0	0
Dist. of Col.	1	2	2	1	6	13,308,100	21,625,100
Florida	3	1	0	0	4	3,500,000	3,500,000
Georgia	1	0	0	0	1	1,000,000	0
Hawaii	1	0	0	0	1	1,000,000	700,000
Idaho	0	0	0	0	0	0	0
Illinois	1	4	1	0	6	8,847,000	15,707,000
Indiana	0	0	0	0	0	0	0
Iowa	0	0	0	0	0	0	0
Kansas	0	0	0	0	0	0	0
Kentucky	0	1	0	0	1	1,456,591	1,600,000
Louisiana	0	0	1	0	1	2,700,010	3,119,549
Maine	0	0	0	0	0	0	0
Maryland	2	0	0	0	2	1,015,000	1,250,000
Massachusetts	1	0	0	0	1	500,000	1,500,000
Michigan	0	2	2	0	4	7,528,443	14,808,000
Minnesota	0	0	0	1	1	7,342,662	10,000,000
Mississippi	1	0	0	0	1	1,258,100	0
Missouri	0	0	0	0	0	0	0
Montana	0	0	0	0	0	0	0
Nebraska	0	0	0	0	0	0	0
Nevada	0	0	0	0	0	0	0
New Hampshire	0	0	0	0	0	0	0
New Jersey	4	1	0	0	5	5,499,000	3,105,000
New Mexico	0	1	0	0	1	707,000	1,700,000
New York	14	18	5	4	41	73,632,102	123,420,179
North Carolina	0	0	0	0	0	0	0
North Dakota	0	0	0	0	0	0	0
Ohio	2	0	0	0	2	1,500,000	500,000
Oklahoma	0	0	0	0	0	0	0
Oregon	0	0	0	0	0	0	0
Pennsylvania	1	1	1	0	3	4,586,783	4,930,000
Puerto Rico	0	1	0	0	1	750,000	2,250,000
Rhode Island	0	0	0	0	0	0	0
South Carolina	0	0	0	0	0	0	0
South Dakota	0	0	0	0	0	0	0
Tennessee	6	0	0	0	6	5,232,000	2,750,000
Texas	1	5	1	0	7	9,455,900	13,704,000
Utah	0	0	0	0	0	0	0
Vermont	0	0	0	0	0	0	0
Virginia	2	1	0	0	3	2,005,000	3,500,000
Washington	0	0	0	0	0	0	0
West Virginia	0	0	0	0	0	0	0
Wisconsin	0	1	0	0	1	1,020,000	1,000,000
Wyoming	0	0	0	0	0	0	0
TOTAL	53	53	16	6	128	184,148,945	278,469,448

FORM D

OMB APPROVAL
OMB Number: 3235-0076
Expires: August 31, 1989

U.S. SECURITIES AND EXCHANGE COMMISSION
Washington, D.C. 20549

NOTICE OF SALE OF SECURITIES
PURSUANT TO REGULATION D,
SECTION 4(6), AND/OR
UNIFORM LIMITED OFFERING EXEMPTION

SEC USE ONLY

Prefix | Serial

DATE RECEIVED

Name of Offering   (☐ check if this is an amendment and name has changed, and indicate change.)

Filing Under (Check box(es) that apply):   ☐ Rule 504   ☐ Rule 505   ☐ Rule 506   ☐ Section 4(6)   ☐ ULOE

Type of Filing: ☐ New Filing   ☐ Amendment

A. BASIC IDENTIFICATION DATA

1. Enter the information requested about the issuer

Name of Issuer   (☐ check if this is an amendment and name has changed, and indicate change.)

Address of Executive Offices (Number and Street, City, State, Zip Code)	Telephone Number (Including Area Code)
Address of Principal Business Operations (Number and Street, City, State, Zip Code) (if different from Executive Offices)	Telephone Number (Including Area Code)

Brief Description of Business

Type of Business Organization
☐ corporation   ☐ limited partnership, already formed   ☐ other (please specify):
☐ business trust   ☐ limited partnership, to be formed

Month   Year

Actual or Estimated Date of Incorporation or Organization: ☐☐ ☐☐   ☐ Actual   ☐ Estimated

Jurisdiction of Incorporation or Organization: (Enter two-letter U.S. Postal Service abbreviation for State: CN for Canada; FN for other foreign jurisdiction)   ☐☐

GENERAL INSTRUCTIONS

Federal:

Who Must File: All issuers making an offering of securities in reliance on an exemption under Regulation D or Section 4(6), 17 CFR 230.501 et seq. or 15 U.S.C. 77d(6).

When To File: A notice must be filed no later than 15 days after the first sale of securities in the offering. A notice is deemed filed with the U.S. Securities and Exchange Commission (SEC) on the earlier of the date it is received by the SEC at the address given below or, if received at that address after the date on which it is due, on the date it was mailed by United States registered or certified mail to that address.

Where to File: U.S. Securities and Exchange Commission, 450 Fifth Street, N.W., Washington, D.C. 20549.

Copies Required: Five (5) copies of this notice must be filed with the SEC, one of which must be manually signed. Any copies not manually signed must be photocopies of the manually signed copy or bear typed or printed signatures.

Information Required: A new filing must contain all information requested. Amendments need only report the name of the issuer and offering, any changes thereto, the information requested in Part C, and any material changes from the information previously supplied in Parts A and B. Part E and the Appendix need not be filed with the SEC.

Filing Fee: There is no federal filing fee.

State:

This notice shall be used to indicate reliance on the Uniform Limited Offering Exemption (ULOE) for sales of securities in those states that have adopted ULOE and that have adopted this form. Issuers relying on ULOE must file a separate notice with the Securities Administrator in each state where sales are to be, or have been made. If a state requires the payment of a fee as a precondition to the claim for the exemption, a fee in the proper amount shall accompany this form. This notice shall be filed in the appropriate states in accordance with state law. The Appendix to the notice constitutes a part of this notice and must be completed.

──── **ATTENTION** ────
Failure to file notice in the appropriate states will not result in a loss of the federal exemption. Conversely, failure to file the appropriate federal notice will not result in a loss of an available state exemption unless such exemption is predicated on the filing of a federal notice.

SEC 1972 (5-87)

A. BASIC IDENTIFICATION DATA

2. Enter the information requested for the following:

- Each promoter of the issuer, if the issuer has been organized within the past five years;
- Each beneficial owner having the power to vote or dispose, or direct the vote or disposition of, 10% or more of a class of equity securities of the issuer;
- Each executive officer and director of corporate issuers and of corporate general and managing partners of partnership issuers; and
- Each general and managing partner of partnership issuers.

Check Box(es) that Apply: ☐ Promoter ☐ Beneficial Owner ☐ Executive Officer ☐ Director ☐ General and/or Managing Partner

Full Name (Last name first, if individual)

Business or Residence Address (Number and Street, City, State, Zip Code)

Check Box(es) that Apply: ☐ Promoter ☐ Beneficial Owner ☐ Executive Officer ☐ Director ☐ General and/or Managing Partner

Full Name (Last name first, if individual)

Business or Residence Address (Number and Street, City, State, Zip Code)

Check Box(es) that Apply: ☐ Promoter ☐ Beneficial Owner ☐ Executive Officer ☐ Director ☐ General and/or Managing Partner

Full Name (Last name first, if individual)

Business or Residence Address (Number and Street, City, State, Zip Code)

Check Box(es) that Apply: ☐ Promoter ☐ Beneficial Owner ☐ Executive Officer ☐ Director ☐ General and/or Managing Partner

Full Name (Last name first, if individual)

Business or Residence Address (Number and Street, City, State, Zip Code)

Check Box(es) that Apply: ☐ Promoter ☐ Beneficial Owner ☐ Executive Officer ☐ Director ☐ General and/or Managing Partner

Full Name (Last name first, if individual)

Business or Residence Address (Number and Street, City, State, Zip Code)

Check Box(es) that Apply: ☐ Promoter ☐ Beneficial Owner ☐ Executive Officer ☐ Director ☐ General and/or Managing Partner

Full Name (Last name first, if individual)

Business or Residence Address (Number and Street, City, State, Zip Code)

Check Box(es) that Apply: ☐ Promoter ☐ Beneficial Owner ☐ Executive Officer ☐ Director ☐ General and/or Managing Partner

Full Name (Last name first, if individual)

Business or Residence Address (Number and Street, City, State, Zip Code)

(Use blank sheet, or copy and use additional copies of this sheet, as necessary.)

2

	Yes	No
1. Has the issuer sold, or does the issuer intend to sell, to non-accredited investors in this offering?.................	☐	☐

Answer also in Appendix, Column 2, if filing under ULOE.

2. What is the minimum investment that will be accepted from any individual? .... $_____

	Yes	No
3. Does the offering permit joint ownership of a single unit?	☐	☐

4. Enter the information requested for each person who has been or will be paid or given, directly or indirectly, any commission or similar remuneration for solicitation of purchasers in connection with sales of securities in the offering. If a person to be listed is an associated person or agent of a broker or dealer registered with the SEC and/or with a state or states, list the name of the broker or dealer. If more than five (5) persons to be listed are associated persons of such a broker or dealer, you may set forth the information for that broker or dealer only.

Full Name (Last name first, if individual)

Business or Residence Address (Number and Street, City, State, Zip Code)

Name of Associated Broker or Dealer

States in Which Person Listed Has Solicited or Intends to Solicit Purchasers

(Check "All States" or check individual States) .... ☐ All States

[AL]	[AK]	[AZ]	[AR]	[CA]	[CO]	[CT]	[DE]	[DC]	[FL]	[GA]	[HI]	[ID]
[IL]	[IN]	[IA]	[KS]	[KY]	[LA]	[ME]	[MD]	[MA]	[MI]	[MN]	[MS]	[MO]
[MT]	[NE]	[NV]	[NH]	[NJ]	[NM]	[NY]	[NC]	[ND]	[OH]	[OK]	[OR]	[PA]
[RI]	[SC]	[SD]	[TN]	[TX]	[UT]	[VT]	[VA]	[WA]	[WV]	[WI]	[WY]	[PR]

Full Name (Last name first, if individual)

Business or Residence Address (Number and Street, City, State, Zip Code)

Name of Associated Broker or Dealer

States in Which Person Listed Has Solicited or Intends to Solicit Purchasers

(Check "All States" or check individual States) .... ☐ All States

[AL]	[AK]	[AZ]	[AR]	[CA]	[CO]	[CT]	[DE]	[DC]	[FL]	[GA]	[HI]	[ID]
[IL]	[IN]	[IA]	[KS]	[KY]	[LA]	[ME]	[MD]	[MA]	[MI]	[MN]	[MS]	[MO]
[MT]	[NE]	[NV]	[NH]	[NJ]	[NM]	[NY]	[NC]	[ND]	[OH]	[OK]	[OR]	[PA]
[RI]	[SC]	[SD]	[TN]	[TX]	[UT]	[VT]	[VA]	[WA]	[WV]	[WI]	[WY]	[PR]

Full Name (Last name first, if individual)

Business or Residence Address (Number and Street, City, State, Zip Code)

Name of Associated Broker or Dealer

States in Which Person Listed Has Solicited or Intends to Solicit Purchasers

(Check "All States" or check individual States) .... ☐ All States

[AL]	[AK]	[AZ]	[AR]	[CA]	[CO]	[CT]	[DE]	[DC]	[FL]	[GA]	[HI]	[ID]
[IL]	[IN]	[IA]	[KS]	[KY]	[LA]	[ME]	[MD]	[MA]	[MI]	[MN]	[MS]	[MO]
[MT]	[NE]	[NV]	[NH]	[NJ]	[NM]	[NY]	[NC]	[ND]	[OH]	[OK]	[OR]	[PA]
[RI]	[SC]	[SD]	[TN]	[TX]	[UT]	[VT]	[VA]	[WA]	[WV]	[WI]	[WY]	[PR]

(Use blank sheet, or copy and use additional copies of this sheet, as necessary.)

1. Enter the aggregate offering price of securities included in this offering and the total amount already sold. Enter "0" if answer is "none" or "zero." If the transaction is an exchange offering, check this box ☐ and indicate in the columns below the amounts of the securities offered for exchange and already exchanged.

Type of Security	Aggregate Offering Price	Amount Already Sold
Debt	$_____	$_____
Equity	$_____	$_____
☐ Common ☐ Preferred		
Convertible Securities (including warrants)	$_____	$_____
Partnership Interests	$_____	$_____
Other (Specify _____)	$_____	$_____
Total	$_____	$_____

Answer also in Appendix, Column 3, if filing under ULOE.

2. Enter the number of accredited and non-accredited investors who have purchased securities in this offering and the aggregate dollar amounts of their purchases. For offerings under Rule 504, indicate the number of persons who have purchased securities and the aggregate dollar amount of their purchases on the total lines. Enter "0" if answer is "none" or "zero."

	Number Investors	Aggregate Dollar Amount of Purchases
Accredited Investors	_____	$_____
Non-accredited Investors	_____	$_____
Total (for filings under Rule 504 only)	_____	$_____

Answer also in Appendix, Column 4, if filing under ULOE.

3. If this filing is for an offering under Rule 504 or 505, enter the information requested for all securities sold by the issuer, to date, in offerings of the types indicated, in the twelve (12) months prior to the first sale of securities in this offering. Classify securities by type listed in Part C - Question 1.

Type of offering	Type of Security	Dollar Amount Sold
Rule 505	_____	$_____
Regulation A	_____	$_____
Rule 504	_____	$_____
Total	_____	$_____

4. a. Furnish a statement of all expenses in connection with the issuance and distribution of the securities in this offering. Exclude amounts relating solely to organization expenses of the issuer. The information may be given as subject to future contingencies. If the amount of an expenditure is not known, furnish an estimate and check the box to the left of the estimate.

Transfer Agent's Fees	☐	$_____
Printing and Engraving Costs	☐	$_____
Legal Fees	☐	$_____
Accounting Fees	☐	$_____
Engineering Fees	☐	$_____
Sales Commissions (specify finders' fees separately)	☐	$_____
Other Expenses (identify) _____	☐	$_____
Total	☐	$_____

b. Enter the difference between the aggregate offering price given in response to Part C - Question 1 and total expenses furnished in response to Part C - Question 4.a. This difference is the "adjusted gross proceeds to the issuer." . . . . $_____

5. Indicate below the amount of the adjusted gross proceeds to the issuer used or proposed to be used for each of the purposes shown. If the amount for any purpose is not known, furnish an estimate and check the box to the left of the estimate. The total of the payments listed must equal the adjusted gross proceeds to the issuer set forth in response to Part C - Question 4.b above.

	Payments to Officers, Directors, & Affiliates	Payments To Others
Salaries and fees	☐ $_____	☐ $_____
Purchase of real estate	☐ $_____	☐ $_____
Purchase, rental or leasing and installation of machinery and equipment	☐ $_____	☐ $_____
Construction or leasing of plant buildings and facilities	☐ $_____	☐ $_____
Acquisition of other businesses (including the value of securities involved in this offering that may be used in exchange for the assets or securities of another issuer pursuant to a merger)	☐ $_____	☐ $_____
Repayment of indebtedness	☐ $_____	☐ $_____
Working capital	☐ $_____	☐ $_____
Other (specify): _____	☐ $_____	☐ $_____
_____	☐ $_____	☐ $_____
Column Totals	☐ $_____	☐ $_____
Total Payments Listed (column totals added)	☐ $_____	

The issuer has duly caused this notice to be signed by the undersigned duly authorized person. If this notice is filed under Rule 505, the following signature constitutes an undertaking by the issuer to furnish to the U.S. Securities and Exchange Commission, upon written request of its staff, the information furnished by the issuer to any non-accredited investor pursuant to paragraph (b)(2) of Rule 502.

Issuer (Print or Type)	Signature	Date
Name of Signer (Print or Type)	Title of Signer (Print or Type)	

─────ATTENTION─────
Intentional misstatements or omissions of fact constitute federal criminal violations. (See 18 U.S.C. 1001.)

1. Is any party described in 17 CFR 230.252(c), (d), (e) or (f) presently subject to any of the disqualification provisions   Yes   No
   of such rule? ....   ☐   ☐

See Appendix, Column 5, for state response.

2. The undersigned issuer hereby undertakes to furnish to any state administrator of any state in which this notice is filed, a notice on Form D (17 CFR 239.500) at such times as required by state law.

3. The undersigned issuer hereby undertakes to furnish to the state administrators, upon written request, information furnished by the issuer to offerees.

4. The undersigned issuer represents that the issuer is familiar with the conditions that must be satisfied to be entitled to the Uniform limited Offering Exemption (ULOE) of the state in which this notice is filed and understands that the issuer claiming the availability of this exemption has the burden of establishing that these conditions have been satisfied.

The issuer has read this notification and knows the contents to be true and has duly caused this notice to be signed on its behalf by the undersigned duly authorized person.

Issuer (Print or Type)	Signature	Date
Name (Print or Type)	Title (Print or Type)	

Instruction:
Print the name and title of the signing representative under his signature for the state portion of this form. One copy of every notice on Form D must be manually signed. Any copies not manually signed must be photocopies of the manually signed copy or bear typed or printed signatures.

1	2		3	4				5	
	Intend to sell to non-accredited investors in State (Part B-Item 1)		Type of security and aggregate offering price offered in state (Part C-Item1)	Type of investor and amount purchased in State (Part C-Item 2)				Disqualification under State ULOE (if yes, attach explanation of waiver granted) (Part E-Item1)	
State	Yes	No		Number of Accredited Investors	Amount	Number of Non-Accredited Investors	Amount	Yes	No
AL									
AK									
AZ									
AR									
CA									
CO									
CT									
DE									
DC									
FL									
GA									
HI									
ID									
IL									
IN									
IA									
KS									
KY									
LA									
ME									
MD									
MA									
MI									
MN									
MS									
MO									

1	2		3	4				5	
	Intend to sell to non-accredited investors in State (Part B-Item 1)		Type of security and aggregate offering price offered in state (Part C-Item1)	Type of investor and amount purchased in State (Part C-Item 2)				Disqualification under State ULOE (if yes, attach explanation of waiver granted) (Part E-Item1)	
State	Yes	No		Number of Accredited Investors	Amount	Number of Non-Accredited Investors	Amount	Yes	No
MT									
NE									
NV									
NH									
NJ									
NM									
NY									
NC									
ND									
OH									
OK									
OR									
PA									
RI									
SC									
SD									
TN									
TX									
UT									
VT									
VA									
WA									
WV									
WI									
WY									
PR									

SECURITIES AND EXCHANGE COMMISSION
Washington, D.C. 20549

FORM S-18

REGISTRATION STATEMENT UNDER THE SECURITIES ACT OF 1933

_____

(Exact name of registrant as specified in its charter)

_____

(State or other jurisdiction of incorporation or organization)

_____

(Primary Standard Industrial Classification Code Number)

_____

(I.R.S. Employer Identification Number)

_____

(Address, including zip code, and telephone number, including area code, of registrant's principal executive offices)

_____

(Address of principal place of business or intended principal place of business)

_____

(Name, address, including zip code, and telephone number, including area code, of agent for service)

_____

(Approximate date of commencement of proposed sale to the public)

Calculation of Registration Fee

Title of Each Class of Securities to be Registered	Amount to be Registered	Proposed Maximum Offering Price Per Unit	Proposed Maximum Aggregate Offering Price	Amount of Registration Fee

SEC 1766 (2-87)

Exhibit 12-6

The registrant hereby amends this registration statement on such date or dates as may be necessary to delay its effective date until the registrant shall file a further amendment which specifically states that this registration statement shall thereafter become effective in accordance with Section 8(a) of the Securities Act of 1933 or until the registration statement shall become effective on such date as the Commission, acting pursuant to said Section 8(a), may determine.*

*Inclusion of this paragraph is optional. See Rule 473. (Each page of this document, including exhibits and attachments, shall be numbered sequentially from this page. as page 1, through the last page of the document.)

I. **Rule as to Use of Form S-18.**

   A. This form is to be used for the registration of securities not to exceed an aggregate offering price of $7.5 million which are to be sold for cash, installments for cash and/or cash assessments and assumptions by partners of partnership debt, by the registrant, or for the account of security holders in accordance with paragraph B, provided such registrant:

   (1) Is organized under the laws of the United States or Canada or any State or Province thereof, and has or proposes to have its principal business operations in the United States, if a domestic issuer, or Canada or the United States if a Canadian issuer;

   (2) Is not subject to the reporting provisions of the Securities Exchange Act of 1934 pursuant to Section 12 or 15(d) of that Act;

   (3) Is not an investment company;

   (4) Is not an insurance company which is exempt from the provisions of Section 12 of the Securities Exchange Act of 1934 in reliance upon Section 12(g)(2)(G) thereof; and

   (5) Is not a majority owned subsidiary of a registrant which does not meet the qualifications for use of the form, as specified herein.

   B. This form may be used for the registration of securities to be sold for the account of any person other than the registrant, *provided:* (i) the aggregate offering price of such securities by any such persons does not exceed $1.5 million and (ii) the aggregate offering price of such securities together with the aggregate offering price of any securities to be sold by the registrant does not exceed $7.5 million.

   C. For purposes of computing the $7.5 million ceiling specified above, there shall be included in the aggregate offering price of the securities registered herein, the aggregate offering price of all securities sold: (i) by the registrant within one year prior to the commencement of the proposed offering in violation of Section 5(a) of the Securities Act; (ii) by the registrant within one year prior to the commencement of the proposed offering pursuant to a registration statement filed on Form S-18; and (iii) which would be deemed integrated with the proposed offering. (*See* Securities Act Release No. 4552 (November 6, 1962) [27 FR 11316].) In computing the $7.5 million ceiling amount, the aggregate price of all securities sold which fall in more than one of the above-described categories need be counted only once.

   D. Notwithstanding the provisions of paragraph (A)(2), a registrant which has had a prior offering on Form S-18 may, during the remainder of the fiscal year in which the prior registration statement was made effective, use the form to register additional securities until the offering limit as computed in paragraph C has been met.

II. **Place of Filing**

   A. At the election of the registrant, all registration statements on Form S-18 and related papers filed with the Commission should be filed either at its principal office in Washington, D.C. or in the Regional Office for the region in which the registrant's principal business operations are conducted, or are proposed to be conducted; *Provided, however,* that if the registrant's principal business operations are conducted or are proposed to be conducted in the region covered by the Philadelphia Regional Office, the registration statement may be filed either with the Atlanta or the New York Regional Office. The registration statement of any registrant having or proposing to have its principal business operations in Canada may file with the Regional Office nearest the place where the registrant's principal business operations are conducted, or are proposed to be conducted; *Provided, however,* that if the offering is to be made through a principal underwriter located in the United States, the registration statement may be filed with the Regional Office for the region in which such underwriter has its principal office.

If the application of the previous sentence would require a filing with the Philadelphia Regional Office, such filing may be made with the Atlanta or the New York Regional Office.

B. The Commission will endeavor to process From S-18 registration statements at the place of filing. However, due to workload or other special consideration, the Commission may refer processing to a different Commission office.

C. All post-effective amendments to the Form S-18 registration statement shall be filed in the office where the corresponding Form S-18 registration statement was declared effective.

III. Application of General Rules and Regulations.

A. Attention is directed to the General Rules and Regulations under the Act, particularly those comprising Regulation C [17 CFR 230.400 to 230.494], which contains general requirements regarding the preparation and filing of a registration statement.

B. Attention is directed to Rule 463 [17 CFR 230.463] and Form SR [17 CFR 239.61] which is required to be filed by first-time registrants under the Securities Act showing sales of registered securities and the use of proceeds therefrom. Form SR shall be filed at the same office where the registration statement was declared effective.

C. Attention is directed to Regulation S-K [17 CFR 229.001 et seq.] relating to registration statement content. Where this form specifically references an item within that Regulation, the information need only be furnished to the extent appropriate. Special attention also is directed to paragraphs (b) and (c) of §229.10 of Regulation S-K which outline the Commission's policies on projections and securities ratings, respectively.

D. Attention is directed to disclosure provisions set forth in the Industry Guides which are listed in §229.801 of Regulation S-K [17 CFR 229.801]. These Industry Guides represent Division practices with respect to the disclosure to be provided by the affected industries in registration statements.

E. Attention is directed to Rule 15c2-8 [17 CFR 240.15c2-8] regarding prior delivery of preliminary prospectuses by registrants not subject to the reporting requirements of the Exchange Act.

F. Attention is directed to From S-11 [17 CFR 239.18] which relates to the registration of securities of certain real estate companies, and particularly Item 13 [Investment Policies of Registrant], Item 14 [Description of Real Estate], and Item 15 [Operating Data] contained therein. To the extent that these items offer enhanced guide lines for disclosure by real estate entities, registrants engaged or to be engaged in real estate operations may wish to consider these items for use in a Form S-18 offering.

PART I—INFORMATION REQUIRED IN PROSPECTUS

Item 1. Forepart of the Registration Statement and Outside Front Cover Page of Prospectus.

Set forth in the forepart of the registration statement and on the outside front cover page of the prospectus the information required by Item 501 of Regulation S-K [17 CFR 229.501].

Item 2. Inside Front and Outside Back Cover Pages of Prospectus.

Set forth on the inside front cover page of the prospectus or, where permitted, on the outside back cover page, the information required by Item 502 of Regulation S-K [17 CFR 229.502].

Item 3. Summary Information and Risk Factors.

Furnish the information required by Item 503(a), (b), and (c) of Regulation S-K [17 CFR 229.503(a), (b) and (c)].

Item 4. Use of Proceeds.

Furnish the information required by Item 504 of Regulation S-K [17 CFR 229.504].

Item 5. Determination of Offering Price.

Furnish the information required by Item 505 of Regulation S-K [17 CFR 229.505].

Item 6. Dilution.

Furnish the information required by Item 506 of Regulation S-K [17 CFR 229.506].

Item 7. Selling Security Holders.

Furnish the information required by Item 507 of Regulation S-K [17 CFR 229.507].

Item 8. Plan of Distribution.

Furnish the information required by Item 508 of Regulation S-K [17 CFR 229.508], except the information specified in Item 508(c)(1), (3), and (d).

Item 9. Legal Proceedings.

Furnish the information required by Item 103 of Regulation S-K [17 CFR 229.103].

Item 10. Directors and Executive Officers.

Furnish the information required by Item 401 of Regulation S-K [17 CFR 229.401].

Item 11. Security Ownership of Certain Beneficial Owners and Management.

Furnish the information required by Item 403 of Regulation S-K [17 CFR 229.403].

Item 12. Description of the Securities To Be Registered.

Furnish the information required by Item 202 of Regulation S-K [17 CFR 229.202].

Item 13. Interest of Named Experts and Counsel.

Furnish the information required by Item 509 of Regulation S-K [17 CFR 229.509].

Item 14. Statement as to Indemnification.

Furnish the information required by Item 510 of Regulation S-K [17 CFR 229.510].

Item 15. Organization Within Five Years.

If the registrant was organized within the past five years, furnish the following information:

(a) State the names of the promoters, the nature and amount of anything of value (including money, property, contracts, options or rights of any kind) received or to be received by each promoter directly or indirectly from the registrant, and the nature and amount of any assets, services or other consideration therefor received or to be received by the registrant. The term "promoter" is defined in Rule 405 under the Act.

(b) As to any assets acquired or to be acquired by the registrant from a promoter, state the amount at which acquired or to be acquired and the principal followed or to be followed in determining the amount. Identify the persons making the determination and state their relationship, if any, with the registrant or any promoter. If the assets were acquired by the promoter within two years prior to their transfer to the registrant, state the cost thereof to the promoter.

(c) List all parents of the registrant showing the basis of control and as to each parent, the percentage of voting securities owned or other basis of control by its immediate parent if any.

Instruction. Include the registrant and show the percentage of its voting securities owned or other basis of control by its immediate parent.

Item 16. Description of Business.

   (a) *General development of business.* Describe the general development of the business of the registrant, its subsidiaries and any predecessor(s) during the past five years, or such shorter period as the registrant may have been engaged in business. Information shall be disclosed for earlier periods if material to an understanding of the general development of the business.

     (1) In describing developments, information shall be given as to matters such as the following: the year in which the registrant was organized and its form of organization; the nature and results of any bankruptcy, receivership or similar proceedings with respect to the registrant or any of its significant subsidiaries; the nature and results of any other material reclassification, merger or consolidation of the registrant or any of its significant subsidiaries; the acquisition or disposition of any material amount of assets otherwise than in the ordinary course of business; and any material changes in the mode of conducting the business.

     Instruction: The following requirement in paragraph (2) applies only to registrants (including predecessors) which have not received revenue from operations during each of the three fiscal years immediately prior to the filing of the registration statement.

     (2) Describe, if formulated, the registrant's plan of operation for the remainder of the fiscal year, if the registration statement is filed prior to the end of the registrant's second fiscal quarter. Describe, if formulated, the registrant's plan of operation for the remainder of the fiscal year and for the first six months of the next fiscal year if the registration statement is filed subsequent to the end of the second fiscal quarter. If such information is not available, the reasons for its not being available shall be stated. Disclosure relating to any plan should include such matters as:

       (i) A statement in narrative form indicating the registrant's opinion as to the period of time that the proceeds from the offering will satisfy cash requirements and whether in the next six months it will be necessary to raise additional funds to meet the expenditures required for operating the business of the registrant. The specific reasons for such opinion shall be set forth and categories of expenditures and sources of cash resources shall be identified; however, amounts of expenditure and cash resources need not be provided. In addition, if the narrative statement is based on a cash budget, such budget should be furnished to the Commission as supplemental information, but not as a part of the registration statement.

       (ii) An explanation of material product research and development to be performed during the period covered in the plan.

       (iii) Any anticipated material acquisition of plant and equipment and the capacity thereof.

       (iv) Any anticipated material changes in number of employees in the various departments such as research and development production, sales or administration.

       (v) Other material areas which may be peculiar to the registrant's business.

   (b) *Narrative description of business.*

     (1) Describe the business done and intended to be done by the registrant and its subsidiaries. Such description should include, if material to an understanding of the registrant's business, a discussion of:

       (a) the principal products produced and services rendered and the principal markets for and methods of distribution of such products and services.

       (b) the status of a product or service if the issuer has made public information about a new product or service which would require the investment of a material amount of the assets of the registrant or is otherwise material.

       (c) the estimated amount spent during each of the last two fiscal years on company-sponsored research and development activities determined in accordance with generally accepted accounting principles. In addition, state the estimated dollar amount spent during each of such years on material customer-sponsored research activities relating to the development of new products, services or techniques or the improvement of existing products, services or techniques.

       (d) the number of persons employed by the registrant indicating the number employed full time.

(e) the material effects that compliance with Federal, State and local provisions which have been enacted or adopted regulating the discharge of materials into the environment, or otherwise relating to the protection of the environment, may have upon the capital expenditures, earnings and competitive position of the registrant and its subsidiaries. The registrant shall disclose any material estimated capital expenditures for environmental control facilities for the remainder of its current fiscal year and for such further periods as the registrant may deem material.

(2) The registrant should also describe those distinctive or special characteristics of the registrant's operations or industry which may have a material impact upon the registrant's future financial performance. Examples of factors which might be discussed include dependence on one or a few major customers or suppliers (including suppliers of raw materials or financing), existing or probable governmental regulation, expiration of material labor contracts or patents, trademarks, licenses, franchises, concessions or royalty agreements, unusual competitive conditions in the industry, cyclicality of the industry and anticipated raw material or energy shortages to the extent management may not be able to secure a continuing source of supply.

(c) *Segment data.* If the registrant is required to include segment information in its financial statements, such information may be disclosed in the description of business or in the financial statements. If such information is included in the financial statements, an appropriate cross reference shall be included in the description of business.

Item 17. Description of Property.

State briefly the location and general character of the principal plants, and other materially important physical properties of the registrant and its subsidiaries. If any such property is not held in fee or is held subject to any major encumbrance, so state and briefly describe how held.

Instruction: What is required is information essential to an investor's appraisal of the securities being registered. Such information should be furnished as will reasonably inform investors as to the suitability, adequacy, productive capacity and extent of utilization of the facilities used in the enterprise. Detailed descriptions of the physical characteristics of individual properties or legal descriptions by metes and bounds are not required and should not be given.

Item 17A. Description of Property—Issuers Engaged or to be Engaged in Significant Mining Operations.

(a) *Definitions:* The following definitions apply to registrants engaged or to be engaged in significant mining operations:

(1) *Reserve:* That part of a mineral deposit which could be economically and legally extracted or produced at the time of the reserve determination. *Note:* Reserves are customarily stated in terms of "ore" when dealing with metalliferous minerals; when other materials such as coal, oil shale, tar sands, limestone, etc. are involved, an appropriate term such as "recoverable coal" may be substituted.

(2) *Proven (Measured) Reserves:* Reserves for which (a) quantity is computed from dimensions revealed in outcrops, trenches, workings, or drill holes; grade and/or quality are computed from the results of detailed sampling and (b) the sites for inspection, sampling and measurement are spaced so closely and the geologic character is so well-defined that size, shape, depth, and mineral content of reserves are well-established.

(3) *Probable (Indicated) Reserves:* Reserves for which quantity and grade and/or quality are computed from information similar to that used for proven (measured) reserves, but the sites for inspection, sampling, and measurement are farther apart or are otherwise less adequately spaced. The degree of assurance, although lower than that for proven (measured) reserves, is high enough to assume continuity between points of observation.

(4) (i) *Exploration Stage*—includes all issuers engaged in the search for mineral deposits (reserves) which are not in either the development or production stage.

(ii) *Development Stage*—includes all issuers engaged in the preparation of an established commercially mineable deposit (reserves) for its extraction which are not in the production stage.

(iii) *Production Stage*—includes all issuers engaged in the exploitation of a mineral deposit (reserve).
Instruction: Mining companies in the exploration stage should not refer to themselves as development stage companies in the financial statements, even though such companies should comply with FASB Statement No. 7, if applicable.

(b) *Mining Operations Disclosure*—Furnish the following information as to each of the mines, plants and other significant properties owned or operated, or presently intended to be owned or operated, by the registrant:

6

(1) The location of and means of access to the property.

(2) A brief description of the title, claim, lease or option under which the registrant and its subsidiaries have or will have the right to hold or operate the property, indicating any conditions which the registrant must meet in order to obtain or retain the property. If held by leases or options, the expiration dates of such leases or options should be stated. Appropriate maps may be used to portray the locations of significant properties.

(3) A brief history of previous operations, including the names of previous operators, insofar as known.

(4) (a) A brief description of the present condition of the property, the work completed by the registrant on the property, the registrant's proposed program of exploration and development, and the current state of exploration and/or development of the property. Mines should be identified as either open-pit or underground. If the property is without known reserves and the proposed program is exploratory in nature, a statement to that effect shall be made.

(b) The age, details as to modernization and physical condition of the plant and equipment, including sub-surface improvements and equipment. Further, the total cost for each property and its associated plant and equipment should be stated. The source of power utilized with respect to each property should also be disclosed.

(5) A brief description of the rock formations and mineralization of existing or potential economic significance on the property, including the identity of the principal metallic or other constituents insofar as known. If proven (measured) or probable (indicated) reserves have been established, state (i) the estimated tonnages and grades (or quality, where appropriate) of such classes of reserves, and (ii) the name of the person making the estimates and the nature of his relationship to the registrant.

Instructions:

1. It should be stated whether the reserve estimate is of in-place material or of recoverable material. Any in-place estimate should be qualified to show the anticipated losses resulting from mining methods and beneficiation or preparation.

2. The summation of proven (measured) and probable (indicated) ore reserves is acceptable if the difference in degree of assurance between the two classes of reserves cannot be reliably defined.

3. Estimates other than proven (measured) or probable (indicated) reserves, and any estimated values of such reserves shall not be disclosed unless such information is required to be disclosed by foreign or state law; provided, however, that where such estimates previously have been provided to a person (or any of its affiliates) that is offering to acquire, merge, or consolidate with, the registrant or otherwise to acquire the registrant's securities, such estimates may be included.

(6) If technical terms relating to geology, mining or related matters whose definitions cannot be readily found in conventional dictionaries (as opposed to technical dictionaries or glossaries) are used, an appropriate glossary should be included in the registration statement.

(7) Detailed geologic maps and reports, feasibility studies and other highly technical data should not be included in the registration statement but should be, to the degree appropriate and necessary for the Commission's understanding of the registrant's presentation of business and property matters, furnished as supplemental information.

(c) *Supplemental Information:*

(1) If an estimate of proven (measured) or probable (indicated) reserves is set forth in the registration statement, furnish:

(i) maps drawn to scale showing any mine workings and the outlines of reserve blocks involved together with the pertinent sample-assay thereon,

(ii) all pertinent drill data and related maps,

(iii) the calculations whereby the basic sample-assay or drill data were translated into the estimates made of the grade and tonnage of reserves in each block and in the complete reserve estimate.

Instructions: Maps and other drawings submitted to the staff should include:

1. A legend or explanation showing, by means of pattern or symbol, every pattern or symbol used on the map or drawing; the use of the symbols used by the U.S. Geological Survey is encouraged;

2. A graphical bar scale should be included; additional representations of scale such as "one inch equals one mile" may be utilized provided the original scale of the map has not been altered;

3. A north arrow on maps;

4. An index map showing where the property is situated in relationship to the state or province, etc., in which it was located;

5. A title of the map or drawing and the date on which it was drawn;

6. In the event interpretive data is submitted in conjunction with any map, the identity of the geologist or engineer that prepared such data;

7. Any drawing should be simple enough or of sufficiently large scale to clearly show all features on the drawing.

(2) Furnish a complete copy of every material engineering, geological or metalurgical report concerning the registrant's property, including governmental reports, which are known and available to the registrant. Every such report should include the name of its author and the date of its preparation, if known to the registrant.

Any of the above-required reports as to which the staff has access need not be submitted. In this regard, issuers should consult with the staff prior to filing the registration statement. Any reports not submitted should be identified in a list furnished to the staff. This list should also identify any known governmental reports concerning the registrant's property.

(3) Furnish copies of all documents such as title documents, operating permits and easements needed to support representations made in the registration statement.

Item 17B. Supplementary Financial Information about Oil and Gas Producing Activities.

Registrants engaged in oil and gas producing activities shall follow the disclosure standards specified in paragraph (c) of Item 302 of Regulation S-K [17 CFR 229.302] with respect to such activities.

Item 18. Interest of Management and Others in Certain Transactions.

Describe briefly any transactions during the previous two years or any presently proposed transactions, to which the registrant or any of its subsidiaries was or is to be a party, in which any of the following persons had or is to have a direct or indirect material interest, naming such person and stating his relationship to the issuer, the nature of his interest in the transaction and, where practicable, the amount of such interest:

(1) Any director or executive officer of the issuer;

(2) Any nominee for election as a director;

(3) Any security holder named in answer to Item 11; or

(4) Any member of the immediate family of any of the foregoing persons.

Instructions:

1. See Instruction 2 to Item 20(a)(i). No information need be given in response to this Item as to any remuneration or other transaction reported in response to Item 20 or specifically excluded from Item 20.

2. No information need be given in answer to this Item as to any transaction where:

   (a) the rates or charges involved in the transaction are determined by competitive bids, or the transaction involves the rendering of services as a common or contract carrier, or public utility, at rates or charges fixed in conformity with law or governmental authority;

   (b) the transaction involves services as a bank depositary of funds, transfer agent, registrar, trustee under a trust indenture, or similar services;

   (c) the amount involved in the transaction or a series of similar transactions, including all periodic installments in the case of any lease or other agreement providing for periodic payments or installments, does not exceed $60,000; or

(d) the interest of the specified person arises solely from the ownership of securities of the issuer and the specified person receives no extra or special benefit not shared on a pro rata basis by all holders of securities of the class.

3. It should be noted that this item calls for disclosure of indirect, as well as direct, material interests in transactions. A person who has a position or relationship with a firm, corporation, or other entity, which engages in a transaction with the issuer or its subsidiaries may have an indirect interest in such transaction by reason of such position or relationship. However, a person shall be deemed not to have a material indirect interest in a transaction within the meaning of this Item where:

(a) the interest arises only (i) from such person's position as a director of another corporation or organization (other than a partnership) which is a party to the transaction, or (ii) from the direct or indirect ownership by such person and all other persons specified in subparagraphs (1) through (3) above, in the aggregate, of less than a 10 percent equity interest in another person (other than a partnership) which is a party to the transaction, or (iii) from both such position and ownership.

(b) the interest arises only from such person's position as a limited partner in a partnership in which he and all other persons specified in (1) through (4) above had an interest of less than 10 percent; or

(c) the interest of such person arises solely from the holding of an equity interest (including a limited partnership interest but excluding a general partnership interest) or a creditor interest in another person which is a party to the transaction with the issuer or any of its subsidiaries and the transaction is not material to such other person.

4. Include the name of each person whose interest in any transaction is described and the nature of the relationship by reason of which such interest is required to be described. The amount of the interest of any specified person shall be computed without regard to the amount of the profit or loss involved in the transaction. Where it is not practicable to state the approximate amount of the interest, the approximate amount involved in the transaction shall be disclosed.

5. Information should be included as to any material underwriting discounts and commissions upon the sale of securities by the registrant where any of the specified persons was or is to be a principal underwriter or is a controlling person, or member, of a firm which was or is to be a principal underwriter. Information need not be given concerning ordinary management fees paid by underwriters to a managing underwriter pursuant to an agreement among underwriters the parties to which do not include the registrant or its subsidiaries.

6. As to any transaction involving the purchase or sale of assets by or to the registrant or any subsidiary, otherwise than in the ordinary course of business, state the cost of the assets to the purchaser and if acquired by the seller within two years prior to the transaction, the cost thereof to the seller.

7. Information shall be furnished in answer to this item with respect to transactions not excluded above which involve remuneration from the registrant or its subsidiaries, directly or indirectly, to any of the specified persons for services in any capacity unless the interest of such persons arises solely from the ownership individually and in the aggregate of less than 10% of any class of equity securities of another corporation furnishing the services to the registrant or its subsidiaries.

8. The foregoing instructions specify certain transactions and interests as to which information may be omitted in answering this item. There may be situations where, although the foregoing instructions do not expressly authorize nondisclosure, the interest of a specified person in the particular transaction or series of transactions is not a material interest. In that case, information regarding such interest and transaction is not required to be disclosed in response to this item. The materiality of any interest or transaction is to be determined on the basis of the significance of the information to investors in light of all of the circumstances of the particular transaction. The importance of the interest to the person having the interest, the relationship of the parties to the transaction to each other and the amount involved in the transaction are among the factors to be considered in determining the significance of the information to investors.

9. For purposes of this item, a person's immediate family shall include such person's spouse; parents; children; siblings; mothers and fathers-in-law; sons and daughters-in-law; and brothers and sisters-in-law.

Item 19. Certain Market Information.

Furnish the information required by Item 201(a)(2) of Regulation S-K [17 CFR 229.201(a)(2)].

Item 20. Executive Compensation.

(a) (1) *Cash compensation.* Furnish, in substantially the tabular form specified, all cash compensation paid to the following persons through the latest practicable date for services rendered in all capacities to the registrant and its subsidiaries during the registrant's last fiscal year.

    (i) Each of the registrant's five most highly compensated executive officers whose cash compensation required to be disclosed pursuant to this paragraph exceeds $60,000, naming each person; and

    (ii) All executive officers as a group, stating the number of persons in the group without naming them.

Cash Compensation Table

A	B	C
Name of individual or number in group	Capacities in which served	Cash Compensation

Instructions:

1. The Cash Compensation Table shall include:)i) all cash bonuses to be paid for services rendered during the last fiscal year unless such amounts have not been allocated at such time as the registration statement is filed, and (ii) all compensation that would have been paid in cash but for the fact the payment of such compensation was deferred.

2. Paragraph (a) applies to any person who was an executive officer of the registrant at any time during the period specified. However, information need not be given for any portion of the period during which such person was not an executive officer of the registrant, provided a statement to that effect is made.

(b) (1) *Compensation pursuant to plans.* Describe briefly all plans, pursuant to which cash or non-cash compensation was paid or distributed during the last fiscal year, stating such amounts, and all plans pursuant to which cash or non-cash is proposed to be paid or distributed in the future, to the named individuals and group specified in paragraph (a) of this section. Information need not be given with respect to any group life, health, hospitalization, medical reimbursement or relocation plans that do not discriminate, in scope, terms, or operation in favor of officers or directors of the registrant and that are available generally to all salaried employees. Information relating to pension or retirement benefits need not be disclosed if the amounts to be paid are computed on an actuarial basis under any plan which provides for fixed benefits in the event of retirement at a specified age or after a specified number of years of service.

(2) *Stock option plans.* In addition to providing the information required by paragraph (b)(1) of this section, furnish:

    (i) With respect to stock options granted during the last fiscal year: (A) the title and aggregate amount of securities subject to options; (B) the average per share exercise price; and (C) if such option exercise price was less than 100 percent of the market value of the security on the date of grant, such fact and the market price on such date.

    (ii) With respect to stock options exercised during the last fiscal year, regardless of the year such options were granted, the net value realized upon such exercise, calculated by subtracting the exercise price from the market value.

(c) *Other compensation.* Describe, stating amounts, any other compensation not covered by paragraphs (a) or (b) of this section, such as personal benefits, securities or property, that was paid or distributed during the last fiscal year to the named individuals and group specified in paragraph (a) of this section unless:

    (1) With respect to any named individual, the aggregate amount of such other compensation is the lesser of $25,000 or 10 percent of the compensation reported in the Cash Compensation Table of such person pursuant to paragraph (a) of this section or

    (2) With respect to the group, the aggregate amount of such other compensation is the lesser of $25,000 times the number of persons in the group or 10 percent of the compensation reported in the Cash Compensation Table for the group pursuant to paragraph (a) of this section and a statement to that effect is made.

Instruction: Compensation within paragraph (c) shall be valued on the basis of the registrant's and subsidiaries' aggregate incremental cost.

(d) *Compensation of directors.* Describe briefly, stating amounts, all compensation received by directors of the registrant for all services as a director.

Item 21. Financial Statements.

(a) General

(1) The financial statements of the registrant, or the registrant and its predecessors or any businesses to which the registrant is a successor, which are to be filed as part of the registration statement shall be prepared in accordance with generally accepted accounting principles (GAAP) in the United States or in the case of a Canadian registrant, a reconciliation to such U.S. GAAP shall be included in a note or schedule to the financial statements.

(2) Regulation S-X [17 CFR 210.1-210.12], Form and Content of and Requirements for Financial Statements, shall not apply to the preparation of such financial statements, except that the report and qualifications of the independent accountant shall comply with the requirements of Article 2 of Regulation S-X [17 CFR 210.2], and registrants engaged in oil and gas producing activities shall follow the financial accounting and reporting standards specified in Article 4-10 of Regulation S-X [17 CFR 210.4-10] with respect to such activities. However, to the extent that Article 10 [17 CFR 210.10] (Interim Financial Statements), Article 11-01 [17 CFR 210.11-01] (Pro Forma Presentation Requirements) and Article 11-02 [17 CFR 210.11-02] (Pro Forma Preparation Requirements) offer enhanced guidelines for the preparation, presentation and disclosure of condensed financial statements and pro forma financial information, registrants may wish to consider these items for use in a Form S-18 offering.

(3) The Commission may, upon the informal written request of the registrant, and where consistent with the protection of investors, permit the omission of one or more of the financial statements herein required or the filing in substitution therefor of appropriate statements of comparable character. The Commission may also by informal written notice require the filing of other financial statements in addition to, or in substitution for, the statements herein required in any case where such statements are necessary or appropriate for adequate presentation of the financial condition of any person whose financial statements are required, or whose statements are otherwise necessary for the protection of investors.

(b) Consolidated Balance Sheets

(1) The registrant and its subsidiaries consolidated shall file an audited balance sheet as of the end of the most recent fiscal year, or as of a date within 135 days of the date of filing the registration statement if the registrant (including predecessors) existed for a period less than one fiscal year.

(2) When the filing date of the registration statement falls after 134 days subsequent to the end of the registrant's most recent fiscal year, a balance sheet as of an interim date within 135 days of the filing date also shall be included in the registration statement. Such balance sheet need not be audited and may be in condensed form.

(c) Consolidated Statements of Income, Changes in Financial Condition and Stockholder's Equity.

(1) There shall be filed for the registrant and its subsidiaries consolidated statements of income, changes in financial position and stockholders equity for each of the two fiscal years preceding the date of the most recent audited balance sheet being filed (or for such shorter period as the registrant has been in business), and for the interim period, if any, between the end of the most recent fiscal year and the date of the most recent balance sheet being filed. These statements should be audited to the date of the most recent audited balance sheet being filed. Any interim financial statements may be in condensed form.

(2) If an income statement is filed for an interim period there shall also be filed, except for registrants in the development stage as defined by GAAP, an income statement for a comparable period of the prior year.

(3) Any unaudited interim financial statements furnished shall reflect all adjustments which are, in the opinion of management, necessary to a fair statement of the results for the interim periods presented. A statement to that effect shall be included. Such adjustments shall include, for example, appropriate estimated provisions for bonus and profit sharing arrangements normally determined or settled at year-end. If all such adjustments are of a normal recurring nature, a statement to that effect shall be made; otherwise, there shall be furnished information describing in appropriate detail the nature and amount of any adjustments other than normal recurring adjustments entering into the determination of the results shown.

11

(d) **Financial Statements of Businesses Acquired or to be Acquired.**

  (1) Financial statements for the periods specified in (3) below should be furnished if any of the following conditions exist:

    (i) Consummation of a significant business combination accounted for as a purchase has occurred or is probable (for purposes of this rule, the term "purchase" encompasses the purchase of an interest in a business accounted for by the equity method); or

    (ii) Consummation of a significant business combination to be accounted for as a pooling of interests is probable.

  (2) A business combination shall be considered significant if a comparison of the most recent annual financial statements of the business acquired or to be acquired and the registrant's most recent annual consolidated financial statements filed at or prior to the date of acquisition indicates that the business would be a significant subsidiary pursuant to the conditions specified in Rule 405 of Regulation C [17 CFR 230.405].

  (3) (i) The financial statements shall be furnished for the periods up to the date of acquisition, for those periods for which the registrant is required to furnish financial statements as specified in paragraph (b) and (c)(1).

    (ii) The financial statements covering fiscal years shall be audited.

    (iii) A separate audited balance sheet of the acquired business is not required when the registrant's most recent audited balance sheet filed is for a date after the acquisition was consummated.

    (iv) If none of the conditions in the definitions of significant subsidiary in Rule 405 exceeds 20%, income statements of the acquired business for only the most recent fiscal year and any interim period need be filed.

  (4) If consummation of more than one transaction has occurred or is probable, the tests of significance shall be made using the aggregate impact of the business and the required financial statements may be presented on a combined basis, if appropriate.

  (5) This paragraph (d) shall not apply to a business which is totally held by the registrant prior to consummation of the transaction.

(e) **Pro Forma Financial Information.**

  (1) Pro forma information shall be furnished if any of the following conditions exist (for purposes of this rule, the term "purchase" encompasses the purchase of an interest in a business accounted for by the equity method):

    (i) During the most recent fiscal year or subsequent interim period for which a balance sheet is required by paragraph (b), a significant business combination accounted for as a purchase has occurred.

    (ii) After the date of the most recent balance sheet filed pursuant to paragraph (b), consummation of a significant business combination to be accounted for by either the purchase method or pooling of interests method of accounting has occurred or is probable.

  (2) The provisions of paragraph (d)(2), (4) and (5) apply to this paragraph (e).

  (3) Pro forma statements shall ordinarily be in columnar form showing condensed historical statements, pro forma adjustments, and the pro forma results and should include the following:

    (i) If the transaction was consummated during the most recent fiscal year or in the subsequent interim period, pro forma statements of income reflecting the combined operations of the entities for the latest fiscal year and interim period, if any; or

    (ii) If consummation of the transaction has occurred or is probable after the date of the most recent balance sheet, a pro forma balance sheet giving effect to the combination as of the date of the most recent balance sheet required by paragraph (b). For a purchase, pro forma statements of income reflecting the combined operations of the entities for the latest fiscal year and interim period, if any, and for a pooling of interests, pro forma statements of income for all periods for which income statements of the registrant are required.

12

(f) Age of Financial Statements at Effective Date of Registration Statement.

(1) If the financial statements are as of a date 135 days or more prior to the date the registration statement is expected to become effected the financial statements shall be updated with a balance sheet as of an interim date within 135 days and with statements of income and changes in financial position for the interim period between the end of the most recent fiscal year and the date of the interim balance sheet. There shall also be filed, except for registrants in the development stage, an income statement for a corresponding period of the preceding fiscal year. Such interim financial statements need not be audited and may be in condensed form.

(2) When the anticipated effective date of the registration statement falls within 45 days subsequent to the end of the fiscal year, the registration statement need not include financial statements more current than as of the end of the third fiscal quarter of the most recently completed fiscal year: *Provided, however,* That if the audited financial statements for such fiscal year are available they must be included in the registration statement. If the anticipated effective date falls after 45 days subsequent to the end of the fiscal year the registration statement must include audited financial statements for the most recently completed fiscal year.

(3) When the filing date of the registration statement is near the end of a fiscal year and the audited financial statements for that fiscal year are not included in the registration statement, the registration statement shall be updated with such financial statements if they become available prior to the anticipated effective date.

(g) Special Instructions for Real Estate Operations to be Acquired.

If, during the period for which income statements are required, the registrant (a) has acquired one or more properties which in the aggregate are significant, or (b) since the date of the latest balance sheet required, has acquired or proposes to acquire one or more properties which in the aggregate are significant, the following shall be furnished with respect to such properties.

(1) Audited income statements (not including earnings per unit) for the two most recent years, which shall exclude items not comparable to the proposed future operations of the property such as mortgage interest, leasehold rental, depreciation, corporate expenses and Federal and state income taxes: *Provided, however,* That such audited statements need be presented for only the most recent fiscal year if (i) the property is not acquired from a related party; (ii) material factors considered by the registrant in assessing the property are described with specificity in the prospectus with regard to the property, including sources of revenue (including, but not limited to, competition in the rental market, comparative rents, occupancy rates) and expense (including, but not limited to, utility rates, *ad valorem* tax rates, maintenance expenses, capital improvements anticipated); and (iii) the registrant indicates in the prospectus that, after reasonable inquiry, the registrant is not aware of any material factors relating to that specific property other than those discussed in response to paragraph (1)(ii) of this section that would cause the reported financial information not to be necessarily indicative of future operating results.

(2) If the property is to be operated by the registrant there shall be furnished a statement showing the estimated taxable operating results of the registrant based on the most recent twelve month period including such adjustments as can be factually supported. If the property is to be acquired subject to a net lease the estimated taxable operating results shall be based on the rent to be paid for the first year of the lease. In either case, the estimated amount of cash to be made available by operations shall be shown. There shall be stated in an introductory paragraph the principal assumptions which have been made in preparing the statements of estimated taxable operating results and cash to be made available by operations.

(3) If appropriate under the circumstances, there shall be given in tabular form for a limited number of years the estimated cash distribution per unit showing the portion thereof reportable as taxable income and the portion representing a return of capital together with an explanation of annual variations, if any. If taxable net income per unit will become greater than the cash available for distribution per unit, that fact and approximate year of occurrence shall be stated, if significant.

(h) Special Instructions for Limited Partnerships.

(1) In addition to the financial reporting requirements in paragraphs (a) through (g), registrants which are limited partnerships are required also to file the balance sheets of the general partners as described in subparagraphs (2) through (4), below.

(2) Where a general partner of the limited partnership is a corporation there shall be filed an audited balance sheet of such corporation as of the end of its most recently completed fiscal year. Receivables from the parent or affiliate of the general partner (including notes receivable, but excluding trade receivables), should

13

be presented as deductions from the shareholders' equity of the general partner. Where a parent or affiliate of the general partner has committed itself to increase or maintain the general partner's capital then there shall also be filed an audited balance sheet of such parent or affiliate as of the end of its most recently completed fiscal year.

(3) Where a general partner of the limited partnership is a partnership there shall be filed an audited balance sheet of such partnership as of the end of its most recently completed fiscal year.

(4) Where a general partner of the limited partnership is a natural person there shall be filed, as supplemental information, a balance sheet of such natural person as of a recent date. Such balance sheet need not be audited. The assets and liabilities on such balance sheet should be carried at estimated fair market value, with provisions for estimated income taxes on unrealized gains. The net worth of such general partner(s), based on the estimated fair market value of their assets and liabilities, singly or in the aggregate, shall be disclosed in the text of the prospectus.

(i) Special Instructions for Registrants Engaged in Mining Operations.

With respect to companies engaged or to be engaged in the mining business, attention is directed to the instruction to Item 17A concerning the appropriate classification of issuers engaged in the exploratory, development and production stage of mining.

(j) Special Instructions for Companies Engaged in Marketing Computer Software.

(1) Companies shall not capitalize costs of internally developing (other than under a contractual arrangement for which accounting for contracts is appropriate) computer software as a product or process (or a part of a product or process) to be sold, leased, or otherwise marketed to others in financial statements included in documents prepared pursuant to rules adopted pursuant to either the Securities Act of 1933 or the Securities Exchange Act of 1934 and filed with or furnished to the Commission after April 14, 1983, unless they had disclosed the practice of capitalizing software costs in either: (i) audited financial statements issued prior to April 14, 1983; (ii) a report or registration statement filed with the Commission prior to April 14, 1983; or (iii) a document for an offering of securities by the issuer, other than a registration statement, which document was used in such offering prior to April 14, 1983.

(2) Because the term "product" also encompasses services that are sold, leased, or otherwise marketed to others, the prohibition in paragraph (1) of this section applies, for example, to a data processing service bureau or a computer time-sharing company.

(3) A company which, pursuant to paragraph (1) of this section, continues to follow the practice of capitalizing costs of internally developing computer software as a product or process to be sold, leased, or otherwise marketed to others, shall disclose for each period for which an income statement is required to be presented, the net amount of such costs capitalized during the period.

(k) Furnish the information required by Item 304 of Regulation S-K (§239.304 of this chapter), changes in and disagreements with accountants on accounting and financial disclosure.

NOTE: The requirements of this item shall not apply to financial statements which reflect the provisions of a prounouncement adopted after August 4, 1983 by the Financial Accounting Standards Board which provides specific accounting guidance in this area.

Part II—INFORMATION NOT REQUIRED IN PROSPECTUS

Item 22. Indemnification of Directors and Officers.

Furnish the information called for by Item 702 of Regulation S-K [17 CFR 229.702].

Item 23. Other Expenses of Issuance and Distribution.

Furnish the information called for by Item 511 of Regulation S-K [17 CFR 229.511].

Item 24. Recent Sales of Unregistered Securities.

Furnish the information called for by Item 701 of Regulation S-K [17 CFR 229.701].

14

Item 25. Exhibits.

Furnish the exhibits as required by Item 601 of Regulation S-K [17 CFR 229.601].

Item 26. Undertakings.

Furnish the undertakings required by Item 512 of Regulation S-K [17 CFR 229.512].

SIGNATURES

Pursuant to the requirements of the Securities Act of 1933, the registrant certifies that it has reasonable grounds to believe that it meets all of the requirements for filing on Form S-18 and has duly caused this registration statement to be signed on its behalf by the undersigned, thereunto duly authorized, in the City of_____,
State of _____, on _____, 19_____.

_____
(Registrant)

By _____
(Signature and Title)

Pursuant to the requirements of the Securities Act of 1933, this registration statement has been signed by the following persons in the capacities and on the dates indicated.

_____
(Signature)

_____
(Title)

_____
(Date)

Instructions:

1. The registration statement shall be signed by the registrant, its principal executive officer or officers, its principal financial officer, its controller or principal accounting officer and by at least a majority of the board of directors or persons performing similar functions. If the registrant is a Canadian person, the registration statement shall also be signed by its authorized representative in the United States. Where the registrant is a limited partnership, the registration statement shall be signed by a majority of the board of directors of any corporate general partner signing the registration statement.

2. The name of each person who signs the registration statement shall be typed or printed beneath his signature. Any person who occupies more than one of the specified positions shall indicate each capacity in which he signs the registration statement. Attention is directed to Rule 402 concerning manual signatures and to the exhibit requirements concerning signatures pursuant to powers of attorney.

SECURITIES AND EXCHANGE COMMISSION
Washington, D.C. 20549

FORM S-1

REGISTRATION STATEMENT UNDER THE SECURITIES ACT OF 1933

. . . .

(Exact name of registrant as specified in its charter)

. . . .

(State or other jurisdiction of incorporation or organization)

. . . .

(Primary Standard Industrial Classification Code Number)

. . . .

(I.R.S. Employer Identification Number)

. . . .

(Address, including zip code, and telephone number,
including area code, of registrant's principal executive offices)

. . . .

(Name, address, including zip code, and telephone number,
including area code, of agent for service)

. . . .

(Approximate date of commencement of proposed sale to the public)

. . . .

If any of the securities being registered on this Form are to be offered on a delayed or continuous basis pursuant to Rule 415 under the Securities Act of 1933 check the following box: ☐

(Calculation of Registration Fee)

Title of Each Class of Securities to be Registered	Amount to be Registered	Proposed Maximum Offering Price Per Unit	Proposed Maximum Aggregate Offering Price	Amount of Registration Fee

SEC 870 (2-87)

Exhibit 12-7

GENERAL INSTRUCTIONS

I. Eligibility Requirements for Use of Form S-1

This Form shall be used for the registration under the Securities Act of 1933 ("Securities Act") of securities of all registrants for which no other form is authorized or prescribed, except that this Form shall not be used for securities of foreign governments or political subdivisions thereof.

II. Application of General Rules and Regulations

A. Attention is directed to the General Rules and Regulations under the Securities Act, particularly those comprising Regulation C (17 CFR 230.400 to 230.494) thereunder. That Regulation contains general requirements regarding the preparation and filing of the registration statement.

B. Attention is directed to Regulation S-K (17 CFR Part 229) for the requirements applicable to the content of the non-financial statement portions of registration statements under the Securities Act. Where this Form directs the registrant to furnish information required by Regulation S-K and the item of Regulation S-K so provides, information need only be furnished to the extent appropriate.

III. Exchange Offers

If any of the securities being registered are to be offered in exchange for securities of any other issuer, the prospectus shall also include the information which would be required by Item 11 if the securities of such other issuer were registered on this Form. There shall also be included the information concerning such securities of such other issuer which would be called for by Item 9 if such securities were being registered. In connection with this instruction, reference is made to Rule 409.

PART 1—INFORMATION REQUIRED IN PROSPECTUS

Item 1.   Forepart of the Registration Statement and Outside Front Cover Page of Prospectus.

Set forth in the forepart of the registration statement and on the outside front cover page of the prospectus the information required by Item 501 of Regulation S-K (§229.501 of this chapter).

Item 2.   Inside Front and Outside Back Cover Pages of Prospectus.

Set forth on the inside front cover page of the prospectus or, where permitted, on the outside back cover page, the information required by Item 502 of Regulation S-K (§229.502 of this chapter).

Item 3.   Summary Information, Risk Factors and Ratio of Earnings to Fixed Charges.

Furnish the information required by Item 503 of Regulation S-K (§229.503 of this chapter).

Item 4.   Use of Proceeds.

Furnish the information required by Item 504 of Regulation S-K (§229.504 of this chapter).

Item 5.   Determination of Offering Price.

Furnish the information required by Item 505 of Regulation S-K (§229.505 of this chapter).

Item 6.   Dilution.

Furnish the information required by Item 506 of Regulation S-K (§229.506 of this chapter).

Item 7.   Selling Security Holders.

Furnish the information required by Item 507 of Regulation S-K (§229.507 of this chapter).

Item 8.   Plan of Distribution.

Furnish the information required by Item 508 of Regulation S-K (§229.508 of this chapter).

Item 9.   Description of Securities to be Registered.

Furnish the information required by Item 202 of Regulation S-K (§229.202 of this chapter).

Item 10.   Interests of Named Experts and Counsel.

Furnish the information required by Item 509 of Regulation S-K (§229.509 of this chapter).

Item 11.   Information with Respect to the Registrant.

Furnish the following information with respect to the registrant:

(a) Information required by Item 101 of Regulation S-K (§229.101 of this chapter), description of business;

(b) Information required by Item 102 of Regulation S-K (§229.102 of this chapter), description of property;

(c) Information required by Item l03 of Regulation S-K (§229.103 of this chapter), legal proceedings;

(d) Where common equity securities are being offered, information required by Item 201 of Regulation S-K (§229.201 of this chapter), market price of and dividends on the registrant's common equity and related stockholder matters;

(e) Financial statements meeting the requirements of Regulation S-X (17 CFR Part 210) (Schedules required under Regulation S-X shall be filed as "Financial Statement Schedules" pursuant to Item 15, Exhibits and Financial Statement Schedules, of this Form), as well as any financial information required by Rule 3-05 and Article 11 of Regulation S-X;

(f) Information required by Item 301 of Regulation S-K (§229.301 of this chapter), selected financial data;

(g) Information required by Item 302 of Regulation S-K (§229.302 of this chapter), supplementary financial information;

(h) Information required by Item 303 of Regulation S-K (§229.303 of this chapter), management's discussion and analysis of financial condition and results of operations;

(i) Information required by Item 304 of Regulation S-K (§229.304 of this chapter), changes in and disagreements with accountants on accounting and financial disclosure;

(j) Information required by Item 401 of Regulation S-K (§229.401 of this chapter), directors and executive officers;

(k) Information required by Item 402 of Regulation S-K (§229.402 of this chapter), executive compensation;

(l) Information required by Item 403 of Regulation S-K (§229.403 of this chapter), security ownership of certain beneficial owners and management; and

(m) Information required by Item 404 of Regulation S-K (§229.404 of this chapter), certain relationships and related transactions.

Item 12.   Disclosure of Commission Position on Indemnification for Securities Act Liabilities.

Furnish the information required by Item 510 of Regulation S-K (§229.510 of this chapter).

PART II—INFORMATION NOT REQUIRED IN PROSPECTUS

Item 13.   Other Expenses of Issuance and Distribution.

Furnish the information required by Item 511 of Regulation S-K (§229.511 of this chapter).

Item 14.   Indemnification of Directors and Officers.

Furnish the information required by Item 702 of Regulation S-K (§229.702 of this chapter).

Item 15.   Recent Sales of Unregistered Securities.

Furnish the information required by Item 701 of Regulation S-K (§229.701 of this chapter).

Item 16.   Exhibits and Financial Statement Schedules.

(a) Subject to the rules regarding incorporation by reference, furnish the exhibits as required by Item 601 of Regulation S-K (§229.601 of this chapter).

(b) Furnish the financial statement schedules required by Regulation S-X (17 CFR Part 210) and Item 11(e) of this Form. These schedules shall be lettered or numbered in the manner described for exhibits in paragraph (a).

Item 17.   Undertakings.

Furnish the undertakings required by Item 512 of Regulation S-K (§229.512 of this chapter).

SIGNATURES

Pursuant to the requirements of the Securities Act of 1933, the registrant has duly caused this registration statement to be signed on its behalf by the undersigned, thereunto duly authorized in the City of ....,

State of ...., on ...., 19 ....

(Registrant)

....

By (Signature and Title)

....

Pursuant to the requirements of the Securities Act of 1933, this registration statement has been signed by the following persons in the capacities and on the dates indicated.

(Signature)

....

(Title)

....

(Date)

....

Instructions.

1. The registration statement shall be signed by the registrant, its principal executive officer or officers, its principal financial officer, its controller or principal accounting officer and by at least a majority of the board of directors or persons performing similar functions. If the registrant is a foreign person, the registration statement shall also be signed by its authorized representative in the United States. Where the registrant is a limited partnership, the registration statement shall be signed by a majority of the board of directors of any corporate general partner signing the registration statement.

2. The name of each person who signs the registration statement shall be typed or printed beneath his signature. Any person who occupies more than one of the specified positions shall indicate each capacity in which he signs the registration statement. Attention is directed to Rule 402 concerning manual signatures and to Item 601 of Regulation S-K concerning signatures pursuant to powers of attorney.

INSTRUCTIONS AS TO SUMMARY PROSPECTUSES

1. A summary prospectus used pursuant to Rule 431 (§230.431 of this chapter), shall at the time of its use contain such of the information specified below as is then included in the registration statement. All other information and documents contained in the registration statement may be omitted.

   (a) As to Item 1, the aggregate offering price to the public, the aggregate underwriting discounts and commissions and the offering price per unit to the public;

   (b) As to Item 4, a brief statement of the principal purposes for which the proceeds are to be used;

   (c) As to Item 7, a statement as to the amount of the offering, if any, to be made for the account of security holders;

   (d) As to Item 8, the name of the managing underwriter or underwriters and a brief statement as to the nature of the underwriter's obligation to take the securities; if any securities to be registered are to be offered otherwise than through underwriters, a brief statement as to the manner of distribution; and, if securities are to be offered otherwise than for cash, a brief statement as to the general purposes of the distribution, the basis upon which the securities are to be offered, the amount of compensation and other expenses of distribution, and by whom they are to be borne;

   (e) As to Item 9, a brief statement as to dividend rights, voting rights, conversion rights, interest, maturity;

   (f) As to Item 11, a brief statement of the general character of the business done and intended to be done, the selected financial data (Item 301 of Regulation S-K (§229.301 of this chapter)) and a brief statement of the nature and present status of any material pending legal proceedings; and

   (g) A tabular presentation of notes payable, long term debt, deferred credits, minority interests, if material, and the equity section of the latest balance sheet filed, as may be appropriate.

2. The summary prospectus shall not contain a summary or condensation of any other required financial information except as provided above.

3. Where securities being registered are to be offered in exchange for securities of any other issuer, the summary prospectus also shall contain that information as to Items 9 and 11 specified in paragraphs (e) and (f) above which would be required if the securities of such other issuer were registered on this Form.

4. The Commission may, upon the request of the registrant, and where consistent with the protection of investors, permit the omission of any of the information herein required or the furnishing in substitution therefor of appropriate information of comparable character. The Commission may also require the inclusion of other information in addition to, or in substitution for, the information herein required in any case where such information is necessary or appropriate for the protection of investors.

WESTAMCO INVESTMENT COMPANY

8929 WILSHIRE BLVD. SUITE 400 BEVERLY HILLS, CALIFORNIA 90211

(213) 652-8288

A FEDERAL LICENSEE UNDER THE
SMALL BUSINESS INVESTMENT ACT OF 1958

April 30, 1987

Mr. Gary Brenner
President, BEC Group, Inc.
3609 Mt. Everest Blvd.
San Diego, CA 92111

Dear Mr. Brenner:

Westamco Investment Company is a Small Business Investment Company
(SBIC) licensed by the Small Business Administration (SBA) to provide equity capital and/or long-term loans to Small Business Companies (SBIC's) in accordance with the provisions of the Small
Business Act and Regulations issued by the SBA.

We are currently in our 26th year as an SBIC and have substantial
funds available to invest. Our professional management has almost
30 years experience in this business. The following is a broad
prospectus of our current investment policy and type of financing
we offer.

THE SMALL BUSINESS COMPANY: A Small Business Company (SBIC) is
defined as a business that has a net worth under Six Million
Dollars ($6,000,000.00), and average after-tax earnings of less
than Two Million Dollars ($2,000,000.00) during the past two (2)
years. In addition, a firm may qualify as a small business
either under an employment standard or amount of annual sales.
Both these standards vary from industry to industry.

THE FORM OF INVESTMENTS: Every single SBIC financing is tailored
individually to meet your needs and make the best use of our
available SBIC funds. We normally purchase interest-bearing
Subordinated Debentures, with detachable warrants for a percentage
of the equity in the SBC. Legally, we are also permitted to purchase common stock, preferred stock, convertible debentures, or
limited partnership interests. Additionally, we make straight
loans.

THE SIZE OF INVESTMENTS: As a matter of policy, we prefer investments in the range of $30,000.00 to $500,000.00, due to the size of
our staff and portfolio. We also participate with other venture
companies and SBIC's for larger investments.

EQUITY INTEREST: Equity interest is required - usually in the form
of detachable warrants to purchase a percentage of the equity in
the SBC. The percentage of equity is negotiable, ranging from 5%
to 49%. The conversion price is also negotiable, ranging from 1¢
per share to diluted book value per share at time of original investment.

DISPOSING OF EQUITY INTERESTS: This is done usually by sale to
other owners, private placement with other investors, sale to the
public after registration, or sale or exchange with other companies
in the event the SBC is sold or merged. Unregistered, publicly
traded securities may be sold in the open market under certain
circumstances.

CURRENT RETURNS: Current returns in interest and dividends are
required - since we borrow the equivalent funds to invest and
must pay interest in addition to meeting normal operating expenses. The fixed interest rate is usually set at a few points
over prime at time of closing.

Exhibit 12-8

THE MATTER OF FEES: Fees are minimal. We accept directors' fees so long as it is the SBC policy to pay them. (All outside directors are paid the same.) We may charge consulting fees, but only to the extent such service is requested by the SBC and the fees are agreed to in advance.

REPAYMENT/REDEMPTION TERMS: Terms are generally 5 to 8 years - with a moratorium on the first 2 to 3 years, depending upon the SBC projections and needs. The overall term must be at least 5 years.

COLLATERAL REQUIREMENTS: We may take collateral to the extent it is available and prudent, which includes first or second liens on the assets of the SBC, pledging of the stock in the SBC, or personal signatures as dictated by the risk involved.

SBC LIMITATIONS: A minimum current ratio and net-worth and maximum debt-to-equity ratio is always negotiated at the time of the original investment. Limitations may also be placed on dividends, officers' compensation, capital additions and other activities considered prudently necessary to safeguard our investment. Generally, these same limitations are inherent in loan agreements with banks and other conventional lending sources. All of these limitations may be waived under the proper circumstances.

BOARD REPRESENTATION: The SBIC must be represented by at least one director, in most cases. We encourage active, periodic board meetings. We prefer to stay very close to our portfolio companies, but without interfering in management.

REGISTRATION RIGHTS: Registration rights are required - but generally as a "piggy back" with corporate registration.

CLOSING COSTS: They are always paid by the SBC, including our legal expenses.

FINDERS' FEES: We permit the SBC to pay finders' fees. In fact, we require a disclosure that all such fees are either paid or arranged at time of closing.

STATEMENTS: Audited statements are required - both initially and annually, and annually thereafter. We also require the right to approve the CPA selected by the SBC. Statements are usually on a monthly basis - but in some cases quarterly statements might be appropriate.

INVESTMENT ISSUES: We prohibit investments in lending or reinvestment situations such as leasing and finance companies. Passive investment situations such as apartment buildings and commercial or industrial buildings held for lease are also prohibited.

Real estate investments can be considered - to the extent there is a going business, such as land development, construction and sale of properties or even apartment buildings in the process of conversion for sale as condominiums.

We do invest in limited partnerships - but never as a general partner.

Leverage buy-outs are considered - but any new management is carefully scrutinized.

PROPOSAL REQUIREMENTS: Each situation is different - but at least the following information musr be addressed in any proposal:

- Funds requested (and proposed use)
- Company history
- Product description and patents
- Marketing and sales plan
- Competition
- Suppliers

PROPOSAL REQUIREMENTS: (continued)

- Facilities and equipment (including appraisal
  if available)
- Labor
- Organization
- Stockholders
- Debt schedule and terms
- Executive resumes and compensation
- Five-year business plan (including net income,
  cash flow and balance sheets, projections, with
  appropriate commentary)
- Five years of historical financial statements,
  to extent available.

Should you require any further information, please do not hesitate
to contact me.

Very truly yours,

WESTAMCO INVESTMENT COMPANY

Scott T. Van Every

mw

Chapter 13

TAX SAVINGS AND TAX PITFALLS IN YOUR BUSINESS

Going into business will expose you to a different set of tax laws. Some of these laws were enacted to encourage individuals to start their own business. By their very design they should benefit you. Other laws were passed for various reasons and could help or hinder you depending on how you run your business. This chapter explains how to:

* Use a corporation as a tax shelter
* Shelter profits on export sales
* Withdraw funds from an incorporated business
* Deduct expenses that relate to your business
* Choose the best taxable year for your business
* Select a tax accounting method
* Identify tax problems unique to corporations
* Plan for your estate when your business accounts for a large portion of your personal net worth
* Receive tax credits for hiring certain economically disadvantaged groups
* Put your spouse on the payroll
* Save on unemployment taxes

USING A CORPORATION AS A TAX SHELTER

Corporate Form

The decision to use the corporate form of business organization may provide tax benefits to the owners of the corporation, who are the shareholders. For example, shareholders have the opportunity to be treated as employees for tax purposes if they render services to the corporation. This, in effect, may shift income from the corporation to the employee. Forms of payment that may be offered to employees include the items listed below. They may be deductible as business expenses by the corporation if they meet the requirements discussed below, and when added to other forms of payment are reasonable in amount and provide the corporation with a business expense deduction.

Examples of Fringe Benefits

*   Group term life insurance covering the lives of the corporate officers and employees who designate their own beneficiaries, if the corporation does not retain any incidents of ownership and is not directly or indirectly the beneficiary. (*Note*: An employee, unless disabled, may have to include in his or her income the cost of group term life insurance coverage that is more than the cost of $50,000 of the insurance plus any amount paid by the employee toward its purchase. Also, a key employee may have to include in income the cost of the first $50,000 of this insurance. For more information, we recommend you read chapter 8 of IRS Publication No. 535, *Business Expenses*. This free government publication provides an excellent, easy-to-read discussion on fringe benefits and is a valuable source of information for entrepreneurs beginning their first business.)
*   Group hospitalization and medical care premiums paid for the benefit of employees.
*   Payments made under wages continuation, accident, or health plans for employees.
*   Payments made for employees' tuition, fees, books, course supplies, and similar items under a qualified educational assistance program. The courses must be required for their job.
*   Payments for employee child care or disabled dependent care services to allow employees to work.
*   Payments for employees' meals and lodging related to their job.
*   Payments to a qualified group prepaid legal service plan, which provides legal services for an employee or an employee's spouse.
*   Cafeteria plans that allow employees to choose among two or more benefits consisting of cash and nontaxable benefits.

Nondiscrimination Rules

The 1986 Tax Reform Act established a comprehensive set of nondiscrimination rules for certain statutory fringe benefits plans and cafeteria plans. Under certain conditions part of the fringe benefits may be included in the income of the employee. As a general guideline, employees must include in their income an amount equal to their employer-provided benefit *unless*:

*   The plan is in writing.
*   The employees' rights under the plan are legally enforceable.
*   Employees are given reasonable notification of benefits available under the plan.
*   The plan is maintained for the exclusive benefit of the employees.
*   The plan was established with the intention of being maintained indefinitely.

These requirements apply to statutory fringe benefits, tuition reduction programs, cafeteria plans, fringe benefit programs providing no additional cost services, employee discounts, employer provided operating facilities and welfare benefit plans.

The amount included is the fair market value of the benefit, less the amount, if any, the employee paid for it and less the amount specifically excluded from gross income. For more information about fringe benefits, see IRS Publication No. 525, *Taxable and Nontaxable Income*. Also, we strongly recommend you consult with your tax advisor before implementing any tax-sheltered fringe benefits.

An example of how employee benefits might impact on an employee's take home pay is shown below.

Corporation		Employee	
Net sales	$ 1,000	Wages	$20
Less: cost of goods sold	400	Employee benefits	1
Gross profit	600		
Less:selling and		Total wages reported	
administrative expenses		on form W-2	21
Salaries	150	Less: federal and	
Payroll taxes	30	state taxes	5
Rent	20		
Advertising	10		
Interest	5	Net wages	$16
Maintenance and repairs	5		
Employee benefits	2		
Telephone	2		
Office expense	1		
	226		
Net income before taxes	374		
Federal and state taxes	165		
Net income after taxes	$ 209		

SHELTERING PROFITS ON EXPORT SALES: DISCS AND FSCS

DISC stands for domestic international sales corporation, while FSC stands for foreign sales corporation. Congress, in an effort to stimulate exports, has granted certain special tax breaks to firms that sell to foreign countries.

DISC

Internal Revenue Code section 992 describes the qualification requirements of a DISC and how a corporation can elect to be treated as a DISC. Essentially, a DISC is a domestic corporation that derives a large percentage of its income from export sales and rentals. The tax code allows the corporation to defer paying tax on a portion of that income. The DISC itself is not taxed, instead the shareholders are taxed when they receive the income through dividends. The tax laws make a slight distinction between corporate shareholders and individual shareholders. Approximately six percent of the DISC's income is taxed if it is distributed to corporate shareholders.

For a corporation to qualify as a DISC, it must meet the following requirements:

* At least 95 percent of its gross receipts must be qualified export receipts.
* At least 95 percent of its assets must be qualified export assets.
* It must not have more than one class of stock.
* It must have minimum capital of at least $2,500 on each day of its taxable year.
* It must have an election in effect for the tax year, which must be consented to by each person who is a shareholder on the first day of the corporation's first taxable year as a DISC.
* It must not be a member of any controlled group in which a foreign sales corporation is a member.

The Tax Reform Act of 1984 changed the rules concerning the DISC so that it now favors small business rather than large corporations. This change was a direct result of pressure placed on the United States by the European Economic Community (EEC) which argued that DISCs constituted an illegal export subsidy which was in violation of the General Agreement on Tariffs and Trade (GATT). Currently, DISC gross receipts which are below $10 million will still receive preferential tax treatment but gross receipts that are in excess of $10 million will be fully taxed.

FSC

In response to pressure from the EEC, Congress created the foreign sales corporation, which is replacing DISCs for corporations that have gross receipts exceeding $10 million in an attempt to adhere to GATT guidelines but at the same time not allow U.S. corporations to suffer a competitive disadvantage.

A percentage of foreign trade income for an FSC is exempt from corporate income tax provided a portion of its income is derived from a foreign presence in a qualifying country, which means the corporation must be organized under the laws of a foreign country that has an international agreement with the United States to exchange tax information. A list of foreign countries in which an FSC may be incorporated is contained in Temporary Regulation Section 1.922-1T(e). Among other requirements, the corporation must maintain a foreign office and the board of directors must include at least one member who does not reside in the United States.

The TRA has made several changes to the FSC rules with the intention of clarifying some of the ambiguities concerning issues associated with income earned while not adhering to administrative pricing rules, deduction for dividends from earnings, and profits resulting from foreign trade income, and whether a U.S. possession may impose a tax on FSC income for certain types of transactions. We recommend you see your tax advisor if you are considering a DISC or FSC.

HOW TO WITHDRAW FUNDS FROM AN INCORPORATED BUSINESS

This section shows you six methods in which corporate earnings can be transmitted to shareholders while at the same time remain deductible to the corporation. **Warning:** Before proceeding with any of these methods, you must see your tax advisor for advice on whether any of these methods applies to your situation.

Employee Compensation

One method used to withdraw funds from a corporation by a shareholder/employee is in the form of compensation. However, the compensation must meet the reasonableness test, which is based on surrounding facts and circumstances. Exhibit 13-1 shows the case of *Edwin's, Inc.* v. *United States*, which addressed the issue of whether or not compensation was reasonable.

Making Loans to the Business

The second method is to reduce the amount of equity capital invested by increasing the corporate debt obligations. The IRS may contend that the capital structure is unrealistic and the debt is not bona fide and as a result disallow the corporate interest deduction. Furthermore, if the debt instrument has too many features of stock, the principal and interest payments will be considered dividends. The debt should have the following characteristics:

* Be in proper legal form
* Bear a legitimate rate of interest
* Have a definite maturity date
* Be repaid on a timely basis

Debt should not be subordinated to other liabilities nor should debt payments be contingent upon earnings. Also, proportionate holdings of stock and debt should be avoided.

Leasing Shareholder Property

The third method involves the corporation leasing shareholder-owned property. Again, the IRS might disallow the rental deductions by classifying the rents as disguised dividends.

Accumulated Earnings

The fourth method is to accumulate earnings in the corporation. However, if the IRS considers the accumulations unreasonable in light of the business's "reasonably" anticipated needs, it may impose an accumulated earnings tax. The IRS will have a difficult time imposing the accumulated earnings tax if a corporation's funds are invested in assets essential to the needs of the business. These anticipated needs must be specific, definite, and feasible. Examples of legitimate reasons include:

* Business expansion
* Replacement of plant and facilities
* Business acquisition
* Retirement of debt
* Providing working capital
* Investment
* Loans to suppliers or customers
* Self-insurance
* Business contingencies
* Key-employee life insurance

> * Post-death redemption requirements
> * Future product liability losses

Loans to Shareholders

The fifth method is through loans to shareholders. Once again, the IRS could argue that the loan was a taxable dividend or assess an accumulated earnings tax for unreasonable accumulation of earnings. You need to be careful when you attempt this type of transaction. We recommend you consult with your attorney or tax advisor.

Issuing Stock to Children

The sixth method is to issue stock to the children of the shareholders in order to reduce each family's aggregate tax liability by shifting dividend income to the children. For children under the age of fourteen, net unearned income is taxed at the parents' rate—that is, as if the parent had received the income. This applies even if the property was given to the child before 1987. The under-fourteen rules remain applicable until the child reaches age fourteen. For children fourteen and over, generally all unearned income is taxed at the child's rate.

For example, a boy, age thirteen, has $1,400 of unearned income. The $1,400 is first reduced by his standard deduction of $500. Of the remaining $900, $500 is taxed at the child's rate and the remaining $400 is taxed at the top rate of his parents.

In summary, children under the age of fourteen will be taxed at their parents' rate on their "net unearned income " (NUI). To determine the amount of income for a child under the age of fourteen, use the following formula:

> NUI = child's net unearned income - $500 + the greater of $500 of the standard
> deduction or $500 of itemized deductions *or* the deductions allowed the child
> which are directly connected with the production of the child's unearned income.

See your tax advisor before implementing any of the tax strategies listed above because proper tax planning may prevent additional taxes and penalties.

DEDUCTING EXPENSES THAT RELATE TO YOUR BUSINESS

What Are Business Expenses?

Business expenses are the normal and current costs of operating a business. They include outflows of assets or incurrence of liabilities during a period to generate revenue. To be deductible, a business expense must be both ordinary in your business and necessary for its operation.

> * An ordinary expense is one that is common and accepted in your field of business.
> * A necessary expense is one that is helpful and appropriate for your business.

Business expenses must be kept separate from personal expenses. Only the business expenses are deductible. For examples of business expenses, see part (e) of this section. Examples of deductions that are not considered business expenses include owner's draw, commuting expenses, and 20 percent personal part of business meals and business entertainment.

Capitalization vs. Expensing

Some costs must be capitalized rather than expensed. These costs are part of your investment in the business and are called *capital expenditures*. The cost of a capital expenditure can be recovered by subtracting it from revenue over time. Examples of a capital expenditure are:

* Going into business or start-up costs, such as advertising, traveling, utilities, repairs.
* Business assets, such as land, building, machinery, furniture, vehicles, equipment, tools, patents, and franchise rights.
* Improvements, if they add to the value of the asset or materially lengthen the asset's life or adapt the asset to a different use—the cost of the improvement usually is added to the basis of the improved property. Examples of improvements that are capitalized are new electric wiring, new roof, new floor, new plumbing, strengthening a wall, and new lighting.

How Much Expense Can Be Deducted?

There is usually no limit on how much you can deduct, provided the amount is reasonable. Although your deductions may be large enough to produce a net business loss for the year, the amount of tax loss may be limited. The issue of net business losses is a red flag which may draw an audit by the IRS or your state taxing agency, or both; therefore, we recommend you consult with your tax advisor on this matter.

Timing

Under the cash method of accounting, business expenses are deducted when they are paid regardless of when they were incurred.

Under the accrual method of accounting, business expenses are deductible when they are incurred regardless of when they are paid.

Examples of deductible expenses

* Cost of goods sold
* Employees' pay
* Rent expense
* Depreciation
* Amortization and depletion
* Bad debts
* Travel, entertainment, and gift expenses
* Interest expense
* Insurance
* Taxes
* Advertising
* Business use of your home
* Charitable contributions
* Dues and subscriptions
* Education expenses

* Professional fees
* Licenses and regulatory fees
* Lobbying expenses
* Medical expenses
* Political contributions
* Repairs and maintenance
* Supplies and materials

We recommend you review IRS Form 1040 Schedule C, IRS Form 1065, IRS Form 1120, and IRS Form 1120S for examples of deductible expenses.

Also see Exhibit 13-2, which contains an example of a business situation of a sole proprietorship and a completed IRS Form 1040 Schedule C. Exhibit 13-3 contains an example of a business situation for a partnership and a completed IRS Form 1065. Exhibit 13-4 contains an example of a business situation for a corporation that has elected S Corporation status and a completed IRS Form 1120S.

If you want more information concerning business expenses, we recommend you get a hold of the following IRS publications:

No. 334 *Tax Guide for Small Business*

No. 535 *Business Expenses*

Both of these publications are free and contain plenty of useful information.

CHOOSING THE BEST TAXABLE YEAR FOR YOUR BUSINESS

A tax return is filed on the basis of an annual accounting period called a *tax year*. A tax year is usually twelve consecutive months and may be either a calendar year or a fiscal year. In order to file on a fiscal year basis, your books must be kept on that basis. A short tax year is less than twelve months and arises if:

The taxpayer is not in existence for an entire tax year, or

The taxpayer changes tax years.

Corporate returns are due by the fifteenth day of the third month after the close of the taxable year. Other taxpayers' returns are due by the fifteenth day of the fourth month after the close of the taxable year.

If you have never filed a tax return, you may adopt either a calendar or fiscal year subject to the following restriction: You must use the calendar year: (1) if you do not maintain a set of books, or (2) if you have no annual accounting period, or (3) if the business year you have established does not qualify as a fiscal year.

Sole Proprietorship: You establish your tax year when you file your first income tax return. If, later, you begin business as a sole proprietorship, you must continue to use the same tax year as when your first return was filed, unless you get permission to change by filing Form 1128.

Partnerships: As a general rule, partnerships must conform their tax years to the tax years of their partners.

Corporations: A new corporation establishes its tax year when it files its first income tax return. The first tax year may not extend beyond the twelfth month of corporate existence. For a subchapter S corporation, it must use the calendar year unless the corporation can establish a business purpose for having a different tax year.

In order to change your tax year, you must obtain approval of the IRS by filing IRS Form 1128. (See Exhibit 13-5.) For more information on this topic, we recommend that you read IRS Publication No. 538, *Accounting Periods and Methods.*

SELECTING A TAX ACCOUNTING METHOD

What Is an Accounting Method?

An accounting method is a set of rules to decide when and how to record income and expenses on the books. These rules are also used to prepare an income statement for the accounting period.

Possible Methods

The Internal Revenue Code requires taxable income to be computed under the method of accounting regularly employed by the taxpayer in keeping his or her books. The method must clearly reflect income. Permissible methods are:

* Cash method
* Accrual method
* Hybrid method (combination of cash and accrual)

You may use any of these three methods; however, you are required to use the accrual method if inventories are an income-producing factor, for example, if your business is that of a merchandiser or manufacturer. In other words, the accrual method is required if inventories are necessary to clearly show income when the production, purchase, or sale of merchandise is income producing. For certain items such as research and development costs, carrying charges, intangible drilling costs, exploration costs, circulation costs, and depreciation, you may use a method other than the general accounting method used for books and records. For example, the items listed previously represent costs that you can choose to deduct or to capitalize. See your tax advisor for a discussion of Internal Revenue Code section 179, deduction for fixed assets.

Note: If you do not have an accounting method or if the method does not clearly reflect income, the IRS will compute income under the method it feels most clearly shows that income.

Cash Method

This method is used by small businesses with no inventories. Under this method, revenue is recorded when cash is either actually received or constructively received. Constructive receipt is when an amount is made available without restriction as to the time and manner of payment. You do not need to have possession of it.

Accrual Method

Under this method, income and expenses are matched when earned and incurred, respectively, in the correct accounting period. When cash is received and/or paid it has no effect on accrual income and expenses.

As mentioned earlier, if inventories are necessary to show income correctly, you will be required to use the accrual method for purchases and sales.

Hybrid Method

This method is a combination of cash and accrual. You may use the hybrid method if the combination clearly reflects income and is used in a consistent manner.

Miscellaneous Items

If more than one business is operated by the same individual, he or she may use a different accounting method for each.

You may, without prior consent of the IRS, choose any appropriate accounting method for your first return. Subsequently, any change of accounting method requires prior consent of the IRS. This is done on IRS Form 3115. (See Exhibit 13-6.)

Note: The cash method may not be used by the following:

* Any C corporation (regular corporation as opposed to an S corporation)
* Any partnership having a C corporation as a partner
* Any tax shelter

However, this rule does not apply to: (1) farm businesses, (2) qualified personal service corporations, or (3) any corporation or partnership having average gross receipts of $5 million or less for prior tax years beginning after 1985.

Summary

The accounting method you select must clearly reflect income and be used consistently. However, even under this constraint, it does not preclude you from proper tax planning in order to minimize your tax liability.

TAX PROBLEMS UNIQUE TO CORPORATIONS

Individual vs. Corporations

Rules on income and deductions that apply to individuals generally apply to corporations as well. However, a corporation is entitled to several special deductions in determining its taxable income.

Corporations may deduct, subject to certain limitations, 80 percent of the dividends it receives from taxable domestic corporations. They also may claim a deduction, subject to certain limits, for charitable contributions made in cash or other property. To be deductible, the contribution must meet certain requirements. The organization to which you make a contribution should be able to tell you if the contribution is deductible.

Corporations are not entitled to claim a credit for certain political contributions. Moreover, a deduction will be disallowed if any of the earnings of the organization receiving the contribution are used for the benefit of any private shareholder or individual.

Reallocating Income and Deductions

Under certain conditions, the IRS may reallocate income and deductions between two or more businesses that are directly or indirectly controlled by the same interests.

Estimated Tax Payments

Corporations are required to make estimated tax payments if their estimated tax is expected to be $40 or more. In addition, corporations must take into account both the .12 percent environmental tax and the alternative minimum tax in determining estimated taxes.

Accumulated Earnings Tax

Corporations may be subject to an accumulated earnings tax if earnings are allowed to accumulate beyond the reasonable needs of the business.

Corporations performing services in the fields of health, law, engineering, architecture, accounting, actuarial science, performing arts, or consulting have a $150,000 limit on accumulated earnings.

For other corporations, an accumulation of $250,000 is considered within the reasonable needs of the business. Reasonable needs of a business include:

* Specific, definite, and feasible plans for the use of the accumulation in the business,
* The amount necessary to redeem the corporation's stock in a deceased shareholder's gross estate.

The IRS has held that the mere existence of tax avoidance in accumulating earnings is sufficient for imposition of the accumulated earnings tax. Use your corporate minutes to document plans for the use of accumulations.

Dividends Withholdings

Generally, corporate distributions made out of earnings and profits to stockholders are considered dividends. However, this distribution is not a taxable dividend if it is a return of capital to the stockholder. Backup withholding may require corporations to withhold a tax equal to 20 percent of dividends paid to certain shareholders. For further information on this topic, we recommend you see IRS Publication No. 550, "Investment Income and Expenses."

Alternative Minimum Tax

Often, a corporation that has no tax liability under a straight calculation will owe taxes under the alternative minimum tax formula. Corporations are subject to an alternative minimum tax (AMT). The calculation is:

AMT = regular taxable income + tax preferences - certain deductions

This rule ensures that corporate taxpayers pay tax equal to at least 20% of their economic income above the exemption amount. The amount of minimum tax owed is the amount by which the tentative minimum tax exceeds the regular tax. The law in this area has been changed radically because of recent tax bills. If you are thinking of incorporating your business, we strongly recommend you see your tax advisor for additional information in this area.

"S" Corporation Election

Some corporations may elect not to be subject to income tax, which avoids double taxation. If a corporation qualifies as an S corporation, a corporation's income usually will be taxed to its shareholders. This topic was explained in Chapter 5. For additional information on S corporations, we recommend you obtain IRS Publication No. 589, "Tax Information on S Corporations," from the IRS. It is free and contains valuable information about the S corporation election.

In summary, this overview of tax problems unique to corporations is intended to illustrate the importance of adequate tax planning. See your tax advisor prior to incorporating. Also, we urge you to obtain from the IRS a free copy of its Publication No. 542 "Tax Information on Corporations".

HOW TO PLAN FOR YOUR ESTATE WHEN YOUR BUSINESS ACCOUNTS FOR A LARGE PORTION OF YOUR PERSONAL NET WORTH

Set Your Goals

Estate planning is best done with an estate planning team consisting of your CPA, attorney, trust officer, insurance advisor, and investment manager, with one acting as team leader. Your goals will determine the nature of your estate plan and the tools you will select. In addition, you will want to ensure your plan is properly implemented so that your objectives can be reached, which is the reason for an estate planning team.

Estate Planning Techniques

There is a variety of techniques you can use to reach your objectives. Below are examples of estate planning techniques that should be discussed with your estate planning team.

Intervivos gifts

Intervivos gifts are direct gifts during your lifetime and offer advantages which include the following:

* Appreciation in value of an asset subsequent to transfer escapes taxation in the decedent's estate.
* Retention of annual gift exclusion ($10,000 per donee per year and if spouse joins in making gift, $20,000 per donee per year).
* Income produced from gifts of income producing assets can be shifted to a taxpayer with a lower marginal tax rate.

* Gift taxes paid during life on transferred property will not be included in the donor's gross estate for estate tax purposes and yet will be credited against the unified tax due after death.

Trusts

Trusts are one of the most flexible legal instruments available for estate planning. A trust is a legal device whereby legal title to property is held by one person (a trustee) for the benefit of a beneficiary, usually another person. A beneficiary is a person who is to receive the benefits from the trust. You, yourself, may be the beneficiary of your own trust, although the beneficiary is usually another individual.

The money or property given to the trust is called the trust fund or principal. A trust fund may consist of stocks, real estate, cash, insurance policies, or even a going business. The assets that are in the trust fund may change from time to time, depending on the investments made by the trustee as well as restrictions and instructions placed on the trustee from time to time.

The trustee who accepts the responsibility for handling the trust fund is required to account for all money or assets received and will be held liable in a civil lawsuit for mishandling trust funds. There is no rule governing how large a trust should be. The size usually varies with the purpose of the trust.

Using a trust to plan your estate provides several advantages:

* It will avoid the delays and cost of probate. The cost to create a trust is usually less than the cost of bond premiums and court costs required in the probate process.
* It will permit the continuance of an asset management program, even after the death of the person who established the trust. For example, if you are going to leave a substantial sum of cash, either through accumulated wealth or because of life insurance, to someone who is inexperienced, that individual may be unable to take care of the money and may quickly spend it. If property is given as an outright bequest through a will, it may be quickly dissipated or attached by the recipient's creditors. Trusts are often used when property, such as cash or stocks, is to be passed down to children who are minors.
* It is a private matter among trustor, trustee, and beneficiary. By using a trust, you can be reasonably assured that the details of your estate and its subsequent disposition will never be disclosed to the general public.
* It allows you to retain considerable flexibility in the handling of your estate. As the trustor, you retain the right to change the trustee at any time. The trustor can also change the method of distributing trust proceeds at any time.

The TRA eliminates income splitting by use of a Clifford or spousal remainder trust. If you have sufficient assets to enable you to part with complete control over a portion of them, an irrevocable lifetime trust should be considered. This transfer serves to remove assets from the gross estate. The most common type is an irrevocable trust funded with life insurance.

Marital trusts can be used for management of assets for the surviving spouse and control over the principal.

The best known marital trust is called the *qualified terminable interest property trust* (QTIP trust), which is a special type of marital trust through which a special election allows the QTIP assets to qualify for the marital deduction. (These assets escape estate taxation until the second spouse dies.)

Another type of trust is called the *Crummey trust,* which is appropriate for wealthy individuals who want to reduce their estates by making gifts but who are concerned about the recipient's ability to handle money. (Trust income and principal are distributed at the trustee's discretion.)

Will and Marital Deduction Clause

The marital deduction offers a significant tax planning opportunity. (This is a deduction allowed upon the transfer of property from one spouse to another.) This deduction makes possible a substantial bequest to a surviving spouse without incurring any estate tax.

The couple's estate also may be divided between two spouses in order to maximize the total amount of assets that can be transferred to the next generation.

The tax planning utility of the marital deduction centers around the ability of the tax planner to design a will that will significantly increase the amount of assets passing to the children, and provide a direct benefit to the surviving spouse.

Tax Shelter Investments

Carefully chosen, the tax shelter investment may be an attractive vehicle. The income tax losses provided by such an investment can shield a substantial proportion of your salary from a high marginal tax rate. (It is imperative, however, that you consult your tax advisor because of changes in this area brought about by the TRA specifically the passive loss rule.)

In evaluating such investments, the first rule is to evaluate the underlying economics of the transaction. Other factors include:

* Whether the project will have any residual value after the loss period;
* The amount of syndication proceeds or other distributions being paid to the promoters; and
* Liquidity potential of the investment.

A major disadvantage for estate planning purposes is that tax shelter investments tend to be illiquid. (Such assets might be included in your gross estate but cannot be disposed of in order to meet the estate's cash requirements.)

Life Insurance

All life insurance may be divided into two fundamental categories: term insurance and whole life insurance.

Term life insurance is an agreement by the insurance company to pay a specified amount (called the face amount of the policy) if the named individual (called the insured) dies during the policy term.

Term insurance has no loan value, no cash surrender value, and no investment value. In essence, it is similar to auto or fire insurance in that it covers a particular risk for a specified period of time. Furthermore, because the likelihood of death increases each year, term insurance becomes more expensive the longer you retain it. This expense is manifested by either the face amount of the insurance declining or the amount of the premium increasing.

Whole life insurance is actually a combination of insurance and investment. A portion of each year's premium is allocated to the policy's cash value and the balance of the premium is allocated to the actual insurance protection. As the cash value of the policy increases each year, a larger portion of the premium is allocated to investment and a smaller portion to insurance protection.

Term life insurance is usually much less expensive than whole life. Often it is used by young parents to insure against the risk of premature death. In this sense, term insurance for head of a household is a temporary insurance used to cover the risk of death before the children are grown and before there are sufficient accumulated assets to provide for the family. However, because term life insurance premiums necessarily become more expensive with advancing age, it is not considered a satisfactory vehicle for fulfilling permanent insurance objectives. Life insurance can provide liquidity to provide funds to pay funeral and administrative expenses as well as estate and inheritance taxes, thereby avoiding the need to sell other assets of the estate. The heirs are thus able to avoid additional capital gains taxes and can retain assets that have good investment possibilities.

Life insurance proceeds must be included in the decedent's estate if policy proceeds are receivable by, or for, the benefit of the estate, or if proceeds are receivable by other beneficiaries and the decedent possessed, either alone or in conjunction with others, the incidents of ownership in the policy. To remove life insurance proceeds from the decedent's estate, the estate cannot be named as policy beneficiary and another named beneficiary cannot be encumbered with an obligation running in favor of the estate.

Proceeds must be included in the insured's gross estate if any of the following powers exist:

* Power to change beneficiary
* Power to surrender or cancel policy
* Power to assign policy
* Power to revoke an assignment
* Power to pledge policy for a loan
* Power to obtain from the insurance compay a loan against the cash surrender value of the policy

Two basic questions estate planners will ask concerning life insurance are, "How much coverage is advisable?" and "Who should be designated the beneficiary?" For example, if an irrevocable insurance trust is named beneficiary, the trustee can be given the power to make loans to the executor for payment of estate taxes.

Executive Compensation Estate Planning

Recognizing an Income in Respect of Decedent Problem. Any review of estate planning for compensation plans must begin with an understanding of the concept of income in respect of a decedent (IRD). IRD represents income earned by a decedent at the time of death but not reportable on the final income tax return because of the method of accounting utilized. This income is included in the gross estate and will be taxed to the eventual recipient. Note that the recipient will be allowed an income tax deduction for the estate tax attributable to the income. An example is in the case of a cash basis taxpayer, who made loans prior to his or her death. Regardless of when the taxpayer dies, the accrued interest is income in respect to a decedent and is includible in the gross estate. The accrued interest is reported as interest income on the fiduciary return.

The recognition of IRD will be precipitated by the receipt of the IRD income or the transfer of the IRD receivable.

The death of a decedent in which income transfers from the IRS receivable to an estate is not a triggering event, and the distribution of an IRD receivable to a beneficiary who has inherited it is not considered to be a transfer requiring the recognition of income.

IRD will be created by most compensation-related items. If the item of compensation is also taxable for estate tax purposes, a double tax burden will result because the same compensation related receivable will be subject to both estate taxation and income taxation.

The Internal Revenue Code provides limited relief from double taxation in the form of an income tax deduction for the estate tax payable with respect to the IRD.

If you think your estate will be subject to double taxation, see your tax advisor to determine whether limited relief provided by the Internal Revenue Code will be applicable.

Deferred Compensation

This compensation plan generally consists of a corporate employer's unsecured and unfunded obligation to pay compensation at some future time, usually in installments, beginning upon the executive's retirement, death, or termination of employment.

A tax-qualified plan cannot discriminate in favor of officers, shareholders, or highly compensated employees.

Note: Deferral is not permitted for income tax purposes if any of the following exist:

* The employee has the right to receive currently amounts set aside for his or her benefit;
* The obligation is a cash equivalent; or
* The obligation is funded and set aside separately in a trust or escrow account.

While planning your estate, you should consider the wisdom of participating in such a fund. Factors to consider include:

* If the plan's primary goal is income tax savings, can savings be reasonably expected?
* What is the percent value of the income to be deferred?
* What is the economic risk of postponing recognition of the income?

Qualified Plans

Executives in both public and closely-held companies usually are participants in 401(K) qualified pensions, profit sharing, or stock bonus plans. These plans are described in detail in Chapter 16. Briefly, these plans are described below.

* 401(K) plans defer the receipt of income on the amounts contributed by the employer to the plan until distributions are made to participants.
* ESOPs provide the employee with ownership rights in the corporate employer's stock. Controversy has arisen from a provision of the TRA that allows estate executors to reduce estate tax by selling stock to an ESOP. It is recommended that this topic be discussed with your estate and tax planners.

In general, qualified pension or profit-sharing plans will be taxed to the recipient under the rules relating to income taxation of annuities. This means distributions will be taxable to the recipient as received, to the extent attributable to employer contributions.

The Internal Revenue Code provides for a $100,000 estate tax exclusion for the value of an annuity receivable by a beneficiary under a qualified plan. If you are contemplating qualifying for this exclusion, see your tax advisor for the requirements that need to be satisfied.

Individual Retirement Accounts (IRA)

Under the TRA, setting aside your nest egg is not only more difficult but more expensive. You have less flexibility in choosing among retirement plans and you won't be able to "salt away" as much tax-deferred income as in the past.

Currently, a working taxpayer not covered by another retirement plan may deduct individual retirement account (IRA) contributions. However, a working taxpayer covered by another retirement plan may deduct IRA contributions if adjusted gross income (AGI) is less than $25,000 a year ($40,000 for married couples filing jointly). In addition, a working taxpayer covered by another retirement plan may not make deductible IRA contributions if his or her AGI exceeds $35,000 a year ($50,000 for joint filers). Any nondeductible contributions to an IRA must be reported on IRS Form 8606.

The problem of record keeping under the new IRA rules has become more complex. You should consult with your tax advisor before investing in an IRA.

Constructing a Plan to Pass Your Estate on to Loved Ones

For many individuals, the ownership of a business interest constitutes the single largest asset in their estate. To successfully plan on how their estate will pass to their loved ones, it is necessary to make the following determinations:

STEP 1: You must determine the type of business interest you have.

Sole proprietorship —This is a singly-owned business. Generally, the owner is the manager and is the recipient of all the income, deductions, and credits for federal and state income tax purposes.

Partnership—There are two types of partnerships: limited and general. In most states, there must be a partnership agreement signed by all of the partners and a certificate of limited partnership filed with the Secretary of State. The advantage of the limited partnership is that the limited partner is viewed under the eyes of the law as only an investor. Thus, unless the limited partner participates in control of the partnership business, he or she will not be held personally liable for the partnership's debts. Often there are restrictions on the transfer of partnership interests as well as provisions that explain how partnership interests will be valued.

In a general partnership, a general partner takes an active role in the affairs of the business but also is held personally liable for the debts of the business. As a rule, income, deductions, and credits of the partnership will generally pass through to the partners in proportion to their partnership interests.

Corporation—This type of business organization is considered a separate legal entity. Most often if the corporation is closely held, which is defined by Internal Revenue Code 6166(b), all the stock will be owned either by one person or spread among only a few persons. If the stock is owned by more than one person, the bylaws of the corporation or a shareholders' agreement usually provide restrictions on the transfer of any shares of the corporation either during the shareholder's lifetime or at death.

STEP 2: You must value your business interest.

Valuation of a business interest is a gray area. Generally the rule is that the interest must be valued at fair market value. Treasury Department regulations 20.2031–1(b) and 25.2512–1 define fair market value as the price at which property would change hands between a willing buyer and a willing seller, neither party being under any compulsion to buy or sell and both parties having reasonable knowledge of relevant facts. Treasury regulation 20.2031-3 also states that various factors are to be used to determine the value of a business, such as appraisal of assets, demonstrated earning capacity, dividend paying capacity, goodwill, economic outlook, quality of management, degree of control represented by business interest, values of similar publicly traded businesses.

To help individuals to determine the actual value of a closely held business, the IRS has provided guidelines that elaborate upon Treasury regulation 20.2031–3. The guidelines can be found in Revenue Ruling 59–60, 1959–1 Cumulative Bulletin 237 modified by Revenue Ruling 83–120, 1983–2 Cumulative Bulletin 130. For instance, Revenue Ruling 59–60 lists the following factors that need to be examined in valuing any closely held business.

 a. Nature and history of the enterprise

 b. Economic outlook in general and in the specific industry

 c. Book value and financial conditions

 d. Earning capacity

 e. Dividend paying capacity*

 f. Goodwill or other intangible value**

Undervaluation: Beware

What happens if you undervalue your business interest? A significant undervaluation of a business interest that results in an underpayment of federal estate or gift tax is subject to a penalty, which is imposed under Internal Revenue Code section 6660. The following table provides general guidelines of the penalties that may be incurred.

	Valuation Claimed	**Penalty[a]**
1.	Is less than 40% of the current valuation	30%
2.	Is more than 40% but less than 50%	20%
3.	Is more than 50% but less than 66 2/3%	10%
4.	Is more than 66 2/3% or underpayment is less than $1,000	0%

[a] Penalty represents a percentage of the underpayment of tax.

 * Revenue Ruling 59–60 distinguishes actual dividends that have been paid from potential dividends that could be paid. The IRS reasons that most closely held corporations avoid having to pay dividends by increasing the salaries and other fringe benefits of owner–employees.

 ** Goodwill, as defined by Revenue Ruling 59–60, is the excess of net earnings over a fair return on net tangible assets. The IRS reasons that if a business is earning more than a "reasonable return" on its tangible assets, the additional return must be attributable to such factors as location, name, etc. For more information, we recommend you see Revenue Ruling 68–609, 1968–2 Cumulative Bulletin 327, which provides an actual formula for the valuation of goodwill.

STEP 3: You must decide whether you want to liquidate your interest in the business before you retire or sell the business and receive installment payments.

Liquidation. Your main concern is your ability to withdraw your interest in the business in the form of cash. For a sole proprietorship, it means selling off assets and paying off creditors. For a partnership and a closely held corporation, the most popular approach, and some say the best because of the nature of many business assets, is to be bought out.

Buy-out agreements. One method that is often used in corporations and partnerships is the buy-out agreement, which is either mandatory or optional. A mandatory buy-out agreement makes the repurchase of an individual's interest in the business mandatory upon retirement. For partnerships, these types of agreements are common and present little or no legal problems; however, for a corporation, even if it is closely held, there are certain legal hurdles that must be overcome.

For instance, many states impose limitations on the amount of corporate funds that can be spent in the purchase of shares from an owner of the business, especially if it results in the corporation being unable to satisfy its liabilities as they become due. Moreover, any stockholder who receives assets and who knows that it is prohibited is liable to the corporation for the amount of the assets plus interest. Because it is often difficult to forecast the financial condition of the firm far in advance many corporations choose to use an optional buy-out agreement because it gives the corporation flexibility. At the same time, however, it creates uncertainty for the owner who wants to sell his or her interest.

Numerous tax issues arise whenever there is a buy-out agreement, and, as a consequence, you should consult your tax advisor. Some of the issues you may need to consider are listed below.

* Payment terms—in particular, the interest rate charged to finance the purchase.
* Capital gains treatment of your corporate distribution if you have capital losses in excess of $3,000 and you wish to make the deduction in the same year.
* Attribution rule—in particular, where you are a parent and both you and your child are stockholders/employees, but your child has acquired his or her stock from you as a result of a gift or sale.
* Purchase of the stock - may be viewed as a dividend by the IRS.
* Whether your stock is considered "small business stock" and therefore exempt from state income tax.

Selling the business. This issue arises most often in a sole proprietorship, partnership in which the partners cannot agree on a buy-out agreement, or corporation in which a buy- out agreement may cause a violation of a regulation or law. Some individuals prefer to have the business continue after they retire, and as such, instead of liquidating their interest by selling off the assets, search for a new owner—that is, an outsider to take over the business. There are various reasons for choosing this route. Perhaps the reason most often given is a sense of moral obligation to provide continued employment for loved ones, friends, and loyal employees. Second, it may be the only way the owner(s) can extract his or her entire investment from the business without taking a loss.

In most instances, the owner or owners will have to finance the purchase themselves. The buyer of the business will make payments on an installment basis, usually, for a period of five to ten years. Because the source of the payment will be revenues generated from the business, it is necessary to have the buyer sign a security agreement as well as a promissory note. A security interest in the assets of the business that is perfected may offer at least some protection in the event the buyer defaults in making payments.

HOW TO RECEIVE TAX CREDITS FOR HIRING CERTAIN ECONOMICALLY DISADVANTAGED GROUPS

If, as an employer, you hire certain employees, you may be able to take the targeted jobs credit to reduce your federal income tax. The credit may be taken only for wages you incur or pay to employees selected from specified targeted groups.

An individual is a member of a targeted group if he or she falls within one of the following classifications:

* Vocational rehabilitation referral
* Economically disadvantaged youth
* Economically disadvantaged Vietnam-era veteran
* Supplemental security income (SSI) recipient
* General assistance recipient
* Youth participating in a cooperative education program
* Economically disadvantaged ex-convict
* Eligible work incentive employee
* Qualified summer youth employee

To utilize this program, it will be necessary to obtain certification, which can be made by a designated local agency (local offices of a state employment security agency), or by the participating school in the case of a cooperative education student.

There are some additional rules you should know as well. You cannot claim a credit for wages paid to a related individual. A credit cannot be taken on wages paid to an eligible employee who works less than 90 days or 120 hours. In the case of a qualified summer youth, the cutoff is 14 days or 20 hours. Wages qualify for the credit only if more than one-half of the wages are for work done in your business. The credit cannot reduce your tax liability below zero. Unused credits can be carried back three years or forward fifteen years. See Exhibit 13-7, which shows IRS Form 5884.

PUTTING YOUR SPOUSE AND CHILDREN ON THE PAYROLL

Despite the TRA, there are still some advantages in placing your spouse and children on the payroll. *Caution:* You must actually pay your spouse and children, and the amounts must be reasonable. Remember to issue W-2 forms for your spouse and children.

There are other favorable aspects in placing your spouse or child on the payroll:

* No FICA or FUTA taxes are owed on spouse's or children's pay if your are a proprietor. Children must be under age 18, however.
* You can deduct up to $2,000 for IRA pay-ins that your spouse makes. See your tax advisor for IRA pay-in limitations.
* A child's salary or wages are taxed at the child's rate.
* A child also gets the benefit of a standard deduction.

* A sole proprietorship can deduct salary and wages of spouse and children.

Some of these advantages may disappear in the near future. For example, the Treasury Department wants FICA and FUTA taxes on spouse's salary and wages. Furthermore, pay of children under 18 may be subject to FICA and FUTA taxes.

HOW TO SAVE ON UNEMPLOYMENT TAXES

The topic of unemployment taxes was first explained in Chapter 6. The purpose of this section is to explain how you can save on unemployment taxes.

In review, the Federal unemployment tax rate is (6.2 percent – 5.4 percent) = .8 percent of the first $7,000 in wages paid to a covered employee.

State unemployment tax varies, based on the employer's experience, up to 5.4 percent of the first $7,000 in wages. If your state tax rate happens to be less than 5.4 percent, you are still allowed the 95.4 percent credit against the federal 6.2 percent rate.

As a rule, state unemployment insurance is payable to covered employees who satisfy the following requirements:

* Unemployed through no fault of their own
* Able to work
* Available for work
* Actively seeking employment
* Have met all of the eligibility requirements of the law

The weekly benefit amount is based on the amount of wages paid in the highest quarter of the claimant's base period. The following actions of the claimant may favorably affect the employer's experience rating:

* Quit without good cause
* Was discharged for misconduct connected with his or her work
* Left work because of a trade dispute
* Is working full time
* Is not physically able to work
* Is not available for or is not seeking work
* Refused to take suitable employment
* Made false statements to obtain benefits
* Is a school employee who has reasonable assurance of returning to work after a recess period
* Is receiving a pension which is paid under a plan that was maintained or contributed to by the employer

Filing a claim for unemployment insurance benefits starts a chain of action which results in one or more employers becoming interested parties. The employer should respond to the first claim notice with any facts that may affect the claimant's eligibility for benefits.

Whenever an issue regarding the claimant's eligibility is raised, a determination is made before benefits are paid. If the employer contends the claimant voluntarily quit or is otherwise ineligible for benefits, he or she must give the reason for such contention.

A ruling, issued by the state agency, which is based on the circumstances surrounding a claimant's separation, advises the employer if his or her reserve account will or will not be relieved of charges resulting from benefits paid.

A favorable ruling is one that finds the claimant:

* Quit without good cause
* Was discharged for misconduct
* Is continuously employed on a part-time basis
* Was a student employed temporarily during vacation period
* Quit to join or accompany a spouse to an area from which it is impractical to commute, to which a transfer is not available, or where the spouse has secured other employment

On a favorable ruling, the employer's reserve account will not be charged for benefits based on the wages paid for the term of the employment on which the ruling is made. If an unfavorable ruling results, the employer's reserve account will be charged for benefits paid. An appeal process is available if you believe findings are contrary to the law or facts. We recommend you see your attorney before you attend the state agency hearing because once the official has made his or her decision, it will be extremely difficult to have his or her findings of fact overturned. In most states, there is an automatic presumption in favor of the party who received the ruling even if the matter is heard de novo.

Chapter 13 Exhibits

Exhibit 13.1 Was Compensation Reasonable? *Edwin's,
Inc. v. United States*

Exhibit 13.2 Completed with Explanation: Profit or Loss
From Business or Profession Schedule C (Form 1040)

Exhibit 13.3 Completed with Explanation: U.S.
Partnership Return of Income (Form 1065)

Exhibit 13.4 Completed with Explanation: U.S. Income Tax
Return for S Corporation (IRS Form 1120S)

Exhibit 13.5 Application for Change in Accounting
Period (IRS Form 1128)

Exhibit 13.6 Application for Change in Accounting
Method (IRS Form 3115)

Exhibit 13.7 Jobs Credit (IRS Form 5884)

Was Compensation Reasonable?

Edwin's, Inc. v. United States 501 F.2d 675 (1974)

Facts:

The taxpayer, Edwin's Incorporated, is a women's specialty store in Eau Claire, Wisconsin. Edwin and Rose Marcus originally purchased the store in 1950 and operated it as a partnership. Assets were turned over to the taxpayer corporation with Edwin and Rose each taking 50% of the taxpayer's stock.

During the period in question, Edwin Marcus was the taxpayer's president and acted as its general manager, credit manager, buyer, financial director, and merchandise manager. Rose Marcus was the taxpayer's vice-president and acted as store manager when Edwin was absent; managed the Bridal Shop; wrote, directed, and performed in the taxpayer's television advertising; and purchased certain merchandise for the store. Rose and Edwin's son, Jeff Marcus, worked for the taxpayer as assistant manager.

During the fiscal years ending January 1, 1966 and 1967, the taxpayer paid Edwin and Rose each a salary of $24,000 per year. In addition, Edwin and Rose eached received an annual bonus equal to 20% of the corporation's net income before taxes. Jeff Marcus was paid a straight salary of $15,000 in 1966 and $18,000 in 1967 but received no bonus. The taxpayer also contributed amounts to a pension plan for all three Marcuses, the total of such pension payments being $8,905.01 in 1966 and $12,322.49 in 1967. The total deductions taken by the taxpayer as compensation on behalf of the Marcuses were $88,277.47 in 1966 and $93,041.35 in 1967. The Commissioner determined that reasonable compensation would be $65,200.00 for each year. The taxpayer paid the additional tax assertedly due and sued for a refund.

Following a bench trial, the district court found that the salaries and bonuses paid to Edwin and Rose and the salaries paid to Jeff were reasonable. The Government appealed.

Holding and Reasoning:

In determining whether compensation is reasonable, a number of factors must be considered, including: the type and extent of the services rendered; the scarcity of qualified employees; the qualifications and prior earning capacity of the employee; the contributions of the employee to the business venture; the net earnings of the taxpayer; the prevailing compensation paid to employees of comparable jobs and the peculiar characteristics of the taxpayer's business.

Exhibit 13-1

The evidence indicated that all the Marcuses worked long hours and performed their jobs exceedingly well. All three Marcuses worked 60 to 70 hours a week at the store and performed work which would normally require five or six persons. At least one member of the Marcus family was always present at the store duirng business hours. Each of the Marcuses, moreover, had considerable experience in the field of merchandising. Even before they bought the store in 1950, Edwin and Rose had each worked in women's apparel. After purchasing the store, Edwin and Rose both worked there full-time. Jeff Marcus had worked at his parents' store after school and during summers while he was growing up and had gained substantial experience in the business. Furthermore, Rose Marcus was actively involved in advertising the store. She prepared the scripts and memorized them after store hours. She worked with photographers. The commercials were generally run five evenings a week. She established an unusual personal relationship in this line of merchandising which itself is highly personal and not to be equated with the sale of faded jeans. Customers would come in especially to see her. She perhaps unwittingly anticipated a popular recent television jingle, for as she put it, "I closed my program with holding the merchandise toward the camera, and the camera came in on it, and I would say, 'Try it on' " The skill and time which the Marcuses devoted to the store were clearly reflected in the store's success. The gross sales increased from $50,000 in 1950, when the Marcuses purchased the store, to $650,000 in the years in question. The inventory at the store, furthermore, turned over at a significantly faster rate than in the average specialty store. The net profit was in excess of 20% of the invested capital.

Having reviewed the record, we affirm that part of the district court's ruling which found the salaries and bonuses paid to the Marcuses to be reasonable compensation and, therefore, deductible by the taxpayer.

SCHEDULE C (Form 1040) - Profit or Loss From Business

As the sole proprietor of an unincorporated business, you report income on Schedule C. In our example, Sue Z. Kew owns and operates Sue Z's Apparel, a ladies ready-to-wear apparel shop. She uses the accrual method and evaluates inventory at cost.

Sue sold $795,484 of retail goods and suffered returns/allowances of $2,884. In calculating her cost of goods sold, Sue reports beginning inventory of $85,686, ending inventory of $87,492 and purchases of $480,504.

For deductions, Sue claims the following expenses: Advertising of $7,000, bank service charges of $360 and car/truck expenses of $4,500. Sue suffered bad debts of $958. She claims $5,462 in depreciation on fixed assets. Insurance cost Sue $1,900 and interest on borrowings ran $5,266. Office expense was $432 and rent for the store totalled $24,000. Repairs were $3,552 and supplies cost $2,406. Sales taxes were $11,604 and telephone expense was $7,140. Sue paid her staff $126,900 and earned a Jobs Credit of $8,800. Miscellaneous expenses included window washing of $476, trash removal for $3,200, credit card company discount fee of $12,000 and Chamber of Commerce fee of $120.

For other examples of the construction of Schedule C (Form 1040) Profit or Loss from Business, refer to the Department of the Treasury, Internal Revenue Service Publication 334 (Rev. Nov. 88). Every line and every box of this form is explained in detail in this publication.

Exhibit 13-2

SCHEDULE C
(Form 1040)

Department of the Treasury
Internal Revenue Service (O)

Profit or Loss From Business
(Sole Proprietorship)
Partnerships, Joint Ventures, Etc., Must File Form 1065.
▶ Attach to Form 1040, Form 1041, or Form 1041S. ▶ See Instructions for Schedule C (Form 1040).

OMB No. 1545-0074

1988

Attachment
Sequence No. **09**

Name of proprietor SUE Z. KEW	Social security number (SSN) 123 45 6789

A Principal business or profession, including product or service (see Instructions)
LADIES APPAREL RETAIL

B Principal business code (from Part IV) ▶ 3 9 1 1 3

C Business name and address ▶ SUE Z'S APPAREL
123 ELM ST., FRANKLIN, NY 18725

D Employer ID number (Not SSN) 9 5 1 2 3 4 5 6 7

E Method(s) used to value closing inventory:
  (1) ☒ Cost (2) ☐ Lower of cost or market (3) ☐ Other (attach explanation)

F Accounting method: (1) ☐ Cash (2) ☒ Accrual (3) ☐ Other (specify) ▶ ....

		Yes	No
G	Was there any change in determining quantities, costs, or valuations between opening and closing inventory? (If "Yes," attach explanation.)		X
H	Are you deducting expenses for business use of your home? (If "Yes," see Instructions for limitations.)		X
I	Did you "materially participate" in the operation of this business during 1988? (If "No," see Instructions for limitations on losses.)	X	

J If this schedule includes a loss, credit, deduction, income, or other tax benefit relating to a tax shelter required to be registered, check here . ▶ ☐
If you check this box, you MUST attach **Form 8271**.

Part I Income

1a	Gross receipts or sales	**1a**	795,484
b	Less: Returns and allowances	**1b**	2,884
c	Subtract line 1b from line 1a. Enter the result here	**1c**	792,600
2	Cost of goods sold and/or operations (from Part III, line 8)	**2**	478,698
3	Subtract line 2 from line 1c and enter the **gross profit** here	**3**	313,902
4	Other income (including windfall profit tax credit or refund received in 1988)	**4**	-0-
5	Add lines 3 and 4. This is the **gross income** ▶	**5**	313,902

Part II Deductions

6	Advertising	**6**	7,000		**23**	Repairs	**23**	3,552
7	Bad debts from sales or services (see Instructions)	**7**	958		**24**	Supplies (not included in Part III)	**24**	2,406
8	Bank service charges	**8**	360		**25**	Taxes	**25**	11,604
9	Car and truck expenses	**9**	4,500		**26**	Travel, meals, and entertainment:		
10	Commissions	**10**			**a**	Travel	**26a**	
11	Depletion	**11**			**b**	Meals and entertainment		
12	Depreciation and section 179 deduction from Form 4562 (not included in Part III)	**12**	5,462		**c**	Enter 20% of line 26b subject to limitations (see Instructions)		
13	Dues and publications	**13**			**d**	Subtract line 26c from 26b	**26d**	
14	Employee benefit programs	**14**			**27**	Utilities and telephone	**27**	7,140
15	Freight (not included in Part III)	**15**			**28a**	Wages	126,900	
16	Insurance	**16**	1,900		**b**	Jobs credit	8,800	
17	Interest:				**c**	Subtract line 28b from 28a	**28c**	118,100
a	Mortgage (paid to banks, etc.)	**17a**			**29**	Other expenses (list type and amount):		
b	Other	**17b**	5,266			WINDOW WASH 476		
18	Laundry and cleaning	**18**				TRASH 3200		
19	Legal and professional services	**19**				FEE: CREDIT CARD 12,000		
20	Office expense	**20**	432			CHAMBER OF		
21	Pension and profit-sharing plans	**21**				COMMERCE 120		
22	Rent on business property	**22**	24,000				**29**	15,796

30	Add amounts in columns for lines 6 through 29. These are the **total deductions** ▶	**30**	208,476
31	**Net profit or (loss).** Subtract line 30 from line 5. If a profit, enter here and on Form 1040, line 12, and on Schedule SE, line 2. If a loss, you MUST go on to line 32. (Fiduciaries, see instructions.)	**31**	105,426

32 If you have a loss, you MUST check the box that describes your investment in this activity (see Instructions)
    32a ☐ All investment is at risk.
    32b ☐ Some investment is not at risk.

If you checked 32a, enter the loss on Form 1040, line 12, and Schedule SE, line 2. If you checked 32b, you MUST attach **Form 6198**.

For Paperwork Reduction Act Notice, see Form 1040 Instructions.

Schedule C (Form 1040) 1988

Part III　Cost of Goods Sold and/or Operations (See Schedule C Instructions for Part III)

1	Inventory at beginning of year. (If different from last year's closing inventory, attach explanation.)	1	85,686
2	Purchases less cost of items withdrawn for personal use	2	480,504
3	Cost of labor. (Do not include salary paid to yourself.)	3	–0–
4	Materials and supplies	4	–0–
5	Other costs	5	–0–
6	Add lines 1 through 5	6	566,190
7	Less: Inventory at end of year	7	87,492
8	**Cost of goods sold and/or operations.** Subtract line 7 from line 6. Enter the result here and in Part I, line 2.	8	478,698

Part IV　Codes for Principal Business or Professional Activity

Locate the major business category that best describes your activity (for example, Retail Trade, Services, etc.). Within the major category, select the activity code that identifies (or most closely identifies) the business or profession that is the principal source of your sales or receipts. **Enter this 4-digit code on line B on page 1 of Schedule C.** (**Note:** If your principal source of income is from farming activities, you should file **Schedule F (Form 1040), Farm Income and Expenses.**)

Construction
Code
- 0018 Operative builders (building for own account)

General contractors
- 0034 Residential building
- 0059 Nonresidential building
- 0075 Highway and street construction
- 3889 Other heavy construction (pipe laying, bridge construction, etc.)

Building trade contractors, including repairs
- 0232 Plumbing, heating, air conditioning
- 0257 Painting and paper hanging
- 0273 Electrical work
- 0299 Masonry, dry wall, stone, tile
- 0414 Carpentering and flooring
- 0430 Roofing, siding, and sheet metal
- 0455 Concrete work
- 0471 Water well drilling
- 0885 Other building trade contractors (excavation, glazing, etc.)

Manufacturing, Including Printing and Publishing
- 0612 Bakeries selling at retail
- 0638 Other food products and beverages
- 0653 Textile mill products
- 0679 Apparel and other textile products
- 0695 Leather, footware, handbags, etc.
- 0810 Furniture and fixtures
- 0836 Lumber and other wood products
- 0851 Printing and publishing
- 0877 Paper and allied products
- 0893 Chemicals and allied products
- 1016 Rubber and plastics products
- 1032 Stone, clay, and glass products
- 1057 Primary metal industries
- 1073 Fabricated metal products
- 1099 Machinery and machine shops
- 1115 Electric and electronic equipment
- 1313 Transportation equipment
- 1339 Instruments and related products
- 1883 Other manufacturing industries

Mining and Mineral Extraction
- 1511 Metal mining
- 1537 Coal mining
- 1552 Oil and gas
- 1719 Quarrying and nonmetallic mining

Agricultural Services, Forestry, and Fishing
- 1917 Soil preparation services
- 1933 Crop services
- 1958 Veterinary services, including pets
- 1974 Livestock breeding
- 1990 Other animal services
- 2113 Farm labor and management services
- 2212 Horticulture and landscaping
- 2238 Forestry, except logging
- 0836 Logging
- 2279 Fishing, hunting, and trapping

Wholesale Trade—Selling Goods to Other Businesses, Government, or Institutions, Etc.
Durable goods, including machinery, equipment, wood, metals, etc.
- 2618 Selling for your own account

Code
- 2634 Agent or broker for other firms— more than 50% of gross sales on commission

Nondurable goods, including food, fiber, chemicals, etc.
- 2659 Selling for your own account
- 2675 Agent or broker for other firms— more than 50% of gross sales on commission

Retail Trade—Selling Goods to Individuals and Households
- 3012 Selling door-to-door, by telephone or party plan, or from mobile unit
- 3038 Catalog or mail order
- 3053 Vending machine selling

Selling From Store, Showroom, or Other Fixed Location
Food, beverages, and drugs
- 3079 Eating places (meals or snacks)
- 3095 Drinking places (alcoholic beverages)
- 3210 Grocery stores (general line)
- 0612 Bakeries selling at retail
- 3236 Other food stores (meat, produce, candy, etc.)
- 3251 Liquor stores
- 3277 Drug stores

Automotive and service stations
- 3319 New car dealers (franchised)
- 3335 Used car dealers
- 3517 Other automotive dealers (motorcycles, recreational vehicles, etc.)
- 3533 Tires, accessories, and parts
- 3558 Gasoline service stations

General merchandise, apparel, and furniture
- 3715 Variety stores
- 3731 Other general merchandise stores
- 3756 Shoe stores
- 3772 Men's and boys' clothing stores
- 3913 Women's ready-to-wear stores
- 3921 Women's accessory and specialty stores and furriers
- 3939 Family clothing stores
- 3954 Other apparel and accessory stores
- 3970 Furniture stores
- 3996 TV, audio, and electronics
- 3988 Computer and software stores
- 4119 Household appliance stores
- 4317 Other home furnishing stores (china, floor coverings, drapes, etc.)
- 4333 Music and record stores

Building, hardware, and garden supply
- 4416 Building materials dealers
- 4432 Paint, glass, and wallpaper stores
- 4457 Hardware stores
- 4473 Nurseries and garden supply stores

Other retail stores
- 4614 Used merchandise and antique stores (except used motor vehicle parts)
- 4630 Gift, novelty, and souvenir shops
- 4655 Florists
- 4671 Jewelry stores

Code
- 4697 Sporting goods and bicycle shops
- 4812 Boat dealers
- 4838 Hobby, toy, and game shops
- 4853 Camera and photo supply stores
- 4879 Optical goods stores
- 4895 Luggage and leather goods stores
- 5017 Book stores, excluding newsstands
- 5033 Stationery stores
- 5058 Fabric and needlework stores
- 5074 Mobile home dealers
- 5090 Fuel dealers (except gasoline)
- 5884 Other retail stores

Real Estate, Insurance, Finance, and Related Services
- 5512 Real estate agents and managers
- 5538 Operators and lessors of buildings (except developers)
- 5553 Operators and lessors of other real property (except developers)
- 5710 Subdividers and developers, except cemeteries
- 5736 Insurance agents and services
- 5751 Security and commodity brokers, dealers, and investment services
- 5777 Other real estate, insurance, and financial activities

Transportation, Communications, Public Utilities, and Related Services
- 6114 Taxicabs
- 6312 Bus and limousine transportation
- 6338 Trucking (except trash collection)
- 6510 Trash collection without own dump
- 6536 Public warehousing
- 6551 Water transportation
- 6619 Air transportation
- 6635 Travel agents and tour operators
- 6650 Other transportation and related services
- 6676 Communication services
- 6692 Utilities, including dumps, snowplowing, road cleaning, etc.

Services (Providing Personal, Professional, and Business Services)
Hotels and other lodging places
- 7096 Hotels, motels, and tourist homes
- 7211 Rooming and boarding houses
- 7237 Camps and camping parks

Laundry and cleaning services
- 7419 Coin-operated laundries and dry cleaning
- 7435 Other laundry, dry cleaning, and garment services
- 7450 Carpet and upholstery cleaning
- 7476 Janitorial and related services (building, house, and window cleaning)

Business and/or personal services
- 7617 Legal services (or lawyer)
- 7633 Income tax preparation
- 7658 Accounting and bookkeeping
- 7674 Engineering, surveying, and architectural

Code
- 7690 Management, consulting, and public relations
- 7716 Advertising, except direct mail
- 7732 Employment agencies and personnel supply
- 7757 Computer and data processing, including repair and leasing
- 7773 Equipment rental and leasing (except computer or automotive)
- 7914 Investigative and protective services
- 7880 Other business services

Personal services
- 8110 Beauty shops (or beautician)
- 8318 Barber shop (or barber)
- 8334 Photographic portrait studios
- 8516 Shoe repair and shine services
- 8532 Funeral services and crematories
- 8714 Child day care
- 8730 Teaching or tutoring
- 8755 Counseling (except health practitioners)
- 8771 Ministers and chaplains
- 6882 Other personal services

Automotive services
- 8813 Automotive rental or leasing, without driver
- 8839 Parking, except valet
- 8854 General automotive repairs
- 8870 Specialized automotive repairs (brake, body repairs, paint, etc.)
- 8896 Other automotive services (wash, towing, etc.)

Miscellaneous repair, except computers
- 9019 TV and audio equipment repair
- 9035 Other electrical equipment repair
- 9050 Reupholstery and furniture repair
- 2881 Other equipment repair

Medical and health services
- 9217 Offices and clinics of medical doctors (MDs)
- 9233 Offices and clinics of dentists
- 9258 Osteopathic physicians and surgeons
- 9274 Chiropractors
- 9290 Optometrists
- 9415 Registered and practical nurses
- 9431 Other licensed health practitioners
- 9456 Dental laboratories
- 9472 Nursing and personal care facilities
- 9886 Other health services

Amusement and recreational services
- 8557 Physical fitness facilities
- 9613 Videotape rental stores
- 9639 Motion picture theaters
- 9654 Other motion picture and TV film and tape activities
- 9670 Bowling alleys
- 9696 Professional sports and racing, including promoters and managers
- 9811 Theatrical performers, musicians, agents, producers, and related services
- 9837 Other amusement and recreational services

- 8888 Unable to classify

SCHEDULE C (Form 1040) - Profit or Loss From Business

As the sole proprietor of an unincorporated business, you report income on Schedule C. In our example, Sue Z. Kew owns and operates Sue Z's Apparel, a ladies ready-to-wear apparel shop. She uses the accrual method and evaluates inventory at cost.

Sue sold $795,484 of retail goods and suffered returns/allowances of $2,884. In calculating her cost of goods sold, Sue reports beginning inventory of $85,686, ending inventory of $87,492 and purchases of $480,504.

For deductions, Sue claims the following expenses: Advertising of $7,000, bank service charges of $360 and car/truck expenses of $4,500. Sue suffered bad debts of $958. She claims $5,462 in depreciation on fixed assets. Insurance cost Sue $1,900 and interest on borrowings ran $5,266. Office expense was $432 and rent for the store totalled $24,000. Repairs were $3,552 and supplies cost $2,406. Sales taxes were $11,604 and telephone expense was $7,140. Sue paid her staff $126,900 and earned a Jobs Credit of $8,800. Miscellaneous expenses included window washing of $476, trash removal for $3,200, credit card company discount fee of $12,000 and Chamber of Commerce fee of $120.

For other examples of the construction of Schedule C (Form 1040) Profit or Loss from Business, refer to the Department of the Treasury, Internal Revenue Service Publication 334 (Rev. Nov. 88). Every line and every box of this form is explained in detail in this publication.

FORM 1065 - U.S. Partnership Return of Income

In this section, we will demonstrate the method of filling in Form 1065 for XYZ Wholesale Company, a general partnership formed by Albert Jones and Jim Smith. The partnership uses the accrual method of accounting and uses a calendar year end for reporting income or loss. Mr. Jones devotes all of his time to the business and Mr. Smith devotes 25% of his time to it. The partnership agreement states that Mr. Jones is to receive a yearly guaranteed payment of $15,000 and that Mr. Smith is to receive a guaranteed payment of $5,000. Any profit or losses are to be shared equally by the partners. Both partners are general partners and are, therefore, personally liable for all partnership liabilities. Both partners are involved with the operation of the business on a regular, continuous and substantial basis.

For 1988, XYZ had gross sales of $850,150 and returns/allowances of $10,400. The beginning inventory was $100,522 and the ending inventory was $99,476. The company made purchases of $551,632 during 1988. The company earned $1,525 in interest from its money market account which it classifies as other income. The company paid salaries/wages of $86,650 to its employees. The rent for the company's premisis was $20,000 and interest expense for the company's loans was $25,211. The company paid sales and other non-income taxes of $4,525. During 1988, the company experienced bad debts in the extention of trade credit in the amount of $12,596. The company spent $4,525 for the repair of various pieces of equipment and charged depreciation on equipment and furniture and fixtures at the rate of $15,010. The company had miscellaneous deductions including insurance, telephone, postage, supplies etc. in the amount of $37,322 for all of 1988. The company contributed $1,300 to the Boys' Club during the year. In addition to the above normal revenues and expenses, the company has owns investment assets that generated dividend income of $150. It, also, sold two of these assets experiencing a short term gain of $100 and a long term gain of $200. During the year, Mr. Jones contributed $700 to the partnership.

For other examples of the construction of Form 1065 U. S. Partnership Return of Income, refer to the Department of the Treasury, Internal Revenue Service Publication 334 (Rev. Nov. 88). Every line and every box of this form is explained in detail in this publication.

Exhibit 13-3

Form **1065**

Department of the Treasury
Internal Revenue Service

U.S. Partnership Return of Income

▶ For Paperwork Reduction Act Notice, see Form 1065 Instructions.

For calendar year 1988, or fiscal year beginning _____, 1988, and ending _____, 19 ___

OMB No. 1545-0099

1988

A Principal business activity

WHOLESALE

B Principal product or service

SUNDRIES

C Business code number

5001

Use IRS label. Otherwise, please print or type.

Name

XYZ WHOLESALE COMPANY

Number and street (or P.O. Box number if mail is not delivered to street address)

334 WEST OVERSHOE ST.

City or town, state, and ZIP code

SAN DIEGO, CA 92555

D Employer identification number

95-9876543

E Date business started

10-1-78

F Enter total assets at end of tax year

$ 389,113

		Yes	No
G Check accounting method: (1) ☐ Cash (2) ☒ Accrual (3) ☐ Other			
H Check applicable boxes: (1) ☐ Final return (2) ☐ Change in address (3) ☐ Amended return			
I Number of partners in this partnership ▶ 2			
J Is this partnership a limited partnership (see the Instructions)?			X
K Are any partners in this partnership also partnerships?			X
L Is this partnership a partner in another partnership?			X
M Does the partnership meet all the requirements shown in the Instructions for **Question M**?			X
N Was there a distribution of property or a transfer (for example, by sale or death) of a partnership interest during the tax year? If "Yes," see the Instructions concerning an election to adjust the basis of the partnership's assets under section 754.			X
O (1) Does the partnership have any foreign partners?			X
(2) If so, were any distributions made to foreign partners during the tax year?			

	Yes	No
P At any time during the tax year, did the partnership have an interest in or a signature or other authority over a financial account in a foreign country (such as a bank account, securities account, or other financial account)? (See the Instructions for exceptions and filing requirements for Form TD F 90-22.1.) If "Yes," write the name of the foreign country. ▶ _____		X
Q Was the partnership the grantor of, or transferor to, a foreign trust which existed during the current tax year, whether or not the partnership or any partner has any beneficial interest in it? If "Yes," you may have to file Form 3520, 3520-A, or 926		X
R Check this box if the partnership has filed or is required to file Form 8264, Application for Registration of a Tax Shelter	☐	
S Check this box if this is a partnership subject to the consolidated partnership audit procedures of TEFRA. (See the Instructions.)	☐	
T Check this box if the partnership is a publicly traded partnership as defined in section 469(k)(2)	☐	

Caution: Include only trade or business income and expenses on lines 1a–21 below. See the instructions for more information.

Income

1a	Gross receipts or sales $ 850,150 1b Minus returns and allowances $ 10,400 Balance ▶	1c	839,750	
2	Cost of goods sold and/or operations (Schedule A, line 7)	2	552,678	
3	Gross profit (subtract line 2 from line 1c)	3	287,072	
4	Ordinary income (loss) from other partnerships and fiduciaries (attach schedule)	4		
5	Net farm profit (loss) (attach Schedule F (Form 1040))	5		
6	Net gain (loss) (Form 4797, line 18)	6		
7	Other income (loss)	7	1525	
8	**TOTAL** income (loss) (combine lines 3 through 7)	8	288,597	

Deductions (see instructions for limitations)

9a	Salaries and wages (other than to partners) $ 86,650 9b Minus jobs credit $ _____ Balance ▶	9c	86,650	
10	Guaranteed payments to partners	10	20,000	
11	Rent	11	18,000	
12	Deductible interest expense not claimed elsewhere on return (see Instructions)	12	25,211	
13	Taxes	13	4525	
14	Bad debts	14	12,596	
15	Repairs	15	4525	
16a	Depreciation from Form 4562 (attach Form 4562) $ 15,010 16b Minus depreciation claimed on Schedule A and elsewhere on return $ —0— Balance ▶	16c	15,010	
17	Depletion (**Do not deduct oil and gas depletion.**)	17		
18a	Retirement plans, etc.	18a		
b	Employee benefit programs	18b		
19	Other deductions (attach schedule)	19	37,322	
20	**TOTAL** deductions (add amounts in column for lines 9c through 19)	20	223,839	
21	Ordinary income (loss) from trade or business activity(ies) (subtract line 20 from line 8)	21	64,758	

Please Sign Here

Under penalties of perjury, I declare that I have examined this return, including accompanying schedules and statements, and to the best of my knowledge and belief, it is true, correct, and complete. Declaration of preparer (other than taxpayer) is based on all information of which preparer has any knowledge.

▶ _Albert E. Jones_
Signature of general partner

▶ 4-3-89
Date

Paid Preparer's Use Only

Preparer's signature ▶		Date	Check if self-employed ▶ ☐	Preparer's social security no.
Firm's name (or yours if self-employed) and address ▶			E.I. No. ▶	
			ZIP code ▶	

Schedule A · Cost of Goods Sold and/or Operations

1	Inventory at beginning of year.	1	100,522
2	Purchases minus cost of items withdrawn for personal use	2	551,632
3	Cost of labor.	3	—0—
4a	Additional section 263A costs (attach schedule) (see instructions)	4a	—0—
b	Other costs (attach schedule)	4b	—0—
5	Total (add lines 1 through 4b).	5	652,154
6	Inventory at end of year.	6	99,476
7	Cost of goods sold (subtract line 6 from line 5). Enter here and on page 1, line 2	7	552,678

8a Check all methods used for valuing closing inventory:

(I) ☐ Cost

(II) ☐ Lower of cost or market as described in regulations section 1.471-4

(III) ☐ Writedown of "subnormal" goods as described in regulations section 1.471-2(c)

(Iv) ☐ Other (specify method used and attach explanation) ▶ ....

b Check if the LIFO inventory method was adopted this tax year for any goods (if checked, attach Form 970) . . . . ☐

c Do the rules of section 263A (with respect to property produced or acquired for resale) apply to the partnership? . . ☐ Yes ☐ No

d Was there any change in determining quantities, cost, or valuations between opening and closing inventory? If "Yes," attach explanation . . . . ☐ Yes ☐ No

Schedule H · Income (Loss) From Rental Real Estate Activity(ies)

1 In the space provided below, show the kind and location of each rental property. Attach a schedule if more space is needed.

Property A ....

Property B ....

Property C

Rental Real Estate Income		Properties			Totals (Add columns A, B, C, and amounts from any attached schedule)	
		A	B	C		
2 Gross Income	2				2	
Rental Real Estate Expenses						
3 Advertising	3					
4 Auto and travel	4					
5 Cleaning and maintenance	5					
6 Commissions	6					
7 Insurance	7					
8 Legal and other professional fees	8					
9 Interest expense	9					
10 Repairs	10					
11 Taxes	11					
12 Utilities	12					
13 Wages and salaries	13					
14 Depreciation from Form 4562	14					
15 Other (list)						
....						
....						
16 Total expenses. Add lines 3 through 15	16				16	
17 Net income (loss) from rental real estate activity(ies). Subtract line 16 from line 2. Enter total net income (loss) from all properties on Schedule K, line 2.	17				17	

Schedule K	Partners' Shares of Income, Credits, Deductions, etc.		
	(a) Distributive share items		**(b) Total amount**

	(a) Distributive share items		(b) Total amount
Income (Loss)	**1** Ordinary income (loss) from trade or business activity(ies) (page 1, line 21)	**1**	64,758
	2 Net income (loss) from rental real estate activity(ies) (Schedule H, line 17)	**2**	
	3a Gross income from other rental activity(ies) **3a**		
	b Minus expenses (attach schedule) **3b**		
	c Balance: net income (loss) from other rental activity(ies) ▶	**3c**	
	4 Portfolio income (loss) (see instructions):		
	a Interest income	**4a**	
	b Dividend income	**4b**	150
	c Royalty income	**4c**	
	d Net short-term capital gain (loss) (Schedule D, line 4)	**4d**	100
	e Net long-term capital gain (loss) (Schedule D, line 9)	**4e**	200
	f Other portfolio income (loss) (attach schedule)	**4f**	
	5 Guaranteed payments	**5**	20,000
	6 Net gain (loss) under section 1231 (other than due to casualty or theft) (see instructions)	**6**	
	7 Other (attach schedule)	**7**	
Deductions	**8** Charitable contributions (attach list)	**8**	1,300
	9 Expense deduction for recovery property (section 179) (attach schedule)	**9**	
	10 Deductions related to portfolio income (do not include investment interest expense)	**10**	
	11 Other (attach schedule)	**11**	
Credits	**12a** Credit for income tax withheld	**12a**	
	b Low-income housing credit: (1) Partnerships to which section 42(j)(5) applies	**12b(1)**	
	(2) Other	**12b(2)**	
	c Qualified rehabilitation expenditures related to rental real estate activity(ies) (attach schedule)	**12c**	
	d Credit(s) related to rental real estate activity(ies) other than 12b and 12c (attach schedule)	**12d**	
	e Credit(s) related to other rental activity(ies) (see instructions) (attach schedule)	**12e**	
	13 Other (attach schedule)	**13**	
Self-Employment	**14a** Net earnings (loss) from self-employment	**14a**	84,758
	b Gross farming or fishing income	**14b**	
	c Gross nonfarm income	**14c**	84,758
Tax Preference Items	**15a** Accelerated depreciation of real property placed in service before 1/1/87	**15a**	
	b Accelerated depreciation of leased personal property placed in service before 1/1/87	**15b**	
	c Depreciation adjustment on property placed in service after 12/31/86	**15c**	
	d Depletion (other than oil and gas)	**15d**	
	e (1) Gross income from oil, gas, and geothermal properties	**15e(1)**	
	(2) Deductions allocable to oil, gas, and geothermal properties	**15e(2)**	
	f Other (attach schedule)	**15f**	
Investment Interest	**16a** Interest expense on investment debts	**16a**	
	b (1) Investment income included on lines 4a through 4f, Schedule K	**16b(1)**	450
	(2) Investment expenses included on line 10, Schedule K	**16b(2)**	
Foreign Taxes	**17a** Type of income		
	b Foreign country or U.S. possession		
	c Total gross income from sources outside the U.S. (attach schedule)	**17c**	
	d Total applicable deductions and losses (attach schedule)	**17d**	
	e Total foreign taxes (check one): ▶ ☐ Paid ☐ Accrued	**17e**	
	f Reduction in taxes available for credit (attach schedule)	**17f**	
	g Other (attach schedule)	**17g**	
Other	**18a** Total expenditures to which a section 59(e) election may apply (attach schedule)	**18a**	
	b Attach schedule for other items and amounts not reported above (see instructions)		
Analysis	**19a** Total distributive income/payment items (combine lines 1 through 5, above)	**19a**	
	b Analysis by type of partner:		

	(a) Corporate	(b) Individual		(c) Partnership	(d) Exempt organization	(e) Nominee/Other
		i. active	ii. passive			
1. General partners						
2. Limited partners						

Schedule L Balance Sheets

(See the Instructions for Question M Before Completing Schedules L and M.)

Assets	Beginning of tax year (a)	(b)	End of tax year (c)	(d)
1 Cash		40 350		62 538
2 Trade notes and accounts receivable	150 137		170 350	
a Minus allowance for bad debts		150 137		170 350
3 Inventories		100 522		99 476
4 Federal and state government obligations				
5 Other current assets (attach schedule)				
6 Mortgage and real estate loans				
7 Other investments (attach schedule)		3 000		2 000
8 Buildings and other depreciable assets	75 437		75 437	
a Minus accumulated depreciation	13 203	60 234	28 213	47 274
9 Depletable assets				
a Minus accumulated depletion				
10 Land (net of any amortization)				
11 Intangible assets (amortizable only)				
a Minus accumulated amortization				
12 Other assets (attach schedule)		10 525		7 475
13 TOTAL assets		362 768		389 113
Liabilities and Capital				
14 Accounts payable		89 521		88 589
15 Mortgages, notes, bonds payable in less than 1 year		50 000		75 000
16 Other current liabilities (attach schedule)		3 543		4 276
17 All nonrecourse loans				
18 Mortgages, notes, bonds payable in 1 year or more		100,000		86 535
19 Other liabilities (attach schedule)				
20 Partners' capital accounts		119 704		134 713
21 TOTAL liabilities and capital		362 768		389 113

Schedule M Reconciliation of Partners' Capital Accounts

(Show reconciliation of each partner's capital account on Schedule K-1 (Form 1065), Question K.)

(a) Capital account at beginning of year	(b) Capital contributed during year	(c) Income (loss) from lines 1,2, 3c, and 4 of Sch. K	(d) Income not included in column (c), plus nontaxable income	(e) Losses not included in column (c), plus unallowable deductions	(f) Withdrawals and distributions	(g) Capital account at end of year
119 704	700	65 208		1300	49599	134 713

Designation of Tax Matters Partner

The following general partner is hereby designated as the tax matters partner (TMP) for the tax year for which this partnership return is filed:

Name of designated TMP ▶ ALBERT E. JONES

Identifying number of TMP ▶ 549-64-8483

Address of designated TMP ▶ 10953 COOL TERRACE
SAN DIEGO, CA 92128

FORM 1120S - S Corporation Form

We will now demonstrate the use of S Corporation Form 1120S with an example of JEE Manufacturing, Inc. This company fabricates various plastic products. It uses the accrual method of accounting and files its returns on the basis of the calendar year end. The company elected S Corporation status on December 31, 1987 and has three stockholders.

During 1988, the company had gross sales of $4,001,532 and returns/allowances of $43,657. For schedule A purposes, the company had a beginning inventory of $506,320 and an ending inventory of $459,622. Purchases during the year were $1,992,406 and labor costs for Schedule A were $810,516. Schedule A depreciation was $175,000. The company revalued its beginning inventory upward $10,015, which is considered Other Income.

In the deduction section, we find the following expenses. Officer compensation totalled $167,000, while salaries/wages totalled $254,163. Repairs to machinery totalled $14,175. Specific accounts charged to bad debts during the year were $29,684. Rent for the year was $75,000 while taxes amounted to $12,000. Interest on company debt was $110,000. Total depreciation for the company was $202,500 with $175,000 taken in Schedule A. The company spent $17,000 for advertising. Other expenses, which include supplies, sales commissions, legal fees, insurance, etc. amounted to $56,530.

The company had other investments valued at cost equal to $100,000. Form these investments, the company earned dividends of $16,000. The company earned $4,000 from its bank account. The company donated $24,000 to the YMCA as a charitable contribution. The company took advantage of federal job programs and earned a Jobs Credit of $6,000.

For Schedule M calculations, Other Additions amount to $20,000 made up of $4,000 of interest and $16,000 of dividend income. The owners received a total of $65,000 of distributions in materials and property (this value is, also, entered on Schedule K). Other reductions amounted to $30,000 made up of $24,000 of charitable contributions and $6,000 of Jobs Credits. The company received $5,000 of tax free income from municipal bonds.

For other examples of the construction of Form 1120S - S Corporation return, refer to the Department of the Treasury, Internal Revenue Service Publication 334 (Rev. Nov. 88). Every line and every box of this form is explained in detail in this publication.

Exhibit 13-4

Form **1120S**
Department of the Treasury
Internal Revenue Service

U.S. Income Tax Return for an S Corporation

For the calendar year 1988 or tax year beginning _____, 1988, ending _____, 19 ____

▶ For Paperwork Reduction Act Notice, see page 1 of the instructions.

OMB No. 1545-0130

1988

A Date of election as an S corporation 12-31-87	Use IRS label. Otherwise, please print or type.	**Name** JEE MANUFACTURING, INC.	**C** Employer identification number 95-1234567
B Business code no. (see Specific Instructions) 3070		Number and street (P.O. Box number if mail is not delivered to street address) 123 'A' STREET	**D** Date incorporated 3-1-1972
		City or town, state, and ZIP code ELM CITY CA 95555	**E** Total assets (see Specific Instructions) Dollars $270 8505 Cents

F Check applicable boxes: (1) ☐ Initial return (2) ☐ Final return (3) ☐ Change in address (4) ☐ Amended return

G Check this box if this is an S corporation subject to the consolidated audit procedures of sections 6241 through 6245 (see instructions) . . . . ▶ ☐

H Enter number of shareholders in the corporation at end of the tax year . . . . ▶ 3

Caution: Include **only** trade or business income and expenses on lines 1a through 21. See the instructions for more information.

Income

1a Gross receipts or sales	4001 532	**b** Less returns and allowances 43 657	**c** Bal ▶ **1c** 3 957 875
2 Cost of goods sold and/or operations (Schedule A, line 7).			**2** 3 024 620
3 Gross profit (subtract line 2 from line 1c)			**3** 933 255
4 Net gain (or loss) from Form 4797, line 18 (see instructions)			**4** —0—
5 Other income (see instructions—attach schedule). . . .			**5** 10 015
6 Total income (loss)—Combine lines 3, 4, and 5 and enter here . . . . . . ▶			**6** 943 270

Deductions (See instructions for limitations.)

7 Compensation of officers		**7** 167 000
8a Salaries and wages 254 163 **b** Less jobs credit		**c** Bal ▶ **8c** 254 163
9 Repairs.		**9** 14 175
10 Bad debts (see instructions)		**10** 29 684
11 Rents		**11** 75 000
12 Taxes		**12** 12 000
13 Deductible interest expense not claimed or reported elsewhere on return (see instructions) . .		**13** 110 000
14a Depreciation from Form 4562 (attach Form 4562). **14a** 202 500		
b Depreciation reported on Schedule A and elsewhere on return . **14b** 175 000		
c Subtract line 14b from line 14a		**14c** 27 500
15 Depletion (**Do not deduct oil and gas depletion.** See instructions.) . . .		**15** —0—
16 Advertising		**16** 12 000
17 Pension, profit-sharing, etc. plans		**17** —0—
18 Employee benefit programs		**18** —0—
19 Other deductions (attach schedule)		**19** 56 530
20 Total deductions—Add lines 7 through 19 and enter here . . . . . . ▶		**20** 763 052
21 Ordinary income (loss) from trade or business activity(ies)—Subtract line 20 from line 6 . . .		**21** 180 278

Tax and Payments

22 Tax:		
a Excess net passive income tax (attach schedule) **22a**		
b Tax from Schedule D (Form 1120S) **22b**		
c Add lines 22a and 22b		**22c** —0—
23 Payments:		
a Tax deposited with Form 7004 . . . . . . **23a**		
b Credit for Federal tax on fuels (attach Form 4136) . . **23b**		
c Add lines 23a and 23b		**23c** —0—
24 Tax due (subtract line 23c from line 22c). See instructions for Paying the Tax . . . . . ▶		**24** —0—
25 Overpayment (subtract line 22c from line 23c) . . . . ▶		**25** —0—

Please Sign Here

Under penalties of perjury, I declare that I have examined this return, including accompanying schedules and statements, and to the best of my knowledge and belief, it is true, correct, and complete. Declaration of preparer (other than taxpayer) is based on all information of which preparer has any knowledge.

Signature of officer: *John Everette Evans*	Date: 3-9-89	Title: President

Paid Preparer's Use Only

Preparer's signature ▶	Date	Check if self-employed ▶ ☐	Preparer's social security number
Firm's name (or yours if self-employed) and address ▶		E.I. No. ▶	
		ZIP code ▶	

Form **1120S** (1988)

Schedule A Cost of Goods Sold and/or Operations (See instructions for Schedule A.)

1	Inventory at beginning of year	1	506 320
2	Purchases	2	1992 406
3	Cost of labor	3	810 516
4a	Additional section 263A costs (attach schedule) (see instructions)	4a	—0—
b	Other costs (attach schedule)	4b	175,000
5	Total—Add lines 1 through 4b	5	3 484 242
6	Inventory at end of year	6	459 622
7	Cost of goods sold and/or operations—Subtract line 6 from line 5. Enter here and on line 2, page 1	7	3 024 620

8a Check all methods used for valuing closing inventory:
   (i) ☒ Cost
   (ii) ☐ Lower of cost or market as described in Regulations section 1.471-4
   (iii) ☐ Writedown of "subnormal" goods as described in Regulations section 1.471-2(c)
   (iv) ☐ Other (Specify method used and attach explanation) ▶ _____

   b Check this box if the LIFO inventory method was adopted this tax year for any goods (if checked, attach Form 970) . . . . ☐

   c If the LIFO inventory method was used for this tax year, enter percentage (or amounts) of closing inventory computed under LIFO . . . . | 8c |

   d Do the rules of section 263A (with respect to property produced or acquired for resale) apply to the corporation? . . . ☐ Yes ☒ No

   e Was there any change in determining quantities, cost, or valuations between opening and closing inventory? (If "Yes," attach explanation.) . . . . ☐ Yes ☒ No

Additional Information Required

		Yes	No
I	Did you at the end of the tax year own, directly or indirectly, 50% or more of the voting stock of a domestic corporation? (For rules of attribution, see section 267(c).) If "Yes," attach a schedule showing: (1) name, address, and employer identification number; and (2) percentage owned.		X
J	Refer to the listing of business activity codes at the end of the Instructions for Form 1120S and state your principal. (1) Business activity ▶ _____ ; (2) Product or service ▶ _____		
K	Were you a member of a controlled group subject to the provisions of section 1561?		X
L	At any time during the tax year, did you have an interest in or a signature or other authority over a financial account in a foreign country (such as a bank account, securities account, or other financial account)? (See instructions for exceptions and filing requirements for form TD F 90-22.1.)		X
	If "Yes," enter the name of the foreign country ▶ _____		
M	Were you the grantor of, or transferor to, a foreign trust which existed during the current tax year, whether or not you have any beneficial interest in it? If "Yes," you may have to file Forms 3520, 3520-A, or 926.		X
N	During this tax year did you maintain any part of your accounting/tax records on a computerized system?		X
O	Check method of accounting: (1) ☐ Cash (2) ☐ Accrual (3) ☐ Other (specify) ▶ _____		
P	Check this box if the S corporation has filed or is required to file Form 8264, Application for Registration of a Tax Shelter . . . . ▶ ☐		
Q	Check this box if the corporation issued publicly offered debt instruments with original issue discount . . . . ▶ ☐		
	If so, the corporation may have to file Form 8281, Information Return for Publicly Offered Original Issue Discount Instruments.		
R	If the corporation: (1) filed its election to be an S corporation after December 31, 1986, (2) was a C corporation prior to making the election, and (3) at the beginning of the tax year has net unrealized built-in gain as defined in section 1374(d)(1), enter the net unrealized built-in gain (see instructions) ▶		

Designation of Tax Matters Person (See instructions.)

The following shareholder is hereby designated as the tax matters person (TMP) for the tax year for which this tax return is filed:

Name of designated TMP ▶ JOHN EVERRETTE EVANS   Identifying number of TMP ▶ 123-45-6789

Address of designated TMP ▶ 4340 HOLMES PARKWAY
ELM CITY CA 95555

Schedule K   Shareholders' Shares of Income, Credits, Deductions, Etc. (See Instructions.)

(a) Distributive share items		(b) Total amount

Income (Loss) and Deductions

1	Ordinary income (loss) from trade or business activity(ies) (page 1, line 21)	1	180 278
2a	Gross income from rental real estate activity(ies). 2a		
b	Minus expenses (attach schedule) 2b		
c	Balance: net income (loss) from rental real estate activity(ies).	2c	
3a	Gross income from other rental activity(ies) 3a		
b	Minus expenses (attach schedule) 3b		
c	Balance: net income (loss) from other rental activity(ies)	3c	
4	Portfolio income (loss):		
a	Interest income	4a	4 000
b	Dividend income	4b	16 000
c	Royalty income	4c	
d	Net short-term capital gain (loss) (Schedule D (Form 1120S)).	4d	
e	Net long-term capital gain (loss) (Schedule D (Form 1120S))	4e	
f	Other portfolio income (loss) (attach schedule)	4f	
5	Net gain (loss) under section 1231 (other than due to casualty or theft) (see instructions) . . .	5	
6	Other income (loss) (attach schedule)	6	
7	Charitable contributions (attach list)	7	24000
8	Section 179 expense deduction (attach schedule)	8	
9	Expenses related to portfolio income (loss) (attach schedule) (see instructions) . . .	9	
10	Other deductions (attach schedule)	10	

Credits

11a	Jobs credit	11a	6000
b	Low-income housing credit: (1) Partnership to which section 42(j)(5) applies	11b(1)	
	(2) Other.	11b(2)	
c	Qualified rehabilitation expenditures related to rental real estate activity(ies) (attach schedule) . .	11c	
d	Credits related to rental real estate activity(ies) other than on lines 11b and 11c (attach schedule)	11d	
e	Credit(s) related to other rental activity(ies) (see instructions) (attach schedule)	11e	
12	Other credits (attach schedule)	12	

Investment Interest

13a	Interest expense on investment debts	13a	
b	(1) Investment income included on lines 4a through 4f, Schedule K	13b(1)	20 000
	(2) Investment expenses included on line 9, Schedule K	13b(2)	

Tax Preference and Adjustment Items

14a	Accelerated depreciation of real property placed in service before 1987	14a	
b	Accelerated depreciation of leased personal property placed in service before 1987	14b	
c	Depreciation adjustment on property placed in service after 1986	14c	
d	Depletion (other than oil and gas)	14d	
e	(1) Gross income from oil, gas, or geothermal properties	14e(1)	
	(2) Gross deductions allocable to oil, gas, or geothermal properties	14e(2)	
f	Other items (attach schedule)	14f	

Foreign Taxes

15a	Type of income		
b	Name of foreign country or U.S. possession		
c	Total gross income from sources outside the U.S. (attach schedule)	15c	
d	Total applicable deductions and losses (attach schedule)	15d	
e	Total foreign taxes (check one): ▶ ☐ Paid ☐ Accrued	15e	
f	Reduction in taxes available for credit (attach schedule)	15f	
g	Other (attach schedule)	15g	

Other Items

16	Total property distributions (including cash) other than dividends reported on line 18, Schedule K	16	65000
17	Other items and amounts not included in lines 1 through 16, Schedule K, that are required to be reported separately to shareholders (attach schedule).		
18	Total dividend distributions paid from accumulated earnings and profits contained in other retained earnings (line 26 of Schedule L)	18	

Schedule L　Balance Sheets

Assets	Beginning of tax year (a)	(b)	End of tax year (c)	(d)
1 Cash		354 010		454 343
2 Trade notes and accounts receivable . . .	495 150		503 340	
a Less allowance for bad debts		495 150		503 340
3 Inventories		506 320		459 622
4 Federal and state government obligations . .				
5 Other current assets (attach schedule) . .				
6 Loans to shareholders				
7 Mortgage and real estate loans				
8 Other investments (attach schedule) . . .		100 000		100 000
9 Buildings and other depreciable assets . .	1 525 700		1 725 700	
a Less accumulated depreciation . . .	350 000	1 175 700	552 500	1 173 200
10 Depletable assets				
a Less accumulated depletion				
11 Land (net of any amortization)				
12 Intangible assets (amortizable only) . . .				
a Less accumulated amortization				
13 Other assets (attach schedule)		15 000		18 000
14 Total assets		2 646 180		2 708 505
Liabilities and Shareholders' Equity				
15 Accounts payable		123 788		125 835
16 Mortgages, notes, bonds payable in less than 1 year		150 000		150 000
17 Other current liabilities (attach schedule) . .		100 000		200 000
18 Loans from shareholders				
19 Mortgages, notes, bonds payable in 1 year or more		900 000		750 000
20 Other liabilities (attach schedule) . . .				
21 Capital stock		500 000		500 000
22 Paid-in or capital surplus				
23 Accumulated adjustments account . . .	–0–		105 278	
24 Other adjustments account			5000	
25 Shareholders' undistributed taxable income previously taxed				
26 Other retained earnings (see instructions) .	872 392		872 392	
Check this box if the corporation has sub-chapter C earnings and profits at the close of the tax year ▶ ☐ (see instructions)				
27 Total retained earnings per books—Combine amounts on lines 23 through 26, columns (a) and (c) (see instructions)		872 392		982 670
28 Less cost of treasury stock.	( )		( )	
29 Total liabilities and shareholders' equity . .		2 646 180		2 708 505

Schedule M　Analysis of Accumulated Adjustments Account, Other Adjustments Account, and Shareholders' Undistributed Taxable Income Previously Taxed (If Schedule L, column (c), amounts for lines 23, 24, or 25 are not the same as corresponding amounts on line 9 of Schedule M, attach a schedule explaining any differences. See instructions.)

	Accumulated adjustments account	Other adjustments account	Shareholders' undistributed taxable income previously taxed
1 Balance at beginning of year	–0–	–0–	
2 Ordinary income from page 1, line 21 . . .	180 278		
3 Other additions	20 000	5000	
4 Total of lines 1, 2, and 3	200 278	5000	
5 Distributions other than dividend distributions	65 000	–0–	
6 Loss from page 1, line 21	–0–		
7 Other reductions	30 000	–0–	
8 Add lines 5, 6, and 7	95 000	–0–	
9 Balance at end of tax year—Subtract line 8 from line 4	105 278	5000	

Form **1128**
(Rev. June 1987)
Department of the Treasury
Internal Revenue Service

Application for Change in Accounting Period

▶ For Paperwork Reduction Act Notice, see page 1 of separate instructions.

OMB No. 1545-0134
Expires 6-30-89

Please Type or Print	Name of applicant (if joint return is filed, also show your spouse's name)
	Address (Number and street)
	City or town, state, and ZIP code
	Name of person to contact (see specific instructions)

Identifying number (See specific instructions)
Service Center where return will be filed
Applicant's telephone number ( )
Telephone number of contact person ( )

Check one:
- ☐ Individual
- ☐ Partnership
- ☐ Estate
- ☐ Trust
- ☐ Corporation
- ☐ S Corporation
- ☐ Personal Service Corporation
- ☐ IC-DISC
- ☐ Cooperative (Sec. 1381(a))
- ☐ Tax-Exempt Organization
- ☐ Controlled Foreign Corp.
- ☐ FSC
- ☐ Foreign Corp.

DO NOT FILE FORM 1128 if you meet any of the exceptions under General Instruction B.

DO NOT CHANGE YOUR TAX YEAR UNTIL THE COMMISSIONER HAS APPROVED YOUR REQUEST.

SECTION A.—All Filers

1a Present tax year ends

1b Permission is requested to change to a tax year ending

1c Permission is requested to adopt tax year ending

2 The period change will require a return for a short period

Beginning , 19   Ending , 19

3 Nature of business or principal source of income

		Yes	No
4	What is your overall method of accounting? ☐ Cash receipts and disbursements ☐ Accrual ☐ Other (explain) ▶		
5	Are you an individual requesting a change from a fiscal year to a calendar year under Rev. Proc. 66-50, 1966-2 C.B. 1260? (If "Yes," file Form 1128 with the applicable Service Center. See General Instruction C.)		
6	In the last 6 years have you changed or requested permission to change your accounting period, your overall method of accounting or the accounting treatment of any item?		
	If "Yes" and there was a ruling letter issued granting permission to make the change, attach a copy. If a copy of the ruling letter is not available, explain and give the date permission was granted. If a ruling letter was not required, e.g., corporations using Rev. Proc. 84-34, 1984-1 C.B. 508 or Regulations section 1.442-1(c), explain the facts and give the date the change was implemented.		
	If a change in accounting period was granted within the last 6 years, explain in detail the unusual circumstances requiring this change.		
7	Do you have pending any accounting method, accounting period, ruling, or technical advice request in the National Office?		
	If "Yes," attach a statement explaining the type of request (method, period, etc.) and the specific issues involved in each request.		
8	Enter the taxable income* or (loss) for the three tax years immediately before the short period and for the short period. If necessary, estimate the amount for the short period.		
	Third preceding year $_____ Second preceding year $_____ First preceding year $_____ Short period $_____		
	Individuals enter adjusted gross income. Partnerships and S corporations enter ordinary income. Section 501(c) organizations enter unrelated business taxable income.		
9	Are you a member of a partnership, a beneficiary of a trust or estate, a shareholder of an S corporation, or a shareholder of an Interest Charge Domestic International Sales Corporation (IC-DISC) or a shareholder in a FSC?		
	If "Yes," attach a statement showing the name, address, identifying number, tax year, percentage of interest in capital and profits, or percentage of interest of each IC-DISC and the amount of income received from each partnership, trust, estate, S corporation, IC-DISC, or FSC for the first preceding year and the short period.		
10	Are you an unincorporated syndicate, group, pool, or joint venture that has elected, under the provisions of regulations section 1.761-2(b), not to be treated as a partnership?		
	If yes, provide a copy of the statement described in regulations section 1.761-2(b). If no formal election was made, describe in detail why you are not considered a partnership for Federal income tax purposes.		

Form **1128** (Rev. 6-87)

Exhibit 13-5

SECTION A.—All Filers (continued)

	Yes	No

11 Are you a U.S. shareholder in a controlled foreign corporation (CFC)? . . . .
If "Yes," attach a statement for each CFC stating the name, address, identifying number, tax year, your percentage of total combined voting power, and the amount of income included in your gross income under section 951 for the three tax years immediately before the short period and for the short period.

12 State the reasons for requesting the change. (Attach a separate sheet if you need more space.) _____

SECTION B.—Estates or Trusts

1 **Attach a statement showing the following information:**
 a Name, identifying number, address, and tax year of each beneficiary and each person who is an owner or treated as an owner of any portion of the trust.
 b Based on the taxable income of the estate or trust entered in Section A, item 8, show the distribution deduction and the taxable amounts distributable to each beneficiary for the 2 tax years immediately before the short period and for the **short period.**
 c If the trust is a member of a common trust fund, show name and tax year of that fund.
2 Are you filing for a simple trust as defined in section 651? . . . .
3 Are you filing for a complex trust as defined in section 661? . . . .
4 Are you requesting a change for a trust under Rev. Proc. 68-41, 1968-2 C.B. 943? (If "Yes," file Form 1128 with the applicable Service Center. See General Instruction C.) . . . .
5 Are you filing for a grantor trust as described in regulations section 1.671-1? . . . .

SECTION C.—Partnerships

1 Date business began. (See specific instructions for Section C.) ▶
2 Is any partner applying for a corresponding change in accounting period? . . . .
3 Attach a statement showing each partner's name, type of partner (e.g., individual, partnership, estate, trust, corporation, S corporation, IC-DISC, etc.), address, identifying number, tax year, the percentage of interest in capital and profits, and how the interest was acquired.
4 Is any partner of this partnership a member of a personal service corporation as defined in section 269A? . . . .
If "Yes," attach a separate sheet providing the name, address, identifying number, tax year, percentage of interest in capital and profits, and the amount of income received from each personal service corporation for the first preceding year and the short period.

SECTION D.—All Corporations

1 Date of incorporation ▶
2 Is the change being requested by a subsidiary who became a member of an affiliated group to join with the parent corporation in the filing of a consolidated return for the short period? . . . .
If "Yes," DO NOT FILE THIS FORM. SEE "EXCEPTIONS" IN GENERAL INSTRUCTION B.
3 Is the corporation a member of an affiliated group filing a consolidated return? . . . .
If "Yes," attach a statement showing (a) the name, address, identifying number used on the consolidated return, the tax year, and the Internal Revenue Service Center where the taxpayer files the return; and (b) the name, address, and identifying number of each member of the affiliated group. Designate the parent corporation and the taxable income (loss) of each member for the 3 years immediately before the short period and for the short period.
4 Did the corporation pay any dividends to its shareholders during the short period? . . . .
If "Yes," furnish the following information:
 (a) Taxable dividends . . . . $ _____
 (b) Nontaxable dividends (explain how determined) . . . . $ _____
5 Are you requesting a change for a corporation under Rev. Proc. 84-34? (If "Yes," file Form 1128 with the applicable Service Center. See General Instruction C.) . . . .
6 If you are a personal service corporation, attach a statement showing each shareholder's name, address, identification number, tax year, percentage of ownership, and type of entity (e.g., individual, partnership, corporation, etc.)

SECTION E.—S Corporations

		Yes	No
1	Date of election ▶		
2	Attach a statement showing each shareholder's name, address, identifying number, tax year, percentage of ownership, and type of entity (e.g., individual, estate, trust, or qualified Subchapter S Trust as defined in section 1361(d)(3)).		
3	Is the corporation a newly electing S corporation required to file Form 2553, Election by a Small Business Corporation, to adopt, retain or change its accounting period?		
	If "Yes," do not file this form. See "Exceptions" in General Instruction B.		

SECTION F.—Tax-Exempt Organizations

		Yes	No
1	Form of organization: ☐ Corporation　☐ Trust　☐ Other (specify) ▶		
2	Date of organization ▶		
3	Code section under which you are recognized as exempt ▶		
4	Are you required to file an annual return on either Form 990, 990-C, 990-PF, 990-T, 1120-H, or 1120-POL?		
5	Date exemption was granted ▶ _ . Attach a copy of the ruling letter granting exemption. If a copy of the letter is not available, attach explanation.		
6	If a private foundation, is the foundation terminating its status under section 507?		
7	Are you requesting a change for a tax-exempt organization under Rev. Proc. 85-58, 1985-2 C.B. 740, or 76-10, 1976-1 C.B. 548? (If "Yes," see General Instruction C.)		

SECTION G.—Interest Charge Domestic International Sales Corporations or Foreign Sales Corporations

		Yes	No
1	Date of election ▶		
2	Attach a statement stating the name, address, identifying number, tax year, and the percentage of ownership and percentage of voting power of each shareholder.		

SECTION H.—Controlled Foreign Corporation

		Yes	No
1	Enter the tax year that was used for tax purposes ▶		
2	Attach a statement for each U.S. shareholder (as defined in section 951(b)) stating the name, address, identifying number, tax year, percentage of total combined voting power, and the amount of income included in the gross income under section 951 for the three tax years immediately before the short period and for the short period.		

Signature—ALL FILERS (See specific instructions)

Under penalties of perjury, I declare that I have examined this application, including accompanying schedules and statements, and to the best of my knowledge and belief it is true, correct, and complete. Declaration of preparer (other than applicant) is based on all information of which preparer has any knowledge.

Applicant's name

Date

Signature

Title

Signing official's name (Please print or type)

Date

Signature of officer of the parent corporation, if applicable

----
Title

Signature of individual or firm preparing the application other than applicant

----
Date

Firm or preparer's name

Form 3115
(Rev. April 1986)

Department of the Treasury
Internal Revenue Service

Application for Change in Accounting Method

Note: *If you are applying for a change in accounting period, use Form 1128.*

▶ **See separate instructions.**

OMB No. 1545-0152
Expires 12-31-88

Name of applicant (if joint return is filed, show names of you and your spouse)	Identifying Number (See Instructions)
Address (Number and street)	Applicant's area code and telephone number
City or town, state, and ZIP code	District Director's office having jurisdiction
Name of person to contact (Please type or print)	Telephone number of contact person

Check one: ☐ Individual ☐ Partnership; No. of Partners _____ ☐ Corporation ☐ S Corporation; No. of Shareholders _____
☐ Cooperative (Section 1381(a)) ☐ Ins. Co. (Sec. 801) ☐ Ins. Co. (Sec. 821) ☐ Ins. Co. (Sec. 831)
☐ Exempt organization; Enter code section _____
☐ Other (specify) ▶ _____

NOTE: *Are you making an election under section 458 or 466?* . . . . ☐ **Yes** ☐ **No**
If "Yes," see Specific Instructions for Section J. Do not fill in Section A. If "No", you must complete Section A.

Section A. Applicable to All Filers Other Than Those Answering "Yes" to "Note" Above

1 a Tax year of change begins (mo., day, yr.) ▶ _____ and ends (mo., day, yr.) ▶ _____

  b Enter the 180th day of your tax year ▶ _____ If this date is earlier than date you signed this Form 3115 on page 6, see General Instruction for "Late Applications" before proceeding any further.

2 Nature of business and principal source of income (including type of business designated on your latest income tax return) ▶ _____
_____

3 The following change in accounting method is requested (check and complete appropriate spaces):

  a ☐ Overall method of accounting : from ▶ _____ to _____

  b ☐ The accounting treatment of (identify item) ▶ _____
   from (present method) ▶ _____ to (new method) ▶ _____
   Attach a separate statement providing all relevant facts, including a detailed description of your present and proposed methods. See also item 14 of Section A on page 2 regarding the "legal basis" for the proposed change.

  c If a change is requested under 3b above, check the present overall method of accounting:
   ☐ Accrual ☐ Cash ☐ Hybrid (if a hybrid method is used, explain the overall hybrid method in detail in a separate statement)

		Yes	No
d	Is your use of your present method specifically not permitted by the Internal Revenue Code, the Income Tax Regulations, or by a decision of the U.S. Supreme Court? See sections 4, 5, and 6 of Rev. Proc. 84-74		
e	Are you currently under examination, or were you or any member of the affiliated group contacted in any manner by a representative of the Internal Revenue Service for the purpose of scheduling an examination of your Federal tax return(s) prior to the filing of this application, or do you have an examination under consideration by an appeals officer or before any Federal court, or is any criminal investigation pending? See sections 4 and 6 of Rev. Proc. 84-74. . . .		
f	Are you a manufacturer to whom Regulations section 1.471-11 applies? If "Yes," complete Section E-2 on page 4		
4	In the last 10 years have you requested permission to change your accounting period, your overall method of accounting, or the accounting treatment of any item? (Members of an affiliated group of corporations filing a consolidated return, see item 7d on page 2.) . . .		
a	If "Yes," was a ruling letter granting permission to make the change issued? If "Yes," attach a copy of the letter. If "No," attach an explanation . . .		
b	Regardless of your response to 4a, do you or an affiliated corporation have pending any accounting method or period ruling or technical advice request in the National Office?		

  c If 4b is "Yes," indicate the type of request (method, period, etc.) and the specific issue involved in each request ▶ _____

5 If engaged in a business or profession: **a** Enter your taxable income or (loss)* from operations for tax purposes for the five (5) tax years preceding the year of change: (See Specific Instructions for Section A.)

1st preceding year ended: mo. yr.	2nd preceding year ended: mo. yr.	3rd preceding year ended: mo. yr.	4th preceding year ended: mo. yr.	5th preceding year ended: mo. yr.
$	$	$	$	$

b	Enter the amount of net operating loss to be carried over to the year of change, if any	$
c	Amount of investment credit carryover to year of change, if any	$
d	Other credit carryover, if any. (Identify) ▶	$

*Individuals enter net profit or (loss) from business; partnerships enter ordinary income or (loss); members of an affiliated group filing a consolidated return, see item 7a on page 2.

For Paperwork Reduction Act Notice, see separate instructions.

Form **3115** (Rev. 4-86)

Exhibit 13-6

	Yes	No
6 Do you have more than one trade or business?		
a If "Yes," do you account for each trade or business separately?		
b If "Yes," see Specific Instructions for Section A.		
7 Is applicant a member of an affiliated group filing a consolidated return for the tax year of change?		
a If 7 is "Yes," state parent corporation's name, identifying number, address, tax year, and Service Center where return is filed and provide the information requested in item 5 on a consolidated basis ▶ _____ _____		
b If 7 is "Yes," do all other members of the affiliated group employ the method of accounting for which the change is requested? If "No," explain ▶ _____		
c If 7 is "Yes," are any of the items involved in the calculation of the net section 481(a) adjustment attributable to transactions between members of the affiliated group?. If "Yes," attach explanation.		
d If 7 is "Yes," provide the information requested in items 4a, 4b, and 4c for each member of the affiliated group. Also, see General Instructions for "Signature."		
8 Is applicant a member of an affiliated group not filing a consolidated return for the tax year of change? If "Yes," are any of the items involved in the calculation of the net section 481(a) adjustment attributable to transactions between members of the affiliated group or other related parties? (If "Yes," attach explanation.)		
9 If change is granted, will the new method be used for financial reporting purposes? If "No," attach an explanation. Such explanation should include a discussion of whether your new method of accounting conforms to generally accepted accounting principles and why it will clearly reflect income.		

10 Enter the net section 481(a) adjustment for the year of change, and the net section 481(a) adjustment that would have been required if the requested change had been made for each of the 3 preceding tax years preceding the year of change. (See Specific Instructions for Section A.)

At the beginning of the year of change ending, enter: mo. yr.	At the beginning of the 1st preceding year ended, enter: mo. yr.	At the beginning of the 2nd preceding year ended, enter: mo. yr.	At the beginning of the 3rd preceding year ended, enter: mo. yr.
$	$	$	$

	Yes	No
11 Has net adjustment under section 481(a) for the year of change been reduced in any way by a pre-1954 amount?		
12 Number of tax years present method has been used for which the change is requested in item 3a or 3b. (See Specific Instructions for Section A.) ▶ _____		
13 Has your present method been designated by Rev. Rul. or Rev. Proc. more than 2 years before filing this Form 3115 as a change in method of accounting to which section 5.12(2) of Rev. Proc. 84-74 applies?		

14 State the reason(s) including the legal basis (statutes, regulation, published rulings, etc.) why you believe approval to make this change should be granted. See section 7 of Rev. Proc. 84-74. _____

Section B. Change in Overall Method of Accounting

1 The following amounts should be stated as of the end of the tax year **preceding** the year of change. If none, state "None." (Although some of the items listed below may not have been required in the computation of your taxable income due to your present method of accounting, it is necessary that they be entered here for this form to be complete. Show amounts attributable to long-term contracts on page 4, Section G-1.) Provide on a schedule the breakdown of the individual items which make up the "Amount" for lines 1a through 1h. See Rev. Proc. 85-36 and Rev. Proc. 85-37 for rules to make this change expeditiously.

	Amount	Show by (✓) how treated on last year's return	
		Included in income or deducted as expense	Excluded from income or not deducted as expense
a Income accrued but not received	$		
b Income received before the date on which it was earned. State nature of income. If discount on installment loans, see Section C below. For advance payments for goods and services, see Specific Instructions for Section B. ▶ _____ _____			
c Expenses accrued but not paid			
d Other (specify) ▶ _____			
e Prepaid expense previously deducted			
f Supplies on hand previously deducted			
g Inventory on hand . . . . $_____ Inventory reported on your return $_____ Difference.			
h Reserve for bad debts (See instructions)			
I **Net adjustment** (combine lines 1a through 1h)	$		

2　Nature of inventory ▶ _____

3　Method used to value inventory ☐ Cost　☐ Cost or market, whichever is lower　☐ Other (attach explanation)

4　Method of identifying costs in inventory　☐ Specific identification　　　☐ FIFO　☐ LIFO

5　Have any receivables been sold in the past three years? . . . . . ☐ Yes ☐ No	1st preceding year ended, enter: mo. yr.	2nd preceding year ended, enter: mo. yr.	3rd preceding year ended, enter: mo. yr.
If "Yes," enter the amounts sold for each of the three years . . .	$	$	$

6　Attach copies of Profit And Loss Statement (Schedule F (Form 1040) in the case of farmers) and Balance Sheet, if applicable, as of the close of the tax year preceding the year of change. State accounting method used when preparing balance sheet. If books of account are not kept, attach copy of the business schedule provided with your Federal income tax return or return of income for that period. If amounts in 1 above do not agree with those shown on profit and loss statement and balance sheet, explain on separate page.

Section C.　Change in Method of Reporting Interest (Discount) on Installment and Other Loans

1　Change with respect to interest on ☐ Installment loans,　☐ Commercial loans, and ☐ Other loans (explain) ▶ _____

_____

2　Do any of these loans cover a period in excess of 60 months? . . . . ☐ **Yes** ☐ **No**

If "Yes," please attach an explanation. (See Rev. Rul. 83-84 and Rev. Proc. 83-40.)

If you wish to change from the sum of the months digits method (rule of 78's) to the economic accrual of interest method for reporting interest (discount) under Rev. Rul. 83-84, see Rev. Procs. 84-27, 84-28, 84-29, and 84-30.

3　Amount of earned or realized interest that has not been reported on your return as of the end of the tax year preceding the year of change . . . . $ _____

4　Amount of unearned or unrealized interest that has been reported on your return as of the end of the tax year preceding the year of change . . . . $ _____

5　Method of rebating in event of prepayment of loans ▶

Section D.　Change in Method of Reporting Bad Debts
(See Specific Instructions for Section D before completing item 2.)

1　If a change to the Reserve Method is requested and applicant has installment sales, are such sales reported on the installment method?　☐ **Yes** ☐ **No**

If "Yes," show whether change relates to: ☐ Installment sales,　☐ Sales other than installment sales, or ☐ Both.

2　If a change to the Reserve Method is requested, provide the following information for the five tax years preceding the year of change:

	1st preceding year	2nd preceding year	3rd preceding year	4th preceding year	5th preceding year
Total sales					
Deductions for specific bad debts charged off [1] . .					
Recoveries of bad debts deducted in prior years					
Year-end balances:					
Trade accounts receivable					
Trade notes receivable [2].					
Installment accounts receivable [3] . .					
Other receivables (explain in detail) . .					

3　If a change to the method of deducting specific bad debt items is requested, enter the amount in reserve for bad debts at end of the year preceding the year of change . . . . $ _____

[1] If your return was examined, enter amount allowed as a result of the examination.
[2] If loan company, enter only capital portion.
[3] Applicable only to receivables attributable to sales reported on installment method. Enter only the capital portion of such receivables.

Section E-1.　Change in Method of Valuing Inventories. *(See Specific Instructions for Section E-1.)*

1　Nature of all inventories ▶ _____

2　Method of identifying costs in inventory . . . . ☐ Specific identification　☐ FIFO　☐ LIFO

If "LIFO," attach copy of Form 970 adopting that method and copies of any Forms 970 filed to extend the use of the method.

3　Method used to value inventory: ☐ Cost ☐ Cost or market, whichever is lower ☐ Retail cost ☐ Retail lower cost or market

　　　　☐ Other (attach explanation)

4　Method of allocating indirect production costs: ☐ Standard cost method ☐ Burden method ☐ Other (attach explanation)

5　Show method and value of all inventories at the end of the tax year preceding the year of change under:

　a　Present method ▶ _____ $ _____

　b　New method ▶ _____ $ _____

　c　If changing to cost method, are you going to elect LIFO for identifying costs? . . . . ☐ Yes ☐ No

Section E-2. Change in Method of Inventory Costing by Manufacturers and Processors.
(See Specific Instructions for Section E-2.)

Please check (✓) the appropriate boxes showing which costs are included in inventoriable costs, under both the present and proposed methods, of all costs listed in Regulations sections 1.471-11(b)(2), (c)(2)(i), and (c)(2)(ii) for Federal income tax purposes, and all costs listed in or subject to Regulations section 1.471-11(c)(2)(iii) for tax and financial statement reporting purposes. If any boxes are not checked, it is assumed that these costs are excluded from inventoriable costs. If certain costs are not incurred , please mark "N/A" in the appropriate box.

Part I Direct Production Costs (Regulations section 1.471-11(b)(2))	Federal income tax purposes	
	Present method	Proposed method
	Included (✓)	Included (✓)
1 Material.		
2 Labor.		

Part II Indirect Production Costs:		
1 Category One Costs (Regulations section 1.471-11(c)(2)(i)	////	////
a Repairs		
b Maintenance		
c Utilities		
d Rent		
e Indirect labor and production supervisory wages		
f Indirect materials and supplies		
g Small tools and equipment		
h Quality control and inspection		
2 Category Two Costs (Regulations section 1.471-11(c)(2)(ii) (See also Rev. Rul. 79-25))	////	////
a Marketing		
b Advertising		
c Selling		
d Other distribution expenses		
e Interest		
f Research and experimental		
g Section 165 losses		
h Percentage depletion in excess of cost depletion		
i Depreciation and amortization for Federal tax purposes in excess of financial report depreciation and amortization		
j Local and foreign income taxes		
k Past service costs of pensions		
l Administrative (general)		
m Other salaries (general)		

3 Category Three Costs (Regulations section 1.471-11(c)(2)(iii)). (See also Rev. Proc. 75-40 and attach the data required by either section 5.02 or 5.03 of Rev. Proc. 75-40.)	Federal Income Tax Purposes		Financial Statements	
	Present method	Proposed method	Present method	Proposed method
	Included (✓)	Included (✓)	Included (✓)	Included (✓)
a Taxes under section 164 (other than local and foreign income taxes).				
b Financial statement depreciation and cost depletion				
c Employee benefits				
d Costs of strikes, rework labor, scrap, and spoilage				
e Factory administrative expenses				
f Officers' salaries (manufacturing)				
g Insurance costs (manufacturing)				

Section F. Change in Method of Treating Vacation Pay

1 Is the plan(s) fully vested as of the end of the tax year preceding the year of the change? ☐ Yes ☐ No
2 If "Yes," enter the amount of accrued vacation pay as of the end of the tax year preceding the year of change $ _____
3 Number of tax years plan(s) has been vested ▶

Section G-1. Change in Method of Reporting Income from Contracts

1 Are your contracts long-term contracts as defined in Regulations section 1.451-3? ☐ Yes ☐ No
2 Is the same method used for reporting all long-term contracts regardless of duration? If "No," explain ☐ Yes ☐ No
3 Do you have extended period long-term contracts as defined in Regulations section 1.451-3(b)(3)? ☐ Yes ☐ No
4 Net adjustment required under section 481(a) $ _____

Section G-2. Change to the Completed Contract Method or Change in Allocation of Costs

Please check (✓) the appropriate boxes showing which costs are allocable to long-term contracts to the extent required by Regulations sections 1.451-3(d)(5) and (6) for Federal income tax purposes. Please mark "N/A" in boxes for costs that do not apply to the taxpayer.

	Tax Purposes			
	Non-Extended Period		Extended Period	
	Present Method	Proposed Method	Present Method	Proposed Method
	Included (✓)	Included (✓)	Included (✓)	Included (✓)
Direct Material				
Direct Labor				
Repairs				
Maintenance				
Utilities				
Rent				
Indirect labor and contract supervisory wages				
Indirect material and supplies				
Tools and equipment				
Quality control and inspection				
Taxes under section 164 (other than local and foreign income taxes)				
Financial statement depreciation and cost depletion				
Percentage depletion in excess of cost depletion				
Depreciation and amortization for Federal tax purposes in excess of financial report depreciation and amortization for equipment and facilities in use				
Administrative costs				
Other administrative, service, or support costs				
Officers' salaries attributable to long-term contract activities				
Insurance				
Employee benefits				
Research and experimental expenses attributable to extended period long-term contracts	▨	▨		
Other research and experimental expenses				
Rework labor, scrap, and spoilage				
Bidding expenses incurred in the solicitation of extended period long-term contracts	▨	▨		
Other bidding expenses				
Marketing, selling, and advertising				
Interest				
Other general and administrative costs				
Section 165 losses				
Income taxes				
Cost of strikes				

Section H. Change in Overall Method of Reporting Income of Farmers to Cash Receipts and Disbursements Method

Note: *Also complete Section B.*

1 Is the taxpayer a corporation? . . . . ☐ **Yes** ☐ **No**

2 Is the taxpayer a partnership with a corporation as a partner? . . . . ☐ **Yes** ☐ **No**

3 If either 1 or 2 is "Yes," has the taxpayer had gross receipts of $1,000,000 or less in each of its tax years beginning after 1975? . . . . ☐ **Yes** ☐ **No**
   If "No," attach a schedule showing which years the taxpayer's receipts were more than $1,000,000.

4 Provide the following information for the five tax years before the year of change:

	1st preceding yr.	2nd preceding yr.	3rd preceding yr.	4th preceding yr.	5th preceding yr.
a Gross receipts from farming					
b Inventory: Crops, etc.					
Livestock held for sale:					
Purchased					
Raised					
Livestock held for draft breeding, sport, or dairy purposes:					
Purchased					
Raised					
Total inventory					

5   Method used to value inventory *(check appropriate block):*

☐ Cost ☐ Cost or market, whichever is lower ☐ Farm price ☐ Unit livestock price ☐ Other (explain on separate page)

Section I. Change in Method of Accounting for Depreciation

Applicants desiring to change their method of accounting for depreciation must complete this section. This information must be supplied for each account for which a change is requested. **Note:** *Certain changes in methods of accounting for depreciation may be filed with the Service Center where your return will be filed. See Rev. Proc. 74-11 for the methods covered.*

1   Date of acquisition ▶ . . . .

2   **a** Are you the original owner or the first user of the property? . . . . ☐ **Yes** ☐ **No**

   b If residential property, did you live in the home before renting it? . . . . ☐ **Yes** ☐ **No**

3   Is depreciation claimed under Regulations section 1.167(a)-11 (CLADR)? . . . . ☐ **Yes** ☐ **No**

   If ''Yes,'' the only changes permitted are under Regulations section 1.167(a)-11(c)(1)(iii). Identify these changes on the tax return for the year of change.

4   Is the property public utility property? . . . . ☐ **Yes** ☐ **No**

5   Location of the property (city and state) ▶ . . . .

6   Type or character of the property ▶ . . . .

7   Cost or other basis of the property and adjustments thereto (exclude land) . . . . | $ _____

8   Depreciation claimed in prior tax years (depreciation reserve) . . . . | $ _____

9   Estimated salvage value . . . . | $ _____

10   Estimated remaining useful life of the property ▶ . . . .

11   If the declining balance method is requested, show percentage of straight-line rate ▶ . . . .

12   Other information, if any ▶ . . . .
. . . .

Section J. Change in Method of Accounting Not Listed Above *(See Specific Instructions for Section J.)*

. . . .
. . . .
. . . .
. . . .
. . . .

Signature—All Filers *(See instructions.)*

Under penalties of perjury, I declare that I have examined this application, including accompanying schedules and statements, and to the best of my knowledge and belief, it is true, correct and complete. Declaration of preparer (other than applicant) is based on all information of which preparer has any knowledge.

Applicant's name	Signature and title	Date
Signing official's name (Please print or type)	Signature and title of officer of the parent corporation, if applicable	Date
Signature of individual or firm preparing the application		Date

☆U.S. GOVERNMENT PRINTING OFFICE: 1986-491-473:20137

Form 5884

Form 5884

Department of the Treasury
Internal Revenue Service

Jobs Credit

▶ **Attach to your tax return.**

OMB No. 1545-0219

1988

Attachment
Sequence No. **77**

Name(s) as shown on return

Identifying number

Part I — Jobs Credit

1 Enter the number of employees and total qualified wages paid or incurred during the tax year (up to $6,000 for each employee) for services of employees who are certified as members of a targeted group. **See instructions for special rules on qualified summer youth employees.**

	Number of employees		Total qualified wages	
First year employees	**a**		**b**	
Qualified summer youth employees	**c**		**d**	

2 Enter 40% of line 1b **2**

3 Enter 85% of line 1d (fiscal year filers see instructions if line 1d contains wages of employees that began work after 12-31-88) **3**

4 Current year jobs credit—Add lines 2 and 3. Enter here and include on Schedule C (Form 1040), line 28b; Form 1120, line 13(b), page 1; or the corresponding line on other returns. (Members of a group of trades or businesses under common control, see Specific Instructions.) **4**

5 Flow-through jobs credits from other entities . . .

If you are a—	Then enter total of current year jobs credit(s) from—
a Shareholder . .	Schedule K-1 (Form 1120S), lines 11 or 12 .
b Partner . . .	Schedule K-1 (Form 1065), lines 12d, 12e, or 13
c Beneficiary . .	Schedule K-1 (Form 1041), line 11 . . .
d Patron	(see instructions for line 5d)

5

6 Total jobs credit for current year—Add lines 4 and 5 (S corporations, partnerships, estates, trusts, and cooperatives, see instructions for line 6.) **6**

Note: *If you have a 1988 investment credit (Form 3468), credit for alcohol used as fuel (Form 6478), research credit (Form 6765), or low-income housing credit (Form 8586) in addition to your 1988 jobs credit, or if you have a carryback or carryforward of any of these credits, stop here and go to* **Form 3800**, *General Business Credit, to claim your 1988 jobs credit. If you have only a 1988 jobs credit, you may continue with lines 7 through 14 to claim your credit.*

Part II — Tax Liability Limitation

7 **a** Individuals—From Form 1040, enter amount from line 40 . . . .
　b Corporations—From Form 1120, Schedule J, enter tax from line 3 (or Form 1120-A, Part I, line 1)
　c Other filers—Enter income tax before credits from return **7**

8 **a** Individuals—From Form 1040, enter credits from lines 41, 42, and 43, plus any orphan drug credit, mortgage interest credit, and nonconventional source fuel credit included on line 46 . .
　b Corporations—From Form 1120, Schedule J, enter credits from lines 4(a) through 4(d) (Form 1120-A filers, enter zero) . . . .
　c Other filers—See instructions for line 8c **8**

9 Income tax liability as adjusted (subtract line 8 from line 7) **9**

10 Tentative minimum tax—
　a Individuals—From Form 6251, enter amount from line 17 . . . .
　b Corporations—From Form 4626, enter amount from line 13 . . . .
　c Estates and trusts—From Form 8656, enter amount from Part III, line 10 . . . . **10**

11 Net income tax—
　a Individuals—Enter the sum of line 9, above, and line 19 of Form 6251 . . . . .
　b Corporations—Enter the sum of line 9, above, and line 16 of Form 4626 . . . . .
　c Other filers—See instructions for line 11c **11**

12 If line 9 is more than $25,000—Enter 25% of the excess (See instructions) **12**

13 Enter—Line 11 less whichever is greater, line 10 or line 12. (If the result is less than zero, enter zero.) **13**

14 Total allowed jobs credit—Enter the smaller of line 6 or line 13. This is your **General Business Credit** for 1988. Enter here and on Form 1040, line 44; Form 1120, Schedule J, line 4(e); Form 1120-A, Part I, line 2a; or the proper line of other returns **14**

General Instructions

(Section references are to the Internal Revenue Code.)

Paperwork Reduction Act Notice.—We ask for this information to carry out the Internal Revenue laws of the United States. We need it to ensure that taxpayers are complying with these laws and to allow us to figure and collect the right amount of tax. You are required to give us this information.

The time needed to complete and file this form will vary depending on individual circumstances. The estimated average time is:

Recordkeeping	4 hrs., 4 min.
Learning about the law or the form	2 hrs., 20 min.
Preparing the form	7 hrs., 10 min.
Copying, assembling, and sending the form to IRS	1 hr., 20 min.

If you have comments concerning the accuracy of these time estimates or suggestions for making this form more simple, we would be happy to hear from you. You can write to either IRS or the Office of Management and Budget at the addresses listed in the instructions of the tax return with which this form is filed.

Changes You Should Note

The Technical and Miscellaneous Revenue Act of 1988 made the following changes in the law:

Form **5884** (1988)

Exhibit 13-7

- The targeted jobs credit is extended to qualified wages paid or accrued to employees who begin work for the employer before January 1, 1990.
- For economically disadvantaged youth employees who begin work for the employer after December 31, 1988, the youth must be at least age 18 but less than age 23 on the date they are hired.
- For summer youth employees who begin work for the employer after December 31, 1988, the credit is reduced from 85 percent to 40 percent of qualified wages.

General Business Credit.—The general business credit consists of the investment credit, jobs credit, credit for alcohol used as fuel, research credit, and low-income housing credit. If you have more than one of these credits or a carryback or carryforward of any of these credits, you must attach the appropriate credit forms and summarize them on **Form 3800**, General Business Credit. If you have only a 1988 jobs credit, you do not have to file Form 3800 this year.

Purpose of Form.— Use Form 5884 if you had jobs credit employees and take an income tax credit for wages you paid or accrued for them during the tax year.

Mutual savings institutions, regulated investment companies, and real estate investment trusts can take a limited credit. See section 52(e) and the related regulations.

You can take or revoke the jobs credit any time within 3 years from the due date of your return. Take the credit either on your original return or on an amended return.

For more information, see **Publication 572**, General Business Credit.

How To Figure the Credit.—In general, figure your jobs credit based on the employee's wages subject to the Federal Unemployment Tax Act (FUTA). Jobs credit wages, however, are limited to $6,000 for each employee ($3,000 for each qualified summer youth employee). Special rules apply in the following cases:

(1) You can take a jobs credit for *agricultural employees* who meet the other tests if their services qualify under FUTA as agricultural labor during more than half of any pay period. Base your credit for each employee on the first $6,000 in wages subject to social security (FICA) tax you paid or accrued for that person during the year.

(2) You can take a credit for *railroad employees* who meet the other tests if their wages qualify under the Railroad Unemployment Insurance Act (RUIA). Base your credit for each employee on the first $500 a month you paid or accrued for that person during the year in wages subject to RUIA tax.

(3) Wages for *youths in a cooperative education program* are not subject to FUTA, but include their wages in the amount you use to figure your jobs credit. Base your credit for each youth on the first $6,000 in wages you paid or accrued for that person during the year.

Your credit is based on a percentage of the wages for each employee in the following targeted groups:

- Referrals by a vocational rehabilitation program.
- Economically disadvantaged Vietnam-era veterans.
- Economically disadvantaged youths.
- Supplemental Security Income (SSI) recipients.
- General assistance recipients.
- Youths in a cooperative education program, who belong to an economically disadvantaged family.
- Economically disadvantaged ex-convicts.
- Eligible work incentive employees.
- Qualified summer youth employees, age 16 or 17, who work for you between May 1 and September 15.

In addition, to claim a jobs credit on an employee's wages:

(1) more than half the wages received from you must be for working in your trade or business;

(2) the employee must be certified, as explained below, as belonging to a targeted group;

(3) you may not claim a credit on wages that were repaid by a federally funded on-the-job training program, or for which you received work supplementation payments under the Social Security Act;

(4) the employee cannot be your relative or dependent (see section 51(i));

(5) the employee cannot be your rehired employee if he or she was not a targeted group member when employed earlier;

(6) the employee must have worked for you for at least 90 days (14 days for a summer youth employee) or completed at least 120 hours of services (20 hours for a summer youth employee); and

(7) the wages cannot be for services of replacement workers during a strike or walkout.

Certification is done by a local agency, generally an office of the State Employment Security Agency (Jobs Service). The agency gives the employer a form certifying that the employee is in a targeted group. The certification must be completed or the employer must request, in writing, a certification from the certifying agency by the date the employee begins work (or within 5 days if the employer has received a written preliminary determination that the employee is in a targeted group).

Certification of a Youth in a Cooperative Education Program.—The certification is completed by the school administering the cooperative program. The school gives the employer a completed **Form 6199,** Certification of Youth Participating in a Qualified Cooperative Education Program.

Specific Instructions

Part I

On lines 1 through 4 figure your credit for wages you paid or accrued. If you have credits only from sources that shared a jobs credit (S corporations, partnerships, estates, trusts, or cooperatives), skip lines 1 through 4.

Whether or not you complete lines 1 through 4, enter on line 5 any credits you received from sources that share the credit. Complete the rest of the form to figure the credit to enter on your income tax return.

Controlled groups: The group member proportionately contributing the most first-year wages figures the group credit in Part I and skips Part II. See sections 52(a) and 1563.

On separate Forms 5884, that member and every other member of the group skips lines 1 through 3 and enters its share of the group credit on line 4. Each member then completes lines 5 through 14 on its separate form. Each group member attaches to its Form 5884 a schedule showing how the group credit was divided among all the members. The members share the credit in the same proportion that they contributed qualifying wages.

Line 1a.—Enter the number of employees for whom you have first-year wages.

Line 1b.—Enter the first-year wages. They are limited to $6,000 of each employee's first-year wages. If you paid first-year wages to any of these employees last year, subtract those wages from the $6,000 limit.

For example, if a jobs credit employee began working in your business on September 1, 1987, and you are a calendar year taxpayer, you would have figured your 1987 jobs credit based on the first-year wages you paid between September 1 and December 31, 1987. You would have figured your 1988 credit on the rest of the first-year wages you paid between January 1 and August 31, 1988.

Line 1d.—For each qualified summer youth employee, wages are limited to those paid for any 90-day period between May 1 and September 15,

up to $3,000. You cannot claim a credit for an employee who was your employee in any prior period. Also, the summer youth employee must have worked for you at least 14 days, or completed at least 20 hours of services.

Line 3.—Taxpayers with qualified summer youth employees.—Include 85% of the first $3,000 of wages paid to each qualified employee who began working for you before January 1, 1989. For qualified employees who begin working for you after December 31, 1988, the rate is reduced to 40%.

Line 4.—In general, you must subtract your current year jobs credit on line 4 from the deduction on your return for salaries and wages you paid or owe for 1988. This is true even if you cannot take the full credit this year and must carry part of it back or forward.

An exception is a credit based on salaries and wages you capitalize for depreciation. If you have such a credit, reduce the amount on which you figure depreciation by the part of the current year jobs credit on line 4 that applies to the jobs credit wages you capitalize.

Another exception involves the full absorption method of inventory costing. See the regulations under section 280C to reduce your basis in inventory for the jobs credit.

If either exception applies to you, attach a statement to your return to explain why the amount on line 4 differs from the amount you subtract from your salary and wage deduction. See Publication 572 for details.

Line 5d.—If you belong to a cooperative that has an excess jobs credit, the cooperative should have given you a statement showing your share of the excess. Include on line 5 your total excess jobs credit from all cooperatives to which you belong.

Line 6.—If you have credits from passive activities, see **Form 8582-CR,** Passive Activity Credit Limitations, or **Form 8810,** Corporate Passive Activity Loss and Credit Limitations, before completing the remainder of this form.

Estates and trusts: The jobs credit on line 6 is shared between the estate or trust itself and the beneficiaries in proportion to the income allocable to each. On the dotted line to the left of the amount on line 6, the estate or trust should enter its own part of the total jobs credit. Label it "1041 PORTION" and use *this amount* in Part II to figure the jobs credit to take on Form 1041.

S corporations and partnerships: Prorate the jobs credit on line 6 among the shareholders or partners. Attach Form 5884 to the return and on Schedule K-1 show the credit for each shareholder or partner.

Cooperatives: Most tax-exempt organizations cannot take the jobs credit; but a cooperative described in section 1381(a) takes the jobs credit to the extent it has tax liability. Any excess is shared among its patrons.

Carrybacks and carryforwards: If you cannot use part of the credit because of the tax liability limitations, you may carry it back 3 years, then forward 15 years. Use Form 3800.

Part II

Line 8c. Other filers.—Before you can claim the jobs credit (which will be your general business credit for 1988) against your income tax liability, you must reduce this tax liability by the credits listed below:

- Personal credits (child and dependent care credit, credit for the elderly or disabled, and credit for interest on certain home mortgages)
- Foreign tax credit
- Possessions corporation tax credit
- Orphan drug credit
- Nonconventional source fuel credit

Line 11c. Other filers.—Enter the sum of line 9 and your alternative minimum tax from whichever alternative minimum tax form you file.

Line 12. Limitation.—See section 38(c)(3) for special rules for married couples filing separate returns, for controlled corporate groups, and for estates and trusts.

PART THREE

GETTING THE MOST FROM YOUR BUSINESS

Chapter 14

OPERATING YOUR BUSINESS

To get the most from your business, you want your business to operate at peak efficiency. There are a variety of tools that you can use to increase revenues and lower costs. The object of this chapter is to explain some of the better known tools and how they can be used in your business. The following topics will be discussed in this chapter:

* How to forecast sales
* How to forecast asset needs
* Understanding ratio analysis and why it is important
* Selling on credit
* Managing your accounts receivable
* Why you must closely monitor your inventory
* Determining the amount of inventory you should carry
* How to value your inventory
* How to estimate ending inventory
* Using trade credit to your advantage
* The importance of the breakeven point
* How to evaluate your competition
* How to select and train personnel

HOW TO FORECAST SALES

Sales forecasts are critical. You need to forecast sales in order to determine the amount of assets necessary in the immediate future, near future, and far future. For instance, suppose you manufacture product A and your sales forecast overestimated the amount of product you were going to sell. Based on the expected demand, you stocked up on raw materials and purchased extra equipment. Of course, these assets have to be financed. Net result: much of your plant and equipment stands idle; your inventory sits on the shelf; and your overhead costs in relation to your sales are intolerable. The flipside of the forecast could be just as bad. Suppose you underestimated the strength of consumer demand. Accordingly, you would not be able to keep up with your customers' needs because you do not have sufficient amounts of equipment and new materials. Orders would begin to get backlogged, delivery time would increase, repair and installations would become more difficult to schedule, and customers would eventually turn elsewhere because they have lost patience. Thus, not only have you lost out on an excellent opportunity to increase revenues but you have soured the public on your product.

There are several approaches you can take to forecast sales. The easiest approach is to solicit a marketing research firm to perform a cursory study of the market. Prices usually range from $800 to $5,000. Many of these firms usually provide such services as marketing research, consultation, feasibility studies, and market planning. The other two approaches involve conducting the sales forecast yourself.

Forecasting First-Time Sales

The following approach is a method that is commonly used to forecast first-time sales. It is a two step procedure.

Step One—Determine Market Potential

Generally, most markets are not homogeneous but are composed of groups of individuals and organizations that have diverse needs. These groups are called market segments. To maximize your sales, you must define each segment and be able to articulate the needs of that segment. Once that is accomplished, you should then tailor your approach to that segment so that the segment perceives your product or service as meeting its needs.

For instance, if you were in the business of providing facilities and catering services for various social functions, your market could be segmented as follows:

* *Corporations*—Many of the larger organizations often have seminars, meetings, banquets, and parties.
* *Wedding Receptions*—This segment of the market can be further segmented based upon ethnic background, religious beliefs, culture, income etc.
* *Charitable and Political Fundraisers*
* *Quinceneras*—In the Hispanic community a celebration occurs in honor of a girl's fifteenth birthday which begins her traditional entrance into society.
* *Bar and Bat Mitvahs*—In the Jewish community there is a celebration when a boy or girl reaches the age of thirteen.

If you decide to segment the social functions market in the manner described above then it must be followed by defining the needs of each segment. This will take some research but it is well worth the effort because once accomplished you will be able to tailor your approach to satisfy the needs of each segment.

Once you have defined the segments of the market, you will need to estimate the potential number of sales for each segment. Take, for example, the social functions market. You would have to survey corporations in the area and inquire as to whether they have meetings, banquets, seminars, etc. A good source for locating many of these corporations is the local chamber of commerce. Often the chamber of commerce will publish a directory that lists its corporate members and includes both phone numbers and names of some of the corporate officers. Once you complete your survey, you will have a good estimate of the market potential for that particular segment of the market. Then you would move to the next segment: wedding receptions. Find out how many marriage licenses are issued and use that as your base. Quinceneras can be estimated by using census information for your area. The information is free and you can find it in a public library.

We will use Quinceneras as an example. The way to estimate the potential market for Quinceneras would be to examine the census tracts that are in your standard metropolitan statistical area (SMSA).

The 1980 census gathered information according to SMSA. The concept of SMSA is as follows: The United States is composed of numerous population nuclei which have adjacent communities with a high degree of social and economic integration within the population center. Most SMSAs have at least one population center although some may have more. Within the SMSA, there are numerous subdivisions which are called tracts or census tracts. Your objective, therefore, would be to examine the tracts in your SMSA to determine the number of individuals who identify themselves as Hispanics.

Using San Diego SMSA for race and Spanish origin, which is shown in Exhibit 14-1, we can see that as of 1980, 275,177 individuals identified themselves as being of Spanish origin. Of that total, 227,177 identified themselves as being of Mexican ancestry, which is approximately 82% of all persons of Spanish origin. Your next step would be to examine the general characteristics of Spanish origin persons, which are contained in the census tracts. Exhibit 14-2 is an example. For instance, in San Diego County, there were 13,521 females of Spanish origin who were listed in the age range of 10 to 14 years of age, and 14,823 females of Spanish origin who fell within the age range of 15 to 19 years of age. By now you should have a good idea of your market potential for Quinceneras. If you intend to limit your market geographically then you would need to examine each tract to determine which areas within the SMSA contain the largest portion of females of Spanish origin near the age of fifteen.

For example, Exhibit 14-3 shows various tracts within San Diego County and the population of females that fall within this category. Once you have analyzed each segment of the social functions market, using your various sources, you will then add all the segments together. The total is your market potential.

By now you have probably concluded that the census is an excellent source of information. You are right. Over the years, the census has become more probing and sophisticated in its quest for information. It asks questions such as language spoken at home, the amount of the mortgage, how the home is heated, as well as income, sex, and race.

Step Two — Determine Market Penetration

Once you have estimated the potential sales of your market, the next step is to determine the percentage of the market you intend to capture.

You should begin by first analyzing the competition for each segment you intend to enter. Your analysis should include the following factors:

* Features of the product or service
* Pricing
* Credit policies
* Advertising (amount and type of media used)
* Personal selling
* Services following the sale

Once you have analyzed the competition for each segment, your next step is to make an estimate of each segment. Your estimate should be realistic and conservative. Some businesses, in order to supplement their estimates, conduct a market test, which consists of making the product/service available to buyers on a limited basis and then measuring the buyers' responses to price, advertising, or the product or service itself. The advantage of market testing is that it provides you with information concerning actual purchases rather than intended purchases.

Forecasting Sales of an Existing Business

If you have purchased an existing business there is another method you can use to forecast sales: time series analysis. This technique uses historical sales data in an attempt to determine whether there is a pattern in the sales of the business over a period of time. If a pattern can be determined then it can be used to forecast sales. Many companies that have stable sales patterns have used this technique, and it has proven to be highly accurate. This forecasting method, however, assumes that past sales patterns can be used to predict the future. Because of this underlying assumption you must not close your eyes to events around you.

There are three types of time series analysis. Each method attempts to isolate a pattern of sales associated with a unit of time. The table below shows how these three methods are distinguished:

Method	Data Analyzed	Units of Time Analyzed
Seasonal	Daily sales	Week/month increment
Cyclical	Monthly sales	3/4/5 year increment
Trend	Annual sales	5/8/10+ year increment

For many businesses, sales trends are linear, which means they approximate a straight line and can be computed easily. The formula for describing a straight line relationship is :

$$Yc = a + bX$$

where: Yc = the projected value of the Y variable
a = the Y intercept, that is, it is the estimated value of Y when $X = 0$
b = the slope of the line
X = the value of X that is selected and is always expressed as a unit of time

in which:

$$a = \frac{\text{Sum of } Y}{n}$$

$$b = \frac{\text{Sum of } XY}{\text{Sum of } X^2}$$

Example:

Suppose the business you purchased had the following sales history. How much revenue will your business generate for 1990?

Year	Sales in Millions of Dollars
1984	$ 7
1985	10
1986	9
1987	11
1988	13

This question can be answered using a two-step procedure.

First: Construct a least squares table such as the one below:

Year	Sales	X	XY	X^2
1985	7	-2	-14	4
1986	10	-1	-10	1
1987	9	0	0	0
1988	11	1	11	1
1989	13	2	26	4
	50		13	10

Second: Plug the numbers you have just calculated from the least squares table into the formula:

$$a = \frac{50}{5} = 10$$

$$b = \frac{13}{10} = 1.3$$

$$Yc = a + bX$$
$$Yc = 10 + 1.3(3)$$
$$Yc = 13.9$$

Thus, for 1990 the sales forecast would be $13.9 million.

HOW TO FORECAST ASSET NEEDS

To run a profitable business, you must have the appropriate asset base. Too few assets will doom the business to failure and too many assets are simply wasted investment potential. This important exercise requires you to make an accurate sales forecast. In the previous section, we discussed this requirement and provided you with two forecasting methods. Armed with a sales forecast and a number of additional variables, we can approximate the asset side of the balance sheet. For an on-going business, many of these variables will be available as a matter of historical record; however, some of these variables will need to be altered as you incorporate your management methods and ideas. For the start-up business, this historical information will not be available. We suggest, therefore, the use of industry standard data as found in trade journals, industry statistics, and in the RMA. In our discussion, we will rely heavily on the RMA financial statistics which are classified according to the SIC code.

In any business a number of interrelated factors need to be considered. A partial list of these factors includes the following.

Capital Intensity. This refers to the amount of capital required, for example, machinery, automotive and plant equipment . An example of a capital-intensive business is a foundry industry or a machine shop. An example of a noncapital intensive business would be a retail store. The amount of capital will determine the type and quantity of investment required.

Trade Credit Requirements. Is it necessary to extend credit to your customers and create accounts receivable? Creation of receivables requires significant sums of cash, especially if traditional trade terms are long, for example, sixty or ninety days net.

Inventory Requirements. Some industries can exist on a day's worth of inventory while others require vast amounts of inventory to meet demand. Inventory also can eat up large amounts of cash.

Cash Needs. How much operating cash is necessary to support on-going operations including rent, insurance, payroll, etc.? In a start-up, you must be very sensitive to this requirement. It is the quickest way to get into hot water.

Miscellaneous Needs. This catch-all category includes supplies, goodwill purchased (if any), and deposits which generally need to be prepaid.

With our sales forecast and the RMA in hand, we will take a look at an example of the method employed in projecting asset needs for a wine, liquor and beer wholesaler, SIC code 5181.

In our example we note a few of the quirks of this business. Notably, most wholesalers are not capital intensive, in this case about 25 percent of total assets are fixed assets. As expected, inventory makes up a rather large percentage of the total assets at 28 percent. We would also expect accounts receivable to be low at 20 days worth of sales. This says simply that standard terms for this industry are about fifteen days, which also makes sense since beer and wine are rather liquid in nature (no pun intended) and are hard to repossess. The value of receivables as a percentage of total assets happens to be 20 percent. A recap of total assets from RMA would look like this:

Cash	12%
Accounts Receivable	20%
Inventory	28%
Fixed Assets	25%
Other	15%
	100%

Note that for simplicity sake, we have rounded these percentages to whole digits and have lumped small categories of assets into "other." As you get closer to the start-up or purchase of the business, these percentages will be altered by you to suit your needs and, therefore, are presented only as a guide to application of our method of determining asset needs.

Now, how do you go from percentages to dollars required? The next step requires looking at projected sales for the firm and the cost of those sales. The RMA establishes numerous useful relationships between balance sheet accounts (assets) and income statement accounts (sales and cost of sales). By using these relationships, we hope to move from percentages to dollars. The RMA relationships of interest are:

Account Receivable Turnover. This is the ratio of accounts receivable to sales for a given period. This ratio is measured in days and is a measure of the effectiveness of the management of accounts receivable. We will assume you will do at least as well as the industry average.

Inventory Turnover. This is the ratio of inventory to cost of sales for a given period. This ratio is, also, measured in days and is a measure of the effectiveness of the management of inventory. Again, we will assume that you will do at least as well as the industry average.

We have nearly all of the information required to generate an asset requirements list. There are just two more items needed: We must extract from RMA cost of goods sold as a percentage of sales and from our own business plan the sales forecast. For our example, we will forecast annual sales of $900,000 and from RMA we see that cost of sales should be 75 percent or $675,000 (.75 x 900,000). After one last ratio from RMA, we will be on our way: that ratio is the accounts receivable turnover ratio which in this case is 18 days.

Solution:

Since:

$$\text{Accounts receivable turnover} = \frac{(\text{accounts receivable x 360 days})}{\text{sales}}$$

and:

$$\text{Accounts receivable turnover (A/R turn)} = 18 \text{ days}$$

then it follows:

$$\text{Accounts receivable} = \frac{(\text{A/R turn x sales})}{360 \text{ days}}$$

or

$$\text{Accounts Receivable} = \frac{(18 \text{ days x } \$900,000)}{60 \text{ days}}$$

or

$$\text{Accounts receivable} = \$45,000$$

Now let's see what inventory level will be required to support this level of sales. From RMA, we see that inventory turnover is 33 days.

Solution:

Since:

$$\text{Inventory turnover} = \frac{(\text{inventory x 360 days})}{\text{cost of sales}}$$

and:

$$\text{Inventory turnover} = 33 \text{ days}$$

Then it follows:

$$\text{Inventory} = \frac{\text{(inventory turn x cost of sales)}}{360 \text{ days}}$$

or

$$\text{Inventory} = \frac{\text{(33 days x \$675,000)}}{360 \text{ days}}$$

or

$$\text{Inventory} = \$61,880$$

With the knowledge that accounts receivable have a value of $45,000 and represent 20 percent of the asset base, we can solve for the total asset base required to support your business in our example. The total asset base is, therefore, $225,000 or $45,000 divided by 20 percent. If these figures are correct, we should be able to check our estimate by performing the same mathematical operation on the inventory figure. Upon division of the inventory figure of $61,880 by 28 percent, we find that total assets should be $221,000. Not bad! The $4,000 difference is due to the rounding of the RMA figures mentioned earlier. Suffice it to say that since this is an estimate, we need not be accurate to the penny.

Based on a total asset base of $225,000 and rounded RMA percentages, the asset side of our balance sheet would look like this:

Cash	12%	$ 27,000
Accounts receivable	20%	45,000
Inventory	28%	63,000
Fixed assets	25%	6,250
Other	15%	33,750
Total	100%	$225,000

Note that these estimates are based on an on-going business operating at a $900,000 annual sales rate, however, they are a good first approximation of asset needs. To cross check this result, we strongly suggest you create a cash flow spread sheet for the first twelve months on a month-by-month basis factoring in the growth of sales estimated in your business plan. This will give you a clear picture as to when and how much cash will be required. Chapter 9 explained how you can construct a cash flow spread sheet.

As before, below are a few rules of thumb that can be used to estimate your asset needs.

Cash. For retail firms, cash should equal out-of-pocket expenses for one inventory turnover period. This will cover such items as rent, payroll, and overhead expenses. Service firms should carry sufficient cash to cover out-of-pocket expenses for three months.

Accounts Receivable. Each industry has its own traditional credit terms. You will need assets to cover 1.5 to 2 times the maximum credit period. Simply stated, if you sell on 30-day terms, expect to collect receivables on average between 45 to 60 days from invoice date.

Fixed Assets. Assess the cash flows and investments required in analysis of your business. If the cash required to purchase fixed assets strains cash availability, consider leasing or renting these fixed assets. It is not necessary to buy a building, computer, furniture, or other types of fixed assets to go into business.

As you can see, the required asset base is a function of the forecast and industry variables. Weigh all factors and determine the asset mix that will support your operation. Remember, RMA is simply an estimating tool. It is a good tool but must be weighed against cash flow projections before meaningful information will be yielded. Once the asset requirements are known, you can start to determine from which sources these assets will be funded: trade credit, accruals, short- or long-term bank debt or contributed capital, all of which were discussed in Chapter 12.

UNDERSTANDING RATIO ANALYSIS AND WHY IT IS IMPORTANT

Financial ratio analysis was designed to provide a formalized system of relating elements of the balance sheet to the income statement. The benefit of this formalized analysis is that it allows you, your creditors, and your investors to analyze your performance. It also allows you to analyze a business or franchise to determine whether it is a wise investment. It is our intention to provide you with the following: (1) why ratio analysis is important; (2) a list of the important and commonly used ratios; and (3) how to calculate various ratios and the significance of their meaning.

Why is ratio analysis important? There are numerous reasons, but the five we consider most important are discussed below:

Trend Analysis. Since the mathematical effect of creating a ratio is to eliminate the importance of the absolute numbers involved, a manager can analyze his or her company's performance as it grows or shrinks in size. This makes ratio analysis a valuable tool since it makes it easier to remove the bias created by large numbers over small ones. That is, say you earned $100,000 on $1 million of sales in year 1 and $150,000 on $2 million of sales in year 2. An analysis of the absolute numbers leads you to believe that year 2 was superior. However, under closer analysis (ratio analysis) you find that year 1 was more efficient having earned a 10 percent return on sales (100,000 / 1,000,000) versus the 7.5 percent return on sales (150,000 / 2,000,000) earned in year 2. Further, you can use ratio analysis to identify emerging trends of either a positive or negative nature. Once identified, these trends can be corrected or exploited to your company's benefit.

Cross Comparison with Industry Standard. By performing ratio analysis, managers can compare their performance with their peers in the industry. Sources of industry average ratios includes Dun & Bradstreet, RMA, trade associations and the FTC's quarterly financial report for manufacturing corporations. For an example of RMA's industry average ratios see Exhibit 14-4. Comparisons can reveal to us methods of operation or problems in given areas of asset management. These comparisons are also good "report cards" of your ability to perform versus the industry leaders.

Acquisition Evaluation. Ratio analysis allows us to chart a target company's performance historically as well as determine the corporate philosophy regarding important aspects of business such as asset turnover management or return on equity performance.

Your Banker Knows It. If your banker knows it, you had better know it. He or she will perform this type of analysis on your company using software now available with certain popular electronic spread sheets. You must be prepared to discuss and mitigate (if necessary) any trends the business is experiencing.

Projections. Ratio analysis allows businesspeople to project asset needs based on historical ratios. This realistic approach can keep you out of trouble or explain why growth expectations are unrealistic.

The reasons above should convince you to follow through with the rest of this section. Your next task is to learn the basic categories of ratios that are most commonly used. We have provided examples of each category. Of particular concern is to determine which ratios are the most important.

Liquidity Ratios

These ratios are the most common of all the ratios and are designed to measure your firm's ability to meet its short-term obligations as they come due—that is, will the firm be able to generate sufficient cash in the short run to pay its short-term bills.

Current Ratio. This ratio measures current assets to current liabilities. Remember, "current liability" means an obligation is due and payable within one year. For assets, the term "current" refers to those assets that can be sold, consumed, or converted to cash within one year. Current assets, therefore, include cash, marketable securities, accounts receivable, inventory and short-term notes receivable. Current liabilities include trade payables, accruals, current portion of long-term debt and short-term notes payable. Mathematically, the current ratio is simply current assets divided by current liabilities. The current ratio should be greater than 1 to 1; otherwise, it is an indication of short-term insolvency. As the current ratio gets higher, creditors feel better about your company's ability to repay short-term credit. If the current ratio gets too high it can be an indication of inefficient or improper asset management.

Acid or Quick Ratio. This ratio is designed to remove the least liquid and most highly suspect asset, inventory, from the current asset base. The ratio is simply current assets less inventory divided by current liabilities. Financial analysts have long known that inventory is the asset most subject to manipulation. Inventory can be overvalued, undervalued, missing, and very illiquid. By removing this asset, the analyst can determine the underlying health of your company and its ability to "quickly" liquidate its other current assets to satisfy current liabilities. A quick ratio of 1 to 1 could be considered very good. A quick ratio below 1 to 1 is not necessarily a negative factor.

Leverage Ratios

There are two main methods of financing the asset side of the balance sheet: funds obtained from others (debt) or funds obtained from the investors (equity). The use of leverage ratios helps to measure the relationship between debt and equity so as to provide a measure of your firm's risk to a creditor or an investor. The creditor is interested in being repaid with interest, and as such, is interested in a buffer provided by the owners in the form of equity. The investor is interested in receiving a fair return for his or her investment but realizes he or she must wait in line behind the creditors. Therefore, an investor also will be reviewing your leverage ratios to determine risk associated with the investment.

Debt Ratio. The debt ratio is mathematically the total debt from all sources divided by total assets. This ratio tells us simply what fraction of assets are financed by debt. The lower the debt ratio the higher the amount of equity used to finance assets, and the larger the buffer the creditors have to depend on. As the debt ratio increases, the margin of safety provided creditors decreases and so does the creditors' propensity to extend credit.

Times Interest Earned (TIE). This ratio was designed to provide a measure of the interest coverage available from a company's *earnings before interest and taxes* (EBIT). Mathematically, the ratio is EBIT divided by interest expense. Note that since interest is a deductible expense, we treat the ratio in pretax terms. On the one hand, as the TIE increases, creditors become more comfortable. On the other hand, if TIE gets too high, you may not be aggressive enough in your use of debt to maximize stockholders' wealth.

Fixed Charge Coverage Ratio. Similar to TIE, this ratio measures your business's ability to cover interest, lease payments, and loan principal repayment. Since operating lease payments are treated as tax-deductible expenses, we need to add them back to EBIT as cash available to service fixed charges. The fixed charges are interest expense, lease payments, and pretax equivalent principal payments. We need to gross up the principal repayment to a pretax basis since principal payments are not tax-deductible expenses. That is, we need to create an equivalent amount of pretax flows to support repayment of principal which comes from after-tax cash flows. This is achieved by dividing the principal repayment by the amount of 1 minus the corporate tax rate. The resultant equation will look like this:

$$\text{Fixed charge coverage} = \frac{\text{EBIT} + \text{lease payments}}{\text{interest} + \text{lease payments} + \dfrac{\text{principal}}{1 - \text{tax rate}}}$$

Activity Ratios

In the first two categories of ratios, the ability of your business was measured to provide a level of comfort to creditors and investors. This section discusses the ratios that are intended to measure the efficiency of investment in assets, which are resources. We are vitally interested in these ratios since the resources of your business, if it is like most other businesses, are limited. Maximization of your wealth can only occur with efficient employment of those resources. Also, resources supplied to your business have some cost either in the form of interest to creditors or return on investment to the owner.

For this category of ratios, information from both the balance sheet and the income statement is used to arrive at the comparisons of interest. This information is used to determine how fast assets can be converted to sales.

Inventory Turnover (ITO). This is perhaps the most important activity ratio because inventory is usually the single largest asset and the one in which mistakes are most easily made. The wrong type of inventory has caused many businesses to go under. The ITO inventory is determined by dividing the cost of sales with the result multiplied by the number of days in the period of interest. If you are looking at one quarter, we recommend you use ninety days. If you are looking at one year, we recommend you use 360 days. The optimum ITO would be the level of inventory that just meets each day's demand as it occurs. Just-in-time (JIT) inventory meets this criteria and is practiced by the automobile companies of Japan. Ideally, we would like to practice JIT like the Japanese auto makers; however, because many of us will not have that type of leverage, we need to keep an eye on inventory management through ITO.

Note: Instead of using average inventory, ending inventory is used since the idea is to identify trends. If consistent time frames are chosen, the comparison will be valid. Also, as a matter of mathematical ease, use 360 days or 30 days per month. This note is also applicable to the next ratio.

Average Collection Period. This ratio is also known as accounts receivable turnover (A/R Turn). This ratio measures efficiency of accounts receivable management. Many sales are made on credit. As a result, this ratio has a great deal of meaning. The object is to compare all credit sales occurring in a particular period to accounts receivable at the end of that period. Once again, be consistent in the period or periods you are comparing. A/R turn is the result of dividing accounts receivable at the end of a period by sales for that period and multiplying the result by the number of days in the period. The lower the A/R turn in days the better. A low number of days indicates a good collection effort and effective credit policy. A high number of days indicates just the opposite. If A/R turn becomes too low, however, it could mean that credit criteria for your business are too strict and you may be losing sales as a result.

Total Asset Turnover. This ratio aggregates all categories of assets and provides an overall level of management effectiveness in the asset investment decision. Mathematically, the ratio is sales divided by total assets. A low turnover ratio indicates your business is not generating sufficient sales from the investment in assets. In other words, your business is investing in the wrong assets.

Profitability Ratios

As an entrepreneur, your goal is to maximize your wealth. To measure your overall effectiveness, we introduce the concept of profitability. You can measure profitability in a number of ways to determine how well your business is performing in the aggregate.

Gross Margin. This margin is the relationship of gross profit to sales. Gross profit is defined as sales less direct costs of sales including direct labor, direct materials, and direct factory overhead. This margin can be used to measure period-to-period efficiency of cost of producing sales.

Net Margin. This margin is the relationship between net income, which is sales less all direct and indirect expenses and taxes, and sales themselves. This number should be positive and is used to perform self comparison of overall effectiveness of the business endeavor.

Return on Assets (ROA). Also known as ROI or return on investment, this ratio compares net income after tax and total assets. It measures both the effectiveness of investing and financing decisions.

Return on Equity (ROE). Also known as return on net worth, this measure is important because this ratio is based on your investment contribution as well as the retention of earnings in your business. Mathematically the ratio is earnings divided after tax by net worth. The higher this value the better.

Earnings Per Share (EPS). While many of you will have only one shareholder (you!), some of you may decide to seek additional funds by bringing in other investors. As the number of investors increases, this ratio takes on more importance. Simply divide net income by the number of shares outstanding. The higher the EPS, the better.

This list of ratios will give you a fair cross section of the important ratios in use today. This list is by no means complete. There are other ratios available to measure the success of your business; however, we believe the ratios we have selected will allow you to analyze, with a high degree of accuracy, the strengths and weaknesses of your business. If you are ever confronted with an unfamiliar ratio, simply ask for a definition and proceed from there.

How to Calculate Ratios and Determine Their Meanings

To calculate ratios, a balance sheet and income statement information are necessary. Following are an income statement and balance sheet for 1988 and 1989. Two year's of statements are provided to give you some practice in the calculations as well as allowing you to look at trends.

The following information is provided as the raw data for the calculations used in the income statement and balance sheet:

YourCorp
Balance Sheet

	December 31, 1988 (000) Omitted	December 31, 1989 (000) Omitted
Assets		
Cash	$40	$ 25
Marketable securities	0	15
Accounts receivable	300	350
Inventory	160	200
Prepaid expense	10	20
Total current assets	510	610
Machinery and equipment	80	100
Plant and land	300	300
Transport equipment	80	100
Leasehold improvement	30	50
Less: accumulated depreciation	(70)	(150)
Net fixed assets	420	400
Covenant	55	50
Goodwill	55	50
Total Noncurrent assets	110	100
Total Assets	$1040	$1110
	=====	=====
Liabilities and net worth		
Accounts payable	$ 115	$ 125
Notes payable	140	100
Miscellaneous accruals	70	50
Current portion of long-term debt	15	15
Total current liabilities	340	290
Long-term debt	215	200
Deferred taxes	45	50
Notes payable	100	100
Total non-current liabilities	360	350
Common stock	100	100
Capital surplus	50	50
Treasury stock	(10)	(10)
Retained earnings	200	330
Total net worth	340	470
Total liabilities and net worth	$1040	$1110
	=====	=====

A fairly detailed set of balance sheets for the following ratio analysis exercises has been provided. The income statements, on the other hand, will be relatively devoid of detail for our analysis because we are mainly concerned with the net effects of the income statement as it relates to the balance sheet. It must be clear, however, that as a concerned entrepreneur, you will want to compare the various elements of your income statement on a periodic basis. The best method available is *common sizing*. Common sizing is the method by which each item on the income statement is converted into a percentage of the sales figure. The creation of these percentages eliminates the problem of relative magnitude and restates all expenses as a percent of total sales. Use of this method will allow you to concentrate your efforts in the areas that will yield the highest return. As an example of this method, an income statement for the years 1988 and 1989 cast in the common sized method is shown below.

YourCorp
Income Statement
for the twelve months ended

	December 31, 1988		December 31, 1989	
	(000 Omitted)		(000 Omitted)	
Net sales	$2,830	100.0%	$3,000	100.0%
Cost of goods sold	1,415	50.0	1,460	48.7
Gross profit	1,415	50.0	1,540	51.3
Operating expenses	1,210	42.8	1,268	42.2
Earnings before				
interest and taxes	205	7.2	272	9.1
Interest expense	40	1.4	47	1.6
Earnings before taxes	165	5.8	225	7.5
Tax at 40%	66	2.3	90	3.0
Net income	$ 99	3.5	$ 135	4.5

Assume the following information is given in the footnotes of the financial statement:

* Operating expenses include lease payments of $15,000 in 1988 and $17,000 in 1989.
* Principal debt service for 1988 is $12,000 and for 1989 is $15,000.
* Shares of common stock outstanding in each year are 100,000.

Common sizing yields much information if you know how to recognize it. We will take a look at a few appropriate items and determine the underlying meaning.

Gross Profit Growth. Gross profit has grown from 50 percent to 51.3 percent—which is good. An increase in gross profit can be caused by two factors: (1) your business is able to increase prices while maintaining cost of goods sold or (2) your business has held its prices while at the same time cutting its costs.

Operating Expenses. Note that these expenses have decreased from 42.8 percent to 42.2 percent of sales. Although the drop is not a large one, any drop is considered good because it reflects a management control of indirect costs and higher efficiency of operation. This improvement tells us we are operating in an efficient area above the breakeven point.

Net Income Growth. As a result of the factors mentioned above, net income has grown from 3.5 percent to 4.5 percent of sales. This indicates that the firm is in excellent control of prices and direct and indirect costs.

At this point, we are ready to look at the specific ratios for YourCorp, compare them with a fictitious set of industry standards, and interpret the meanings of the trends indicated. First, however, the formulas of interest are provided:

Liquidity Ratios

$$\text{Current ratio} = \frac{\text{Current assets}}{\text{Current liabilities}}$$

$$\text{Acid ratio} = \frac{\text{current assets - inventory}}{\text{current liabilities}}$$

Leverage Ratios

$$\text{Debt ratio} = \frac{\text{Total liabilities}}{\text{total assets}}$$

$$\text{Times interest earned} = \frac{\text{EBIT}}{\text{interest charges}}$$

Note: EBIT = earnings before interest and taxes

$$\text{Fixed charge coverage} = \frac{\text{EBIT + lease payments}}{\text{interest + lease payments} + \frac{\text{principal}}{\text{1-tax rate}}}$$

Activity Ratios

$$\text{Inventory turnover} = \frac{\text{inventory x 360}}{\text{cost of goods sold}}$$

$$\text{Average collection period} = \frac{\text{Accounts Receivable x 360}}{\text{Sales}}$$

Note: Both activity ratios are calculated for a one year period. For any other period simply replace 360 with the appropriate days in the period of interest.

$$\text{Total Asset Turnover} = \frac{\text{Sales}}{\text{Total Assets}}$$

Profitability Ratios

$$\text{Gross Margin} = \frac{\text{Gross Profit}}{\text{Sales}}$$

$$\text{Net Margin} = \frac{\text{Net Income}}{\text{Sales}}$$

$$\text{Return on Assets} = \frac{\text{Net Income}}{\text{Total Assets}}$$

$$\text{Return on Equity} = \frac{\text{Net Income}}{\text{Net Worth}}$$

$$\text{Earnings per Share} = \frac{\text{Net Income}}{\text{Shares Outstanding}}$$

The following calculations are the result of the above formulas applied to the figures presented in the balance sheet and income statement of YourCorp:

Ratio   (000) Omitted

	1988	1989	Industry
Liquidity			
Current	$\frac{510}{340} = 1.5$	$\frac{610}{290} = 2.1$	1.4 times
Acid	$\frac{510 - 160}{340} = 1.03$	$\frac{610 - 200}{290} = 1.41$	0.8 times
Leverage			
Debt	$\frac{700}{340} = 2.06$	$\frac{640}{470} = 1.36$	2.1 times
Times interest earned	$\frac{205}{40} = 5.1$	$\frac{272}{47} = 5.8$	3.2 times
Fixed charge coverage	$\frac{205 + 15}{40 + 15 + \frac{12}{1 - .4}} = 2.93$	$\frac{272 + 17}{47 + 17 + \frac{15}{1 - .4}} = 3.25$	2.7 times
Activity			
Inventory turnover	$\frac{160 \times 360}{1,415} = 40.7$	$\frac{200 \times 360}{1,460} = 49.3$	44 days
Average collection period	$\frac{300 \times 160}{2,830} = 38.2$	$\frac{350 \times 360}{3,000} = 42$	40 days
Total asset turnover	$\frac{2,830}{1,040} = 2.72$	$\frac{3,000}{1,110} = 2.70$	2.9 times
Profitability			
Gross margin	$\frac{1,415}{2,830} = 50\%$	$\frac{1,540}{3,000} = 51.3\%$	48%
Net margin	$\frac{99}{2,830} = 3.5\%$	$\frac{135}{3,000} = 4.5\%$	2.9%
Return on assets	$\frac{99}{1,040} = 9.5\%$	$\frac{135}{1,110} = 12.2\%$	10.3%

Return on equity	$\dfrac{99}{340} = 29.1\%$	$\dfrac{135}{470} = 28.7\%$	22.3%
Earnings per share	$\dfrac{99}{100} = \$.99$	$\dfrac{135}{100} = \$1.35$	N/A

Now that two years' worth of ratios have been calculated, we can analyze them for trends and compare them with industry standards. For ease of analysis, we will look at the ratios in topical groups.

Liquidity Ratios. YourCorp has managed to increase the liquidity of the firm and compares favorably with the industry standard for both current and acid ratios. Note, however, that YourCorp exceeds both ratios by considerable margins. Although liquidity is a sign of health to creditors, it can be a sign of inefficiency to the owners. Remember, liquidity is comprised of assets such as inventory, accounts receivable and cash. Too much cash can be an underutilization of assets—that is, even if cash is invested at money market rates, it may not be earning at a rate consistent with the returns available from the business. Inventory and accounts receivable should be kept as low as is consistent with efficient operation of the business.

Too much liquidity has a price, which is reflected in the cost of carrying inventory and accounts receivable, and therefore can lead to a reduction in return on assets and return on equity. To determine if YourCorp is too liquid we need to look at other ratios—specifically the activity ratios.

Activity Ratios. The inventory turnover rate has increased from 40.7 to 49.3 days and exceeds the industry standard of 44 days. This fact sheds some light on what happened to the firm's liquidity. YourCorp has experienced an inventory build up; as a result, liquidity was affected because inventory is a current asset. This ratio deserves close attention by the owner since it appears that too much inventory or the wrong type of inventory is being purchased. Average collection period has also increased from 38.2 to 42 days and now exceeds the industry average of 40 days. Again, liquidity was affected by the growth in this accounts receivable. There are two relationships that explain this situation: (1) diminished collection effort or (2) reduced credit standards which may have aided in reaching the increased level of sales. The owner must promptly investigate what has gone wrong in the area of accounts receivable and take action to correct it.

The last of the activity ratios is total asset turnover. Based on previous observations it should come as no surprise that this ratio has declined from 2.72 to 2.70 times and is below the industry average of 2.9 times. Simply stated, YourCorp is not as effective as its peers in creating sales from its investment in assets. The owner needs to review assets, in general, and inventory and accounts receivable, in specific, for improved performance.

Debt Ratio. This ratio shows a decline from 67.3 to 57.7% and is below the industry average of 60.2%. This ratio tells us that YourCorp has chosen to use equity in the form of retained earnings to finance asset growth from $1,040,000 to $1,110,000. Creditors will like this trend since it increases their "buffer" if a liquidation occurs. The positive by-product of a low debt ratio is reduced interest expense. The negative by-product is that the return on equity might suffer because there exists in the United States tax code a legitimate tax shelter in the form of interest expense. That is, the effective cost of debt is reduced by the tax savings caused by deducting interest from pretax earnings.

The next debt ratio is the times interest earned (TIE) ratio. TIE has increased from 5.1 to 5.8 times and is well above the industry standard of 4.1 times. This goes hand in hand with the debt ratio. Generally, when the debt ratio decreases, the TIE will increase because lower debt implies lower interest expense. The fixed charge coverage ratio reflects the same trend as TIE and is healthy at 3.25 times versus the industry average of 2.7 times.

Profitability Ratios. These ratios show whether YourCorp has been successful in the creation of profits through operations. The gross margin has grown from 50 to 51.3% and exceeds the industry standard of 48%. This reflects the owner's ability to (1) increase its prices while holding constant its cost of goods sold or (2) decrease its costs of goods sold while holding constant its prices. In either event, YourCorp has done well. The net margin provides further evidence of the owner's ability to control costs or prices or both. In the area of ROA, even though ownership did not turn assets as well as it should have, it counteracted this effect by improving profitability. Continued efforts of management to reduce the asset base while maintaining this sales level or a higher level of sales will further increase ROA. YourCorp did not fare as well in the area of ROE because it fell from 29.1 to 28.7%. Even though the company exceeds industry average of 22.3%, a minor negative trend is indicated. Although a reduction in the asset base liquidity will provide cash with which to pay a dividend, it will also reduce net worth and increase ROE. The last ratio is earnings per share (EPS). Stockholders will be happy to note the significant growth in EPS from $0.99 to $1.35 per share indicating a very successful year.

As you can see, an extremely profitable company can have areas of weaknesses. As an entrepreneur, you must be prepared to address these issues as they become known. Ratio analysis can provide you with the tools necessary to keep your business thriving. *Beware:* Ratio analysis is only a tool, as such it will help you identify both positive and negative aspects of your business, but it will not solve your problems.

Sources of Industry Ratios

Throughout our discussion of ratio analysis, we have stated that you should use comparisons with the industry your business is in. Now we will provide you with a detailed list of the sources of those comparison ratios.

Dun & Bradstreet, Inc. D & B has been in existence for many years and provides "key business ratios" on a monthly basis in *Dun's Review*. This monthly periodical covers specific retail, wholesale, and industrial lines of business. Annually, D & B compiles "cost of doing business" from the IRS's "Statistics of Income." For further information, D & B is located at 99 Church Street, New York, NY 10007.

Robert Morris Associates. RMA is a national association of bank loan and credit officers. The stated purpose of the RMA is to maintain and advance the standards of correct credit practice. RMA provides ratio studies of over 350 lines of business. For further information, RMA is located in the Philadelphia National Bank Building, Philadelphia, PA 19107.

Accounting Corporation of America. ACA publishes the "Barometer of Small Business" on a semiannual basis. This publication is based on various industry groups by gross sales volume, which rarely exceeds $300,000. For further information, ACA is located at 1929 First Avenue, San Diego, CA 92101.

Bank of America. The Bank of America publishes a series of pamphlets known as the "Small Business Reporter," which deals with a number of generic topics as well as specifics related to chosen industries. For further information write to Bank of America at Department 3120, P.O. Box 37000, San Francisco, CA.

Trade Associations. The list is too numerous to publish here. Suffice it to say that most industries have trade associations, and most trade associations publish some form of industry-specific data. The best method of tapping into this information is to use a trade association reference book which contains a list of trade associations and their addresses. Most public libraries have this book in their reference section.

Government Sources. By far the largest data processor in the world, our federal government through its various bureaus produces reams of useful information. The bureaus that publish financial ratios are: Federal Trade Commission, the Interstate Commerce Commission, the United States Department of Commerce, the United States Department of Agriculture, the Civil Aeronautics Board, the Federal Communications Commission, the Federal Power Commission, and the Securities and Exchange Commission. One bureau that deserves mention in its own right is the Bureau of the Census, which publishes limited ratio and financial information.

Besides the variety of sources listed above, doing a little research at your local public library or at a local chamber of commerce will aid you in your search for the information sources that will mean the most to you. Good luck in your search.

SHOULD YOU SELL ON CREDIT?

To compete effectively, you will find that most of the time you will have to sell your product or service on credit. Large creditworthy customers will not buy your goods or services on a COD basis unless you happen to be the only supplier around. To determine whether or not you should sell on credit, you should weigh the pros and cons of credit as it relates to your philosophy. To assist you in making this determination, a brief list of the factors you should consider is given below.

Why Firms Prefer to Buy on Credit

* The number of firms that buy on credit are significantly larger than those who are willing to buy on a COD basis.
* Companies prefer to handle the payment of invoices through a controlled environment which allows for accounting for the receipt of goods and a verification of the quality required. They also prefer to use your funds during this set of events.
* No cash will change hands in the shipping department; therefore, the chance of "cash shrinkage" is reduced.

Negative Aspects of Granting Trade Credit

Costs associated with granting credit include:

* Credit checking
* Bookkeeping costs
* Stationery costs
* Postage expense
* Interest charges on borrowings used to support accounts receivable
* Collection costs for delinquent accounts
* Bad debts

If a customer owes you money, he or she can use it as leverage to extract additional performance, which you would not otherwise provide.

The issue of credit is neither black nor white. That is, you should neither seek to avoid the use of credit at all costs nor should you grant credit to everyone who walks through the door. Credit, when administered properly, will both increase sales and profits. The proper administration of credit is discussed in the next section.

ACCOUNTS RECEIVABLE: THE LIFEBLOOD OF THE BUSINESS

Once you are convinced that selling on credit is essential, you must manage your credit program so that it does not end up managing you out of business. Should you decide to sell on a COD or all cash basis, you may move to the next section; otherwise welcome to the land of trade credit.

Credit Application Process

Accounts receivable does not begin when the sale is made; instead, it begins when your customer orders your product and requests that you sell it to him or her on credit. We are extremely interested in this first crucial step, since a mistake here can result in a bad debt at worst or a collection account at best. You should take a number of steps before granting credit:

* Have the applicant fill out a credit application that includes such basic information as:
    - Name of the business (include fictitious business name, if any) and address
    - Type of business (SIC code if known)
    - Years in business and number of employees
    - Bank references for five years including bank officer name, account numbers, and loans, if any
    - At least three trade references
    - Names, addresses ,and social security numbers of principals for closely held firms
* Check applicant's credit with local credit bureaus and regional and national credit agencies such as Dun & Bradstreet and TRW. Obtain TRW reports on principals. Check trade references for performance as a measure of both character and capacity.
* Analyze information provided to determine acceptability of customer and limits you would be willing to provide.
* Follow new credit accounts closely until a track record has been established. If payment is prompt, then consider extending additional credit, if not, pull credit line and require COD basis shipping.

Once you have approved your customer's credit, you are ready to accept his or her order.

Once you accept the order, a sale is created. The order is then memorialized by an invoice. The invoice is a special document that has value. It is the record of the transfer of goods from your ownership to your customer's ownership in exchange for the promise to pay an agreed upon amount. Since it is such an important document, we recommend it contain at least the following information:

* Name and address of customer
* Your company's name, address, and telephone number
* The date the invoice is prepared
* A unique serial number to identify and track invoices
* A description of the goods shipped
* A price per unit and extension of total price
* Shipping method and cost (if customer pays)
* The trade credit terms

Trade Credit Terms

The terms of the trade credit outline the timing of required payment and the amount to be paid. For instance, if terms are "net 10" on a $100 invoice, you will expect receipt of $100 within 10 days of invoice date and some amount greater than $100 if your terms call for a late charge. If the terms are "2%/10 net 30" on that same $100 invoice, you would expect to receive $98 if the invoice was paid within 10 days of the date of the invoice or the net amount ($100) if the invoice was paid anytime between the 11th and the 30th day from invoice date. *Note:* It would be unwise to pay on any day but the 30th day if you allow the invoice to remain unpaid by the 10th day. If a customer has failed to pay on or before the 30th day, the customer is delinquent in his obligation. Tracking the delinquency problem with one customer and one invoice would be simple if you had one customer; however, if your business is successful, you will be sending out scores of invoices each month to customers. How do you control this situation? We recommend the use of a tried and true method known as the aged report or the aging of accounts receivable.

The Aged Report: Aging of Accounts Receivable

The aged report is simply what it says, a chronological listing of all unpaid invoices of the firm, grouped by period. An aged report should consist of at least the following:

* Customer name
* Balance by period for each customer
* Totals of all period balances

Aged reports can contain many other items including customer address, assigned customer identification number, open invoice numbers, and credits.

An example of an aged report of YourCorp, which sells its goods on the following terms: "net 30," follows.

YourCorp
Aging of Accounts Receivable
December 31, 1989

Customer Name	Balance	Current	0-30 Days	31-60 Days	61-90 Days	Over 90 Days
ABC Corp.	$10,000	$ 8,500	$1,500			
XYZ Limited	15,000	15,000				
Delinc Inc.	6,000	-	-	$1,000	$2,000	$3,000
Ontime Co.	25,000	25,000				
Flakey Corp.	10,000	-	1,000	3,000	5,000	1,000
Totals	$66,000	$48,500	$2,500	$4,000	$7,000	$4,000
Percentage	100%	73.4%	3.8%	6.1%	10.6%	6.1%

As you can see, YourCorp has a couple of customers who are not abiding by the required credit terms. This leads us into the last area of accounts receivable management, namely collections.

Collection Procedures

A collection department is established to follow up on invoices that are due and unpaid. Usually when an entrepreneur is first starting a business, he or she is the collection department. The job of collecting money is one of the most thankless jobs existing in business today. The customer can become downright abusive. However, collection should not be pushed aside. If you hire a bookkeeper to assist you in collecting your receivables, try to fill the position with someone who is rather hardened to the abuse and excuses to which he or she may become exposed.

A tight collection procedure usually goes something like this:

* Mail first statement within ten days after invoice payment is due.
* Mail second statement at end of first month after invoice payment is due with a "benefit of the doubt" statement such as: "Perhaps our first statement was not received, please remit balance due at once."
* At forty-five days past due, telephone customer. Some businesses will call much sooner.
* At seventy-five days past due, you should send a *Demand* letter stating that you will be forced to turn the account over to your attorney unless payment is made immediately.
* At 90–120 days, turn account over to collection agent or attorney for legal action.

How to Manage Accounts Receivable

In the management of accounts receivable, you must be somewhat flexible. There will be occasions when an otherwise fast paying customer will need extended terms. As long as customers are communicative and forthright with you, you must be prepared to extend repayment terms. One crucial point to remember when contacting customers for payment is to obtain a commitment as to when the payment can be expected. It is also a good technique to get the customer to sign a statement acknowledging that commitment. (Studies have shown that many individuals will follow through with a commitment once they sign a document that states their commitment.) Never be afraid to call on customers to pay monies due, since the creation of accounts receivable is an investment on your part in them. That investment is not free and becomes more costly as you wait to collect your money. The more delinquent your receivables become, the greater your investment.

In the area of accounts receivable management, three other tactics can be employed:

First. Establish or tighten your credit policy to eliminate slow paying customers. The obvious problem with this tactic is that you may eliminate some slow paying customers that are loyal and have provided you with much business. Each industry has its share of larger companies that take advantage of small entrepreneurial firms. This is a fact in business. It seems foolhardy to exclude a company from shipment when sales are profitable and represent a substantial portion of your revenue.

Second. Hold future shipments on customers whose payments are past due. The worst you can do is lose the balance of what is owed to you, and the best you can do is save yourself from suffering an even larger bad debt.

Third. On marginal credit quality accounts or new accounts, ship on a prepaid or COD basis. This is common place for new companies.

How to Finance Accounts Receivable

Accounts receivable was described as an investment in an asset. As such you must determine how you will finance this asset. There are two methods: debt or equity. The use of equity is most probably the method you will use in a fledgling business. The other method involves the use of debt, which is someone else's money. As your business grows, you will find numerous debt funding sources:

* Permanent working capital in the form of a long-term (greater than two years) loan with a principal repayment schedule that includes principal and interest. This type of loan is designed to be repaid out of profits.

* Accounts receivable financing through a revolving line of credit. Generally one year in duration, this type of loan represents an advance of funds on a formula basis determined by some advance rate which looks to your accounts receivable at the end of each month.

* Factoring. This method uses a discount technique in which each invoice generates an advance of funds; the amount of which is based on credit quality of both buyer and seller.

Due to its capital-intensive nature, accounts receivable need to be managed very closely. The importance of this statement becomes self-evident when you look at the amount of cash necessary to support a modest sales effort when the collection of receivables lags beyond what is expected. To illustrate the importance of this concept, we will show you, through a cash flow analysis, how slipshod management of accounts receivable can adversely affect your business.

Example:

Your terms are net 30 days, and if the rule of thumb holds for your industry, you can expect the following cash collection flow: 60–65 percent of accounts receivable will be collected in the next month (30 days); 20–25 percent of accounts receivable in the second month after sale; about 15–18 percent in the third month after sale; and about 1 percent in the fourth month after sale. For the purposes of this example, assume that 1 percent of sales are never collected. Assume also that only credit sales are analyzed. Your cash receipts schedule would look something like the following:

CASH RECEIPTS OF ACCOUNTS RECEIVABLE
(000 omitted)

	Month 1	Month 2	Month 3	Month 4	Month 5	Month 6
Sales	$100	$120	$120	$130	$100	$110
Approximate cash receipts						
First month	$ 0	$ 60	$ 72	$ 72	$ 78	$ 60
Second month (20%)	0	0	20	24	24	26
Third month (18%)	0	0	0	18	22	22
Fourth month (1%)	0	0	0	0	1	1
Total	$ -0-	$ 60	$ 92	$114	$125	$109

As you can see, it becomes obvious that very little cash flows into the company coffers during the first ninety days. In fact, the company above will receive only $152,000 on sales of $340,000 or 45 percent of sales recorded in the first ninety days. Assuming the business has a net cash margin of 10 percent and it had to pay cash for labor, materials, and rent, 90% of sales or $306,000 will be paid out during the first ninety days of operations. Of this amount, only $152,000 will be collected, which will leave a cash deficit of $154,000. This deficit will have to be made up from sources other than the collection of receivables.

In the example above, certain assumptions were made regarding the terms under which accounts receivable were collected. We assumed all sales were made on thirty day net terms. Now assume that you wish to use a time-honored method for speeding up the collection of your receivables: the trade discount. A typical trade discount used in many industries is 2%/10 net 30 which literally means: "pay 98 percent of the invoice amount within ten days of invoice date or pay 100 percent of the invoice amount within thirty days of the invoice date." If you assume only 10 percent (which is a conservative figure) of your customers take advantage of your discounted terms, let's see what happens to accounts receivable collections. Note that you had to forego 2 percent of the amount otherwise due. The impact of using this trade discount can be seen below:

CASH RECEIPTS OF ACCOUNTS RECEIVABLE
(000 omitted)

	Month 1	Month 2	Month 3	Month 4	Month 5	Month 6
Sales	$100.0	$120.0	$120.0	$130.0	$100.0	$110.0
Approximate cash receipts:						
Month of shipment	$ 9.8	$ 11.8	$ 11.8	$ 12.7	$ 9.8	10.8
First month (60%)	0	54.0	64.8	64.87	0.2	54.0
Second month (20%)	0	0	18.0	21.6	21.6	23.4
Third month (18%)	0	0	0	16.2	19.4	19.4
Fourth month (1%)	0	0	0	0	.9	1.1
Total	$ 9.8	$ 65.8	$ 94.6	$115.3	$121.9	$108.7
Cash receipts without discount:	$ 0	$ 60	$ 92	$114	$125	$109

Like it or not, to compete in today's business environment, you will probably have to extend credit. Credit, in and of itself, is not bad but it must be monitored closely to avoid loss of control and the inevitable disaster that follows. We suggest you exercise a good tight reign on granting credit and the process of collection. It is always less difficult to ease up on credit policies than to tighten them. In the collection process the golden rule is to "ask and ask often and ye shall receive."

WHY YOU MUST CLOSELY MONITOR YOUR INVENTORY

Inventories are assets held for sale in the ordinary course of business, or assets that will be used in the production of other goods which will be sold. There are various reasons that you should monitor your inventory:

* In many businesses, inventories represent the single largest current asset.
* In manufacturing and retail entities, the sale of inventory at a price greater than cost is the primary source of revenue.
* Net income is determined by matching inventory cost against revenue.
* Inventory affects both the balance sheet and the income statement.

As a business owner, you should participate in inventory planning and control because (1) inventory is frequently the largest current asset and therefore will probably constitute a material part of the total assets; (2) unsaleable inventory items contain a potential loss; (3) sales may be lost if products are not available in the desired style, quality, and quantity; (4) insufficient purchasing procedures, faulty manufacturing techniques, and inadequate sales efforts will be manifested by excessive and unsaleable inventory; and (5) failure to monitor inventory levels may result in high financing costs because your business may be stuck with having to carry a large amount of inventory.

Inventories are very sensitive to business cycles. During prosperous times, merchandise can be disposed of and quantities on hand may not appear excessive. However, during cyclical downtimes, inventory begins to move slowly and piles up to the point where the problem of obsolescence may become a reality. The major objective of inventory management is to discover and maintain the optimum level of inventory investment. If inventory levels are too high, there are unnecessary carrying costs, risks of spoilage, and risks of obsolescence. If levels are too low, production may be disrupted or sales permanently lost.

There is a variety of costs associated with inventory. Some costs are associated with carrying too much inventory, others are associated with not carrying enough.

Costs associated with carrying too much inventory include:

* Reduction of desired rate of return on investment
* Risk of obsolescence
* Space for storage
* Awkward handling for transfer
* Unnecessary clerical and/or paperwork
* Increased personal property taxes
* Higher volume necessitates higher insurance costs

Costs associated with not carrying enough inventory include:

* Lost quantity discounts
* Lost fortuitous purchases
* Contribution margin on lost sales
* Loss of customer goodwill
* Extra purchasing or transportation costs
* Extra costs of uneconomical production runs, overtime, setups, and training

There are two questions you must always ask whenever you buy inventory:

(1) How much to order at a time?
(2) When to order?

Mathematical decision models are used to answer these questions because they replace "hunches" with explicit assumptions and criteria. The next section shows you the purpose of inventory and how to use a mathematical model to estimate how much inventory to order each time as well as when the orders should be made.

HOW MUCH INVENTORY SHOULD YOUR BUSINESS CARRY?

Business owners often ask, "How much inventory should my business carry?" Your business should carry only enough inventory to service customers' needs. Although this answer appears to be flippant, in reality, it is the best answer. Ideally, a business would want to have only enough inventory to meet the demand of one day so that it would be possible to have a zero investment in inventory as well as zero expense to carry inventory. However, this ideal situation is not possible because a typical business is faced with the following shortfalls:

* Customer demand is not perfectly known.
* The desired mix of inventory to support a perfectly known demand is not available on an instantaneous basis. Even if it was, the cost of delivery would probably be prohibitive.

Some of you may say, "What about JIT inventory methods practiced by some automobile manufacturers, notably the Japanese?" The answer is, yes, certain large companies may be able to approach the perfect inventory levels discussed earlier in the chapter. However, most start-ups do not have the leverage necessary to use this method. The Japanese automobile manufacturers may control their demand for raw materials, yet they cannot control consumers' demand for the finished product. Thus, even at the level of sophistication practiced by some Japanese firms, the perfect inventory level is not attainable.

What Is Inventory?

Before inventory is discussed further, the question, "What is inventory?" must first be answered. Inventory can take many forms: raw materials, work-in-process (WIP), or finished goods. No matter what form it takes, the main purpose of inventory is to supply a demand. That demand could be a manufacturing process demand or the demand of an ultimate enduser. The amount of inventory you carry will be a function of these types of demands. Before this idea is explored further, it is necessary to discuss the characteristics and purposes of inventory.

The first form of inventory, raw materials, is made up of the goods/commodities or subassemblies purchased from suppliers to support the next step in the manufacturing process. Raw materials include basic commodities such as metals, wood products and chemicals. Raw materials also include semifinished products such as motors, semiconductors, and chassis.

The second form of inventory, WIP, consists of the partially completed products of the manufacturing process. The WIP has three components: raw materials employed, labor added, and overhead allocated in the conversion process. This type of inventory fills the manufacturing pipeline and will ultimately end up as finished goods.

The last form of inventory, finished goods, is the goods your company will endeavor to sell to the ultimate enduser. Although not all business types, such as retailers and wholesalers, have raw material or WIP inventories, all businesses have finished goods. The demand for finished goods is what drives all other forms of inventory.

Now that the characteristics of inventory have been defined, the purposes of carrying various types of inventory will be discussed next.

Purposes of Inventory

Raw Materials

* Variations in demand require a buffer of raw materials inventory to be held in order to service fluctuations in demand requirements.
* Fewer orders reduce order costs.
* Fewer and larger shipments reduce per unit freight costs.
* Inconsistency of supply makes it impossible to expect consistent response to demand.
* Volume purchases can provide for favorable purchasing terms, which can translate into a lower selling price.
* Larger loads are more efficient to handle.

Work-In-Process

* Batch processing can be achieved and therefore the costs associated with materials can be reduced.
* Flow of work is kept moving through the various processing steps.
* Piecework operators are kept active, which will avoid a slow down caused by process backlog.
* Flexibility in planning process can be maintained in situations in which processes are independent of one another.

Finished Goods

* It is extremely difficult to manufacture a product to meet immediate customer demand.
* A safety stock acts as a buffer, which will permit you to satisfy fluctuating customer demand.
* Emergency production/ordering is inefficient and costly.
* Customer order backlogs may be unacceptable, and unfilled orders will mean lost sales and customers.
* There is a need for display or sample items in order to sell the goods.
* Emergency production or ordering is inefficient and costly.

Inventory Costs

Many of the reasons, both positive and negative, for having inventory have been discussed. Inventory is a necessary evil; therefore, the reasons for minimizing it must be discussed. The reasons all center around cost. According to a report issued by the U.S. Department of Commerce, the average carrying costs amount to 25 percent of the value of the cost of inventory. That 25 percent is broken down as follows:

Obsolescence	9.00%
Deterioration/theft	5.00
Finance charges	8.50
Handling	1.00
Taxes	.50
Insurance	.25
Storage/rent	.75
	25.00%

You will recall from earlier discussions of asset needs that inventory represents a substantial investment of funds. It is in your best interests to make this investment a wise one. Making this type of investment, however, will place you between the proverbial rock and a hard place. On the one hand, you cannot be out of inventory for fear of losing sales or disrupting your manufacturing flow. On the other hand, if you are afraid to lose a single sale, you will tie up valuable and limited resources in inventory. To resolve this seemingly impossible issue you are required to analyze the costs involved. These costs will be discussed in reverse order of importance.

Production Cost. This cost addresses the start-up and shut down of a production line. Although production cost is defined as actual cost, it will be ignored in our discussion since many factors, such as slowing down the line or creating increased work-in-process, can be employed in the short run to eliminate this problem. Further, this type of problem usually occurs in larger, longer-run production process situations.

Opportunity Cost of Lost Sales. Although you will not experience out-of-pocket expenses in this situation, you will experience a loss of revenue inflows. One of the methods typically employed is the backorder. The backorder may or may not be acceptable. In those situations where it is not acceptable, lack of inventory will cause an opportunity cost of lost sales. This cost will be discussed in more detail later.

Ordering Cost. Literally speaking, this is the cost involved in placing the order for inventory. The elements of ordering cost are:

- Typing the purchase order
- Stationery, stamps, etc.
- Expediting costs
- Warehousing labor for handling each incoming order
- Record keeping of inventory
- Receiving department costs
- Purchase department costs

Some of the costs listed above are variable, which means they vary with the number of orders placed. These variable costs will impact upon your annual ordering costs. The relationship is expressed as:

Annual ordering cost = (orders per year) x (cost of placing each order)

Carrying Cost. This cost includes the following items: obsolescence, deterioration, finance charges, handling charges, taxes, insurance, and storage. The carrying cost varies directly with the size of your inventory. The relationship is expressed as:

Annual carrying cost = (average total inventory) x (carrying cost in units)

Where carrying cost is expressed as dollars per unit per year the following relationship exists:

Carrying cost = inventory cost per unit x carrying cost as percent of inventory cost

Economic Order Quantity Model

Many businesses, to reduce inventory costs, use a formula called the economic order quantity or EOQ. The EOQ is a mathematically derived quantity that minimizes total cost of carrying inventory subject to certain assumptions:

* There is no penalty for stock outs—that is, there is no opportunity cost for lost sales.
* There are no available quantity discounts.
* Inventory is used at a uniform, constant rate.
* Annual demand, ordering costs, and carrying costs are estimated with a high degree of accuracy.
* There is no order lead time—that is, orders are filled instantaneously.
* Average annual inventory will be the EOQ divided by 2.

Some of these assumptions may seem a bit unrealistic, but in order to create the model, these assumptions are necessary. Once the basic model has been created, these assumptions can be relaxed and replaced with more realistic ones. The result will be answers that fit into today's business world. Before deriving the model, we must define the variables that will be used:

$$D \quad = \quad \text{annual demand of an item of inventory expressed in units per year}$$
$$Q \quad = \quad \text{quantity to be ordered expressed in units per order}$$
$$S \quad = \quad \text{average order cost expressed in dollars per order}$$
$$C \quad = \quad \text{average cost to carry inventory expressed in dollars per unit per year}$$
$$TSC \ = \quad \text{total annual stocking cost expressed in dollars per year}$$

As we mentioned previously:

$$\text{Annual carrying costs} = (\text{average annual inventory}) \times (\text{carrying cost})$$

or

$$\text{Annual carrying costs} = (Q/2) \times C = \frac{QC}{2}$$

and

$$\text{Annual ordering costs} = (\text{orders per year}) \times (\text{cost per order})$$

or

$$\text{Annual ordering costs} = (D/Q) \times S = \frac{DS}{Q}$$

and

$$\text{Total annual stocking cost} = (\text{annual carry cost}) + (\text{annual order cost})$$

or

$$\text{Total annual stocking cost} = \frac{QC}{2} + \frac{DS}{Q}$$

The graph for total annual stocking cost looks something like this:

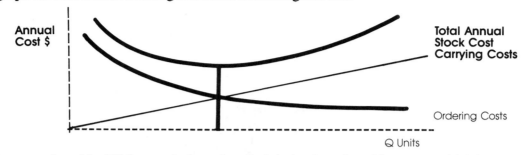

The lowest point of the TSC curve is the point of minimization of stocking costs, which in turn defines the EOQ for this set of criteria. To solve for the lowest point on the TSC curve, only the first derivative of the TSC formula with respect to Q needs to be calculated. The resultant formula, after taking the first derivative, is:

$$0 = \frac{C}{2} - \frac{DS}{Q^2}$$

Solving for Q, we get:

$$Q^2 = \frac{2DS}{C} \quad \text{or} \quad Q = \sqrt{\frac{2DS}{C}}$$

and finally:

$$EOQ = \sqrt{\frac{2DS}{C}}$$

A diagram of the model would look like this:

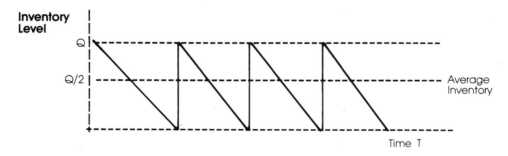

As you can see, all the assumptions are in effect. When inventory level reaches zero, a purchase is made that causes inventory to instantaneously increase to level Q.

To help you solidify the mathematics, let's look at an example. Assume annual sales in units for your product is 1,000; your ordering costs are $2 per order; and the cost to carry your inventory is $3 per unit. The solution for EOQ would be:

$$\text{EOQ} = \sqrt{\frac{2DS}{C}} = \sqrt{\frac{2 \times 1,000 \times 2}{3}}$$

EOQ = 36.51 units per order
EOQ = 37 units per order (rounded)

and the TSC will be:

$$\text{TSC} = \frac{QC}{2} + \frac{DS}{Q} = \frac{37 \times 3}{2} + \frac{1,000 \times 2}{37}$$

$$\text{TSC} = \$109.55$$

Note: Some professional texts state that total inventory cost must be computed by adding TSC to the actual cost of purchasing the inventory. Our method allows you to calculate your total inventory cost by using sales and carrying cost per unit. For example, if we assume your percentage cost to carry is 25 percent, then the carrying cost per unit would be $12.00 ($3.00/.25). Knowing that value, you only need to multiply it times your annual sales, as expressed in units. In this case, total inventory cost would be:

Total inventory cost   =   TSC + (carrying cost x annual sales)

or

Total inventory cost   = $109.55 + ($12 x 1,000)
                        = $12,109.55

Instantaneous Delivery. As stated earlier, the assumptions of the basic EOQ model are fairly restrictive. We will now take a look at the model after we ease one of the constraints. The first constraint is the instantaneous delivery constraint. We will now assume that delivery occurs within a known period of time called lead time. By knowing the lead time and the usage rate of inventory, you can determine an order point (OP) such that the order will arrive at the point that you will experience as a stock-out. The formula that describes the OP is:

OP = (usage rate per day x lead time in days)

The graph for this model looks like this:

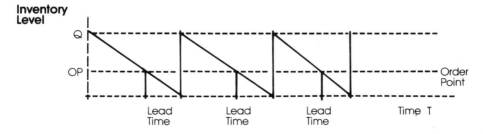

Note that the EOQ is not affected by the lead time constraint but will affect your operation in terms of when you will place your order.

Quantity Discounts. The next constraint to be relaxed is quantity discount. Quantity discounts are real everyday occurrences. Suppliers will offer discounts for any of a number of reasons including:

* Desire to move goods from overstocked shelves.
* Desire to minimize handling and associated costs.

That is, they wish to ship a quantity that does not involve breaking an original carton size.

As is the case with our model, the EOQ size may not be consistent with the amount necessary to receive a quantity discount. In this situation, you will need to employ a trial-and-error method and should be guided by total inventory cost in determining what quantity will be purchased.

Let'sgo back to the example: Annual demand for the product is 1,000, ordering costs are $2 per order and the cost to carry is $3 per unit. Assume the following quantity discount prices are offered:

Quantity (units)	Price/unit ($)
0 – 25	12.00
26 – 50	11.50
51 +	11.00

Note that the price/unit under the quantity discount must be converted to a cost to carry in order to utilize the EOQ formula. The conversion formula is:

$$\text{Cost to carry} = \frac{\text{inventory cost}}{\text{unit}} \times \frac{\text{percentage cost}}{\text{year}}$$

In the example, assume an inventory carrying cost percentage that is consistent with the Department of Commerce findings, which is 25 percent of the cost of inventory. Thus, in order to employ the EOQ model, you simply let C equal the product of 25 percent and the quantity discount price per unit. Solving for EOQ at each level of price in the quantity discount table will allow you to determine the following: (1) whether the EOQ will fit within the quantity discount parameters, and (2) which EOQ is the optimum when used in conjunction with the total inventory cost formula.

The calculation below is an illustration of the concept:

$$\text{EOQ (\$12.00)} = \sqrt{\frac{2 \times 1,000 \times 2}{.25 \times 12.00}} = 36.51 \text{ units}$$

$$\text{EOQ (\$11.50)} = \sqrt{\frac{2 \times 1,000 \times 2}{.25 \times 11.50}} = 37.30 \text{ units}$$

$$\text{EOQ (\$11.00)} = \sqrt{\frac{2 \times 1,000 \times 2}{.25 \times 11.00}} = 38.14 \text{ units}$$

As you can see, the first EOQ at $12.00 is not possible since 36.51 units lie outside of the 0–25 unit range offered. Therefore, we must discard this EOQ and try the next two. Note that the third EOQ, at $11.00, is also outside of the offered range. However, in this case we need to investigate the EOQ further since it lies outside of the range on the low side and not the high side. As a result, the effect of price might outweigh the effect of ordering and carrying. Next, we calculate the total inventory cost. To solve the total inventory cost for EOQ, at $11.00, we must set the EOQ equal to 51, which is the minimum amount that must be ordered at that price. Note the solved EOQ at $11.00 is equal to $38.14 which falls below the minimum order necessary to receive the $11.00 per unit discount price. See the calculations below.

For EOQ at $11.50:

$$\text{Total inventory cost} = \frac{38 \times .25 \times \$11.50}{2} + \frac{1,000 \times 3}{38} + (1,000 \times \$11.50)$$

Total inventory cost = $11,688.20

For EOQ at $11.00:

$$\text{Total inventory cost} = \frac{51 \times .25 \times \$11.00}{2} + \frac{1,000 \times 3}{51} + (1,000 \times \$11.00)$$

Total inventory cost = $11,128.95

As you can see, it pays to buy the higher quantity. Also, notice that the EOQ model gives an approximate answer in this situation, which you must then test further. In this example, you will purchase 51 units with each order since total inventory costs are minimized at this level.

Using Inventory at a Constant Rate. Of all of the constraints, this is the one which is most likely to be violated. There are two variables to consider:

* Fluctuation of demand
* Opportunity cost of lost sales

There are three approaches to factoring in these two variables:

* Given extreme fluctuation of demand and no opportunity cost of lost sales, you can establish an average level of demand and solve for EOQ accordingly.
* Given extremely high opportunity cost of lost sales and little or no fluctuation of demand, you can establish a safety stock equal in cost to the opportunity cost of lost sales.
* Given extreme fluctuation of demand and extremely high opportunity cost of lost sales, you can establish an average level of demand that provides a chosen degree of certainty of occurrence and set a safety stock equal in cost to the opportunity cost of lost sales.

Since the last approach is the most complex and encompasses all we wish to discuss, we will show you how it works. The first assumption takes into consideration fluctuation of demand. Our solution involves determining a level of demand that provides a chosen degree of certainty of occurrence. Therefore, the first step involves studying the daily sales for the item of interest over a period of time. As a rule, when we take a sufficiently large sample of daily sales to analyze demand, we can invoke the central limit theorem, which will allow us to assume that daily sales are normally distributed about some mean average. Based on this normal distribution, we can forecast demand with a degree of certainty expressed as a percentage. The result of this method is that we can arbitrarily select a daily sales figure and then estimate the likelihood that future daily sales will be less than or equal to the figure we selected.

For example: Assume annual sales of your product are 1,000 units and there are 250 selling days in the year. On an average, you sold 4 units per day. The next step is to determine the standard deviation, which is a measure of dispersion about the mean. The standard deviation is then used to calculate the variability of a normally distributed sample through a formula which produces a "Z score." For now, assume you have calculated the standard deviation, and it is two units per day. Essentially, you sold on an average four units per day. Actually, on some days you sold more than four units and on some days you sold less than four units. On an average, the range was plus or minus two units.

Given these three factors: (1) a normal distribution, (2) a mean, and (3) a standard deviation, we can arbitrarily select a daily sales figure in which we can be 90 percent, 95 percent, or even 99 percent certain that future daily sales will be equal to or less than the daily demand we have selected. The method for accomplishing this end involves a calculation which results in the Z score. Assuming that we want to be 95 percent certain of our forecast, we would make the following calculations:

Estimated daily demand = average daily demand + (Z score x standard deviation)

Estimated daily demand = 4 + (1.65 x 2)

Estimated daily demand = 7.3 units per day

Note: The Z score for 95 percent degree of certainty for this type of problem is 1.65. Most financial management, statistics, or calculus texts contain a table that will provide you with the necessary Z score.

This amount, 7.3 units per day, tells us that with a 95 percent degree of certainty, all daily sales will be less than or equal to 7.3 units per day. Another way of saying this is that daily sales will be larger that 7.3 units per day only 5 percent of the time. Based on this forecast, we can now estimate the safety stock level necessary to cover those times when we have underestimated demand.

Now let's look at opportunity cost of lost sales in more detail. In order to quantify the safety stock level, a relationship between the cost of carrying the safety stock and the cost of a stock-out must be established. That relationship is:

Stock-out cost = carrying cost of safety stock

The cost of carrying safety stock is simply the quantity of safety stock carried times the annual dollar cost of carrying inventory. The stock-out cost, however, is a different story. It is defined as:

Stock-out cost = (probability of possible stock-out) x (inventory cycles per year) x (stock-out units) x (unit stock-out cost)

In order to proceed with the solution of the level of safety stock required, the elements of the stock-out cost equation must be defined. These elements are:

Probability of Stock-out. This is the probability of a possible stock-out—that is, based on the distribution of daily usages and their probability, the percentage of stock outs that could possibly occur.

Inventory Cycles per Year. This is the annual demand (D) divided by the EOQ (Q).

Stock-out Units. This is the difference between the maximum daily usage during lead time and the order point without a safety stock.

Unit Stock-out Cost. This is the value of the "loss" estimated as a result of the failure to consummate the sale. It could be represented as lost profit or lost profit plus a penalty, or any other additional amount that may seem appropriate for loss of a sale.

Now let's employ these equations in our example and create a safety stock that meets our requirements. The following variables are presented:

* Annual usage is 1,000.
* Average daily usage is four.
* Lead time is a relatively constant eight days.
* EOQ based on the quantity discount of $11.00 is 51.
* Cost to carry inventory is $2.75 per unit per year (.25 x 11.00).
* Maximum average daily usage is 7.5.
* Company calculates the opportunity cost of lost sale at $3.00.
* Order point is 32 (8 days x 4 per day).
* Probability of a possible stock-out is .05 which was selected arbitrarily.

Now we are ready to calculate the safety stock for this set of circumstances.

Solution:

$$\text{Cost of carrying safety stock} = \text{carrying cost} \times SS$$

where SS stands for safety stock, or

$$\text{Cost of carrying safety stock} = \$2.75 \times SS$$

$$\text{Stock-out cost} = (\text{probability of a possible stock-out}) \times$$
$$(\text{inventory cycles per year}) \times$$
$$(\text{stock-out units}) \times (\text{unit stock-out cost})$$

First, solve for the value of stock-out units:

$$\text{Stock-out units} = (7.5 \times 8) - 32$$

$$\text{Stock-out units} = 28$$

Second, solve for stock-out cost:

$$\text{Stock-out cost} = .05 \times \frac{1,000}{51} \times 28 \times 3.00$$
$$\text{Stock-out cost} = 82.35$$

Third, set the cost of carrying safety stock equal to the stock-out cost and solve:

Cost of carrying safety stock = stock-out cost

$$2.75 \times SS = 82.35$$

or

$$SS = 29.9 \text{ units}$$

$$SS = 30 \text{ units}$$

The new order point, therefore, will be equal to the old order point plus the safety stock:

New order point = 32 + 30

New order point = 62

Note: The first order will be 62 and succeeding orders will be the EOQ quantity of 51.

This level of safety stock will keep the company supplied with adequate stock of inventory ninety-five percent of the time. Whenever inventory falls to 62 units, the company will automatically place an order for 51 units.

You must strike the proper balance between too much and too little inventory. You must balance the cost of carrying inventory against the cost of losing sales. Vigilance is the key word in the management of this important asset. The more you understand how inventory costs operate, the better your chances are in successfully managing this asset.

HOW TO VALUE YOUR INVENTORY

The method used to value inventory is important because it impacts directly on taxable income through cost of goods sold. IRS rules state that a new business may use any inventory method explained below if the method applies to the business and clearly reflects income.

A new business usually shows the inventory method selected by determining income under that method in the first income tax return filed for the period in which the business began.

Specific Identification

This method is used to identify items in an inventory with their costs by matching the item with the income. This method calls for identifying each item sold and each item in inventory. It is used where it is practical to physically separate the various purchases. It can be used in situations where a small number of costly, easily distinguishable items are purchased.

Average Cost

This method prices items on the basis of the average cost of all similar items available during the period. Methods of average cost computation are:

- Weighted-average method
- Moving-average method

See your accountant for further information on these computations.

First-in First-out

This method assumes that the first items purchased or produced are the first items sold. This means that the items in ending inventory are valued as the items most recently purchased or produced. Generally, if there is intermingling of the same type of goods in inventory so that they cannot be identified with specific invoices, either first-in first-out (FIFO) or last-in first-out (LIFO) must be used. One objective of FIFO is to follow an approximation of the physical flow of goods. An advantage of this method is that the ending inventory is stated in terms of approximate current cost. A disadvantage is that current costs are not matched against current revenues.

Last-in First-out

This method assumes that the last items of inventory are sold or removed from inventory first. This means that items included in ending inventory are considered to be those from the beginning inventory plus those items purchased in LIFO order. Note that this method allocates costs based on the assumption that the cost of the last goods purchased is matched against revenue first. When this method is used, inventory must be valued at cost regardless of its market value. To adapt the LIFO method, you are required to file IRS Form 970, "Application to Use LIFO Inventory Method", or a statement that has all the information required in Form 970. (See Exhibit 14-5.) The taxpayer must file the statement with a timely based filed tax return for the year in which LIFO is first used.

Furthermore, if LIFO is used for tax purposes, it generally must also be used in preparing annual financial statements for credit purposes or for the purpose of reports to stockholders, partners, or proprietors. For more information, see the regulations under section 472 of the Internal Revenue Code.

Note: You must include in the cost of inventory:

- Direct costs of inventoriable property
- Proper share of most indirect costs (including taxes) allocable to such property

FIFO and LIFO produce different income results depending on price level trends. During inflationary times, LIFO will produce a larger cost of goods sold and a lower ending inventory. FIFO will produce a lower cost of goods sold and a higher ending inventory. During a falling price level, the results will be reversed.

The example below illustrates the results of computing costs of goods sold under both FIFO and LIFO.

Example:

Beginning inventory	1,000 units
Made up of	
500 units bought in 1982 at $1.00	
500 units bought in 1984 at $1.50	
Purchases during current year	500 units
200 units bought in March at $2.00	
300 units bought in August at $3.00	
Ending inventory	250 units
Current year sales	1,250 units

		FIFO	LIFO
Sales		$ 3,300	$3,300
Less: cost of goods sold			
Beginning inventory			
500 units @ $1.00	$500		
500 units @ $1.50	750	1250	1250
Add: purchases			
200 units @ $2.00	400		
300 units @ $3.00	900	1300	1300
Good available for sale		2,550	2,550
Less:ending inventory (1,500-1,250=250)			
250 units @ $3.00		750	
250 units @ $1.00		—	250
Cost of goods sold		1,800	2,300
Gross profit		1,500	1,000
Less: operating expenses		1,000	1,000
Net income before taxes		500	—
Income taxes		123	—
Net income after taxes		$377	$—

HOW TO ESTIMATE ENDING INVENTORY

Why Is It Necessary ?

On occasion it may be necessary to estimate the amount of ending inventory. For example:

* To determine inventory amounts for interim financial reporting.
* To test inventory for reasonableness when cost was derived by some other method.
* To determine inventory amounts where inventory and inventory records were destroyed.

Gross Profit Method

The gross profit method estimates the value of inventory by assuming an average gross profit percentage earned on sales. The average gross profit percentage may be based on either prior years' experience or on current markup.

This method makes the following assumptions:

• Total goods available = beginning inventory + purchases
• Goods not sold are on hand
• Ending inventory = goods available - sales reduced to cost

For example, assume an average gross profit of 40 percent, then:

Sales		$ 100,000
Gross profit (40% of $100,000)		40,000
Cost of goods sold		60,000
Beginning inventory	$20,000	
Purchases	50,000	
Goods available for sale		70,000
Ending inventory at cost		$10,000

Note: Several cautions should be observed when using the gross profit method. These include:

* This method provides an estimate; therefore, a physical inventory should be taken at least once a year to verify the amount.
* Care should be exercised in applying a blanket gross profit rate. Note that a change in either the quantity of one line of merchandise relative to another or in the markup of one line can lead to an inaccurate ending inventory estimate.
* If past gross profit percentages are used, the accountant should adjust the percentages as appropriate to reflect the current rate.
* This method is not normally acceptable for financial reporting purposes or for tax purposes.

Retail Method

The retail method estimates the value of inventory by ascertaining the ratios between costs and selling prices of purchases, including the beginning inventory, and applying this percentage to net sales to obtain cost of goods sold. Markups, markdowns, and revisions of both also enter into the computation. This method is used by department and other retail stores.

This method requires records to be kept of: (1) total cost and retail value of goods purchased, (2) total cost and retail value of goods available for sale, and (3) period sales.

The cost and retail price of goods available for sale are used to calculate a cost–price ratio. This ratio is then used to convert the retail price of ending inventory to approximate cost.

Assume a cost–price ratio of 70 percent, then:

Example 1:

Beginning inventory		$ 23,500
Add: Net purchases	$97,250	
Markups	6,000	
Markdown cancellations	3,500	106,750
Deduct: Net sales	94,250	
Markup cancellations	1,500	
Markdowns	8,000	103,750
Ending inventory		$26,500

Example 2:

	Cost	Retail
Beginning inventory	7,000	10,000
Purchases	31,500	45,000
Goods available	$ 38,500	55,000
Deduct: Net sales		(42,500)
Ending inventory at retail		$12,500
Ratio of cost to retail ($38,500 - 55,000)		70%
Ending inventory at cost (70% x $12,500)		$8,750

Because retail method uses an average cost-price ratio, its applicability is based on two assumptions:

* The markup percentage remains constant during the year.
* The ending inventory consists of the types and proportions of goods available during the year.

Uses of this method include:

• Computing net income without a physical count

• Determining inventory shortages

• Regulating quantities of merchandise on hand

• Determining information needed for insurance purposes

The retail method has the blessing of the accounting profession, Internal Revenue Service, and various retail associations.

See your accountant for further considerations of the retail method including LIFO retail, LIFO retail stable prices, and dollar value LIFO retail fluctuating prices. Other items to consider include freight-in, purchase returns and allowances, purchase discounts, sales returns and allowances, sales discounts, transfers-in, "normal" shortages, "abnormal" shortages, and employee discounts.

USING TRADE CREDIT TO YOUR ADVANTAGE

Trade credit is defined as the offering of payment terms by the seller such that payment is not due at time of delivery.

The seller who is extending trade credit is essentially "lending" to its buyer an amount equal to the invoice amount. The buyer, therefore, has use of the goods or service for some defined period of time prior to payment. The seller is also assuming a risk-and-loss potential through the extension of this credit. Trade credit is practical and serves as an incentive to buy.

The operative portion of trade credit is the terms under which the credit is offered and the goods are shipped. These terms can vary from very strict, such as cash before delivery, to very lenient, such as net 90 days. If you are a small player, there is not much you can do to change these terms and you will have to work with them. Since trade credit can represent up to 40 percent of your current liabilities, keeping your trade creditors happy is an essential element in doing business. There will be times, however, when cash flow delays will necessitate delaying payments to suppliers until your cash inflows match required cash outflows. In general, suppliers are sensitive to industry trends and will bend somewhat to help good customers. The use of trade credit to ease company cash flow problems is known as "stretching payables."

At the other extreme, your suppliers may offer terms that will motivate you to pay early. As a matter of fact, some companies will expect to receive payment by the tenth day while others will accept payment that has been mailed by the tenth day. Be sure to clarify what your supplier expects. Furthermore, most companies will not provide a discount for the freight portion of the bill. If you choose to pay after ten days, however, you will pay the full invoice amount and this must be done by the thirtieth day after the invoice date. For instance, say the supplier has offered you terms of 2/10 net 30. What is he or she saying? These terms mean that if you pay the invoice within 10 days of invoice date, you may deduct 2% from the invoice amount.

The example shows how the discount works. The facts are as follows:

* Goods are invoiced to you at $5,000
* Freight cost for this invoice is $25
* The terms of the transaction are 2/10 net 30

Example:

If you pay by the tenth day after invoice date, the remittance would be:

$$\begin{array}{ll} \$5,000 \times .98 = & \$4,900 \\ \text{Freight} & \underline{\quad 25} \\ \text{You pay} & \$4,925 \end{array}$$

If you pay after the tenth day after invoice date, the remittance would be $5,025.

As you can readily see, by taking the discount you can save $100 on the cost of the cost of your inventory. Of course, you could probably say "If I pay early the money has to come from somewhere." That certainly is correct. The monies may need to come from the cash account or from borrowings. If you borrow the money to pay the discount, you will have to pay interest. If you withdraw cash from the cash account, you will have to forego other investment opportunities. To determine whether you should take the discount, it is necessary to perform a cost-benefit analysis. First, you will need to determine the interest rate to borrow funds. Second, you will need to determine the cost of not taking the discount.

The formula you can use, which converts a discount into an annual percentage, is:

$$X = \frac{D}{1-D} \times \frac{365}{t}$$

where:

X = Cost of credit expressed as an annual percentage if discount not taken

D = Cash discount as a decimal

t = The number of days earlier you must pay to get the discount. In this case 20 days (30 - 10).

$$X = \frac{.02}{1-.02} \times \frac{365}{20}$$

$$X = 37.24\%$$

This is an astounding annual interest rate. Banks do not charge that much. Moreover, if you are going to withdraw cash from your cash account, your savings by taking the discount represents a return of 37.24 percent. Therefore, any investment you may be considering, and thereby foregoing the discount, would have to give you a return of 37.24 percent or greater. The cost benefit is clear in this case.

Trade credit is a fragile relationship. Great care should be taken to cultivate major suppliers and keep them apprised of your needs. They are your "bank" for related trade transactions. When possible, take the discount because it can mean large dollar savings. Also, use trade credit to help out in those slow periods when cash flows do not measure up to your needs. Finally, in all cases, use trade credit wisely.

IMPORTANCE OF THE BREAKEVEN POINT

One of the cardinal rules of business is that an endeavor should create profit or else it should be abandoned. To determine the viability of an enterprise, you must gather all the salient facts about costs and evaluate those costs in light of your projected sales revenues. By performing this analysis, known as breakeven analysis, you can determine whether or not a viable quantity–price relationship exists, and if so, what quantity–price combination will satisfy your minimum requirement that revenues at least equal costs.

To accomplish this goal, you need to learn the various elements of the breakeven equation:

P = Price The price at which a unit of product will be sold. This is generally the unknown, however, it can be established and then used to solve for other variables.

Q = Quantity This is the amount in units that needs to be sold to generate revenues sufficient to cover various costs. This quantity must have the same unit measurement as price. That is, you can deal in gross, individual units, hundredweights, etc. but you must be consistent.

F = Fixed Costs Those costs are present regardless of whether or not you produce one unit or one thousand. Note that the fixed costs are fixed only to some maximum level of quantity (Q) production. When that level is exceeded, you must increase F. For example, you can build 1000 widgets per year in a 10,000 square-foot plant, but to build 1001 widgets you need to expand. Thus, F increases. Fixed costs include items such as rent, heat, lighting, insurance, administrative salaries, indirect labor expense, and the cost of machinery.

V = Variable These costs are associated with each unit of production in a direct one-to-one relationship. These costs are incurred only when the item is produced. Variable costs typically include direct labor expense, raw material expense and sales commissions.

PF = Profit This is the reason you are in business. When you solve for the breakeven level of sales, profit is equal to zero.

Now that all the elements of the breakeven equation have been defined, let's proceed with the equation itself. The basic equation in verbal form is:

Profit = sales revenue - fixed costs - total variable costs

At this point, further equations are necessary:

Sales revenue = (quantity sold) x (price per unit)

or

Sales revenue = QP
Total variable costs = (quantity sold) x (variable cost per unit)

or

Total variable costs = QV

You are now ready to state the breakeven equation in its general abbreviated form:

PF = QP - F - QV

You will recall that the breakeven point of sales occurs when revenues equal total costs. Our general equation, however, has a term for profit. We inserted profit to allow you flexibility in determining a level of sales required to provide you with a desired amount of profit. At this point, however, let's adjust the general breakeven equation to solve for a breakeven pricing level. Since the breakeven level of sales is that point at which revenues just equal total costs, it is, also, the point at which profit equals zero. Therefore, our general equation now looks like this:

0 = PF = QP - F - QV

or

0 = QP - F - QV

Solving the equation for P, we get:

$$P = \frac{F + QV}{Q}$$

Note: We can also solve the equation for Q:

$$Q = \frac{F}{P - V}$$

The following graph presents the entire concept of breakeven analysis. The three lines are labeled as follows:

F	=	fixed cost to produce Q units
TC	=	total cost to produce Q units
R	=	sales revenue generated by selling Q units

The point labeled B is the breakeven level of sales. Above point B, your business will make a profit equal to the distance between line R and line TC. Below point B the firm suffers a loss equal to the distance between line TC and line R.

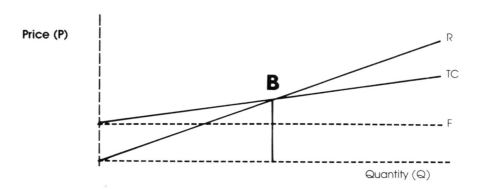

Let's take a look at four examples of the use of breakeven analysis.

Example 1:

Assume your business can sell everything it produces and that it produces at maximum capacity, which is 100,000 units per year. Fixed costs for your business are $500,000 per year and variable costs are $3.00 per unit. This is a relatively high fixed cost business.

Question: If your business produces and sells at maximum output, what is the breakeven price?

Solution: Because you are looking for breakeven price, you employ the breakeven equation solved for price:

$$P = \frac{F + QV}{Q}$$

where: F = $500,000
Q = 100,000
V = $3

Therefore:

$$P = \frac{500,000 + 100,000(3)}{100,000}$$

$$P = \$8.00 \text{ per unit}$$

At $8.00 per unit, your business will just cover fixed and total variable costs.

Example 2:

Assume the same set of circumstances as in Example 1, however, each unit is sold at $9.25 per unit.

Question: What is the breakeven quantity at this price level?

Solution: Because you are looking for the breakeven quantity, you need to employ the second form of the breakeven equation solving for quantity:

$$Q = \frac{F}{P - V}$$

where:

$$F = \$500,000$$
$$P = \$9.25$$
$$V = \$3.00$$

Therefore:

$$Q = \frac{500,000}{9.25 - 3}$$

$$Q = 80,000 \text{ units}$$

At a price of $9.25 per unit, your business can operate at below maximum capacity and still break even.

If your business operates at full capacity or 100,000 units and sells all these units, will it make a profit? Yes, since, by definition, any sales above the breakeven point will cause your business to earn a profit. The amount of the profit is a function of the relationship known as the *contribution margin*. The contribution margin is defined as the difference between the price per unit and its variable cost per unit. In this example, the contribution margin is $6.25 ($9.25 -$3.00). Thus, for every unit above the breakeven point, your business earns $6.25 of profit. This relationship simply relates the fact that all of your fixed overhead is absorbed at the breakeven point.

Example 3:

Assume the same set of circumstances as Example 1, however, your goal is to earn a profit of $100,000 when your business is operating at full capacity.

Question: What is the price you must charge?

Solution: This variation assumes profit is not equal to zero as it was in Examples 1 and 2. In fact, profit is $100,000 and you must go back to the general formula in order to solve this equation:

$$PF = QP - F - QV$$

Solve the equation for P:

$$P = \frac{PF + F + QV}{Q}$$

where:

$$F = \$500,000$$
$$PF = \$100,000$$
$$Q = 100,000$$
$$V = \$3.00$$

Therefore:

$$P = \frac{100,000 + 500,000 + 100,000(3)}{100,000}$$

P = $9.00 per unit

Example 4:

Let's take a look at a slightly different set of circumstances. The examples above deal with a high level of fixed cost. We will now look at a low fixed cost structure. Assume that fixed costs per year are $50,000; variable costs are $.25 per unit; and sales are estimated to be 10,000,000 units per year.

Question: What price must you charge to breakeven?

Solution: Because you are looking for the breakeven price per unit, you will use the first form of the breakeven equation and solve for price:

$$P = \frac{F + QV}{Q}$$

where:

$$F = \$50,000$$
$$Q = 10,000,000$$
$$V = \$.25$$

Therefore:

$$P = \frac{50,000 + 10,000,000(.25)}{10,000,000}$$
$$P = \$.255 \text{ per unit}$$

As you can see, at a price equal to $.255 per unit, the markup necessary to cover your fixed costs is slight because of the enormous volume of sales. Should you wish to perform "what if" situations, you need only change one or more of the variables and solve the equation.

The use of breakeven analysis provides you with a great deal of latitude in the analysis of your pricing strategy. It allows you to manipulate many variations or combinations of variables to ascertain levels of production/sales, levels of cost, or levels of price necessary to make a desired profit. It will give you that all important point above which you will create profit and below which you will suffer losses. Knowledge of where this point is located can be extremely important to the entrepreneur in the pursuit of his or her market. It will identify products that are profitable to produce and those that need to be returned.

Note that although the primary examples have been of a manufacturing company, the breakeven method will work just as well for wholesalers and retailers. You need only define the appropriate terms, which are fixed costs, variable costs, and selling price or quantity, in order to arrive at the unknown of interest.

We believe that the calculation of fixed and variable costs should be a simple task for the entrepreneur. The key unknown will often be the quantity sold/produced. In constructing your marketing plan, you will want to project or forecast the demand for your product or service at various levels of price. This all important forecast will provide you with a quantity which can then be used to test your price and vice versa.

HOW TO EVALUATE YOUR COMPETITION

Rarely will you have the luxury of operating in an economic vacuum. Recognizing that there are other competitors in the market will allow you to adjust your product/service or your approach to avoid head-on competition, or at the very least, avoid some of the intense heat of competition.

Types of Competitive Environments

There are four types of market situations in which your business can fall:

Monopoly—a firm makes a product or service that has no close substitutes. In certain instances, the barrier that keeps other potential competitors from entering into the market can be perfectly legal, such as a patent or copyright. If you are recreating a new product you may be able to get government protection which will allow you to establish a monopoly.

Oligopoly—only a few competitors control the supply of the product/service. Most often, oligopolies emerge because only a few firms have the special technical skills to produce or sell a certain product/service.

Monopolistic Competition—many competitors sell virtually the same product/service yet one or two firms are able to firmly embed the image of their product/service in the buyers' mind to such an extent that buyers will not substitute. Firms strive to be in this enviable position through a combination of trademarks, design, advertising, image, etc. For instance, there are many bluejeans but only one Levi's; there are many tissues but only one Kleenex; there are many photocopiers but only one Xerox.

Pure Competition—there are many competitors, all of which are selling virtually the same product/service yet none of them can significantly influence the price or supply.

Factor to Consider in Evaluating Your Competition

The best environment for your business is to have a monopoly on the product/service that you sell. Unfortunately that rarely happens. Instead, the normal course of events is that you produce a better product/service, it then becomes successful and attracts competition. In anticipation of this eventuality, your best approach is to methodically analyze each competitor. In essence, you want to know where you stand in relation to everyone else so that you can position your product/service in a way that will be perceived by the segment of the market as best fulfilling its needs. The following table can help you in assessing your competition.

	DEGREE OF COMPETITION		
	High	Medium	Low
Competitor's Name:			
Product			
Quality			
Features			
Options			
Style			
Packaging			
Sizes			
Services			
Warranties			
Returns			
Price			
List price			
Discounts			
Allowances			
Payment period			
Credit terms			
Promotion			
Advertising			
Personal selling			
Sales promotion			
Publicity			
Distribution			
Locations			
Delivery			
Amount of			
Inventory			

HOW TO SELECT AND TRAIN PERSONNEL

Sources of Employees

There are two sources from which you can draw prospective employees: internal and external.
Internal sources can be used by businesses that are already established. However, if you are starting your own business you will not be able to hire from within. You will need to seek outside sources. The list of sources below will aid you in finding prospective employees for your business:

- Colleges and universities
- Technical schools
- Professional organizations
- Religious organizations
- Newspaper advertising
- Specialized employment agencies
- Temporary help

How To Determine Whether the Prospective Employee Is Right for the Job

There is a three-step procedure that many employers use:

Step One: You should determine which skills are necessary to do the job well. A basic business assessment table follows:

Skill	Critical	DEGREE OF IMPORTANCE	
		Helpful	Not Necessary
Technical expertise			
Accurate/detail oriented			
Communicates effectively			
Cooperates with others			
Works without supervision			
Maintains good relations with customers			
Performs under pressure			
Motivates others to perform			

Each job may be different and therefore requires a different set of skills. Thus, it is incumbent upon you, as the entrepreneur, to think about which skills are necessary to do the job and then list those skills so that you will have a guide to follow when you analyze prospective employees.

Step Two: Interview each prospective employee. Your interview process should begin by assessing the basics. Your goal is to screen out the obvious misfit: Is the person unkempt, or lacking serious interest in the job or the opportunity that it provides, or physically unable to do the job? However, you must be careful not to ask the types of questions that will violate the law. Most states have enacted a comprehensive set of laws that protect job applicants from employment discrimination. For instance, in California, statutory law limits certain types of inquiries made by the employer. The statute is Government Code section 12940(d) and it expressly prohibits the following:

> Any nonjob-related inquiry, either verbal or through the use of an application form, which expresses, directly or indirectly, any limitation, specification, or discrimination as to race, religious creed, color, national origin, ancestry, physical handicap, medical condition, marital status or sex, or any interest to make such limitation, specification or discrimination.

Moreover, inquiries about arrests or detentions that did not result in convictions, other than an arrest for which the prospective employee is out on bail on his or her own recognizance pending trial are, with a few exceptions, prohibited. So are a host of other type questions. Below is a list of some of the questions you should not ask job applicants until you have spoken with your lawyer:

* Maiden name
* Whether an applicant owns or rents his or her home
* Any question that tends to identify applicants over the age of forty
* Language commonly spoken by applicant
* Nationality, lineage, ancestry, national origin, descent, or parentage of applicant, applicant's parents, or spouse
* How applicant acquired ability to read, write, or speak a foreign language
* Number and /or ages of children or dependents
* Provisions for child care
* Any questions regarding birth control
* Applicant's race, complexion, color of skin, eyes, hair
* Applicant's religion or religious days observed
* Questions concerning physical disabilities or handicaps
* Military service and type of discharge
* List of organizations, clubs, societies, or lodges to which applicant belongs
* Applicant's current or past assets, liabilities, or credit rating, including bankruptcy or garnishment

Step Three: Next, you should assess an individual's past performance. This is the step in which you examine education, training records, technical background, and experience. This data is available from the application form that you had the prospective employee complete or from work records, military records and similar sources.

Step Four: Your last step is to verify the data that was presented to you by the prospective employee. The two most effective references are academic transcripts and previous employers.

Academic Transcripts—Many firms request transcripts to determine whether the individual successfully passed the courses or attended the schools claimed on the application. In addition, transcripts may be useful as a predictor of success for individuals going into a specialized job.

Previous Employers—Ideally, you want to get a measure of a person's ability to get along with others, productivity, reliability, etc. Work references can be an invaluable source of this kind of information. However, this reference check my be difficult to accomplish. A growing number of prospective employers have found that former employers will not give out any information about former workers for fear of being sued for defamation.

This fear has been exacerbated by a series of court cases, the most far reaching from the Minnesota Supreme Court: *Lewis* v. *Equitable Life Assurance Society*. The case concerned four women who worked as dental claim approvers. They were told by the company that their expense account reports were inflated. The women disputed the company's assertion and claimed that the expenses were accurate and incurred in the good faith performance of their job. Nonetheless, the four women paid the company the amounts in dispute, which totaled $400, but did so under protest. The company subsequently fired all four of them for "gross insubordination." The court, which decided the case in July 1986, stated that employees fired on false charges of bad conduct can sue their former employers for defamation even if it was the workers themselves who revealed the charges to prospective employers. The court reasoned that the former employer should have known the former workers would be forced to disclose the reasons for their termination when they applied for new jobs. The four women were initially awarded $1 million in damages, but the state supreme court lowered it to $575,000.

Training Employees

There may be a variety of subject matter in which you want your employees trained, such as job skills, safety, orientation to your policies, etc.

Following is a brief description of the various techniques organizations use to train their employees.

Apprenticeship Training—This represents a combination of classroom theory and supervised work experience, in which the ratio is usually fifteen hours of supervised work experience for every hour of classroom theory. The concept of apprenticeship training usually goes hand in hand with those types of jobs that demand certain specialized skills that can only be obtained through a long period of practice and experience.

On-the-Job Training (OJT)—This type of training is the most common method used by employers. There is no class theory. The employee immediately begins the job after some brief instructions, and the supervisor watches and provides guidance as the job is being performed. The advantage to this method is the employee begins to produce immediately while learning how to perform the job.

Simulated Work Conditions—Sometimes OJT is not effective because the type of work that is demanded from employees does not allow an inexperienced individual to quickly learn the necessary skills without substantially disrupting the workflow. Instead, the work environment is simulated: the employee learns the necessary skills while production continues uninterrupted.

Classroom Instruction—The theory behind this approach is that many times complicated information cannot be effectively assimilated on the job because there are too many distractions and interruptions. This learning must occur, however, if successful job performance is to be realized. As a result, employees are placed into a classroom where they are allowed to concentrate on information presented to them. The concept of classroom instruction in the business environment is becoming more popular. Many organizations now have training classrooms in which to teach employees processes and techniques that will increase productivity.

Chapter 14 Exhibits

Exhibit 14.1   Census Tracts: San Diego SMSA (Race and
Spanish Origin)

Exhibit 14.2   Census Tracts: San Diego SMSA (General
Characteristics of Spanish Origin Persons)

Exhibit 14.3   Census Tracts: San Diego SMSA (General
Characteristics of Spanish Origin Persons)

Exhibit 14.4* Robert Morris Associations
Wholesalers–Hardware and Paints

Exhibit 14.5   Application to Use Lifo Inventory Method
(IRS Form 970)

*Interpretation of Statement Studies Figures

RMA cautions that the studies be regarded only as a general guideline and not as an absolute industry norm. This is due to limited samples within categories, the categorization of companies by their primary Standard Industrial Classification (SIC) number only, and different methods of operations by companies within the same industry. For these reasons, RMA recommends that the figures be used only as general guidelines in addition to other methods of financial analysis.

Table P-7. Race and Spanish Origin: 1980

[For meaning of symbols, see Introduction. For definitions of terms, see appendixes A and B]

Census Tracts

	The SMSA	San Diego County									
		Total	Cardiff-by-the-Sea (CDP)	Carlsbad city	Casa de Oro-Mount Helix (CDP)	Castle Park-Otay (CDP)	Chula Vista city	Coronado city	El Cajon city	Encinitas (CDP)	Escondido city
RACE											
Total persons	1 861 846	1 861 846	10 054	35 490	19 651	21 049	83 927	16 859	73 892	10 796	64 355
White	1 514 006	1 514 006	9 182	31 881	18 682	15 440	69 086	15 703	68 992	9 749	57 721
Black	104 452	104 452	29	232	245	781	1 678	314	749	30	276
American Indian, Eskimo, and Aleut	14 616	14 616	66	150	65	144	542	73	600	55	712
American Indian	14 355	14 355	65	145	65	143	527	72	590	51	706
Eskimo	115	115	–	2	–	–	8	–	6	3	2
Aleut	146	146	1	3	–	1	7	1	4	1	4
Asian and Pacific Islander[1]	89 861	89 861	199	810	215	1 085	5 075	459	1 092	300	1 165
Japanese	12 410	12 410	90	244	70	258	996	58	195	118	213
Chinese	7 800	7 800	43	211	33	54	251	57	193	66	134
Filipino	48 658	48 658	38	120	60	578	2 977	285	249	28	242
Korean	2 394	2 394	8	44	3	51	156	10	32	21	73
Asian Indian	1 831	1 831	12	66	6	9	54	13	61	25	68
Vietnamese	7 307	7 307	1	49	20	40	126	5	209	31	310
Hawaiian	2 464	2 464	6	34	3	30	112	10	51	10	41
Guamanian	4 190	4 190	–	3	15	57	308	16	82	–	70
Samoan	2 807	2 807	1	39	5	8	95	5	20	1	14
Other	138 911	138 911	578	2 417	444	3 599	7 546	310	2 459	662	4 481
SPANISH ORIGIN[2]											
Persons of Spanish origin	275 177	275 177	1 181	4 790	1 060	8 637	19 624	782	5 862	1 340	9 378
Mexican	227 943	227 943	986	4 195	792	7 926	16 987	492	4 424	1 212	8 256
Puerto Rican	6 007	6 007	19	60	26	65	310	40	159	10	135
Cuban	1 531	1 531	7	5	10	10	72	8	60	11	27
Other Spanish	39 696	39 696	169	530	232	636	2 255	242	1 219	107	960
Persons of Spanish origin	275 177	275 177	1 181	4 790	1 060	8 637	19 624	782	5 862	1 340	9 378
White	139 357	139 357	633	2 431	708	4 960	11 954	529	3 622	689	4 917
Black	2 287	2 287	1	19	–	40	61	8	24	1	13
Other races	133 533	133 533	547	2 340	352	3 637	7 609	245	2 216	650	4 448

Census Tracts

	San Diego County—Con.												
	Fallbrook (CDP)	Imperial Beach city	Lakeside (CDP)	La Mesa city	Lemon Grove city	National City city	Oceanside city	Poway (CDP)	San Diego city	San Marcos city	Santee (CDP)	Solana Beach (CDP)	Spring Valley (CDP)
RACE													
Total persons	14 041	22 689	23 921	50 308	20 780	48 772	76 698	32 263	875 538	17 479	47 080	13 047	40 191
White	11 880	18 058	22 899	47 018	17 808	27 922	58 157	30 019	666 863	15 915	44 129	11 767	33 802
Black	114	658	62	890	985	4 375	5 759	412	77 700	77	355	41	1 751
American Indian, Eskimo, and Aleut	90	239	214	270	144	375	672	209	5 065	131	374	37	304
American Indian	88	227	214	267	141	372	664	209	4 923	131	364	36	300
Eskimo	–	7	–	–	–	1	5	–	63	–	5	–	1
Aleut	2	5	–	3	3	2	3	–	79	–	5	1	3
Asian and Pacific Islander[1]	174	1 601	223	799	624	6 042	3 717	929	57 207	287	701	258	2 067
Japanese	57	246	52	210	163	340	849	210	6 099	75	148	95	283
Chinese	22	54	16	129	58	82	198	117	5 343	20	72	116	127
Filipino	39	1 075	70	166	231	4 725	1 041	414	33 084	75	256	13	1 255
Korean	15	21	15	34	11	62	100	38	1 449	6	31	3	26
Asian Indian	6	6	8	55	5	22	67	48	1 046	28	17	22	18
Vietnamese	7	102	13	104	18	75	193	21	5 536	49	52	2	62
Hawaiian	21	46	31	35	25	82	249	48	1 189	11	75	4	226
Guamanian	7	40	16	59	96	453	141	24	2 297	16	40	1	37
Samoan	–	11	2	7	17	201	879	9	1 164	7	10	2	37
Other	1 783	2 133	523	1 331	1 219	10 058	8 393	694	68 703	1 069	1 521	944	2 267
SPANISH ORIGIN[2]													
Persons of Spanish origin	2 837	4 831	1 645	3 177	2 909	18 708	14 118	1 686	130 613	2 233	3 448	1 545	5 367
Mexican	2 607	4 065	1 243	2 276	2 369	16 322	11 885	1 171	106 274	1 965	2 518	1 375	4 150
Puerto Rican	28	95	16	70	65	387	527	58	2 943	24	120	11	124
Cuban	3	18	7	30	18	45	61	18	887	7	9	16	37
Other Spanish	199	653	379	801	457	1 954	1 645	439	20 509	237	801	143	1 056
Persons of Spanish origin	2 837	4 831	1 645	3 177	2 909	18 708	14 118	1 686	130 613	2 233	3 448	1 545	5 367
White	1 088	2 713	1 161	2 053	1 708	8 242	5 647	1 057	64 903	1 201	2 086	611	2 985
Black	1	21	4	6	22	137	161	7	1 513	1	6	10	45
Other races	1 748	2 097	480	1 118	1 179	10 329	8 310	622	64 197	1 031	1 356	924	2 337

[1]Excludes ''Other Asian and Pacific Islander'' groups identified in sample tabulations.
[2]Persons of Spanish origin may be of any race.

Exhibit 14-1

[For meaning of symbols, see Introduction. For definitions of terms, see appendixes A and B]

Census Tracts [400 or More Spanish Origin Persons]	The SMSA	San Diego County									
		Total	Cardiff-by-the-Sea (CDP)	Carlsbad city	Casa de Oro-Mount Helix (CDP)	Castle Park-Otay (CDP)	Chula Vista city	Coronado city	El Cajon city	Encinitas (CDP)	Escondido city
AGE											
Total persons	275 177	275 177	1 181	4 790	1 060	8 637	19 624	782	5 862	1 340	9 378
Under 5 years	31 601	31 601	109	515	80	1 025	2 053	60	737	131	1 238
5 to 9 years	28 851	28 851	112	378	101	917	2 097	51	587	118	1 057
10 to 14 years	27 088	27 088	116	367	121	819	2 121	41	526	119	953
15 to 19 years	32 406	32 406	134	539	151	951	2 233	64	685	160	1 143
20 to 24 years	36 030	36 030	159	709	92	1 104	2 092	144	823	202	1 164
25 to 34 years	48 013	48 013	227	913	148	1 431	3 320	164	980	245	1 575
35 to 44 years	27 226	27 226	121	484	151	806	2 182	82	598	146	933
45 to 54 years	20 704	20 704	96	411	119	714	1 723	71	408	106	597
55 to 64 years	12 956	12 956	63	278	65	463	1 035	62	272	60	370
65 to 74 years	6 705	6 705	25	129	18	262	500	30	157	40	232
75 years and over	3 597	3 597	19	67	14	145	268	13	89	13	116
3 and 4 years	11 924	11 924	46	181	32	381	747	21	286	54	486
16 years and over	181 948	181 948	819	3 450	728	5 707	12 948	619	3 881	941	5 914
18 years and over	169 826	169 826	768	3 251	659	5 304	12 032	602	3 631	873	5 485
21 years and over	147 380	147 380	672	2 837	589	4 690	10 686	539	3 169	771	4 743
60 years and over	15 424	15 424	72	297	55	598	1 176	68	351	80	478
62 years and over	13 086	13 086	63	260	43	521	985	57	304	65	414
Median	22.3	22.3	23.4	24.1	24.3	22.6	23.1	26.5	22.4	23.4	21.2
Female	135 307	135 307	586	2 164	544	4 479	10 300	363	3 031	620	4 591
Under 5 years	15 629	15 629	58	248	42	509	993	28	373	69	594
5 to 9 years	14 194	14 194	62	201	47	449	1 025	26	267	60	479
10 to 14 years	13 521	13 521	54	178	59	433	1 072	24	264	55	494
15 to 19 years	14 823	14 823	65	228	78	465	1 120	33	364	61	557
20 to 24 years	15 653	15 653	72	276	40	557	1 103	42	402	74	553
25 to 34 years	23 266	23 266	108	375	83	704	1 799	73	494	119	753
35 to 44 years	14 375	14 375	63	213	81	456	1 197	36	334	72	499
45 to 54 years	10 910	10 910	52	198	68	406	950	36	226	54	292
55 to 64 years	6 839	6 839	30	134	29	249	562	39	152	28	182
65 to 74 years	3 901	3 901	10	74	10	166	303	18	101	22	121
75 years and over	2 196	2 196	12	39	7	85	176	8	54	6	67
3 and 4 years	5 941	5 941	22	87	19	176	373	11	137	26	233
16 years and over	89 124	89 124	398	1 491	380	3 004	7 027	280	2 057	427	2 914
18 years and over	83 375	83 375	376	1 404	345	2 803	6 553	270	1 921	399	2 706
21 years and over	73 821	73 821	334	1 252	311	2 500	5 850	241	1 684	356	2 347
60 years and over	8 853	8 853	36	171	26	363	705	45	208	44	255
62 years and over	7 605	7 605	32	149	20	316	603	37	182	34	219
Median	22.9	22.9	23.5	24.0	25.9	23.3	24.2	28.4	23.0	24.2	21.5
HOUSEHOLD TYPE AND RELATIONSHIP											
Total persons	275 177	275 177	1 181	4 790	1 060	8 637	19 624	782	5 862	1 340	9 378
In households	260 712	260 712	1 116	4 127	1 058	8 634	19 582	666	5 801	1 247	9 176
Householder	69 549	69 549	285	1 164	241	2 317	5 212	238	1 726	318	2 372
Family householder	55 844	55 844	213	919	204	1 931	4 327	147	1 315	252	1 965
Nonfamily householder	13 705	13 705	72	245	37	386	885	91	411	66	407
Living alone	9 809	9 809	43	169	22	306	693	73	275	37	278
Spouse	45 789	45 789	175	774	218	1 526	3 754	135	1 032	206	1 561
Other relatives	133 362	133 362	547	1 932	521	4 567	10 046	243	2 718	626	4 761
Nonrelatives	12 012	12 012	109	257	78	224	570	50	325	97	482
Inmate of institution	1 539	1 539	–	–	2	3	37	–	55	2	6
Other, in group quarters	12 926	12 926	65	663	–	–	5	116	6	91	196
Persons per household	3.50	3.50	3.65	3.34	3.45	3.58	3.47	2.46	3.07	3.74	3.69
Persons per family	3.93	3.93	4.09	3.73	3.77	3.99	3.86	3.12	3.50	4.10	4.03
Persons 65 years and over	10 302	10 302	44	196	32	407	768	43	246	53	348
In households	10 013	10 013	44	192	32	407	756	43	213	50	341
Householder	5 851	5 851	21	122	11	232	411	32	130	31	212
Nonfamily householder	2 322	2 322	7	50	2	72	170	17	66	9	70
Living alone	2 180	2 180	7	46	2	65	161	16	61	9	64
Spouse	1 866	1 866	9	41	9	73	134	7	43	10	65
Other relatives	2 021	2 021	10	26	8	92	193	3	37	9	54
Nonrelatives	275	275	4	3	4	10	18	1	3	1	10
Inmate of institution	207	207	–	–	–	–	12	–	33	2	4
Other, in group quarters	82	82	–	4	–	–	–	–	–	1	3
FAMILY TYPE BY PRESENCE OF OWN CHILDREN											
Families	55 844	55 844	213	919	204	1 931	4 327	147	1 315	252	1 965
With own children under 18 years	38 744	38 744	140	592	143	1 298	2 959	69	914	176	1 363
Number of own children under 18 years	94 378	94 378	337	1 325	365	3 037	6 959	162	2 035	409	3 434
Married-couple families	42 449	42 449	157	719	175	1 464	3 374	108	938	196	1 516
With own children under 18 years	29 731	29 731	109	454	121	1 000	2 319	51	644	137	1 074
Number of own children under 18 years	74 776	74 776	281	1 037	315	2 401	5 635	127	1 482	331	2 761
Female householder, no husband present	10 518	10 518	41	145	19	393	778	29	304	40	315
With own children under 18 years	7 730	7 730	27	113	16	275	562	15	226	33	234
Number of own children under 18 years	17 084	17 084	49	245	38	600	1 175	30	476	70	542
MARITAL STATUS											
Male, 15 years and over	95 674	95 674	432	1 993	362	2 788	6 143	345	1 885	536	3 106
Single	38 057	38 057	188	770	149	989	2 073	149	690	247	1 117
Now married, except separated	50 160	50 160	204	1 081	186	1 600	3 572	160	984	256	1 760
Separated	1 965	1 965	8	37	7	62	137	15	48	12	51
Widowed	1 088	1 088	5	25	5	16	50	3	26	1	40
Divorced	4 404	4 404	27	80	15	121	311	18	137	20	138
Female, 15 years and over	91 963	91 963	412	1 537	396	3 088	7 210	285	2 127	436	3 024
Single	25 387	25 387	131	376	117	806	1 878	75	555	128	804
Now married, except separated	49 582	49 582	207	888	231	1 669	4 017	146	1 095	235	1 692
Separated	3 859	3 859	19	64	12	137	269	13	90	12	129
Widowed	5 836	5 836	19	92	9	247	461	27	135	20	179
Divorced	7 299	7 299	36	117	27	229	585	24	252	41	220

Exhibit 14-2

[For meaning of symbols, see Introduction. For definitions of terms, see appendixes A and B]

Census Tracts [400 or More Spanish Origin Persons]

San Diego city, San Diego County—Con.

	Tract 0045	Tract 0046	Tract 0047	Tract 0048	Tract 0049	Tract 0050	Tract 0051	Tract 0053	Tract 0058	Tract 0063	Tract 0064	Tract 0065	Tract 0075
AGE													
Total persons	1 475	903	1 831	2 564	3 097	1 430	1 019	957	504	762	707	483	401
Under 5 years	219	116	269	385	393	167	105	2	65	–	–	45	39
5 to 9 years	124	87	215	339	361	170	121	2	38	–	–	35	31
10 to 14 years	91	54	177	253	293	158	103	4	34	–	2	34	17
15 to 19 years	135	101	176	282	372	146	114	92	49	429	353	58	36
20 to 24 years	241	127	238	318	343	140	89	274	83	251	245	77	84
25 to 34 years	316	183	292	429	444	193	145	298	103	78	88	79	113
35 to 44 years	111	67	174	209	245	137	98	107	50	4	15	40	31
45 to 54 years	90	73	131	158	256	129	104	83	30	–	4	42	19
55 to 64 years	63	44	91	93	171	81	79	49	25	–	–	33	13
65 to 74 years	48	31	46	70	141	65	33	29	14	–	–	22	11
75 years and over	37	20	22	28	78	44	28	17	13	–	–	18	7
3 and 4 years	74	39	92	155	154	65	44	1	25	–	–	18	13
16 years and over	1 019	634	1 137	1 538	1 975	899	667	947	359	762	705	355	308
18 years and over	985	593	1 064	1 425	1 819	843	618	931	338	675	651	331	299
21 years and over	870	518	947	1 234	1 594	757	559	797	306	239	256	300	270
60 years and over	109	62	106	134	298	151	87	55	35	–	–	54	26
62 years and over	·96	59	87	121	262	131	78	49	33	–	–	49	24
Median	23.5	23.6	21.7	20.3	21.7	22.6	23.1	27.7	23.8	19.7	20.0	24.4	24.7
Female	751	446	907	1 318	1 574	730	506	83	244	9	31	251	185
Under 5 years	107	58	130	190	206	87	55	–	31	–	–	20	21
5 to 9 years	60	41	94	185	160	82	69	1	22	–	–	18	17
10 to 14 years	43	24	94	119	127	85	50	1	19	–	–	18	10
15 to 19 years	76	48	79	129	186	74	55	5	27	3	13	28	21
20 to 24 years	123	68	119	153	164	67	41	18	37	5	14	36	33
25 to 34 years	143	76	128	229	233	98	72	26	47	1	4	36	42
35 to 44 years	58	33	93	105	137	58	48	11	24	–	–	23	16
45 to 54 years	49	41	78	90	137	74	50	6	13	–	–	23	6
55 to 64 years	39	28	49	60	84	42	37	5	12	–	–	23	8
65 to 74 years	30	16	30	42	88	41	15	7	6	–	–	14	6
75 years and over	23	13	13	16	52	22	14	3	6	–	–	12	5
3 and 4 years	33	22	47	75	75	32	21	–	13	–	–	9	6
16 years and over	528	316	575	799	1 047	456	321	80	167	9	31	188	134
18 years and over	509	293	536	746	967	431	301	79	154	9	30	177	129
21 years and over	445	262	490	665	849	387	268	72	139	5	15	160	111
60 years and over	69	35	65	78	181	88	37	10	17	–	–	34	16
62 years and over	62	34	53	69	164	75	34	10	16	–	–	31	15
Median	23.8	23.6	22.4	21.1	23.2	22.5	22.6	30.9	22.9	21.3	20.8	26.6	23.9
HOUSEHOLD TYPE AND RELATIONSHIP													
Total persons	1 475	903	1 831	2 564	3 097	1 430	1 019	957	504	762	707	483	401
In households	1 464	903	1 828	2 560	3 097	1 430	1 019	207	504	–	1	483	401
Householder	485	321	493	621	791	406	304	189	162	–	–	170	173
Family householder	342	190	391	522	666	304	204	7	107	–	–	108	78
Nonfamily householder	143	131	102	99	125	102	100	182	55	–	–	62	95
Living alone	105	97	72	68	104	89	95	175	42	–	–	50	61
Spouse	236	117	256	361	468	196	139	6	70	–	–	75	56
Other relatives	634	393	974	1 473	1 718	775	534	5	220	–	1	190	115
Nonrelatives	109	72	105	105	120	53	42	7	52	–	–	48	57
Inmate of institution	5	–	–	2	–	–	–	720	–	–	–	–	–
Other, in group quarters	6	–	3	2	–	–	–	30	–	762	706	–	–
Persons per household	2.85	2.79	3.68	4.09	3.90	3.48	3.29	1.10	2.98	–	–	2.69	2.19
Persons per family	3.34	3.61	4.13	4.48	4.26	4.17	4.24	2.57	3.51	–	–	3.32	2.94
Persons 65 years and over	85	51	68	98	219	109	61	46	27	–	–	40	18
In households	83	51	68	98	219	109	61	44	27	–	–	40	18
Householder	51	37	43	65	151	72	43	43	20	–	–	28	13
Nonfamily householder	25	23	20	22	64	35	24	43	9	–	–	15	9
Living alone	25	22	18	20	59	33	23	43	8	–	–	15	8
Spouse	11	6	11	9	32	12	7	–	5	–	–	6	4
Other relatives	18	4	9	20	24	16	8	1	2	–	–	5	1
Nonrelatives	3	4	5	4	12	9	3	1	–	–	–	1	–
Inmate of institution	2	–	–	–	–	–	–	2	–	–	–	–	–
Other, in group quarters	–	–	–	–	–	–	–	–	–	–	–	–	–
FAMILY TYPE BY PRESENCE OF OWN CHILDREN													
Families	342	190	391	522	666	304	204	7	107	–	–	108	78
With own children under 18 years	227	134	270	386	444	197	145	–	67	–	–	55	47
Number of own children under 18 years	434	282	673	996	1 134	522	363	–	138	–	–	123	91
Married-couple families	217	111	256	354	463	193	134	6	68	–	–	67	55
With own children under 18 years	150	80	180	287	319	142	102	–	42	–	–	37	30
Number of own children under 18 years	296	169	467	770	839	394	285	–	90	–	–	91	64
Female householder, no husband present	95	55	108	131	155	83	56	–	25	–	–	25	14
With own children under 18 years	66	41	83	85	108	45	42	–	18	–	–	15	12
Number of own children under 18 years	122	88	185	187	253	93	77	–	39	–	–	28	21
MARITAL STATUS													
Male, 15 years and over	500	323	581	763	969	459	358	868	195	753	674	174	177
Single	192	136	235	299	372	163	143	421	77	598	562	75	92
Now married, except separated	247	146	310	419	532	228	162	301	89	125	83	72	58
Separated	19	14	14	16	14	18	19	38	8	12	9	7	5
Widowed	6	7	8	8	23	24	8	13	6	1	–	4	5
Divorced	36	20	14	21	28	26	26	95	15	17	20	16	17
Female, 15 years and over	541	323	589	824	1 081	476	332	81	172	9	31	195	137
Single	154	106	171	251	330	138	95	33	45	7	25	54	44
Now married, except separated	261	134	282	405	513	220	157	16	84	1	4	85	58
Separated	31	25	46	52	54	27	18	10	20	1	–	18	3
Widowed	44	33	49	58	112	54	39	8	9	–	–	16	14
Divorced	51	25	41	58	72	37	23	14	14	–	2	22	18

Exhibit 14-3

	Current Data						Comparative Historical Data				
	9	48	20	1	78	**Type of Statement** Unqualified		104	74	78
	1	7	2		10	Qualified		14	7	10
	35	60			95	Reviewed	DATA NOT AVAILABLE	107	103	95
	71	42		2	115	Compiled		92	98	115
	22	26	1	2	51	Other		58	47	51
	125(6/30-9/30/86)		224(10/1/86-3/31/87)				6/30/82-3/31/83	6/30/83-3/31/84	6/30/84-3/31/85	6/30/85-3/31/86	6/30/86-3/31/87

0-1MM 138	1-10MM 183	10-50MM 25	50-100MM 3	ALL 349	ASSET SIZE NUMBER OF STATEMENTS	ALL 343	ALL 318	ALL 375	ALL 329	ALL 349
%	%	%	%	%	**ASSETS**	%	%	%	%	%
5.3	5.3	7.2		5.5	Cash & Equivalents	7.3	6.4	6.2	5.2	5.5
31.9	33.1	27.8		32.2	Trade Receivables - (net)	30.8	31.4	33.6	32.1	32.2
44.4	42.9	37.7		43.0	Inventory	41.5	43.6	40.9	43.6	43.0
1.7	1.2	4.2		1.6	All Other Current	1.3	1.1	1.7	1.3	1.6
83.3	82.5	77.0		82.3	Total Current	80.9	82.5	82.4	82.2	82.3
11.4	11.3	15.0		11.7	Fixed Assets (net)	13.0	12.1	11.2	12.5	11.7
.9	1.0	.9		.9	Intangibles (net)	.5	.6	.6	.6	.9
4.4	5.2	7.2		5.0	All Other Non-Current	5.6	4.8	5.8	4.7	5.0
100.0	100.0	100.0		100.0	Total	100.0	100.0	100.0	.100.0	100.0
					LIABILITIES					
14.8	15.8	10.5		14.9	Notes Payable-Short Term	12.3	13.7	12.9	15.8	14.9
4.4	2.1	1.3		3.0	Cur. Mat.-L/T/D	3.3	2.5	2.4	2.7	3.0
23.8	22.0	21.7		22.7	Trade Payables	21.9	21.8	24.3	23.4	22.7
1.1	1.2	.7		1.2	Income Taxes Payable	–	–	1.2	.7	1.2
6.8	8.3	5.1		7.4	All Other Current	8.6	8.4	8.2	7.1	7.4
50.9	49.4	39.3		49.1	Total Current	46.1	46.3	49.0	49.8	49.1
11.8	7.5	13.2		9.8	Long Term Debt	10.8	11.1	11.2	10.0	9.8
.2	.3	1.7		.3	Deferred Taxes	–	–	.5	.4	.3
2.7	2.0	2.7		2.3	All Other Non-Current	2.2	3.0	1.4	1.6	2.3
34.4	40.8	43.1		38.4	Net Worth	40.8	39.6	38.0	38.2	38.4
100.0	100.0	100.0		100.0	Total Liabilities & Net Worth	100.0	100.0	100.0	100.0	100.0
					INCOME DATA					
100.0	100.0	100.0		100.0	Net Sales	100.0	100.0	100.0	100.0	100.0
31.8	28.4	23.7		29.5	Gross Profit	30.3	30.1	29.7	30.3	29.5
28.7	25.4	19.7		26.4	Operating Expenses	27.8	27.5	26.3	27.0	26.4
3.1	3.0	4.0		3.1	Operating Profit	2.5	2.6	3.4	3.4	3.1
.8	.4	.2		.5	All Other Expenses (net)	1.1	1.0	.8	.9	.5
2.2	2.6	3.8		2.6	Profit Before Taxes	1.4	1.5	2.6	2.5	2.6
					RATIOS					
2.2	2.4	3.0		2.4	Current	2.7	2.7	2.4	2.5	2.4
1.7	1.7	2.0		1.7		1.8	1.8	1.7	1.6	1.7
1.4	1.3	1.7		1.3		1.3	1.4	1.3	1.3	1.3
1.2	1.1	1.4		1.2	Quick	1.3	1.2	1.2	1.1	1.2
.7	.8	1.0		.8		.8	.8	.8	.7	.8
.5	.5	.6		.5		.5	.6	.6	.5	.5
29 12.6	35 10.5	39 9.4		33 11.0	Sales/Receivables	32 11.3	36 10.2	34 10.7	33 11.1	33 11.0
40 9.2	43 8.4	47 7.7		42 8.6		41 9.0	43 8.4	43 8.5	43 8.5	42 8.6
54 6.8	57 6.4	57 6.4		57 6.4		52 7.0	54 6.7	53 6.9	51 7.1	57 6.4
54 6.7	58 6.3	51 7.2		56 6.5	Cost of Sales/Inventory	55 6.6	60 6.1	51 7.2	54 6.7	56 6.5
89 4.1	85 4.3	72 5.1		87 4.2		83 4.4	94 3.9	76 4.8	85 4.3	87 4.2
140 2.6	114 3.2	111 3.3		126 2.9		118 3.1	126 2.9	118 3.1	126 2.9	126 2.9
24 15.3	26 14.1	33 11.0		26 14.1	Cost of Sales/Payables	25 14.8	26 14.3	26 13.8	25 14.5	26 14.1
41 8.9	38 9.7	46 7.9		40 9.2		39 9.4	42 8.7	41 9.0	42 8.6	40 9.2
65 5.6	60 6.1	58 6.3		62 5.9		60 6.1	62 5.9	61 6.0	61 6.0	62 5.9
5.6	5.2	4.0		5.3	Sales/Working Capital	5.1	4.6	5.4	5.5	5.3
8.2	8.4	6.2		7.9		7.7	7.2	8.3	8.6	7.9
16.1	15.5	9.0		15.5		12.7	12.9	14.7	15.9	15.5
6.8	10.3	10.1		8.5	EBIT/Interest	4.7	5.0	7.0	6.7	8.5
(123) 2.7	(169) 3.0	(21) 3.6		(316) 3.0		(296) 1.8	(282) 2.2	(324) 2.8	(289) 2.4	(316) 3.0
1.2	1.5	1.7		1.5		1.0	1.1	1.4	1.4	1.5
4.7	7.3	13.0		6.3	Net Profit + Depr., Dep., Amort./Cur. Mat. L/T/D	4.4	4.6	6.4	6.1	6.3
(65) 1.8	(98) 2.8	(18) 5.7		(184) 2.9		(194) 1.6	(172) 2.4	(187) 2.8	(183) 3.0	(184) 2.9
.5	1.1	1.6		.9		.5	.4	1.2	1.1	.9
.1	.1	.2		.1	Fixed/Worth	.1	.1	.1	.1	.1
.3	.2	.3		.3		.3	.3	.3	.3	.3
.7	.5	.5		.5		.7	.6	.5	.6	.5
1.0	.7	.8		.8	Debt/Worth	.7	.8	.9	.8	.8
2.0	1.8	1.2		1.9		1.6	1.5	1.6	1.9	1.9
3.9	3.4	3.0		3.6		2.9	3.3	3.6	3.8	3.6
33.9	32.1	32.2		32.8	% Profit Before Taxes/Tangible Net Worth	21.6	22.6	36.8	33.4	32.8
(124) 18.0	(178) 15.2	14.3		(330) 16.3		(325) 9.2	(308) 10.8	(360) 16.8	(315) 15.5	(330) 16.3
5.8	4.8	8.1		5.6		1.2	2.0	6.4	3.7	5.6
11.6	11.2	14.9		11.6	% Profit Before Taxes/Total Assets	8.8	9.3	12.7	11.9	11.6
5.9	5.7	6.6		5.9		3.6	4.2	5.9	4.9	5.9
.6	1.6	2.6		1.5		.2	.5	2.0	1.3	1.5
72.9	55.3	37.3		60.3	Sales/Net Fixed Assets	52.1	57.7	62.8	53.7	60.3
33.9	31.6	21.8		31.5		27.4	28.0	34.2	29.1	31.5
16.9	17.6	12.4		16.7		14.7	15.0	17.6	14.8	16.7
3.5	3.1	2.6		3.2	Sales/Total Assets	3.1	3.0	3.4	3.3	3.2
2.7	2.6	2.3		2.6		2.6	2.5	2.7	2.7	2.6
2.0	2.1	1.9		2.0		2.1	2.0	2.2	2.1	2.0
.7	.6	.6		.6	% Depr., Dep., Amort./Sales	.6	.6	.6	.6	.6
(114) 1.2	(160) .9	(24) .8		(301) 1.0		(321) .9	(288) 1.0	(332) .9	(298) 1.0	(301) 1.0
2.0	1.4	1.4		1.7		1.4	1.5	1.3	1.5	1.7
3.3	2.1			2.6	% Officers' Comp/Sales	2.2	2.6	2.2	1.9	2.6
(75) 5.8	(80) 3.5			(157) 4.1		(131) 3.7	(134) 3.9	(160) 4.1	(136) 3.7	(157) 4.1
7.8	5.3			6.6		5.3	6.2	5.7		6.6
196960M	1450729M	1209936M	342686M	3200311M	Net Sales ($)	3476693M	3009909M	3745333M	3243790M	3200311M
71800M	554024M	547875M	173597M	1347296M	Total Assets ($)	1374642M	1203771M	1579739M	1302667M	1347296M

©Robert Morris Associates 1987

M = $thousand   MM = $million
See Pages 1 through 13 for Explanation of Ratios and Data

Exhibit 14-4

RETAILERS - RESTAURANTS SIC# 5812

Current Data					Type of Statement	Comparative Historical Data				
28	59	34	15	136	Unqualified			148	117	136
3	4	3		10	Qualified			15	14	10
103	67	6	1	177	Reviewed	DATA NOT AVAILABLE		162	137	177
347	86	2		435	Compiled			288	334	435
121	70	7	5	203	Other			185	153	203
392(6/30-9/30/86)		569(10/1/86-3/31/87)				6/30/82-3/31/83	6/30/83-3/31/84	6/30/84-3/31/85	6/30/85-3/31/86	6/30/86-3/31/87
0-1MM	1-10MM	10-50MM	50-100MM	ALL	ASSET SIZE	ALL	ALL	ALL	ALL	ALL
602	286	52	21	961	NUMBER OF STATEMENTS	805	653	798	755	961
%	%	%	%	%	**ASSETS**	%	%	%	%	%
12.3	11.0	7.6	9.1	11.6	Cash & Equivalents	10.9	10.2	10.4	11.2	11.6
4.0	4.1	4.6	5.6	4.1	Trade Receivables - (net)	5.0	4.9	4.6	4.5	4.1
7.8	5.2	3.9	5.1	6.7	Inventory	6.8	6.5	6.9	7.1	6.7
2.8	1.9	2.1	2.3	2.5	All Other Current	2.0	2.4	2.5	2.5	2.5
26.9	22.2	18.2	22.1	24.9	Total Current	24.6	24.0	24.4	25.3	24.9
54.7	59.1	60.5	60.7	56.5	Fixed Assets (net)	58.7	59.9	59.0	57.0	56.5
5.6	5.2	5.3	7.2	5.5	Intangibles (net)	3.9	4.1	4.0	4.3	5.5
12.8	13.5	16.0	10.0	13.1	All Other Non-Current	12.8	12.0	12.5	13.4	13.1
100.0	100.0	100.0	100.0	100.0	Total	100.0	100.0	100.0	100.0	100.0
					LIABILITIES					
8.8	3.9	4.2	3.2	7.0	Notes Payable-Short Term	5.8	5.8	6.7	6.7	7.0
6.6	6.5	5.7	3.3	6.5	Cur. Mat.-L/T/D	6.1	5.8	5.8	6.3	6.5
11.8	10.3	9.2	8.9	11.1	Trade Payables	11.5	11.3	11.2	11.6	11.1
1.3	.9	.7	.9	1.1	Income Taxes Payable	—	—	1.3	1.2	1.1
13.0	10.7	6.4	6.1	11.8	All Other Current	13.4	13.4	11.7	10.7	11.8
41.5	32.3	26.3	22.4	37.5	Total Current	36.7	36.2	36.7	36.6	37.5
31.3	34.8	39.4	27.3	32.7	Long Term Debt	30.2	31.6	32.5	32.1	32.7
.3	1.0	1.8	2.8	.6	Deferred Taxes	—	—	.6	.5	.6
2.1	2.3	3.2	3.0	2.2	All Other Non-Current	3.8	3.7	2.5	2.9	2.2
24.9	29.6	29.4	44.6	27.0	Net Worth	29.3	28.5	27.6	27.8	27.0
100.0	100.0	100.0	100.0	100.0	Total Liabilities & Net Worth	100.0	100.0	100.0	100.0	100.0
					INCOME DATA					
100.0	100.0	100.0	100.0	100.0	Net Sales	100.0	100.0	100.0	100.0	100.0
56.4	55.8	49.0	53.2	55.7	Gross Profit	54.8	53.8	54.1	54.9	55.7
53.1	51.2	44.5	45.3	51.9	Operating Expenses	49.5	49.2	49.4	50.9	51.9
3.3	4.6	4.5	7.9	3.9	Operating Profit	5.2	4.6	4.7	4.1	3.9
1.5	2.1	1.9	3.3	1.7	All Other Expenses (net)	2.1	1.6	2.1	1.9	1.7
1.8	2.5	2.6	4.6	2.1	Profit Before Taxes	3.1	3.0	2.7	2.2	2.1
					RATIOS					
1.4	1.2	1.0	1.8	1.3	Current	1.2	1.2	1.2	1.3	1.3
.7	.6	.6	1.1	.7		.7	.7	.6	.7	.7
.3	.3	.3	.6	.3		.3	.3	.3	.4	.3
.9	.8	.7	1.2	.8	Quick	.9	.8	.8	.8	.8
(597) .4	(285) .4	.4	.7	(955) .4		(796) .4	(646) .4	(787) .4	(748) .4	(955) .4
.1	.2	.2	.3	.1		.1	.2	.2	.2	.1
0 INF	0 999.8	2 222.2	1 267.9	0 INF	Sales/Receivables	0 INF	0 INF	0 INF	0 INF	0 INF
0 999.8	1 261.5	6 59.7	5 68.6	1 387.0		2 172.6	2 188.3	2 237.7	2 215.0	1 387.0
4 89.8	6 58.2	13 27.5	9 40.3	5 70.0		7 51.7	7 51.7	7 51.0	6 59.3	5 70.0
8 45.7	7 48.8	7 54.8	9 39.1	8 47.5	Cost of Sales/Inventory	9 42.8	9 42.2	9 42.2	8 45.5	8 47.5
13 28.0	11 32.1	11 32.3	18 20.6	13 29.0		14 26.5	13 27.5	14 26.1	13 27.6	13 29.0
21 17.2	20 18.4	29 12.4	38 9.6	22 16.9		23 16.2	23 16.1	22 16.5	23 15.7	22 16.9
8 45.7	17 21.7	21 17.6	35 10.5	12 31.3	Cost of Sales/Payables	14 25.4	15 23.6	13 27.8	12 30.9	12 31.3
22 16.9	31 11.8	39 9.3	42 8.7	26 14.2		27 13.5	29 12.7	26 13.8	25 14.5	26 14.2
40 9.2	50 7.3	66 5.5	74 4.9	45 8.1		45 8.2	46 8.0	45 8.1	47 7.8	45 8.1
44.4	67.9	±INF	12.3	50.1	Sales/Working Capital	59.3	51.2	66.1	47.8	50.1
-37.0	-25.2	-18.6	98.6	-31.8		-32.6	-29.4	-29.8	-38.5	-31.8
-11.8	-10.1	-9.9	-16.7	-10.9		-10.9	-11.3	-10.8	-11.9	-10.9
5.3	4.5	4.3	7.4	5.0	EBIT/Interest	5.0	5.1	5.2	4.8	5.0
(530) 2.2	(255) 2.4	(45) 1.6	(18) 2.5	(848) 2.2		(686) 2.2	(580) 2.4	(689) 2.2	(661) 2.0	(848) 2.2
.4	1.1	.7	.9	.7		1.0	1.0	.9	.6	.7
3.8	4.3	3.0	8.6	3.9	Net Profit + Depr., Dep., Amort./Cur. Mat. L/T/D	5.5	4.7	5.1	4.6	3.9
(239) 1.8	(177) 2.0	(43) 1.9	(18) 2.3	(477) 1.9		(375) 2.3	(352) 2.1	(400) 2.4	(383) 2.2	(477) 1.9
.8	1.1	1.1	.9	1.0		1.2	1.1	1.1	1.0	1.0
1.0	1.2	1.8	1.0	1.1	Fixed/Worth	1.1	1.2	1.2	1.1	1.1
2.7	2.7	2.7	1.6	2.6		2.1	2.4	2.4	2.4	2.6
-36.9	13.7	5.0	2.3	25.2		10.5	9.1	15.3	27.1	25.2
1.0	1.3	1.9	.9	1.1	Debt/Worth	1.0	1.2	1.2	1.1	1.1
3.2	2.9	3.6	1.6	3.1		2.5	2.6	2.9	2.8	3.1
-77.3	20.2	6.9	2.7	37.6		13.1	12.5	19.2	31.0	37.6
63.5	51.4	49.9	31.2	56.6	% Profit Before Taxes/Tangible Net Worth	54.9	60.3	54.3	52.1	56.6
(446) 22.7	(230) 23.2	(47) 21.1	(20) 23.0	(743) 22.5		(657) 27.4	(529) 25.7	(635) 24.6	(589) 20.2	(743) 22.5
.7	7.5	3.4	8.1	3.6		6.8	6.9	4.6	4.9	3.6
15.5	11.8	12.2	15.1	13.9	% Profit Before Taxes/Total Assets	16.6	16.0	15.6	14.9	13.9
6.2	6.0	4.0	10.5	5.9		7.3	8.0	6.9	5.4	5.9
-3.9	.8	-.7	1.4	-1.5		.0	.3	-.2	-1.5	-1.5
13.8	6.6	5.0	2.9	10.6	Sales/Net Fixed Assets	9.4	8.3	9.7	10.4	10.6
7.1	4.2	2.6	2.1	5.4		5.2	4.8	4.9	5.3	5.4
3.6	2.5	1.9	1.9	2.9		2.7	2.6	2.6	2.7	2.9
5.2	3.4	2.0	1.7	4.5	Sales/Total Assets	4.1	4.0	4.4	4.6	4.5
3.6	2.4	1.7	1.4	2.9		2.8	2.7	2.8	2.9	2.9
2.4	1.6	1.2	1.2	1.8		1.8	1.8	1.8	1.8	1.8
2.3	2.7	3.8	2.8	2.5	% Depr., Dep., Amort./Sales	2.2	2.3	2.3	2.5	2.5
(553) 3.4	(271) 3.9	(50) 4.7	(20) 4.1	(894) 3.7		(751) 3.3	(610) 3.5	(753) 3.5	(697) 3.7	(894) 3.7
5.0	5.2	5.4	5.6	5.1		4.7	4.8	4.7	5.2	5.1
2.9	2.3			2.6	% Officers' Comp/Sales	3.1	2.9	2.7	2.9	2.6
(270) 4.7	(93) 3.7			(371) 4.5		(339) 5.0	(245) 5.0	(306) 4.9	(292) 5.0	(371) 4.5
8.9	6.8			7.7		7.5	7.3	7.2	8.1	7.7
765636M	2125785M	1831227M	2596887M	7319535M	Net Sales ($)	7072588M	6610038M	7170353M	5252028M	7319535M
216355M	884074M	1099971M	1450823M	3651223M	Total Assets ($)	3595183M	3701365M	3329698M	2884571M	3651223M

M = $thousand   MM = $million
See Pages 1 through 13 for Explanation of Ratios and Data

Form **970**	**Application To Use LIFO Inventory Method**	OMB No. 1545-0042
(Rev. April 1987)	▶ **Attach to your tax return.**	Expires 3-31-90
Department of the Treasury Internal Revenue Service	▶ **For Paperwork Reduction Act Notice, see instructions on back.**	

Name	Identifying number (See instructions)

Address (Number, street, city, state and ZIP code)	CHECK ONE: ☐ Initial Election ☐ Subsequent Election

Statement of Election and Other Information:

A The taxpayer applies to adopt and use the LIFO inventory method provided by section 472. The taxpayer will use this method for the first time (or modify this method) as of (date tax year ends) _____, for the following goods (give details as explained in instructions; use more sheets if necessary):

B The taxpayer agrees to make any adjustments that the District Director of Internal Revenue may require, on examination of the taxpayer's return, to reflect income clearly for the years involved in changing to or from the LIFO method or in using it.

1 Nature of business

2 a Inventory method used until now

   b Will inventory be taken at actual cost regardless of market value? If "No," attach explanation . . . . ☐ Yes ☐ No

3 a Was the inventory of the specified goods valued at cost as of the beginning of the first tax year to which this application refers, as required by section 472(d)? If "No," attach explanation . . . . ☐ Yes ☐ No

   b Will you include in income over 3 tax years any adjustments that resulted from changing to LIFO? If "No," attach explanation . . . . ☐ Yes ☐ No

4 a List goods subject to inventory that are not to be inventoried under the LIFO method.

   b Were the goods of the specified type included in opening inventory counted as acquired at the same time and at a unit cost equal to the actual cost of the total divided by the number of units on hand? If "No," attach explanation ☐ Yes ☐ No

5 a Did you issue credit statements, or reports to shareholders, partners, other proprietors, or beneficiaries covering the first tax year to which this application refers? . . . . ☐ Yes ☐ No

   b If "Yes," state to whom, and on what dates.

   c Show the inventory method used in determining income, profit, or loss in those statements.

6 a Check method used to figure the cost of the goods in the closing inventory over those in the opening inventory. (See instructions.)
    ☐ Most recent purchases   ☐ Earliest acquisitions during the year
    ☐ Average cost of purchases during the year   ☐ Other—Attach explanation

   b The taxpayer selects the month of _____ as the appropriate representative month to be used in selecting the index or indexes to be used in determining the current-year cost of the taxpayer's inventory pool(s) under regulations section 1.472-8(e)(2)(ii) (see instructions).

7 Method used in valuing LIFO inventories: ☐ Unit method   ☐ Dollar-value method

8 a If you use pools, list and describe contents of each pool and, if applicable, the consumer or producer price index or indexes selected for each pool.

   b ☐ As an eligible small business, the taxpayer has elected under section 474 to use the Simplified Dollar-Value LIFO Method.

   c ☐ As a retailer, wholesaler, jobber, or distributor, the taxpayer selects the pooling method authorized by regulations section 1.472-8(e)(3)(iv).

   d Describe briefly the cost system used.

   e Method used in computing LIFO value of dollar-value pools (see instructions and attach required information):
    ☐ Double extension method   ☐ Published price index (describe)
    ☐ Other method (describe and justify)

9 Did you change your method of valuing inventories for this tax year with the Commissioner's permission? . . . . . ☐ Yes ☐ No
If "Yes," attach a copy of the National Office's "grant letter" to this Form 970.

10 Were you ever on LIFO before? . . . . ☐ Yes ☐ No
If "Yes," attach a statement to list the tax years you used LIFO and to explain why you discontinued it.

Under penalties of perjury, I declare that I have examined this application, including any accompanying schedules and statements, and to the best of my knowledge and belief, it is true, correct, and complete.

Date	Signature of taxpayer	
Date	Signature of officer	Title

Form **970** (Rev. 4-87)

Exhibit 14-5

General Instructions

(Section references are to the Internal Revenue Code unless otherwise noted.)

Paperwork Reduction Act Notice.— We ask for this information to carry out the Internal Revenue laws of the United States. We need it to ensure that taxpayers are complying with these laws and to allow us to figure and collect the right amount of tax. You are required to give us this information.

Purpose of Form.—Form 970 is an optional form that you can file with your income tax return to adopt or expand the LIFO inventory method described in section 472. If you prefer, you can file a statement that gives the information asked for on Form 970. (See regulations section 1.472-3(a).) File the application with your return for the first tax year for which you intend to use or expand the LIFO method.

New Simplified Dollar-Value LIFO Method Available to Certain Small Businesses (Item 8b).—The Tax Reform Act of 1986 added a new category to the LIFO inventory method, Simplified Dollar-Value LIFO method. Only small businesses whose average annual gross receipts for the three preceding tax years did not exceed $5,000,000 may elect to use this method. If the taxpayer is a member of a controlled group, the gross receipts of the group are used to determine if the taxpayer qualifies. The new method requires that the taxpayer maintain a separate inventory pool for items in each major category in the applicable Government price index, and that the taxpayer make adjustments to each separate pool based on changes from the preceding tax year in the component of such index for the major category. The qualified taxpayer does not need the consent of the Secretary to elect these provisions. The election is in effect for the first year the election is made and for each succeeding year the taxpayer qualifies as an eligible small business. The election may be revoked only with the consent of the Secretary. The Simplified Dollar-Value LIFO method applies for tax years beginning after 1986.

Protective Election.—A protective election in connection with section 95 of the Tax Reform Act of 1984 (P.L. 98-369) may be made by completing and filing Form 970 as specified in temporary regulations section 5h.4(g). Write "Protective Election Under Regulations 5h.4(g)" at the top of the Form 970 you file to make this election. This election must be made for your first tax year beginning after July 18, 1984.

Change from LIFO Method.—Once you adopt the LIFO method, it is irrevocable unless the Commissioner allows you to change to another method.

Specific Instructions

Identifying Number.—An individual's identifying number is the social security number. For all others it is the employer identification number.

Initial Election or Subsequent Election.—If this is your first election to use the LIFO method, check the box for Initial Election. If you are expanding a prior LIFO election, check the box for Subsequent Election.

Statement of Election and Other Information.—If this is an initial election, enter the tax year you will first use the LIFO method and specify the goods to which you will apply it. If this is a subsequent election, enter the tax year you will expand the LIFO method and specify the goods to which the LIFO method is being expanded.

Attach a detailed analysis of all your inventories as of the beginning and end of the first tax year for which you will use the LIFO method (tax year for which the LIFO method is being expanded if this is a subsequent election) and as of the beginning of the preceding tax year. Also, include the ending inventory reported on your return for the preceding tax year. Regulations sections 1.472-2 and 1.472-3 give more information about preparing this analysis.

Item 6a.—See regulations sections 1.472-2 and 1.472-8(e) for more information.

Item 6b.—See regulations section 1.472-8(e)(3)(iii)(C) before completing item 6b.

Item 8a.—To adopt and use the inventory price index computation method provided by regulations section 1.472-8(e)(3), you must enter in item 8a a list of each inventory pool, the type of goods included in each pool, and the consumer or producer price index or indexes selected for each inventory pool. If more space is needed, attach a schedule showing the information.

Item 8b.—Check item 8b if you have made the section 474 election to use the Simplified Dollar-Value LIFO method. See section 474 for additional details.

Item 8c.—Check item 8c to select the pooling method authorized by regulations section 1.472-8(e)(3)(iv). See the regulations for additional details.

Item 8e.—You may use the "dollar-value" LIFO method to determine the cost of your LIFO inventories as long as you use it consistently and it clearly reflects income. Regulations section 1.472-8 gives details about this method.

If you are a wholesaler, retailer, jobber, or distributor, see regulations section 1.472-8(c) for guidelines on establishing dollar-value LIFO pools.

To figure the LIFO value of a dollar-value pool, use a method described in regulations section 1.472–8(e). If you do not use the "double-extension" or "index" method, attach a detailed statement to explain the method you do use and how it is justified under regulations section 1.472-8(e)(1). For example, if you use a "link-chain" method, your statement should explain why the nature of the pool makes the other two methods impractical or unsuitable.

Signature.—Form 970 must be signed. If you are filing for a corporation, the form must be signed by the president, vice president, treasurer, assistant treasurer, chief accounting officer, or other corporate officer (such as tax officer) authorized to sign.

☆ U.S. Government Printing Office: 1987—181-447/40141

Chapter 15

WILL YOU NEED A COMPUTER FOR YOUR BUSINESS?

Purchasing a computer may consume a majority of your precious budget when you are getting started. Because your resources are limited and expenses will inevitably be incurred for other items, many of which are unplanned, it is important for you to question the necessity of purchasing or leasing a computer in the beginning stage of your business. This chapter explains:

* How to assess your needs
* Types of software
* Components of a computer system
* Ten of the most commonly used computer terms

HOW TO ASSESS YOUR NEEDS

You should always know your needs and what you can afford before you talk to a computer salesperson. A computer salesperson's objective is to sell you a computer and software, which may or may not satisfy the needs of your business.

Your first step is to determine the needs of your business—that is, you must ask yourself, in what areas of your business will a computer increase revenues or lower costs. The use of a computer must be justified; otherwise, it is only an expensive toy. Costs associated with a computer include hardware, software, printer, diskettes, container for the diskettes, ribbons, paper, additional electricity consumed, lost time and expense in learning how to use the computer, lost time and expense in learning how to use the software, lost time and expense if the computer, printer, or software malfunctions, and additional wages that must be paid to find people with the skills to operate the hardware and software. These costs must be estimated and then balanced against any alleged benefits the computer will provide.

The computer has been proven to be effective for businesses that have the following needs:

* Carry large amounts of inventory spread over thousands of items;

* Make hundreds or thousands of their sales on credit and must monitor accounts receivable;
* Have large payrolls and must account for each individual's paycheck and taxes; or
* Generate large amounts of correspondence or internal memorandums.

Your second step is to determine the software you will need. The software determines the make, model, and size of the computer you will buy. Software is either packaged or custom made. Packaged software is the type sold in stores. It has been developed and tested by the manufacturer and is in use by hundreds, perhaps thousands of purchasers who use it in their businesses. Custom software is developed specifically for a particular business. To properly program software, an individual must have a background in programming, which usually means education and experience. Although there are many computer consultants that have the requisite skills in writing a software program for your business, there are also many charlatans who masquerade as experts. The expense and risk involved in choosing the custom software route is much greater than if you were to rely on packaged software.

Types of Software

There are two types of software: application and operative. Application software performs the specific functions which will satisfy the needs of your business. Operative software, also known as systems software, controls the operation of the computer.

Below are the most common types of software that businesses use:

Spread Sheet

The spread sheet allows you to shorten computational time because of its ability to perform various mathematical functions. These packages, as a rule, contain the word "Calc" in their titles, such as VisiCalc, SuperCalc, or GeoCalc. The value of the spread sheet is that information can be entered into a table format, which then can be changed to analyze the "what if's." For instance, budgets lend themselves to spread sheet analysis. A budget is a comprehensive financial plan that sets forth the expected revenues and costs of running a business. There are various reasons why you would want a budget: (1) it enhances your perspective of the business; (2) it will give you advance warning of problems; (3) it will state exactly what objectives must be reached by various departments or divisions within your business; and (4) it will allow you to accurately measure performance. Once your budget is entered on a spread sheet, it will allow you to analyze any adjustments that have to be made. If revenues change or costs need to be increased or decreased, the spread sheet can tell you the effect it will have on operations within seconds.

The two major features you will need to compare are the speed of calculation and the maximum number of rows and columns that can be carried. Also, remember that the more information you have and the more complicated your analysis, the more random access memory (RAM) your computer will need. RAM is the temporary memory accessed by the processor during operations. Processors come in 8-bit, 16-bit, and 32-bit formats. A bit is a binary number digit. An 8-bit processor can only directly access 64,000 bytes, which is eight bits of information or one type written character, of RAM at any one time. The 16-bit processor, however, can access 640,000 bytes of RAM.

Word Processing

This program allows you to enter and edit text material and is best suited if you have large amounts of written communications. The better software programs contain features such as spellcheck, global search and replace, and mailing lists. To be effective, however, a word processing software package will require a printer.

The three most popular types of printers are dot matrix, daisy wheel, and laser.

Dot Matrix—This printer has a strikehead which consists of a matrix of dot hammers. Letters and numbers are formed by a command which causes the dot hammers to strike the paper. The speed with which this occurs is very fast because of the short distance the hammer must travel to reach the paper. Many printers are available in a range of speeds, from 200–550 characters per second (CPS) and are priced below a thousand dollars.

Daisy Wheel—The printing operation is analogous to the typewriter: a letter or number is formed by a hammer striking the ink ribbon onto the paper. The daisy wheel derives its name from the way the characters are mounted on a wheel. The advantage of a daisy wheel printer is that print communication looks professional, unlike the dot matrix printer, and the wheel can be changed to alter type style. The disadvantages of the daisy wheel are noise, speed, and cost. Regardless of what the advertisements tell you, the noise can be almost deafening, and it can be a challenge just to maintain your concentration. You will probably need an acoustical desktop enclosure to reduce printer noise if you share office space with anyone or if the walls are thin. Speed is also a factor. Although some of the more expensive daisy wheel printers can operate between 50 and 60 characters per second, this is still slower than the lowest priced dot matrix models. Finally, cost is a factor that cannot be ignored. Daisy wheel printers, as a rule, are much more expensive than dot matrix printers.

Laser—The third most popular type of printer is the laser, which now sells for less than $1,700. Laser printers are fast, between 400 and 500 CPS, and are of letter quality. The crisp clear lettering even exceeds the daisy wheel and is much quieter as well.

Data Base

If you need to maintain vast quantities of information that must be searched out on a daily basis, then you should investigate data base software. In essence, the computer acts as a warehouse for your information inputs. You can file and store information and then retrieve it when you need it. The storage and sorting of information can be conducted in a variety of ways. For instance, if you have a customer base of several thousand names, which you use for mailing brochures or circulars, then you may want to sort your customers by zip code. This will allow you to better analyze your customers by geographic area as well as assist the post office in mailing your advertisements. Many of the data base software packages are menu driven, which means that you are given a menu of choices to select from whenever you need certain operations performed. Once the selection is made, the computer does the rest. Data base is often used by businesses that carry large amounts of different types of inventory or want to keep track of their customers.

COMPONENTS OF A COMPUTER SYSTEM

A computer system should be designed to perform the following functions:

- Accept input
- Process input
- File and store results
- Display the results
- Print the results

Accept Input—Your computer will accept input through the use of a keyboard.

Process Input—Information is processed through a CPU which is a group of electronic on/off switches. Often the CPU is housed inside the unit that contains the keyboard.

File and Store Results—A diskette is used to store information. Think of a diskette as a file cabinet. Like a file cabinet, information is retrieved, used, and perhaps revised. Afterwards, it is placed back into the file cabinet from where it originated. The diskette allows you to perform the same function. The advantage of a diskette is that it allows vast quantities of information to be stored on a small space. The unit that allows the computer to transfer its information to the diskette is called the *disk drive*.

Display the Results—A screen is necessary to determine the type of information you are processing. A screen can be a television set or a standard cathode ray tube (CRT). When a keyboard and screen are connected, it is called a *terminal*.

Print the Results—This allows you to produce a source document so you can have a record of the information to show others. The device that performs this function is called a *printer*.

Thus, the components for a system, which is called the hardware, are: (1) keyboard and CPU, (2) disk drive, (3) CRT, and (4) printer.

TEN OF THE MOST COMMONLY USED COMPUTER TERMS

As with any industry or profession, the computer business has its share of jargon and acronyms to master in order to understand the thought being communicated. Below is a handy list of ten of the most commonly used terms so that you can better understand the workings of a computer.

Bit: A computer processes and stores all its information using electrical impulses. The impulses are channeled through an electrical on/off switch, which is called a bit, and operates under a binary number system: the value will either be 0 or 1 and represents the position of the switch.

Byte: As a rule, it takes eight bits or switches to make a byte. A byte is the smallest unit that will allow the computer to form a letter or digit.

Central Processing Unit (CPU): This unit processes and executes the instructions given to the computer.

Cathode Ray Tube (CRT): Also known as monitor, video display screen, or terminal, this is a display device similar to your television set which allows you to view both input and output information.

Disk: This is a magnetic device which allows the computer to store information. The computer program you use, on a disk as well as input data you type into the computer through your keyboard, will be processed on a disk. The necessity of a disk is that it retains information once the computer has been turned off.

File/File Structure: A file is information that is grouped together and considered a unit of information. The way information is stored and retrieved by the computer is called file structure. There are two systems used to file information: random and sequential. Random means the computer does not have to process the records in sequence and thus allows almost instantaneous access to information. Sequential, however, means that information must be accessed in a certain order before you will be able to get the exact information you need. The advantage of a sequential file structure is that it is simpler to understand, relatively inexpensive, and can be efficient and economical.

Hardware: The physical equipment of the computer, such as CPU, keyboard, printer, and disk drive.

Memory: Ability of the computer to accept information, hold it, and then deliver on demand. Memory is controlled by the CPU. RAM refers to the computer's ability to directly retrieve information regardless of the location within the storage facility. It is in RAM that software and program results are stored. Read only memory (ROM) is a solid-state storage chip that is programed at the time it is manufactured. ROM is normally used to store the information the computer needs to get itself running once the power is turned on as well as allow the computer to perform other certain functions.

Modem: A device that allows information to be transmitted over the telephone lines from one computer to another.

Operating System: Software commands that control the overall operations of the computer.

Chapter 16

HOW TO SQUEEZE MORE BENEFITS FROM YOUR BUSINESS FOR YOU AND YOUR EMPLOYEES

When it comes to providing additional benefits, such as deferred compensation plans and fringe benefits, many entrepreneurs have asked which legal form is the best, for example "Should you incorporate your business and treat yourself as an employee, or should you remain a sole proprietor?"

This chapter will explain the various programs available, some of which apply to corporations and some of which apply to sole proprietorships. The chapter begins with deferred compensation plans and ends with fringe benefits. By the time you have finished reading this chapter, you should have a good idea of how each program works and whether it will fit within your plans. This chapter explains:

* Employee benefit plans: how they work
* Defined contribution plans
* Defined benefit plans
* Qualifying a benefit plan
* Simplified employee pensions
* Self-employed retirement plans
* Fringe benefits

Note: The 1986 TRA made many changes in the deferred compensation area. These changes have numerous and varied dates as to when they take effect. Therefore, it is imperative that you exercise caution with respect to these new changes because many of them became effective after 1988.

EMPLOYEE BENEFIT PLANS: HOW THEY WORK

There is a variety of available benefit plans which will allow you and your employees to either defer compensation, establish a retirement plan, or receive fringe benefits. The chief tax advantage of these plans, as long as they are qualified, is that the Internal Revenue Code allows you, as the employer, to take a current deduction for the contributions that you make to these plans. At the same time, employees do not have to recognize those contributions as part of their gross income. For deferred compensation and retirement plans, recognition of income for tax purposes occurs only when employees actually begin to receive distributions from the plan. Moreover, there are certain instances when employees can rollover part or all of what they receive into another qualified plan to postpone taxation.

What happens if the plan is not qualified? If the IRS disqualifies your plan, you may still be able to deduct the contributions you have made if you maintain a separate account for each employee, but your employees will have to include those contributions into their gross income.

Your first step in selecting a plan for your business is to determine your objectives. Below is a list of goals you may want to consider.

* Provide maximum retirement benefits for older employees, younger employees, or highly paid employees.
* Provide retirement benefits to merely supplement employees' other retirement income.
* Provide retirement benefits of a certain amount that employees can rely on.
* Provide benefits that are payable before retirement or termination of employment.
* Provide benefits to employees' survivors.
* Provide benefits based on disability.
* Reduce estate taxes.
* Reduce gift taxes.
* Allow flexibility in the amount of employer contribution.
* Create incentives to improve employees' productivity.

Once you have determined your objectives, the next step is to match the plan to the objective. Below is a description of the more popular plans.

Defined Contribution Plans

These types of plans call for specified contributions to be credited to a separate account maintained for each employee. The employee will then be entitled to the amount that is in that account at the occurrence of some specified event.

There are three advantages of using a defined contribution plan: First, the employer's cost can be forecasted with relative certainty because it is usually based on a percentage of profits or percentage of payroll. Second, a contribution plan can be structured to allow withdrawals or loans for purchase of a home or for children's education and therefore are flexible in satisfying employees' needs. Third, governmental regulation under the Employee Retirement Income Security Act of 1974 (ERISA) is less severe than a defined benefit plan.

Profit Sharing

Profit sharing allows your employees or their beneficiaries to share in the profits of your business. You make contributions to the plan from current or retained earnings. To qualify the plan, however, you must provide a definite predetermined formula for allocating the contributions made to the plan among participating employees and distributing the funds upon the occurrence of a certain event. Events that would trigger payment are: (a) fixed number of years, (b) attainment of a stated age, (c) layoff, (d) illness, (e) retirement, (f) disability, or (g) death.

A profit-sharing plan allows flexibility for you as the employer. It does not guarantee any fixed level of benefits. Contributions are limited to profits. It is not necessary for you to contribute every year, or to contribute the same amount, or that you maintain the same percentage; however, your contributions must be substantial and recurring in order to qualify the plan. Forfeitures, which are amounts that were contributed by you but did not become a vested right of the employee because of the premature termination of employment, can also be used to reduce your contributions or to increase the accounts of your other employees. Finally, although your plan must have a predetermined formula, it does not have to provide for a fixed contribution. Thus, you can allocate in proportion to your employees' compensation or for years of service or both.

One other advantage of a profit sharing plan is that it provides an incentive to employees. Unlike a pension plan, in which amounts are usually fixed, profit sharing allows for increased contributions when profits increase; as a result, employees are motivated to increase productivity and become more efficient.

Stock Bonus and Employee Stock Ownership Programs

This method has often been used by employers as a method to motivate employees as well as to compensate them. However, it was not until the enactment of ERISA in 1974 that the concept of stock bonus became a standard employee benefit. Congress, in an effort to promote employee stock ownership, created new tax benefits for stock bonus plans as well as variants which are similar in concept to the stock bonus plan.

To date, the two most popular plans are the stock bonus plan and the employee stock ownership programs (ESOPs). The plans are similar but there are different rules and restrictions for each.

A stock bonus plan is much like a profit-sharing program except that benefits are paid in the form of your company's stock, and your contribution as an employer need not depend on profits. Moreover, your contribution to the plan may be made in cash or stock, and there is no requirement that your plan contain a definite formula for making contributions; although to be qualified, the contributions must be recurring and substantial. Stock bonus plans are most popular with employers that would like to establish a cash or deferred arrangement (CODA) but do not have the current or accumulated profits.

An ESOP, which is either a stock bonus plan or a combination stock bonus and money purchase pension plan, is designed to invest primarily in the employer's securities, which results in employees having significant equity ownership in the company that employs them. Under an ESOP, employees receive their benefits only upon leaving the company, or retiring, or after reaching the age of 59 1/2. Much of the controversy surrounding ESOPs is their use as a financing tool. In essence, the plan borrows funds from a lending institution to purchase the company's stock with the company signing a guaranty to repay the loan in the event of a default. The stock itself serves as collateral for the loan. The plan then uses the proceeds of the loan to purchase the employer's stock. The loan is repaid out of future employer contributions to the plan which are tax deductible. As the loan is repaid, the stock is released to each employee's account, which is then distributed to him or her when his or her employment terminates. Moreover, to induce lending institutions to provide loans to ESOPs, Congress has allowed lenders to exclude 50 percent of interest they receive on the loans from gross income.

Cash or Deferred Arrangements

Also known as Section 401(K) plan, CODA allows an employee who participates in a qualified profit-sharing or stock bonus plan to elect whether to receive certain employer contributions in cash or to have them paid into a qualified plan. The advantage to the employee is that it allows him or her to save for retirement on a pretax basis. The advantage to you as the employer is that it allows you to offer a substantial benefit, which is relatively low in cost.

There are two major drawbacks in using CODAs: First, the tax exclusion for amounts contributed has been limited under the TRA to $7,000 per year. Second, you must pay careful attention to highly compensated employees who are defined as: (a) 5 percent owners of the employer; (b) having received compensation from the employer; (c) having received compensation from the employer in excess of $75,000; (d) having received compensation from the employer in excess of $50,000 and was among the 20 percent of the highest paid employees during that year; or (e) having been an officer of the employer and received compensation in excess of $45,000. To qualify a CODA, according to Internal Revenue Code section 401, one of two requirements must be satisfied:

* The average percentage of income deferred by highly compensated employees does not exceed the average percentage deferred by all other eligible employees by a factor of more than 1.25, or
* The average percentage of income deferred by highly compensated employees does not exceed the average percentage deferred by all other eligible employees by more than two percentage points and does not exceed such average by a factor of more than two.

Money Purchase

This type of plan is really a pension plan and as such must satisfy U.S. Treasury regulations, which state that a pension plan must be "established and maintained by an employer primarily to provide systematically for payment of definitely determinable benefits to his or her employees over a period of years, usually for life, after retirement." As a consequence, contributions to this type of plan are based on a predetermined formula that is not subject to your discretion nor can it be based on your profits.

However, unlike a defined pension plan, in which the retirement benefits are determined in advance by a formula specified in the plan and thus may require you to make ever-increasing contributions, the money purchase requires only that you contribute according to a fixed formula. Retirement benefits received by your employees are dependent on your contributions and not the other way around. Thus, the cost of funding a retirement plan is a variable you can control, which is a very important advantage.

Defined Benefit Plans

Any qualified employee benefit plan that is not a defined contribution plan is classified as a defined benefit plan. As a rule, a defined benefit plan must provide definitely determinable benefits, and therefore, it is the benefit and not the contribution that must be calculated by the time the plan is put into effect. The advantage to the defined benefit plan is that it permits the greatest amount of annual deductible contributions. It is usually the older, highly compensated employee who benefits most from this type of situation because retirement benefits are usually calculated as a percentage of the employee's pay at the time he or she retires.

Pensions

Any plan established to provide systematically for the payment of definitely determinable benefits is a pension plan. The cost of those benefits to you as the employer is determined actuarially, which is a calculation that computes the amount of your contribution based on the benefits that are granted under the plan.

The single biggest drawback to this type of plan is that the cost of funding cannot be controlled. If investments that are made with controlled dollars are not performing as forecasted, then the amount of the contribution must be increased accordingly. Furthermore, ERISA imposes a contingent liability on the employer. If a pension plan is terminated and later found to be underfunded, the employer may be held liable to make up the difference.

Annuities

This method allows you to purchase an annuity or insurance contract directly from an insurance company or some other financial institution. Many businesses tend to lean toward this type of plan. The usual insurance company contract provides for guaranteed rates of return for a fixed period. Insurance companies are able to make this guarantee because they invest their money in government bonds.

The drawback to this type of plan is that you cannot withdraw your money if interest rates increase. Thus, an insurance contract consists of a glorified bet between you and the insurance company. You are betting the interest rates will fall, which means you win because your interest rate is locked in. The insurance company is betting that interest rates will rise, which allows it to reinvest while having to pay back only the fixed rate of return.

Qualifying a Benefit Plan

To set up a self-employed retirement plan, you may adopt your own written plan, or a written program prepared by specified sponsoring organizations that have received prior approval from the IRS on the plan form. (Master or Prototype Plans) If you decide to adopt your own plan, it may become necessary to qualify the plan with the IRS.

A qualified employee benefit plan is a written plan that you, as the employer, establish for the exclusive benefit of your employees and their beneficiaries. Contributions to a qualified plan by you are deductible when made. Generally, employees are not taxed on their contributions to the plan or earnings on those contributions until they are distributed to them. To be a qualified plan, the plan must meet numerous requirements.

Requirements for Qualification

The requirements for qualifying include the following:

Exclusive benefit requirement. A plan must be created by an employer for the exclusive benefit of employees or their beneficiaries. The IRS specifies that:

- The cost of the investment must not exceed the fair market value at the time of purchase.
- A fair return commensurate with prevailing rates must be provided.
- Sufficient liquidity must be maintained to permit distributions in accordance with the terms of the qualified plan. The safeguards and diversity that a prudent investor would adhere to must be present.

Nondiscrimination rules. To qualify a plan, contributions or benefits under such a plan must not discriminate in favor of employees who are officers, shareholders, or highly compensated individuals. Section 89 of the Internal Revenue Code requires that every employee benefit plan be tested for compliance with nondiscrimination rules. Penalties for noncompliance are severe. We recommend you see your tax advisor for help in implementing the requirements.

Participation and coverage requirements. A minimum participation requirement of a qualified plan is that all employees 21 years old in the covered group are eligible to participate after completing one year of service. If the plan provides 100 percent vesting of the employee's accrued benefits upon starting participation, the participation may be postponed until the later of three years or three years from date of employment or age 21. After the age and service requirements are met, the employee must participate no later than the earlier of:

* The first day of the first plan year beginning after the date upon which the requirements were satisfied.

* Six months after the date on which the requirements were satisfied.

* In January 1, 1989 a new participation requirement was imposed which states, "A plan will not be a qualified plan unless it benefits no fewer than the lesser of 50 employees or 40 percent or more of all employees."

Vesting requirements. The purpose of vesting requirements is to protect employees who have worked a reasonable period of time for an employer from losing employee contributions because of being fired or changing jobs. The three vesting schedules under prior law (10-year rule, 5 to 15 year graded, rule of 45) were replaced by two new schedules. The first schedule is satisfied if plan participants have a nonforfeitable right to 100 percent of their accrued benefits derived from employer contributions on completion of five years of service. The second schedule requires that participants be vested in 20 percent of their employer derived contributions after three years of service, with an additional 20 percent vesting each year thereafter until the participant is 100 percent vested after seven years of service. The law also provides that a plan may require two years of service (down from three) as a condition of eligibility to participate if the plan provides for 100 percent vesting on participation.

Distribution requirements. Prior to January 1, 1989 the required commencement date for distribution is April 1 of the calendar year following the calendar year in which the participant attains age 70 or retires, whichever is later. After 1989, distributions must begin no later than April 1 of the calendar year following the calendar year in which the participant attains age 70 1/2.

Note: The commencement date is unaffected by the actual date of retirement or termination. A 50 percent nondeductible excise tax on the excess on any taxable year of the amount that should have been distributed over the amount that actually was distributed is imposed on the payee. If a taxpayer receives an early distribution from a qualified plan, a 10 percent additional tax is levied on the amount includable in gross income. Finally, there is a 15 percent excise tax imposed on excess distributions from qualified plans. This tax is reduced by the amount of the tax imposed on early distributions, to the extent attributable to the excess distribution.

Obtaining an IRS Determination Letter

Determination letters are written for individually designed plans and are issued by the IRS Key District Office. The IRS will issue a determination letter regarding a plan's qualification as it is written, not as it operates. However, the IRS will not issue a determination letter if an employer adopts a master or prototype plan that was previously approved and if the plan's provisions are followed. If a plan is amended, a determination letter may be requested to see if the plan continues to qualify after amendment. A determination letter may be requested by an employer or a plan administrator of an individually designed plan. Determination letter requests should be made on one of the following forms, depending on the plan type:

IRS Form 5300, Application for Determination for Defined Benefit Plan for Pension Plans Other Than Money Purchase Plans. (See Exhibit 16-1.) *Note:* According to the IRS instructional booklet, the estimated average time to complete Form 5300 is 5 hours and 19 minutes. Included, as part of Exhibit 16-1, is *instructions for Forms 5300 and 5301* to assist you in the completion of these forms. Because of the complicated nature of the material, we recommend you seek the assistance of your tax advisor in completing these forms.

Schedule T (IRS Form 5300), Supplemental Application for Approval of Employee Benefit Plans Under TEFRA, TRA 1984 and REA. See Exhibit 16-2. *Note:* According to the IRS instructional booklet, the estimated average time to complete Form 5300 is 2 hours and 40 minutes.

IRS Form 5301, Application for Determination for Defined Contribution Plan for Profit-Sharing, Stock Bonus and Money Purchase Plans. See Exhibit 16-3. *Note:* According to the IRS instructional booklet, the estimated average time to complete Form 5301 is 6 hours and 34 minutes.

IRS Form 5303, Application for Determination for Collectively Bargained Plan. (See Exhibit 16–4.)

Employee Census. IRS Form 5302 must be filed with IRS Form 5300 or 5301 and may be required with IRS Form 5303. These forms are filed with the key district director for the employer's main office. See Exhibit 16-5.

Reporting and Disclosure Requirements

ERISA requires annual reports be filed by employers and plan administrators with the IRS, Department of Labor (DOL), and Pension Benefit Guaranty Corporation (PBGC). Filing of the 5500 series of forms with the IRS generally satisfies the annual reporting requirements of the IRS, DOL, and PBGC. However, there are exceptions as noted in IRS Publication 1048. See Exhibit 16-6, which is an excellent government publication that explains who must file Form 5500 series returns/reports, kinds of plans, which forms to file, when the forms must be filed, where the forms must be filed, PBGC filing requirements, and where to file IRS determination or notification letters. Below is a list of reporting requirements:

IRS Form 5500, *Annual Return/Report of Employee Benefit Plan.* Filed annually for plans with 100 or more participants at the start of the plan year. (See Exhibit 16-7.)

IRS Form 5500-C, *Return/Report of Employee Benefit Plan.* Generally filed once every three years for plans that, when the plan year started, had fewer than 100 participants. (See Exhibit 16-8.) (Form 5500-R is filed in the intervening years.)

IRS Form 5500-R, *Registration Statement of Employee Benefit Plan.* Filed for years when Form 5500-C is not filed, and for sole participant plans. (See Exhibit 16-9.)

IRS Form 5500-EZ, *Annual Return of One-Participant Pension Benefit Plan.* Filed for plans that are one-participant plans which cover only you or you and your spouse, and the business is wholly owned by you or you and your spouse or only partners in a business partnership or the partners and their spouses. (See Exhibit 16-10.)

Schedule A (Form 5500), *Insurance Information.* Attached to Form 5500, 5500-C, or 5500-R if any plan benefits are provided by an insurance company, insurance service, or similar organization. (See Exhibit 16-11.)

Schedule B (Form 5500), *Actuarial Information.* Attached to Form 5500, 5500-C, or 5500-R for most deferred benefit plans.

Schedule P (Form 5500), *Annual Return of Fiduciary of Employee Benefit Trust.* Filed by a trustee or custodian of an organization that qualifies under code section 401(a) and is exempt from tax under section 501(a) who wants to protect the organization under the statute of limitations provided in section 6501(a). (See Exhibit 16-12.)

Schedule SSA (Form 5500), *Annual Registration Statement Identifying Separated Participants With Deferred Vested Benefits.* Attached to Form 5500, 5500-C, or 5500-R for certain separated participants. (See Exhibit 16-13.)

All required annual report forms and schedules must be filed for each plan by the last day of the seventh month following the end of the plan year. File all forms and schedules with the IRS center shown on the form instructions.

Note: The record keeping, understanding of the forms, preparing of the forms, and copying, assembling, and sending of the forms to the IRS is complicated and time-consuming. The following table shows the estimated average time that the federal government believes it will take you to satisfy the requirements associated with these forms.

	Record keeping	Learning	Preparing	Copying, Assembling, Sending
Form 5500	82 hrs.	9 hrs.	13 hrs.	3/4 hr.
Schedule A	17 1/2 hrs.	1/2 hr.	1 3/4 hrs.	1/4 hr.
Schedule B	25 3/4 hrs.	1 hr.	1 1/2 hrs.	1 1/2 hrs.
Schedule C	5 hrs.	1/20 hr.	1/6 hr.	
Schedule P	2 1/6 hrs.	1 1/2 hrs.	1 1/2 hrs.	
Schedule SSA	6 3/4 hrs.	1/4 hr.	1/5 hr.	

Master and Prototype Plans

A master plan is one that has a single trust or custodial account. All employers who adopt a master plan use the single trust or custodial account. A prototype plan has separate trusts or custodial accounts for each employer who adopts the plan.

It may be more convenient for you to adopt an already existing master or prototype retirement plan than to set up a separate original plan. Master and prototype plans are sponsored only by trade or professional organizations, banks, insurance companies, or regulated investment companies. Normally, these organizations have applied for and received an opinion letter on the plan from the IRS. Your plan must still meet all the requirements in order to qualify.

Taxation of the Distribution

The tax treatment of a distribution depends on whether it is a lump sum distribution or a distribution other than a lump sum. A lump sum distribution is a payment of the entire balance to the credit of a participant in a qualified plan. Distribution from a qualified retirement plan must begin no later than April 1 following the calendar year in which the employee reaches age 70 1/2. The 1986 TRA changed the tax treatment of lump sum distributions. Capital gains treatment is phased out, except for certain distributions made to individuals who were at least 50 years old on January 1, 1986. This means that lump-sum distributions are treated as ordinary income.

The entire amount of the lump sum distribution may not be subject to taxation. To determine the taxable portion of a lump sum distribution, the following amounts must be subtracted from the total amount of the distribution:

First—nondeductible amounts contributed to the plan by the participant, and
Second—net unrealized appreciation of employer securities.

The recipient of a lump sum distribution may elect a special five-year averaging rule for the ordinary income portion of the distribution. This rule can be elected only once after attaining age 59 1/2 and the distributee must have been a plan participant for five or more years before the taxable year of the lump sum distribution. The above age requirement for five-year averaging does not apply to individuals who were at least 50 years old on December 31, 1985.

Tax treatment of a distribution other than a lump sum distribution depends on whether or not the distribution is received in the form of an annuity. Under the 1986 TRA, the three-year recovery rule has been repealed except for employees whose annuity starting date is before July 1, 1986. This means that annuity payments will be taxed by employing the exclusion ratio formula. Under this formula, the tax-free portion of annuity income is spread evenly over the annuitant's life expectancy. An employee's total exclusion is limited to the amount the employee contributed. The 1986 TRA also changed the timing of the taxability of benefits under qualified annuity plans. Now these benefits are taxable only when they are actually distributed.

In distributions that are neither lump sum distributions nor distributions in the form of an annuity, they will be taxed only to the extent that these distributions exceed the participant's investment in the contract. In other words, these distributions are treated partially as taxable employer contributions and income, and partially as nontaxable employee contributions.

It should be noted that there is a 10% tax on early distributions from any qualified retirement plan, qualified annuity, IRA, or tax sheltered annuity before the recipient reaches age 59 1/2.

SIMPLIFIED EMPLOYEE PENSION

The simplified employee pension (SEP) section 408(K) is ideal for small businesses and start-ups. Furthermore, a self-employed individual may establish and contribute into an SEP. Internal Revenue Code section 408(k) allows an employer to establish a pension plan that is exempt from many of the ERISA reporting and disclosure requirements as long as the employer makes certain disclosures regarding the plan to its employees.

In essence, the plan calls for either a direct contribution to be made by the employer or a salary reduction arrangement, called an elective deferral, whereby the employer diverts part of the employee's salary into an SEP. The SEP is an individual retirement account (IRA) which has been set up with a bank, insurance company, or any other organization that has been qualified. If an employee chooses an elective deferral arrangement, the most he or she can defer from income is $7,000. To be eligible for this type of arrangement, however, certain requirements must be met:

* At least 50 percent of your employees must choose to have amounts contributed to the SEP.
* You must have no more than 25 employees at any time during the preceding year.
* The amount deferred each year by a highly compensated employee* can be no more than 125 percent of the average deferral percentage of all other employees.

---

*A highly compensated employee is an employee who during the year or preceding year is one of the following: (1) owns more than 5 percent of the capital, outstanding stock, total voting power, or profits interest in your business; (2) received annual compensation in excess of $75,000; (3) received annual compensation in excess of $50,000 and was a member of the top-paid group of employees during the year; (4) is an officer in your corporation whose annual compensation exceeds 150 percent of the limit on the annual additions under a defined contribution plan.

Under the 1986 TRA, you as the employer must allow each employee to participate who:

- Is twenty one years or older.
- Performed services for you in the current calendar year and at least three of the five preceding calendar years.
- Received at least $300 in compensation from you for the year.

In addition, your contribution to each employee's account must have some relationship to that employee's total compensation.

Internal Revenue Code section 402 allows the employer to contribute into each employee's account up to 15 percent of the employee's compensation or $30,000, whichever is less. This includes any amounts that may have come from salary reductions. Contributions that you make into the SEP on behalf of your employees are no longer included in your employee's income in the calendar year in which the contributions are made and do not appear on Form W-2, "Wage and Tax Statement"; however, those amounts attributed to a salary reduction arrangement will have to be reported on Form W-2 and must be used in the computation of social security and unemployment tax.

SELF-EMPLOYMENT RETIREMENT PLANS (KEOGH OR H.R. 10 PLANS)

How Much to Deduct

Individuals who are self-employed are subject to limits that affect both employer contributions and the amount deductible on Form 1040. The limits differ depending on whether the plan is a defined contribution or defined benefit. Plans will not qualify for tax benefits unless certain requirements are met. These include a provision that contributions or benefits may not exceed certain limits.

Annual contributions and other additions to the account of a participant in a defined contribution plan may not exceed the smaller of:

- $30,000
- 25 percent of the participant's compensation

There are contribution deduction limits for both types of plans. The deduction for contributions to a defined contribution plan that is a profit-sharing plan may not be more than 15 percent (25 percent for a money purchase pension plan) of the employee's compensation from the business that has the plan.

The table states the maximum deductible contributions to defined contribution plans:

Plan Type	Lesser of
Profit sharing	15% or $30,000
Money purchase	25% or $30,000
Both	25% or $30,000

The deduction for contributions to a defined benefit plan is generally limited to the total contribution needed to produce your allowable benefits that accrued for the year under the plan. For plan purposes, compensation means net earnings from self-employment.

The 1986 TRA makes it clear that the earned income of a self-employed worker is determined without regard to the deductions allowable for Keogh contributions, solely for the purpose of determining to the extent the contributions are ordinary and necessary. However, net earnings are figured with regard to the deduction for contributions on behalf of common-law employees. These net earnings do not include items that are excluded by law from gross income, nor the deductions related to these items.

When to Deduct Contributions

Contributions to a plan are generally applied to the current year but may be applied to the previous year if the following conditions occur:

- The employer makes contributions by the due date of his or her tax return for the previous year, including extensions.
- The plan treats the contributions as though it had received them on the last day of the previous year.
- Either of the following conditions are satisfied: (1) The employer specifies in writing to the plan administrator or trustee that the contributions apply to the previous year, or (2) the employer deducts the contributions on the tax return for the previous year.

Sole proprietors may deduct contributions to a plan on behalf of common law employees subject to limitations mentioned above. Deductions are reported on Schedule C of IRS Form 1040. A partnership passes its deduction through to its partners on Schedule K-1 of IRS Form 1065. The partners then deduct them on Form 1040.

Qualifying Your Plan

Requirements of self-employed retirement plans are similar to those of other qualified plans. Included in plan requirements are the following:

Employee Leasing

Special rules require that all employees of employers that stand in certain relationship to one another be treated as employed by a single employer. This includes leased employees. Included in plan requirements are:

- Nondiscrimination in coverage, contributions, and benefits
- Minimum age and service requirements
- Vesting
- Limits on contributions and benefits
- Top-heavy plan requirements

A qualified plan must be a written program which is communicated to the employees and established and maintained by the employer.

Contributions must be for the exclusive benefit of employees. Contributions by the employer, or employees, or both, or by another employer that is entitled to deduct contributions to a profit-sharing plan must be for the purpose of distributing to the employees or their beneficiaries the corpus and accumulated income under the plan terms.

Plan assets may not be diverted. It must be impossible under the plan, prior to the satisfaction of all liabilities with regard to employees and their beneficiaries, for the plan's assets to be used for, or diverted to, purposes other than for their benefit.

In addition, there are minimum age and service requirements for participation. A plan may not require, as a condition of participation, that an employee have a period of service beyond the later of:

- The date the employee reaches 21 or
- The date the employee completes one year of service.

This rule does not prevent the plan from setting conditions, other than those relating to age and service, for employee participation.

Minimum Coverage

A qualified plan must meet either the percentage test or the classification test. The percentage test is met if the plan benefits either 70 percent or more of all employees or 80 percent or more of all employees who are eligible to benefit under the plan if 70 percent or more of all the employees are eligible to benefit under the plan.

The classification test is met if the plan benefits employees who qualify under an employee classification of employees that the IRS finds not to discriminate in favor of highly compensated employees.

Contributions or Benefits

Neither contributions nor benefits may discriminate in favor of highly compensated employees. A plan will not be considered discriminatory merely because contributions or benefits of, or on behalf of, employees either (1) bear a uniform relationship tu the employee's compensation or rate of compensation, or (2) the contributions or benefits based on the part of an employee's pay that is excluded from social security taxation differ from the contributions or benefits based on that part of an employee's pay not so excluded.

Limits on Contributions and Benefits

Plan contributions or benefits may not exceed certain limits. These limits apply to annual contributions and other additions to the account of a participant in a defined contribution plan and to the annual benefit payable to a participant in a defined benefit plan.

Minimum Vesting Standards

An employee's rights to his or her normal retirement benefit must be nonforfeitable upon reaching normal retirement age. Normal retirement age means the earlier of: (a) normal retirement age under the plan, or (b) the later of: (1) the time a participant reaches age 55, or (2) the tenth anniversary of the date the person began to participate in the plan.

Excluded Service

Generally, all years of service with the employer or employers maintaining the plan must be taken into account for participation and vesting purposes.

Commencement of Benefits

A plan must provide that, unless the participant otherwise elects, the payment of benefits to the participant must begin within sixty days after the close of the latest of either: (a) the plan year in which the participant reaches the earlier of age 65 or the normal retirement age, (b) the plan year in which occurs the tenth anniversary of the year in which the participant came under the plan, or (c) the plan year in which the participant separated from service.

Required Distributions

The employee's entire interest must be distributed by April 1 of the calendar year following the later of the calendar year in which the employee attains age 70 1/2 or, the calendar year in which the employee retires.

Joint and Survivor Annuity

A defined benefit and certain money purchase pension plans are required to provide automatic survivor benefits in the following cases:

- A participant who retires under the plan, in the form of a qualified joint and survivor annuity.
- A vested participant who dies before the annuity starting date and who has a surviving spouse, in the form of a qualified preretirement survivor annuity.

Requirements in the Cases of Merger, Consolidation, or Transfer of Assets

A plan must provide that in the case above, each participant would afterwards receive a benefit equal to or more than the benefit he or she would have been entitled to receive just before the merger, consolidation, or transfer of assets.

Benefits May Not Be Assigned or Alienated

This rule does not apply to a voluntary and revocable assignment by the participant of not more than 10 percent of a benefit payment and if the assignment or alienation is not to defray administration costs. There must be no benefit reduction for social security increases.

Special Rules for Plans Covering Owner–Employees

- All plans of controlled trades or businesses must be combined into a single plan for purposes of determining whether or not the plan requirements are met.
- Contributions and benefits provided for employees must be as favorable as those provided for owner–employees under the plan.
- The plan must provide that contributions to it on behalf of an owner–employee may be made only with respect to his or her earned income that is derived from the trade or business with respect to which the plan is established.

Top-heavy Plan Requirements

There are additional requirements that apply to a defined benefit plan where, as of the determination date, the present value of the cumulative accrued benefits for key employees for the plan exceed 60 percent of the present value of the cumulative accrued benefits for all employees. A defined contribution plan, if it is a top-heavy plan, which occurs when on the determination date, the sum of the account balances of key employees for the plan year exceed 60 percent of the sum of the account balances of all employees. For more information on the topic of top heavy plans, we suggest you see IRS Publication 560, *Self-Employed Retirement Plans*.

FRINGE BENEFITS

There will be times when you will want to compensate your employees in an indirect manner, such as insurance, hospitalization, moving expenses, dependent care, athletic facilities, etc. These indirect forms of payment are called fringe benefits. As a rule, they are deductible as legitimate business expenses if they are ordinary, necessary, and reasonable. Moreover, many of these fringe benefits are not counted as part of your employees' compensation for income tax purposes. Many employees consider these types of benefits to be critically important. As a result, if used correctly, fringe benefits can serve as powerful motivators which have a positive effect on hiring, retention, and productivity of employees.

Fringe benefits, however, are subject to regulation by the Department of Labor Title 29 of the Code of Federal Regulation Part 2520, which is a part of ERISA and spells out the requirements an employer must follow. Generally, ERISA divides employee benefits into two groups: (1) pension plans, such as pension and profit-sharing plans; and (2) welfare plans, which are the typical fringe benefits, such as life insurance, health insurance, and disability.

The regulations for welfare plans are not as complex or as time consuming as those for pension plans. If you are an employer with less than 100 employees and you may be eligible for fringe benefits, the most important requirement is that you disclose certain information, which means you must prepare a summary plan description. The summary plan description must be distributed to each employee within ninety days of that employee becoming a participant in the plan or 120 days after the plan first takes effect. The summary plan description must disclose the following information:

* Name of the plan
* Name and address of employer or employee organization that maintains the plan
* Employer identification number assigned by the IRS
* The plan's requirements regarding eligibility for participation, such as age or years of service
* A description or summary of the benefits
* A statement that clearly identifies circumstances which may result in disqualification, ineligibility or denial, loss or forfeiture or suspension of benefits that a participant may otherwise reasonably expect the plan to provide on the basis of the description of benefits
* The sources of contributions to the plan
* The procedures to be followed in presenting claims for benefits under the plan and the remedies available under the plan for redress of claims which are denied in whole or in part
* A statement of ERISA rights which must conform to 29 Code of Federal Regulations section 2520.102-3

If your business has over 100 employees covered by a plan then you must not only disclose the preceding information to your employees but you must do the following: file a copy of the summary description plan with the DOL; file Form 5500 with the IRS; and distribute a summary annual report to each employee.

Life Insurance

One of the most common fringe benefits employers sponsor is life insurance. Group term life insurance generally allows the employer to provide life insurance coverage on a tax-free basis to employees while deducting the premiums as a business expense. However, the really big advantage is that any death benefit the beneficiary receives will be wholly excludable from the beneficiary's gross income. It does not matter whether the beneficiary is a corporation, partnership, or family of the insured.

As a rule, insurance companies determine the amount of premiums the employer will have to pay based on the following factors:

- Nature of the work the employees perform
- Whether or not the company is reputable and financially stable
- Whether at least 75 percent of the employees will be enrolled (which may be legally required in some states)
- The amount of insurance coverage (for instance, some employers want coverage of up to four to five times each employee's salary, which will cause premiums to rapidly escalate).

For tax purposes, there are certain limitations to deductibility of premiums. Life insurance premiums are not deductible if paid on any policy covering the life of an officer of a corporation or any employee in which the employer and not the insured individual has the right to proceeds of the insurance. For example, if you purchased a life insurance contract for your employees but the contract states they are to assign the policies to you and grant you the right to terminate the policies and collect the cash values, then you would not be allowed to deduct the premiums as a tax expense. There is a slight exception to this rule: key employee insurance. Premiums that you pay on a policy covering a corporate officer or key employee are deductible only if you can prove the following:

- * The payments are an ordinary and necessary business expense in the nature of additional compensation.
- * The total amount of all compensation including insurance premiums paid to that person is reasonable.
- * The policy is not beneficial to the employer either directly or indirectly.

Finally, the IRS treats key person insurance policies as wages subject to withholding.

Another limitation is Internal Revenue Code section 79(d) which states that a group life insurance plan must not discriminate in favor of key employees either in eligibility to participate or in the type or amounts of insurance benefits provided. A key employee is defined as an employee who falls within any of the following categories at anytime during the five previous years:

- Officer of the employer earning more than $45,000 per year.
- Received more than $75,000 in annual compensation from the employer.
- Owner of more than 5 percent of the stock of the employer.
- Received more than $50,000 in annual compensation from the employer and was a member of the top-paid group of the employer during the same year. (The IRS classifies an employee in the top-paid group if the employee is in the group which consists of the top 20 percent of the employees on the basis of compensation.)

In addition to certain federal tax restrictions, you must also pay attention to state law. Each state has its own group life insurance laws that prescribe who can purchase life insurance, whether employees must be covered, grace periods for renewal, assignments of ownership by the employee, the right of the employee to name the beneficiary, and the right of the employee to obtain individual ordinary life insurance once his or her coverage under a group term life insurance policy terminates.

Health Insurance

Health insurance is comprised of two categories: basic health insurance and major medical insurance. Basic health insurance represents "first dollar coverage." As a rule, there is no deductible and the plan consists of basic services covered rather than a dollar limit. Within basic health insurance, there are two plans that are most commonly used: basic hospitalization and basic medical/surgical coverage. Hospitalization plans, such as Blue Cross, Blue Shield, usually limit their coverage to certain member hospitals. These plans will cover diagnosis and treatment of conditions covered under the plan. Typical hospital plans offer the following benefits:

- Psychiatric care
- Accidental injury
- Alcoholism treatment
- Outpatient surgery
- Home care following hospitalization
- Diagnostic services

Medical/surgical coverage pays for services of physicians and surgeons usually in a fixed payment for each type of service rendered. Many insurance companies use a standard fee schedule called *usual, customary,* and *reasonable* fees (UCR). This fee schedule establishes a maximum payment for specified procedures and is often used by numerous insurance companies. It is based on the average fee charged by physicians within a particular geographical area for a given service.

Major medical insurance represents a "second dollar coverage." It is often purchased as a supplement to basic insurance to cover those premiums that go unreimbursed by a basic plan. When major medical is used, there is a substantial deductible for services performed. Many employers are now relying solely on major medical plans by using them as a combination of a basic and supplemental plan. This combination is called a comprehensive major medical program. When an employer makes this decision, it results in lower premiums. Insurance costs for this type of plan are lower because of the deductible. It has been observed that many people will not want to pay a deductible for what they perceive as a simple visit to the doctor; an observation not lost on the insurance companies.

Whatever plan you choose, remember that group hospitalization and medical care premiums that are paid for the benefit of employees are treated as deductible expenses. However, for plans that begin after 1987, health insurance cannot discriminate in favor of highly compensated employees either in eligibility to participate or in the type or amounts of insurance benefits provided. In addition, premiums cannot be deducted if the insurance plan differentiates in the benefits it provides between individuals requiring major medical services and those who do not.

Disability

Congress encourages employers to provide employees with a disability plan. As a consequence, the Internal Revenue Code provides that a premium paid by an employer to purchase an insurance plan which will provide benefits to an employee in the event of disability constitutes an ordinary and necessary business expense and therefore is deductible.

Educational Expenses

When an employer pays the tuition expense of an employee who is enrolled in a course that is not required for his or her job or is not job-related, the tuition must be included in the gross income of the employee and therefore is subject to FICA, FUTA, and income tax withholding.

Dependent Care Assistance

Many times, employees, to be able to work, must have someone take care of their children or disabled spouse. To assist these individuals, Congress has declared that an employer who pays for child care or disabled dependent care services for employees shall be allowed to exclude the amount that is spent, up to $5,000, from the employee's gross income. In order for this fringe benefit to be excluded from employees' wages, however, it must not discriminate in favor of officers, owners, or highly compensated employees.

Moving Expenses

Moving expenses are deductible by the employer if they are ordinary, necessary, and reasonable. If you pay an employee an allowance or reimbursement in connection with a move from one job site to another you must decide whether your employee will be allowed a deduction for moving expenses in computing his or her income tax. If it is reasonable to believe that he or she will not be allowed a deduction then you must treat any amount you have paid as gross income and withhold for FICA, FUTA, and income tax. If it is reasonable to believe that the employee will be allowed a deduction then the amount paid will be included in gross income but will not be subject to FUTA, FICA, or income tax withholding.

Supplemental Unemployment Benefits

This fringe benefit is growing in popularity. The question of how much to deduct and when to deduct payments you have made as an employer depends on whether or not you have contributed to an independently controlled trust fund or made your payment directly to your former employee under some type of plan.

If the payments were made to an independently controlled trust fund that was created solely to furnish supplemental unemployment benefits for eligible employees then your payments are considered an ordinary and necessary business expense, and you may deduct the amount of the payments in the year in which they are made or accrued depending on your method of accounting.

If the payments were made directly to your former employee under a plan that is funded from amounts set aside by you then you may deduct only the actual payments that have been made or when the liability to make payment becomes fixed. Amounts you set aside to fund the plan cannot be deducted.

Athletic Facilities

More and more employers are providing athletic facilities for their employees. It is a benefit many employees enjoy, and the money spent to build and maintain a facility is deductible as long as certain requirements are met. Furthermore, an on-premises athletic facility provided to employees for their use may be excluded from an employee's gross income provided that mostly employees, their spouses, or dependents use the facility. Facilities that have been approved by Congress are gyms, swimming pools, tennis courts, and golf courses.

Cafeteria Plans

Taxable and Nontaxable Benefits

Frequently, employees are permitted to choose from a package of employer provided fringe benefits. These cafeteria plans are benefit packages that offer employee participants a choice between taking cash and other taxable benefits or taking nontaxable benefits. If the employee participant chooses taxable benefits, they are includable in the employee's gross income as compensation. If nontaxable benefits are chosen, they are excludable from the employee's gross income to the extent allowed by law. Nontaxable benefits include accident and health coverage and group term life insurance coverage.

A cafeteria plan must limit its offering of benefits only between cash or statutory nontaxable benefits specifically excluded from gross income. Examples are scholarship grants, qualified transportation, educational assistance benefits and excludable fringe benefits per Internal Revenue Code section 132.

Nondiscrimination Rules

Such a plan must cover a fair cross section of employees. It cannot discriminate with respect to coverage, eligibility for participation, contributions, and benefits. The rules mentioned above do not apply to highly compensated employees with respect to any benefit attributable to a plan year in which the plan discriminates in favor of such employees with respect to participation, contributions and benefits. Also, the rules mentioned above do not apply to any benefit attributable to a plan year in which the statutory nontaxable benefits provided to key employees exceed 25 percent of the total of such benefits provided to all employees under the plan. Such benefits must be included in the gross income of the highly compensated employee or key employee for the tax year in which the plan year ends.

Reporting Requirements

Internal Revenue Code section 6039-D requires reports to be filed by the employer on cafeteria plans. They are due the last day of the seventh month following the end of the plan year. IRS Form 5500-C must be filed for the first plan year. For subsequent years, Form 5500-R should be filed. Forms 5500-C and 5500-R are filed for pension benefit plans with fewer than 100 employees. For plans with more than 100 employees, Form 5500 must be filed annually. If you are interested in establishing a cafeteria plan, we recommend you read IRS Publication 1048, *Filing Requirements for Employee Benefit Plans*, IRS Publication 104B.

Employers' records should include the following information for filing purposes:

- Number of employees
- Number of eligible employees to participate in the plan
- Number of employees participating under the plan

- Total cost of the plan for the tax year
- Name, address, and tax identification number of the employer
- Type of business in which the employer is engaged

Chapter 16 Exhibits

Exhibit 16.1 Application for Determination for Defined
Benefit Plan: for Pension Plans Other Than Money
Purchase Plans (IRS Form 5300); Instructions for IRS
Forms 5300 and 5301

Exhibit 16.2 Supplemental Application for Approval of
Employee Benefit Plans Under TEFRA 1984, REA, and
TRA 1986 (Schedule T)

Exhibit 16.3 Application for Determination of Defined
Contribution Plan: for Profit-Sharing, Stock Bonus and
Money Purchase Plans (IRS Form 5301)

Exhibit 16.4 Application for Determination for
Collectively Bargained Plan Under Sections 401(a) and
510 (a) of the Internal Revenue Code (Form IRS 5303)

Exhibit 16.5 Employee Census (IRS Form 5302)

Exhibit 16.6 Filing Requirements for Employee Benefit
Plans (IRS Publication 1048)

Exhibit 16.7 Annual Return/Report of Employee Benefit
Plan (with 100 or More Participants) (IRS Form 5500)

Exhibit 16.8 Return/Report of Employee Benefit Plan
(with Fewer Than 100 Participants) (IRS Form 5500-C)

Exhibit 16.9 Registration Statement of Employee Benefit
Plan (with Fewer Than 100 Participants) (IRS Form
5500-R)

Exhibit 16.10 Annual Return of One-Participant (Owners
and Their Spouses) Pension Benefit Plan (IRS Form
5500EZ)

Exhibit 16.11 Insurance Information Schedule A (IRS
Form 5500)

Exhibit 16.12 Annual Return of Fiduciary of Employee
Benefit Trust Schedule P (IRS Form 5500)

Exhibit 16.13 Annual Registration Statement Identifying
Separated Participants with Deferred Vested Benefits
(Schedule SSA)

Application for
Determination for Defined Benefit Plan

For Pension Plans Other Than Money Purchase Plans
(Under sections 401(a) and 501(a) of the Internal Revenue Code)

OMB No. 1545-0197
Expires 6-30-91

For IRS Use Only
File folder number ▶
Case number ▶

▶ Church and governmental plans not subject to ERISA need not complete lines 10, 11, 12b, 12c, and 15.

▶ **Caution:** All other plans must complete all lines except as indicated on specific lines. For example, if you answer "No" to line 7, you need not complete lines 7a and 7b since they require responses only if you answer "Yes" to line 7. N/A is only an acceptable answer if an N/A block is provided. All applications are now computer screened, therefore it is important that you provide all the information requested and have the application signed by the employer, plan administrator, or authorized representative. Otherwise, we may need to correspond with you or return your application for completion, which will delay its processing.

1 a	Name of plan sponsor (employer if single employer plan)	1 b	Employer identification no.
	Address (number and street)	1 c	Employer's tax year ends Month ☐ N/A
	City or town, state, and ZIP code		Telephone number ( )

2 Person to be contacted if more information is needed (see Specific Instructions). If same as 1a, enter "same as 1a."

Name	Telephone number ( )
Address	

3 a Determination requested for (check applicable box(es)): See Instruction B. "What To File."

(i) ☐ Initial qualification—Date plan signed _____ Date plan effective _____

(ii) ☐ Amendment after initial qualification—Is plan restated? ☐ Yes ☐ No   Date amendment signed_____

Date amendment effective _____ Date plan effective_____

(iii)☐ Affiliated service group status (section 414(m))— Date effective _____ Date plan effective _____

(iv)☐ Partial termination— Date effective _____ Date plan effective _____

b Enter IRS file folder number shown on the last determination letter issued to the plan sponsor _____ ☐ N/A

c Is this application also expected to satisfy the notice requirement for this plan for merger, consolidation, or transfer of plan assets or liabilities involving another plan? See Specific Instructions. . . . . ☐ Yes ☐ No

d Were employees who are interested parties given the required notification of the filing of this application? . . . . ☐ Yes ☐ No

e Is this plan or trust currently under examination, or is any issue related to this plan or trust currently pending before the Internal Revenue Service, the Department of Labor, the Pension Benefit Guaranty Corporation, or any court?. . . . . . ☐ Yes ☐ No
If "Yes," attach explanation.

4 a	Name of plan	b	Plan number ▶ _____
		c	Plan year ends ▶ _____

5 Are there other qualified plans? (Do not consider plans that were established under union-negotiated agreements that involved other employers.) . . . . ☐ Yes ☐ No

If "Yes," enter for each other qualified plan you maintain:

a Name of plan ▶ _____

b Type of plan ▶ _____

c Rate of employer contribution ▶ _____ ☐ N/A

d Allocation formula ▶ _____ ☐ N/A

e Benefit formula or monthly benefit ▶ _____ ☐ N/A

f Number of participants ▶ _____

6 Type of entity (check only one box). (If **b**, **c**, or **d** is checked, see instructions.):

a ☐ Corporation   **b** ☐ Subchapter S corporation   **c** ☐ Sole proprietor   **d** ☐ Partnership

e ☐ Tax exempt organization   **f** ☐ Church   **g** ☐ Governmental organization

h ☐ Other (specify) ▶

7 Is this an adoption of a master or prototype plan? . . . . ☐ Yes ☐ No
If "Yes," complete **a** and **b**.

a	Name of plan	b	Notification letter no.

8 a	Type of plan: (i) ☐ Fixed benefit (ii) ☐ Unit benefit	b	Does plan provide for variable
	(iii)☐ Flat benefit (iv)☐ Other (specify) ▶		benefits?. . . . ☐ Yes ☐ No

c Is this a defined benefit plan covered under the Pension Benefit Guaranty Corporation insurance program? . . . . ☐ Yes ☐ No ☐ Not determined

Under penalties of perjury, I declare that I have examined this application, including accompanying statements, and to the best of my knowledge and belief, it is true, correct, and complete.

Signature	Title	Date

For Paperwork Reduction Act Notice, see page 1 of the instructions.

Form **5300** (Rev. 8-88)

Exhibit 16-1

(Section references are to the Internal Revenue Code, unless otherwise noted.)

Where applicable, indicate the article or section and page number of the plan or trust where the following provisions are contained. N/A (not applicable) is an appropriate response only if an "N/A" block is provided.

		Section and Page Number
9 a	General eligibility requirements: (Check box (i), (ii), (iii), or (iv), and complete (v), (vi), and (vii).)	
	(i) ☐ All employees (ii) ☐ Hourly rate employees only (iii) ☐ Salaried employees only	
	(iv) ☐ Other (specify) ▶...	
	(v) Length of service (number of years) ▶................ ☐ N/A	
	(vi) Minimum age (specify) ▶................ ☐ N/A	
	(vii) Maximum age (specify) ▶................ ☐ N/A	
b	Does any plan amendment since the last determination letter change the method of crediting service for eligibility? . . . . ☐ Yes ☐ No ☐ N/A	

		Yes	No	Not certain
10	Participation (see Specific Instructions):			
a	(i) Is the employer a member of an affiliated service group? . . . . . . : . . . . . . If your answer is "No," go to 10b.			
	(ii) Did a prior ruling letter rule on what organizations were members of the employer's affiliated service group, or did the employer receive a determination letter on this plan that considered the effect of section 414(m) on this plan?			
	(iii) If (ii) is "Yes," have the facts on which that letter was based materially changed?			
b	Is the employer a member of a controlled group of corporations or a group of trades or businesses under common control?			

		Number Enter "0" if N/A
11	Coverage of plan at (give date) .... (Attach Form(s) 5302 as necessary—see instructions.) (If the employer is a member of an affiliated service group, controlled group of corporations, or a group of trades or businesses under common control, employees of all members of the group must be considered in completing the following schedule.)	
a	Total employed (see Specific Instructions) (include all self-employed individuals)	
b	Statutory exclusions under this plan (do not count an employee more than once):	
	(i) Number excluded because of age or years of service required	
	(ii) Number excluded because of employees included in collective bargaining	
	(iii) Number of other employees excluded (specify)	
c	Total statutory exclusions under this plan (add lines b(i) through (iii))	
d	Employees not excluded under the statute (subtract line c from line a)	
e	Other employees ineligible under terms of this plan (do not count an employee included in line b)	
f	Employees eligible to participate (subtract line e from line d)	
g	Number of employees participating in this plan	
h	Percent of nonexcluded employees who are participating (divide line g by line d) . . . . . . %	
	If line h is 70% or more, go to line k.	
i	Percent of nonexcluded employees who are eligible to participate (divide line f by line d) . . . . %	
j	Percent of eligible employees who are participating (divide line g by line f) . . . . %	
	If lines h and i are less than 70% or line j is less than 80%, see Specific Instructions and attach schedule of information.	
k	Total number of participants in this plan (include certain retired and terminated employees (see Specific Instructions))	
l	Has a plan amendment since the last determination letter resulted in exclusion of previously covered employees? . . . . ☐ Yes ☐ No ☐ N/A	

		Yes	No	N/A	Section and Page Number
12	Does the plan define the following terms:				
a	Compensation (earned income if applicable)?				
b	Break in service?				
c	Hour of service (under Department of Labor Regulations)?				
d	Joint and survivor annuity?				
e	Normal retirement age?				
f	Year of service?				
g	Entry date?				

		Yes	No	N/A	Section and Page Number
13	Employee contributions:				
a	(i) Does the plan document allow voluntary deductible employee contributions?			▨	
	(ii) If "Yes," are the voluntary deductible employee contributions appropriately limited? . .			▨	
b	Are voluntary nondeductible contributions limited for all qualified plans to 10% or less of compensation?				
c	Are employee contributions nonforfeitable?				
14	Integration:			▨	
	Is this plan integrated with social security or railroad retirement?				
	If "Yes," attach a schedule of compliance with Rev. Rul. 71-446 (see Specific Instructions).	▨	▨	▨	
15	Vesting:				
a	Are years of service with other members of a controlled group of corporations, trades or businesses under common control, or an affiliated service group counted for vesting and eligibility to participate?				
b	Is employee's right to normal retirement benefits nonforfeitable on reaching normal retirement age as defined in section 411(a)(8)?			▨	
c	Does any amendment to the plan decrease any participant's accrued benefit?				
d	Does any amendment to the plan directly or indirectly affect the computation of the nonforfeitable percentage of a participant's accrued benefit?				
e	Does the plan preclude forfeiture of an employee's vested benefits for cause?			▨	

f Check only one of these boxes to indicate the vesting provisions of the plan:
- (i) ☐ Full and immediate.
- (ii) ☐ Full vesting after 10 years of service, i.e., no vesting for the first 9 years, 100% vesting after 10 years (section 411(a)(2)(A)).
- (iii) ☐ 5- to 15-year vesting (section 411(a)(2)(B)).
- (iv) ☐ Rule of 45 (section 411(a)(2)(C)).
- (v) ☐ 4/40 vesting (Rev. Procs. 75-49 and 76-11).
- (vi) ☐ 10% vesting for each year of service (not to exceed 100%).
- (vii) ☐ Other (specify—see Specific Instructions and attach schedule).

16 Administration:

a Type of funding entity:
- (i) ☐ Trust (benefits provided in whole from trust funds).
- (ii) ☐ Custodial account described in section 401(f) and not included in (iv) below.
- (iii) ☐ Trust or arrangement providing benefits partially through insurance and/or annuity contracts.
- (iv) ☐ Trust arrangement providing benefits exclusively through insurance and/or annuity contracts.
- (v) ☐ Other (specify) ▶ _____

		Yes	No	N/A	
b	Does the trust agreement prohibit reversion of funds to the employer (Rev. Rul. 77-200)? . .			▨	
17	Benefits and requirements for benefits:				
a	Normal retirement age is ▶ _____ If applicable, years of service/participation required _____	▨	▨	▨	
b	Does the plan contain an early retirement provision?			▨	
	If "Yes," (i) Early retirement age is ▶ _____	▨	▨		
	(ii) Years of service/participation required ▶ _____ . .	▨	▨		
c	Does the plan provide for payment of benefits according to section 401(a)(14)?			▨	
d	Method of determining accrued benefit ▶ _____	▨	▨	▨	
	(i) Benefit formula at normal retirement age is ▶ _____	▨	▨	▨	
	(ii) Benefit formula at early retirement age is ▶ _____	▨	▨		
	(iii) Normal form of retirement benefits is ▶ _____	▨	▨	▨	
e	Does the plan comply with the payment of benefits provisions of section 401(a)(11)? . . .			▨	
f	Are benefits under the plan definitely determinable at all times (section 401(a)(25))? . . .			▨	
g	Are benefits computed on the basis of total compensation?			▨	
	If "No," see instructions and attach schedule.	▨	▨	▨	
h	If participants may withdraw their mandatory contributions or earnings, may withdrawal be made without forfeiting vested benefits based on employer contributions?	▨	▨	▨	

		Yes	No	N/A	Section and Page Number
17	Benefits and requirements for benefits—*(Continued)*				
i	Does the plan disregard service attributable to a distribution in computing the employer-derived accrued benefit?			▨	
j	If line i is "Yes," does the plan contain provisions that satisfy Regulations section 1.411(a)-7(d)(4) or (6)?				
k	Are distributions limited so that no more than incidental death benefits are provided? . . .			▨	
l	Does the plan provide for maximum limitation under section 415?			▨	
m	Does the plan meet the requirements of section 401(a)(12)?			▨	
n	Does the plan prohibit the assignment or alienation of benefits?			▨	
o	Does the plan prohibit distribution of benefits except for retirement, disability, death, plan termination, or termination of employment?			▨	
p	As a result of a plan amendment, has the amount of benefit or rate of accrual of the benefit been reduced?				
18	Termination of plan or trust:			▨	
a	Are the participants' rights to benefits under the plan nonforfeitable (to the extent funded) on termination or partial termination of the plan?			▨	
b	Has the early termination rule been included in the plan (Regulations section 1.401-4(c))? .			▨	

Caution: The following Procedural Requirements Checklist identifies certain basic data that will facilitate the processing of your application. While no response is required to the questions, you may find that answering them will ensure that your application is processed without the need for contact to obtain missing information. If the answer to any of the questions is "No," your application is incomplete. Incomplete applications are identified through a computer screening system for return to the applicant. **This checksheet should be detached before submitting the application.**

Procedural Requirements Checklist

		Yes	No	N/A
1	**General requirements**			
a	If this application is made by a representative on behalf of the employer or plan administrator, has a current power of attorney been submitted with this application (see "Signature" under General Information)?			
b	If notices or other communications are to be sent to someone other than the employer, have you provided proper authorization by attaching a completed **Form 2848**, Power of Attorney and Declaration of Representative, or by attaching a statement that contains all the information required (see Specific Instructions)?			▨
c	Have you completed and attached Form(s) 5302?			▨
d	Have you signed the application?			▨
e	Have you completed and attached Schedule T (Form 5300)?			▨
2	**Specific requirements**			
a	If this is a request for a determination letter on initial qualification of the plan, have the following documents been attached:			
	(i) Copies of all instruments constituting the plan?			
	(ii) Copies of trust indentures, group annuity contracts, or custodial agreements?			
b	If this is a request for a determination letter on the effect of an amendment on the plan after initial qualification, have the following documents been attached:			
	(i) A copy of the plan amendment(s)?			
	(ii) A description of the amendment covering the changes to the plan sections?			
	(iii) An explanation of the plan sections before the amendment?			
	(iv) An explanation of the effect of the amendment on the provisions of the plan?			
c	If this is a request for a determination letter on the qualification of the entire plan, as amended after initial qualification, have the following documents been included:			
	(i) A copy of the plan incorporating all amendments made to the date of the application?			
	(ii) A statement indicating that the copy of the plan is complete in all respects and that a determination letter is being requested on the qualification of the entire plan?			
	(iii) A copy of trust indentures, group annuity contracts, or custodial agreements if there has been any change since copies were last furnished to IRS?			
d	For partial termination:			
	(i) Have you completed line 3a according to the Specific Instructions?			
	(ii) Have you attached the information requested for a partial termination in General Instruction B?			
e	For a plan adopted by one or more members of a controlled group:			
	(i) Have you attached the statements requested in the Specific Instructions for line 10b?			
	(ii) Have you completed line 11 according to General Instruction B and the Specific Instructions?			
f	For a multiple-employer plan that does not involve collective bargaining:			
	(i) Have you submitted one fully completed application (Form 5300 or 5301, whichever is appropriate) for all adopting employers?			
	(ii) Have you attached a Form 5300 or 5301 (as applicable) with only lines 1 through 11 completed, and a Form 5302 for each employer who adopted the plan?			
g	For a plan that contains a cash or deferred arrangement, have you submitted the appropriate information requested for line 11?			
h	For governmental and church plans, have you completed Form 5300 or 5301 according to General Instruction B?			
i	For notice of merger, consolidation, or transfer of plan assets or liabilities, have you submitted the information requested in the Specific Instructions for line 3c?			
j	For a plan that is or may be sponsored by a member of an affiliated service group:			
	(i) Have you completed lines 3a, 10, and 11 according to the Specific Instructions?			
	(ii) Have you attached the information requested in the Specific Instructions for lines 10a(ii) and (iii)?			▨
3	**Miscellaneous requirements:**			
a	Have you entered the plan sponsor's 9-digit employer identification number on line 1b?			
b	If a determination letter was previously issued to this sponsor for any plan, have you entered the file folder number on line 3b?			▨
c	Have you answered line 3d?			
d	If this plan has been amended at least four times since the last determination letter on the entire plan was issued, have you attached a copy of the plan that includes all amendments made to the plan since that determination letter was issued?			▨
e	Have you entered the effective date of the plan in the space provided by the block you checked for line 3a?			▨
f	If applicable, have you attached schedules or other documentation required by:			
	(i) Form 5300, lines 2, 3e, 6, 11j, 14, 15f(vii), and 17g?			
	(ii) Form 5301, lines 2, 3e, 11j, 14, 15f(viii), 17k, 17l, 17m, and 17s?			

**Department of the Treasury
Internal Revenue Service**

Instructions for Forms 5300 and 5301

(Revised August 1988)

Application for Determination for Defined Benefit Plan and for Defined Contribution Plan

(Section references are to the Internal Revenue Code, unless otherwise noted.)

General Information

Paperwork Reduction Act Notice.—We ask for this information to carry out the Internal Revenue laws of the United States. We need it to determine whether you meet the legal requirements for plan approval. If you want to have your plan approved by IRS, you are required to give us this information.

The estimated average times needed to complete these forms, depending on individual circumstances, are as follows:

Form 5300 – 5 hours and 19 minutes
Schedule T (Form 5300) – 2 hours and 40 minutes
Form 5301 – 6 hours and 34 minutes

If you have comments concerning the accuracy of these time estimates or suggestions for making these forms more simple, we would be happy to hear from you. You can send your comments to the Internal Revenue Service, Washington, DC 20224, Attention: IRS Reports Clearance Officer TR:FP; or the Office of Information and Regulatory Affairs, Office of Management and Budget, Washington, DC 20503, Attention: Desk Officer for Internal Revenue Service.

Purpose of Forms.—Forms 5300 and 5301 may be used for the following reasons:

1. To request a determination letter on initial qualification; on amendment after initial qualification; on affiliated service group status; or on the effect of section 414(m) on the plan.

2. To request a determination letter regarding the effect of a potential partial termination on the plan's qualification.

3. To give notice of merger, consolidation, or transfer of plan assets or liabilities (required by section 6058(b)) and request a determination on the remaining plan(s). (See Instruction B. "What To File.", and item 3c under Specific Instructions.)

Form 5301 may also be used to obtain a determination letter on whether a defined contribution plan contains a qualified cash or deferred arrangement within the meaning of section 401(k).

User Fees.—The Revenue Act of 1987 requires payment of a user fee for determination letter requests submitted to the Internal Revenue Service. Use **Form 8717**, User Fee for Employee Plan Determination Letter Request, to make payment of the fee. Form 8717 must accompany each determination letter request submitted after January 31, 1988.

Public Inspection.—The application is open to public inspection if there are more than 25 participants. Therefore, it is important that the total number of participants be shown on line 11k. See the Specific Instructions for line 11k for the definition of participant.

Disclosure Requested by Taxpayers.—See item 2 under Specific Instructions for the information the request should include.

Signature.—The application must be signed by the employer, plan administrator, or an authorized representative who must be either an attorney, a certified public accountant, or a person enrolled to practice before the IRS. (See Treasury Department Circular No. 230 (Revised).) An application made by a representative on behalf of an employer or plan administrator must be accompanied by:

1. a power of attorney specifically authorizing representation in this matter (you may use **Form 2848**, Power of Attorney and Declaration of Representative); or

2. a written declaration that the representative is a currently qualified attorney, certified public accountant, or is currently enrolled to practice before the IRS (include either the enrollment number or the expiration date of the enrollment card); and is authorized to represent the employer or plan administrator.

General Instructions

A determination letter may be requested from the IRS for the qualification of a defined benefit plan or a defined contribution plan and the exempt status of any related trust. A defined contribution plan is a plan that provides for an individual account for each participant and for benefits based solely on the amount contributed to the participant's account, and any income, expenses, gains and losses, and any forfeitures of accounts of other participants which may be allocated to the participant's account. A defined benefit plan is any plan that is not a defined contribution plan.

Determination applications are now screened for completeness by computer. For this reason, it is important that an appropriate response

be entered for each line item except as indicated in 5 below. In completing the application, be sure to pay careful attention to the following:

1. N/A (not applicable) is accepted as a response only if an N/A block is provided.

2. If an item requests a numeric response, a number must be entered.

3. If an item provides a choice of boxes to be checked, only one box should be checked unless instructed otherwise.

4. If an item provides a box or boxes to be checked, written responses are not acceptable.

5. If the Church or Governmental organization block is checked for line item 6, certain line items need not be completed. In this regard, please refer to General Instruction B. "What To File.", to determine which items to complete if this application is for a church or government plan.

Only one copy of the application must be filed. ATTACH ONLY ONE COPY OF EACH DOCUMENT AND STATEMENT REQUESTED BY THE FORM OR INSTRUCTIONS (SEE THE PROCEDURAL REQUIREMENTS CHECKLIST). If more space is needed for any item, attach additional sheets, preferably of the same size as the form.

The key district office may request additional information or return the application for completion if the application and attachments do not contain enough information to make a determination. In either case, the result will be a delay in issuing a determination letter.

A. Who May File.—1. Any employer, including a sole proprietor, a partnership which has adopted an individually designed plan, a plan sponsor or a plan administrator desiring a determination letter on an initial qualification, amendment, partial termination of a plan, affiliated services group status, or the effect of section 414(m) on the plan (all five items referred to as "determination request").

2. Any plan sponsor or plan administrator desiring a determination letter for a "determination request" that involves a plan of a controlled group of corporations (section 414(b)), or trades or businesses under common control (section 414(c)), hereafter referred to as "controlled group," or an affiliated service group (section 414(m)).

3. Any plan sponsor or plan administator desiring a determination letter for a "determination request" of a multiple-employer plan (a plan maintained by more than one employer but not a controlled group nor an affiliated service group).

4. Any employer, plan sponsor, or plan administrator desiring a determination letter for compliance with the applicable requirements of a foreign situs trust for the taxability of beneficiaries (section 402(c)) and deductions for employer contributions (section 404(a)(4)).

Note: *This form may not be filed by anyone desiring approval of a plan that covers only employees covered by a collective-bargaining agreement, including employees of the representative labor union or any plan(s) for union members or a multiemployer plan. Also, it may not be filed by anyone desiring approval of the adoption of a master or prototype plan, or a uniform plan.*

B. What To File.—Any plan sponsor or plan administrator making a determination request for a plan of a single employer should file one Form 5300 or 5301 with one **Form 5302**, Employee Census. A **Schedule T (Form 5300)**, Supplemental Application for Approval of Employee Benefit Plans Under TEFRA, TRA 1984, REA and TRA 1986, should be attached to each application. Only one application should be filed for each plan maintained by a single employer, i.e., if there are two separate plans, two separate applications should be filed, etc. A separate application must also be filed for each defined benefit plan and for each defined contribution plan.

The following specifies what to file when requesting a determination letter:

For initial qualification (Rev. Proc. 80-30, 1980-1 C.B. 685), file the application form and a copy of the appropriate documents and statements summarized in items 1, 2a(i), and 3 of the Procedural Requirements Checklist.

For the effect of an amendment on the plan (Rev. Proc. 81-19, 1981-1 C.B. 689), file the application form and a copy of the appropriate documents and statements summarized in items 1, 2b(iii), and 3 of the Procedural Requirements Checklist. A restated plan is required if four or more amendments have been made since the last restated plan was submitted. For restatement purposes, an amendment making only non-substantive plan changes need not be counted as a plan amendment. A non-substantive change will not affect the plan's qualification, for example: a change in name, address, or trustee of a corporate type plan.

Note: *In lieu of Form 5300 or 5301, a **Form 6406,** Short Form Application for Determination for Amendment of Employee Benefit Plan, may be used when requesting a determination letter on the effect of an amendment on a plan which received or was issued a favorable determination letter under the Employee Retirement Income Security Act of 1974 (ERISA). See Rev. Proc. 81-19 for further explanation on who may file Form 6406.*

For qualification of the entire plan as amended after initial qualification (Rev. Proc. 81-19), file the application form and a copy of the appropriate documents and statements summarized in items 1, 2b(iii), and 3 of the Procedural Requirements Checklist.

For partial termination (Rev. Proc. 80-30), file the application form and the appropriate documents and statements summarized in items 1, 2, and 3 of the Procedural Requirements Checklist (see the Specific Instructions and the Note for line 3a).

In addition:

(a) Attach a statement indicating whether a partial termination may have occurred or might occur as a result of proposed actions.

(b) Using the format that follows, submit a schedule of information for the plan year in which the partial (or potential partial) termination began or during which the multiemployer plan terminated. Also, submit a schedule for the next plan year, as well as for the two prior plan years, to the extent the information is available. If this is a plan maintained by more than one employer (when all employers in each affiliated service group or controlled group are considered one employer), in addition to completing (i)(e) for the entire plan, on an attached sheet show this information for each such single employer in the same format as (i)(e).

	19	19	Year of partial termination 19	19 ....
(i) Participants employed: (a) Number at beginning of plan year				
(b) Number added during the plan year				
(c) Total, add lines (a) and (b)				
(d) Number dropped during the plan year				
(e) Number at end of plan year, subtract (d) from (c)				
(f) Total number of participants in this plan separated from service without full vesting .				
(ii) Present value (as of a date during the year) of:				
(a) Plan assets				
(b) Accrued benefits . . .				
(c) Vested benefits				

(c) Submit a description of the actions that may have resulted or might result in a partial termination. Include an explanation of how the plan meets the requirements of section 411(d)(3).

For a plan sponsored by a member of an affiliated service group (Rev. Proc. 85-43, 1985-2 C.B. 501), file the application and a copy of the appropriate documents and statements listed in lines 10a(ii) and (iii) of these instructions, as well as any of the appropriate items summarized in the Procedural Requirements Checklist.

For a plan adopted by one or more members of a controlled group, file the appropriate documents and statements as summarized in the Procedural Requirements Checklist. In addition, attach a list of the member employers and explain in detail their relationship, the types of plans each member has, and the plans common to all member employers (See instructions for line 10b). For purposes of these instructions, a controlled group is considered a single entity.

Line 11 on Form 5300 or 5301 for a plan which includes one or more members of a controlled group must be completed as if the group were a single entity. If more than one member of a controlled group adopts the same plan, only one application for determination should be submitted for the controlled group. The controlled group should designate the parent corporation or a member of the group to act as the applicant for the controlled group and to furnish the names of the members who adopt the plan. The parent corporation or a member of the controlled group must have employees who are eligible to participate before adopting the qualified plan of the group.

For a multiple-employer plan that does not involve collective bargaining, file one application. In addition, attach a Form 5300 or 5301 (complete only lines 1 through 11) and a Form 5302 for each employer who adopted the plan, when all employers in each affiliated service group or controlled group are considered one employer. The applications for the individual employers must be signed by the respective employers.

For a plan that contains a cash or deferred arrangement (section 401(k)), file the appropriate documents and statements summarized in the Procedural Requirements Checklist. Also submit the information requested for line 11. See the Specific Instructions for that line.

Page 2

For governmental and church plans, the plan administrator may request a determination by filing the appropriate application. If the request is for a plan that is subject to ERISA, complete all items of the application. If the request is for a plan that is not subject to ERISA, omit the following lines on the appropriate application form:

On Form 5300, omit lines 10, 11, 12b, 12c, and 15.

On Form 5301, omit lines 10, 11, 12b, 12c, 15, 17g, 17l, and 18b.

For merger, consolidation, or transfer of plan assets or liabilities, if this application is also intended to satisfy the notice requirement of section 6058(b), attach the information requested in line 3c of the Specific Instructions.

For terminations, file Form 5310, Application for Determination Upon Termination, to request a determination letter for the complete termination of a defined benefit plan or a defined contribution plan, except that Form 5303 should be filed to request a determination letter involving the complete termination of a multiemployer plan covered by the PBGC insurance program.

Note: *If a defined benefit plan is amended to become a defined contribution plan, or if the merger of a defined benefit plan with a defined contribution plan results solely in a defined contribution plan, the defined benefit plan is considered terminated.*

C. Where To File.—File this form as follows:

(i) Single Employer Plans.—Send the forms to the District Director for the key district in which the employer's or employee organization's principal place of business is located.

(ii) Plan Maintained by More Than One Employer.—Send the forms to the District Director for the key district in which the principal place of business of the plan sponsor is located. This means the principal place of business of the association, committee, joint board of trustees, or other similar group or representatives of those who established or maintain the plan.

If the principal office of the plan sponsor is located in the following IRS District ▼	Send your fee and application to the address below ▼
Brooklyn, Albany, Augusta, Boston, Buffalo, Burlington, Hartford, Manhattan, Portsmouth, Providence	Internal Revenue Service EP/EO Division P. O. Box 1680, GPO Brooklyn, NY 11202
Baltimore, District of Columbia, Pittsburgh, Richmond, Newark, Philadelphia, Wilmington, any U.S. possession or foreign country	Internal Revenue Service EP/EO Division P. O. Box 17010 Baltimore, MD 21203
Cincinnati, Cleveland, Detroit, Indianapolis, Louisville, Parkersburg	Internal Revenue Service EP/EO Division P. O. Box 3159 Cincinnati, OH 45201
Dallas, Albuquerque, Austin, Cheyenne, Denver, Houston, Oklahoma City, Phoenix, Salt Lake City, Wichita	Internal Revenue Service EP/EO Division Mail Code 4950 DAL 1100 Commerce Street Dallas, TX 75242
Atlanta, Birmingham, Columbia, Ft. Lauderdale, Greensboro, Jackson, Jacksonville, Little Rock, Nashville, New Orleans	Internal Revenue Service EP/EO Division Room 1112 P.O. Box 941 Atlanta, GA 30301
Honolulu, Laguna Niguel, Las Vegas, Los Angeles, San Jose,	Internal Revenue Service EP Application Receiving Room 5127, P. O. Box 536 Los Angeles, CA 90053-0536
Chicago, Aberdeen, Des Moines, Fargo, Helena, Milwaukee, Omaha, St. Louis, St. Paul, Springfield	Internal Revenue Service EP/EO Division 230 S. Dearborn DPN 20-6 Chicago, IL 60604
Sacramento, San Francisco	Internal Revenue Service EP Application Receiving Stop SF 4446 P. O. Box 36001 San Francisco, CA 94102
Anchorage, Boise, Portland, Seattle	Internal Revenue Service EP Application Receiving P. O. Box 21224 Seattle, WA 98111

Domestic employers adopting foreign situs trusts should file with the District Director for the key district in which the principal place of business of the employer is located.

Foreign employers should file with the Baltimore key district.

Determination requests for industry plans established or proposed by subscribing employers with principal places of business located within the jurisdiction of more than one District Director, should be addressed to the Director for the key district where the trustee's principal place of business is located. If the plans have more than one trustee, the request should be filed with the Director for the key district where the trustees usually meet.

Specific Instructions

Use the following instructions to complete Forms 5300 and 5301. If any item requests a date or number, the RESPONSE MUST BE A DATE OR A NUMBER. N/A (not applicable) IS ACCEPTABLE ONLY IF AN N/A BLOCK IS PROVIDED.

The following instructions are keyed to the line items on the forms.

1a. Enter the name and address of the plan sponsor. If a plan covers the employees of only one employer, "plan sponsor" means the employer. For plans maintained by two or more employers (other than a plan sponsored by two or more members of a controlled group of corporations), plan sponsor means the association, committee, joint board of trustees or other similar group of representatives of those who established or maintain the plan.

For a plan sponsored by two or more members of a controlled group of corporations, "plan sponsor" means one of the members participating in the plan.

Be sure to include enough information in 1a to describe the sponsor accurately.

1b. Enter the 9-digit employer identification number (EIN) assigned to the plan sponsor. This should be the same EIN that was used or will be used when Form 5500 series returns/reports are filed for the plan.

Controlled groups of corporations whose sponsor is more than one of the members of the controlled group should insert only the EIN of one of the sponsoring members. This EIN must be used in all subsequent filings of determination letter requests for the controlled group. This is also the EIN used for filing annual returns/reports.

1c. If this application is for a single employer plan, enter the month the employer's tax year ends. For plans of more than one employer, check the N/A box.

2. The Tax Reform Act of 1976 permits a taxpayer to request IRS to disclose and discuss his or her return and/or return information with any person(s) the taxpayer designates in a written request. If you want to designate a person or persons to assist in matters relating to an application for a determination, you must give the IRS office of jurisdiction a written statement containing certain information:

(i) Your name, address, employer identification number, and plan number(s).

(ii) A paragraph that clearly identifies the person or persons you have authorized to receive the return and/or return information. It must include the name, address, and telephone number(s), and social security number(s) of the authorized person(s).

(iii) A paragraph that clearly and explicitly describes the return and/or return information that you authorize the IRS to discuss.

(iv) You must sign the request as the taxpayer making the authorization. As an alternative to providing the statement, you may substitute **Form 2848**, Power of Attorney and Declaration of Representative, or **Form 2848-D**, Tax Information Authorization and Declaration of Representative.

3a. Check applicable box(es). In the place indicated, enter the date the plan or amendment was signed. If a determination is requested based on a proposed plan or amendment, enter 9/9/99. Enter the effective date where requested. The term "effective date" means the date the plan, amendment, affiliated service group status, or partial termination becomes operative, takes effect, or changes. The EFFECTIVE DATE OF THE PLAN is a required entry for all submissions. For example, if a determination is requested for an amendment to the plan, enter the date the plan is effective as well as the date the amendment is effective.

(i) Check this box if the IRS has not previously issued a determination letter for this plan.

(ii) Check this box if this application is for an amendment to a plan for which the IRS has previously issued a determination letter.

(iii) Check this box if a determination letter is desired with regard to the effect of section 414(m) on the plan being submitted. This box should also be checked if a determination letter is desired because of a change in the affiliated service group membership.

(iv) Check this box if a determination letter is desired on the effect of a potential partial termination on the plan's qualification.

Note: For 3a(iii) and (iv), also check box 3a(i) or (ii), as applicable, unless: (1) IRS has previously issued a determination letter on this plan, and (2) an amendment is not involved in this request for a determination letter.

3b. Enter the file folder number shown on the last determination letter, if any, issued to this sponsor. For example, if the sponsor maintains two plans and previously received a determination letter for plan number 001, the file folder number shown on that determination letter should be entered on line 3b when an application is submitted with regard to plan number 002.

3c. This form may be used for applications for a determination letter only in the situations provided in line 3a. However, in the case of a merger, consolidation, or transfer of plan assets or liabilities, a plan sponsor may request a determination letter on a plan involved in such activity and may simultaneously give notice of the merger, consolidation,

or transfer of plan assets or liabilities as required by section 6058(b). Each sponsor or administrator of a plan involved in a merger, consolidation, or transfer of plan assets or liabilities must provide the notice 30 days before such event takes place. If the plan does not desire a determination letter on such a plan, Form 5310 must be filed to provide this notice. A plan sponsor who requests a determination letter on the qualified status of a plan that was involved in a merger, consolidation, or transfer of plan assets or liabilities may use Form 5300, 5301, or 5303 to simultaneously give the required notice and request a determination letter for that plan by:

(1) submitting this application not less than 30 days prior to the date of the merger, consolidation, or transfer of plan assets or liabilities, and

(2) attaching a statement containing the plan name(s) and number(s), the name(s) of the plan sponsor(s), and the employer identification number(s) for the other plan(s) involved in the merger, consolidation, or transfer. The statement should include the date of the transaction and, for a defined benefit plan, an actuarial statement of valuation for the plan showing compliance with the requirements of sections 401(a)(12) and 414(l) and the related regulations.

3d. Section 3001 of ERISA states that the applicant must provide evidence that each employee who qualifies as an interested party has been notified of the application. Check "Yes" only if you have notified each employee as required by regulations under section 7476. Rules defining "interested parties" and providing for the form of notification are contained in the regulations. **Note:** An example of an acceptable format can be found in Rev. Proc. 80-30.

4a. Enter the name you designated for your plan.

4b. You should assign a three-digit number beginning with "001", and continuing in numerical sequence, to each plan you adopt. This numbering will differentiate your plans. Enter your three-digit number here. The number that is assigned to a plan must not be changed or used for any other plan.

4c. Plan year means the calendar, policy, or fiscal year on which the records of the plan are kept.

6. Check only one box. All subchapter S corporations, check box (b). If the plan involves more than one employer, check box (h) and enter an appropriate explanation, i.e., controlled group of corporations, employers under common control, or non-controlled group of employers, such as multiple employers.

10. You should complete line 10 for the plan sponsor filing this application. However, for a multiple-employer plan, consider line 10 separately for each employer to determine the employers for whom information must be attached. In addition, answer line 10a(i) "Yes" if the answer is yes for any employer participating in the plan.

If the plan sponsor is a member of an affiliated service group described in section 414(m), all employees of the affiliated service group members will be treated as employed by a single employer for purposes of certain qualification requirements such as coverage. See Rev. Proc. 85-43, 1985-2 C.B. 501, for procedures on submission of an application to the key district office for a determination letter on the effect of section 414(m). Also see Rev. Rul. 81-105, 1981-1 C.B. 256, regarding the application of section 414(m).

10a(ii) and (iii). If you or any member (or possible member) of the affiliated service group received a ruling or determination letter regarding section 414(m), attach a copy of the letter to the application. If you are uncertain as to whether or not you are a member of an affiliated service group, and no affiliated service group ruling or determination letter is available, or if the facts have changed since the ruling or determination letter was issued, attach the following information:

(1) A description of the nature of the business of the employer, specifically discussing whether it is a service organization or an organization whose principal business is the performance of management functions for another organization, including the reasons therefor;

(2) The identification of other members (or possible members) of the affiliated service group;

(3) A description of the nature of the business of each member (or possible member) of the affiliated service group describing the type of organization (corporation, partnership, etc.) and indicating whether such member is a service organization or an organization whose principal business is the performance of management functions for the other group member(s);

(4) The ownership interests between the employer and the members (or possible members) of the affiliated service group (including ownership interests as described in section 414(m)(2)(B);

(5) A description of services performed for the employers by the members (or possible members) of the affiliated services group, or vice versa (including the percentage of each member's or possible member's gross receipts and service receipts provided by such services, if available, and data as to whether their services are a significant portion of the member's business) and whether or not, as of December 13, 1980, it was unusual for the services to be performed by employees of organizations in that service field in the United States;

(6) A description of how the employer and the members (or possible members) of the affiliated service group associate in performing services for other parties;

(7) A description of management functions, if any, performed by the employer for the member(s) (or possible member(s)) of the affiliated service group, or received by the employer from any other member(s) (or possible member(s)) of the group (including data as to whether such management functions are performed on a regular and continuous basis) and whether or not it is unusual for such management functions to be performed by employees of organizations in the employer's business field in the United States;

(8) If management functions are performed by the employer for the member(s) (or possible member(s)) of the affiliated service group, a description as to what part of the employer's business constitutes the performance of management functions for the member(s) (or possible member(s)) of the group (including the percentage of gross receipts derived from management activities as compared to the gross receipts from other activities);

(9) A brief description of any other plan(s) maintained by the member(s) (or possible member(s)) of the affiliated service group, if such other plan(s) is designated as a unit for qualification purposes with the plan for which a determination letter has been requested;

(10) A description of how the plan(s) satisfies the coverage requirements of section 410(b) if the member(s) (or possible member(s)) of the affiliated service group is considered part of an affiliated service group with the employer.

10b. If the adopting employer is a member of a controlled group, attach a statement showing in detail all members of the group, their relationship to the adopting employer, the types of plans each member has, and the plans common to all members.

11. Enter the total number of employees as of the date given on line 11. Include all self-employed individuals. If the answer to 10a is "Yes," or "Not certain," or the answer to 10b is "Yes," complete the coverage information (line 11) as if the employees of all the member(s) (or possible member(s)) of the controlled group or affiliated service group are employees of a single employer. If the plan involves more than one such group, a separate line 11 should be attached for each such group. Total employed should include any individual considered a leased employee of the employer within the meaning of section 414(n). For a plan in which more than one employer participates (a multiple-employer plan) that does not involve a controlled group or an affiliated service group, answer a through I of line 11 separately for each employer participating in the plan. For a plan that contains a cash or deferred arrangement (section 401(k)), complete line 11 as stated above. In addition, if the plan does not contain a provision for fail-safe devices or other mechanisms that will assure compliance with the antidiscrimination requirements of section 401(k) (including provisions in the Tax Reform Act of 1984), submit a demonstration of how the discrimination tests in section 401(a)(4) and 410(b) will be satisfied. This may require a schedule of the proposed employee allocations as of the end of the plan year in which the cash or deferred arrangements will become effective, or a schedule of the actual allocations as of the end of the latest year of operation.

11b. *Employees included in collective bargaining.*—Section 410(b)(3)(A) provides that a plan may exclude certain employees who are included in a unit of employees covered by an agreement which the Secretary of Labor finds to be a collective bargaining agreement between employee representatives and one or more employers, if there is evidence that retirement benefits were the subject of good faith bargaining between such employee representatives and such employer or employers.

Nonresident aliens. Section 410(b)(3) provides that a plan may exclude nonresident alien employees who receive no earned income from the employer which constitutes income from sources within the United States.

11e. Enter the number of employees ineligible under the terms of the plan for reasons such as minimum pay, hourly pay, maximum age, etc. Do not include persons excluded under line 11b. Also, do not include individuals who are ineligible solely because they elect not to be covered by the plan, or do not make mandatory contributions to the plan, or those who are not eligible because they are employed by a member of a controlled group or affiliated service group that has not adopted the plan.

11j. The percentage test of section 410(b)(1)(A) is met only if: (1) line 11h is 70% or more; or (2) line 11i is 70% or more and line 11j is 80% or more.

If the plan does not meet the percentage test, you must submit a schedule using the format below to show that the plan meets the requirements of section 410(b)(1)(B). The question of acceptable classification is a continuing one and must be met in all following years as well. You should review your classification at the time you submit your annual return/report. If the plan does not, by itself, satisfy the coverage requirements, other plans may be designated as a unit for this purpose. If any other plan is considered in combination with this plan, attach a schedule that follows the format of line 11. Complete the schedule as though the combined plans were a single plan. Also attach a brief description of the other plans considered.

1		2	3	4	5
*Compensation range		Employees not excluded (see note)	Employees ineligible to participate	Employees participating	Participants who are officers or shareholders
At least	But not more than				
Totals					

*The compensation brackets used must reflect the employer's pay pattern.
Note: *In column 2, enter the total number of employees less exclusions under section 410(b)(2) if provided in the plan.*

11k. The term "participant" includes retirees and other former employees and the beneficiaries of both who are receiving benefits under the plan, or will at some future date receive benefits under the plan. Thus, the figure to enter on this line is the total of: the number of employees who are participating in the plan, (2) former employees who are receiving benefits under the plan, or will at some future date receive benefits under the plan, and (3) beneficiaries of former employees who are receiving benefits under the plan. This means one beneficiary for each former employee regardless of the number of individuals receiving benefits. For example, payment of a former employee's benefits to three children is considered as a payment to one beneficiary.

14, Form 5300—all integrated plans. Form 5301—integrated target benefit plans. Show that the integration limit actually used by the plan cannot exceed the allowable plan integration limit. In determining the allowable integration limit, take into account all plan features that require an adjustment (for example, preretirement death benefit, normal form of payment other than life annuity, average compensation of less than 5 years).

15a. For a definition of a controlled group or trades or businesses under common control, see sections 414(b) and (c). For a definition of an affiliated service group, see section 414(m).

15d. This includes any amendment to a vesting schedule or any plan amendment that directly or indirectly affects the computation of the nonforfeitable percentage of a participant's accrued benefit, for example, each change in the plan which affects either the vesting percentages for years of service or the computation of years of service. See Regulations section 1.411(a)-8(c).

15f(vii), Form 5301. A class year plan is a plan in which the amount of vesting is determined separately with respect to each year's contributions and each contribution becomes 100% vested no later than the 5th plan year following the plan year for which the contributions were made.

15f(vii), Form 5300 and 15f(viii), Form 5301. Check one box to indicate the regular (not top-heavy) vesting schedule used in the plan. If box "Other" is checked and the vesting schedule is less rapid than 15f(v), submit a schedule of turnover of employees or provide enough facts upon which a determination can be made that the vesting schedule of the plan is satisfactory. See Rev. Proc. 76-11, 1976-1 C.B. 550, or its successor, if any. Note that this is a requirement for all initial qualifications.

17g, Form 5300. If compensation other than "total compensation" (generally Form W-2 pay) is used to determine benefits, you must submit with this application a schedule similar in format to the one in 17k (below) if there are more than 25 participants in the plan.

17i, Form 5301. See Regulations sections 1.401-1(b)(1)(ii) and (iii) for an explanation of distributions that will not affect the qualified status of a profit-sharing or stock bonus plan. An example of another event permitting distributions in a profit-sharing or stock bonus plan would be a hardship distribution within two years from the date of the contribution.

17k, Form 5301. If other than "total compensation" (generally Form W-2 pay) is used as the basis for allocating the employer's contributions, you must submit with this application a schedule in similar format to the following, if there are more than 25 participants in the plan.

1		2	3	4	5
*Brackets based on total compensation		Number of employees in bracket	Total compensation for employees included in compensation bracket	Amount of compensation used to determine benefits	Percentage of total (col. 4 divided by col. 3)
At least	But not more than				
Totals					

*The compensation brackets used must reflect the employer's pay pattern.

Before submitting your application, be sure that it conforms to the Procedural Requirements Checklist in the Form 5300 or 5301.

☆U.S. Government Printing Office: 1988-242-473/80008

SCHEDULE T	**Supplemental Application for Approval**	OMB No. 1545-0197
(Form 5300)	**of Employee Benefit Plans Under TEFRA,**	Expires 9-30-88
(Rev. February 1987)	**TRA 1984, REA, and TRA 1986**	
Department of the Treasury Internal Revenue Service	▶ Section references are to the Internal Revenue Code unless otherwise noted.	**For IRS Use Only File Folder Number**

Caution: Schedule T must be attached to all determination requests made on Form 5300, 5301, 5303, 5307, or 6406, including requests by adopters of master or prototype plans of self-employed individuals except: (1) adopters of master or prototype plans who received favorable opinion letters after June 19, 1984, that have only one plan, or (2) adopters of uniform plans who received notification letters after December 31, 1984, the effective date of Revenue Procedure 84-86, and that have only one plan.

This form is designed to get a response of "N/A" if a line would otherwise be answered "No," and to get an entry in the "Article or Section and Page Number" column if the answer would be "Yes."

1a	Name of plan sponsor (employer if single employer)	1b	Employer Identification Number
	Address (number and street)		
	City or town, state, and ZIP code		

Answer items 2 through 27 either by checking "N/A" if the item does not apply, or by entering the Article or Section and Page Number of the plan where the provision is found in the plan.	N/A	Article or Section and Page Number
2a Is the plan:		
(i) A collectively-bargained plan that has never been top-heavy as defined in section 416, and that covers only employees who are covered by a collective bargaining agreement under which retirement benefits were the subject of good faith bargaining, or employees of employee representatives, or		
(ii) A governmental plan?		
If (i) or (ii) is "Yes," do not complete items 3-11 or 24e.		
b Is the plan:		
(i) A master or prototype plan which received a favorable opinion letter after June 19, 1984, and the applicant has more than one plan, or		
(ii) A uniform plan which received a notification letter after December 31, 1984, and the applicant has more than one plan?		
If (i) or (ii) is "Yes," complete only items 10, 24c, and 24d.		
3a Does the plan limit the compensation that can be taken into account for any employee to $200,000 for any year in which the plan is top-heavy?		
b Does the plan provide vesting which is at least as favorable as is required under section 416(b)? . .		
4 For a defined benefit plan:		
a Are minimum benefits provided for each non-key employee which are not less than 2% of the employee's average high 5 consecutive years of compensation per year of service (not to exceed 20% in total)?		
b Does each non-key employee obtain the minimum benefit if such non-key employee has 1,000 hours of service during an accrual computation period without exception?		
5 For defined contribution plans only:		
a Does the plan provide for a minimum contribution (allocation) which is not less than the lower of 3% of compensation or the highest rate of contribution applicable to any key employee?		
b Does the plan provide that, in determining the highest rate of contribution applicable to any key employee, amounts that a key employee elects to defer under a qualified section 401(k) arrangement are counted for purposes of section 416?		
c Will a non-key employee receive a minimum contribution if that employee has not separated from service at the end of the plan year?		
6 Are account balances attributable to minimum contributions fully nonforfeitable even though a non-key employee withdraws mandatory contributions?		
7 Are the plan provisions described in item 4 or 5 (whichever is applicable) and items 3 and 6 operative for each year regardless of whether the plan is actually top-heavy?		
If "Yes," do not complete items 8 and 9.		
8 Testing for top-heaviness:		
a Does the plan define:		
(i) Determination date?		
(ii) Valuation date?		
(iii) Required aggregation?		

For Paperwork Reduction Act Notice, see the Instructions for Form 5300.　　　　　　　　　　　Schedule T (Form 5300) (Rev. 2-87)

Exhibit 16-2

Answer all items either by checking "N/A" if the item does not apply, or by entering the Article or Section and Page Number of the plan where the provision is found in the plan.	N/A	Article or Section and Page Number
8 Testing for top-heaviness (continued):		
(iv) Permissive aggregation?		
(v) Top-heavy ratio?		
(vi) Key employee?		
(vii) Non-key employee?		
b If this is a defined benefit plan, are the actuarial assumptions used to determine the present value of accrued benefits:	/////	/////
(i) Specified in the plan?		
(ii) Identical for all defined benefit plans being tested?		
9 Does the plan provide that the accrued benefits and account balances that are to be taken into account in order to determine top-heaviness must relate to the proper determination date (see instructions)? . .	/////	/////
10 Answer 10 only if the employer maintains or has maintained more than one plan.		
a If this plan is a defined benefit plan, does it provide the top-heavy minimum benefit?		
b If both defined contribution and defined benefit plans have been or are being maintained, is the top-heavy minimum contribution for each non-key employee participating in both plans comparable to the top-heavy minimum benefit?		
c Does a floor offset arrangement apply with the floor being the top-heavy defined benefit minimum?		
d If both defined contribution and defined benefit plans have been or are being maintained, is a minimum 5% of compensation provided for each non-key employee participating in both plans? . .		
e If both defined contribution and defined benefit plans have been or are being maintained, is a minimum 2% of compensation provided for each non-key employee who participates solely in the defined benefit plan?		
11a Does this plan always use a factor for purposes of determining the fractions under section 415(e) of 1.0 times the applicable dollar limitation? If "Yes," do not answer 11b or c		
b Does this plan use a limitation of 1.0 times the dollar limitation if the top-heavy ratio is greater than 90%?		
c If the top-heavy ratio is between 60% and 90%, and the plan uses a factor of 1.25 times the dollar limitation, does the plan provide for one of the following:	/////	/////
(i) If this is a defined benefit plan, a defined benefit minimum of 3% in lieu of the 2% minimum described in 4a (not to exceed 30% in total)?		
(ii) If this is a defined contribution plan, a defined contribution minimum of 4% in lieu of the 3% described in 5a?		
d When a non-key employee is covered by both a defined benefit plan and a defined contribution plan, both of which are top-heavy, and the employer wants to use the 1.25 factor, then does such an employee receive one of the following:	/////	/////
(i) A defined contribution minimum comparable to a 3% defined benefit minimum?		
(ii) A floor offset in a defined benefit plan with the floor being a 3% minimum described in 11c(i)?		
(iii) If this is a defined contribution plan, and this plan and a defined benefit plan of the employer are both top-heavy, a defined contribution minimum of 7½% of compensation for each non-key employee covered under both plans?		
12 If this is a profit-sharing plan, are employer contributions on behalf of permanently and totally disabled employees nonforfeitable when made?		
13 Does the plan provide that the minimum age required for participation may not exceed age 21? . .		
14 Does the plan count years of service upon attainment of age 18 for vesting purposes?		
15 Does the plan require at least five consecutive 1-year breaks in service in order to disregard:		
a Post-break service for pre-break vested accrued benefits (see instructions)?		
b In the case of a nonvested participant, pre-break service for participation or vesting?		
16 Are hours of service credited, during maternity or paternity absence, for purposes of determining whether a break in service has occurred?		
17 If the plan provides for disregarding service attributable to a cash out, does it meet the requirements of Code section 411(a)(7)(C)?		
18 Does the plan (if a pension plan) provide for the payment of benefits in the form of a qualified joint and survivor annuity and a qualified preretirement survivor annuity?		
19 If the answer to 18 is "N/A," and this is a profit-sharing or stock bonus plan, does it provide:	/////	/////
a The participant's nonforfeitable account balance will be paid on the death of the participant to the surviving spouse or, if the surviving spouse consents, or if there is no surviving spouse, to a designated beneficiary of the participant?		

Answer all items either by checking "N/A" if the item does not apply, or by entering the Article or Section and Page Number of the plan where the provision is found in the plan.	N/A	Article or Section and Page Number

19 (Continued):

b If a life annuity is offered and elected by the participant, the participant's benefits will be paid in the form of a qualified joint and survivor annuity? . . . .

c If the plan is, or may become, a direct or indirect transferee, that the survivor annuity benefit described in 18 will be provided with respect to the participant who received the transfer? . . .

20 Does the plan provide a procedure for the participant to waive the qualified joint and survivor annuity and the qualified preretirement survivor annuity during the election period? . . . . .

a In the case of the qualified joint and survivor annuity, does the election period begin no later than 90 days before the annuity starting date? . . . .

b In the case of a qualified preretirement survivor annuity, does the election period begin on the first day of the plan year in which the participant attains age 35 and end on the date of the plan participant's death? . . . .

c Does any waiver require the written consent of the participant's spouse to the waiver? . . . . . .

21 Does the plan provide that if the present value of the vested accrued benefit of a participant exceeds $3,500, then the benefit cannot be paid out immediately without the consent of the participant? . . . .

22 If this is a defined benefit plan, are the actuarial assumptions used to determine the amount of any benefit specified in the plan so as to preclude employer discretion? . . . .

23 If this application relates to an amendment to an existing plan, does the amendment preclude either:

a The elimination or reduction of an early retirement benefit or a subsidy that continues after retirement? . . . .

b Elimination of an optional form of benefit? . . . .

24 Does the plan provide for the following within the limitations of section 415:

a For a defined contribution plan:

   (i) Definition and limitation of annual additions according to the Code and regulations? . . . .

   (ii) A mechanism by which excess annual additions due to a reasonable estimate of a participant's annual compensation or an allocation of forfeitures are reduced according to one of the methods described in the regulations? . . . .

b For a defined benefit plan:

   (i) An annual benefit to which a participant may be entitled, limited to the lesser of (a) 100% of the participant's average compensation for his or her high 3 years of service, or (b) $90,000 (or other amounts as adjusted for cost of living increases under section 415(d))? . . . . .

   (ii) If the plan provides a retirement benefit beginning on or after age 55 but before social security retirement age, is the benefit limited to the greater of (a) the actuarial equivalent of a $90,000 (or the adjusted dollar limitation in item 24b(i) above) annual benefit beginning at social security retirement age, or (b) $75,000? . . . .

   (iii) If the plan provides a retirement benefit beginning before age 55, is the benefit limited to the greater of (a) the actuarial equivalent of a $75,000 annual benefit beginning at age 55, or (b) the actuarial equivalent of a $90,000 (or the adjusted dollar limitation in 24b(i) above) annual benefit beginning at social security retirement age? . . . .

   (iv) Are the actuarial equivalents in 24b(ii) and (iii) based on an interest rate not less than the greater of 5% or the rate specified in the plan? . . . .

   (v) If the retirement benefit under the plan begins after social security retirement age, provision for an increase in the maximum dollar limitation on benefits to the actuarial equivalent of a $90,000 (or the adjusted dollar limitation in 24b(i) above) annual benefit beginning at social security retirement age, using an interest assumption no greater than the lesser of 5% or the rate specified in the plan? . . . .

   (vi) If the employer maintains, or at one time maintained, another qualified defined benefit plan, the plan or plans preclude the possibility that the limitations of 24b(i)-(v) will be exceeded when all such defined benefit plans are treated as one plan? . . . .

   (vii) If the plan is a pre-TEFRA defined benefit plan, does it preserve a participant's accrued benefit that was properly accrued under pre-TEFRA law? . . . .

c If the employer maintains another qualified defined contribution plan (or a defined benefit plan to which nondeductible employee contributions are made), the plan or plans preclude the possibility that the limitations of 24a(i) and/or 24b(i) will be exceeded when all such defined contribution plans and/or defined benefit plans are treated as one plan? . . . .

Answer all items either by checking "N/A" if the item does not apply, or by entering the Article or Section and Page Number of the plan where the provision is found in the plan.	N/A	Article or Section and Page Number
24 (Continued):		
d If this plan is a defined contribution plan and the employer maintains, or at any time maintained, a qualified defined benefit plan, or if this plan is a defined benefit plan and the employer maintains, or at any time maintained, a qualified defined contribution plan, do the provisions of the plan preclude the possibility that, with respect to any participant for a limitation year, the sum of the defined benefit plan fraction and the defined contribution plan fraction will exceed 1.0?		
e If the plan is or becomes a top-heavy plan subject to the requirement of section 416(h)(1), the required adjustment to the computation of the defined benefit and defined contribution fraction denominators will be made?		
25 If this is an integrated defined contribution plan, does the contribution rate satisfy section 401(l)? .		
26a Does the employer receive services from any leased employees within the meaning of section 414(n)?		
b If "Yes," are the leased employees included as employees in the employee data given for the plan? .		
27a Distributions before death:		
(i) Does the plan require that distributions to a participant other than a 5% owner begin not later than April 1 of the calendar year following the later of the calendar year in which the participant attains age 70½ or the calendar year in which the participant retires?		
(ii) Does the plan require that distributions to a 5% owner begin not later than April 1 following the calendar year in which he or she attains age 70½?		
(iii) Will distribution(s) of the participant's entire interest be made in one of the following ways: in a lump sum; over the life of the participant; over the life of the participant and a designated beneficiary; over a period certain not extending beyond the life expectancy of the participant; or over a period certain not extending beyond the joint life and last survivor expectancy of the participant and a designated beneficiary?		
b Distributions after death:		
(i) Does the plan provide that, if distribution has started before the participant's death, the remaining interest will be distributed at least as rapidly as under the method being used as of the date of the participant's death?		
(ii) Does the plan provide that, if the participant dies before distribution begins, the portion of the participant's interest that is not payable to a beneficiary designated by the participant will be distributed within 5 years after such participant's death?		
(iii) Does the plan provide that, if the participant dies before distribution begins, any portion of the participant's interest that is payable to a beneficiary designated by the participant will be distributed over the life of such beneficiary (or over a period not to exceed the life expectancy of the beneficiary) beginning not later than the later of one year after the participant's death, or if the designated beneficiary is the participant's surviving spouse, the date on which the participant would have attained age 70½?		
c Transitional rule:		
If the plan permits an employee to designate before January 1, 1984, a method of distribution that does not satisfy section 401(a)(9), as in effect on January 1, 1985, does the method satisfy the requirements of section 401(a) as in effect before January 1, 1984?		

Reminder: *If this request relates to the adoption of a master or prototype or uniform plan, you must attach the latest opinion or notification letter issued to the sponsor. If this request relates to an amendment of an individually designed plan, you must attach a copy of the latest determination letter.*

Instructions

(Section references are to the Internal Revenue Code unless otherwise noted.)

Purpose of Form.—Schedule T (Form 5300) is used by applicants requesting a favorable determination letter on the qualified status of certain retirement plans to provide information under the Tax Equity and Fiscal Responsibility Act of 1982 (TEFRA), the Tax Reform Act of 1984 (TRA), Retirement Equity Act of 1984 (REA), and the Tax Reform Act of 1986 (TRA 1986).

It should be attached to a Form 5300, 5301, 5303, 5307, or 6406 (whichever is appropriate) in order for the application to be complete. However, if you previously submitted a Schedule T with an application covering amendments under TEFRA, TRA of 1984, and REA, and received a favorable determination letter covering the amendments, and you are now making amendments not under these laws; attach a photocopy of the previous Schedule T and a brief explanation that your amendments under these laws have been approved by IRS (give date approved) and a new Schedule T is not required under these circumstances.

Note: *Determination letters pursuant to the submission of this form apply to changes under the Tax Reform Act of 1986 only to the extent that they are made to incorporate changes under sections 415(b)(2) and 416(g)(4) as amended by TRA of 1986.*

1. Enter the name, address, and EIN of the plan sponsor as shown on the Form 5300, 5301, 5303, 5307, or 6406 to which this schedule is attached.

2. Plans are not required to contain section 416 provisions, except for 416(h) in cases of multiple plans, if the plans contain a single benefit structure that satisfies the requirements of section 416(b), (c), and (d). Also, certain collectively-bargained plans and government plans need not contain section 416 provisions. See T-36, T-37, and T-38 of Section 1.416 of the Income Tax Regulations. Unless the above applies, the plan must contain provisions that are effective in any plan year in which the plan is top-heavy. The contributions must satisfy the vesting requirement of section 416(b), the minimum benefit provision of section 416(c), the compensation limits of section 416(d), and the adjustment to section 415 limits in section 416(h). The plan must also preclude any change in the plan's benefit structure (including vesting) resulting from a change in the plan's top-heavy status from violating section 411(a)(10).

4a. See sections 416(c)(1)(A) and (B).

4b. See M-4 of regulations section 1.416, effective for plan years beginning after December 31,1983.

5b. Effective for plan years beginning after December 31, 1984, see T-29 of regulations section 1.416.

8. A qualified plan must contain some mechanism by which the plan administrator can implement the section 416 minimum requirements if the plan becomes top-heavy. A defined benefit plan is top-heavy when the ratio of the present value of accrued benefits for key employees to the present value of accrued benefits for all employees (including beneficiaries but excluding former key employees who are now non-key employees) exceeds 60%. All distributions that were made during the 5-year period ending on the most recent determination date must be taken into account. For plan years beginning after December 31, 1984, if an individual has not received compensation as an employee with respect to any plan of the employer at any time during the five-year period ending on the determination date for such (top-heaviness) testing, then any accrued benefit or account balance of the individual is disregarded.

Employee contributions, whether mandatory or voluntary, must be taken into account (except for deductible employee contributions).

If the employer maintains other qualified plans (including a Simplified Employee Plan), benefits from all plans in the required aggregation group must be taken into account for purposes of determining the top-heavy ratio.

For more complete definitions of the terms in Item 8, see section 416 and regulations section 1.416.

9. For plan years beginning after December 31, 1986, accrued benefits will be treated as accruing ratably for purposes of determining whether the plan is top-heavy.

10. See M-12 of regulations section 1.416.

11. See T-37, M-12, and M-14 of regulations section 1.416.

12. This item is effective for tax years beginning after 1981.

13. REA amended section 410(a)(1)(A)(i) to provide that a plan cannot exclude from participation employees who have attained age 21, effective for plan years beginning after December 31, 1984.

14. REA amended section 411(a)(4)(A) to provide that a plan must count, for vesting purposes, years of service completed after the employee has attained age 18. This change is effective for plan years beginning after December 31, 1984.

15. See sections 410(a)(5)(D) and 411(a)(6)(C) and (D) as amended by REA. Effective for plan years beginning after December 31, 1984.

16. Sections 410(a)(5)(E) and 411(a)(6)(E) were added to the Code by REA to provide, in general, that a maximum of 501 hours of service must be credited to an individual who is on maternity or paternity leave, effective for plan years beginning after December 31, 1984.

18-20. See section 401(a)(11) as amended by REA, effective for plan years beginning after December 31, 1984.

21. See section 411(a)(7)(B) as amended by REA and effective for plan years beginning after December 31, 1984.

22. See section 401(a)(25) and Rev. Rul. 79-90, 1979-1 C.B. 155.

23. See section 411(d)(6) and Rev. Rul. 81-12, 1981-1 C.B. 228.

24. TEFRA decreased the maximum dollar limitations applicable to qualified defined contribution and defined benefit plans. These new limits apply to limitation years ending after July 1, 1982, for plans not in existence on that date; and apply to limitation years beginning after December 31, 1982, for all other plans. Plans may continue to have "Cost of Living" language even though no adjustments will be made with respect to any calendar year beginning before 1988. See T-1 and T-7 of Notice 83-10, 1983-1 C.B. 536. Also see sections 415, 415(b)(2)(C), (D), and (E); and 415(d)(2)(A) and 415(d)(3) as amended by TRA of 1984.

26. Section 414(n) (added by TEFRA) deals with persons who are the employees of any employee leasing organization, but who perform services during the course of their employment for a separate trade or business (a recipient organization). Such leased employees are to be considered employees of the recipient organization at certain times and for certain qualification requirements unless the leasing organization adopts and maintains the type of qualified plan specified in section 414(n)(5).

Section 414(n)(5) provides a safe harbor for a recipient organization if the leasing organization maintains a qualified, nonintegrated, money purchase pension plan that provides for immediate participation, full and immediate vesting, and an annual contribution of at least 7½% of compensation. In general, if these requirements are met, the leased employee does not have to be counted for any purpose pertaining to the qualified plans of the recipient organization. However, the TRA of 1984 clarified section 414(n) to emphasize that common-law employer-employee principles are applicable in this area.

27a and b. The TRA of 1984 amended section 401(a)(9), as in effect prior to the amendments made by TEFRA. This means that for distributions in calendar years prior to calendar year 1985, distributions will be made according to section 401(a)(9) as constituted prior to TEFRA. For plan years beginning after 12/31/84, the TRA of 1984 distribution rules are effective. Also, if an employee designated a method of distribution before January 1, 1984, as allowed by TEFRA, which met the requirements of section 401(a)(9) as in effect on December 31, 1983, then it will be considered a valid method.

✿U.S. G.P.O. 1987 181-447/40109

Application for
Determination for Defined Contribution Plan
For Profit-sharing, Stock Bonus and Money Purchase Plans
(Under Sections 401(a), 401(k), and 501(a) of the Internal Revenue Code)

OMB No. 1545-0197
Expires 6-30-91

For IRS Use Only
File folder number ▶
Case number ▶

Caution: Church and governmental plans not subject to ERISA need not complete items 10, 11, 12b, 12c, 15, 17g, 17l, and 18b. All other plans must complete all items except as indicated on specific lines. For example, if you answer "No" to line 7, you need not complete lines 7a and 7b since they require responses only if you answer "Yes" to line 7. N/A is only an acceptable answer if an N/A block is provided. All applications are now computer screened, therefore it is important that you provide all the information requested and have the application signed by the employer, plan administrator, or authorized representative. Otherwise, we may need to correspond with you or return your application for completion, which will delay its processing.

1 a	Name of plan sponsor (employer if a single employer plan)	1b	Employer identification number
	Address (number and street)	1c	Employer's tax year ends Month ☐ N/A
	City or town, state and ZIP code		Telephone number ( )

2 Person to be contacted if more information is needed (If same as 1a, enter "same as 1a"). (See Specific Instructions.)
Name _____ Telephone number ( )
Address _____

3 a Determination requested for (check applicable boxes): (See Instruction B. "What To File.")
- *(i)* ☐ Initial qualification—Date plan signed _____ Date plan effective _____
- *(ii)* ☐ Amendment after initial qualification—Is plan restated? ☐ Yes ☐ No Date amendment signed _____
   Date amendment effective _____ Date plan effective _____
- *(iii)* ☐ Affiliated service group status (section 414(m))—Date effective _____ Date plan effective _____
- *(iv)* ☐ Partial termination—Date effective_____ Date plan effective _____

b Enter IRS file folder number shown on the last determination letter issued to the plan sponsor _____ ☐ N/A

c Is this application also expected to satisfy the notice requirement for this plan for merger, consolidation, or transfer of plan assets or liabilities involving another plan? (See Specific Instructions.) . . . . ☐ Yes ☐ No

d Were employees who are interested parties given the required notification of the filing of this application? . . ☐ Yes ☐ No

e Is this plan or trust currently under examination or is any issue related to this plan or trust currently pending before the Internal Revenue Service, the Department of Labor, the Pension Benefit Guaranty Corporation, or any court? . . . . ☐ Yes ☐ No
If "Yes," attach explanation.

f Does your plan contain cash or deferred arrangements described in section 401(k)? . . . . ☐ Yes ☐ No
If "Yes," is a determination also requested on the qualification of those provisions? (See Instruction B.) . . . ☐ Yes ☐ No

4 a	Name of Plan	b Plan number ▶ _____
		c Plan year ends ▶

5 Are there other qualified plans? (Do not consider plans that were established under union-negotiated agreements that involved other employers.) . . . . ☐ Yes ☐ No
- **a** Name of plan ▶ _____
- **b** Type of plan ▶ _____
- **c** Rate of employer contribution ▶_____ ☐ N/A
- **d** Allocation formula ▶_____ ☐ N/A
- **e** Benefit formula or monthly benefit ▶ _____ ☐ N/A
- **f** Number of participants ▶

6 Type of entity (check only one box):
- **a** ☐ Corporation **b** ☐ Subchapter S corporation **c** ☐ Sole proprietor **d** ☐ Partnership
- **e** ☐ Tax exempt organization **f** ☐ Church **g** ☐ Governmental organization
- **h** ☐ Other (specify) ▶

7 Is this an adoption of a master or prototype plan? ☐ Yes ☐ No. If "Yes," complete **a** and **b**
- **a** Name of plan **b** Notification letter no.

8 Type of plan: **a** ☐ Profit-sharing **b** ☐ Stock bonus **c** ☐ Money purchase **d** ☐ Target benefit
e ☐ Other (specify) ▶

Under penalties of perjury, I declare that I have examined this application, including accompanying statements, and to the best of my knowledge and belief, it is true, correct, and complete.

Signature ▶ _____ Title ▶ _____ Date ▶ _____

For Paperwork Reduction Act Notice, see page 1 of the instructions. Form **5301** (Rev. 8-88)

Exhibit 16-3

ction references are to the Internal Revenue Code, unless otherwise noted.)*

Where applicable, indicate the article or section and page number of the plan or trust where the following provisions are contained. N/A (not applicable) is an appropriate response only if an N/A block is provided.

		Section and Page Number
9 a	General eligibility requirements: (Check box (i), (ii), (iii) or (iv), and complete (v), (vi) and (vii).)	
	(i) ☐ All employees *(ii)* ☐ Hourly rate employees only *(iii)* ☐ Salaried employees only	
	(iv) ☐ Other (specify) ▶	
	(v) Length of service (number of years) ▶ .... ☐ N/A	
	(vi) Minimum age (specify) ▶ .... ☐ N/A	
	(vii) Maximum age (specify) ▶ .... ☐ N/A	
b	Does any plan amendment since the last determination letter change the method of crediting service for eligibility? . . . ☐ Yes ☐ No ☐ N/A	

		Yes	No	Not Certain
10	Participation (see Specific Instructions):			
a	*(i)* Is the employer a member of an affiliated service group? . . .	▨	▨	▨
	If your answer is "No," go to 10b.			
	(ii) Did a prior ruling letter rule on what organizations were members of the employer's affiliated service group or did the employer receive a determination letter that considered the effect of section 414(m) on this plan? . . .			
	(iii) If (ii) is "Yes," have the facts on which that letter was based materially changed?			
b	Is the employer a member of a controlled group of corporations or a group of trades or businesses under common control? . . .			

		Number Enter "0" if N/A
11	Coverage of plan at (give date) .... (attach Form(s) 5302—see instructions)	
	(If the employer is a member of an affiliated service group, a controlled group of corporations, or a group of trades or businesses under common control, employees of all members of the group must be considered in completing the following schedule.) If your plan contains cash or deferred arrangements described in section 401(k), see the Specific Instructions for line 11.	▨
a	Total employed (see Specific Instructions) (include all self-employed individuals) . . .	
b	Statutory exclusions under this plan (do not count an employee more than once)	
	(i) Number excluded because of age or years of service required . . .	
	(ii) Number excluded because of employees included in collective bargaining . . .	
	(iii) Number of other employees excluded (specify)..........	
c	Total statutory exclusions under this plan (add lines b(i) through (iii)) . . .	
d	Employees not excluded under the statute (subtract line c from line a) . . .	
e	Other employees ineligible under terms of this plan (do not count an employee included in line b) . . .	
f	Employees eligible to participate (subtract line e from line d) . . .	
g	Number of employees participating in this plan . . .	
h	Percent of nonexcluded employees who are participating (divide line g by line d) . . . ▨ %	
	If line h is 70% or more, go to line k.	
i	Percent of nonexcluded employees who are eligible to participate (divide line f by line d) . . . . %	
j	Percent of eligible employees who are participating (divide line g by line f) . . . . %	
	If lines h and i are less than 70% or line j is less than 80%, see Specific Instructions and attach schedule of information.	
k	Total number of participants (include certain retired and terminated employees (see Specific Instructions)).	
l	Has a plan amendment since the last determination letter resulted in exclusion of previously covered employees? . . . ☐ Yes ☐ No ☐ N/A	

		Yes	No	N/A	Section and Page Number
12	Does the plan define the following terms—				
a	Compensation (earned income if applicable)? . . .			▨	
b	Break in service? . . .				
c	Hour of service (under Department of Labor Regulations)? . . .			▨	
d	Joint and survivor annuity? . . .				
e	Normal retirement age? . . .			▨	
f	Year of service? . . .				
g	Entry date? . . .			▨	
13 a	Employee contributions:				
	(i) Does the plan allow voluntary deductible employee contributions? . . .				
	(ii) If "Yes," are the voluntary deductible employee contributions appropriately limited? . .			▨	
	(iii) Are voluntary nondeductible contributions limited for all qualified plans to 10%, or less, of compensation? . . .				
	(iv) Are employee contributions nonforfeitable? . . .				

				N/A	Section and Page Number

13 *(Continued)*

b Employer contributions: (Response required in either (i), (ii), (iii) or (iv).)

   (i) Profit-sharing or stock bonus plan contributions are determined under:

      ☐ A definite formula   ☐ An indefinite formula   ☐ Both

   (ii) Profit-sharing or stock bonus plan contributions are limited to:

      ☐ Current earnings   ☐ Accumulated earnings   ☐ Combination

   (iii) Money purchase—Enter rate of contribution ▶ ....

   (iv) State target benefit formula, if applicable ▶

			Yes	No	N/A	

14 Integration:

Is this plan integrated with social security or railroad retirement? . . . .

If "Yes" and this is a target benefit plan, attach a schedule of compliance with Rev. Rul. 71-446 (see Specific Instructions).

15 Vesting:

a Are years of service with other members of a controlled group of corporations, trades or businesses under common control, or an affiliated service group counted for vesting and eligibility to participate? . . . .

b Are employee's rights to normal retirement benefits nonforfeitable on reaching normal retirement age as defined in section 411(a)(8)? . . . .

c Does any amendment to the plan decrease any participant's accrued benefit? . . . . .

d Does any amendment to the plan directly or indirectly affect the computation of the non-forfeitable percentage of a participant's accrued benefit? . . . .

e Does the plan preclude forfeiture of an employee's vested benefits for cause? . . . . .

f Check only one of the boxes to indicate the vesting provisions of the plan:

   (i) ☐ Full and immediate.

   (ii) ☐ Full vesting after 10 years of service; i.e., no vesting for the first 9 years, 100% after 10 years (section 411(a)(2)(A)).

   (iii) ☐ 5- to 15-year vesting (section 411(a)(2)(B)).

   (iv) ☐ Rule of 45 (section 411(a)(2)(C)).

   (v) ☐ 4/40 vesting (Rev. Procs. 75-49 and 76-11).

   (vi) ☐ 10% vesting for each year of service (not to exceed 100%).

   (vii) ☐ 100% vesting within 5 years after contributions are made (class year plans only).

   (viii) ☐ Other (specify—see Specific Instructions and attach schedule).

16 Administration: **a** Type of funding entity:

   (i) ☐ Trust (benefits provided in whole from trust funds).

   (ii) ☐ Custodial account described in section 401(f) and not included in (iv) below.

   (iii) ☐ Trust or arrangement providing benefits partially through insurance and/or annuity contracts.

   (iv) ☐ Trust or arrangement providing benefits exclusively through insurance and/or annuity contracts.

   (v) ☐ Other (specify) ▶ ....

b Does the trust agreement prohibit reversion of funds to the employer? (Rev. Rul. 77-200) . .

c Are limits placed on the purchase of insurance contracts? . . . .

If "Yes," complete (i), (ii) or (iii), below

   (i) Ordinary life ▶ ....

   (ii) Term insurance ▶ ....

   (iii) Other (specify) ▶ ....

d If the trustees may earmark specific investments, including insurance contracts, are such investments subject to the employee's consent, or purchased ratably when employee consent is not required? . . . .

e Are loans to participants limited to their vested interests? . . . .

17 Requirements for benefits—distributions—allocations:

a Normal retirement age is ▶ .... If applicable, years of service/participation required ▶ ....

b Does the plan contain an early retirement provision? . . . .

If "Yes," (i) Early retirement age is ▶ ....

   (ii) Years of service participation required ▶ ....

c Does the plan provide for payment of benefits according to section 401(a)(14)? . . . . .

	Yes	No	N/A	**Section and Page Number**
17 (Continued)				
d Distribution of account balances may be made in:				
(i) ☐ Lump sum (ii) ☐ Annuity contracts				
(iii) ☐ Substantially equal annual installments—not more than ▶ .... years				
(iv) ☐ Other (specify) ▶				
e If distributions are made in installments, they are credited with:				
(i) ☐ Fund earnings				
(ii) ☐ Interest at a rate of ▶.............. % per year				
(iii) ☐ Other (specify) ▶..............				
f Does the plan comply with the payment of benefits provisions of section 401(a)(11)? . . .				
g If this is a stock bonus plan, are distributions made in employer stock?				
h If this is a pension plan, does it permit distribution only on death, disability, plan termination, or termination of employment?				
i If this is a profit-sharing or stock bonus plan, what other events permit distributions?				
--				
j If participants withdraw their mandatory contributions or earnings, may withdrawal be made without forfeiting vested benefits based on employer contributions?				
k Are contributions allocated on the basis of total compensation?				
If "No," see Specific Instructions and attach schedule.				
l Are forfeitures allocated, in case of a profit-sharing or stock bonus plan, on basis of total compensation? If "No," explain how they are allocated				
m Are trust earnings and losses allocated on the basis of account balances?				
If "No," explain how they are allocated.				
n For target benefit or other money purchase plan, are forfeitures applied to reduce employer contributions?				
o Does the plan provide for maximum limitation under section 415?				
p Does the plan prohibit the assignment or alienation of benefits?				
q Does the plan meet the requirements of section 401(a)(12)?				
r Are trust assets valued at fair market value?.				
s Are trust assets valued at least annually on a specific date?				
If "No," explain.				
18 Termination of plan or trust:				
a Are the participants' rights to benefits under the plan nonforfeitable (to the extent funded) upon termination or partial termination of the plan?				
b Are employees' rights under the plan nonforfeitable on complete discontinuance of contributions under a profit-sharing or stock bonus plan?				

Procedural Requirements Checklist

Caution: The following Procedural Requirements Checklist identifies certain basic data that will facilitate the processing of your application. While no response is required to the questions, you may find that answering them will ensure that your application is processed without the need for contact to obtain missing information. If the answer to any of the questions is "No," your application may be incomplete. Incomplete applications are identified through a computer screening system for return to the applicant. **This checksheet should be detached before submitting the application.**

		Yes	No	N/A
1	General requirements			
a	If this application is made by a representative on behalf of the employer or plan administrator, has a current power of attorney been submitted with this application (see "Signature" under General Information)?			
b	If notices or other communications are to be sent to someone other than the employer, have you provided proper authorization by attaching a completed **Form 2848,** Power of Attorney and Declaration of Representative, or by attaching a statement that contains all the information required (see Specific Instructions)?			▨
c	Have you completed and attached Form(s) 5302?			▨
d	Have you signed the application?			▨
e	Have you completed and attached Schedule T (Form 5300)?			▨
2	Specific requirements			
a	If this is a request for a determination letter on initial qualification of the plan, have the following documents been attached:			
	(i) Copies of all instruments constituting the plan?			
	(ii) Copies of trust indentures, group annuity contracts, or custodial agreements?			
b	If this is a request for a determination letter on the effect of an amendment on the plan after initial qualification, have the following documents been attached:			
	(i) A copy of the plan amendments?			
	(ii) A description of the amendment covering the changes to the plan sections?			
	(iii) An explanation of the plan sections before the amendment?			
	(iv) An explanation of the effect of the amendment on the provisions of the plan sections?			
c	If this is a request for a determination letter on the qualification of the entire plan, as amended after initial qualification, have the following documents been included:			
	(i) A copy of the plan incorporating all amendments made to the date of the application?			
	(ii) A statement indicating that the copy of the plan is complete in all respects and that a determination letter is being requested on the qualification of the entire plan?			
	(iii) A copy of trust indentures, group annuity contracts, or custodial agreements, if there has been any change since copies were last furnished to IRS?			
d	For partial termination:			
	(i) Have you completed line 3a according to the Specific Instructions?			
	(ii) Have you attached the information requested for a partial termination in General Instruction B?			
e	For a plan adopted by one or more members of a controlled group:			
	(i) Have you attached the statement requested in the Specific Instructions for line 10b?			
	(ii) Have you completed line 11 according to General Instruction B and the Specific Instructions?			
f	For a multiple-employer plan that does not involve collective bargaining:			
	(i) Have you submitted one fully completed application (Form 5300 or 5301, whichever is appropriate) for all adopting employers?			
	(ii) Have you attached a Form 5300 or 5301 (as applicable) with only line items 1 through 11 completed, and a Form 5302 for each employer who adopted the plan?			
g	For a plan that contains a cash or deferred arrangement, have you submitted the appropriate information requested for line 11?			
h	For governmental and church plans, have you completed Form 5300 or 5301 according to General Instruction B?			
i	For notice of merger, consolidation, or transfer of plan assets or liabilities, have you submitted the information requested in the Specific Instructions for line 3c?			
j	For a plan that is or may be sponsored by a member of an affiliated service group:			
	(i) Have you completed lines 3a, 10, and 11 according to the Specific Instructions?			
	(ii) Have you attached the information requested in the instructions for lines 10a(ii) and (iii)?			▨
3	Miscellaneous requirements—			
a	Have you entered the plan sponsor's 9-digit employer identification number in line 1b?			▨
b	If a determination letter was previously issued to this sponsor for any plan, have you entered the file folder number on line 3b?			▨
c	Have you answered line 3d?			
d	If this plan has been amended at least four times since the last determination letter on the entire plan was issued, have you attached a copy of the plan that includes all amendments made to the plan since that determination letter was issued?			▨
e	Have you entered the effective date of the plan in the space provided by the block you checked for line 3a?			
f	If applicable, have you attached schedules or other documentation as required by:			
	(i) Form 5301—Lines 2, 3e, 11j, 14, 15f(viii), 17k, 17l, 17m, and 17s?			
	(ii) Form 5300—Lines 2, 3e, 6, 11j, 14, 15f(viii), and 17g?			

Form 5303
(Rev. March 1986)

Department of the Treasury
Internal Revenue Service

Application for
Determination for Collectively Bargained Plan

(Under Sections 401(a) and 501(a) of the Internal Revenue Code)

(Section references are to the Internal Revenue Code.)

OMB No. 1545-0534
Expires 3-30-89

For IRS Use Only
File folder number ▶
Case number ▶

Church and governmental plans not subject to ERISA need not complete items 9, 10b, 10c, 13, 15g, 15l, and 17c.

All other plans must complete all items except as indicated on specific lines. For example, if you answer "No" to line 7b, you need not complete line 11b since it requires a response only if you answer "Yes" to line 7b. N/A is only an acceptable answer if an N/A block is provided. All applications are now computer screened, therefore it is important that you provide all the information requested and have the application signed by the employer, plan administrator, or authorized representative. Otherwise, we may need to correspond with you or return your application for completion, which will delay its processing.

1a Name of plan sponsor (employer if a single employer plan)	**1b** Employer identification number
Address (number and street)	**1c** Employer's tax year ends Month ☐ N/A
City or town, state and ZIP code	Telephone number ( )

2 Person to be contacted if more information is needed. (If same as 1a, enter "same as 1a.") (See Specific Instructions.)
Name _____
Address _____   Telephone number ( )

3a Determination requested for (Check applicable boxes):   (See Instruction B. "What to File.")
　　(i) ☐ Initial qualification—Date plan signed _____   Date plan effective _____
　　(ii) ☐ Amendment after initial qualification—Is plan restated? ☐ Yes ☐ No   Date amendment signed _____
　　　　Date amendment effective _____   Date plan effective _____
　　(iii) ☐ Partial termination—Date effective _____   Date plan effective _____
　　(iv) ☐ Termination of multiemployer plan covered by PBGC insurance. . . .   Date effective _____
　　　　　　Date plan effective _____

b Enter IRS file folder number shown on the last determination letter issued to the plan sponsor _____ ☐ N/A

c Is this application also expected to satisfy the notice requirement for this plan for merger, consolidation, or transfer of plan assets or liabilities involving another plan (see Specific Instructions)? . . . . ☐ Yes ☐ No

d Were employees who are interested parties given the required notification of the filing of this application? . . . . ☐ Yes ☐ No

e Is this plan or trust currently under examination or is any issue related to this plan or trust currently pending before the Internal Revenue Service, the Department of Labor, the Pension Benefit Guaranty Corporation, or any court? . . . . . . ☐ Yes ☐ No
If "Yes," attach explanation.

f Does your plan contain cash or deferred arrangements described in section 401(k)? . . . . ☐ Yes ☐ No

g If 3f is "Yes," is a determination also requested with regard to the qualifications of those provisions (see Instruction B)? . . . . ☐ Yes ☐ No

4a Name of plan	**b** Plan number ▶ _____ **c** Plan year ends ▶

5 Check proper box for the type of plan entity: **a** ☐ Single employer plan
b ☐ Plan of controlled group of corporations or trades or businesses under common control   **c** ☐ Multiemployer plan
d ☐ Multiple-employer-collectively-bargained plan (other than a multiemployer plan)   **e** ☐ Church plan
f ☐ Governmental plan   **g** ☐ Other (specify) ▶

6 Is this an adoption of a master or prototype plan? ☐ Yes ☐ No—If "Yes," complete 6a and 6b

a Name of plan	**b** Letter serial number

7a Is this a defined benefit plan? . . . . ☐ Yes ☐ No—If "Yes," indicate whether:
　　(i) ☐ Unit benefit   (ii) ☐ Fixed benefit   (iii) ☐ Flat benefit   (iv) ☐ Other (specify) _____

b Is this a defined contribution plan? . . . . . ☐ Yes ☐ No—If "Yes," indicate whether: (i) ☐ Profit-sharing
　　(ii) ☐ Stock bonus   (iii) ☐ Money purchase   (iv) ☐ Target benefit   (v) ☐ Other (specify) _____

c Does plan provide for variable benefits?   ☐ Yes ☐ No ☐ N/A

d Is this plan, or was this plan before amendment, a defined benefit plan covered under the Pension Benefit Guaranty Corporation termination insurance program? . . . . . . ☐ Yes ☐ No ☐ Not determined

Under penalties of perjury, I declare that I have examined this application, including accompanying statements, and to the best of my knowledge and belief it is true, correct, and complete.

Signature ▶ _____   Title ▶ _____   Date ▶ _____

Signature ▶ _____   Title ▶ _____   Date ▶ _____

For Paperwork Reduction Act Notice, see page 1 of the instructions.   Form **5303** (Rev. 3-86)

Exhibit 16-4

Where applicable, indicate the article or section and page number of the plan or other document (trust or collective-bargaining agreement) where the following provisions are contained. N/A is an appropriate response only if a check block is provided.

		Section and Page Number
8a	General eligibility requirements: (Check box (i), (ii), (iii) or (iv), and complete (v), (vi) and (vii).)	
	(i) ☐ All employees (ii) ☐ Hourly rate employees only (iii) ☐ Salaried employees only	
	(iv) ☐ Other (specify) ▶	
	(v) Length of service (number of years) ▶ .... ☐ N/A	
	(vi) Minimum age (specify) ▶ .... ☐ N/A	
	(vii) Maximum age (specify) ▶ .... ☐ N/A	
b	Does any plan amendment since the last determination letter alter the method of crediting service for eligibility? . . . . ☐ Yes ☐ No ☐ N/A	

		Number Enter "0" if N/A (see instructions)
9	Coverage of plan at (give date) ▶	
a	(i) Total number of participants, including certain retired and terminated employees (see Specific Instructions).	
	(ii) Participants whose benefits or accounts are fully vested	
	(iii) Number of contributing employers	
b	Does this plan cover employees of the representative labor union(s) or of any plan(s) for union members? . . . . ☐ Yes ☐ No	
c	Complete only if **b** is "Yes" (see Specific Instructions).	
	(i) Total employed by union or plan	
	(ii) Exclusions—	
	a. Minimum age or years of service required (specify which) ▶	
	b. Nonresident aliens who receive no earned income from United States sources	
	c. Other (specify) ▶	
	(iii) Total exclusions (add (ii) a through c)	
	(iv) Employees not excluded under the statute (subtract (iii) from (i))	
	(v) Employees who do not meet plan eligibility requirements	
	(vi) Employees eligible to participate (subtract (v) from (iv)).	
	(vii) Employees participating in the plan	
d	If **b** is "Yes," attach a separate completed Form 5302 for employees of such union or plan.	
e	Has a plan amendment since the last determination letter resulted in exclusion of previously covered employees? . . . . ☐ Yes ☐ No ☐ N/A	

		Yes	No	N/A	Section and Page Number
10	Does the plan define the following terms—				
a	Compensation?				
b	Break in service?				
c	Hour of service (under Department of Labor Regulations)?				
d	Joint and survivor annuity?				
e	Normal retirement age?				
f	Year of service?				
g	Entry date?				
11a	Employee contributions:				
	(i) Does the plan document allow voluntary deductible employee contributions?				
	(ii) If "Yes," are the voluntary deductible employee contributions appropriately limited? . .				
	(iii) Are voluntary nondeductible contributions limited for all qualified plans to 10%, or less, of compensation?				
	(iv) Are employee contributions nonforfeitable?				

b	Employer contributions: If line 7b is "Yes," complete (i), (ii), (iii), or (iv) below:
	(i) Profit-sharing or stock bonus plan contributions are determined under:
	☐ A definite formula ☐ An indefinite formula ☐ Both
	(ii) Profit-sharing or stock bonus plan contributions are limited to:
	☐ Current earnings ☐ Accumulated earnings ☐ Combination
	(iii) Money purchase—Enter rate of contribution ▶ ....
	(iv) State target benefit formula, if applicable ▶

12	Integration:
	Is this plan integrated with social security or railroad retirement? . . . .
	If "Yes," and this is a defined benefit plan or a target benefit plan, attach a schedule of compliance with Rev. Rul. 71-446 (see Specific Instructions).

		Yes	No	N/A	Section and Page Number
13	**Vesting:**				
a	Are years of service with other members of a controlled group of corporations, trades or businesses under common control, or an affiliated service group counted for purposes of vesting and eligibility to participate?.				
b	Are employee's rights to normal retirement benefits nonforfeitable on reaching normal retirement age as defined in section 411(a)(8)?			▨	
c	Does any amendment to the plan decrease any participant's accrued benefits?				
d	Does any amendment to the plan directly or indirectly affect the computation of the nonforfeitable percentage of a participant's accrued benefit?				
e	Does the plan preclude forfeiture of an employee's vested benefits for cause?			▨	
f	Check only one of the boxes to indicate the vesting provisions of the plan:	▨	▨	▨	
	(i) ☐ Full and immediate.				
	(ii) ☐ Full vesting after 10 years of service; i.e., no vesting for the first 9 years, 100% after 10 years (section 411(a)(2)(A)).				
	(iii) ☐ 5- to 15-year vesting as defined in section 411(a)(2)(B).				
	(iv) ☐ Rule of 45 (section 411(a)(2)(C)).				
	(v) ☐ 4/40 vesting (Rev. Procs. 75-49 and 76-11).				
	(vi) ☐ 10% vesting for each year of service (not to exceed 100%).				
	(vii) ☐ 100% vesting within 5 years after contributions are made (class year plans only).				
	(viii) ☐ Other (specify—see Specific Instructions and attach schedule).				
14	**Administration:**	▨	▨	▨	
a	Type of funding entity:				
	(i) ☐ Trust (benefits provided in whole from trust funds).				
	(ii) ☐ Custodial account described in section 401(f) and not included in (iv) below.				
	(iii) ☐ Trust or arrangement providing benefits partially through insurance and/or annuity contracts.				
	(iv) ☐ Trust or arrangement providing benefits exclusively through insurance and/or annuity contracts.				
	(v) ☐ Other (specify). ▶_____				
b	Does the trust agreement prohibit reversion of funds to the employer?			▨	
c	Are limits placed on the purchase of insurance contracts? If "Yes," specify the limits in (i), (ii) or (iii).				
	(i) Ordinary life ▶_____	▨			
	(ii) Term insurance ▶_____	▨			
	(iii) Other (specify) ▶_____	▨			
d	If the trustees may earmark specific investments including insurance contracts, are such investments subject to the employee's consent, or purchased ratably when employee consent is not required?	▨	▨	▨	
e	Are loans to participants limited to their vested interests?				
15	**Requirements for benefits—distributions—allocations:**	▨		▨	
a	Normal retirement age is ▶ . . . . . . If applicable, years of service/participation required ▶	▨		▨	
b	Does the plan contain an early retirement provision? If "Yes,"				
	(i) Early retirement age is ▶	▨		▨	
	(ii) Years of service/participation required ▶	▨			
c	Does the plan provide for payment of benefits according to section 401(a)(14)?			▨	
	Note: *Complete **d** and **e** only if this plan is a defined contribution plan.*	▨	▨	▨	
d	Distribution of account balances may be made in:				
	(i) ☐ Lump-sum *(ii)* ☐ Annuity contracts				
	(iii) ☐ Substantially equal annual installments—not more than ▶ . . . . years				
	(iv) ☐ Other (specify) ▶_____				
e	If distributions are made in installments, they are credited with:				
	(i) ☐ Fund earnings				
	(ii) ☐ Interest at a rate of ▶ . . . . % per year				
	(iii) ☐ Other (specify) ▶_____				
f	Does this plan comply with the payment of benefits provisions of section 401(a)(11)?				
g	If this is a stock bonus plan, are distributions made in employer stock?				
h	If this is a pension plan, does it permit distribution before normal retirement age only on death, disability, plan termination, or termination of employment?				
i	If this is a profit-sharing or stock bonus plan, what other events permit distributions?	▨	▨	▨	

	Yes	No	N/A	Section and Page Number
15 Requirements for benefits—distributions—allocations: (continued)				
j If participants may withdraw their mandatory contributions or earnings, may withdrawal be made without forfeiting vested benefits based on employer contributions?				
k Are contributions allocated or benefits computed on the basis of total compensation?				
If "No," see instructions and attach schedule.				
l Are forfeitures allocated, in case of a profit-sharing or stock bonus plan, on the basis of total compensation?				
If "No," explain how they are allocated. _____				
m Are trust earnings and losses allocated on the basis of account balances?				
If "No," explain how they are allocated. _____				
n In case of target benefit or other money purchase plan, are forfeitures applied to reduce employer contributions?				
o Does the plan provide for maximum limitation under section 415?				
p Does the plan prohibit the assignment or alienation of benefits?				
q Does the plan meet the requirements of section 401(a)(12)?				
r Are trust assets valued at fair market value?				
s Are trust assets valued at least annually on a specified date?				
If "No," explain.				
16 Additional information for defined benefit plans only:				
a Method of determining accrued benefit ▶ _____				
(i) Benefit formula at normal retirement age is ▶ _____				
(ii) Benefit formula at early retirement age is ▶ _____				
(iii) Normal form of retirement benefits is ▶ _____				
_____				
b Are benefits under the plan definitely determinable at all times (see Rev. Rul. 79-90)? . . .				
c Does the plan disregard service attributable to a distribution in computing the employer-derived accrued benefit?				
d If **c** is "Yes," does the plan contain provisions that satisfy regulations section 1.411(a)-7(d)(4) or (6)?				
e Are distributions limited so that no more than incidental death benefits are provided?				
f As a result of a plan amendment, has the amount of benefit or rate of accrual of the benefit been reduced?				
17 Termination of plan or trust:				
a Are the participants' rights to benefits under the plan nonforfeitable (to the extent funded) upon termination or partial termination of the plan?				
b If this is a defined benefit plan, has the early termination rule been included in the plan (see regulations section 1.401-4(c))?				
c Upon complete discontinuance of contributions under a profit-sharing or stock bonus plan are the employees' rights under the plan nonforfeitable?				

Caution

The following Procedural Requirements Checklist identifies certain basic data that will facilitate the processing of your application. While no response is required to the questions, you may find that answering them will ensure that your application is processed without the need for contact to obtain missing information. If the answer to any of the questions is "No," your application may be incomplete. INCOMPLETE APPLICATIONS ARE IDENTIFIED THROUGH A COMPUTER SCREENING SYSTEM FOR RETURN TO THE APPLICANT. Detach this checksheet before submitting the application. You may wish to keep it for your records. DO NOT SEND THIS CHECKSHEET TO IRS.

Procedural Requirements Checklist

		Yes	No	N/A
1	General requirements:			
a	If this application is made by a representative on behalf of the plan sponsor or plan administrator, has a current power of attorney been submitted with this application (see "Signature" under General Information)?			
b	If notices or other communications are to be sent to someone other than the plan sponsor, have you provided proper authorization by attaching a completed **Form 2848**, Power of Attorney and Declaration of Representative, or by attaching a statement that contains all the information required (see Specific Instructions)?			
c	If applicable, have you completed and attached Form(s) 5302?			░
d	Have you signed the application?			░
e	Have you completed and attached Schedule T (Form 5300)?			░
2	Specific requirements:	░	░	░
a	If this is a request for a determination letter on initial qualification of the plan, have you attached the following documents:	░	░	░
	(i) Copies of all instruments constituting the plan?			
	(ii) Copies of trust indentures, group annuity contracts, or custodial agreements?			
b	If this is a request for a determination letter on the effect an amendment will have on the plan after initial qualification, have you attached the following documents:	░	░	░
	(i) A copy of the plan amendments?			
	(ii) A description of the amendment covering the changes to the plan sections?			
	(iii) An explanation of the plan sections before the amendment?			
	(iv) An explanation of the effect of the amendment on the provisions of the plan sections?			
c	If this is a request for a determination letter on the qualification of the entire plan, as amended after initial qualification, have you included the following documents:	░	░	░
	(i) A copy of the plan incorporating all amendments made to the date of the application?			
	(ii) A statement indicating that the copy of the plan is complete in all respects and that a determination letter is being requested on the qualification of the entire plan?			
	(iii) A copy of trust indentures, group annuity contracts, or custodial agreements, if there has been any change since copies were last furnished to IRS?			
d	For partial termination:			
	(i) Have you completed line 3a according to the Specific Instructions?			
	(ii) Have you attached the information for a partial termination requested in General Instruction B?			
e	For a plan that contains a cash or deferred arrangement, have you submitted the appropriate information requested for line 9?			
f	For governmental and church plans, have you completed Form 5303 according to General Instruction B?			
g	For notice of merger, consolidation, or transfer of plan assets or liabilities, have you submitted the information requested in the Specific Instructions for line 3c?			
3	Miscellaneous requirements:			░
a	Have you entered the plan sponsor's 9-digit employer identification number in item 1b?			
b	If a determination letter was previously issued to this sponsor for any plan, have you entered the file folder number on line 3b?			
c	Have you answered item 3d?			░
d	If this plan has been amended at least four times since the last determination letter on the entire plan was issued, have you attached a copy of the plan that includes all amendments made to the plan since that determination letter was issued?			
e	Have you entered the effective date of the plan in the space provided by the block you checked for line 3a?			░
f	If applicable, have you attached schedules or other documentation as required by line items 2, 3e, 9d, 12, 13f(viii), 15k, 15l, 15m, and 15s?			

Form 5302 — Employee Census

Form 5302 (Rev. November 1987)
Department of the Treasury
Internal Revenue Service

Employee Census

▶ Attach to application for determination—defined benefit and defined contribution plans.   (Round off to nearest dollar)

Schedule of 25 highest paid participating employees for 12-month period ended ▶

OMB No. 1545-0416
Expires 11-30-90

This Form is NOT Open to Public Inspection

Name of employer

Employer identification number

Line no.	Participant's last name and initials (See instructions) (a)	Check: Officer, shareholder, or self-employed (b)	Check: Percent of voting stock or business owned (c)	Age (d)	Years of service (e)	Annual Nondeferred Compensation: Used in computing benefits or employee's share of contributions (f)	Annual Nondeferred Compensation: Excluded (g)	Annual Nondeferred Compensation: Total (h)	Employee contributions under the plan (i)	Defined Benefit: Annual benefit expected under this plan (j)	Defined Benefit: Annual benefit under each other qualified defined benefit plan of deferred compensation (k)	Defined Contribution: Employer contribution allocated (l)	Defined Contribution: Number of units, if any (m)	Defined Contribution: Forfeitures allocated in the year (n)	Defined Contribution: Amount allocated under each other defined contribution plan of deferred compensation (o)
1															
2															
3															
4															
5															
6															
7															
8															
9															
10															
11															
12															
13															
14															
15															
16															
17															
18															
19															
20															
21															
22															
23															
24															
25															

Total for above . . . .

Totals for all others (specify number ▶   ) . .

Total for all participants

For Paperwork Reduction Act Notice, see back of this form.

See instructions on the back of this form.

Form **5302** (Rev. 11-87)

Exhibit 16-5

Department of the Treasury
Internal Revenue Service

Publication 1048
(Rev. March 1987)

Filing Requirements for Employee Benefit Plans

Department of the Treasury Internal Revenue Service

Department of Labor Pension and Welfare Benefits Administration

Pension Benefit Guaranty Corporation

Introduction

Under the Employee Retirement Income Security Act of 1974, Public Law 93-406 (ERISA), employers and administrators of public and private retirement plans must file certain annual returns or reports with the Internal Revenue Service (IRS), the Department of Labor (DOL), and the Pension Benefit Guaranty Corporation (PBGC). To reduce duplication of reporting, IRS, DOL, and PBGC have designed consolidated annual return/report forms, the Form 5500 series. These forms are filed with IRS and satisfy the annual report requirements of IRS, DOL, and PBGC. However, these agencies may require special reports if certain events occur. For example, see the discussion of *Filing for Reportable Events* under *PBGC Filing Requirements,* later.

In addition, pension benefit plans covered by PBGC insurance must file PBGC Form 1 with PBGC to pay premiums. Other PBGC reporting requirements, including those that apply only to multiemployer plans covered by PBGC insurance, are described later.

Note. There are new filing requirements for single-employer plan terminations. IRS/PBGC Form 5310 is no longer used to file the notice of intent to terminate. Instead, a written notice of intent to terminate must be provided to parties affected by the termination. Form 5310, together with an enrolled actuary certification and a plan administrator certification, must be filed with the PBGC later as part of the termination procedure. Because of these changes, the "one-stop" service program (listed on the Form 5310 under Box C of "Reason for filing") is no longer generally available. In addition, the PBGC is reviewing its termination procedures and may change its filing requirements in the future. See *Additional Information for Filing with IRS,* and *Filing for Reportable Events* (under *PBGC Filing Requirements*), later, for more information on the one-stop service program and plan termination procedures.

This publication tells you who must file, what forms to file, the due dates for filing, and where to file. It tells you how to apply to IRS for a determination or opinion letter regarding the tax qualification of a plan. Also included is a list of the forms generally filed by, and related to, employee plans.

You may get the 5500 series forms and instructions from the Internal Revenue Service. The other forms and instructions used specifically by each agency are available from that particular agency. The instructions for each form include additional information for filing.

Summary plan description. Certain employee benefit plans are required to file a summary plan description with DOL and furnish a copy of this description to their participants and beneficiaries. For information on this, contact the Department of Labor, Pension and Welfare Benefits Administration, 200 Constitution Avenue, N.W., Washington, DC 20210.

Who Must File Form 5500 Series Returns/Reports

Pension benefit plans. Each plan administrator or employer who maintains an employee pension benefit plan (defined benefit or defined contribution plan) must file an annual return/report.

The return/report must be filed for each plan, whether or not it is a qualified plan. A return/report must be filed for each plan even if benefits no longer accrue (as in a "frozen plan") or contributions to it are no longer made (as in a "wasting trust").

In addition, an annual return/report must be filed for the following:

1) Tax-sheltered annuity programs maintained by certain exempt organizations. For excep-

tions, see the instructions to the forms.

2) Custodial accounts for regulated investment company stock, under section 403(b)(7) of the Internal Revenue Code, maintained by certain exempt organizations.

3) Individual retirement account trusts maintained by employers for employees.

4) Church plans choosing coverage under section 410(d) of the Code.

5) Plans maintained outside the United States primarily for nonresident aliens if the plan is maintained by:
   a) A domestic employer, or
   b) A foreign employer with income derived from sources within the United States, including foreign subsidiaries of domestic employers.

   However, this applies only if the employer is claiming a deduction on its U.S. income tax return for contributions made to the plan. See *Plans excluded from filing,* later.

6) Plans that cover residents of Puerto Rico, the Virgin Islands, Guam, Wake Island, or American Samoa. This includes a plan that chooses to have the provisions of section 1022(i)(2) of ERISA apply.

Welfare benefit plans. Each administrator or sponsor of a welfare benefit plan covered by Part 1 of Title I of ERISA must file an annual return/report.

Exception for certain plans with fewer than 100 participants. A welfare benefit plan with fewer than 100 participants at the start of the plan year does not have to file an annual return/report if:

1) Benefits are paid as needed only from the general assets of the employer or employee organization maintaining the plan,

2) Benefits are provided only through insurance contracts or policies, or

3) Benefits are provided through a combination of the methods described in (1) and (2).

These insurance contracts or policies must be issued by an insurance company or similar organization, such as Blue Cross, Blue Shield, or a health maintenance organization, that can legally do business in any state. The premiums for these contracts or policies must be paid either directly by the employer or employee organization from its general assets, or partly from its general assets and partly from contribution by its employees or members. The employer or employee organization must forward the premiums within 3 months of receipt.

Exception for group insurance arrangements. A welfare benefit plan that is part of a group insurance arrangement does not have to file a separate return/report if a consolidated report for all the plans in the arrangement is filed by the trust or equivalent body according to DOL Regulations 29 CFR 2520.104–43.

Exception for apprenticeship and other training plans. A welfare benefit plan that provides only apprenticeship or other training benefits, or a combination of both, is not required to file reports if the plan administrator:

1) Files a notice with DOL containing the name of the plan, the employer identification number of the plan sponsor, the name of the plan administrator, and the name and location of an office or person with information about courses and enrollment.

2) Takes steps reasonably designed to make sure that employees of employers contributing to the plan who may be eligible to enroll are aware of the information in the notice, and

3) Makes the notice available to employees upon request.

Fringe benefit plans. Any employer maintaining a fringe benefit plan described in Code section

Exhibit 16-6

6039D must file an annual return/report. For this purpose, a fringe benefit plan includes only a cafeteria plan (in which participants may choose among the benefits), a qualified group legal services plan, and an educational assistance program. Educational assistance programs that provide *only* job-related training need not file returns/reports.

If a cafeteria plan includes a pension benefit plan described in Code section 401(k) as one of its components, separate returns/reports must be filed for the pension benefit plan and for the remaining plan features of the cafeteria plan.

Plans excluded from filing. Returns/reports are not required for the following plans (provided the plans are not fringe benefit plans required to file under code section 6039D):

1) Unfunded pension benefit plans and unfunded or insured welfare benefit plans maintained by an employer to provide benefits for only a select group of management or highly compensated employees, and which satisfy the requirements of Department of Labor Regulations 29 CFR 2520.104–23 and 2520.104–24.

2) Plans maintained only to comply with workmen's compensation, unemployment compensation, or disability insurance laws.

3) Unfunded excess benefit plans.

4) Welfare benefit plans maintained outside the United States if most of the participants are nonresident aliens.

5) A pension benefit plan maintained outside the United States if it is a qualified foreign plan within the meaning of Code section 404A(e) that does not qualify for the treatment provided in Code section 402(c).

6) Church plans that do not choose coverage under Section 410(d) of the Code, or governmental plans.

7) Tax-sheltered annuity arrangements described in 29 CFR 2510.3–2(f).

Kinds of Plans

One-participant plan. A one-participant plan is a pension benefit plan that covers only an individual or an individual and his or her spouse who wholly own a trade or business (whether incorporated or unincorporated). It also includes a plan covering only a partner in a partnership, or the partner and the partner's spouse.

Note. For plan years beginning in 1986, Form 5500EZ may be filed for one-participant plans. See the discussion on *What Annual Return/ Report Forms to File with IRS,* later, for more information.

Single employer plan. A single employer plan is a plan maintained by one employer, by one employee organization, or by both. One annual return/report must be filed for each single employer plan. A member of a controlled group of corporations or a group of trades or businesses under common control that maintains its own plan is required to file a separate return/report for that plan, if the plan does not involve other members of the controlled group.

If several employers participate in a program of benefits in which the funds from each employer are available only to pay benefits to that employer's employees, each employer must file a separate return/report.

Plan for a controlled group of corporations or for a group of trades or businesses under common control. A plan only for members of one of these groups is a plan maintained by the group, and each group is treated as a single employer. One annual return/report must be filed for each such plan. An individual employer must not file any return/report for this type of plan.

For a plan that includes a controlled group of corporations or a group of trades or businesses

under common control and also includes one or more employers who are not members of the group, one annual return/report must be filed for the group and one annual return/report for each employer who is not a member of the group.

Note. If the benefits are payable to employees covered by the plan from the plan's total assets without regard to their respective employer's contributions, one annual return/report must be filed for the plan as a whole. In addition, each employer who is a member of the controlled group must file either Form 5500–C, regardless of the number of participants, completing only certain items, or Form 5500–R, whichever applies.

Multiemployer plan. This is a plan defined in section 414(f) of the Internal Revenue Code or section 3(37) or 4001(a)(3) of ERISA. One annual return/report must be filed for each multiemployer plan. Contributing employers do not file individually for these plans.

Multiple-employers, collectively bargained plan. This is a plan that involves more than one employer, is collectively bargained, is collectively funded, and for which an election had been made before September 27, 1981, not to treat it as a multiemployer plan under section 414(f)(5) of the Code or sections 3(37) and 4001(a)(3) of ERISA. One annual return/report must be filed for each such plan. Participating employers do not file individually for these plans.

Multiple-employer plan (other). A multiple-employers plan (other) involves more than one employer and is not one of the plans already described. A multiple-employer plan (other) includes only those plans whose individual employer contributions are available to pay benefits to all participants. One annual return/report must be filed for each such plan. In addition, for pension benefit plans, each participating employer must file either Form 5500–C, regardless of the number of participants, completing only certain items, or Form 5500–R, whichever applies.

If more than one employer participates in a plan and the plan provides that each employer's contributions are available to pay benefits only for that employer's employees who are covered by the plan, one annual return/report must be filed for each participating employer. These filers will be considered single employers and should complete the entire form.

Group insurance arrangement. This is an arrangement that provides benefits to the employees of two or more unaffiliated employers (not in connection with a multiemployer plan or a multiple-employer, collectively bargained plan). It fully insures one or more welfare plans of each participating employer. A trust or other entity, such as a trade association, holds the insurance contracts and acts as the conduit for paying the premiums to the insurance company.

If the trust or entity files a single consolidated annual return/report for all welfare benefit plans in the group insurance arrangement, administrators of participating welfare benefit plans need not file separate annual returns/reports for them as single employer plans. 29 CFR 2520.103–2 requires that the annual return/report Form 5500 be part of the consolidated report.

Master trust. A master trust is a trust in which assets of the plans of one employer or a group of employers under common control are held. It is a trust for which a regulated financial institution, such as a bank, trust company, or similar financial institution, services as trustee or custodian. The asset of a master trust are considered to be held in one or more "investment accounts."

The plan administrator or its designee must file certain master trust information with DOL, as explained in the Form 5500 series instructions. In addition, the plan will have to file Form 5500 or 5500–C and, if they apply, any Schedules with IRS.

Other investment entity. This is an entity that holds the assets of two or more plans that are not members of a "related group" of benefit plan investors. Such an entity must file a report directly with DOL, as explained in the Forms instructions, while the plans' Forms 5500 or 5500–C and (if applicable) any Schedules must be filed with the IRS.

What Annual Return/Report Forms to File With IRS

Form 5500, *Annual Return/Report of Employee Benefit Plan.* Each plan with 100 or more participants at the beginning of the plan year must file this form annually.

Form 5500–C, *Return/Report of Employee Benefit Plan.* Each pension benefit plan with more than one but fewer than 100 participants (one-participant plans, see Form 5500 EZ, later) at the start of the plan year must file this form at least once every three years.

Each welfare benefit plan with fewer than 100 participants at the start of the plan year must also file this form at least once every three years. See the exceptions, discussed earlier, under *Welfare benefit plans.*

File Form 5500–C only if:

1) This is the plan's first year,
2) This is the year a final return/report is due, or
3) Form 5500–R has been filed for both of the prior 2 years.

For more information, see the instructions to Form 5500–C.

Form 5500–R, *Registration Statement of Employee Benefit Plan.* Pension or welfare benefit plans with more than one but fewer than 100 participants (one-participant plans, see Form 5500EZ, below) at the start of the plan year will generally have to file Form 5500–C once every three years. Form 5500–R should be filed for plan years when Form 5500–C is not required. However, for years during which Form 5500–R would normally be filed, adminstrators or sponsors may instead choose to file Form 5500–C. Do not file Form 5500–R in place of Form 5500 or when Form 5500–R has been filed for the previous two plan years by plans with more than one participant.

Generally, Form 5500–R should be filed by plans with more than one participant if:

1) It is not for the plan's first year,
2) It is not for the year a final return/report is due, and
3) Form 5500–C has been filed for one of the previous 2 plan years.

For more information, see the instructions for Form 5500–R.

Exception for plans with 80 to 120 participants. Generally, under the filing requirements explained above, if the number of plan participants increases from under 100 to 100 or more or decreases from 100 or more to under 100, from one year to the next, you would have to file a different form from that filed the previous year. However, there is an exception to this rule. You may file the same form you filed last year, even if the number of participants changed, provided that at the beginning of this plan year the plan had at least 80 participants, but not more than 120.

Form 5500EZ, *Annual Return of One-Participant Pension Benefit Plan.* Most one-participant pension plans should file new Form 5500EZ annually for plan years beginning after 1985. See the definition of one-participant plan, discussed earlier, under *Kinds of Plans.*

Do not file Form 5500EZ if the plan covers a business that is a member of:

1) An affiliated service group,

2) A controlled group of corporations, or

3) A group of businesses under common control.

Also, a plan that covers a business that leases employees may not file this form.

If Form 5500EZ cannot be used, the one-participant plan must use Form 5500–C or 5500–R, whichever applies.

One-participant defined contribution plans do not have to file annual information returns if all of the following requirements are met:

1) No employer contributions were made or required to be made for this year or the prior 2 plan years,
2) The total assets of the plan do not exceed $25,000,
3) No plan assets were held by a party-in-interest for this year or the prior 2 years, and
4) The plan had no party-in-interest transactions this year or the prior 2 years.

For further information on Form 5500EZ and for the meaning of party-in-interest, see the instructions for Form 5500EZ.

Schedule A (Form 5500), *Insurance Information.* Attach this schedule to Form 5500, 5500–C, or 5500–R if any benefits under the plan are provided by an insurance company, insurance service, or similar organization, such as Blue Cross, Blue Shield, or a health maintenance organization.

Exception. Schedule A (Form 5500) does not have to be filed for a one-participant plan (as defined earlier).

Schedule B (Form 5500), *Actuarial Information.* Attach this schedule to Form 5500, 5500–C, 5500–R, or 5500EZ for most defined benefit plans. See the instructions to Schedule B.

Schedule P (Form 5500), *Annual Return of Fiduciary of Employee Benefit Trust.* A fiduciary (trustee or custodian) of an organization that is qualified under section 401(a) of the Code and exempt from tax under section 501(a) may want to protect the organization under the statute of limitations provided in section 6501(a). To do so, the fiduciary should file, under section 6033(a), Schedule P as an *attachment* to Form 5500, 5500–C, 5500–R, or 5500EZ for the plan year in which the trust ends. Schedule P cannot be filed separately. Refer to the instructions to Schedule P for further information.

Schedule SSA (Form 5500), *Annual Registration Statement Identifying Separated Participants With Deferred Vested Benefits.* This schedule must be filed as an attachment to Form 5500, 5500–C, or 5500–R for certain separated participants. See the instructions to Schedule SSA.

Note. Form 5498, *Individual Retirement Arrangement Information,* must be filed to show the contributions that were made to an individual retirement arrangement (IRA) or simplified employee pension (SEP) for the year. This includes contributions for the year that are actually made after the end of the year but by the due date for the individual's tax return for that year.

Form 5498 is due by May 31 of the year following the year for which the contributions were made. For issuers and trustees of IRAs and SEPs, this due date applies both to filing Form 5498 with IRS and to providing the annual statements to participants. Late filing penalties are based on the May 31 due date. For 1987, Form 5498 is due by June 1, 1987 because May 31 falls on a Sunday.

To file Form 5498, use Form 1096, *Annual Summary and Transmittal of U.S. Information Returns.*

Summary of Filing Requirements for Employers and Plan Administrators (File forms ONLY with IRS)

Type of plan	What to file	When to file
Certain pension benefit plans with one participant or one participant and that participant's spouse	Form 5500EZ	File all required forms and schedules for each plan by the last day of the 7th month after the plan year ends.
Pension plan with fewer than 100 participants	Form 5500–C or 5500–R	
Pension plan with 100 or more participants	Form 5500	
Annuity under Code section 403(b)(1) or trust under Code section 408(c)	Form 5500, 5500–C, or 5500–R	
Custodial account under Code section 403(b)(7)	Form 5500, 5500–C, or 5500–R	
Welfare or fringe benefit plan with 100 or more participants	Form 5500	
Welfare or fringe benefit plan with fewer than 100 participants	Form 5500–C or 5500–R	
Plan with 100 or more participants (see DOL regulations for exemptions)	Financial statements, schedules, and accountant's opinion	
Pension or welfare plan with benefits provided by an insurance company or similar organization	Schedule A (Form 5500)	
Pension plan that requires actuarial information	Schedule B (Form 5500)	
Pension plan filing a registration statement identifying separated participants with deferred vested benefits from a pension plan	Schedule SSA (Form 5500)	

When to File Annual Returns/Reports with IRS

File all required annual report forms and schedules for each plan by the last day of the 7th month following the end of the plan year.

Extension of time to file. You may be granted an extension of up to 2½ months for filing returns/reports. Use Form 5558, *Application for Extension of Time to File Certain Employee Plan Returns,* to request the extension.

Exception. Single employer plans and plans of controlled groups of corporations that file consolidated federal income tax returns may be entitled to an automatic extension of time to file Form 5500, 5500–C, 5500–R, or 5500EZ, whichever applies. The time for filing is extended to the due date of the federal income tax return of the single employer or controlled group of corporations. The automatic extension applies if *all* of the following conditions are met:

1) The plan year and the tax year are the same,
2) The single employer or the controlled group has been granted an extension of time to file its federal income tax return to a date later than the normal due date for filing Form 5500, 5500–C, 5500–R, or 5500EZ and
3) A copy of the approved IRS extension of time to file the federal income tax return is attached to each Form 5500, 5500–C, 5500–R, or 5500EZ filed with the IRS.

Note. An extension of time to file the return/report does not operate as an extension of time to file the PBGC Form 1.

Short plan year. File a return/report and applicable schedules for a short plan year by the last day of the 7th month following the end of the short plan year.

Where to File

File all annual return/report forms and schedules with the Internal Revenue Service Centers shown in the instructions to the forms

Note. Send the annual statement of assets and liabilities of a common/collective trust or a pooled separate account submitted by a bank or insurance company in accordance with 29 CFR 2520.103–9(b)(3) to: Common/Collective Trust or Pooled Separate Account, Pension and Welfare Benefits Adminstration, U.S. Department of Labor, 200 Constitution Avenue, N.W., Washington, DC 20210.

Additional Information for Filing with IRS

Plan identification. Internal Revenue records are kept by the employer identification number, the plan number, the name of plan sponsor, and the month in which the plan year ends. Therefore, it is important that each of these items be consistent from year to year on your return/report. See *Employer Identification Numbers (EINs),* later, for additional information on the consistent use of EINs to identify pension plans.

Final return/report. If all assets under the plan, including insurance/annuity contracts, have been distributed to the participants and beneficiaries, check the "Final Return" box at the top of the return/report filed for the plan. The year of complete distribution is the last year a return/report must be filed for the plan.

For a terminating defined benefit plan, which is insured by PBGC and for which PBGC eventually becomes trustee, a complete distribution will occur in the year in which PBGC becomes trustee of the plan's assets. *See When to file and pay premium,* under *PBGC Filing Requirements,* later for information on filing PBGC Form 1 upon termination of the plan.

You may request an IRS qualification determination upon your plan's termination, if a determination is desired, by filing IRS/PBGC Form 5310. Form 5303 must be used by multiemployer plans covered by PBGC insurance that are terminating.

For purposes of the return/report, the plan year ends upon the complete distribution of the assets of the plan.

Penalties. ERISA imposes the following penalties for not giving complete information and not filing statements and returns/reports:

1) $25 a day (up to $15,000) for not filing returns for certain plans of deferred compensation, certain trusts and annuities, and bond purchase plans by the due date. This penalty also applies to returns/reports required of fringe benefit plans.
2) $1,000 for not filing an actuarial report. If more than one person is responsible for filing

3

the report as a plan administrator and no report is filed, all plan administrators involved are jointly and individually responsible for paying the $1,000 penalty. See Code section 6692 and the regulations under that section for more information about the penalty.

3) $1 a day (up to $5,000) for each participant for whom a registrant statement is required but not filed.

4) $1 a day (up to $1,000) for not filing a notification of change of status of a plan.

The above penalties may be waived if you can show reasonable cause for the failure to file the necessary forms.

Caution. The following penalties imposed by ERISA may be applied upon conviction:

1) If you, as an individual, willfully violate any provision of Part I of Title 1 of ERISA, you may be fined not more than $5,000 or imprisoned not more than one year, or both.

2) If you knowingly make any false statement or representation of fact, or knowingly conceal or fail to disclose any fact required by ERISA, you may be fined up to $10,000 or imprisoned for 5 years, or both.

Signature and date. The plan administrator must sign and date all returns/reports. In addition, the employers must sign a return/report filed for a single employer plan or a fringe benefit plan required to file a report.

When the plan sponsor or the plan administrator is a joint employer-union board or committee, at least one employer representative and one union representative must sign and date the return/report.

Participating employers in a multiple-employer plan (other), who are required to file Form 5500–C or 5500–R, must sign the return/report. The plan adminstrator need not sign the Form 5500–C or 5500–R filed by the participating employer.

Reproductions. You should file original returns/reports, if possible. However, you may file legible copies of the completed forms. All signatures on the forms must be original signatures, signed after the copies have been made.

Change of plan year. To change a plan year of certain qualified employee pension benefit plans, you should get prior approval from IRS by filing Form 5308, *Request for Change in Plan/Trust Year.*

Amended return/report. If you file an amended return/report, check the "amended" box at the top of the form. When filing an amended return, be sure to put a circle around the line number of the items that have been amended.

Notification of termination, merger, or consolidation. Filing the return/report and showing that the plan was terminated satisfies the notification required by section 6057(b)(3) of the Code. Filing IRS/PBGC Form 5310, *Application for Determination Upon Termination; Notice of Merger, Consolidation or Transfer of Plan Assets or Liabilities; Notice of Intent to Terminate,* to show that the plan was merged or consolidated with another plan, or that the plan was divided into two or more plans, satisfies the notification required by section 6058(b) of the Code.

Form 5310 or Form 5303, if appropriate, may also be used if the administrator of a plan being terminated wishes to get an IRS determination on the plan's qualification status upon its termination. See *Where to File IRS Determination, Notification, Opinion, and Ruling Letter Requests,* later, for information on how to file directly with IRS for such a determination. An application for an IRS determination upon plan termination generally may not be filed with the PBGC under the "one-stop" service program (see Form 5310, "Reason for filing", Box C), because of the revised filing requirements for single-employer plan terminations, discussed later in *Filing for*

Reportable Events, under *PBGC Filing Requirements.* One-stop service was initiated to allow terminating non-multiemployer pension plans to file duplicate copies of the completed Form 5310 and required attachments with the PBGC, only, to satisfy both the PBGC's and the IRS's requirements relating to the plan's termination. Until final revisions to termination procedures are completed, this program is limited to plans terminating in "distress terminations" in which plan assets are not sufficient to provide the benefits guaranteed by the PBGC.

Income tax withholding. You must generally withhold income tax on designated distributions, unless the recipient chooses to have no tax withheld by filing with the payer or administrator Form W-4P, *Withholding Certificate for Pension or Annuity Payments.* For more information on the withholding requirements, and the tables used to figure the withholding, see Publication 15, Circular E, *Employer's Tax Guide,* and Publication 493, *Alternative Tax Withholding Methods and Tables* (for withholding from qualified total distributions).

Employer Identification Numbers (EINs)

As a plan sponsor or administrator, you must enter the proper identification numbers on all forms. In particular, you must enter the correct employer identification number (EIN) and plan number (PN) on the Form 5500 series returns/reports. You must use the same EIN/PN to identify a plan on the PBGC Form 1 or other correspondence with PBGC that you use on the Form 5500 series returns/reports. This number is needed to correct misfilings by plan administrators and to reduce administrative costs for plan administrators and the PBGC. For more information, see Publication 1004, *Identification Numbers Under ERISA.*

Although employer identification numbers (EINs) for funds (trusts or custodial accounts) associated with employee benefit plans are not needed on the Form 5300 series applications or the Form 5500 series returns for the plans, IRS will issue EINs for these funds for other reporting purposes. You may obtain EINs by filing Form SS–4 with your Internal Revenue Service Center.

PBGC Filing Requirements

Note. The Administration has proposed a revision in the premium structure for single-employer plans for the plan years beginning on or after January 1, 1988. If enacted, the proposal would charge a higher premium, based on plan funding status, to plans that pose the greatest risk of loss to the insurance program.

Annual Filing for Premium Payments

PBGC requires annual filing only of PBGC Form 1, *Annual Premium Payment,* which is used to pay PBGC insurance premiums. **File this form with PBGC only.** Do *not* file it with IRS.

Who must file. The plan administrator of a defined benefit plan insured by PBGC under Title IV of ERISA must file a PBGC Form 1.

When to file and pay premium. The due date for filing PBGC Form 1 and paying the premium depends on the size of the plan, whether the plan is newly covered, and whether there has been a change in plan year.

Large plans. Plans with 500 or more participants are considered large plans. Large plans must file PBGC Form 1 and pay a premium using either an estimated or final participant count by the last day of the second month following the close of the previous plan year (the PBGC calls this the Original Filing Due Date). If a large plan pays its premium using an estimated participant count, it must make a reconciliation filing by the last day of the seventh month following the close of the previous plan year (the PBGC calls this the

Reconciliation Due Date). If the plan pays its premium using a final participant count by the Original Filing Due Date and *so indicates* in Item 12 of the PBGC Form 1, a reconciliation filing is not required.

A large plan will incur a late payment penalty if it does not pay, by its Original Filing Due Date, an amount which either (1) is at least 90% of the full premium ultimately due for the plan year, or (2) is based on the participant count reported on its previous Form 1 filing. However, even if the plan does not incur a late payment *penalty* charge, it will still incur an *interest* charge on any part of the premium ultimately due on the plan's Reconciliation Due Date that it does not pay by the Original Filing Due Date.

Small plans. All plans other than large plans must file PBGC Form 1 and pay their premiums by the last day of the seventh month following the close of the previous plan year (for these plans, the PBGC calls this the Final Filing Due Date).

New plans. For new plans or existing plans newly covered by section 4021 of ERISA, regardless of the number of plan participants, file the form and pay the premium by the *latest* of the following dates:

1) The last day of the seventh month following the *beginning* of the plan year, or

2) 90 days after the date of the plan's adoption, or

3) 90 days after the date the plan became effective for benefit accruals for future service, or

4) 90 days after the date the plan became covered under section 4021 of ERISA.

Change in plan year. When you change your plan year, you have an old (or short) plan year followed by the new plan year. You must file a PBGC Form 1 for each of these years. For large plans that change their plan year, separate reconciliations may also be due for each of the years involved.

The PBGC Form 1 and premium payment for the short plan year is due by the Original or Final Filing Due Dates for that plan year, as explained earlier under *Large plans* and *Small plans,* respectively. For the new plan year, small plans must file the PBGC Form 1 and pay their premium by either the last day of the seventh month following the close of the short plan year, *or* the 30th day after the date on which they adopt the plan amendment changing the plan year, *whichever is later.*

Large plans must file the PBGC Form 1 and pay a premium, using either an estimated or final participant count, for the new plan year by either the last day of the *second* month following the close of the short plan year, or the 30th day after the date on which they adopt the plan amendment changing the plan year, *whichever is later.* In all other respects the rules for large plans filing with estimated or final participant counts are the same as those discussed earlier.

Each filing must reflect a full 12-month plan year on item 13 of PBGC Form 1. You must also figure and pay the premium for each filing for a full plan year without prorating it. Therefore, a change in plan year usually results in a duplicate or overlapping premium payment. You may request a refund in such a case by writing to: Pension Benefit Guaranty Corporation, FOD/Premium Operations Division (33700), 2020 K St., N.W., Washington, DC 20006-1860.

Plan termination. If the plan is being terminated, the plan administrator must continue to file the PBGC Form 1 and pay the required premium through the plan year in which either the plan's assets are distributed under section 4044 of ERISA and PBGC's regulations, or a trustee is appointed to administer the plan under section 4042 of ERISA.

Late premium payments. If the premium amount due for a plan year is paid after its due date, or, in the case of large plans, is underpaid on the Original Filing Due Date, you may be assessed late payment interest and penalty charges. See PBGC Form 1 Instructions.

However, plan administrators may apply to PBGC before the premium due date for a waiver of the late payment penalty charge if they can show substantial hardship. If a waiver is granted, the PBGC will not impose the late payment penalty charge for any payment made within 60 days of the due date. For other waiver provisions, see the PBGC's regulation on *Payment of Premiums,* 29 CFR Part 2610. However, even if PBGC grants a waiver of the penalty charge, it will still charge late payment interest from the due date through the date the payment is made. You may request a waiver of the late payment penalty charge by writing, **before the filing due date,** to: Pension Benefit Guaranty Corporation, FOD/Financial Programs Division (33600), 2020 K St., N.W., Washington, DC 20006-1860.

If IRS has granted you an extension of the due date for filing any of the 5500 series forms, this does **not** extend the filing due date for PBGC Form 1.

Where to file. Mail PBGC Form 1 and your premium payment to:

Pension Benefit Guaranty Corporation
P.O. Box 105655
Atlanta, GA 30348–5655

Complete information. The Package of PBGC Form 1 and Instructions, as revised for calendar year 1987, contains more detailed instructions and specific examples for use in completing and filing this form. This package may be obtained from the Premium Operations Division, at the address given above.

Filing for Reportable Events

The plan administrator of a covered **single-employer plan** must notify PBGC of certain **reportable events** within 30 days of their occurrence. See PBGC's regulation on *Reportable Events,* 29 CFR Part 2615, and PBGC's booklet, *Reportable Events,* for more information on reportable event notification requirements.

Single-employer plan termination procedures. The Single-Employer Pension Plan Amendments Act of 1986 ("SEPPAA"), which became law on April 7, 1986, made substantial changes in the filing requirements for terminating single-employer plans, effective as of January 1, 1986. The PBGC will be revising its regulations and accompanying forms during 1987, in light of SEPPAA. Temporary procedures were established by the PBGC and published in the *Federal Register* on April 10, 1986, as a "Notice of interim procedures" (51 FR 12491). You may obtain a copy from the PBGC. The following information summarizes the procedure to be followed in order to terminate single-employer plans during the interim period.

SEPPAA provides for two types of voluntary termination of a single-employer plan insured by the PBGC: (1) standard termination, for which the plan must have sufficient assets to provide **all** "benefit commitments" under the plan (these include, generally, all nonforfeitable benefits, including early retirement supplements or subsidies and plant closing benefits), and (2) distress termination, for which certain statutory distress criteria must be met. A plan that is not fully funded for all benefit commitments may be voluntarily terminated only in a distress termination.

For either a standard or distress termination, the plan administrator must give the following notices:

Notice of Intent to Terminate (NOIT). The plan administrator must give written personal notice of the proposed termination, including the proposed termination date, to affected parties at least 60 days before the proposed termination date. Affected parties are:

- the plan participants, beneficiaries of deceased participants, and alternative payees,
- any employee organization representing participants, and
- for **distress terminations only,** the PBGC.

Notice to the PBGC. As soon as practicable after providing the NOIT as required, the plan administrator must submit a notice to the PBGC (a second notice, in the case of a distress termination), containing the following:

1) For a standard termination, an enrolled actuary's certification that the plan is projected to be sufficient for all benefit commitments as of the proposed date of final distribution of plan assets or, for a distress termination, a certification concerning the degree to which the plan is funded, *i.e.,* whether, as of the proposed termination date, the plan is sufficient for benefit commitments, guaranteed benefits, or neither,

2) For a distress termination, information sufficient to enable the PBGC to determine that the criteria for a distress termination are met, and

3) For either type of termination, the plan administrator's certification that the information on which the enrolled actuary based his or her certification and any additional information required to be submitted to the PBGC is accurate and complete.

For a standard termination, the plan administrator must use the IRS/PBGC Form 5310 and PBGC Forms 444 and 445, modified for this notice. For a distress termination, the plan administrator should use Form 5310 for the second notice to the PBGC, including additional information as necessary, and may use Forms 444 and 445 for the required certifications by the enrolled actuary and the plan administrator, if they are further modified to fit the facts of the particular plan. These forms are available from the PBGC, and Form 5310 is also available at most local IRS offices. The "Notice of interim procedures", referred to earlier, describes the necessary modifications to these forms. The instructions for the forms (*Instructions for Form 5310; PBGC Form 446* [instructions for Forms 444 and 445]) should be followed, subject to these modifications.

Note. The PBGC is reviewing its termination procedures in light of SEPPAA and, consequently, may change these filing requirements in the future.

Second notice to plan participants or beneficiaries. For standard terminations only, a notice containing information about his or her benefit commitments must be given to each plan participant or beneficiary of a deceased participant, no later than the date the notice to the PBGC (described above) is given.

The PBGC has assigned specially trained staff to answer questions dealing with SEPPAA and the revised termination procedures. You may reach these individuals between 8:30 a.m. and 5:00 p.m. every weekday by calling (202) 778-8800 or (202) 778-8859 for TTY and TTD.

For additional information on termination of single-employer plans, see the PBGC's regulations on *Determination of Plan Sufficiency and Termination of Sufficient Plans,* 29 CFR Part 2617, and *Notice of Intent to Terminate for Non-Multiemployer Pension Plans,* 29 CFR Part 2616, which are still in effect to the extent they are not inconsistent with SEPPAA.

For PBGC purposes, a single-employer plan is any defined benefit pension plan (including a multiple-employer plan), other than a multiemployer plan, covered by Title IV of ERISA.

Multiemployer plan filings. The plan sponsor of a covered **multiemployer plan** must notify PBGC of the plan's termination within 30 days after the

termination. In case of a merger, spin-off, or transfer of assets or liabilities with or to another multiemployer plan, the plan sponsor must notify PBGC at least 120 days **in advance of** the event.

In addition, the sponsor of an ongoing covered multiemployer plan must notify the PBGC and the Secretary of the Treasury that the plan is or may become insolvent, within 30 days after such insolvency is determined. The notification must state the level of benefits the plan will pay in each year of insolvency. In the case of a multiemployer plan that has been terminated by mass withdrawal, the plan sponsor must notify the PBGC: (1) if the plan is required to reduce benefits, or (2) if the plan becomes insolvent and is required to suspend benefit payments. For more information on these notice requirements, see the PBGC's regulations on *Mergers and Transfers Between Multiemployer Plans,* 29 CFR Part 2672; *Notice of Termination for Multiemployer Plans,* 29 CFR Part 2673; *Notice of Insolvency,* 29 CFR Part 2674; and *Powers and Duties of Plan Sponsor of Plan Terminated by Mass Withdrawal; Notice of Benefit Reductions and Suspensions,* 29 CFR Part 2675.

Where to send PBGC notices. Send the notices referred to in this section to:

Pension Benefit Guaranty Corporation
Insurance Operations Department
Room 5300A, (25420) CC
2020 K Street, N.W.
Washington, DC 20006-1860

For further information about PBGC's filing requirements, write to PBGC at this address or call (202) 778-8800.

Where to File IRS Determination, Notification, Opinion, and Ruling Letter Requests

Requests for determination or notification letters. Send these to the key District Director specified as follows:

1) For a plan of a single employer, send the request to the District Director for the key district in which the employer's principal place of business is located.

2) For a plan of more than one employer, send the request to the District Director for the key district in which the principal place of business of the employer or plan administrator is located.

3) For an industry plan established or proposed by subscribing employers having principal places of business within the jurisdiction of more than one key district, send the request to the District Director for the key district in which the trustee's principal place of business is located. If the plan has more than one trustee, send the request to the District Director for the key district where the trustees usually meet.

The addresses of all key District Directors to whom you should send your requests for determination or notification letters are included in the instructions for most of the forms listed under *What Forms to File for Requests,* later.

Foreign situs trust, foreign employers, and pooled fund arrangements. U.S. employers adopting a foreign situs trust, foreign employers, and pooled fund arrangements should refer to Revenue Procedure 80–30 to find out where to send requests.

Employers or plan administrators who request determination letters from IRS do not have to notify PBGC separately that they have made the request.

Opinion letter and employer-sponsored IRA and SEP ruling letter requests. Sponsors of plans should file opinion letter requests and requests for rulings on employer-sponsored IRAs and SEPs with the Commissioner of Internal Revenue, 1111 Constitution Avenue, N.W., Washington, DC 20224, Attention: OP:E:EP:Q:E.

Sponsoring organizations should furnish a copy of the approved master or prototype plan and the Internal Revenue Service opinion letter to the key District Director, specified under *Requests for determination or notification letters*, previously discussed, in whose jurisdiction there are employers who adopt these plans.

What Forms to File for Requests

The following is a list of forms that are filed with IRS by most employee benefit plans to request determination, notification, opinion, or ruling letters. See the specific forms and their instructions for filing requirements.

General Types of Plans	Defined Benefit Plan	Defined Contribution Plan
A) *Individually designed:*		
1) Keogh (H.R. 10) plan (not collectively bargained)	5300 and 5302	5301 and 5302
2) Employee stock ownership plan (ESOP) or tax credit employee stock and ownership plan	—	5301,** 5303, or 5307,** and 5309
3) Pension plan other than a money purchase plan (not collectively bargained)	5300 and 5302	
4) Profit-sharing, stock bonus, target benefit, and money purchase plan (not collectively bargained)	—	5301 and 5302
5) Plan that involves a controlled group of corporations, employers under common control, or an affiliated service group (not collectively bargained)	5300 and 5302	5301 and 5302
6) Multiple-employer plan (not collectively bargained)	5300 and 5302*	5301 and 5302*
B) *Collectively bargained plan*	5303**	5303**

	Sponsors File	Adopters File
C) *Master or prototype plan:*		
1) Defined contribution plan including a plan covering self-employed individuals (not collectively bargained)	4461	5307*** and 5302***
2) Defined benefit plan including a plan covering self-employed individuals (not collectively bargained)	4461-A	5307*** and 5302***
3) Individual retirement arrangement (IRA)	5306	—
4) Simplified employee pension (SEP)	5306-SEP	—
D) *Individual retirement account*—employer or employee association sponsored	5306	—
E) *Uniform plans*—notification letter requested by sponsor (i.e., law firm) and determination letter requested by adopter	4461 or 4461-A	5037****

F) *Termination of plan*	Partial	Full
	5300, 5301, or 5303†	5310 and 6088, or 5303†

*Plan administrator should file one application and, in addition, attach Form 5300 or 5301 and Form 5302 for each employer who adopted the plan.
** Form 5302 may also be required. See Forms 5301, 5303, or 5307 and their instructions.
*** Generally, these forms will not be filed for plans treated as "paired plans" or "standardized form plans"; see Revenue Procedure 84-23 for details.
**** Includes plans previously defined as "pattern," "field prototype," and/or "basic plans." See

Revenue Procedure 84-86 for details.
†Form 5303 is required if the plan is a multiemployer plan.

Note. Form 6406, *Short Form Application for Determination for Amendment of Employee Benefit Plan,* may be filed to amend a plan on which a favorable determination letter has been issued under ERISA. For more information, see the instructions for Form 6406.

List of Forms and Titles

The following forms concern employee benefit plans:

Pension Benefit Guaranty Corporation

PBGC Form 1, *Annual Premium Payment*

PBGC Form 444, *Enrolled Actuary Certification*

PBGC Form 445, *Plan Administrator Certification*

PBGC Form 446, *Instructions for Filing under the Enrolled Actuary Certification Program*

Internal Revenue Service/Pension Benefit Guaranty Corporation

5310, *Application for Determination Upon Termination; Notice of Merger, Consolidation, or Transfer of Plan Assets or Liabilities; Notice of Intent to Terminate*

Department of Labor/Internal Revenue Service/Pension Benefit Guaranty Corporation

5500, *Annual Return/Report of Employee Benefit Plan (With 100 or more participants)*

5500–C, *Return/Report of Employee Benefit Plan (With fewer than 100 participants)*

5500EZ, *Annual Return of One-Participant Pension Benefit Plan*

5500–R, *Registration Statement of Employee Benefit Plan (With fewer than 100 participants)*

Schedule A (Form 5500), *Insurance Information*

Schedule B (Form 5500), *Actuarial Information*

Schedule P (Form 5500), *Annual Return of Fiduciary of Employee Benefit Trust*

Schedule SSA (Form 5500), *Annual Registration Statement Identifying Separated Participants With Deferred Vested Benefits*

Internal Revenue Service

SS–4, *Application of Employer Identification Number*

W–2P, *Statement for Recipients of Annuities, Pensions, Retired Pay, or IRA Payments*

W–4P, *Withholding Certificate for Pension or Annuity Payments*

1099–R, *Statement for Recipients of Total Distributions from Profit-Sharing, Retirement Plans, Individual Retirement Arrangements, Etc.*

4461, *Application for Approval of Master or Prototype Defined Contribution Plan*

4461–A, *Application for Approval of Master or Prototype Defined Benefit Plan*

5300, *Application for Determination for Defined Benefit Plan For Pension Plans Other Than Money Purchase Plans*

Schedule T (Form 5300), *Supplemental Applications for Approval of Employee Benefit Plans Under TEFRA, TRA 1984, and REA (Later revisions of Form 5300 may eliminate the need for this schedule in the future.)*

5301, *Application for Determination for Defined Contribution Plan for Profit-Sharing, Stock Bonus and Money Purchase Plans*

5302, *Employee Census*

5303, *Application for Determination for Collectively Bargained Plan*

5305, *Individual Retirement Trust Account*

5305–A, *Individual Retirement Custodial Account*

5305-SEP, *Simplified Employee Pension-Individual Retirement Accounts Contribution Agreement*

5306, *Application for Approval of Prototype or Employer Sponsored Individual Retirement Account*

5306-SEP, *Application for Approval of Prototype Simplified Employee Pension-SEP*

5307, *Short Form Application for Determination for Employee Benefit Plan (Other than Collectively Bargained Plans)*

5308, *Request for Change in Plan/Trust Year*

5309, *Application for Determination of Employee Stock Ownership Plan*

5329, *Return for Individual Retirement Arrangement Taxes*

5330, *Return of Excise Taxes Related to Employee Benefit Plans*

5498, *Individual Retirement Arrangement Information*

5558, *Application for Extension of Time to File Certain Employee Plan Returns*

6088, *Distributable Benefits from Employee Pension Benefit Plans*

6406, *Short Form Application for Determination for Amendment of Employee Benefit Plan (Under sections 401(a) and 501(a) of the Internal Revenue Code)*

Form **5500**	**Annual Return/Report of Employee Benefit Plan**	OMB No. 1210-0016
Department of the Treasury Internal Revenue Service	**(With 100 or more participants)** This form is required to be filed under sections 104 and 4065 of the Employee Retirement Income Security Act of 1974 and sections 6039D,	**1988**
Department of Labor Pension and Welfare Benefits Administration	6057(b), and 6058(a) of the Internal Revenue Code, referred to as the Code.	**This form is open**
Pension Benefit Guaranty Corporation	▶ **For Paperwork Reduction Act Notice, see page 1 of the instructions.**	**to public inspection.**

For the calendar plan year 1988 or fiscal plan year beginning _____ , 1988, and ending _____ , 19____ .

If your plan year changed since the last return/report filed, check this box ▶ . . . . □

Type or print in ink all entries on the form, schedules, and attachments. If an item does not apply, enter "N/A." File the originals.

If (i) through (iii) do not apply to this year's return/report, leave the boxes unmarked. This return/report is:

(i) □ the first return/report filed for the plan;   (ii) □ an amended return/report; or   (iii) □ the final return/report filed for the plan.

▶ Welfare benefit plans and fringe benefit plans need only complete certain items—see the instructions "What To File."

▶ If you have been granted an extension of time to file this form, you must attach a copy of the approved extension to this form.

Use IRS label. Other- wise, please print or type.	**1a** Name of plan sponsor (employer if for a single-employer plan)	**1b** Employer identification number
	Address (number and street)	**1c** Telephone number of sponsor ( )
	City or town, state, and ZIP code	**1d** Business code number

2a Name of plan administrator (if same as plan sponsor, enter "Same")	**1e** CUSIP issuer number
Address (number and street)	**2b** Administrator's employer identification no.
City or town, state, and ZIP code	**2c** Telephone number of administrator ( )

3 Are the name, address, and employer identification number (EIN) of the plan sponsor and/or plan administrator the same as they appeared on the last return/report filed for this plan? □ Yes □ No. If "No," enter the information from the last return/report in **a** and/or **b**, and complete **c**.

a Sponsor ▶ _____ EIN _____ Plan number _____

b Administrator ▶ _____ EIN _____

c If **a** indicates a change in the sponsor's name and EIN, is this a change in sponsorship only? (See specific instructions for definition of sponsorship.) □ Yes □ No

4 Check the appropriate box to indicate the type of plan entity (check only one box):

a □ Single-employer plan   **c** □ Multiemployer plan   **e** □ Multiple-employer plan (other)

b □ Plan of controlled group of corporations or common control employers   **d** □ Multiple-employer-collectively-bargained plan   **f** □ Group insurance arrangement (of welfare plans)

5a (i) Name of plan ▶ _____

(ii) □ Check if name of plan changed since last return/report

5b Effective date of plan ▶
5c Enter three-digit plan number . . ▶

6a □ Welfare benefit plan (plan numbers 501 through 999) must check applicable items (A) through (P) and 6c.

(i) □ Type

(A) □ Health (other than dental or vision)   (F) □ Temporary disability (accident & sickness)   (K) □ Scholarship (funded)

(B) □ Life insurance   (G) □ Prepaid legal   (L) □ Death benefits other than life insurance

(C) □ Supplemental unemployment   (H) □ Long-term disability   (M) □ Code section 120 (group legal services plan)

(D) □ Dental   (I) □ Severance pay   (N) □ Code section 125 (cafeteria plan)

(E) □ Vision   (J) □ Apprenticeship & training   (O) □ Code section 127 (educational assistance program)

(P) □ Other (specify) ▶ _____

(ii) If you checked (M), (N), or (O), check if plan is: □ funded or □ unfunded.

6b □ Pension benefit plan (plan numbers 001 through 500) must check applicable items in (i) through (vii) and answer 6c through 6f.

(i) □ Defined benefit plan

(ii) □ Defined contribution plan—(indicate type of defined contribution):   (A) □ Profit-sharing   (B) □ Stock bonus

(C) □ Target benefit   (D) □ Other money purchase   (E) □ Other (specify) ▶ _____

(iii) □ Defined benefit plan with benefits based partly on balance of separate account of participant (Code section 414(k))

(iv) □ Annuity arrangement of certain exempt organizations (Code section 403(b)(1))

(v) □ Custodial account for regulated investment company stock (Code section 403(b)(7))

(vi) □ Pension plan utilizing individual retirement accounts or annuities (described in Code section 408) as the sole funding vehicle for providing benefits

(vii) □ Other (specify) ▶

▶ **Caution: A penalty for the late or incomplete filing of this return/report will be assessed unless reasonable cause is established.**

Under penalties of perjury and other penalties set forth in the instructions, I declare that I have examined this return/report, including accompanying schedules and statements, and to the best of my knowledge and belief, it is true, correct, and complete.

Date ▶ _____   Signature of employer/plan sponsor ▶ _____

Date ▶ _____   Signature of plan administrator ▶ _____

Form **5500** (1988)

Exhibit 16-7

6c Other plan features: (i) ☐ ESOP   (ii) ☐ Leveraged ESOP   (iii) ☐ Participant-directed account plan
  (iv) ☐ Pension plan maintained outside the United States   (v) ☐ Master trust (see instructions)
  (vi) ☐ 103-12 investment entity (see instructions)   (vii) ☐ Common/collective trust   (viii) ☐ Pooled separate account

----

		Yes	No
d Single-employer plans enter the tax year end of the employer in which this plan year ends ▶ Month .... Day .... Year........			
e Is the employer a member of an affiliated service group?			
f Does this plan contain a cash or deferred arrangement described in Code section 401(k)?			

7 Number of participants as of the end of the plan year (welfare plans complete only a(iv), b, c, and d):

a Active participants: (i) Number fully vested . . . . **a(i)**		
(ii) Number partially vested . . . . **(ii)**		
(iii) Number nonvested . . . . **(iii)**		
(iv) Total . . . . **(iv)**		
b Retired or separated participants receiving benefits . . . . **b**		
c Retired or separated participants entitled to future benefits . . . . **c**		
d Subtotal (add a(iv), b, and c) . . . . **d**		
e Deceased participants whose beneficiaries are receiving or are entitled to receive benefits . . . . **e**		
f Total (add d and e). . . . . **f**		

		Yes	No
g (i) Was any participant(s) separated from service with a deferred vested benefit for which a Schedule SSA (Form 5500) is required to be attached to this form?	**g(i)**		
(ii) If "Yes," enter the number of separated participants required to be reported ▶			

		Yes	No
8a Were any plan amendments adopted during the plan year?	**8a**		
b Did any amendment result in the retroactive reduction of accrued benefits for any participant?	**b**		
c Enter the date the most recent amendment was adopted ▶ Month .... Day .... Year			
d If **a** is "Yes," did any amendment change the information contained in the latest summary plan descriptions or summary description of modifications available at the time of the amendment?	**d**		
e If **d** is "Yes," has a summary plan description or summary description of modifications that reflects the plan amendments referred to in **d** been furnished to participants and filed with the Department of Labor?	**e**		

9a Was this plan terminated during this plan year or any prior plan year? If "Yes," enter the year ▶_____	**9a**	
b Were all plan assets either distributed to participants or beneficiaries, transferred to another plan, or brought under the control of PBGC?	**b**	
c Was a resolution to terminate this plan adopted during this plan year or any prior plan year?	**c**	
d If **a** or **c** is "Yes," have you received a favorable determination letter from IRS for the termination?	**d**	
e If **d** is "No," has a determination letter been requested from IRS?	**e**	
f If **a** or **c** is "Yes," have participants and beneficiaries been notified of the termination or the proposed termination? .	**f**	
g If **a** is "Yes" and the plan is covered by PBGC, is the plan continuing to file a PBGC Form 1 and pay premiums until the end of the plan year in which assets are distributed or brought under the control of PBGC?	**g**	
h During this plan year, did any trust assets revert to the employer for which the Code section 4980 excise tax is due? . .	**h**	
i If **h** is "Yes," enter the amount of tax paid with your Form 5330 ▶		

10a In this plan year, was this plan merged or consolidated into another plan(s), or were assets or liabilities transferred to another plan(s)? . . . . ☐ **Yes** ☐ **No**
  If "Yes," identify other plan(s)

b Name of plan(s) ▶	**c** Employer identification number(s)	**d** Plan number(s)
-------------------------------	--------------------------	-------------------

e Has Form 5310 been filed? . . . . ☐ **Yes** ☐ **No**

11 Enter the plan funding arrangement code (see instructions)	**12** Enter the plan benefit arrangement code (see instructions)

		Yes	No
13a Is this a plan established or maintained pursuant to one or more collective bargaining agreements?	**13a**		
b If **a** is "Yes," enter the appropriate six-digit LM number(s) of the sponsoring labor organization(s) (see instructions): ▶ (i) (ii) (iii)			

14 If any benefits are provided by an insurance company, insurance service, or similar organization, enter the number of **Schedules A** (Form 5500), Insurance Information, that are attached. If none, enter "-0-." ▶

WELFARE PLANS DO NOT COMPLETE ITEMS 15 THROUGH 27. GO TO ITEM 28

		Yes	No
15a If this is a defined benefit plan, is it subject to the minimum funding standards for this plan year?	**15a**		
If "Yes," attach **Schedule B** (Form 5500).			
b If this is a defined contribution plan, i.e., money purchase or target benefit, is it subject to the minimum funding standards? (If a waiver was granted, see instructions.)	**b**		

If "Yes," complete (i), (ii), and (iii) below:

(i) Amount of employer contribution required for the plan year under Code section 412	**b(i)**	$
(ii) Amount of contribution paid by the employer for the plan year	**b(ii)**	$
Enter date of last payment by employer ▶ Month _____ Day _____ Year _____		
(iii) If (i) is greater than (ii), subtract (ii) from (i) and enter the funding deficiency here; otherwise, enter zero. (If you have a funding deficiency, file Form 5330.) .	**b(iii)**	$

		Yes	No
16 Has the plan been top-heavy at any time beginning with the 1984 plan year?	**16**		
17 Has the plan accepted any transfers or rollovers with respect to a participant who had attained age 70½?	**17**		
18a If the plan distributed any annuity contracts this year, did these contracts contain a requirement that the spouse consent before any distributions under the contract are made in a form other than a qualified joint and survivor annuity?	**18a**		
b Did the plan make distributions to participants or spouses in a form other than a qualified joint and survivor annuity (a life annuity if a single person) or qualified preretirement survivor annuity (exclude deferred annuity contracts)?	**b**		
c Did the plan make distributions or loans to married participants and beneficiaries without the required consent of the participant's spouse?	**c**		
d Upon plan amendment or termination, do the accrued benefits of every participant include the subsidized benefits that the participant may become entitled to receive subsequent to the plan amendment or termination?	**d**		
19 Were the spousal consent requirements for distributions under Code section 417(e) complied with?	**19**		
20 Have any contributions been made or benefits accrued in excess of the Code section 415 limits, as amended by the Tax Reform Act of 1986?	**20**		
21 Has the plan made the required distributions in 1988 under Code section 401(a)(9)?	**21**		

		Number
22a Does the plan satisfy the percentage test of Code section 410(b)(1)(A)?	**22a**	
If **a** is "Yes," complete **b** through **i**. If "No," complete only **b** and **c** below and see specific instructions.		
b (i) Number of employees who are aggregated with employees of the employer as a result of the employer being aggregated with any employer covered by this plan under Code section 414(b), (c), or (m)	**b(i)**	
(ii) Number of individuals who performed services as leased employees under Code section 414(n) including leased employees of employers in (i).	**b(ii)**	
c Total number of employees (including any employees aggregated in **b**)	**c**	
d Number of employees excluded under the plan because of (i) minimum age or years of service, (ii) employees on whose behalf retirement benefits were the subject of collective bargaining, or (iii) nonresident aliens who receive no earned income from United States sources	**d**	
e Total number of employees not excluded (subtract **d** from **c**)	**e**	
f Employees ineligible (specify reason) ▶ _____	**f**	
g Employees eligible to participate (subtract **f** from **e**)	**g**	
h Employees eligible but not participating	**h**	
i Employees participating (subtract **h** from **g**)	**i**	

		Yes	No
23a Is it intended that this plan qualify under Code section 401(a)?	**23a**		
If "Yes," complete **b** and **c**.			
b Enter the date of the most recent IRS determination letter . . . . Month _____ Year _____			
c Is a determination letter request pending with IRS?	**c**		
24a If this is a plan with Employee Stock Ownership features, was a current appraisal of the value of the stock made immediately before any contribution of stock or the purchase of the stock by the trust for the plan year covered by this return/report?	**24a**		
b If **a** is "Yes," was the appraisal made by an unrelated third party?	**b**		
25 Is this plan integrated with social security or railroad retirement?	**25**		
26 Does the employer/sponsor listed in **1a** of this form maintain other qualified pension benefit plans?	**26**		
If "Yes," enter the total number of plans, including this plan ▶			
27 If this plan is an adoption of a master, prototype, or uniform plan, indicate which type by checking the appropriate box: **a** ☐ Master　　　　　**b** ☐ Prototype　　　　　**c** ☐ Uniform			

		Yes	No

28a Did any person who rendered services to the plan receive directly or indirectly $5,000 or more in compensation from the plan during the plan year (except for employees of the plan who were paid less than $1,000 in each month)? . . . **28a**

  If "Yes," complete Part I of **Schedule C** (Form 5500).

  b Did the plan have any trustees who must be listed in Part II of Schedule C (Form 5500)? . . . . **b**

  c Has there been a termination in the appointment of any person listed in **d** below? . . . . **c**

  d If **c** is "Yes," check the appropriate box(es), answer **e** and **f**, and complete Part III of Schedule C (Form 5500):

    (i) ☐ Accountant   *(ii)* ☐ Enrolled actuary   *(iii)* ☐ Insurance carrier   *(iv)* ☐ Custodian

    (v) ☐ Administrator   *(vi)* ☐ Investment manager   *(vii)* ☐ Trustee

  e Have there been any outstanding material disputes or matters of disagreement concerning the above termination? **e**

  f If an accountant or enrolled actuary has been terminated during the plan year, has the terminated accountant/actuary been provided a copy of the explanation required by Part III of Schedule C (Form 5500) with a notice advising them of their opportunity to submit comments on the explanation directly to DOL? . . . . . . **f**

  g Enter the number of Schedules C (Form 5500) that are attached. If none, enter -0- ▶

29a Is this plan exempt from the requirement to engage an independent qualified public accountant? **29a**

  b If **a** is "No," attach the accountant's opinion to this return/report and check the appropriate box. This opinion is:

    (i) ☐ Unqualified

    (ii) ☐ Qualified/disclaimer per Department of Labor Regulations 29 CFR 2520.103-8 and/or 2520.103-12(d)

    (iii) ☐ Qualified/disclaimer other

    (iv) ☐ Adverse

    (v) ☐ Other (explain)

  c If **a** is "No," do the financial statements or notes to the financial statements attached to this return/report disclose *(i)* a loss contingency indicating that assets are impaired or liability incurred; *(ii)* significant real estate or other transactions in which the plan and (A) the sponsor, (B) plan administrator, (C) the employer(s), or (D) the employee organization(s) are jointly involved; *(iii)* that the plan has participated in any related party transactions; or, *(iv)* any unusual or infrequent events or transactions occurring subsequent to the plan year-end that might significantly affect the usefulness of the financial statements in assessing the plan's present or future ability to pay benefits? . . . . **c**

  d If **c** is "Yes," provide the total amount involved in such disclosure ▶

30 If **29a** is "No," during the plan year

  a Did the plan have assets held for investment? **30a**

  b Were any loans by the plan or fixed income obligations due the plan in default as of the close of the plan year or classified during the year as uncollectible? . . . . **b**

  c Were any leases to which the plan was a party in default or classified during the year as uncollectible? . . . . **c**

  d Were any plan transactions or series of transactions in excess of 5% of the current value of plan assets? . . . . **d**

  e Do the notes to the financial statements accompanying the accountant's opinion disclose any nonexempt transactions with parties-in-interest? . . . . **e**

  f Did the plan engage in any nonexempt transactions with parties-in-interest not reported in **e**? . . . . **f**

  g Did the plan hold qualifying employer securities that are not publicly traded? . . . . **g**

  h Did the plan purchase or receive any nonpublicly traded securities that were not appraised in writing by an unrelated third party within 3 months prior to their receipt? . . . . **h**

  i Did any person manage plan assets who had a financial interest worth more than 10% in any party providing services to the plan or receive anything of value from any party providing services to the plan? . . . . . . **i**

  If **a, b, c, d, e,** or **f** is checked "Yes," schedules of those items in the format set forth in the instructions are required to be attached to this return/report.

31 Did the plan acquire individual whole life insurance contracts during the plan year? **31**

32 During the plan year:

  a *(i)* Was this plan covered by a fidelity bond? **32a**

    (ii) If **(i)** is "Yes," enter amount of bond ▶ _____

  b *(i)* Was there any loss to the plan, whether or not reimbursed, caused by fraud or dishonesty? . . . . . . **b**

    (ii) If **(i)** is "Yes," enter amount of loss ▶

33a Is the plan covered under the Pension Benefit Guaranty Corporation termination insurance program?

    ☐ Yes   ☐ No   ☐ Not determined

  b If **a** is "Yes" or "Not determined," enter the employer identification number and the plan number used to identify it.

    Employer identification number ▶   Plan number ▶

34 Current value of plan assets and liabilities at the beginning and end of the plan year. Combine the value of plan assets held in more than one trust. Allocate the value of the plan's interest in a commingled trust containing the assets of more than one plan on a line-by-line basis unless the trust meets one of the specific exceptions described in the instructions. Do not enter the value of that portion of an insurance contract which guarantees, during this plan year, to pay a specific dollar benefit at a future date. **Round off amounts to the nearest dollar.** Plans with no assets at the beginning and the end of the plan year, enter zero on line 34f.

Assets		(a) Beginning of year	(b) End of Year
a Total noninterest-bearing cash	a		
b Receivables (net):			
(i) Employer contributions	b(i)		
(ii) Participant contributions	(ii)		
(iii) Income	(iii)		
(iv) Other	(iv)		
(v) Total	(v)		
c General investments:			
(i) Interest-bearing cash (including money market funds)	c(i)		
(ii) Certificates of deposit	(ii)		
(iii) U.S. Government securities	(iii)		
(iv) Corporate debt instruments	(iv)		
(v) Corporate stocks:			
(A) Preferred	(v)(A)		
(B) Common	(B)		
(vi) Partnership/joint venture interests	(vi)		
(vii) Real estate:			
(A) Income-producing	(vii)(A)		
(B) Nonincome-producing	(B)		
(viii) Loans (other than to participants) secured by mortgages:			
(A) Residential	(viii)(A)		
(B) Commercial	(B)		
(ix) Loans to participants:			
(A) Mortgages	(ix)(A)		
(B) Other	(B)		
(x) Other loans	(x)		
(xi) Value of interest in certain investment arrangements (see instructions)	(xi)		
(xii) Value of funds held in insurance company general account (unallocated contracts)	(xii)		
(xiii) Other	(xiii)		
(xiv) Total	(xiv)		
d Employer-related investments:			
(i) Employer securities	d(i)		
(ii) Employer real property	(ii)		
e Buildings and other property used in plan operation	e		
f Total assets	f		
Liabilities			
g Benefit claims payable	g		
h Operating payables	h		
i Acquisition indebtedness	i		
j Other liabilities	j		
k Total liabilities	k		
Net Assets			
l Line **f** minus line **k**	l		

35 Plan income, expenses, and changes in net assets for the plan year.
Include all income and expenses of the plan, including any trust(s) or separately maintained fund(s), and any payments/receipts to/from insurance carriers. **Round off amounts to the nearest dollar.**

	Income		(a) Amount	(b) Total
a	Contributions:			
	(i)	Received or receivable from:		
		(A) Employers	a(i)(A)	
		(B) Participants	(B)	
		(C) Others	(C)	
	(ii)	Noncash contributions	(ii)	
b	Earnings on investments:			
	(i)	Interest:		
		(A) Interest-bearing cash (including money market funds)	b(i)(A)	
		(B) Certificates of deposit	(B)	
		(C) U.S. Government securities	(C)	
		(D) Corporate debt instruments	(D)	
		(E) Mortgage loans	(E)	
		(F) Other loans	(F)	
		(G) Other	(G)	
	(ii)	Dividends:		
		(A) Preferred stock	b(ii)(A)	
		(B) Common stock	(B)	
	(iii)	Rents	(iii)	
	(iv)	Net gain (loss) on sale of assets:		
		(A) Aggregate proceeds	b(iv)(A)	
		(B) Aggregate costs	(B)	
	(v)	Unrealized appreciation (depreciation) of assets	(v)	
	(vi)	Net investment gain (loss) from certain investment arrangements—see instructions	(vi)	
c	Other income	c	
d	Total income (add **a**, **b**, and **c**)	d	
	Expenses			
e	Benefit payment and payments to provide benefits:			
	(i)	Directly to participants or beneficiaries	e(i)	
	(ii)	To insurance carriers for the provision of benefits	(ii)	
	(iii)	Other	(iii)	
f	Interest expense	f	
g	Administrative expenses:			
	(i)	Salaries and allowances	g(i)	
	(ii)	Accounting fees	(ii)	
	(iii)	Actuarial fees	(iii)	
	(iv)	Contract administrator fees	(iv)	
	(v)	Investment advisory and management fees	(v)	
	(vi)	Legal fees	(vi)	
	(vii)	Valuation/appraisal fees	(vii)	
	(viii)	Trustees fees/expenses (including travel, seminars, meetings, etc.)	(viii)	
	(ix)	Other	(ix)	
h	Total expenses (add **e**, **f**, and **g**)	h	
i	Net income (loss) (**d** minus **h**)	i	
j	Transfers to (from) the plan (see instructions)	j	
k	Net assets at beginning of year (line **34l**, column (a))	k	
l	Net assets at end of year (line **34l**, column (b))	l	

		Yes	No
36	Did any employer sponsoring the plan pay any of the administrative expenses of the plan that were not reported in **35g**?		

Form **5500-C**

Department of the Treasury
Internal Revenue Service

Department of Labor
Pension and Welfare Benefits Administration

Pension Benefit Guaranty Corporation

Return/Report of Employee Benefit Plan
(With fewer than 100 participants)

This form is required to be filed under sections 104 and 4065 of the Employee Retirement Income Security Act of 1974 and sections 6039D, 6057(b), and 6058(a) of the Internal Revenue Code, referred to as the Code.

OMB No. 1210-0016

1988

This Form Is Open to Public Inspection.

For the calendar plan year 1988 or fiscal plan year beginning _____ , 1988, and ending _____ , 19___

If your plan year changed since the last return/report filed, check this box ▶ . . . . ☐

Type or print in ink all entries on the form, schedules, and attachments. If an item does not apply, enter "N/A." File the originals.

If (i) through (iii) do not apply to this year's return/report, leave the boxes unmarked. This return/report is:

(i) ☐ the first return/report filed for the plan;   (ii) ☐ an amended return/report; or   (iii) ☐ the final return/report filed for the plan.

▶ Welfare benefit plans and fringe benefit plans need only complete certain items or may not be required to file—see instructions "What to File."

▶ One-participant plans file Form 5500EZ for 1988.

▶ If you have been granted an extension of time to file this form, you must attach a copy of the approved extension to this form.

Use IRS label. Otherwise, please print or type.	**1a** Name of plan sponsor (employer, if for a single-employer plan)	**1b** Employer identification number
	Address (number and street)	**1c** Telephone number of sponsor ( )
	City or town, state, and ZIP code	**1d** Business code number

2a Name of plan administrator (if same as plan sponsor, enter "Same") | **1e** CUSIP issuer number

Address (number and street) | **2b** Administrator's employer identification no.

City or town, state, and ZIP code | **2c** Telephone number of administrator ( )

3 Are the name, address, and employer identification number (EIN) of the plan sponsor and/or plan administrator the same as they appeared on the last return/report filed for this plan? ☐ Yes ☐ No If "No," enter the information from the last return/report in a and/or b, and complete c.

a Sponsor ▶ _____ EIN _____ Plan number _____

b Administrator ▶ _____ EIN _____

c If a indicates a change in the sponsor's name and EIN, is this a change in sponsorship only? (See specific instructions for definition of sponsorship.)
☐ Yes ☐ No

4 Check box to indicate the type of plan entity (check only one box):
a ☐ Single-employer plan
b ☐ Plan of controlled group of corporations or common control employers
c ☐ Multiemployer plan
d ☐ Multiple-employer-collectively-bargained plan
e ☐ Multiple-employer plan (other)
f ☐ Exceptions to (b) and (e). (See instructions for line 4f.)

5a (i) Name of plan ▶ _____
_____
(ii) ☐ Check if name of plan changed since the last return/report
(iii) ☐ Check this box if this plan covers self-employed participants

5b Effective date of plan

5c Enter three-digit plan number . . . . ▶

6a ☐ Welfare benefit plan (plan numbers 501 through 999) must check applicable items A through P and 6c

(i) ☐ Type
   A ☐ Health (other than dental or vision)
   B ☐ Life insurance
   C ☐ Supplemental unemployment
   D ☐ Dental
   E ☐ Vision
   F ☐ Temporary disability (accident and sickness)
   G ☐ Prepaid legal
   H ☐ Long-term disability
   I ☐ Severance pay
   J ☐ Apprenticeship and training
   K ☐ Scholarship (funded)
   L ☐ Death benefits other than life insurance
   M ☐ Code section 120 (group legal services plan)
   N ☐ Code section 125 (cafeteria plan)
   O ☐ Code section 127 (educational assistance plan)
   P ☐ Other (specify) _____

(ii) If you checked M, N, or O, check if plan is: ☐ funded or ☐ unfunded

6b ☐ Pension benefit plan (plan numbers 001 through 500) must check applicable items in (i) through (vii) and answer 6c through 6f.

(i) ☐ Defined benefit plan

(ii) ☐ Defined contribution plan—(indicate type of defined contribution): (A) ☐ Profit-sharing (B) ☐ Stock bonus (C) ☐ Target benefit
(D) ☐ Other money purchase (E) ☐ Other (specify) ▶ _____

(iii) ☐ Defined benefit plan with benefits based partly on balance of separate account of participant (Code section 414(k))

(iv) ☐ Annuity arrangement of certain exempt organizations (Code section 403(b)(1))

(v) ☐ Custodial account for regulated investment company stock (Code section 403(b)(7))

(vi) ☐ Pension plan utilizing individual retirement accounts or annuities (described in Code section 408) as the sole funding vehicle for providing benefits

(vii) ☐ Other (specify) ▶

Under penalties of perjury and other penalties set forth in the instructions, I declare that I have examined this return/report, including accompanying schedules and statements, and to the best of my knowledge and belief it is true, correct, and complete.

Date ▶ _____ Signature of employer/plan sponsor ▶ _____

Date ▶ _____ Signature of plan administrator ▶ _____

For Paperwork Reduction Act Notice, see page 1 of the Instructions.

Form **5500-C** (1988)

Exhibit 16-8

		Yes	No

6c Other plan features: *(i)* ☐ ESOP   *(ii)* ☐ Leveraged ESOP   *(iii)* ☐ Participant-directed account plan
  (iv) ☐ Pension plan maintained outside the United States   *(v)* ☐ Master trust (see instructions)
  (vi) ☐ 103-12 investment entity (see instructions)   *(vii)* ☐ Common/Collective trust   *(viii)* ☐ Pooled separate account

----

----

d Single-employer plans enter the tax year end of the employer in which this plan year ends ▶ Month _____ Day_____ Year _____

e Is the employer a member of an affiliated service group? . . . . **e**

f Does this plan contain a cash or deferred arrangement described in Code section 401(k)? . . . . **f**

7a Total participants: *(i)* Beginning of plan year_____   *(ii)* End of plan year_____

b *(i)* Were any participants in the pension benefit plan separated from service with a deferred vested benefit for which a Schedule SSA (Form 5500) is required to be attached? . . . . **(i)**

  (ii) If "Yes," enter the number of separated participants required to be reported ▶

8a Were any plan amendments adopted during the plan year? . . . . **a**

b Did any amendment result in the retroactive reduction of accrued benefits for any participant?. . . . . **b**

c Enter the date the most recent amendment was adopted   . . ▶ Month _____ Day _____ Year _____

d If a is "Yes," did any amendment change the information contained in the latest summary plan descriptions or summary description of modifications available at the time of the amendment? . . . . **d**

e Has a summary plan description or summary description of modifications that reflects the plan amendments referred to in d been furnished to participants and filed with the Department of Labor?. . . . . **e**

9a Was this plan terminated during this plan year or any prior plan year? If "Yes," enter year ▶ _____ **9a**

b Were all plan assets either distributed to participants or beneficiaries, transferred to another plan, or brought under the control of PBGC? . . . . **b**

c Was a resolution to terminate this plan adopted during this plan year or any prior plan year? . . . . **c**

d If a or c is "Yes," have you received a favorable determination letter from IRS for the termination? . . . . . . **d**

e If d is "No," has a determination letter been requested from IRS? . . . . **e**

f If a or c is "Yes," have participants and beneficiaries been notified of the termination or the proposed termination? . . . . . **f**

g If a is "Yes" and the plan is covered by PBGC, is the plan continuing to file a PBGC Form 1 and pay premiums until the end of the plan year in which assets are distributed or brought under the control of PBGC? . . . . **g**

h During this plan year, did any trust assets revert to the employer for which the Code section 4980 excise tax is due? . . . . **h**

i If h is "Yes," enter the amount of tax paid with your Form 5330 ▶

10a Was this plan merged or consolidated into another plan(s), or were assets or liabilities transferred to another plan(s) since the end of the plan year covered by the last return/report Form 5500 or 5500-C which was filed for this plan (or during this plan year if this is the initial return/report)? **10a**

If "Yes," identify the other plan(s):   **c** Employer identification number(s)   **d** Plan number(s)

b Name of plan(s) ▶ _____   _____   _____

e Has Form 5310 been filed? . . . . ☐ Yes ☐ No

11 Enter the plan funding arrangement code (see instructions) ▶	**12** Enter the plan benefit arrangement code (see instructions) ▶

		Yes	No

13 Is this a plan established or maintained pursuant to one or more collective bargaining agreements? **13**

14 If any benefits are provided by an insurance company, insurance service, or similar organization, enter the number of Schedules A (Form 5500), Insurance Information, that are attached. If none, enter "-0-" ▶

Welfare Plans Do Not Complete Items 15 Through 28. Skip to item 29.

15a If this is a defined benefit plan, is it subject to the minimum funding standards for this plan year? . . . . **a**

If "Yes," attach Schedule B (Form 5500).

b If this is a defined contribution plan, i.e., money purchase or target benefit, is it subject to the minimum funding standards (if a waiver was granted, see instructions)? . . . . **b**

If "Yes," complete *(i)*, *(ii)*, and *(iii)* below:

  (i) Amount of employer contribution required for the plan year under Code section 412 . . . **(i)** $

  (ii) Amount of contribution paid by the employer for the plan year . . . . **(ii)** $

    Enter date of last payment by employer ▶ Month _____ Day _____Year _____

  (iii) If *(i)* is greater than *(ii)*, subtract *(ii)* from *(i)* and enter the funding deficiency here. Otherwise, enter zero. (If you have a funding deficiency, file Form 5330.) . . . . . . **(iii)** $

16 Has the plan been top-heavy at any time beginning with the 1984 plan year? **16**

17 Has the plan accepted any transfers or rollovers with respect to a participant who has attained age 70½? **17**

		Yes	No
18a If the plan distributed any annuity contracts this year, did these contracts contain a requirement that the spouse consent before any distributions under the contract are made in a form other than a qualified joint and survivor annuity?	**18a**		
b Did the plan make distributions to participants or beneficiaries in a form other than a qualified joint and survivor annuity (a life annuity if a single person) or qualified preretirement survivor annuity (exclude deferred annuity contracts)?	**b**		
c Did the plan make distributions or loans to married participants and beneficiaries without the required consent of the participant's spouse?	**c**		
d Upon plan amendment or termination, do the accrued benefits of every participant include the subsidized benefits that the participant may become entitled to receive subsequent to the plan amendment or termination?	**d**		
19 Were distributions made in accordance with the requirements of Code section 417(e)? (See instructions.)	**19**		
20 Have any contributions been made or benefits accrued in excess of the Code section 415 limits, as amended by the Tax Reform Act of 1986?	**20**		
21 Has the plan made the required distributions in 1988 under Code section 401(a)(9)?	**21**		

22a Does the plan satisfy the percentage test of Code section 410(b)(1)(A)? . . . .

If a is "Yes," complete b through i. If "No," complete only b and c below and see Specific Instructions.

		Number
22a		
b *(i)* Number of employees who are aggregated with employees of the employer as a result of being an affiliated service group under Code section 414(b), (c), or (m)	**(i)**	
(ii) Number of individuals who performed services as leased employees under Code section 414(n) including leased employees of employers in (i)	**(ii)**	
c Total number of employees (including any employees aggregated in b)	**c**	
d Number of employees excluded under the plan because of *(i)* minimum age or years of service, *(ii)* employees on whose behalf retirement benefits were the subject of collective bargaining, or *(iii)* nonresident aliens who received no earned income from United States sources	**d**	
e Total number of employees not excluded (subtract d from c)	**e**	
f Employees ineligible (specify reason)	**f**	
g Employees eligible to participate (subtract f from e)	**g**	
h Employees eligible but not participating	**h**	
i Employees participating (subtract h from g)	**i**	

		Yes	No
23a Is it intended that this plan qualify under Code section 401(a)?	**23a**		
If "Yes," complete b and c.			
b Enter the date of the most recent IRS determination letter—Month _____ Year _____			
c Is a determination letter request pending with IRS?	**c**		
24a If this is a plan with Employee Stock Ownership features, was a current appraisal of the value of the stock made immediately before any contribution of stock or the purchase of the stock by the trust for the plan year covered by this return/report? . . .	**24a**		
b If a is "Yes," was the appraisal made by an unrelated third party?	**b**		
25 Is this plan integrated with social security or railroad retirement?	**25**		
26 Does the employer/sponsor listed in 1a of this form maintain other qualified pension benefit plans?	**26**		
If "Yes," enter the total number of plans including this plan ▶			

27 Is this plan an adoption of a master, prototype or uniform plan? Indicate which type by checking the appropriate box:

  a ☐ Master **b** ☐ Prototype plan **c** ☐ Uniform plan

28a Is the plan covered under the Pension Benefit Guaranty Corporation termination insurance program? ☐ **Yes**   ☐ **No**   ☐ **Not determined**

  b If a is "Yes" or "Not determined," enter the employer identification number and the plan number used to identify it.

  Employer identification number ▶   Plan number ▶

29 During the plan year:		Yes	No	Amount
a Was this plan covered by a fidelity bond?	**29a**			
b Was there any loss to the plan, whether or not reimbursed, caused by fraud or dishonesty?	**b**			
c Was there any sale, exchange, or lease of any property between the plan and the employer, any fiduciary, any of the five most highly paid employees of the employer, any owner of a 10% or more interest in the employer, or relatives of any such persons?	**c**			
d Was there any loan or extension of credit by the plan to the employer, any fiduciary, any of the five most highly paid employees of the employer, any owner of a 10% or more interest in the employer, or relatives of any such persons?	**d**			
e Did the plan acquire or hold any employer security or employer real property?	**e**			
f Has the plan granted an extension on any delinquent loan owed to the plan?	**f**			
g Has the employer owed contributions to the plan which are more than 3 months overdue?	**g**			
h Were any loans by the plan or fixed income obligations due the plan classified as uncollectible or in default as of the close of the plan year?	**h**			

			Yes	No	Amount
i	Has any plan fiduciary had a financial interest in excess of 10% in any party providing services to the plan or received anything of value from any such party?	29i			
j	Did the plan at any time hold 20% or more of its assets in any single security, debt, mortgage, parcel of real estate, or partnership/joint venture interests?	j			
k	Did the plan at any time engage in any transaction or series of related transactions involving 20% or more of the current value of plan assets?	k			
l	Were there any noncash contributions made to the plan whose value was set without an appraisal by an independent third party?	l			
m	Were there any purchases of nonpublicly traded securities by the plan whose value was set without an appraisal by an independent third party?	m			
n	Has the plan failed to provide any benefit when due under the terms of the plan because of insufficient assets?	n			

30 Current value of plan assets and liabilities at the beginning and end of the plan year. Combine the value of plan assets held in more than one trust. Allocate the value of the plan's interest in a commingled trust containing the assets of more than one plan on a line-by-line basis unless the trust meets one of the specific exceptions described in the instructions. Do not enter the value of that portion of an insurance contract which guarantees during this plan year to pay a specific dollar benefit at a future date. Round off amounts to the nearest dollar.

Assets

			(a) Beginning of year	(b) End of year
a	Cash	a		
b	Receivables	b		
c	Investments:			
	(i) U.S. Government securities	(i)		
	(ii) Corporate debt and equity instruments	(ii)		
	(iii) Real estate and mortgages (other than to participants)	(iii)		
	(iv) Loans to participants:			
	A Mortgages	A		
	B Other	B		
	(v) Other	(v)		
	(vi) Total investments (add (i) through (v))	(vi)		
d	Buildings and other property used in plan operations	d		
e	Other assets	e		
f	Total assets	f		

Liabilities

g	Payables	g		
h	Acquisition indebtedness	h		
i	Other liabilities	i		
j	Total liabilities	j		
k	Net assets (f minus j)	k		

31 Plan income, expenses, and changes in net assets for the plan year. Include all income and expenses of the plan including any trust(s) or separately maintained fund(s) and payments/receipts to/from insurance carriers.

Income

			(a) Amount	(b) Total
a	Contributions received or receivable in cash from:			
	(i) Employer(s) (including contributions on behalf of self-employed individuals)	(i)		
	(ii) Employees	(ii)		
	(iii) Others	(iii)		
b	Noncash contributions	b		
c	Earnings from investments (interest, dividends, rents, royalties)	c		
d	Net realized gain (loss) on sale or exchange of assets	d		
e	Other income (specify) ▶ _____	e		
f	Total income (add a through e)	f		

Expenses

g	Distribution of benefits and payments to provide benefits:			
	(i) Directly to participants or their beneficiaries	(i)		
	(ii) Other	(ii)		
h	Administrative expenses (salaries, fees, commissions, insurance premiums)	h		
i	Other expenses (specify) ▶ _____	i		
j	Total expenses (add g through i)	j		
k	Net income (loss) (subtract j from f)	k		

★U.S.GPO:1989-0-205-302

Form **5500-R**

Department of the Treasury
Internal Revenue Service

Department of Labor
Pension and Welfare Benefits Administration

Pension Benefit Guaranty Corporation

Registration Statement of Employee Benefit Plan

(With fewer than 100 participants)

This form is required to be filed under sections 104 and 4065 of the
Employee Retirement Income Security Act of 1974 and sections
6039D and 6058 of the Internal Revenue Code.

OMB No. 1210-0016

1988

Amended ☐

**This Form is Open
to Public Inspection**

For the calendar plan year 1988 or fiscal plan year beginning _____ , 1988, and ending _____ , 19 ____ .

One-participant plans file Form 5500EZ (see the instructions).

Plans described in Code section 6039D, complete the applicable box 6d, 6e, or 6f, and see the instructions.

Do NOT file this form for the plan's first year or for the plan's final return/report. Instead file Form 5500-C.

Check this box if an extension of time to file this return is attached . . . . ▶ ☐

▶ **If you have been granted an extension of time to file this form, you must attach a copy of the approved extension to this form.**

▶ **Type or complete in ink and file the original. If any item does not apply, enter "N/A."**

Use IRS label. Otherwise, please print or type.	**1a** Name of plan sponsor (employer, if for a single employer plan)	**1b** Employer identification number
	Address (number and street)	**1c** Sponsor's telephone number ( )
	City or town, state, and ZIP code	**1d** If plan year changed since last return/report, check here . . ▶ ☐

2a Name of plan administrator (if same as plan sponsor, enter "Same")	**2b** Administrator's employer identification number
Address (number and street)	**2c** Administrator's telephone number ( )
City or town, state, and ZIP code	

3 Are the name, address, and identification number of the plan sponsor and/or plan administrator the same as they appeared on the last return/report filed for this plan? . . . . ☐ **Yes** ☐ **No**

If "No," enter the information from the last return/report in a and/or b, and complete c.

a Sponsor ▶ _____ EIN _____ Plan number _____

b Administrator ▶ _____ EIN _____

c If **a** is completed, is this a change in sponsorship only? (See specific instructions for definition of sponsorship.) ☐ **Yes** ☐ **No**

4 Check appropriate box to indicate the type of plan entity (check only one box):

a ☐ Single-employer plan

b ☐ Plan of controlled group of corporations or common control employers

c ☐ Multiemployer plan

d ☐ Multiple-employer-collectively-bargained plan

e ☐ Multiple-employer plan (other)

f ☐ Exceptions to (b) and (e). (See instructions for line 4f.)

5a(i) Name of plan ▶ _____

(ii) ☐ Check if name of plan changed since last return/report
(iii) ☐ Check this box if this plan covers self-employed participants

5b Effective date of plan ▶

5c Enter three-digit plan number . . . ▶

6 Type of plan (check applicable boxes):

a ☐ Defined benefit

b ☐ Defined contribution (money purchase or profit-sharing)

c ☐ Welfare benefit

d ☐ Code section 120 (group legal services plan)

e ☐ Code section 125 (cafeteria plan)

f ☐ Code section 127 (educational assistance program)

g ☐ Master trust

h ☐ Common/collective trust

i ☐ Pooled separate account

j ☐ Other (specify) ▶ _____

k If you checked d, e, or f, check if plan is:
☐ funded or ☐ unfunded

		Yes	No
7a Total participants: (i) Beginning of plan year _____ (ii) End of plan year _____			
b (i) Was any pension benefit plan participant(s) separated from service with deferred vested benefits for which a Schedule SSA (Form 5500) is required to be attached to this form?	**7b(I)**		
(ii) If "Yes," enter the number of separated participants required to be reported ▶			

Under penalties of perjury and other penalties set forth in the instructions, I declare that I have examined this return/report, including accompanying schedules and statements, and to the best of my knowledge and belief, it is true, correct and complete.

Date ▶ _____ Signature of employer/plan sponsor ▶ _____

Date ▶ _____ Signature of plan administrator ▶ _____

For Paperwork Reduction Act Notice, see page 1 of Form 5500-R Instructions.

Form **5500-R** (1988)

Exhibit 16-9

		Yes	No
8a	Was this plan terminated during this plan year or any prior plan year? If "Yes," enter the year _____ **8a**		
b	Were all the plan assets either distributed to participants or beneficiaries, transferred to another plan, or brought under the control of PBGC? **8b**		
c	If **a** is "Yes" and the plan is covered by PBGC, is the plan continuing to file PBGC Form 1 and pay premiums until the end of the plan year in which assets are distributed or brought under the control of PBGC? **8c**		
9	Is this a plan established or maintained pursuant to one or more collective bargaining agreements? **9**		
10	If any benefits are provided by an insurance company, insurance service, or similar organization, enter the number of Schedules A (Form 5500), Insurance Information, that are attached. (If none, enter "-0-") ▶		
11a	Were any plan amendments adopted during the plan year? **11a**		
b	If **a** is "Yes," did any amendment result in a retroactive reduction of accrued benefits for any participant? **11b**		
c	If **a** is "Yes," did any amendment change the information contained in the latest summary plan description or summary description of modifications available at the time of the amendment? **11c**		
d	Has a summary plan description or summary description of modifications that reflects the plan amendments referred to in 11c been furnished to participants and filed with the Department of Labor? **11d**		
12a	If this is a pension benefit plan subject to the minimum funding standards, has the plan experienced a funding deficiency for this plan year (defined benefit plans must answer this question and, attach Schedule B (Form 5500))? **12a**		
b	If **a** is "Yes," have you filed Form 5330 to pay the excise tax? **12b**		
13a	Total plan assets as of the beginning _____ and end _____ of the plan year.		
b	Total liabilities as of the beginning _____ and end _____ of the plan year.		
c	Net assets as of the beginning _____ and end _____ of the plan year.		
14	For this plan year, enter: **a** Plan income _____		
b	Expenses _____ **c** Net income (loss) _____		
d	Plan contributions _____ **e** Total benefits paid _____		

		Yes	No	Amount
15	During this plan year:			
a	Was this plan covered by a fidelity bond? **15a**			
b	Was there any loss to the plan, whether or not reimbursed, caused by fraud or dishonesty? . . . **15b**			
c	Was there any sale, exchange, or lease of any property between the plan and the employer, any fiduciary, any of the five most highly paid employees of the employer, any owner of a 10% or more interest in the employer, or relatives of any such persons? **15c**			
d	Was there any loan or extension of credit by the plan to the employer, any fiduciary, any of the five most highly paid employees of the employer, any owner of a 10% or more interest in the employer, or relatives of any such persons? **15d**			
e	Did the plan acquire or hold any employer security or employer real property? **15e**			
f	Has the plan granted an extension on any delinquent loan owed to the plan? **15f**			
g	Has the employer owed contributions to the plan which are more than 3 months overdue? . . . **15g**			
h	Were any loans by the plan or fixed income obligations due the plan classified as uncollectible or in default as of the close of the plan year? **15h**			
i	Has any plan fiduciary had a financial interest in excess of 10% in any party providing services to the plan or received anything of value from any such party? **15i**			
j	Did the plan hold at any time 20% or more of its assets in any single security, debt, mortgage, parcel of real estate, or partnership/joint venture interests? **15j**			
k	Did the plan at any time engage in any transaction or series of related transactions involving 20% or more of the current value of plan assets? **15k**			
l	Were there any noncash contributions made to the plan the value of which was set without an appraisal by an independent third party? **15l**			
m	Were there any purchases of nonpublicly traded securities by the plan the value of which was set without an appraisal by an independent third party? **15m**			
n	Has the plan failed to provide any benefit when due under the terms of the plan because of insufficient assets? **15n**			

16a Is the plan covered under the Pension Benefit Guaranty Corporation termination insurance program?
☐ Yes   ☐ No   ☐ Not determined

b If **a** is "Yes" or "Not determined," enter the employer identification number and the plan number used to identify it.
Employer identification number ▶   Plan number ▶

★ U.S. GPO: 1988 — 205-306

Form 5500EZ

Annual Return of One-Participant (Owners and Their Spouses) Pension Benefit Plan

Department of the Treasury
Internal Revenue Service

For the calendar year 1988 or fiscal plan year beginning _____ , 19 ___ ,
and ending _____ , 19 ___

OMB No. 1545-0956

1988

Please type or machine print

5588

► For Paperwork Reduction Act Notice, see page 1 of the instructions.

This Form is Open to Public Inspection

This return is: *(i)* ☐ the first return filed *(ii)* ☐ an amended return *(iii)* ☐ the final return *(iv)* ☐ filed for identification purposes

Use IRS label. Otherwise, please type or machine print.		
1a Name of employer	**1b** Employer identification number	
Address (number and street)	**1c** Telephone number of employer	
City or town, state, and ZIP code	**1d** If plan year has changed since last return, check here . . . . . ►☐	

2a *(i)* Name of plan ► ---

(ii) ☐ Check if name of plan has changed since last return

2b Date plan first became effective

Month | Day | Year

2c Enter three-digit plan number . . ► ☐☐☐

				Yes	No
3a Enter the date the most recent plan amendment was adopted	Month ☐	Year ☐ .			
b Enter the date of the most recent IRS determination letter	Month ☐	Year ☐			
c Is a determination letter request pending with IRS?					

4 Enter the number of other qualified pension benefit plans maintained by the employer . . . . ► _____

5 Type of plan: *a* ☐ Defined benefit pension plan (attach Schedule B (Form 5500)) *b* ☐ Money purchase plan
c ☐ Profit-sharing plan *d* ☐ Stock bonus or ESOP plan

6 Were there any noncash contributions made to the plan during the plan year? . . . .

7 Enter the number of participants in each category listed below:

		Number
a Less than age 59½ at the end of the plan year	**7a**	
b Age 59½ or more at the end of the plan year, but less than age 70½ at the beginning of the plan year . . .	**b**	
c Age 70½ or more at the beginning of the plan year.	**c**	

8a A fully insured plan with no trust and which is funded entirely by allocated insurance contracts that fully guarantee the amount of benefit payments should check the box at the right and not complete 8b through 10d . . . . ☐

b Contributions received for this plan year	**8b**	
c Net plan income other than from contributions	**c**	
d Plan distributions	**d**	
e Plan expenses other than distributions	**e**	

Note: *Do not complete 9 through 12 if this plan completed items 8 through 12 as applicable on the 1986 or 1987 Form 5500EZ.*

9a Total plan assets at the end of the year	**9a**	
b Total plan liabilities at the end of the year	**b**	

10 During the plan year, if any of the following transactions took place between the plan and a party-in-interest (see instructions), check "Yes" and enter amount. Otherwise, check "No."

		Yes	Amount	No
a Sale, exchange, or lease of property	**10a**			
b Loan or extension of credit	**b**			
c Acquisition or holding of employer securities	**c**			
d Payment by the plan for services	**d**			

		Yes	No
11a Does your business have any employees other than you and your spouse (and your partners and their spouses)? . . . If "No," do NOT complete the rest of this question; go to question 12.			
b Total number of employees (including you and your spouse and your partners and their spouses) ► _____			
c Does this plan meet the percentage tests of Code section 410(b)(1)(A)? . . . . See the specific instructions for line 11c.			

12 Answer this question only if there was a benefit payment, loan, or distribution of an annuity contract made during the plan year and the plan is subject to the spousal consent requirements (see instructions).

a Was there consent of the participant's spouse to any benefit payment or loan within the 90-day period prior to such payment or loan? . . . . .

b If "No," check the reason for no consent: *(i)* ☐ the participant was not married
(ii) ☐ the benefit payment made was part of a qualified joint and survivor annuity *(iii)* ☐ other
c Were any annuity contracts purchased by the plan and distributed to the participants? . . . .

Under penalties of perjury and other penalties set forth in the instructions, I declare that I have examined this return, including accompanying schedules and statements, and to the best of my knowledge and belief, it is true, correct, and complete.

Date ► ------------------ Signature of employer/plan sponsor ► ------------------

For IRS Use Only

☐ 1 1 1 1 1 1 | ☐ 2 2 2 2 2 2 | ☐ 3 | ☐ 4 4 4 4 | ☐ 5 | ☐ 6 | ☐ 7 | ☐ 8 ☐☐☐

★ U.S.GPO:1988-0-205-304

Exhibit 16-10

SCHEDULE A
(Form 5500)

Department of the Treasury
Internal Revenue Service

Department of Labor
Pension and Welfare Benefits Administration

Pension Benefit Guaranty Corporation

Insurance Information

This schedule is required to be filed under section 104 of the Employee Retirement Income Security Act of 1974.

▶ **File as an Attachment to Forms 5500, 5500-C, or 5500-R.**

▶ Insurance companies are required to provide this information as per ERISA section 103(a)(2).

OMB No. 1210-0016

1988

This Form Is Open to Public Inspection

For calendar year 1988 or fiscal plan year beginning _____, 1988 and ending _____, 19 ___

▶ Part I must be completed for all plans required to file this schedule.
▶ Part II must be completed for all insured pension plans.
▶ Part III must be completed for all insured welfare plans.

▶ Enter master trust or 103-12 IE name in place of "sponsor" and specify investment account or 103-12 IE in place of "plan" if filing with DOL for a master trust or 103-12 IE.

Name of plan sponsor as shown on line 1a of Form 5500, 5500-C, or 5500-R

Employer identification number

Name of plan

Enter three-digit plan number ▶

Part I — Summary of All Insurance Contracts Included in Parts II and III

Group all contracts in the same manner as in Parts II and III.

1 Check appropriate box: **a** ☐ Welfare plan **b** ☐ Pension plan **c** ☐ Combination pension and welfare plan

2 Coverage:

(a) Name of insurance carrier	(b) Contract or identification number	(c) Approximate number of persons covered at end of policy or contract year	Policy or contract year	
			(d) From	(e) To

3 Insurance fees and commissions paid to agents and brokers:

(a) Contract or identification number	(b) Name and address of the agents or brokers to whom commissions or fees were paid	(c) Amount of commissions paid	(d) Fees paid	
			Amount	Purpose

Total

4 Premiums due and unpaid at end of the plan year ▶ $ _____ : Contract or identification number ▶ _____

Part II — Insured Pension Plans

Provide information for each contract on a separate Part II. Where individual contracts are provided, the entire group of such individual contracts with each carrier may be treated as a unit for purposes of this report.

▶ Contract or identification number ▶

5 Contracts with allocated funds, for example, individual policies or group deferred annuity contracts:

  a State the basis of premium rates ▶

  b Total premiums paid to carrier .

  c If the carrier, service, or other organization incurred any specific costs in connection with the acquisition or retention of the contract or policy, other than reported in 3 above, enter amount .

  Specify nature of costs ▶

6 Contracts with unallocated funds, for example, deposit administration or immediate participation guarantee contracts. Do not include portions of these contracts maintained in separate accounts:

  a Balance at the end of the previous policy year .

  b Additions: (i) Contributions deposited during year .

    (ii) Dividends and credits .

    (iii) Interest credited during the year .

    (iv) Transferred from separate account .

    (v) Other (specify) ▶

    (vi) Total additions .

  c Total of balance and additions, add **a** and **b**(vi) .

  d Deductions:

    (i) Disbursed from fund to pay benefits or purchase annuities during year .

    (ii) Administration charge made by carrier .

    (iii) Transferred to separate account .

    (iv) Other (specify) ▶

    (v) Total deductions .

  e Balance at end of current policy year, subtract **d**(v) from **c** .

7 Separate accounts: Current value of plan's interest in separate accounts at year end .

For Paperwork Reduction Act Notice, see page 1 of the Instructions for Form 5500 or 5500-C.

Schedule A (Form 5500) 1988

Exhibit 16-11

Part III Insured Welfare Plans

Provide information for each contract on a separate Part III. If more than one contract covers the same group of employees of the same employer(s) or members of the same employee organization(s), the information may be combined for reporting purposes if such contracts are experience-rated as a unit. Where individual contracts are provided, the entire group of such individual contracts with each carrier may be treated as a unit for purposes of this report.

8	**(a)** Contract or identification number	**(b)** Type of benefit	**(c)** List gross premium for each contract	**(d)** Premium rate or subscription charge

9 Experience-rated contracts: **a** Premiums: *(i)* Amount received . . . .

    (ii) Increase (decrease) in amount due but unpaid . . . .

    (iii) Increase (decrease) in unearned premium reserve . . . .

    (iv) Premiums earned, add (i) and (ii), and subtract (iii) . . . .

  b Benefit charges: *(i)* Claims paid . . . .

    (ii) Increase (decrease) in claim reserves . . . .

    (iii) Incurred claims, add (i) and (ii) . . . .

    (iv) Claims charged . . . .

  c Remainder of premium: *(i)* Retention charges (on an accrual basis)—(A) Commissions .

    (B) Administrative service or other fees . . . .

    (C) Other specific acquisition costs . . . .

    (D) Other expenses . . . .

    (E) Taxes . . . .

    (F) Charges for risks or contingencies . . . .

    (G) Other retention charges . . . .

    (H) Total retention . . . .

    (ii) Dividends or retroactive rate refunds. (These amounts were ☐ paid in cash, or ☐ credited.) . . . .

  d Status of policyholder reserves at end of year: *(i)* Amount held to provide benefits after retirement . . . .

    (ii) Claim reserves . . . .

    (iii) Other reserves . . . .

  e Dividends or retroactive rate refunds due (do not include amount entered in **c**(ii)) . . . .

10 Nonexperience-rated contracts: **a** Total premiums or subscription charges paid to carrier . . . .

  b If the carrier, service, or other organization incurred any specific costs in connection with the acquisition or retention of the contract or policy, other than reported in 3 above, report amount . . . .

    Specify nature of costs ▶ --

If additional space is required for any item, attach additional sheets the same size as this form.

General Instructions

This schedule must be attached to Form 5500, 5500-C, or 5500-R for every defined benefit, defined contribution, and welfare benefit plan where any benefits under the plan are provided by an insurance company, insurance service, or other similar organization.

Specific Instructions

(References are to the line items on the form.)

Include only contracts with policy or contract years ending with or within the plan year (for reporting purposes a year cannot exceed 12 months). Data on Schedule A (Form 5500) should be reported only for such policy or contract years. **Exception:** *If the insurance company maintains records on the basis of a plan year rather than policy or contract year, data on Schedule A (Form 5500) may be reported for the plan year.*

Include only the contracts issued to the plan for which this return/report is being filed.

Plans Participating in Master Trust(s) and 103-12 IEs—See the Form 5500 or Form 5500-C instructions for "Reporting Requirements for Investment Arrangements Filing With DOL."

2(c).—Since the plan coverage may fluctuate during the year, the number of persons entered should be that which the administrator determines will most reasonably reflect the number covered by the plan at the end of the policy or contract year.

Where contracts covering individual employees are grouped, entries should be determined as of the end of the plan year.

2(d) and (e).—Enter the beginning and ending dates of the policy year for each contract listed under column (b). Where separate contracts covering individual employees are grouped, enter "N/A" in column (d).

3.—All sales commissions are to be reported in column (c) regardless of the identity of the recipient. Override commissions, salaries, bonuses, etc., paid to a general agent or manager for managing an agency, or for performing other administrative functions, are not to be reported.

Fees to be reported in column (d) represent payments by insurance carriers to agents and brokers for items other than commissions (e.g., service fees, consulting fees, and finders fees).

Note: *For purposes of this item, commissions and fees include amounts paid by an insurance company on the basis of the aggregate value*

(e.g., policy amounts, premiums) of contracts or policies (or classes thereof) placed or retained. The amount (or pro rata share of the total) of such commissions or fees attributable to the contract or policy placed with or retained by the plan must be reported in column (c) or (d), as appropriate.

Fees paid by insurance carriers to persons other than agents and brokers should be reported in Parts II and III on Schedule A (Form 5500) as acquisition costs, administrative charges, etc., as appropriate. For plans with 100 or more participants, fees paid by employee benefit plans to agents, brokers, and other persons are to be reported on Schedule C (Form 5500).

5a.—The rate information called for here may be furnished by attachment of appropriate schedules of current rates filed with appropriate state insurance departments or by a statement as to the basis of the rates.

6.—Show deposit fund amounts rather than experience credit records when both are maintained.

8(d).—The rate information called for here may be furnished by attachment of appropriate schedules of current rates or by a statement as to the basis of the rates.

SCHEDULE P (Form 5500)	Annual Return of Fiduciary of Employee Benefit Trust	OMB No. 1210-0016
Department of the Treasury Internal Revenue Service	▶ File as an attachment to Form 5500, 5500-C, 5500-R, or 5500EZ. ▶ For the Paperwork Reduction Notice, see page 1 of the Form 5500 Instructions.	1988

For trust calendar year 1988 or fiscal year beginning   , 1988, and ending   , 19

Please type or print

1 a Name of trustee or custodian

  b Address (number and street)

  c City or town, state, and ZIP code

2 Name of trust

3 Name of plan if different from name of trust

4 Have you furnished the participating employee benefit plan(s) with the trust financial information required to be reported by the plan(s)? . . . . ☐ **Yes** ☐ **No**

5 Enter the plan sponsor's employer identification number as shown on the form to which this schedule is attached . . . . ▶

Under penalties of perjury, I declare that I have examined this schedule, and to the best of my knowledge and belief it is true, correct, and complete.

Date ▶   Signature of fiduciary ▶

Instructions

(Section references are to the Internal Revenue Code.)

A. Purpose of Form
You may use this schedule to satisfy the requirements under section 6033(a) for an annual information return from every section 401(a) organization exempt from tax under section 501(a).

The filing of this form will also start the running of the statute of limitations under section 6501(a) for any trust described in section 401(a) which is exempt from tax under section 501(a).

B. Who May File
(1) Every trustee of a trust described in section 401(a) which was created as part of an employee benefit plan.
(2) Every custodian of a custodial account described in section 401(f).

C. How To File
File Schedule P (Form 5500) for the trust year ending with or within any participating plan's plan year as an attachment to the Form 5500, 5500-C, 5500-R, or 5500EZ filed by the plan for that plan year.

Schedule P (Form 5500) may be filed only as an attachment to a Form 5500, 5500-C, 5500-R, or 5500EZ. A separately filed Schedule P (Form 5500) will not be accepted.

If the trust or custodial account is used by more than one plan, file only one Schedule P (Form 5500). It must be filed as an attachment to one of the participating plan's returns/reports. If a plan uses more than one trust or custodial account for its funds, file one Schedule P (Form 5500) for each trust or custodial account.

D. Signature
The fiduciary (trustee or custodian) must sign this schedule. If there is more than one fiduciary, one of them, authorized by the others, may sign.

E. Other Returns and Forms That May Be Required
(1) Form 990-T.—For trusts described in section 401(a), a tax is imposed on income derived from business that is unrelated to the purpose for which the trust received a tax exemption. Report such income and tax on **Form 990-T,** Exempt Organization Business Income Tax Return. (See sections 511 through 514 and related regulations.)
(2) Forms W-2P and 1099-R.—If you made payments or distributions to individual beneficiaries of a plan, report these payments on Forms W-2P or 1099-R. (See sections 6041 and 6047 and related regulations.)
(3) Forms 941 or 941E.—If you made payments of distributions to individual beneficiaries of a plan, you are required to withhold income tax from those payments unless the payee elects not to have the tax withheld. Report this withholding on Form 941 or 941E. (See Forms 941 or 941E and Circular E, Publication 15.)

Schedule P (Form 5500) 1988

Exhibit 16-12

Annual Registration Statement Identifying Separated Participants With Deferred Vested Benefits

Under Section 6057(a) of the Internal Revenue Code

▶ File as an attachment to Form 5500, 5500-C, or 5500-R.

▶ For Paperwork Reduction Act Notice, see page 1 of the instructions for Form 5500 or 5500-C.

OMB No. 1210-0016

1988

This Form Is NOT Open to Public Inspection

For the calendar year 1988 or fiscal plan year beginning _____, 1988, and ending _____, 19___

▶ **This form must be filed for each plan year in which one or more participants with deferred vested benefit rights separated from the service covered by the plan. See instructions on when to report a separated employee.**

1a Name of sponsor (employer if for a single employer plan)	1b Sponsor's employer identification number
Address (number and street)	1c Is this a plan to which more than one employer contributes? . . ☐ Yes ☐ No
City or town, state, and ZIP code	
2a Name of plan administrator (if other than sponsor)	2b Administrator's employer identification no.
Address (number and street)	
City or town, state, and ZIP code	

3a Name of plan	3b Plan number ▶

4 Have you notified each separated participant of his or her deferred benefit? . . . . ☐ Yes ☐ No

5 Separated participants with deferred vested benefits (if additional space is required, see instruction, "What To File"):

(a) Social Security Number	(b) Name of participant	Enter code for nature and form of benefit		Amount of vested benefit			(h) Plan year in which participant separated
		(c) Type of annuity	(d) Payment frequency	(e) Defined benefit plan—periodic payment	Defined contribution plan		
					(f) Units or shares	(g) Total value of account	

The Following Information Is Optional (See Specific Instruction 6)

6 Use this item to report (i) separated participants with deferred vested benefits who were previously reported on Schedule SSA (Form 5500) and who have received part or all of their vested benefits or who have forfeited their benefits during the plan year for which this form is being filed, and (ii) to delete participants erroneously reported on a prior Schedule SSA (Form 5500):

Note: *Participants listed in this item, because they have received part of their vested benefits, must also be reported in item 5 above listing their remaining vested benefits.*

(a) Social Security Number	(b) Name of participant	Enter code for nature and form of benefit		Amount of vested benefit			(h) Plan year in which participant separated
		(c) Type of annuity	(d) Payment frequency	(e) Defined benefit plan—periodic payment	Defined contribution plan		
					(f) Units or shares	(g) Total value of account	

Under penalties of perjury, I declare that I have examined this report, and to the best of my knowledge and belief, it is true, correct, and complete.

_____   _____
Date   Signature of plan administrator

Exhibit 16-13

General Instructions

Note: *Please type or print all information and submit original copy only.*

Who Must File.—The plan administrator must file this form for any plan year for which a separated plan participant is reported under "When To Report a Separated Participant" below.

What To File.—File this schedule and complete all items. If you need more space, use additional copies of Schedule SSA, completing only items 1, 3, 5, and 6 of the additional copies.

A machine-generated computer listing showing the information required in items 5 and 6 may be submitted in lieu of completing items 5 and 6 on the schedule. Complete items 1 through 4 on Schedule SSA and enter in items 5 and 6 a statement that a list is attached. On each page of the computer list, enter the name of the sponsor, the EIN, the plan name, and the plan number. The list must be in the same format as items 5 and 6.

How To File.—File as an attachment to Form 5500, 5500-C, or 5500-R.

When To Report a Separated Participant.—

In general, **for a plan to which only one employer contributes,** a participant must be reported on Schedule SSA if:

(1) The participant separates from service covered by the plan in a plan year, and

(2) The participant is entitled to a deferred vested benefit under the plan.

The separated participant must be reported no later than on the Schedule SSA filed for the plan year following the plan year in which separation occurred. The participant may be reported earlier (i.e., on the Schedule SSA filed for the plan year in which separation occurred). Once separated participants have been reported on a Schedule SSA they should not be reported on a subsequent year's Schedule SSA.

However, a participant is not required to be reported on Schedule SSA if, before the date the Schedule SSA is required to be filed (including any extension of time for filing), the participant:

(1) Is paid some or all of the deferred vested retirement benefit,

(2) Returns to service covered by the plan, or

(3) Forfeits all of the deferred vested retirement benefit.

In general, **for a plan to which more than one employer contributes,** a participant must be reported on Schedule SSA if:

(1) The participant incurs two successive one-year breaks in service (as defined in the plan for vesting purposes) in service computation periods, and

(2) The participant is (or may be) entitled to a deferred vested benefit under the plan.

The participant must be reported no later than on the Schedule SSA filed for the plan year in which the participant completed the second of the two consecutive one-year breaks in service. The participant may be reported earlier (i.e., on the Schedule SSA filed for the plan year in which he or she separated from service or completed the first one-year break in service).

However, a participant is not required to be reported on Schedule SSA if, before the date the Schedule SSA is required to be filed (including any extension of time for filing), the participant:

(1) Is paid some or all of the deferred vested retirement benefit,

(2) Accrues additional retirement benefits under the plan, or

(3) Forfeits all of the deferred vested retirement benefit.

Cessation of Payment of Benefits.—As described above in "When To Report a Separated Participant," a participant is not required to be reported on Schedule SSA if, before the date the Schedule SSA is required to be filed, some of the deferred vested benefit to which the participant is entitled is paid to the participant. If payment of the deferred vested benefit ceases before all of the benefit is paid to the participant, the benefit to which the participant remains entitled must be reported on the Schedule SSA filed for the plan year following the last plan year within which any of the benefit was paid to the participant. However, a participant is not required to be reported on Schedule SSA on account of a cessation of payment of benefits if, before the date the schedule is required to be filed (including any extension of time for filing), the participant:

(1) Returns to service covered by the plan,

(2) Accrues additional retirement benefits under the plan, or

(3) Forfeits the remaining benefit.

Separation of a Re-employed Employee.— The deferred vested benefit reported on the current Schedule SSA for a re-employed employee who is again separated from service must include only the benefit not previously reported in or for prior years. Generally, the benefit to be shown on the current filing will be the benefit earned during the re-employment period.

Caution: *A penalty may be assessed if Schedule SSA (Form 5500) is not timely filed.*

Specific Instructions

4. Check "Yes" if you have complied with the requirements of Code section 6057(e). The notification to each participant must include the information set forth on this schedule and the information with respect to any contributions made by the participant and not withdrawn by the end of the plan year. Any benefits that are forfeitable if the participant dies before a certain date must be shown on the statement.

5(a). Please be careful to enter the exact social security number of each participant listed.

If the participant is a foreign national employed outside of the United States who does not have a social security number, enter the participant's nationality.

5(b). Enter each participant's name exactly as it appears on the participant's social security card or the employer's payroll records for purposes of reporting to the Social Security Administration.

5(c). From the following list, select the code that describes the type of annuity that will be provided for the participant. The type of annuity to be entered is the type that normally accrues under the plan at the time of the participant's separation from service covered by the plan (or for a plan to which more than one employer contributes at the time the participant incurs the second consecutive one-year break in service under the plan).

A A single sum

B Annuity payable over fixed number of years

C Life annuity

D Life annuity with period certain

E Cash refund life annuity

F Modified cash refund life annuity

G Joint and last survivor life annuity

M Other

5(d). From the following list, select the code that describes the benefit payment frequency during a 12-month period.

A Lump sum

B Annually

C Semiannually

D Quarterly

E Monthly

M Other

5(e). For a defined benefit plan, enter the amount of the periodic payment that a participant would normally be entitled to receive under 5(c), commencing at normal retirement age. However, if it is more expedient to show the amount of periodic payment the participant would be entitled to receive at early retirement date, enter that amount.

For a plan to which more than one employer contributes, if the amount of the periodic payment cannot be accurately determined because the plan administrator does not maintain complete records of covered service, enter an estimated amount and add the letter "X" in column 5(c) in addition to the annuity code to indicate that it is an estimate. If, from records maintained by the plan administrator, it cannot be determined whether the participant is entitled to any deferred vested benefit, but there is reason to believe he or she may be entitled, leave column 5(e) blank and enter "Y" in column 5(c) in addition to the annuity code.

5(f). For a defined contribution plan, if the plan states that a participant's share of the fund will be determined on the basis of units, enter the number of units credited to the participant.

If, under the plan, participation is determined on the basis of shares of stock of the employer, enter the number of shares and add the letter "S" to indicate shares. A number without the "S" will be interpreted to mean units.

5(g). For defined contribution plans, enter the value of the participant's account at the time of separation.

6. If, after a participant has been reported on Schedule SSA, the participant:

(1) is paid some or all of the deferred vested retirement benefit, or

(2) forfeits all of the deferred vested retirement benefit,

the plan administrator may, at its option, request that the participant's deferred vested benefit be deleted from Social Security Administration's records. Information reported in item 6, columns (a) through (g), is to be the exact information previously reported on Schedule SSA for the participant.

If this option is chosen because the participant is paid some of the deferred vested benefit, the reporting requirements described in "Cessation of Payment of Benefits" above apply if payment of the benefit ceases before all of the benefit is paid to the participant.

Also, if a person was erroneously reported on a prior Schedule SSA, use item 6 to delete this information from Social Security Administration's records.

Signature.—This form must be signed by the plan administrator. If more than one Schedule SSA is filed for one plan, only page one should be signed.

Chapter 17

PROTECTING YOUR IDEAS AND YOUR PRODUCTS

One of the keys to success in a competitive environment is to distinguish your product or service from those of your competitors so that buyers will seek you out. The law recognizes the need for business people to have their hard work and efforts protected from unscrupulous imitators who often attempt to take advantage of someone else's name or product. The imitators attempt either to sell their product with the exact name or a confusingly similar name of the well known competitor or attempt to sell an exact copy of the competitor's product to unsuspecting customers who do not know the difference. Usually, they attempt to do both. The body of law that has grown around the concept of protecting the marketing and production efforts of others is called *intellectual property law*. This chapter explains:

* Branding as a marketing tool
* Protecting your brand through trademarks and service marks
* Copyrights
* Patents
* Trade secrets

BRANDING: THE WAY TO INCREASE SALES AND PROFITS

How Brands Are Used as a Marketing Tool

Increasing sales and profits will often depend on your ability to distinguish your service or product from your competitors'. One method that has proven to be effective is called *branding*. The concept goes back to at least the Middle Ages and was used to identify the source of the product. Today, buyers use brands to identify specific products they like and thus make the purchase decision easier. Moreover, brands have been used to create a guide for quality and have served as a symbol of status.

From the seller's viewpoint, a known brand helps to develop a loyal following which protects against competition. The stronger the brand loyalty the more latitude you have to charge a premium price. In addition, a brand can improve your business image. As your product or service becomes better known, it facilitates the acceptance of future products or services that you may develop.

When a business sells more than one product or service it must decide on one of two branding strategies: family branding or individual branding.

Family branding means that each product will receive the same brand name. Sara Lee, Campbell, and Kraft are examples of successful family branding strategies. The advantage to this approach is that the promotion of one product indirectly promotes the others because they all share the same brand. This approach allows for lower promotion costs and may make it easier to introduce new items.

Individual branding means that each product will have its own brand. There are two advantages to using this strategy. First, it may be easier to aim your product at a specific segment of the market. Each segment may have different characteristics, and you want to tailor your brand to reflect those characteristics. A family brand may start to resemble a shotgun approach to the market which is ineffective if the market is composed of various segments. Second, if the product you are introducing does not do well in the market because of poor quality, poor packaging, etc., the negative connotations associated with the product and that particular brand do not spill over to the rest of your products because each brand operates in isolation.

Legally Protecting Your Brand: Trademarks and Servicemarks

A brand is a name, term, symbol, design, or a combination of these used to identify a product. The legal protection to prevent an imitator from using your brand is called *trademark* or *service mark*.

Federal law covering trademarks and service marks is found in the Federal Trademark Act of 1946, and a series of amendments, the most recent of which is the Trademark Law Revision Act of 1988. (See 15 United States Code 1051 et seq.) These acts are read as one and are commonly referred to as the Trademark Act. According to the Federal Trademark Act, a trademark may be "any word, symbol, device, or combination thereof adopted and used by a manufacturer or merchant to identify and distinguish his or her goods, including a unique product, from those manufactured or sold by others and to indicate the source of the goods, even if that source is unknown."

A trademark is used to identify a product. If the trademark is used to identify a service it is called a service mark. Generally, the word or design that appears on the product or its packaging is called a trademark, while the word or design that is used in advertising to identify the owner's services is called a service mark. The law concerning trademarks closely parallels the law of service marks.

Types of Trademarks

Trademarks are classified as arbitrary, suggestive, or descriptive.

Arbitrary Mark—This trademark may have no established usage in any context other than as a trademark, such as XEROX or Kodak (which results in the strongest type of mark and usually the easiest to protect), or it may have an independent and recognizeable meaning because it is part of the current language but it provides no indication of the nature or quality of the product. The relationship between the mark and the product is arbitrary. Examples are BOLD detergent, Gulf gasoline, Camel cigarettes, or Arrow shirts. If you choose this type of mark, the potential drawback is that others may also be using it for different types of products. As a consequence, you could be limited if you decide to apply the mark to other products or services.

Suggestive Mark—This trademark suggests some characteristic of the product without explicitly describing the product itself. Examples are Rapid Shave shaving cream, Roach Motel insect trap, and Beetle fishing lure.

Descriptive Mark—This trademark describes the intended use or characteristic of the product. This type of mark is the most difficult to protect. To register the trademark, it is necessary to demonstrate that a descriptive mark has acquired a "secondary meaning" within the consuming public. Secondary meaning requires that there is a second meaning, other than the standard English language meaning of the word, which serves to distinguish the trademark owner's product from the products of others.

One term that does not receive any trademark protection is the *generic* term. A generic term refers to the general type or class of product. A hazard that various businesses have had to contend with is the generic use of a trademark as the generic name for the product or service. Once that occurs, trademark protection is lost. Examples of products that once had trademark protection but lost it because they were declared to be generic words are: cellophane, linoleum, shredded wheat, aspirin, and escalator. Many companies in order to combat this potential problem always include in their advertisements the word brand after the product's trademark or that its brand is a trademark and should not be used generically. See Exhibit 17-1 for an example of how Xerox Corporation treats this problem.

Benefits of Federal Registration

Although there are approximately 600,000 active trademarks registered with the United States Patent and Trademark Office, it is not necessary for you to have your trademark registered on the principal register with the U.S. Patent and Trademark Office to receive trademark protection. Trademarks may be obtained by use under the common law. Moreover, a trademark not used in interstate commerce cannot be registered with the United States Patent and Trademark Office. Therefore, should you decide to establish protection for your mark, and you have decided not to market your product or service that contains your mark in interstate commerce, we strongly recommend you register your mark in the state in which is used. By registering your mark with the state, it will put on notice anyone who is conducting a search for your particular mark that you have stated a claim for that particular mark. Every state has a registration process for trademarks and service marks. See Exhibit 17-2 which contains a notice of trademark registration from the state of California and is the type of correspondence you will receive from the state in which you register your mark.

If you decide that you are going to conduct interstate business with your mark, then you should consider its registration with the United States Patent and Trademark Office because of the various benefits it provides. For instance, if your trademark is not federally registered, and another business uses your mark or another mark that is confusingly similar in connection with the same or closely related product or service that you sell, that business can develop common law rights to use its mark, at the very least, on a local basis.

Some of the benefits of federal registration are the following:

* The right to sue in federal court for trademark infringement.
* The right to claim constructive notice of claim of ownership which prevents the invocation of a "good faith adoption" defense by a subsequent user.
* Recovery of profits, damages, and costs in a federal action for infringement and the possibility of treble damages and attorneys' fees.
* The right to deposit the registration with U.S. Customs in order to stop the importation of goods bearing a mark that infringes upon the protected mark.
* A basis for filing trademark applications in foreign countries.
* Availability of criminal penalties in an action for counterfeiting a registered trademark.

The term of a federal trademark is ten years with ten-year renewal terms. Between the fifth and sixth year after the date of registration, the registrant must file an affidavit with the U.S. Patent and Trademark Office stating that the mark is currently in use in commerce. If no affidavit is filed the registration will be cancelled. Unlike a copyright or patent, a trademark can last indefinitely if it can be shown that the mark continues to perform a source-indicating function.

Once federal registration is issued, there are several ways you may give notice of registration:

- The symbol ®
- The phrase "Registered in U.S. Patent and Trademark Office"
- The phrase "Reg. U.S. Pat.& Tm. Off."

Care should be taken, however, to distinguish the use of ® and ™. The ® symbol may only be used if the trademark has actually been registered with the United States Trademark and Patent Office. If the ® symbol is used prior to registration, for instance , a federal application is pending, it may result in the rejection of the application or it may be determined that the owner of the mark has perpetrated fraud on the public. If the trademark is not registered then the symbol ™ should be used or ^{SM} if it is an unregistered service mark.

Trademark registration, both at the federal and state level, will provide you with a number of advantages: (1) It often acts as a deterrent to subsequent users, (2) it is easier to obtain a cease and desist order from the court to enjoin an infringer; and (3) it establishes prima facie evidence of your prior claim.

Why an Application May Be Rejected

When a trademark is approved, it is published in The *Trademark Official Gazette,* which is a weekly publication of the U.S. Patent and Trademark Office. See Exhibit 17-3, which shows a page of the gazette. After publication, any party has thirty days to oppose the registration of the mark. If no opposition is filed, a registration is issued and the mark is placed on the principal register approximately twelve weeks from the date the mark was published.

Not all applications for trademark registration are accepted by the U.S. Patent and Trademark Office for placement on the principal register, however. The trademark may be rejected by the trademark examining attorney, who initially approves the application, for a variety of reasons including if the trademark:

- Is immoral, deceptive, or scandalous.
- May disparage or falsely suggest a connection with persons, institutions, beliefs, or national symbols, or bring them into contempt or disrepute.
- Consists of or simulates the flag or coat of arms or other insignia of the United States, or a state, a municipality, or any foreign nation.
- Is the name, portrait, or signature of a particular living individual, unless he or she has given written consent; or is the name, signature, or portrait of a deceased president of the United States during the life of his widow, unless she has given her consent.
- So resembles a mark already registered by the U.S. Patent and Trademark Office as to be likely, when applied to the goods of the applicant, to cause confusion, or to cause mistake, or to deceive.
- Does not function as a trademark to identify the goods or services as coming from a particular source; for example, the matter applied for is merely ornamentation;* merely descriptive or deceptively misdescriptive of the goods or services.*
- Is primarily geographically descriptive or deceptively misdescriptive of the goods or services of the applicant.*

• Is primarily a surname.*

Trademark Search

Before attempting to register your trademark, it is advisable to conduct a search of the trademark to determine whether your mark may be infringing the trademark rights of another party. A record of all active registrations and pending applications is maintained by the U.S. Patent and Trademark Office. The library is located at Crystal Plaza 3, 2021 Jefferson Davis Highway, Arlington, Virginia and is open to the public free of charge from Monday through Friday. As a rule, the U.S. Patent and Trademark Office will not advise you as to whether or not a particular trademark is available. You must first file an application. As a consequence, many individuals prior to filing an application hire a private search firm or an attorney to conduct a trademark search. Often a search can be done quickly and inexpensively and will provide information on state and federal registered trademarks. If a mark has been registered either at the federal or state level, the following information will be provided:

- The mark.
- The product or service used in connection with the mark.
- The identity of the trademark owner.
- The date on which the trademark was first used.

The most difficult aspect of the trademark search are trademarks that have been established through common law, which means they have been used in commerce but have not been registered or were once registered and then cancelled. We recommend that if a trademark search is conducted, it should include the following:

* A search of all federal registers (including pending applications, registered trademarks, unregistered published marks, expired registrations, assignments, cancellations, abandonments, renewals, and any oppositions related to the mark)
* A search of all registers for all fifty states
* A search of all common law marks (including business name listings, periodicals, telephone directories, and trade journals)
* A search of all litigated trademarks

Applying for Federal Trademark Registration

When applying for federal trademark registration, you may fill out the application yourself, although it is advisable to seek the assistance of an attorney. An application for the federal register consists of the following: (1) a written application form, (2) a drawing of the mark (there are special rules regarding the form and size of the drawing), (3) five actual specimens of the mark in connection with the product or service, such as labels, tags, containers, or displays (if you claim existing use in interstate commerce as the basis for registration), and (4) the filing fee. You must file a separate application for each trademark that you wish to have registered.

---

*Although these particular reasons may be sufficient to deny a mark from becoming placed on the principal register, they may be entitled to be placed on the supplemental register. The supplemental register contains terms or designs considered capable of distinguishing the applicant's goods or services but do not yet do so. If your mark is registered on the supplemental register, you may still bring a suit in federal court for trademark infringement or use the registration as a basis for filing in some foreign countries.

Under the Trademark Law Revision Act of 1988, there are two ways you can attempt federal trademark registration. One method is to file with the U.S. Patent and Trademark Office a written application which contains the following information: (1) verification by the applicant, (2) domicile and citizenship of the applicant, (3) statement of applicant's bona fide intention to use the mark in commerce, (4) description of the goods or services that are connected with the mark, (5) mode or manner in which the goods or services connected with the mark are intended to be used, (6) statement by applicant that to the best of his or her knowledge no other person, firm, or organization has the right to use such mark in commerce either in the identical form or in such near resemblance as to cause confusion, mistakes, or deception, and (7) a drawing of the mark.

Assuming the information that is filed is approved by the trademark examining attorney, the mark will be published in the official gazette for opposition. If, after thirty days, no opposition is filed with the U.S. Patent and Trademark Office, then a Notice of Allowance will be issued. Upon receipt of a Notice of Allowance, you will have six months in which to file the following: (1) a verified statement that the mark is in use in commerce, the date the mark was first used in commerce, the nature of the goods or services described in the Notice of Allowance, and the mode or manner in which the goods or services that are connected with the mark are used, and (2) specimens or facsimiles of the mark as used in commerce. Upon examination and acceptance of the statement of use, the mark will be registered in the U.S. Patent and Trademark Office, a certificate of registration shall be issued for those goods or services recited in the statement of use for which the mark is entitled to registration, and notice of registration will be published in the official gazette.

The second way to attempt trademark registration is to employ the method that was in use before the Trademark Law Revision Act of 1988. You will need to send in a completed application. (For an example of the application see Exhibit 17-4, which shows a trademark application for the principal register by an individual, and Exhibit 17-5, which shows a trademark application for the principal register by a corporation.) There is a two-step process in using this method to apply for federal registration.

The first step of the process involves the trademark examining attorney making a determination as to the suitability of your mark for registration. It usually takes about three months for an initial determination to be issued. If the trademark examining attorney rejects the mark as being unsuitable for registration, then you will have six months to respond to the Trademark Examining Attorney. If the trademark examining attorney remains unconvinced and makes a final refusal of the registration, then you must appeal your application to the Trademark Trial and Appeal Board.

If your mark receives approval for registration, then the second step of the process begins. Your mark is published in the official gazette. A thirty-day period then begins to allow opposition to be filed with the Trademark Trial and Appeal Board. If there is no opposition to your mark, then a registration is issued approximately twelve weeks from the date your mark was first published in the official gazette.

What You Must Prove When You Claim Infringement

To establish liability for infringement under trademark law, the trademark owner who claims that his or her mark has been infringed must show the following:

- The validity of the trademark (a federally registered trademark establishes prima facie validity)
- Priority of usage of the mark
- A likelihood of confusion in the minds of potential purchasers of the product in question. Factors include: (1) the similarity or dissimilarity between the two marks as to appearance, sound, connotation, and commercial impression; (2) the similarity or dissimilarity between respective goods or services sold under two markets; (3) the marketing conditions or

channels of trade under which the goods or services are distributed and sold; (4) the popularity of the prior mark, as evidenced by the extent of sales and advertising and the length of use; (5) the extent of use of similar marks by third parties with respect to related products or services; and (6) the nature and extent of any actual confusion in the market place

An excellent discussion and application of these factors can be found in the federal case *AMF INC*. v. *Sleekcraft Boats* 599 F.2d 341 (1979).

You must be vigilante if you are serious about protecting your mark. Your employees should be instructed to notify you whenever they sight a similar mark. In addition, there are trademark search companies that provide watch services in which they review various types of literature and then report to you any potential infringement. An example of a trademark search company that provides this service is Trademark Service Corporation, 747 Third Avenue, New York, NY 10017.

Tradenames

A tradename is the name or designation that an organization uses to conduct business. A fictitious name is any name used in a trade or business that does not fully identify the user.

The federal trademark law defines a tradename as:

The terms *tradename* and *commercial name* include individual names and surnames, firm names, and tradenames used by manufacturers, industrialists, merchants, agriculturalists, and others to identify their businesses, vocations, or occupations; the names or titles lawfully adopted and used by persons, firms, associations, corporations, companies, unions, and any manufacturing, industrial, commercial, agricultural, or other organizations engaged in trade or commerce and capable of suing or being sued in a court of law.

Thus, there is no federal registration provision for a tradename; however, if a tradename is used as a trademark it may be registered with the appropriate government agencies. An example of a tradename used as a trademark is Ford Thunderbird. Under common law, however, there is the broader question as to whether a company's name which appears on the package or label is entitled to trademark protection. As a rule, the determining factor is whether or not consumers view the company name as identifying and distinguishing the product or simply identifying and distinguishing the company. If it is the former then a good case for trademark protection can be made, however, if it is the latter then no protection will be afforded.

COPYRIGHTS: THEY APPLY TO MORE THAN ONLY BOOKS AND RECORDS

When most people hear the term copyright they think in terms of books, records, and motion pictures. However copyright protection extends beyond these three items to cover all original works of authorship fixed in any tangible medium of expression, now known or later developed, from which they can be perceived, reproduced, or otherwise communicated, either directly or with the aid of a machine or device. As a result, items such as computer programs, music, shop manuals, jewelry, plans of processes, compilations of data, or works of art can be protected.

A copyright offers the following exclusive rights to the copyright holder:

- To make copies of the work
- To make derivatives of the work based on the copyrighted work, such as a revised version, a translation, or an abridgement
- To sell or license the work

Furthermore, these rights are independent of each other and therefore can be divided.

Applications of Copyright Protection

Copyright laws protect what is termed "expression." It does not protect an idea, procedure, process, system, method of operation, concept, principle, or discovery. Instead it protects the expression of the idea, procedure, process, system, method of operation, etc. The table below illustrates this concept.

Subject	Nature of Protection
Machine	Written description of the machine
Manufacturing process	Written description of the process
Story	Written text of the story
Business idea	Written description of the idea

Because the emphasis is on authorship of original work fixed in a tangible medium of expression, the following works have been determined to qualify for copyright protection:

- Computer programs
- Manuals, training material
- Data bases (if there is evidence that creator exercised selectivity, creativity, and judgment in compiling the data base)
- Newsletters, circulars, technical reviews
- Computer-generated movies
- Computer-generated sound effects
- Charts
- Directories
- Catalogs
- Reports and speeches

Copyright protection is not available for names, titles, short phrases, or expressions even if they are novel or distinctive. Moreover, the copyright office cannot register claims to exclusive rights in brief combinations of words, such as:

* Names of products or services
* Names of businesses, organizations, or groups (including the name of a group of performers)
* Names of pseudonyms of individuals (including a pen name or stage name)
* Titles of works
* Catch words, catch phrases, mottoes, slogans, or short expressions

There are three basic requirements that must be satisfied before copyright protection will be awarded:

First. There must be at least some originality.
Second. The work must be created by the author. *Note:* The term "creator" is not synonymous with the term "author." If the creator of the work prepared the work as an activity that was within the scope of his

or her employment then the employer is considered to be the author or owner of the copyright under the "work-for-hire" doctrine. This rule even extends to volunteers in many circumstances.

Third. The work must assume some permanent or stable form so that it can be perceived, reproduced, or communicated for more than one transitory period in any medium of expression.

The work need not be novel, however. This requirement, which differs from the requirement of a patent, can become a double-edged sword. Although it is easier to receive copyright protection than patent protection, copyright protection does not go to the extent of protecting the creator as does a patent. Generally, copyright laws only protect against copying. They do not protect against someone creating a similar or identical product independently of the creator. A patent, however, would offer this protection.

Another limitation of copyright laws is the doctrine of "fair use." According to the Copyright Revision Act of 1976, "the . . . fair use of a copyrighted work, including such use by reproduction in copies or phonorecords or by any other means . . . for purposes such as criticism, comment, news reporting, teaching (including multiple copies for classroom use), scholarship, or research, is not an infringement of copyright." In determining whether the use made of a copyrighted work is fair use of that work, the act states that the following factors will be considered:

- The purpose and character of the use, including whether such use is of a commercial nature or is for nonprofit educational purposes
- The nature of the copyrighted work
- The amount and substantiality of the portion used in relation to the copyrighted work as a whole
- The effect of the use upon the potential market for or value of the copyrighted work

For work that was copyrighted after January 1, 1978, copyright life is measured by the life of the author plus fifty years. When a joint work has been prepared by two or more authors, the life of the copyright is measured by the life of the last surviving author plus fifty years. If the copyrighted work was authored under the work-for-hire doctrine the life of the copyright is seventy-five years from the date of the first publication or 100 years from the date of the creation, whichever comes first.

How to Apply for Copyright Protection

Copyright protection becomes crucial if you decide to "publish" your work. The law defines the term "publish" as the distribution of copies of the work to the public by sale or other transfer of ownership, or by leasing or distributing copies of the work for the purpose of further distribution. However, registration with the U.S. Copyright Office is not a prerequisite to own a valid copyright. The easiest and least costly method to obtain a copyright is to place the required copyright notice on all copies of the work. According to the copyright act, the copyright notice consists of the following:

- The symbol © or the word "Copyright", or the abbreviation "Copr.".
- The year of the first publication of the work; in the case of compilations or derivative works incorporating previously published material, the year date of the first publication of the compilation or derivative work is sufficient. The year date may be omitted where a pictorial, graphic, or sculptural work, with accompanying text matter, if any, is reproduced in or on greeting cards, postcards, stationery, jewelry, dolls, toys, or any useful articles.
- The name of the owner of copyright in the work, or an abbreviation by which the name can be recognized, or a generally known alternative designation by the owner.

The copyright notice must be affixed to the copies of the work in a manner and location which will give reasonable notice of the claim of the copyright.

Although a work is copyrighted, there are valid reasons you would want to register your claim to a copyright.

First. No legal action for infringement of copyright can be brought until registration of the copyright claim has been made, unless the copyrighted work consists of live radio or television broadcasts.

Second. If the work is registered before or within five years of its first publication, the certificate of registration constitutes prima facie evidence of the validity of the copyright.

The actual process of registering your work is straightforward. The copyright office will supply the necessary applications depending on the nature of the work you wish to have copyrighted. The five most common forms are described below.

Form TX—Used for all published and unpublished nondramatic literary works which include books, manuals, computer programs, data bases, compilers, assemblers, interpreters, instruction sheets, circulars, newsletters. Exhibit 17-6 shows an example of Form TX and the instructions that accompany Form TX.

Form PA—Used for all published and unpublished works that involve moving sequential images, which include motion pictures, video or computer games, computer-generated display screens, and music.

Form SE—Used for articles, newsletters and journals. Exhibit 17-7 gives an example of Form SE and the instructions that accompany it.

Form VA—Used for graphs, graphics, stills, symbolic flow charts.

Form SR—Used for sounds marketed separately from accompanying visual effects.

Once you complete the application for copyright protection return it along with a fee, which the copyright office establishes, and one copy of your work if it is unpublished, or two copies which bear the necessary copyright notice if the work is about to be published. The submission of copies of your work satisfy the "deposit requirement." The reasons for the deposit rule are to allow the copyright office to determine that your work satisfies the copyright requirements and to serve as an identifier for your work in the event there is a dispute concerning the copyrighted work.

Deposit rules also apply to software protection, however, there are certain variations you need to be aware of if you decide to copyright software. Exhibit 17-8 shows Circular R61, Copyright Registration for Computer Programs, which is published by the copyright office, and explains in general terms the deposit requirements for computer software. However, an in-depth discussion concerning these rules is beyond the scope of this book, and you will need to consult the advice of an attorney. Below is a list of software-related products, each of which have separate deposit rules.

- Object code program
- Source code program
- Data base input instructions
- Data base output: single file
- Data base output: multifile
- Manuals
- Flowcharts (textual and graphic)
- Computer game screens
- Musical compositions or sound recordings

Semiconductor Chip Protection Act of 1984

The copyright laws of 1984 were amended to include semiconductor chip products. In particular, the act addresses semiconductor chip products and mask works. According to Title 17 of the United States Code, a semiconductor chip product is the final or intermediate form of any product having two or more layers of metallic, insulating, or semiconductor material, deposited or otherwise placed on, or etched away or otherwise removed from, a piece of semiconductor material in accordance with a predetermined pattern and intended to perform electronic circuitry functions.

A mask work is defined as a series of related images, however fixed or encoded, having or representing the predetermined, three-dimensional pattern of metallic, insulating, or semiconductor material present or removed from the layers of a semiconductor chip product, and in which series the relation of the images to one another is that each image has the pattern of the surface of one form of the semiconductor chip product. A mask work is "fixed" in a semiconductor chip product when its embodiment in the product is sufficiently permanent or stable to permit the mask work to be perceived or reproduced from the product for a period of more than transitory duration.

The owner of a mask work has the exclusive right to do and authorize any of the following:

- Reproduce the mask work by optical, electronic, or any other means.
- Import or distribute a semiconductor chip product in which the mask work is embodied.
- Induce or knowingly cause another person to either reproduce the mask or import or distribute a chip product that carries the mask.

The Semiconductor Chip Protection Act of 1984 has several limitations, however. For instance, protection is not available for the following:

- Reverse engineering if it is done solely for the purpose of teaching, analyzing, or evaluating the concepts and techniques embodied in the mask work, circuitry, logic flow, or organization of components used in the mask work.
- Mask work that is not original.
- Mask work that consists of designs that are staple, commonplace, or familiar in the semiconductor industry, or variations of such designs, combined in a way that when considered as a whole is not original.

Microcodes: *NEC Corporation* v. *Intel Corporation*

At the time of this writing the most recent case concerning microcodes is the NEC Corporation case which was handed down by Judge William P. Gray of the United States District Court for the northern district of California. This case was a landmark decision because of the issues involved and the reputation of the jurist who made the decision and wrote the opinion. Because of the importance of this case, its application to entrepreneurs who are engaged in work relating to computers, and the excellent discussion by Judge Gray on the law of copyright, we have included below major excerpts of Judge Gray's memorandum of decision. The decision:

Judgment

For reasons set forth in the Memorandum of Decision filed on this date, IT IS ADJUDGED that:

1. The Intel microcode for its 8086 and 8088 microprocessors...were proper subjects for protection under United States copyright laws.

2. Intel did forfeit the above copyrights it had obtained because more than a relatively small number of copies of product, distributed by its authority did not contain the copyright notice prescribed by 17 U.S.C section 401, because Intel failed to make a reasonable effort to cause such notice to be added to those copies after the omission had been discovered within the meaning of 17 U.S.C section 405, and because those copies were distributed at times when no express requirement in writing, within the meaning of 17 U.S.C. section 405, mandated such marking.

3. The microcodes that NEC produced for its V20, V30, V40, and V50 microprocessors do not infringe on the Intel copyrights for its 8086 and 8088 microcodes.

4. NEC's V20 and V30 microprocessors are not simply "improvements" upon its uPD 8086 and uPD 8088 microprocessors, which were licensed by Intel under its copyrights.

Each party shall bear its own costs.

No. C-84-20799
United States District Court
Northern District of California
February 7, 1989

MEMORANDUM OF DECISION

In this action, NEC seeks a declaration that Intel's copyrights on its 8086 and 8088 microcodes are invalid and/or are not infringed by NEC. Intel has filed a counterclaim for infringement of its copyrights on those microcodes. This case was tried without a jury for eighteen days between April 25 and July 18, 1988... The issues to be determined and the decision that the court now renders on each are as follows:

1. Are Intel's microcodes for its 8086 and 8088 processors proper subject matter for protection under United States copyright laws (17 U.S.C. section 101 et seq.)? This question is answered in the affirmative.

2. Did Intel forfeit the copyrights that it had obtained for its 8086 and 8088 microcodes because more than a relatively small number of copies of product distributed by its authority did not contain the copyright notice prescribed by 17 U.S.C. section 401, because it failed to make a reasonable effort to cause such notice to be added to those copies after the omission had been discovered, within the meaning of 17 U.S.C section 405, and because those copies were distributed at times when no express requirement in writing, within the meaning of 17 U.S.C. section 405, mandated such marking? This court concludes that Intel did so forfeit its copyrights.

4. Are NEC's V20 and V30 microprocessors no more than "improvements" upon its uPD 8086 and uPD 8088 microprocessors, which were licensed by Intel under its copyrights? NEC's V20 and V30 microprocessors are not simply "improvements" upon its uPD 8086 and uPD 8088 microprocessors.

The reasons for the foregoing decision are contained in the following discussion:

I. THE COPYRIGHTABILITY OF INTEL'S MICROCODE

A microcode consists of a series of instructions that tell a microprocessor which of its thousands of transistors to actuate in order to perform the tasks directed by the macro instruction set. As such, it comes squarely within the definition of a "computer program," which Congress added to the Copyright Act of 1980, namely, "a set of statements or instructions to be used directly or indirectly in a computer in order to bring about a certain result. . . .

A computer program, even though articulated in object code, is afforded copyright protection as a "literary work" under section 101, which includes works "expressed in words, numbers, or other verbal or numerical symbols or indicia, regardless of the nature of the material objects with which they are embodied." . . . For a particular literary work to be copyrightable, two requirements must be satisfied: the work must be "fixed in any tangible medium of expression," and it must be "original." . . . It is undisputed that Intel's microcode is fixed in a tangible medium of expression. However, NEC challenges the originality of Intel's microcode, and urges two other bases for denying copyright protection.

A. Originality

NEC contends that many of Intel's microsequences are not copyrightable because they consist only of a few obvious steps and thus lack the originality required for copyright protection. . . . It may well be that, considered alone, several of the microsequences in Intel's microcode consist of "forms of expression directed solely by functional considerations" lacking even "minimal creativity." But these examples are only a small segment of the copyrighted microcode. As Intel points out, any copyrighted work, be it a poem, novel, or computer program, can be chopped into parts that could be said to have very few creative steps.

However for purposes of copyrightability, "[o]riginality means only that the work owes its origin to the author, i.e., is independently created, and not copied from other works," and that the work contains a modicum of originality, i.e., "exceeds that required for a fragmentary work or short phrase.". . . The Intel microcode fully meets this test. There is no evidence that Intel's microcode was other than an independent effort and, overall, Intel's microcode exceeds a modicum of originality.

B. Microcode as Part of the Computer

As stated above, the copyright act defines a computer program as "a set of statements or instructions to be used in a computer.". . . NEC contends that Intel's microcode does not come within the definition of a computer program because it cannot be used in a computer and also be a defining part of the computer. But, as stated at the outset, Intel's microcode is within the statutory definition of a "computer program," and NEC's semisemantical argument runs counter to the authority cited by Intel....

II. THE FORFEITURE BY INTEL OF ITS MICROCODE COPYRIGHT

The copyright act provides that "[w]henever a work protected under this title is published . . . by authority of the copyright owner, a notice of copyright . . . shall be placed on all publicly distributed copies." 17 U.S.C. section 401(a). The failure by the copyright owner to affix such notice invalidates the copyright, unless as provided in section 405(a):

1. the notice has been omitted from no more than a relatively small number of copies distributed to the public; or

2. a reasonable effort is made to add notice to all copies that are distributed to the public . . . after the omission has been discovered; or

3. this notice has been omitted in violation of an express requirement in writing that . . . the . . . copies . . . bear the prescribed notice.

As is discussed below, this court finds that Intel allowed a relatively large number of copies of its microcode to be distributed to the public without the prescribed copyright notice; upon learning of such omission, Intel did not make a "reasonable effort" to correct its oversight; and the omission of the notice by Intel's licensees was not in violation of "an express requirement in writing.". . .

A. The Required Copyright Notice Was Omitted from More Than a Relatively Small Number of Copies

Intel admits that out of approximately 28,000,000 copies of its microcode that were distributed to the public between May 1978 and May 1986, 2,984,000, or about 10.6%, did not contain the required copyright notice. It seems to me that almost 3,000,000 copies of any merchandised article constitute a very substantial number in an absolute sense. However, in using the words "relatively small number," the statute appears to require a comparison between the number of copies without the notice and the total number distributed, in other words, a percentage.

An examination of twenty federal court decisions that have considered the matter discloses none in which 10.6% was held to be a relatively small number. The highest percentage found to have been within the exception is 9%, but in that case the number of items without the affixed notice was only 208, as compared with almost 3,000,000 here involved . . . .

The foregoing authorities are in harmony with my own conclusion that 10.6% of 28,000,000 cannot reasonably be considered to constitute a relatively small number. Accordingly, the section 405(a)(1) exception does not apply. This conclusion makes it unnecessary to adjudicate NEC's contention that, as of December 1984, when this action was filed, 7,940,000 unmarked or improperly marked copies of the Intel microcode had been distributed under license, or 46% of a total of 17,151,000. . . .

1. When Discovery Occurred

Intel licensed twelve companies to manufacture, use, and sell its 8086/8088 microprocessors containing its microcode. The initial licenses to Fujitsu, NEC, and Mitsubishi, which were issued between August 1981 and April 1984, contained no mention to affix a copyright notice . . . . In about October 1981, Intel engineers examined one of Fujitsu's licensed products and made a report to Intel's counsel. The engineers either failed to observe the absence of a copyright notice or neglected to report such fact to counsel, and the matter made no inquiry of the engineers concerning the matter . . . On September 5, 1984, Intel's general counsel met with a representative of NEC, and in the course of the discussion asked if NEC was placing the copyright notice on its licensed products. The NEC representative said that he did not know but would check. Intel received no further response and made no further inquiry until six months later, after this action was filed . . . .

PATENTS: DOES YOUR NEW PRODUCT VIOLATE SOMEONE'S PATENT?

Reasons to Seek Patent Protection

The patent system was established to carry out the U.S. Constitution's goal of promoting the arts and sciences. From a policy perspective, the founding fathers, many of whom were inventors themselves, wanted to encourage an inventor to make full public disclosure in exchange for the right to exclude others from making, using, or selling the invention during a limited period of time.

The value of a patent is that it gives evidence of one's right to exclude others from making, using, or selling a particular invention. There are various reasons entrepreneurs seek patent protection:

- It offers the only protection against a competitor who independently makes the same invention.
- It is often considered a valuable asset by potential creditors and investors.
- It allows the purchase from U.S. Customs Service of the names and addresses of importers of products which appear to infringe.
- It may be used in a cross-licensing agreement in the event there is a patent infringement claim made by a competitor.

Thus, whenever you discover or invent a "new" product, you may find that you have infringed upon the patent rights of another inventor.

Title 35 of the United States Code sets forth the federal statutory law of patents. According to Title 35 section 101, there are four classes of invention for which a patent can be obtained. If an invention falls outside of these four categories, it will not receive patent protection from the U.S. Patent Office. The four classes are:

Machine--includes a wide variety of mechanisms and mechanical elements.
Article of Manufacture--products other than machines and compositions of matter.
Composition of Matter--elements such as new molecules, chemical compounds, mixtures, alloys, etc.
Process--encompasses procedures leading to useful results.

Because of these four statutory classes, many inventions or commercial ideas, such as mixtures of ingredients, factual compilations, mental steps, printed matter, problem-solving techniques, laws of nature, and scientific principles have been refused patent protection.

Types of Patents

Utility Patents. This type of patent is granted to protect new, useful, and unobvious processes, machines, compositions of matter, and articles of manufacture. A utility patent has a term of seventeen years measured from the date in which the patent right is issued.

Design Patent. Subject matter that may be protected using this type of patent are new, original, ornamental, and unobvious designs for articles of manufacture. Design patents have a 14 year life span. Like the utility patent, the design patent allows the owner to exclude others from making, using, or selling an article that infringes upon the patent.

Plant Patent. Any distinct and new variety of plant asexually reproduced may be patented for 17 years. Patentable plants must be reproduced by means other than seeds, such as by the rooting of cuttings, by layering, budding, grafting, or inarching.

A patent is evidenced by a document that is issued by the U.S. Patent and Trademark Office in which the description of the invention is explained in detail and there are one or more claims that explicitly state the subject matter for which protection has been obtained. Exhibit 17-9 is an example of utility patents that were issued by the U.S. Patent and Trademark Office for general and mechanical, chemical, and electrical articles. Moreover, when a patent has been issued it will appear in the *Official Gazette* which is published by the U.S. Trademark and Patent Office. The *Official Gazette* is published weekly and contains a synopsis of the patents issued during a particular week.

Requirements for a Patent

There are two major groups of hurdles you must consider if you are thinking about applying for a patent:

Statutory Class. The invention must fall within one of the four statutory classes: process, machine, article of manufacture, and composition of matter.

35 U.S.C. 102. Title 35 section 102 of the United States Code lists a variety of hurdles which are interrelated in several aspects. Requirements that the invention be new, useful, and unobvious are included as well as the requirement that the invention not be in public use or on sale in the United States more than one year prior to the date of the application for the patent.

According to section 102, an invention cannot be patented if any of the following occur:

(a) the invention was known or used by others in this country, or patented or described in a printed publication in this or a foreign country, before the invention thereof by the applicant for patent, or

(b) the invention was patented or described in a printed publication in this or a foreign country or in public use or on sale in this country, more than one year prior to the date of the application for patent in the United States, or

(c) (the inventor) has abandoned the invention, or

(d) the invention was first patented or caused to be patented, or was the subject of an inventor's certificate, by the applicant or his legal representatives or assigns in a foreign country prior to the date of the application for patent or inventor's certificate filed more than twelve months before the filing of the application in the United States, or

(e) the invention was described in a patent granted on an application for patent by another filed in the United States before the invention thereof by the applicant for patent, or on an international application by another who has fulfilled the requirements of paragraphs (1),(2), and (4) of section 371(c) of this title before the invention thereof by the applicant for patent, or

(f) (the person) did not himself invent the subject matter sought to be patented, or

(g) before the applicant's invention thereof the invention was made in this country by another who had not abandoned, suppressed, or concealed it. In determining priority of invention there shall be considered not only the respective dates of conception and reduction to practice of the invention, but also reasonable diligence of one who was first to conceive and last to reduce to practice, from a time prior to conception by the other.

Applying for a Patent

Your first step in applying for a patent should begin with a patentability search. This step should be taken before you attempt to complete the patent application. The patent search serves several objectives:

- Helps to determine whether your invention infringes upon another's patent;
- Assists in the drafting of the patent application which helps to avoid complications when the invention is subjected to the scrutiny of patent examination.

Your second step is to prepare the patent application. A patent application contains the following components:

- Written specification
- Drawing, if it is necessary for understanding the invention

- Oath or declaration (See Exhibit 17-10)
- Filing fee

The written specification must include a written description of the invention. The well drafted patent application often includes a description of the invention and how it is used; the nature of the problems the invention overcomes; the closest prior invention known to the inventor; how the invention differs from other inventions; the advantages the invention offers; and the best mode known to the inventor for carrying out the invention. In addition, the written portion should contain in its conclusion one or more claims which explicitly discusses that subject matter which the inventor asserts in his or her invention. The drafting of the inventor's claim is extremely important because many patentability issues are determined by an examination of the claims that are made by the inventor.

A patent application can at times be a difficult document to complete correctly. Because of the complexity of patent procedure and patent law and the need for clear articulation in drafting the application, it is strongly advised that you seek the assistance of a patent attorney, which is an attorney who possesses certain legal, technical, and scientific qualifications necessary to practice before the U.S. Patent and Trademark Office. The U.S. Patent and Trademark Office maintains a register of patent attorneys and patent agents.

The filing fee of an application, except in design and plant cases, is comprised of one basic fee and additional fees. The basic fee is $370.00 which entitles each applicant to present twenty claims, including not more than three in independent form. An additional fee is required for each claim in independent form which is in excess of three and an additional fee of $12.00 is required for each claim which is in excess of twenty claims.

Small Entity Status

On October 1, 1982, fees for applications were reduced by 50 percent if the applicant was an individual inventor, nonprofit organization, or small business.

To qualify for small entity status, the applicant must file a verified statement. (See Exhibit 17-11.)Small entity status includes:

* A sole inventor who has not transferred his or her rights and is under no obligation to transfer these rights to an entity that fails to qualify.
* Joint investors where no one among them has transferred his or her rights and is under no obligation to transfer his or her rights to an entity that fails to qualify.
* A nonprofit organization such as an institution of higher education or an Internal Revenue Service-qualified and exempted nonprofit organization.
* A small business that does not have more than 500 employees during the fiscal year of the business entity in question.

Disadvantages of a Patent

Although a patent offers the inventor the right to have a monopoly or to prevent others from making, using, or selling the invention without permission, even if the invention was created independently, it requires full public disclosure. Thus, once an inventor opts for the patent route and the patent is granted, the intricacies of the invention are no longer kept secret. Moreover, the scope of the patent claim(s) may be very narrow, which would allow competitors leeway in devising a method to produce the "protected" product without infringing the patent. It has often been said that patents which completely preclude the existence of competitors are rare. Many times a competitor is able to discover a way of performing the same function and solving the same problem without violating the patent claim. As a result, many businesses prefer to rely on trade secret laws for protection of their ideas and products.

TRADE SECRETS: AN ALTERNATIVE TO PATENTS

How Trade Secrets Differ from Patents

Courts differ as to whether a particular idea, process, formula, or type of information should be considered a trade secret. As a rule, courts have declared that a trade secret must constitute information that is not generally known in a trade. The definition most often used by the courts is the *restatement of torts*:

A trade secret may consist of any formula, pattern, device, or compilation of information used in one's business, which gives him an opportunity to obtain an advantage over competitors who do not know or use it. It may be a formula for a chemical compound, a process of manufacturing, treating or preserving materials, a pattern for a machine or other device, or a list of customers. A trade secret is a process or device for continuous use in the operation of the business. Generally it relates to the production of goods, as for example, a machine or formula for an article. It may, however, relate to the sale of goods or to other operations in the business, such as a code for determining discounts, rebates, or other concessions in a price list or catalogue, or a list of specialized customers, or a method of bookkeeping or other office management.

Thus, a trade secret can result from a combination of information which may have been in the public domain but has been assembled in such a manner as to constitute a method or process not generally known to competitors. This combination in and of itself is a valuable asset because it permits one firm to gain an economic advantage over the other firms.

In many states, trade secret law is still based on common law and not statutory provisions. As a result, the courts examine each situation on a case-by-case basis. Factors the courts will examine in order to render a decision are:

- Money, time, and effort in developing the secret
- Novelty of the secret
- Value of the secret to the owner's business
- Effort made by the owner to keep the information a secret

Thus, courts have ruled that a trade secret can be a marketing plan, industrial idea, invention, food or drug formula, manufacturing technique, pattern machines, processes for preparing a product, sources of supply, customer list, or other types of information. A trade secret does not have to be an invention that is patentable. In fact, many trade secrets would not qualify for patent protection. Trade secret protection is available, however, only when a trade secret can be exploited without having to disclose the secret to competitors or to the public. Another feature that distinguishes a trade secret from a patent is that, unlike a patent, which requires the subject matter to be completely novel, unobvious, and have utility, a trade secret only requires that the subject matter not be generally known in the trade or readily discernible.

Information disclosure is another topic in which there are significant differences: patents and trade secrets are mutually exclusive. Once a patent is granted, the federal government makes public all information about the invention. A trade secret, however, remains a secret unless it is disclosed. A dilemma that many inventors face if they have a patentable invention is whether to seek patent protection or utilize the available trade secret laws. Title 35 section 112 of the United States Code requires that the written specification of a patent application state the best mode contemplated by the inventor in carrying out his or her invention. Many inventors, however, are tempted to withhold this information and treat it as a trade secret, which is a direct violation of patent law and could result in the patent being declared invalid for insufficiency of disclosure. In addition, courts, when faced with this situation, have been known to strike down any trade secret protection that may have existed because of the inventor's willful failure to make a complete disclosure on the patent application.

There are other aspects of the two forms of protection which create differences. A comparison of a trade secret and a patent is discussed below.

Subject Matter
Trade secret. Manufacturing techniques, business methods, customer lists, sources of supply, advertising schemes, literary and entertainment schemes, certain commercial formulas, certain industrial formulas, chemical processes, computer software, confidential sales data, confidential bidding procedures, confidential financing plans, research and development reports, confidential negotiations with customers, salaries of key employees, and patentable inventions.

Patent. Must fall within one of the four statutory classes: processes, machines, articles of manufacture, and composition of matter.

Duration of Protection
Trade secret. Ceases when subject matter is no longer a secret.
Patent. It lasts seventeen years from the date the patent is issued.

Independent Discovery
Trade secret. Independent inventor cannot be prosecuted. Only those persons who exploit information derived from trade secret owner while under a duty to remain silent can be prosecuted.
Patent. Everyone except the patent owner is excluded from using, making, or selling patented information, which includes independent inventors.

Public Use or Publication
Trade secret. Any public use, sale, or disclosure destroys the trade secret.
Patent. Public use, sale, or disclosure prior to filing the application will not jeopardize the right if the filing occurs within twelve months of commercial application, although right to foreign patent may be destroyed.

Remedies
Trade secret. Damages, which may include punitive damages, and an injunction. Moreover, there may be criminal sanctions. Many states have begun to include provisions in their criminal code for trade secret theft. For instance California Penal Code Section 499c states, in part:

> (b) Every person is guilty of theft who, with the intent to deprive or withhold from the owner thereof the control of a trade secret, or with an intent to appropriate a trade secret to his own use or to the use of another, does any of the following:
> (1) Steals, takes, or carries away any article representing a trade secret.
> (2) Fraudulently appropriates any article representing a trade secret entrusted to him.
> (3) Having unlawfully obtained access to the article, without authority makes or causes to be made a copy of any article representing a trade secret.
> (4) Having obtained access to the article through a relationship of trust and confidence, without authority and in breach of the obligations created by such relationship makes or causes to be made, directly from and in the presence of the article, a copy of any article representing a trade secret.

In addition, like numerous other states, California law also contains criminal sanctions against anyone who induces, bribes, or rewards former agents, employees, or servants of an employer to procure and turn over a trade secret obtained while working for that employer.

Patent. Damages and injunction, courts may treble damages and award attorney's fees to prevailing party.

How to Discourage a Consultant from Disclosing Your Idea

A challenging problem many entrepreneurs face is the unauthorized use of their ideas. Many times this problem arises when an entrepreneur has an idea but needs technical assistance as to the feasibility or implementation of the idea. The entrepreneur seeks out the advice of a computer consultant, consulting engineer, or business consultant and then discusses his or her idea and thoughts to that person. Later, after the idea has been articulated in the form of drawings, description, or business plan, the consultant then takes the idea for his or her own use.

In order for the idea to receive protection as a trade secret, it must first fall within the definition of a trade secret and then it must be shown that reasonable efforts were used to maintain the secrecy. There have been various cases which have discussed the issue of "reasonable efforts" to maintain secrecy. Many of these cases point to the use of a nondisclosure agreement that must be signed by any party that comes into contact with the secret, in addition to other measures, such as locking up the secret in a locked filing cabinet or safe, limiting the access to the trade secret, coded terminology, etc.

Therefore, to protect your idea from being used by another, you must not make any public disclosures of the idea and should demand that a nondisclosure agreement be signed by the consultant before any discussion concerning idea begins. The agreement should state that the consultant shall hold in strictest confidence and in trust for your sole and exclusive benefit any information concerning your business plan, product line, source of supply, marketing data, etc. disclosed by you or discovered by the consultant as a result of his or her relationship with you.

Finally, you should not forget to recover any written information that was given to the consultant once the need for that information has concluded. Failure to do so could jeopardize any claim you may have against the consultant if the consultant uses the information for his own benefit.

Protecting against Trade Secret Theft

Dealing with consultants should not be the only instance in which you should exercise "reasonable efforts" to maintain secrecy. You should establish a program of affirmatively protecting your trade secrets; otherwise, you may find it extremely difficult to convince a court that the information taken was not general knowledge but valuable proprietary information.

The list of suggestions below have proven to be effective deterrents in preventing trade secret theft:

- Limit access to all trade secrets.
- Escort visitors.
- Label all trade secret documents as such and utilize "confidential" stamps.
- Require all files to be signed out before removal.
- Check credentials of all repair and equipment maintenance personnel and building maintenance personnel.
- Secrets that are not being used should be locked in a safe or a filing cabinet.
- Do not allow any single employee from having access to all of your trade secrets.

- Carefully screen individuals before you hire them and ensure they understand you have trade secret controls and a policy that you enforce.
- Have each employee sign and date a nondisclosure agreement in which he or she promises not to disclose trade secret information.

Entrepreneurs Beware: Soliciting Trade Secrets to Begin Your New Business May Invite a Lawsuit

Many entrepreneurs attempt to hire away key employees from a competitor with the expectation that they will divulge trade secrets. Unfortunately, these entrepreneurs often invite a lawsuit instead. Even if the employee has not signed an agreement concerning his or her employer's trade secrets, the courts will often declare there was an implied agreement if it can be shown that the following fact pattern occurred: there existed a valuable trade secret; the secret was made available to the employee because of his or her employment relationship; the employee knew the information was a secret or that the employer considered it a secret; and the use of the secret would have a detrimental effect on the employer.

Although many states have passed statutes voiding clauses in employment contracts which contain a covenant not to compete, for example California has Business and Professions Code section 16600, the statutes, as a rule, do not affect covenants to protect trade secrets or confidential information. As a result, employers have been somewhat successful in obtaining injunctive relief to prevent their former employees from accepting competitive employment under a claim of unfair competition rather than breach of covenant not to compete.

Chapter 17 Exhibits

Exhibit 17.1 Xerox Advertisements

Exhibit 17.2 Notice of Trademark Registration From the
State of California

Exhibit 17.3 Page from Official Gazette

Exhibit 17.4 Trademark Application Individual (Form
PTO-1476FB)

Exhibit 17.5 Trademark Application Corporation (Form
PTO-1478FB)

Exhibit 17.6 Copyright Application (Form TX);
Instructions for Completing Application Form TX

Exhibit 17.7 Copyright Application (Form SE);
Instructions for Completing Application Form SE

Exhibit 17.8 Circular R61: Copyright Registration for
Computer Programs

Exhibit 17.9 Patents Granted (General and Mechanical,
Chemical, Electrical)

Exhibit 17.10 Declaration for Patent Application

Exhibit 17.11 Verified Statement Claiming Small Entity
Status (Form PTO-FB-A410)

Just a little reminder from Xerox.

XEROX

You may have heard a phrase like, "I Xeroxed my recipe for you" or "Please Xerox this for me." And they may seem harmless enough.

But they're not. Because they overlook the fact that Xerox is a registered trademark of Xerox Corporation. And trademarks should not be used as verbs.

As a brand name, Xerox should be used as an adjective followed by a word or phrase describing the particular product.

Like the Xerox 1075 Copier. The Xerox 640 Memorywriter. Or the Xerox 9700 Electronic Printing System.

Our brand name is very valuable to us. And to you, too. Because the proper use of our name is the best way to ensure you'll always get a Xerox product when you ask for one.

So, please remember that our trademark starts with an "X."

And ends with an "®."

Exhibit 17-1

Once a trademark, not always a trademark.

They were once proud trademarks, now they're just names. They failed to take precautions that would have helped them have a long and prosperous life.

We need your help to stay out of there. Whenever you use our name, please use it as a proper adjective in conjunction with our products and services: e.g., Xerox copiers or Xerox financial services. And never as a verb: "to Xerox" in place of "to copy," or as a noun: "Xeroxes" in place of "copies."

With your help and a precaution or two on our part, it's "Once the Xerox trademark, always the Xerox trademark."

Team Xerox. We document the world.

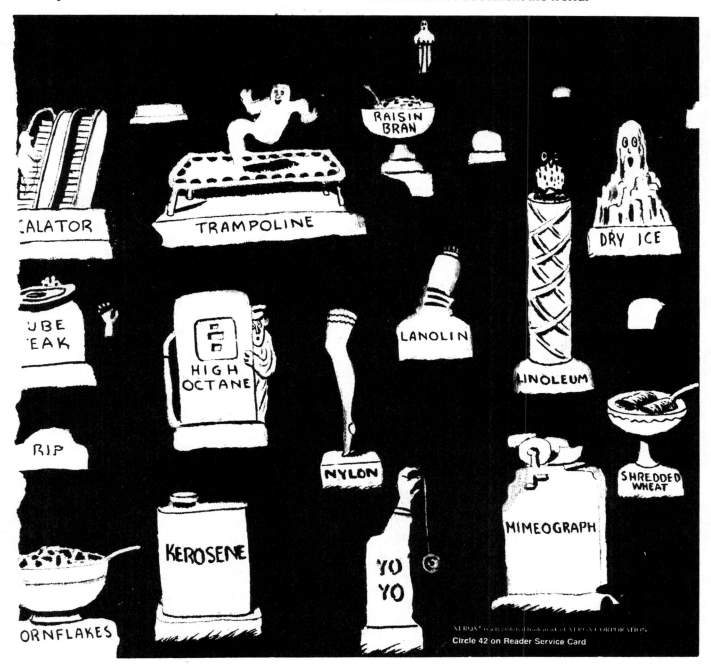

Office of

March Fong Eu

Secretary of State
SACRAMENTO

As Secretary of State, it is my pleasure to notify you that the mark you submitted has been registered in this office.

Please be advised that Section 14220(f) of the Business and Professions Code specifies that a mark shall not be registered if it so resembles a mark or trade name already registered or used in this state by another and not abandoned, as to be likely, when applied to the goods or services of the applicant, to cause confusion or mistake or to deceive.

My office has conducted a search of California trademark and service mark registrations. Your mark does not appear to resemble any previous registration.

Please be advised, however, that there may be unregistered marks or California trade names used by corporations and partnerships, fictitious names, and names under which individuals conduct business which may resemble your registration. A check for such names is beyond the scope of the review of this office in registering marks.

Most sincerely,

MARCH FONG EU

Exhibit 17-2

CLASS 9—(Continued).

SN 730,470. TEXAS VETERINARY MEDICAL DIAGNOSTIC LABORATORY, COLLEGE STATION, TX. FILED 5-16-1988.

NO CLAIM IS MADE TO THE EXCLUSIVE RIGHT TO USE THE REPRESENTATION OF A CADUCEUS, APART FROM THE MARK AS SHOWN.

FOR COMPUTER PROGRAMS FOR VETERINARY DIAGNOSTICS (U.S. CL. 38).

FIRST USE 6-1-1987; IN COMMERCE 1-6-1988.

SN 731,423. MICRO PALM COMPUTERS, INC., CLEARWATER, FL. FILED 5-31-1988.

NO CLAIM IS MADE TO THE EXCLUSIVE RIGHT TO USE "MICRO", APART FROM THE MARK AS SHOWN.

THE LINING IN THE MARK ON THE DRAWING IS A FEATURE OF THE MARK AND IS NOT INTENDED TO INDICATE COLOR.

THE MARK COMPRISES "MICRO PALM" AND DESIGNS OF A PALM TREE AND HORIZONTAL BAR.

FOR HAND-HELD COMPUTERS (U.S. CL. 26).

FIRST USE 4-29-1988; IN COMMERCE 4-29-1988.

SN 732,339. SHARED MEDICAL SYSTEMS CORPORATION, MALVERN, PA. FILED 6-3-1988.

ALLEGRA

FOR COMPUTER PROGRAMS AND COMPUTERS PROVIDED AS A UNIT TO HOSPITALS AND OTHER HEALTHCARE INSTITUTIONS FOR USE IN PROCESSING FINANCIAL AND CLINICAL DATA (U.S. CLS. 26 AND 38).

FIRST USE 3-11-1988; IN COMMERCE 3-11-1988.

CLASS 9—(Continued).

SN 733,800. INSTRUMENTATION NORTHWEST, INC., REDMOND, WA. FILED 6-13-1988.

INSTRUMENTATION NORTHWEST

NO CLAIM IS MADE TO THE EXCLUSIVE RIGHT TO USE "INSTRUMENTATION", APART FROM THE MARK AS SHOWN.

FOR ELECTRONIC SENSORS, GROUND WATER SAMPLING PUMPS FOR POLLUTION MONITORING AND GROUND WATER MONITORING UNITS (U.S. CLS. 23 AND 26).

FIRST USE 3-24-1984; IN COMMERCE 3-24-1984.

SN 733,873. UNITED STATES SHOE CORPORATION, THE, CINCINNATI, OH. FILED 6-13-1988.

ARPEGGIOS SEASONS

OWNER OF U.S. REG. NOS. 686,698, 1,292,393 AND 1,430,961.

FOR EYEGLASSES AND FRAMES FOR SPECTACLES (U.S. CL. 26).

FIRST USE 4-14-1988; IN COMMERCE 4-14-1988.

SN 734,321. REUNION RECORDS, INC., NASHVILLE, TN. FILED 6-13-1988.

THE LINING IN THE DRAWING IS A FEATURE OF THE MARK AND IS NOT INTENDED TO INDICATE COLOR.

FOR PHONOGRAPH RECORDS AND PRERECORDED AUDIO CASSETTES (U.S. CL. 36).

FIRST USE 1-25-1986; IN COMMERCE 1-25-1986.

Exhibit 17-3

<table>
<tr>
<td rowspan="2">

TRADEMARK APPLICATION, PRINCIPAL REGISTER, WITH DECLARATION
(Individual)
</td>
<td>MARK *(identify the mark)*</td>
</tr>
<tr>
<td>CLASS NO. *(if known)*</td>
</tr>
</table>

TO THE COMMISSIONER OF PATENTS AND TRADEMARKS:

NAME OF APPLICANT, AND BUSINESS TRADE NAME, IF ANY	TELEPHONE AREA CODE NUMBER

BUSINESS ADDRESS

RESIDENCE ADDRESS

CITIZENSHIP OF APPLICANT

The above identified applicant has adopted and is using the trademark shown in the accompanying drawing for the following

goods: _____

_____

and requests that said mark be registered in the United States Patent and Trademark Office on the Principal Register established by the Act of July 5, 1946.

The trademark was first used on the goods on _____ ; was first used on the goods in
                                                        (date)

_____ commerce on _____ ; and is now in use in such
        (type of commerce)   *(date)*

commerce.

The mark is used by applying it to _____

_____

and five specimens showing the mark as actually used are presented herewith.

_____
(name of applicant)

being hereby warned that willful false statements and the like so made are punishable by fine or imprisonment, or both, under Section 1001 of Title 18 of the United States Code and that such willful false statements may jeopardize the validity of the application or any registration resulting therefrom, declares that he/she believes himself/herself to be the owner of the trademark sought to be registered; to the best of his/her knowledge and belief no other person, firm, corporation, or association has the right to use said mark in commerce, either in the identical form or in such near resemblance thereto as may be likely, when applied to the goods of such other person, to cause confusion, or to cause mistake, or to deceive; the facts set forth in this application are true; and all statements made of his/her own knowledge are true and all statements made on information and belief are believed to be true.

_____
(signature of applicant)

_____
(date)

FORM PTO-1476FB (REV. 4-87)   U.S. DEPARTMENT OF COMMERCE/Patent and Trademark Office

Exhibit 17-4

Goods

1	Chemicals used in industry, science, photography, as well as in agriculture, horticulture, and forestry; unprocessed artificial resins; unprocessed plastics; manures; fire extinguishing compositions; tempering and soldering preparations; chemical substances for preserving foodstuffs; tanning substances; adhesives used in industry.
2	Paints, varnishes, lacquers; preservatives against rust and against deterioration of wood; colourants; mordants; raw natural resins; metals in foil and powder form for painters, decorators, printers and artists.
3	Bleaching preparations and other substances for laundry use; cleaning, polishing, scouring and abrasive preparations; soaps; perfumery, essential oils, cosmetics, hair lotions; dentifrices.
4	Industrial oils and greases; lubricants; dust absorbing, wetting and binding compositions; fuels (including motor spirit) and illuminants; candles, wicks.
5	Pharmaceutical, veterinary, and sanitary preparations; dietetic substances adapted for medical use, food for babies; plasters, materials for dressings material for stopping teeth, dental wax, disinfectants; preparations for destroying vermin; fungicides, herbicides.
6	Common metals and their alloys; metal building materials; transportable buildings of metal; materials of metal for railway tracks; non-electric cables and wires of common metal; ironmongery, small items of metal hardware; pipes and tubes of metal; safes; goods of common metal not included in other classes; ores.
7	Machines and machine tools; motors (except for land vehicles); machine coupling and belting (except for land vehicles); agricultural implements; incubators for eggs.
8	Hand tools and implements (hand operated); cutlery; side arms; razors.
9	Scientific, nautical, surveying, electric, photographic, cinematographic, optical, weighing, measuring, signalling, checking (supervision), life-saving and teaching apparatus and instruments; apparatus for recording transmission or reproduction of sound or images; magnetic data carriers, recording discs; automatic vending machines and mechanisms for coin-operated apparatus; cash registers, calculating machines, data processing equipment and computers; fire-extinguishing apparatus.
10	Surgical, medical, dental, and veterinary apparatus and instruments, artificial limbs, eyes and teeth; orthopedic articles; suture materials.
11	Apparatus for lighting, heating, steam generating, cooking, refrigerating, drying, ventilating, water supply, and sanitary purposes.
12	Vehicles; apparatus for locomotion by land, air or water.
13	Firearms; ammunition and projectiles; explosives; fireworks.
14	Precious metals and their alloys and goods in precious metals or coated therewith, not included in other classes; jewelry, precious stones; horological and other chronometric instruments.
15	Musical instruments.
16	Paper and cardboard and goods made from these materials, not included in other classes; printed matter; bookbinding material; photographs; stationery; adhesives for stationery or household purposes; artists' materials; paint brushes; typewriters and office requisites (except furniture); instructional and teaching material (except apparatus); plastic materials for packaging (not included on other classes); playing cards; printers' type; printing blocks.
17	Rubber, gutta-percha, gum, asbestos, mica and goods made from these materials and not included in other classes; plastics in extruded form for use in manufacture; packing, stopping and insulating materials; flexible pipes, not of metal.
18	Leather and imitations of leather, and goods made from these materials and not included in other classes; animal skins, hides; trunks and travelling bags; umbrellas, parasols and walking sticks; whips, harness and saddlery.
19	Building materials (non-metallic); non-metallic rigid pipes for building; asphalt, pitch and bitumen; non-metallic transportable buildings; monuments, not of metal.
20	Furniture, mirrors, picture frames; goods (not included in other classes) of wood, cork, reed, cane, wicker, horn, bone, ivory, whalebone, shell, amber, mother-of-pearl, meerschaum and substitutes for all these materials, or of plastics.
21	Household or kitchen utensils and containers (not of precious metal or coated therewith); combs and sponges; brushes (except paint brushes); brush-making materials; articles for cleaning purposes; steel wool; unworked or semi-worked glass (except glass used in building); glassware, porcelain and earthenware, not included in other classes.
22	Ropes, string, nets, tents, awnings, tarpaulins, sails, sacks; and bags (not included other classes); padding and stuffing materials (except of rubber or plastics); raw fibrous textile materials.
23	Yarns and threads, for textile use.
24	Textile and textile goods, not included in other classes; bed and table covers.
25	Clothing, footwear, headgear.
26	Lace and embroidery, ribbons and braid; buttons, hooks and eyes, pins and needles; artificial flowers.
27	Carpets, rugs, mats and matting; linoleum and other materials for covering existing floors; wall hangings (non-textile).
28	Games and playthings; gymnastic and sporting articles not included in other classes; decorations for Christmas trees.
29	Meats, fish, poultry and game; meat extracts; preserved, dried and cooked fruits and vegetables; jellies, jams; eggs, milk and milk products; edible oils and fats; salad dressings; preserves.
30	Coffee, tea, cocoa, sugar, rice, tapioca, sago, artificial coffee; flour, and preparations made from cereals, bread, pastry and confectionery, ices; honey, treacle; yeast, baking-powder; salt, mustard, vinegar, sauces, (except salad dressings) spices; ice.
31	Agricultural, horticultural and forestry products and grains not included in other classes; living animals; fresh fruits and vegetables; seeds, natural plants and flowers; foodstuffs for animals, malt.
32	Beers; mineral and aerated waters and other non-alcoholic drinks; fruit drinks and fruit juices; syrups and other preparations for making beverages.
33	Alcholic beverages (except beers).
34	Tobacco; smokers' articles; matches.

Services

35	Advertising and business.
36	Insurance and financial.
37	Construction and repair.
38	Communication.
39	Transportation and storage.
40	Material treatment.
41	Education and entertainment.
42	Miscellaneous.

TRADEMARK APPLICATION, PRINCIPAL REGISTER, WITH DECLARATION (Corporation)	MARK *(identify the mark)*
	CLASS NO. *(if known)*

TO THE COMMISSIONER OF PATENTS AND TRADEMARKS:

NAME OF CORPORATION

STATE OR COUNTRY OF INCORPORATION

BUSINESS ADDRESS OF CORPORATION	TELEPHONE AREA CODE NUMBER

The above identified applicant has adopted and is using the trademark shown in the accompanying drawing for the following

goods: _____

_____

and requests that said mark be registered in the United States Patent and Trademark Office on the Principal Register established by the Act of July 5, 1946.

The trademark was first used on the goods on _____ ; was first used on the goods in

(date)

_____ commerce on _____ ; and is now in use in such

(type of commerce) *(date)*

commerce.

The mark is used by applying it to _____

_____

and five specimens showing the mark as actually used are presented herewith.

_____

(name of officer of corporation)

being hereby warned that willful false statements and the like so made are punishable by fine or imprisonment, or both, under Section 1001 of Title 18 of the United States Code and that such willful false statements may jeopardize the validity of the application or any registration resulting therefrom, declares that he/she is

_____

(official title)

of applicant corporation and is authorized to execute this instrument on behalf of said corporation; he/she believes said corporation to be the owner of the trademark sought to be registered; to the best of his/her knowledge and belief no other person, firm, corporation, or association has the right to use said mark in commerce, either in the identical form or in such near resemblance thereto as may be likely, when applied to the goods of such other person, to cause confusion, or to cause mistake, or to deceive; the facts set forth in this application are true; and all statements made of his/her own knowledge are true and all statements made on information and belief are believed to be true.

_____

(name of corporation)

By _____

(signature of officer of corporation, and official title of officer)

_____

(date)

Exhibit 17-5

International schedule of classes of goods and services

Goods

1 Chemicals used in industry, science, photography, as well as in agriculture, horticulture, and forestry; unprocessed artificial resins; unprocessed plastics; manures; fire extinguishing compositions; tempering and soldering preparations; chemical substances for preserving foodstuffs; tanning substances; adhesives used in industry.

2 Paints, varnishes, lacquers; preservatives against rust and against deterioration of wood; colourants; mordants; raw natural resins; metals in foil and powder form for painters, decorators, printers and artists.

3 Bleaching preparations and other substances for laundry use; cleaning, polishing, scouring and abrasive preparations; soaps; perfumery, essential oils, cosmetics, hair lotions; dentifrices.

4 Industrial oils and greases; lubricants; dust absorbing, wetting and binding compositions; fuels (including motor spirit) and illuminants; candles, wicks.

5 Pharmaceutical, veterinary, and sanitary preparations; dietetic substances adapted for medical use, food for babies; plasters, materials for dressings material for stopping teeth, dental wax, disinfectants; preparations for destroying vermin; fungicides, herbicides.

6 Common metals and their alloys; metal building materials; transportable buildings of metal; materials of metal for railway tracks; non-electric cables and wires of common metal; ironmongery, small items of metal hardware; pipes and tubes of metal; safes; goods of common metal not included in other classes; ores

7 Machines and machine tools; motors (except for land vehicles); machine coupling and belting (except for land vehicles); agricultural implements; incubators for eggs.

8 Hand tools and implements (hand operated); cutlery; side arms; razors.

9 Scientific, nautical, surveying, electric, photographic, cinematographic, optical, weighing, measuring, signalling, checking (supervision), life-saving and teaching apparatus and instruments; apparatus for recording transmission or reproduction of sound or images; magnetic data carriers, recording discs; automatic vending machines and mechanisms for coin-operated apparatus; cash registers, calculating machines, data processing equipment and computers; fire-extinguishing apparatus.

10 Surgical, medical, dental, and veterinary apparatus and instruments, artificial limbs, eyes and teeth; orthopedic articles; suture materials.

11 Apparatus for lighting, heating, steam generating, cooking, refrigerating, drying, ventilating, water supply, and sanitary purposes.

12 Vehicles; apparatus for locomotion by land, air or water.

13 Firearms; ammunition and projectiles; explosives; fireworks.

14 Precious metals and their alloys and goods in precious metals or coated therewith, not included in other classes; jewelry, precious stones; horological and other chronometric instruments.

15 Musical instruments.

16 Paper and cardboard and goods made from these materials, not included in other classes; printed matter; bookbinding material; photographs; stationery; adhesives for stationery or household purposes; artists' materials; paint brushes; typewriters and office requisites (except furniture); instructional and teaching material (except apparatus); plastic materials for packaging (not included on other classes); playing cards; printers' type; printing blocks.

17 Rubber, gutta-percha, gum, asbestos, mica and goods made from these materials and not included in other classes; plastics in extruded form for use in manufacture; packing, stopping and insulating materials; flexible pipes, not of metal.

18 Leather and imitations of leather, and goods made from these materials and not included in other classes; animal skins, hides; trunks and travelling bags; umbrellas, parasols and walking sticks; whips, harness and saddlery.

19 Building materials (non-metallic); non-metallic rigid pipes for building; asphalt, pitch and bitumen; non-metallic transportable buildings; monuments, not of metal.

20 Furniture, mirrors, picture frames; goods (not included in other classes) of wood, cork, reed, cane, wicker, horn, bone, ivory, whalebone, shell, amber, mother-of-pearl, meerschaum and substitutes for all these materials, or of plastics.

21 Household or kitchen utensils and containers (not of precious metal or coated therewith); combs and sponges; brushes (except paint brushes); brush-making materials; articles for cleaning purposes; steel wool; unworked or semi-worked glass (except glass used in building); glassware, porcelain and earthenware, not included in other classes.

22 Ropes, string, nets, tents, awnings, tarpaulins, sails, sacks; and bags (not included other classes); padding and stuffing materials (except of rubber or plastics); raw fibrous textile materials.

23 Yarns and threads, for textile use.

24 Textile and textile goods, not included in other classes; bed and table covers.

25 Clothing, footwear, headgear.

26 Lace and embroidery, ribbons and braid; buttons, hooks and eyes, pins and needles; artificial flowers.

27 Carpets, rugs, mats and matting; linoleum and other materials for covering existing floors; wall hangings (non-textile).

28 Games and playthings; gymnastic and sporting articles not included in other classes; decorations for Christmas trees.

29 Meats, fish, poultry and game; meat extracts; preserved, dried and cooked fruits and vegetables; jellies, jams; eggs, milk and milk products; edible oils and fats; salad dressings; preserves.

30 Coffee, tea, cocoa, sugar, rice, tapioca, sago, artificial coffee; flour, and preparations made from cereals, bread, pastry and confectionery, ices; honey, treacle; yeast, baking-powder; salt, mustard, vinegar, sauces, (except salad dressings) spices; ice.

31 Agricultural, horticultural and forestry products and grains not included in other classes; living animals; fresh fruits and vegetables; seeds, natural plants and flowers; foodstuffs for animals, malt.

32 Beers; mineral and aerated waters and other non-alcoholic drinks; fruit drinks and fruit juices; syrups and other preparations for making beverages.

33 Alcholic beverages (except beers).

34 Tobacco; smokers' articles; matches.

Services

35 Advertising and business.

36 Insurance and financial.

37 Construction and repair.

38 Communication.

39 Transportation and storage.

40 Material treatment.

41 Education and entertainment.

42 Miscellaneous.

FORM TX
UNITED STATES COPYRIGHT OFFICE

REGISTRATION NUMBER

_____

TX _____ TXU _____

EFFECTIVE DATE OF REGISTRATION

_____

Month   Day   Year

DO NOT WRITE ABOVE THIS LINE. IF YOU NEED MORE SPACE, USE A SEPARATE CONTINUATION SHEET.

1

TITLE OF THIS WORK ▼

PREVIOUS OR ALTERNATIVE TITLES ▼

PUBLICATION AS A CONTRIBUTION   If this work was published as a contribution to a periodical, serial, or collection, give information about the collective work in which the contribution appeared.   **Title of Collective Work ▼**

If published in a periodical or serial give: **Volume ▼**   **Number ▼**   **Issue Date ▼**   **On Pages ▼**

2

a

NAME OF AUTHOR ▼

DATES OF BIRTH AND DEATH
Year Born ▼   Year Died ▼

Was this contribution to the work a "work made for hire"?
☐ Yes
☐ No

AUTHOR'S NATIONALITY OR DOMICILE
Name of Country
OR { Citizen of ▶ _____
Domiciled in ▶ _____

WAS THIS AUTHOR'S CONTRIBUTION TO THE WORK
Anonymous?   ☐ Yes ☐ No
Pseudonymous?   ☐ Yes ☐ No
If the answer to either of these questions is "Yes," see detailed instructions.

NATURE OF AUTHORSHIP   Briefly describe nature of the material created by this author in which copyright is claimed. ▼

NOTE

Under the law, the "author" of a "work made for hire" is generally the employer, not the employee (see instructions). For any part of this work that was "made for hire" check "Yes" in the space provided, give the employer (or other person for whom the work was prepared) as "Author" of that part, and leave the space for dates of birth and death blank.

b

NAME OF AUTHOR ▼

DATES OF BIRTH AND DEATH
Year Born ▼   Year Died ▼

Was this contribution to the work a "work made for hire"?
☐ Yes
☐ No

AUTHOR'S NATIONALITY OR DOMICILE
Name of country
OR { Citizen of ▶ _____
Domiciled in ▶ _____

WAS THIS AUTHOR'S CONTRIBUTION TO THE WORK
Anonymous?   ☐ Yes ☐ No
Pseudonymous?   ☐ Yes ☐ No
If the answer to either of these questions is "Yes," see detailed instructions.

NATURE OF AUTHORSHIP   Briefly describe nature of the material created by this author in which copyright is claimed. ▼

c

NAME OF AUTHOR ▼

DATES OF BIRTH AND DEATH
Year Born ▼   Year Died ▼

Was this contribution to the work a "work made for hire"?
☐ Yes
☐ No

AUTHOR'S NATIONALITY OR DOMICILE
Name of Country
OR { Citizen of ▶ _____
Domiciled in ▶ _____

WAS THIS AUTHOR'S CONTRIBUTION TO THE WORK
Anonymous?   ☐ Yes ☐ No
Pseudonymous?   ☐ Yes ☐ No
If the answer to either of these questions is "Yes," see detailed instructions.

NATURE OF AUTHORSHIP   Briefly describe nature of the material created by this author in which copyright is claimed. ▼

3

YEAR IN WHICH CREATION OF THIS WORK WAS COMPLETED This information must be given in all cases.
◀ Year

DATE AND NATION OF FIRST PUBLICATION OF THIS PARTICULAR WORK
Complete this information ONLY if this work has been published.
Month ▶ _____ Day ▶ _____ Year ▶ _____ ◀ Nation

4

See instructions before completing this space.

COPYRIGHT CLAIMANT(S) Name and address must be given even if the claimant is the same as the author given in space 2.▼

TRANSFER If the claimant(s) named here in space 4 are different from the author(s) named in space 2, give a brief statement of how the claimant(s) obtained ownership of the copyright.▼

APPLICATION RECEIVED

ONE DEPOSIT RECEIVED

TWO DEPOSITS RECEIVED

REMITTANCE NUMBER AND DATE

DO NOT WRITE HERE OFFICE USE ONLY

MORE ON BACK ▶   • Complete all applicable spaces (numbers 5-11) on the reverse side of this page.   • See detailed instructions.   • Sign the form at line 10.

DO NOT WRITE HERE

Page 1 of _____ pages

Exhibit 17-6

DO NOT WRITE ABOVE THIS LINE. IF YOU NEED MORE SPACE, USE A SEPARATE CONTINUATION SHEET.

PREVIOUS REGISTRATION Has registration for this work, or for an earlier version of this work, already been made in the Copyright Office?

☐ Yes ☐ No If your answer is "Yes," why is another registration being sought? (Check appropriate box) ▼

☐ This is the first published edition of a work previously registered in unpublished form.

☐ This is the first application submitted by this author as copyright claimant.

☐ This is a changed version of the work, as shown by space 6 on this application.

If your answer is "Yes," give: **Previous Registration Number** ▼   **Year of Registration** ▼

5

DERIVATIVE WORK OR COMPILATION Complete both space 6a & 6b for a derivative work; complete only 6b for a compilation.

a. Preexisting Material Identify any preexisting work or works that this work is based on or incorporates. ▼

b. Material Added to This Work Give a brief, general statement of the material that has been added to this work and in which copyright is claimed. ▼

See instructions
before completing
this space.

6

MANUFACTURERS AND LOCATIONS If this is a published work consisting preponderantly of nondramatic literary material in English, the law may require that the copies be manufactured in the United States or Canada for full protection. If so, the names of the manufacturers who performed certain processes, and the places where these processes were performed **must** be given. See instructions for details.

Names of Manufacturers ▼   **Places of Manufacture** ▼

7

REPRODUCTION FOR USE OF BLIND OR PHYSICALLY HANDICAPPED INDIVIDUALS   A signature on this form at space 10, and a check in one of the boxes here in space 8, constitutes a non-exclusive grant of permission to the Library of Congress to reproduce and distribute solely for the blind and physically handicapped and under the conditions and limitations prescribed by the regulations of the Copyright Office: (1) copies of the work identified in space 1 of this application in Braille (or similar tactile symbols); or (2) phonorecords embodying a fixation of a reading of that work; or (3) both.

a ☐ Copies and Phonorecords   b ☐ Copies Only   c ☐ Phonorecords Only

See instructions.

8

DEPOSIT ACCOUNT If the registration fee is to be charged to a Deposit Account established in the Copyright Office, give name and number of Account.

Name ▼   **Account Number** ▼

9

CORRESPONDENCE Give name and address to which correspondence about this application should be sent. Name/Address/Apt/City/State/Zip ▼

Area Code & Telephone Number ▶

Be sure to
give your
daytime phone
◀ number.

CERTIFICATION* I, the undersigned, hereby certify that I am the

Check one ▶

☐ author
☐ other copyright claimant
☐ owner of exclusive right(s)
☐ authorized agent of _____

of the work identified in this application and that the statements made by me in this application are correct to the best of my knowledge.

Name of author or other copyright claimant, or owner of exclusive right(s) ▲

10

Typed or printed name and date ▼ If this is a published work, this date must be the same as or later than the date of publication given in space 3.

_____ date ▶ _____

☞ Handwritten signature (X) ▼

MAIL CERTIFI-CATE TO

Name ▼

Number/Street/Apartment Number ▼

City/State/ZIP ▼

Certificate will be mailed in window envelope

Have you:
• Completed all necessary spaces?
• Signed your application in space 10?
• Enclosed check or money order for $10 payable to *Register of Copyrights*?
• Enclosed your deposit material with the application and fee?

MAIL TO: Register of Copyrights, Library of Congress, Washington, D.C. 20559.

11

Filling Out Application Form TX

Detach and read these instructions before completing this form. Make sure all applicable spaces have been filled in before you return this form.

BASIC INFORMATION

When to Use This Form: Use Form TX for registration of published or unpublished non-dramatic literary works, excluding periodicals or serial issues. This class includes a wide variety of works: fiction, non-fiction, poetry, textbooks, reference works, directories, catalogs, advertising copy, compilations of information, and computer programs. For periodicals and serials, use Form SE.

Deposit to Accompany Application: An application for copyright registration must be accompanied by a deposit consisting of copies or phonorecords representing the entire work for which registration is to be made. The following are the general deposit requirements as set forth in the statute:

Unpublished Work: Deposit one complete copy (or phonorecord).

Published Work: Deposit two complete copies (or phonorecords) of the best edition.

Work First Published Outside the United States: Deposit one complete copy (or phonorecord) of the first foreign edition.

Contribution to a Collective Work: Deposit one complete copy (or phonorecord) of the best edition of the collective work.

The Copyright Notice: For published works, the law provides that a copyright notice in a specified form "shall be placed on all publicly distributed copies from which the work can be visually perceived." Use of the copyright notice is the responsibility of the copyright owner and does not require advance permission from the Copyright Office. The required form of the notice for copies generally consists of three elements: (1) the symbol "©", or the word "Copyright," or the abbreviation "Copr."; (2) the year of first publication; and (3) the name of the owner of copyright. For example: "© 1981 Constance Porter." The notice is to be affixed to the copies "in such manner and location as to give reasonable notice of the claim of copyright."

For further information about copyright registration, notice, or special questions relating to copyright problems, write:

Information and Publications Section, LM-455
Copyright Office
Library of Congress
Washington, D.C. 20559

LINE-BY-LINE INSTRUCTIONS

1 SPACE 1: Title

Title of This Work: Every work submitted for copyright registration must be given a title to identify that particular work. If the copies or phonorecords of the work bear a title (or an identifying phrase that could serve as a title), transcribe that wording *completely* and *exactly* on the application. Indexing of the registration and future identification of the work will depend on the information you give here.

Previous or Alternative Titles: Complete this space if there are any additional titles for the work under which someone searching for the registration might be likely to look, or under which a document pertaining to the work might be recorded.

Publication as a Contribution: If the work being registered is a contribution to a periodical, serial, or collection, give the title of the contribution in the "Title of this Work" space. Then, in the line headed "Publication as a Contribution," give information about the collective work in which the contribution appeared.

2 SPACE 2: Author(s)

General Instructions: After reading these instructions, decide who are the "authors" of this work for copyright purposes. Then, unless the work is a "collective work," give the requested information about every "author" who contributed any appreciable amount of copyrightable matter to this version of the work. If you need further space, request additional Continuation sheets. In the case of a collective work, such as an anthology, collection of essays, or encyclopedia, give information about the author of the collective work as a whole.

Name of Author: The fullest form of the author's name should be given. Unless the work was "made for hire," the individual who actually created the work is its "author." In the case of a work made for hire, the statute provides that "the employer or other person for whom the work was prepared is considered the author."

What is a "Work Made for Hire"? A "work made for hire" is defined as: (1) "a work prepared by an employee within the scope of his or her employment"; or (2) "a work specially ordered or commissioned for use as a contribution to a collective work, as a part of a motion picture or other audiovisual work, as a translation, as a supplementary work, as a compilation, as an instructional text, as a test, as answer material for a test, or as an atlas, if the parties expressly agree in a written instrument signed by them that the work shall be considered a work made for hire." If you have checked "Yes" to indicate that the work was "made for hire," you must give the full legal name of the employer (or other person for whom the work was prepared). You may also include the name of the employee along with the name of the employer (for example: "Elster Publishing Co., employer for hire of John Ferguson").

"Anonymous" or "Pseudonymous" Work: An author's contribution to a work is "anonymous" if that author is not identified on the copies or phonorecords of the work. An author's contribution to a work is "pseudonymous" if that author is identified on the copies or phonorecords under a fictitious name. If the work is "anonymous" you may: (1) leave the line blank; or (2) state " anonymous" on the line; or (3) reveal the author's identity. If the work is "pseudonymous" you may : (1) leave the line blank; or (2) give the pseudonym and identify it as such (for example: "Huntley Haverstock, pseudonym"); or (3) reveal the author's name, making clear which is the real name and which is the pseudonym (for example: "Judith Barton, whose pseudonym is Madeline Elster"). However, the citizenship or domicile of the author **must** be given in all cases.

Dates of Birth and Death: If the author is dead, the statute requires that the year of death be included in the application unless the work is anonymous or pseudonymous. The author's birth date is optional, but is useful as a form of identification. Leave this space blank if the author's contribution was a "work made for hire."

Author's Nationality or Domicile: Give the country of which the author is a citizen, or the country in which the author is domiciled. Nationality or domicile **must** be given in all cases.

Nature of Authorship: After the words "Nature of Authorship" give a brief general statement of the nature of this particular author's contribution to the work. Examples: "Entire text"; "Coauthor of entire text"; "Chapters 11-14"; "Editorial revisions"; "Compilation and English translation"; "New text."

3 SPACE 3: Creation and Publication

General Instructions: Do not confuse "creation" with "publication." Every application for copyright registration must state "the year in which creation of the work was completed." Give the date and nation of first publication only if the work has been published.

Creation: Under the statute, a work is "created" when it is fixed in a copy or phonorecord for the first time. Where a work has been prepared over a period of time, the part of the work existing in fixed form on a particular date constitutes the created work on that date. The date you give here should be the year in which the author completed the particular version for which registration is now being sought, even if other versions exist or if further changes or additions are planned.

Publication: The statute defines "publication" as "the distribution of copies or phonorecords of a work to the public by sale or other transfer of ownership, or by rental, lease, or lending"; a work is also "published" if there has been an "offering to distribute copies or phonorecords to a group of persons for purposes of further distribution, public performance, or public display." Give the full date (month, day, year) when, and the country where, publication first occurred. If first publication took place simultaneously in the United States and other countries, it is sufficient to state "U.S.A."

4 SPACE 4: Claimant(s)

Name(s) and Address(es) of Copyright Claimant(s): Give the name(s) and address(es) of the copyright claimant(s) in this work even if the claimant is the same as the author. Copyright in a work belongs initially to the author of the work (including, in the case of a work made for hire, the employer or other person for whom the work was prepared). The copyright claimant is either the author of the work or a person or organization to whom the copyright initially belonging to the author has been transferred.

Transfer: The statute provides that, if the copyright claimant is not the author, the application for registration must contain "a brief statement of how the claimant obtained ownership of the copyright." If any copyright claimant named in space 4 is not an author named in space 2, give a brief, general statement summarizing the means by which that claimant obtained ownership of the copyright. Examples: "By written contract"; "Transfer of all rights by author"; "Assignment"; "By will." Do not attach transfer documents or other attachments or riders.

5 SPACE 5: Previous Registration

General Instructions: The questions in space 5 are intended to find out whether an earlier registration has been made for this work and, if so, whether there is any basis for a new registration. As a general rule, only one basic copyright registration can be made for the same version of a particular work.

Same Version: If this version is substantially the same as the work covered by a previous registration, a second registration is not generally possible unless: (1) the work has been registered in unpublished form and a second registration is now being sought to cover this first published edition; or (2) someone other than the author is identified as copyright claimant in the earlier registration, and the author is now seeking registration in his or her own name. If either of these two exceptions apply, check the appropriate box and give the earlier registration number and date. Otherwise, do not submit Form TX; instead, write the Copyright Office for information about supplementary registration or recordation of transfers of copyright ownership.

Changed Version: If the work has been changed, and you are now seeking registration to cover the additions or revisions, check the last box in space 5, give the earlier registration number and date, and complete both parts of space 6 in accordance with the instructions below.

Previous Registration Number and Date: If more than one previous registration has been made for the work, give the number and date of the latest registration.

6 SPACE 6: Derivative Work or Compilation

General Instructions: Complete space 6 if this work is a "changed version," "compilation," or "derivative work," and if it incorporates one or more earlier works that have already been published or registered for copyright, or that have fallen into the public domain. A "compilation" is defined as "a work formed by the collection and assembling of preexisting materials or of data that are selected, coordinated, or arranged in such a way that the resulting work as a whole constitutes an original work of authorship." A "derivative work" is "a work based on one or more preexisting works." Examples of derivative works include translations, fictionalizations, abridgments, condensations, or "any other form in which a work may be recast, transformed, or adapted." Derivative works also include works "consisting of editorial revisions, annotations, or other modifications" if these changes, as a whole, represent an original work of authorship.

Preexisting Material (space 6a): For derivative works, complete this space **and** space 6b. In space 6a identify the preexisting work that has been recast, transformed, or adapted. An example of preexisting material might be: "Russian version of Goncharov's 'Oblomov'." Do not complete space 6a for compilations.

Material Added to This Work (space 6b): Give a brief, general statement of the new material covered by the copyright claim for which registration is sought. Derivative work examples include: "Foreword, editing, critical annotations"; "Translation"; "Chapters 11-17." If the work is a **compilation**, describe both the compilation itself and the material that has been compiled. Example: "Compilation of certain 1917 Speeches by Woodrow Wilson." A work may be both a derivative work and compilation, in which case a sample statement might be: "Compilation and additional new material."

7 SPACE 7: Manufacturing Provisions

General Instructions: The copyright statute currently provides, as a general rule, that the copies of a published work "consisting preponderantly of nondramatic literary material in the English language" be manufactured in the United States or Canada in order to be lawfully imported and publicly distributed in the United States. If the work being registered is unpublished or not in English, leave this space blank. Complete this space if registration is sought for a published work "consisting preponderantly of nondramatic literary material that is in the English language." Identify those who manufactured the copies and where those manufacturing processes were performed. As an exception to the manufacturing provisions, the statute prescribes that, where manufacture has taken place outside the United States or Canada, a maximum of 2000 copies of the foreign edition may be imported into the United States without affecting the copyright owners' rights. For this purpose, the Copyright Office will issue an Import Statement upon request and payment of a fee of $3 at the time of registration or at any later time. For further information about import statements, write for Form IS.

8 SPACE 8: Reproduction for Use of Blind or Physically Handicapped Individuals

General Instructions: One of the major programs of the Library of Congress is to provide Braille editions and special recordings of works for the exclusive use of the blind and physically handicapped. In an effort to simplify and speed up the copyright licensing procedures that are a necessary part of this program, section 710 of the copyright statute provides for the establishment of a voluntary licensing system to be tied in with copyright registration. Copyright Office regulations provide that you may grant a license for such reproduction and distribution solely for the use of persons who are certified by competent authority as unable to read normal printed material as a result of physical limitations. The license is entirely voluntary, nonexclusive, and may be terminated upon 90 days notice.

How to Grant the License: If you wish to grant it, check one of the three boxes in space 8. Your check in one of these boxes, together with your signature in space 10, will mean that the Library of Congress can proceed to reproduce and distribute under the license without further paperwork. For further information, write for Circular R63.

9,10,11 SPACE 9, 10, 11: Fee, Correspondence, Certification, Return Address

Deposit Account: If you maintain a Deposit Account in the Copyright Office, identify it in space 9. Otherwise leave the space blank and send the fee of $10 with your application and deposit.

Correspondence (space 9): This space should contain the name, address, area code, and telephone number of the person to be consulted if correspondence about this application becomes necessary.

Certification (space 10): The application can not be accepted unless it bears the date and the **handwritten signature** of the author or other copyright claimant, or of the owner of exclusive right(s), or of the duly authorized agent of author, claimant, or owner of exclusive right(s).

Address for Return of Certificate (space 11): The address box must be completed legibly since the certificate will be returned in a window envelope.

FORM SE
UNITED STATES COPYRIGHT OFFICE

REGISTRATION NUMBER

U

EFFECTIVE DATE OF REGISTRATION

| Month | Day | Year |

DO NOT WRITE ABOVE THIS LINE. IF YOU NEED MORE SPACE, USE A SEPARATE CONTINUATION SHEET.

1 TITLE OF THIS SERIAL ▼

Volume ▼   Number ▼   Date on Copies ▼   Frequency of Publication ▼

PREVIOUS OR ALTERNATIVE TITLES ▼

2

a NAME OF AUTHOR ▼

DATES OF BIRTH AND DEATH
Year Born ▼   Year Died ▼

Was this contribution to the work a "work made for hire"?
☐ Yes
☐ No

AUTHOR'S NATIONALITY OR DOMICILE
Name of Country
OR { Citizen of ▶
Domiciled in ▶

WAS THIS AUTHOR'S CONTRIBUTION TO THE WORK
Anonymous? ☐ Yes ☐ No
Pseudonymous? ☐ Yes ☐ No

If the answer to either of these questions is "Yes," see detailed instructions.

NATURE OF AUTHORSHIP   Briefly describe nature of the material created by this author in which copyright is claimed. ▼
☐ Collective Work   Other:

NOTE

Under the law, the "author" of a "work made for hire" is generally the employer, not the employee (see instructions). For any part of this work that was "made for hire" check "Yes" in the space provided, give the employer (or other person for whom the work was prepared) as "Author" of that part, and leave the space for dates of birth and death blank.

b NAME OF AUTHOR ▼

DATES OF BIRTH AND DEATH
Year Born ▼   Year Died ▼

Was this contribution to the work a "work made for hire"?
☐ Yes
☐ No

AUTHOR'S NATIONALITY OR DOMICILE
Name of country
OR { Citizen of ▶
Domiciled in ▶

WAS THIS AUTHOR'S CONTRIBUTION TO THE WORK
Anonymous? ☐ Yes ☐ No
Pseudonymous? ☐ Yes ☐ No

If the answer to either of these questions is "Yes," see detailed instructions.

NATURE OF AUTHORSHIP   Briefly describe nature of the material created by this author in which copyright is claimed. ▼
☐ Collective Work   Other:

c NAME OF AUTHOR ▼

DATES OF BIRTH AND DEATH
Year Born ▼   Year Died ▼

Was this contribution to the work a "work made for hire"?
☐ Yes
☐ No

AUTHOR'S NATIONALITY OR DOMICILE
Name of Country
OR { Citizen of ▶
Domiciled in ▶

WAS THIS AUTHOR'S CONTRIBUTION TO THE WORK
Anonymous? ☐ Yes ☐ No
Pseudonymous? ☐ Yes ☐ No

If the answer to either of these questions is "Yes," see detailed instructions.

NATURE OF AUTHORSHIP   Briefly describe nature of the material created by this author in which copyright is claimed. ▼
☐ Collective Work   Other:

3

YEAR IN WHICH CREATION OF THIS ISSUE WAS COMPLETED   This information must be given in all cases.
◀ Year

DATE AND NATION OF FIRST PUBLICATION OF THIS PARTICULAR ISSUE
Complete this information ONLY if this work has been published.
Month ▶   Day ▶   Year ▶   ◀ Nation

4

COPYRIGHT CLAIMANT(S) Name and address must be given even if the claimant is the same as the author given in space 2.▼

See instructions before completing this space.

TRANSFER If the claimant(s) named here in space 4 are different from the author(s) named in space 2, give a brief statement of how the claimant(s) obtained ownership of the copyright.▼

DO NOT WRITE HERE OFFICE USE ONLY

APPLICATION RECEIVED

ONE DEPOSIT RECEIVED

TWO DEPOSITS RECEIVED

REMITTANCE NUMBER AND DATE

MORE ON BACK ▶
- Complete all applicable spaces (numbers 5-11) on the reverse side of this page.
- See detailed instructions.
- Sign the form at line 10.

DO NOT WRITE HERE

Page 1 of_____ pages

Exhibit 17-7

EXAMINED BY

CHECKED BY

☐ CORRESPONDENCE
  Yes

☐ DEPOSIT ACCOUNT
  FUNDS USED

FORM SE

FOR
COPYRIGHT
OFFICE
USE
ONLY

DO NOT WRITE ABOVE THIS LINE. IF YOU NEED MORE SPACE, USE A SEPARATE CONTINUATION SHEET.

PREVIOUS REGISTRATION   Has registration for this issue, or for an earlier version of this particular issue, already been made in the Copyright Office?

☐ **Yes** ☐ **No**   If your answer is "Yes," why is another registration being sought? (Check appropriate box) ▼

a. ☐ This is the first published version of an issue previously registered in unpublished form.

b. ☐ This is the first application submitted by this author as copyright claimant.

c. ☐ This is a changed version of this issue, as shown by space 6 on this application.

If your answer is "Yes," give: **Previous Registration Number** ▼   **Year of Registration** ▼

5

DERIVATIVE WORK OR COMPILATION   Complete both space 6a & 6b for a derivative work; complete only 6b for a compilation.

a. Preexisting Material   Identify any preexisting work or works that this work is based on or incorporates. ▼

b. Material Added to This Work   Give a brief, general statement of the material that has been added to this work and in which copyright is claimed. ▼

6

See instructions
before completing
this space.

MANUFACTURERS AND LOCATIONS   If this is a published work consisting preponderantly of nondramatic literary material in English, the law may require that the copies be manufactured in the United States or Canada for full protection. If so, the names of the manufacturers who performed certain processes, and the places where these processes were performed **must** be given. See instructions for details.

Names of Manufacturers ▼   **Places of Manufacture** ▼

7

REPRODUCTION FOR USE OF BLIND OR PHYSICALLY HANDICAPPED INDIVIDUALS   A signature on this form at space 10, and a check in one of the boxes here in space 8, constitutes a non-exclusive grant of permission to the Library of Congress to reproduce and distribute solely for the blind and physically handicapped and under the conditions and limitations prescribed by the regulations of the Copyright Office: (1) copies of the work identified in space 1 of this application in Braille (or similar tactile symbols); or (2) phonorecords embodying a fixation of a reading of that work; or (3) both.

a ☐ Copies and Phonorecords   **b** ☐ Copies Only   **c** ☐ Phonorecords Only

8

See instructions.

DEPOSIT ACCOUNT   If the registration fee is to be charged to a Deposit Account established in the Copyright Office, give name and number of Account.

Name ▼   **Account Number** ▼

CORRESPONDENCE   Give name and address to which correspondence about this application should be sent.   Name/Address/Apt/City/State/Zip ▼

Area Code & Telephone Number ▶

9

Be sure to
give your
daytime phone
◀ number.

CERTIFICATION*   I, the undersigned, hereby certify that I am the

Check one ▶

☐ author
☐ other copyright claimant
☐ owner of exclusive right(s)
☐ authorized agent of _____

of the work identified in this application and that the statements made by me in this application are correct to the best of my knowledge.

Name of author or other copyright claimant, or owner of exclusive right(s) ▲

Typed or printed name and date ▼ If this is a published work, this date must be the same as or later than the date of publication given in space 3.

_____ date ▶ _____

☞   Handwritten signature (X) ▼

10

MAIL CERTIFI-CATE TO

Certificate will be mailed in window envelope

Name ▼

Number/Street/Apartment Number ▼

City/State/ZIP ▼

Have you:
● Completed all necessary spaces?
● Signed your application in space 10?
● Enclosed check or money order for $10 payable to *Register of Copyrights*?
● Enclosed your deposit material with the application and fee?

MAIL TO: Register of Copyrights, Library of Congress, Washington, D.C. 20559.

11

Filling Out Application Form SE

Detach and read these instructions before completing this form. Make sure all applicable spaces have been filled in before you return this form.

BASIC INFORMATION

When To Use This Form: Use a separate Form SE for registration of each individual issue of a serial, Class SE. A serial is defined as a work issued or intended to be issued in successive parts bearing numerical or chronological designations and intended to be continued indefinitely. This class includes a variety of works: periodicals; newspapers; annuals; the journals, proceedings, transactions, etc., of societies. Do not use Form SE to register an individual contribution to a serial. Request Form TX for such contributions.

Deposit to Accompany Application: An application for copyright registration must be accompanied by a deposit consisting of copies or phonorecords representing the entire work for which registration is to be made. The following are the general deposit requirements as set forth in the statute:

Unpublished Work: Deposit one complete copy (or phonorecord).

Published Work: Deposit two complete copies (or phonorecords) of the best edition.

Work First Published Outside the United States: Deposit one complete copy (or phonorecord) of the first foreign edition.

Mailing Requirements: It is important that you send the application, the deposit copy or copies, and the $10 fee together in the same envelope or package. The Copyright Office cannot process them unless they are received together. Send to: *Register of Copyrights, Library of Congress, Washington, D.C. 20559.*

The Copyright Notice: For published works, the law provides that a copyright notice in a specified form "shall be placed on all publicly distributed copies from which the work can be visually perceived." Use of the copyright notice is the responsibility of the copyright owner and does not require advance permission from the Copyright Office. The required form of the notice for copies generally consists of three elements: (1) the symbol "©"; or the word "Copyright," or the abbreviation "Copr."; (2) the year of first publication; and (3) the name of the owner of copyright. For example: "© 1981 National News Publishers, Inc." The notice is to be affixed to the copies "in such manner and location as to give reasonable notice of the claim of copyright." For further information about copyright registration, notice, or special questions relating to copyright problems, write:

Information and Publications Section, LM-455
Copyright Office, Library of Congress, Washington, D.C. 20559

LINE-BY-LINE INSTRUCTIONS

1 SPACE 1: Title

Title of This Serial: Every work submitted for copyright registration must be given a title to identify that particular work. If the copies or phonorecords of the work bear a title (or an identifying phrase that could serve as a title), copy that wording *completely* and *exactly* on the application. Give the volume and number of the periodical issue for which you are seeking registration. The "Date on copies" in space 1 should be the date appearing on the actual copies (for example: "June 1981," "Winter 1981"). Indexing of the registration and future identification of the work will depend on the information you give here.

Previous or Alternative Titles: Complete this space only if there are any additional titles for the serial under which someone searching for the registration might be likely to look, or under which a document pertaining to the work might be recorded.

2 SPACE 2: Author(s)

General Instructions: After reading these instructions, decide who are the "authors" of this work for copyright purposes. In the case of a serial issue, the organization which directs the creation of the serial issue as a whole is generally considered the author of the "collective work" (see "Nature of Authorship") whether it employs a staff or uses the efforts of volunteers. Where, however, an individual is independently responsible for the serial issue, name that person as author of the "collective work."

Name of Author: The fullest form of the author's name should be given. In the case of a "work made for hire," the statute provides that "the employer or other person for whom the work was prepared is considered the author." If this issue is a "work made for hire," the author's name will be the full legal name of the hiring organization, corporation, or individual. The title of the periodical should not ordinarily be listed as "author" because the title itself does not usually correspond to a legal entity capable of authorship. When an individual creates an issue of a serial independently and not as an "employee" of an organization or corporation, that individual should be listed as the "author."

Author's Nationality or Domicile: Give the country of which the author is a citizen, or the country in which the author is domiciled. Nationality or domicile **must** be given in all cases. The citizenship of an organization formed under United States Federal or state law should be stated as "U.S.A."

What is a "Work Made for Hire"? A "work made for hire" is defined as: (1) "a work prepared by an employee within the scope of his or her employment"; or (2) "a work specially ordered or commissioned for use as a contribution to a collective work, as a part of a motion picture or other audiovisual work, as a translation, as a supplementary work, as a compilation, as an instructional text, as a test, as answer material for a test, or as an atlas, if the parties expressly agree in a written instrument signed by them that the work shall be considered a work made for hire." An organization that uses the efforts of volunteers in the creation of a "collective work" (see "Nature of Authorship") may also be considered the author of a "work made for hire" even though those volunteers were not specifically paid by the organization. In the case of a "work made for hire," give the full legal name of the employer and check "Yes" to indicate that the work was made for hire. You may also include the name of the employee along with the name of the employer (for example: "Elster Publishing Co., employer for hire of John Ferguson").

"Anonymous" or "Pseudonymous" Work: Leave this space **blank** if the serial is a "work made for hire." An author's contribution to a work is "anonymous" if that author is not identified on the copies or phonorecords of the work. An author's contribution to a work is "pseudonymous" if that author is identified on the copies or phonorecords under a fictitious name. If the work is "anonymous" you may: (1) leave the line blank; or (2) state "anonymous" on the line; or (3) reveal the author's identity. If the work is "pseudonymous" you may: (1) leave the line blank; or (2) give the pseudonym and identify it as such (for example: "Huntley Haverstock, pseudonym"); or (3) reveal the author's name, making clear which is the real name and which is the pseudonym (for example: "Judith Barton, whose pseudonym is Madeline Elster"). However, the citizenship or domicile of the author **must** be given in all cases.

Dates of Birth and Death: Leave this space blank if the author's contribution was a "work made for hire." If the author is dead, the statute requires that the year of death be included in the application unless the work is anonymous or pseudonymous. The author's birth date is optional, but is useful as a form of identification.

Nature of Authorship: Give a brief statement of the nature of the particular author's contribution to the work. If an organization directed, controlled, and supervised the creation of the serial issue as a whole, check the box "collective work." The term "collective work" means that the author is responsible for compilation and editorial revision, and may also be responsible for certain individual contributions to the serial issue. Further examples of "Authorship" which may apply both to organizational and to individual authors are "Entire text"; "Entire text and/or illustrations"; "Editorial revision, compilation, plus additional new material."

3 SPACE 3: Creation and Publication

General Instructions: Do not confuse "creation" with "publication." Every application for copyright registration must state "the year in which creation of the work was completed." Give the date and nation of first publication only if the work has been published.

Creation: Under the statute, a work is "created" when it is fixed in a copy or phonorecord for the first time. Where a work has been prepared over a period of time, the part of the work existing in fixed form on a particular date constitutes the created work on that date. The date you give here should be the year in which this particular issue was completed.

Publication: The statute defines "publication" as "the distribution of copies or phonorecords of a work to the public by sale or other transfer of ownership, or by rental, lease, or lending"; a work is also "published" if there has been an "offering to distribute copies or phonorecords to a group of persons for purposes of further distribution, public performance, or public display." Give the full date (month, day, year) when, and the country where, publication of this particular issue first occurred. If first publication took place simultaneously in the United States and other countries, it is sufficient to state "U.S.A."

4 SPACE 4: Claimant(s)

Name(s) and Address(es) of Copyright Claimant(s): This space must be completed. Give the name(s) and address(es) of the copyright claimant(s) of this work even if the claimant is the same as the author named in space 2. Copyright in a work belongs initially to the author of the work (including, in the case of a work made for hire, the employer or other person for whom the work was prepared). The copyright claimant is either the author of the work or a person or organization to whom the copyright initially belonging to the author has been transferred.

Transfer: The statute provides that, if the copyright claimant is not the author, the application for registration must contain "a brief statement of how the claimant obtained ownership of the copyright." A transfer of copyright ownership (other than one brought about by operation of law) must be in writing. If any copyright claimant named in space 4 is not an author named in space 2, give a brief, general statement describing the means by which that claimant obtained ownership of the copyright from the original author. Examples: "By written contract"; "Written transfer of all rights by author"; "Assignment"; "Inherited by will." Do not attach the actual document of transfer or other attachments or riders.

5 SPACE 5: Previous Registration

General Instructions: This space applies only rarely to serials. Complete space 5 if this particular issue has been registered earlier or if it contains a substantial amount of material that has been previously registered. Do not complete this space if the previous registrations are simply those made for earlier issues.

Previous Registration:
a. Check this box if this issue has been registered in unpublished form and a second registration is now sought to cover the first published edition.
b. Check this box if someone other than the author is identified as copyright claimant in the earlier registration and the author is now seeking registration in his or her own name. If the work in question is a contribution to a collective work, as opposed to the issue as a whole, file Form TX, not Form SE.
c. Check this box (and complete space 6) if this particular issue, or a substantial portion of the material in it, has been previously registered and you are now seeking registration for the additions and revisions which appear in this issue for the first time.

Previous Registration Number and Date: Complete this line if you checked one of the boxes above. If more than one previous registration has been made for the issue or for material in it, give only the number and year date for the latest registration.

6 SPACE 6: Derivative Work or Compilation

General Instructions: Complete space 6 if this issue is a "changed version," "compilation," or "derivative work," which incorporates one or more earlier works that have already been published or registered for copyright, or that have fallen into the public domain. Do not complete space 6 for an issue consisting of entirely new material appearing for the first time, such as a new issue of a continuing serial. A "compilation" is defined as "a work formed by the collection and assembling of preexisting materials or of data that are se-

lected, coordinated, or arranged in such a way that the resulting work as a whole constitutes an original work of authorship." A "derivative work" is "a work based on one or more preexisting works." Examples of derivative works include translations, fictionalizations, abridgments, condensations, or "any other form in which a work may be recast, transformed, or adapted." Derivative works also include works "consisting of editorial revisions, annotations, or other modifications" if these changes, as a whole, represent an original work of authorship.

Preexisting Material (space 6a): For derivative works, complete this space and space 6b. In space 6a identify the preexisting work that has been recast, transformed, adapted, or updated. Example: "1978 Morgan Co. Sales Catalog." Do not complete space 6a for compilations.

Material Added to This Work (space 6b): Give a brief, general statement of the new material covered by the copyright claim for which registration is sought. **Derivative work** examples include: "Editorial revisions and additions to the Catalog"; "Translation"; "Additional material." If a periodical issue is a **compilation**, describe both the compilation itself and the material that has been compiled. Examples: "Compilation of previously published journal articles"; "Compilation of previously published data." An issue may be both a derivative work and a compilation, in which case a sample statement might be: "Compilation of [describe] and additional new material."

7 SPACE 7: Manufacturing Provisions

General Instructions: The copyright statute currently provides, as a general rule, that the copies of a published work "consisting preponderantly of nondramatic literary material in the English language" be manufactured in the United States or Canada in order to be lawfully imported and publicly distributed in the United States. If the work being registered is unpublished or not in English, leave this space blank. Complete this space if registration is sought for a published work "consisting preponderantly of nondramatic literary material that is in the English language." Identify those who manufactured the copies and where those manufacturing processes were performed. As an exception to the manufacturing provisions, the statute prescribes that, where manufacture has taken place outside the United States or Canada, a maximum of 2000 copies of the foreign edition may be imported into the United States without affecting the copyright owners' rights. For this purpose, the Copyright Office will issue an Import Statement upon request and payment of a fee of $3 at the time of registration or at any later time. For further information about import statements, write for Form IS.

8 SPACE 8: Reproduction for Use of Blind or Physically Handicapped Individuals

General Instructions: One of the major programs of the Library of Congress is to provide Braille editions and special recordings of works for the exclusive use of the blind and physically handicapped. In an effort to simplify and speed up the copyright licensing procedures that are a necessary part of this program, section 710 of the copyright statute provides for the establishment of a voluntary licensing system to be tied in with copyright registration. Copyright Office regulations provide that you may grant a license for such reproduction and distribution solely for the use of persons who are certified by competent authority as unable to read normal printed material as a result of physical limitations. The license is entirely voluntary, nonexclusive, and may be terminated upon 90 days notice.

How to Grant the License: If you wish to grant it, check one of the three boxes in space 8. Your check in one of these boxes, together with your signature in space 10, will mean that the Library of Congress can proceed to reproduce and distribute under the license without further paperwork. For further information, write for Circular R63.

9,10,11 SPACE 9, 10, 11: Fee, Correspondence, Certification, Return Address

Deposit Account: If you maintain a Deposit Account in the Copyright Office, identify it in space 9. Otherwise leave the space blank and send the fee of $10 with your application and deposit.

Correspondence (space 9): This space should contain the name, address, area code, and telephone number of the person to be consulted if correspondence about this application becomes necessary.

Certification (space 10): The application cannot be accepted unless it bears the date and the **handwritten signature** of the author or other copyright claimant, or of the owner of exclusive right(s), or of the duly authorized agent of the author, claimant, or owner of exclusive right(s).

Address for Return of Certificate (space 11): The address box must be completed legibly since the certificate will be returned in a window envelope.

DEFINITION

"A 'computer program' is a set of statements or instructions to be used directly or indirectly in a computer in order to bring about a certain result."

WHAT TO SEND

- A Completed Form TX
- A $10.00 Non-refundable Filing Fee Payable to the Register of Copyrights
- One Copy of Identifying Material (See Below)

EXTENT OF COPYRIGHT PROTECTION

Copyright protection extends to the literary or textual expression contained in the computer program. Copyright protection is not available for ideas, program logic, algorithms, systems, methods, concepts, or layouts.

DESCRIBING BASIS OF CLAIM ON FORM TX

- Space 2. In the "Author of" space identify the copyrightable authorship in the computer program for which registration is sought; for example, AUTHOR OF "Text of computer program," "Text of user's manual and computer program text," etc. (Do not include in the claim any reference to design, physical form, or hardware.)
- Space 6. Complete this space only if the computer program contains a substantial amount of previously published, registered, or public domain material (for example, subroutines, modules, or textual material).

DEPOSIT REQUIREMENTS

For published or unpublished computer programs, one copy of identifying portions of the program, (first 25 and last 25 pages), reproduced in a form visually perceptible without the aid of a machine or device, either on paper or in microform, together with the page or equivalent unit containing the copyright notice, if any.

For a program less than 50 pages in length, a visually perceptible copy of the entire program. For a revised version of a program which has been previously published, previously registered, or which is in the public domain, if the revisions occur throughout the entire program, the first 25 and last 25 pages. If the revisions are not contained in the first and last 25 pages, any 50 pages representative of the revised material in the new program, together with the page or equivalent unit containing the copyright notice for the revised version, if any.

The Copyright Office believes that the best representation of the authorship in a computer program is a listing of the program in source code.

Where the applicant is unable or unwilling to deposit a source code listing, registration will proceed under our RULE OF DOUBT policy upon receipt of written assurance from the applicant that the work as deposited in object code contains copyrightable authorship.

If a published user's manual (or other printed documentation) accompanies the computer program, deposit one copy of the user's manual along with one copy of the identifying portion of the program.

SPECIAL RELIEF AND TRADE SECRETS

When a computer program contains trade secrets or other confidential material that the applicant is unwilling to disclose by depositing the first and last 25 pages in source code, the Copyright Office is willing to consider special relief requests enabling the applicant to deposit less than or other than the usual 50 pages of source code. Special relief requests for the following three deposit options are presently being granted upon receipt of the applicant's written request to the Chief, Examining Division for special relief:

- first and last 25 pages of source code with some portions blocked out, provided that the blocked-out portions are proportionately less than the material still remaining;

- at least the first and last ten pages of source code alone, with no blocked-out portions; or

- first and last 25 pages of object code plus any ten or more consecutive pages of source code, with no blocked-out portions.

Exhibit 17-8

LOCATION OF COPYRIGHT NOTICE
Section 201.20(g), 37 C.F.R.

(g) WORKS REPRODUCED IN MACHINE-READABLE COPIES

For works reproduced in machine-readable copies (such as magnetic tapes or disks, punched cards, or the like), from which the work cannot ordinarily be visually perceived except with the aid of a machine or device,[1] each of the following constitute examples of acceptable methods of affixation and position of notice:

(1) A notice embodied in the copies in machine-readable form in such a manner that on visually perceptible printouts it appears either with or near the title, or at the end of the work;

(2) A notice that is displayed at the user's terminal at sign on;

(3) A notice that is continuously on terminal display; or

(4) A legible notice reproduced durably, so as to withstand normal use, on a gummed or other label securely affixed to the copies or to a box, reel, cartridge, cassette, or other container used as a permanent receptacle for the copies.

FORM OF COPYRIGHT NOTICE

Form of Notice for Visually Perceptible Copies

The notice for visually perceptible copies should contain all of the following three elements:

1. *The symbol* © (the letter C in a circle), or the word "Copyright," or the abbreviation "Copr."

2. *The year of first publication* of the work. In the case of compilations of derivative works incorporating previously published material, the year date of first publication of the compilation or derivative work is sufficient.

---

[1] Works published in a form requiring the use of a machine or device for purposes of optical enlargement (such as film, filmstrips, slide films, and works published in any variety of microform), and works published in visually perceptible form but used in connection with optical scanning devices, are not within this category.

3. *The name of the owner of copyright* in the work, or an abbreviation by which the name can be recognized, or a generally known alternative designation of the owner.
Example: © 1986 John Doe

FURTHER QUESTIONS:

If you have general information questions and wish to talk to an information specialist, call 202-479-0700.

TO ORDER FORMS:

Write to the Publications Section, LM-455, Copyright Office, Library of Congress, Washington, D.C. 20559 or call 202-287-9100, the Forms and Publications Hotline.

Please note that a copyright registration is effective on the date of receipt in the Copyright Office of all the required elements in acceptable form, regardless of the length of time it takes thereafter to process the application and mail the certificate of registration. The length of time required by the Copyright Office to process an application varies from time to time, depending on the amount of material received and the personnel available to handle it. It must also be kept in mind that it may take a number of days for mailed material to reach the Copyright Office and for the certificate of registration to reach the recipient after being mailed by the Copyright Office.

If you are filing an application for copyright registration in the Copyright Office, you will not receive an acknowledgement that your application has been received (the Office receives more than 500,000 applications annually), but you can expect:

- A letter or telephone call from a copyright examiner if further information is needed;
- A certificate of registration to indicate the work has been registered, or if the application cannot be accepted, a letter explaining why it has been rejected.

You may not receive either of these until 90 days have passed.

If you want to know when the Copyright Office received your material, you should send it via registered or certified mail and request a return receipt.

Copyright Office • Library of Congress • Washington, D.C. 20559

May 1987—6,000

☆U.S. GOVERNMENT PRINTING OFFICE: 1987: 181-532/40,017

GENERAL AND MECHANICAL

4,390,995
SHOCK DAMPING FACE GUARD STRAP FOR FOOTBALL HELMETS
Vernon R. Walck, 267 Bonita Dr., Bakersfield, Calif. 93305
Filed Mar. 3, 1982, Ser. No. 354,169
Int. Cl.³ A41D *13/00;* A42B *3/00*
U.S. Cl. 2—9   13 Claims

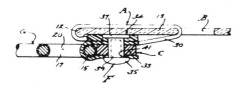

1. Shock damping anchor straps for a face guard mounted on a transverse horizontal axis to a brow portion of a protective helmet, the face guard having a mounting bar rotatably mounted to the helmet on said axis and extending rearward at opposite sides of the helmet, and the face guard having opposite side anchor bars depending from the mounting bar at the front edges of opposite side ear portions of the helmet, there being an ear hole through each side ear portion of the helmet, and each anchor strap including a flexible body with inner and outer loop portions continuing one into the other from one end provided with a hole therethrough and to a terminal end, the hole at said one end being engaged over a fastener means and the inner loop portion formed into an inner loop wrapped around the front edge of the ear portion and passing through the ear hole of the helmet and secured by a second hole therethrough engaged over the fastener means, and the outer loop portion formed into an outer loop wrapped over the anchor bar and the said terminal end secured by a third hole therethrough engaged over and held by said fastener means.

4,390,996
GARMENT
Stuart W. Read, 87 Malvern Rd., St. Johns, Worcester, England
Filed Aug. 17, 1981, Ser. No. 293,673
Claims priority, application United Kingdom, Sep. 2, 1980, 8028302
Int. Cl.³ A41B *1/12*
U.S. Cl. 2—70   10 Claims

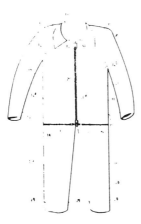

1. A garment comprises a jacket and a trouser part, the jacket comprising a body having a lower edge at or above crotch level, two arms extending from the body, the trouser part comprising two legs, part of the upper edge of each leg being permanently attached to the lower edge of the body and the remainder of the upper edge being releasably attached to the lower edge of the body by fastening means thereby to provide a one piece suit, the jacket and trouser part each having co-operable retaining means whereby, when the fastening means are released and the trouser part folded relative to the jacket, the trouser part may be retained between the upper and lower edges of the body by said retaining means, whereby the garment may be worn as a jacket only.

4,390,997
HEAT PROTECTION GARMENT
Claus-Dieter Hinz, Lübeck, and Adalbert Pasternack, Bad Schwartau, both of Fed. Rep. of Germany, assignors to Drägerwerk Aktiengesellschaft, Fed. Rep. of Germany
Filed Jan. 16, 1981, Ser. No. 225,656
Claims priority, application Fed. Rep. of Germany, Feb. 2, 1980, 3004593
Int. Cl.³ A41D *13/00*
U.S. Cl. 2—81   6 Claims

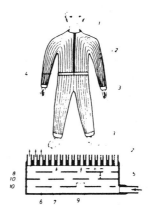

1. A heat protection garment comprising:
at least one manifold having opposite parallel end walls defining a mixing chamber;
at least one header having opposite parallel end walls defining a mixing chamber;
a plurality of coolant tubes connecting the manifold and header mixing chambers, the tubes connected to one end wall of each of the manifold and header;
at least one coolant supply conduit connected to the manifold mixing chamber at a location spaced from the coolant tubes connected thereto;
at least one coolant discharge conduit connected to the header mixing chamber at a location spaced from the coolant tubes connected thereto; and
a plurality of parallel rows of connecting pieces extending across the manifold and header mixing chambers respectively, between the conduits and the coolant tubes and parallel to the end walls of the manifold and header respectively;
the ratio, in each of the manifold and header of the number of coolant tubes to the number of parallel rows of connecting pieces to the number of coolant conduits being approximately equal to or smaller than 12:3:1; and
the ratio in each of the manifold and header of the spacing between the parallel rows of connecting pieces to the

Exhibit 17-9

4,392,005
TEMPERATURE SENSOR
Raymond F. Mohrman, St. Louis, Mo., assignor to Mon-a-therm, Inc., St. Louis, Mo.
Filed Nov. 2, 1981, Ser. No. 317,128
Int. Cl.³ H01L 35/06
U.S. Cl. 136—235
21 Claims

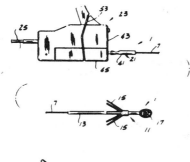

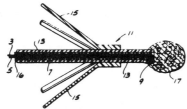

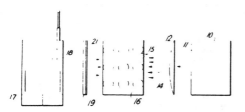

1. A temperature sensor comprising a pair of dissimilar metallic conductors electrically insulated one from the other along the lengths thereof but electrically connected at one of their ends to form a thermojunction, and a connector comprising an elongate backing strip of dielectric sheet material, the other ends of the conductors being positioned to extend generally transversely across one face of the strip and being spaced apart longitudinally of the strip, and facing strip means on the backing strip comprising a first facing strip of dielectric material on said one face of the backing strip overlying said other ends of the conductors, said first facing strip having openings therein exposing bare uninsulated portions of said other ends of the conductors to provide electrical contacts whereby on insertion of said connector into a mating connector said contacts are adapted to be engaged by corresponding contacts in the mating connector for making respective electrical connections.

4,392,006
SOLAR CELL ACTIVATION SYSTEM
Lawrence Apelian, 51 S. Coleman Rd., Centereach, N.Y. 11720
Filed Aug. 17, 1981, Ser. No. 293,280
Int. Cl.³ H01L 31/04
U.S. Cl. 136—246
8 Claims

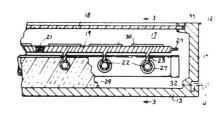

1. A solar cell activation system comprising:
a substantially flat board-like transparent member having a coating of a light emitting substance on one surface thereof to emit light rays therefrom,

a thin magnifying lens mounted adjacent the coated member to focus the light rays emitted from the coated member,
a substantially flat member having a plurality of solar cells mounted and interconnected thereon and positioned at a predetermined distance from the lens to receive the focused light rays therefrom for purposes of activation, and,
a one-sided mirror mounted adjacent the solar cells and on the side opposite the lens to reflect the focussed light passing through said cells back onto said cells and means coupled to the solar cells to receive the output therefrom.

4,392,007
SOLAR GENERATOR PROVIDING ELECTRICITY AND HEAT
Gerard Barkats, Mandelieu; Alain Girard, Cros de Cagnes; Jean Marchal, Peymeinade, and Charles Morel, Le Cannet, all of France, assignors to Societe Nationale Industrielle Aerospatiale, Paris, France
Filed Sep. 23, 1981, Ser. No. 304,853
Claims priority, application France, Oct. 9, 1980, 80 21595
Int. Cl.³ H01L 31/04; F24J 3/02
U.S. Cl. 136—248
7 Claims

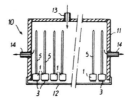

1. A solar energy collecting device comprising:
a plurality of photovoltaic cells;
a plurality of heat pipes;
said photovoltaic cells being carried by said heat pipes in heat transfer relationship therewith; and
a fluid-tight cooling chamber provided with a cold fluid inlet and hot fluid outlet and enclosing at least said plurality of heat pipes.

4,392,008
COMBINED ELECTRICAL AND THERMAL SOLAR COLLECTOR
Herbert M. Cullis, Silver Spring, and Reinhard Stamminger, Gaithersburg, both of Md., assignors to Monegon, Ltd., Gaithersburg, Md.
Filed Nov. 13, 1981, Ser. No. 320,946
Int. Cl.³ H01L 31/04; F24J 3/02
U.S. Cl. 136—248
9 Claims

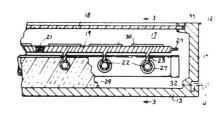

1. A solar panel assembly comprising support means defining an enclosure, flat solar collector plate means mounted in said enclosure, photovoltaic cell means including at least one thin semi-conductor wafer mounted on said plate means, flow tube means in the enclosure below said plate means, thin perpendicularly depending heat-conductive web means rigidly connecting said plate means to said flow tube means and being located

CHEMICAL

4,391,601
WRITING PARCHMENT AND METHODS FOR THE PRODUCTION THEREOF
Shmuel Y. Herman, 65 Hapisga St. Bayit Vegan, Jerusalem, Israel
Filed Dec. 7, 1981, Ser. No. 328,070
Claims priority, application Israel, Dec. 26, 1980, 61809
Int. Cl.³ C14C 1/00
U.S. Cl. 8—94.15   8 Claims

1. Fine writing parchment made from the skins of turkeys.

4,391,602
PROCESS FOR SMOOTHING AND DRYING WASHED SHAPED ARTICLES OF MIXED FABRIC
Otto Stichnoth, and Andreas Stichnoth, both of Schiefer Weg 21, 3400 Gottingen, Fed. Rep. of Germany
Filed Sep. 23, 1980, Ser. No. 190,078
Claims priority, application Fed. Rep. of Germany, Oct. 2, 1979, 2939870
Int. Cl.³ D06B 3/30
U.S. Cl. 8—149.1   20 Claims

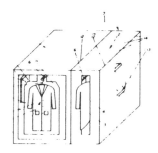

1. A process for smoothing shaped articles of mixed fabric having both synthetic and natural fibers, comprising the steps of:

(a) washing said articles at a first temperature;

(b) conveying said washed articles through a heating chamber until said articles are a temperature at least equal to said first temperature and substantially isothermal throughout;

wherein atmosphere within said heating chamber is maintained at a substantially uniform wet bulb temperature at least equal to said first temperature by introduction of steam and air therein;

(c) drying said heated washed articles by conveying said articles through a plurality serially disposed drying chamber sections and directing drying air at said articles within each of said drying chamber sections at sufficient velocity to agitate said articles and thereby tighten, smooth and dry said fabric by:

i. introducing a stream of drying air first into the drying chamber section lastly encountered by said articles upon conveying through said drying chamber sections and thereafter serially into said drying chamber sections in order reverse from that traversed by said articles during conveyance thereof through said drying chamber sections;

ii. heating said drying air intermediate each of said drying chamber sections of said plurality;

iii. introducing said stream of heated drying air leaving a drying chamber section which is first encountered by said articles during conveyance thereof through said serially disposed drying chamber sections into said heating chamber as high humidity heating air by discharging said stream of heated drying air through a steam environment into said heating chamber;

iv. discharging said high humidity heating air from said heating chamber

v. removing condensate from said high humidity heating air;

vi. cooling said high humidity heated thereby reducing relative humidity thereof to produce relatively dry cooler air;

vii. heating said relatively dry cooler air to produce heated relatively dry air for repeated serial passage through said drying chamber sections

wherein the steps of element c are performed repetitively and serially in the order recited.

4,391,603
HYDROXYL DERIVATIVES OF BENZALDEHYDE FOR COLORING KERATIN FIBRES IN THE ABSENCE OF OXIDIZING AGENT
Georges Rosenbaum, Asnieres; Jean F. Grollier, Paris, and Jean Cotteret, Franconville, all of France, assignors to L'Oreal, Paris, France
Filed Apr. 15, 1981, Ser. No. 254,514
Claims priority, application France, Apr. 17, 1980, 80 08645
Int. Cl.³ A61K 7/13
U.S. Cl. 8—424   17 Claims

1. Process for colouring keratin fibres in the absence of an oxidising agent, which comprises applying thereto at least one composition containing a cosmetically acceptable medium and a dyestuff corresponding to the formula:

$$(RO)_m \underset{\text{CHO}}{\underbrace{\bigcirc}} (OH)_n \qquad (I)$$

in which R denotes a linear or branched lower alkyl group which is optionally substituted by one or two hydroxyl groups, n is equal to 1, 2 or 3, m is equal to 0, 1 or 2 such that n+m is equal to 2 or 3, with the proviso that (i) if m is equal to 0 (and n is equal to 2 or 3), the OH groups occupy the following positions of the ring:

2	3	4	5	6
	OH	OH		
OH		OH		
	OH		OH	
OH	OH	OH		
OH	OH			OH
OH	OH		OH	
OH		OH		OH
	OH	OH	OH	
OH				OH

and (ii) if m and n both denote 1, the substituents occupy the following positions of the rings:

2	3	4	5	6
OH				OR
OR	OH			
	OH	OR		
	OH		OR	
OH			OR	
OH	OCH₂CH₂OH (3)			
OH			OCH₂CHCH₂ OHOH (5)	
OH	OC₂H₅			

or a bisulphite adduct thereof.

DECLARATION FOR PATENT APPLICATION

Docket No. _____

As a below named inventor, I hereby declare that:

My residence, post office address and citizenship are as stated below next to my name.

I believe I am the original, first and sole inventor (if only one name is listed below) or an original, first and joint inventor (if plural names are listed below) of the subject matter which is claimed and for which a patent is sought on the invention entitled
_____, the specification of which

(check one) ☐ is attached hereto.
         ☐ was filed on _____ as
         Application Serial No. _____
         and was amended on _____ (if applicable).

I hereby state that I have reviewed and understand the contents of the above identified specification, including the claims, as amended by any amendment referred to above.

I acknowledge the duty to disclose information which is material to the examination of this application in accordance with Title 37, Code of Federal Regulations, §1.56(a).

I hereby claim foreign priority benefits under Title 35, United States Code, §119 of any foreign application(s) for patent or inventor's certificate listed below and have also identified below any foreign application for patent or inventor's certificate having a filing date before that of the application on which priority is claimed:

Prior Foreign Application(s)   Priority Claimed

(Number)	(Country)	(Day/Month/Year Filed)	Yes	No
(Number)	(Country)	(Day/Month/Year Filed)	Yes	No
(Number)	(Country)	(Day/Month/Year Filed)	Yes	No

I hereby claim the benefit under Title 35, United States Code, §120 of any United States application(s) listed below and, insofar as the subject matter of each of the claims of this application is not disclosed in the prior United States application in the manner provided by the first paragraph of Title 35, United States Code, §112, I acknowledge the duty to disclose material information as defined in Title 37, Code of Federal Regulations, §1.56(a) which occurred between the filing date of the prior application and the national or PCT international filing date of this application:

(Application Serial No.)	(Filing Date)	(Status—patented, pending, abandoned)
(Application Serial No.)	(Filing Date)	(Status—patented, pending, abandoned)

I hereby appoint the following attorney(s) and/or agent(s) to prosecute this application and to transact all business in the Patent and Trademark Office connected therewith:

_____.

Address all telephone calls to _____ at telephone no. _____.
Address all correspondence to _____
_____
_____
_____.

I hereby declare that all statements made herein of my own knowledge are true and that all statements made on information and belief are believed to be true; and further that these statements were made with the knowledge that willful false statements and the like so made are punishable by fine or imprisonment, or both, under Section 1001 of Title 18 of the United States Code and that such willful false statements may jeopardize the validity of the application or any patent issued thereon.

Full name of sole or first inventor _____
Inventor's signature _____ Date _____
Residence _____ Citizenship _____
Post Office Address _____

Full name of second joint inventor, if any _____
Second Inventor's signature _____ Date _____
Residence _____ Citizenship _____
Post Office Address _____

(Supply similar information and signature for third and subsequent joint inventors.)

Form PTO-FB-A110 (8-83)

Exhibit 17-10

Applicant or Patentee: _____ Attorney's
Serial or Patent No.: _____ Docket No.: _____
Filed or Issued: _____
For: _____

VERIFIED STATEMENT (DECLARATION) CLAIMING SMALL ENTITY
STATUS (37 CFR 1.9 (f) and 1.27 (b)) — INDEPENDENT INVENTOR

As a below named inventor, I hereby declare that I qualify as an independent inventor as defined in 37 CFR 1.9 (c) for purposes of paying reduced fees under section 41 (a) and (b) of Title 35, United States Code, to the Patent and Trademark Office with regard to the invention entitled _____
described in

[ ] the specification filed herewith
[ ] application serial no. _____ , filed _____ .
[ ] patent no. _____ , issued _____ .

I have not assigned, granted, conveyed or licensed and am under no obligation under contract or law to assign, grant, convey or license, any rights in the invention to any person who could not be classified as an independent inventor under 37 CFR 1.9 (c) if that person had made the invention, or to any concern which would not qualify as a small business concern under 37 CFR 1.9 (d) or a nonprofit organization under 37 CFR 1.9 (e).

Each person, concern or organization to which I have assigned, granted, conveyed, or licensed or am under an obligation under contract or law to assign, grant, convey, or license any rights in the invention is listed below:

[ ] no such person, concern, or organization
[ ] persons, concerns or organizations listed below*

    *NOTE: Separate verified statements are required from each named person, concern or organization having rights to the invention averring to their status as small entities. (37 CFR 1.27)

FULL NAME _____
ADDRESS _____
    [ ] INDIVIDUAL   [ ] SMALL BUSINESS CONCERN   [ ] NONPROFIT ORGANIZATION

FULL NAME _____
ADDRESS _____
    [ ] INDIVIDUAL   [ ] SMALL BUSINESS CONCERN   [ ] NONPROFIT ORGANIZATION

FULL NAME _____
ADDRESS _____
    [ ] INDIVIDUAL   [ ] SMALL BUSINESS CONCERN   [ ] NONPROFIT ORGANIZATION

I acknowledge the duty to file, in this application or patent, notification of any change in status resulting in loss of entitlement to small entity status prior to paying, or at the time of paying, the earliest of the issue fee or any maintenance fee due after the date on which status as a small entity is no longer appropriate. (37 CFR 1.28 (b))

I hereby declare that all statements made herein of my own knowledge are true and that all statements made on information and belief are believed to be true; and further that these statements were made with the knowledge that willful false statements and the like so made are punishable by fine or imprisonment, or both, under section 1001 of Title 18 of the United States Code, and that such willful false statements may jeopardize the validity of the application, any patent issuing thereon, or any patent to which this verified statement is directed.

NAME OF INVENTOR	NAME OF INVENTOR	NAME OF INVENTOR
Signature of Inventor	Signature of Inventor	Signature of Inventor
Date	Date	Date

Form PTO-FB-A410 (8-83)

Exhibit 17-11

Chapter 18

SHOULD YOU HIRE INDEPENDENT CONTRACTORS OR EMPLOYEES?

Often when entrepreneurs begin a business they are surprised and angered when they discover the hidden costs associated with hiring employees. There are extra taxes as well as additional insurance premiums that must be paid. As entrepreneurs attempt to budget their costs and look for ways to reduce expenses, the question inevitably is asked, "Is the person who works for me an employee or independent contractor?" These two terms represent important legal distinctions. This chapter explains:

* Significant legal distinctions between independent contractor and employee
* Tax considerations
* Independent contractors and your business operation

SIGNIFICANT LEGAL DISTINCTIONS

There are various labor and tax-related issues which may arise while running your business that will determine whether the individual who works for you is an employee or an independent contractor. Many of these issues are directly related to the costs of doing business. Some of the more important issues are:

- Whether or not you are legally liable for a worker's actions
- Whether or not you are subject to minimum wage and overtime requirements
- Whether or not your workers have the right to form a union
- Whether or not your workers are classified as employees for the purpose of unemployment insurance
- Whether or not you must make certain deductions from wages for state and federal tax purposes
- Whether or not you must pay workers' compensation insurance

Liability for Workers' Actions

One area of law that affects all employers is called *agency*. An agency relationship occurs whenever two persons agree that one is to act on behalf of the other. The person authorized to act on behalf of the other is called the *agent*. The principal is the person who authorizes the agent to act on his or her behalf. As a rule, the principal will be held liable for the agent's actions if the agent acts within the scope of the agent's authority. For an agency relationship to exist, however, the principal must have the right to control the acts of the agent. It is irrelevant that the principal does not actually invoke the right to exercise control. All that is necessary is for the right to exist. The rule concerning independent contractors, however, is different. An independent contractor hired to accomplish some task is not an agent because he or she does not submit to the control of the person who has hired him or her. An independent contractor acts independently. As a result, liability is not attached to the hiring party. When an independent contractor, while performing his or her duties, injures another individual the person who hired him or her, as a rule, is not held liable.

Again, the issue of control is all important. Even though you enter into a contract that states the person you have employed is an independent contractor, you will still be held liable for his actions if you exercise supervision and control over that individual.

Minimum Wage and Overtime Payments

The requirements and protections of wage and hour laws both at the state and federal levels apply only when an employer–employee relationship exists. Without this relationship, an individual will not receive the governmental protection of minimum wage or overtime pay. The criteria used to determine the existence of such a relationship for the purpose of wage and hour laws differ, however, in certain instances from the standards used to determine whether or not an employer–employee relationship exists for the purpose of income tax, social security, unemployment insurance, and labor unions.

According to the Federal Labor Standards Act (FLSA), an employee is any individual who is "suffered or permitted to work" by an employer. The term "suffered or permitted to work" is not defined at either the state or federal level. As a result, federal governmental agencies examine the realities of the situation to determine whether or not an individual is actually an employee. The need for this type of determination often arises when an individual is characterized as one of the following:

- Independent contractor
- Employees of an independent contractor
- Volunteers
- Partners and shareholders
- Special-duty nurses and sitters
- Training programs for persons not on the employer's payroll
- Graduate students

In the case of an independent contractor, the courts examine the facts and circumstances of the relationship between the company and the individual doing the work. In certain instances, the courts have held that an individual may be considered an independent contractor for some purposes, such as minimum wage law, but not for others. Moreover, many companies mistakenly believe that when a contract is entered into between an individual and a company, which states that the relationship between the two is that of work-for-hire–independent contractor, it will automatically relieve the company of any liability. Although the intention of the parties is a relevant factor, the courts often look beyond the contract itself and examine the actual nature of the relationship.

Perhaps the single most important factor that the courts will examine is whether or not the company has the control or right to control the following: the individual, the work to be done, and the manner in which the work is to be performed. There are a number of other factors that the courts have used in determining the nature of the relationship. Although these factors individually would not be controlling, a combination of them in any given situation have been deemed sufficient to convince a court that an individual classified as an independent contractor was really an employee. Factors that are considered are as follows:

* The extent to which the individual's services are an integral part of the employer's business
* The amount of investment the individual has in the facilities and equipment
* The amount of initiative, judgment, or foresight required for the success of any supposed independent enterprise in open market competition
* The permanency of the relationship
* The nature and degree of control of the employer versus the nature of the independent business organization and operation
* The individual's opportunities for profit and loss
* Whether or not the individual is listed on the payroll and whether or not tax deductions are withheld
* Whether or not payments to the individual are charged to the labor and salary account, instead of the account to which attorneys' and accountants' fees and the like are charged
* Whether or not the employer has to approve of any employees of the alleged independent contractor.

Unionization and Unfair Labor Practices

The statutes that have the most impact on labor–managment relations are the National Labor Relations Act (NLRA) and the Labor–Management Relations Act (LMRA). Both the NLRA and LMRA, as a rule, will preempt any state labor laws if the employer is engaged in interstate or foreign commerce. The NLRA declares that the national labor policy is to encourage collective bargaining and to protect "the exercise by workers of full freedom of association, self organization, and designation of representatives of their own choosing, for the purpose of negotiating the terms and conditions of their employment or other mutual aid or protection."

The administrative body in charge of interpreting and enforcing the NLRA's provisions is the National Labor Relations Board (NLRB). The NLRB has the authority to remedy and prevent unfair labor practices. Unfair labor practices include both union and employer interference with employees' protected activities.

The principal unfair labor practices for employers are:

• Refusing to bargain with the employees' representative.
• Interfering with, restraining, or coercing employees in the exercise of their rights guaranteed by the NLRA.
• Discriminating among employers to encourage or discourage union membership.
• Discriminating against or discharging employees for testifying or bringing charges before the NLRB.

Not all individuals are covered by the NLRA provisions, however. As a result, these individuals are not entitled to the protections of the NLRA, which includes the right to join a union. The two largest groups that are excluded are: (a) supervisors and managerial employees, and (b) independent contractors.

Supervisors and managerial employees. A supervisor is defined as an individual who has the authority in the name of the employer to perform certain functions requiring the use of independent judgment, including hiring, transferring, suspending, laying-off, recalling, promoting, discharging, assigning, rewarding, or disciplining other employees or adjusting their grievances, or effectively recommending any of these actions. In particular, the NLRB looks to whether or not the individual had the authority to perform these functions as opposed to exercising them.

Independent contractors. The NLRA does not define the term independent contractor. Instead the courts and the NLRB have crafted a definition which has undergone some refinement as cases have been decided. At present, the approach used to define an independent contractor is called the *right-to-control test* as applied using the "totality of the circumstances." "Right to control" means whether or not the factors indicate that a company has the right not only to control the results of the work but also the methods by which those results are achieved. In addition, factors such as an individual's risk of loss, opportunity for profit, and degree of proprietary interest in the business are examined to determine whether or not an individual crosses the threshold from independent contractor to employee or vice versa.

Below is a list of factors taken from the Second Restatement of Agency 220, which affect contractor–employee status.

- Extent of employer's control over details of work
- Whether or not service provider is engaged in a distinct operation or business
- Whether or not the kind of work is usually done by a specialist without supervision
- The amount of skill required
- Whether or not the employer supplies instrumentalities, tools, and place of work
- Whether or not method of payment is based on time or on the job
- Nature of the work as compared to the employer's regular business
- Whether or not the individual is free to work for others
- Whether or not the individual is free to set the hours of work
- Whether or not there is a formal agreement between the individual and the employer

TAXES ARE ALSO A FACTOR

A worker should consider many factors before deciding if independent contractor (self-employed) status is preferable to employee status:

Record keeping and filing requirements for various types of taxes can be burdensome.

One of the most expensive considerations is social security tax versus self-employment tax. For 1989, the social security tax rate is 7.51 percent for both employers and employees and a taxable wage base of $48,000. Self-employment (SE) taxes are 13.02 percent (15.02 percent less 2.0 percent credit) on earnings through $48,000. No SE taxes are payable if annual net earnings are less than $400. See Exhibit 18-1, which shows Schedule SE (IRS Form 1040).

It is advantageous to deduct one's business expenses for adjusted gross income. A self-employed individual is required to file Schedule C of Form 1040.

A self-employed individual is required to make quarterly estimated tax payments which include both estimated federal income tax and self-employment tax as well as state income tax.

Determining Independent Contractors for Tax Purposes

Anyone who performs services is an employee if the employer controls what will be done and how it will be done. This is true even when the employer gives the employee freedom of action. What matters is that the employer has the legal right to control the method and result of the service. Two of the usual characteristics of an employer–employee relationship are:

* The employer has the right to discharge the employee.
* The employer supplies tools and a place to work.

People in business for themselves are not employees—that is, people in an independent trade in which they offer their services to the public. Independent contractors generally are listed in the yellow pages and are licensed. Examples include accountants, doctors, lawyers, veterinarians, construction contractors, and others in an independent trade in which they offer their services to the public.

If an employer–employee relationship exists, it does not matter what it is called: partner, agent, independent contractor. Also, it does not matter how payments are measured or paid, what they are called, or whether the employee works full or part time.

If an employer treats a worker other than as an employee, he or she will not be liable for employment taxes on payments to the worker. This relief is not available for any arrangement for services provided by certain technical personnel such as engineers, computer programmers, drafters, systems analysts, and designers. In Revenue Ruling 87–41, the IRS stated that when an agency hires employees, pays their wages, and can fire them and bar their working for clients for three months after an assignment, they are agency employees. The agency must withhold payroll taxes and pay FICA and FUTA.

There are twenty factors the IRS can look at to determine if a worker is an employee. Not all factors apply in every circumstance. If you want a decision about whether or not a worker is an employee, file IRS Form SS-8, "Information for Use in Determining Whether a Worker Is an Employee for Federal Employment Taxes and Income Tax Withholding." (See Exhibit 18-2.) Among these factors are training, supervision, setting hours of work, whose place of business, and salaried or hourly wages. These factors also affect salespeople, carpenters, truckers, nurses, and physicians for hospitals.

Tax Reports Necessary for Independent Contractors

At year end, various federal and state tax forms must be filed on behalf of independent contractors.

Generally, employers must issue IRS Form 1099 to independent contractors to report $600 or more for services performed for a trade or business. Exhibit 18-3 shows a completed IRS Form 1096 and Form 1099. Form 1099 must be mailed to independent contractors by February 1. Transmittal IRS Form 1096 is due to the IRS by February 28. Copies of IRS Form 1099 must accompany the transmittal. There are penalties for not filing the transmittal in a timely manner.

Warning to Employers

If the IRS determines that the independent contractors you hired are in fact employees, you as an employer will be subject to the payment of back payroll taxes plus penalties and interest. Also, there is a penalty for failure to file Form 1099.

THE INDEPENDENT CONTRACTOR AND YOUR OPERATION

Now that the legal and tax ramifications of the independent contractor have been explained, let's take a look at the operational or practical side of the matter. As a small business entrepreneur, you will be called upon to solve all types of problems: legal, accounting, tax, management, and operational. We have consistently recommended that you use professionals to tackle your legal, accounting, and tax issues. These professionals, lawyers and accountants, are in essence your independent contractors. Your use of professionals need not stop there. In all fields of endeavor, there are specialists, who generally refer to themselves as consultants, who can help you solve special nonrecurring business problems. These people are independent contractors.

Contractors provide many valuable services and benefits. Some of those benefits are:

- They provide a specific area and level of expertise which is not present on your staff.
- They are nonpermanent "employees" who are used on a temporary basis.
- Employers need not pay for fringe benefits.
- There is no training required.
- Contractors can be a potential employment source.
- Contractors can be severed without fear of wrongful termination actions.

On the other side of the coin, there are certain disadvantages when you use contractors:

- They are not always available when you need them.
- They are more expensive than full-time employees.
- They may "over" represent their skills.
- There is no consistent professional regulation of consultants.
- Consultants are not necessarily loyal to your firm.

Contractors fill an important niche in the business community. They provide the expertise and knowledge necessary to solve peculiar business problems. Contractors offer solutions to short-term business needs. Consider using the contractor when the problem requires expert ability or is short-term in nature.

Chapter 18 Exhibits

Exhibit 18.1   Explanation: Computation of Social Security
              Self-Employment Tax (Schedule SE IRS Form 1040)

Exhibit 18.2   Information for Use in Determination
              Whether a Worker Is an Employee for Federal
              Employment Taxes and Income Tax Withholding (IRS
              Form SS-8)

Exhibit 18.3   Completed with Explanation: Miscellaneous
              Income (Form 1099-Misc); Annual Summary and
              Transmittal of U.S. Information Returns (Form 1096)

SCHEDULE SE (FORM 1040) - Social Security Self-Employment Tax

This form has a short and long version. Use the short version unless you are one of the following taxpayer types:

a. Ministers not taxed on ministry earnings but who owe self-employment tax on other earnings.

b. Government employees subject only to the medicare part of social security tax.

c. Employees of a church or church-controlled organization that elected exemption from social security taxes.

d. Individuals with tip income subject to social security tax that was not reported to their employers.

e. Individuals who want to use one of the optional methods to figure self-employment tax.

As an example, refer to Schedule C (Form 1040) previously provided. Sue Z. Kew earned $105,426 in self-employment income.

For other examples of the construction of Schedule SE (Form 1040) Social Security Self-Employment Tax, refer to the Department of the Treasury, Internal Revenue Service Publication 334 (Rev. Nov. 88). Every line and every box of this form is explained in detail in this publication.

Exhibit 18-1

SCHEDULE SE	**Social Security Self-Employment Tax**	OMB No. 1545-0074
(Form 1040)	▶ See Instructions for Schedule SE (Form 1040).	19**88**
Department of the Treasury Internal Revenue Service (O)	▶ Attach to Form 1040.	Attachment Sequence No. **18**

Name of person with **self-employment** income (as shown on social security card)	Social security number of person with **self-employment** income ▶	

Who Must File Schedule SE

You must file Schedule SE if:

● Your net earnings from self-employment were $400 or more (or you had wages of $100 or more from an electing church or church organization); AND

● You did not have wages (subject to social security or railroad retirement tax) of $45,000 or more.

For more information about Schedule SE, see the Instructions.

Note: *Most taxpayers can now use the new short Schedule SE on this page. But, you may have to use the longer Schedule SE that is on the back.*

Who MUST Use the Long Schedule SE (Section B)

You must use Section B if ANY of the following applies:

● You choose the "optional method" to figure your self-employment tax. See Section B, Part II;

● You are a minister, member of a religious order, or Christian Science practitioner and received IRS approval (from **Form 4361**) not to be taxed on your earnings from these sources, but you owe self-employment tax on other earnings;

● You are an employee of a church or church organization that chose by law not to pay employer social security taxes;

● You have tip income that is subject to social security tax, but you did not report those tips to your employer; OR

● You are a government employee with wages subject ONLY to the 1.45% medicare part of the social security tax.

Section A—Short Schedule SE

(Read above to see if you must use the long Schedule SE on the back (Section B).)

1	Net farm profit or (loss) from Schedule F (Form 1040), line 39, and farm partnerships, Schedule K-1 (Form 1065), line 14a	**1**		
2	Net profit or (loss) from Schedule C (Form 1040), line 31, and Schedule K-1 (Form 1065), line 14a (other than farming). See the Instructions for other income to report	**2**		
3	Add lines 1 and 2. Enter the total. If the total is less than $400, **do not** file this schedule	**3**		
4	The largest amount of combined wages and self-employment earnings subject to social security or railroad retirement tax (tier 1) for 1988 is	**4**	$45,000	00
5	Total social security wages and tips from Forms W-2 and railroad retirement compensation (tier 1)	**5**		
6	Subtract line 5 from line 4. Enter the result. (If the result is zero or less, **do not** file this schedule.) . . .	**6**		
7	Enter the **smaller** of line 3 or line 6	**7**		
	If line 7 is $45,000, enter $5,859 on line 8. Otherwise, multiply line 7 by .1302 and enter the result on line 8		× .1302	
8	Self-employment tax. Enter this amount on Form 1040, line 48	**8**		

For Paperwork Reduction Act Notice, see Form 1040 Instructions.   Schedule SE (Form 1040) 1988

Name of person with **self-employment** income (as shown on social security card)	Social security number of person with **self-employment** income ▶	

Section B—Long Schedule SE

(Before completing, see if you can use the short Schedule SE on the other side (Section A).)

A If your only self-employment income was from earnings as a minister, member of a religious order, or Christian Science practitioner, AND you filed **Form 4361**, then DO NOT file Schedule SE. Instead, write "Exempt-Form 4361" on Form 1040, line 48. However, if you filed Form 4361, but have $400 or more of other earnings subject to self-employment tax, continue with Part I and check here.   ▶ ☐

B If your only earnings subject to self-employment tax are wages from an electing church or church-controlled organization that is exempt from employer social security taxes and you are not a minister or a member of a religious order, skip lines 1–3b. Enter zero on line 3c and go on to line 5a.

Part I   Figure Social Security Self-Employment Tax

1	Net farm profit or (loss) from Schedule F (Form 1040), line 39, and farm partnerships, Schedule K-1 (Form 1065), line 14a	**1**		
2	Net profit or (loss) from Schedule C (Form 1040), line 31, and Schedule K-1 (Form 1065), line 14a (other than farming). (See Instructions for other income to report.) Employees of an electing church or church-controlled organization **do not** enter your Form W-2 wages on line 2. See the Instructions . . .	**2**		
3a	Enter the amount from line 1 (**or,** if you elected the farm optional method, Part II, line 10)	**3a**		
b	Enter the amount from line 2 (**or,** if you elected the nonfarm optional method, Part II, line 12)	**3b**		
c	Add lines 3a and 3b. Enter the total. If the total is less than $400, **do not** file this schedule. *(Exception: If you are an employee of an electing church or church-controlled organization and the total of lines 3a and 3b is less than $400, enter zero and complete the rest of this schedule.)*	**3c**		
4	The largest amount of combined wages and self-employment earnings subject to social security or railroad retirement tax (tier 1) for 1988 is	**4**	$45,000	00
5a	Total social security wages and tips from Forms W-2 and railroad retirement compensation (tier 1). **Note:** *Government employees whose wages are subject only to the 1.45% medicare tax and employees of certain church or church-controlled organizations should **not** include those wages on this line. See Instructions* **5a**			
b	Unreported tips subject to social security tax from Form 4137, line 9, or to railroad retirement tax (tier 1) **5b**			
c	Add lines 5a and 5b. Enter the total	**5c**		
6a	Subtract line 5c from line 4. Enter the result. (If the result is zero or less, enter zero.)	**6a**		
b	Enter your medicare qualified government wages if you are required to use the worksheet in the Instructions . . . **6b**			
c	Enter your Form W-2 wages of $100 or more from an electing church or church-controlled organization . . . **6c**			
d	Add lines 3c and 6c. Enter the total	**6d**		
7	Enter the **smaller** of line 6a or line 6d	**7**		
	If line 7 is $45,000, enter $5,859 on line 8. Otherwise, multiply line 7 by .1302 and enter the result on line 8		×.1302	
8	Self-employment tax. Enter this amount on Form 1040, line 48	**8**		

Part II   Optional Method To Figure Net Earnings (See "Who Can File Schedule SE" in the Instructions.)

See Instructions for limitations. Generally, you may use this part **only** if:

A Your **gross** farm income[1] was not more than $2,400; **or**

B Your **gross** farm income[1] was more than $2,400 and your **net** farm profits[2] were **less** than $1,600; **or**

C Your **net** nonfarm profits[3] were less than $1,600 and also **less** than two-thirds (⅔) of your **gross** nonfarm income.[4]

Note: *If line 2 above is two-thirds (⅔) or more of your gross nonfarm income[4], or if line 2 is $1,600 or more, you may **not** use the optional method.*

[1]From Schedule F (Form 1040), line 12, and Schedule K-1 (Form 1065), line 14b.   [3]From Schedule C (Form 1040), line 31, and Schedule K-1 (Form 1065), line 14a.
[2]From Schedule F (Form 1040), line 39, and Schedule K-1 (Form 1065), line 14a.   [4]From Schedule C (Form 1040), line 5, and Schedule K-1 (Form 1065), line 14c.

9	Maximum income for optional methods	**9**	$1,600	00
10	**Farm Optional Method**—If you meet test A or B above, enter the **smaller** of: two-thirds (⅔) of gross farm income from Schedule F (Form 1040), line 12, and farm partnerships, Schedule K-1 (Form 1065), line 14b; **or** $1,600. Also enter this amount on line 3a above	**10**		
11	Subtract line 10 from line 9. Enter the result	**11**		
12	**Nonfarm Optional Method**—If you meet test C above, enter the **smallest** of: two-thirds (⅔) of gross nonfarm income from Schedule C (Form 1040), line 5, and Schedule K-1 (Form 1065), line 14c (other than farming); **or** $1,600; **or,** if you elected the farm optional method, the amount on line 11. Also enter this amount on line 3b above	**12**		

For Paperwork Reduction Act Notice, see Form 1040 Instructions.   ☆U.S. GPO: 1988—205-134   **Schedule SE (Form 1040) 1988**

Information for Use In Determining Whether a Worker Is an Employee for Federal Employment Taxes and Income Tax Withholding

OMB No. 1545-0004
Expires 12-31-90

Paperwork Reduction Act Notice.—We ask for this information to carry out the Internal Revenue laws of the United States. We need it to ensure that taxpayers are complying with these laws and to allow us to figure and collect the right amount of tax. If you want a determination on employment status, you are required to give us this information.

Instructions

This form should be completed carefully. If the firm is completing the form, it should be completed for **ONE** individual who is representative of the class of workers whose status is in question.

If a written determination is desired for more than one class of workers, a separate Form SS-8 should be completed for one worker from each class whose status is typical of that class. A written determination for any worker will be applicable to other workers of the same class if the facts are not materially different from those of the worker whose status was ruled upon.

Please return Form SS-8 to the Internal Revenue Service office that provided the form. If the Internal Revenue Service did not ask you to complete this form but you wish a determination on whether a worker is an employee, file Form SS-8 with your District Director.

Name of firm (or person) for whom the worker performed services	Name of worker
Address of firm (include street address, city, state, and ZIP code)	Address of worker (include street address, city, state, and ZIP code)

Trade name	Telephone number	Worker's social security number

Telephone number	Firm's taxpayer identification number	

Check type of firm

☐ **Individual**   ☐ **Partnership**   ☐ **Corporation**   ☐ **Other** (specify) ▶

This form is being completed by   ☐ FIRM   ☐ WORKER

If the form is being completed by the worker, do you object to disclosing your name or the information on this form to the firm? . . . . ☐ **Yes**   ☐ **No**

(If your answer is YES, we are not able to furnish you a determination on the basis of this form. You may write to your District Director for further information. **Do not complete the rest of the form, unless the IRS requests it.**)

All items must be answered or marked "Unknown" or "Not Applicable" (NA). **If you need more space, attach another sheet.** This form is designed to cover many work activities, so some of the questions may not pertain to you.

Total number of workers in this class (if more than one, please see item 19) ▶ _____

This information is about services performed by the worker from ▶ _____ to _____
(Month, day, year)   (Month, day, year)

What was the first date on which the worker performed services of any kind for the firm? ▶ _____
(Month, day, year)

Is the worker still performing services for the firm? . . . . ☐ **Yes**   ☐ **No**
If "No," what was the date of termination? ▶ _____
(Month, day, year)

In which IRS district are you located? _____

1a   Describe the firm's business _____
_____
_____

b   Describe the work done by the worker _____
_____
_____
_____

2a   If the work is done under a written agreement between the firm and the worker, attach a copy.
b   If the agreement is not in writing, describe the terms and conditions of the work arrangement _____
_____
_____
_____
_____

Form **SS-8** (Rev. 1-88)

Exhibit 18-2

  c If the actual working arrangement differs in any way from the agreement, explain the differences and why they occur ....

3a Is the worker given training by the firm?. . . . . □ **Yes** □ **No**

      If yes:

          What kind? ....

          How often? ....

  b Is the worker given instructions in the way the work is to be done? . . . . □ **Yes** □ **No**

      If yes, give specific examples. ....

  c Attach representative copies of any written instructions or procedures.

  d Does the firm have the right to change the methods used by the worker or direct that person on how to do the work? □ **Yes** □ **No**

      Explain your answer ....

----

  e Does the operation of the firm's business require that the worker be supervised or controlled in the performance of

      the service?. . . . . □ **Yes** □ **No**

      Explain your answer ....

4a The firm engages the worker:

      □ To perform and complete a particular job only.

      □ To work at a job for an indefinite period of time.

      □ Other (explain) ....

  b Is the worker required to follow a routine or a schedule established by the firm? . . . . □ **Yes** □ **No**

      If yes, what is the routine or schedule? ....

----

  c Does the worker report to the firm or its representative? . . . . □ **Yes** □ **No**

      If yes:

          How often? ....

          For what purpose? ....

          In what manner (in person, in writing, by telephone, etc.)? ....

          Attach copies of report forms used in reporting to the firm.

  d Does the worker furnish a time record to the firm? . . . . □ **Yes** □ **No**

      If yes, attach copies of time records.

5a State the kind and value of tools and equipment furnished by:

      The firm ....

      The worker ....

----

  b State the kind and value of supplies and materials furnished by:

      The firm ....

      The worker ....

----

  c What expenses are incurred by the worker in the performance of services for the firm?

----

  d Does the firm reimburse the worker for any expenses? . . . . □ **Yes** □ **No**

      If yes, specify the reimbursed expenses ....

6a Is it understood that the worker will perform the services personally? . . . . □ **Yes** □ **No**

  b Does the worker have helpers? . . . . □ **Yes** □ **No**

      If yes: Are the helpers hired by: □ Firm □ Worker

      If hired by the worker, is the firm's approval necessary? . . . . □ **Yes** □ **No**

      Who pays the helpers? □ Firm □ Worker

      Are social security taxes and Federal income tax withheld from the helpers' wages? . . . . □ **Yes** □ **No**

      If yes: Who reports and pays these taxes? □ Firm □ Worker

      Who reports the helpers' incomes to the Internal Revenue Service? □ Firm □ Worker

      If the worker pays the helpers, does the firm repay the worker? . . . . □ **Yes** □ **No**

      What services do the helpers perform?

7 At what location are the services performed? ☐ Firm's ☐ Worker's ☐ Other (specify) ....

8a Type of pay worker receives:

    ☐ Salary   ☐ Commission   ☐ Hourly wage   ☐ Piecework   ☐ Lump sum   ☐ Other (specify) ....

   b Does the firm guarantee a minimum amount of pay to the worker? . . . . ☐ Yes   ☐ No

   c Does the firm allow the worker a drawing account or advances against pay?. . . . . ☐ Yes   ☐ No

      If yes: Is the worker paid such advances on a regular basis?. ☐ Yes   ☐ No

        How does the worker repay such advances? ....

9a Is the worker eligible for a pension, bonuses, paid vacations, sick pay, etc.? . . . . ☐ Yes   ☐ No

      If yes specify ....

   b Does the firm carry workmen's compensation insurance on the worker? . . . . ☐ Yes   ☐ No

   c Does the firm deduct social security tax from amounts paid the worker? . . . . ☐ Yes   ☐ No

   d Does the firm deduct Federal income taxes from amounts paid the worker? . . . . ☐ Yes   ☐ No

   e How does the firm report the worker's income to the Internal Revenue Service?

      ☐ Form W-2   ☐ Form 1099   ☐ Does not report   ☐ Other (specify) ....

   f Does the firm bond the worker?. . . . . ☐ Yes   ☐ No

10a Approximately how many hours a day does the worker perform services for the firm? ....

   b Does the worker perform similar services for others? . . . . ☐ Yes   ☐ No   ☐ Unknown

      If yes: Are these services performed on a daily basis for other firms?   . . . . . . ☐ Yes   ☐ No   ☐ Unknown

      Percentage of time spent in performing these services for:

      This firm ....%   Other firms.........%   ☐ **Unknown**

      Does the firm have priority on the worker's time? . . . . ☐ Yes   ☐ No

      If no, explain ....

   c Is the worker prohibited from competing with the firm either while performing services or during any later period? . . ☐ Yes   ☐ No

11a Can the firm discharge the worker at any time without incurring a liability? . . . . ☐ Yes   ☐ No

      If no, explain ....

   b Can the worker terminate the services at any time without incurring a liability? . . . . ☐ Yes   ☐ No

      If no, explain ....

12a Does the worker perform services for the firm under:

      ☐ The firm's business name   ☐ The worker's own business name   ☐ Other (specify) ....

   b Does the worker advertise or maintain a business listing in the telephone directory, a trade journal, etc.? ☐ Yes   ☐ No ☐Unknown

      If yes, specify ....

   c Does the worker represent himself or herself to the public as being in business to perform the

      same or similar services?   ☐ Yes   ☐ No ☐Unknown

      If yes, how?..

   d Does the worker have his or her own shop or office? . . . . ☐ Yes   ☐ No ☐Unknown

      If yes, where?..

   e Does the firm represent the worker as an employee of the firm to its customers? . . . . ☐ Yes   ☐ No

      If no, how is the worker represented? ....

   f How did the firm learn of the worker's services? ....

13 Is a license necessary for the work? . . . . ☐ Yes   ☐ No ☐Unknown

      If yes, what kind of license is required? ....

      By whom is it issued? ....

      By whom is the license fee paid?...

14 Does the worker have a financial investment in a business related to the services performed? . . . . ☐ Yes   ☐ No ☐Unknown

      If yes, specify and give amounts of the investment ....

15 Can the worker incur a loss in the performance of the service for the firm? . . . . ☐ Yes   ☐ No

      If yes, how?..

16a Has any other government agency ruled on the status of the firm's workers? . . . . ☐ Yes   ☐ No

      If yes, attach a copy of the ruling.

   b Is the same issue being considered by any IRS office in connection with the audit of the worker's tax return or the

      firm's tax return, or has it recently been considered? . . . . ☐ Yes   ☐ No

      If yes, for which year(s)? ....

17 Does the worker assemble or process a product at home or away from the firm's place of business?. . . . . ☐ Yes   ☐ No

      If yes:

          Who furnishes materials or goods used by the worker?   ☐ Firm   ☐ Worker

          Is the worker furnished a pattern or given instructions to follow in making the product? . . . . ☐ Yes   ☐ No

          Is the worker required to return the finished product to the firm or to someone designated by the firm? . . . . . ☐ Yes   ☐ No

Answer items 18a through n if the worker is a salesman or provides a service directly to customers.

18a　Are leads to prospective customers furnished by the firm? . . . . ☐ **Yes** ☐ **No** ☐ **Does not apply**

 b　Is the worker required to pursue or report on leads? . . . . ☐ **Yes** ☐ **No** ☐ **Does not apply**

 c　Is the worker required to adhere to prices, terms, and conditions of sale established by the firm? . . . . ☐ **Yes** ☐ **No**

 d　Are orders submitted to and subject to approval by the firm? . . . . ☐ **Yes** ☐ **No**

 e　Is the worker expected to attend sales meetings? . . . . ☐ **Yes** ☐ **No**

　　If yes: Is the worker subject to any kind of penalty for failing to attend? . . . . ☐ **Yes** ☐ **No**

 f　Does the firm assign a specific territory to the worker? . . . . ☐ **Yes** ☐ **No** ☐ **Does not apply**

 g　Who does the customer pay? ☐ Firm ☐ Worker

　　If worker, does the worker remit the total amount to the firm? . . . . ☐ **Yes** ☐ **No**

 h　Does the worker sell a consumer product in a home or establishment other than a permanent retail establishment? . ☐ **Yes** ☐ **No**

 i　List the products and/or services distributed by the worker, such as meat, vegetables, fruit, bakery products, beverages (other than milk), or laundry or dry cleaning services. If more than one type of product and/or service is distributed, specify the principal one. _____

 j　Were the route or territory and a list of customers assigned to the worker by the firm or another person? . . . . . ☐ **Yes** ☐ **No**

　　If yes, please identify the person who made the assignment. _____

 k　Did the worker pay the firm or person for the privilege of serving customers on the route or in the territory? . . . . ☐ **Yes** ☐ **No**

　　If yes, how much did the worker pay (not including any amount paid for a truck or racks, etc.)? $ _____

　　What factors were considered in determining the value of the route or territory? _____

 l　How are new customers obtained by the worker? Explain fully, showing whether the new customers called the firm for service, were solicited by the worker, or both. _____

 m　Does the worker sell life insurance? . . . . ☐ **Yes** ☐ **No**

　　If yes:

　　　　Is the selling of life insurance or annuity contracts for the firm the worker's entire business activity? . . . . . ☐ **Yes** ☐ **No**

　　　　If no, state the extent of the worker's other business activities _____

　　　　Does the worker sell other types of insurance for the firm? . . . . ☐ **Yes** ☐ **No**

　　　　If yes, state the percentage of the worker's total working time spent in selling such other types of insurance _____ %

　　　　State if, at the time the contract was entered into between the firm and the worker, their intention was that the worker would be considered as selling life insurance for the firm (a) on a full-time basis, or (b) on a part-time basis. State the manner in which such intention was expressed. _____

 n　Is the worker a traveling salesperson or city salesperson? . . . . ☐ **Yes** ☐ **No**

　　If yes:

　　　　Specify from whom the worker principally solicits orders on behalf of the firm. _____

　　　　If the worker solicits orders from wholesalers, retailers, contractors, or operators of hotels, restaurants, or other similar establishments, specify the percentage of the worker's time spent in such solicitation. _____ %

　　　　Is the merchandise purchased by the customers for resale, or is it purchased for use in their business operations? If used by the customers in their business operations, describe the merchandise and state whether it is equipment that is installed on their premises or is a consumable supply. _____

19　Attach the names and addresses of the total number of workers in this class from page 1, or the names and addresses of 10 such workers if there are more than 10.

20　Attach a detailed explanation for any other reason why you believe the worker is an independent contractor or is an employee of the firm.

IMPORTANT INFORMATION NEEDED TO PROCESS YOUR REQUEST

Under section 6110 of the Internal Revenue Code, the text and related background file documents of any ruling, determination letter, or technical advice memorandum will be open to public inspection. This section provides that before the text and background file documents are made public, identifying and certain other information must be deleted.

Are the names, addresses, and taxpayer identifying numbers the only items you want deleted? . . . . ☐ **Yes** ☐ **No**

If you checked No and believe additional deletions should be made, we cannot process your request unless you submit a copy of this form and copies of all supporting documents indicating, in brackets, those parts you believe should be deleted in accordance with section 6110(c) of the Code. Attach a separate statement indicating which specific exemption provided by section 6110(c) applies to each bracketed part.

Under penalties of perjury, I declare that I have examined this request, including accompanying documents, and to the best of my knowledge and belief, the facts presented are true, correct, and complete.

Signature ▶ _____　　　Title ▶ _____　　　Date ▶ _____

If this form is used by the firm in requesting a written determination, the form should be signed by an officer or member of the firm.
If this form is used by the worker in requesting a written determination, the form should be signed by the worker. If the worker wants a written determination with respect to services performed for two or more firms, a separate form should be furnished for each firm.
Additional copies of this form may be obtained from any Internal Revenue Service office.

MISCELLANEOUS INCOME (FORM 1099-MISC); ANNUAL SUMMARY AND
TRANSMITTAL OF U.S. INFORMATION RETURNS (FORM 1096)

EXAMPLE:

During tax season, Harry hired Ni U Pi as an independent
contractor and paid him $2,000. Since the amount paid Mr. Pi was
over $600, Harry is required to prepare IRS Form 1099-MISC and
related transmittal IRS Form 1096.

On the left side of IRS Form 1099-MISC, Harry enters required
information for the payer and for the recipient. On the right
side, Harry enters $2,000 in box 7, nonemployee compensation.
Since Harry hired only one independent contractor, he completes
only the 1099-MISC, at the top of the page. The two additional
forms on the page are marked void.

IRS Form 1099-MISC is really a packet of three forms, Copy A,
Copy B, and Copy C. The entire page of Copy A is mailed to the
IRS along with the transmittal IRS Form 1096. Copy B is given the
recipient, and Copy C is kept by Harry. IRS Forms 1096 and 1099-
MISC are mailed to the District office of the IRS. For Harry, it
is Ogden, Utah.

Harry will receive a peel-off label from the IRS to place on
Form 1096. This label identifies the filer and filer's address.
Harry will place the label on IRS Form 1096. Next, he enters his
EIN in box 1. The EIN was assigned to Harry as a result of filing
IRS Form SS-4, "Application for Employer Identification Number."
The total number of completed documents is entered in box 3 and
the relevant information entered in boxes 4 and 5. Harry checks
the box 1099-MISC to indicate the type of forms being transmitted.

After reviewing the form for completeness, Harry is ready to
sign, date, and enter his title as "owner."

Additional information may be obtained by requesting IRS
Publication 916, "Information Returns."

Exhibit 18-3

9595 ☐ VOID ☐ CORRECTED For Official Use Only

Type or machine print PAYER'S name street address, city, state, and ZIP code	1 Rents	OMB No. 1545-0115	**Miscellaneous Income**
HARRY P. KAYHILL, CPA 1 KESINGTON RD. SACRAMENTO, CA 95691	$	19**88**	
	2 Royalties $	Statement for Recipients of	

PAYER'S Federal identification number 33-0177583	RECIPIENT'S identification number 987-65-4321	3 Prizes and awards $	4 Federal income tax withheld $	**Copy A For Internal**
Type or machine print RECIPIENT'S name (first, middle, last) Ni U Pi	5 Fishing boat proceeds $	6 Medical and health care payments $	**Revenue Service Center**
	7 Nonemployee compensation $ 2,000	8 Substitute payments in lieu of dividends or interest $	For Paperwork Reduction Act Notice and instructions for completing this form, see Instructions for Forms 1099, 1098, 5498, 1096, and W-2G.
Street address 678 HOME AVE		
City, state, and ZIP code SAN JOSE, CA 95916	9 Payer made direct sales of $5,000 or more of consumer products to a buyer (recipient) for resale . . . . ▶ ☐
Account number (optional)	10 The amount in Box 7 is crop insurance proceeds . . ▶ ☐

Form **1099-MISC**   Do NOT Cut or Separate Forms on This Page   Department of the Treasury - Internal Revenue Service

---

9595 ☒ VOID ☐ CORRECTED For Official Use Only

Type or machine print PAYER'S name street address, city, state, and ZIP code	1 Rents	OMB No. 1545-0115	**Miscellaneous Income**
	$	19**88**	
	2 Royalties $	Statement for Recipients of	

PAYER'S Federal identification number	RECIPIENT'S identification number	3 Prizes and awards $	4 Federal income tax withheld $	**Copy A For Internal**
Type or machine print RECIPIENT'S name (first, middle, last)	5 Fishing boat proceeds $	6 Medical and health care payments $	**Revenue Service Center**
	7 Nonemployee compensation	8 Substitute payments in lieu of dividends or interest	For Paperwork Reduction Act Notice and instructions for completing this form, see Instructions for Forms 1099, 1098, 5498, 1096, and W-2G.
Street address	$	$
City, state, and ZIP code	9 Payer made direct sales of $5,000 or more of consumer products to a buyer (recipient) for resale . . . . ▶ ☐
Account number (optional)	10 The amount in Box 7 is crop insurance proceeds . . ▶ ☐

Form **1099-MISC**   Do NOT Cut or Separate Forms on This Page   Department of the Treasury - Internal Revenue Service

---

9595 ☒ VOID ☐ CORRECTED For Official Use Only

Type or machine print PAYER'S name street address, city, state, and ZIP code	1 Rents	OMB No. 1545-0115	**Miscellaneous Income**
	$	19**88**	
	2 Royalties $	Statement for Recipients of	

PAYER'S Federal identification number	RECIPIENT'S identification number	3 Prizes and awards $	4 Federal income tax withheld $	**Copy A For Internal**
Type or machine print RECIPIENT'S name (first, middle, last)	5 Fishing boat proceeds $	6 Medical and health care payments $	**Revenue Service Center**
	7 Nonemployee compensation	8 Substitute payments in lieu of dividends or interest	For Paperwork Reduction Act Notice and instructions for completing this form, see Instructions for Forms 1099, 1098, 5498, 1096, and W-2G.
Street address	$	$
City, state, and ZIP code	9 Payer made direct sales of $5,000 or more of consumer products to a buyer (recipient) for resale . . . . ▶ ☐
Account number (optional)	10 The amount in Box 7 is crop insurance proceeds . . ▶ ☐

Form **1099-MISC**   Department of the Treasury - Internal Revenue Service

DO NOT STAPLE   6969   ☐ CORRECTED

| Form **1096**
Department of the Treasury
Internal Revenue Service | **Annual Summary and Transmittal of
U.S. Information Returns** | OMB No. 1545-0108
19**88** |

⌐ Type or machine print FILER'S name (or attach label)

Street address   **PLACE LABEL HERE**

City, state, and ZIP code
⌐

Paperwork Reduction Act Notice
We ask for this information to carry out the Internal Revenue laws of the United States. We need it to ensure that taxpayers are complying with these laws and to allow us to figure and collect the right amount of tax. You are required to give us this information.

If you are not using a preprinted label, enter in Box 1 or 2 below the identification number you used as the filer on the information returns being transmitted. Do not fill in both Boxes 1 and 2.

For Official Use Only

| 1 Employer identification number
33-0177583 | 2 Social security number | 3 Total number of documents
1 | 4 Federal income tax withheld
$ 0 | 5 Total amount reported with this Form 1096
$ 2,000 |

Check only one box below to indicate the type of forms being transmitted.

☐	☐	☐	☐	☐	☐	☐	☒	☐	☐	☐	☐	☐
W-2G 32	1098 81	1099-A 80	1099-B 79	1099-DIV 91	1099-G 86	1099-INT 92	1099-MISC 95	1099-OID 96	1099-PATR 97	1099-R 98	1099-S 75	5498 28

Under penalties of perjury, I declare that I have examined this return and accompanying documents and, to the best of my knowledge and belief, they are true, correct, and complete. In the case of documents without recipients' identification numbers, I have complied with the requirements of the law in attempting to secure such numbers from the recipients.

Signature ▶ *Henry P. Kayhuff*   Title ▶ *OWNER*   Date ▶ *1-28-90*

Please return this entire page to the Internal Revenue Service. Photocopies are NOT acceptable.

Instructions

Change You Should Note.—Form 1096 is now used to transmit new **Form 1099-S,** Statement for Recipients of Proceeds From Real Estate Transactions.

Purpose of Form.—Use this form to transmit Forms W-2G, 1098, 1099, and 5498 to the Internal Revenue Service.

Completing Form 1096.—If you have received a preprinted label from IRS, place it in the name and address area of the form using the brackets as indicators. Make any necessary corrections to your name and address on the label. However, do not use the label if the taxpayer identification number (TIN) shown is incorrect. If you are not using a preprinted label, enter the filer's name, address, and TIN in the spaces provided on the form. A filer includes a payer, a recipient of mortgage interest payments, a broker, a barter exchange, a person reporting real estate transactions, a trustee or issuer of an individual retirement arrangement (including an IRA or SEP), and a lender who acquires an interest in secured property or who has reason to know that the property has been abandoned. Individuals not in a trade or business should enter their social security number in Box 2; sole proprietors and all others should enter their employer identification number in Box 1. However, sole proprietors who are not required to have an employer identification number should enter their social security number in Box 2.

Group the forms by form number and submit each group with a separate Form 1096. For example, if you must file both Forms 1099-DIV and Forms 1099-INT, complete one Form 1096 to transmit your Forms 1099-DIV and another Form 1096 to transmit your Forms 1099-INT.

In Box 3, enter the number of forms you are transmitting with this Form 1096. Do not include blank or voided forms in your total. Enter the number of correctly completed forms, not the number of pages, being transmitted. For example, if you send one page of three-to-a-page Forms 5498 with a Form 1096 and you have correctly completed two Forms 5498 on that page, enter 2 in Box 3 of Form 1096. Check the appropriate box to indicate the type of form you are transmitting.

No entry is required in Box 5 if you are filing Form 1099-A or 1099-G. For all other forms, enter in Box 5 of Form 1096 the total of the amounts from the specific boxes of the forms listed below:

Form W-2G	Box 1
Form 1098	Box 1
Form 1099-B	Boxes 2, 3, and 6
Form 1099-DIV	Boxes 1, 8, and 9
Form 1099-INT	Boxes 1 and 3
Form 1099-MISC	Boxes 1, 2, 3, 5, 6, 7, and 8
Form 1099-OID	Boxes 1 and 2
Form 1099-PATR	Boxes 1, 2, 3, and 5
Form 1099-R	Boxes 1 and 8
Form 1099-S	Box 2
Form 5498	Boxes 1 and 2

If you are filing a Form 1096 for corrected information returns, enter an "X" in the CORRECTED box at the top of this form.

For more information about filing, see the separate Instructions for Forms 1099, 1098, 5498, 1096, and W-2G.

Form **1096** (1988)

Chapter 19

RESEARCH AND DEVELOPMENT PARTNERSHIPS

The use of limited partnerships, known as *research and development partnerships,* has become a common method of raising funds for many highly technical projects. Although this method of financing is relatively new, it has substantially impacted on research and development in the United States. This chapter explains:

* Origin of research and development partnership
* The most common types of research and development partnerships
* Advantages and disadvantages of using research and development partnerships
* Securities laws and disclosure
* Tax aspects to consider

ORIGIN OF THE RESEARCH AND DEVELOPMENT PARTNERSHIP

Research and development partnership (R & D partnership) is a limited partnership that is used as a vehicle for financing the development of new products and new technologies. This method of attracting funds is gaining popularity as ever increasing numbers of entrepreneurs look beyond traditional capital sources for funding of their projects.

R & D Partnerships, as they now exist, trace their origins to the landmark U.S. Supreme Court decision in 1974, *Snow* v. *Commissioner* 416 U.S. 500 (1974). In that case, the IRS attempted to disallow deductions taken by an R & D partnership under Internal Revenue Code Section 174 because it was not engaged in a "trade or business." The IRS reasoned that only a trade or business should be allowed to take advantage of the rule that allowed a taxpayer the option to either capitalize research and development expenditures or expense them as they were incurred or paid.

The taxpayer, Snow, was a R & D partnership but its "product" was under development and had not been successfully manufactured or sold. The IRS took the position that Snow was not in a trade or business and therefore could not elect to deduct research and development expenses as they occurred. The U.S.

Tax Court sided with the IRS. Snow appealed the case to the U.S. Supreme Court. The Supreme Court reversed the tax court's decision and allowed the research and development deduction and stated that Internal Revenue Code section 174 should not be limited to established businesses. Shortly afterwards, thousands of R & D partnerships emerged. Many of them were private placements but there have been numerous public offerings that have raised millions of dollars.

In 1986, R&D Partnerships went through a dramatic change as a result of the Tax Reform Act of 1986. For the individual investor, research and development expenditures now constitute a passive loss, which may be offset only against passive income. Moreover, in determining the alternative minimum tax, only 10 percent of the passive loss can be deducted.

THE MOST COMMON TYPES OF R & D PARTNERSHIPS

Most R & D partnerships fall within two classes: royalty and equity. In both instances, the partnership is limited in which the general partner, for a fee and/or a share of the profits, manages the partnership and accepts all operational risks. Furthermore, the general partner, in most cases, contracts out the actual research and development work through an R & D agreement to a third party, which either is a non profit research institute or a for-profit company that is seeking funds for its projects.

Royalty R & D Partnerships

This arrangement is used by start-up companies that wish to develop a high risk product, process, or technology. The usual course of events is as follows: A company wants to develop a product. It approaches an R & D partnership for funds. An agreement is struck in which the R & D partnership pays a sponsor fee for the research and development, and the resultant product is owned by the R & D partnership. Usually as part of the agreement, the partnership will grant the company a license to manufacture and sell the product in return for royalties based on sales.

Equity R & D Partnerships

This arrangement is also used by start-ups, especially inventors. It follows a typical pattern: Inventor has an idea and transfers his or her intellectual property to the general partnership, which is a corporation, in return for stock in the general partner. The general partner then transfers the property interest to the R & D partnership. The R & D partnership is an active business that actually conducts the research and development. Upon successful completion of the research and development, the general partner and limited partners in the R & D partnership transfer their partnership interests to a newly created corporation in exchange for stock of the new corporation. The transaction is a tax free exchange pursuant to Internal Revenue Code section 351. Each limited partner usually receives convertible preferred stock, while the general partner receives common stock.

ADVANTAGES AND DISADVANTAGES OF USING AN R & D PARTNERSHIP

Retention of Control

The R & D partnership is a limited partnership, and as such, the limited partners are restricted in their input into the decision-making process. If the state in which the R & D partnership has been formed adheres to the Uniform Limited Partnership Act or Revised Uniform Limited Partnership Act (which has been adopted by most states) then the limited partners are not permitted to participate in the management of the partnership. As a result, the general partner, which is usually the sponsoring company, retains control over the research and development activities. Another aspect of retention and control is that the R & D partnership by its very nature does not issue stock or borrow funds to raise its funds. Therefore, equity of the sponsoring company is not diluted because no shares of stock are ever issued, and creditors' demands and restrictions, as well as interest payments, are not a factor to contend with because no money is borrowed.

Tax Treatment Is an Incentive for Some

Passive losses generated in an R & D partnership flow through to the limited partners. Although the Tax Reform Act of 1986 limits passive loss offsets to passive income, the losses generated in the early years of the R & D partnership can be used to shelter income in the later years as the partnership becomes successful. Moreover, any passive loss that results from the R & D partnership can be applied by the limited partner to other passive income. An additional factor to consider is that many limited partners that are C corporations, which are not classified as personal service corporations, are not subject to the one-tenth rule in computing their alternative minimum tax. As a result, passive losses from R & D expenditures, which are absorbed by these corporations are fully deductible despite the alternative minimum tax computation.

Shifting the Risk

Whenever a start-up business or an established firm develops a new product, especially one that is technologically advanced, there is the ever-present risk of failure. For some businesses, the risk of product failure may be so high that it is better to shift the risk to investors. Thus, by starting an R & D partnership, there is a trade-off: the business is able to raise funds for the development of a new product without jeopardizing its own resources, although it will have to accord preferential treatment regardless if the product is successful, and the limited partners in exchange for tax benefits and the preferential right to royalty income underwrite much of the risk associated with the product from conception to production.

Permits "Off Balance Sheet" Financing

Using an R & D partnership to raise funds to develop a new product allows a business to avoid having to borrow money. Any type of debt financing will immediately appear on the balance sheet as a liability. Moreover, the interest payments on the debt as well as the immediate expensing of R & D expenditures under Internal Revenue Code section 174, could severely depress cash flow and net income, respectively. By establishing an R & D partnership, the sponsoring company can raise the necessary funds and develop its product without having to borrow funds or issue stock.

Royalty Payments Are Burdensome

In a typical R & D partnership, the limited partners are paid a percentage based on gross sales—not profit. As a consequence, if a company seeks a second round of funding for further development or marketing of the product, potential traditional investors may be turned off because the product is burdened with royalty obligations which are independent of profit performance.

Complexity of Formation

R & D partnerships are expensive to form because they are so complex. Legal, tax, and accounting considerations are complicated and need careful planning. The professional fees associated with formation are very high.

SECURITIES LAWS AND DISCLOSURES

Soliciting investors for an R & D partnership will be subject to both state and federal securities laws. Limited partners, are by definition, passive investors, much like shareholders, with little or no say in how the business enterprise will operate. Thus, the offering of a limited partnership interests are classified as securities within the meaning of the Securities Act of 1933, and as such, are subject to the scrutiny of state and federal regulations.

To offer a limited partnership interest, it is necessary for the offering to be registered or exempt from the registration process. For a public offering, the registration process, at the very least, entails the completion of federal Form S-1, or if the offering does not exceed $7.5 million, Form S-18. These two forms are designed to ensure that all material facts concerning the partnership are disclosed to the investing public. If the registration process is ignored, the limited partnership along with those individuals who are involved with the offering may be subject to civil and criminal penalties as well as actions for rescission and fraud.

Many limited partnerships are not registered, however, because they are small private offerings which are exempt from registration. There are three categories of exemptions: Regulation D, Intrastate Offering Exemption (Rule 147), and Statutory Private Offering Exemption. You will need to consult with your attorney for a thorough understanding of the requirements of each exemption.

TAX ASPECTS

Research expenditures may be amortized or deducted as a business expense. These costs may be treated as deferred expenses and amortized in equal amounts over a period of not less than sixty months or deducted currently as business expenses. These costs exclude expenditures for land, oil or gas exploration, or for depreciable property used in experimental work.

The amortization deduction is an election that applies to costs, which are:

- Paid or incurred in connection with a trade or business
- Not currently deducted
- Chargeable to a capital account

If the costs have no determinable useful life, the 60-month amortization may be elected. If they have a determinable useful life, they must be capitalized and depreciated over their useful lives. For example, expenses for investigating and acquiring a license must be capitalized and depreciated over the life of the license.

The amortization period should be selected at the time the election to amortize is made. A different amortization period may be elected for two or more separate projects. The amortization period begins with the month in which benefits from the costs are first realized.

Research expenditures include those expenses incurred in relation to a trade or business that are research and development costs in the experimental or laboratory sense. Examples include:

* Costs incidental to the development of an experimental or pilot model, a plant process, a product, a formula, or an invention.
* The improvement of already existing property of the types mentioned above.

Nonqualifying costs include costs incurred in the ordinary testing or inspection of materials or products for quality control or costs for efficiency surveys, management studies, consumer surveys, advertising, or promotions.

If you decide to deduct research and development expenditures now, simply claim them as an expense deduction on your income tax return for the year in which they are first incurred. If a choice is to be made after the first year, permission must be obtained from the IRS. Your request must be in writing and addressed to:

Commissioner of Internal Revenue

Attention: CC:C:C

Washington, DC 20224

Your request must also include the following information:

• Your name and address
• The first tax year for which the request is made
• A description of the project

The request must be signed and filed not later than the last day of the first tax year for which the change is requested.

Note that research and development expenditures are a tax preference item for noncorporate taxpayers, S corporations, and personal holding companies. However, if individual taxpayers elect to capitalize such costs and amortize them over a ten-year period, such costs are not treated as an alternative minimum tax preference item by individuals.

No matter how research and development expenditures are treated, some or all may qualify for a tax credit.

In February 1989, Congress extended the research tax credit for eligible expenses paid or incurred through December 31, 1989. The law also reduced the R & D credit to 20 percent of the excess of qualified research expenses over average research expenses in the base period. The 1986 TRA defines the base period as the three-tax-year period ending with the tax year immediately preceding the first tax year of the taxpayer beginning after December 31, 1983.

To be eligible for the credit, research expenses: (1) must qualify for expensing or amortization under section 174 of the Internal Revenue Code, (2) be conducted in the United States, (3) be paid by the taxpayer (not funded by government grant), (4) be research and development in the experimental or laboratory sense, and (5) pass a new three-part test (see your accountant for an explanation of the three-part test requirements and how they are to be applied).

There are special rules for internal-use computer software. The software must be used in qualified research (other than the development of the software itself) or in a production process that involves a credit-eligible component. Treasury regulations also prescribe that internal-use software must: (1) be innovative, (2) involve significant economic risk, and (3) not be commercially available elsewhere.

Research expenses related to any of the following do not qualify for the credit:

- Style, taste, cosmetic, or seasonal design factors
- Social sciences, arts, or humanities
- Efficiency surveys, management studies, market research, routine data collection, and routine quality control testing or inspection
- Expenses incurred after commercial production has begun; costs of ascertaining the existence, location, extent, or quality of any ore or mineral deposit (including oil and gas)
- Development of any plant process, machinery, or technique for the commercial production of a business component, unless the process is technologically new or improved
- Adoption of a business component to suit a particular customer's needs
- Partial or complete reproduction of an existing business component from plans, specifications, a physical examination, or publicly available information

Note: Some expenses listed above may qualify for expensing or 60-month amortization even though they are not eligible for the credit. See your accountant for details.

For tax years beginning after 1986, the TRA introduced a new tax credit equal to 20 percent of all basic research expenses in excess of a special base amount. The new credit is available to any C corporation. It is not available to S corporations. Basic research means any original investigation for the advancement of scientific knowledge not having a specific commercial objective. Research does not have to be conducted in the same field as the taxpayer's business. The expenses are not deductible until actually paid in cash under a written agreement between the taxpayer and qualifying organization, such as most colleges, universities, tax-exempt scientific research organizations, and certain tax-exempt grant organizations. See your accountant for steps in computing the 20 percent credit.

Note: Basic research expenses eligible for the new 20 percent credit are not eligible for the regular 20 percent credit. Moreover, there are credit limitations which include the following:

- Credits can offset only 75 percent of tax liability over $25,000.
- Research credits for sole proprietors, partners, beneficiaries of an estate or trust, and shareholders of S corporations may offset only the tax attributable to the taxpayer's interest in the trade or business that generated the credit.
- Any unused credits may be carried back three years and forward fifteen years.

File IRS Form 6765, Credit for Increasing Research Activities, with your tax return to claim the credit. For an example of this form, see Exhibit 19-1. If you have other business credits in addition to the research credit, you also must file IRS Form 3800, General Business Credit. See Exhibit 19-2 for an example of this form. For additional information on the research credit see IRS Publication 906, Jobs and Research Credits.

Chapter 19 Exhibits

Exhibit 19.1 Credit for Increasing Research Activities
(IRS Form 6765)

Exhibit 16.2 General Business Credit (IRS Form 3800)

Form **6765**	**Credit for Increasing Research Activities**	OMB No. 1545-0619
Department of the Treasury Internal Revenue Service	(or for claiming the orphan drug credit) ▶ **Attach to your tax return**	19**88** Attachment Sequence No. **81**

Name(s) as shown on return	Identifying number

Part I Orphan Drug Credit

1 Qualified clinical testing expenses (do not include any amounts claimed as current year research expenses in 15(a) below) **1**

2 Enter 50% of line 1 (see instructions) **2**

3 Flow-through orphan drug credit(s) from a partnership, S corporation, estate, or trust **3**

4 Total—Add lines 2 and 3 . . . . **4**

Part II Tax Liability Limitation—For Figuring Orphan Drug and Research Credits

5a Individuals—From Form 1040, enter amount from line 40 . . . .
 b Corporations—From Form 1120, Schedule J, enter tax from line 3 (Form 1120-A filers claiming the research credit, enter amount from Form 1120-A, Part I, line 1) **5**
 c Other filers—Enter income tax before credits from return . . . .

6a Individuals—From Form 1040, enter credits from lines 41, 42, and 43 plus any mortgage interest credit
 b Corporations—From Form 1120, Schedule J, enter any credits from lines 4(a) and 4(b) (Form 1120-A filers, enter zero) . . **6**
 c Other filers—Enter any personal credits, foreign tax credit, and possessions tax credit . . . .

7 Income tax liability as adjusted (subtract line 6 from line 5) **7**

8 Tentative minimum tax—
 a Individuals—From Form 6251, enter amount from line 17 . . . .
 b Corporations—From Form 4626, enter amount from line 13 . . . . **8**
 c Estates and Trusts—From Form 8656, enter amount from Part III, line 10 . . . .

9 Excess of income tax liability over tentative minimum tax—Subtract line 8 from 7 . . . . . . **9**

Part III Allowed Orphan Drug Credit

10 Orphan drug credit—Enter here and on the appropriate line of your return the smaller of line 4 or line 9 **10**

Part IV Research Credit

		(a) Current tax year	**(b)** Base period
11	Wages for qualified services (do not include wages used in figuring the jobs credit) **11**		
12	Cost of supplies used in conducting qualified research **12**		
13	Rental or lease costs of computers used in conducting qualified research . . **13**		
14	65% of contract expenses for qualified research (but see line 20 below) . . . **14**		
15	Total qualified research expenses (add lines 11 through 14 in columns (a) and (b)) **15**		
16	Subtract line 15 column (b) from line 15 column (a) **16**		
17	Limitation—Enter 50% of line 15 column (a) **17**		
18	Enter the smaller of line 16 or line 17 . . . . **18**		
19	University basic research payments paid in cash during year (corporations only) **19**		
20	Base period amount (see instructions). **20**		
21	Subtract line 20 from line 19. . . . . **21**		
22	Add line 18 and line 21. . . . . **22**		
23	Tentative credit—Enter 20% of line 22 . . . . **23**		
24	Flow-through research credit(s) from a partnership, S corporation, estate or trust **24**		
25	Total allowable research credit—Add lines 23 and 24. . . . . **25**		

Note: *If you have a 1988 investment credit (Form 3468), jobs credit (Form 5884), credit for alcohol used as fuel (Form 6478), or low-income housing credit (Form 8586) in addition to your 1988 research credit, or if you have a carryback or carryforward of any general business credit, stop here and go to **Form 3800**, General Business Credit, to claim your 1988 research credit. If you have only a 1988 research credit, you may continue with lines 26 through 31 to claim your credit.*

See Paperwork Reduction Act Notice on page 1 of the separate instructions. Form **6765** (1988)

Exhibit 19-1

Form **3800**	**General Business Credit**	OMB No. 1545-0895
Department of the Treasury Internal Revenue Service	▶ **Attach to your tax return.**	19**88** Attachment Sequence No. **24**

Name(s) as shown on return	Identifying number

Part I **Tentative Credit**

1	Investment credit (Form 3468, line 8)	**1**	
2	Jobs credit (Form 5884, line 6)	**2**	
3	Credit for alcohol used as fuel (Form 6478, line 11)	**3**	
4	Credit for increasing research activities (Form 6765, line 25)	**4**	
5	Low-income housing credit (Form 8586, line 6)	**5**	
6	**Current year general business credit**—Add lines 1 through 5	**6**	
7	Carryforward of general business credit (investment (see instructions), WIN, jobs, alcohol fuel, research, ESOP, or low-income housing credits)	**7**	
8	Carryback of general business credit to 1988	**8**	
9	Tentative general business credit—Add lines 6, 7, and 8	**9**	

Part II **Tax Liability Limitations**

10a	Individuals—From Form 1040, enter amount from line 40		
b	Corporations—From Form 1120, Schedule J, enter tax from line 3 (or Form 1120-A, Part I, line 1)		
c	Other filers—Enter income tax before credits from return	**10**	
11a	Individuals—From Form 1040, enter credits from lines 41, 42, and 43, plus any orphan drug credit, mortgage interest credit, and nonconventional source fuel credit included on line 46 . .		
b	Corporations—From Form 1120, Schedule J, enter credits from lines 4a through 4d (Form 1120-A filers, enter zero)		
c	Other filers—See instructions for line 11c	**11**	
12	Income tax liability as adjusted—Subtract line 11 from line 10	**12**	
13	Tentative minimum tax—		
a	Individuals—From Form 6251, enter amount from line 17		
b	Corporations—From Form 4626, enter amount from line 13		
c	Estates and Trusts—From Form 8656, enter amount from Part III, line 10	**13**	
14	Net income tax—		
a	Individuals—Enter the sum of line 12, above, and line 19 of Form 6251		
b	Corporations—Enter the sum of line 12, above, and line 16 of Form 4626		
c	Other filers—See instructions for line 14c	**14**	
15	If line 12 is more than $25,000—Enter 25% of the excess	**15**	
16	Enter—Line 14 less whichever is greater, line 13 or line 15 (if less than zero, enter zero)	**16**	
17	General business credit—Enter the smaller of line 9, or line 16 (corporations, see instructions) here and on Form 1040, line 44; Form 1120, Schedule J, line 4e; Form 1120-A, Part I, line 2a; or the proper line on other returns	**17**	

For Paperwork Reduction Act Notice, see page 1 of the separate Instructions to this form.

Form **3800** (1988)

☆U.S. Government Printing Office: 1988-205-260

Exhibit 19-2

Chapter 20

LICENSING AGREEMENTS

Many entrepreneurs have found they can increase their revenues by entering into a licensing agreement. In some instances, entrepreneurs ask others if they may have permission to market certain products or services upon which they will pay a royalty, thus making them licensees. In other instances, entrepreneurs seek out other businesses that will produce and sell their product or service for them and pay them a royalty; as a result they are termed licensors. Licensing agreements represent an excellent channel of distribution for products, services, and even trademarks. This chapter explains:

* Advantages and disadvantages of using licenses
* Types of licensing rights
* Types of property that can be licensed
* How to analyze prospective licensees
* Issues to consider in any licensing agreement
* OEM and VAR arrangements
* Product licensing information

WHY ENTREPRENEURS USE LICENSES

When you grant a license it permits others to use your property without granting them ownership in it. A license agreement can include any type of personal property. Most licenses, however, are granted for the use of intellectual property, such as trademarks, trade secrets, know-how, show-how, copyrights, patents, patentable inventions, or mask works for semiconductor chip products.

Many entrepreneurs have discovered that a licensing agreement allows them to tap into a source of revenue which would ordinarily not be available because of the entrepreneur's limited resources. Generally, the situation is as follows: Entrepreneur grants a company a license to manufacture the entrepreneur's patent or trade secret, which is then sold in several different varieties by the company. The company then pays the entrepreneur a royalty for each unit that the company manufactures and sells. The royalty usually ranges from 15 to 35 percent of the pretax net profit, although other percentages may be agreed upon depending on whether or not the entrepreneur has a history of successful licensing agreements and is known to defend his or her intellectual property rights vigorously against infringers. *Note:* Sometimes the company will insist that the royalty be calculated as a percentage of net invoiced sales. Frequently, firms are apprehensive about releasing profit figures but will gladly disclose sales data. The royalty rate on net invoiced sales may range from 1 to 10 percent. Below is a schedule of the most common rates.

Annual Net Sales	Royalty Rate
0 – $500,000	10%
$500,000 – $1,000,000	8
$1,000,000 – $2,000,000	6
$2,000,000 – $5,000,000	3
$5,000,000 +	1

Advantages

As an entrepreneur, you should plan the licensing of your property based on the advantages that the licensing agreement brings. Below are some of the advantages you should take into account.

Quickly Recoup Research and Development Costs: Competition may become intense once the product becomes known in the market. If your resources are limited it may be more advantageous to license your product to a larger organization, which can introduce your product quickly with maximum penetration. This situation could allow both you and the licensee to practice a pricing policy known as "price skimming," which calls for a hefty price tag in the beginning of the product's life cycle so that you can quickly recoup your research and development costs.

Increase Market Share: Ideally, you want a wide distribution of your product. By increasing the number of outlets in which your product is sold or used, you increase your market share and therefore increase sales. However, to reach this objective, you will need to have ample resources at your disposal, which by then could be too late because of competitive forces moving into the market. A larger organization could bring your product to market on a large scale thereby increasing public recognition and customer acceptance of your product.

Engage in Technological Exchange: Some entrepreneurs insist as part of the licensing agreement that they be allowed to share in technology developed by the licensee. This type of arrangement usually results in the entrepreneur saving large sums of money in research and development expenditures because duplication of efforts is avoided. Moreover, the entrepreneur has access to the benefits of research and development of another organization which could help the entrepreneur produce additional products.

Disadvantages

The use of licensing arrangements are not without their danger. Some of these potential traps could destroy your business if you are not careful. Below are some of the more common situations entrepreneurs have been faced with:

Piracy: Unauthorized exploitation is a constant risk. Often the piracy is committed by either the licensee, employees of the licensee, or customers of the licensee. It is extremely difficult to practice any type of effective containment policy once the intellectual property leaves your control.

Creation of Competition: By showing another business how to perform a certain procedure or make a certain product, the entrepreneur may be creating a future competitor. There may come a time when the licensee will decide it no longer wants to pay royalties and will attempt to break out from its arrangement.

Loss of Quality Control: In most agreements, the licensee will insist upon controlling production, quality control, and marketing. As a result, the entrepreneur loses control over maintaining the quality of the product. From a products liability standpoint, the risks associated with the use of the product and the resultant potential liability and legal costs associated with defending a lawsuit may outweigh any potential royalty revenue derived from the license.

Hidden Administrative Costs: Many types of license agreements call for the rendering of technical assistance by the licensor, which often means technical instruction, supervision, supply of information, and hand holding. The costs associated with providing these services can quickly add up and cause the licensing agreement to become unprofitable.

TYPES OF LICENSING RIGHTS

Many entrepreneurs are under the assumption that a license automatically permits any type of "use" of the intellectual property being transferred. However, this is not the case. There are many separate rights associated with a license, which may or may not be included in the license agreement. Some of these rights include:

- Right to use
- Right to disclose through publication
- Right to lease
- Right to distribute or sell
- Right to copy
- Right to manufacture
- Right to modify, enhance, or improve
- Right to advertise
- Right to sublicense

TYPES OF PROPERTY THAT CAN BE LICENSED

Various types of intellectual property easily lend themselves to licensing agreements. Below is a list of different types of property which have been successfully licensed by entrepreneurs:

- Trade Secrets
- Patent Applications
- Patents
- Trademarks
- Know-How
- Show-How

Often entrepreneurs will ask, "What is the difference between know-how and show-how?"

Know-how has two features: (1) it represents a body of knowledge which is not readily available to the public and (2) it has value. Usually, know-how consists of either a trade secret or some process or compilation of facts and figures that have been distilled from the mountains of information which are disseminated each year to the public through text books, college courses, periodicals, etc. Examples of know-how that have been licensed are marketing plans, compilations of data, operating instructions, formulas, teaching manuals, patterns, blueprints, manufacturing technique, specifications, bills of materials, designs and drawings.

Show-how is the teaching aspect of know-how. Essentially, the entrepreneur gives instructions on how to apply certain knowledge: for instance, how to build and operate a plant; how to test and interpret quality control data; how to maintain high productivity in a manufacturing process; how to implement a marketing plan; how to merchandise a retail operation; or how to manage and control inventory.

CHECKLIST TO ANALYZE PROSPECTIVE LICENSEES

If you decide to use licensing as a method of distribution, you should carefully analyze each prospective licensee to determine whether the organization you choose benefits or hinders the distribution of your product or service. You do not want to get stuck with a licensee who is sloppy in the manufacturing of your product, does not market your product correctly, or has financial problems which may affect you.

The following list contains issues you should analyze in order to determine who to grant your license to.

*   How strong of a relationship does the prospective licensee have with its bank?
*   Does the prospective licensee have a consistent positive cash flow?
*   What are the current and long-term liabilities of the prospective licensee?
*   Does the prospective licensee have unfettered access to sources of raw materials and labor?
*   Has the prospective licensee experienced labor unrest ,which could later disrupt its operations?
*   Does the prospective licensee produce quality work?
*   How many other licenses does the prospective licensee have, with whom, and are they successful?
*   Does the prospective licensee have an established market or will the prospective licensee need assistance in breaking into the market, and, if so, what type of assistance will be necessary?
*   Will the prospective licensee pay for advertising and promotion and how much will be spent?
*   Will there be cross-licensing possibilities with the prospective licensee?
*   Will the prospective licensee pay for technical support in advance as a retainer?
*   Will the prospective licensee agree not to disclose any proprietary information received from you, the licensor?
*   Does the prospective licensee have a high turnover in its sales personnel or marketing representatives?
*   Has the prospective licensee ever been sued for injuring an individual based on products liability or negligence in the manufacture of the product?
*   Has the prospective licensee ever been sued for breach of a licensing agreement because of a royalty dispute?
*   Has the prospective licensee ever been issued a cease and desist order by a court or government agency?
*   Has the prospective licensee shown you a business plan that clearly explains how the prospective licensee intends to: (1) produce and deliver your product or service, (2)

finance the production of your product or service, and (3) market your product or service?

* Will the prospective licensee agree to a specifically defined market, such as geographical or customer type?
* Will the prospective licensee make an initial license payment?
* Will the prospective licensee guarantee a minimum royalty?
* Does the prospective licensee carry sufficient amounts of insurance and will it indemnify you in the event it causes injury to an end user because of negligence in the production or installation of the product?

LICENSING AGREEMENTS: ISSUES TO CONSIDER

When you enter into negotiations with a prospective licensee you want to make sure you cover as many of the issues as possible. It is always best to discuss the issues before you sign any agreement so that there is room for negotiation or disassociation and each party clearly knows where the other stands. We strongly recommend you seek the advice of a business lawyer when you begin negotiating a licensing agreement and that any licensing agreement be memorialized in writing.

Below is a checklist which serves as a guideline for the issues you must consider. However, this checklist is not intended to act as a substitute for an attorney.

- Royalty rate (percentage of gross sales, net sales, gross income or net income)
- Payment for the license (initial payment or downstream payment)
- Rights to sublicense (condition based on consent by licensor)
- Restrictions on the use of licensing technology
- Territorial limits to sell licensed product or service
- Exclusive license (excludes licensor, excludes everyone but licensor, excludes others from certain territories, or nonexclusive)
- Selling price of product or service
- Term of license
- Assignment of license by licensee
- Quantity restrictions of product or service
- Inspection rights of licensor (accounting records and operations)
- Nondisclosure of proprietary information
- Cross-licensing
- Patent markings on product
- Notice of trademark on products
- Notice of Copyright on products (the Berne Convention Treaty, which was signed by the U.S. to take effect March 1989, does not require notice of copyright. However, it is recommended that copyright notice be used nonetheless).
- Altering of the product or process
- Minimum annual royalty
- Technical assistance (how the price will be determined and who will pay for it)
- Promotion and advertisement of the product or service (how it will be conducted and who will pay for the marketing effort)
- Future research and development costs (who will pay for it)

- Insurance and indemnification in the event of a loss through a claim
- Patent rights (new patentable inventions, indemnification for infringement of patent claim, warranty of patent, prosecution of patent infringers)
- Payment of royalties (accounting of the royalties, inspection of accounting records, audit, who will perform the audit, who will pay for the audit, and if there is a material variance)
- Termination of the license (cancellation by the licensor and cancellation by the licensee)
- Quality control in production of the product
- Best efforts by licensee to market licensor's product or sell through advertising and promotion
- Choice of law and choice of jurisdiction to hear dispute
- Remedies for material breach of licensing agreement (definition of material breach, provisional and equitable remedies, liquidated damages)

ORIGINAL EQUIPMENT MANUFACTURER AND VALUE ADDED RESELLER ARRANGEMENTS: ANOTHER AVENUE OF DISTRIBUTION

Component parts are often marketed through an original equipment manufacturer (OEM) or value added reseller (VAR).

In an OEM arrangement, two manufacturers, A and B enter into an agreement in which A licenses to B certain components made by A which will be used in the manufacture of B's products. B will sell its products under its own name. Usually, the public will never know that some of A's components are tucked into B's products.

A VAR arrangement occurs when A and B agree that B will resell A's products but with value added by B. For instance, B may install additional equipment or make certain design modifications which enhance the value of A's product. Unlike OEM license agreements, in which the original manufacturer is rarely disclosed to the public, a VAR arrangement usually calls for the licensor's product to remain clearly identifiable even though certain pronounced changes have been made.

The component part industry allows a manufacturer another source of distribution in addition to its own. In many cases, a firm just beginning will bid on a component parts contract while building its own distribution chain. The result of taking this approach is that it gives the new manufacturer sales stability and will increase its cash flow because there is a predetermined demand for its product.

There are numerous factors you will need to be alert to if you intend to enter this market. It is well known that OEM and VAR customers have certain strict requirements and you must be prepared to satisfy those requirements if you anticipate breaking into this market. Some of these requirements are:

- Absolute adherence to customer specifications
- Certainty of delivery because of its impact on customer's production timetable
- Quantity of parts that are needed
- Maintaining certain quality standards
- Return provisions for faulty components

The OEM and VAR market is only one avenue that manufacturers can use to sell their products. To be successful as an entrepreneur who manufacturers products, you should be cognizant of other channels of distribution that may be available to you. A channel of distribution is the path your product takes before reaching the end user. Often, it is necessary to use a middleman or intermediary to distribute your goods.

Intermediaries, such as wholesalers and agents, are used by many manufacturers to increase distribution of their products. Following is a brief description of how wholesalers and agents are used by manufacturers.

Wholesalers: As a rule, wholesalers buy from the manufacturer and sell to the industrial buyer. The wholesaler provides a variety of services: (1) it will usually offer both field sales and inside sales, for telephone and walk-in sales; (2) it will advertise the product and sometimes drum up publicity; (3) it warehouses the product and handles the product for the manufacturer; (4) it delivers the product to the customer; (5) it extends credit to the customer; and (6) it has direct contact with the customer and therefore is a valuable source of information about the market for the manufacturer.

Agents: Agents provide fewer services than the wholesaler. The most common type of agent is the manufacturer's representative. A manufacturer's representative will usually represent several sellers and offer a complete product line to a customer. Most manufacturer's representatives operate in strictly defined territory which is established in its legal relationship with the manufacturer. A manufacturer's representative does not take possession or title to the product or become involved in financing or storage of the product. In essence, the manufacturer's representative assumes almost no risk. Its sole job is to sell product by taking orders and relaying those orders to the manufacturer.

PRODUCT LICENSING INFORMATION

There are numerous publications that cover licensing opportunities. The quality of these publications varies in regard to depth, accuracy, and timeliness of the information. Below are three of the best known publications:

Government Inventions Available for Licensing
National Technical Information Service
U.S. Department of Commerce
P.O. Box 1533
Springfield, VA 22151

Technology Mart
Thomas Publishing Company
250 West 34th Street
New York, NY 10001

American Bulletin of International Technology Transfer
554 Wilshire Boulevard
Los Angeles, CA 90036

Chapter 21

LEASING VERSUS BUYING EQUIPMENT

Leasing has become a popular method of obtaining fixed assets for use in a business without having to make a purchase. Regardless of what leasing agents will tell you or what you may read in an advertisement, there are certain advantages as well disadvantages in leasing assets. As a consequence, you must carefully look at your own situation and then analyze whether or not the benefit of the leased asset outweighs its cost. This chapter explains:

* Advantages and disadvantages of leasing equipment
* Operating lease versus capital lease
* Analysis of operating lease versus capital lease
* How to analyze the cost of a lease
* How to negotiate a lease
* Understanding the terms of a lease contract

ADVANTAGES AND DISADVANTAGES OF LEASING EQUIPMENT

Leasing assets presents certain advantages over owning the assets. Advantages of leasing include:

Leasing is a way to conserve cash. Leases are often signed without requiring any money down. Furthermore, lease payments frequently remain fixed. This fixed payment protects the lessee against inflation and cost of money increases.

Reduces borrowing. Leasing can save credit lines for other purposes and can help strengthen the balance sheet. For example, lessees can use credit lines saved, for financing inventories. Also, certain types of leases do not add debt on the balance sheet, do not affect financial ratios, and as a result, may add to borrowing capacity.

Protects against obsolescence. Leasing permits rapid changes in equipment and may pass the risk in residual value to the lessor. If a better item of equipment comes along, the lessee can trade in the old one.

739

More flexible than buying. Lease agreements may contain less restrictive provisions than other debt agreements. Leases can be tailored to the special needs of a company. For example, lease payments can be structured to meet the timing of cash revenues.

Tax advantages. Start-up companies, depressed industries, or companies in low tax brackets may lease as a way of claiming tax benefits that might otherwise be lost. The lessee shifts the write-off to the lessor, who, in turn, may share benefits with the user, in the form of lower rental payments.

Corporate minimum tax gives leasing an edge over buying. Leasing circumvents tax traps related to the corporate minimum tax by avoiding transactions hit by the tax. Note that certain tax breaks such as accelerated depreciation can trigger this 20% tax. If book profit exceeds taxable income, the corporate minimum tax comes into play.

However, in some situations, buying offers advantages over leasing.

If a firm has excess cash. If the cash is not needed for operations or cannot be invested profitably, then buying may be advantageous.

Tax advantages. If the firm has high earnings, which it wants to offset with depreciation or if the firm qualifies for the Internal Revenue Code section 179 election, which treats all or part of asset cost as a currently deductible expense in the placed in service year, buying should be considered.

No obsolescence. Buying offers an advantage when obsolescence isn't a worry and slow growth is expected.

Pride of ownership. In some cases, pride of ownership has tilted the scales toward buying.

Miscellaneous considerations. It is possible to lease almost any type of capital asset. Currently, computers and telecommunications gear are popular; you can rent such assets as furniture, material handling equipment, earth moving equipment, trucks, and robots.

No "easy" way exists for determining whether to lease or buy. You will need to compare actual numbers—that is: (1) cost of leasing versus buying, (2) interest expense versus rental fees, and (3) fees and other miscellaneous charges associated with leasing. To assist you in making a decision about whether to buy or lease your asset, we have provided a method that is often used to analyze the cost of a lease. We recommend you follow this method when making your decision because it will produce some hard numbers that you can study and compare.

HOW TO ANALYZE THE COST OF THE LEASE

Before a lease can be analyzed, the different types of leases available to you as a lessee must first be explained. Should your business be the leasing business, there are many good sources of information. The recognized leader in lease education and consulting is Amembal & Isom of Salt Lake City, Utah. However, most entrepreneurs will participate in a lease as the lessee and will encounter two types of leases: the operating and capital.

Operating Lease vs. Capital Lease

The determination of lease type depends on four criteria set out in Financial Accounting Standards Board (FASB) statement number 13. If any one of these criteria are met then the lease is a capital lease, and if none are met, then it is an operating lease. Those criteria are:

* Ownership of the asset transfers automatically at the end of the lease.
* The lease has a bargain purchase option. That is, at the end of the lease, transfer of ownership is affected by a less than fair market value (FMV) price.
* The lease term is equal to or greater than 75 percent of the asset's economic life. Economic life means the asset's life in the hands of all users.

   * The present value of the minimum lease payments is equal to or greater than 90 percent of the asset's fair market value.

In the criteria listed above, several terms were introduced which may be unfamiliar to you. They are defined below.

Fair Market Value (FMV). This is the amount paid for an asset by a willing buyer to a willing seller in an arm's length transaction.

Bargain Purchase Option. The measure of this criteria is rather subjective. However, the true test is if the purchase option is so small that it will be exercised in any event, then that option is a bargain purchase option.

Present Value Criteria. This criteria requires the use of a discount rate to calculate the present value of the minimum lease payments required. As a lessee, your discount rate is the incremental, pretax, coterminous, secured installment borrowing rate. In short, this is the rate the bank would charge you to lend you the funds to buy the asset.

Minimum Lease Payments. These are simply all of the payments contractually required by the lease.

From a balance sheet perspective, the operating lease is neither an asset nor a liability. It is commonly known as an "off-balance sheet liability." From an income statement perspective, the operating lease payments are treated as pure expense.

Unlike the operating lease, the capital lease is less straightforward. Since the lease is little more than a financing tool in the eyes of FASB, the asset as well as its related liability must be carried on the balance sheet. As a capital asset, the leased equipment must be depreciated and the payment must be treated as a combination of principal and interest for expense purposes.

The purpose of this discussion is not to convince you that leasing is superior to the buy option or vice versa, rather it is intended to provide you with a method of analysis. Changing depreciation rules, tax laws and costs of financing will periodically favor one option over the other.

We will look at two examples. In the first example, the operating lease will be compared with the purchase option. In the second example, the capital lease will be compared with the purchase option.

Example 1: Analysis of the Operating Lease

In our example, let's make the following assumptions:

FMV	= $80,000
Depreciable life	= 6 years
Economic life	= 8 years
Lease term	= 48 months
Lessee's coterminous borrowing rate	= 12%
Lease payments	= $1950/month
Advance payments	= First and Last
Company tax rate	= 50%

Lessor assumes a residual value of $20,000 after the equipment is given back from the lessee at lease term.

Given the information above, we must verify certain criteria which are necessary to satisfy ourselves that this is indeed an operating lease:

- There is no automatic transfer of ownership.
- There is no bargain purchase option.
- The lease term is less than 75 percent of the economic life.
- The present value of lease payments is less than 90% of FMV. This criterion must be checked even more carefully.

$$90 \text{ percent of FMV} = .9 \times \$80,000 = \$72,000.$$

- The present value of 46 payments of $1,950 at 12 percent is $71,618.

Therefore, all criteria have been met, and this is indeed an operating lease.

If the same piece of equipment were to be purchased for the same four year-period, the transaction might look something like this:

Loan downpayment	= 20%
Four year loan payments	= $1,685/month
Straight line depreciation (6 years)	= $13,333/year

At the end of the four-year period, the company will sell the equipment for the same $20,000, which is the amount the equipment lessor expects the equipment to be worth.

For the sake of simplicity in this analysis, the following reasonable assumptions have been made:

* Income generated from the machine will be the same regardless of which financing scenario we choose.
* Insurance, maintenance, and repair expenses are identical.
* The company has these choices.

The next step is to analyze the cash outflow process that occurs under each method and create a present value based on a chosen discount rate of 10 percent.

For the operating lease, the following cash flows are found:

	Year 1	Year 2	Year 3	Year 4
First and last payment	$ 3,800			
Payments	21,450	23,400	23,400	21,450
Total cash outflow	25,250	23,400	23,40	21,450
Tax saving (50%)[a]	12,625	11,700	11,700	10,725
Net cash outflow	$12,625	$11,700	$11,700	$10,725

[a]Your tax rate may differ depending on the form or profitability of your business.

The present value of these outflows is:

Year 1	$11,477
Year 2	9,669
Year 3	8,970
Year 4	7,325
	$37,441

Now let's take a look at the cash flows for the purchase option. We have assumed a fully amortized bank loan with a term of forty-eight months, original principal (after downpayment) of $64,000 at 12 percent with monthly principal and interest payments of $1685 (rounded). The principal and interest paid in each year will be:

Year End	Principal Balance	Principal Paid	Interest Paid
1	$50,742	$13,258	$6,962
2	35,803	14,939	5,281
3	18,969	16,834	3,386
4	0	18,969	1,251

At the end of the loan period, assume the equipment will be sold for the same value the lessor attaches to the equipment ($20,000). Not only does this assumption allow us to compare options on the same criteria, it is reasonable because retention of the equipment would automatically favor the purchase—that is, we are assuming some sort of technical obsolescence in this case. Because we are employing straight line depreciation of $13,333 per year and we have an original cost of $80,000, it will result at the end of four years of operation in a book basis of $26,668 (80,000 - 53,332). If the machine is sold for $20,000, we will incur a book loss of $6,668 which results in a tax saving of $3,334, and of course, a cash inflow of $20,000. Thus, the cash flow impact on a sale of this sort would be $23,334. With these facts in mind, the cash flow for the purchase options looks like this:

	Year 1	Year 2	Year 3	Year 4
Depreciation	$13,333	$13,333	$13,333	$13,333
Interest expense	6,962	5,281	3,386	1,251
Book expense	20,295	18,614	16,719	14,584
Tax saving	10,148	9,307	8,360	7,292
Net book expense	10,148	9,307	8,360	7,292
Add back depreciation	13,333	13,333	13,333	13,333
Principal payments	13,258	14,939	16,834	18,969
Net cash outflow	10,073	10,913	11,867	12,928
Net effect of equipment sale				23,343
Net cash outflow	$10,073	$10,913	$11,867	
Net cash inflow				$10,415

The present value of these cash flows, discounted at the assumed rate of 10 percent is:

Year 0 (Downpayment)	($16,000)
Year 1	(9,157)
Year 2	(9,019)
Year 3	(8,916)
Year 4	7,113
Total	($35,974)

Given these two choices, the purchase option is better because its outgoing cash flows are less. However, you must remember there is risk associated with the purchase option regarding the ultimate sale of the equipment. What if the sale is not possible at the assumed level? The cost of the purchase option would, in that case, be higher by some amount and the lease option might be better. Therefore, the difference between the two options is tied to the lessor's assumption of residual value risk on the lesee's behalf.

Example 2: Analysis of the Capital Lease

The assumptions used for the operating lease example will be used in this example except for the following capital lease differences:

Lease payment	= $2,100
Purchase option	= $1.

From an accounting point of view, the capital lease is essentially the same as the purchase option. That is, the asset will be carried in a fixed asset account, the asset will be depreciated, and the lease obligation will be carried as a liability. In order to book the capital lease into the proper accounts, a "gross up" of the lease based on the lease terms and the coterminous borrowing rate of the lessee must be performed. This is done by taking the present value of the lease payments over the term discounted by the lessee's coterminous borrowing rate (in this case 12 percent). FASB requires that the lower of the present value of the lease payment stream or FMV of the asset be used in the recording of the asset on the books. In this example, the present value of forty-eight payments of $2,100 @ 12% is $79,745. This is the amount that will be entered in the accounting records and depreciated. In this case, assume the same depreciation period (six years) and the same disposal price ($20,000) as provided in the purchase option. As a result, the depreciation per year will be $13,291 (79,745 / 6 years). The amortization of the "grossed up" amount will occur as follows:

Year End	Principal Balance	Principal Paid	Interest Paid
1	$63,226	$16,519	$8,681
2	44,611	18,615	6,585
3	23,656	20,955	4,245
4	0	23,656	1,544

Note that the lease calls for first and last payments. From an accounting perspective, the first payment was due and the last payment takes the form of a noncurrent prepayment that will be associated with the last month of the lease.

Now let's construct a cash flow analysis for the capital lease option:

	Year 1	Year 2	Year 3	Year 4
Depreciation	$13,291	$13,291	$13,291	$13,291
Interest expense	8,681	6,585	4,245	1,544
Book expense	21,972	19,876	17,536	14,835
Tax saving	10,986	9,938	8,768	7,418
Net book expense	10,986	9,938	8,768	7,418
Add back depreciation	13,291	13,291	13,291	13,291
Principal payments	16,519	18,615	20,955	23,656
Net effect of sale				23,291[a]
Net cash outflow	$14,214	$15,286	$16,432	
Net cash inflow				$ 5,508

[a] Sold for $20,000 with a basis of $26,581 ($79,745 - $53,164) or a loss of $6,581. The loss saves $3,291 in taxes. This savings plus the $20,000 inflow from the sale equals $23,291.

Now let's take the present value of these cash flows at our assumed discount rate of 10 percent:

Year 0 (last payment)	($ 2,100)
Year 1	(12,922)
Year 2	(12,633)
Year 3	(12,346)
Year 4	3,762
Total	($36,239)

In this case the purchase option is better by $260. This decision would be a close call. The difference may boil down to the cash outflow at time 0. In the purchase option, time zero outflow is $16,000, while for the lease option, time zero outflow is $4,200 (first and last payment).

We have provided you with a method of cost analysis that will allow you to determine which financing option is better for you. The final decision may rest on the intangibles of the choices. However, it is beneficial to be aware of the quantitative elements of the choices available. We strongly recommend that when you enter the capital market for equipment purchases, you perform at least a cursory analysis of the alternatives.

If these calculations overwhelm you, your accountant should be able to perform them for you. The vendor should also be able to help you in this regard.

HOW TO NEGOTIATE A LEASE

To negotiate a lease, you will need to know what your options are. Earlier, we discussed the analysis of the lease versus buy option. By knowing the present value of the total cost to purchase, you can negotiate the lease intelligently. There are numerous other factors to be aware of:

* Will the equipment be obsolete within a foreseeable period of time? If so, is it an item you would not want to purchase? This situation favors the lease and thus puts you at a disadvantage in the negotiations.

* Is this piece of capital equipment maintenance-sensitive? Will you be able to maintain it for a lower cost than the leasing company? If so, the buy option may be favored, if not, the lease option is preferred.

* Is your business in an alternate minimum tax (AMT) position? If so, an operating lease will not aggravate the AMT position and is preferred.

* Is your business in need of quick machinery write-offs to offset a tax liability? Latest tax laws favor leases over purchases since modified accelerated cost recovery system (MACRS) has stretched out depreciation periods on most pieces of capital equipment. For instance, if a machine is within the classification of six-year MACRS, the depreciation will be taken over a seven-year period under the purchase option. For a capital lease, the same piece of equipment will be expensed and depreciated over the lease period which will be somewhat less than seven years.

* Leasing is a very competitive business; therefore, shop around for the best price. Leasing at the low end—that is, under $25,000, is a prime source of credit for those firms who cannot yet get credit at a bank. If your credit is good, you then have significant negotiating power. If not, then the reverse is true.

* In most cases, a bank loan will require 25 to 30 percent of the purchase price as downpayment on a capital piece of equipment. Leasing terms can run from first and last payment and a security deposit to first payment only. In most cases, however, the worst initial cash payment will be no more than 15 percent of the purchase price. If you have strong credit, then demand smaller rather than greater initial cash payment and avoid the security deposit for the following three reasons: (1) you do not know if the leasing company will be in business five years from now, (2) the security deposit is a hook to get you to buy the machine at the end of the lease., and (3) you can put the money to better use rather than giving it to the leasing company.

* Certain leasing companies are specialists in specific areas of capital equipment and as such offer better terms because of their area of expertise. Equipment lessors will also specialize by industry and could provide potential savings to your company. Seek out these specialists.

* The vendor will often have lessors lined up to provide the financing, much the way a car dealer lines up financing sources. Be aware: these arrangements can be of a cooperative nature such that the vendor gets a "commission," also known as a kickback. This arrangement will result in a higher leasing price to you. Your negotiating tool is your good credit and the threat of taking your business to a competitor who can provide reasonable credit terms for a comparable piece of equipment. Remember, at the low ticket end of the capital equipment market, these vendors are looking to move product quickly. Their sources, therefore, are set up to handle the gamut of credit worthy customers.

* At various times and at various places, lessors will be "hungry" for leasing business. If you are lucky enough to encounter this situation, there will be a window of opportunity. Take advantage of it. This phenomenon occurs because various lending institutions find themselves with excess cash to invest and a very willing market that can absorb their funds.

* Avoid the stampede that many vendors will give you regarding price and financing rates. Do not jump at the first offer. There are very few scenarios where the vendor is in complete control of the "game."

The key to negotiating a lease or anything else for that matter is to give the appearance that you at least have a palatable alternative to the seller's product or financing vehicle. This alternative can be either real or a bluff, but it must be perceived that you have this alternative or you will be at the seller's mercy. Your relative advantage will be reflected in the pricing and terms offered you. Accept only what you believe is fair and never the first offer.

UNDERSTANDING THE TERMS OF A LEASE CONTRACT

Most leases are made up of standard terms and conditions generally accepted in the industry. Many of these terms and conditions are discussed in this section. Be sure you understand the terms and conditions of the lease before you agree to it. We strongly recommend you show any proposed lease contract to your attorney and have him or her review it.

In general, the standard leasing rental agreement will contain the following elements:

Full legal name and address of lessee. The lessee's legal name and status are determined by both parties during the application process. The organizational status of the company will determine whether or not a guaranty will be required.

Full description of the leased equipment. This will include serial numbers, model numbers, and any other pertinent identification. From this information the lessor will perfect his or her lien via a UCC filing.

Name and address of supplier. The lease is somewhat like an escrow transaction. The lessee agrees to a purchase price and delivery date of equipment from a supplier. Upon approval of credit, either by the ultimate funding source or lessor, a simultaneous transaction occurs. The funding source pays the supplier in the name of the lessor who then becomes the legal owner. The funding source takes assignment of the lease as collateral and the lessee takes physical (not legal ownership) possession of the equipment.

Location of the leased equipment. The location is listed if it is different from the legal address.

Monthly rental payment. This is the lessee's monthly obligation for the duration of the lease. In most cases, this payment will remain constant for the life of the lease, which can be beneficial or detrimental depending on the variability of interest rates. Suffice it to say that the overwhelming majority of leases are fixed rate in nature. Note also that as a lessee you will be responsible for this payment for the life of the lease since most leases are non-cancellable.

Sales tax. Because a lease involves a change of ownership from vendor to lessor, a taxable event has occurred, and state sales tax is due and payable on the transaction. This sales tax will be passed along to you as the lessee. The payment of the tax depends on how the lease is viewed by the state. If the lease is viewed as a conditional sale by the state, sales tax must be paid on the payment amount; however, if the lease is viewed as a lease, sales tax must be paid only on the sales price. In the latter case, the lessee can generally opt to either pay the tax as part of the initial payment or include it in the lease principal amount. In many states, the determination of lease versus conditional sale is based on the purchase option made available. As long as the purchase option is considered to be fair market value or greater, the state will usually view the transaction as a lease. There are, of course, other issues regarding the definition of a lease for state purposes. However, this criterion is most often the deciding factor.

Term of the lease. This is both the duration of the lease and the number of payments you must make. Typically the lease term is thirty-six to sixty months.

Advance payments required. Since leasing is a financing tool, the yield of the lease is a function of the stream of payments and the timing of their receipt. A lessor can increase his or her yield on any given payment stream by collecting more of the payments in advance. In general, you as the lessee, will be faced with first and last payments at lease inception. Since payments on a lease are due in advance, the first and last payment scenario represents only one advance payment. Under a sixty-month lease, the last payment will be payment number sixty.

Security deposit. The security deposit has four functions. First, it ensures performance of the lessee. Second, it increases the yield of the lease. The lessor has use of those funds for the life of the lease at no interest cost. Third, it can be used as a lever by the lessor to entice the buyer to keep the equipment at the end of the lease term. That is, the lessor will offer the equipment to the lessee in exchange for forfeiture of the security deposit plus some minor consideration. The fourth function, also, benefits the lessor in that he or she can use the security deposit to return the equipment to a normal state of repair should the lessee abuse the equipment. As you can imagine, this topic is an area of contention since normal wear and tear is in the eye of the beholder. Therefore, as lessee, you may want to avoid the security deposit since it serves to benefit only the lessor.

Annual renewal rental fee. Some leases provide that at the end of the lease term, the lessee has the option to continue renting the equipment for another year at some predetermined rate.

No warranties by lessor. The lessor will deny any guaranty as to the condition, merchantability, or fitness for a particular purpose. This clause places the responsibility solely on the shoulders of the lessee to know to the extent of his or her obligations. In practicality, the lessee will accept the equipment in the name of the lessor and is responsible for proper installation and performance. The lessee has great leverage on the vendor at this point since the lessor will not pay the vendor until the lessee unconditionally accepts the equipment.

Liens and taxes. The lessee is not allowed to encumber the leased equipment and is responsible for all taxes on the equipment including the annual property tax. In some states, such as California, this tax is levied on equipment owned on March 1 and is due and payable August 31 of each year. The lessor will bill the lessee for this tax and will normally include a nominal handling charge. The actual tax varies from county to county but runs in the area of 1.2 percent of the equipment cost depreciated by 10 percent for each year of ownership.

Repairs and alterations. Lessee is responsible for the proper maintenance of leased equipment unless lessee has purchased a maintenance contract in conjunction with the lease. Lessees are only allowed to alter the equipment with approval of lessor.

Ownership. The equipment is in fact owned by the lessor much the same way you "own" your mortgaged home. The lessor does have the right to sell the property to settle his or her obligation to the funding source should the lessee default.

Insurance. Lessee is responsible, at his or her expense, for insurance to cover lessor's interests.

Late charges and interest. Lessor may charge a fixed late charge or a late charge tied to a percentage of payment amount. Most lessors will allow a ten-day grace period from due date and mail statements fifteen days prior to due date.

Default. There are numerous events of default, some of which are: bankruptcy, failure to make payments, misrepresentation or false statements, and insolvency. As a result of default, the lessor may be entitled to repossess his or her equipment or accelerate all remaining payments due.

Costs and legal fees of enforcement. Most lessors will require lessee to pay the costs of enforcement of the lease including collection fees and attorney's fees.

In addition to the commonly used terms and conditions of the lease contract, there are other terms and conditions that you should be aware of. They are:

- Should you decide to return the equipment at the end of the lease term, you will be responsible for all freight and carting expenses. This, often times, is more costly than keeping the equipment.

- Make sure that the purchase option, should one exist, is spelled out in detail and in writing. If the option is not spelled out in the lease contract, the option is assumed to be a fair market value option, which means the amount that a willing buyer will pay a willing seller. The purchase option, if given, must be in writing. You do not want to rely on the lessor's memory regarding the terms of a transaction that may have occurred years ago. In addition, you will probably have a statute of frauds problem in the enforcement of the agreement. Again, we recommend your lawyer review any proposed agreement been.

- Determine whether or not there is a clause regarding noncancellability of the lease. Most leases have this type of clause. However, lessors may be willing to release the lessee should an upgrade in equipment be the reason for the cancellation. Find out what options you have prior to signing the lease and get them in writing.

We believe that leasing is just one of many financing vehicles available to you in the operation of your business. It has many positive aspects as well as negative ones. Analyze each lease carefully to determine whether or not the terms and conditions of the lease are in your best interests.

INDEX

A

Academic transcripts, personnel, 573
Accelerated Cost Recovery System (ACRS), 271-73
Accounting Corporation of America, 540
Accounting systems, 257-86
    cash flow management, 276-86
    CPAs, use of, 267-68
    depreciation, 268-73
    double-entry system, 266-67
    financial statements, 258-66
    internal accounting controls, 273-76
    reasons for establishing, 9-10
    single-entry system, 266
Accounts payable, 317
    payment of, 284-85
Accounts receivable, 542-46
    aged reports, 543
    as asset, 317
    as asset need, 530
    collection procedures, 544
    credit application process, 542
    factoring, 345-46
    financing of, 545-46
    managing of, 544
    trade credit terms, 543
Accounts receivable financing, 319
Accounts receivable turnover, forecasting of, 529
Accountants, locating businesses for sale through, 15
Accrual method of accounting, 477, 480
Achievers, psychographic profile, 211
Acid/quick ratio, 532
Acquisition evaluation, 531
Activity ratios, 533-34, 539
Administrative expenses, 260
    licensing agreements and, 733
Advertising, 215-20
    of businesses for sale, 15
    direct mail, 217-18
    legal aspects, 219-20
    magazines/technical journals, 217
    newspapers, 216-17
    radio, 218
    television, 218-19
Age discrimination, 123
Aged reports, 543
Airlines, trade show information, 244
Alcohol, tobacco, and firearms tax, 297
AMF Inc. v. Sleekcraft Boats, 665

Annual Summary of Injuries and Illnesses notice, 126
Apprenticeship training, 573
Arbitron Index, 219
Assets, 316-17
    accounts receivable as, 317
    bonds as, 317
    cash in banks as, 316
    certificates of deposit (CDs) as, 317
    current assets, 258
    fixed assets, 258
    motor vehicles as, 317
    noncurrent assets, 258
    notes receivable as, 317
    real estate as, 317
    return on assets (ROA), 534
    sale of, 23
    stock as, 317
    total asset turnover, 534
Attorneys, locating businesses for sale through, 15
Audits, 267
Automobile insurance, 307-8
Average collection period, 533

B

Balance sheet, 258-59
    sample, 259
Balance sheet comparison worksheet, 35-36
Bank of America, 540
Bankers:
    bank loans, 319
    how to deal with, 316
    locating businesses for sale through, 15
    what bankers look for, 318
Bargain purchase option, 741
Bit, 586
Bonds, 328-29
    as assets, 317
    compared to stocks, 327-29
Book value, 17
Branding, 659-65
    brands as marketing tools, 659-60
    trademarks/servicemarks, 660-65
Breakeven analysis, 231-36
Breakeven point, 564-69
Brokers, 225

Budget, product/service promotion, 222-23
Bulk Transfer Act, compliance with, 25-26
Burglary insurance, 309
Business brokers, 15
Business corporations, 88
Businesses:
    location, 226-29
        metropolitan area, 227-28
        state, 227
    Tax Reform Act (1986) and, 90-97
        fringe benefits, 93-94
        income splitting, 92
        passive activities, 97
        retirement plans, 92-93
        Subchapter S corporations, 95-97
    types of, 83-90
        corporations, 86-90
        partnerships, 84-86
        sole proprietorships, 83-84
Business history, business plans, 179, 337
Business insurance, *See* Insurance
Business interruption insurance, 309
Business location, marketing and, 226-29
Business plans, 177-93, 337-38
    contents of, 178-80
    need for, 177-78
    presentation of, 180-81
    sample, 182-93
        cover page, 183
        financial plan, 192-93
        industry/company/services, 186-93
        management team, 187-88
        marketing plan, 191-92
        market research/analysis, 188-91
        summary, 185
        table of contents, 184
    strategy building through, 181-82
Buying on credit, 541
Buy-out agreements, 489
Byte, 586

C

Cafeteria plans, 606-7
    nondiscrimination rules, 606
    reporting requirements, 606-7
    taxable/nontaxable benefits, 606
CAL/OSHA, 116-18

Capital expenditures, 477
Capital intensity, forecasting of, 528
Capitalization method, of purchase
    price determination, 17-18
Capital lease, 740-41
    cost analysis, 744-45
Carrying cost, inventory, 550
Cash, as asset need, 530
Cash in banks, as asset, 316
Cash flow management, 276-86
    accounts payable, payment of, 284-85
    capital infusion, 285-87
    cash flow statement
        construction of, 276-80
        protecting future cash flows,
          281-83
    collection of accounts receivable,
        283-84
    debt repayment, 285
Cash method of accounting, 477, 479
Cash needs, forecasting of, 528
Cathode ray tube (CRT), 586
Census tracts, 211-14
    analyzing a typical metropolitan
        area, 212-14
    demographics, 212
    marketing and, 211-14
    TIGER data base, 214
Central processing unit (CPU), 586
Certificates of deposit (CDs), as asset,
    317
Certified Development Companies
    (CDCs), loans, 326-27
Certified public accountants (CPAs):
    accounting services, 267-68
        audits, 267
        compilations, 268
        reviews, 268
Chainstyle franchises, 51
Chambers of Commerce:
    locating businesses for sale through,
        15
    trade show information, 244
Citations, for health/safety violations,
    127
Classroom instruction, 573
Clifford trust, 483
Coinsurance, 303
Collection procedures, 544
    average collection period, 533
Commissioner of Internal Revenue,
    address, 725
Commission merchants, 225-26
Commission selling agents, 226
Common stock, 327
    advantages of issuing, 328
    disadvantages of issuing, 328
    types of, 327
Competition:
    competitive environments, types, 569
    evaluation of, 569-70
        factors to consider, 569-70
Competitive market, 230
Compilation method, of purchase price
    determination, 19-20
Compilations, 268
The Complete Handbook of Franchises,
    49
Computer use, 583-87

assessing your needs, 583-85
computer system components, 585-86
    printers, 585
    software, types of, 584-85
    terms, 586-87
Consumer market, 207-8
    demographic segmentation method,
        209-10
    geographic segmentation method,
        210
    market segmentation, 209-11
    product-related segmentation
        method, 211
    psychographic segmentation
        method, 210-11
Continental Franchise Review, 49
Conversion costing method, of pricing,
    240-41
Convertible bonds, 329
Copyrights, 665-72
    applying for, 667-68
    microcodes, 669-72
    Semiconductor Chip Protection Act
        of 1984, 669
    what copyrights protect, 666-67
Corporations, 86-90, 487
    advantages of business form, 88
    disadvantages of business form,
        88-90
    fictitious business names and, 108
    tax year, 479
    types of, 86-87
        business corporations, 88
        domestic versus foreign, 87
        professional corporations, 87-88
        profit versus nonprofit, 87
Cost analysis:
    capital lease, 744-45
    leasing of equipment, 740-45
        operating lease versus capital
          lease, 740-41
Cover page, business plans, 183
Credit application process, 542
Credit sales, 127-28
Crime insurance, 309-10
Cross comparison with industry
    standard, 531
Crude oil windfall profit tax, 297
Crummey trust, 483
Current assets, 258
Current liabilities, 258
Current ratio, 532
Customer relations, 222

D

Daisy wheel printers, 585
Data base programs, 585
Debentures, 329
Debt ratio, 532, 539
Debt repayment, 285
Debt securities, See Bonds
Deferred compensation, 486
Defined benefit plans, 93
Defined contribution plans, 93
Demographics, 209-10
    census tracts, 212
Department of Housing and Urban
    Development (HUD), loans, 323

Dependent care assistance, 605
Depreciation, 268-73
    Accelerated Cost Recovery System
        (ACRS), 271-73
    double declining balance (DDB)
        method, 270-71
    straight-line depreciation, 269
    sum of the year's digits (SYD)
        method, 269-70
Design patents, 673
Direct approach, to locating businesses
    for sale, 15
Direct mail advertising, 217-18
Directory of Franchising Organizations,
    49
Disability, 605
Disability insurance, 311
    notice, 127
Discrimination, 120-22
    age discrimination, 123
Distribution of product, 224-26
Distributorships, 51
Dothard v. Rawlinson, 120-22
Dot matrix printers, 585
Double declining balance (DDB)
    method, of depreciation, 270-71
Double-entry accounting system, 266-67
Dun & Bradstreet, Inc., 540

E

Earnings before interest and taxes
    (EBIT), 532
Earnings per share (EPS), 534
Economic Development Administration
    (EDA), loans, 323
Economic order quantity (EOQ) model,
    551-58
    instantaneous delivery, 553
    inventory cycles per year, 556
    probability of stock-out, 556
    quantity discounts, 554-55
    stock-out units, 556
    unit stock-out cost, 557-58
    using inventory at a constant rate,
        555-56
Educational expenses, 605
Edwin's, Inc. v. United States, 475
Embezzlement, 275-76
Employee benefit plans, 589-97
    defined benefit plans, 592-93
        annuities, 593
        pensions, 592-93
    defined contribution plans, 590-92
        cash/deferred arrangements,
          591-92
        employee stock ownership plans
          (ESOPs), 591
        money purchase, 592
        profit sharing, 590-91
        stock bonus programs, 591
    master/prototype plans, 596
    qualification of, 593-96
        distribution requirements, 594
        exclusive benefit requirement, 593
        IRS determination letter, 594-95
        nondiscrimination rules, 593
        participation and coverage
          requirements, 593-94

reporting/disclosure
        requirements, 595-96
vesting requirements, 594
taxation of distribution, 596-97
Employee safety/health regulations,
    115-19
    federal, 115-16
        recordkeeping, 116
        reporting, 115
    inspection checklist, 118-19
    state, 116-18
        recordkeeping, 117-18
        reporting, 118
Employees Retirement Income Security
    Act of 1974 (ERISA), 311
Employee stock ownership plans
    (ESOPs), 93, 486
Employee testing, 122
"Employment Eligibility Verification"
    (Form I-9), 124
Ending inventory estimation, 560-62
    gross profit method, 560-61
    retail method, 561-62
Equal Employment Opportunity Act,
    120
Equal Employment Opportunity Notice,
    126
Equipment purchase, versus leasing,
    739-49
Equity R&D partnerships, 722
Equity securities, *See* Stocks
Escrow, use of, 28
Estate planning, 482-90
    passing estate on to loved ones,
        487-90
    setting goals, 482
    techniques, 482-87
        deferred compensation, 486
        executive compensation estate
            planning, 485-86
        individual retirement accounts
            (IRAs), 486-87
        intervivos gifts, 482-83
        life insurance, 484-85
        qualified plans, 486
        tax shelter investments, 484
        trusts, 483
        will and marital deduction
            clause, 484
Ethical highbrows, psychographic
    profile, 210
Evaluating your skills, worksheet, 31
Executive compensation estate
    planning, 485-86
Executive summary, business plans, 337
Exhibit Designers and Producers
    Association, 243
Exhibition Validation Council (EVC),
    trade show information, 243
Exhibits schedule, trade show
    information, 243
Existing business purchase, 13-40
    advantages/disadvantages, 14
    determining best type of business for
        you, 15-16
    escrow, use of, 28
    locating businesses for sale, 14-15
    negotiations, 16-17
    purchase price determination, 17-20

taxation, 21-28
    allocating price, 21
    Bulk Transfer Act compliance,
        25-26
    cost allocation rules, 21-22
    employment release, 26-27
    federal tax liens, 27
    future requirements, 22-23
    hidden liabilities, 23
    potential product liability claims,
        27-28
    sale of assets versus sale of stock,
        23-24
    sales and use tax release, 26-27
    security interest, 24-25
    transferring lease to new owner,
        28-29
Expectations:
    defining your, 3-6
    sales volume required to support
        expected return, 5-6
Exposition Service Contractor
    Association, 243
External crime, 274-75

F

Facilities and service taxes, 296
Factoring, 345-46
Fair Employment Practices Act, 120
Fair Labor Standards Act (FLSA), 119-20
Fair market value (FMV), 741
Farmers Home Administration
    (FMHA), loans, 323-24
Federal Age Discrimination in
    Employment Act (1967), 123
Federal employee protection laws,
    119-23
Federal excise taxes, 295-97
Federal Labor Standards Act (FLSA), 705
Federal tax deposit coupons, 110-11, 113
Federal tax liens, 27
Federal unemployment tax (FUTA),
    113-14
Fictitious business names, 108-9
    name check, 108
    reasons for using, 108
File/file structure, 586
Financial data description, business
    plans, 180, 337
Financial investment, estimating your, 4
Financial plan, 192-93
Financial statements, 258-66
    balance sheet, 258-59
    income statement, 260-62
    statement of sources and uses of
        funds (post July 1, 1988),
        264-66
    statement of sources and uses of
        funds (pre-July 1, 1988),
        262-64
Financing sources, 313-46
    assets, 316-17
    borrowing money, 316
    finding sufficient capital, 313-14
    five "Cs" of credit, 315
    funding request refusals, 314-15
    going public, 339-42
    net worth, 318-19

private placements, 329-20
selling securities, 327-29
venture capital, 334-39
Finished goods inventory, 549
First-in, first-out method, inventory, 559
Five "Cs" of credit, 31, 315
Fixed assets, 258
Fixed charge coverage ratio, 533
401(K) plans, 93, 486
403(b) plans, 93
Franchise agreement, 55
Franchise Index/Profile, 49
Franchise offering circular, 55
Franchise Opportunities Handbook, 49
Franchises, 47-59
    advantages/disadvantages, 49
    assistance, types of, 48-49
    chainstyle franchises, 51
    definition of, 50
    disclosure/registration, 51-55
        federal requirements for, 52-55
        FTC rule, 52
        state law, 51
    distributorships, 51
    franchise contract, 55-56
    franchisor control, 48
    legal aspects, 50-56
    locating, 49-50
    manufacturing/processing
        franchises, 51
    questions to ask franchisors, 49
    taxation, 56-58
        key issue, 56
        tax law, 57-58
    types of, 50-51
Franchising, 49
Franchisors, what to expect from, 58-59
Fringe benefits, 602-7
    athletic facilities, 606
    cafeteria plans, 606-7
    dependent care assistance, 605
    disability, 605
    educational expenses, 605
    health insurance, 604
    life insurance, 603-4
    moving expenses, 605
    supplemental unemployment
        benefits, 605
Funding request refusals, 314-15

G

General Agreement on Tariffs and Trade
    (GATT), 474
General expenses, 260
Generalist venture capitalists, 336
General partnerships, 84-85
GeoCalc, 584
Geographic method, of market
    segmentation, 210
Glass insurance, 310
Going public, 339-42
    advantages/disadvantages, 340-41
    investment banking process, 341-42
    registration statement, 342
Government notices, displaying of,
    125-27
Government sources, of industry ratios,
    540-41

Griggs v. Duke Power Company, 122
Gross margin, 534
Gross profit growth, 536
Group health insurance, 311

H

Handbook for Employers (Immigration
    and Naturalization Service), 125
Hardware, computers, 586
Hazardous Conditions and Equipment
    Notice, 127
Health insurance, 604
Highway use tax, 297
Horizontal buyers/sellers, 244-45
H.R. 10 plans, *See* Self-employment
    retirement plans
Hybrid method of accounting, 480

I

Immigration Reform and Control Act
    (1986), 124-25
Income in respect of a decedent (IRD),
    485-86
Income statement, 260-62
    sample, 261
Income taxes, 260
    reporting withholding from
        employees' wages, 112-13
Incremental cost-base method, of
    pricing, 240
Indemnity provision, Purchase and Sale
    Agreement, 27
Indemnity/right of subrogation, 303
Indentures, 329
Independent contractors:
    definition of, 707
    tax reports necessary for, 708
    versus employees, 704-10
        legal distinctions, 704-7
        operational view, 709
        taxation, 707-8
        warning to employers, 708
Individual retirement accounts (IRAs),
    92-93, 486-87
Industrial market, 207-8, 211
Industrial Welfare Commission Orders,
    126
Industrial Welfare Commission (State of
    California), 123-24
Initial Public Offerings (IPOs), 339
Inspection checklist, employee
    safety/health regulations,
    118-19
Insurance, 301-12
    cash surrender value of life
        insurance, as asset, 317
    health insurance, 604
    insurance checklist, 305-12
    key provisions, 302
    nature of, 302
    reducing your risk, 304
    terms/definitions, 302-4
    types of, 304-12
        automobile insurance, 307-8
        business interruption insurance,
          309
        crime insurance, 309-10

disability insurance, 311
    employee benefit coverage, 310
    employee insurance, 312
    glass insurance, 310
    group health insurance, 311
    liability insurance, 307
    rent insurance, 310
    retirement income, 311
    worker's compensation, 308
    unanticipated events, types of, 301-2
Intellectual property law, 659
Internal accounting controls, 273-76
    components of, 274
    embezzlement, 275-76
    external crime, 274-75
    function of, 273-74
    internal crime, 273
    mechanics of, 274
Internal crime, 273
International Exhibitors Association, 243
Intervivos gifts, 482-83
Introduction, business plans, 179
Inventory:
    carrying cost, 550
    definition of, 548
    economic order quantity (EOQ)
        model, 551-58
    ending inventory estimation, 560-62
    financing, 319
    finished goods, 549
    inventory costs, 549-50
    inventory turnover (ITO), 533
        forecasting of, 529
    monitoring of, 546-48
    new businesses, 11
    opportunity cost of lost sales, 550
    ordering cost, 550
    production costs, 550
    purposes of, 549
    raw materials, 549
    requirements, forecasting of, 528
    valuation, 558-62
    work-in-process, 549
Investment bankers, 333
Investment return/internal rate of
    return, 336
Irrevocable lifetime trusts, 483

J

Job method, of pricing, 241-42

K

Keogh plan, *See* Self-employment
    retirement plans
Key person insurance, 303
Know-how, license agreements, 733-34

L

Labor Dispute Notice, 127
Labor-Management Relations Act
    (LMRA), 706
Laser printers, 585
Lease, transfer to new owner, 28-29
Leasing of equipment:
    advantages/disadvantages, 739-40

cost analysis, 740-45
    operating lease versus capital
        lease, 740-41
    lease contract terms, 747-49
    negotiation of, 745-47
    versus buying, 739-49
Leverage ratios, 532-33
Lewis v. Equitable Life Assurance
    Society, 573
Liabilities, 317
    current liabilities, 258
    hidden, in existing business
        purchase, 23
    noncurrent liabilities, 258
Liability insurance, 307
Licensing agreements, 731-37
    advantages of, 732
    creation of competition, 733
    disadvantages, 732-33
    hidden administrative costs, 733
    increase in market share, 732
    information, addresses for, 737
    issue to consider, 735-36
    licensing rights, types of, 733
    loss of quality control, 733
    original equipment
        manufacturer/value added
        reseller arrangements,
        736-37
    piracy, 732-33
    property that can be licensed, 733-34
    prospective licensees' checklist,
        734-35
    purpose of, 731-33
    recoup of R&D costs, 732
    technological exchange, 732
Life insurance, 484-85, 603-4
    See also Insurance
Limited partnerships, 85-86
Liquidation, 489
Liquidity ratios, 532, 539
Loans, 320-26
    Certified Development Companies
        (CDCs), 326-27
    Department of Housing and Urban
        Development (HUD), 323
    Economic Development
        Administration (EDA), 323
    Farmers Home Administration
        (FMHA), 323-24
    Local Development Companies
        (LDCs), 326
    Small Business Administration
        (SBA), 320-23
    Small Business Investment
        Companies (SBICs), 324-25
Loans against real estate, 319
Local Development Companies (LDCs),
    loans, 326
Local license, 109
Location:
    businesses, 226-29
    metropolitan area, 227-28
    state, 227

M

Magazines, advertising in, 217
Management team, 187-88

Managerial employees, definition of, 707
Manufacturer's representatives, 225
Manufacturers taxes, 296
Manufacturing businesses:
 location of, 229
 pricing methods, 239-41
  conversion costing method,
   240-41
  incremental cost-base method,
   240
  markup on full cost method,
   239-40
Manufacturing franchises, 51
Manufacturing plan, business plans,
 179, 337
Market analysis/strategy, business
 plans, 179, 337
Marketing, 205-45
 business location, 226-29
 census tracts, 211-14
 consumer market, 207
 industrial market, 207-8
 marketing research, 205-11
  learning industry needs, 206-7
  library use, 206
 market segmentation, 208-11
 new businesses, 10-11
 product/service promotion, 215-45
 reseller market, 208
 target market, selection of, 215
 trade shows, 242-45
Marketing plan, 191-92
Market markup method, of pricing, 237
Market segmentation, 208-11
 consumer market, 209-11
  demographic method, 209-10
  geographic method, 210
  product-related method, 211
  psychographic method, 210-11
 industrial market, 211
 reseller market, 211
Markup on full cost method, of pricing,
 239-40
Markup percentage method, of pricing,
 236-37
Memory, computers, 586
Microcodes, 669-72
Minimum lease payments, 741
Minimum Wage Notice, 126
Minimum wages, 705-6
Miscellaneous needs, forecasting of, 528
Modem, 587
Modified accelerated cost recovery
 system (MACRS), 748
Monopoly market, 230
Mortgage bonds, 329
Motor vehicles, as assets, 317
Moving expenses, paid as fringe benefit,
 605
Multiplier method, of pricing, 241

N

Name check, fictitious business names
 and, 108
National Association of Exposition
 Managers (NAEM), 243

National Association of Small Business
 Investment Companies
 (NASBIC), 339
National Labor Relations Act (NLRA),
 706-7
National Labor Relations Board (NLRB),
 706
National Venture Capital Association
 (NVCA), 339
Negotiation:
 of equipment lease contract, 745-47
 for existing business purchase, 16-17
Net income, 261
Net income growth, 537-39
Net margin, 534
Net unearned income (NUI), 476
Net worth, 259, 318-19
New businesses, 7-12
 accounting aspects, 9-10
 advantages/disadvantages, 7-11
 banking, 11
 employees, 11
 equipment, 11
 inventory, 11
 legal issues, 8-9
 location, 11
 marketing, 10-11
 supplies, 11
 taxation, 8-9
Newspapers:
 advertising in, 216-17
 locating businesses for sale through,
  15
Nielsen Station Index (NSI), 219
Noncurrent assets, 258
Noncurrent liabilities, 258
Nondiscrimination rules, cafeteria
 plans, 606
Notes payable, 317
Notes receivable, as asset, 317

O

Objectives, establishment of, 4
Occupational Safety and Health Act
 (1970), 115-19
Office of Small Business Policy (SEC),
 333
Oligopolistic market, 230
On-the-job training (OJT), 573
Operating expenses, 260, 536
Operating lease, 740-41
 cost analysis, 741-44
Operating systems, computers, 587
Overtime payments, 705-6
Owner's equity, 259

P

Parties to an insurance policy, definition
 of, 302
Partnerships, 84-86, 487
 fictitious business names and, 108
 general partnerships, 84-85
 limited partnerships, 85-86
 tax year, 478

See also Research and development
 (R&D) partnerships
Patent application, license agreements,
 733
Patents, 672-76
 applying for, 674-75
 disadvantages of, 675-76
 license agreements, 733
 reasons to seek patent protection,
  672-73
 requirements for, 674
 small entity status, 675
 types of, 673-74
Paydays notice, 127
Permit to Conduct Hazardous Business
 notice, 126
Personal financial statement,
 construction of, 316
Personal selling, 221
Personal skills, taking stock of, 4
Personnel, 570-74
 new businesses, 11
 sources of, 570-73
 training of, 573
Personnel plan, business plans, 179-80,
 337
Piracy, licensing agreements and, 732-33
Plant patents, 673-74
Pleasure-oriented males, psychographic
 profile, 210
Preferred stock, 328
Premiums, insurance, 302
Present value criteria, 741
Previous employers, personnel, 573
Pricing methods:
 manufacturing businesses, 239-41
  conversion costing method,
   240-41
  incremental cost-base method,
   240
  markup on full cost method,
   239-40
Pricing strategy, 229-37
 breakeven analysis, 231-36
 commonly used pricing methods,
  236-42
  manufacturing, 239-41
  retailers, 236-37
  service sector, 241-42
  wholesalers, 237-39
 nature of market and, 229-31
Printers, 585
Privately published lists, trade show
 information, 244
Private placements, 329-20
Processing franchises, 51
Production costs, inventory, 550
Product liability claims, 27-28
Product-related method, of market
 segmentation, 211
Product/service, pricing, 229-37
Product/service description, business
 plans, 179, 337
Product/service promotion, 215-45
 advertising, 215-20
 budget, 222-23
 customer relations, 222
 personal selling, 221

promotion campaigns, 221
publicity, 220-21
trade shows, 242-45
Professional corporations, 87-88
Profitability ratios, 540
Profit and loss worksheet, 33-34
Projections, 531
Pro rata clause, insurance, 303
Protection of ideas/products, 659-79
    branding, 659-65
    copyrights, 665-72
    patents, 672-76
    trade secrets, 676-79
Psychographic method, of market
        segmentation, 210-11
Publicity, 220-21
    subject matter, 220-21
Purchase price determination:
    existing business
        book value, 17
        capitalization approach, 17-18
        compilation approach, 19-20
        multipliers, 18-19
        replacement cost approach, 18

Q

Qualified plans, 486
Qualified terminable interest property
        trust (QTIP trust), 483
Quarterly Federal Excise Tax Return
        (Form 720), 295
Quick ratio, 532

R

Rack jobbers, 225
Radio advertising, 218
Random access memory (RAM), 584
Ratio analysis, 531-41
    activity ratios, 533-34
    calculating ratios and their
        meanings, 534-40
    industry ratios, sources of, 540-41
    leverage ratios, 532-33
    liquidity ratios, 532
Raw materials, inventory, 549
Real estate, as asset, 317
Real estate loans, 317
Realtors, 15
Registration statement, 342
Regulation A, Securities and Exchange
        Commission (SEC), 331
Rent insurance, 310
Replacement cost method, of purchase
        price determination, 18
Research and development (R&D)
        description, business plans,
        180, 337
Research and development (R&D)
        partnerships, 721-27
    advantages/disadvantages, 722-24
        complexity of formation, 724
        "off balance sheet" financing, 723
        retention of control, 722-23
        royalty payments, 723
        shifting of risk, 723

    tax treatment, 723
    origin of, 721-22
    securities laws/disclosures, 724
    taxation, 724-26
    types of, 722
    See also Partnerships
Reseller market, 208, 211
Reserve accounts, 345
Retail businesses:
    location of, 228
    pricing methods, 236-37
        market markup method, 237
        markup percentage method,
            236-37
Retail and use taxes, 297
Retirement income, 311
Return on assets (ROA), 534
Return on equity (ROE), 534
Revenues, 260
Reviews, of CPAs, 268
Robert Morris Associates, 540
Royalty R&D partnerships, 722

S

Safety and Health Protection on the Job
        notice, 126
Salaried salespeople, 226
Sale of assets, 23
Sales forecasting, 523-41
    asset needs, 527-31
    existing business, 526-27
    first-time sales, 524-26
Sale of stock, 23-24
Sales and use tax:
    permits, 110-11
    state agencies, 37-40
Secured loans, 319
Securities and Exchange Commission
        (SEC), 330-33
    intrastate offering exemption, 330-31
    Regulation A, 331
    Rule 504, 331
    Rule 505, 332
    Rule 506, 332
Security interest, 24-25
    perfecting, 24
Seed funds, 336
Self-distribution, cost of, 224
Self-employment retirement plans,
        598-602
    how much to deduct, 598-99
    qualifying the plan, 599-602
        assigned/alienated benefits, 601
        commencement of benefits, 601
        contributions/benefits, 600
        employee leasing, 599-600
        excluded service, 600
        joint/survivor annuity, 601
        minimum coverage, 600
        minimum vesting standards, 600
        required distributions, 601
        rules covering owner-employees,
            601
        top-heavy requirements, 601-2
    when to deduct contributions, 599
Self-employment tax (SE tax),
        estimation of, 110-11

Selling the business, 489-90
Selling expenses, 260
Semiconductor Chip Protection Act of
        1984, 669
SEP-IRA, 93
Service businesses:
    location of, 229
    pricing methods, 241-42
        job method, 241-42
        multiplier method, 241
Servicemarks, 660-65
Show-how, license agreements, 733-74
Simplified employee pensions (SEP),
        597-98
Simulated work conditions, 573
Single-entry accounting system, 266
Small Business Administration (SBA),
        loans, 320-23
Small Business Innovation Research
        (SBIR) Program, 343-44
Small Business Investment Companies
        (SBICs), loans, 324
Snow v. Commissioner, 721
Social Security:
    how to obtain numbers, 111-12
    reporting withholding from
        employees' wages, 112-13
Software:
    types of, 584-85
        data bases, 585
        spread sheets, 584
        word processing, 584-85
Sole proprietorships, 83-84, 487
    advantages, 83-84
    disadvantages, 84
    fictitious business names and, 108
    tax year, 478
Specialist venture capitalists, 336
Split borrowing, 315
Spouse remainder trust, 483
Spread sheet programs, 584
Standard metropolitan statistical area,
        525
Starting a business from scratch, See
        New businesses
State agencies, sales and use tax, 37-40
State employee protection laws, 123-24
State license, 109-10
Statement of sources and uses of funds
        (post July 1, 1988), 264-66
Statement of sources and uses of funds
        (pre-July 1, 1988), 262-64
Stocks, 327-29
    as assets, 317
    common stock, 327
    compared to bonds, 327-29
    issuance of, 329
    preferred stock, 328
Straight-line depreciation, 269
Subchapter S corporations, 95-97
Successful Meeting magazine, 243
Sum of the year's digits (SYD) method,
        of depreciation, 269-70
SuperCalc, 584
Supervisors, definition of, 707
Supplemental unemployment benefits,
        605
Supplies, new businesses, 11

T

Table of contents, business plans, 184
Target market, selection of, 215
Taxation, 417-93
    accounting methods, 479-80
        accrual method, 480
        cash method, 479
        hybrid method, 480
    corporation as tax shelter, 471-73
        corporate form, 471-72
        fringe benefits, 472
        nondiscrimination rules, 472-73
    deductible expenses, 476-78
        business expenses, 476
        capitalization versus expensing, 477
        examples, 477-78
        how much can be deducted, 477
        tax years, 478-79
        timing, 477
    estate planning, 482-90
    export sales, 473-74
        domestic international sales corporation (DISC), 473-74
        foreign sales corporation (FSC), 474
    new businesses, 8-9
    problems unique to corporations, 480-82
        accumulated earnings tax, 481
        alternative minimum tax, 481-82
        dividends withholding, 481
        estimated tax payments, 481
        individual versus corporations, 480-81
        reallocating income and deductions, 481
        S corporation election, 482
    spouse/children on payroll, 490-91
    tax credits, 490
    unemployment taxes, 491-92
    withdrawing funds from incorporated businesses, 474-76
        accumulated earnings, 475-76
        employee compensation, 475
        issuing stock to children, 475
        leasing shareholder property, 475
        loans to shareholders, 476
        making loans to the business, 475
Tax credits, 490
Taxes payable, 317

Tax Reform Act (1986):
    fringe benefits, 93-94
    income splitting, 92
    passive activities, 97
    R&D partnerships, 723
    retirement plans, 92-93
    Subchapter S corporations, 95-97
Tax shelter investments, 484
Technical journals, advertising in, 217
Television advertising, 218-19
Term life insurance, 484-85
TIGER data base, 214
Time Off for Voting Notice, 127
Times interest earned (TIE), 532
Title page, business plans, 179, 337
Total asset turnover, 534
Trade association publications, 243
Trade associations, as source of industry ratios, 540
Trade credit, 562-64
    granting of, 541
    requirements, forecasting of, 528
    terms, 543
Trademarks, 660-65
    applying for, 663-64
    benefits of, 661-62
    license agreements, 733
    proving infringement, 664-65
    rejection of applications, 662-63
    trademark search, 663
    tradename, 665
    types of, 660-61
        descriptive mark, 660-61
        suggestive mark, 660
Trade publications, locating businesses for sale through, 15
Trade secrets, 676-79
    compared to patents, 676-78
    license agreements, 733
    projecting against theft, 678-79
    solicitation of, 679
Trade shows, 242-45
    exhibits, 242
    information sources on, 242-44
    locating franchises through, 50
Tradeshow Week, 243
Trade suppliers, locating businesses for sale through, 15
Traditionalists, psychographic profile, 210
Trend analysis, 531
Trusts, 483

U

Undervaluation, of business interest, 488
Underwriters, 333
    insurance, 302
Unemployment taxes, 113-14, 491-92
Unfair labor practices, 706-7
Uniform Franchise Offering Circular (UFOC), 52
Unionization, 706-7
Unlisted stocks, 339
Unsecured loans, 319
U.S. Department of Commerce (DOC), trade show information, 243
Utility patents, 673

V

Valuation:
    of business interest, 487-88
    inventory, 558-62
        average cost, 558-59
        first-in, first-out method, 559
        last-in, last-out method, 559-60
        specific identification, 558
Venture capital, 334-39
    advantages/disadvantages, 334-35
    analysis sheet, 338-39
    business plan, 337-38
    industry, 335
    investment return/internal rate of return, 336
    locating venture capitalists, 339
    riskless investments, 335-36
Vertical buyers/sellers, 244-45
VisiCalc, 584

W

Wagering taxes, 297
Whole life insurance, 484
Wholesale businesses:
    location of, 229
    pricing methods, 237-40
Wholesalers, 225
Will and marital deduction clause, 484
Word processing programs, 584-85
Workers' actions, liability for, 705
Worker's compensation, 308
Worker's compensation insurance, 114-15
Worker's Compensation Notice, 127